ISBN 978-1-333-87232-8
PIBN 10650082

FB &c Ltd, Dalton House, 60 Windsor Avenue, London, SW19 2RR.
Company number 08720141. Registered in England and Wales.

For support please visit www.forgottenbooks.com

THE WOMAN'S BOOK

CONTAINS EVERYTHING A WOMAN OUGHT TO KNOW

EDITED BY FLORENCE B. JACK, LATE PRINCIPAL OF THE SCHOOL OF THE DOMESTIC ARTS, EDINBURGH, AND RITA STRAUSS, ASSISTED BY MANY EXPERT CONTRIBUTORS

LONDON: T. C. & E. C. JACK
16 HENRIETTA STREET, W.C. : AND EDINBURGH
1911

30825 buf HQ

U0555X2

PREFACE

We have been asked to address a few words to our readers before the Woman's Book goes to press. Its preparation has been no light task, and we have attempted so much that it is with some reason we fear some omissions and not a few mistakes will be discovered by our critics. But, defects notwithstanding, we are confident that the book is valuable, and we look forward hopefully to new editions being called for, when any suggestions and corrections sent us can be effected.

We have done our best to provide a Reference Book dealing with all subjects of special interest to women. A glance at the Contents will show how varied a list it is. And now that our work is finished and we look back on the book as a whole, thoughts about women's work in general force themselves upon us. Our work would have been mechanically done if they did not.

We have noted the variety of the work undertaken by women. It is matter for congratulation that so many new spheres of usefulness have been opened for women within recent years; but we look forward to the time when capacity for work will be the only test of competence to undertake it. To have the work well done—that is the end to be aimed at, whether it be done by men or by women.

It is often urged that the limited outlook and training of women in the past have left them insufficiently developed in mental capacity and judgment for certain responsible spheres of work. But it seems to us that, if the test of the educative value of work is the number of faculties it calls into play, woman's work, even in the past—the work of the domestic woman—called forth faculties of the highest order. It has taken months of hard work to write an intelligible book on woman's work. A considerable part of the book is devoted to the ordering of a household, and this portion has not been the easiest to write. In writing it we have discovered afresh that the qualities that are demanded of a field-marshal, and a few not unimportant qualities in addition, are the necessary qualifications of a model wife and mother. Instinct in selecting subordinates, tact in managing them, organising of daily work, financial ability in handling the household budget, the taste that imparts charm to a home—these are not common faculties. But the training of the child makes the highest demand upon

a woman. Patience, wisdom, self-sacrifice are called for at every hour of the day. Morally as well as intellectually the domestic woman's life is rich in opportunity.

While, however, we cannot appreciate too highly the value of the work done by the domestic woman, it is absurd to regard that as woman's only sphere. Many have not the opportunity of such a life: many have not the aptitude for it. We have therefore endeavoured to take the widest possible view of Woman's sphere. Everything she can do well, *that* she is entitled to have the opportunity of doing. We hope that the information given in the volume about the various kinds of work now open to women, and the various agencies at work to qualify women for the work they can do, will be found useful; and we hope, too, that the manner in which we have presented the domestic information may lead to a higher standard of attainment in woman's greatest industry—the home.

F. B. J.
R. S.

LONDON,
April 1911.

LIST OF CONTENTS

	PAGE
THE HOUSE—CHOICE, CONSTRUCTION, FITTINGS	1
MISTRESS AND SERVANTS	41
GUIDE TO HOUSEHOLD WORK	58
FOOD AND THE KITCHEN	87
GUIDE TO COOKERY	116
THE TABLE	236
HOUSEHOLD LINEN	257
GUIDE TO LAUNDRY WORK	271
DRESS—ITS CHOICE AND CARE	301
ETIQUETTE AND SOCIAL GUIDE	325
MANAGEMENT OF MONEY AND LEGAL GUIDE	362
PLAIN SEWING AND MENDING	387
HOME DRESSMAKING	419
HOME MILLINERY	432
HEALTH AND THE TOILET	447
THE CHILD	466
HOLIDAYS AND TRAVEL	498
HOME PETS	507
POULTRY-KEEPING	517
RECREATIONS	524
HOME NURSING AND "FIRST AID"	548
HOME GARDENING	580
HOUSEHOLD REPAIRS AND UPHOLSTERY	604
CAREERS FOR WOMEN	615
LITERARY AND SECRETARIAL WORK	625
MEDICINE AND NURSING	633
WOMEN IN HORTICULTURE AND IN AGRICULTURE	647
DOMESTIC SCIENCE	658
WOMEN IN BUSINESS	665
CIVIL SERVICE AND PUBLIC WORK	678
ARTS AND CRAFTS	682
SOCIAL AND PHILANTHROPIC WORK	691
WOMEN IN POLITICS	696
MISCELLANEOUS FACTS AND FIGURES	699

THE

H CO ORS

ollege, Hamp-

.a's College of Housecraft, London.

. Teacher, Dressmaking and Millinery,
ol c Cookery, London.

R.B .A.

CHNAN, Ph. Chem., M.P.S., President of
nen Pharmacists.

D, rincipal of Colne Engaine Farm, Earl's

resient of the Ladies' Poultry Club and
ultr Farm, Gloucestershire.

TE, Teacher of and Lecturer on "Bee-

THE WOMAN'S BOOK

THE HO'SE

THERE is nothing that requires more careful consid ation than the choosing of a house—there are so many points to be studied, so many side issues tcemember; yet many people set about selecting what to them must henceforth spell the magic woı " home " in the most casual manner, giving never a thought to position, site, aspect, ventilatioı sanitary arrangements, or any of the other important matters which are so necessary to ensure ıe health, comfort, and general well-being of the inmates of a dwelling. It is more often through iлorance, however, than through wilful neglect that the house is chosen in so thoughtless a manner, ›r the English are proverbially a home-loving nation, and, in spite of all that has been said to theontrary, it is the home life above all others which appeals to the average Englishwoman. In ıis chapter all the important considerations which should govern (1) the choice of a house, (2) its ecoration, and (3) the selection of its furniture, are dealt with in a manner which, it is trusted, will beelpful to many a young housewife, and more especially to those whose choice must in many way be restricted by the limitations of a slender purse.

First Considerations.—The first point for the would-be householder to consider is what rent can be afforded, or, if she wishes to purchase the house, what sum can be devoted to this purpose. She should be as exact as possible in her calculations before she makes up her mind whether to buy or rent a dwelling. Rates and taxes have to be considered in both cases. The purchase money, it must be remembered, represents r ney which otherwise invested would have b t in a rate of interest. The loss of t he reckoned as equival xpenditure, added to and repairs, of a house let to speak of t ownership of h proposed to sc which w the c taken to see to will amount course of the should be avoided however, and many the houses are let up these circumstances it portant that the house be and repair before the new session.

n some leases a stipulation is made that the ladlord will attend to all outside repairs, whilst aenant will be held responsible for inside reprs; but the ideal arrangement is undoubtedly tat in which the landlord undertakes to do *all* rpairs, even though the rent may be a little bher in consequence. There are many imprtant legal points involved in the drawing up a lease or a deed of purchase (see Law of Landlord and Tenant, p. 379). It is always advisable, therefore, for the would-be householder to secure the service of a good and reliable house agent to act for her in the transaction. She might also find it expedient to consult her lawyer.

A small amount expended upon agent's and 's fees has often been the means of saving of money, and it is worse than folly holder without any elementary law in regard to landlord and ricacies of a contract of sale th the legal technicalities se or lease without any es possess some know- etter for her to have are found in leases trained legal mind otter to be on the e Agents' Fees,

a house, this edium of a

A

SOME OF THE CONTRIBUTORS

MRS. BERNARD MOLE, Principal, St. Mary's Nursery College, Hampstead.

MISS FEDDEN, Principal, St. Martha's College of Housecraft, London.

MISS MAUD COOKES, Head Teacher, Dressmaking and Millinery, National Training School of Cookery, London.

MISS ALICE LEMON, M.R.B.W.A.

MISS MARGARET E. BUCHANAN, Ph. Chem., M.P.S., President of the Association of Women Pharmacists.

MISS K. M. COURTAULD, Principal of Colne Engaine Farm, Earl's Colne, Essex.

MISS N. EDWARDS, President of the Ladies' Poultry Club and Principal of Coaley Poultry Farm, Gloucestershire.

MISS BERTHA LA MOTHE, Teacher of and Lecturer on "Bee-keeping."

THE WOMAN'S BOOK

THE HOUSE

There is nothing that requires more careful consideration than the choosing of a house—there are so many points to be studied, so many side issues to remember; yet many people set about selecting what to them must henceforth spell the magic word "home" in the most casual manner, giving never a thought to position, site, aspect, ventilation, sanitary arrangements, or any of the other important matters which are so necessary to ensure the health, comfort, and general well-being of the inmates of a dwelling. It is more often through ignorance, however, than through wilful neglect that the house is chosen in so thoughtless a manner, for the English are proverbially a home-loving nation, and, in spite of all that has been said to the contrary, it is the home life above all others which appeals to the average Englishwoman. In this chapter all the important considerations which should govern (1) the choice of a house, (2) its decoration, and (3) the selection of its furniture, are dealt with in a manner which, it is trusted, will be helpful to many a young housewife, and more especially to those whose choice must in many ways be restricted by the limitations of a slender purse.

First Considerations.—The first point for the would-be householder to consider is what rent can be afforded, or, if she wishes to purchase the house, what sum can be devoted to this purpose. She should be as exact as possible in her calculations before she makes up her mind whether to buy or rent a dwelling. Rates and taxes have to be considered in both cases. The purchase money, it must be remembered, represents money which otherwise invested would have brought in a yearly rate of interest. The loss of this yearly interest must be reckoned as equivalent to annual out-of-pocket expenditure, added to which must be the cost of upkeep and repairs, and those taxes which, in the case of a house let on lease, are paid by the landlord, not to speak of the many other expenses which the ownership of house property involves.

If it is proposed to lease a house there are several points which would increase or decrease the expenditure as the case may be. If it is taken on a repairing lease, the tenant will have to see to all repairs both inside and out. This will amount to not a little expenditure in the course of the year, and therefore repairing leases should be avoided where possible. In London, however, and many other large towns most of the houses are let upon repairing leases. In these circumstances it is more than ever important that the house be in thorough condition and repair before the new tenant takes possession.

In some leases a stipulation is made that the landlord will attend to all outside repairs, whilst a tenant will be held responsible for inside repairs; but the ideal arrangement is undoubtedly that in which the landlord undertakes to do *all* repairs, even though the rent may be a little higher in consequence. There are many important legal points involved in the drawing up of a lease or a deed of purchase (see Law of Landlord and Tenant, p. 379). It is always advisable, therefore, for the would-be householder to secure the service of a good and reliable house agent to act for her in the transaction. She might also find it expedient to consult her lawyer.

A small amount expended upon agent's and lawyer's fees has often been the means of saving large sums of money, and it is worse than folly for the householder without any elementary knowledge of the law in regard to landlord and tenant, or of the intricacies of a contract of sale to hope to cope with the legal technicalities involved in a purchase or lease without any advice. Even if she does possess some knowledge of the law, it is better for her to have expert advice; often flaws are found in leases or agreements which only a trained legal mind can detect, and it is always better to be on the safe side in these matters. (See Agents' Fees, p. 383.)

In regard to the purchase of a house, this may often be done through the medium of a good "Building Society." A Building Society advances to its members loans for the purpose of acquiring houses, or of acquiring land for building purposes. In return for the loan, the house or land so acquired is mortgaged to the Society. When the loan is repaid, the house becomes the absolute property of the member. The fund out of which the Society grants the loans is provided by the subscription of the members themselves.

Locality.—Having calculated to the nearest figure the sum of money she is justified in spending, or the annual amount for rent, rates, and taxes which she can afford to allot out of her yearly income, the householder must consider in what locality she is most likely to obtain a house which will best meet with her requirements. If members of the family have to go into the city daily, then the residence should be one from which the city is of easy access. House rents in towns are higher than in the suburbs, but where a residence in the suburbs is selected, train and omnibus fares will have to be added to the yearly expenditure, so that in the long run the difference may not be so great. Very often in some parts of a town rents will be found to be on a cheaper scale than elsewhere, but this is mostly the case in streets which do not bear the best of reputations; the character of the locality should therefore be well inquired into before deciding to profit by a seeming bargain in the rental of a town house.

Where there is a family of children, it is better as a rule to choose a house in some accessible suburb rather than in a town itself. In the suburbs good roomy houses with gardens can be had at quite moderate rentals. Houses with gardens are rare in town, except at very high rentals, whilst in many towns even a high rental cannot secure the most minute amount of garden space.

A suburb where there is a good train service should be selected, and the house should be as near as possible to the station. This last is of the utmost importance. Some people, whilst being careful to select an easily accessible spot within twenty minutes' train journey of town, choose a residence of about half-an-hour's walk from the station. If they had chosen a home near the station in one of the more remote suburbs, they would have been better off. The time spent in going backwards and forwards would have been the same, and the drawback of the long walk to and from the house in inclement weather would have been avoided.

Many of the smaller towns, it is true, combine the advantages of town and suburban life in that good dwelling-houses may be had with gardens at fairly moderate rentals. These towns, however, are not great centres of activity, and the foregoing remarks must only apply, of course, to those cases where paterfamilias has to earn his livelihood in one of our large towns or cities.

In many cases, it will be argued on behalf of the children, that educational facilities in town are so much greater and cheaper than in the suburbs or in the country. Nowadays, however, good educational establishments are to be found everywhere, and in regard to specialised subjects such as these included in commercial training, many of the large town establishments have opened branches in most parts of the country. Then, again, if the suburb has been selected with due regard to railway facilities, cheap fares, &c., there is nothing easier than to let the young people go into town for their special lessons if necessary. In the selection of a house, educational facilities for the children should never be overlooked, and for this reason it is always better to inquire whether there are good schools in the neighbourhood.

The same argument must prevail if the house is selected in some country place. In many cases, apart from all question of low rental, &c., the love of paterfamilias for the country is so great, that not all the tedium and discomfort of the long train journey twice daily will deter him from pitching his tent "far from the madding crowd." If he is prepared to endure the discomfort, well and good, but the welfare of the children from the point of view of education must be considered, and for this reason he should take care to be near some good educational centre, unless the plan of sending the children to a boarding-school is adopted.

If one decides to pitch one's tent in the country, care should be taken to find out if there are one or two good reliable medical men within easy distance. In case of illness, the fact of having to send two or more miles for medical aid may at times amount to actual calamity. Such risks should therefore be avoided. It is advisable also that the house should not be too far away from a village where food and other commodities can be purchased.

The chief drawback to residence in the country lies in the fact that up-to-date arrangements in regard to sanitation, water supply, and lighting are not always to be found, and although many charms are to be found in life in a country cottage, there are also in many cases disadvantages which will more than counterbalance these charms if great care and discrimination are not exercised in the choice of both locality and dwelling.

House versus Flat.—The comparative merits of houses and flats as places of residence will ever be a debatable subject. There is no doubt, however, that as regards town life, for people of moderate means, flats represent the minimum amount of annual outlay. It is much easier for a woman to regulate her expenditure when she knows that the sums she pays yearly for her flat will cover not only rent, but also rates and taxes. As the latter usually amount to a third of the rental, this is a most important consideration. Then there is an old saying that "a large house is a big thief," and many a weary householder, harassed at the thought of high wages claimed by servants, large sums spent in cleaning and keeping the house in repair, has proved the truth of this old adage.

With a flat expenditure is kept within easy bounds; none of the thousand and one odd expenses are liable to crop up in various unexpected quarters as in the case of a house, and all the rooms being on one floor, one's housework is reduced to a minimum, and the amount spent on servants' wages is correspondingly decreased.

There is also the additional advantage of security, for one feels quite safe when leaving for the annual holiday in locking up the flat and placing the key in the care of the doorkeeper. It can also be locked up during the daytime, when one wishes to go out, without the necessity of leaving any one in charge.

On the other hand, a flat nas many disadvantages as compared with a complete dwelling-house. The rooms are small, in many cases dark, the larder and cellar accommodation poor —dress cupboards are generally conspicuous by their absence, and in even the best and most expensive of flats the servant's room, where there is one, is little better than a cupboard in size. Then, again, flats at the lower rentals are always on the top or second top stories of a building or else in the basement. In the case of the luxurious buildings which are let out in flats at high rentals a lift will be provided, but this is seldom the case in regard to the buildings at which flats are let out at moderate rents. In the absence of a lift there will be the weary climb up high flights of stone steps before one can reach one's dwelling, a disadvantage which does much to counterbalance the advantage of the rooms being on one floor. But even with this disadvantage, top floor flats are preferable to flats in the basement in regard to light and ventilation.

In a flat it is impossible to maintain the same degree of privacy as in a house. One's slumbers are apt to be disturbed in the small hours of the morning by the efforts of some conscientious youngster laboriously practising five finger exercises in the flat below, or else a "musical evening" in the flat opposite continued far into the night, though very enjoyable to those whom it may concern, succeeds in robbing you of those precious hours of "beauty sleep" which you prize so highly. In case of contagious illness also the danger of infection is greater, as isolation is more difficult.

On the whole, there are many things to be said for and against flat life; but it may be taken as a general rule that for the young couple beginning housekeeping on strictly limited means, a flat is always best from the point of view of keeping down expenditure; whilst in the case of a family of young children, flat life is incompatible with comfort owing to the limited space available, and the very fact of all the rooms being on one floor is in these circumstances a positive disadvantage.

Site and Soil.—Absence of damp is of the utmost importance to health, and in this respect a great deal will depend on the soil upon which the house is built. A gravel soil or chalk soil above the water level is best. A clay soil, being non-porous, retains moisture and should be avoided.

On the other hand, the position of the site is an important factor in determining the advantage or disadvantage of the soil upon which it is built. Generally speaking, a house should never stand low: it often happens that a house standing on high ground, although built on clay soil, is dryer than a low-lying dwelling situated in a valley upon gravel soil. Trees are desirable, if not too near the house, as they aid in drying the soil, certain trees such as eucalyptus, plane, and poplar being specially useful.

What is known as "made-up ground" is about the worst soil upon which a house can be built. The word "made" is true in its actual sense, for the ground consists of holes and hollows which have been literally filled up with all sorts of rubbish and refuse to make a foundation. The danger of building on such a soil, which will in many cases be largely composed of organic matter from which noxious gases emanate and force their way upwards, is obvious. Careful inquiry should therefore be made in regard to this important question of soil before selecting a dwelling.

Construction.—The absence of damp will also depend to a great extent upon the construction of the house, proper construction tending to minimise many of the disadvantages of an unsuitable soil. Houses built on clay soil should be well raised above the ground level, and should possess neither cellars nor basements. Houses with basements must be very carefully constructed with the view of preventing the damp from rising up the floor and lower walls. The subsoil should be drained by means of subsoil drain-pipes, which consist of short earthenware pipes laid in trenches several feet below the surface (see p. 4). To prevent dampness rising through the floor of the basement, the floor should be built upon a bed of concrete, whilst to prevent moisture from rising up the lower walls, these should not only be constructed upon a foundation of concrete, but what is known as a "damp course" should be provided. A "damp course" consists of an impervious layer of cement, slate, asphalt, or bitumen, which is placed in the brick-work of the wall above the ground level, but below the floor. Houses with basements should always be separated from the street by an area.

A great deal of the comfort and well-being of the inhabitants of a house will depend upon the plan upon which it is built. Houses with basements always entail work for servants in going up and down stairs between the dining-room and the kitchen. On the other hand, in houses where the kitchen and dining-room are on one floor, care should be taken that the kitchen is not situated in such close proximity to the other rooms as to make the smell of cooking go all over the house. The ideal plan is to have the kitchen and pantry shut off from the rest of the rooms on the first floor by a separate little passage and door, the passage running between the kitchen and pantry, the latter being placed at the back of the dining-room, with a hatch, *i.e.* a small cupboard like an aperture in the wall itself opening from the pantry into the dining-room, through which dishes may be passed to the servant waiting at table. When not in use, this little cupboard can be kept closed and will not be noticeable. A lift from the kitchen to the dining-room where there is a basement is a very great help; but these are as a rule expensive to fit in and are luxuries not within the reach of the many. Plenty of cupboards are also desirable, including a hot-air cupboard for the airing of linen. If the house is a high one, water should be laid on one of the upper landings in addition to the bath-room. There should in all cases be a housemaid's pantry on one of the upper landings in which she can keep pails and brushes.

Too much stress cannot be laid upon the necessity of the house being thoroughly dry: for this reason it is never wise to take up residence too soon in a newly-built house, as the walls are usually damp. Fires should be kept burning in all the rooms for as long a period as possible before going into a new house.

A little wall-peeling and discoloration in the case of a new house is almost unavoidable, but if, when looking over a house which has been built for some time, the paper is seen to be discoloured, this may be taken as a sure sign of damp, and the house should be avoided. In these cases a musty damp smell will almost invariably be present; a house of this kind cannot possibly be healthy, and residence in damp dwellings is a most prolific cause of all kinds of illness. Many a case of chronic rheumatism can be traced to residence in a damp house. Care should also be taken to find out if the roof is in good condition, as dampness in the upper rooms may often be traced to some defect in the roof. Though for the purpose of drainage of the soil it is well to have trees near the house, they must not be too near, as

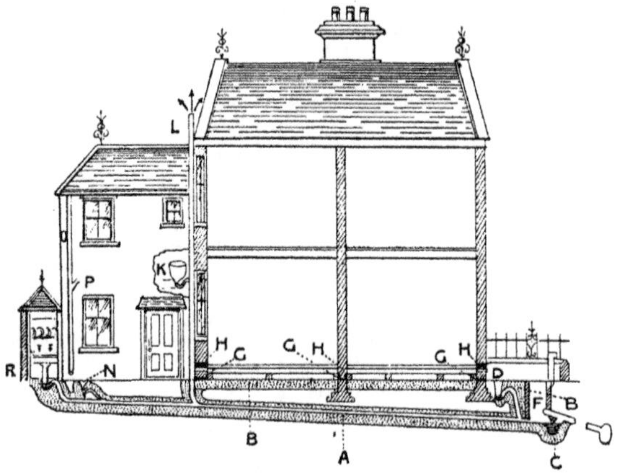

Illustration showing Concrete Foundation of a House with Damp Course and Drainage System.

A. House drain.
B. Concrete foundation.
C. Intercepting trap.
D, N. Gulleys.
F. Dry area.
G, H. Damp proof course.
K. W.C.
L. Soil pipe.
O. Rainwater pipe.
P. Bath waste-water pipe.
R. Sink.

in this case they are liable to make it damp. Ivy growing up the walls of the house, though very pretty and decorative in appearance, is also a cause of damp.

Aspect.—A house should also be carefully selected in regard to its aspect. Generally speaking, the front should face south-west or south-east. The front bedrooms and sitting-rooms will in this way catch the morning sun, whilst the back rooms will have the afternoon sun. For this reason it is advisable to have as many bedrooms in the front as possible. The breakfast-room should also have a sunny aspect; where there is no breakfast-room, the dining-room should be in the front of the house in order that the cheering influence of the morning sun may be enjoyed at breakfast, whilst the drawing-room will do well in a position where it receives the sunshine in the afternoon. It is not advisable, as a rule, to choose a house facing due north; the rooms will be dark through absence of sunlight, and the house will be cold, requiring a much greater degree of artificial warmth in winter to make it habitable than in the case of a south-west or south-east aspect.

DRAINAGE

A house should not be purchased nor an agreement for a lease entered into before the purchaser or lessee is satisfied that the drainage system is in thorough order. To make sure of this, it is essential to take independent expert advice upon the subject and to have the premises examined by a sanitary engineer. Failing this, it would be advisable to insist upon a written guarantee from the vendor or landlord that the drains have been recently tested and are in good condition. It is well, however, to always have an independent opinion, therefore the former plan is the better of the two, and by adopting it the intending purchaser or tenant protects himself from becoming saddled with a house where insanitary conditions prevail.

However well a house may be constructed in regard to light and ventilation, if the drainage is wrong, sickness and disease will invariably follow, and a little trouble and expense in investigating this important matter in the first instance will save no end of trouble and expense in the long run.

The most usual system of drainage or disposal of sewage prevailing in towns and almost all but remote country places is that known as the "water-carriage system" by which all the sewage is carried off underground in pipes called drains. The following drain-pipes are to be found in the average house—

The sink pipe for taking away water from the sink; the water pipe for taking away the bath water; the soil pipe (discharging from the water-closets), with its ventilating pipe carried above the roof; the outer drain pipe for carrying off superfluous water.

These pipes all lead to the house drain which, in its turn, is connected with the street sewer. It is not only important that all drains should be properly constructed, but also that they be kept in good condition if the house is to be healthy. To this end they should be regularly examined and all defects put right with the least delay possible.

Good drains should be (1) water-tight; (2) well ventilated; (3) without direct connection between those carrying sewage and those carrying waste from baths, basins, and the like; (4) well flushed.

(1) In order to be water-tight, the drain-pipes are best made of iron, but owing to the expense this involves they are generally made of earthenware. Long iron pipes with lead joints constitute the most water-tight system invented so far. The bed in which the pipes are laid must not be liable to sink, or the joints will give, even although firmly cemented. For this purpose, care must be taken not to sink the original trenches deeper than is necessary, as any filling in with fresh earth promotes consequent sagging.

(2) The ventilation must be very thorough, or sewer gas will find its way into the house in spite of the most careful traps to prevent it.

(3) The waste pipes from baths, &c., should never open directly into the sewer, even although the connection is guarded by a trap. They should pour their water into an open receiver or gully placed outside the house, and the gully should be connected with the sewer. Then if any sewer gas escapes from the gully, it will pass off in the open air without being conducted into the house. In the case of all pipes connection with the sewer must be guarded by a trap. Traps are devised to prevent the escape of sewer gas from the drain into the house. Many of the older traps had the drawback that they allowed filth to accumulate in them. U- or S-shaped traps are the ones now chiefly used. By having it of either shape, whenever the drain is flushed some water is retained in the bent part or trap, which then prevents the passage of gas through this portion of the pipe. The water used to flush the water-closet should not come direct from the chief cistern, but from a special small cistern, the water of which is never used for drinking purposes. By this means, if sewer gas passes into the small cistern, it will be absorbed by the water in it without passing on to the chief water-drinking cistern.

(4) In order that a drain may be well flushed, not only must an ample supply of water pass down it, but the drain must be laid at such an incline that the flow is sufficiently rapid. It must be fairly narrow and as straight as possible for the same reason; and, again, friction must be reduced by making the internal surface

smooth. By these means the accumulation of filth is reduced to a minimum.

Testing the drains is done by plugging the outlet of the suspected drain at the nearest manhole and then filling it with water from the nearest water-closet. If a leak is present, the water soon sinks, and if many leaks are present, it may not be possible to fill the drain at all. Suspected leaks may also be tested by pouring down strong oil of peppermint or assafetida in hot water, whilst a second person in the room below determines whether the odour escapes or not, but this method is not so thorough as the former test, though more easily performed by the householder.

The water-closet must be of such a pattern that it is always clean and efficiently trapped, has no direct connection with the drinking-water cistern, and is flushed by a special cistern of its own which should hold from two to three gallons. The "wash-out" closet and the "valve" closet are two of the best patterns in use at present—a "hopper" closet is commonly used, and it is satisfactory if a short hopper is used, but a long hopper is to be condemned for its lack of cleanliness. What is known as the "pan" closet is an old form of closet which cannot be too strongly condemned. The traps should be furnished with anti-siphonage pipes to prevent them becoming unsealed. In well-built houses water-closets are always separated from the other portion of the house by a small passage, and where there are two or three they are placed on the different landings one above the other. In properly constructed houses all places where water is laid on, such as the bath-room, lavatories, house-maid's sinks, should come one over the other on the various floors.

The Earth System.—In the country, where a sufficient water-supply is not always available for a complete water-borne system of drainage, what is known as the "Earth" system is the most sanitary to adopt. In this system earth is used instead of water in the closet pails, and the contents of the latter are buried at intervals in the garden.

The principle of the earth system is founded on the well-known power possessed by dry earth of deodorising and disinfecting fæcal matter—a given quantity of earth, if applied in detail to *fresh* excrement, destroying all smell and absorbing all noxious vapours. Where sufficient earth is not available, ashes should be used. Moule's earth closets are amongst the best-known sanitary appliances used in connection with this system.

Removal of Refuse.—All the dry refuse of a house which does not come under the designation of "sewage," is removed by dustmen in the employ of the local authorities at regular intervals. The most sanitary dustbins are made of zinc. The dustbin should be kept closed to keep out rain and damp, otherwise the contents will quickly decompose, and noxious odours will be the result. It should not be kept too near the wall of the house, but should be at least six feet away from it. Only dry refuse should be placed in the dustbin. All vegetable matter, such as potato parings, &c., should be burnt if noxious and unsanitary odours are to be avoided. (See Kitchen Refuse, p. 94.)

WATER-SUPPLY

A pure and abundant water-supply is a necessity in every house. Care must be taken, therefore, to find out (1) if the supply is good; (2) if it is constant or intermittent; (3) if the latter, whether the cisterns are adequate for the storage of the water and are in good condition.

In regard to the purity of the water, this should be ascertained by applying to the county or borough analyst for an analysis. The usual fee for this analysis is one guinea. As a rule the water-supply in large towns is pure. When, as in country districts, the water is derived from wells, the utmost precautions should be taken. All well water should be boiled before use, as it is very liable to pollution. If a well is shallow the risk of contamination is often considerable. A well should be deep and have its sides protected by some waterproof material to prevent the surface water from entering it. The best wells are those which are driven through the first impervious stratum so as to tap the one lying below.

Filters are largely used for purifying water, but a number of those in domestic use are not so effective as is generally supposed. Many stop some of the germs, which then flourish in the substance of the filter and infect all subsequent water that passes through. Hence purification of the water by boiling is a much safer method. Among the more reliable filters are the Pasteur-Chamberland and the Berkefeld. In the Pasteur-Chamberland filter the water passes through a thick-walled unglazed earthenware tube, which stops germs. It has been recommended to clean this by brushing the outside with a stiff brush; as, however, the germs are not only outside but probably also distributed through the substance of the porcelain, to be thoroughly cleansed it should be boiled or a new tube substituted. All filters require thorough and constant cleansing if they are to be effective. A dirty filter will do more harm than good.

In most towns there is now what is called a "constant water-supply." The constant supply system renders cisterns for the storage of water unnecessary, excepting in connection with the hot-water supply. Where there is what is known as an "intermittent supply" the water is turned off for a certain time each day. In these circumstances the intending householder should find out if the cisterns are large enough for the adequate storage of the water during those hours in which the supply is cut off, and also if the cisterns are clean and in thoroughly good condition. Cisterns should never under any circumstances be left uncovered, but should be provided with a well-fitting lid. No house should be taken until it has been ascertained that all cisterns have been thoroughly cleaned by the plumber. This cleaning should be repeated at regular intervals. The cisterns should be made of galvanised iron. An overflow pipe should be provided for any overflow of water that might arise; this pipe should discharge into the open air and never into a soil pipe or drain, or pollution of the water by sewage gases is likely to result. Cisterns from which drinking water is drawn should be as far as possible from water-closets and drains. The simple precaution of letting the water run a little before drawing it in the morning for drinking purposes should always be taken, as it should be remembered that the water has been stationary in the pipes all night, and the supply is therefore not so pure as when constantly drawn from during the day.

Hot-Water Supply.—A good hot-water supply is a necessity in every household, and a great deal of the comfort of the house depends upon this supply being adequate to the demands made upon it.

In most houses the water is heated by the kitchen range, at the back of which is a boiler; from this hot water is conveyed to the hot-water tank by means of circulation pipes. The supply of hot water will depend to a great extent upon the efficacy of the kitchen range and the supply system installed. The two best-known systems in this connection are the "tank" and the "cylinder" system. In the first system a tank is supplied for storage of hot water, while a cylinder takes the place of the tank in connection with the second system. Before taking a house, care should be taken to ascertain whether the hot-water system is in thorough working order.

Hot-water Circulator.

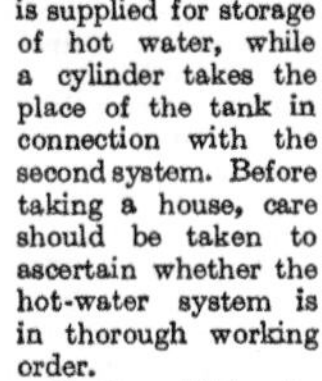

Heating Water by Gas.—There are other methods, however, of securing a hot-water supply independent of the kitchen-range. There has been placed upon the market within recent years an apparatus known as a "Circulator." This is a small boiler heated by gas which can easily be connected to the "flow" and "return" pipes from the coal-range boiler, and will then with a quite moderate consumption of gas supply hot water to the circulating tank, either independently of, or in conjunction with, the coal-range boiler, the working of the latter, in the event of the kitchen fire being lighted, being in no way interfered with. These circulators are specially adapted for use in flats, and in villas where the length of the circulating pipes are not abnormal.

In small houses and flats where gas is used exclusively as fuel, many people obtain their supply of water for the bath by installing a geyser in the bath-room for the purpose of heating the bath water, whilst the water for kitchen and other purposes is boiled on the gas stove. Geysers for the purpose can be hired from all the gas companies. The geyser, however, does not give a storage of hot water throughout the house, and does not therefore fully take the place of the range boiler as does the circulator. It is a useful accessory to the bath-room, however, in summer, as hot water for the bath can be obtained by this means independently of the kitchen range.

VENTILATION

A supply of fresh pure air is essential to health, hence it follows that homes should be well ventilated. Good air must be admitted and bad air expelled. Ventilation is the renewal of the air contained in a room. The necessity for such renewal increases with the number of people occupying it, and the number of lights burning in it. Both lights and people alike use up the oxygen of the air and discharge into it a certain amount of carbon-dioxide; but the human breath has a more noxious effect than the flame of an ordinary lamp or gas jet, for it emits a certain quantity of highly poisonous organic matter, and it is chiefly this which vitiates the air and gives it the well-known "stuffy" odour.

Every one is aware that air that has been breathed is warm, and that warm air rises. Many people think that if a room is sufficiently lofty the bad air will all accumulate near the roof and the air near the floor will not be vitiated for many hours. This is a great mistake, for unless some means of letting out the bad air is provided, its warmth will soon become lost and its moisture will condense, causing the bad air to become heavier than the fresh air, when it will sink and mingle with the latter and a vitiated atmosphere will be the result. As a matter of fact, the bad air rarely rises higher than twelve feet before it becomes cool and descends.

Every room, therefore, that is to be adequately ventilated requires both an inlet for good and an outlet for bad air.

To secure the ventilation of a dwelling-room we require no ceiling to be higher than twelve feet, but the windows should reach the ceiling and be open at the top. A fire-place should always be present and the chimney register should never be closed. The window and the chimney are the two readiest means of ventilation.

The ventilation should be arranged so that the fresh air is let in with its current directed upwards, and the bad air let out near the ceiling. It is an error to ventilate the room into the passage by leaving the door open and the window closed. "Windows were made to be opened, doors to be shut." Bedroom windows, especially, should never be altogether closed at the top. Care should be taken that the bed is placed so that the cold air does not beat down upon the sleeper.

The danger of draughts, however, must be reckoned with in many cases, and for delicate

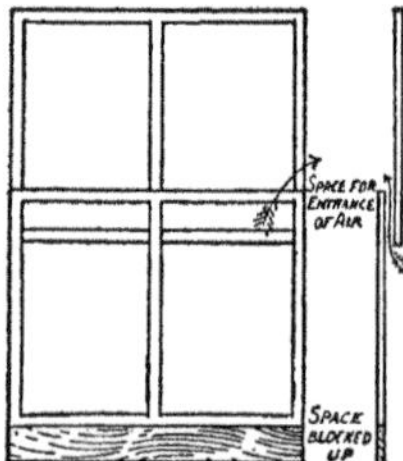

The Hinckes-Bird Method of Ventilation.

people wide-open windows in winter are not always advisable. In these circumstances a very simple system of ventilation known as the Hinckes-Bird method should be adopted. It consists in raising the lower sash of a window a few inches, and blocking up the opening with a piece of boarding as long as the width of the window and about six inches broad, thus allowing the fresh air to enter the room, but only between the two sashes, and with an upper current.

The proper ventilation of a house will depend to a great extent upon its warming arrangements. Some grates are constructed so that the fire burning in them serves to warm the air before it enters the room. A Galton's grate, for instance, has an air-space behind the chimney communicating below with the outside air and above with the interior of the room, the heat of the chimney being in this way used to warm the incoming air.

A very simple means of ventilating ordinary dwelling-houses is found in what is known as the "Sheringham Valve," which is a metal guard placed around an aperture in the wall, so arranged as to direct the incoming air upwards and made to work on a hinge so as to show the opening when desired.

A *Tobin's Tube* is a pipe the lower end of which communicates through an opening in the wall with the outside air, whilst the upper end opens into the room about six feet above the floor.

Among other simple aids to ventilation without draught are the following :—

Perforated Bricks, communicating with the room by gratings, which serve to break up the current and thus prevent the draught from being felt.

Boyle's Valve inserted in the chimney near the ceiling. This contrivance consists of an aperture leading into the chimney with two talc flaps, forming a valve, which permits the air of the room to enter the chimney, but prevents the smoke from entering the room.

Louvre Panes, consisting of slips of glass placed obliquely in an oblong opening cut in the window pane. They are commonly used in shop windows that do not open. The Cooper rose ventilator is on the same principle.

LIGHTING

The proper lighting of a house is essential not only from the point of view of the health, but also for the comfort of its inhabitants. A person is more influenced by his or her surroundings than one would think—good temper and cheeriness come naturally amid cheerful surroundings, whereas dark, gloomy, and ill-lighted premises tend to have a most depressing effect upon even the most optimistic of individuals.

Good natural light during the daytime may be secured by a wise choice of aspect (see p. 5). Stained-glass windows should be avoided in living rooms. Many people elect to have the lower sashes of their dining-rooms, for instance, of stained glass. The effect may be imposing, perhaps, but it is certainly not cheerful, and grandeur is dearly bought at the expense of the light and cheeriness of a room. Then, again, creepers should not be allowed to grow over the front of the house in such a way as to overshadow the windows, nor should the light be shut out by the too close proximity of trees. It must be remembered that plenty of light is essential to our health, and care should be taken therefore to secure it.

Artificial Lighting.—In towns electric light and gas form the chief artificial illuminants. Gas is also supplied in a large number of country places, but where this is not to be had, lamps are generally used. In large country houses, however, air gas is often made from a plant on the premises.

Electric Light as an illuminant has many advantages. It is cleanly, hygienic, and convenient; and if care is taken in regulating its use, the quarterly electric light bill may be kept well within bounds. It is very little trouble to switch off the light when one leaves the room, and if this is done not once in a way, but as a general rule, a substantial saving on the electric light bill is the result. Low candle-power lights should be used in the bedrooms, one or two 7 or 8 candle-power lamps being usually sufficient for each room.

Economy may also be exercised by means of the electric lamps selected. Tantalum and many of the other metallic filament lamps, whilst giving a much brighter light than the ordinary incandescent lamps with carbon filaments, consume much less current than the latter, and are therefore more economical.

In connection with the installation of an electric plant for lighting in country mansions situated in localities where there is no public supply, the initial outlay will necessarily be higher. Where a public supply is available the only expense will be that of wiring the premises and purchasing the necessary fixtures. In most cases the latter may be hired from the electric light company by payment of a fixed sum every year. The cost of electric light varies in different towns. In London it averages from 4d. to 5d. per unit for lighting, whilst for heating purposes the cost is 1d. per unit.

Coal Gas is obtained by the distillation of coal in large chambers or retorts. The distillation proceeds for about four hours under a great heat, and the products are broadly coke, gas, and coal tar. The gas is then cooled, washed with water, and treated with slaked lime to remove impurities.

The large cylindrical vessels so prominent in all gas works are the gas-holders, from which the supply issues to the consumers. These holders rise and sink in a tank of water by their own weight and the upward pressure of the gas inside. The gas is conveyed from the holder by mains and from the mains to the consumer by service pipes.

The use of coal gas as an illuminant is almost universal, and many important improvements in regard to fittings have been made within recent years which have increased its usefulness to a remarkable degree.

Meters are used to measure the gas consumed, and it is important that every householder should know how to read and check the meter. Gas meters are usually lent on hire to the consumer by the gas company. It is important that the supply of gas to the burner should be regulated. This can always be done by means of a regulator or "governor" on the main pipes or governor burners.

Incandescent Gas.—This is by far the most superior and effective method of gas lighting. It is used in connection with special burners which admit air to be burned with the gas, a most brilliant effect being achieved by the illumination of the white mantle which is used in conjunction with the burner. The burner is usually fitted with a by-pass for lowering and raising the light. By means of this by-pass the gas may be left turned on at the stop-cock, whilst only the faintest flicker of a flame is left on the burner. The Veritas and Welsbach mantles are amongst the best known and most effective to use with incandescent gas.

Amongst the latest improvements in connection with gas lighting may be classed the Pneumatic Gas Switch, by means of which gas can be switched on in the same manner as electric light. With this simple apparatus any number of gas lights can be switched on or off, separately or together. It consists of three parts—a switch, a valve and a coil of small tubing. The switch turns the gas up or down from any position or distance. The valve with by-pass complete screws on to any ordinary gas bracket or chandelier at the burner, which is easily done without tools of any kind, whilst the tube, which is as small and flexible as a bell wire, conducts the air pressure from the switch to the valve, and is attached to the wall or woodwork with small staples supplied with the sets. By touching the switch, air pressure is sent through the fine tube, and the light is thus turned either on or off as desired. One of the special features of the gas switch is the fact that no batteries or chemicals of any kind whatever are required. It is self-contained and requires no further attention when fitted. Another advantage to be found in using this switch lies in the fact that incandescent mantles will be found to last much longer owing to the fact that the gas switches on easily; it does away with the slight explosion which always takes place when a match or taper is applied when lighting the gas in the usual way.

Air Gas.—In large country houses where there is no public gas-supply, air gas is largely used for lighting purposes. This is manufactured from a plant on the premises, and there are many apparatus for the purpose on the market. One of the best apparatus for manufacturing air gas is that sold by Messrs. W. A. S. Benson and Co., Ltd., of 82 and 83 New Bond Street, London, W. It is known as the "Aeos" Gas Apparatus. The light given by "Aeos" gas, whilst being brilliant and pure white, is exceedingly soft and restful. The apparatus is exceedingly simple, as the plant is wholly automatic; it is also absolutely safe to use, being non-explosive.

The price for a 25-light apparatus capable

of supplying 25–26 candle-power burners would be as follows :—

Apparatus	£42 0 0
Pump and Tank	5 10 0
Carriage, including return of empties, about	3 10 0
	£51 0 0

whilst the cost of installing would be about £1 per point. Once the initial cost of installation has been borne this gas proves one of the most economical illuminants it is possible to have.

Electric Light, Gas and Oil Fittings.—A great deal of the beauty of a room depends upon the choice and position of suitable lighting fittings.

In the dining-room there should always be a centre light coming over the dinner-table in addition to any other bracket lights necessary. With electric fittings it is as well to have one or two lamps to the centre light which are switched on by different switches, so that either one or more of the lamps can be lighted at will. A red silk shade over the centre light has a most softening and soothing effect. The metal work is most effective when of antique copper or brass.

In the drawing-room which is lighted by electricity, the centre pendant is of different design, usually consisting of a number of lights, each with separate ornamental glass shades. A high electric standard lamp, with a pretty silk shade of a light colour to tone with the general decorative scheme of the room, gives a very pretty effect, as do small lamps to be placed on mantelpiece, table, or piano as desired.

The hall should be provided with a hanging centre lamp of lantern design, whilst, especially in houses built in the Queen Anne style, a plain old-time iron lantern should be hung outside the porch.

In the billiard-room the lights over the table should have plain green shades. In the library or study a centre light with one or two small metal table standard lamps with soft silk shades should be provided.

In the bedrooms there should always be a light in front of the toilet table and one over the bed, the latter to be turned on by a switch at the side of the bed. Pretty soft silk shades of a light bright colour to tone with the colouring of the room should be used; pale pink and pale green shades are very effective.

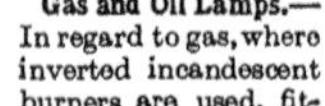

Bray's Inverted Burner.

Gas and Oil Lamps.—In regard to gas, where inverted incandescent burners are used, fittings for centre lights and bracket lights may be very similar to those used for electric light, and where the "switch on" system is installed, the illusion can be made almost complete.

Many of the disadvantages connected with the use of oil for house lighting can be minimised by means of suitable fittings. Pendant lamps should be used as much as possible. In the hall a lantern lamp is most effective. The dining-room lamp can be provided with a pretty silk shade, or, where it is preferred, a plain white glass shade, and can be carried out in wrought iron metal work or polished brass. (For Care of Lamps, see p. 77.)

Bracket lamps for hanging on walls are also made in many pretty and effective designs.

Warming the House.—The comfort of the house will depend not a little upon the method of artificial heating adopted during the cold season. Warming should always be considered in relation to ventilation as there is a very close connection between the two.

Rooms may be warmed either by open fire-places, closed stoves (for burning of coal or coke, gas and oil), or by hot-water pipes and radiators.

The old-fashioned open grate will always be popular in English homes. There is something very cheery and comforting about a good bright coal fire that is lacking with closed-in stoves and other methods of heating. It is true it consumes a large amount of fuel for the heat it yields, as most of the heat goes up the chimney, but it makes the chimney a valuable ventilation shaft, which many more economical grates do not. A great deal of the heat-giving capacity of a fire will, of course, depend upon the construction of the grate. The best heating fire-places have the back and sides of brick and not of iron, as brick radiates back the heat, whilst iron lets heat slip through it up the chimney. The back should lean over the fire, not away from it. The slits in the grid that the coal rests on should be narrow so that cinders may not fall through and be wasted. The bars in front of the grate should also be narrow, and the space beneath the fire should be closed up in front by means of an iron shield. Again, the grate should be wider in front than at the back. All these principles of construction are to be found in the grates devised by Pridgin Teale and Lionel Teale; the Teale system, in fact, has formed the basis of all the latest improvements in fire-grates. Many fire-places are now made almost entirely of glazed briquette, this material covering both the hearth and fire-place surround. This is undoubtedly one of the most artistic as well as one of the most heat-giving styles of grate.

An adjustable canopy is in most cases fitted to the top of modern grates.

Many of the newer types of grate are constructed without the front bars. Of these the Wells fire-grates are perhaps the best known. The "Burkono" patent barless fire is another also of excellent design; both grates are so constructed as to give the maximum of heat with a mimimum consumption of fuel.

Stoves.—Closed stoves greatly economise fuel at the expense of ventilation. They often give the room a stuffy odour, probably from organic matter in the air being charred by contact with the stove, and also from the fact that hot iron is porous and permits the escape of some of the gaseous products of combustion through it. They also tend to make the atmosphere unpleasantly dry. This latter defect can be remedied to a certain extent, however, by keeping trays of water around the stove. The ventilating stoves specially constructed to admit air by means of pipes or tubes are the best kind to use. Various kinds of fuel are used for burning in these stoves, chief amongst which are coal, coke, and anthracite coal.

The last-named is a slow-burning natural coal which has three times the heating power of ordinary bituminous coal, and is absolutely smokeless. The fuel is very expensive, costing about £2 per ton, but as one fire will last for hours, an anthracite stove will really prove an economy in the long run. It has been calculated that the average cost for fuel for twelve hours continuous burning will not amount to more than 1½d. Anthracite stoves are best fitted in front of fire-places. Where there is no fire-place, it is always necessary that the flue pipe should be carried to a chimney.

Heating by Gas.—The open gas fires, consisting of jets of flame distributed amongst lumps of asbestos and burning in an ordinary grate with

An Anthracite Stove.

the chimney just as open as for a coal fire, form the healthiest method of heating rooms by gas in ordinary dwelling-houses.

The most careful ventilation of the room is necessary when any means of heating by gas is employed. Whenever gas is used as fuel, whether in open fires or stoves, trays of water should be kept near the fire-place or stove to prevent excessive drying of the atmosphere.

The convenience of gas fires as labour-saving

Boudoir Grate.

devices is undoubted, and for bedrooms especially they form an easy and convenient method of warming, the fact that they can be turned off as soon as the room is sufficiently warmed adding not a little to their usefulness. There are some people, however, who, although they quite appreciate the many good points about gas fires, refrain from adopting them from purely sentimental motives, the coal fire representing to them the essence of homeliness and cheeriness. Gas stove manufacturers are quite aware of the existence of this feeling, and are continually inventing new devices calculated to render the gas fire as near as possible in appearance to the coal fire. In a new gas fire-grate sold by Messrs. Davis & Sons, and known as the "Boudoir Grate," an almost perfect imitation of a homely log fire is achieved. In the "Boudoir" fire imitation logs are fitted; and the marked resemblance to the effect of the old-fashioned wood log fire is so great as to almost make the illusion complete. This grate, it is interesting to note, was designed by a woman—Miss Helen Edden, of the Gas Light & Coke Company, London.

Electric Radiators.—Where electric light is laid on in a house the electric radiator stoves make very convenient, cleanly, and useful heating apparatus. They can be switched on and off at will as in the case of electric light. The initial cost is small, very good radiators being procurable for an outlay of 35s. and upwards; but they have the drawback of consuming a great amount of current, and for this reason, unless great care and discrimination are exercised in their use, they are apt to prove expensive.

Oil-Stoves.—Where no other method of heating is available oil-stoves are very useful, but at the same time they have many disadvantages. From the point of view of ventilation they are not hygienic, as they use up a good amount of pure air; and being nearly always used in rooms which contain no fire-place there is no outlet for the fumes which pass into the room and vitiate the atmosphere.

Oil-stoves require constant attention in the way of cleaning and trimming; they have a tendency to smell unpleasantly, and this tendency is particularly marked when their care in either of the above respects is neglected. The prices of these stoves range from three or four shillings to two and a half guineas. Very useful little stoves may be purchased for an outlay of ten to eleven shillings. The more expensive varieties are of course the best. They burn a good deal of oil, however, and for this reason, if burning constantly, the weekly outlay on oil for a stove would represent in many instances more than the outlay on coal for a fire.

Hot-Water Pipes.—This system of heating is mostly restricted to large houses and public buildings and institutions. The heat is diffused by means of hot water circulated through the house by pipes and radiators. The installing of a hot-water system amounts to a considerable sum in the first instance. The disadvantage of this heating arrangement lies in the fact that it is not easy to regulate the temperature, and a stuffy atmosphere is usually the result. Very often in large houses a hot-water system is installed for heating the hall and landings, whilst the rooms are heated with fires in the ordinary way. There is no doubt that many colds and other similar ills may often be attributed to the fact that people are apt to overlook the danger of loitering in a cold and draughty hall after coming out of a warm room. Some method of heating the hall to make it of uniform temperature with the rooms is therefore highly desirable, and no more efficient method than that of a hot-water system could be devised for the purpose.

General Condition of the House.—Before renting or purchasing a house, careful investigation should be also made into the general condition of the premises.

The roofs should be examined by a builder for any defect that might give rise to damp and other similar ills; walls, flooring, and ceilings should be looked into for cracks and other imperfections. Care should be taken to find out that doors fit well, opening and shutting easily, on their hinges; also that locks are in good condition. Windows should be examined to see that cords are good, and that they open both top and bottom; also that they are properly fitted with bolts, and that the shutters (if any) are in working order.

Defects in chimneys should be looked for; these are often indicated by discoloration by smoke of the marble of the mantelpieces. The kitchen range and boiler should be tested, care being taken to find out if a good supply of hot water can be ensured. In some houses it is only after a regular furnace has been blazing in the kitchen grate for some hours that the water begins to show any signs of warmth; this points to some defect in the boiler, and a plumber should at once be called in to put matters right.

If the kitchen fire-place is of an obsolete type, the landlord should be asked to put in a modern range. All pipes should be attended to and put in repair.

Care should be taken to see that the principal rooms are fitted with bells, and if so, whether the latter are in good condition. Needless to say, the house should be thoroughly clean and in every way fit for the occupation of the incoming tenant. The latter must be careful to ascertain that this is the case, and also that it is not infested by rats, mice, beetles, or other vermin of an even more disagreeable kind.

No pains should be spared in attending to all these matters, and seeing that attention is paid to everything that makes for comfort. The landlord who wishes to let a house is a much better-tempered and amenable person than the landlord who has actually "caught" his tenant. Insist on everything being put in order before you take over the premises. If matters are allowed to slide a great deal of future expense will be entailed, more especially where the house is taken upon a "repairing" lease. The need for caution before making a purchase is none the less imperative, or else the purchaser will find that what with the cost of putting the premises into repair in the first instance and the amount expended subsequently upon the general upkeep of the house, he will have made a very bad bargain indeed.

It should be remembered that, excepting in the case of houses let furnished, a landlord is not bound in law to put the premises in a state of repair or even into a habitable condition before the tenantry commences unless he has entered into an agreement to do so with the incoming tenant.

HOUSE DECORATION

Once a house has been taken and all the necessary cleaning and repairs have been duly carried out, the important question of decoration will have to be entered into.

Many women look upon the selection of wall-paper as a tedious task which is best avoided where possible, and leave the entire scheme of papering and decoration to the discretion of the landlord, with very often lamentable results. True, in some instances, the latter may be a man of taste and may take sufficient pride in his property to select papers suitable for the aspect of the various rooms and the purpose for which they are intended. But such a landlord will prove an exception to the general rule. The idea which ranks paramount in the mind of the average landlord is how to save himself expense. In these circumstances it may be taken for granted that if the selection is left to him his choice will be governed by no other consideration that that of his pocket.

The policy of leaving the selection of wall-papers to a landlord is therefore an altogether fallacious one, and should never be adopted. If he has arranged to paper and decorate the premises for the incoming tenant he will be only too pleased for the latter to make his selection, provided however that he keeps within a certain stipulated sum. If the tenant wishes to obtain papers of a better quality than those procurable for the sum allotted, all that he will have to do will be to make up the difference. A landlord will always consent to an arrangement of this kind.

It should be ascertained that the walls are thoroughly dry and clean before the new paper is put on. The practice of pasting a new paper over an old one cannot be too highly condemned from the point of view of cleanliness and sanitation. Care should also be taken that the paper is fixed to the wall with material that does not turn sour; bad size used for this purpose is particularly noxious. A great deal of illness has been traced to the hanging of wall-papers with bad paste or size. The walls of newly-built houses should not be properly papered for six or eight months, as they will not be thoroughly dry before that time. A temporary papering should be provided during this period.

The decorative scheme should be carefully considered both in regard to the shape, size, light, and aspect of the various rooms, and also in regard to the style of furniture which they will contain. Rooms that are furnished according to a special period scheme, for instance, must be papered in conformity with the style of this period. Wall-papers must always act as a suitable background for the furniture of a room both in regard to pattern, style, and colouring, and this fact should never be lost sight of in making a choice. Then, again, the aspect of a room must influence the choice of the colour selected; what are known as warm colours should not be selected for a room with a south or south-east aspect, whilst all "cold" colours should be avoided in the decoration of rooms facing north or north-east. Yellow and red, for instance, are warm colours, whilst blue is what is known as a cold colour. These three colours are known as the "primary" colours.

Any child who has experimented with a box of paints will know that blue and yellow mixed make green, whilst red and blue make purple. The secondary colours so made may be either warm or cold colours according to the proportion in which their primary colours are mixed. In green, for instance, if the blue preponderates over the yellow the result is a "cold" colour; but many shades of green in which the yellow preponderates will result in an almost warm colour, the warmth of the original yellow being judiciously tempered by the admixture of the cold colour blue. Certain tones of very pale green should always be avoided, because their colour is due to an injurious white pigment containing arsenic. At an inquest held in London a short time ago on the body of a man it was found that his death was due to arsenical poisoning from the cheap green paper on his bedroom wall. Fires in the bedroom had caused the fluff from the paper to be distributed over the room, and as the man was in a weak state of health the poison germs proved fatal.

Just because some greens are dangerous, however, it does not follow that green should be tabooed in house decoration. It is only the cheap pale cold greens which should be shunned. Dark green is one of the most useful colours that can be selected in room decoration, as most other colours tone or contrast well with it. Several delicate greens may also be had which have no injurious ingredients in their composition.

Dadoes and friezes enter largely into the scheme of present-day wall-paper decoration, but their choice must depend upon the size and height of the room. In small low-ceilinged rooms dadoes should never be used, as they only make small rooms look smaller. In regard to friezes, there is a certain difference of opinion amongst furniture experts. Some say that they should not be used at all in low small rooms, whilst others maintain that an unbroken line of wall-paper from floor to ceiling, far from adding to the apparent height of a low room, only serves to diminish it, whilst if the line is broken by means of a narrow frieze, the effect is to make the room more lofty. It may be said as a general rule, however, that the striped self-coloured papers are the best to use in small low-ceilinged rooms, as the stripes tend to give an impression of height. All papers with large patterns should be avoided on the walls of small rooms, although, if judiciously chosen, when used in large lofty rooms they are very effective. Before choosing a wall-paper it is always as well to see it in the piece, and to try the effect of a piece held against the wall before making the final selection.

One important thing to remember in the decoration of rooms is that the various decorations should not match each other in monotonous fashion. The colour scheme is always more effective, for instance, when carpets or table coverings or both form a pleasing contrast to the wall-papers. Where there is a pattern on the wall-paper, let the curtains be of absolutely plain material; never repeat the pattern of a wall-paper in the chintz of curtains or chair coverings.

Ceilings should always be in light tones and cornices should harmonise with the ceiling, whilst all woodwork, including wall skirting, insides of doors, and windows, should be painted in a tint to match the principal tones of the wall-paper—with light delicate papers white woodwork is always suitable. In bedrooms, the designs of which should be always light where possible, light woodwork is also an advantage.

On the whole it may be said that the absolutely plain papers are those which form the most effective background for both pictures and furniture, providing of course that suitable colourings are chosen. Where a number of pictures are to be hung, elaborate designs should never be used. Papers with dull surfaces show off good pictures to the best advantage. Picture rails or mouldings from which the pictures can be hung by means of picture-hooks should be included in the decoration of all the reception rooms. These mouldings not only form an additional ornament to the room, but do away altogether with the necessity of adopting the old-fashioned method of suspending the pictures from large nails in the wall, a method which is certainly not conducive to the long life of the wall-paper.

Picture-hook.

Different Kinds of Papers.—Amongst the most effective of present-day wall-papers may be classed the plain silk fibre papers in uniform tints. These have a softness of surface which is peculiarly pleasing and effective. Pretty friezes in floral and other designs are sold to match these papers.

The most pleasing effects with all plain papers, however, are achieved by means of floral borders, which are not only utilised as friezes, but are carried down the walls at certain intervals to form wide panels. These plain papers with border effects form the most fashionable designs at the present moment. The silk fibre papers may be had from 1s. 6d. per piece, an especially good quality being obtainable for 2s. 6d.

The plain ingrain papers are also very effective; they have a somewhat rougher surface than the silk fibre papers, and may be had from 1s. 6d. per piece.

The moiré papers have a surface resembling the silk after which they are named, and may be had from 1s. 6d. a piece. They are especially effective when thrown into relief by a pretty frieze or border.

Very artistic also are the satin stripe papers. These are in uniform colourings consisting of satin-like stripes alternating with stripes of a duller surface. Their effect in pink, blue, and all the lighter shades is dainty in the extreme; whilst carried out in alternate stripes of white and silver they make a particularly effective drawing-room decoration, especially when used as a background for seventeenth-century furniture.

Patterned wall-papers, where they are preferred, can be very effective if judiciously selected, but the principle that large and bold designs are only suitable for large lofty rooms should never be lost sight of. Several very pretty designs may be had in the chintz wall-papers. Stencilled papers are much more expensive than the other varieties. They are very handsome in effect, but on the whole are more suitable for the decoration of large public buildings than for that of private houses.

The plain sanitary washable papers are especially useful for nursery decoration when finished with pretty friezes and borders illustrating nursery rhymes, fairy stories, or representing various farmyard animals or any other objects calculated to appeal to the childish mind.

Tiled walls form an ideal decoration for the bath-room, but these are necessarily expensive and beyond the reach of the average purse. A very good substitute for tiles is to be had in the material known as "Emdeca," which consists of an alloy of tin enamelled and is sold at prices ranging from 2s. 4d. the piece ($16\frac{1}{2} \times 22$ inches) and upwards. This, however, would also form a somewhat costly decoration for a bath-room when regarded from the point of view of only a moderately filled purse, but it can be used as a dado, the upper part of the walls being painted with "muraline" or some other washable preparation. Emdeca is also very useful for fixing in sheets at the back of wash-stands and sinks, its appearance being very cleanly and dainty.

Painting and Distemper.—The usefulness of paint in wall decoration must not be overlooked, especially when quite plain walls are required. It does not show damp or dirt in the same degree as plain wall-paper, nor is it liable to fade when exposed to the glare of the sun in a room with a sunny aspect.

Of the various preparations for painting walls "Ripolin" is one of the most satisfactory. The Flat Ripolin has a dull velvety surface which is very soft and pleasing in effect. Ripolin may be had in any colour. It should be finished off where possible with a paper border or frieze, and a dado of lincrusta or other material where the decoration scheme of the room admits of it.

Sanalene is also an excellent paint for wall decoration. Ripolin Gloss and Sanalene Gloss are especially good decorations for nurseries, bath-rooms, larders, kitchens, &c., as they are washable. Both Ripolin and Sanalene are also very useful for painting the woodwork of a room. Plain distempered walls can also be very effective. Hall's Sanitary Washable Distemper is one of the best to use. It is easily washed when the walls begin to show signs of dirt, and proves one cf the cheapest and most economical wall decorations it is possible to have. A pretty paper frieze can be used with advantage to finish off the decoration of distempered walls.

Dadoes, Panelling and Relief Work.—Dadoes make a very effective finish to wall decoration, being especially suited to rooms with lofty walls. The Japanese leather papers sold at from 3s. 6d. a yard are often used in dado work. Lincrusta is another good material which can be had at prices varying from 1s. a yard and upwards, a very good quality being procurable for 3s. or 4s. per yard. The brown lincrusta is much used for dining-room dadoes. "Anaglypta" is also a very useful material both for dadoes and ceiling relief work. It may be had in all designs and qualities, 4s. a yard representing a good average price for ordinary purposes. A pretty dado of white anaglypta makes a very graceful finish to drawing-room walls.

Dadoes should always be finished with ornamental mouldings called dado rails. These serve not only to set them off to advantage, but also as a protection to the lower part of the walls from the knocks of chairs and other furniture.

Wood panelling makes a very effective decoration for dining-room, library, or study where the rooms are large and lofty. A panelling is carried much higher up the walls than a dado, a deep frieze being as a rule the only other wall decoration required. Oak, mahogany, and cedar panellings give a most handsome effect. The cheapest oak panelling is 1s. 6d. a foot. Good English oak may be had from 2s. 3d. a foot, whilst mahogany panelling may be had from 2s. a foot. Though the initial expense is necessarily very great, yet from the point of view of wear wood panellings are unequalled. They are easy to keep clean, and can be bodily removed and fitted in other rooms if desired. Wood panelling enamelled or painted white is often used in drawing-room decoration. In very elaborately decorated period drawing-rooms the wood is often carried up the walls in very narrow panels, alternating with panels of silk in delicate tints. Such an elaborate scheme of decoration, however, would only be suitable in very large and luxuriously furnished dwellings. Where white wood panelling is used in the drawing-room of the average household it is only carried to the height of a dado. Needless to say, in very small rooms panelling of any kind would look altogether out of place. (For Chimney-piece Decorations, see p. 22.)

COLOUR SCHEMES FOR DIFFERENT ROOMS

The Dining-Room.—For the decoration of a dining-room reds, yellows, buffs, dark greens, and russet browns are the colours most often selected. There is a certain tradition in regard to the decoration of a dining-room which dies hard. Everything about the room must be imposing, hence a rich red is a very favourite colour. It is, however, not so fashionable for this purpose as of yore, its use being to a certain extent superseded by the present vogue for papers of buff and russet tints, which are now being used extensively in the dining-room decoration of the most tastefully furnished houses.

The choice of colour must of course be guided by the aspect of the room—red, yellow, and the warmer shades being the most suitable where it has a north-east aspect, whilst cool dark greens and mauves are ideal colourings for rooms with sunny aspects. Red and green, russet and green, and buff, brown and green, mauve and grey make admirable dining-room colour schemes. For instance, a dining-room papered in red might have dark green curtains, a dark green table-cover, and an Axminster carpet in which dark green is the prevailing tone, or else one of these many-toned oriental carpets, the soft tones of which combine so well with almost any scheme of colouring; russet-coloured walls would look well with green curtains, green table-cloth, and a warm red carpet-square over a dark parquet or polished wood flooring.

A plain patternless buff paper thrown into relief by a rich brown dado would make an exceptionally handsome background for mahogany furniture and pictures in dark brown frames, whilst walls papered in soft mauve with a frieze of silver grey, mauve curtains, a tapestry carpet-square with a subdued pattern on a grey ground, and a tapestry table-cover to tone with the carpet, would set off a dining-room suite of oak in Queen Anne style.

The Drawing-Room.—The drawing-room is the room of all others which lends itself to light and delicate treatment. The general effects of the decorative scheme should be one of brightness and cheerfulness, and, above all, of refinement. Delicate mauves, soft greens, turquoise blues, white, pinks, are all suitable colours for wall decoration. The aspect of the room must of course be considered. Warm soft pinks and yellows are best for rooms facing north-east, whilst soft cool greys, blues and greens form ideal colourings for rooms with sunny aspects. White is particularly suitable in small rooms, as it gives an impression of greater space. As a background for Adam's or Empire furniture it is especially effective. Pretty striped papers in light colours with floral friezes go well with Hepplewhite furniture.

A drawing-room papered or painted in white would look well with a frieze or floral border of a pretty shade of blue green with a carpet and curtains in the same colouring. The entire woodwork of the room, including mantelpiece, overmantel, and dado (if any) would also be white.

A drawing-room with a north-east aspect would look well with a pink satin stripe paper in a soft tone, an art green pile carpet, and curtains of the same shade of green.

Soft grey wall-paper with a rose-coloured floral frieze, rose curtains, and rose and grey in the colour of the carpet would make another effective colour scheme.

Nothing could be calculated to set off drawing-room furniture to better advantage than a light well-polished parquet flooring adorned here and there by one or two choice oriental rugs. The cost is, however, prohibitive to those who are not superabundantly supplied with this world's riches.

Many people who have carpet-squares or rugs as floor coverings in all the other rooms of the house prefer a fitted carpet in the drawing-room. Where square carpets are used "parquet" makes the best surround, but this is necessarily expensive. Failing parquet a good floor stain should be applied to the surround. Many good stains are sold to imitate oak, dark oak, light oak, walnut, rosewood, satinwood, and other woods. Both parquet and stained floorings require to be kept well polished (see p. 66).

The Library.—The library should be painted or papered in sober colours such as brown, red, tan, and dark green, in keeping with the dignity of the room. To paper a library in the pale art shades of blue or green would be to go against every law of what is fitting and proper. A good soft Turkey carpet forms a favourite floor covering for this room. The shades of Turkey and other oriental carpets are so skilfully interwoven that they will tone with almost any colour. Brown walls and a deep red carpet and curtains are very effective. All the wood should be in brown. Oak and other wood panellings are largely used for wall decoration in the libraries of the rich. They have a very handsome and imposing effect. Dadoes in dark shades of anaglypta or lincrusta are very suitable. Red is a favourite colour in library decoration. Walls papered in red with brown woodwork, a carpet in deep tones of green and red, and curtains to match makes a very effective background.

Breakfast-Room.—The colour treatment of a breakfast-room will, of course, depend upon its aspect. In well-planned houses it usually has a sunny position. A paper with an unobtrusive rose floral pattern on a white ground would tone well with an art blue carpet-square. A plain blue paper with white woodwork, pretty chintz or cretonne curtains with a pink floral pattern on a white ground, a pretty cord carpet with a rose pattern on a fawn ground would also be very suitable.

Bedrooms.—The bedroom papers should be bright and cheerful-looking; never heavy, and, above all, intricate designs should be avoided. These are apt to be particularly irritating to an invalid who is forced to spend a number of days in bed, and worrying over the intricacies of a wall-paper can at times have an almost maddening effect upon a person so situated. As illness is a factor which will have to be reckoned with in almost every household, let the bedroom paper be bright yet restful in design; in fact, nothing can be better than an absolutely plain wall-paper. Washable distemper also forms an admirable decoration, and can be had in all the best and most artistic shades. Distempered walls, however, should always be finished off with a pretty frieze. A plain white paper or distemper, with a pretty floral border of roses to form a panelled effect, would go well with a green art square carpet, rose curtains, and ivory-white woodwork: soft blue paper would tone well with a pretty tapestry carpet with a rose design on a fawn ground, whilst pretty white and rose chintz curtains would complete the colour scheme. White papers with pretty floral friezes and borders to tone with the rest of the decorative scheme form the most characteristic feature of present-day bedroom decoration; a plain white paper with a very deep wisteria frieze is especially effective and would look well with a mauve carpet and mauve curtains.

The Hall.—It is a mistake to think that gloomy colouring is essential to the decoration of a hall—so much depends upon whether it is a bright hall or a dark one. Plain papers or distemper are as a rule the best to use unless the hall is a very lofty one. Warm shades of red and terra-cotta are very suitable, or green where the hall is a particularly bright one. White dadoes, friezes, and woodwork will go a long way towards brightening up a dark hall. Very deep friezes can be used with good effect. A rich pile carpet to tone with the stair carpet and laid over linoleum is a very effective floor covering. When the hall is separated from the outer door by a small vestibule, the door of the latter should be draped with curtains to tone with the rest of the colour scheme. Where linoleum is used as floor covering it should be of a simple parquetry pattern. Any valued trophies, such as swords, other armour, fox brushes, &c., &c., form most suitable decorations for the walls of a hall.

FURNISHING THE HOME

The choice of furniture for the home should not be undertaken lightly. It is a matter which calls for the exercise of much discrimination and forethought, careful consideration of ways and means, and, above all, much ingenuity in cutting one's coat according to one's cloth, and at the same time getting the best possible value for money expended.

The requirements of the different rooms in the house should first be carefully studied, and a list made out of every piece of furniture necessary for each separate room, including carpet, fire-irons, window-curtains, curtain rods, blinds, &c.

It may take some time to make out a thoroughly comprehensive list, but it will prove to be time well expended. To go to a furniture shop with only a vague idea of the general wants of the different rooms is to court disaster at the outset. Money which should have been expended upon essentials goes to purchase articles which may be ornamental, it is true, but which are totally unnecessary for use, whilst the important essentials that make for comfort are either overlooked, or else remembered too late.

It is most important, therefore, to set about buying furniture in a business-like way. Lack of method in buying will inevitably result in chaos, and the shopping for the home, instead of being a pleasure, as it should be if undertaken in the proper spirit, will prove a positive ordeal for the unfortunate shoppers.

Many people who have only a very small sum to spend upon furniture make the mistake of taking little interest in their shopping, resigning themselves to the purchase *of anything*, no matter how ugly, so long as it is cheap. Never was there a greater fallacy. Good taste should be the guiding spirit in the furnishing of the home, and good taste goes a great deal further than mere money in this respect. The most beautiful homes are not necessarily those which have been furnished without any regard to cost; rather are they those upon which care and trouble have been expended in making a judicious and tasteful selection.

A woman of refinement and taste will make a room in which the furniture largely consists of the results of her own handiwork and skill look better and much more desirable than the room of the woman with unlimited wealth at her command, who does not possess the necessary taste to guide her in steering clear of mere vulgar display. Money is a most important factor in the furnishing of a home, it is true, but a very little money can be made to go a long way if only a little trouble and care are exercised in the spending of it. A great deal, of course, will depend upon the resourcefulness of the young couple. Some men, for instance, have a taste for carpentering and carving, then how can this taste be more satisfactorily employed than in the furnishing of the home? Pretty shelves and book-cases and even tables can be made in this way at a very trifling cost. Ordinary orange or soap boxes can be turned into wall brackets, boot cupboards, and even book-cases. Cosy window-seats and pretty ottomans can be turned out by the home upholsterer and carpenter at a trifling cost. It is wonderful what can be done with a few yards of chintz and a liberal supply of enamel. Dainty hangings for impromptu curtain cupboards, wall draperies to hide ugly corners, cushions and window-curtains can be fashioned from the chintz by deft and skilful fingers, whilst ordinary deal tables and shelves may be converted into very dainty pieces of furniture indeed by means of a good coating of enamel well applied. As a general rule, the homes which require the exercise of so much care, ingenuity, and ability to make a sum of money go a long way in the furnishing are those that give the most real satisfaction to their occupants, and what greater pleasure can there be than in the realisation of the fact that the little pinchings and contrivings have brought their reward. The young wife who hears a friend congratulate her on the appearance of a pretty rug which she has fashioned from a piece of carpet bought as a traveller's sample for a few shillings at a furniture shop, will experience a much more genuine thrill of pleasure than will her richer sister who is complimented upon any article of furniture upon the purchase of which she has not expended a single thought.

It should be every woman's aim, therefore, however small a sum she may have to invest on the purchase of furniture, to see that it is expended to the best advantage, both from the point of view of taste and also from that of suitability and wear. Do not aim at handsome effects which cannot be achieved with the small sum at your command; cheap imitations should also be shunned. Let what you have be good of its kind. It is better to buy one or two really *good* pieces of simple and unpretentious furniture and add to them by degrees, than to buy a quantity of cheap imitation which will be shabby in a year.

A good deal of furniture is sold upon the hire system nowadays; that is to say, that, after the payment of a certain stipulated small sum as a deposit by the purchaser the furniture is delivered at his premises, and is paid for in monthly instalments until the purchase is complete. When a hire contract is entered into with a good and reliable firm the transaction often proves satisfactory, and for people who have not the command of a sum of ready money, however small, with which to buy their furniture it is a most convenient method, but in many other respects the hire system is open to objection. To begin with, it will mean a great strain upon the income of the young husband during the years in which he is first beginning to realise his added responsibilities, a strain which is apt to become a veritable burden in the case of those ups and downs of fortune to which every one more or less is liable. Should any reverse of fortune occur owing to which for a time he is obliged to suspend his payments, he is confronted with the probability of having the furniture taken away, even though he should have paid off all but the last few instalments. Again, when a person has a fixed sum to spend, he knows he must keep within its limits, whereas when it is a question of payment by degrees he often ends by buying more than he can afford. As a matter of principle, therefore, from the point of view of the young couple who are just starting upon the management of a home, the hire system has much in its disfavour, and, however small the sum available, it is better to pay outright for the furniture, beginning married life clear of the money responsibilities which would be otherwise involved. One can always begin in a small way, launching out further as the savings accumulate or the income increases.

A small flat with two bedrooms, a sitting-room, bath-room, and a kitchen can be very well furnished for £50, and much less than that if the young couple are adept at contriving in the way already described.

Young engaged couples who have to set about choosing furniture for their new home would do well to get some assistance in drawing up a list of their requirements. Knowledge of the ins and outs of furnishing is best attained by experience, and for this reason the bride's mother will often be able to make many useful suggestions.

Having made out their list it must next be their aim to divide up the sum to be spent upon the various rooms in suitable proportions. For this they will have to acquire some knowledge of the prices of the various articles, and for information in regard to this point they cannot do better than send for the catalogues of one or two of the best furnishing firms. Furniture catalogues in these enlightened days are not only true objects of art in regard to illustrations, but they usually contain all possible information in regard to the question of furniture, which makes it exceptionally easy for the buyer to make a suitable selection. Comprehensive lists are drawn up containing details in regard to each article necessary in furnishing the home from the table in the dining-room to the saucepans in the kitchen, and all the prices are marked in plain figures.

In addition, people are advised as to how to spend certain sums of money on their furniture to the best advantage. Nearly every furniture list contains schemes for furnishing flats and houses for sums varying from £50 to £500 and upwards. These schemes are drawn up especially for the use of people of average means who have a certain sum to spend and must keep within its limits.

Furthermore, all the large firms show model houses on their premises completely furnished in accordance with the details in their catalogues. A visit to any of these model houses is an education in itself, and nothing is calculated to be of greater assistance in giving reliable guidance to the shopper as to how her money may be spent. The model dwellings are completely furnished in every detail, and in each room a list is usually hung up in some prominent position giving full particulars in regard to every piece of furniture necessary with the price of each separate article. The decorative scheme is complete, including fire-place and fire-irons, window drapery, curtains and wall paper, though the estimate in most cases does not include the latter. A careful study of these rooms both in regard to the colour scheme and also to the arrangement of their actual contents cannot fail to be a useful guide to any purchaser as to her requirements.

Not only one but three or four furniture show-rooms should be visited. The shopper can have no better opportunity of studying really practical furniture schemes, and even though she cannot afford to purchase furniture of the kind so displayed, she will gain many helpful ideas in planning out her own little furniture scheme according to the limitations of her purse. (See Maples' Ninety Guinea Flat, p. 35.)

FLOORING AND FLOOR COVERINGS

Parquetry. — It should be ascertained that the floors are well levelled, smooth, and free from cracks and holes before laying down carpets. Plasticity and elasticity are very necessary attributes to all good flooring. It should also have a good surface capable of easy polish. Particularly where the floor, or at any rate the borders of the floors, are stained and polished is the last quality necessary. Parquetry is the ideal flooring for hall and reception rooms, but its cost is very great, and for this reason it is a luxury to be enjoyed only by the favoured few. The cost of laying parquetry flooring in a moderately sized square hall of the kind so often seen in modern houses and flats might in many instances be met by economies practised in the general furnishing of the rooms. The first impressions gained of the interior of the house upon entering the hall goes a long way to help the visitor to form an opinion of the whole, and for this reason the question of hall decoration should never be relegated to the background when the decorative scheme is planned.

Where parquetry is used for the entire flooring it should be of the best. The thin makes are, however, quite effective as surrounds for central carpets. They can be purchased at prices ranging from 3d. per foot and upwards.

Carpets.—The choice of carpets for a house must first of all depend upon the sum of money to be allotted to their purchase. This should not amount to more than one-sixth of the sum allowed for furnishing. Where a house or flat has to be furnished for £90 to £100, for instance, not more than £15 should be spent on carpets, whereas out of a sum of £200 for furniture, the outlay on carpets should not be more than £30.

It requires the exercise of no little forethought to make a small sum of money go a long way in the purchase of floor coverings. First and foremost cheap showy carpets should be avoided. One cannot expect good wear out of a very cheap carpet. It will very soon become faded and shabby looking, and nothing tends more to spoil the appearance of a room than a shabby carpet. For those with limited purses there can be no more economical and, at the same time, more durable floor coverings than plain felts and linoleums.

Felts are now largely used as entire fitted floor carpets. They wear much better, and are much more effective in every way than the cheaper varieties of carpets, for whereas the latter are very seldom obtainable in really good colourings, the plain felts are to be had in all the best art shades and are most soft and harmonious in effect. They lend themselves admirably to the soft subdued colour schemes now so greatly in vogue, and act as a very effective background to furniture. When felt is used as a floor covering there should always be in addition one or two pretty rugs scattered here and there about the room. Felt is also largely used as a surround for a square carpet, many people preferring it to linoleum owing to the fact that it gives the room an appearance of greater warmth in winter. Oriental rugs show up especially well upon a plain felt carpet. Brussels, Wilton, and Axminster rugs are also very effective. Many a bargain in rugs may be picked up at the annual sales of any large furniture establishment. In many cases the large furnishing firms and carpet manufacturers sell what are known as "traveller's samples" of carpet. These run at times into lengths of a yard and over. They only require to be finished off with a little gallon, and very pretty and handsome rugs are thus made at the cost of a few shillings. Pieces of the very best Brussels, Axminster, and other well-known makes may be had in this way, and when the buyer is able to make a good selection, she will find that she has a much better rug than it would have been possible for her to procure when buying in the ordinary way.

Carpets wear much longer if an underlay is provided to keep them from direct contact with the floor. Plain grey felt is admirable for the purpose, and serves not only to preserve the carpet, but also to make it softer to the tread. A good underfelt may be had from 1s. to 1s. 4½d. per yard running from 46 to 54 inches in width. Brown paper also makes a very good underlay, and may be purchased for 2d. a yard. What is known as felt paper is also suitable and costs 3d. per yard. A species of coarse canvas is also used for putting under carpet and may be purchased for 4½d. a yard.

Art square carpets as a rule do not require fastening to the floor, as the heavy furniture of a room would keep them in place. Heavy rich pile carpets, however, require to be fastened here and there. The most handy fastening for a square carpet consists of a patent brass nail which fixes into a groove of the same metal. The groove is screwed into the floor, a hole being drilled into the latter to receive it. The carpet can thus be lifted when necessary with very little trouble, the nails coming easily out of the grooves when it is pulled gently upwards (see illustration).

Patent Carpet Nail.

Measuring Rooms for Carpets.—Most carpet manufacturers send representatives to take the measurements of their customers' rooms for carpets, but long distances and various other circumstances sometimes make it impossible

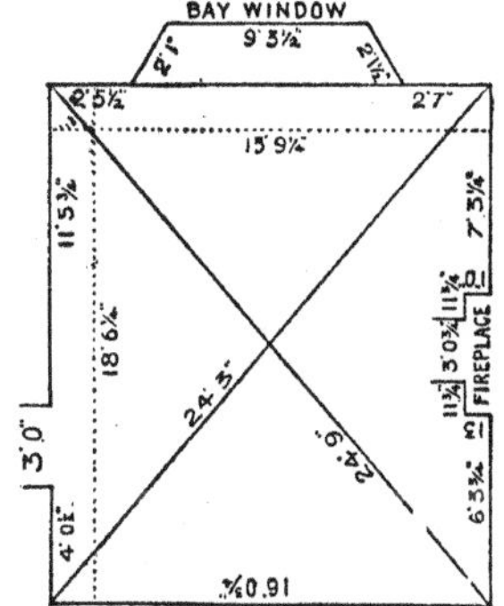

Plan showing Method of Measuring Room for Carpet.

for them to do so. The diagram here given shows how a room should be measured for carpet and surround. When ordering carpets a similar plan should be sent showing position of windows, doors, and fire-place, and giving the measurements in feet and inches. The dimensions should be accurately taken, though the plan need not be drawn to scale; carpets of any kind can be made up from such a drawing.

Different Kinds of Carpets.—For good wear, artistic colouring, and handsome appearance generally the various oriental carpets are unequalled. They are hand-made and the design and colouring are so skilfully interwoven that they will be found to tone well with almost any colour scheme. Skill in designing is almost a tradition with the peasants of the East, for the various designs are handed down from father to son, and are woven from memory, the keen eye for designing and colouring being thus an hereditary gift.

The carpets are sold in the eastern bazaars. Most large carpet-dealers in Europe have agents in the various well-known centres of the carpet industry who are entrusted with the purchase of carpets on behalf of their firm. Turkey carpets are very rich and handsome in appearance. They are favourite carpets for the dining-room, library, or study. The Anatolian Turkey carpets are particularly noted for their delicate colourings, especially in the lighter shades suitable for drawing-room carpets. Persian carpets have a particularly varied range of colouring from the handsome rich tints suitable for dining-room and study, to the soft delicate tints for drawing-room use. They are also durable, being very close in texture. Indian carpets are lower in quality and consequently less expensive than most other oriental carpets. The patterns are worked on various light grounds for drawing-room wear and also darker grounds suitable for dining-room and library. The cheapest varieties should not be chosen as they do not wear well. The better qualities are, however, very satisfactory, as the pile of these is close and deep and the colouring light and harmonious.

Brussels Carpets seem to retain a perennial hold upon the public favour. They make very beautiful and durable floor coverings, but a fair price should always be paid for them. Increase of competition in the carpet trade has induced many manufacturers to place very cheap carpets upon the market, advertising them as "Best Brussels" and quoting very low prices for them. It is impossible to obtain a good "Brussels" at a low price; 4s. 9d. a yard represents a good average figure for best Brussels carpets, and as a general rule not less than 3s. 9d. a yard should be paid if a really good quality carpet is desired. The pattern of a Brussels carpet always shows through on the wrong side. The carpets are made by weaving thread through a canvas over wires, the latter being withdrawn after the carpet is woven, leaving the loops which form the pile of the carpet. A good quality Brussels carpet can always be judged by the length of the loops or pile. These carpets may be bought by the yard or in seamless woven squares.

Axminster.—The real hand-made Axminster carpets make luxurious and therefore costly floor coverings. They take their name from the town of Axminster in Devonshire where they were first made. They have a rich deep pile and are woven in the most beautiful designs and colourings. More within the reach of the average purse are the machine-made Axminster Pile Carpets. These are to be had in many qualities and in a great variety of colourings—in light tones suitable for drawing-room use, and in the deeper colourings suitable for dining-room and library, and may be purchased for from 4s. 6d. per yard. The patent Axminster and the Crompton Axminster are the best of the machine-made varieties.

Wilton Carpets.—The Wilton carpets are noted for their soft appearance and plush-like surface. They are closer in texture, though shorter in pile than the Axminster carpets. They are made in a very similar manner to Brussels carpets with the exception that the wires are not taken away until the loops are cut. They are made in a variety of designs and colourings, the design in self colours being especially beautiful. Wilton carpets may be purchased by the yard or in seamless woven squares.

Kidderminster Carpets.—These are reversible carpets without pile. They are mostly suitable for bedrooms. It is never advisable, however, to use them as fitted carpets, as the dirt gets very quickly through the carpet to the floor, remaining there in thick layers if the carpet is not frequently lifted. Kidderminster squares, with linoleum surrounds, are the best to use.

Seamless Kidderminster squares are now sold under a great many different names, each manufacturer having his own name for his special make of carpet. The carpets known as "Roman Squares" are well-known varieties of the Kidderminsters, as also are the Cheviot and Shetland squares.

Tapestry Carpets are not unlike Brussels in appearance, but the pattern does not show through on the wrong side. They are inexpensive, and may be had in many pretty designs, but are not suitable for hard wear.

Velvet Pile Carpets.—Many varieties of velvet pile carpets are manufactured in imitation of Wilton carpets. They are inexpensive, but unsuitable for hard wear.

Stair Carpets.—Stair carpets require to be very carefully laid over underfelt or stair-pads. A sufficient quantity should be bought to ensure an extra half yard for each flight of stairs. This will allow for a periodical shifting of the carpets at the treads about four times a year so that the wear is evenly distributed, the extra half yard being always kept neatly folded under the last tread of each flight or under the carpet on the landing. The carpets will be found to wear much longer if this simple precaution is taken.

It is always advisable if a saving can be

effected elsewhere to spend a little more money on stair carpets and to have them of as good a quality as possible. They are subjected to an enormous amount of wear and tear, and the very cheap kinds will soon become shabby looking. Good pile carpets are the best for wear, Brussels, Wilton, and Axminster stair carpets being very effective. Tapestry carpets are also suitable and may be had at moderate prices.

Plain felt in one of the art shades makes a very effective and economical stair covering especially suitable for a house furnished in soft subdued tones.

Those to whom an inexpensive carpet is a *sine quâ non* cannot do better than try the cord stair carpets sold by the Abingdon Carpet Co., of Thames Wharf, Abingdon, which are both cheap and durable.

Stair Rods for keeping the carpet in place on each tread are indispensable to the staircase equipment. They are usually of brass and fit

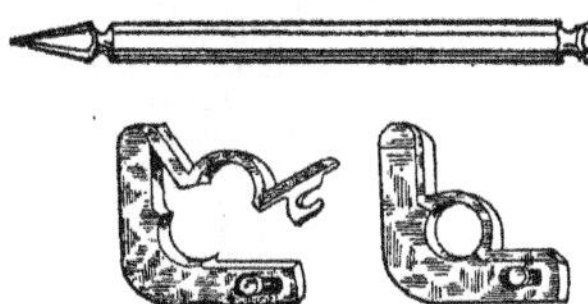

Stair Rod and Eyelets.

into specially made eyelets. The thin round rods are the least expensive; the price varies with the degree of their thickness. The flat sexagonal brass rods are the most handsome, and add not a little to the appearance of a well-carpeted staircase.

LINOLEUMS

The inlaid linoleums are the best, as their colourings and designs are so worked into the materials that they cannot wear off or be obliterated. One of the best of the inlaid linoleums is that known as "Greenwich Linoleum." "Duroleum" is also very good and durable.

The entire hall can be covered to advantage with Greenwich linoleum or duroleum. The pattern should be very judiciously selected. Needless to say, floral patterns are quite out of place, the most suitable being the simple geometrical patterns in imitation of tiles or parquetry. Linoleum requires to be very carefully laid and should be pasted to the floor with the edges of each breadth fastened by a few headless brads.

In many houses linoleum is largely used instead of carpets in all the bedrooms. It is certainly the most hygienic floor covering for a bedroom, as it does not accumulate dust and can be easily swept and washed, and it is at the same time the least expensive. In bedrooms carpeted with linoleum rugs are usually placed at either side of the bed and in front of the toilet table. Twelve square yards will be required to carpet a room 12 feet by 9 feet. The outlay will therefore be most moderate, and to those with inelastic purses this is a very important consideration.

Linoleum is also a suitable floor covering for bath-rooms and nurseries. Cork carpet is also largely used for these rooms. It has the advantage of being noiseless to the tread, and in the opinion of many has a warmer appearance than linoleum. It may be had at 2s. 2d. per yard, the shades in dark green and dark blue being particularly effective.

CURTAINS AND BLINDS

The decorative effect of a room can be made or marred by the selection of its curtains in regard to material, colour, and suitability to the various rooms in which they are placed.

In dining-room and library, for instance, there should always be curtains of tapestry, chenille, velvet, serge, or other similar materials. In the drawing-room curtains of dainty materials such as lace or silk and the various art linens

Portière Curtains.

are most appropriate, whilst light chintz, cretonne, lace, muslin, and all other light washable curtains are suitable for the bedrooms.

The cornice poles from which the curtains are to be hung must also be suitably chosen. These will form an item in the general cost of window decoration which should not be overlooked. Ninepence per foot represents an average price for a brass pole one inch in diameter. For brass poles three inches in diameter 3s. 3d. per foot would represent a fair price. White enamelled cornice poles are suitable for drawing-room and other brightly furnished rooms and are cheaper than the brass ones. Mahogany poles three inches in diameter suitable for dining-room and study may be had for 1s. per foot. For bay windows

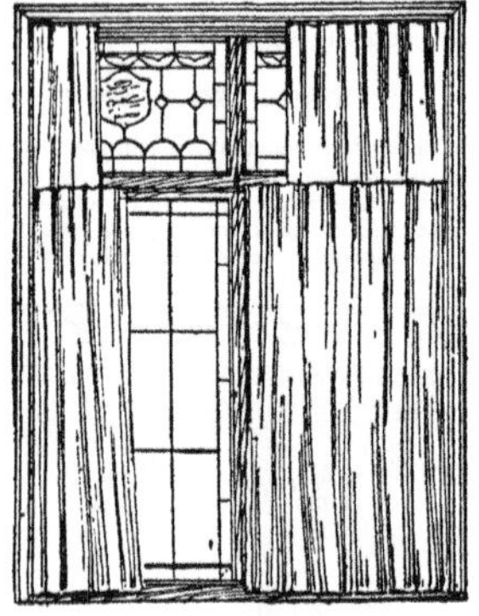

Casement Curtains.

the prices are higher. Rings to match these poles are sold at prices also varying with their sizes.

Portière curtains are often hung over doors, both for decorative purposes and the exclusion of draughts. They should be of materials such as chenille, velvet, silk, or serge, and should be hung by means of rings to a rod across which they can easily be drawn backwards and forwards. Where there are curtain cupboards in the bedrooms, the hangings should always be of cretonne, linen, or other firm washable material substantial enough to keep out the dust.

Casement Curtains, are now largely used instead of the ordinary roller blind, so casement blinds would be the more correct name to give them. They present a very pretty and decorative appearance and look best with casement windows, but can also be used with sash windows. In the latter case there must always be separate blinds for both upper and lower sash. The casement curtains (or blinds) only reach to the window sills, and the ordinary side curtains are used with them. Cretonne, chintz, casement cloths, silk and Bolton sheeting are the best materials for these blinds. The selection of both material and colour will of course depend upon the decoration and upholstery of the room in which they are used.

Arrangement of Curtains.—Much may be done to improve an ugly-looking window by the manner in which the curtains are arranged. A very narrow straight window may be made to look wider by extending the cornice pole a few inches beyond the window on each side. From this the curtains should hang straight without being looped up in any way. When two or three very narrow little windows come close to each other a top valance can be made to include them as one wide window. From either side should hang curtains of the same material as the valance, whilst lace casement curtains hung over the divisions of the other windows would serve to complete the one window illusion, giving a pretty casement effect to the whole. The casement window lends itself more readily than any other to decorative treatment. Special fabrics are sold by all furniture dealers for this favourite type of window. In this connection it is interesting to note the great revival in old-fashioned fabrics including the actual repetition of the patterns of the quaint chintzes and printed linens which were in vogue during the seventeenth and eighteenth centuries.

The alcoved casement window is always the most effective. Pretty casement curtains in two tiers can adorn the windows, whilst the broad recess may be occupied by a quaint old-world window-seat of the same material as the curtains and valance by which the alcove is enclosed.

Blinds.—Venetian blinds, if of good quality, are always suitable and useful as the laths can be easily cleaned. Their use has to a great extent been superseded however by the more ornamental linen or holland blinds trimmed with lace edging and insertion and working on spring rollers. Very good quality blinds may be had for eight or nine shillings each, the cost of the roller depending upon the particular patent used. Inexpensive linen blinds suitable for bedrooms may be had for about four shillings. With most firms the prices quoted for the blinds include both the measuring and fitting. Blind materials are also sold by the yard for people who prefer to make and fix their blinds themselves. Furniture firms usually send pattern books of these materials when applied for, giving the price per yard and also the price of the whole blinds including making and fixing.

Mantelpiece Decoration.—The decoration of the mantelpiece and its surroundings must conform with the general decorative scheme of the room. Period furnishing requires that the chimney-piece decoration should have a special treatment, and its decoration should therefore be placed in the hands of the firm which is supplying the rest of the furniture.

The ugly gilt-edged mirror which formed the conventional chimney-piece decoration of the time of our grandmothers is now mercifully buried in oblivion. Artistic wooden chimney-pieces and overmantles combined now form part of the decorative equipment of most tastefully furnished houses. These are constructed of mahogany and oak or in other dark woodwork for dining-room and library, and in wood painted white for drawing-room and morning-room. The mantelpieces of bedrooms do not require the elaborate treatment given to those

Illustration showing Artistic Chimney-piece and Club Curb.

of the reception rooms. Either a picture or a small overmantle may be placed over the chimney-piece of the latter, and where the woodwork is carried up over the mantelpiece it is only carried up to a very small height.

Where there are no fitted overmantles in connection with the chimney-pieces of the reception rooms the latter must be bought separately. Very pretty overmantles may be purchased in oak, walnut, mahogany, and wood painted white.

Mantelpiece drapery is seldom seen now, but at times it is absolutely necessary to hide an ugly chimney-piece. In these circumstances the material used should be as light and graceful in appearance as possible. Pretty liberty silks and satins in the delicate art shades make most effective draperies.

Tiled hearths and marble fenders are much favoured in present-day house decoration. Brass and steel fenders should always be kept well polished. A very ornamental type of fender is that known as the "Club Curb." This consists of plain brass or iron rails which reach at times to a height of two feet and which are surmounted by an upholstered seat, usually of morocco. Sometimes the upholstery goes all round the top of the curb, but more usually the seats are only at the sides and corners. A pair of fire-dogs and the necessary fire-irons, *i.e.* shovel, poker, and tongs, should form part of the equipment of the fire-place. Very useful for morning-room, study, and bedrooms are the little combination set of fire-irons now sold, which fit on to a specially constructed stand. These are inexpensive to buy and look very well. As the stand is of a good height the fire-irons can easily be taken from it without having to stoop as in the case of the ordinary fire-dogs.

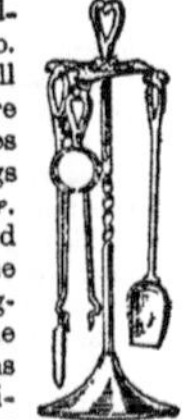

Fire-Irons.

FURNISHING THE VARIOUS ROOMS

The Drawing-Room.—This is essentially the domain of the house mistress, and it is stamped as it were with her own individuality. The woman of refinement and taste makes her personality felt not only in the general furniture scheme of the room, but in the many dainty little finishing touches without which there always seems to be something lacking in even the best furnished drawing-rooms. This something is invariably absent from the drawing-room of the wealthy uncultured woman, who, though she may have had the good sense to give *carte blanche* to a reliable furniture dealer in regard to the choice of furniture, yet fails utterly in imparting that atmosphere of refinement conveyed by the subtle touch in the arrangement of details which is always characteristic of the drawing-room of the gentlewoman, however poorly furnished it may be.

All stiffness and awkwardness of arrangement in drawing-room furniture should be avoided. There should be an air of daintiness and grace and at the same time of cosiness about the room. The drawing-room of to-day is not a room for show but a room for use. It is no longer thrown open on strictly state occasions, nor are children nowadays trained to look upon it as a sort of Bluebeard's chamber only to be entered upon occasions when both Sunday frocks and Sunday manners must be donned and the maxim "Little children may be seen, but not heard," most rigorously observed. There are still some middle-class people who keep their drawing-room as a show-room, only using it on "At Home" days and for other similar functions; but such rooms always wear an air of stiffness and lack of comfort which is often reflected in the manner of the house mistress upon the rare occasions when she is called upon to sit in it in state to do honour to her guests.

Pretty occasional tables and daintily upholstered tapestry settees, one or two cosy tapestry easy-chairs, a tea-table, a drawing-room cabinet, an escritoire, and a piano should be present in every well-furnished drawing-room, to say nothing of such ornamental accessories as tapestry screens, flower-pots on stands, and the innumerable trifles which go to complete the furnishing of a really cosy room. Needless to say, heavy furniture of all kinds should be banished; everything in the room should be as dainty and artistic as possible.

Inlaid mahogany and rosewood are largely used in the construction of present-day drawing-room furniture. There is much that is French in the modern style, which is of graceful and refined design. Furniture manufacturers seem to have taken as their groundwork some of the best characteristics of the old world styles,

Corner Chair.

Occasional Table.

evolving from them a style particularly suitable for present-day needs. Drawing-room chairs are of a dainty spindle-legged design, the pretty little corner chair being especially typical of present-day drawing-room suites. Tables are small, light, and graceful. The needs of the slender purse are particularly well catered for by the modern furniture dealer. People of average means are no longer compelled to furnish their drawing-rooms with all sorts of odds and ends, and chairs which quarrel with each other in both colour and design are now seldom seen in even the most poorly furnished rooms, as complete furniture suites in inlaid mahogany or satinwood can be purchased for quite a moderate sum. The less expensive suites do not contain so many pieces as the more expensive kinds; sometimes only a settee, two small chairs, two corner chairs, and a round table are provided. In these circumstances the furnishing scheme must be completed by purchasing by degrees one or two upholstered arm-chairs, and, if possible, a small sum should be expended upon one or two dainty little occasional tables to match the rest of the suite. A cabinet and an escritoire might also be added as soon as the purse allows. The settees provided with drawing-room suites are always of the same spindle-legged pattern as the chairs, and an added air of cosiness will therefore be imparted by the addition of a pretty drawing-room Chesterfield or some other similar type of softly upholstered settee or couch. A jardinière to match the furniture will also be effective; and where a brass standard lamp with a soft delicately coloured silk shade, may be had, the effect of the pretty subdued light it gives at night is very pleasing. A little "tea companion," upon which plates of cake and bread and butter may be handed round at afternoon tea, is a piece of furniture the usefulness of which must be by no means overlooked. A tasteful fire-screen, preferably one draped in delicate silk, liberty style, should be placed before the grate. The clock should be in keeping with the general daintiness of the room. Very pretty designs may be had in the refined Sheraton and Chippendale styles for quite a moderate outlay. An art tapestry screen in a framework of mahogany or any other wood of which the furniture may be composed may also be added with effect. The drawing-room is essentially a room to which little extras may be added by degrees, but—and this is very important—the additions must always be in keeping with the general furniture scheme.

The larger the room the more advantageously can the daintiness of drawing-room furniture be displayed. It is a mistake, however, to crowd too much furniture into a small room, not only from the point of view of space, but owing to the fact that its effect will be completely lost and the room made to look smaller than it is.

A small drawing-room should, if possible, be papered in white. A white satin striped paper with a very narrow floral frieze would be effective. (For Drawing-room Decoration, see p. 15.) Water-colour sketches and delicate engravings are the most suitable pictures for drawing-room walls.

A pretty Indian carpet with a light ground makes a very effective floor covering. Wilton, Brussels, and Axminster carpets in the lighter tones are also suitable (see carpets, p. 20). Where a seamless woven square carpet is used in a small room plain Japanese matting will be found to make a very good surround.

Many drawing-rooms are furnished nowadays in reproductions of famous period styles such as Chippendale, Adam, Sheraton, Hepplewhite, Louis XV., or Louis XVI. Needless to say, where such a style is adopted everything must be in keeping. Chairs of one period must not be mixed up with tables of another, and a bureau of still another epoch; wall papers and carpets must also be chosen in accordance with the particular furniture scheme.

Arrangement of Furniture.—A great deal will depend upon the suitable arrangement of the room. The position of a piano, for instance, has spoiled the effect of many otherwise well-arranged drawing-rooms. Very often it is necessary to place an upright piano against the wall through exigencies of space. A more graceful effect, however, is usually obtained by placing it at a convenient angle. Where it is an old and shabby-looking instrument the face of it can be turned towards a corner of the room hidden from all but the pianist, whilst the back can be draped in silk of a delicate art shade. Whenever an upright piano is placed with its back turned away from the wall it should be draped in this manner.

Grand pianos give an air of "finish" to a drawing-room which is achieved by no other means. A pretty silk cover should be kept over the top if photographs or ornaments of any kind are to stand upon it. It is bad taste to have too many ornaments or photographs on a piano, a panel photograph in a very handsome frame and one or two choice ornaments being quite sufficient. It requires a very large room to show off a grand piano to advantage. Demi-grands look very well, and the "Baby Grands" are very suitable both for large and moderately sized rooms. Piano-stools are not now inartistic as of yore. The high round piano-stools are things of the past; more attention is now paid to both comfort and appearance in regard to this piece of furniture. The design pictured in our illustration is much in vogue at present.

Piano-Stool.

Choice of a Piano.—In choosing a piano four important things must be considered, *i.e.* size, volume of sound, tone, and touch. In connection with the first two the size of the room must be taken into consideration so that both size and volume of sound are in proportion. In regard to tone, where singing is an accomplishment in the family it must be seen that the piano has a good singing tone. The pianist of the family should also try it before it is purchased to see that it is in every way to his (or her) satisfaction in regard to touch. There are many makes of pianos noted for their soft beautiful tones, such as those bearing the names of Rud Ibach, Sohn; Bechstein, Erard, and innumerable others.

Hall, Staircase, and Landings.—Within recent years good taste in hall furniture has decidedly increased. There is a leaning towards the artistic in every way. Instead of the one time conventional combined hat-rack and umbrella-stand we find the quaint, old world monk's settle and the separate umbrella-stand and neat wall rack for hats and coats. Oak is a very favourite wood for hall furniture. Imposing looking richly carved oak settles with chairs to match are pieces of furniture upon which very large sums of money may be spent, but the needs of the shopper with the slender purse have been by no means overlooked in this connection. Plain artistically designed settles may be had in fumed oak for as small a sum as £1, 1s.; a neat fumed oak umbrella-stand can be purchased for six or seven shillings, whilst high-backed oak chairs may also be had for very moderate prices. Where there is an outer hall or vestibule both hat-rack and umbrella-stand should be placed there. A grandfather's clock is a very effective piece of hall furniture. It should always occupy a prominent position near the staircase. Mats to be placed outside the various room doors should not be overlooked when furnishing the hall. There should also be a good fibre mat in the vestibule.

Hat-Rack.

If the hall is a bright one some pictures can be displayed to advantage upon the walls, also any military or hunting trophies (see Hall Decoration, p. 16). Where there is a high white dado crowned with a projecting rail or shelf, one or two good pieces of china might be displayed upon this.

Umbrella-Stand.

Where the hall is carpeted staircase and landing carpets should match the hall carpet. In high houses, however, the flight of stairs leading to the servants' room may be covered with oilcloth. If a tenant is fortunate enough to secure a house with a tiled hall, she will be spared the expense of purchasing a floor-covering of any kind, for a few mats will be all that is necessary. One or two pictures may be hung on the walls of the stairway if the light is sufficiently good for them to be properly seen.

Where there are good landings these are capable of tasteful decorative treatment. In houses where there is a large alcoved landing leading from the first flight of stairs to a side wing of the house, the alcove should be prettily draped with curtains. A low-standing book-case enamelled white could be placed upon the side facing the stairs with one or two choice pieces of art pottery displayed upon it. A small table and two chairs could occupy the curtained recess to the left. Those who are the fortunate possessors of some good piece of statuary might display it here to advantage. One or two tall jardinières containing palms

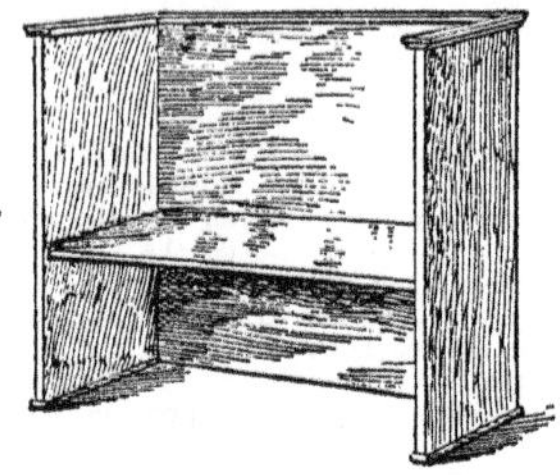

Monk's Settle.

would also be effective. Such a landing, if cosily furnished, can easily be used as a smoking lounge. We do not all possess large square landings, however, but even very tiny landings, if of the proper shape, can be gracefully treated by means of hangings and appropriately placed jardinières.

There are so very many different types of halls and landings that it is rather difficult to lay down hard and fast rules for their treatment. The ordinary passage hall does not lend itself to much decoration. Very often there is only room for settle, hat-rack, and umbrella-stand. Chairs are really unnecessary where there is a good oak settle, but they should always form part of the hall furniture where there is none.

The Lounge Hall.—This description covers two widely different types of hall. The large square hall of the country mansion, with its carved wood panelling, deep wide staircase, and handsome furniture, need not here be dealt with. Such halls are only possessed as a rule by people with whom money is no object and who can afford to pay for the most expert advice upon the question of furnishing. But there is another type of square hall which is often met with nowadays, *i.e.* that which forms a characteristic feature of the modern type of bungalow or flat. In the smaller flats where there is only one sitting-room a hall of this kind has to do duty as another sitting-room or lounge. In these circumstances it should be furnished as much like a room as possible. Screens should be used to keep off the draught from the front door, whilst curtains should hang from the doors of the rooms which lead out into the hall. A cork carpet in a shade of art green could be used as a floor-covering, with two or three warm cosy-looking mats scattered over it. Umbrella-stand and hat-rack should be banished away in some hidden corner. Near the fire-place might be placed a glass-fronted cupboard, painted white, in which either dinner or tea-set could be displayed. If space permits there might also be a low white enamelled book-case, upon which one or two pretty vases in Wedgwood blue could stand. Two low chairs and a cushioned settee would complete the "sitting-room" illusion. A bright fire burning in the grate in winter will increase the homely and comfortable appearance of the hall sitting-room. In flats with only one sitting-room such an arrangement will be found not only cosy but convenient. Care must be taken, however, to reduce draughts to a minimum. All doors leading on the hall should be kept closed when it is in use and the portières drawn well over them.

Dining-Room.—Large sums of money are very often spent upon dining-room furniture with very poor results. There is a tradition with most people that the dining-room must be sombre and heavy looking, and in the effort of living up to that tradition they often succeed in turning out a room which is so gloomy in appearance that to spend any amount of time in it is to become hopelessly depressed.

This is a great mistake. The dining-room, it is true, must be furnished in a dignified manner, but cheerfulness must not be banished from it. We have gone past the days of the ponderous Victorian sideboard and hideous horse-hair chairs. All should realise the fact that our dining-rooms may be dignified and at the same time pleasing and artistic.

There was a time when the cost of furnishing the simplest type of dining-room was so great that people of slender means could seldom afford to furnish the room outright, but were forced to purchase the various articles by degrees. Nowadays things have changed—furniture manufacturers supply complete suites at reasonable prices, as a visit to any of their show-rooms can prove, and, what is more, the workmanship is good and the design excellent.

In former times the design of cheap furniture was seldom good, hence the public belief in the "cheap and nasty" theory which is still so widely spread. It is true that to obtain really good furniture one must pay a good price, but the fact remains that manufacturers and dealers

Model Dining-Room for small Flat (*Maple*).

A Simple Bedroom (*Heal & Sons*).

are studying more and more the needs of those to whom money is an object, recognising that it is not of people with unlimited wealth at their disposal with which to indulge their most extravagant tastes that the major part of the great army of shoppers is composed, but rather of those who have only a certain sum to spend and who must necessarily keep within its limits.

Dinner-Waggon.

First of all, the dining-room must be suitabl[illegible] decorated (see p. 15). A few well-chosen oi[illegible] paintings and family portraits (if any) may ador[illegible] the walls. Failing these some very good en[illegible]gravings in frames of the same wood as th[illegible] furniture. A good Turkey carpet is the carp[illegible] *par excellence* for a dining-room, but we c[illegible] all afford to indulge in luxuries of th[illegible]
Let the carpet at any rate be as [illegible]
appearance as possible, with a good pi[illegible]
mahogany, and walnut are the princ[illegible]
utilised in the manufacture of dining-[illegible]
ture. Especially inexpensive, and [illegible]
time good, furniture may be had [illegible]
known as "fumed oak."

At one time even the cheap[illegible]
sideboards cost a fair sum, and [illegible]
this article of furniture had to b[illegible]
the list of many a young coupl[illegible]
very small means. Nowadays [illegible]
style of fumed oak sideboard, [illegible]
to a Welsh dresser in app[illegible]
obtained for an outlay of on[illegible]
This type of sideboard is very [illegible]
room decoration. It is a [illegible]
very fashionable at the pre[illegible]
two pieces of china should [illegible]
on the shelves. Dutch fa[illegible]
and white china looks p[illegible]
the expensive sideboards [illegible]
fashion of curving is [illegible]
in front of these glass [illegible]
conspicuous by its abse[illegible]
A dining-room can [illegible]
cost of between £18 [illegible]
including all necessari[illegible]

the kind described, some high-backed fumed oak chairs neatly upholstered in green leather, a good oak dining-table, a dinner-waggon, or butler's tray, an easy-chair, a small writing-table, and the necessary equipment in the way of cloth table-cover, curtains, cornice pole, fender, fire-irons, coal-scuttle, carpet and surround hearthrug. Where strict economy has to be practised the easy-chair and the writing-table may be omitted. Very inexpensive black iron coal-scuttles, gipsy pattern, may be purchased for a few shillings, and can be made to do duty where a better kind cannot be afforded. A pretty cloth or art serge table-cover can be made at home for a very small outlay, and casement curtains may also be made for a trifling cost by the clever home worker. (See Furnishing Lists, p. 36.)

Morning and Breakfast-Room.—These two titles are bracketed together because in the generality of houses, where there are but three or four reception rooms at most, the terms "morning-room" and "breakfast-room" are synonymous. The "breakfast" or "morning" room may be taken to indicate the most generally useful room in the house. It is writing-room, sewing-room, and school-room in turn. Many a morning is spent in this room by the busy house mistress in writing letters, going over accounts, and attending to innu[illegible]able small household details. It is also [illegible]he room where the elder children, em[illegible] from the nursery, prepare their less[illegible] partake of that ever favourite meal [illegible]od—the fi[illegible]lock tea.

The furnit[illegible] morning-ro[illegible] fast-room [illegible]fore be ch[illegible]

as a good one may be purchased for about £3. Fumed oak chairs with rush seats may be purchased for from 12s. each. In addition, there should be a large lounge easy-chair or two small tapestry arm-chairs, a small writing-table for the special use of the house mistress, and a book-case or some book-shelves for the children's school books.

Where there are no children, the morning-room will be probably utilised as her own special room by the mistress of the house. In these circumstances she will be able to give full scope to her taste for dainty and graceful effects. Chairs may be upholstered in tapestry, pretty engravings can be hung upon the walls, and, apart from the sideboard, which is a necessity in a breakfast-room, the whole scheme of furnishing may be such that it might be aptly termed a "boudoir."

There are many possibilities in the furnishing of a morning-room, possibilities which must always, however, be guided by individual circumstances.

The Library.—There should be an air of restfulness about the library, conducive to reading and study. A flat leather top desk with drawers on either side should be placed in a good light. The writing equipment should be complete in every way—inkstand, pen-rest, blotter and letter weight, a stand for notepaper and envelopes and telegram forms and postcards should all be there and should be kept neat and tidy. To go with this desk there should be a low desk-chair—the round leather upholstered revolving-chair is the most comfortable type. A very large arm-chair in which the master of the house can lounge at ease while reading one of his favourite works is also

Flat Library Desk

n the well-furnished library. Near ɔuld be one of the ever-handy re-cases from which the reader may me at will. A large stationary also be necessary. This should ble shelves in order that books ›e placed upon it. A very good ng book-case may be purchased · £3. One or two high-backed chairs should also be in the room, and a good hassock footstool should be placed near the easy-chair.

In houses where there is little money to spend upon book-cases and other similar articles of furniture, much may be done by the home worker towards its equipment. With a little knowledge of carpentering inexpensive shelves can be made and fitted round the walls. These should always have some sort of border, not only as a finish but to keep off the dust. It may be often found advantageous to purchase the writing-table from one of the large office-furnishing firms, as very often these firms have second-hand goods which they are willing to sell at quite a moderate sum. Desk-chairs may often also be purchased in this way. A little smokers' cabinet should also find a place upon the wall.

Revolving Book-case.

There should always be dark curtains in the library—red or green are particularly suitable. Where there is a portière over the door it should be of the same colour as the window curtains. (For Library Decoration, see p. 16.)

Bedroom Furniture.—The stiffness, ugliness, and lack of comfort generally which characterised the furniture of the early Victorian era, was in no way more clearly demonstrated than in regard to furniture for the bedroom. Happily the heavy, cumbersome high chest of drawers, the ungainly wardrobe, and the deal muslin-bedecked table which, surmounted by a looking-glass of the most conventional pattern, did duty as toilet-table in even the best rooms of the average middle-class household, are now things of the past, at any rate with all those who prefer the present-day artistic furniture to the atrocities of the early Victorian tradition. There are still some people, it is true, who, whilst sparing neither trouble nor expense in the suitable furnishing of dining-room, drawing-room, and other reception rooms, barely give a thought to the furnishing of their bedrooms. So long as the reception rooms are nice anything will do for the bedrooms seems to be their guiding principle, and whilst money is spent ungrudgingly upon the decoration of the other rooms a totally inadequate sum is set apart for the furnishing of those rooms in which after all they spend a very considerable portion of the twenty-four hours.

Happily in these enlightened days there are comparatively few people who take so decidedly unenlightened a view of things. With those who do, it must be presumed that tradition dies hard and that they are simply carrying on the tastes of their grandmothers. Sensible are studying more and more the needs of those to whom money is an object, recognising that it is not of people with unlimited wealth at their disposal with which to indulge their most extravagant tastes that the major part of the great army of shoppers is composed, but rather of those who have only a certain sum to spend, and who must necessarily keep within its limits.

Dinner-Waggon.

First of all, the dining-room must be suitably decorated (see p. 15). A few well-chosen oil-paintings and family portraits (if any) may adorn the walls. Failing these some very good engravings in frames of the same wood as the furniture. A good Turkey carpet is the carpet *par excellence* for a dining-room, but we cannot all afford to indulge in luxuries of the kind. Let the carpet at any rate be as soft in appearance as possible, with a good pile. Oak, mahogany, and walnut are the principal woods utilised in the manufacture of dining-room furniture. Especially inexpensive, and at the same time good, furniture may be had in what is known as "fumed oak."

At one time even the cheapest makes of sideboards cost a fair sum, and so very often this article of furniture had to be banished from the list of many a young couple furnishing on very small means. Nowadays a most artistic style of fumed oak sideboard, something akin to a Welsh dresser in appearance, may be obtained for an outlay of only a few pounds. This type of sideboard is very effective in dining-room decoration. It is a type also which is very fashionable at the present time. One or two pieces of china should always be displayed on the shelves, Dutch fashion. Blue or blue and white china looks prettiest with oak. Of the expensive sideboards in the old Dutch styles richness of carving is the chief characteristic. In most of these glass in any shape or form is conspicuous by its absence.

A dining-room can be well furnished at a cost of between £18 and £20, the furniture including an inexpensive fumed oak dresser of the kind described, some high-backed fumed oak chairs neatly upholstered in green leather, a good oak dining-table, a dinner-waggon, or butler's tray, an easy-chair, a small writing-table, and the necessary equipment in the way of cloth table-cover, curtains, cornice pole, fender, fire-irons, coal-scuttle, carpet and surround hearthrug. Where strict economy has to be practised the easy-chair and the writing-table may be omitted. Very inexpensive black iron coal-scuttles, gipsy pattern, may be purchased for a few shillings, and can be made to do duty where a better kind cannot be afforded. A pretty cloth or art serge table-cover can be made at home for a very small outlay, and casement curtains may also be made for a trifling cost by the clever home worker. (See Furnishing Lists, p. 36.)

Morning and Breakfast-Room.—These two titles are bracketed together because in the generality of houses, where there are but three or four reception rooms at most, the terms "morning-room" and "breakfast-room" are synonymous. The "breakfast" or "morning" room may be taken to indicate the most generally useful room in the house. It is writing-room, sewing-room, and school-room in turn. Many a morning is spent in this room by the busy house mistress in writing letters, going over accounts, and attending to innumerable small household details. It is also often the room where the elder children, emancipated from the nursery, prepare their lessons, and partake of that ever favourite meal of childhood—the five o'clock tea.

The furniture for the morning-room or breakfast-room must therefore be chosen with due

Gate-legged Table.

regard to the uses to which it will be put. As meals are to be served in this room a sideboard will be necessary. This can be much smaller and of lighter design than that of the dining-room. Then there must be a table—a fair-sized round gate-leg table of fumed oak would be useful and at the same time inexpensive, as a good one may be purchased for about £3. Fumed oak chairs with rush seats may be purchased for from 12s. each. In addition, there should be a large lounge easy-chair or two small tapestry arm-chairs, a small writing-table for the special use of the house mistress, and a book-case or some book-shelves for the children's school books.

Where there are no children, the morning-room will be probably utilised as her own special room by the mistress of the house. In these circumstances she will be able to give full scope to her taste for dainty and graceful effects. Chairs may be upholstered in tapestry, pretty engravings can be hung upon the walls, and, apart from the sideboard, which is a necessity in a breakfast-room, the whole scheme of furnishing may be such that it might be aptly termed a "boudoir."

There are many possibilities in the furnishing of a morning-room, possibilities which must always, however, be guided by individual circumstances.

The Library.—There should be an air of restfulness about the library, conducive to reading and study. A flat leather top desk with drawers on either side should be placed in a good light. The writing equipment should be complete in every way—inkstand, pen-rest, blotter and letter weight, a stand for notepaper and envelopes and telegram forms and postcards should all be there and should be kept neat and tidy. To go with this desk there should be a low desk-chair—the round leather upholstered revolving-chair is the most comfortable type. A very large arm-chair in which the master of the house can lounge at ease while reading one of his favourite works is also

Flat Library Desk

a necessity in the well-furnished library. Near this chair should be one of the ever-handy revolving book-cases from which the reader may select a volume at will. A large stationary book-case will also be necessary. This should be with adjustable shelves in order that books of all sizes can be placed upon it. A very good sectional extending book-case may be purchased for a little over £3. One or two high-backed chairs should also be in the room, and a good hassock footstool should be placed near the easy-chair.

In houses where there is little money to spend upon book-cases and other similar articles of furniture, much may be done by the home worker towards its equipment. With a little knowledge of carpentering inexpensive shelves can be made and fitted round the walls. These should always have some sort of border, not only as a finish but to keep off the dust. It may be often found advantageous to purchase the writing-table from one of the large office-furnishing firms, as very often these firms have second-hand goods which they are willing to sell at quite a moderate sum. Desk-chairs may often also be purchased in this way. A little smokers' cabinet should also find a place upon the wall.

Revolving Book-case.

There should always be dark curtains in the library—red or green are particularly suitable. Where there is a portière over the door it should be of the same colour as the window curtains. (For Library Decoration, see p. 16.)

Bedroom Furniture.—The stiffness, ugliness, and lack of comfort generally which characterised the furniture of the early Victorian era, was in no way more clearly demonstrated than in regard to furniture for the bedroom. Happily the heavy, cumbersome high chest of drawers, the ungainly wardrobe, and the deal muslin-bedecked table which, surmounted by a looking-glass of the most conventional pattern, did duty as toilet-table in even the best rooms of the average middle-class household, are now things of the past, at any rate with all those who prefer the present-day artistic furniture to the atrocities of the early Victorian tradition. There are still some people, it is true, who, whilst sparing neither trouble nor expense in the suitable furnishing of dining-room, drawing-room, and other reception rooms, barely give a thought to the furnishing of their bedrooms. So long as the reception rooms are nice anything will do for the bedrooms seems to be their guiding principle, and whilst money is spent ungrudgingly upon the decoration of the other rooms a totally inadequate sum is set apart for the furnishing of those rooms in which after all they spend a very considerable portion of the twenty-four hours.

Happily in these enlightened days there are comparatively few people who take so decidedly unenlightened a view of things. With those who do, it must be presumed that tradition dies hard and that they are simply carrying on the tastes of their grandmothers. Sensible people are keenly alive to the fact that, apart from the usual number of hours spent in the bedroom, intervals of illness are apt to occur in the lives of every one of us. In these circumstances should not our bedrooms be as bright, cheery, and as pleasing to the eye as possible? Neither ungainly inartistic furniture nor hideous wall paper will be conducive to the cheerfulness of an invalid in that period of convalescence, during which a morbid and depressed state of mind will do more than anything else to retard recovery. On the other hand, a prettily decorated room, with a bright pleasing wall paper, tasteful furniture, however simple, and a cheery aspect have more influence in keeping up the spirits of the invalid and assisting her to a speedy recovery than one would generally suppose.

The ideal bedroom has a sunny aspect. There is something especially exhilarating about the morning sun. Care should be taken, however, to see that the rays of the sun do not beat down direct upon the forehead of the sleeper on those summer mornings when sunrise occurs at a time when she has not completed more than three-quarters of her full amount of sleep. Needless to say, suitable blinds should be provided for every bedroom, and these should be kept well lowered, or, if there is a casement window, the curtains should be drawn. When the plan of the room allows of such an arrangement, the bed should be placed so that the window does not face, but comes to one side of it. In this way the discomfort of the early morning glare will be avoided.

It is also essential that the bed should not be placed in a draught. The head of the bed should never be facing the window, for instance, neither should the fire-place be on the same side of the room as the door. If only for purposes of ventilation, there should always be a fire-place in the bedroom—an open gas-fire is especially useful, as it does away with the labour of setting fires and carrying up coals, and can be turned off and on as required without involving any trouble.

When taking a house a woman should be careful in looking over the bedrooms to note if they contain any fitted cupboards. These are a boon in every household, and, painted a pretty white to match the woodwork, they add considerably to the ornamentation of the room. The presence or absence of these cupboards should always form a consideration in the taking of a house. It is also advisable to study the structure of the walls. In many cases where cupboards are lacking there may be convenient alcoves where these may easily be fitted, or, if money is a consideration, they may be utilised for making pretty curtain cupboards. Suitably placed alcoves are capable of treatment, by which they may add considerably to the decoration of a room. An alcove just over the bed, for instance, lends itself to tasteful curtain drapery. Where one occurs over the window it may be treated in the same way.

In the Queen Anne style of house especially, many of the quaint old-world casement windows are set into deep alcoves. What prettier effect may be obtained than by furnishing the window with a dainty chintz-covered window-seat, and draping the alcove with head valance and curtains of chintz to match that used in the upholstering of the seat?

The furnishing of the bedroom should be studied first of all from the point of view of hygiene and comfort. Where there is a fitted carpet to the room, or a square carpet which goes under the bed, it should be seen that the mattress of the latter stands at a sufficient height from the floor to enable the dust to be easily taken from underneath it. There are many makes of bedsteads nowadays, more especially those of the various modern French styles, which are so low as to almost touch the floor, leaving little or no space between the floor and the mattress. Such a style of bed may be artistic, but it is certainly far from comfortable, and in no circumstances should comfort be made to give way to art, the ideal furniture being essentially that in which art and comfort are combined.

Medical authorities have laid much stress upon the fact that carpets in bedrooms are merely harbingers of dust and dirt, and therefore unhygienic. They maintain that there should be no carpets under beds, as these cannot always be moved every day for sweeping purposes and dust is apt to accumulate there because unseen. Bedroom manufacturers have, however, found a way out of this difficulty, and Messrs. Heal & Sons, of Tottenham Court Road, London, sell beds which are furnished with patent rails upon which they can be moved with the greatest ease.

There is no doubt that linoleum is the best floor covering for a bedroom from the point of hygiene. It can be easily swept and washed, and one or two nice rugs will serve as a concession to the claims of comfort and warmth.

The next best thing would of course be a square carpet with a linoleum or a stained floor surround. There are people who object, however, to the cold look of the bare boards or of linoleum even if they only appear on the border of the room. In these circumstances a plain felt surround to tone with the carpet is very useful.

The brass bedstead is much in vogue at the present day. It is not the cumbersome-looking object of yore, but a well-designed and useful piece of furniture. When fitted with swinging Italian wings it can be prettily draped with dainty cretonne or other artistic hangings to tone with the colour scheme of the room. Draperies of this kind suspended from wings, and wall draperies hung in artistic fashion from the wall against which the head of the bed stands, are the only form of bed-curtains used nowadays, excepting in the case of the old-time four-poster

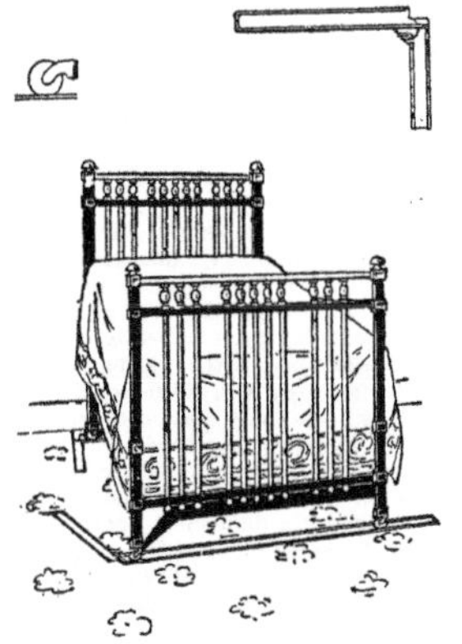

Bedstead on Metal Tramway.

which is still to be found in many homes, and revivals of which many bed manufacturers are placing upon the market. Valances are as a rule limited to the latter type of bedstead.

The wooden bedsteads now on the market are artistic in every way and free from that ugliness which characterised those of Victorian days. They are no longer ungainly, cumbersome pieces of furniture, too heavy to move and consequently difficult to clean. Fitted with all the most up to date improvements, including iron frames and wire mattresses, they do not now act as harbingers of dust and dirt. To the many hygienic disadvantages of the old-time wooden bedstead may be ascribed the subsequent craze for *anything* in metal, however ugly in pattern. Some of the most ornamental wooden bedsteads are those of inlaid mahogany in Sheraton style. Iron bedsteads can be had for the most moderate outlay. A white enamelled iron bedstead always looks dainty and clean. It is one of the best and most useful types of inexpensive bedsteads, and looks especially well with brass tops. The ordinary low iron bedsteads are very suitable for servants' rooms.

Bedding.—It is of the utmost importance that the bedding should be of the best. Many people are apt to study show more than comfort when furnishing their bedrooms, with the result that the important question of bedding is very often neglected. It never answers to purchase very cheap bedding, for the latter is apt to prove only too dear in the long run. A cheap mattress is not only uncomfortable, but it is an actual menace to the health.

Woven wire spring mattresses with good horse-hair or wool over mattresses should be used where possible. Good hair mattresses, however, are apt to be somewhat costly, and therefore are not always within reach of the average purse. Good wool mattresses are infinitely preferable to cheap hair ones. They should in all cases be purchased from a reliable furniture dealer, preferably from a firm who make a speciality of bedroom furniture and bedding, for in this case good value is assured.

In buying mattresses never be misled by an attractive covering, which too often hides much that is deficient in the quality of the material of which it is comprised. For this reason it is seldom advisable to purchase what are described as "bargains" at sales. The common qualities of horse-hair mattresses are filled with various sorts of "short hair" which afford no hold to the "ties," and therefore tend to move and work into those uncomfortable "lumps" which so often turn a bed into a regular instrument of torture. On the other hand, the fine long horse-hair used in good

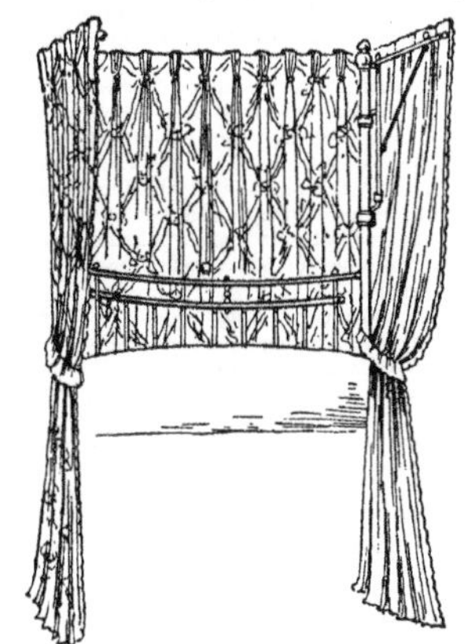

Italian Wing-Drapery.

mattresses gives a proper hold to the "ties" and is kept in place by them. The French mattresses, which contain a special quality of hair mixed with white wool, are exceedingly soft and comfortable. Cheap flock mattresses, which are made up from any sort of rags, should be always avoided.

The wire mattress should be covered with a piece of ticking or Hessian to prevent it from rubbing the hair mattress which is placed over it.

The colour scheme of a bedroom should be as bright and cheery as possible, and always chosen with due regard to the aspect of the room and to the furniture which it will contain (see p. 16). Where the hygienic method of covering the floor with linoleum or cork carpet is adopted, care should be taken to prevent the room from having a bare appearance by putting down a number of warm and cosy-looking rugs of as good a quality as can be procured for the sum available. Everything that tends to harbour dust and dirt should be absent from the bedroom. There should never be an excess of ornamental trifles and knick-knacks about the room. Girls are especially prone to collect these little ornaments, to the despair of many a hard-working housemaid.

Furniture.—The best-designed bedroom furniture of to-day combines much of the artistic effects of the famous epochs in furniture history with a strict attention to convenience of construction as necessitated by modern needs. Modern bedroom furniture manufacturers also make a special feature of reproductions from the antique. Needless to say, when a bedroom is furnished in accordance with a certain period, decoration, carpet, hangings, all must conform with this furniture scheme.

Oak, mahogany, satinwood, rosewood are very favourite materials for bedroom suites. There is also a great vogue at present for white enamelled furniture. This fashion comes as something in the nature of a blessing in disguise for the woman with a slender purse, as the white enamelled suites show a wide range of prices, the cheaper kinds being procurable for a few pounds.

Every furniture suite should comprise a wardrobe, a dressing-table, a wash-stand and two chairs, although in some of the more inexpensive suites only toilet table, chest of drawers, and wash-stand are included. When the latter is not fitted with rails for towels a towel-horse should be provided. It should be ascertained that the locks of drawers and wardrobe cupboards are in order, that the drawers open and shut easily, and that the inside of each piece of furniture is in as good condition as the outside. The wash-stand should have a marble top and be tiled at the back. A sheet of emdeca might also be fixed up at the back of the wash-stand instead of the ordinary "splasher" for the protection of the wall. A cosy easy-chair and a table should also be included in the bedroom furniture where possible. Very daintily upholstered little tapestry arm-chairs may be obtained at quite moderate prices. For an inexpensively furnished room an ordinary basket chair painted to tone with the furniture and with pretty cretonne cushions can be made to answer the purpose. A box ottoman daintily upholstered in cretonne is a most useful piece of furniture, more especially in flats where the cupboard accommodation is necessarily limited. This may be either purchased from a furniture shop or fashioned by the deft fingers of the home upholsterer. Pretty cretonne, chintz, lace, or other washable curtains are the most suitable for the bedroom. Heavy hangings of any kind should be avoided. The walls should not be covered with pictures—one or two engravings in light-coloured frames will be sufficient.

The toilet-table linen should always be fresh and spotless. The pretty duchesse sets consisting of a narrow lace-edged or hem-stitched toilet cover and mats are the most suitable for the present-day type of table. These sets are often used also for the wash-stand. They are apt to get very wet, however, if they are left on during the toilet ablutions, and for this reason most people prefer to do without them. The general equipment of the toilet-table in regard to pin-cushions (well supplied with pins), hat-pin and hair-pin tidies must not be neglected. Any silver displayed on the table should be kept clean and well polished. All these are details, attention to which will go a long way to securing the cosy effect in bedroom decorations which some people find it so hard to achieve.

THE DRESSING-ROOM

The decoration of a dressing-room should conform with that of the bedroom which it adjoins. It should contain a good roomy gentleman's wardrobe, a shaving-stand with mirror, also washstand and suit-case stand. A shaving-stand is to be preferred to the ordinary toilet-table, not only because it takes up much less room, though this is an important consideration as dressing-room space is usually limited, but also because a shaving-glass is much more easily adjusted to the correct angle required by the person shaving, and, being very light, it is easily moved to any convenient position.

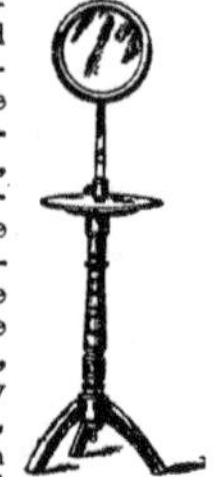

Shaving-Mirror

Toilet Ware.—Over-elaboration of design in toilet ware should be avoided in tastefully furnished homes. Artistic yet simple patterns should be chosen. Patterns after the style of Wedgwood and Spode are much favoured by those whose furnishing is on artistic lines. Plain colours and simple shapes go best with the present-day style of bedroom furniture. The self-coloured art wares are largely used, and with these the quaintly shaped ewer with a spout like that of a teapot is often seen. On the whole, the ewers of a more conventional design are preferable to these.

In addition to the regular toilet set there should be a white china slop-pail, a water-bottle, and a glass in every bedroom.

THE BATH-ROOM

In the bath-room the sanitary fittings should be beyond reproach. In a rented house this will of course be the landlord's affair, so when looking over a house particular attention should be paid to the bath-room fittings. A good fitted iron bath of the latest type with taps for hot and cold water and waste and without any wooden casing is the best. Iron baths are preferable to the more luxurious porcelain, as the latter take a great deal of heat from the water, taxing the capacity of the kitchen range to the utmost, whereas with iron baths the heat of the water is retained. There are several methods of covering and finishing the interior surface of iron baths. Of these the porcelain enamel process is perhaps the most effective. Where this process has been applied the interior of the bath presents the same enamelled surface as earthenware—the enamel is also very durable.

A fitted lavatory basin with hot and cold water-supply is very desirable in a bath-room. Beyond the actual fittings very little furniture is required. There should be a towel-rail, a cane-seated chair, a stool, and a rack for sponges and soap to be hung on the wall next to the bath. One of the new bath-racks which fit across the centre of the bath to act as receptacle for the soap and sponge which the bather is actually using is also useful, as it does away with the necessity of reaching up whenever anything is required to the rack on the wall. A cork bath-mat and one or two warm bath-rugs are also necessary. There should also be a mirror on the wall, preferably the regulation bath-room mirror, with a drawer for brushes and combs. Cork carpet or linoleum are the best floor coverings for bath-rooms. (For Bath-room Wall Coverings, see p. 14.)

FURNISHING A BED-SITTING-ROOM

The bed-sitting-room represents the home of many a woman worker, who often takes more pride in the arrangement of the few simple articles she can call her own and the purchase of which in many instances have involved several little acts of self-sacrifice than does the possessor of the most luxurious furniture which money can buy.

It is wonderful what good results may be achieved with comparatively little outlay in the furnishing of a room of the kind, but necessity nearly always proves "the mother of invention," as the many ingenious yet simple contrivances which can be resorted to in furnishing a bed-sitting-room will go very far to prove.

The great object to be attained in furnishing a bed-sitting-room is to arrange it in such a manner that it gives no idea of a bedroom during the daytime. This result is not so difficult to achieve as one would suppose. Before taking the room, first of all ascertain that the wall-paper is not one of those glaring atrocities so often met with in the present-day lodging-house. If the room is suitable in every way and the wall-paper is the only drawback try and get the landlady to have it re-papered. If she is not disposed to do so offer to share part of the expense, which will not be much. Very simple and effective paper may be bought for an ordinary-sized room at an entire cost of from 15s. to 20s., including the work of hanging, and rather than put up with ugly wall-paper it will be found better in the long run to bear the cost oneself, if the landlady is obdurate on the point.

It is well to observe when taking the room if there are any cupboard fitments. A good

The "Divan" Bed.

roomy cupboard will save the purchase of a wardrobe which, besides being somewhat expensive to buy, would go a long way towards destroying the sitting-room illusion during the day. If a wardrobe is a necessity then one of the plain inexpensive bamboo cupboards without any glass in front would be the best to purchase. If the cost of a carpet cannot be afforded, stain the floor with permanganate of potash and polish it with bees'-wax and turpentine—the cost of this will be very trifling if you do the whole work yourself. Two or three pretty rugs may be purchased for a few shillings each. A fairly good art square carpet for a small room may be purchased for about 25s.; with this only the surround of the floor need be stained.

The furniture should include a bed which can be made to look as much like a couch in the daytime as possible—a perfectly flat bed of the camp variety without any upstanding head or foot-piece would do. With this there should be a good soft wool mattress. The bed should always be placed against the wall. In the daytime the bed-clothes can be neatly folded up and placed underneath the mattress, and the whole can be covered with a pretty Indian rug. Arrange on this one or two cushions and the result is a very cosy and effective-looking eastern divan. Special couch beds are now largely sold by furniture manufacturers.

A small plain deal table with one or two drawers may be purchased for five or six shillings. This should be stained a shade corresponding

Dwarf Cupboard.

with the rest of the furniture of the room and placed against the wall, and a good-sized looking-glass hung on the wall directly over it. The table will do duty as both toilet-table and writing-table. In the daytime the brushes and hand-mirror, together with the toilet-cover and mats, may be put aside in the drawer, their places being taken by a neat blotting-pad, an ink-stand, and the necessary writing materials. A dwarf cupboard could be made to do duty as a washstand, the toilet ware being placed inside the cupboard during the daytime; or, if the conventional wash-stand is preferred, this could be placed in a corner of the room and completely hidden by a large screen.

Then there must be a table large enough for meals. A round deal gate-leg table would be very useful, as the flaps can be let down and the table put on one side when the meal is not in progress. A large box ottoman in which clothes may be kept should also form part of the furniture; one or two smaller ones made out of sugar-boxes and upholstered in cretonne to match that of the ottoman would also be useful, acting as handy receptacles for millinery.

At one side of the room there should be a low table or cupboard which can do duty as a sideboard. The usefulness of corner brackets and shelves in a room of this kind cannot be too highly estimated. A hanging corner cupboard with a glass door would be especially useful for the display of a dainty afternoon tea service which cannot safely be trusted downstairs. Very many large general stores, such as Whiteley's in London, make a special feature of the sale of white wood articles for carving, poker work, or enamelling. Very well-designed pieces of furniture may be had in this white wood at a comparatively small cost. Thirty shillings will purchase a pretty china cabinet in white wood, whilst a small book-case with glass doors may be had for even less, and a hanging bookcase 27 inches high would cost from twelve to fifteen shillings. Small book-shelves and wall-brackets may be bought for from 1s. 11d. and upwards. When properly stained or enamelled this furniture looks very well indeed. For an extra change it can be stained at the shop where it is purchased

Three or four small chairs and one or two easy-chairs will complete the furniture of the room. Upholstered tapestry arm-chairs may now be had for as little as fifteen shillings. Wicker chairs when prettily upholstered can be made to look very cosy. When bought ready upholstered they necessarily cost more than when the work is undertaken at home. In the section upon home carpentery and upholstery many useful hints are given in regard to the making of inexpensive little odds and ends for the home which the proud possessor of a bed-sitting-room would do well to study. Pretty curtains and draperies, dainty table-

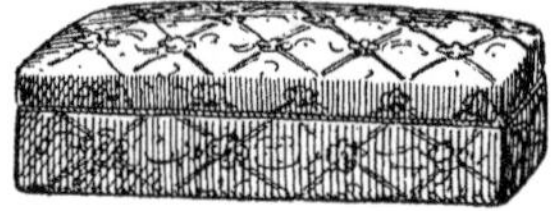

Ottoman

cloths, all can be made by the deft fingers of the woman who takes a pride in making her surroundings as cosy and dainty as possible, however heavily she may be handicapped in regard to means.

Period Furniture.—Distinctive style in furniture is becoming cultivated to a very great extent nowadays, and people who have the means with which to indulge their taste in this direction like to furnish at least one room in their house in accordance with one of the famous furniture periods. Genuine "antiques" can as a rule be only indulged in by those with well-filled purses. Other people, however, may be fortunate enough to possess one or two pieces of really good antique furniture which has come to them by inheritance. These should be cherished as articles of real value, and placed amongst surroundings in keeping with their character.

A good piece of furniture is apt to prove somewhat costly at times in the expenditure entailed by living up to it. A Louis XVI. cabinet, for instance, will demand that not only the rest of the furniture in the room but also the decoration be in the same style. It seems superfluous to remark that no woman of taste would allow such a piece of furniture to be placed in a room furnished in accordance with the early Victorian tradition.

All women should have at least an elementary knowledge of the characteristics of the various styles of furniture belonging to the famous epochs. Without this knowledge they are apt to make somewhat glaring errors when attempting to furnish their rooms in accordance with any particular period. The study of the evolution of furniture has a fascination peculiarly its own. Through it the manners and customs of our forefathers may be traced step by step from the time when primitive man first began to carve out of wood or stone those crude implements suited to his needs, through the centuries of progression marked by the Gothic, Tudor, Jacobean and Georgian periods to the Victorian era (which last, strangely enough, marked a time of positive decadence in the art of furniture designs), and thence to the present day.

The connoisseur does not need to concern herself with the styles of furniture which prevailed prior to the fourteenth century, however. The needs of our ancestors in those days were too simple for the evolution of any really characteristic style, which could be adapted to present-day needs. The real evolution of artistic furniture in this country began with the Tudor period. Many Italian craftsmen settled in England during Henry VIII.'s reign, and the influence of the Italian Renaissance has left its mark upon the furniture of the period. The furniture of the "Jacobean" period has a dignity all its own. Many people like their dining-rooms furnished in this particular style, which prevailed during the reign of James I., 1603—until the end of the reign of James II., 1685. It was during the eighteenth century, however, that English furniture reached its greatest degree of artistic perfection, and it is with this period, therefore, that collectors are most concerned. It gave birth to such artist-craftsmen as Chippendale, Adam, Hepplewhite, and Sheraton, whose names will ever live in the annals of furniture design. Contemporaneous with these famous English styles were the French styles of Louis XV., Louis XVI., the Directoire, and the First Empire.

As has been already remarked, during the Victorian era art in furniture went through a marked decadence. The furniture of this recent period is marked by its stiffness, ungainliness, and general air of discomfort. It may safely be said that connoisseurs of the future will not readily advocate a revival of the Victorian style.

Those who wish to make a study of the characteristics of the best periods in furniture cannot do better than read some good books upon the subject. Mr. Edwin Foley, in his book entitled "Decorative Furniture," traces the evolution of artistic furniture from the most remote times, explaining the main characteristics which distinguish the art of each particular period. Much valuable assistance is given to the collector by the many coloured illustrations of the various styles which are to be found throughout the book. She should also make a point of visiting museums and other places where specimens of old furniture may be seen; such as the Victoria and Albert Museum, South Kensington, London; the Royal Scottish Museum, Edinburgh, and the Dublin Museum. For French decorative furniture in particular the Jones Collection, South Kensington Museum and the Wallace Collection, Hertford House, Manchester Square, should be visited.

SOME FURNISHING ESTIMATES

The following lists, giving suggestions in regard to the best way of spending two fairly representative sums of money on the furnishing of a small house or flat, will prove useful to the young couple who are about to furnish a home, and who require guidance not only as to the furniture to be purchased, but also in regard to the cost of the various articles. The first list of this has been compiled by Messrs. Maple in connection with a ninety guinea model flat displayed at their show-rooms. The second scheme for furnishing a house for £300 has also been largely compiled from information obtained from the same firm—

THE NINETY GUINEA FLAT

The sum of ninety guineas is apportioned amongst the various rooms as follows:—

	£	s.	d.
Dining-room	18	5	3
Drawing-room	22	17	6
Bedroom	20	19	1
Servant's room	4	3	3
Bath-room		17	3
Hall	3	4	3
Kitchen	2	1	5½
Linens, blankets, &c.	7	8	4
China and glass	3	6	7½
Electro-plate and cutlery	5	5	2
Ironmongery	6	1	10
	£94	10	0

The following lists give detailed expenditure for the various rooms:—

Dining-Room

	£	s.	d.
Seamless tapestry carpet (12 ft. by 9 ft.)	2	6	6
Linoleum surround (say) 8 yds. at 1s. 1½d.		9	0
2 pairs casement curtains with rod and fittings		17	6
Cloth table-cover		10	0
Black curb fender		7	6

	£	s.	d.
Set of fire-irons		4	6
Coal-scoop		10	0
Fumed oak sideboard	4	8	6
Dining-table (3 ft. 6 in. by 5 ft.)	2	5	0
1 Elbow-chair with rush seat	1	2	6
4 Small chairs with rush seat at 13s. 9d.	2	15	0
Oak side-table		17	6
1 Lounge easy-chair	1	3	6
Hearth-rug		8	3
	£18	5	3

Drawing-Room

	£	s.	d.
Axminster pile carpet (12 ft. by 9 ft.)	4	4	0
Linoleum surround (say) 10 yds. at 1s. 1½d.		11	3
2 pairs of Mapleton damask curtains with rods and fittings	1	6	0
Curb fender		7	6
Set of fire-irons		4	6
Brass coal-scoop		10	0
2 "Neston" easy-chairs upholstered in tapestry at 22s. 6d.	2	5	0
1 "Neston" settee upholstered in tapestry	1	18	6
1 Arm-chair with tapestry seat	1	1	0
2 Small chairs with tapestry seat at 13s. 9d.	1	7	6
Inlaid mahogany cabinet	4	15	0
Inlaid mahogany centre table	1	12	6
Inlaid mahogany occasional table		9	9
Mahogany escritoire	2	5	0
	£22	17	6

Bedroom

	£	s.	d.
Felt carpet planned to room (say) 12 yds. at 3s. 9d.	2	5	0
2 pairs cretonne casement curtains with rods and fittings		18	4
Curb fender		7	6
Set of fire-irons		4	6
4 ft. 6 ins. Bedstead, white and brass	1	8	9
Wire-woven mattress		10	6
Sanitary pad		5	9
Extra thick wool mattress	1	11	6
Feather bolster		10	0
2 Pillows at 6s. 9d.		13	6
Decorated white bedroom suite, comprising dressing-chest with jewel drawers, double wash-stand, wardrobe, bevel plate glass mirror, pedestal cupboard, towel-horse, and 2 chairs	10	5	0
Double set toilet ware		13	6
Easy-chair		12	9
Bed furniture		12	6
	£20	19	1

Servant's Bedroom

	£	s.	d.
Linoleum for covering floor		9	9
Bedside rug		3	9
2 ft. 6 in. iron bedstead and wire mattress, wool mattress, pad bolster, and pillow complete	1	7	9
Japanned oak wash-stand		5	3
Simple set of toilet ware		3	6
Japanned oak chest of drawers with dressing-glass fixed	1	5	6
Cane-seated chair		2	6
Japanned oak towel-rail		1	9
Fender		3	6
	£4	3	3

Bath-Room

	£	s.	d.
Covering floor with linoleum		4	6
Cane-seated chair		3	6
1 pair casement curtains with rod and fittings		5	6
Bath-mat		3	9
		17	3

Hall

	£	s.	d.
1 pair casement curtains with rod and fittings		6	0
Fumed oak umbrella-stand		15	0
Fumed oak hat-rack		6	6
Linoleum for covering floor (say)		11	3
Black fender		4	6
Fumed oak settee	1	1	0
	£3	4	3

Kitchen

	£	s.	d.
15½ yds. linoleum at 1s. 1d.		16	3
4 ft. kitchen table		13	6
2 Kitchen chairs at 2s. 10d.		5	8
Kitchen fender		5	6
	£2	0	11

Linens, Blankets, &c.

	£	s.	d.
1 pair blankets (84 by 104 in.)		17	9
1 Under-blanket		4	6
1 White quilt		12	9
1 Down quilt		17	6
2 pairs cotton sheets at 10s. 6d.	1	1	0
2 pairs pillow-cases at 2s. 4d.		4	8
1 pair blankets for servant's bed		8	11
1 Under-blanket		2	11
1 Coloured quilt		3	11
2 pairs cotton sheets at 5s. 11d.		11	10
1 pair pillow-cases		1	11

	£	s.	d.
2 Damask table-cloths (2½ by 2 yds.) at 5s. 11d.		11	10
6 Napkins for		3	9
6 Huckaback towels for		4	9
3 Bath towels at 1s. 1½d.		3	4½
6 Servants' towels at 6½d.		3	5
6 Tea-cloths for		2	11
6 Glass-cloths for		2	6
6 Dusters for		2	0
2 Kitchen table-cloths at 1s. 11½d.		3	11
2 Roller towels at 1s. 1½d.		2	3
	£7	8	4½

CUTLERY

	£	s.	d.
6 Table knives for		6	3
6 Small knives for		5	3
1 pair meat-carvers		4	9
1 pair game-carvers		4	9
1 Steel		2	0
6 Electro-plated table forks for		11	3
6 Electro-plated dessert forks for		8	3
4 Electro-plated table spoons for		7	6
6 Electro-plated dessert spoons for		8	3
6 Electro-plated tea spoons for		5	3
2 Egg spoons		1	8
1 Butter knife		2	6
1 pair sugar tongs		2	0
2 Electro-plated sauce ladles at 2s. 6d.		5	0
1 Electro-plated cruet with mustard spoon		13	6
2 Electro-plated salt spoons at 9d.		1	6
Electro-plated teapot		15	6
	£5	5	2

CHINA AND GLASS

	£	s.	d.
Dinner service for six persons		16	0
Tea and breakfast service for six persons	1	2	0
Service of glass for 6 persons, viz.: 6 port glasses, 6 tumblers, 6 sherry glasses, 2 decanters complete		9	3
Water-bottles and glass for bedroom		1	5
Water-bottles and glass for servant			10
China and glass for kitchen use—			
6 Plates, assorted sizes		1	6
1 Vegetable dish		2	3
3 Dishes for		2	9
1 Sauce boat			6
2 Breakfast cups and saucers at 5½d.			11
2 Plates at 3d.			6
1 Sugar basin			4
1 Milk jug			7
1 Salt cellar			3½
2 Tumblers			5
1 Set of 3 jugs		1	3
2 Pie dishes		1	6
2 Pudding bowls		1	2
1 Teapot 6d., 2 store jars for 1s. 5d.		1	11
1 Bread pan		1	3
	£3	6	7½

IRONMONGERY (*Kitchen List*)

	£	s.	d.
1 Bath (galvanised)		2	6
1 Bowl (hand)		1	0
1 Bread grater			7
1 Cake tin			8
1 Chopping board		1	4
1 Clothes horse		5	0
1 Coal scuttle		1	11
1 Coffee canister		1	0
1 Coffee pot		1	9
1 Corkscrew			6
1 Colander		1	0
1 Set of dish mats		1	11
3 Dish covers: 1 each, 3s. 6d., 6s. 3d., 7s.		16	9
1 Dust pan		1	0
1 Egg slice			8
1 Egg whisk			6
1 Fish kettle		3	3
1 Fish slice			8
2 Iron spoons for			6
3 Tea spoons			7
1 Set steps		7	0
1 Slop-pail		3	0
1 Tea canister		1	3
1 Tea tray		2	9
1 Tin-opener			6
1 Toasting fork			6
1 Glass tub (pulp)		2	6
1 Nutmeg grater			2
1 Gravy strainer		1	2
1 Housemaid's box		2	9
1 Tin kettle		1	2
1 Iron kettle		3	0
1 Knife board			7
1 Knife tray		1	8
3 Knives and forks (table)		2	9
1 Galvanised pail			10
2 Flat irons for		1	6
1 Flat iron stand			6
1 Flour dredger			6
1 Flour tub		2	9
1 Frying pan		1	0
1 Funnel			3
1 Paste board		2	3
1 dozen patty pans			4
1 Pepperbox			4
1 Plate basket		3	0
2 Plate leathers		2	0
1 Kitchen poker			9
1 Rolling pin			6
1 Salt box		1	9
3 Iron saucepans, 1 each, 1s. 4d., 1s. 9d., 2s. 9d.		5	10

	£	s.	d.
1 Enamelled saucepan		1	3
1 Set skewers			7
1 Soap-dish			4
1 Towel roller and brackets		1	0
1 Wire sieve			10
3 Wood spoons			7
Brushes—			
1 Hair banister brush		1	3
1 Whisk brush		1	1
1 Long hair broom		2	6
1 Carpet broom		2	6
1 Dusting brush		1	0
1 Nail brush			4
1 Scrubbing brush		1	3
1 Bass scrubbing brush			8
2 Plate brushes for		1	9
1 Set shoe brushes		2	9
1 Set stove brushes		2	9
1 Sweep's brush			9
	£6	1	10

£300 HOUSE

Summary

	£	s.	d.
Hall	9	13	3
Dining-room	55	4	0
Drawing-room (with piano)	84	13	3
Morning-room	18	14	11
Best bedroom	32	16	8
Spare bedroom	19	8	5
2nd spare bedroom	14	17	11
Servants' bedroom	9	13	0
Kitchen	4	7	2½
Bath-room	1	14	3
Plate and cutlery	9	0	0
Linen and blankets	17	18	5
China and glass	8	0	0
Ironmongery and extra fittings	10	0	0
	£296	1	3½

This leaves a balance of £3, 18s. 8½d., which will go towards any extra expenditure upon clocks, cushions, portières, and fancy table-covers which have not been included in our lists.

DETAILED LISTS

Hall

	£	s.	d.
18 yds. stair and landing carpet at 4s.	3	12	0
2 doz. rods, eyes and pins		16	0
Covering floor with linoleum (say) 12 yds. at 1s. 6d.		18	0
Hat-rack		8	6
Fumed oak settle	1	1	0
Fumed oak umbrella-stand	1	8	9
Rug		17	6
1 pair casement curtains with rod and fittings		7	0
Fender		4	6
	£9	13	3

Dining-Room

	£	s.	d.
Axminster pile carpet 12 ft. by 12 ft.	6	4	0
Linoleum surround (say) 12 yds. at 1s. 1½d.		13	6
2 pairs casement curtains with rod and fittings	1	3	6
Table-cover	1	5	0
Pierced steel fender	1	1	0
Set of fire-irons		9	0
Coal-scoop		11	0
Mahogany sideboard	8	17	6
Mahogany 2-tier serving-table	2	10	0
Dining-table	4	12	6
6 mahogany small chairs upholstered in morocco at 22s. 6d.	6	15	0
Easy-chair upholstered in tapestry	4	4	0
Easy-chair upholstered in tapestry	3	5	0
Mahogany occasional table	1	11	6
Mahogany escritoire	4	11	6
Mahogany book-case	7	10	0
	£55	4	0

Morning-Room

	£	s.	d.
Seamless tapestry square carpet 12 ft. by 9 ft.	2	6	6
Linoleum surround		9	0
2 pairs curtains with rod and fittings		17	6
Curb fender		7	6
Set of fire-irons		10	0
Coal-scoop		5	0
4 small rush-seated fumed oak chairs at 13s. 9d. each	2	15	0
Fumed oak sideboard	4	8	6
Easy-chair	1	5	0
Hearth-rug		8	3
Gate-leg table	2	0	0
Sectional book-case	3	2	8
	£18	14	11

Drawing-Room

	£	s.	d.
Axminster pile carpet 10 ft. 6 ins. by 9 ft.	4	4	0
Felt surround (say) 12 yds. at 3s. 9d.	2	5	0
Pierced fender	1	1	0
Set of fire-irons		12	0
Brass coal-scoop		11	0
2 pairs casement curtains with rod and fittings	1	3	6

	£	s.	d.
Inlaid mahogany Sheraton cabinet	8	17	6
Inlaid mahogany writing	2	17	6
Piano	40	0	0
Piano-stool with velvet cushion	1	2	6
Inlaid mahogany circular table	2	5	0
Settee upholstered in tapestry	5	7	6
Easy-chair	2	12	0
1 Inlaid mahogany elbow-chair	1	17	6
4 Inlaid mahogany small chairs at 22s. 6d.	4	10	0
1 Inlaid mahogany occasional table	1	6	9
Hearth-rug		18	0
Screen	3	2	6
	£84	13	3

Kitchen

	£	s.	d.
Covering floor with linoleum	1	5	0
4 ft. kitchen table		17	9
2 Kitchen chairs at 6s. 6d.		13	0
1 Windsor chair		8	0
1 Carpet deck-chair		6	6
Alarm clock		5	6
Coal hod		2	2
Strong shovel		2	3½
Kitchen poker		1	6
Rug		5	6
	£4	7	2½

Bath-Room

	£	s.	d.
Covering floor with linoleum		10	0
Cane-seated chair		3	6
Glass with drawer for brush and comb		11	6
Bath rack		5	6
Bath mat		3	9
	£1	14	3

Best Bedroom

	£	s.	d.
Gobelin carpet 12 ft. by 12 ft.	3	12	0
Linoleum surround (say) 12 yds. at 1s. 1½d.		13	6
Curb fender		7	6
Set of fire-irons		4	6
2 pairs casement curtains with rod and fittings	1	0	0
4 ft. 6 in. brass bedstead	3	5	6
Wire-woven mattress		10	6
Sanitary pad		5	9
Hair mattress	2	3	9
Feather bolster		10	0
2 Pillows		18	0
Inlaid mahogany bedroom suite, comprising: — Wardrobe, dressing-chest with glass, washstand fitted with cupboard, and towel-rail and two chairs	12	15	6
Double set of toilet ware		15	0
Easy-chair		12	9
Hearth-rug		8	9
Occasional table		14	9
1 set of bed draperies to match curtains		18	6
Oval Sheraton mirror	1	5	0
Screen	1	9	6
Linen basket		5	11
	£32	16	8

Spare Bedroom

	£	s.	d.
Caledon carpet 12 ft. by 9 ft.	2	14	0
Linoleum surround (say) 10 yds. at 1s. 1d.		10	10
2 pairs Mapleton damask curtains with rod and fittings	1	0	0
1 set of bed draperies to match		17	6
Fender		7	6
Set of fire-irons		4	6
3 ft. White and brass bedstead	1	5	0
Wire-woven mattress		7	9
Sanitary pad		3	9
Hair mattress	1	7	6
Bolster		6	0
Feather pillow		9	0
White bedroom suite, comprising:— Wardrobe, dressing-chest, with glass, washstand fitted with towel-rail and 2 chairs	7	10	0
Single set toilet ware		7	11
Hearth-rug		8	9
Easy-chair		12	9
Occasional table		9	9
Linen basket		5	11
	£19	8	5

Second Spare Bedroom

	£	s.	d.
Fumed oak bedstead with wire spring mattress	2	4	9
Sanitary pad		3	9
Hair mattress	1	7	6
Bolster		6	0
Feather pillow		9	0
Fumed oak suite comprising:—2 ft. 6 ins. wardrobe, 2ft. 6 ins. dressing-table, washstand, and one chair	4	10	0
Oak shaving-stand	1	9	6
Easy-chair		12	9
Set of toilet ware		6	9
2 pairs casement curtains with rod and fittings	1	0	0
Clothes-basket		2	11
Linoleum to cover floor (12 by 9)	1	10	0
2 Rugs at 7s. 6d. each		15	0
	£14	17	11

SERVANTS' BEDROOM (2 *maids*)

	£	s.	d.
Covering floor with linoleum . . .		9	9
2 Bedside rugs		6	0
Two 2 ft. 6 ins. iron bedsteads and wire mattresses, wool mattresses, pads, bolsters, and pillows complete at £1, 7s. 9d. each . . .	2	15	6
2 Painted chests of drawers at £1, 9s. 6d. each	2	19	0
2 Painted washstands at 12s. 6d. . .	1	5	0
2 Painted dressing-glasses at 4s. 6d. each		8	9
2 Painted chairs at 4s. 3d. each . .		8	6
Double set of toilet ware		7	0
Fender		3	6
1 pair casement curtains with rod and fittings		10	0
	£9	13	0

(For Ironmongery, see p. 37.)
(For China and Glass, see p. 37.)
(For Electro-plate and Cutlery, see p. 37.)

LETTING A FURNISHED HOUSE

Speaking generally, it is unadvisable to let a well-furnished house. To do so is to place your precious household goods at the mercy of strangers, who will not appreciate them or care for them as you do. Dilapidations and breakages of various kinds are bound to occur, and even if their money value is received, there are some things that cannot be replaced in the owner's estimation.

Very often, however, a woman finds it absolutely necessary to let her house. She may be called abroad, and might not care to leave the house shut up or in charge of a caretaker. Again, the finances for the annual holiday might depend to a great extent upon her ability to let it. In these circumstances, therefore, she must take the utmost precautions to ensure that it is let to careful tenants. The house should be put in the hands of a good agent, who will see that all the formalities in regard to suitable references from the prospective tenant are proceeded with, and who can make judicious inquiries apart from these references.

The agent will charge a commission upon the amount received for rental, together with fees for drawing up agreement and taking inventory. An inventory has always to be taken of every piece of furniture, plate, and linen left in the house. Where the house is large it may sometimes take a whole day to go over this carefully. The mistress of the house should see that this important piece of work is properly done, drawing the agent's attention particularly to articles she wishes to be carefully noted.

It is usual to leave a certain small supply of plate and linen; but the bulk of this with other cherished articles should be locked carefully away. A very large cupboard or a room, sometimes both, should be reserved for locking-up purposes, and the agent should see that the doors of these are carefully sealed.

If the furniture is very good, never let the house to people with young children, as these are often responsible for a great deal of damage. Dogs, if not under proper control, also often cause a large amount of wear and tear. It is as well to have a clause inserted in the agreement that no dogs must be kept without the landlord's consent. This consent should not, however, be unreasonably withheld. Many people would not dream of taking a house without taking their pets with them. Let it be impressed upon the tenants, therefore, that they will be held responsible for any additional wear and tear which the keeping of these pets might entail.

Before letting the house it should be thoroughly cleaned from cellar to attic, and the chimneys should be swept. The tenant should also leave it as clean in every way as when he (or she) took up the tenancy.

QUARTER DAYS

English		*Scotch*	
Lady Day	Mar. 25	Candlemas	Feb. 2
Midsummer	June 24	Whitsuntide	May 15
Michaelmas	Sep. 29	Lammas	Aug. 1
Christmas	Dec. 25	Martinmas	Nov. 11

Half-Quarter Days

Feb. 8, May 9, Aug. 11, and Nov. 11.

MISTRESS AND SERVANTS

There is an old and very true saying that "knowledge is power." Nowhere does this maxim more fittingly apply than in the case of the woman who is thoroughly acquainted with every detail of the work of the home, and knows how the various domestic duties can be most efficiently and, at the same time, most expeditiously performed.

Even to the woman who is so comfortably endowed with this world's goods that she can afford to maintain a staff of highly trained servants at liberal wages, a knowledge of housewifery is an invaluable asset. Then hers must be the brain to supervise and direct the smooth running of the household machinery, to see that each servant performs conscientiously and efficiently the work allotted to her, that the whole establishment is maintained in that perfect working order which is a typical feature of the good housewife's régime.

In this section each phase of the servant question is carefully considered. The duties of the mistress in regard to the treatment and management of servants and the proper organisation and supervision of their work are clearly outlined, as are also the duties of each servant in accordance with the number kept. Useful information is also included in regard to the engagement of servants, prevailing scale of wages, allowances and holidays.

DUTIES OF THE MISTRESS

Knowledge of Housewifery Advisable.—Like every other profession the profession of home-making requires a certain amount of training and apprenticeship. It is quite a mistaken notion to think that housewifery comes instinctively and naturally to every woman, and that the woman who is unfitted for any other career in life can stay at home and "keep house." Domestic skill can only be acquired by training.

Whatever other calling a girl or woman may choose to select, be it nursing, teaching, medicine, art, or any other of the professions open to women, both time and money are expended in order to qualify her for her career. Why should housekeeping be left out when training in this is just as essential, seeing that the happiness and comfort of so many will depend upon her fulfilling her duties in an intelligent manner? A woman who has no knowledge of the right way to manage a house has no more right to marry and be responsible for her husband's worldly goods than a man would have to accept a post the duties of which he was quite ignorant.

A servant is quick to grasp the fact when her mistress is not versed in the arts of domestic science, and quicker still to take advantage of the ignorance thus displayed. She knows that there is no trained eye to detect flaws in her work; that a room half dusted will seldom evoke a protest—a table carelessly or slovenly laid will as often as not pass unheeded. The mistress will be made to suffer in many little ways for her ignorance in respect to household duties until by bitter experience she will awaken to the realisation of the fact that knowledge is indeed power, and strive to learn what she should have known when she first began to reign as mistress of her own home.

To the girl who is destined to begin married life in such humble circumstances that she will not be able to afford to keep even a general servant, ignorance of the rules of household work is apt to become something in the nature of a calamity. An untidy, ill-kept home, to say nothing of ill-cooked meals, is not conducive to the good temper or cheerfulness of a husband, more especially when he comes home after a hard day's work to find chaos reigning supreme, and that atmosphere of discomfort which few can analyse, and only those who have experienced it can understand. Indeed, it may be said that many a little "rift within the lute" has been occasioned by nothing less prosaic than the lamentable ignorance of her household duties displayed by the young wife.

Training in housekeeping may be acquired in different ways. Firstly, a young girl may be trained in her own home under a good mother or guardian, and this is the best training of all. The training may be given gradually throughout early life by allotting her little home duties to perform and teaching her the importance of the small things on which the comfort of the home depends. Or, if the greater part of the girl's life has been spent away from home in a boarding-school, then the training may be given in a more concentrated form when the school life is over. The practical nature of a real home training is of much greater value than any isolated courses of lessons, which may be taken later on in life. Training can also be acquired at one of the numerous schools of Domestic Science now established in various parts of the country, and if only sufficient time is allowed this is another excellent way of learning various branches of household routine. Finally, knowledge can be gained by experience, but this unfortunately may be at the expense of needless worry and anxiety not only to oneself, but to the other members of the household as well.

Modern housekeeping requires an expert and not an ignoramus, and there should be nothing degrading about having to look to the ways of one's household. In fact, it will generally be found that the better educated and the more intelligent a woman is, the higher will be her housekeeping capacities. A sound knowledge of household details does not tie one more to one's own four walls, but it enables one to get the best results with the least expenditure of time and energy.

Oversight and Inspection.—It is the duty of the mistress to see that her house is kept as spotlessly clean as it is possible to make it. Each part must receive her attention, not only the principal rooms of the house, such as the sitting-rooms and bedrooms, but the kitchen, scullery and servants' bedrooms as well.

She must also see that food is neither wasted nor thrown away. This will necessitate a daily visit to the larder (see p. 101), and even the scrap-pail and dust-bin must not escape her notice. Constant watchfulness in this respect is all-important, and if a mistress thoroughly understands what ought to be, she will detect waste from the beginning and be able to put it right.

Sinks and lavatories must also be included in the tour of inspection, and if there is any unpleasant smell it must be seen to at once.

It will also be the duty of the mistress to see that the locking up of the house at night is attended to—that all low windows and doors of unused rooms are locked and back and front doors bolted. She must see that silver is carefully put away, and that all fires are in a safe condition to leave.

Order and Arrangement.—The wheels of domestic machinery will not run smoothly unless the mistress is orderly and methodical in all her arrangements.

She must first of all have a clear idea of what she wishes to have done, and then make her plan accordingly, so apportioning the work among the different workers that for each detail some one person is responsible. There must be a fair division of labour, so that too much does not fall to one person and not sufficient to another.

There must also be a proper time for everything and everything should be done in its time. Punctuality and method will contribute essentially to the comfort of the home, and if household work is systematised there will be little fear of friction or neglect.

It is impossible to draw out a model plan which will suit the requirements of all households, so much depends upon the size of the house, the number of the family, the style of living, and the means at disposal; it therefore rests with each mistress to devise her own particular working scheme. She may not always succeed in attaining her ideal, but she can at least have a certain standard at which she aims and which she does her best to attain. This amount of method must not prevent departure from routine should circumstances require it. It must always be remembered that rules are made for people not people for rules, and the mistake must not be made of subordinating everything to the keeping of the ménage.

If there is one thing worse than an uncomfortable and disorderly home, it is the household where order and system are carried to such a pitch that all those pleasantly diverting pursuits, which tend at times to upset the general arrangement of things, are reduced to a minimum in order to avoid unnecessary work, to save the carpets, keep the furniture in good condition, or something else of a like nature. This is to make a desert of a home.

Order and system should be silent factors which do not obtrude themselves, necessities which are best kept out of sight, but which act none the less as drops of oil on the machinery of domestic routine.

Daily Duties.—The duties of the mistress of a household are very numerous and very varied, and it will be well for her to try to draw out a plan and time-table of her own daily routine.

The extent of her duties will naturally depend upon her income, the staff of servants at her disposal, and the size of her household.

To house the members of her household in comfort and health, to feed them properly and nurse them in sickness, to keep household accounts, to engage servants and allot to each their proper share of work, and to do the work herself when occasion requires, are among a few of the duties which will rest upon her shoulders.

Details of the various branches of work for which she will be responsible will be found under their respective headings, such as The House, The Table, Nursing, &c., and it is hoped that the instructions there given will prove helpful to the woman who desires to be a real home-maker.

The Duty of Cheerfulness.—Cheerfulness is one of the most valuable of possessions; it is really the sunshine of life, the promoter of health and happiness. To be able to keep up the spirits of those around us not only adds to the brightness of the home, but helps to make all duties comparatively light and easy. It is a woman's duty to make the life of the home as happy and gay as possible, and however depressed she may sometimes feel she ought to struggle against the feeling and not damp the spirits of those around her.

No one can be more trying than the person who continually gives way to low spirits, going about with a martyr-like expression, and making a habit of airing her grievances at every meal or family gathering. Such a person is a constant source of irritation to the other members of the household.

Unfortunately, it is often upon the home-loving woman that the little worries, the small contretemps of daily life weigh most heavily. She takes it too much to heart if her house is not so spotlessly clean as she would like, or if her well-planned arrangements have been upset, and she finds it difficult to look at things from a right perspective.

It requires some strength of will to grapple against this spirit of worrying and getting depressed, but the home-maker ought to think of others before herself and do her utmost to keep these little troubles in the background.

Health and happiness are a thousand times more important than all the spotless homes in the world, and to worry over every speck of dust, over every broken dish, or such-like trifles will only result in greater miseries, broken-down nerves, and premature wrinkles and old age.

Home Touches.—The duties of the mistress are not finished when the routine of household work is set agoing and cleanliness and order have been established. The little finishing touches, the small elegances, the tasteful arrangement, the special provision made for individual comfort must come from her or be wanting altogether. She must endeavour to make the rooms as pretty as possible and give to them an air of repose and restfulness. Who does not know the difference between a room that is merely kept in order by a servant and one in which the lady of the house takes an interest as well. It is perhaps attention to the small things of the house that has the most to do with the comfort of it, and it is just these minor details that require the most thought, as they are outside the ordinary routine. If they are neglected or forgotten all the cosiness, all the home feeling and soothing influence will be gone and bare utility alone will remain.

The true home-maker is also one who has the intuitive power of divining the tastes and feelings of others and who is ever ready to minister to their needs. With a ready tact she will put herself in the place of those around her, will be able to perceive their unspoken worries and disappointments, and sympathise with them without remark. She will even be able when occasion arises to shield them from unkindly notice or an ungenerous remark. Tact of this kind is perhaps innate, and yet much of it may be acquired by observation and kindly feeling.

Women are the real home-makers, and it rests with them to make the four walls in which they live something more than a mere dwelling.

Happy is the woman who can so surround her own fireside with the true spirit of home, as to make it the spot where the brightest and most desirable of everything is to be found, a harbour from all outside cares and worries; she will find that not alone to herself, but to those around her as well, it has become the best place in the world.

Duty towards Herself.—Last but not least, it is the duty of the mistress to take care of herself and attend to her health. However busy she may be, she ought to contrive to have a period of leisure and to be out of doors for some time every day. Self-sacrifice in the cause of duty may become almost a fetich with many women. No woman, however, is justified in making herself a domestic drudge. She confers no benefit upon any one by being a slave to her family and to her home. The best house-mistress is undoubtedly the one who allows herself time for both relaxation and diversion, realising that without it not only her health, but also her nerves and her temper would suffer in the long run.

The head of the house must also find time for her own toilet and make the best of her personal appearance. There is no occasion for her to wear costly apparel unless she can afford it, but she must always be neat and wear what suits her and looks attractive. A lady cannot expect servants to look up to her and pay attention to their dress if she herself goes about in slovenly attire; in this, as in everything else, she must be the example to be copied.

Beyond the Home.—We often hear it said that if a woman does her duty in her own home this is all that can be expected of her. But this is a very narrow view to take of life, and such a limited existence is bad not only for the woman herself, but for the other members of her household as well. In fact, the reason that so many heads of families break down in health is because they wrap themselves up too much in the cares of their own household and worry so much over every trifle that it ends in their requiring a rest cure or something of the kind.

A woman ought, as a responsible member of society, to use her powers to help and encourage those beyond the borders of her own home. If she did this, even to a small extent, she would find that the strain of constantly thinking of household affairs was very much relieved, and that she gained strength for renewed effort.

Then there are social duties to perform—the paying of calls, the giving of entertainments, the cultivation of friends, &c., and these are claims which cannot be neglected. If we shut ourselves up from our friends and live entirely within our own small circle we very soon become narrow-minded and end in being forgotten.

ENGAGING SERVANTS

There are several different ways of obtaining servants. If one can be heard of by recommendation, either through friends or through a servant in one's employment, this is certainly the most satisfactory and easiest way, but it is only occasionally that one is favoured by such a chance.

Then there is the registry office, which may or may not be good. While there are offices of high standing, where business is done in an honest and upright manner, there are many others whose dealings can by no means be relied upon. As a rule, city registry offices are of little use for supplying servants for the ordinary middle-class household, as they cater more for hotels and other large establishments; and while they may have on their books a long list of butlers, cooks, lady's-maids, parlourmaids, and other specialists in domestic service, the cook-general, house-parlourmaid, or general rarely seeks for a situation through that channel. A good suburban registry office may, on the other hand, render valuable assistance, especially if a girl belonging to a special district is required.

A well-drawn-up advertisement inserted either in a local paper or in a good general newspaper with a wide circulation is one of the best means, and this method often enables one to have a better choice. The wording of the advertisement must be concise, and at the same time it must neither be vague nor misleading. A few particulars as to requirements should be given, and it should be stated whether the applicant is to write or to apply in person and at what hour. The following specimen advertisements may serve as a guide to those who are inexperienced in this work:—

General Servant.—For small flat, three in family, must understand plain cooking, no washing. Wages £16–£18. Good health and references essential. Apply after 4 P.M.

Cook General.—Wanted immediately, small house, four in family. Wages £18–£20. Late dinner. Age 25–30. Apply after 7 P.M.

Parlour-maid.—Wanted 1st July, good at silver and needlework, a little housework. Age 22–28. Wages £20–£25. Three servants. Apply ——

Young girls trained in domestic work can also be obtained from charitable institutions, but this plan should not be resorted to unless one is prepared to devote a considerable amount of time and trouble to their training. Although the girls have had training of a kind in their institution, they are as a rule quite unaccustomed to the niceties of a private house, and are apt to be very uncouth in their manners. There is difficulty, too, in getting other servants to take kindly to a girl of this class, and not infrequently it proves an unhappy arrangement on both sides.

It is always wise to have a personal interview with a servant before engaging her. This not only helps the mistress to judge of her character by her appearance, but it also enables the girl to see the house to which she may be asked to come, and gives her a better idea of the work that will be expected of her.

The mistress should begin the interview by asking the maid some questions as to what experience she has had, how long she remained in her last place, and what reason she had for leaving it—what wage she had been having, and what she would now expect. Some inquiries should be made regarding the girl's family and also whether she has good health or not. Attention should also be paid to her personal appearance, whether she is clean and tidy in her person, neatly and suitably dressed, and of a prepossessing manner. If the information thus obtained is in the main satisfactory, the mistress should next give an outline of the duties she would expect her to perform, and if after a little mutual conversation the arrangement seems likely to suit both parties, details may be entered into a little more fully.

A servant must never be engaged under false pretences, and it is never a wise plan to make things appear better than they really are. It is better policy to make it quite clear what will be expected in the way of work, so that there may be no chance of future misunderstanding.

Some information should be given as regards the habits and customs of the family, the number of servants kept, and the amount of entertaining likely to be done. The mistress should also state her wishes as regards dress, caps, aprons, &c., and whether she will allow visitors or not. The question of wages must also be discussed and a clear statement must be given as to what time will be allowed off and what holiday will be given, also what notice must be given should either party wish to terminate the engagement. If a cook is being engaged, there should be a clear understanding about perquisites.

The first conversation in a matter of this kind counts for a great deal, and there is nothing like making everything clear at the outset.

If a maid has been asked to come some distance in order to have this interview, it is usual to pay her expenses.

With regard to references, a personal interview with the maid's last employer should be obtained if possible. There are a few occasions on which a written character may be safely accepted, but these should be the exception and not the rule, and written particulars should be accepted with a certain amount of caution. Besides, ladies will always give more information verbally than they will by writing, and there is always something to be gained by seeing the house in which the girl has been previously employed, as this also serves as an index as to what has been expected of her in the way of service. In fact, it is never a very wise plan to take a servant who has been employed in a house out of one's own rank in life. For instance, a servant who has been employed by a lodging-house keeper, by small trades-people, or even in an hotel is not suitable for private service with gentlefolk, as she would be unaccustomed to the ways of refined people. Each branch of service has its own standard, and what may be ideal in one line of life, falls very far below the ideal in another.

During the above interview the mistress should ascertain the reasons for the maid leaving her place and also her capacity for work. She must also make inquiries as to her moral character, whether she is clean, neat, good-tempered, also whether she has good health and is an early riser.

If the answers to such inquiries prove to be satisfactory and the mistress considers the girl likely to suit her requirements, the next step is to write to the maid or to ask for another interview in order to fix the date of arrival, and to make the final terms of engagement. In Scotland and the North there is an old-fashioned custom of giving arles or earnest money as a token of engagement. The sum of 2s. or 2s. 6d. is given to the maid as sealing the contract. But this is merely an old custom and not a necessity.

The usual custom of hiring a servant is from month to month; this means that they are paid once a month and the engagement can be terminated on a month's notice. (See Law of Master and Servant, p. 377.)

Character-giving.—Although a mistress cannot be compelled to give her servant a character, it is customary to do so when a girl is leaving her employment. The fact of refusing to grant a reference would almost imply inability to testify to any good qualities in the girl's character, and this would be most prejudicial to her future career.

A character must not, however, be given lightly; it is essential to state only what is true. There must be no exaggeration either of the good or of the bad points, and the mistress in search of a maid must be considered as much as the maid herself.

A mistress has no right to hide some serious fault from a desire to give the girl a better chance, but she must be absolutely frank and impartial in every way. (See Law of Master and Servant, p. 377.)

WAGES, ALLOWANCES, AND HOLIDAYS

Wages.—The wages of an indoor servant should be paid monthly, dating from the day the maid enters your service. Or, for convenience sake, where there are several servants, a fixed date may be chosen, say the 1st of the month as general pay-day. In this case, the odd days when a girl arrives would have to be paid for separately. Wages must always be paid regularly, and under no circumstances should a servant be obliged to wait for her money.

The amount payable as wages varies very much in different localities, and one has to conform very much to custom in a thing of this kind. The wages in town are usually higher than those paid in the country.

The following table may serve as an approximate guide as to what is usually paid :—

Butler	£45—£90
Housekeeper	30— 80
Cook	20— 40
Cook-general	18— 25
Parlour-maid	16— 25
Housemaid	16— 20
House-Parlour-maid	15— 25
Kitchen-maid	12— 20
Scullery-maid	8— 14
General Servant	10— 25
Lady's-maid	25— 50
Footman	20— 30
Valet	30— 50
Tweeney	10— 16
Hall Boy	9— 12

Licences.—An annual licence is required for each man-servant in addition to wages (see p. 384).

Board Wages.—When servants are left in charge of a house during the absence of the family, or if they are sent away temporarily for the same reason, it is usual to put them on board wages. This means that in addition to their regular wage they are paid a sum ranging from 7s. 6d. to 12s. 6d. for a woman-servant, and from 12s. to 15s. for a man-servant per week as food money. The amount varies according to the style of living, and the district in which they are living. When several servants are left it is very usual for them to club together and for one, generally the cook, to do the catering; but this is a matter of arrangement amongst themselves. If they are obliged to find their own accommodation as well as board, an extra allowance should be paid for lodging or the fare paid to their own homes.

Food Allowances.—In a small household where only one or two servants are kept it is not usual to have food allowances. In fact, the less difference there is made between the meals of the family and those of the servants the better.

When there are several servants it is very customary to make an allowance of such articles as tea, butter, and sugar, but here, again, unless there is a large establishment it is seldom wise to make a difference in the quality of these commodities, unless it be tea, where a special brand such as China tea is frequently used for the dining-room and another, better liked by the domestics, is given for kitchen use. Otherwise to give an inferior quality of anything to the servants only leads to discontent, and the saving of expense is scarcely noticeable.

The usual allowances for tea, butter, and sugar are the following :—¼ lb. tea, ½ lb. butter, and 1 lb. sugar per week for each servant.

As regards the different meals, the following is a very usual rate of allowances :—

Breakfast.—Tea, bread and butter and porridge (if wished) with some little addition, such as dried fish, egg, or boiled bacon. There are some houses where this addition is not granted, but this is poor fare when we consider that a girl is expected to do a morning's work on the strength of this early meal.

Lunch.—This is not a recognised meal, but when breakfast is taken very early, a little bread and butter, with a cup of milk or a cup of cocoa, should not be denied, especially as some girls are unable to take much breakfast.

Dinner.—This meal is usually the same as the dining-room lunch or early dinner, and consists of meat with at least one vegetable, and pudding, or soup and cold meat with a little cheese or stewed fruit.

Tea.—Bread and butter with a little jam or dripping cake in addition to tea.

Supper.—Cocoa or coffee with bread and butter and cheese, or the remains of any salad, savoury, or simple pudding left from dinner. Meat is never given unless there are men-servants, but a basin of soup may sometimes take the place of the cocoa or coffee.

Laundry Allowance.—If the washing is not done at home, servants are usually allowed from 1s. to 1s. 6d. for their laundry bill ; if the lesser sum, some of the smaller articles would require to be washed by themselves.

Holidays and Time Off Duty.—There is no hard-and-fast rule as regards this, and it is best for each mistress to arrange the matter with her maids. The usual allowance is an evening or afternoon once a week with an afternoon and evening on alternate Sundays ; while a fortnight's holiday in the year is very general.

TREATMENT OF SERVANTS

It is most important that when a new servant arrives, the house, or her department of it at least, should be in good order. It is very disheartening to have to commence by cleaning out cupboards and clearing away some one else's disorder before any good work can be started.

In small houses the mistress should take the maid round and show her where her work will be. and where she will find the necessary implements to perform it. A list of her duties should be written on a card and hung in some convenient place, such as the kitchen or pantry, and it will be just as well to have the time off duty stated on the same card. The details of the maid's work should be given her by degrees. There is no use confusing the girl's mind by telling her too much at once; the necessary instructions for the first day's work will be quite sufficient to begin with. For the first few days a little patience and forbearance will be necessary until the girl learns the ways of the household and the wishes of her employer, and allowance must be made if everything is not done exactly as one would wish.

Then, later on, though a mistress cannot expect perfection, it is her duty to see that the work is properly and regularly done, and if anything is wrong, to speak about it at once and not allow it to slip. This should always be done in a kindly spirit and without any show of temper. In fact, if she is very much annoyed about anything, it is much better to wait until the first feeling of vexation has passed over and she is able to speak calmly and firmly without showing unnecessary vexation.

A servant should never be corrected before a third person, neither should a message of reprimand be sent through a child or a fellow-servant.

Then, again, it is a bad plan to be constantly going after a servant and doing oneself any work that may have been slurred over or omitted. This is frequently done to save oneself the trouble of speaking, but it will not make a capable nor a reliable maid. A girl ought to be given a reasonable amount of work to do and then held responsible for its fulfilment ; if it is found to be more than she can properly do it is much wiser to relieve her of some of it than to have the constant feeling of dissatisfaction.

Above all things, a mistress must make an effort to be absolutely fair and consistent, and there should be nothing underhand in her dealings. By these means she will have a better chance of obtaining faithful service. A good servant likes to feel that there is a firm hand over her, and that the mistress notices whether her work is well or badly done.

While reproof should be given when necessary, praise must not be withheld when work is well done. A word of commendation is very welcome to all of us. To those who clean our rooms, cook our food, brush our boots, &c., we cannot be too grateful, as, at the best, it is monotonous work, and one's maids are certainly due more consideration than is frequently given. They are not all demons trying to " do us " at every turn, but human, often very human, and they should certainly be treated reasonably and their rights respected.

As we exact and expect civility and courtesy from our maids it is only fair that we should render them the same. A fear of familiarity should never be an excuse for a curt answer, nor justify the omission of " please " from our requests, nor a word of thanks for any service rendered. Neither should we be reluctant to wish them the common salutations of " good morning " and " good night."

Servants who are treated with this courtesy of manner will, as a rule, like their place and try to render faithful service.

It is also fitting that well-performed duties which tend to make the home happy and comfortable should be rewarded by little kindnesses—a gift now and then in acknowledgment of some special service or at a special season, such as Christmas or on return from a holiday, or an occasional holiday or treat. A little encouragement of this kind goes a long way towards making the drudgery of housework pleasant and easy.

One should not be backward either in raising the wages of a girl who has worked well. If she has been in our service for a year or eighteen months, she is worth more than when she first came, and the rise will be appreciated so much more if it is given unsought. Then when a gift is given, let it be something that shows a little kindly thought—a length of print, a muslin apron, or a pair of stockings are very useful and sensible, but they are not pretty, and every girl who is earning a fair wage ought to be able to afford these necessaries. How much nicer would be a little handbag and purse, a pretty work-basket, a set of toilet brushes in a case, or something which she would not likely buy herself, which would show the friendly thought and serve as a little keepsake.

There is much said nowadays about the dislike of the lower classes for domestic service. One reason to account for this is the increased education which they receive in the elementary schools. This naturally creates a spirit of independence and a wish to rise in the social scale, which is not altogether unworthy. An employer, to be successful, must therefore take this new spirit into consideration and make allowances for it by respecting the rights of those who serve. Many mistresses fail to move with the times, and cannot see that the requirements of the working-classes are altering, and that more liberty and more wages is demanded.

Fortunately, much is being done to raise domestic service to a higher level, and it depends very much upon the employers whether these efforts succeed or not. If the mistress herself despises household work, and allows it to be seen that she looks down upon those who do it, it will not be surprising if her domestics cultivate the same ideas. On the contrary, she ought to be able when necessary to take part in the household work without in any way losing her dignity.

A lack of leisure and want of privacy are other reasons for making domestic service unpopular. It frequently happens that a maid has no time she can call her own, and that she is continually under the eye of her employer. Now although there is no limit regarding the working hours of a servant, beyond the fact that she must be allowed a sufficient time to sleep, this does not entitle us to demand service without relaxation. A certain amount of leisure must be granted and then strictly adhered to. An effort, too, should be made to make this leisure time happy by letting servants have a comfortable place to sit in. Often the only means of freedom from work is to go out of the house, no matter what the weather is like. A few books or magazines or even the daily paper sometimes might be passed on to the kitchen with advantage.

Then a certain amount of privacy is due, especially at meal times. Servants have a right to take their meals free from interruption, and they should not be called away if it can possibly be avoided. Although a mistress should feel free to enter her kitchen at any time, she ought to choose her times for doing so and not be continually passing in and out.

Allowing a servant her independence does not prevent a mistress from taking a kindly interest in her affairs, and she must remember, too, that from the time the girl enters her house until the hour she leaves it, she is morally, although not legally, her guardian. It is an exception when a girl resents being spoken to as a fellow-woman, and yet some mistresses hesitate to do this and thus fail to win respect and affection. Servants should be encouraged to tell their little ailments, and to say at once when they are not feeling well. It should be seen that they go to bed in good time and that they take proper and sufficient food.

It is especially necessary in the case of a young servant to exercise this supervision, and particularly so if she has been brought a long way from her own home and her own people. Then it will be the duty of the mistress to ascertain where she is going to spend her time off. In fact an "evening out" should scarcely be granted unless she has friends to go to or can go out with a fellow-servant. An effort should rather be made to let her go out during the day until she has made the acquaintance of some respectable girls with whom she can be trusted.

A word might be said here about servants' bedrooms. The places in which some maids are asked to sleep are a disgrace to civilisation, and not infrequently it is in the houses of the wealthy that the worst accommodation is found—underground bedrooms which, besides being dark and airless, are sometimes damp and insanitary as well. For her own sake as well as theirs a mistress should see that her maids are provided with proper sleeping quarters, and each servant must have her own bed, a good mattress, and sufficient covering. The room itself should be light and airy, and it must be cleaned and attended to in the same way as the other rooms of the house. A servant herself is not always fastidious and particular about her room, and will sometimes be lax as regards the cleaning of it, but none the less we must see that sufficient time is given to clean it and that our wishes in this respect are carried out. There is no reason either why the servants' bedroom should be the only ugly room in the house—a place to hang useless pictures and store unsightly pieces of furniture. A pretty wall-paper or, better still, a washable distemper of a nice colour, a nice clean coverlet on the beds, tidy furniture, &c., is a training in itself and helps to increase the girl's self-respect.

And, finally, let us treat our servants with a spirit of trust and confidence, and we shall seldom have reason to regret it. For instance, a too strict locking up of daily necessaries is not always a good plan, as it shows a lack of confidence which a good servant will often resent, while a dishonest one will find a way of being dishonest whatever precautions we may take, and she is better out of the house. Besides, for one's own sake, it is bad to live in an atmosphere of suspicion and watchfulness. Human nature is the same all round; the best in us responds to trust, and the worst rises to the surface if we are constantly being rubbed the wrong way. Servants, like other people, would often do better if they were trusted more.

DUTIES OF SERVANTS

In drawing up a scheme of servants' duties it is not possible to make a plan which will suit all requirements, as every household has its own individual arrangements and no two are exactly alike. All that can be done is to furnish a broad outline of the work which requires to be done, and the following paragraphs must be looked upon as suggestive only. It is to be hoped that they will serve as a guide to the inexperienced and help them with their ménage until they have gained sufficient knowledge to make their own plan.

The amount of work to be done before breakfast by the different maids must depend upon the hour of that meal, and if before 8.30 or 9 o'clock some of the duties put down in the following lists must be delayed until later in the morning.

There has been little or no provision made for home washing, but where this is undertaken it must be looked upon as the special work of the day and time given for it in accordance with the amount to be done.

The exact time for doing the various pieces of work has not been stated, because, as a rule, it is a bad plan to tie a worker down in this way and to say that a certain piece of work has to take a certain time, and so on; it makes her grow into a sort of working machine, and takes away from her all responsibility.

If the servant is active she has no inducement to work quickly if she finds that her spare moments are just filled up with more work, and, on the other hand, if she is slow it is very discouraging to find that her work is never finished at the time expected.

The Cook.—The cook, as her name implies, is the one who prepares and cooks the food of the household. She is the chief servant in the kitchen, where she reigns supreme.

There are different grades of cooks. First we have the *Professed Cook*, who is only found in large establishments. In former years a chef or man cook frequently filled this post, but women cooks have now come more to the fore, and a chef is rarely employed in a private ménage. The professed cook has always one or two maids under her—(kitchen-maid and scullery-maid)—to whom she assigns the cleaning of the kitchen premises, the preparation, and possibly the cooking of vegetables, the cooking and serving of servants' meals and also nursery meals if there are such, while she devotes herself to the higher branches of cookery only, assists the mistress in drawing up the necessary menus, and orders the stores required for her department. She does no cleaning nor housework, but is waited on by her underlings.

Then we have the *Good Plain Cook*, who in large households, where there are a number of meals to be served, will undertake all the cooking that is required and the cleaning of the kitchen and kitchen premises. Sometimes she will have the help of a charwoman once a week to do the heavy cleaning or scrubbing, or that of a "tweeney," a young girl who divides her time between the house and the kitchen, working generally under the housemaid in the morning and under the cook from lunch time onwards. She may or may not undertake the cleaning of her own bedroom, but beyond that will do no work in other parts of the house.

And finally we have the *Cook-General*, who is usually found in middle-class households, where only two or three servants are kept. Her duties extend somewhat beyond the kitchen. She is expected to take some share in housework proper, such as the cleaning of the dining-room or library, the cleaning of the front hall, door-step, and brasses, and to give some assistance to the housemaid.

Qualifications Necessary.—There are certain qualities necessary to the making of a good cook, whatever her grade may be. She must first of all have some knowledge of cookery more or less extensive according to what is required of her. She should at least know thoroughly what she professes, and if it be only the simplest cookery, it must be good of its kind, palatable, and nicely served. She must also be punctual in all her duties, and especially so in the serving of meals. There is nothing which upsets the ways of a household so much as having meals served at uncertain hours, and for this the cook is usually responsible.

It is also important that a cook be clean and tidy in her work. All the kitchen premises and utensils should be kept spotlessly clean, and while cooking is going on there should be tidying up and clearing away at the same time. An untidy and littered kitchen is very dispiriting for other servants, even if the cook herself does not mind the disorder. No good work can be done in a muddle; in fact, the best cooks make the least mess and use the fewest utensils. The kitchen should be tidied up after every meal and made to look as bright and comfortable as possible, especially in the afternoon when the heavy part of the day's work is usually over.

A cook should also be an early riser. With her rests the lighting of the kitchen fire, upon which the hot-water supply for early morning baths, &c., depends, not to speak of the cooking of the breakfast. The amount of actual work done before breakfast will naturally depend upon the hour at which the meal is served, but unless an early start is made the cooking of the breakfast will be hurried and unsatisfactory, the water will only be tepid, and the rest of the work will be behindhand all day. The other servants, too, look to the cook as an example of what is required in this respect, and if she rises late the others will doubtless follow her lead.

Method and forethought are also valuable qualities for a cook to possess, as by their practice the labours of the day can often be considerably lightened. In cooking so many little things can be prepared in advance, and if the bill of fare is known a day beforehand one day's work can often be fitted in with another's. Then, when it comes to the actual cooking of the meal, the cook must consider carefully what dish requires the longest time, and so arrange that everything is ready at the hour appointed. Forethought, too, in the ordering of stores and provisions may save many a worry and bustle at the last minute. Then, again, in the matter of breakfast it is often possible to prepare what has to be cooked the night before, so that if anything should happen in the morning to make her a little late, the first meal may still be prepared with a calm mind.

And last, but not least, a cook ought to have consideration for her fellow-servants, and although the kitchen is her domain, there is no reason why it should ever be a place where others are afraid to enter, and where she acts as tyrant. On the contrary, she should do her best to make the place cosy and comfortable for them, as it is often their only resting-place when they have a little leisure to sit down. It is the cook's duty, too, to see that the kitchen meals are served properly, and while it is right that she should have no interference with the larder, she must provide a sufficient supply of well-cooked food and that which has been ordered by the mistress herself. A word of warning, too, is sometimes required to cooks who have young servants working under them, as they are often tempted to put an undue amount upon them, especially of the heavy work, while she herself does only what requires little output of strength.

Personal Appearance.—A cook should pay special attention to her personal appearance, and specially from the point of view of cleanliness and neatness. Her hair must at all times be neat and not allowed to come beyond bounds. There is nothing more revolting than to see a woman preparing food with her hair hanging round her head in an untidy fashion, or, what is worse still, brushing or combing her hair in a kitchen.

A cook should always try to keep her hands in good condition, and they must always be washed before any cooking is commenced. Gloves should be worn when doing any dirty work, such as the fines, the grates, and the cleaning of tins. In winter-time, if the skin is inclined to become very rough, a little glycerine should be rubbed in occasionally.

A dress of washing material, such as print, drill, or galatea should be worn in the early part of the day; in fact, there is a large amount of cooking to be done in the evening, and as the cook is not expected to leave her kitchen, it is very usual for her to remain in her cotton dress. Or she may if she chooses wear a light print dress in the morning, changing to a darker cotton one in the afternoon. Cotton, being easily washed, is a much more suitable material for kitchen use than any woollen stuff. The dress must be short enough to clear the ground by two inches. White linen aprons with bibs should be worn while cooking, and these should be furnished with a good-sized pocket. White linen sleeves, too, are sometimes slipped on, but a shorter dress sleeve or one that can be well rolled up is in many ways preferable, as the white sleeves to the wrist become very soon soiled, and in warm weather are very heating. A strong coarse apron should be donned while doing the rougher work or standing at the sink. A neat and simple cap should also be worn. If the cook has very little cooking to do in the evening, it is usual for her to dress in a dark navy blue or black dress, and to wear a muslin apron like the other house-servants. Tidy and comfortable shoes should be worn at all times.

Duties of the Cook.—It is the duty of the cook to do all the cooking that is required either single-handed or with the help of a kitchen-maid or scullery-maid. Then beyond this her duties will vary according to the number of servants kept and the style of living of the household.

Although it is impossible to draw out a plan which will suit all cases, the following table of duties may serve as a guide where the cook takes a share in the work of the house. In larger establishments where the cook's services are entirely confined to the kitchen it is very easy to delete the other duties, and the order of the remaining work would continue in very much the same way.

Duties of the Cook-General.—Rise at six, strip bed, and leave bedroom airing. Downstairs at 6.30. Open up kitchen premises and air where necessary. Light kitchen fire and clean range. (If the boiler is not a self-filling one, it should be filled the night before.) Fill kettles with water, and if there is anything for breakfast which requires long cooking, such as porridge, put this on to cook before leaving the kitchen and leave other things ready for breakfast as far as possible.

Then go to dining-room, draw up blinds and open windows, clean fire-place and light fire if necessary. Sweep room with carpet-sweeper, dust it carefully and fill coal-box. Sweep and dust hall, clean doorstep and brasses and shake mats.

Then serve kitchen breakfast and prepare what is required for the dining-room. Clean gentlemen's boots and sweep any backstairs or passages.

Clear away dining-room breakfast things, and take up crumbs. Wash all or some of the dishes.

Tidy kitchen and larder, and be ready to receive mistress. In the forenoon prepare and cook early dinner or luncheon and prepare late dinner as far as possible. Dust and tidy cook's bedroom and commence any special work of the day.

Answer the front-door bell until 1 o'clock, while the housemaid is engaged upstairs, and attend to any messages which come to the back-door.

Serve lunch, then kitchen dinner and wash up, leaving kitchen tidy. It is usual for the cook to wash the dinner service used in the dining-room, although glass and silver are done by the housemaid. Finish special work of the day, and dress if there is no late dinner or a very simple one. Kitchen tea.

Prepare and cook late dinner or supper and coffee if ordered. Wash up (this can often be done while the meal is going on, and need not be a troublesome matter). Kitchen supper.

Leave everything tidy for the night and fuel ready for lighting fire in the morning. The back-door should be locked as soon as it is dark and windows the last thing before going to bed. Bed at 10 o'clock.

Special Weekly Duties.—Besides the daily routine some special cleaning should be undertaken each day so as to keep all in order.

This might be arranged in somewhat the following manner:—

Monday—Downstairs windows.
Tuesday—Backstairs and passages.
Wednesday—Clean dining-room and hall alternate weeks.
Thursday—Clean tins, brasses.
Friday—Larder and cupboards.
Saturday—Kitchen (flues before breakfast).

Notes.—The above plan presupposes that the dining-room breakfast is at 8.30; if earlier some of the housework must be left until that meal is over.

It is sometimes customary for the cook-general to help the housemaid with the beds except when there are young ladies in the house, when they generally undertake this piece of work.

The clearing of the breakfast-table and washing of some of the dishes is also frequently done by the ladies of the house, especially if the family is large and only two maids are kept.

The cook-general is often expected to do some washing, such as all the kitchen towels and dusters, her own washing, and sometimes the flannel washing as well. When this is the case, this should be done on Monday or Tuesday and be regarded as the special work of the day. It should be started as early in the forenoon as possible, the cooking being made as simple as possible that day, and a little extra help might be given by members of the household.

The cook-general is also expected to take the housemaid's duties when the latter has her evening out or her free time.

The Nurse.—See under Section "The Child."

The Housemaid.—A housemaid is employed to do work about the house and more especially in the bedrooms and sitting-rooms. This work will vary according to the number of servants kept and the style of living. In larger establishments where there are many bedrooms and a constant coming and going of visitors, there may be several housemaids—an upper housemaid and two or three under-housemaids. In this case the upper housemaid would be responsible for and supervise all the work done in the bedrooms and sitting-rooms, although most of the actual cleaning and all the rough work would be undertaken by the junior maids.

The upper housemaid would do the lighter and more difficult work in the principal rooms, would see that the bedrooms were properly prepared for guests, answer the bedroom bells, and attend to the wants of the ladies of the house. Sometimes she is required to act as lady's-maid to her mistress if there is no special maid for this purpose. She would take charge of the bed-linen, giving out the necessary supplies, and keeping an accurate account of the stock. She would also take charge of all curtains and hangings, cushion-covers and table-covers, see that the suitable articles were in use and all kept in good order. She might also have time for some of the mending.

It would be her duty to take early tea and water into the principal rooms in the morning, and again give the necessary attendance in these rooms throughout the day and in the evening.

Some of the locking up at night might also fall to her share.

The under housemaids would do all the cleaning proper, such as the sweeping, dusting, and scrubbing. The cleaning of the bathrooms, lavatories, and housemaids' pantry, the cleaning of all grates and the lighting of fires. If there is a school-room or nursery it would be the duty of one of them to do all the cleaning and waiting required in that department. The junior maid would also have charge of the servants' bedrooms and back staircase. The boot cleaning, too, would be shared by the under-housemaid unless there was a boy or man employed for the purpose.

In smaller households where only two or three servants are kept, the housemaid will have to do the work of the bedrooms single-handed, and the sitting-rooms are generally divided between the different maids. She may or may not have some mending to do; this will depend upon the extent of her other duties.

A single housemaid is also expected to give the parlour-maid some assistance in waiting at table and answering of bells, and to take her duties during off-duty times.

She will also have the cleaning of ladies' and any children's boots.

The House-parlourmaid combines the duties of housemaid and tablemaid, and, in addition to her house duties, she will have charge of the table, *i.e.* the setting and clearing of the table for all meals, all the waiting required, and the washing of the silver, glass, and china. She should answer all front-door bells after one o'clock and might have to undertake a little washing. The cook may or may not give some assistance with the housework.

Qualifications Necessary.—A housemaid must be clean, orderly, and an early riser. Much of the comfort of the household depends upon getting a fair amount of cleaning done before breakfast. She must be quiet and unobtrusive in her work and make as little disturbance as possible with her cleaning. She must be polite and courteous in her manner and always respectful. She must also be methodical, arranging her work so that too much does not fall to one day and not sufficient to others.

Dress and Appearance.—A housemaid should at all times be neat and tidy in appearance, and pay particular attention to her hair and the cleanliness and freshness of her person.

In the morning she should be dressed in a neat print dress with a plain white apron with bib, a linen collar, and a simple cap with cambric frill. A coarser apron may be put on when doing any rough work, and a pair of gloves while cleaning the grates. In the afternoon the cotton dress should be changed for the orthodox dress of some black woollen material, plainly made, but neat fitting with tight sleeves and of a smart walking length. A muslin apron should then be worn with a becoming cap and turn-down collar and cuffs usually fastened with bows of black ribbons. Quiet shoes should be worn at all times.

Duties of the Housemaid.—(Three maids—cook, housemaid, and parlour-maid.) Rise at 6 or 6.30, dress, turn down bed and leave room airing.

Open up drawing-room or any other sitting-room under her care, clean fire-place, sweep and dust room, and light fire if necessary. Sweep and dust stairs. Take hot water to the bedrooms and early cups of tea if required. Prepare baths. Kitchen breakfast. Clean front hall and doorsteps unless done by cook, clean any boots, make her own bed, and tidy bedroom.

While family are at breakfast go into bedrooms, and see that windows are open and beds left to air. Then empty slops and attend to the wash-stands. Make beds with the parlour-maid's help. Dust bedrooms and put them in order and then do special work of the day.

Kitchen dinner. Dress. In the afternoon finish off any lighter pieces of work which are not dirty, and do mending if required.

Kitchen tea. In the evening take hot water to the bedrooms half-an-hour before dinner is served. Draw down blinds, and light up at dark, closing windows if required.

During dinner it is usual for the housemaid to do the carrying of the dishes from the kitchen to the dining-room and *vice versâ*, so that the parlour-maid may never require to leave the room, and also to give what assistance she can with the waiting. When dinner is over, return to the bedrooms, empty slops, and give fresh supply of water, turn down beds and lay out clothes for the night; remove any dirty boots and see that all is in order.

Kitchen supper. Bed at ten o'clock.

Special Weekly Work

Monday—Clean drawing-room and spare bedroom alternately.
Collect and count washing.
Tuesday—Clean two bedrooms.
Wednesday—Clean servants' bedrooms and housemaid's pantry.
Thursday—Clean bath-room, lavatory, and staircase.
Friday—Clean library or morning-room and front hall, unless done by the cook.
Saturday—Put away linen from washing and make things generally tidy for Sunday.

Duties of the House-parlourmaid.—(Two maids, cook general, and house-parlourmaid.) Rise at 6 or 6.30, dress, turn down bed and leave room to air.

Sweep and dust drawing-room or library, and light fire if required. (The dining-room is done by the cook.)

Sweep and dust stairs. Take hot water to the bedrooms and call the family.

Kitchen breakfast. Lay sitting-room breakfast, and clean boots, serve breakfast. Empty slops and see that beds are left airing. Dust and tidy own bedroom. Clear breakfast-table and wash up, unless this is done by the cook. Make beds with the assistance of the cook or some member of the family.

Dust and tidy bedrooms and proceed to special work of the day. Dress by one o'clock. Set the table and serve lunch or early dinner.

Kitchen dinner. Clear the dining-room table, take up crumbs and leave room tidy. Wash up silver and glass and finish any light work. Answer front-door bell in the afternoon and evening and indoor bells all day.

Prepare and take in afternoon tea. Kitchen tea. Wash up afternoon tea things.

Draw down blinds, close windows (if required), and light up at dusk.

Lay dinner-table and serve dinner. Wait at table, clear and wash up. Serve coffee if required.

Attend to bedrooms, emptying slops, laying down beds, and removing any dirty boots.

Kitchen supper. Bed at ten o'clock.

Special Weekly Duties

Monday—Clean drawing-room or spare bedroom alternately.
Collect and count washing.
Tuesday—Clean one or two bedrooms.
Wednesday—Clean bath-room, lavatory, and staircase.
Thursday—Clean servants' bedroom and pantries
Friday—Clean silver and brasses.
Saturday—Put away washing and tidy up generally.

The Parlour-maid.—A parlour-maid or table-maid's chief duty is to look after the table and see to the serving of all meals. It is a very important position, and one which would be filled by a butler in houses where men-servants were employed.

The parlour-maid takes the sole charge of the silver, glass, china, and other valuables in daily use, and is mistress of the pantry. She also has charge of the sideboard, the wine, cake, fruit, &c., and sees that fresh supplies are ordered as required.

The care of the table-linen will be another of her duties. She must see that the table is sufficiently supplied, and that an accurate account is kept of the stock. The mending, too, might be done by her if time permitted.

A parlour-maid usually undertakes the cleaning of one or two sitting-rooms, usually the drawing-room and one other smaller room as well. She attends to the sitting-room fires, and lamps and candles if used.

She answers the front-door bell throughout the day, unless relieved for part of the time by the housemaid, and announces all visitors.

She may also be responsible for the floral decorations of the table and for the arrangement of flowers and plants throughout the house, unless the mistress herself undertakes this piece of work.

If there is no man-servant the parlour-maid valets her master, attending to the brushing of his clothes and the cleaning of his boots. If there is no lady's-maid she may be called upon to wash up and do lace and other fine articles belonging to her mistress and also any fancy articles, such as d'oyleys and tray-cloths for table use.

She might also be called upon to assist the housemaid with bed-making, and would do housemaid's duties in the latter's off-duty times. She is usually responsible for the shutting of the sitting-room windows at night and the front door, unless done by some member of the family.

Personal Appearance and Requirements.—A parlour-maid should be tall and elegant in appearance and rather slight, so that she can move about easily and be graceful in her movements. The dress, which is similar to that worn by the housemaid, must be neatly made and fit well, and the apron, collar, cuffs, and cap must always be spotlessly clean, and especially so when the maid is waiting at table.

A parlour-maid should pay particular attention to her hands, in order to have them nice for giving attendance to the members of the family, and her hair should be neatly done without being too elaborate or fussy in style. She must be orderly and punctual in all her doings, and have a thorough knowledge of waiting at table and other table requirements.

As a parlour-maid comes into such close contact with the family, the post can only be filled by a woman who is capable and conscientious, and who has the interests of her master and mistress at heart. Her manner must be pleasant and respectful at all times, she must know how to receive and address people of refinement, and be able to give in an intelligent way any information that may be required.

Daily Duties of Parlour-maid.—Rise at 6 or 6.30, according to time of breakfast. Dress, turn down bed and leave room to air.

Open up sitting-rooms under her charge, light fires if necessary, and do the sweeping and dusting. Give any attendance required by the master of the house and clean his boots.

Kitchen breakfast. Then set sitting-room breakfast-table and make toast, tea and coffee unless done by the cook. Serve breakfast and wait if required. Finish any work in the sitting-rooms. Clear breakfast-table, take up crumbs, and leave room in order. Help housemaid with beds. (This might be done before the clearing of the table if breakfast is a very prolonged meal, but at the same time the beds should be left sufficient time to air.)

Dust and put in order her own bedroom, unless done by the housemaid. Wash up dishes, including silver. See that all cruets are filled ready for the next meal, also jam and sugar dishes attended to, and butter rolled or made into pats. Attend to the sideboard and see that the necessary wine is decanted, and that fruit and cake dishes are clean and tidy. Make a note of any stores required. Attend to any floral decorations and water-plants. Attend to lamps and candles if used in the sitting-rooms.

Dress by one o'clock, in time to lay luncheon table. Make up sitting-room fire, and put room in order before setting the table. Serve luncheon and wait as required.

Kitchen dinner. After dinner clear luncheon from sitting-room table, leave room in order, and wash up. If time permits, do mending in the afternoon or a little ironing. Take in afternoon tea and attend to all visitors. Light up sitting-rooms at dusk and draw down blinds.

Kitchen tea. Prepare for dinner, lay table, and at the appointed time announce the meal in the drawing-room or sound a bell or gong. Wait at table either alone or assisted by the housemaid. Carve if required. Then clear and wash up. Serve coffee or any other refreshment that may be required.

Kitchen supper. Bed at ten P.M.

Special Weekly Duties

Monday—Collect and count table linen, wash out towels, dusters, wash-leathers, &c., and give special attention to plants.

Tuesday—Clean drawing-room or other sitting-room.

Wednesday—Clean second sitting-room (morning-room or library) or assist housemaid with special cleaning.

Thursday—Clean silver.

Friday—Clean pantry and her own bedroom, or any brasses and other ornaments.

Saturday—Count and put away washing, general tidying up and preparations for Sunday.

The General Servant.—The general servant is employed to do the entire work of the house, except that which is undertaken by the mistress herself or some other member of the family.

If the household consist of more than two or three persons it will be necessary for the mistress to give a considerable amount of help, if the work is to be done properly. She may either do the cooking or the lighter parts of the housework, such as dusting, laying the table, washing of silver and glass, &c.; this depends entirely upon her own tastes and inclinations.

Although a general servant cannot be expected to be an expert in all branches of household work, she ought to have a good all-round knowledge and be able to cook simple dishes in a wholesome and appetising manner.

Her work need not necessarily be harder than that of another servant who only performs special duties, but it must be systematically arranged, and she must be quick and active if the day's proceedings are to be carried through in a satisfactory manner. A general servant is not infrequently looked down upon as holding an inferior position, a sort of "jack of all trades and master of none"; but this entirely depends upon the maid herself and upon the house in which she serves. If she does her work well, she is a most valuable person, and her position, if conscientiously filled, may become one of trust. If she has the good fortune to be employed by a kind and considerate mistress, her life should be a very happy one. She will enter into much closer relationship with the family than it is possible to do where there are several servants, and she will get full credit for all her work. A good general is always particular about her personal appearance; the fact of being busy should never be an excuse for having a dirty and dishevelled appearance; in fact, this state only denotes a slovenly worker. It ought also to be a source of pleasure to be dressed in good time in the afternoon. The dress should be that worn by any other house servant, *i.e.* a nice print dress in the morning, with a white linen apron, linen collar, and cap, and a black or dark blue dress in the afternoon with a muslin apron and more dressy cap. A coarse apron or overall should always be kept at hand to slip on when doing any dirty work.

Daily Duties.—Rise at 6 or 6.30, dress, turn down bed and leave room to air. Unbolt door, draw up blinds and open kitchen and sitting-room windows. Light kitchen fire and tidy grate. Fill kettle and put on porridge if required. Clean boots, sweep and dust sitting-room, lighting fire if necessary. Sweep and dust hall and clean doorstep and brasses. (If breakfast is at an early hour this may be left until later.) Prepare sitting-room breakfast and have kitchen breakfast.

Empty slops and air bedrooms. Tidy and dust her own bedroom. Clear breakfast-table, wash up and tidy kitchen. Take orders for the day.

Make beds with assistance, dust and tidy bedrooms, and sweep and dust stairs. Prepare early dinner or lunch and do special work for the day. (If late dinner is the rule, the mid-day meal should be as simple as possible, and most of the cooking should be prepared in the morning.)

Serve lunch and have early dinner. Clear and wash up. When kitchen has been tidied, change dress, attend to any light duties in the afternoon, and serve tea. Attend to all bells promptly. Serve supper or dinner at the hour appointed, and do what waiting is required. Clear and wash up and have kitchen supper.

Light up at dusk, draw down blinds, and close windows as required. After dinner turn down beds and attend to the bedrooms. Collect sticks and coals for the morning. Bed at ten P.M.

SPECIAL WEEKLY DUTIES

Monday—Wash towels and dusters, &c. (Heavy washing can scarcely be undertaken unless the maid is relieved of most of her other work for the forenoon.)
Tuesday—Clean drawing-room and dining-room alternate weeks.
Wednesday—Clean bath-room, staircase, and hall.
Thursday—Clean bedrooms.
Friday—Clean pantry, larder, and any back premises, also silver and tins alternate weeks.
Saturday—Clean kitchen.

The Housekeeper.—The housekeeper is the representative of her mistress, and in large households she fulfils the duties which naturally fall to the mistress herself in a smaller ménage. This leaves the lady of the house free to attend to social and other claims.

The housekeeper is second in command, and answerable only to the head of the house. She engages and dismisses servants and pays their wages—with the exception of the nurse and lady's-maid—arranges their work, and is responsible in every way for their appearance and behaviour and the fulfilment of their duties.

The housekeeper is responsible for the proper keeping of the house in every part, and she sees to the needs and comfort of the whole family and domestic staff.

She orders and gives out all stores, keeps accounts, and pays the bills. If there is a butler he relieves her of some of those duties, and he is always responsible for the men-servants.

The housekeeper should see her employer at stated times in order to give in a report of the various departments, and also to receive her instructions and learn her wishes.

The housekeeper has always her own sitting-room in which her meals are served by one of the under-maids, except dinner, which she usually takes with the other servants.

Her sitting-room may be shared by some of the upper servants, such as the lady's-maid, the butler, and the valet.

The Butler.—The position of butler is usually one of great trust. He is head of the men-servants, is responsible for the work of those under him, arranges their off-duty time, and often engages them as well.

He has sole charge of the wine cellar, and gives out the wine required, keeping a note of the stock, and frequently seeing to the buying in of supplies.

To his care is confided the silver and other articles of value in daily use.

He is responsible for the arrangement of all meals and the table appointments. He announces when meals are ready, puts the dishes on the table or does the carving, pours out the wine, and waits assisted by a footman or parlour-maid.

He is responsible for the care of the billiard-room and smoking-room or library, and the fires and lighting arrangements of the other rooms.

If single-handed, his duties would be very much the same as those already detailed for the house-parlourmaid. If there is no valet he waits upon his master. He also looks after any carriage or motor rugs and lamps, and in the country would be responsible for shooting and picnic lunches.

When there is no housekeeper the butler frequently pays the bills and does the marketing. He usually goes out every day.

The butler is also responsible for the shutting up of the house.

In the early part of the day his dress should be dark trousers and waistcoat and black tail coat, with a white front and collar and black tie —in the evening the regulation dress suit with a white tie.

The Footman.—The footman is generally an all-round useful man and his duties may be very varied. If there is a butler, he would work under him, but in houses where he is the only man-servant his duties might be somewhat after the following:—

He would clean boots and shoes, knives and windows, fetch coal and see to the filling of coal-scuttles and the keeping up of fires.

He would lay the table and wait, assisted by a parlour-maid or housemaid, and wash up the silver, glass, and china after each meal.

He would valet his master and go out with the carriage if required, attending to any rugs.

The charge of lamps and window-plants would also fall to his share. He would answer bells, announce visitors, and take in afternoon tea.

He would also be responsible for the locking up of the house at night.

A footman may or may not wear livery. If this is not supplied it is usual to give two suits in the year, either new or from his master's wardrobe.

The Lady's-maid.—The lady's-maid devotes herself to the personal requirements of her mistress and looks after her needs in every way.

She undertakes the charge of her wardrobe and sees that all her belongings are kept in good order and proper repair.

She assists her mistress with her toilet, helps her to dress and undress, brushes and dresses her hair, selects and lays out the clothes she is going to wear.

She does any packing and unpacking and travels with her mistress when required.

She requires a bedroom for herself, which is sometimes fitted as a bed-sitting-room, where she can do her sewing and other work.

She will keep her own and her mistress's room in order, do the dusting, and make the beds with some assistance; but she will not be expected to clean grates nor do any hard cleaning, and she will take no part in general housework.

If well filled the post of lady's-maid is no sinecure, as a varied knowledge is necessary to do all that is required. A woman who undertakes this work must be able to sew well in order that she may both make and mend neatly. She must also have some knowledge of dressmaking and millinery so as to be able to alter and renovate, to change the style of an evening dress, to make a tasteful bow, retrim a hat or bonnet, or give the necessary finishing touches to a lady's toilet. She must be a woman of taste, and be able to give advice as to the choice of dresses, &c.

She ought to know enough laundry work to enable her to wash and do up laces and silks and muslin, wash shawls and feather boas, and other fancy articles.

She must be a good hair-dresser, and if a fashionable coiffure is required, it is a good plan to take a lesson occasionally from a first-class hairdresser in order to learn the newest modes.

If she travels with her mistress a knowledge of languages, especially French, is invaluable, and she should know how to make travelling arrangements, see to tickets and luggage, and be responsible for the exchange of money.

A lady's-maid wears no uniform, but ought to be quietly and neatly dressed when in attendance on her mistress.

Her manner must be pleasant and respectful, and she must know how to exercise self-control. As she comes into such close contact with the private life of her mistress, it is her duty to give her faithful and loyal service as long as she remains in her employment.

The Valet.—The valet attends to the personal wants of his master just as the lady's-maid waits upon her mistress. He helps him with his dressing, and takes full charge of his wardrobe, brushes his clothes, cleans his boots, and attends to any repairs.

He sees that his master's wash-stand and toilet-table are supplied with the necessary requisites, and is responsible for all his belongings being kept in order and in the proper place.

He must know how to pack and unpack, and if he travels with his master he must know how to make all arrangements, take tickets, and see to luggage, &c.

The valet is sometimes expected to give assistance in waiting at table.

The Laundry-maid.—The laundry-maid is responsible for the washing and dressing of the household linen.

She will have full charge of the laundry, seeing that it is kept clean and in perfect order. She will also be responsible for all the linen confided to her care.

If the family is not large, she may be expected to take part in some of the housework as well. (For fuller details of her duties see Guide to Laundry Work, p. 271.)

The Scullery-maid.—The scullery-maid ranks lowest amongst the kitchen servants, and if there is a kitchen-maid she works under her.

A scullery-maid is employed primarily for cleaning all the dishes and utensils used in the kitchen; she washes the kitchen floors and does the scrubbing. She will assist with the preparation of vegetables and be responsible for the keeping up of the kitchen fire.

If there is no kitchen-maid, the scullery-maid will assist the cook and work under her direction.

Although the work may be somewhat laborious, it is a good beginning for a young girl who aspires to be cook, and if she is quick and willing she may learn a great deal, and gradually rise to a better position.

The Kitchen-maid.—A kitchen-maid is employed to work under a cook, to be her apprentice as it were. She is responsible for many of the plainer dishes, thus leaving the cook free for more important duties. She prepares and serves the kitchen meals, and also cooks for the nursery and school-room if required.

If there is no scullery-maid, the kitchen-maid will also undertake the cleaning of the kitchen utensils, the kitchen stove, and some of the kitchen premises.

Provided a kitchen-maid serves under a good cook, this is the best way for her to learn the art of cooking.

The Tweeny.—This is a title given to a young girl who divides her time between the house and the kitchen. In the forenoon she may work under the housemaid or the nurse and do the housework, and from lunch time onwards assist the cook. She does all the odd jobs and must be ready to make herself generally useful.

The Hall Boy.—The hall boy or boy in buttons is sometimes kept in place of a single man-servant, and if clever and willing he may be an extremely useful member of the household.

He will be found of special value in the house of a professional man, such as a doctor or dentist, where there is much answering of bells required, and perhaps running of messages as well.

A capable boy will soon learn to clean knives, boots, and windows, to fill coal-scuttles and look after fires. He will also be able to set the table, do some waiting and most of the washing up.

The boy in buttons must be provided with clothes; a livery suit of some dark cloth, navy serge, dark green, or dark crimson with the coat buttoning to the neck, and for doing cleaning or rough work he should have a cotton jacket of dark blue or striped drill or strong holland and some good stout aprons.

HOUSEKEEPING WITHOUT A SERVANT

In these days of flat life, when accommodation for housing a servant is very limited, it is often found more convenient to do without one altogether, or to manage with either daily help or the services of a thoroughly competent worker once or twice a week.

It ought to be quite possible for a newly married lady to undertake the work of a small flat with perhaps the occasional help of a charwoman, and to have time for other interests as well. Or if, as is often the case, two sisters or two friends live together, the work should be all the more easy to manage, as each can take her share of the household duties.

Some knowledge of housekeeping is, however, necessary for the successful management of a "no servant" ménage, and if one is entirely ignorant of the ways of doing things, it should scarcely be attempted unless absolutely necessary, as the results are not likely to be satisfactory.

Good health is also a *sine qua non*, although no great physical strength is required; so much is done nowadays to make the work of a house simple, and especially the work in a flat. There are no stairs nor front door-step to keep in order, the cooking and water heating can be done by gas, and all provisions, &c., can be brought to the very door without the trouble of going up and down stairs. Yet with all the conveniences possible, success in the undertaking will depend to a large extent upon the order and method displayed in its organisation. The work must be planned carefully, or one will either be in a constant muddle, or be continually at it, and have time for nothing beyond the daily round of house duties.

To begin with, the woman who does her own work must dress suitably when performing her household duties—a short skirt, a cotton or other washing blouse, and a big apron or overall is the most suitable attire; or a complete washing dress might be worn if the weather is warm. A large overall to slip on over a good afternoon dress will also be found useful.

It will be well also to secure as many labour-saving apparatus as possible, such as gas-cooker, carpet-sweeper, knife-cleaner, mop for washing dishes, &c.

Care, too, must be taken of the hands. Because a woman is her own maid-of-all-work this is no excuse for her being careless in this respect. Gloves should be worn as much as possible, and after doing washing up the hands should be well dried and a few drops of glycerine and rose-water should be rubbed into the skin.

Do not commence by doing too much before breakfast. Unless one has been accustomed to early rising it is apt to knock one up for the rest of the day without any reason. Do not attempt to light fires and clean out a sitting-room before a meal has been taken. Sometimes it may be possible to prepare a certain amount the night before, and in any case there should be a small gas or even an oil-stove upon which the morning meal can be prepared. If the sitting-room has not a stove which can be lit without much trouble, there is no reason why the kitchen should not be pretty enough and tidy enough for the first meal to be taken there.

On rising in the morning put on a large kettle of water. If there is porridge for breakfast this should have been soaked over-night in a double cooker. Put a light under this also. Then dress, and when ready let breakfast have the first attention, taking time to have this meal leisurely and in comfort. Next collect the dishes and clear the table, and either put the dishes to one side while the bedrooms and sitting-room are being done, or wash them up straight away.

The sitting-room should be done next, as it will be as well to let the bedrooms air as long as possible. If a fire has to be laid, do this with order and method. Go over the floor with a carpet-sweeper, then dust every part and leave the window open. Next turn your attention to the bedrooms, put these in order, and then sweep and dust the passage. Now return to the kitchen, wash up all the dishes, and sweep and dust. If breakfast has not been very late, all the cleaning should be finished by eleven o'clock, unless some special work has to be done, such as the thorough cleaning of a room, silver, brasses, &c., but if any help is given with the work this could also be fitted in.

The cooking for the day should now be thought of, and although it is always possible to have meals at a restaurant, or to order various dishes from a caterer's, it must be remembered that this is an expensive way of living, and with the necessary knowledge of cookery it should be quite possible to have dainty little meals at home, and so feed well with very little trouble. The woman who does her own work will not require to spend much time considering what is in her larder; she will no doubt have arranged in her own mind what the different meals have to be whilst doing her other work. All the cookery required should either be done in the morning or at least prepared as far as possible, so that what must be left for the evening will take very little time to get ready when required. Light utensils should be used, such as aluminium, enamelled tin, or earthenware saucepans, as they are easier to handle and keep in order. One or two steamers would also be invaluable, as so much cooking can be done in these without trouble and attention.

After the mid-day meal it is a good plan to rest, even if only for half-an-hour, and then, after dressing, one ought to feel quite fresh to go out and turn one's thoughts in a different channel. The afternoon should be free from household cares.

If the evening meal has been prepared in the morning it will not take long to get it ready, and half-an-hour as an ordinary rule should be sufficient. Then if washing up in the evening is found awkward, there is no occasion to do more than the silver, which it is never wise to leave, and the other dishes, if they are not required in the morning, could be packed up and washed with the breakfast dishes.

Marketing.—The time for doing this will depend upon circumstances, and need not be rigidly fixed. If it is inconvenient to go out in the morning in the midst of the other work it may be possible to order in the afternoon for the following day, or another way is to arrange for the tradesmen to call, and for everything to be brought to the door at a certain time.

Outside Help.—This may be obtained either daily or once or twice a week, according to circumstances and individual needs. If a young girl is engaged to come in for an hour or two every morning, she might do the washing up, prepare the vegetables, and attend to the other kitchen work, also clean the boots and stoves and assist with the rooms as well. Many prefer, however, to have more competent help even if it is not so often. A good worker for half a day could do all the hard cleaning, including the stoves, scrubbing of the kitchen, and thoroughly clean one or two rooms each visit. If the rooms can be prepared for her, and any ornaments and other trifles dusted and afterwards arranged, it will be a great saving of time, and in this way half the rooms could be cleaned one week, and the other half the next.

Advantages.—Besides the actual saving of board and wages of an indoor servant there will be a feeling of independence. It will be possible to leave home for a day or a week without any need for worrying about the house. There will also be freedom from that feeling of close proximity to a servant which is impossible to avoid in a flat, and which destroys the sense of liberty which is essential to the happiness of both parties.

Warning.—It must be remembered that housework must not crowd out everything else; one must have time to read a little, rest a little, and keep in touch with the outside world as well. The economy that saves money at the expense of health and the capability of enjoyment is in reality one of the worst extravagances.

Another point is that the housekeeper must remember to feed herself. If the mid-day meal is taken alone, she is only too apt to make it as meagre as possible to save trouble, and also to take it too quickly, whereas time would be well spent in eating something really nutritious, and if the quantity is small the quality should be all the more carefully considered.

One must also learn to do without many things, and not expect to live in the same style as those who have plenty of servants at their command, but this can quite well be done without falling into a slovenly way of living and losing any of the refinement of life.

WAGES TABLE

Giving the rates per Month, Week, and Day of Yearly Incomes from £10 to £50

Year.			Month.			Week.			Day.			Year.			Month.			Week.			Day.		
£	s.	d.	£	s.	d.	£	s.	d.	£	s.	d.	£	s.	d.	£	s.	d.	£	s.	d.	£	s.	d.
10	0	0	0	16	8	0	3	10¼	0	0	6½	17	0	0	1	8	4	0	6	6½	0	0	11¼
10	10	0	0	17	6	0	4	0½	0	0	7	17	10	0	1	9	2	0	6	8¾	0	0	11½
11	0	0	0	18	4	0	4	2¾	0	0	7¼	17	17	0	1	9	9	0	6	10½	0	0	11¾
11	10	0	0	19	2	0	4	5	0	0	7½	18	0	0	1	10	0	0	6	11	0	0	11¾
11	11	0	0	19	3	0	4	5¼	0	0	7½	18	10	0	1	10	10	0	7	1½	0	1	0¼
12	0	0	1	0	0	0	4	7½	0	0	8	18	18	0	1	11	6	0	7	3¼	0	1	0½
12	10	0	1	0	10	0	4	9¾	0	0	8¼	19	0	0	1	11	8	0	7	3¾	0	1	0½
12	12	0	1	1	0	0	4	10¼	0	0	8½	19	10	0	1	12	6	0	7	6	0	1	0¾
13	0	0	1	1	8	0	5	0	0	0	8½	19	19	0	1	13	3	0	7	8	0	1	1
13	10	0	1	2	6	0	5	2¼	0	0	9	20	0	0	1	13	4	0	7	8¼	0	1	1¼
13	13	0	1	2	9	0	5	3	0	0	9	21	0	0	1	15	0	0	8	1	0	1	1¾
14	0	0	1	3	4	0	5	4½	0	0	9¼	22	0	0	1	16	8	0	8	5½	0	1	2½
14	10	0	1	4	2	0	5	7	0	0	9½	23	0	0	1	18	4	0	8	10¼	0	1	3
14	14	0	1	4	6	0	5	7¾	0	0	9¾	24	0	0	2	0	0	0	9	2¾	0	1	3¾
15	0	0	1	5	0	0	5	9¼	0	0	9¾	25	0	0	2	1	8	0	9	7½	0	1	4½
15	10	0	1	5	10	0	5	11¼	0	0	10¼	30	0	0	2	10	0	0	11	6½	0	1	7¾
15	15	0	1	6	3	0	6	0¾	0	0	10¼	35	0	0	2	18	4	0	13	5½	0	1	11
16	0	0	1	6	8	0	6	1¾	0	0	10½	40	0	0	3	6	8	0	15	4½	0	2	2¼
16	10	0	1	7	6	0	6	4¼	0	0	10¾	45	0	0	3	15	0	0	17	3¾	0	2	5½
16	16	0	1	8	0	0	6	5½	0	0	11	50	0	0	4	3	4	0	19	2¾	0	2	9

GUIDE TO HOUSEHOLD WORK

The object of the following pages is to furnish the housewife with directions for the performance of such details of household work as are not dealt with under special headings.

The directions are the result of many years practical experience of everything pertaining to household management.

The various details of household work are dealt with separately under their own headings, and the many useful hints with regard to cleaning, &c., are the result of actual test.

It is hoped that the information given will afford valuable help to the harassed housewife in the little difficulties which are continually cropping up in the course of daily duties. If it does this the mission of this section of the book will be abundantly fulfilled.

THE CLEANING OF ROOMS

Before beginning to clean a room of any kind it is very important that everything required for the work should be collected together, so that there need be no unnecessary running about to seek for this or that duster or brush. So first consider what has to be cleaned, and then take with you the necessary implements, seeing that everything is in order for the work to be carried out satisfactorily and systematically, with the least possible waste of time.

TO CLEAN AND TIDY A BEDROOM

Daily Work.—First draw up the blinds as far as they will go, being careful to keep them straight, and open the windows top and bottom. Then turn down the bed and spread out any night garments on a chair. Allow the room to air for an hour at least before the bed is made. During this time the slops may be emptied, towels hung up evenly, and any clothing or other articles left lying about the room put away in their places. It is always better if two people can make the bed. When this is neatly finished, fold up the night-dress or sleeping-suit, put it in a neat case, and lay it on the bed just beneath the pillow.

If there has been a fire in the room attend to the grate next, being careful to make as little dust as possible.

It will not be necessary to sweep the room every day, but the floor must be gone over with a short brush and shovel or with a carpet-sweeper, so as to take up any pieces or surface dust. Be careful too that all fluff is removed from underneath the bed. Some people prefer to have the carpet wiped over with a slightly damp cloth or leather.

Then dust the room. Commence at one corner and go steadily round, dusting each article until every part has been done. Pay particular attention to the toilet table. Lift each article and dust underneath it, arranging everything with order and taste.

If the edges of the floor are polished or covered with linoleum, rub them round with a slightly damp duster, or, better still, with the flannel or cloth which has been used to rub up a polished floor. The latter will have the remains of a little wax upon it, and will keep the floor in good condition.

If a candlestick has been used, see that this is in order, putting in a fresh candle if required, and removing any old matches.

Finally fill up the ewer and water-jug with fresh cold water, and lower the blinds and windows a little if desired. Look round the room to see that everything is in order and that no duster or brush is being left behind, and close the door quietly on leaving.

Weekly or Thorough Cleaning.—Once a week, or at least once a fortnight, a bedroom will require a more thorough cleaning if it is in constant use.

After the slops have been emptied, the bedroom ware and any gas globes should be carried away to a bathroom or housemaid's pantry, where they can be washed. If this is not convenient, they must be covered over and washed afterwards in the room.

Before making the bed, brush the mattress on both sides and well round the edges, as this is one of the best means of keeping away moths. Dust also the bedstead under the mattress and then make the bed, but do not put on the top cover; this is better kept off until the cleaning is finished. Tuck up the valance all round, if there is one, and brush and pin back any curtains out of the way.

Next lay some sheets of clean paper or a large towel on the top of the bed. Dust all ornaments (keeping aside any that may require washing) and other small articles, and lay them on the top of the bed over the paper, or towel. Shake and fold up the toilet cover, and all table-cloths and towels; shake and remove any short window-blinds, and lay these also on the bed. Cover all with a large dust-sheet, which will hang well over the sides.

Dust and remove from the room as many as possible of the small articles of furniture, and cover over what is left with dust-sheets or old newspapers. If any of the chairs are upholstered, these should be brushed with a furniture brush before being covered. All clothing must be taken down from the back of doors and kept out of the room or under cover.

Roll up all rugs or mats, and take them outside to be beaten later on. If this cannot be done they must be brushed with a short brush in the room and then removed.

If there has been a fire in the room, remove all the cinders and dust, but do not polish the grate until the room has been swept. Next close all windows and doors, and see that drawers too are shut.

Sprinkle the carpet with tea-leaves or bran, and sweep it thoroughly. When the dust has all been collected in a shovel, the window should be thrown open and the room left for a little while to allow the dust to settle.

Meanwhile the dust in the dust-pan should be taken away and burnt at once. If left lying about it is very apt to be knocked over and the contents perhaps scattered around. The articles that have been outside can also have attention. The rugs should be brushed or beaten outside and carried back in readiness to be laid down, the ware in the bathroom washed, and the small furniture rubbed up.

Then return to the room and finish off the fireplace, using a hearth-cloth.

Roll up the dust-sheets, which should afterwards be shaken in the open air. One word about dust-sheets—too often these are used until they reach such a dirty state as to be rendered almost useless. They should be washed whenever necessary.

The dusting may now be commenced. First mount a pair of steps, dusting all out-of-reach places, such as blinds, curtain poles, inside of windows, pictures, top of wardrobe and door, &c. Then dust and polish, if necessary, the furniture that remains in the room; also dust round the skirting board, panels of doors and floor where it is uncarpeted.

When the dust has as far as possible been removed from the room, it is time to do any necessary washing. Wash the top of the wash-stand if it is marble, the tiles round the fire-place, the window ledges if they require it, and any finger-marks off doors. The windows and mirrors too if they require special cleaning should now have attention. Also finish off the edges of the floor in a suitable manner, according to whether they are linoleum, varnish, or matting.

Now put back in their places the articles which were laid on the bed, let down the bed valance, and put the bed in order.

Then bring back the things from outside and arrange everything in order. Supply the wash-stand with fresh water and new soap if required.

Spare Bedrooms.—These will not require to be cleaned so often as the rooms that are in constant use. If they are aired and dusted regularly they ought to keep in good order without being turned out more than perhaps once a month. Of course, this depends a good deal upon the locality in which a house is situated. A room in a smoky city will require much more cleaning than one in a fresh country district.

Note.—For details of the various operations, see under special headings.

TO CLEAN A SITTING-ROOM

The order and method for this is very much the same as for a bedroom, except of course there is not the bed and wash-stand to attend to.

Daily Work.—Draw up the blinds and open the window. Remove any table-covers, shake them and fold them up, and roll up the rugs (sometimes this is done over-night).

If there has been a fire in the room, attend to that first. Lay down the hearth-cloth before commencing, and finish off the grate completely.

Then with a dust-pan and short brush—or, better still, with a carpet-sweeper—go over the floor, taking up any crumbs and pieces and all surface dust. Be careful to make as little dust as possible. Lay down the rugs and brush them over also.

Then take away the dust and burn it at once, also the contents of the waste-paper basket.

Next dust the room carefully, commencing at one corner and going steadily round.

If there is a polished or linoleum surround to the carpet, wipe this round with a *slightly* damp duster and then with a dry one. Dust at the same time the skirting-boards. Replace the table-covers, and see that cushions, books, &c., are all in order.

To "Thorough-Clean" a Sitting-room.—A room that is in constant use will require to be cleaned more thoroughly once a week. A drawing-room or room that is only used occasionally will not require it so often. The mistress of the house must decide for herself how often it is necessary to turn it out.

To Prepare the Room.—First remove all plants and flowers, and these should be attended to and arranged outside before they are brought back into the room.

Pull up the blinds as far as they will go. Shake or brush the curtains, and pin them high up out of the way. Remove any short window-curtains, shake them and fold them up.

Then dust thoroughly all ornaments, odd books, music, &c., and either remove them from the room or cover them over on a table or side-board inside.

Dust also and remove, if possible, all small articles of furniture.

Roll up all rugs, and have them taken out of doors to be shaken or beaten later on.

Take off all table-cloths and antimacassars, shake them and fold them up. Beat all cushions, but not too roughly, and then cover all these small things with a dust-sheet.

Upholstered furniture and footstools should be brushed, and all furniture which cannot be removed should be covered over with large clean dust-sheets.

To Clean the Room.—Follow the same order for sweeping, dusting, and doing the grate as for a bedroom. (See 59.)

After sweeping, and while the dust is settling, the things outside should be seen to. Rugs should be shaken, dirty ornaments and glass globes washed or cleaned, and any necessary polishing done.

After the inside dusting is done, put back the furniture in its place, and put on table-cloths and antimacassars. Bring back all ornaments, &c., take down the curtains and see that all is in order.

Finally replace any plants and flower decorations.

CLEANING OF HALL AND STAIRCASE

Before commencing to clean these, close all doors leading into them. Take up all mats and have them shaken outside the house. In houses where there is much going up and down stairs the latter will require to be swept down daily, but with a quiet household it may be sufficient to sweep them two or three times a week, and to simply dust them on the other days.

Begin at the top landing and work downwards. If there is a long stretch of landing on any of the floors, this should be swept with a long broom or carpet-sweeper instead of the short brush, as it will save unnecessary kneeling.

To sweep the stairs, take a banister or stair-brush and a dust-pan. A double brush, with bristles on one side and hair on the other, is the most convenient for the purpose. Sweep the top and front of each step, catching the dust in the dust-pan. Use the bristle side of the brush for the carpet and the soft hair side for the paint or varnish.

When the bottom of the stair is reached take the dust away at once and have it burnt; if left lying in the dust-pan it is very liable to be knocked over and spilt. And here a word of warning may be given about the danger of leaving cleaning materials on a stair; most serious accidents have happened owing to carelessness in this respect.

Allow the dust to settle before doing the dusting. Stairs and banisters will require to be dusted thoroughly every day, and each banister rail should be done separately.

The varnished or painted sides of stair and landing should be wiped first with a *slightly* damp rubber, as this will prevent the dust flying about, and then polished with a dry one.

Doors, door-handles, and window ledges must also have attention. Lay down the mats last of all.

Weekly Cleaning.—Once a week the stairs will require a more thorough cleaning.

When sweeping the steps, pull out the ends of the rods and sweep away the dust from underneath. The banisters too, if they are of wood, should be carefully brushed. If made of painted iron, they may be washed after the sweeping is finished with a wash leather wrung out of warm water and a very little soap. Care must be taken to wring the leather rather firmly, so as to prevent drops of water falling on the steps.

After the stairs have been thoroughly swept, and while the dust is settling, the rods may be cleaned. While doing this an old newspaper or large duster should be laid on the steps to protect the carpet, and not more than one or two rods must be taken out at one time.

Then after the steps and banisters have been carefully dusted, polish the hand-rail with a little furniture polish and the sides of the stairs and landing with floor polish, or bees'-wax and turpentine. If of varnished wood, or if of enamelled white paint, wash them carefully with a little plain soap and water, and rub up with a dry cloth.

A stair carpet will require lifting more frequently than other carpets; twice a year at least, and oftener, if there is much going up and down. When the carpet is up, the steps should be well scrubbed with a little carbolic soap before it is relaid.

If there is a linen drugget over the stair carpet, this should be lifted frequently. Roll it up as gently as possible so as not to disturb the dust. Then have it taken out of doors, well brushed and rubbed over with a damp cloth. The carpet underneath should be well brushed before laying it down again. Change the position of the drugget a little each time it is relaid, so as to ensure equal wear.

To Clean the Hall.—The rugs having been removed, sweep the floor carefully, keeping the dust down as much as possible. Take the dust up in a dust-pan and have it burnt. Then allow the dust that has risen to settle, and dust all the furniture, skirting-boards and doors. If the hall is tiled or covered with linoleum, it ought to be washed once or twice a week, or as often as necessary.

The hall mats should be shaken or beaten outside the back-door if possible, and they must not be relaid until the floor is dry. The door-steps must be washed every day (see p. 73), and as early in the morning as possible. If there is not time for much work before breakfast, then the steps can be done first and the hall left until later in the day. Empty the scraper, and blacklead it brightly. Polish all brass door-handles and plates; those inside once a week and those outside every day.

Once a week the furniture in the hall should be well rubbed up, all brass or other ornaments cleaned, gas globes washed, gas bracket dusted, and any windows and mirrors cleaned.

Note.—For details of the various operations, see under special headings.

THE BATHROOM AND LAVATORY

To Clean Baths.—All baths should be thoroughly well rinsed and wiped out after having been used. If the soapy scum which rises on the top of the water is allowed to lie on them, they will be found much more difficult to clean.

Enamelled Baths.—Empty or run out all the soapy water, and then let in some clean warm water. Take a flannel or soft brush and wash the sides and all over with this, using a little soft soap, or Sunlight soap if necessary; but if the bath is in constant use this will not likely be required every day. If the enamel becomes stained or discoloured, dip the flannel in a little dry salt before applying it. Rinse with clean warm water if soap has been used, and then dry with a cloth. This treatment should be sufficient to keep the bath in order, but if the enamel becomes very dirty use a little Sapolio along with the ordinary soap. Care must always be taken not to roughen the surface of tho enamel, because if once the polish is spoilt it is much more difficult to keep it in order.

A Porcelain Bath can be treated in the same way as above, but Brooke's soap may be used instead of Sapolio if the ordinary soap and water is not sufficient to make it clean.

A Zinc Bath is a little more difficult to keep in order. It should be washed out as above, and, if much soiled, rubbed with a mixture of soft soap and Brooke's soap. Shred down some Brooke's soap and mix it in a saucer with some soft soap. Apply this to the bath with a flannel, rubbing it well in, rinse and dry thoroughly. Fine bath-brick dust mixed with a little paraffin is also an excellent thing for cleaning zinc, but it requires a lot of rinsing to get rid of the smell.

The Water-closet Pan.—This should be well flushed out with water every day and brushed round with a special brush, which is kept for this purpose only. Then once a week at least a good pailful of hot soda-water should be poured in and the brush used again.

If the pan has become discoloured or a coating of fur collected on the sides, empty out as much of the cold water as possible and scrub it well with sand and soft soap, or use a little coarse salt. If this is not sufficient to bring it into good condition, dissolve a pennyworth of spirits of salt in one quart of boiling water; pour this into the pan and allow it to remain there for a short time. Then brush round vigorously and rinse. Care must be taken that the mixture does not touch the hands, as it is very poisonous and liable to burn.

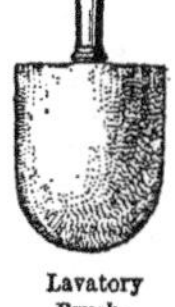
Lavatory Brush.

The lavatory brush should, if possible, be hung on a nail outside the window. Each lavatory should also be provided with a towel hung on to a nail by a loop.

It is very important that no rubbish be put down the lavatory, such as burnt matches, hair combings, faded flowers, pieces of orange peel, &c. It must be remembered that the pipes are usually made with a bend, and such articles would be likely to obstruct them. Young servants should always be warned against throwing any scraps they find in the bedrooms into the slop-pail.

The window of the lavatory should always be kept open and the door shut.

The Lavatory Basin.—If this is emptied immediately after use and rinsed with a little cold water, it will be easily kept in order. It is when dirty soapy water is allowed to remain in the basin that it becomes more difficult to clean. When necessary wash with hot water, soap, and a brush, using a little Brooke's soap or Sapolio if required for any stains; rinse with cold water and dry with a cloth. Every day the taps ought to be dried and rubbed with a duster, and twice a week at least they should be polished with a little metal polish to keep them bright and shining.

CARE OF CARPETS AND RUGS

To Sweep a Carpet.—In these days of carpet-sweepers and suction dust-lifters much of the old-fashioned hand-switching has been done away with. A carpet-sweeper is now to be seen in almost every house, and it is certainly an immense saving of labour. The price varies from 10s. 6d. upwards. It is quick and simple, and takes up the dust where it lies instead of raising it to float about the room in an unhygienic way. It must be rolled across the carpet with even strokes, and there is no occasion to press too heavily. Care must be taken not to use it near heavy furniture, so as to avoid knocking it, and a brush will always be required as well to brush all corners and places where

Carpet-Sweeper.

the sweeper cannot reach. The sweeper must be emptied each day after use, and any fluff, hairs, or thread ends removed from the brushes. If attention is not paid to this the sweeper will very soon become clogged and out of order.

When cleaning a carpet which has a thick pile, such as an Axminster, it is better to use a brush in preference to a sweeper, as the rollers on the latter are liable to leave marks on the soft surface.

Patent suction dust-lifters or vacuum cleaners are also coming into use, but the really practical ones are still much too expensive for the ordinary private house.

When none of these patent cleaners are available, then a carpet must be swept. It will not be necessary to sweep it with a hard broom every day; it will be sufficient just to go over it with a short-handled brush and dust-pan, taking up any pieces or surface dust. Then once a week, or once a fortnight, according to how much the room is used, the carpet must be brushed more thoroughly.

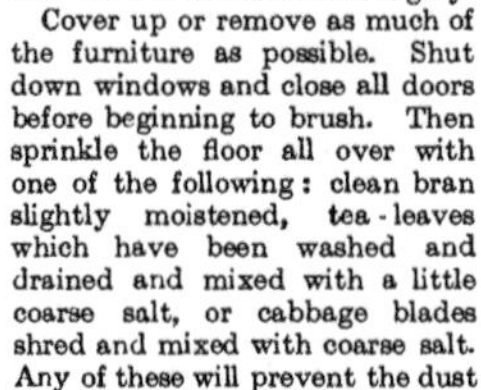

Short-handled Brush.

Cover up or remove as much of the furniture as possible. Shut down windows and close all doors before beginning to brush. Then sprinkle the floor all over with one of the following: clean bran slightly moistened, tea-leaves which have been washed and drained and mixed with a little coarse salt, or cabbage blades shred and mixed with coarse salt. Any of these will prevent the dust from flying about the room unnecessarily and also help to freshen the carpet.

Then take a carpet broom or switch and brush all over the floor with short sharp strokes. Commence at one of the corners and work methodically, sweeping all the dust towards the fireplace or door. Sweep in such a direction as to flatten the pile, or the carpet will have a rough appearance and be apt to collect dust. The brush ought to be turned occasionally so as to wear it equally. The dust must be kept together as much as possible and not sent flying over the room. When brushing a thick pile carpet, such as an Axminster or Turkey, be particular to brush the way of the pile, or the dust will only be swept into it. Collect all the dust together in a heap, brush into a shovel and take it away to be burnt. Then open the window, and leave the room for a short time before doing any dusting.

To Revive the Colour.—If the carpet is old and somewhat faded, the colour may be somewhat revived by washing it over with a flannel wrung out of ammonia and water; or if the carpet is soiled as well, wash over first with carbolic or Sunlight soap and water, and rinse with ammonia and water.

To Remove Stains.—*Ink.*—As much as possible should at once be absorbed with a piece of blotting-paper. Then pour on some fresh milk, rub it in, and off, then take some more milk and repeat the process, finally washing with a little clean warm water. If this fails, which may be the case if the ink has been on the carpet for some time, try Sanitas, or one tea-spoonful of oxalic acid mixed in half a teacupful of water.

Grease.—If it is candle grease, remove as much as possible with a spoon or bone paper-knife; then place a piece of thick brown or blotting-paper over the stain and apply the point of a hot iron, allowing the grease to sink into the paper. Move the paper and repeat the process. Other grease stains may be removed by covering them with a paste made of Fuller's earth and water. Allow this to remain for twenty-four hours and then brush off. *Black-lead* stains can also be removed with Fuller's earth.

Chiver's carpet soap is also very good for removing stains.

To Beat Carpets.—If a carpet has to be beaten at home it should be taken into the garden and carried as far from the house as possible. If the distance cannot be very great, all windows and outside doors should be closed while the beating is going on to prevent the dust entering the house. Hang the carpet over a clothes-line with the wrong side out, and beat it well with strong canes or carpet-beaters. Care must be taken that there are no sharp points in the sticks which would be likely to injure the carpet. When the wrong side seems clean and no more dust rises, turn the carpet and repeat the same process on the right side. Then if there is some nice clean grass, spread the carpet over it and sweep off the surface-dust with a strong broom. The carpet may even be drawn over the grass to freshen it.

Rugs should if possible be taken out of doors to be beaten or brushed. If they are too heavy to be shaken by hand, they should be hung over a rope and beaten with a stick, or laid on the grass and brushed thoroughly. When there is no garden or yard they must be swept in the room to which they belong. If much soiled, wash them over in the same way as carpets.

White Skin Rugs.—If these are large it is wise to send them to a professional cleaner to be cleaned, as it is too much of an undertaking to attempt them at home, and the result is not likely to be satisfactory. A small skin rug can, however, be washed without much trouble. Prepare a tub of warm water and make a strong lather with melted soap or soap powder, adding enough ammonia to make the water smell rather strongly. Put the rug into this and knead it well with the hands, or put it on to a washing-board and brush with a brush. Repeat the process in a second soapy water if the first is not sufficient to clean the rug. Rinse thoroughly in warm soapy water; put it two or three times through the wringing-machine. It is always better to leave a little soap in the skin, as this helps to keep it soft. Shake the rug well, in the open air if possible, and dry in a good wind or indoors in a warm atmosphere, but not too near a fire. Whilst drying the rug should be shaken and rubbed occasionally to keep the skin soft.

Cocoanut-Fibre Door-Mats.—These should be beaten right side downwards, and on a green if possible. When very dirty, wash them with hot water and soda and a very strong brush. Then dip the brush in salt and water and wash over again. The salt will help to keep the fibre stiff.

GENERAL DIRECTIONS FOR DUSTING

It is very important that all dust should be removed from our rooms, not only because dusty rooms are uncomfortable and unpleasant to look upon, but also because dust is one of the sources of disease when we inhale it into our lungs.

The first point in dusting is to be provided with the proper sort of duster. This should be made of some soft material that will gather up the dust, and something smooth that leaves no fluff. In large families there is generally some old material that can be used for the purpose, such as remains of old curtains, or print dresses, old window-blinds, or even thin bed-covers, which have become too shabby to serve their original purpose. Cotton is as a rule better than linen. A duster must always be hemmed. A ragged duster should never be used for fine work, as it is very likely to catch on to some ornament or pointed furniture and cause an accident. Old dusters can always be used up in the cleaning of grates, brasses, and the like.

It is a good plan when dusting a room to work with two dusters, one slightly damp to gather up the dust, and the other dry to follow after and polish up. The aim in dusting must be to remove the dust and not merely to flick it from one part of the room to another. The duster ought to be rolled up into a sort of pad, the dust collected in it and then shaken out of the window from time to time. The work must be done on some distinct plan to ensure every part of the room having attention. Commence at one corner of the room and work steadily round it until every article has been dusted. High and out-of-reach places should be dusted first, as then any dust falling from the upper part will be removed when the lower part is being done. It is not only the tops of furniture and the places that are seen that require dusting, the backs of chairs, chair and table legs, the ledges of wainscoting, and other out-of-the-way places all require attention. When dusting a chimney-piece or table where small ornaments, &c., are placed, lift each article separately, dust it and also the surface underneath it before laying it down again. A furniture brush should be used for the dusting of ornamental furniture.

THE CLEANING OF FURNITURE

All furniture requires regular dusting to keep it in good order. A soft duster is necessary; in fact, it is best when dusting and polishing to work with two dusters, one with which to hold the article of furniture, and the other to do the dusting and rubbing up. A soft brush will be a help for any twisted or ornamental parts.

Upholstered furniture will also require a brush, and especial attention must be given to the crevices, and folds and buttons on chairs. Furniture brushes can be bought in many different patterns, and it is as well to choose the one that is best suited to the work to be done.

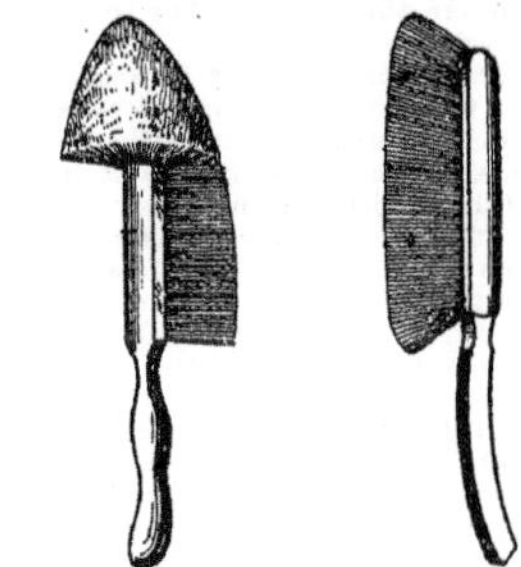

Furniture Brushes.

It must be remembered when dusting and rubbing up furniture that more can be done by plenty of "elbow grease" than by any amount of furniture polish; in fact, this latter is often used in far too lavish a manner.

In addition to the regular dusting a more thorough cleaning and rubbing up will be required at periodic intervals, and then some furniture polish may be applied. This may be prepared at home in one of the following ways:—

(1) Put into a bottle equal quantities of boiled linseed oil and brown vinegar—shake together and use as required. This is very simple and very good.

(2) Take equal quantities of linseed oil, turpentine, brown vinegar and methylated spirits and mix all together in a bottle.

Many other formulæ might be given, and melted bees'-wax is a very favourite ingredient, but although a good thing it requires an amount of very hard rubbing to remove the effect of its sticky properties. Furniture polishes may be bought ready prepared, and many of these are so good and so inexpensive that it is just a question whether it is worth one's while to go to the trouble of making one's own.

Furniture polish must never be used until the furniture has been well dusted, or it will smear and clog. Shake the bottle before beginning, and apply a little with a flannel or soft cotton pad. Rub it well into the wood, and evenly according to the grain. It should never be used in excess. Afterwards rub off with a soft duster and polish with a second duster or chamois leather.

When working with furniture polish be careful to place the bottle where it is not likely to be knocked over.

At spring-cleaning time, or at least once a year, most furniture will be improved by being washed before polishing.

Mahogany Furniture should be washed either with cold tea or with vinegar and water. Use a soft flannel or sponge for the plain pieces and a soft brush for any carved or ornamental parts. Dry and then polish as above.

Oak Furniture.—A little warm beer is the best thing for washing this, as it improves the colour. This is better than soap and water, and especially for old oak, as soap would spoil the appearance of the wood. When dry, polish with furniture cream.

Highly Polished Furniture should be washed with methylated spirits and water. Put two table-spoonfuls of methylated spirits into three breakfast-cupfuls of warm water, wring a small sponge out of this and wash the furniture all over. Dry and polish with a chamois leather. No further polishing will be necessary.

Pitch-Pine Furniture may be washed with warm water and a little soap, but care must be taken not to make it too wet.

Stains on Furniture.—*White Stains*, which are due to hot dishes having been placed upon the wood, can be removed with spirits of camphor. Rub well in with a soft rag and then polish the wood in the usual way. *Ink Stains* can be removed by rubbing them with a little oxalic acid. Do not spread the acid over the wood more than is necessary. A cork is a good thing to use for the application. Wash off with warm water and then polish.

Upholstered Furniture.—To clean this thoroughly it should be well beaten and brushed in the open air. If the material with which it is covered becomes soiled and dirty, it may be considerably restored by rubbing it over with warm bran or fig-dust, which can be bought from any corn-dealers. Benzine will probably remove any obstinate stains.

Leather Chairs.—These can be washed when dirty simply with soap and tepid water. Rub very lightly with a sponge, and then wipe off the soap and dry with a soft cloth. Very little water must be used. When dry, polish with the linseed oil and vinegar polish, or with an application of white of egg slightly beaten.

White Wicker Chairs.—Wash with soap and warm water and a soft brush. Rinse off the soap, and rub the cane over with equal quantities of lemon juice and water, or with a pennyworth of oxalic acid mixed in two cupfuls of water; this will help to whiten the cane. Put the chairs in the open air to dry.

Grease stains may be removed from wicker by rubbing them with a little methylated spirits.

FIRES AND FIREPLACES

Before beginning to lay a fire or clean a grate, the hearth-rug, if there is one, should be rolled up and put on one side and a hearth-cloth laid down over the carpet. Any coarse close material will do for this, such as sacking, tick, or an old cretonne curtain; but care must be taken to spread always the clean side next the carpet.

Have at hand everything that will be required for the cleaning of the grate and the laying of the fire. Some old newspaper, dry sticks, and a supply of small coal; a sweep's brush or grate brush, a small shovel, black-lead or other stove polish, with brushes for putting it on and polishing; one or two dusters, the necessary materials for cleaning steel or brass, and a pair of gloves. The best plan is to keep all these in readiness in a housemaid's box, which is usually fitted with small divisions for keeping the different requisites, and is sometimes provided with a cinder-sifter as well. A pair of gloves should always be worn, as there is nothing worse than black-lead for the hands, and there is no occasion to have them unnecessarily spoilt.

First remove the fire-irons and place them on the hearth-cloth. Then clean out the fireplace, using a piece of stick for the purpose, as this will make less noise than the poker. Be careful to make as little dust as possible. Next brush the back of the grate and inside the fireplace with the sweep's brush, and remove all ashes and cinders. The latter must be reserved for laying the fire, or if there are too many, burnt in the kitchen or boiler stove. The grate must now be thoroughly dusted before any black-leading or polishing takes place.

Sweep's Brush.

If the stove requires black-leading, apply a very little black-lead that has been moistened with water and a few drops of turpentine, by means of the black-lead brush. Or instead of black-lead a specially prepared stove polish may be used, such as Nixelene or Enameline; and this is almost simpler and cleaner, as there is no danger of it being splashed over any surrounding tiles, or even on the carpet. Brush off with a polishing brush, and then finish off with a firm polisher. There is no occasion to use much black-lead or polish; in fact, if a stove is in constant use, it will not likely be required every day; a rub up with the polishing brushes will be sufficient, except

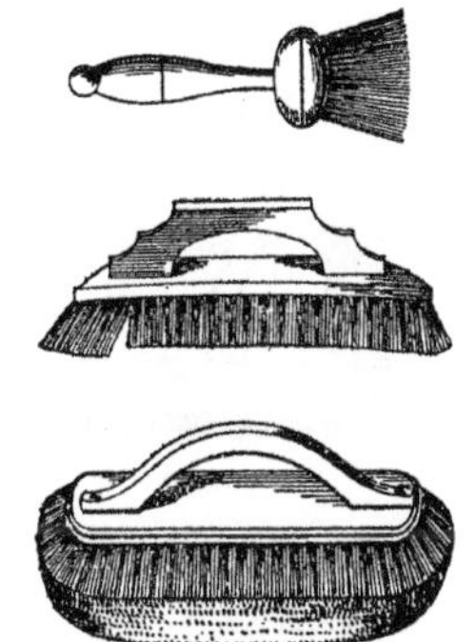

Black-lead Brushes.

perhaps once a week when the room is having a more thorough cleaning.

The bars of the grate will always require a little extra attention, and may require to be blackened more often.

Next lay the fire. Many people never succeed in laying a fire that will burn well, because they pack it too tightly and do not leave enough space for the air to get through between the paper and sticks. Commence by laying a few cinders at the foot of the grate with some lightly crumpled paper on the top. Next place in some sticks crossways, allowing some of the ends to rest on the bars of the grate, and then some more large cinders or small pieces of coal on the top. The fire should be made to slope backwards, so that when it is first lighted the smoke will not blow into the room. Fire-lighters may be used instead of ordinary sticks; they are resined and burn up very quickly.

If the front and sides of the grate are tiled, rub these over daily with a duster, and occasionally wash them with a flannel wrung out of warm water and a little sunlight soap; rinse, dry with cloth, and polish with a chamois leather. If the tiles are stained, a little Sapolio rubbed on the flannel and applied rather dry will generally remove the marks; then wash over and finish as before. Do not use too much water when doing the cleaning, as it will be liable to sink into the cement and ultimately loosen the tiles.

Then finally clean the fender curb and fire-irons. If these are of brass, copper or steel, it will be sufficient to rub them well with a dry duster or chamois leather each day, and to give them a more thorough cleaning, say once a week. (See cleaning of brass, steel or copper, p. 72.) If they are made partly of iron and partly of steel, &c., the iron part may be brushed over with the polishing brushes, or a little Brunswick black may be used to the fender if it becomes very shabby. Black-lead must on no account be put on the handles of fire-irons.

If an iron grate is not to be used for some time, it is a good plan to rub it up with a little Ronuk; this will not only keep it looking bright, but will prevent rust. Directions for use are given with each tin.

If by any chance the grate has become rusty, rub well with a mixture of bath-brick dust and paraffin, then wash off and dry before polishing. Grates that are seldom used are sometimes painted with Brunswick black to keep them in good condition.

CARE OF CHIMNEYS

Chimney on Fire.—This can to a large extent be prevented by keeping the chimneys clean. Every chimney should be swept once or twice a year at least, and oftener if the fireplace is in constant use. Kitchen chimneys should be swept oftener; three or four times a year will not be too much if large fires are kept burning daily.

In addition to the thorough cleaning given by the sweep, any soot which accumulates near the fireplace should be swept away with the sweep's brush when the different grates are cleaned.

If the chimney should catch fire the first thing to do is to close the door and window to prevent a strong current of air from increasing the flames. Then throw over the fire a few handfuls of salt, when it will as a rule burn itself out in a very short time.

HOW TO SCRUB A ROOM

The room must first be cleared of as much furniture as convenient, and all rugs and pieces of carpet rolled up and put on one side. Then sweep the room with a soft broom, and remove all the dust in a shovel.

Have ready a kneeling-mat, a pail of warm water, a scrubbing brush, a piece of house flannel or a swab, and a little soft soap.

Commence at the corner of the room farthest from the door. Wring the flannel out of the

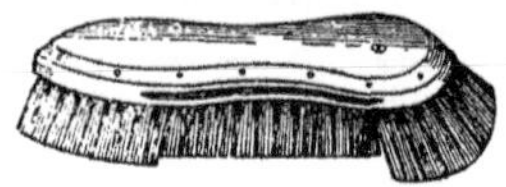

Scrubbing-Brush.

water, and wet as much of the boards as the arm can conveniently reach. Put a little soap on the brush and scrub each piece thoroughly backwards and forwards, and with the grain of the wood. This loosens the dirt, and it is now important to have it removed. Wring the flannel again out of the water and wipe the portion of board that was scrubbed until all the soap is gathered up; then dry with a coarse cloth. Do not make the boards wetter than is necessary to make them clean, especially if it is a floor that has a ceiling underneath, and change the water as soon as it becomes dirty. Work methodically over every part of the floor until all is finished.

If the wood is greasy, a little soda may be added to the water, and when washing boards that are much soiled a little sand used along with the soap will be a help. A bad stain can be usually removed from a floor by spreading it with a paste made of Fuller's earth and hot water, allowing it to remain overnight and then washing off.

When finished, allow a good current of air to pass through the room to dry it; or on a damp day it is better to have a fire burning, more especially if it is a bedroom or a room that will be used immediately.

CARE OF POLISHED FLOORS

These should be swept and dusted every day. First remove as much as possible of the surface dust with a soft short-handled broom and dust-pan, or, if there is a large surface of flooring under treatment, a long broom can be used. Then rub the floor with a dry duster, or what is better still, with a floor-duster. If there is much polished flooring to be kept in order, it is very important that the worker should not do it on

Floor-Duster.

her knees. Then once a week the floor should be polished.

To Prepare Floor Polish.—Shred down ¼ lb. bees'-wax, and put it into a jar with ½ pint turpentine; allow this to melt slowly in the oven or on the side of the stove, stirring occasionally with a wooden stick.

Rub a little of this on to the floor with a piece of flannel and then polish with a pad, which can be bought for the purpose, or with a floor-polisher.

Special floor polishes can also be bought prepared, such as Ronuk, Jackson's Camphorated

Floor-Polisher.

Polish, &c., and the use of one of these would of course save the trouble of making, but it would come a little more expensive than the simple bees'-wax and turpentine.

TO CLEAN LINOLEUM OR FLOOR-CLOTH

Much washing and scrubbing is bad for the ordinary linoleum. It should be well swept every day, and only washed when necessary. Take a pail of warm water, some plain yellow soap, and a piece of house flannel, and wash the linoleum with this. Wring out the flannel and take up as much of the moisture as possible. Then dry with a clean dry towel. If the linoleum is very dirty and requires a brush, then a soft one only must be used. The use of soda, ammonia, or washing powders must be avoided.

Greenwich Linoleum, which has the pattern all the way through, can be washed with warm water, a flannel, and a little Brook's soap. This revives the colour and makes it look like new. To give the linoleum a more finished appearance, it may be rubbed over with a little skimmed milk after washing and finished with a dry cloth; or with a little glue water made thus :—Take one ounce of glue powder or shredded glue, dissolve it in one pint of boiling water and allow it to melt, stirring occasionally with a stick. The linoleum may of course be polished if a brighter gloss is desired. (See Polished Floors, p. 66.)

Indian Matting.—This should be washed on the floor with a strong solution of salt and water and then dried quickly with a soft cloth. Or, if it becomes very much soiled, take it up and scrub with soap and water and a moderately hard brush. Rinse on both sides and dry with a cloth or in the open air. If there are stains on the matting a little ammonia might be added to the water or some benzine applied to the spot.

Care of Tiled Floors.—Sweep every day with a soft broom; and once or twice a week, or oftener if necessary, wash them over with soap and water. Take some water in a pail and add to it a little soap powder or melted soap. Use either a house flannel or brush to wash with. If the tiles are very dirty a brush will be required. Rinse off the soap, and then make as dry as possible with the flannel. A little Brook's soap or Sapolio will be useful for removing any stains. If it is desired to have a polish on the tiles, they may be rubbed over with a little milk after washing, or with linseed oil and turpentine mixed in equal quantities.

THE MAKING AND CARE OF BEDS

However well chosen and hygienic a bed may be, if it is not well made, the comfort of it will be greatly reduced, if not altogether spoilt.

A bed must be thoroughly well aired every day for an hour at least before making. The windows of the bedroom should first be thrown open top and bottom, the bed-curtains drawn back, if there are any, then the clothes stripped off the bed one at a time and placed over the back of a chair or chairs. The pillows and bolster must be well shaken and beaten, and placed near the open window if possible, and then the mattress raised on its two ends so as to form an arch for the air to pass through. If there is a feather mattress, this should be laid over the end of the bed.

In making a bed individual taste should always be considered. Some like all the surplus length of blanket doubled over at the top, while others like the covering only to reach to the shoulders; and in the case of a feather-bed some like the bed made so as to slope towards the foot, and others prefer it perfectly flat, and so on. These may appear fads, but it entails no extra trouble to give in to them—only a little thought; and attention to these small details may add very much to the comfort and real repose of the sleeper.

It is always better and more expeditious if two people can be engaged in the making of the beds; and needless to say their hands should be spotlessly clean, and they should each wear a clean apron or overall.

The mattress must be turned each morning —one day from top to bottom, and the next from side to side—so as to ensure equal wear.

If there is a feather-bed, it must be thoroughly shaken to prevent lumps. Take the two opposite corners and shake the feathers towards the centre, then the other two corners and do the same, and next the sides. When the feathers seem perfectly light and free from lumps, smooth the mattress over, being particular to fill the corners with feathers. If any feathers should come out during the process, it will generally be from a hole in the seam, and this should at once be attended to and sewn together with a needle and cotton.

In laying the clothes on the bed each article must be put on separately, and not thrown on in a mass to save time. They must be put on evenly, allowing the same amount to come over each side of the bed and be tucked in all round. It is also most important to have them free from wrinkles or folds of any kind.

When the mattress is arranged, next put on the binder or under-blanket. This should be wide enough to tuck in well at the sides of the bed, when it will hold the mattress together and make the bed smoother and more comfortable. The under-sheet is now put on and tucked in all round, and the bolster laid on the top at the head of the bed, unless no bolster-slip is used, when the under-sheet must be left long enough to fold over the bolster and completely cover it, but this is not such a comfortable arrangement. Next, place on the top sheet with the wrong side uppermost, and the widest hem at the top to turn over the blankets. On the top of the sheets lay the blankets with the open end at the top (as it is easy then to throw off one fold if the occupant of the bed should find it too hot). Then a coverlet or sheet should cover all, and must be light in weight, as it is meant for night use. This should be turned in over the blankets at the top, and the end of the sheet turned over it; the blankets are thus preserved from dust, and the bed has a more inviting appearance when it is turned down for the night. Then slip in the pillow or pillows on the top of the bolster without flattening them down, and on a double bed place the opening of the slip to the inside of the bed. Lastly may be put on a pretty counterpane, which is removed at night. This should not be tucked in, but allowed to hang over the sides in graceful folds. If there is a centre pattern, be sure that this comes to the centre of the bed, and any surplus length may be laid in folds at the foot. If carefully folded up at night and always in the same folds, the counterpane will keep clean for quite a long time, and it adds very much to the dainty appearance of the bedroom during the day.

If an eider-down is used it should be rolled up or folded double at the foot of the bed. Those who like warmth without weight will find it a great advantage to make the bed with the eider-down between the upper sheet and the blankets. The warmth is thereby sensibly increased, and if the eider-down is well ventilated it is not unhealthy.

If pillow shams and sheet shams are used, the pillows should be placed on the outside of the counterpane during the day, and the sheet sham slipped under the bed-clothes and arranged so that the embroidered edge rests on the counterpane.

If there are curtains, draw these back and arrange the ends neatly on the pillows.

Turning down a Bed.—First remove the eider-down; then take off the counterpane and sheet and pillow shams, if there are such, and fold all these up very carefully, and place them where they will not be crushed nor sat upon. Then turn down the clothes about a foot or a foot and a half at the top of the bed, and one corner, or two corners if it is a double bed, may be turned back again towards the centre, but this is a matter of taste. It is also a question of taste whether the clothes be left tucked in at the sides or loosened. Let down and draw any curtains. See that pillows are nice and smooth and all straight and even, and then replace the eider-down, spreading it out over the bed this time.

Care of Beds.—The strictest cleanliness must be observed as regards beds, not merely in the changing of the linen, but in the bed itself and everything about it.

One hears of beds the spars of which are never dusted except at the annual period of spring cleaning, and sometimes not even then. We ought to remember that the dust in our houses, and especially in our bedrooms, is not only earth dust, soot, fraying of carpets and curtains, &c., but that there is a large admixture of animal matter, for our outer skin or cuticle is constantly peeling off and being removed; and added to that, this dust if not removed becomes impregnated with noxious gases exhaled from our lungs and from the pores of our bodies, and poisons the air we breathe, thereby greatly lessening the beneficial effects of sleep. Every part of the bedstead should be carefully dusted once a week, a small brush being used if necessary. The best time for this will be before the bed is made on the day the room is thoroughly cleaned.

The bedstead itself, and especially the under-part, should be washed with warm water and carbolic soap at least once a year. If at any time insects should appear, the bedstead should be rubbed over with paraffin or very strong ammonia.

Japanned bedsteads may be revived by rubbing them over with a little paraffin, and then polishing with a leather or soft duster.

Brass bedsteads should be dusted daily, and occasionally rubbed over with a little sweet oil and polished with a leather. Metal polish should not be used, as the brass is lacquered. If this wears off it will require special treatment.

If the mattresses and pillows have been covered with cotton slips (see p. 258), it is very easy to have these taken off and washed as soon as they become soiled. The bedding can then be thoroughly brushed and beaten, special attention being paid to the edges and to the little corners where the mattress is tacked down. If this can be done out of doors, so much the better.

The mattresses ought to be taken to pieces and re-made every few years—not merely because they will, even with the most careful treatment, eventually form into hard lumps and hollows, but because they will really require to be purified from animal matter. Although it is possible to do this at home, this course is scarcely to be recommended. It is much wiser and simpler to send them to a good upholsterer.

Blankets, too, must be washed or cleaned whenever they require it. Once or twice a year will be sufficient under ordinary circumstances, provided they have proper care in the way of airing, shaking, and being kept covered from dust; but if they have been used in the case of illness they must of course be washed specially, and if the illness is an infectious one, disinfected as well.

EMPTYING OF SLOPS AND CARE OF THE WASH-STAND

The appliances necessary for this portion of household work are: a slop-pail, a can of boiling water in which a little soda has been dissolved, a small mop, two slop-cloths, and a glass-towel. The slop-pail used for carrying about is best made of enamelled tin, as it is easily kept in order and there is no danger of its breaking. It should always be fitted with a lid.

Slop-Pail.

The slop-cloths should be of some thin open material, which can be washed and dried easily. One must be used for the basin and wash-stand and the second for the chamber and bedroom slop-pail. It is important to keep each cloth for its special purpose.

Commence by emptying everything into the slop-pail. Pour a little of the hot soda-water into the chamber, and allow it to remain there while the wash-stand is being put in order.

Rinse out the basin with clean water, using a little of the soda-water if necessary to remove any stain or soap-suds. Then pour a little clean water into the basin and rinse the tumbler and water-bottle, and dry them with the glass-towel.

Next rinse any sponges or loofahs, &c., and either hang them up to dry or place them in a sponge basket. Then pour out the water, and wipe the basin thoroughly with its special cloth. Empty the ewer and wash it out if necessary. If rain water is used there is frequently a considerable amount of sediment which settles at the foot of the jug.

Wipe also the wash-stand, lifting each article and wiping it clean. Pay particular attention to the soap-dish.

Wash the chamber with the mop, using the water that has been standing in it; rinse and dry with the special cloth. If there is a slop-pail belonging to the room, empty this also, wash with hot water, using the mop. Then rinse with cold, and dry with the chamber cloth.

Finally fill up the ewer and water-bottle with fresh water. The former with soft water if available, and the latter with drinking water. It is very important that the ewer should be quite emptied every day; if old water is allowed to remain and just a little fresh added, the water will very soon begin to smell. So let it all be *fresh*.

Cover the slop-pail before taking it from the room, and have the contents emptied at once. Care too must be taken to keep this pail very clean and fresh. It should be rinsed out every day with hot soda-water; rinsed, dried, and then left with the lid off to air. The lid should have the same treatment, and then be hung up until required again.

The two slop-cloths should be washed every day and hung up to dry. The glass-towel if properly used ought to last a week.

Once a week, usually on the day the bedroom is being turned out, the wash-stand, &c., will require a more thorough cleaning.

The ware should be taken out of the room if possible and well washed in the housemaid's pantry or bath-room. Use hot water and a little paraffin soap or soap-powder. Pay particular attention to the handles of ewer and chamber, and use small brush for the corners, if necessary. The inside of the ewer too must be washed as well as the outside, and a little soda-water may be required to remove discoloration.

If the water-bottle has become stained and dim, it ought to have special treatment. (See p. 75.)

Wash the wash-stand with a little soap and water, using a washing flannel or soft brush; wipe off the soap and rub up with a towel. Then replace the ware, and supply with water and soap too if required.

TO CLEAN WALLS AND CEILINGS

Papered Walls, when they become dirty, should be thoroughly dusted. To do this, tie a clean soft duster over the head of a long-handled broom. Any soft broom will do, provided the wall is not very high, in which case it is almost necessary to have a special wall-broom, or Turk's-head broom, which has a jointed bamboo handle, and can be shortened or lengthened as required. Sweep every part of the wall, moving the brush up and down in long straight lines, and be particular to remove all dust from any cornice or mouldings. The duster must be changed when it becomes dirty.

Turk's-head Broom.

If the paper has still a soiled appearance after dusting, it may be further improved by rubbing it all over with stale bread. Cut a plain dry loaf in four pieces, and rub the paper all over with it. It will be necessary to mount on a pair of steps to do this. Commence at one of the top corners and rub with light even strokes, undertaking about a yard at a time. There is no need to rub very hard; too much vigour would only destroy the surface of the paper. Go over each piece in a careful methodical way, and in the order most convenient to yourself. This manner of cleaning will make a considerable difference to dirty wall-paper.

The *ceiling* of a room can be cleaned in the same way, and special attention must be given to the corners, where cobwebs so frequently lodge.

Varnished Paper and Painted Walls may be washed *after* dusting. Take a pail of tepid water, and add to it enough melted soap to make a light lather. Use a sponge, and wash the wall all over with this. Then carefully remove the soap with a second sponge or chamois leather wrung out of clear cold water. Leave the wall to dry without any further wiping.

TO CLEAN WINDOWS

Windows must never be cleaned in frosty weather, as the glass is then very brittle and would be liable to break as soon as moisture were applied. Choose a dull dry day when the sun is not shining upon them.

First dust the windows inside and out, and also the woodwork surrounding them. A painter's brush or any other soft brush is the best thing for the purpose. Then take some tepid water and add enough liquid ammonia to it to make it smell slightly, or a small quantity of paraffin. Wring a sponge or chamois leather out of this and wash over the window with it, paying particular attention to the sides and corners. Finish off with a linen duster or a dry chamois leather. No material of a fluffy nature must be used. Clean soft newspaper makes a very good polishing-pad. Commence always at the top and work downwards.

Painter's Brush.

Paint or other stains can be removed from the glass with a little vinegar or oxalic acid.

Various powders are now sold for cleaning windows without water, and these in many cases are found quite satisfactory. Directions for use are given with each special make.

It must be remembered that no woman is allowed to sit or stand outside an upstairs window in order to clean it; so that for large windows which cannot be cleaned from the inside, it will be necessary to employ a man. These men usually bring their own apparatus. The usual charge for cleaning is about 2d. a window.

TO CLEAN BLINDS

Venetian Blinds.—These ought to be thoroughly dusted once a week. Let the blinds down, and by means of a pair of steps, dust all the webbing and the cords. Then with a soft duster dust each lath separately. Commence at the top and work downwards. Do one side first, all the way down, then turn the blind and dust the other side. Put the duster over the finger and rub well round the cords where they pass through the laths.

Once a year, or even oftener, Venetian blinds should be washed. Take a basin or small pail of warm water in which a little soap and borax have been dissolved, wring a sponge out of this, and wash each lath separately. Then dip the sponge into clean warm water and rub the soap off the wood. Dry with a soft towel. Or, if found easier, the laths may be removed. To do this, undo the knot at the foot of the cord which runs through the blind. Then pull out the cord and remove the laths. Wash them as above, and when thoroughly dry, put them back in their place and lace the cord through them.

Linen or Holland Blinds.—These should be dusted weekly. Let the blind down as far as it will go and with a soft duster wipe it well on both sides. Dust also the cord and roller.

To clean them more thoroughly they should be taken down, laid flat on a table and well dusted on both sides. Then take some stale bread or bran, and rub this lightly and quickly all over the material. Dust off with a clean duster. If this is not sufficient to clean them, they will require to be washed. Unless the blinds are small in size, it is not wise to attempt this at home, as they really require special washing to give them a good gloss and keep them in shape.

TO WASH PAINT

Dust the paint first, using a soft brush for the purpose, as this is less likely to drive the dirt into the wood than a cloth. Then have ready at hand a pail of warm soft water, to which a little dissolved soap has been added, and a soft flannel; a second pail of cold or tepid water with a sponge, and a soft cloth or chamois leather for drying. Wring the flannel out of the soapy water, and wash the paint gently with it. Do not use the flannel too wet, and be careful to avoid splashing the surrounding wall. Then rinse off the dirty soap with the sponge and tepid water, and this will prevent the wood having a smeary appearance. Finish off with the dry cloth or leather.

Do not wet too much of the paint at one time; if there is a large quantity of woodwork to be done it will be a great advantage if two can be engaged at the work; one to wash, and the second to follow and do the rinsing and drying. The water must be changed as soon as it becomes dirty.

For *varnished paint* use tepid water only; in fact for any paint care must be taken not to have the water too hot.

Soda must never be used, but a little borax may be added with safety to water that is hard. Care must be taken, too, that the soap used is of a pure and simple kind. Good yellow soap, mottled soap, or carbolic soap are to be recommended. Then as regards the flannel, the ordinary house flannel is too rough, and housekeepers would do well to save up any pieces of old flannel, woven under-garments, old blankets, &c., for this purpose. The towels, too, that are used must not be of a fluffy nature; old huckaback bedroom towels are excellent for the purpose.

The woodwork in a house should be washed at least twice a year. Flies and other insects lay their eggs along the crevices of doors and windows, and by keeping these clean we can do much to avoid the arrival of these unwelcome visitors. Finger-marks and other marks should, of course, be removed as need arises; a little benzine applied on a flannel, or simply a gentle rub with a soapy sponge, will be sufficient. All hard rubbing must be avoided.

White Enamel Paint.—The following is a very good preparation for cleaning this special kind of paint:—

Take one gill of vinegar, one gill paraffin, and half-gill linseed oil, and shake them together in a bottle. Apply this to the paint with a clean sponge or soft flannel and the result will be excellent. No washing is required.

TO CLEAN MARBLE

When marble is in good condition, it can be kept in order by simply washing it with soap and water, rinsed off and then dried. This would apply to marble wash-stands and slabs which are in frequent use.

A chimney-piece which is not cleaned so often may require a little stronger treatment. Dust it first, and in this case a little shredded Brook's soap or Sapolia used along with ordinary yellow soap or soft soap will be efficacious, and a brush should be used for any ornamental parts. Always rinse off the soap, and take a second water if necessary. Dry with a cloth and polish with a chamois leather. Black or grey marble may be rubbed over with a little linseed oil after washing to give it a gloss.

If the marble is stained, the appearance of it may be improved by the following treatment:—Take 1 oz. powdered chalk, 1 oz. powdered pumice-stone and 2 ozs. soda—pound these together and pass them through a sieve. Then make them into a paste with boiling water, and spread this over the marble, especially over the stained parts. Allow it to remain overnight, and wash off as before.

Another way of cleaning marble is to coat it all over with a layer of thick hot-water starch (see p. 280). This starch penetrates into all the crevices and absorbs the surface dirt. When dry it will scale off in large pieces, bringing the dirt away with it. Then wash with soap and water and dry as before.

Oxalic acid, too, will sometimes remove a stain, but it must be rubbed on and washed off again very quickly, as it will discolour the marble if allowed to remain. If a stain is very deep-seated the only sure way of eradicating it is to have the marble repolished.

Marble Statuary should be washed with soap and water only. Sunlight or paraffin soap is good, but nothing of a gritty nature must be used. The washing should be done with soft brushes, small ones being used for any corners or intricate parts. The water must be changed whenever it becomes dirty, and care must be taken to rinse off all soap. Allow the marble to dry, and then polish with a leather or soft dry brush.

Marble statuary may also be cleaned with a paste of starch as above.

TO CLEAN PICTURES

The Glass.—To clean the glass of pictures, dust it first with a soft silk or muslin duster. Then put one tablespoonful of methylated spirits into a small basin of warm water (about two breakfast-cupfuls), wring a sponge out of this and wash the picture glass all over. Be careful not to wet the frame when cleaning the corners and edges. Pay particular attention to any fly-marks or other stains. Then dry with a fine towel and polish with a chamois leather.

Oil-Paintings.—These require very careful treatment. They should be dusted frequently with an old silk handkerchief or feather brush, but if the latter is used one must make sure there are no sharp pieces of quill or wire fastenings which might scratch the canvas. The picture must be taken down to be cleaned thoroughly. First of all it should be dusted, back and front. Then sponge the oil-painting very carefully with a fine sponge or piece of cotton-wool wrung out of lukewarm water. Soap must on no account be used. Rub the surface over lightly and quickly, and do not allow it to remain wet longer than is needful. Dry with a fine cloth or chamois leather. This can of course only be done to oil-paintings that have a coating of varnish over them, as it is the varnish only that will bear the washing. If this gets rubbed or worn off, the picture must be dusted only. If an oil-painting becomes very much discoloured and dirty through age, it is better to send it to an expert to have scientific treatment, as trying different things at home might easily end in injuring the picture.

Brass Picture-Chains.—These become very dirty after they have been exposed to the atmosphere for some time, but they can be made to look quite fresh again by the following treatment:—Brush them first with a soft brush, so as to remove as much of the dust as possible. Then plunge them into a pail of boiling water to which a good handful of soda has been added, and allow them to remain until that is cold. Next wash them in clean hot water with soap and a brush, rinse and hang them up to dry. Finally they may have a rub with the chamois leather.

Gilt Picture-Frames.—If the frames are made of inferior gilt they will not endure much cleaning. Dust them carefully with a soft brush, and if the gilt has chipped off in places it may be touched up with a little gold paint, which can be bought at any oil-shop.

To clean good English gilt frames, dust them first with a soft brush or silk handkerchief, then wash gently with a small fine sponge wrung out of equal quantities of methylated spirits and water. Or a camel's-hair brush may be used instead of the sponge. Dry with a chamois leather.

A little onion water applied with a sponge

sometimes helps to restore the colour of the gilding, and also keeps off flies.

Prepare it thus:—Remove the skin from two or three onions and boil them in two breakfast-cupfuls of water until all the goodness is extracted. Strain through a very fine strainer or piece of muslin and use warm.

JAPANESE TRAYS OR PAPIER-MACHÉ ARTICLES

Clean these by washing them gently with a sponge wrung out of tepid water. Then dry with a cloth and polish with a little dry flour rubbed on with a soft duster or chamois leather.

TO CLEAN MIRRORS

First remove all dust. Then take a basin of tepid water and add enough ammonia to make it smell slightly. Wring a sponge or chamois leather out of this, and wash the glass all over, going carefully round the edges and into the corners to avoid wetting the frame, and especially if it is a gilded one.

Dry with a soft towel, and polish with a chamois leather or old silk handkerchief.

If the mirror has not been cleaned for some time, and is smeared and stained, instead of washing it, make a paste with fine whitening and methylated spirits, and rub this well over the glass with a piece of flannel. When dry, rub off with a duster and polish as before.

For gilt frames see p. 71.

TO CLEAN STEEL

If steel is rubbed daily with a dry duster or leather, and so kept free from dust and moisture, it ought to retain its brightness for a considerable time. When it requires extra cleaning, use very fine emery paper; No. 0 is best. Rub the steel backwards and forwards with this, and always in the one direction. Cross-rubbing will not polish properly. Emery powder, fine bath-brick dust or crocus powder made into a paste with paraffin or methylated spirits are all good things for the cleaning of steel. These should be applied with a piece of flannel and well rubbed on to the metal. Then a little of the dry powder used for polishing and the chamois leather for the final rub up.

The emery paper is, however, cleaner and simpler to use, and unless the steel is allowed to get into bad condition, it ought to be sufficient to keep it in excellent order.

TO CLEAN BRASS

There are many different materials used for the cleaning of brass, but perhaps nothing is better than fine bath-brick dust or powdered rotten-stone made into a paste with a little paraffin or oil of turpentine. Apply this with a flannel, rubbing the brass well; then rub off with a second flannel, using a little dry powder, and polish with a duster or chamois leather. There are also many modern polishes that can be used, but with some of them the result, although good to begin with, is not lasting; the brass tarnishes and becomes dim very rapidly.

The "Blue-bell" polish is one to be recommended, and it has the advantage of being very clean to use. Directions for its use are given with each tin. If a paste of any kind is used, care must be taken that none of it is left sticking to the brass.

Outside brasses may be kept from tarnishing by rubbing them over with a little vaseline after cleaning.

Benares Brass should be washed in very hot soapy water, and well rubbed with a flannel or soft brush. If the brass is greasy, add a little borax to the water, then rinse in hot water and dry with a towel. If the brass still remains stained or discoloured, rub it over with the squeezed half of a lemon and wash again. Finally polish with a chamois leather. It is better not to use any polishing paste for chased work, as it is almost impossible to remove it entirely; but a little dry whitening may be used to polish with, if it is very carefully brushed off.

Lacquered Brass requires very careful treatment, and especially so if it is not of a very good quality, as the application of paste and a great deal of rubbing would then be liable to remove the lacquer, which is only a sort of varnish which can quickly be worn off.

Lacquered articles should be rubbed up frequently with a leather, and if this is not sufficient to keep them in order, wash them in warm water with soap and a flannel. Then dry and polish. Soda must never be used when washing lacquered goods, but a little borax may be added if the water is hard.

THE CLEANING OF BOOKS

Books should be kept as free from dust as possible. If the book-case is covered with glass this is comparatively easy, but when the books are placed on open shelves they will require more attention. Care should be taken to always cover them with a dust-sheet before any sweeping is done in the room. Then from time to time, or as often as necessary, the books should be removed from the shelves and thoroughly dusted. Take them two at a time, and clap them together to disperse the dust, then dust them gently with a very light duster or soft clothes'-brush. The dust must not be rubbed into the leaves. The shelves, too, should be dusted before the books are returned to them.

THE CARE OF A PIANO

The most important point is to protect it from all damp. It should never be in a temperature under 60 degs. Fahrenheit, therefore it is unwise to have it standing in a room where there is no fire in winter. Great heat is also injurious.

A piano should never be placed against an outside wall, unless it can be protected in some way, neither should it stand in a direct draught.

A strip of felt or a pad of silk is sometimes placed over the keyboard to protect it from damp and dust.

It is a bad plan to pile books and ornaments on the top of a piano, as any weight is apt to spoil the tone of the instrument. A flower vase with water should be especially avoided, as there is always the danger of the water being spilt and soaking between the keys.

Pianos should be carefully dusted with a soft cloth or silk duster, and polished when necessary with a chamois leather. Any marks on the keyboard may be removed with a damp chamois leather, but soap and water should never be used.

A piano, whether it is in use or not, should be tuned regularly by a competent tuner. An arrangement can be made for this to be done periodically, generally four times a year, for a very moderate charge. This will preserve the instrument and keep it at the necessary pitch.

BRASS CHANDELIERS OR GAS BRACKETS

Keep these free from dust with a soft brush or duster. When they become soiled, wash with a sponge wrung out of vinegar and water. Dry with a soft cloth, and polish with a chamois leather.

TO CLEAN BRONZE ORNAMENTS

These must never be *washed.* Dust with a muslin or silk duster, and use a soft brush for any ornamental part. If this is not sufficient to make them clean, sponge the ornaments with stale beer, using a small sponge, and when dry, polish with a chamois leather.

TO CLEAN IVORY

Wash in lukewarm water with plain yellow soap, using a soft brush if necessary to remove dirt from any carved parts. Rinse and dry. Then polish with a chamois leather. If the ivory is stained, rub with a little salt and vinegar, or salt and lemon juice, after washing; rinse and dry as before.

Or, if the ivory is discoloured, lift it out of the soapy water and stand it in the sun. Before it becomes dry, repeat the process if necessary. It must not be allowed to remain dry in a hot sun, or it will warp. Rinse and dry as before.

TO CLEAN DOOR-STEPS

First sweep away all the dust with an old broom kept for the purpose. Then take a pail of cold or tepid water, a piece of strong floor-cloth or swab, and some rough hearth-stone, which can be bought at the rate of two or three pieces for a penny. A kneeling-mat must always be used. Wring the cloth out of the water, and wet over as much as is convenient of the steps at one time. Then rub over with the stone evenly backwards and forwards, and not in curves.

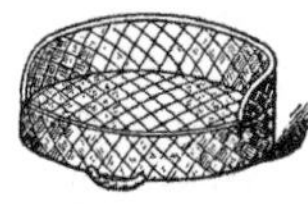

Kneeling-Mat.

Next wring the cloth again out of the water, and wipe the stone again to prevent it having a patchy appearance when dry. Then go on to the next piece of step and do it in the same way, and so on until all is finished. The sides and front of the steps must also have attention.

In frosty weather a handful of salt should be put in the water, and this will prevent its freezing.

GENERAL DIRECTIONS FOR "WASHING UP"

Before commencing the actual washing of dishes, &c., a certain amount of preliminary arrangement is necessary. First of all, one must see that a plentiful supply of hot water is available. If there is a hot-water supply in the house, this is a simple matter if the fire is first attended to, but if only a side boiler or kettles are to be relied on, some looking ahead will be necessary to see that these are filled in time, and then refilled, when once they have been emptied, in order to cause no delay in having to wait for the water to boil.

Then everything that requires washing must be collected together and put within easy reach. The contents of dishes on which food has been served must be put away on clean plates or basins. All scraps of food, crumbs, remains of mustard or jam, &c., must be removed from plates; slops must be poured out of teacups or coffee-cups; remains of tea and tea leaves from the teapot, and so on.

If this were not done before starting the washing, the water would not only become unnecessarily dirty and require more frequent changing, but the work itself would be disagreeable.

Arrange all articles of one kind together, plates of different sizes in neat piles, saucers by themselves in another pile, cups by themselves, and so on.

Silver and glass ought to be kept apart on a tray, or in the case of the former in a plate-basket, until they can be washed. They must not be mixed up with other dishes.

Knives should be placed blades downwards in a washer or jug of hot water. (See p. 76.)

If attention is paid to these small points, "washing up" will be a much simpler affair than if it were just started in a muddle. Much time too will be saved, as all unnecessary turning round and walking about with wet and soapy hands will be avoided.

Two basins or small tubs will be necessary for the washing, one for hot water and the second for a cold or tepid rinsing water. For silver, glass and fine china, a small wooden or pulp-ware tub is best, as this is less liable to scratch or break fine articles; but for ordinary dishes, and especially greasy dishes, zinc or tin is preferable, as it can be kept clean more easily.

If the water is hard, it must be softened with a little soda or borax, and a little soap or soap-powder must be used if required. Care must, however, be taken to avoid unnecessary extravagance in the employment of these materials; there is frequently considerable waste caused by their needless use, and this must be guarded against.

With regard to dish-cloths, these are best made of some open material which will not retain the grease, such as thin old towelling, or a cheap canvas-like material sold for the purpose.

Some people prefer a mop or dish-brush instead of the dish-cloth, and both are useful.

When all is arranged, commence with the glass and silver, and when these are out of the way start on the cleanest and least greasy of the dishes. If there are two people to do the work, then one can wash while the other does the drying.

The water must be changed whenever it becomes dirty; continuing to wash in the dirty water would only result in smeary dishes, with probably an unpleasant smell. This is one of the most important points to pay attention to.

Another very important point is the use of dry and clean towels. The thickness of the towel must be regulated according to the kind of article being dried. Glass, silver, and china will require fine smooth towels without a fluffy surface, while coarser dishes will require a coarse and stronger material. In all cases the towels must be clean and free from grease, and as they become wet should be hung near the fire to dry.

Finally, when the "washing up" is finished and everything put away in its place, the dish-cloths or flannels that have been used must be washed out and hung up to dry, and also any towels that require it. The tub or basin must be well washed and rinsed and set on end to air. All then will be clean and ready when wanted again, and a good worker is recognised by attention to these small details.

See also detailed directions under special articles.

For the washing of kitchen utensils, see pp. 92–94.

CARE OF SILVER

The daily care of silver is much more important than the thorough cleaning which is given to it at stated intervals. In fact, if a little extra time were spent over the regular washing and drying, the "thorough cleaning," as it is called, need not be oftener than once in three weeks or a month.

The keeping of silver requires a good deal of care, but it is not difficult if the work is done with method, and attention paid to a few special points.

Table silver should be washed as soon as possible after it has been used. A papier mâché or wooden tub is the best for the purpose, as then there will be little danger of it scratching the silver. Take water as hot as the hand can bear, add a few drops of ammonia and enough melted soap, "lux" or soap-powder to make a nice lather. Wash the silver in this, using a piece of flannel or soft towelling to rub it with. Rinse in clean hot water, and dry with a fine towel while the silver is still warm. If allowed to lie wet, it will be difficult to remove the water-marks. For this reason, if a large quantity of silver is being done, it is better not to start it all at one time, but one lot can be finished as far as the rinsing, and the second lot put to soak in the soapy water while the first lot is being dried. When dry give each article a good rub up with a chamois leather, and then arrange the silver neatly and in order in the plate-basket, or on a tray ready to put away.

Throughout the process the greatest care must be taken not to scratch the silver, and with this in view it is really better if forks can be kept by themselves. In the case of real silver, a careful worker will first lay a towel or piece of flannel on the tray on which the silver is drained, and, in fact, never allow it to touch a hard surface, which might be liable to injure it.

Another important point to remember is, that both towel and lather must be perfectly clean and free from grease, and in the case of the former it must be changed when it becomes too damp. A wet towel is practically useless.

From time to time the silver will be improved by having a more special cleaning. One of the best things to use for this is fine Spanish whitening or some good plate powder and liquid ammonia.[1] Put a little whitening (not more than one dessert-spoonful at a time) into a saucer and mix into a perfectly smooth paste with the ammonia. It should be of the consistency of thin cream. Apply this to the silver with a piece of soft flannel, rubbing each article well, and especially the parts which are most likely to be

[1] Elkington & Co. Ltd., Birmingham, sell a plate powder which is thoroughly to be recommended. It is free from mercury, and does not contain chalk in any form. Chalk is very injurious to silver and electro-plated articles from its cutting nature, and unfortunately forms the basis of many of the plate powders in existence.

stained. Allow this to dry on the silver, then rub off with a second piece of flannel, using a soft silver brush wherever necessary to remove the whitening. Forks require special attention, as the powder is apt to lodge between the prongs. The "Selvyt" fork polisher is useful for this purpose. Then polish well with the chamois leather. When finished, it must not be handled more than necessary.

Silver Brush.

There are many other plate powders which can be used in place of the whitening, but care must be taken to use one that is thoroughly reliable, as so many of them are mixed with mercury, which is injurious to the plate. Rouge and hartshorn powder are both very good, but unless the former is carefully removed it looks bad. Methylated spirits may be used instead of ammonia, and will be found very satisfactory, but when once a good method is adopted it should be adhered to, as it is easier for the worker and better for the silver.

Silver forks and knives with ivory handles should not be allowed to soak in water, or at least the handles must be kept out of the water, or the heat will melt the cement which fixes them together. The best plan is to hold them in the hand while washing and to place them in a jug for rinsing with enough boiling water to reach just up to the handles.

Egg spoons that have become very much stained with the sulphur from the egg should be rubbed with a little fine dry salt and then washed.

A silver teapot may be washed in the same way, only if it has a wooden handle or wooden or ivory rings on the handle, it must not be allowed to soak in hot water. A teapot must on no account be left standing with the remains of tea and tea-leaves in it, but should be emptied and rinsed out with boiling water as soon as possible after use. When it begins to have a discoloured appearance inside or to smell musty, fill it to the brim with boiling water, and add a piece of washing-soda. Close down the lid and let it remain thus all night. Next day pour out the soda-water, wash with soap and water, using a small brush, and rinse thoroughly. A teapot must be dried inside as well as outside, and left with the lid open until quite free from moisture.

Silver should be exposed as little as possible to the action of the atmosphere, more especially in damp foggy weather, when it will very readily tarnish. That which is in daily use should be kept either in a baize-lined plate-basket and covered with a piece of felt or flannel, or in a baize-lined drawer covered in a similar way.

Articles that are not in constant use should be kept in the lined cases, or in bags made of flannel or chamois leather.

A lump of camphor stored with silver will help to preserve its brilliancy.

Britannia Metal Goods.—Messrs. Dixon and Sons, manufacturers, Sheffield, have kindly supplied the following directions for cleaning:—Rub the article all over with a piece of woollen cloth, moistened with sweet oil, and then apply a little pounded rotten-stone, or polishing paste, with the finger till the polish is produced; after which, wash it well with soap and hot water, and when dry wipe off smartly with soft wash-leather and a little fine whiting. This simple method will effectually preserve the colour.

By attending to the above, Britannia metal goods are warranted to stand their colour any duration of time.

THE WASHING OF GLASS, WATER-BOTTLES, DECANTERS, &c.

Glass requires very special care if we want it to look nice. Tumblers should be washed first in warm water, with a very little soap or a few drops of ammonia, using the fingers or a fine cloth to rub them with. Then rinse them in clear cold water and place them upside down on a tray to drain. Use a very fine towel for drying, as one that is fluffy would leave small particles on the glass. Care must be taken, too, that the towel is dry and free from grease, or it would give the glass a smeared appearance. A final polish with a chamois leather is sometimes given; but this is objected to by some people, because they think it gives the glass a taste. When a tumbler has been used for milk or any other liquid of a greasy nature, it should be filled with cold water as soon as possible to prevent the grease sinking into the glass and making it troublesome to wash.

Wine-glasses should be treated in the same way as tumblers, only the greatest care must be taken in the drying, because of the slender stems.

If a little vinegar is added occasionally to the water in which table glass is rinsed, it will give it an extra brightness.

Moulded or Cut-glass Dishes.—When washing these use a light lather of soap and warm water, and a few drops of ammonia as well, if the articles are very dirty. A soft brush, too, will be found useful for removing any dust or dirt from the crevices. Always rinse well in clear cold water to remove all trace of soap, and dry and polish as before.

Water-bottles and Decanters.—When these become stained or discoloured, they may be treated in one of the following ways:—Fill the bottle half-full of warm soapy water, and put in some pieces of brown paper, some tea-leaves or small pieces of raw potato; let it soak for some time, shaking it occasionally, then pour out, rinse and drain. Crushed egg-shells or fine ashes used along with a little soap are also very good. If none of these are enough to remove the discoloration, try vinegar and coarse salt—one part salt to two parts vinegar, undiluted with water (this can be used more than once); allow them to remain some hours in the bottle, then pour out and rinse and dry as before. Sometimes a brush is an assistance in the washing of decanters.

Bottle-Brushes.

If the *stoppers* become fixed in wine decanters, it is a good plan to pour a few drops of oil round the neck and place the decanter near the fire, and in a short time try to loosen it gently; if it still sticks, wash it in warm water and repeat the process.

Sometimes a few gentle taps with another stopper will help to loosen the fixed one. Glycerine, too, is a good thing to use instead of oil.

Flower Vases should be washed inside with a small brush, and if stained, treated in the same way as decanters.

TO WASH CHINA AND OTHER DISHES

Tea Dishes.—If these are in daily use, it will be sufficient to wash them in hot water with a soft dish-cloth; rinse in cold or tepid water and dry with a fine towel. If the water is very hard, a little borax or soap-powder may be added to it, but soda must never be used for fine-coloured china, and especially if there is any gilt on it. Excessive rubbing, too, must be avoided when finely painted china is under treatment. The water must not be used too hot, and the china should not be put in until the heat has been tested with the hand. If the water is too hot for the hand to rest in, it is too hot for the china. Commence with the cups, then the saucers, and lastly the plates and any jugs or basins. Particular attention must be given to the handles of cups and jugs to see that they are clean.

Care, too, must be taken in the drying of fine china; it will require very gentle handling.

Tea stains may be removed from cups and teapots by rubbing them with a little common salt, or by rubbing a little Brook's soap on a flannel, and then applying it to the mark. This will also remove burnt stains from meat-dishes or pie-dishes.

China Ornaments which are washed only occasionally will require a little more rubbing, and the addition of soap to the water will be a necessity. A soft brush will also be found useful when washing any intricate parts. After washing, rinse well; drain, dry, and polish with a chamois leather.

Dinner Dishes.—As these are stronger and generally more greasy than other china, the addition of a little soda to the water in which they are washed will be advisable, except in the case of gilded ware, when borax or soap-powder must be used instead.

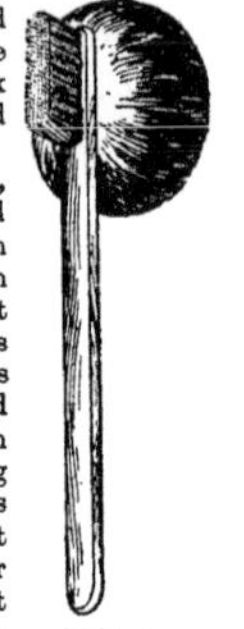

Dish-Mop.

When using soda in the water, it is a good plan to use a small mop instead of a cloth to wash with; the hands will not then require to come into such direct contact with the water. Plates and other dishes must always be washed on both sides, and must always be rinsed in clean cold or tepid water before being put aside to drain. If there is a rack, the plates may be put straight out of the rinsing water into that, and a certain amount of drying will thus be saved. They should be taken down when dry, and rubbed over lightly with a clean dry cloth to give them a polish.

THE CARE OF KNIVES AND STEEL FORKS

Soiled knives must never be put into a basin or tub of hot water and allowed to soak, as this would melt the cement or glue in the handles, and cause the blades to come apart.

Stand them blade downwards in a knife-washer or jug with sufficient hot water to reach just up to the handles, and add a small piece of soda. Allow them to soak for some little time, then wipe them well, handle and blade, with a dish-cloth, and dry them carefully with a towel or coarse cloth kept for the purpose. If an ordinary towel is used, the greatest care must be taken that the knives do not cut it, as this accounts for many holes which appear far too soon in kitchen and pantry towels.

With regard to polishing the knives, this can be done either on a board or in a knife-cleaning machine. These latter can now be bought for a few shillings, and they are certainly a great saving of labour, but care must be taken in their use. The knives must in all cases be put in clean and free from grease, and the machine must be turned gently and not more than is necessary. If the knife-board is used it is a good plan to remove the worst stains from the knives, and especially from the points, before beginning to rub them on the board. This may be done either with a piece of raw potato dipped in bath-brick dust or knife-powder and rubbed on the knife, or with a piece of cork used in the same way. This will lessen the rubbing considerably and lessen the wear and tear of the knife. Then sprinkle the knife-board with a little of the powder, and rub the knife quickly and lightly backwards and forwards on this. Any pressure must be brought to bear on the back of the knife rather than on the sharp edge, and the point must never be rubbed down. The knives must finally be well dusted to free them from all powder, and must be kept in a dry place.

Should the ivory or bone handles of knives become stained or discoloured, they may be improved by rubbing them with a cut lemon and a little dry salt, or vinegar and salt, then wipe off with a damp flannel and dry. Fine emery powder moistened with a little water and applied with a flannel is also a good thing to use for stains.

When knives are not to be used for some time, it is a good plan to rub the blades with sweet oil and then to roll them, one by one, in a piece of flannel or felt, and in such a way that they do not touch each other. This is especially necessary in damp districts, because if once rust is allowed to attack the steel the appearance of the knife is spoilt.

Steel Forks must be treated in the same way as knives, only instead of rubbing them on the board apply the knife-powder or bath-brick with a piece of flannel. Particular care must be taken to dust well between the prongs.

THE CARE OF LAMPS AND OIL-HEATING STOVES

If lamps are used in a household, the care of them should be in the hands of one person, and unless there is a capable maid who has time to devote herself to the work, it is really better for the mistress to undertake this duty herself. The value of a lamp depends upon its being properly attended to, and if it is allowed to smoke and smell, it is not only worse than useless, as far as light is concerned, but there is nothing more disagreeable.

To begin with, lamps must be cleaned and filled by daylight, as there is always a certain amount of danger in working with oil by artificial light. Needless to say, this must not be done on the kitchen table, nor where any fine work is in progress, as lamp-oil stains are very difficult to eradicate. If a small table cannot be reserved for the purpose, then the best plan is to use an old tray or a piece of thick mill-board.

A lamp in daily use should be filled three parts full every morning, as it is dangerous to use when the oil is very low in the reservoir or container. The oil should be poured in by means of a feeder, and not from the can itself, for in the latter case it would be apt to come out by jerks and be spilt over, or the lamp would be made too full. It is very important also to use oil of a good quality. In fact, it is no economy to buy cheap oil, as it not only gives an inferior light and burns more quickly, but it is also more dangerous to use. Good oil should give a white light, have no smell, and be as clear as water.

Then with regard to the wick; it is of the utmost importance that this fits the burner well, and it should be just long enough to reach the bottom of the reservoir. A wick should last for three months, after that time it is best to renew it, when the end to be lighted should be dipped in the oil first. As a rule the wick should not require cutting, but should be turned low and the uneven charred part gently rubbed off with a piece of card-board and the surface made smooth with the top of the tubes. If it still remains uneven, it may then be trimmed carefully with a pair of lamp scissors. After this any black pieces of wick must be removed from the burner, and the outside of the lamp rubbed first with a piece of newspaper and then a soft rag, until free from oil.

From time to time, both the reservoir and the burner will require to be thoroughly cleaned. The reservoir should be emptied of all oil and washed out with warm suds to which a few drops of ammonia have been added. Rinse thoroughly, and then turn upside down in a warm place to dry. When the burner becomes clogged and dirty, it should be taken to pieces (care being taken to notice how it is fixed together), and put into an old saucepan with a lump of soda and enough cold water to cover it. Bring to the boil, and boil for half-an-hour. Then rinse in warm water, and use a brush if necessary to remove any charred wick. When quite clean place in a warm place, or a cool oven to dry. The lamp must not be refilled until both reservoir and burner are quite dry, or the oil will splutter.

Pains must be taken to keep both the chimney glass and the globe very clean and bright. The chimney should never be washed, but may be cleaned with lamp-brushes, or a pad of chamois leather or felt fastened to a stick. The Selvyt lamp-cleaner is a most useful article for this purpose. If the glass becomes marked or very much soiled, a little methylated spirits may be used to remove the stains. The outer globe should be dusted every day and occasionally washed in warm water with a little soap, then rinsed and dried with a glass-cloth.

If a lamp burns badly or smells, it is generally due to one of the following causes :—

(1) It has been filled too full, and the oil when heated expands and runs over the sides.

(2) The receiver and burner have not been wiped after filling.

(3) The wick does not fit properly, or it has been badly trimmed.

(4) Inferior oil has been used.

(5) The lamp-glasses are not clean.

When lighting the lamp, turn up the wick only slightly and keep it burning low until the chimney is thoroughly heated; then turn it up as far as it will go without smoking.

When not in use the wick must be kept low, otherwise the oil oozes up through it and over the sides.

To extinguish a lamp (if there in no patent extinguisher attached), turn down the wick until it is level with the tube, and blow quickly across the top of the chimney.

The best lamps are fitted with a patent burner which permits of the lamp being blown out with safety, or, if overturned, will extinguish itself at once. Should an accident, however, happen and the oil be spilt and catch fire, it must be remembered that water poured over it would only spread the flame. The best thing to do is to throw sand or earth on the burning oil, or to smother the flame with a thick rug. Door and window should immediately be shut.

The same remarks apply to the keeping of oil-stoves. It is almost impossible to prevent their smelling a little, but with proper care this smell should be so reduced as to be almost imperceptible.

TO CLEAN BOOTS

Boots should never be cleaned when damp. If they have been brought in very muddy, they should be wiped with a damp flannel or a small wet brush. Then put on to boot-trees, or if these are not available, stuff the inside with some crumpled newspaper, and this will help to keep the boots in good shape. Never put boots close to the fire to dry, as too rapid drying will harden, and perhaps crack the leather. It is much better if they can be allowed to dry slowly in a warm atmosphere. If the leather should become hard, a little vaseline or sweet oil may be applied. This should be rubbed well in and then off again with a piece of flannel.

It is very important that the inside of boots should be kept clean during the process of cleaning. For this reason it is a good plan to cover the hand that is placed inside the boot with a clean duster. Gloves, too, should be worn to protect the hands. Thanks to the many good boot polishes which can now be obtained, the old-fashioned liquid blacking, which was liable to be splashed or spilt where it was not wanted, is now a thing of the past, and boot-cleaning may be quite a clean and tidy occupation. So much so that many ladies who do not keep a lady's-maid prefer to clean their own shoes, and especially those of a fine quality. In fact all the necessary requisites can be kept in a very small tin box, and cause no inconvenience anywhere.

First remove all dust or mud with a brush—then with a piece of flannel or an old stocking-leg, apply a little boot-polish, rubbing it well in and all over the boot, not forgetting the heels and the back part. Then polish with a polishing-pad; one covered with velvet or selvyt cloth is best.

When boots are new and they are found difficult to polish, a few drops of paraffin added to the paste will be found a help.

Brown Boots should be cleaned in the same way, using brown boot-polish instead of black, or the ordinary bees'-wax and turpentine (see p. 66) does very well. Stains may be removed with lemon-juice or methylated spirits, or with the inside of a banana skin.

Patent Leather Boots require rather different treatment. Wipe them first with a damp sponge and dry them. Then rub over with a flannel dipped in a little milk. When the leather becomes shabby it is better to use one of the special polishes sold for the purpose at any bootmakers; or a small quantity of vaseline well rubbed in will keep them soft and bright. The edges of the soles should be blackened.

White Shoes.—Those made of canvas or drill should be cleaned with pipeclay or whitening mixed to a creamy consistency with cold water, then applied evenly with a sponge or piece of soft rag. Place the shoes in the sun to dry, and then lightly brush off any superfluous powder. White kid shoes should be cleaned with a special dressing sold for the purpose.

CARE OF BRUSHES

House Brushes should all be soaked in cold water for some hours, and then well dried before they are used. This prevents the hairs or bristles from coming out, and increases the durability of the brush.

When house-brooms and such-like become dirty, they should be washed. Put a little boiling water in a pail, and add a handful of soda to it. Then pour in cold or tepid water until the pail is three parts full. Take the brushes one at a time, carefully remove from them all fluff, thread ends, hairs, &c., and work them up and down in the soda-water. Rinse thoroughly in cold water and shake well to get rid of as much moisture as possible. Dry in the open air or hang up in a warm atmosphere.

Brushes should never be left lying or standing on their bristles. Small brushes can be hung up, and the longer brooms should be kept in a rack. No pieces of wool nor fluffy matter should be left sticking to the bristles.

It is also very important that brushes be kept for the special purpose for which they are intended, and not used for all and sundry purposes.

EXTERMINATION OF PESTS

Beetles.—These objectionable insects infest usually the ground floor and kitchen premises of houses. They disappear in the daytime and come out at night through the cracks in the flooring, and they multiply so rapidly that

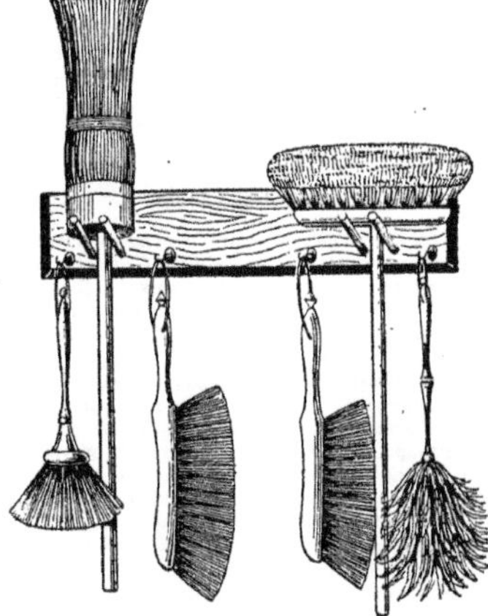

Brush-Rack.

sometimes they can be counted by the thousand. They will attack food of all kinds, and the leather of boots and shoes; in fact, everything that comes in their way.

Many different kinds of traps have been invented, and they all serve their purpose for the time being, but one of the safest and surest methods of extermination is the use of "Blatol." Spread this paste upon pieces of thick paper about three or four inches square. Lay these at night in the places most frequented by the beetles. Remove the papers in the morning and burn them. Lay fresh papers with the paste every night for a week, or more, then every second or third night until all the beetles have disappeared. The "Blatol" so effectively destroys them, and at the same time so completely dries them up, that their dead bodies do not emit the slightest smell.

Fleas.—Strict cleanliness, good ventilation and plenty of light and sunshine are the greatest enemies of this kind of pest. Fleas flourish in warmth, dirt and darkness; these are just the conditions which favour their development.

If a bed becomes infested, the best thing is to have the mattress brought out into the sunshine and thoroughly brushed. The blankets, too, should have the same treatment. Then the bedstead itself should be well washed with carbolic soap and water, and also the flooring under the bed. Throw the windows of the room well open and let it be thoroughly aired. Various powders are also used for the destruction of fleas, and most of these contain the plant substance "Pyrethrum," which has accordingly been popularly known as "Fleabane." This can be bought in powder form from any chemist, and other ready-made insect powders can also be obtained. Lumps of camphor laid between the bedclothes, or carried in a small muslin bag on the person, is also a preventive, but the chief destroyer of all is cleanliness.

Moths.—It is very important that all moths on the wing should be destroyed as soon as they are seen. They lay their eggs in all kinds of woollen materials, carpets, blankets and bedding, upholstered furniture, &c.

Any article that is likely to be attacked should be brushed frequently, and special attention should be paid to them in the month of September, which is about the time when the eggs are laid, and then again in the month of March, when the insect is still in a dormant state.

Care, too, must be taken of woollen things that are laid away for any length of time. They should be well brushed, and then folded up in a newspaper or sewn into cotton with something aromatic, such as cloves, caraway seeds, camphor, naphtha balls, or sprigs of the common bog myrtle put between the folds of the material as preventive. The moths seem to dislike the printer's ink on the newspaper, and they won't eat through cotton. When a mattress or piece of upholstered furniture is once really attacked by moths it will require to be sent away to be professionally stoved and cleaned.

Bugs.—These are rarely found in clean and well-kept houses, although occasionally through accident they may be introduced. They must be attacked at once, as they breed very rapidly. Whenever their presence is noticed in a bedroom, the bedding must have the most careful attention. The mattress should be well brushed, and especially in the corners and crevices, where eggs may possibly be laid. Then the bedstead itself should be taken to pieces, thoroughly washed with hot water and carbolic or paraffin soap. When dry, paint it over with turpentine and allow it to air. Any woodwork too that seems to be infested should be painted over with turpentine.

A formaline lamp left burning in the room is very good for fumigating.

Mice.—The best plan is to starve them out. All eatables should be enclosed, and nothing left uncovered that would supply them with food. A cat or small dog which is a good mouser are also preventives. A trap, too, is often very effectual in catching a stray mouse here and there, and in frightening away others. There are many different kinds, but perhaps the old-fashioned make, which catches the animal alive, are the most humane; others, which are supposed to kill instantaneously, often succeed in only half doing it, and so causing unnecessary suffering.

There are different poisons too which can be bought for the destruction of mice, of which phosphorus paste is perhaps the best; but care must be taken in using them, and especially if there are domestic animals in the house.

Rats.—When rats enter a house, it is often a sign of insanitary drainage, and if that is the case the wrong must be seen to at once, and the necessary repairs carried out. Or it may be that the house is in the close proximity to a stable, and the rats have made their way into the house through some holes. A trap is sometimes of good service for catching the rats, and directions for baiting them are usually given with each special kind. Poisoning is another method; but this must be done with caution, and especially if there are any domestic animals in the house. Another danger of poisoning is that the dead bodies of the rats sometimes decompose under the flooring, and cause a very bad smell. A small dog, a terrier, sometimes keeps them away most effectively.

If the rats become numerous, a rat-catcher should be employed, who will hunt the rats out with trained ferrets. When once the vermin have been got rid of, all holes by which they have entered should be carefully filled up with cement or plaster.

Flies.—When flies are numerous, it is a good plan to wash the windows and window ledges with a strong solution of carbolic, or if the smell is an objection, sprinkle with Persian powder at night, and then sweep up in the morning. Fly-papers will also catch a number, but they are rather disgusting things to use. They should if possible be put in out-of-the-way places, such as the tops of cupboards. A very simple fly-paper can be made by spreading treacle or honey on brown paper, and sprinkling it with Persian powder or other insect poison. Fly-papers prepared with some sticky substance to which the flies adhere and endure a slow torturing death should be avoided. Another good way of getting rid of flies when they become numerous is to disinfect the room with sulphur.

The blow-fly, which is larger than the common house-fly, is the kind most to be dreaded, as it is a great enemy in the larder. It frequently lays its larvæ in meat, which causes it to decompose very quickly. In hot weather all meat should be examined when it is received, and if anything is suspected, it should be carefully washed with a solution of Coudy's fluid and water. The proportions to use will be found printed on the bottle. The meat should then be well sprinkled with pepper or other spice, which will help to keep the flies away. It is a good plan to fasten a piece of muslin or fine gauze over the larder window to prevent the flies entering.

Ants.—These are very troublesome creatures to get rid of when once they infest a house, and sometimes different remedies have to be tried before one succeeds. One of the best is to find the opening through which the ants come, drop in some quicklime, and wash it over with boiling water. A strong solution of carbolic acid or spirits of camphor might also be tried, as ants are very averse to strong smells. Or, again, some petroleum or tobacco juice poured over their nests is sometimes effectual.

SPRING CLEANING

Every year, as soon as the cold days of winter are over, and the promise of fine weather bids fair to be realised, the thoughts of the busy housewife turn towards preparations for the inevitable "Spring Clean." There are still some people who look upon this yearly cleaning as a perfectly unnecessary fetish before which the housewife bows down in deference to a mere time-honoured tradition. This point of view is erroneous, and those who share it show but little knowledge of the art of housewifery. However clean a house is kept, and however regularly the various rooms go through their daily and weekly cleaning, it is always necessary to have a special cleaning from cellar to garret once a year at least. This is not intended to take the place of the daily or weekly cleaning, but rather to supplement it, and to give an opportunity of attending to such matters as can most conveniently be seen to at this season, when all necessary renovation, papering and whitewashing can also be undertaken.

This annual cleaning need not necessarily take place in the *spring*—the time may be arranged according to the convenience of the household; but spring is the season which appeals to most people as being the most natural time for having a good "turn out." After a long winter, things have put on a dark and dingy appearance, and seem very much out of keeping with the fine weather and the bright sunshine. There is a desire to get rid of all dark curtains and other hangings that have been in use all through the wintry months of the year, and to replace them with something light and pretty, and to give things generally a fresher appearance.

The best time for this cleaning is the beginning of May, when fires are required less regularly, and the weather is likely to remain fine. If, however, the autumn or summer suits the arrangements of the household better, it is by no means necessary to adhere to any rigid rule.

A spring cleaning may be hard work while it lasts—a few days of undesirable toil; but there is another side to the picture. What a feeling of satisfaction and air of content there is when all is accomplished, and how fresh and bright the rooms look after they have had their yearly overhauling, and put on their spring dress.

The spring is also the time to see to any repairs and renovations, as, for instance, the re-covering of any furniture which has grown shabby, the re-gilding of any picture-frames which require it, the mending of all locks and door-handles, and so on. Then a new shelf or cupboard might be put up here and there, and any little additions made which might add to the comfort of the home. Deficiencies in stock, too, should be replenished, broken and cracked dishes discarded or given away, and numbers and sets of things made up as completely as possible, so that the work of the house may start anew with a sufficiency of materials and implements.

Importance of Method.—In former times the advent of the annual spring cleaning was looked upon with positive terror by the unfortunate householder. To him it represented a period when he would return home from his hard daily work in the city to find a tired, untidy-looking, cross-tempered wife, furniture heaped pell-mell in all the passages, pails of water and scrubbing brushes at every turn, and curl-papers bristling in the hair, and a liberal display of smuts upon the face of "Mary Jane." His evening meal, more often than not, would have to be taken haphazard in the kitchen, where pots and pans and other culinary paraphernalia in the various stages of the cleaning process would not add to the comfort of his surroundings. Small blame to the man who under these circumstances would seek refuge in the comfort and cheerful society to be found at his club!

In these days of up-to-date cleaning contrivances such a state of affairs should be inexcusable, yet in many houses to-day the words "Spring Cleaning" and "Discomfort" are still synonymous. The extent to which cleaning becomes a nuisance depends very much upon the way in which the work is performed. Some system should be decided on beforehand, and a haphazard way of doing things must be avoided. By the exercise of a little foresight much time and worry may be saved, and method, organisation and thoroughness will bring the work to a speedy conclusion. For instance, if painters, joiners, plumbers, or any other workmen are likely to be required, they ought to be engaged in good time; the services of the sweep too must be retained, and if extra help is required, a charwoman must be engaged.

Before the work is started in real earnest, the housewife should make sure that she has in stock a good supply of all the necessary cleaning materials, such as carbolic soap, soft soap, soda, soap-powder, borax, ammonia, methylated spirits, bees'-wax, &c., and also a sufficiency of towels, cloths, dusters and brushes to carry on the work. Of course the ideal way to do a spring cleaning is to have the house emptied of all its occupants, except only those who are taking part in the work. Then the correct order in which to do it would be to commence at the top of the house, and to work downwards, beginning with the lumber-room, if there is one, then the bedrooms, next the sitting-rooms, bath-room and lavatory, finishing with the kitchen, cellars, and any outhouses. In the case of a flat a different order may perhaps be taken. If this ideal plan cannot be followed, then it is best to do the cleaning by degrees, and not to plunge the whole house into discomfort by undertaking the whole performance at once. In fact, some mistresses find it more convenient to clean half the house in the spring and the other half in the autumn, or even to clean only a single room now and again. In this way it does not seem such a formidable undertaking for servants.

Each day's work should be carefully planned. Too much must not be undertaken at a time, but only what can be done without undue effort. There is never anything to be gained by overtaxing one's strength. A point should be made of having comfortable meals served all the time, as without this the end of each day would simply mean exhaustion.

There will be a great saving of time when the actual cleaning begins if all cupboards and drawers can be turned out beforehand. When they have been emptied of their contents, the insides should be scrubbed out with carbolic soap and warm water, and then left some time to air. Meanwhile the contents should be looked over, and all rubbish disposed of. The remainder should then be dusted, brushed or washed, according to the nature of the various articles, and put in good order. Then the shelves and drawers should be neatly lined with clean paper, and the contents put back in an orderly fashion. Any winter coats or dresses which are not likely to be required for some time should be well brushed, and if possible hung in the open air for some hours; then carefully stored with some preparation which will keep the moth away. (See p. 314.) Winter curtains should undergo the same treatment.

Books, and book-cases too, and stands with music, should all be cleaned and sorted out beforehand, and any magazines or pamphlets that are of no further service destroyed, or sent to some hospital for the use of the patients.

Spring Cleaning a Bedroom.—The first thing to do before having a room spring cleaned is to make it as empty as possible. If it is a bedroom, the bedding should first be seen to. All the coverings, including the covers of mattress and pillows, should be sent either to be cleaned or washed. Then if there is a garden to which things can be taken easily, everything which requires shaking and brushing should be taken outside, such as mattress, pillows, cushions, rugs, upholstered chairs (unless too heavy to be moved), &c.; and after they have been cleaned either left in the open air or in an adjoining passage until the room is ready to receive them.

All pictures, ornaments, and small articles of furniture should be dusted before they are removed from the room, to avoid having dust carried to another part of the house; and that which must be left because of its size or weight must be dusted first, and then carefully covered. If there is a nailed-down carpet, this must be lifted, and folded up carefully to prevent the dust flying about, and then taken away to be cleaned or beaten. The floor should then be sprinkled with a little wet saw-dust or bran, swept with a soft brush, and the dust burnt at once.

Should the chimney require sweeping, this should now be done, the sweep having been engaged beforehand. It is well also to see that the work is properly carried out, and that the brushes have been carried up the whole length of the chimney.

When this is finished, the room is now ready for any papering and painting that may be required, and must perforce be left in the painters' hands until their work is completed. If nothing of this kind is necessary, the cleaning must be done in the following order :—First, get rid of all dust by dusting all walls, curtain poles, blinds, and woodwork; secondly, black-lead and polish the grate; and thirdly, do all the washing that is required, such as woodwork, marble, furniture, including windows, bedsteads, floors, &c. Then the room ought to be left to air and dry with door and window wide open.

Meanwhile the articles of furniture, &c., outside can have attention, and as far as possible everything should be cleaned before it is brought back into the room. When everything is dry, all necessary polishing should be done. Pictures can then be re-hung, and everything as far as possible returned to its proper place. The carpet should of course be re-laid as soon as it is ready; only if this has been sent to the cleaners, it may be necessary to wait for two or three days.

Fresh curtains should then be put up, clean chair-covers, and cushion-covers where they are needed, and dainty touches given to make everything look pretty.

A Sitting-room.—The order in which a sitting-room is "spring cleaned" would be very much the same as that followed for a bedroom (with the exception of the bed), but there will probably be more furniture and odds and ends to attend to.

Hall, Staircase and Bath-room.—It is always well to leave the staircase and bath-room until all the other rooms are finished, as there will of necessity be more tramping up and down the former while the cleaning is going on, and the latter has frequently to be used for the washing of ornaments, bedroom ware, &c. The walls of the bath-room should always be of a washable nature, and then the cleaning is a very easy matter, as it simply means that every part must be washed from the top downwards, finishing with the floor. If the bath itself has become very shabby it should be re-enamelled. This can be done at home, although as a rule home enamelling is not very satisfactory, and if the extra expense can be afforded, it is much better to have it done by a skilled workman. When the washing is finished, the door and window should be left open to dry and air the room, and then the polishing of brasses, woodwork and floor should be undertaken.

The hall and staircase is a more difficult undertaking. The rugs and stair-carpets having been removed, and all pictures, &c., taken from the walls and moved out of the way, the first thing to see to will be the cleaning of the walls. If they are very high, it is scarcely work that can be undertaken by maid-servants, especially if the walls require washing; if it is simply a matter of dusting them down with a long broom, it may be possible. The stairs, railings, and banisters must next be well brushed and washed, and also the floor of the hall and any passages. Wash also any pieces of furniture that require it, including gas globes, flower-pots and ornaments. Next polish all woodwork, stair-rods, brasses and furniture, and lay the carpet and rugs last of all.

The Housemaid's Pantry.—In a well-appointed house where there are several servants there is generally a small room set aside for the housemaid's requirements. It is usually upstairs in close proximity to the bedrooms. This little

Housemaid's Box.

room should contain all that the housemaid will require for cleaning purposes. (See list on page 83.)

It should be fitted up with a sink and be supplied with hot and cold water. There should also be a shelf at a convenient height for holding hot-water cans, hot-water bottles, dust-sheets, &c., and, if room, a rack for hanging brushes and a small pulley or towel-rail for drying the various cloths. It will also be convenient to have a small cupboard in which cleaning materials could be kept in jars, also paper and sticks for lighting fires. A small solid table would also be most useful if space permits, as on this the housemaid could do any special cleaning of silver or brass required for the bedrooms and also the brushing of clothes that come under her care. A few hooks should be put up along the edge of the shelf and at the sink, as they will be found handy for hanging up small articles, such as taper-holder, bottle brushes, sink brush, tin jug, &c.

The following is a list of the articles which the housemaid's pantry might contain :—

A housemaid's box, a slop-pail, a pail for housework, a pair of steps, a kneeling-mat, a dust-pan, hot-water cans, hot-water bottles, a large can for carrying water, a tin jug, a soap-dish.

Brushes.—A carpet switch, a long broom, a small short-handled broom, a banister brush, a wall-broom, a carpet-sweeper, a furniture brush, boot brushes, black-lead brushes, two scrubbing brushes, a bottle brush, hearth brush, clothes' brush.

Cleaning Materials, &c.—Washing soda, Brook's soap or Sapolio, yellow soap, polishing paste, furniture polish, boot polish, turpentine, ammonia, bees'-wax, coarse salt, emery paper, black-lead, paper and sticks, or fire-lighters, matches, taper in holder.

Towels, &c. — Dusters, glass towels, slop-cloths, washing cloth, swabs, coarse towels for drying floors, &c., old soft towels for drying paint, two chamois leathers, pieces of flannel for cleaning purposes, dust sheets, hearth cloth, grate cloths, a pair of gloves.

A REMOVAL

Introductory.—Thanks to modern enterprise on the part of removal contractors, this does not require to be the dreaded affair it was in days gone by. Although a removal is undeniably somewhat of an undertaking, it can be robbed of many of its terrors if it is put into the hands of a reliable firm, and the preliminaries are arranged with some thought and care.

Of course, if money is no object, it is quite possible to step out of the old house in the morning and spend the day enjoyably in town, or with friends, and to walk into the new home in the evening to find there that one's belongings have been bodily transported and placed in position, leaving very little to be done except the arrangement of personal belongings to one's own liking, and other small details.

But this expeditious and easy way of managing the business means money, and we are not all lavishly endowed with this world's riches. People of modest means must be prepared to buckle to when such an important affair as a removal is on hand, and undertake some of the work and arranging themselves.

Thought, advice and experience can, however, do much to lessen discomfort, and prevent chaos, and the more carefully the order of the removal is planned the easier the change of house will be.

Making the Contract.—The first point to decide is how the furniture has to be removed, and by whom. It is always best to choose experienced removers, for although the initial expense may appear more, the ultimate saving in the avoidance of breakages and kindred annoyances is unquestionable. It is better, if possible, to choose a firm near at hand, who will send a representative to look at the things and furnish an estimate free of charge. He will also tell you what arrangements it is necessary to make, and what preliminaries must be attended to. Removals can now be conducted to all parts of the United Kingdom in vans of the most improved construction (pantechnicons), and all risks and responsibilities are undertaken. The charge will depend on the quantity and quality of the furniture, and upon the distance it has to be moved.

Preliminaries in the Old House.—Before the actual removal takes place there are certain preliminaries which must be attended to, both in the old house and in the new.

One very important point to attend to before leaving the old house is to turn out all the rubbish. Clothes that are of no further use, broken and hoarded crockery, damaged and soiled knick-knacks, old saucepans and kettles, empty bottles and jam-pots, all should be disposed of; in fact everything should be done to avoid the carriage of dirt and worthless stuff. Old papers should, however, be kept, as these will be found useful when packing.

Then all the furniture should be sorted out and considered with a view to its place in the new abode, and that which is unsuitable should be sold or otherwise disposed of. It sometimes happens that an incoming tenant will only be too pleased to buy odds and ends of furniture, and even a carpet or two.

Furniture which requires repairing, cleaning or re-covering, and pictures requiring new frames or re-gilding, should be sent away to have the necessary attention, and not returned until the new house is ready to receive them. The decoration and colouring of the new house must of course be borne in mind when choosing any new upholstery, and shades must be chosen which will tone well with the new surroundings.

All carpets should be lifted and sent away to be beaten or cleaned, according to what is necessary. Curtains, too, which require cleaning or dyeing, and any heavy extra washing, such as bed-covers, spare blankets, &c., should be sent from the old house, and returned to the new, as in this way some of the removal expenses will be saved.

Of course this means a certain amount of dismantling beforehand, but upon the whole it is better to have the discomfort before the removal rather than after it has taken place. Once in the new quarters one is naturally anxious to get settled as quickly as possible, and it is annoying to have to wait for this or that to arrive upon the scene.

Preliminaries in the New House.—The business

of a removal can be very much simplified if one can obtain possession of the new house some time before it is necessary to move into it. The house can then be made ready, and entered with comfort.

First of all, every chimney should be swept. Then whatever whitewashing, papering or painting that is necessary should be done. It is fortunate for a new tenant when the landlord undertakes to do up the house throughout, and will give the choice of papers and colouring.

When the workmen have finished, it will next be necessary to have all the floors scrubbed with carbolic soap, soda and a brush, and under no circumstances should one be satisfied with the superficial cleaning given by the painters, or even by the late tenants. Grates and windows can then be cleaned, and if it is winter time, coal should be ordered in and fires put on so as to thoroughly dry and air the rooms. The lighting and heating arrangements should be carefully tested and necessary alterations made, as it is most annoying later on to have to disturb carpets or linoleum for the sake of laying a new gas-pipe or an electric wire. The water-pipes and taps should also be seen to, and the cistern thoroughly cleaned out.

Then the question of floor covering should be considered. It is an immense help if all linoleum and any nailed-down carpets can be laid before the furniture is brought in. This is really the secret of being quickly settled. When once the carpets and linoleum are satisfactorily laid, then the furniture can be brought in with the happy feeling that it will not require to be moved again. Besides, it is much easier to fit and lay down a large carpet in an empty room than it is when heavy furniture has to be lifted and moved from one place to another. Of course, if the carpets consist merely of small squares or large rugs, it would be wiser to defer laying them until later on in the proceedings. Linoleum in any case, and especially that which surrounds a room, should be put in position previous to the moving in of the furniture.

Then with regard to curtains and blinds, if any of these can be put up beforehand, it will greatly add to the comfort of the first few days, even although the old house has to be robbed of them a trifle sooner in consequence.

Packing.—While years ago it was deemed necessary to pack all furniture, to tie wisps of straw round the legs of tables and chairs, and even sew each article into a sheet of sacking in order to preserve it from ill-treatment, now one can confidently leave the tables, chairs, and such-like to the removal men, who are in most cases trained specialists to the work. The large vans, or pantechnicons, take most things, and especially the heavier articles of furniture, just as they are. It is also better to leave the packing of glass, china, and other breakables to the men, who will bring the necessary crates and straw for the purpose. They will be much more likely to avoid breakages than any amateur packer, however careful he (or she) may be. It must be remembered too, that a removal contractor can only be held responsible for things he has packed himself, and not for those packed by the owner.

Of course there are always a few things which can be packed beforehand, and if all small things can be stowed away in portable cases, the actual removal is done in a very short time. Books, for instance, can be safely packed; they should be dusted first, and then put in cases lined with paper. Any precious volumes with fine or delicate bindings should be wrapped separately in paper, in order to prevent them from being scratched or rubbed. In the case of large heavy books, it is better to make them up in bundles, and put a piece of cord round them. If they have a valuable binding, they can be wrapped in paper as well. The packages must not be made too heavy. Music too may be tied up in the same way.

Clothing and personal belongings should also be packed. These will go very well in boxes and drawers. The latter can quite well be utilised, as the men simply carry out the different pieces of the chest, and put them in position again in the van, and nothing can come to harm. A towel or large cover should be laid over the contents and well tucked in. Household linen should be packed away in the same manner. If there is no room for blankets and eider-downs, they can be made into a bale which can easily be lifted. Silver and other valuables should be put in a chest, and securely fastened.

The Removing.—This should always be commenced early in the morning, at six o'clock in the summer, and at eight o'clock in the winter at the very latest. Although everything may be left to the workmen, as a rule, it is better for the members of the household to take a share in order to expedite matters. In fact, if the removal is to be got over rapidly, the only way is for each one to give assistance where he or she can.

Beds and bedding should always be sent in the first van, and placed where they will come to hand easily at the other end. Things should, as far as possible, leave the old house and arrive at the new in the sequence in which it is most convenient to handle them.

As soon as the packing into the van is well on its way, a responsible person should, if possible, act as pioneer and start for the new house, so as to be on the spot when the first van arrives to direct the carrying in of the furniture. If this cannot be done, then each piece of furniture should be marked, or labelled, so as to indicate the room for which it is destined. As far as possible, each article should be carried to its own room and nowhere else; and in fact it may, in many cases, be actually put down in its proper place.

A strip of coarse matting should be laid over each carpet, to prevent the men's feet making marks.

It is a good plan to get every bed that is to be slept in put up and made early in the evening, and then, even if it is ten o'clock before the last vanful of furniture is unloaded, one can shut the door and feel that at least a place of repose is secure. Otherwise, one is inclined to go on working at other things until a late hour, when there is little strength left to make a bed far less put one together.

The question of refreshment on the day of removal is also an important one. It is often a saving of time if the men can be provided with a lunch of bread and cheese, and beer or coffee; and if it is intimated to them beforehand that this will be ready at a certain hour, it will save their time going off to some public-house in order to get refreshments.

A good tea at the other end should also be provided, if at all possible.

For the members of the family, cold refreshments, supplemented by hot drink, must suffice, and those who are not strong enough to support this frugal régime should be out of the way, if possible, on the removal day. Of course it sometimes happens that kind friends come forward and invite the party to a comfortable meal, and this of course is an untold blessing, not only from the point of view of the mere food question, but in regard to the respite afforded from the bustle and hurry of the day's work. Then at the other end, if a maid can be sent over in good time to light a fire and take a picnic basket with her with necessaries for tea, this little meal will prove a comfortable welcome to the new home.

Settling Down.—As soon as the bedrooms have been put fairly straight, it is perhaps best to gi one's first attention to the sitting-rooms and kitchen, as when once these are in order and meals can be served with comfort, the worst of the removal is practically over.

The stair carpet and hall rugs should be put down last of all, when all the carrying and extra walking backwards and forwards is at an end.

Then there will no doubt be extra furniture required, and additions of various kinds to make, but it is just as well not to hurry the buying of new things, as it is much more easy to judge what is needed when everything is in its place, and one has been in the house for a few days.

It will of course be weeks before all the odds and ends are put finally in their places, but these trifles do not matter, and once the real work of removal is over and the new house begins to look ship-shape, it should only be a pleasure to arrange the various trifles and knick-knacks to one's liking.

SHUTTING UP A HOUSE

If a house has to be shut up for three months or longer, it is better to lift all carpets, and to take this opportunity of having them sent away to be cleaned or beaten. Take down all curtains and other hangings, shake them well and fold them up neatly. Remove all chair-covers, table-covers, antimacassars, &c., brush or shake them, and fold them up likewise. Keep the furniture as much as possible to the centre of the room, where it will be safe from damp or soot, and cover everything with dust-sheets or large sheets of paper. Any valuable pictures should either be taken down from the walls or covered with fine gauze or muslin, to preserve them from dust. Light and fragile articles, such as ornaments and clocks, should also be covered in this way.

All soiled linen should be collected and sent to the wash if possible.

Close and fasten all windows, and leave nothing open where rain can enter.

Grease any metal fenders or fire-irons with mutton fat, draw them away from the fire-place, and cover them over.

Turn off the gas from the main, and leave all waste-pipes connected with the water open.

No food must be left behind, which would be likely to smell or encourage mice and other vermin. Kitchen premises especially should be left well swept and as clean as possible.

All valuables, such as silver and jewels, should be packed in a strong box and sent to the bank.

Pull down all blinds, or if there is danger of their being spoilt with the sun, cover the windows with brown paper, fastening it up with strong drawing-pins. Close and bolt the shutters, and shut and lock all doors.

Notice should also be given to the police that the house is closed, and they will give it special attention.

WHAT TO DO IF FIRE OCCURS

Fire accidents, large or small, are liable to occur in every house, and one ought to be prepared to take the necessary precautions to prevent the spreading of the flames.

In the case of a partial fire, speedy action may be the means of putting it out at once. For instance, if a curtain catches fire, which frequently happens owing to its too close proximity to a gas-bracket, it should be pulled down quickly (provided the person who does so is clothed in a woollen dress), and the flames crushed out with a piece of carpet or a rug, or, if the damage has not gone very far, they might be beaten out with a rug or wet cloth.

A wet blanket or cloth is valuable for beating out flames wherever they are, or if the fire is on the ground water may be poured over it. A syphon of soda-water is also a good fire-extinguisher, and in the case of sudden fire, *fire grenades* are excellent, and no large household should be without them. All that is necessary is to break the glass globe and sprinkle the contents over the burning place.

Burning oil, as in the case of a lamp being overturned, should be extinguished by throwing sand, earth, or ashes over it. Water would only help to spread the flames.

If a person's clothing should catch fire the wearer ought to at once throw herself down on the floor and roll over and over, first wrapping herself in a rug or any other heavy woollen article if anything of the kind is handy. If, when the accident occurs, another person is present, the latter should endeavour to extinguish the flames by covering the victim with any heavy woollen articles in reach, pressing them well over her and forcing her to maintain a recumbent position. Heavy table-cloths are amongst the best things to smother the flames. It is a fatal thing for the burning person to rush out and call for help: as long as the upright position is retained the flames will spread, and it is always the face and upper parts which will be the most severely attacked.

In all cases of fire the doors and windows should be kept closed as much as possible, as any draught only helps to fan the flames; smoke follows the current of air, and flames follow the smoke.

If the fire is of a more serious nature, the alarm should be given at once and the fire-engines sent for. Every effort must be made to escape and to help others to escape by the first means of egress. If aroused at night to find the house on fire, wrap yourself in a blanket or rug and get out of the room at once. If the room is full of smoke tie a wet towel or handkerchief or even a wet stocking over the nose and mouth, and this will exclude the smoke and still permit of breathing. If the smoke is so dense that you are unable to stand upright, crawl along on the hands and knees, as the clearest air is always next the floor.

Should the ascent and descent of the stairs be impossible, try to make your way to the window of a front room and if there are others in the house try to get them to do likewise. Unless some one is in the burning room the door should not be opened, and no attempt must be made to extinguish the fire until life has been saved.

On no account should you throw yourself from the window, and if in extremity and no assistance is at hand tear up the sheets and tie the pieces together to form a rope, allowing good ends so that the knots will not slip. Fasten one end to a bedstead or other heavy piece of furniture near the window. Then slip the improvised rope out of the window and let yourself down hand under hand, taking advantage of the knots to keep yourself from slipping too quickly.

Those who are helpless to let themselves down should have the end of the sheet tied round their waist and be lowered through the window. A mattress should if possible be thrown out of the window, as this might be the means of softening a fall if the sheet should happen to be too short.

The most important thing in all cases of fire is not to lose one's presence of mind and not to waste a moment in taking action.

FOOD AND THE KITCHEN

THIS article deals with all that a housewife should know in regard to the management of the culinary department of her household. Useful hints are given as to the suitable furnishing and efficient cleaning of the kitchen premises, care of the kitchen range, and cooking by gas, electricity, and on oil-stoves. Each aspect of the commissariat department has also been considered, including such important questions as the marketing and storing of provisions. The article concludes with a complete calendar of meat, fish, poultry, game, fruit and vegetables in season, which has been compiled for the purposes of easy reference.

HOW TO FURNISH A KITCHEN AND SCULLERY

The furnishings and fittings of the kitchen premises are very important—so much of the comfort of the household depends upon this department and the way in which it is managed that it is well worth while to fit it up comfortably and suitably. When we consider that servants not only have to live in a kitchen as we live in our dining-room and drawing-room, but that their weekly "afternoons" or "evenings out" constitute the only change they have from their surroundings, we ought to try to give the room in which they spend so much of their time as homelike an appearance as possible.

It often happens, however, that people who are most particular about having the other rooms of their house dainty and comfortable grudge the bare necessaries when anything in connection with the kitchen is concerned.

The kitchen itself should be bright, airy, and roomy. Unfortunately, it is not always possible to have all these conditions fulfilled, especially where there are underground premises and an area, and the kitchen-window looks out on to a stone wall, but in such cases the best must be made of a bad job and a few additional inside comforts must make up for the want of outside view. Sometimes the light in premises of this kind may be increased by having the outside wall painted white or a light cream colour.

The ventilation must be good, and in addition to the doors and windows it is well to have a ventilator placed in the wall above the height of the window to allow the fumes of cooking to escape.

The sanitary arrangements should also be carefully attended to, and there must be a good supply of water.

The kitchen ought to be within easy reach of the dining-room, and yet so placed that the odours of cooking do not reach other parts of the house. The larder and storeroom should also be close at hand to avoid any unnecessary going backwards and forwards from one place to the other.

Walls and Ceilings.—The ceiling of the kitchen ought to be smoothly plastered and then whitewashed. This whitewash must be renewed every year, not only for cleanliness, but also to give more light. For the walls glazed tiles are the ideal covering, as they can so easily be washed, or a high-tiled dado with distemper or other suitable finish above. But both these methods of wall-covering prove somewhat expensive, and people of moderate means have to content themselves with something a little cheaper. The walls may be washed all over with a simple distemper, and as this process costs very little the distemper may be renewed whenever it becomes dirty. Pretty light colours, such as buff, pink, pale blue, or pale green are the most effective. Varnished paper makes another appropriate covering; it lasts well, looks bright, and can very easily be cleaned; or, again, the Sanitary or so-called Washable paper might be used—this is less expensive than varnished paper, but it will not last so well nor stand so much cleaning. Specially prepared paints, such as Ripolin, Sanalene, and Muraline are also to be recommended; they are to be had in a variety of shades, and make a kitchen look very pretty. The woodwork in the kitchen should either be painted the same colour as the walls in a darker shade, or with white paint or a light oak stain.

The Floor.—The flooring of a kitchen varies very much according to locality. In some parts of the country we find red flags, in others glazed tiles, in others red or yellow bricks, concrete, or wooden boards, &c. When the floor consists of flags, tiles, or bricks it does not, as a rule, require further covering, as it can be easily washed, and one or two rugs or mats for standing on are all that is necessary. But when there is a wooden floor it is important to cover it with some material that is easily washed, as boards soon become soiled and are very difficult to keep in order. Good linoleum is the best kitchen floor-covering, and one with a pattern is to be preferred to a perfectly plain one, as it does not show marks so quickly. Inlaid linoleum is the best, as its pattern is ingrained in the material, and although the initial outlay is greater it comes cheaper in the end, as it is so much more durable than the other makes. (See also p. 21.)

Fixtures.—The number of immovable fixtures in a kitchen varies considerably with the style of the house—they usually comprise a dresser, shelves, cupboards, a pulley for hanging up towels, &c., a roller for towel, gas or electric fittings, bells, sink and kitchen range or stove.

The dresser is really the kitchen sideboard, and as a rule it is fitted against one of the walls and belongs to the house. If it has to be made to order, take careful measurements of the wall space you can allow and have it made to fit. The upper part is usually made with grooved shelves, on which the plates and dishes of the dinner-service are kept, or it may be fitted with shelves for jars with hooks along the edge of the shelf on which to hang small utensils. The top part of the dresser gives room for soup-tureen, vegetable dishes, sauce-boats, knife-tray, weights and scales, &c. —beneath there should be two or three drawers for holding spoons, knives, &c., and kitchen towels, while the lower part is fitted up with cupboards for holding dishes and the larger cookery utensils. If the kitchen is small, make the most of it by using the walls. It is a good plan to have a shelf carried round all the available wall space, and just as high as a servant can reach. When a number of hooks are required a strip of wood might be fixed below the shelf, and nails or hooks put into that. It is a bad practice to drive nails into the wall itself, as they are sure to come out and bring some of the plaster with them.

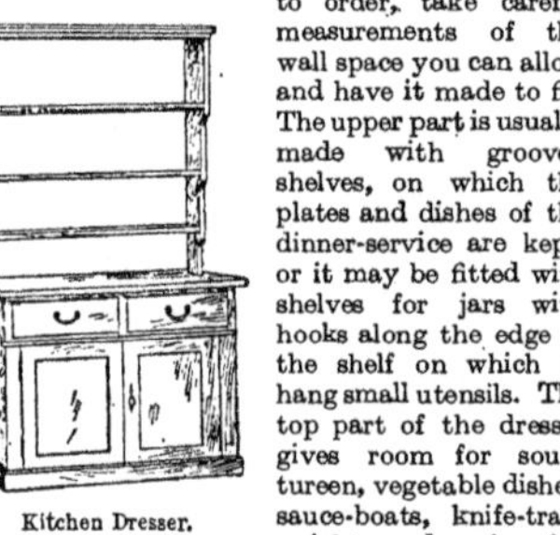

Kitchen Dresser.

Then there should be a well-constructed sink. Stone-ware or tiled sinks are the best, as they are the easiest to clean and keep in good order. The back of the sink should be made of some material which will not spoil with the splashing of the water; if not already fitted with tiles, a sheet of zinc might be fitted up or a sheet of "Emdeca," which is an imitation of tiles and very practical. (See p. 14.) Above the sink should be a plate-rack in which plates can be drained, and the necessity of drying thus avoided. Underneath might be one or two shelves or a small cupboard for keeping cleaning requisites —and at the right-hand side of the sink a sloping grooved board on which to lay dishes, &c., to drain. A flap table might also be arranged at the side on which to place dishes when they are dried if table space is scanty.

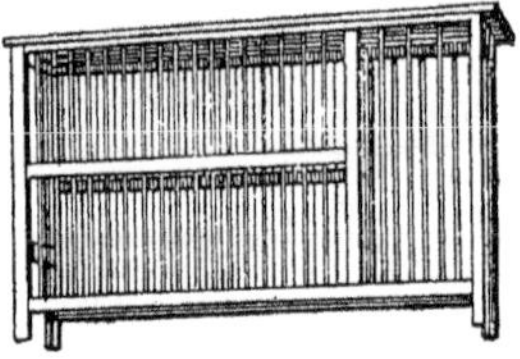
Plate-Rack.

If there is a separate scullery this would naturally contain the sink, &c., and here all the washing up would be done. The walls of the scullery should be lined with shelves, and as much as possible made of the available space. The shelves on which saucepans are placed should be sparred, as this allows the air to get inside to dry them. If there is not much room for shelving, a saucepan-stand which can be placed either in kitchen or scullery is often found most valuable. A small cupboard or shelves underneath the sink will be found useful for keeping cleaning materials. The scullery, like the kitchen, should be light and well ventilated, and unless the floor is tiled or flagged it should be covered in the same way.

Saucepan-Stand.

Cupboard accommodation is also most valuable in a kitchen. If this is inadequate, it is sometimes possible to have a cupboard fitted up on the wall for holding a small store of provisions. A recess or a corner can also be utilised for this purpose, and a joiner will be able to fit up a few shelves with a simple door at a very small cost.

Every kitchen should be supplied with a pulley on which to dry kitchen towels (unless these can be hung elsewhere) and also a roller with brackets on which to hang a roller-towel.

The lighting of the kitchen is another important point, and the light, whether it be gas or electricity, should be so arranged as to make it possible to see clearly both at the table and at the stove.

The Kitchen Range.—The most important fixture of all is the kitchen range. It is impossible to do good cooking without a good stove. The open grate limits one's sphere of work considerably, and there is always the risk of getting food smoky and saucepans dirty. It is certainly best for roasting (a roast never tastes so well as when cooked in front of an open fire), also for broiling and grilling, but with these its merits end. An open range is scarcely to be seen now in modern houses, the kitchener or close range has taken its place.

There is an endless variety of kitcheners, all more or less similar but going under different names. A tenant has not usually a choice in this matter, but before taking a house it should always be seen that a proper stove has been provided and that it is in good working order.

In choosing or buying a stove, do not look out for the cheapest kind procurable, but buy one of a thoroughly good make, and have it well fitted up. The material must be good. Cheap stoves are usually made of some light metal which wears out very quickly, causing great waste of fuel and much annoyance as well, while a well-constructed one will be made of malleable iron, wrought iron or steel.

A good stove should be provided with an adjustable bottom, which can be raised or lowered according to the size of fire required. Thus, when the stove is not being used for cooking purposes the fire may still be kept in and the water warmed, but with a very small consumption of fuel. There should also be a well-ventilated oven, a good boiler and water-supply, and a plate-rack on which to warm dishes.

The best type of stove is usually convertible into an open range, and a cheerful fire can be arranged in the evening by simply sliding back the top plate.

It is a good plan to have a light screen made which can be hooked on to the front of the fire, as this serves as a great protection when any one has to stand near the stove to stir a sauce or do other cooking.

Very often the reason why a kitchen range does not burn well is that it is not understood. It is important, therefore, that both mistress and servant should thoroughly understand the working of it, and also the method of cleaning before the stove is condemned as being inefficient. For cleaning, see p. 91.

Furniture.—For the ordinary kitchen there is very little movable furniture required. The table is the chief article, and this ought to be as large as is convenient. If there is not much floor space available it is better to have it made with flaps, which can easily be put down when not in use. It ought to be made of plain unpainted deal, and should be of a convenient height to work at and very steady on its legs. Kitchen tables are generally made oblong with one or two drawers at the ends, which are always an advantage. Sometimes too a narrow shelf is put underneath on which articles can be placed when cooking is being done, thus keeping the table itself more clear.

In larger kitchens a second table will always be found useful—a smaller and lighter one which can be moved about, or even a collapsible one which can be put aside when necessary.

A fender may also be required and a simple curb is all that is necessary, although one made of steel will of course be more ornamental. In very small kitchens the fender might be dispensed with altogether, and a light screen hooked on to the front of the fire to prevent the cinders falling out will take up much less space. A strong poker, coal shovel and scuttle should also be provided. The best shape of scuttle is that known as a coal-hod; it takes up little room, and is not easily knocked over like the scoop shape. The flue-rake and flue-brush are generally supplied as part of the stove.

Coal-Hod.

The chairs should be of plain varnished wood, and the number will depend upon how many maids there are—there should be one for each and one over. Then if the kitchen is used as the maid's sitting-room, there ought to be one or two comfortable chairs for resting in the evening. Strong wicker ones or the light-coloured Windsor arm-chairs are both suitable—or even camp-chairs with a strong carpet cover might be used, as they can be folded up during the day and put out of the way. In any case it should be remembered that our maids require something a little better than a straight-backed wooden seat when their day's work is over.

Windsor Chair.

One or two strong rugs should also be supplied—something of a nice bright colour. Pieces of stout carpet neatly bound at the edges will serve the purpose very well. A rule should be made that these rugs are rolled up at night and not put down again until the principal work in the kitchen is finished the following day.

A dark serge cloth might also be supplied to cover one of the tables and give it a less forbidding appearance.

The arrangement of the window depends very much upon the style of the house. As a rule, a short muslin curtain across the window is all that is necessary and all there is room for. Madras or strong washing muslin is the best to use for the purpose, or, if preferred, a light casement cloth; but it must be of a material that will wash well and not lose its colour in the tub. The curtain should be simply made with a hem top and bottom. If the window is wide it may be better made in two parts with a division in the middle, but, if narrow, it will look better in one piece. The curtain should be half as wide again as the width of the window to allow for fulness. A light brass rod should be fitted across the window at a convenient height and the curtain fixed to that either by means of small rings or by slipping the rod through the upper hem of the curtain. If the kitchen is large and the window wide, short side-curtains, of some pretty cretonne, linen, or casement cloth might add very much to the comfortable appearance of the room. These are easily washed, and, provided they are not made too long, they will not be found an inconvenience. A simple brass or bamboo rod should be fixed across the window and the curtains attached to that by means of rings sewn on to the upper hem or heading. By this means the curtains can easily be slipped off when they require washing.

A good clock must not be forgotten when furnishing the kitchen—either one to hang on the wall above the kitchen mantelpiece or a small alarm clock, which can easily be carried about or taken to the maid's bedroom at night.

Utensils.—The number and kind of utensils must be determined somewhat by the size and circumstances of the household.

Unless there is a kitchen-maid it is a mistake to buy a large quantity of utensils which require polishing and keeping bright. In fact, it is never wise to buy too many to begin with; the more you have the more there will be to keep in order, and when means are limited and service difficult to procure it is much wiser to start with what is strictly necessary and add by degrees to the supply.

In small houses and flats the kitchen utensils must be reduced to a minimum. Shelf accommodation is scarce and there are few if any cupboards; large and heavy saucepans would then be quite out of place and a multifarious collection of moulds and dishes only in the way. At the same time it is unreasonable to expect dainty cooking to be done without implements, and every facility should be given to those who undertake the work.

It will generally be found that the better the cook the fewer utensils she will require, but still maids have different ways of working, and it is always wise to give them what they ask for within reasonable limits.

And, again, when service is short an effort should be made to give as many labour-saving appliances as possible, such as a knife-cleaner, a mincing machine, a gas stove or gas ring, &c.

Whatever is bought should be good of its kind. Buy plain and well-made articles and they will last a lifetime.

Saucepans.—Except for a large establishment where cooking has to be done in big quantities it is a mistake to invest in a number of heavy iron saucepans. One or two will be quite sufficient. The others might be made of steel, copper, aluminium, enamelled tin, or fire-proof ware.

Both steel and copper saucepans are excellent and very durable, but they are expensive to buy, and those made of copper are liable to verdigris unless well looked after.

The enamelled tin saucepans will be found most useful, but they should be bought in a good quality. The hard grey enamel lasts better than the white, and will stand any amount of hard wear. The cheap make of this kind of saucepan should be avoided, as the lining soon begins to crack and peal off and then they become dangerous to use.

Aluminium saucepans are also to be recommended, and they are rapidly supplanting all others made of metal, as they are absolutely safe from all fear of verdigris and they do not rust. They are easily cleaned (see p. 93), and nothing could be lighter to handle.

Then there are the clay terrines and brown stoneware saucepans, so dear to the heart of the French housewife, and which are coming more and more into favour in this country (see p. 148).

When once a trial has been made of the lighter style of saucepan, there will seldom be a return to the heavy iron make which are such a labour to clean, not to speak of the lifting.

The following list of utensils with approximate prices may prove useful to those who are starting housekeeping for the first time. It is suitable for a small house with one or two servants.

	s.	*d.*
1 Galvanised bath	2	2
1 Galvanised pail		10
1 Tin enamelled basin	1	0
1 Fish-kettle	3	3
1 Frying-pan	1	0
1 Iron stewpan	2	0
1 Iron saucepan	1	9
2 Enamelled saucepans, 1s. 3d., 1s. 9d.	3	0
or 2 Earthenware saucepans	2	0
or 2 Aluminium saucepans	3	6
1 Iron kettle	3	6
1 Tin kettle	1	6
1 Wire sieve	1	2
1 Cooking board	2	3
1 Pot-rest		3
1 Rolling-pin		6
1 Flour dredger		6
1 Sugar dredger		6

	s.	d.
1 Funnel		3
1 Cork-screw		6
1 pair of scissors		10
1 Tin-opener		4
2 Oven tins	1	4
1 Cake tin		8
1 Tray	2	0
1 Sink tidy	*from*	6½
1 Gridiron or hanging grill	1	4½
1 Steamer	6	0
1 Set of skewers		6
1 Grater		7
1 Poker		9
1 Egg whisk		6
1 Soap dish		4
1 Jelly mould	1	0
1 dozen patty pans		4
1 Palette knife	1	0
1 Cook's knife	1	3
2 Table knives and forks	1	10
1 Potato knife		4½
2 Iron spoons		6
2 Wooden spoons		5
2 Dessert spoons		8
2 Tea spoons		4
1 Toasting fork		4½
1 Gravy strainer	1	0
1 Knife-board		10
1 Pepper and salt box		9
1 Shovel		6
1 Coal-scuttle	1	11
1 Roasting tin and stand	1	6
1 Long broom	1	6
1 Yard broom	1	4
1 Set shoe brushes	2	9
1 Set stove brushes	2	9
1 Sweep's brush		9
2 Scrubbing brushes	1	6
1 Nail brush		2
2 Egg-brushes		3
1 Sink brush		6
1 Dish mop		4½
3 Jugs	1	0
2 Pie dishes	1	6
2 Pudding bowls	1	2
1 Large mixing bowl		10
2 Breakfast cups and saucers		11
6 Plates assorted	1	6
3 Dishes	2	9
1 Sugar-basin		4
1 Salt-cellar		3
1 Lemon squeezer		4½

Jars and tins will also be required for kitchen use, but it is seldom necessary to buy these.

The following might be added if means allow—

	s.	d.
1 Mincing machine	4	8
1 Spring balance	5	0
1 Meat-saw	2	6
1 Knife-sharpener		10
1 Box-cutter	1	0
6 Small moulds	1	0
1 Frying basket	1	6
1 Set of steps	5	0
1 Omelet pan	1	6
2 Sandwich cake tins	1	0
1 Preserving pan	4	0
2 Fancy moulds	3	0
1 Pestle and mortar	3	0
1 Fish slice		8
1 Vegetable presser	1	6
1 Flour tub or crock	2	6

The above does not include utensils for laundry work. See under special heading.

If the housemaids' utensils are not separate, the following brushes, &c., will be required in addition for household use :—

	s.	d.
1 Plate brush		9
1 Carpet whisk	2	6
1 Double banister brush	2	9
1 Dust pan	1	0

Note.—If there are several servants they should be allowed inexpensive crockery and glass for their own table use apart from the dishes used for cooking.

The Cleaning of the Kitchen and Kitchen Utensils.—The kitchen may be cleaned either all in one day or by degrees. The latter method is generally found the most convenient, as it is less obtrusive and does not upset the comfort of the house so much. The saucepans and tins may be cleaned one day, cupboards and windows another, larder, passages, and outside premises another, flues and range another, with the scrubbing of the floors and tables, &c., to follow.

This is entirely a matter of arrangement and must be planned to suit the ways and circumstances of each individual household.

An effort should be made to have the cleaning done early in the day or at a time when there is no special cooking to attend to.

Instructions for the various cleaning operations will be found below. (See also Duties of the Cook, p. 49.)

How to Clean a Kitchen Range—Weekly Cleaning.—A large strong apron, or overall, a pair of gloves, and a cap which covers the hair should be worn when doing this piece of work. The kitchen, too, should be prepared by removing or covering with a dust-sheet or sheets of paper anything that is likely to be soiled with dust. Remove any kettles and saucepans from the top of the range and put the fender, plate-rack, and fire-irons to one side. Put down a hearth cloth and have sweep's brush, flue rake and brush, shovel and black-lead brushes in readiness. Commence by raking out the fire, and be particular to pass the rake well to the back to get all the cinders out of the boiler flue. Brush out all cinders and ashes and save the former for making the fire later on.

To clean the flues commence at the top. Open the dampers and the little doors or slides at the entrance to the flue or flues. Pass the flue brush up as far as it will go, then to the sides and then downwards, working it well against the side of the flue. The loose soot will all fall downwards to the back of the stove and will be removed later on. In a large stove there may be two or even three flues and each one must be done in the same way. Brush the top of the dampers and brush the flue doors or slides and put them back in place.

Now remove all rings and tops from the top of the stove and brush all the soot off the top of the oven with the sweep's brush, letting it fall either down the side of the oven or into the fire-place—the former is the simpler. Also pass the flue brush down the sides and back of the oven if there is an opening. Brush the under-side of all the top pieces and put them back in place. If there is a boiler or second oven at the other side of the range the top and sides of this must be cleaned in the same way. Every part must be freed from soot, and always work from the top downwards.

When the top part is finished remove the little door or slide which will be found underneath the oven, put a good-sized shovel below it, pass the flue rake in at the hole and draw out all the soot. Repeat the same at the other side if necessary. The soot must be taken outside at once, and if there is a garden it should be kept for manuring purposes.

Next dust the stove all over, and if the top is greasy wash it with hot water and soda. Thoroughly dust or brush out the oven. If the shelves are greasy wash them out with hot water and soda, then whiten them with a paste of whitening and water, which will give them a nice clean appearance.

To Black-lead the Stove.—Apply the black-lead very lightly with the black-lead brush, commencing with the highest part of the stove and doing a small piece at a time. Brush off with the hard brush and polish with the polisher (see p. 65).

If there are tiles at the back of the stove these must be washed over with a soft cloth, soap, and water, or, if stained, with Brook's soap or sapolio.

Clean all steel parts with fine emery paper or with fine bath-brick dust made into a paste with paraffin (see p. 72).

Lay the fire, using the cinders along with some small coal, sticks, and paper.

Sweep the hearth, wash it over with warm water, and whiten with soft sandstone. Put back the fender, fire-irons, &c., and put a light to the fire if required.

Daily Cleaning.—The fire should be well raked out every day, the top of the stove brushed with the sweep's brush and polished with the stove brushes. Black-leading should not be required more than once a week, except perhaps on the special parts which are much used.

Rub up the steel parts with emery paper, or wipe them with a soft duster or selvyt cloth, and clean the hearth.

If properly done, the flues should not require cleaning more than once a week, but if a large fire is kept constantly burning it may be necessary to brush over the top of the oven more frequently—sometimes, too, in the case of small stoves the fines require cleaning more than once a week. This must be regulated according to how the stove burns.

Cleaning Saucepans.—Clean saucepans form one of the first essentials of good cooking. "You can judge a workman by his tools" cannot be better applied than to a cook, as no woman who has any pride in her profession would put up with such a thing as a dirty saucepan. They ought to be her special pride and care.

Now that saucepans are used almost entirely on gas-stoves and close ranges where there is no smoking from an open fire, there is no excuse for having the outside coated with soot or black grease which comes off on everything that touches it. The handle and outside of the saucepan should receive the same attention as the inside.

As soon as a saucepan is finished with, it should be filled with warm water and left soaking until it can be cleaned.

Care must be taken not to pour cold water into a hot enamelled saucepan or there will be danger of cracking the lining; in fact it is always a risky thing to do if the pan is very hot. Saucepans should be cleaned as soon as possible after they are taken from the fire and never allowed to remain dirty overnight except under very special circumstances.

The method of cleaning will depend somewhat upon the kind of saucepan, but the rule that they must be properly clean and free from taint of any kind applies to all.

If the contents of a saucepan have become burnt boil some hot water and soda in it before attempting to do the cleaning.

No saucepan must be laid away before it is perfectly dry unless it is placed where the air can reach the inside, as on a sparred shelf.

Iron Saucepans.—Wash them well in hot water and soda, scrubbing inside and out with a pot brush. Use a little sand, if necessary, to make them clean. The sand must be used almost dry or it will not have so much power. When clean, rinse thoroughly so as to get rid of any grit and dry with a coarse cloth.

Enamelled Saucepans.—Wash well in hot water and soda, and then apply a little Brook's soap or sapolio to take off any marks or discoloration. Salt or fine silver sand may also be used, or even crushed egg-shells are very good for whitening the enamel. Rinse thoroughly and dry with a cloth.

Tin and Steel Saucepans.—Clean in the same way as enamelled saucepans.

Earthenware Saucepans.—Wash first in hot soapy water, then apply a little fine sand or sapolio, if necessary, to remove any marks. Rinse thoroughly and dry with a stout cloth.

Copper Saucepans.—These require very special care, as, if once neglected, they are apt to harbour verdigris, which is very poisonous. For this reason the tinned linings should always be kept intact, and directly there are signs of wear and the copper begins to show through the saucepans should be sent away to be re-tinned.

Clean the inside of copper saucepans with a mixture of soft soap and Brook's soap or soft soap and fine silver sand applied with a piece of flannel or soft cloth wrung out of warm water. For the outside use the skin of a lemon dipped in bath-brick dust, or salt and vinegar applied with a flannel. Well rinse the saucepan with hot water and dry quickly and thoroughly. The outside may be further polished by rubbing it up with a little dry whitening.

Aluminium Saucepans.—Wash well with hot soapy water, using a little silver sand if necessary to remove any discoloration or burnt matter. Rinse thoroughly first in hot and then in cold water and then dry with a soft cloth. Soda must on no account be used with aluminium ware, and patent cleaning mixtures should also be avoided. The outside may be polished occasionally with metal polish.

The vessels should not be scraped, nor should the light brown enamel which will form inside be disturbed, as it is not only quite harmless, but adds considerably to the life of the articles.

Wooden Articles.—An effort should be made to make kitchen tables, boards, and wooden utensils as white as possible. The following will be required for cleaning them: a pail or basin of warm water, a piece of house flannel, scrubbing brush, sand, soap, and a stout cloth for drying. Wash the wood over with the flannel wrung out of warm water. Rub a little soap on the brush, dip in sand and scrub with the grain of the wood. Rinse well in order to remove all grit and dry quickly with a clean cloth. Soda should not be used, as it tends to discolour the wood. Sand helps to whiten it.

When cleaning a kitchen-table the legs should not be forgotten. If plain wood they may be scrubbed in the same way as the top, but if painted they must only be wiped over with a damp flannel and dried.

Wooden utensils must not be put too near a fire to dry or they will warp; they ought to be placed upright where the air will get round them.

Sieves.—A sieve should be cleaned as soon as possible after it has been used. If any substance is allowed to harden on it the cleaning will be much more difficult. Wash thoroughly with a little hot water and soda and scrub well with a brush. If it is a wire sieve hold it up to the light and see that none of the little holes are blocked up. Be particular also to scrub well round the sides where the rim joins the surface part. Rinse well and dry with a strong cloth. The sieve should then be put in a warm place to dry. If this is not attended to a wire sieve will become rusty and a hair one coated with mildew.

Sieves must always be kept in a dry and clean place.

Tin Lids, Moulds, and Dish Covers.—Hot water with a little soap powder or plain soap should be used for washing these. They must be well rinsed and then dried at once.

Saucepan lids should be washed or at least well wiped with a cloth each time after use. The rim must have special attention, as any grease from a stew or such-like will lodge there. It is a good plan to give all saucepan lids a good washing once a week.

A brush may be used when washing fancy moulds of any kind. When the insides become difficult to clean the moulds should be put into a saucepan with hot water and a little soda, and boiled for half-an-hour. This will loosen any matter or burnt pieces which may adhere to them. They may also be secured with a little silver sand, or Brook's soap may be used to remove any discoloration. Thorough rinsing will be necessary.

All tinned goods must be well dried before being put away, as they are liable to rust.

Polishing.—Tins that are put up for show may be polished to make them look bright, but this should never be attempted before making sure that they are quite free from grease. Make a smooth paste with a little whitening and water—rub this on the tins with a piece of flannel, and, when dry, rub off with a duster. A soft brush may be used to remove the whitening from any corners. The inside of moulds should never be polished.

A few drops of ammonia may be added to the whitening, but as the tinning of some moulds and lids is very thin, strong cleansers should as a rule be avoided.

Zinc.—Sometimes the surround of a sink is covered with zinc, and this may be cleaned in the following way: Scrub first with hot soapy water to which a little soda has been added. Rinse and dry. The zinc may then be polished with a little whitening mixed to a paste with turpentine. Apply with a piece of flannel, and when dry rub off with a duster.

To Clean Floors, Linoleum, &c.—See "Work of the House," p. 66.

Baking Tins.—Wash well in very hot water with a little soda in it, using a strong brush and a little sand if necessary. Rinse well and dry with a coarse cloth. If a roasting-tin has become very brown and is hard to clean, let it soak in hot water and soda for an hour or two to soften the burnt substance.

Kitchen Knives and Forks.—Wipe these with a cloth wrung out of hot water to remove any grease, but do not allow them to lie in hot water, which would tend to loosen the handles. Then rub off any stains with a little Brook's soap or sapolio applied rather dry on a piece of flannel. Rinse off and dry with a knife-cloth. It is not necessary to polish kitchen knives on a knife-board; it only wears them unnecessarily.

Kitchen Cloths.—At the end of the day all cloths which have been used and are soiled should be washed in soapy water with a little soda; then thoroughly rinsed, wrung out, and hung up to dry. At the end of the week they ought to be laid aside in order to have a more thorough washing with the rest of the household linen (see p. 276), and a fresh supply put into use.

Pudding Cloths.—After a pudding cloth has been used it should be thrown into hot water with a little soda and allowed to soak for half-an-hour or so. Then wash out and rinse with care until no trace of the soda water remains. Dry in the open air if possible. Fold up carefully and keep in a clean place. A pudding cloth must only be used for its own special purpose. If the above process is not sufficient to make the cloth clean it ought to be boiled in a saucepan for half-an-hour with hot water and a small piece of soda and then rinsed in the same way. The use of soap and soap powder should be avoided as far as possible.

Jelly Cloths.—Wash in the same way as pudding cloths.

Care of the Sink.—This is a very important matter in the management of the kitchen and scullery, and a sink left in a dirty and greasy state, especially the last thing at night, will at once denote a careless and untidy worker.

Every sink should be provided with a sink basket or tidy and a sink brush. The former is

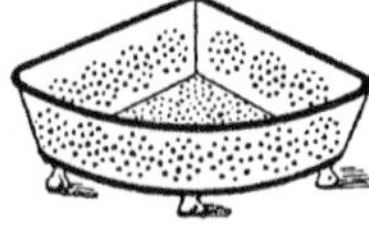

Sink Basket.

used to place over the opening to keep back any tea-leaves, vegetable parings, or other refuse which might block the pipe. An old colander will serve the purpose very well.

Do not throw anything but water down a sink, and if the water is greasy flush it well afterwards with hot soapy water. It is a good plan also to pour down some very hot soda and water when the washing up is finished.

If water in which vegetables have been cooked is not kept for making soup, it should never be poured down a sink, as it would cause an unpleasant smell, but should be emptied straight into a drain or outside in the garden.

An effort should be made to keep the pipe and trap (an elbow-like bend in the pipe just below

Sink Brush.

the sink) in good order by preventing grease and refuse collecting in them. If these become choked and clogged an unnecessary expense must be incurred to have them cleared out, not to speak of the annoyance. Do not be afraid of plenty of hot water when washing up; it is greasy luke-warm water which clogs the pipe sooner than anything.

When the washing up is finished the sink should be well scrubbed out with some hot water and soda and a little soap, rinsed with hot water, and then finally the cold pipe should be allowed to run. If the sink is discoloured, use a little sand or Brook's soap. The sink brush and any dish clothes must also be washed out and hung up to dry. Also any tub or basin that has been used for washing up.

Refuse.—In every household there must necessarily be a certain amount of rubbish to dispose of consisting of ashes, sweepings from floors, broken crockery, old tins, food remains, &c.

Part of this refuse should be put into a dust-bin or ash-pit, with either of which every house should be provided, while the remainder should be burnt.

The ash-pit is more frequently found in country districts where the removal of rubbish cannot be so frequent as in towns. It is usually built of brick or stone and should be well cemented and placed at some distance from the house.

The best kind of dust-bin is one made of galvanised iron and round in shape. The size will depend upon the needs of the household, but it is better to have two, if necessary, of a medium size than one that is too heavy to be lifted. These dust-bins are very often provided by the landlord and belong to the house.

There should always be a lid to fit the dust-bin to prevent damp from entering or dust from flying about. It should be placed at least a few feet from the house and never near a window, and it must be removed and thoroughly emptied by the dustman twice or at least once a week.

Nothing but dry refuse should be put into a dust-bin unless it can be emptied very frequently, as damp favours decomposition and very soon causes an unpleasant and very unhealthy smell. Animal and vegetable refuse in this case is better burnt, and if there is a kitchen range in use it should not be a difficult matter to dispose of all vegetable parings, tea-leaves, and such-like by this means.

There are two ways of burning food remains. They may either be dried slowly at the back of the fire or underneath the grate, after which they will burn quite readily, or they may be put into the stove in small quantities when the fire is very bright and hot enough to consume them quickly. If refuse is put on to a low fire in a damp condition it will cause a most unpleasant smell.

Needless to say, it is the duty of the mistress to see that nothing is thrown out or burnt except that which is absolutely of no value. In some houses the dust-bin is one of the most fruitful sources of waste. (See Law in regard to Removal of Refuse, p. 382.)

COOKING BY GAS

Gas Stoves.—There is much to be said in favour of a gas stove, and if properly managed it can be a great saving of time, labour, and expense. It can either be used to supplement a kitchen range where there is a large amount of cooking to be done, or in small houses it can be made to take the place of a coal stove altogether.

It is especially useful in flats where ladies very often have to do all their own work or the

Breakfast Cooker.

greater part of it themselves, and where actual labour must be reduced to a minimum.

If the whole stove is not required and the oven part would be of little or no use, a small griller or even a gas ring is often a great comfort and saving. It can be placed on the top

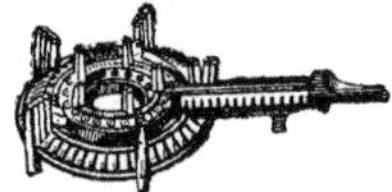

Gas Boiling Ring.

of the range or on a small table in the scullery, and will often save the keeping up of a fire for the sake of boiling a kettle or doing some light cooking in the evening. A little griller would also be found a great boon in the morning when an early breakfast has to be prepared, as it will not only boil a kettle but make toast or grill fish or bacon at the same time. A very nice griller and boiler can be bought for 7s. 6d. or 8s. 6d., while a small boiling ring will only cost two or three shillings plus the india-rubber tubing (6d. to 9d. per foot) required for attaching it to a gas bracket.

Gas stoves can be had in different sizes and various makes. Improvements are constantly being made, and there is great competition among the different makers as to who will produce the most perfect article. Before buying one it is a good plan to go to one of the Gas Company's offices or exhibitions where all the different kinds of stoves are displayed, and where they can often be seen in actual use. The newest make of gas cookers is well raised above the floor, which saves a great deal of unnecessary stooping, and also does away with the necessity of having a slab on which to place the stove for the sake of protection. Those with enamelled linings are the most easily kept in order. The size chosen must depend upon the amount of cooking to be done and the oven space required, and also upon the size of the kitchen. It is a mistake to have one larger than necessary, as it always means a greater consumption of gas to heat the oven, &c.

The price of gas stoves runs from about £4 to £12 according to size, while they can also be hired at a rental of about 2s. 3d. per quarter and upwards. In fact, in many cases it is better to hire than to purchase, as the Gas Company not only supply the stove but keep it in repair, and will change it when desired for one of another description.

It is very important to have a gas stove properly fitted up and to see that there is the necessary ventilation. The work should be put into the hands of a capable workman, because unless the pipe to which the stove is connected is of the right size and there is sufficient pressure of gas, the stove will not work properly. It is sometimes a good plan to have a separate meter for the gas stove in order to regulate the consumption of gas.

How to Use a Gas Stove.—It is also very important to know how to use a gas stove, otherwise there may be great waste of gas and many spoilt dishes.

The Gas Companies give special demonstrations all over the country where the working of the various stoves is fully explained and a cookery lesson given at the same time. They are also beginning to send out lady demonstrators to private houses to show how each part of tho stove should be used in order to secure the best possible results for the smallest consumption of gas; but the hints given below may be of use to those who cannot avail themselves of these special lessons.

Every gas stove is provided with several burners on the top and each burner has a special tap in connection with it. There will also be a special tap for the oven.

A taper is preferable to matches for lighting the gas.

Do not turn on more taps than are actually required at one time, and be careful to turn off the gas directly you have finished using it. When about to use the oven open the door first, turn on the gas, and then apply the light. Be sure that all the little burners inside are lighted and on both sides. If they should become clogged with grease or other matter the little holes must be cleared with a needle or fine wire. Never keep the gas burning longer than is necessary—for instance, when once the contents of a kettle or saucepan have come to the boil the merest flicker of light will keep them simmering.

The large round burner should not be used when the smaller one is sufficient. Then, again, when the griller is being used a saucepan or kettle of water should always be placed on the top to utilise the top heat as well as that of underneath.

Gas may also be economised by using a steamer or patent cooker (see p. 148) in which several different articles can be cooked one above the other with only one jet of gas underneath. It is also a waste of gas to use heavy saucepans, as they require an unnecessary consumption of gas to bring them to the boil. Steel, aluminium, and enamelled saucepans are all suitable, also the fireproof china and the glazed earthenware ones. The saucepans must also be clean at the foot; if there is a coating of soot or black grease it acts as a non-conductor of heat, and this again will cause a waste of gas. It is always better, if possible, to keep a separate set of saucepans for a gas stove and not to use them indiscriminately for a gas cooker and a coal stove.

The flame of gas must not be allowed to blaze up the sides of a saucepan, but only underneath.

When once the oven has been properly heated the light should for most purposes be turned down half way, and in some cases even lower. Then the cooking should be so arranged that when the oven is lighted it should be made use of to the fullest extent, two or three dishes being cooked in it at the same time. For instance, if there is a small roast it may be cooked on a roasting-tin on the bottom shelf, while such things as a milk pudding, potato or macaroni pie, baked potatoes, or stewed fruit might be cooking above. Or, when pastry is being cooked, cakes or scones might be cooked at the same time. It would not, however, do to cook pastry with a roast, as the air of the oven would be too moist. It is a waste of gas to light the oven to cook one dish.

To Grill.—A special grill pan is supplied with every gas stove, and this can be used for many purposes, such as for cooking a chop, steak, kidneys, bacon, fish, or in fact anything that could be cooked on the ordinary grill. Very good toast can also be made under the grill.

Place the grill pan under the griller, light the gas and wait until the griller is red hot before putting the meat or whatever is being cooked underneath. Then proceed as for ordinary grilling (see p. 167), turning the meat and reducing the heat as required.

To Make Toast.—The gas should be turned down after the griller is once hot. The bread must be watched very carefully and turned when necessary. The toast must not be made too quickly or it will be soft and heavy.

To Use the Oven.—A gas oven generally contains two or three grid shelves and always one solid shelf. The latter is used to throw down the heat, and is placed above anything that requires browning. Nothing should be placed on the solid shelf or it will burn, with the exception of liquid things or anything that can be placed in a tin of water. The top of the oven is always the coolest part. When dishes in course of baking are becoming too brown before being sufficiently cooked, the solid shelf should be removed altogether.

It used to be thought necessary to place a tin of water at the foot of the oven, but this is not the case.

When roasting meat the joint should either be hung on a hook attached to a bar which runs across the top of the oven or put on a roasting-tin placed on one of the grid shelves at the lower part of the oven. If the former method is adopted the shelves of the oven will require to be removed and nothing else can be cooked at the same time. The thickest part of the joint must always be hung downwards. Heat the oven well before putting the meat in, and after the first ten minutes reduce the gas one-half or even more according to the amount of pressure; follow in fact the general rules for roasting (see p. 165).

When baking cakes the oven should first be thoroughly heated and then the gas turned down more or less according to the special kind of cake, and whether it requires a moderate or hot oven. Place the cake or cakes on the grid shelf and below the browning shelf, and gradually reduce the heat until the cakes are ready. If the cake is large it may be better to keep out the solid shelf altogether and even to cover it over with a double piece of kitchen paper to prevent its taking too much colour. With large cakes, too, it is a good plan to leave them in the oven for about half-an-hour after the gas has been turned off, and to let them dry slowly in the gradually reducing heat. The same rules will apply to the baking of pastry.

If a little care is taken and attention given to details a gas oven is really very easy to manage, and after a little practice one becomes quite expert at regulating the heat to a nicety.

How to Clean a Gas Stove—Weekly Cleaning.—Put down a hearth-cloth and have in readiness a pail of hot water and soda, one or two strong cloths or swabs, and black-lead brushes, &c., for cleaning purposes. Remove the bars from the top of the stove and wash these in the pail of hot water, using a brush if necessary. Wash the top of the stove, being very careful to make the burners clean; sometimes it may be necessary to clean out the little holes with a piece of wire or a fine skewer if they have become clogged. Wash also the tray under the burners, the oven shelves, the sides of the oven, which are sometimes fitted with movable linings, and the tin which stands at the foot. If there are enamelled linings, as in some of the stoves, a little salt or Brook's soap may be used for cleaning purposes and also for the oven tin to remove any brown marks or other discoloration.

Then black-lead the bars, the top and body of the stove, and put back the different parts in their proper places. Polish the brass taps with metal polish, rub up the steel with fine emery paper, and the stove is finished.

Daily Cleaning.—If the stove is thoroughly cleaned once a week it will not require black-leading the other days; it will be sufficient to give it a good brush over with the harder polishing brush, to wash the tray underneath the burners, and the oven tin if the oven has been used.

Neither grease nor any kind of food which may have been spilled during cooking should ever be allowed to remain on a gas stove, but must be washed off at once with a cloth wrung out of hot water and soda, otherwise an unpleasant smell will be caused the next time the gas is used.

COOKING BY ELECTRICITY

Although we have long been accustomed to electricity as a lighting agent and even for heating purposes, electric cooking stoves have not yet become common. There are, however, several different makes to be had, and the price of some of them is by no means prohibitive.

One of the simplest and most economical stoves on the market is the "Tricity" cooker; it is so simple, so easily regulated, so perfectly controlled and so safe that it cannot fail to appeal to those who try it. There are different types of this stove—The Single Cooker, The Duplex Cooker, and the Extension Cooker, while the ovens are sold separately.

The Single Cooker can be used for grilling, toasting, boiling, steaming, stewing, heating irons, airing clothes, or as a radiator to warm a room. The round plate on the top of the stove is raised to a dull red or lesser heat controlled by means of two switches, and any degree of heat from "very hot" to "low simmering" can be obtained.

Electric current is brought to the stove through a flexible steel-covered cable which ensures absolute safety. The cable is ten feet in length and is attached to a wall-plug. The

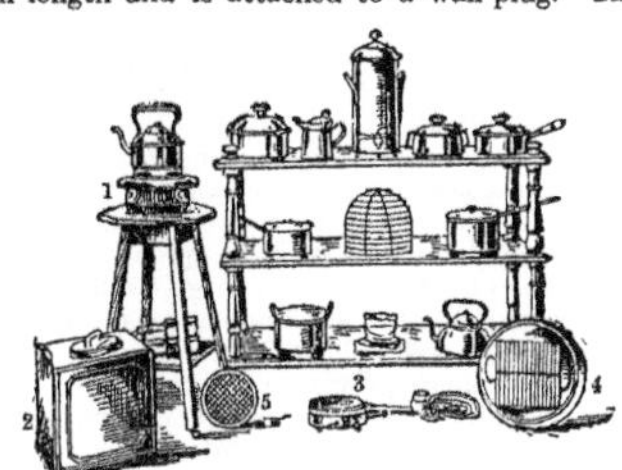

"Tricity" Stove.
1. Single Boiler. 2. Oven. 3. Extension Boiler. 4. Grill Pan. 5. Toaster.

cooker can easily be moved when desired within the range of the length of the cable, and, when in use, should be placed upon a table or on a wooden pedestal as shown in engraving. It should be a convenient height for working at.

Special sets of cooking utensils are sold for use with this cooker. They are quite simple, in both metal and earthenware and without wires of any kind, but one important point about them is that each article is absolutely flat at the base so as to obtain good contact with the hot-plate and thus make the cooking more rapid and economical.

The Duplex Cooker has two hot-plates, and its uses are the same as those of the Single Cooker.

The Extension Cooker has also one hot-plate, and is generally used in conjunction with one of the other cookers or to give top heat to the oven. It is also useful alone for boiling, stewing, and similar simple operations.

Ovens too can be bought in two sizes, and are heated by being placed on the top of a Single or Duplex Cooker. The larger size is quite sufficient for the needs of the average household.

The following is the *working cost* of the "Tricity Cooker" with electricity at a 1d. a unit.

1 Penny runs a "Tricity" hot-plate for 5 hours at lowest heat.

1 Penny runs a "Tricity" hot-plate for 1¼ hours at greatest heat.

Full particulars regarding price, use, &c., can be obtained by writing to the makers, the Berry Construction Co., Ltd., Charing Cross House, London.

COOKING ON OIL STOVES

A small oil stove may sometimes be a convenience when neither gas nor electricity is within reach. In summer, when a big kitchen fire is not required, a stove of this description will often perform all the cooking operations necessary. Being independent of any fittings, it can be moved about at will, and placed wherever it is most convenient. Sometimes, too, in country quarters where the kitchen range is inadequate for the cooking required, an oil stove will be found of valuable assistance, and it can even be used in an out-house if the kitchen is small and inconvenient.

They are to be had in various sizes, ranging from a small stove on which only one saucepan or kettle can be placed, to a large family stove with oven, boiler and accommodation for several saucepans as well. It is important to buy a stove of a thoroughly good make, and of late years there have been so many improvements made in their construction that they are more easily regulated and there is less danger of their smoking than formerly.

It is always well to see the stove at work before buying it, and to obtain full instructions as to its use, as with each special make there are certain points which require explanation. One of the greatest objections to oil stoves is their smell, but this can be to a large extent, if not altogether, avoided by proper management and care.

To secure the best results, care must be taken to keep the stove very clean and to use good oil. The wicks, too, must fit properly and be kept free from all charring. The oil-receivers should be well filled before using the stove, and the oil must not be allowed to burn too low.

It is also important to stand the stove out of a draught, and for this reason, as well as for the sake of convenience, it is better to raise it above the ground. It may be placed either on a simple four-legged stand or if it is a portable stove it is a good plan to have a box made which will serve at the same time as packing-case and a stand upon which to place it when in use. (For Cleaning and Trimming, see p. 77.)

COAL AND OTHER FUEL

Arrangement of the Coal Cellar.—A good-sized coal cellar is always an advantage in a house, as there will then be room to store not only a quantity but also at least two different kinds of coal. The contents of the cellar should be so arranged that each kind can easily be found, and a supply of slack or coal dust should also be kept in one corner.

When a fresh supply of coal is ordered it must not be thrown in on the top of the old dust, but this should first be scraped to one side and used along with the larger pieces. If this is once buried there becomes an accumulation of dust in the cellar which is never used up.

A strong coal shovel should be kept in the cellar, also a hatchet for breaking the coal when necessary. A large lump of coal should always be broken on the ground and not on the top of other coal, which would in all probability produce an unnecessary amount of small coal and dust.

The Buying of Coal.—Coal is always cheaper if it can be bought in large quantities—by the sack or bag is one of the most expensive ways in which it can be procured. Naturally the amount ordered must depend upon the accommodation there is for storing. The prices are generally much cheaper in summer than in winter, and, if convenient, there is a distinct advantage in laying up a store at this time of year. During the months of June, July, and August is the most advantageous time to buy. Sometimes it is possible to make an arrangement with the coal company that if the purchase is made in the summer the coal will only be delivered a ton or half a ton at a time as required.

It is important to buy the right kind of coal for the different ranges or fire-places. Range nuts or cobbles are excellent for kitchen use, and it would be most extravagant to use finer coal for this purpose. Coke, which is cheaper than coal, is often burnt along with the range nuts. A larger and better kind of coal will be required for use in the sitting-rooms. The housekeeper should see that the coal with which she is supplied does not contain too much dust. A careful watch should always be kept on this.

Coal should always be ordered from a good reliable merchant, and, if possible, from a depôt in one's own neighbourhood so as to avoid any extra charge for carriage. The price of coal fluctuates very much according to the supply. It is also affected by labour disputes involving strikes, lock-outs, &c., and is, as a rule, cheaper in localities which are in close proximity to a coal-field.

Householders who live in flats should ask for their coal to be delivered in half-sacks, as these are easier to carry up a number of stairs.

Economy in the Use of Coal.—An extravagant use of coal is one of the greatest sources of waste in a house, but, with careful management, much can be done to economise in this direction without in any way reducing the amount of comfort to be gained from the fires.

Fortunately the construction of stoves and grates has been very much improved of late years, and what are known as slow combustion stoves are fitted up in all the modern houses. Small coal should always be burnt along with the large. A ton of coal always produces a certain amount of dust, but if this is not sufficient an extra amount can always be ordered by the sack.

When a room is not in actual use or when the weather is mild and it is yet advisable that the fire be kept in, a lump of coal should be put on when the fire is rather low and then a good shovelful of damp slack placed on the top.

This is called "backing the fire," and by this means it can be kept in for several hours, and when a blaze is wanted a little breaking up with the poker is all that is necessary. Continual poking is also a cause of waste; the less a fire is touched the better, and if it is desired to keep the room at an equal temperature the fire should never be allowed to burn too low, but a few pieces of coal put on gently from time to time with a sprinkling of dust.

Sometimes the fire-place in a room is unnecessarily large, and this can be remedied by the use of fire-bricks, which will reduce the space and at the same time throw out heat. Clay balls are sometimes used for the same purpose. Briquettes are also used to economise coal. They are made of coal dust moistened and formed into blocks. Used along with a little moistened slack they will keep a fire in for hours, even all night, and they are a great convenience in this way. The only disadvantage to their use is that they cause a lot of dust when broken up.

Cinders should also be utilised. The larger cinders in the room-fires should be used when laying the next fire, while the smaller ones which have been sifted from the ashes can always be used in the kitchen-fire or in a boiler-fire if one is used.

Wood.—Logs of wood are frequently used as fuel, and in country districts a supply of logs can often be had quite cheaply, and they make a nice cheery fire in the winter. In town, however, they are not as a rule any cheaper than coal. Firewood can be bought quite cheaply in bundles, but even with this extravagance should be avoided. One bundle should be made to light two fires; in fact, with care it can be made to serve for three. There are also different kinds of firelighters to be had, and sometimes these are cheaper than the bundles of wood as they light the fire more easily, especially if the coal is of a hard make.

THE LARDER

A house of any considerable size usually contains a larder in which perishable food can be kept, and the importance of this room cannot be over-estimated. The ideal arrangement is to have it in two parts, so that dairy produce may be kept separate from butcher-meat, &c.

Position. — Whenever possible the larder should have a northerly or easterly aspect and comparative absence of bright sunshine. It is important, too, that it should be conveniently near the kitchen, although not near enough to be influenced by the heat of the range. It should never be placed near a lavatory; neither should the window overlook that part of the premises where the gulleys to receive the contents of the waste-pipes are placed.

Arrangement and Fittings.—The ceiling should be lime- or white-washed. The walls too, if they are not tiled, should be lime- or white-washed or painted with some sanitary paint which can easily be washed.

The shelves are best made of stone, marble, or slate, although wooden ones are sometimes fixed. In any case it is well to have a slab of slate or marble on which special things, such as butter and milk, can be placed to keep them cool.

Window-sills should be lined if possible with glazed tiles, and the floor should be of stone or tiles (red flags) or concrete.

Ventilation.—There should be one or more windows with which to ventilate the larder. If there are two one should be glazed to let in light and the other should be fitted with wire gauze or perforated zinc, fine enough to exclude all flies. If there is only one window it should be kept open constantly, and a piece of muslin should be stretched tightly across it to keep out flies and dust. There must be a through ventilation, and sometimes it is advisable to have one of the panels of the door fitted with perforated zinc in order to secure the necessary draught. Or sometimes perforated bricks are let into the walls, which help considerably to ventilate the larder.

The door of the larder should fit securely.

Requisites for the Larder. — Strong hooks securely fixed in the ceiling or hung from rods of iron running from side to side of the larder, from which to hang meat, game, &c.; a few smaller hooks fixed to the shelves or walls; a wire rack, baskets or wooden boxes for vegetables; bags of netting for lemons; a bread-pan, a large earthenware pan for milk with a piece of muslin as a covering; wire covers for cold meat, odd cups, basins, plates and dishes, also a few muslin bags for holding meat, hams, &c., and some improvised meat-safes made of muslin bags stretched out by wooden hoops.

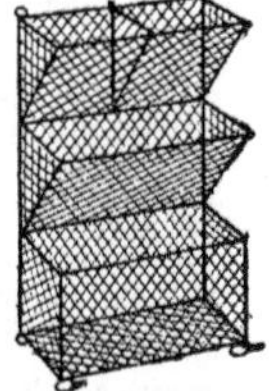

Vegetable-Rack.

A refrigerator is an advantage in a larder but by no means a necessity, except in large establishments or in houses where ices are largely used (see Ices).

Temperature.—This should not exceed 50° Fahr. in summer, nor fall below 38° Fahr. in winter.

Cleaning the Larder.—Absolute cleanliness must be maintained in the larder by daily and weekly cleaning.

Daily Cleaning.—(1) Wipe over the shelves with a damp cloth and put food not being used immediately for cooking on clean plates and dishes.

(2) Wipe over the floor also with a damp cloth or with a brush with a damp cloth or swab

tied over it (sweeping and dusting must never be done while food is in the larder, as it simply raises the dust to let it fall afterwards on the food).

(3) Wipe out the bread-pan.

(4) Burn any scraps not quite fresh of fish, bones, vegetables, &c.

Weekly Cleaning.—A special day should be chosen for this:—

(1) Remove all food from the larder.

(2) Sweep and dust walls and floor; gather up dust and burn.

(3) When dust has settled, dust and scrub shelves, using carbolic soap, or if the weather is hot some disinfectant may be added to the water, such as carbolic, Jeyes' Fluid, Sanitas, or Izol.

(4) Scrub floor with soft soap or carbolic soap and water.

(5) Leave door open to dry floor, &c. When dry replace the food on clean dishes.

(6) Thoroughly wash out bread-pan and leave it to dry and air before returning the bread.

(7) In hot weather place bowls of charcoal or disinfectant and water on the shelves.

Occasionally—

(1) Whitewash or limewash the ceiling about every six months.

(2) Scrub wire gauze or perforated zinc of windows and doors with disinfectant or carbolic soap and water.

(3) Scald and scrub meat-hooks and wire meat-covers.

(4) Wash muslin covers when necessary.

(5) Fill up any cracks or mouse-holes with cement and place traps when necessary.

Treatment of Various Kinds of Food—Meat, Game, and Poultry.—All uncooked meat should be hung. If there is a cut side keep this uppermost to prevent the juice running out. Examine the meat carefully each day and wipe it with a cloth to keep it dry. It may also be dusted over with a little flour. The marrow should be removed from the bone of such joints as a sirloin, ribs of beef or loin of mutton, before the meat is hung up.

If there is any sign of taint cut off the infected part and burn it, then wash the meat with a weak solution of Condy's fluid and water, vinegar and water, or borax and water. If there is a danger of flies attacking the meat, pepper it well and hang it up in muslin; or if there is a danger of the meat not keeping, it may be partially cooked.

Frozen meat should be well thawed before cooking; it should be taken from the larder and kept in a warm kitchen for an hour or two.

Cooked meat should be lifted out of the gravy with which it has been served and put on a dry plate covered over with a meat-screen.

If game or poultry has to be kept some time it should not be plucked, as the feathers are a protection from flies. Tie a piece of string tightly round the neck to exclude the air and hang it up. A little charcoal may also be put inside the vent to help to preserve it. This may be made by putting a piece of wood in the oven and letting it remain until it is quite black. It should be hung in a current of air and well sprinkled with pepper if there is any danger of flies. If there is any sign of taint the feathers should be removed and the bird washed in salt and water or vinegar and water. Repeat if necessary and then rinse in fresh water.

The length of time game should be kept depends partly on the weather and partly on individual taste, some people not caring to eat it until it smells distinctly high, while others prefer to use it comparatively fresh.

To Keep Suet.—If there are any glands or kernels to be seen these should be removed, also any parts which show discoloration, as those very soon become tainted and spoil the rest. If the suet has to be kept for several days it is a good plan to bury it in flour. If it is put into the flour-bin it will not impart any flavour to the contents.

Ham and Sides of Bacon.—Hang in muslin bags dusted with pepper or ginger to keep off the flies. If they are to be kept a long time the bags should be made of calico, or strong brown paper may be used for wrapping them in.

Lard.—Keep in a closely covered crock or basin.

Bones (for stock).—If unable to use at once bake sharply in the oven for a few minutes.

Stock and Soup.—See p. 118.

Fish.—Fish should always be placed in the coolest part of the larder—on a marble or slate slab if possible. It is always better if it can be used fresh, but when necessary to keep it for a day or two sprinkle liberally with salt, or in hot weather it may be wrapped in a piece of muslin wrung out of vinegar and water. Dried fish should be hung on a rod or hook.

Farm Produce—Butter.—Keep in an earthenware crock, cover with a piece of muslin wrung out of salted water and then with a tight-fitting lid. If there is a large quantity of butter to be stored it should be packed very tightly in the crock so as to leave no room for air to get down the sides. Place the crock in a cool, dark, and airy place.

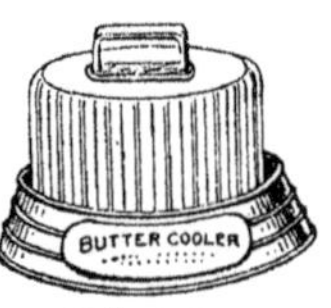

Butter-Cooler.

To keep fresh butter in hot weather a butter-cooler should be used; this is made with a cover into which is poured a little water. Failing a butter-cooler place the butter in a bowl standing in a larger bowl of cold water. Cover it with a piece of muslin, allowing the ends of the muslin to dip into the water. The water, which should be changed daily, is soaked up by the muslin and thus kept constantly wet.

Butter must not be put near any strong-smelling substance as it quickly absorbs any flavour.

Cheese.—A cut piece of cheese should be wrapped in grease-proof paper or in damp muslin and kept in a cheese dish or jar or tin in which there is a little ventilation. A large piece of cheese ought to be turned frequently and the rind rubbed occasionally with a cloth to prevent moisture collecting. A ripe cheese must be watched carefully to see that it is not attacked by the cheese fly.

Milk and Cream.—Strict cleanliness is the first necessity. The jug or basin in which the milk is kept must be thoroughly scalded and rinsed with cold water. Milk should always be kept covered, and, like butter, it should not be put near anything with a strong smell, as it readily absorbs odours. It is a bad plan to mix milk—a fresh lot should never be added to some that has been in the house several hours. In hot weather the milk should be scalded if it has to be kept for several hours. Stand the jug containing it in a large saucepan of water and heat to almost boiling-point, or this may be done in a double saucepan. A pinch of carbonate of soda or powdered borax may be added to the milk to preserve it, but this spoils the flavour. The same care must be taken with cream. If it is scalded as above it will keep sweet for several hours. A lump of sugar will also help to preserve it.

Eggs should be kept in a basket or on an egg-stand where they do not touch each other. If there is room for storing, the thrifty housekeeper will buy a quantity of eggs in the spring and store them for winter use. They can be preserved in one of the following methods :—

(1) Place them in an air-tight box between layers of coarse salt. The small end of the egg should be placed downwards and they must never touch each other. Put a layer of salt two inches deep on the top, cover with a thick piece of calico or strong paper, and then a tight-fitting lid. This must be kept in a cool place.

(2) Grease the eggs (they must be very fresh) over with lard, oil, or any pure fat and place them on a tray with a layer of bran above and below.

(3) Pack in lime, in the same manner as for salt, only this renders them so brittle that they are unfit for boiling.

(4) Lay them in a bath of water glass. Water glass can be bought for about 4d. per pound, and full directions for its use are printed on each tin.

Bread.—Bread should be kept closely covered in an earthenware bread-pan with a lid, or in an enamelled iron bin. It must never be put away while hot, but should be allowed to cool where the air can circulate freely round it.

The pan or crock must be wiped out regularly in order to free it from all musty crumbs, and once a week or once a fortnight thoroughly scalded, and then allowed to become cool and dry before the bread is returned to it.

Bread can also be kept well if it is placed in a clean cloth and placed on a shelf.

What to do when there is no Larder.—In many small houses and flats there is no proper larder, and one cupboard has to serve the purpose of larder and storeroom and sometimes as a place for keeping dishes as well.

When this is the case the quantities ordered must be as small as possible and cleanliness and order are all the more necessary. If the shelves are made of wood it is a good plan to have them covered with white oil-cloth, as this can so easily be wiped over or washed. In addition to this cupboard, a meat-safe should be provided and placed either outside or in a cool place. Needless to say, it should not be placed anywhere near a lavatory. A small meat-safe can occasionally be fixed to the outside ledge of the kitchen window. If it is out of doors the top must be protected from rain by a covering of wood or galvanised iron, and it must be scrubbed out every week and just as carefully as an inside cupboard.

Failing a meat-safe, small cane and muslin cages should be bought in which meat can be hung up in any cool and well-ventilated place. They are very inexpensive to buy, or they can even be simply constructed at home by making a bag of muslin drawn in at top and bottom. Place a plate at the foot and keep out the sides with hoops of cane lightly tacked in position.

Economy in the Larder.—No housekeeper should dispense with a daily visit to the larder. A survey of this department will help her in ordering the meals of the day besides acting as a stimulus to the cook to avoid waste and keep things in good order.

The chief points to notice when inspecting the larder are :—

(1) What food there is left from the previous day's meals, and how best it can be made to reappear at table.

(2) What scraps there are for the stock-pot and odds and ends of fat that can be rendered down.

(3) The condition of any meat or game that is being hung.

(4) The condition of the bread-pan—if there are any scraps that will require to be used up.

(5) What new provisions will be required.

(6) That the larder itself is as tidy and fresh as it ought to be, and that plates on which food rests, as well as any basins and jugs, are all clean.

STORING FRUIT AND VEGETABLES

Vegetables.—When vegetables are only bought in small quantities as required they should be kept in baskets or a vegetable rack and stored in a cool place—the floor of the larder or cellar is the best. Potatoes alone, carrots and turnips together, and green and other special vegetables by themselves. Onions, shalots, chives, and garlic are best hung up by strings or in a net bag and kept away from other food.

Parsley and mint should be kept with the stalks in water, and the water changed every day.

Tomatoes should be kept on a plate or spread out on a shelf without touching each other.

To Store Vegetables.—Although vegetables are at their best when freshly gathered, they can when necessary be kept for a limited period. When potatoes are bought in large quantities and stored through the winter, they should be kept in a dry dark cellar and covered with straw to keep off the frost. If kept in a bright or damp place they will spoil and become milled and withered. Rub off all sprouts and shoots as they appear. Examine frequently and remove any that show signs of decay. In the country potatoes are sometimes stored in a deep hole in the ground lined with straw and banked up with sand.

Artichokes can be treated in the same way.

Carrots, Beetroots, and Parsnips may be preserved in dry sand or earth in a dark cellar.

Turnips should be allowed to lie on the floor of a dark cellar.

Vegetable Marrows and Cucumbers will keep for some time if they are hung up by the stalk in a cool situation.

Small **Cabbages** too, if they are sound and firm and cut before the frost touches them, can be preserved for a few weeks if they are spread on a stone floor in the dark.

Herbs.—If these can be bought fresh in the summer time it is best to dry them quickly beside the kitchen fire. Then strip off the leaves and rub them through a fine sieve. The different kinds should be kept separate and stored in air-tight boxes or bottles.

Fruit.—If only bought in small quantities, such fruit as apples, pears, plums, apricots, and oranges should be wiped and spread out on a tray, on the shelves of the store-room or larder, or on a special fruit-stand.

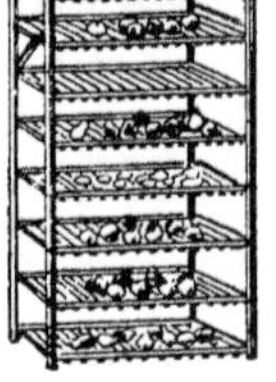

Fruit-Stand.

Bananas and grapes should be hung. Softer fruits, such as currants and berries, should only be bought as required and then used at once.

Lemons should be wiped dry and hung up in nets, or if laid on a shelf they should be turned every day.

All fruit should be kept in a cool place and out of the sun, unless it is a kind which requires further ripening.

When **Apples** have to be stored in large quantities for winter use, they should be dry, sound, and not too ripe. They should be spread out on shelves in a fruit-room or an attic that does not admit too much sunshine. They should not be allowed to touch each other and any decaying ones should be instantly removed. Rough-skinned apples, such as russets, keep best.

Pears, if not ripe, may be kept in the same way or hung up by the stalks.

THE STORE-ROOM OR STORE-CLOSET

If a small room can be set aside for the storage of groceries and other household commodities it will be a great convenience to the careful housewife, and if she has some knowledge as to the stocking and general management of that store-room she will feel a sense of pride in keeping it well plenished and in good order.

A store-room should be dry and airy, tidy and well arranged. A room with a northern or eastern aspect is the best. It should be as near the kitchen as possible in order to avoid unnecessary carrying, and not in the vicinity of a sink or closet.

If a small room is not available a good-sized cupboard can serve the purpose, and goods, &c., must be bought according to the accommodation for keeping them and individual requirements.

Fittings and Arrangements.—The store-room should have its walls and ceiling white-washed or coated with sanitary paint, which can be easily washed. The walls and floor should be examined for any cracks, and if there are such they should be carefully filled up with cement to prevent the entrance of mice, beetles, and other vermin. The floor should be well boarded and either left uncovered or covered with linoleum.

If there is an outside window it should be covered with wire gauze or fine perforated zinc through which no flies can enter.

The walls should be fitted with plenty of shelves, and if these can be graduated in size it will be found an advantage; broader shelves below to hold the bulkier and heavier articles, and narrower ones above for those that are lighter. It is a bad plan to have the shelves so wide that the jars and other receptacles have to be placed one behind the other; it will be a case of "out of sight out of mind," and it will be impossible to see at a glance what the store-room contains. The shelves should be covered with white or brown oilcloth, which is easily wiped down or washed. This can be fastened in position with drawing-pins if there is difficulty in making it lie flat.

If space permits it will be found a great convenience to have a small inner cupboard with one or two drawers, also a strong steady table with a pair of scales or balance.

A few hooks along the edges of the shelves will also be useful for hanging such articles as can be suspended, and they sometimes help to eke out an otherwise limited space.

Requisites.—Besides the stores and provisions it will be found useful to have the following articles in the store-room :—

(1) A dust-pan and brush and one or two dusters for keeping the shelves, floor, &c., in order.

(2) A supply of paper, brown and white, string, pen and ink, and some labels or adhesive papers. A drawer in the table or cupboard might be utilised for these or a special corner of the shelves.

(3) Jars, canisters, boxes, and bottles for keeping the various stores. Any odd jars and boxes, &c., can be used for the purpose as long as they are sound and have tight-fitting lids or saucers to cover the tops very closely. Empty biscuit-boxes, jam or pickle jars, can be utilised for the purpose. For those who can afford something daintier there are many kinds of store jars to be bought both in earthenware and enamelled tin with the names of the various groceries, &c., printed on the outside, from about 1s. each according to size. Glass jars with lids are also nice for groceries that are bought in small quantities, such as almonds, preserved fruits, cocoanut, chocolate, &c., and neat tin boxes or a small chest for keeping the various spices. Receptacles that have no printed name must be neatly labelled to show the nature of the contents.

Store Jar.

(4) A slate and pencil for noting down what stores require replenishing should be hung in a convenient place in the store-room, or a store indicator may be purchased for about 3s. This useful little remembrancer gives a printed list of the different stores on a neat frame, and a system of pegs and holes indicates what is required.

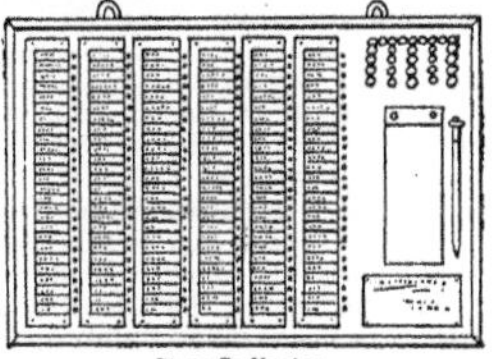
Store Indicator.

(5) A few implements will also be required—a pair of scissors, a cork-screw, a knife, a tin-opener, two or three spoons of different sizes, a few scoops, and a cheese and soap-cutter.

(6) It will also be found useful to keep a small tool-box in the store-room containing a hammer, saw, gimlet, screw-driver, a pair of pincers, chisel, and a useful supply of nails, hooks, and tacks.

Grouping the Stores.—In arranging the store-room the various articles must be grouped methodically according to their kind and in such a way that they can be easily found. Keep a special shelf or corner for cereals, another for the different kinds of sugar, another for jams and preserves, another for bottled goods, and so on.

If there is a small cupboard this might be reserved for a medicine cupboard, or for special articles or poisons, which are better kept under lock and key. There should also be a special corner for wine if there is no separate wine cellar, and a special corner for cleaning requisites.

Then if there are drawers these might be used for kitchen paper, dish papers, cutlet frills, &c., and another one for an extra supply of dusters, dish cloths, floor cloths, &c., while the nails and hooks can be utilised for such articles as can be hung.

Articles such as tea and coffee, cheese and soap, must not be placed near each other, as the smell and flavour may be imparted from one to the other. Nothing must be kept in paper parcels, and every jar, canister, box, &c., must be clearly labelled on the outside. The heavier jars should be placed on the bottom shelf or on the floor, if dry, and those in constant use readiest to hand.

Cleaning the Store-room.—The store-room must be kept very tidy. The jars ought to be taken down periodically and thoroughly dusted, and the shelves dusted and washed over before they are returned. When necessary, the jars should be washed out and well dried before being refilled. The table and floor should also be scrubbed when they require it, and everything kept in good order. If the stores are dropped about in an untidy manner it will only encourage mice and insects. It is important also that the store-room should be well aired.

Giving out Stores.—Stores should be given out regularly, either daily or weekly and at a fixed date. They should be checked when they come in, and the consumption should be strictly regulated, or the method of buying in quantities will be found an extravagant one.

There are two ways of checking consumption : one method is to keep all stores and provisions under lock and key and to give them out by weight and measure. This method is exact, but it does not always answer ; it is more suitable for a public institution or for a large establishment than for a small private house. It is often a cause of worry and annoyance, and is apt to cause friction between mistress and servants. As a rule, good servants will work most willingly in houses where they are trusted, and if we begin by calculating measure for measure with them they will doubtless do the same with us. Servants who are inclined to be wasteful will waste by ounces just as easily as they can by pounds.

Still, it is not wise to have large quantities out at one time for general use. Smaller jars can be filled with the different stores for daily consumption without actually doling them out by the ounce and half ounce and so much for each person. Some things, such as butter, tea, and sugar, it is very usual to measure out for kitchen use, and where there are several servants this is a wise plan and is thought nothing of (see p. 45).

Another way of checking consumption is by means of the weekly bills. Each housekeeper must draw up her own estimate as to how much should be spent upon certain things and then make an effort to keep within its limit (see p. 365).

GENERAL NOTES ON STORING

Tea and Coffee should be kept in air-tight canisters or in a lead-lined chest.

Dry Groceries.—Keep in covered earthenware jars.

Starch.—Keep in a cool place and well covered, as air turns it powdery.

Soda and Salt.—Keep in a wooden or tin box with a lid. Damp is bad for them; it forms them into blocks.

Spices.—Keep in air-tight tins or in a spice chest.

Flour.—Keep in a wooden or enamelled bin. Sometimes the bin is divided, and one portion can be used for household flour and the other for Vienna flour. If the floor is of stone or damp the bin must be raised.

Enamelled Bin.

Jams, Pickles, Bottled Fruits, &c. must be kept in a cool place as they are liable to ferment. If the store-room is hot they should be placed near the floor.

Soap.—Cut in blocks with an old knife or soap-cutter and stack up with a space between each block.

Candles.—If store-room is warm rub with methylated spirits to harden them.

Biscuits and Cakes.—Keep in tin boxes with tight-fitting lid.

CARE OF WINES

Wines require a great deal of attention, and their preservation in a state fit to drink largely depends upon the treatment they receive. Any carelessness or neglect is sure to be followed by deterioration in quality, and the loss of those properties which can only arrive at perfection if the maturing process is allowed to proceed under conditions which are favourable to their growth and development.

The Wine Cellar.—The cellar should be underground if possible, as it will then be less affected by variations in temperature. It should be cool, dry, and well ventilated without any strong draughts. The walls are generally made of brick or stone and white-washed, and the shelves or bins of wood or iron.

Care should be taken to see that the drainage is good and that no foul air enters. The windows or holes to admit light should be small, as any sunshine would raise the temperature which ought to be kept uniform. The thermometer should stand about 55° Fahr. and there should be no variations. If at any time it is necessary to raise the temperature artificially, gas must on no account be employed, as the vitiation of the air which results is injurious to the wine—an oil lamp or small oil stove is better.

Apart from any artificial heating there will always be a slight difference in the degree of warmth between the top bins and the lower ones, owing to the tendency of warm air to rise, and in consequence of this care must be taken to arrange the different varieties of wines in separate parts of the cellar according to their individual requirements as regards heat.

Binning Wines.—Bins are the open divisions in the cellar in which the wine is placed. They may either be fixtures in the cellar or may be bought separately and placed on the floor; if the latter is done, care must be taken that the bin stands steadily or the wine will be disturbed.

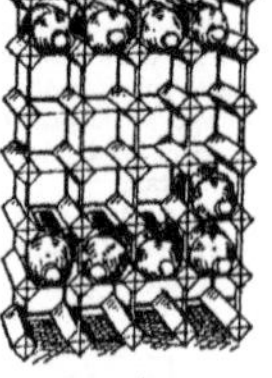

Wine Bin.

In arranging the wines it must be remembered that all wines cannot be treated alike.

As a rule, it is best to bin the light varieties such as Hock, Moselle, and all sparkling varieties at the bottom, Clarets and Burgundies in the middle, and Sherry and Port and other fortified wines at the top.

The bottles must be placed in the bins horizontally, as the wine would soon deteriorate were they allowed to stand upright. When binning port the bottles should be so placed that the chalk or white paint-mark is uppermost on account of the sediment.

The corks of wine bottles should be examined for signs of decay, because if once they become faulty and the air can penetrate the wine will be spoilt.

Wine should be consumed as soon as possible after the bottle has been opened. The lighter wines are hardly fit to drink if they are kept for even two or three days after being decanted, although the fortified wines, such as sherry and port, will last rather longer. (See also Service of Wines, p. 248.)

Ale, Stout, and Cider.—These beverages require

a temperature of about 50° Fahr. The bottles should be allowed to stand upright a few days before use. Stout should not be kept in the house too long, as it is liable to generate too much gas. If beer is kept in a cask, a stand should be provided in order to raise it about a foot from the ground. A cask should be so placed that there is a space all round it to enable of its being examined from time to time. It must also be perfectly steady and wedges of wood used, if necessary, to keep it from shaking.

Spirits (Whisky, brandy, rum, and gin).—Spirits are best stood upright, and when in bottles require very little attention.

Australian Wines.—These wines are easily handled, being sold in flagons with screw stoppers. Care should be taken to keep the stoppers screwed up very tightly, because if the air is allowed to get to the wine it is liable to turn it acid.

When no Wine Cellar is Available.—If there is no wine cellar in which to keep a supply, wine must be bought in smaller quantities and just enough for immediate requirements. A corner of the store cupboard or some downstairs cellar can sometimes be utilised for keeping a moderate supply of bottles, and for convenience sake a small bin might be fitted up. Or a wine cabinet is sometimes found useful, especially in flats and small houses. They are fitted with a strong lock and key, and one to hold four dozen bottles can be bought for about 30s.

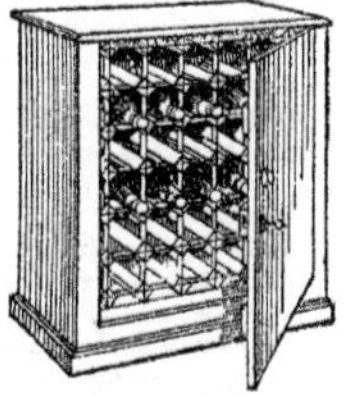

Wine Cabinet.

MARKETING

General Hints.—It requires a considerable amount of forethought and common-sense to do really good marketing, to buy just what is necessary for the needs of the household, to secure the best value for one's money, and to be economical in the true sense of the word without being parsimonious.

Whether we have much money or little at our disposal it always requires some care to lay it out to the best advantage, and the less there is the more necessity there will be to make the most of it.

Money is often wasted and time lost by the housekeeper not knowing how to choose and order food. It requires some experience to do it well, but with common-sense and good will the art of marketing is easily acquired.

Each purchase should be thoughtfully considered, and when means are scarce money must not be frittered away on any trifle which may strike the fancy and has no real value.

It is always best to deal with good reliable shops and not to be continually hunting after the cheapest market. Try, if possible, to patronise the shops in your immediate neighbourhood, and preferably those in which there is a big turnover, where articles are being constantly sold out and renewed. Avoid shops where the goods are not kept in an orderly and cleanly condition, or where they are exposed to the dust and dirt of the street, or to be touched and handled by every passer-by.

However small the income may be, it will never be found economical to buy goods of inferior quality in order to save a few pence. Aim rather at securing good material of its kind and at avoiding luxuries, except as an occasional treat when they can be afforded.

In order to ascertain whether or not you are being charged a fair price for your provisions, try to obtain a price list from two or three good shops and then compare them.

It is the duty of every mistress to see that her merchandise is good; there is no virtue in allowing short weight and inferior quality nor in permitting oneself to be imposed upon in any way. One only gets the best attention by expecting and demanding it.

Previous to making out her order the mistress should go through the larder and store-room and make a note of what is required, always bearing in mind the bill of fare for the day. Sometimes it is possible to order for two days at a time or to order always one day ahead to ensure having the provisions in the house in good time in the morning. This is often necessary in houses where a very early dinner has to be provided for, and it enables the cook, or whoever undertakes the cooking, time to start her preparations directly the breakfast things are cleared away.

Whenever possible, the mistress of the house or housekeeper should do her own shopping, not necessarily every day, but certainly occasionally. In this way the tradesmen get a better idea of her likes and dislikes and can generally serve her better. Variety will be suggested by what she sees in the shops, and a knowledge of what things are in season is more quickly obtained. With meat especially she will get a better joint or more suitable piece of meat for her purpose if she sees it cut and weighed than if she simply left it to the butcher's discretion. At the fishmonger's, too, a personal visit is a wise plan, as the price of fish varies so much, and even from day to day according to the weather and other circumstances. The more plentiful kind will always be the cheapest for the time being, and it will generally be found that it is the best as well.

Shopping should be done as early as possible, as there is generally a better selection in the forenoon and provisions are fresher.

If this personal shopping cannot be managed by the mistress of the household and there is no responsible person to whom the business may be deputed, a duplicate order book should be used. A separate list for each tradesman should be written out in duplicate form, giving exact quantities required and price if possible. The tradesmen can then send for their orders, one list being given to them and the other retained for reference and for the purpose of checking the house books. This is a safer method than that of giving haphazard verbal orders to message boys.

Small vouchers or weight bills should accompany all goods sent from the shops, and these should be used for checking the various items. (For Payment of Bills, House Books, &c., see pp. 365–66.)

GENERAL NOTES ON ORDERING GROCERIES AND PROVISIONS

When ordering stores there are several points to be considered besides the ordering of what is actually required. We must consider in addition what will keep well, what space there is for storing it, what we can afford, and whether or not it is the best season for a large purchase.

The slate or indicator will help us as regards what is wanted, as when each article is finished or nearly so the fact ought to be noted and then that article included in the next order.

It must be remembered that articles bought in small quantities are often dearer in proportion than when purchased in large quantities; not only is the price per pound less, but the weight of paper and paper-bags is saved.

Good-keeping things should always be bought in large quantities where the purse is not very straitened and where space is not a consideration.

As there is generally a cheap and a dear season an attempt should be made to benefit by the former by buying in as large a store as possible of any special commodity that will keep well and for which there is likely to be use.

All things having a strong taste or smell, such as spices, essences, coffee (when ground), &c., should be bought in small quantities, as they are apt to deteriorate.

All **Grains** and **Cereals, Soda** and **Salt,** may be bought in moderate supplies according to the needs of the household.

Sugar may also be bought in considerable quantities, although moist sugar must be watched, as it sometimes becomes infected with sugar mite. Cane sugar is the best for all preserving purposes; jams made with it will keep longer and have a better colour than if beetroot sugar were used. Beetroot sugar is, however, quite good for other sweetening purposes.

Tea should be bought in moderate quantities. It should be well twisted and the leaves not too small. The special blend to use is entirely a matter of taste.

Dried Fruits will also keep well and should be bought in the autumn when the new fruit comes in. Figs, however, must be carefully looked over, as they often become infected with small maggots.

Soap improves with keeping and may safely be ordered in large quantities. The drier it is the less it will waste when used. There are many different kinds—plain yellow soap, mottled soap, paraffin soap, Sunlight soap, and carbolic soap are all useful for household purposes; also the soft soap, which should be bought in large tins and given out as required.

Candles will also improve with keeping.

Tinned Foods.—Choose tins that are in perfect condition and free from rust. There should be no bulges, which are a sign of fermentation; the tops and bottoms should be rather concave. Foods preserved in earthenware or glass jars are better and safer than tinned ones, but they generally cost more money.

Cheese and Butter must always be chosen by the taste. Cheap butter should be avoided—it is better to use good dripping or lard for cooking purposes than inferior butter.

The choice of cheese is entirely a question of taste. For a moderately priced cheese some of the American cheeses similar to our Cheddar cheeses are to be recommended, also the round Dutch cheeses. In choosing such cheeses as Stilton, Gorgonzola, and Roquefort, select one that combines moisture with green mould. Cream cheeses must always be bought very fresh and used at once.

Eggs if fresh are clear when held up to the light; if stale there is a dark spot or cloudy-looking part. They may be tested by putting them in salt and water—1 ounce salt to 1 pint water; eggs that float in this are not good. They should not be too light, and when shaken the inside should not float about. When eggs are cheap it is sometimes a good plan to buy in large quantity and store them for the winter. (See p. 101.)

Ham.—Choose a short thick leg with a moderate amount of fat. The rind should be rather thin and the bone fine. The quality may be tested by running a pointed knife or skewer in close to the bone; when withdrawn it should not be greasy nor have an unpleasant smell, but, on the contrary, be clean and have a good flavour. Hams vary in price according to the manner of curing and special reputation. In England the Yorkshire and Cumberland hams are generally considered the finest and still command a good price, although some of the southern counties prôduce hams by no means inferior. In Scotland, the Dumfries and Galloway hams rank among the best, and Irish hams from Belfast are much prized. Canadian and Danish hams are also in the market in large quantities, and although the flavour is not considered so delicate as that of the home-cured variety, their moderate price recommends them to those who have to study economy.

Bacon must be fresh and free from rustiness. The fat should be very white; the lean should adhere closely to the bone and be of a nice red colour, and there should be as little gristle as possible.

The following diagram will give a general idea of the way in which a side of bacon is usually cut in England; there will of course be subdivisions to make smaller pieces. What is known as "streaky" bacon and the flank are considered the finest, but, being much in demand, they fetch a high price. The back and loin are also prime pieces, while the fore-end and gammon, although not so fine in texture, do excellently for boiled bacon.

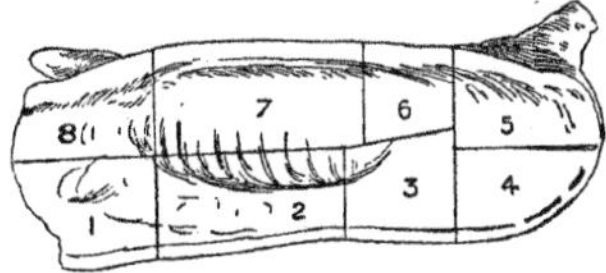

Side of Bacon.

1. Collar.	5. Gammon.
2. Back.	6. Flank.
3. Loin.	7. Streaky.
4. Corner.	8. Fore-end.

HOW TO CHOOSE MEAT

General Hints.—It is very important to buy meat from a good butcher, and one who can be thoroughly trusted.

There are certain signs by which the quality of the meat can generally be judged. The texture should be firm and moderately elastic, and, when pressed, should not leave the imprint of the finger. If the flesh is flabby and moist and has an unpleasant odour it is not good.

The lean part should be finely grained, and the fat, which should not be in any undue proportion, should be free from kernels, brown spots, and streaks of blood.

The meat of most animals that have died a natural death or by accident should be avoided.

Good meat does not waste much in cooking, and when left on a dish the juice should not exude from it in any quantity.

Besidès these general points to be remembered each special kind of meat has its individual character by which it can be judged.

Beef.—The best kind of beef is of a nice red colour, almost a cherry red, and the lean has a marble appearance, being slightly intergrained with fat. The fat is a pale yellow colour, not mottled, and the suet hard and dry. It is fine and smooth in texture, with rather an open grain. There should be little or no gristle between the fat and the lean, as this generally indicates that it is the flesh of an old animal. Beef of a dark colour with very yellow fat should be avoided.

Beef is more nourishing and strengthening than mutton, but not so easy of digestion. Ox beef is better than cow beef and generally fetches a higher price. Bull beef is very coarse, and is never sold by a good butcher.

Beef should be well hung before it is used to make it tender; the time it should hang will depend upon the weather, and it must never be allowed to become high.

Mutton.—The best mutton is plump and small-boned. The quality depends very much upon where the animal has been reared, and also upon the age at which it is killed; the mountain-fed sheep are considered the best, and from four to six years old is the best age for killing, only a farmer can rarely afford to keep his sheép so long, and they are generally killed between two and three years of age.

The lean of mutton is not so red in colour as beef, but hàs a darker and browner hue. It should be firm, close in texture, and not intergrained with fat. The fat should be hard and very white and waxy. Mutton, like beef, should be well hung.

Lamb is paler in colour than mutton, and the fat is pearly white. When fresh, the veins in the neck end of the fore-quarter have a bluish tinge, and when stale these develop a greenish hue. In the hind-quarter the kidneys should be examined; if they are flabby with an unpleasant smell the meat is stale.

A piece of the caul, a thin transparent-looking membrane, should be sent with each joint of lamb to wrap round it and protect it when cooking.

The New Zealand or Canterbury lamb is much cheaper than the home grown, but as far as taste is concerned it is more like mutton, as it seems to lose its characteristic flavour during the process of freezing.

The flesh of lamb is tenderer than that of mutton, but it is more watery ànd not so nutritious. Lamb cannot be hung for very long.

Pork.—Pork requires very careful choosing as it is more subject to disease than perhaps any other animal food, and unless one is sure of its source it is safer to leave it alone. The flesh should be of a pinky white colour, smooth, finely grained, and firm to the touch. The skin must not be too thick. The fat should be pearly white with no black specks nor kernels. Small pork is the best. It is much more difficult to digest than either beef or mutton, as it contains such a large proportion of fat.

Veal is the flesh of the calf. It should be very pale in colour, firm, and closely grained. The fat should be white, and if that which surrounds the kidney is hard and without smell the meat is in good condition. Veal is not so nutritious as beef and it is more difficult of digestion. Like all other young meats, it should not be hung very long.

Venison is the flesh of deer. The lean should be finely grained and dark in colour. The fat should be plentiful and of a creamy white appearance.

The age can be judged by the hoof; in the young animal the cleft is small and smooth, while in the older one it has become much deeper and more rugged.

Venison should be hung as long as possible, but it must be frequently examined. Its freshness can be tested by running a knife or skewer into the bone at the haunch; if when withdrawn it smells well and is not sticky this is a sure sign of good condition.

The flesh of the buck is considered superior to that of the doe.

Suet.—This must be very fresh and of good quality. The solid fat, which surrounds the kidney, either beef or mutton, is considered the best. Beef suet should be cream coloured or pale yellow and mutton suet very white and waxy. Both should be very firm and dry.

Internal Meats.—All inside meats such as tripe, liver, kidneys, sweetbreads, &c., must be bought very fresh and used at once.

CALENDAR OF MEAT IN SEASON

Beef, Mutton, and **Veal** are in season **all** the year round.

Lamb.—House lamb from January to May, grass lamb from May to September, and New Zealand lamb all the year round.

Pork.—All the year round, but best from September to May.

Venison.—Buck venison from May to October, doe venison from October to end of January.

DIFFERENT JOINTS OF MEAT AND THEIR USES

The cutting up of meat varies somewhat according to locality and also according to the special demands of the people with whom the butchers have to deal.

The following diagrams will give an idea of how the different animals are cut up by English butchers, and may also be of assistance to the housewife in knowing what piece to order for the special purpose she has in view.

BEEF

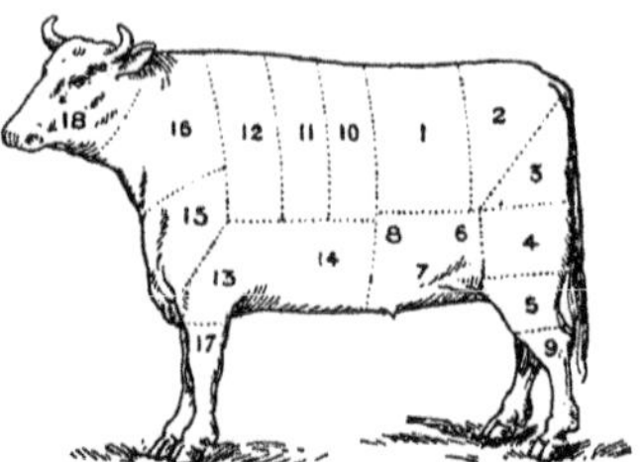

Diagram showing mode of cutting up Beef in England.

1. Sirloin.
2. Rump.
3. Aitchbone.
4. Buttock.
5. Mouse Buttock.
6. Veiny parts.
7. Thick Flank.
8. Thin Flank.
9. Shin.
10. Fore Ribs.
11. Middle Ribs.
12. Chuck Ribs.
13. Leg of Mutton Piece.
14. Brisket.
15. Clod.
16. Neck.
17. Shin.
18. Cheek.

The Sirloin.—This is the best part for roasting, but it is somewhat expensive. It is usually divided into three pieces varying in weight according to the size of the animal. The middle cut is considered the best, as it has the largest amount of undercut. The piece next the ribs has very little undercut, and the one next the rump is a joint difficult to carve, as it has a piece of bone on one side.

The sirloins from both sides of the animal not cut asunder form what is called the baron of beef, corresponding to the saddle in mutton. This is a joint rarely seen nowadays, but was famous at banquets in the days of our ancestors.

The fillet or undercut of the sirloin is the most tender part for entrées or fillets of beef.

Ribs.—The cuts from the ribs are also good for roasting, those nearest the sirloin being the best. Various sizes of joints can be cut according to special requirements. It is more economical to have the bone removed and used for soup and the meat itself rolled. One or two ribs treated in this way make a neat little roast for a small family. When a large cut of the ribs is ordered and roasted whole, it is better to have the thin end cut off and used for a separate dish, otherwise it becomes overcooked before the thicker part is ready. The piece of ribs next the shoulder is better stewed or braised than roasted.

The Rump.—This is divided into three parts—the middle, the silver-side, and the chump end. The middle is an excellent piece of fleshy meat for any purpose. Some of the best steaks are cut from this part; it is also a first-rate cut for pies, for rolled beef, or for a tender stew. The chump end is also good for stewing. The silverside is very often salted and is good for boiling.

Buttock or Round.—This is another very fleshy piece of meat with little bone. It is one of the best pieces for braising or boiling, and is often salted. It can also be roasted, but, although economical, it is not so fine in flavour as the ribs or sirloin.

Aitch Bone, or Edge Bone.—This is a cheap piece of meat, but as it contains a large proportion of bone and wastes very much in cooking it is not really economical. It is an awkwardly shaped joint and very difficult to carve. It is generally boiled and sometimes salted.

Brisket.—This is also sold at a low price, and is used principally for boiling or stewing. It is rather fat, but is excellent when salted and boiled and then served cold.

Flank.—The thick flank is one of the most economical parts to buy, as it contains no bone and very little fat. Suitable for braising, stewing, and boiling. The thin flank contains much more fat, and is best salted, boiled, and eaten cold.

The Clod and Sticking Piece are both somewhat coarse and only suitable for soup or cheap stews.

Shin.—This is also coarse grained and very gelatinous. It is excellent for stock and soup. The top part will also make an economical stew if slowly and carefully cooked.

Cheek.—Only suitable for stews and for making soup. As it contains so much bone it is not really economical.

Cow Heel is very gelatinous, and is used principally for making jelly, or, along with meat, as a foundation for soups. It can also be carefully boiled or stewed and then eaten with a good and piquant sauce.

Tail.—This is somewhat expensive. It is used for making soups, and can also be stewed or braised.

Heart.—This is rather coarse and very indigestible, but it can be made palatable by being stuffed and very carefully roasted or braised.

Tongue is usually salted and then boiled and served cold, or served hot with a good sauce, or cut in slices for an entrée.

Tripe.—The inner lining of the stomach. It is usually sold partially prepared, although in Scotland it requires many hours' boiling. It is very tender and easily digested, and for this reason is frequently ordered for invalids.

There are several different kinds of tripe popularly known as "honeycomb," "blanket," "double" or "book" (because it is like the leaves of a book), and "reed" the dark-coloured portion.

Liver.—This is a cheap piece, and is nutritious for those who can digest it. It requires careful cooking.

Kidneys.—Used for making soup. Can also be stewed, although rather indigestible.

Midriff.—A thin fleshy piece which runs across the middle of the animal. It is rich in flavour and is very good for stews or beef-steak pudding.

Sweetbread.—In the ox this part is coarse, and can only be made palatable by careful cooking.

VEAL

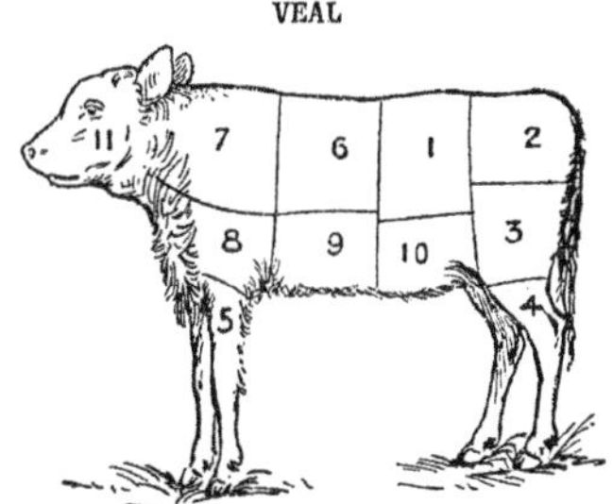

Mode of cutting up a Calf.

1. Loin.
2. Chump end of Loin.
3. Fillet.
4. Hind-knuckle.
5. Fore-knuckle.
6. Neck (best end).
7. Shoulder.
8. Blade-bone.
9. Breast.
10. Flank.
11. Head.

Veal, which is the flesh of the calf, is cut up into the following different joints:—

The Fillet.—One of the finest pieces, very fleshy with little or no bone. Can be used for any purpose. The best cutlets are cut from this part. It is high priced, but not over expensive, as there is practically no waste.

The Breast.—If boned, stuffed and rolled, this part makes a nice little joint for roasting. It can also be braised or stewed. Entrées are also prepared from this piece.

The Loin.—One of the best pieces for roasting, also for chops.

The Neck.—A good joint for braising or stewing. Can also be roasted. The best end may be cut into chops. The scrag-end is more suitable for broth.

Knuckle.—This is a favourite part for soup or broth and is much used in the making of white stock. The fore-knuckle is more tender than the hind-knuckle and is often stewed or boiled and served with a good sauce.

Head and Feet are sometimes served together as a hash, but, being rather insipid in flavour, they require a good sauce. They can also be used for pies, when some ham should be added, and for different entrées. The head is used for soup—Mock Turtle Soup—and the feet for making jelly—Calf's Foot Jelly.

Sweetbread.—This is considered a great delicacy, and is generally expensive. It is much used for entrées, and is a favourite dish for invalids. The throat sweetbread, which is the thymus gland of the calf, is considered inferior in quality to the heart sweetbread.

Kidney.—Generally sold along with a piece of the loin and roasted. Can also be used separately in the same way as sheep's kidneys.

Brains.—A very delicate morsel for entrées.

Liver and Heart.—Can be used in the same way as sheep's liver and heart.

MUTTON

The following diagram will give an idea of the different joints into which mutton is cut:—

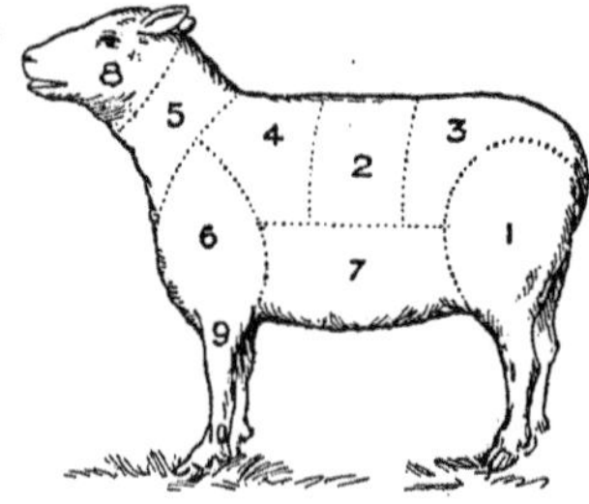

Diagram showing mode of cutting up a Sheep.

1. Leg.
2. Loin.
3. Chump end of the Loin.
4. Neck (best end).
5. Scrag.
6. Shoulder.
7. Breast.
8. Head.
9. Shank.
10. Trotter.

The Leg.—This is one of the most economical cuts for boiling or roasting, as it is lean with a small amount of bone in proportion to its size. It is too large a joint for a small family. It is sometimes a good plan to have it cut in two pieces and to roast one piece and boil or stew the other. When a piece of the loin is cut along with the leg it is called the haunch.

The Loin.—This is generally divided into two parts, the best end and the chump end, or even subdivided into separate cutlets or chops. The loin makes one of the finest and most delicate roasts, but it is not economical owing to the large proportion of fat and bone. If ordering for a roast it must be well jointed by the butcher or it will be found difficult to carve, or sometimes the chine bone, the bone which runs down the centre of the back, is sawn nearly off and then removed altogether after cooking. The double loin from both sides of the animal is called the saddle. It is considered a very fine joint, but too large for an ordinary household.

The Neck.—The best end of the neck is also used for cutlets. It is an excellent piece for broiling and braising, as it is tender and delicate in flavour. The scrag-end, which lies nearer the head, is a cheap piece of an awkward shape and contains a good deal of bone. It is only suitable for broth or plain stews as it is impossible to cut it in neat pieces.

The Shoulder.—This is another good joint for roasting, and some people prefer it to the leg. It is perhaps more delicate in flavour, but is inclined to be fat. It can also be braised or boiled.

The Breast.—Is a cheap piece of mutton with much fat and skin. If boned, stuffed, and rolled it makes quite a nice little roast. It is also very suitable for Irish stew where the potatoes absorb some of the fat.

The Head and Trotters are generally sold at a low price, but they make excellent broth, and can also be served as a dish by themselves with a good sauce or made into a pie and served cold.

The Pluck.—This consists of the heart, liver and lungs, which are often sold together. In Scotland they form the foundation of haggis. The lungs, or lights, are very inferior, and by themselves are seldom used, except perhaps as cats' meat. The heart is sometimes sold by itself, and is very good stuffed and roasted. The liver can also be bought separately, and is generally fried or sautéed along with a little bacon.

Kidneys.—These are very dainty morsels and are a favourite breakfast delicacy. They are generally broiled or stewed, and are also used along with beef in pies and stews. The loin roast often contains one of the kidneys.

LAMB

When lamb is large it is usually cut up and used in the same way as mutton, but when small it is cut in quarters. The fore-quarter consists of the neck, shoulder, and breast, and the hind-quarter of the leg and the loin.

If the hind-quarter makes too large a joint the upper part may be cut into chops and served as one dish, while the lower portion will make a nice little roast or may be steamed and served with a good sauce. Or a larger-sized piece may be cut off the top and made into a stew or braised.

The fore-quarter may be divided in the same way, the breast piece being stewed or braised and the shoulder roasted. The chops from the neck may also be cut off separately and either broiled or fried or used for hotch-potch.

Lamb's Head can be used in the same way as sheep's head and is more delicate in flavour.

Lamb's Fry, consisting of the liver, sweetbread, and heart, is generally cut in slices and fried. The sweetbreads alone are considered a great delicacy and are much used for entrées.

PORK

Diagram showing different cuts of Pork.

1. Spare Rib.
2. Hand.
3. Spring or Belly.
4. Fore-loin.
5. Loin.
6. Leg.

The usual joints of fresh pork are the following:—

The Loin is generally scored and roasted. Pork chops are also cut from this part.

Leg.—Another piece for roasting. The skin must always be scored by the butcher, or it would be impossible to carve the joint. It is sometimes salted and then boiled.

The Hand and Spring or Belly.—These parts are rather fat, and are usually salted. They are best boiled and served cold.

Head.—Usually salted. Can be made into brawn or boiled and served cold.

Feet (Pettitoes) can be cooked in various ways. Usually boiled or stewed.

The Tongue should be pickled and then served in the same way as sheep's tongue.

VENISON

The finest joint for roasting is the **Haunch.** The **Loin** and **Neck** are also good roasting pieces.

The **Shoulder** and **Breast** are better stewed or made into a ragoût. Chops are usually cut from the loin or neck and steaks from the leg.

FROZEN MEAT

Large quantities of meat are now imported from abroad in a frozen condition and sold in this country at a considerably lower price than that of home production. New Zealand, Australia, the United States, S. America, and Canada all send us in supplies.

The prejudice against this kind of meat has to a large extent disappeared, and it is certainly an immense boon to those who cannot afford the high prices asked for our home-fed meat.

Needless to say, this foreign meat does not equal British meat as far as quality and flavour are concerned; the process of freezing apparently takes away from its goodness, but with careful thawing and good cooking it compares very favourably with the more expensive joints, and in many cases it requires an experienced palate to detect the difference.

Mutton and lamb seem to suffer less than beef from the process of freezing. That known as Canterbury lamb is the best. When ordering frozen meat it must be remembered that it will not keep in warm weather without a refrigerator.

HOW TO CHOOSE FISH

General Hints.—Fish to be good ought to be in season.

Moderately-sized fish are better than very large ones, especially those which are thick and plump in proportion to their size. A short thick fish is always better than one that is long and thin.

There are several signs by which its freshness can be judged; the fish should be firm and stiff, and when held up the tail should not droop; but this alone is not sufficient sign, as fish kept on ice will retain its rigidity although several days old, so we must look for other signs as well.

The gills in fresh fish are a bright red, the eyes are bright and not sunken, and the scales also are bright and can be easily removed when rubbed.

A flat fish should never be bought without looking at both sides, and especially the grey side, as this betrays any want of freshness more quickly than the white.

A plaice, for instance, can always be judged by its spots; when fresh they are a bright red, and after it has been kept some time they take a brownish hue.

In choosing cut fish, such as cod, halibut, or salmon, &c., the flesh should have a firm appearance with a close grain; if it looks fibrous and watery it is not good.

Never choose fish that is bruised or has the skin broken, as it will not keep well.

CALENDAR OF FISH IN SEASON

January.—Barbel, bream, brill, carp, cod, dory, eels, flounders, gurnet, haddock, halibut, hake, herring, ling, mackerel, perch, pike, plaice, skate, smelts, soles, sprats, sturgeon, tench, thornback, turbot, whitebait, whiting.

Crabs, crayfish, lobsters, mussels, oysters, scallops, shrimps.

February.—Bream, brill, carp, cod, dory, eels, flounders, gurnets, haddock, halibut, herring, ling, mackerel, mullet, plaice, perch, pike, salmon, skate, smelts, soles, sprats, sturgeon, tench, thornback, trout, turbot, whitebait, whiting.

Crab, crayfish, lobsters, mussels, oysters, prawns, scallops, shrimps.

March.—Bream, brill, carp, cod, eels, flounders, gurnets, haddock, halibut, herring, ling, mackerel, mullet, pike, salmon, skate, smelts, soles, sprats (tench until 15th), thornback, trout, turbot, whiting, whitebait.

Crabs, crayfish, lobsters, mussels, oysters, prawns, scallops, shrimps.

April.—Bream, brill, chub, conger eel, cod, dory, flounders, gurnet, haddock, halibut, herring, ling, mackerel, mullet, plaice, salmon, shad, skate, smelts, soles, sturgeon, turbot, trout, whitebait, whiting.

Crabs, crayfish, lobsters, mussels, oysters, prawns, scallops, shrimps.

May.—Bass, brill, cod, dace, dory, eels, gurnet, hake, halibut, herring, ling, mackerel, mullet, salmon, shad, skate, smelts, soles, sturgeon, trout, turbot, whitebait, whiting.

Crabs, crayfish, lobsters, prawns, scallops, shrimps.

June.—Bass, bream, brill, carp, chub, cod, dace, dory, eels, flounders, gurnets, halibut, hake, haddock, herring, lampreys, mackerel, mullet, perch (after 15th), pike, plaice, salmon, shad, soles, tench, trout, turbot, whitebait, whiting.

Crabs, crayfish, lobsters, prawns, shrimps.

July.—Bass, bream, brill, carp, chub, dace, dory, eels, flounders, gurnets, haddock, hake, halibut, herring, mackerel, mullet, perch, pike, plaice, salmon, sea-bream, shad, smelts, soles, tench, thornback, trout, turbot, whitebait, whiting.

Crabs, crayfish, lobsters, prawns, shrimps.

August.—Bass, bream, brill, carp, chub, dace, dory, eels, flounders, gurnets, haddock, hake, halibut, herring, lamprey, mackerel, mullet, plaice, perch, pike, salmon, sea-bream, shad, soles, tench, trout, turbot, whitebait, whiting.

Crabs, crayfish, lobsters, prawns, shrimps.

September.—Bass, bream, brill, carp, cod, chub, dace, dory, eels, flounders, gurnet, haddock, hake, halibut, herring, lampreys, mackerel, mullet, perch, pike, plaice, salmon, sea-bream, shad, smelts, soles, tench, trout, turbot, whitebait, whiting.

Crabs, crayfish, lobsters, oysters, shrimps.

October.—Bream, brill, carp, cod, dory, eels, flounders, gurnet, haddock, halibut, herring, mackerel, mullet, perch, pike, plaice, salmon, sea-bream, skate, soles, smelts, tench, turbot, whiting.

Crabs, crayfish, lobsters, mussels, oysters, scallops, shrimps.

November.—Bream, brill, carp, cod, dory, flounders, eels, gurnet, haddock, halibut, herring, mackerel, mullet, perch, pike, plaice, salmon (Dutch), skate, smelts, sprats, soles, tench, turbot, whiting.

Crabs, crayfish, lobsters, mussels, oysters, scallops, shrimps.

December.—Brill, carp, cod, eels, flounders, gurnets, haddock, halibut, herring, mackerel, mullet, perch, pike, plaice, salmon (Dutch), sea-bream, skate, smelt, sprats, soles, tench, whiting.

Crabs, crayfish, lobsters, mussels, oysters, scallops, shrimps.

ON CHOOSING GAME AND POULTRY

General Rules for Choosing Poultry.—All poultry when young should have smooth and pliable legs, with the scales overlapping very slightly. The spur on the leg must be short and not prominent, and the feet should be soft and rather moist. If the spur is large and the legs hard and dry the bird is no longer young. The flesh should be smooth and without long hairs. When choosing a bird that has not been plucked it should be seen that the plumage is smooth and downy with soft young feathers under the wing and on the breast. If freshly killed the eyes will be clear and not sunken; there will be no discoloration of the flesh and the vent will be hard and close.

When poultry is bought quite fresh it may be hung for a few days, but should not be drawn until about to be used. It must never be over-hung, and when it shows the least sign of turning green it is unfit for food.

Fowls.—The comb should be smooth and of a bright red colour. For roasting choose a fowl with black or yellow legs, as they are supposed to be more juicy and to possess a better flavour. For boiling, choose one with white legs, as the flesh will likely be whiter.

A fowl for roasting, frying, or grilling should be young and tender, but for boiling, braising, or stewing an older one may be taken, as old birds are generally cheaper, and long slow cooking makes them tender.

Geese and Ducks.—Young birds have yellow feet and bills with few bristles; as they get older they become darker and redder, although the wild duck has small reddish feet even when young. The feet should be white and smooth and without wrinkles. A goose must always be eaten young; when over twelve months old it is not good for table use.

Pigeons.—A dark-coloured one is thought to have the highest flavour, and a light-coloured one the most delicate. The legs should be of a pinkish colour; when they are large and deeply coloured the bird is old. The tame pigeon is smaller than the wild species and is better for cooking. Tame pigeons should be cooked at once as they soon lose their flavour, but wood pigeons may be hung for a few days.

Turkeys.—A good turkey will be recognised by the whiteness of its flesh and its smooth black legs. The wattles should be a bright red, the breast full and the neck long. Beware of those with long hairs and flesh of a violet hue. A moderate-sized bird should be chosen. A hen is preferable for boiling on account of the whiteness of the flesh, and the cock is usually chosen for roasting.

If freshly killed it should be kept for at least three or four days before cooking or it will neither be white not tender. It should be hung up to bleed.

Norfolk turkeys are considered the best.

Game.—It is rather more difficult to choose game than it is to choose poultry, as the birds are usually sold unplucked, but still some of the same signs will hold good. The young birds are known by their smooth and pliable legs and short rounded spurs. The feet should be supple and moist and easily broken. The feathers also help to indicate the age of the bird, as when young there are soft and downy ones under the wing and on the breast. The plumage of the young bird is even and soft, the long feathers of the wings are pointed, while in the older bird these become round and the colours are usually brighter.

The condition of the bird can be judged by turning back the feathers of the breast and seeing if it feels plump and hard; it should also weigh heavy for its size.

As regards the time for keeping game, it is impossible to lay down any definite rules. To begin with it depends very much upon individual taste, those who have it seldom as a rule liking it higher than those who are constantly having it. Then old birds can be hung for a longer time than young ones, and again the weather must be taken into consideration; close muggy days will not be so good for keeping purposes as those which are dry and cold.

Game should be hung unplucked and undrawn and in a current of air if possible. It must be remembered that if it is required to taste high when cooked, it should smell almost offensively so beforehand.

Water birds should always be eaten fresh, as their flesh, being of an oily nature, very soon becomes sour.

Hares and Rabbits.—When young the claws are long and pointed, the cleft in the jaws is very narrow, the teeth are small and white, and the ears can easily be torn. The small nut under the paw should also be well developed. When the animal is old the claws become rounded and rough, the cleft in the jaw deepens, the front teeth are long and yellow, and the ears become tough and dry, and the little nut under the paw disappears.

Rabbits, like poultry, should be used fresh. Choose one that is plump and short-necked, and the flesh should be stiff without any discoloration. Wild rabbits are generally preferred to tame ones, as they are considered to have a better flavour. The flesh of the tame rabbit is white and more delicate. A rabbit should be paunched before it is hung up.

Hares, on the contrary, require to be well hung —at least a week—and should not be paunched until about to be used.

CALENDAR OF POULTRY AND GAME IN SEASON

The following will be found useful for ready reference:—

January. — Capons, capercailzie, chickens, ducks, fowls, geese, hares, larks, landrails, partridges, pheasants, pigeons, pintail, plover, pullets, snipe, turkeys, wild-fowl, widgeon, woodcock.

February. — Capons, capercailzie, chickens, ducks, fowls, geese, hares, larks, landrails, partridges, pheasants, pigeons, pintail, plover, ptarmigan, pullets, prairie-hen, rabbits, snipe, turkeys, teal, wild-fowl, widgeon, woodcock.

March.—Capons, capercailzie, chickens, ducks, fowls, geese, guinea-fowls, hares, landrails, ortolans (partridges, pheasants, and plover until middle of month), prairie-hens, ptarmigan, pigeons, pullets, quail, rabbits, ruffs and reeves, snipe (until 15th), teal, turkeys, widgeon, wild-fowl, woodcock.

April.—Capons, chickens, ducks, ducklings, fowls, guinea-fowls, goslings, hares, leverets, ortolans, prairie-hens, pigeons, ptarmigan, quail, rabbit, ruffs and reeves.

May.—Capons, chickens, ducks, ducklings, fowls, guinea-fowls, goslings, green geese, hares, leverets, ortolans, pigeons, ptarmigan, pullets, quail, rabbits, ruffs and reeves.

June.—Capons, chickens, ducks, ducklings, fowls, guinea-fowls, goslings, green geese, hares, hazel hens, leverets, ortolans, pigeons, pullets, quails, rabbits, ruffs and reeves, turkey poults, wheatears.

July.—Capons, chickens, ducks, ducklings, fowls, green geese, goslings, hares, leverets, ortolans, pigeons, plover, pullets, quail, rabbits, ruffs and reeves, turkey poults, wheatears.

August.—Capercailzie, capons, chickens, wild and tame ducks, ducklings, fowls, geese, goslings, grouse (on 12th), hares, larks, leverets, pigeons, plover, pullets, quails, rabbits, snipe, teal, turkey poults, woodcock, wheatears.

September.—Capercailzie, capons, chickens, wild and tame ducks, fowls, geese, grouse, hares, larks, leverets, moor-game, partridges, pheasants, pigeons, plovers, pullets, rabbits, snipe, turkeys, turkey poults, teal, widgeon, woodcock, wheatears.

October.—Black game, capercailzie, capons, chickens, wild ducks, fowls, geese, grouse, hares, larks, partridges, pheasants, pigeons, pintails, plover, ptarmigan, pullets, rabbits, snipe, turkeys, turkey poults, teal, widgeon, woodcock.

November.—Black game, capercailzie, capons, chickens, wild and tame ducks, fowls, geese, grouse, hares, larks, landrails, partridges, pheasants, pigeons, pintails, plover, ptarmigan, pullets, rabbits, snipe, turkeys, turkey poults, teal, widgeon, woodcock.

December.—Black game, capercailzie (until 20th), capons, chickens, ducks, fowls, geese, grouse (until 18th), hares, landrails, larks, partridges, pheasants, pintail, plover, ptarmigan, rabbits, snipe, teal, turkeys, turkey poults, widgeon, woodcock.

THE CHOOSING OF FRUIT AND VEGETABLES

Although it does not require much experience to tell when fruit and vegetables are fresh, it does require some attention and care to see that one is served with the proper article.

Vegetables are never so good as when procured fresh from a garden, and when one is not the happy possessor of a piece of ground it is sometimes possible to make an arrangement with a gardener or farmer to send a supply two or three times weekly, if not daily.

If vegetables and fruit have to be bought from a shop personal choice is always preferable to a written order. The greengrocer or fruiterer is naturally anxious to get rid of his stock, and it is not to be wondered at if he tries to dispose of the articles he has had longest before selling those which are fresh.

The careful housewife will, however, insist upon getting what is really fresh and will accept nothing that is doubtful.

Salads and other green vegetables especially are only good when newly gathered; if they have been lying packed one on top of the other for any length of time they become unwholesome, and this is often the cause of green vegetables disagreeing with people who have a weak digestion.

Cauliflowers should be close and very white, and those of a medium size are best; avoid those that have a greenish colour.

Brussels Sprouts and Cabbages should be close and firm with plenty of heart. Young cabbages are the most delicate in flavour.

Cucumbers and Vegetable Marrows should also be firm, and those of a medium size and straight in form are to be preferred to the twisted and overgrown specimens.

Tomatoes must not be over-ripe. The home-grown red tomatoes are best for salads and for eating raw, while the foreign ones, which are cheaper, are excellent for cooking purposes.

Peas and Beans are best when they are young, especially if they are to be served separately as vegetables to accompany meat. The older ones can be served in soups and stews.

Celery should be chosen of a medium size, and the stalks must be very stiff and close together. The whiter it is the better.

Root Vegetables, unlike green vegetables, may be kept for some time without suffering in any way; they must, however, be firm and not withered or shrunken. Some kinds, such as potatoes, carrots, turnips, and parsnips can even be stored for winter use (see p. 102). Potatoes, for instance, can often be bought very cheaply by the sack in the summer, and there may be a distinct advantage in laying in a store at this season. There must, of course, be the proper accommodation for keeping them, and the greatest care must be taken to see that they are sound and good when bought.

It is always best to buy the vegetables that are in season; they are then at their cheapest and best. The early and forced varieties rarely have the same flavour as those of maturer growth and should not be bought by the thrifty housewife for the ordinary bill of fare.

The same care must be taken in the choice of fruit, and only that which is perfectly sound should be accepted. When it is to be eaten raw it ought to be fully ripe without being overmuch so.

CALENDAR OF FRUIT IN SEASON

January.—Almonds, apples, bananas, chestnuts, figs, grapes, lemons, medlars, nuts, oranges, pears, pines, Spanish nuts, walnuts, &c.

February.—Almonds, apples, bananas, chestnuts, figs, grapes, lemons, medlars, nuts, oranges, peaches, pears, pines, rhubarb (forced), Spanish nuts, walnuts, &c.

March.—Almonds, apples, bananas, chestnuts, figs, grapes, lemons, melons, nuts, oranges, peaches, pears, pines, rhubarb (forced), Spanish nuts, walnuts, &c.

April.—Almonds, apples, bananas, dried fruits, figs, grapes, nuts, oranges, pines, rhubarb, &c.

May.—Almonds, apples, apricots (forced), bananas, cherries (forced), dried fruits, figs, grapes, green gooseberries, melons, oranges, pears, pines, rhubarb, &c.

June.—Almonds, apples, apricots, bananas, cherries, currants, figs, gooseberries, grapes, melons, nectarines, peaches, pears, pines, raspberries, rhubarb, strawberries, &c.

July.—Almonds, apricots, bananas, cherries, currants, damsons, figs, gooseberries, grapes, melons, nectarines, oranges, peaches, pears, pineapples, plums, raspberries, strawberries, &c.

August.—Almonds, apricots, bananas, cherries, cobnuts, currants, damsons, figs, filberts, grapes, greengages, medlars, melons, mulberries, nectarines, oranges, peaches, pears, pines, plums, raspberries, strawberries, walnuts, &c.

September.—Almonds, apples, apricots, bananas, cherries, cobnuts, damsons, figs, filberts, grapes, greengages, melons, medlars, mulberries, nectarines, oranges, peaches, pears, pines, plums, quinces, walnuts, &c.

October.—Almonds, apples, apricots, bananas, cobnuts, cranberries, cocoanuts, damsons, figs, filberts, grapes, medlars, melons, nectarines, oranges, peaches, pears, pines, quinces, walnuts, &c.

November.—Almonds, apples, bananas, chestnuts, cocoanuts, cranberries, figs, filberts, grapes, melons, nuts (various), pears, pines, pomegranates, plums (Californian), quinces, walnuts, &c.

December.—Almonds, apples, bananas, chestnuts, cocoanuts, cranberries, figs, filberts, grapes, melons, nuts (various), oranges, pears, pines, plums (Californian), pomegranates, rhubarb (forced), walnuts, &c.

CALENDAR OF VEGETABLES IN SEASON.

January.—Artichokes, beetroot, broccoli, Brussels sprouts, cabbage, cardoons, carrots, celery, chervil, cress, cucumbers, endive, leeks, lettuce, onions, parsnips, potatoes, salsify, savoys, spinach, tomatoes, turnips.

February.—Artichokes, beetroot, broccoli, Brussels sprouts, cabbage, celery, chervil, cress, cucumbers, endive, greens, leeks, lettuce, mushrooms, potatoes, onions, parsnips, salsify, Scotch kale, savoys, sorrel, spinach, tomatoes, turnips.

March.—Artichokes, asparagus, beetroot, broccoli, Brussels sprouts, cabbage, cardoons, carrots, cauliflower, celery, chervil, cucumber, endive, greens, horse-radish, leeks, lettuce, mushrooms, onions, parsnips, new potatoes, radishes, savoys, spinach, sea and Scotch kale, turnips, tomatoes, watercress.

April.—Artichokes, asparagus, beetroot, cabbage, cauliflower, celery, cucumber, endive, eschalots, leeks, lettuce, mushrooms, spring onions, parsnips, new potatoes, radishes, sea-kale, spinach, sprouts, tomatoes, turnips.

May.—Artichokes, asparagus, beans, beetroot, cabbage, new carrots, cauliflower, chervil, cucumbers, endive, lettuce, leeks, mushrooms, mustard and cress, peas, new potatoes, spring onions, radishes, sea-kale, spinach, turnips, watercress.

June.—Artichokes, asparagus, beans, beetroot, cabbage, new carrots, cucumbers, endive, greens, leeks, lettuce, mushrooms, parsnips, peas, new potatoes, spring onions, radishes, sea-kale, spinach, tomatoes, turnips, vegetable marrow, watercress.

July.—Artichokes, asparagus, beans, beetroot, broad beans, cabbage, carrots, cauliflower, chervil, cress, cucumber, endive, leeks, lettuce, mushrooms, spring onions, peas, new potatoes, scarlet runners, spinach, tomatoes, turnips, vegetable marrow, watercress.

August.—Artichokes, beans, beetroot, cabbage, carrots, cauliflower, celery, cress, cucumbers, endive, leeks, lettuce, mushrooms, peas, potatoes, salsify, scarlet runners, spinach, tomatoes, turnips, vegetable marrow, watercress.

September.—Artichokes, beans, beetroot, cabbage, carrots, cauliflower, celery, cress, cucumber, endive, leeks, lettuce, mushrooms, parsnips, peas, salsify, scarlet runners, spinach, sprouts, tomatoes, turnips, vegetable marrow, watercress.

October.—Artichokes, beetroot, cabbage, carrots, cauliflower, celery, cucumber, greens, leeks, lettuce, mushrooms, parsnips, savoys, scarlet runners, Spanish onions, spinach, sprouts, tomatoes, turnips, vegetable marrow, watercress.

November.—Artichokes, beetroot, Brussels sprouts, carrots, celery, cress, cucumber, greens, leeks, lettuce, parsnips, savoys, Spanish onions, spinach, tomatoes, turnip tops, watercress.

December.—Artichokes, beetroot, broccoli, Brussels sprouts, cabbage, carrots, cauliflower, celery, cucumber, greens, leeks, parsnips, salsify, savoys, Scotch and sea-kale, Spanish onions, tomatoes, turnip tops, vegetable marrow, watercress.

IMPERIAL WEIGHTS AND MEASURES

Avoirdupois Weight

16 drachms (dr.)	make	1 ounce (oz.).
16 ounces	„	1 pound (lb.).
28 pounds	„	1 quarter (qr.).
4 quarters	„	1 hundredweight (cwt.).
20 hundredweights	„	1 ton.

14 pounds	make	1 stone.
8 stones	„	1 hundredweight.
112 pounds	„	1 hundredweight.

Liquid Measure of Capacity

4 gills	make	1 pint (pt.).
2 pints	„	1 quart (qrt.).
4 quarts	„	1 gallon (gal.).

Dry Measure of Capacity

2 gallons	make	1 peck (pk.).
4 pecks	„	1 bushel (bush.).
8 bushels	„	1 quarter (qr.).

GUIDE TO COOKERY

It is a very mistaken idea that good cooking is necessarily an expensive matter. On the contrary, it is the skilful cook who literally "gathers up the fragments that nothing may be lost," and the careless one who looks upon them as trifles not worthy of consideration.

We as a nation are very much behindhand in our cooking arrangements, and it is only now that we are beginning to realise that training in the subject should form an important branch of every girl's education.

It is Hamerton who says that "Intellectual labour is in its origin as dependent upon the art of cookery as the dissemination of its results is dependent upon paper-making and printing. Cookery in its perfection—the great science of preparing food in the best way suited to our use—is really the most important of all sciences and the mother of the arts."

In the following paragraphs elaborate dishes which require the skill of a professed cook, very expensive dishes and dishes which take a long time to prepare have been purposely excluded, and only those given which are within the power of the amateur and home-worker. It cannot be too emphatically urged, however, that to ensure success great care is needed in the preparation of every dish.

The cook, whether professional or amateur, owes something to the author of the recipes she uses, and that debt is not discharged if the recipes are carelessly read and carelessly followed. Nearly every one has heard the remark, "I am sure I don't know why the dish is like this—the recipe must be wrong." The recipe cannot reply: can only defend itself by success, and so in the interests of fair play it ought to receive just treatment. Accuracy in the weighing and measuring of ingredients must be strongly insisted upon. Cooking may be an art, but it is also a science, and to ensure success we must be exact. There must be no guess-work. An ounce more or less may bring ruin on your labours.

Let all your materials be good of their kind, and do not of set purpose substitute one ingredient for another.

See also that the fire is in good condition for the cooking required of it, or that the oven is in a fair way to be at the right heat by the time you are ready to use it.

Lastly, do not scorn those little details of arrangement which add nothing to the taste, but only to the tastefulness of the dish. A little fresh parsley, a lace-edged paper, a sprinkling of sugar, &c., may make all the difference between a tempting and an untempting dish.

STOCKS, SOUPS, AND PURÉES

General Remarks on Stocks and Soups.—It is quite an art to make a good soup, but it is an art easily mastered if only a little care and trouble are expended upon its acquirement.

There are few things, whether fish, flesh, fowl or vegetable, which will not lend themselves to soup-making. The variety of soups is very great; in fact, it has been reckoned that there are over half a thousand different recipes. This number, however, is obtained by giving a separate title to every separate variation of a combination. For example, clear stock, which is the basis of so many clear soups, will take a different name from each special garnish or flavouring that is added to it, and the same throughout with the other soups—the slightest variations will furnish the occasion for a distinctive name. When the numerous recipes come to be examined, it will be found that, broadly speaking, they can be classified under one of the three following headings:—

(1) Clear Soups and Broths.
(2) Thickened Soups.
(3) Purées.

An explanation of these different classes of soups is given below, along with a few typical recipes, which ought to serve as a guide to the other varieties.

The excellence of the soup will depend to a large extent upon slow and steady cooking and to the judicious introduction of the flavouring. Although all soup should be sufficiently seasoned before it is sent to table, salt must always be added with care, as an over-salted soup can be relished by no one.

In the following recipes the approximate amount of liquid required is always given, but the exact quantity will depend somewhat upon the rate of cooking. If the soup becomes too much reduced by boiling and, consequently, too thick, more water or stock must be added to make up the original allowance.

The vegetables, too, are always spoken of as *prepared*, and full directions for doing this will be found under the heading of "Vegetables."

STOCK

Stock is the foundation of nearly all soups, and it can be made from fresh meat, bones, fish, vegetables, or scraps of cooked meat and bones, &c.

For the better soups, such as clear soup and good white soup, fresh meat is required, while second stock or general stock will serve as the foundation for many of the ordinary soups, and, besides furnishing the liquid part of stews, whether white or brown, it will go a long way towards making gravies and sauces a success.

There are different kinds of stock, *i.e.* brown, white, and fish stock, meat boilings and general stock. Of brown stock and white stock both a first and second stock can be made.

Brown stock is made principally from beef with sometimes a little veal or some chicken bones added.

White stock is made from any white meat such as veal, rabbit, or chicken.

First stock is the first boiling of the meat and vegetables.

Second stock is produced by putting the meat and vegetables on to boil a second time with fresh water.

Fish stock, as its name implies, is made from fish or fish trimmings.

Meat boilings is the name given to the water in which a joint of meat, fowl, or rabbit has been boiled.

General stock is made from scraps of meat, bones, and vegetables, and drawn from a stock-pot.

FIRST STOCK FOR CLEAR AND BROWN SOUPS

Ingredients—

3 lbs. Shin of Beef or 2 lbs. Shin of Beef and 1 lb. Knuckle of Veal.
3 quarts Cold Water.
1 Carrot.
1 Turnip.
1 tea-spoonful Mixed Herbs or a sprig of Thyme, Marjoram, and Basil.
2 small Onions.
2 or 3 sticks of Celery or ½ tea-spoonful Celery Seed.
2 dozen Peppercorns.
8 Cloves.
1 blade of Mace.
2 Bay Leaves.
A few Parsley Stalks.
dessert-spoonful Salt.

Method.—Wipe the meat with a damp cloth, and remove all marrow from the bone. Take a very sharp knife and cut the meat into small pieces, keeping back any fat, but using the skin. Put the bones and meat into a stock-pot or large goblet with the cold water and salt, and if time permits let them soak for half-an-hour; then put the pan on the fire, and bring the contents slowly to the boil. Simmer slowly for half-an-hour, and then remove any scum that may be on the top. If you begin the skimming too soon, the best part of the stock is removed. Next add the vegetables, prepared and cut rather small, and the herbs, celery seed, and peppercorns, &c., tied in a small piece of muslin. Simmer slowly from four and a half to five hours, never letting it go off the boil; then strain through a hair sieve or cloth stretched over a colander into a basin, and stand until cold.

A darker-coloured stock may be obtained by frying the meat in a little dripping or butter before pouring on the water; but the present fashion is to have clear soups pale in colour.

Meat boilings may be used instead of water for making this stock, and any uncooked chicken bones would improve the flavour. Do not throw away the meat and vegetables left after straining, but put them on again with same quantity of water as before, and boil again for *Second Stock.*

FIRST STOCK FOR WHITE SOUPS

Ingredients—

3 lbs. Knuckle of Veal or 2 lbs. Knuckle of Veal and 1 lb. Neck of Mutton.
3 quarts Cold Water.
½ Carrot.
½ Turnip.
1 Onion.
12 White Peppercorns.
1 stick of Celery, or ¼ tea-spoonful Celery Seed.
6 or 8 Cloves.
½ tea-spoonful Mixed Herbs or a small sprig of Thyme, Marjoram, and Basil.
1 blade of Mace.
2 Bay Leaves.
1 dessert-spoonful Salt.

Method.—Make in the same way as first stock for brown soup (see above), but use fewer vegetables, as they tend to discolour the stock. Rabbit or chicken may be used instead of, or along with, the veal. Any white meat will do. A piece of lean ham or a small ham-bone will improve the flavour.

A second stock may be taken from the meat and bones.

SECOND STOCK

After first stock is made, the meat and vegetables should be put on again with the same quantity of water and boiled as before.

It has not the same fresh flavour as first stock, but it is most useful in the making of sauces and gravies, and of many soups for which very good stock is not required.

Second stock is generally a stiffer jelly than first, as more of the gelatine becomes extracted from the bones.

Sometimes the meat and vegetables are fried

in a little dripping first. This gives the stock a darker colour and a richer flavour.

FISH STOCK

Ingredients—

2 lbs. of White Fish or Fish Bones and Trimmings.
2 quarts Cold Water.
1 small Carrot.
1 small Turnip.
1 Onion.
1 stick of Celery or ½ tea-spoonful Celery Seed.
½ tea-spoonful Mixed Herbs or a sprig of Thyme, Marjoram, and Basil.
A few Parsley Stalks.
1 dozen Peppercorns.
3 Cloves.
1 blade of Mace.
1 Bay Leaf.
1 dessert-spoonful Salt.

Method.—Any white fish or trimmings of white fish, such as haddocks, cod, halibut, plaice, flounder, ling, &c., may be used for fish stock. Fish such as mackerel, herring, and salmon are of too oily a nature and too strong in flavour. By fish trimmings is meant the bones, heads, fins, and skins of fish. If a light-coloured stock is wanted, avoid using too much dark-coloured skin. Wash the fish or trimmings thoroughly in cold water, and cut them into small pieces. Put them into a fish-kettle or large goblet with the water and salt. Put the lid on the pan, and bring to the boil; then skim well, and simmer about fifteen minutes before adding the vegetables. As more scum rises remove it, or the stock will be cloudy in appearance. Prepare the vegetables, cut them rather small, and add them to the stock with the herbs, celery seed, peppercorns, &c., tied in a small piece of muslin. Simmer slowly from three to four hours, then strain into a basin.

This stock may be used as a basis for all fish soups and fish sauces.

A whiter stock may be obtained by using half milk and half water, fewer vegetables, and by straining after half-an-hour's slow simmering.

VEGETABLE STOCK

Ingredients—

2 Onions.
2 medium-sized Carrots.
1 medium-sized Turnip.
2 sticks Celery.
2 quarts Water.
Salt.
3 oz. Lentils.
A sprig of Parsley.
" Thyme.
" Marjoram.
12 Black Peppercorns.
1 blade Mace.
3 or 4 Cloves.

Method.—Prepare the vegetables and cut them in pieces. Put them in a saucepan with the water and seasoning, and boil all together for two or three hours. More water must be added if the liquid becomes too much reduced. Skim well, strain, and it is ready for use.

Note.—Almost any kind of vegetable may be used for making this stock, and the more variety the better. The trimmings and even the parings of vegetables can be utilised in this way, only care must be taken to see that they are thoroughly clean and fresh.

GENERAL STOCK—THE STOCK-POT

In every household where meat is used every day a stock-pot should be in general use. A regular stock-pot is made of tinned copper, tinned iron, aluminium, or cast iron. In large houses where much cooking is done it is better to have one fitted with a tap, which will permit of the

Stock-Pot.

liquid being drawn off when required without disturbing the fat, which rises to the top. For small households an ordinary tinned or silicated saucepan will serve the purpose very well, or what is known as a digester, which is made of cast iron with a close-fitting lid. This latter is not expensive, but it has the disadvantage of being very heavy. An earthenware casserole or marmite is also to be recommended for small quantities of stock; it is very clean, and it is easy to keep the contents simmering at a gentle rate.

All scraps of meat, cooked or uncooked, bones and pieces of vegetable, poultry giblets and rinds of bacon, should be kept for making stock.

Earthenware Casserole.

Remains of gravy too should be saved for the same purpose, although no thickened sauce must be added, as it would cloud the stock.

Look over the scraps carefully and see that they are all clean and free from taint. Break up the bones, remove any fat from the meat, and cut the vegetables in small pieces. Put them into the stock-pot with cold water to cover them, or the water in which meat or vegetables (except potatoes or cabbage) have been cooked may be used. Add a little salt, put on the lid, and bring the contents slowly to the boil. Then keep the stock slowly simmering at an even temperature, taking off the lid from time to time in order to remove the scum. A few washed and crushed egg-shells put into the stock will help to clear it. One whole day's cooking will be sufficient, and at night it must be strained through a hair sieve into a basin and allowed to cool. The stock-pot should be thoroughly washed before it is used again.

The bones and any pieces of meat of value may be put on the next day with any fresh scraps, but not the vegetables if they have been boiled for long, because when the flavour of these has been extracted they become worse than useless, and only absorb the meaty flavours.

Nothing must be added to a stock-pot unless it is quite clean and contains some goodness. Little bits must not be added at odd times, but only when the stock-pot is put on for the day; all other pieces should be saved for the next day's use.

Stock should always be made the day before it is required, as by this means the fat can easily be removed.

To Remove Fat from Stock.—Have in readiness two iron spoons, a basin of boiling water, a cloth, and a small basin or dish into which to put the fat.

Heat the spoons in the boiling water, and use first one and then the other to skim off the fat. The spoons, being hot, melt the fat, and make it much more easily removed.

When as much as possible has been taken off with the spoons, dip the end of the cloth into boiling water, and wipe the stock over with this until quite free from grease. If the stock is not a jelly, pieces of kitchen paper must be passed over the top of it instead of the cloth.

Do not remove fat from stock or soup until it is about to be used, as it keeps out the air and helps to preserve it.

GLAZE

Glaze can either be bought by the ounce or made at home from stock. Glaze, as a rule, costs 2d. per ounce, and this quantity will be sufficient to glaze an ox-tongue or a fair-sized piece of meat. Put the glaze into a small saucepan with sufficient water or stock to cover it, and allow it to melt slowly over the fire. Or put it into a jar with a very little water or stock, and stand the jar in a saucepan of boiling water until the glaze is melted. It will then be ready for use.

Home-made glaze can be very easily procured in houses where there are large quantities of stock and bones at disposal. Any good brown stock can be used, and the second boilings from meat and bones is almost preferable to freshly-made stock, as it is more gelatinous. Free the stock from all grease, and put at least one quart into a saucepan. Allow this to boil quickly with the lid off the pan until reduced to about half a pint, skimming when necessary. Then strain through a very fine strainer or piece of muslin, and reduce again in a smaller saucepan until the glaze becomes as thick as treacle, when it will be ready for use.

If not required at once, it should be poured into a jar, and if a little melted lard is poured over the surface the glaze will keep good for weeks. In fact, this is a very good way of preserving any surplus stock, as a little glaze is useful at all times for enriching soups and sauces as well as for coating meat, &c., and, diluted with water, it will again take the form of stock.

To Glaze Meat.—Have the glaze prepared as above and in a melted condition, but not too hot. Use a small paint-brush or egg-brush, and paint the meat all over with it in even straight strokes. If one coating is not sufficient allow the first one to cool, and brush the meat over again as before. Meanwhile keep the glaze in a melted state by putting the pan or jar containing it in a saucepan half full of hot water.

Do not waste any glaze that is left, but pour it carefully into a clean jar ready for future use, and rinse the brush and saucepan with boiling water, which pour into the stock-pot.

CLEAR SOUPS AND BROTHS

Clear Soups (*Consommés*).—The basis of these soups is good brown stock, which is clarified according to directions given on page 120. While first stock is always to be preferred for the purpose, it is quite possible to utilise good second stock, only the soup thus obtained is liable to be rather gelatinous in flavour and somewhat lacking in that fresh meaty taste, which is one of the chief characteristics of good *consommé*.

The different clear soups take their distinctive name from the garnish that is added to them. There may also be some variation in the meat used for the stock—as in clear game, oxtail, or turtle soup, &c.

Clear soups are amongst the most expensive soups to make, and at the same time they are the most generally used, especially if a dinner consists of several courses, as they are light and strengthening without being rich and satisfying.

A good *consommé* should be of a rich amber colour, and this must be obtained without the addition of caramel, which would spoil the flavour.

Broths.—*A Broth* differs from a clear soup in that it is unclarified, and the meat with which it is made is either served in the soup or lifted out and served as a separate course.

There is usually a garnish of rice or barley and cut-up vegetables, or the vegetables may be cut in larger pieces and served as an accompaniment to the meat.

A broth is a very substantial soup and quite

unsuited as the prelude to a long dinner. It forms almost a meal in itself and is excellent as a luncheon dish, especially in cold weather or for a nursery dinner. It is always acceptable too to those who have been working in the open air or engaged in sports. It is one of the most economical forms of soup.

Clear Soup

(*Fr.* Consommé)

Ingredients—

1 quart good Brown or First Stock.	1 lump of Sugar.
6 oz. lean juicy Beef.	1 white and shell of Egg.

Method—Carefully remove all fat from the top of the stock, and put it into a clean lined or copper saucepan. Wipe the beef with a damp cloth, and shred it down finely with a knife, or put it through the mincing machine, removing all fat and skin. Add this to the stock with the white of the egg and the shell well washed. Whisk these over the fire with a wire whisk until the soup just comes to boiling point. Then remove the whisk and let it boil well up. Draw the pan to the side of the fire where the soup will keep warm, but not simmer, and cover it over with a plate or saucepan lid. Let it stand from ten to fifteen minutes. Tie a clean cloth on to a soup-stand or the four legs of a chair turned upside down, letting it fall slightly in the middle so as to form a bag. Pour some boiling water through the cloth into a basin to thoroughly heat the cloth. Put a clean dry basin underneath, and pour the soup gently through the cloth. The soup will not be clear the first time, as it gets shaken with the straining, so change the basin and pour the soup through again, repeating this process until the soup runs through quite clear. In reheating add a lump of sugar, which makes the soup sparkle.

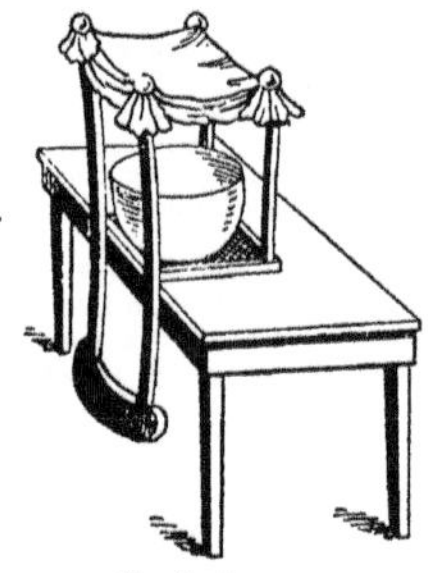

For clearing soup.

Notes.—The various *consommés* take their names from the different garnishes that are added to this soup.

The following are a few of the many varieties:—

Consommé à la Brunoise.—A garnish of cooked carrot, turnip, celery, leeks—cut in dice.

Consommé à la Célestine.—With fine shreds of savoury pancake.

Consommé à la Crécy.—Garnish of little balls of glazed carrot.

Consommé d'Orléans.—Garnish of small green and white quenelles.

Consommé à la Florentine.—With cheese quenelles.

Consommé à l'Impératrice.—Garnish of poached eggs.

Consommé à la Jardinière.—With mixed vegetables cut in pretty shapes.

Consommé Jérusalem.—With little balls of cooked Jerusalem artichokes.

Consommé à la Julienne.—With different vegetables cut in long thin strips.

Consommé aux Pâtes d'Italie.—With Italian paste in fancy shapes.

Consommé à la Printanière.—With spring vegetables and young green peas.

Consommé Royale.—With rounds or dice of custard.

When the garnish is made of vegetables these should be cooked separately and only added to the soup at the last. Root vegetables should be cooked in a little stock and seasoned with salt and a pinch of sugar. The stock should then be allowed to reduce to a glaze. Fine green vegetables, such as green peas, asparagus points, or French beans, should simply be steamed or boiled carefully in a little water.

Various fancy cutters can be bought for cutting vegetables in fancy shapes.

For quenelles use a small quantity of nicely made quenelle meat, put it into a forcing-bag and force out fancy shapes or small balls on a greased tin, then poach in boiling stock or water.

Italian paste or macaroni must also be cooked and rinsed in cold water previous to adding it to the *consommé*, otherwise it would destroy the clearness of the soup. There are scores of garnishes for clear soup besides those given above; in fact, new names are constantly being invented, and a special event or a passing fashion will furnish the occasion for a new name, which in most cases means only a very small variation in a well-known soup.

Chicken Broth

(*Fr.* Bouillon de Poulet)

Ingredients—

1 Chicken.	1 table-spoonful chopped Parsley.
2 or 3 pints Cold Water.	Pepper and salt.
1 table-spoonful Rice or crushed Tapioca.	

Method.—Draw and singe the chicken, and make it very clean. The inferior parts will do quite well for making the broth. The breast may be cut off and reserved for some other dish. Cut the rest of the chicken into joints first, then take all the meat from the bones and cut it into small pieces. Chop the bones and wash any part which does not look perfectly clean. Keep back any soft fat, but use the skin. Wash the neck well, and let it soak in cold water and salt for some time to draw out the blood. Open the gizzard and remove the bag of stones from the inside, then wash it well, pulling off all the fat skin from the outside. Remove the gall-bag very carefully from the liver, cutting it away with a pair of scissors, and wash the liver well. Also wash the heart and scald the feet, letting them lie in boiling water for a short time, and then scrape them well.

Take a clean lined saucepan, put into it the meat, bones, skin, neck, liver, gizzard, heart, and feet. Add the salt and enough cold water to well cover all; the quantity depends upon the size of the fowl used. Put the lid on the pan and bring slowly to the boil, then skim several times until the broth looks quite clear. Allow the broth to simmer from four to five hours until the goodness is well extracted from the bones, &c., skimming when necessary. Strain the broth through a fine strainer or hair sieve, and let it stand till cold. Then remove all fat from the top of the broth, return to a saucepan, and thicken according to taste. If rice is used, wash it well and cook in the broth until tender. If tapioca, bring the broth to the boil, sprinkle in the tapioca, and cook for ten minutes, until quite clear. Season to taste, and add the chopped parsley last. If small pieces of chicken are liked served in the soup, the best plan is to lift some of the nice pieces out of the broth as soon as they are cooked, but before all the goodness is extracted, and reserve these for returning to the broth just before serving. A more economical broth can be made by using a piece of mutton or veal along with the chicken.

Sometimes the chicken is kept whole and served as a separate course; in this case small pieces of vegetable or thinly sliced leeks might be cooked with it, and the rice or tapioca added about half-an-hour before serving.

Note.—A more highly flavoured broth may be made by cooking small pieces of vegetable along with the chicken.

Cockie Leekie

An old cock, along with a plentiful supply of leeks, is generally used for this soup, hence the name. Make in the same way as chicken broth (see above), allowing double the quantity of water and rice and six or eight leeks.

Hotch Potch

Ingredients—

2 quarts Mutton Broth.	1 pint Green Peas.
Equal quantities of young Carrots, Turnips, and Spring Onions.	1 dessert-spoonful chopped Parsley.
1 Lettuce.	1½ lbs. Lamb or small Mutton Cutlets.
1 Cauliflower.	Pepper and Salt.

Method.—Put the mutton broth or water in which some mutton has been boiled into a saucepan, and bring it to the boil. Clean some young carrots, turnips, and onions; cut the carrots and turnips into very small neat pieces, and the onions into thin slices. About one teacupful of each will be required. Put them into the saucepan with the broth, and boil quickly for half-an-hour. Trim the chops neatly, removing most of the fat; add them next with the flower of the cauliflower broken into small pieces, and the lettuce finely shred. Simmer the soup slowly for one hour longer, then add the peas, and cook until they are soft. Add the parsley last, and season with pepper and salt.

Mutton Broth

(*Fr.* Bouillon de Mouton)

Ingredients—

1½ lbs. Neck or Knuckle of Mutton.	1 dessert-spoonful of chopped Parsley.
3 pints Cold Water.	A small piece each of Carrot, Turnip, Onion, and Celery.
1 table-spoonful Rice or Barley.	Pepper and salt.

Method.—Wipe the meat, and cut it away from the bone and into small pieces, removing any superfluous fat. Prepare the vegetables, and cut them into small neat pieces. Put the meat, bones, and water into a saucepan with a little salt, put on the lid, and bring slowly to the boil. Skim well; add the rice well washed, or the barley washed and blanched, and the prepared vegetables. Simmer from two to three hours, or until the vegetables are well cooked. Remove the bones, and any grease from the top of the stock; add the parsley, pepper, and more salt if necessary before serving.

Another way of making this broth is to keep the meat whole and to serve it as a separate course with a little of the liquid broth strained round it. The vegetable should then be added in rather larger pieces and used as a garnish to the meat. The broth itself may also be finished differently. After the meat and vegetables have been removed, switch it for a few minutes with a wire whisk, then beat up an egg in a basin, pour it into the soup-tureen and pour the soup slowly on to it. This makes a very delicious soup.

Pot au Feu

Ingredients—

4 lbs. shin of Beef or shoulder of Beef.	3 sticks of Celery.
4 quarts Cold Water.	3 Leeks.
2 oz. crushed Tapioca or Sago.	A bunch of Herbs.
2 Carrots.	1 Cabbage.
1 Turnip.	20 Black Peppercorns.
1 Parsnip.	6 Cloves.
	1 small blade of Mace.
	Salt.

Method.—Break up the bones, wipe the meat with a damp cloth, and tie it into shape with a piece of tape. Put them into a large saucepan or earthenware casserole with the water, and bring to the boil. Add one dessert-spoonful of salt, and skim well. Then simmer very gently for two hours. Meanwhile have all the vegetables carefully cleaned and prepared, and, with the exception of the cabbage, cut them in moderate-sized pieces and tie them in a piece of muslin. When the meat has simmered the required time, add the vegetables to the pan, with a bunch of herbs and the spices, also tied in a piece of muslin. Simmer gently for two hours more. Then add the cabbage, cleaned and trimmed, cut in two, and tied together with string. Cook again until the cabbage is tender from half to three-quarters of an hour. Then lift out the meat on to a hot dish, undo the tape, garnish with the vegetables, and pour some of the liquid round as gravy. Serve the cabbage separately in a vegetable dish, removing the string. Remove the herbs and spices from the stock in the pan, sprinkle in the sago or tapioca, and cook until transparent about fifteen minutes. Season to taste, skim well, and serve in soup-tureen.

Note.—Pot au Feu is the favourite dish in many French households.

Spring Soup

(*Fr.* Potage Printanière)

Make in the same way as Hotch Potch (p. 121), omitting the meat.

Veal Broth

(*Fr.* Bouillon de Veau)

Make in the same way as Mutton Broth (p. 121).

THICKENED SOUPS

Thickened soups can be made of fish, meat, or vegetables, and they generally have some stock as their basis. The stock may be either brown, white, fish, or vegetable, according to the nature of the soup, or sometimes a mixture of stock and milk, or milk and water is used.

Some starchy or farinaceous material, such as flour, arrow-root, cornflour, tapioca, &c., generally supplies the thickening property, or, in the case of the richer soups, a *liaison* or combination of eggs and cream is used.

Portions of the substance of which the soup is made are frequently served in it as in kidney soup and ox-tail soup. Care must be taken not to make those soups too thick.

Cabbage Soup

Ingredients—

1 Cabbage.	1 tea-spoonful chopped Parsley.
1 small Onion or Leek.	Some croûtons of Toasted Bread.
1 quart Meat Boilings.	White Pepper and Salt.
½ pint Milk.	
1 table-spoonful crushed Tapioca.	

Method.—Wash the cabbage well in cold water, and remove the coarse outside leaves and any hard pieces of stalk. Separate all the leaves, and let them soak in cold water and salt for half-an-hour. Then drain the water away, and shred the leaves finely. Put the shred cabbage into a saucepan of fast-boiling water, salted in the proportion of one dessertspoonful to the quart, boil quickly for five minutes, and then drain. Slice the onion or leek very thinly, and chop it finely, put it into a saucepan with the cabbage and stock or meat boilings, and simmer for twenty minutes. Add the milk and crushed tapioca, and cook for ten minutes longer, or until the tapioca turns quite clear. Add the parsley just before serving, and season to taste with white pepper and salt. Put some small croûtons of toasted bread into the soup-tureen, and pour the soup, boiling hot, over them.

Calf's Tail Soup

(*Fr.* Potage de Queue de Veau)

Ingredients—

2 Tails.	2 Yolks.
3 pints White Stock.	1 gill of Cream.
½ pint Milk.	½ Carrot.
1½ oz. Butter.	A small piece of Turnip.
1½ oz. Flour.	1 Onion.
A Bay Leaf.	6 Cloves.
Some Parsley Stalks.	1 glass of Sherry.
A pinch of Nutmeg.	1 oz. grated Parmesan.

Method.—Wash the tails, and cut them into pieces about 1½ inches long; put them into a saucepan with sufficient cold water to cover them, bring to the boil, and pour the water away. Rinse out the saucepan, and return the pieces of tail to it with the stock, bring to the boil again, and skim well. Add the vegetables all carefully cleaned, and cut in small pieces, the bay leaf, cloves, nutmeg, and parsley stalks. Put the lid on the pan, and simmer slowly from one and a half to two hours, or until the meat will slip quite easily from the bones; then strain through a wire sieve into a basin, and remove all fat from the stock. Melt the butter in a saucepan, but do not brown it, add the flour, and mix smoothly together with a wooden spoon; then pour on the stock, stir over the fire until boiling, and allow it to boil about five minutes.

Beat up the yolks of eggs in a basin with the cream, add the sherry, and strain these into the soup, stirring all the time. Add the pieces of tail and seasoning to taste, but do not boil again. Put the grated cheese into the soup-tureen, and pour the boiling soup on to them.

Note.—The cheese may be omitted.

Cauliflower and Lettuce Soup

(*Fr.* Potage de Choufleur et de Laitues)

Ingredients—

1 large Cauliflower.	1 oz. crushed Tapioca or small Sago.
1 small Lettuce.	1 oz. Butter.
1 quart Meat Boilings or Second White Stock.	White Pepper and Salt.

1 dessert-spoonful chopped Parsley.

Method.—Use the white part only of the

cauliflower. Cut it into small pieces, wash in cold water. Then scald in fast-boiling water for five minutes and drain.

Put the stock into a saucepan, and bring it to the boil. Throw in the pieces of cauliflower, and boil them until tender, about half-an-hour; then add the milk, the butter, and the lettuce cut in fine short shreds. Sprinkle in the tapioca or sago, and cook all together for ten minutes longer, stirring frequently. Season to taste, and add the parsley at the end.

Curry Soup (White)

(*Fr.* Potage au Cari (Blanche))

Ingredients—

1½ pints White Stock or Meat Boilings.	1 table-spoonful chopped Parsley.
1 table-spoonful Curry Powder.	Pepper and Salt.
1 oz. Cornflour.	Squeeze of Lemon Juice.
2 table-spoonfuls Cream.	Small pieces of Chicken or Rabbit.
1 yolk of Egg.	Boiled Rice.

Method.—Any light stock, or the water in which a fowl, rabbit, or piece of veal has been boiled, will do for this soup. Put the stock into a saucepan, and bring it to the boil. Put the curry powder and cornflour into a basin, add the milk gradually to them, mixing with an iron spoon until smooth. Add this to the stock, stir until boiling, and simmer for ten minutes. Then draw the pan to the side of the fire, and strain in the cream and yolk of egg mixed together. Season to taste, and sprinkle in the parsley. If possible, add some small pieces of chicken or rabbit. Stir the soup over the fire until *almost* boiling. Do not boil, or the yolk of egg will curdle. Squeeze in the lemon juice, and pour the soup into a hot soup-tureen. Serve with plain boiled rice, on a separate dish (see p. 157).

Lettuce Soup

(*Fr.* Potage de Laitues)

Ingredients—

2 large Lettuces	2 pints light Stock.
¼ lb. Spinach.	1 or 2 yolks of Eggs.
2 or 4 Spring Onions.	½ gill of Cream.
3 oz. Butter.	

Method.—Wash the vegetables, drain and cut in fine shreds. Put them into a stewpan with the butter and seasoning, and cook them over the fire for ten minutes, stirring all the time with a wooden spoon. Add the stock, which may either be vegetable stock or boilings from meat, and simmer from three-quarters of an hour to one hour. Draw the saucepan to the side of the fire and add the yolk of egg and cream mixed together. The soup must not boil again.

Mock Turtle Soup

(*Fr.* Potage de Fausse Tortue)

Ingredients—

½ Calf's Head.	1 glass Sheery.
¾ quart Cold Water.	¼ tea-spoonful Celery Seed.
½ Carrot.	2 Bay Leaves.
½ Turnip.	1 blade of Mace.
1 Onion.	A sprig of Parsley, Thyme, and Marjoram.
2 oz. Butter.	Pepper and Salt.
2 oz. Cornflour.	A squeeze of Lemon Juice.
6 Cloves.	Force-meat Balls.
3 oz. lean Ham or a Ham-bone.	

Method.—Wash the head well, removing the brains, which are not used in the soup, but may be kept for some small savoury dish. Take away all the gristle from the nostrils, and let the head soak in cold water, with a handful of salt in it, for half-an-hour at least. Then blanch it —that is, put it into a saucepan with cold water to cover it—bring to the boil, pour the water away, and wash the head again in cold water. Cut all the flesh from the bones, and tie it in a piece of muslin. Put it with the bones and water into a large saucepan, and let it simmer gently, skimming occasionally, for three and a half hours. Then strain the stock through a hair sieve, and let it stand till cold. Melt the butter in a saucepan, have the vegetables and ham cut into small pieces, and fry them in it with the herbs and spices. Let them get a nice light brown colour, and stir well to keep them from burning. Then add the cornflour, and mix it smoothly in. Remove all fat from the top of the stock, pour it into the saucepan, and stir until boiling. Add pepper and salt to taste, and simmer slowly for one and a half hours. Remove any scum that may rise. Strain through a hair sieve into a basin, rinse out the saucepan, and return the soup to it to reheat. Add the wine and lemon juice, and serve in it force-meat balls (see p. 179) and small pieces of the head cut into dice.

Oyster Soup

(*Fr.* Potage aux Huîtres)

Ingredients—

2 doz. fresh Oysters or 3 doz. tinned Oysters.	1 gill of Cream.
2 pints White or Fish Stock.	2 yolks of Eggs.
1 oz. Butter.	1 tea-spoonful Anchovy Essence.
1 oz. Flour.	A squeeze of Lemon Juice,
A pinch of Cayenne.	White Pepper and Salt.

Method.—Put the oysters into a small saucepan with their own liquor, bring them almost to the boil, then strain, saving the liquor. Beard the oysters (that is, remove the piece like a fringe that encircles them), cut them in two, and put them aside for serving in the soup. Put the beards into a saucepan with the liquor and the stock, and let them simmer for half-an-hour, to extract all the flavour from them. If the stock is not previously well flavoured, small pieces of the different flavouring vegetables should also be cooked in it. Strain through a fine hair sieve or piece of muslin, and rinse out the saucepan ready for use. First melt in it the butter, being careful it does not brown, add to it the flour, and mix together until quite smooth. Pour on the stock, and stir constantly over the fire until boiling. Skim if necessary. Season to taste with a little white pepper, salt, anchovy essence, and a pinch of cayenne. Beat up the yolks of eggs in a basin with the cream, draw the pan with the soup in it to one side of the fire, and strain them into it, stirring all the time. Reheat, but do not boil again. Add a squeeze of lemon juice. Put the oysters into the soup-tureen, pour the soup over them, and serve.

Sorrel Soup

(*Fr.* Potage d'Oseille)

Ingredients—

½ lb. Sorrel.
2 oz. Butter.
2 oz. Potato Flour.
1½ pints White Stock.
½ pint Milk or 1 gill Cream.
The crust of French Roll.
Pepper and Salt.

Method.—Wash the sorrel very carefully, and then shake it as dry as possible in a sieve or colander. Cut it into fine shreds with a sharp knife. Melt the butter in a saucepan, and, when hot, put in the sorrel, and cook it over the fire for ten minutes. Then add the potato flour, and stir for a few minutes with a wooden spoon, being careful the contents of the pan do not discolour. Add the white stock, and stir until boiling. Put the lid on the pan, and simmer slowly for twenty minutes. Add the milk or cream, and season to taste with white pepper and salt. Remove the crust from a French roll, and dry it in the oven. Then break it in pieces, and put them in a soup-tureen. Pour the soup boiling hot over them, and serve.

Turtle Soup

(*Fr.* Potage à la Tortue)

Ingredients—

1½ lbs. Knuckle of Veal.
1½ lbs. Shin of Beef.
½ lb. sun-dried Turtle.
4 quarts Cold Water.
1 small Carrot.
½ Turnip.
1 Onion.
½ lb. lean Ham.
2 oz. Butter.
24 Black Peppercorns.
8 Cloves.
1 blade of Mace.
2 Bay Leaves.
A sprig of Parsley, Thyme, and Marjoram.
Pepper and Salt.
1 glass Madeira.
A squeeze of Lemon Juice.
2 oz. Cornflour.

Method.—Buy the turtle four or five days before the soup is wanted. Wash it well in warm water, and soak it in water for three days at least, until it is well swollen and comparatively soft. Change the water every twelve hours. On the fourth day commence to make the soup. Wipe the beef and the veal, and cut them both into small pieces, removing as much fat as possible. Put the pieces into a large saucepan with the cold water, the ham cut in small pieces, and the turtle tied in a piece of muslin. Bring slowly to the boil, and skim well. Add all the vegetables, cut in small pieces, and the herbs, and simmer the soup slowly for twelve hours, removing any scum as it rises. Strain through a hair sieve and let it stand till cold. Remove carefully all fat from the top of the stock, and cut the turtle into neat square pieces. Melt the butter in a saucepan, and let it get slightly brown, then add the cornflour and mix until smooth, pour on the stock, and stir until boiling. Boil for a few minutes, and skim if necessary. Season with pepper and salt, and add the wine and lemon-juice. Serve the pieces of turtle and small force-meat balls in the soup (see p. 179).

PURÉES

A purée is perhaps the simplest and most economical kind of soup. It differs from other thickened soups in that its thickening is effected by rubbing the meat, fish, vegetable, or other ingredients of which it is composed through a sieve and serving them in the soup.

A purée can be made of almost any vegetable, whether fresh or dried, and of meat, game, fish, and some farinaceous substances such as rice, barley, macaroni, &c. Either stock, milk, or water, or a mixture of all three will supply the liquid portion.

The ingredients of which a purée is composed must always be simmered slowly until quite soft and pulpy in order to facilitate the sieving process. Although a purée is never so smooth and soft as when rubbed through a hair sieve, when time and labour have to be considered a wire one must suffice. In all cases it will be found advisable to rub the mixture through a wire sieve before putting it through the hair sieve, as the use of the latter alone is a most laborious undertaking. Always when sieving have two spoons in readiness, one to do the rubbing through and the other for scraping the sieve underneath. Stand the sieve with the narrow rim uppermost *within* a basin. The basin must not be so small that the sieve covers the rim. Pour a small quantity of the mixture on the top of the sieve and commence the rubbing through. Put two fingers on the bowl of the spoon and rub through with the edge. Moisten the mixture with some of the liquid part of the soup when necessary, and from time to time remove what adheres to the lower side of the sieve with the second spoon. What comes through is called the purée.

As little as possible should be left on the top of the sieve when the work is finished, and upon the patient rubbing through the success of the soup will depend.

In the case of a meat purée it will simplify

the work if the meat is pounded in a mortar with a little of the liquid before sieving.

A purée can always be rendered richer by the addition of some cream and one or two yolks of eggs just before bringing it to table.

A purée should be of the consistency of thick cream, and is usually served with croûtons of bread, or with "pulled" bread served on a separate dish.

Croûtons of Bread.—Use bread not less than one day old, and rather close in texture. Cut the bread into slices one quarter of an inch thick, take off the crust, then cut it into strips one quarter of an inch wide, and then across into even squares. Or the sliced bread may be cut into fancy shapes with a vegetable cutter. These may either be fried in boiling fat, in clarified butter in a frying-pan, or soaked in stock and browned on a greased tin in the oven. Drain well on kitchen paper before serving. They should be crisp, dry, and of an amber colour.

Croûtons can also be made of scraps of pastry cut in fancy shapes, and either baked or fried. They may, if liked, be sprinkled with a little grated Parmesan.

Pulled Bread.—This may be either bought ready or prepared in the following way: take the inside crumb of a French roll, pull it with the fingers (it must never be cut) into small pieces, and brown these in a slow oven until of a nice amber colour.

PURÉES MADE FROM FRESH VEGETABLES

Artichoke Soup

(*Fr.* Purée d'Artichauts)

Ingredients—

1 lb. Jerusalem Artichokes.	1 small Onion.
1 oz. lean Ham.	1½ pints White Second Stock.
1 stick Celery or ¼ tea-spoonful Celery Seed.	½ pint Milk and 1 tea-spoonful Flour or 1 gill of Cream and 2 yolks of Eggs.
1 oz. Butter.	White Pepper and Salt.
1 Bay Leaf.	
Some Parsley Stalks.	

Method.—First wash and brush the artichokes, then put them into a basin with clean cold water and peel them carefully, changing the water as soon as it becomes dirty. Throw the artichokes as they are peeled into another basin of clean cold water, with a little vinegar or lemon-juice in it, in order to preserve their colour. Skin and slice the onion thinly, wash and brush the celery and cut it into shreds, and cut the ham into small pieces. Melt the butter in a lined or enamelled saucepan, add the artichokes, drained and cut in thin slices, also the onion, ham, celery, bay leaf, and parsley stalks. Put the lid on the pan and cook over the fire for about ten minutes, shaking the pan occasionally to prevent the contents burning. Then add the stock, white pepper and salt, and let all simmer gently from one to one and a half hours, or until the artichokes are quite soft. Rub the soup through a hair sieve into a basin, then rinse out the saucepan and return the soup to it to reheat. Put the flour into a basin, and add the milk gradually to it, mixing until quite smooth. Add this to the soup, and stir over the fire until boiling. Continue boiling for a few minutes, and add more seasoning if necessary.

If cream and yolks of eggs are used for thickening, omit the flour and milk. Beat the yolks of eggs and cream together in a basin, strain them into the soup, stirring all the time, and do not boil the soup again or it will curdle.

Note.—This soup should be white in colour. If it turns green, the artichokes have not been carefully prepared, or it has been made in an iron saucepan.

Carrot Soup and Turnip Soup

(*Fr.* Purée à la Crécy et Purée de Navets)

Both are made in the same way as Potato Soup (p. 126), substituting 1 lb. carrots or 1 lb. turnips for the potatoes. The addition of a little cream will be an improvement to these soups.

Celery Soup

(*Fr.* Purée de Céleri)

Make in the same way as Artichoke Soup (see above), substituting a head of celery for the artichokes. The celery must be very carefully washed and brushed and then cut in fine shreds.

Onion Soup (White)

(*Fr.* Purée aux Oignons)

Ingredients—

3 Spanish Onions.	1 blade of Mace.
1 oz. Butter or Dripping.	1 oz. Flour or Rice Flour.
1 quart Meat Boilings.	½ pint Milk.
1 Bay Leaf.	A few Parsley Stalks.
White Pepper and Salt.	

Method.—Skin and scald the onions in boiling water for a few minutes. Slice them down as thinly as possible from the top to the root. Melt the butter in a saucepan, put into it the onions, bay leaf, blade of mace, and parsley stalks; put the lid on the pan, and cook for ten minutes without browning. Then pour on the meat boilings, simmer until quite soft, about one and a half hours, and rub through a fine wire or hair sieve. Rinse out the saucepan, and return the soup to it. Break the flour gradually with the milk, add this to the soup, and stir over the fire until boiling. Boil five minutes, and season to taste. A little cream is an improvement to this soup, and grated Parmesan cheese may be served with it.

Onion Soup (Brown)

Make according to preceding recipe, but brown the butter or dripping and then brown the

onions in it, being careful they do not blacken or the soup will have a disagreeable taste. Omit the milk, but add the flour broken with a little stock.

Note.—1 dessert-spoonful of sherry may be added.

Parsnip Soup

(*Fr.* Purée de Panais)

Make according to directions given for Potato Soup (see below), using 1 lb. parsnips instead of the potatoes.

Potato Soup

(*Fr.* Purée de Pommes de Terre)

Ingredients—

- 1 lb. Potatoes.
- 1 stick of Celery or ½ tea-spoonful Celery Seed.
- 1 Onion or 2 Leeks.
- 1 Bay Leaf.
- 1 oz. Butter or Dripping.
- 1½ pints Stock or Meat Boilings.
- ½ pint Milk.
- Pepper and Salt.
- A few Parsley Stalks.

Method.—Wash and brush the potatoes, peel them very thinly, removing any black specks, and then weigh them. Cut them down into very thin slices, and let them lie in cold water for a short time. Wash and shred the celery, and skin and slice the onion thinly. Melt the butter or dripping in a saucepan, strain the potatoes, and add them to it with the prepared onion and celery. Put the lid on the pan, and cook over the fire for a few minutes without burning. Then pour on the stock or meat boilings, and simmer slowly from one to one and a half hours, or until the potatoes are quite soft. The soup must be stirred frequently, as it is most liable to burn, and should it become too thick, more water must be added. Then rub as much as possible through a fine wire or hair sieve into a basin, rinse out the saucepan, and return the soup to it to reheat. Add the milk and more seasoning if necessary.

Note.—Any remains of cold cooked potato may be used up in this soup, and a small ham-bone cooked in it is an improvement.

The addition of two or three tomatoes will make a nice change from time to time.

Tomato Soup

(*Fr.* Purée de Tomates)

Ingredients—

- 1 tin or 10 or 12 fresh Tomatoes.
- 3 pints Second Stock or Liquor from the tin.
- 1 Onion.
- ½ Carrot.
- ½ Turnip.
- 1 oz. Butter.
- A squeeze of Lemon Juice.
- 12 Peppercorns.
- 6 Cloves.
- 1 lump of Sugar.
- 1 oz. Rice Flour or crushed Tapioca.
- 1 oz. lean Ham or a small Ham-bone.
- 1 blade of Mace.
- A sprig of Parsley, Thyme, and Marjoram.
- Pepper and Salt.

Method.—Melt the butter in a saucepan, and put into it the ham cut in small pieces, the onion thinly sliced, and the herbs tied together in a bunch. Fry these for a few minutes over the fire, letting them colour slightly. Then add the tomatoes, cutting them into slices if they are fresh, the other vegetables cut into small pieces, and the rice flour, cloves, peppercorns, mace, and salt. Mix these well for a few minutes, and add the stock or liquor from the tin. Allow the soup to simmer slowly from three to four hours, until the vegetables are thoroughly soft, and then rub through a fine wire or hair sieve into a basin. Rinse out the saucepan, and return the soup to it to reheat; add the sugar, lemon juice, and more salt if necessary. A little milk or cream may also be added.

Vegetable Marrow Soup

(*Fr.* Purée de Courge)

Follow the directions given for Potato Soup (see above), substituting vegetable marrow for the potatoes. Wash the marrow, then peel, weigh, and cut it down into thin slices, but do not remove the seeds.

PURÉES WITH NUTS

Almond Soup

(*Fr.* Purée d'Amandes)

Use the recipe given for Chestnut Soup (see below), allowing ½ lb. sweet almonds, weighed after peeling, instead of the chestnuts, and add half a teacupful of bread-crumbs. Blanch and chop the almonds and pound them in a mortar with a few drops of water. Put them into a saucepan with the bread-crumbs, stock, &c., and proceed as in the last recipe.

White Chestnut Soup

(*Fr.* Purée de Marrons)

Ingredients—

- ¾ lb. Chestnuts, weighed after peeling.
- 1 quart White Stock.
- 1 gill of Cream or ½ pint Milk.
- 1 oz. Butter.
- A small blade of Mace.
- White Pepper and Salt.
- A pinch of Cayenne.
- A few Parsley Stalks.

Method.—Wash the chestnuts and cut a small piece off the end of each. Throw them into hot water, and boil for ten minutes. Then skin them and put them into a lined saucepan with the stock and a small blade of mace. Simmer for one hour or more until the chestnuts are quite tender; then rub them through a fine wire or hair sieve, using the stock to moisten them. Rinse out the saucepan, and return the chestnut purée and stock to it. Add the milk or cream, and boil for ten minutes until quite smooth. Add white pepper, salt to taste, and a pinch of cayenne. If too thick, more milk or stock must be added.

PURÉES MADE FROM DRIED SEEDS

Pea Soup

(*Fr.* Purée de Pois)

Ingredients—

½ lb. Split Peas.	A small piece of Carrot and Turnip.
2 pints Cold Water or Meat Boilings.	2 sticks of Celery or ¼ tea-spoonful Celery Seed.
1 oz. Dripping or Butter.	A pinch of Sugar.
1 Onion.	1 Bay Leaf.
A few Parsley Stalks.	

Pepper and Salt.

Method.—Put the peas into a basin, wash them well in cold water, and remove any discoloured ones that float on the surface. Then pour over them the two pints of cold water or meat boilings, cover the basin with a plate, and let them soak overnight. Next day strain off the water and keep it for making the soup with. (A certain amount of nourishment is always drawn out of the peas by soaking, and it would be wasteful to throw this water away.) Prepare the vegetables and cut them into thin slices. Melt the dripping or butter in a saucepan, add to it the peas and sliced vegetables, and stir them over the fire until the fat is thoroughly absorbed. This is called sweating the vegetables; it softens them, and makes them cook more easily. Next pour on the liquid in which the peas were soaked, stir well for a few minutes, and let it come to boiling point. Remove any scum that may rise, add pepper and salt to taste, and if using celery seed, add it now tied in a small piece of muslin. Allow the soup to simmer slowly from two to three hours, or until the peas are quite soft and pulpy. Stir the soup occasionally to prevent it sticking to the foot of the pan and burning, and if it should become too thick whilst cooking, add a little more water. When well cooked, rub through a wire or hair sieve into a basin, rinse out the saucepan, and return the soup to it to reheat. Add more seasoning if necessary, and serve with dried mint finely powdered and sifted.

Note.—A little boiled milk or cream is sometimes added at the end; it has a softening effect. The water in which a piece of ham, pickled pork, or salt beef has been boiled, if not too salt, does very well for making this soup. One tea-spoonful of curry powder may be added.

Both **Lentil** and **Haricot Bean Soup** (*Fr.* Purée de Lentilles et Purée de Haricots Blancs) can be made in the same way as above. For the *Lentil Soup* either the red Egyptian or the green German Lentils can be used, and they will take rather a shorter time to cook than split peas. In making *Haricot Bean Soup* it is as well to omit the carrot and turnip if a very white soup is wanted, and a little boiled milk added at the end is always an improvement.

PURÉES OF FISH

Fish Soup

(*Fr.* Purée de Poisson)

Ingredients—

2 lbs. White Fish or Fish Trimmings.	Some Parsley Stalks.
3 pints Cold Water.	A Bay Leaf.
2 Leeks.	1 oz. Flour.
A small piece of Carrot.	1 oz. Butter or Dripping.
A small piece of Turnip.	1 dessert-spoonful chopped Parsley.
White Pepper and Salt.	1 blade of Mace.
1 stick of Celery.	

Method.—Any white fish can be used for this soup, such as whiting, flounder, haddock, or cod, trimmings of fish or a cod's head. Wash the fish well and cut it into small pieces; put it into a saucepan with the cold water (which should cover it), add a little salt, and bring to the boil. Skim well and boil for about ten minutes. Then remove a few nice pieces of fish, free from skin and bone, and reserve them for serving in the soup. Prepare the vegetables and cut them into small thin pieces, add them to the soup with the bay leaf, parsley stalks, and blade of mace. Let all simmer slowly from one and a half to two hours. If a cod's head is used, longer time will be required. When well cooked, strain through a fine wire sieve into a basin, rubbing through a little of the fish and vegetables, being careful that none of the bones are rubbed through. Rinse out the saucepan and melt the butter or dripping in it, then add the flour and mix smoothly together. Pour in the soup and stir until boiling; add the milk, chopped parsley, and small pieces of fish, and bring to the boil again. Season to taste with white pepper and salt. The yolk of an egg may be put into the soup-tureen and the soup poured boiling hot on to it, stirring all the time; or it may be served with small egg balls in it.

PURÉES OF MEAT

Chicken Soup

(*Fr.* Potage de Volaille)

Ingredients—

1 Chicken.	1 Onion or Leek.
2 quarts Cold Water.	1 gill of Cream, or ¼ pint Boiled Milk.
½ Carrot.	Pepper and Salt.
A small piece of Turnip.	1 Bay Leaf.
1 blade of Mace.	A few Parsley Stalks.
1 oz. Butter.	1 oz. lean Ham or a small Ham-bone.
½ oz. Flour.	
1 stick Celery.	

Method.—Prepare the chicken in the same way as for chicken broth, p. 120, and, if wished, keep back the breast for serving in some other way. Put all together into a clean lined pan, with enough cold water to well cover—about two quarts; add a little salt, and bring slowly to the boil. Then skim well and add the vegetables, cleaned and cut in small pieces, the bay leaf, blade of mace, and parsley stalks. Simmer slowly from five to six hours until reduced about one-third, removing any scum that may rise. When cooked sufficiently, strain through a hair sieve into a basin, and let it stand till cold. Remove all fat from the top of the stock. Take some of the pieces of meat from the chicken, pound them well in a mortar, then rub through a wire sieve, and moisten with some of the liquid whilst rubbing through. Melt the butter in the saucepan, add the flour and mix until smooth. Then pour in the soup and the purée, bring to the boil and pour in the cream or boiled milk. Season to taste with white pepper and salt. A yolk of egg may also be used if liked. Put the yolk in the soup-tureen and pour the hot soup on to it, stirring all the time.

Notes.—The breast of the chicken may be cooked in the soup, and then lifted out, cut into small pieces, and served in the soup when ready.

The soup may be garnished with some cooked green peas, a little finely chopped parsley or chervil.

Rabbit Soup (*Fr.* Purée de Lapin) can be made in the same way, but the rabbit should be allowed to lie in salt and water for an hour before it is cut up, to remove the strong taste. Some nice little pieces of rabbit may be lifted out after they have cooked for about an hour and reserved for serving in the soup.

Hare Soup

(*Fr.* Potage de Lièvre)

Ingredients—

1 Hare.	24 Black Peppercorns.
1 lb. lean Beef,	6 or 8 Cloves.
½ lb. lean Ham.	1 blade of Mace.
2 oz. Butter or Dripping.	1 Bay Leaf.
2 Onions.	2 quarts Cold Water.
A small piece of Turnip.	1 glass Port Wine.
2 sticks of Celery.	½ tea-spoonful Jamaica Pepper.
A bunch of Herbs.	
1½ oz. Flour or 2 oz. Oatmeal.	Salt.

Method.—Skin and paunch the hare, saving the liver and as much of the blood as possible. Then wash the hare, dry it, and cut it into small pieces. Wipe the beef with a damp cloth, and cut it and the ham into small pieces. Melt the butter or dripping in a saucepan, put in the pieces of hare, meat, ham, and onions thinly sliced, and fry all these over the fire from ten to fifteen minutes; then pour in the water, bring to the boil, and skim well. Add the other vegetables cut into small pieces, the herbs, peppercorns, cloves, mace, bay leaf, and a little salt. Let all simmer gently from four to five hours; then strain through a hair sieve into a basin, and let the soup stand until cold. Remove the fat carefully from the top of the stock, put some of the meat from the hare into a mortar, pound it well with a little of the stock, and rub it through a fine wire sieve. Return the soup to the saucepan with the sieved hare. Break the flour with a little of the stock, add it to the soup, and stir until boiling. Boil for a few minutes, adding Jamaica pepper, black pepper, and more salt if necessary. If oatmeal is used for thickening, put it into a basin with half a pint of cold water; let it stand for half-an-hour, stirring occasionally, and then strain off the liquid part into the soup, keeping back the oatmeal; bring to the boil, and boil for a few minutes. The oatmeal gives the soup a soft, velvety taste. The wine and blood should be added to the soup just before serving, but do not boil again, or the soup will curdle.

Serve small force-meat balls (see p. 179), to which the liver of the hare cooked and chopped has been added, in this soup.

PURÉES OF FARINACEOUS FOODS

Cream of Barley Soup

(*Fr.* Potage à la Crème d'Orge)

Ingredients—

1 quart of Chicken or Veal Boilings.	Pepper and Salt.
2 oz. fine Pearl Barley.	1 Onion.
1 oz. Butter.	½ inch Cinnamon Stick.
1 gill of Cream or ¼ pint Boiled Milk.	1 Bay Leaf.
	A few Parsley Stalks.

Method.—Use the fine barley for this soup. Wash it well in cold water. Put it into a saucepan with cold water to cover, bring to the boil, strain and rinse again with cold water. This is to blanch or whiten the barley. Rinse out the saucepan, and return the barley to it with the meat boilings, or thin white stock. (The water in which a fowl, rabbit, or piece of veal has been boiled can be used for this soup.) Add the onion, thinly sliced, the bay leaf, cinnamon, and parsley stalks. Simmer for two hours, or until the barley is quite cooked. Then rub as much as possible through a tammy cloth or hair sieve. Return this purée to the pan with the butter, and add the cream or boiled milk. Season to taste, and stir over the fire until boiling.

A few cooked green peas or asparagus points may be added.

Cream of Rice Soup

(*Fr.* Potage au Riz)

Follow the same directions as for Barley Soup, using half teacupful of Patna rice instead of the barley. The rice will not require to be blanched, and one hour will be sufficient to cook it.

Macaroni Soup

(*Fr.* Potage Macaroni)

Follow the same directions as above, allowing 2 oz. macaroni instead of the barley. The macaroni will not require to be blanched, and one and a half hours will be sufficient to cook it.

PURÉES OF GREEN VEGETABLES

Asparagus Soup

(*Fr.* Purée d'Asperges)

Ingredients—

50 heads of Asparagus.	1 Bay Leaf.
1 quart White Stock.	Pepper and Salt.
1 gill of Cream.	1 oz. lean Ham.
2 yolks of Eggs.	A few Parsley Stalks.
1 oz. Butter.	

Method.—Wash the asparagus in cold water, scraping the stalk ends lightly with a knife. Cut off the points, reserving them for serving in the soup, and slice down the remainder into pieces of about an inch in length. Melt the butter in a saucepan, and add the asparagus to it with the ham cut in small pieces, the bay leaf and parsley stalks. Put the lid on the pan, and shake it gently over the fire for a few minutes until the butter is absorbed. Then pour in the stock, and add a little white pepper and salt. Simmer slowly from one and a half to two hours, or until the asparagus is quite tender. Then rub as much as possible through a hair sieve. Return the soup to the pan to reheat. Beat up the yolks of eggs and cream in a basin with a fork; draw the pan with the soup to the side of the fire, and strain them in, stirring all the time. Then stir carefully over the fire until the yolks thicken, on no account letting the soup boil. Have the asparagus points cooked separately. (Steam them gently about half-an-hour or until tender.) Put them in the soup-tureen and pour the hot soup over them. The soup should be of a delicate green colour, and if necessary a little spinach green must be added—care being taken not to overdo the colouring.

Note.—The yolks of eggs may be omitted and cream only used, or the cream omitted and a little milk added to the yolks.

Brussels Sprout Soup

(*Fr.* Purée de Choux de Bruxelles)

Ingredients—

1 lb. Brussels Sprouts.	1 gill of Cream or ½ pint Boiled Milk.
1 quart White Stock.	

White Pepper and Salt.

Method.—Trim the Brussels sprouts, cutting away any decayed or discoloured leaves. Wash well, and let them steep in a basin of cold water, with a few drops of vinegar, for half-an-hour. Then drain and throw into a saucepan of fast-boiling water (salted in the proportion of one dessert-spoonful to one quart), adding also a small piece of washing soda. Boil quickly with the lid off the pan from fifteen to twenty minutes, removing any scum that may rise. Do not overcook the sprouts, or their colour will be destroyed. When ready, drain and rub through a fine wire sieve. Put the stock into a saucepan, add the Brussels sprout purée, cream or milk and seasoning, and make quite hot, but do not boil again.

Green Pea Soup

(*Fr.* Purée de Petits Pois)

Ingredients—

1 pint Shelled Peas.	3 Spring Onions.
1 handful of Pea Shells.	A sprig of Mint.
1 small Lettuce.	1 lump of Sugar.
A few sprigs of Parsley.	1½ pints Second White Stock.
White Pepper and Salt.	1 gill of Cream.

Method.—Wash the shells well, and cut them into pieces. Wash and shred the lettuce, and wash and slice thinly the onions. Put all these into a saucepan of boiling water salted in the proportion of one dessert-spoonful to a quart, salted; boil for ten minutes, and strain off the water. Put the stock into a saucepan, and bring it to the boil. Add the scalded vegetables, the peas, mint, and parsley, and boil all together until tender, about half-an-hour. Then rub through a hair sieve into a basin. Rinse out the saucepan, and return the soup to it to reheat. Add the cream, and season to taste with white pepper and salt.

Note.—A few leaves of spinach may be added to this soup, and sometimes a few of the peas are cooked separately, and served whole in the soup.

Water-cress Soup

(*Fr.* Potage au Cresson)

Ingredients—

2 bunches Water-cress.	1 quart Cold Water.
1½ small bunch Spring Onions.	1½ oz. Butter.
½ pint Haricot Beans.	1 table-spoonful chopped Parsley.
White Pepper and Salt.	1 or 2 table-spoonfuls Cream.

Method.—Wash the beans in cold water. Put them into a basin with one quart of cold water, cover with a plate, and let them soak overnight. Next day put them into a saucepan with the water in which they were soaked, and boil until quite soft, about three hours. Then rub through a fine wire or hair sieve into a basin, and make up this purée to one quart with boiling water. Wash and pick the water-cress, carefully removing the stalks, and shred it finely with a knife. Wash the onions, removing the roots and most of the green part. Slice them also thinly. Melt the butter in a saucepan, put the greens into it, and stew them gently for about ten minutes, until they are just beginning to change colour. Then pour on the haricot purée, and simmer from fifteen to twenty minutes. Add the cream, pepper, salt, and the chopped parsley just before serving.

Note.—Lettuce, sorrel, endive, or any green vegetable may be shredded and used in the making of this soup.

FISH AND FISH ENTRÉES

How to Clean Fish.—The thorough cleansing of fish is essential to its wholesomeness. When it is bought from a fishmonger it is generally so far prepared, but if caught or obtained from a fisherman it will require very careful cleaning before it can be cooked. Some fish, such as haddock, whiting, or cod, require to be cut open before they can be emptied, while others, such as sole or plaice, can have the entrails drawn out through the gills. Be careful not to disfigure the fish, but clean it thoroughly, and see that no blood or black skin is left inside. If there is a roe this should be allowed to remain if the fish is small, but if large it must be removed and cooked separately. If the fish feels slimy, rub it well with a little salt. Scales should be scraped off with a knife, scraping from the tail upwards, and the fish well rinsed afterwards. If the scales are very hard to remove, as is sometimes the case with fresh-water fish, dip the fish in boiling water for a moment. In cutting off the fins, cut from the tail upwards with a pair of scissors. The fins of turbot and skate may be left on, as they are very gelatinous and are considered a luxury. In taking out the eyes, if the skin over them is tough, cut it first with a pair of scissors, and then the eye can easily be pulled out, or pushed out from the inside. Fish that have a strong muddy flavour should be soaked in salt and water before being cooked.

General Rules for Cooking Fish

Boiling.—Boiling is best suited to large uncut fish or to thick pieces of fish such as salmon, halibut, cod, ling, hake, and turbot. This method of cooking is not to be recommended for small fish or for thin slices of fish. Fish should never be skinned for boiling, and when whole the head is left on with the eyes taken out. Turbot should be scored across on the black side to prevent the white side cracking. All fish, with the exception of salt fish, should be put into water that is *very* hot, but not actually boiling; or it is better still if fish stock can be used instead of water. Salt the liquid in the proportion of 1 oz. of salt to a gallon and two table-spoonfuls of vinegar to the same quantity. The latter is added to keep the flesh white and firm, or lemon juice may be used if preferred. Always weigh the fish before boiling; eight minutes to the pound and eight minutes over is the time usually allowed, but no hard-and-fast rule can be laid down, as the time very much depends upon the shape and thickness of the fish. A fish-kettle is the best utensil to use for boiling fish, where you have a drainer which enables you to lift out the fish easily without breaking it. Have enough water or stock in the fish-kettle to cover the fish and no more; if too much is used the skin of the fish will be liable to crack; and add salt and vinegar in the above proportions. Place the fish on the drainer and lower it gently in. If a fish-kettle is not to be had, a stewpan must be used. An old plate should be placed inside, and the fish tied in a piece of muslin or cheese-cloth. Allow the fish to simmer slowly for the required time. If allowed to cook too quickly the outside will be broken before the inside is ready. All scum that rises must be removed. If allowed to settle on the fish it will spoil its appearance. When the fish is ready, the flesh will have lost its clear appearance, and will look white and opaque. The flesh will also leave the bone easily. Be sure to cook the fish sufficiently, or it will be unwholesome, and at the same time do not overcook it or it will be flavourless. Lift the fish out of the water as soon as it is ready, and drain it well. Never keep it hot in the water. If it has to be kept warm for a time, place the drainer, with the fish on it, across the fish-kettle, and cover over with a clean cloth. Dish on a strainer, and serve with appropriate sauce and garnish.

Steaming.—Fish may be cooked by steam instead of boiling it. It is a slower process, but the flavour of the fish is retained better than by boiling, especially in smaller pieces of fish. The fish is placed in a steamer which fits on to a saucepan, and success depends upon keeping plenty of water boiling under it.

Slices of fish, small skinned whiting, or fillets of fish can be cooked to perfection both as to flavour and substance by steaming, whereas boiling would render them woolly and tasteless. If it is only a small quantity of fish which requires cooking it may be steamed on a plate. Grease the plate with butter and lay the fish neatly on it. Season to taste and squeeze a little lemon juice over the top. Put a piece of well-greased paper on the top and cover with a second plate or the saucepan lid. Place this on the top of a saucepan of boiling water and allow it to remain from twenty to thirty minutes, or until the fish is sufficiently cooked. The liquid on the plate should be served with the fish or made into a sauce with a little flour and butter, and then poured over the fish.

Note.—This is an excellent way of serving fish for an invalid.

Frying (*French or Wet Frying*).—This is cooking in a large quantity of fat, sufficient to cover the article to be fried. Clarified fat, oil or lard may be used for the purpose. The fat must be put into a plain iron stewpan, neither tinned nor enamelled, as the great heat would destroy the lining. Success depends upon getting the fat to the right degree of heat. It must be quite still. If it bubbles it shows that it contains water, which must pass off by evaporation before the fat can reach the required heat. A blue, smoky vapour should also be seen rising from it. It should then be used at once, or drawn back from the fire, to prevent its burning and making an unpleasant smell.

This method of frying is suitable for small fish such as smelts or small pieces of filleted fish, such as filleted haddock, sole or plaice. Larger pieces of fish which require more cooking must be done by a slower process. (See Dry Frying below.)

Fish to be fried must first be made as dry as possible by wiping it gently with a cloth and then by dusting it with flour. Any loose flour which does not adhere should be shaken off. The fish should then be further protected from the fat by being egged and bread-crumbed or dipped in frying batter (see p. 195).

Do not put too many pieces into the pan at one time, as they will cool the fat too much, and always bring it to boiling point again before adding more fish. If the fat is not sufficiently hot, it will soak into the articles fried, and make them greasy instead of crisp. Either a frying-basket or a perforated spoon must be used for lifting out the fish. Let them fry a brown colour, and always drain on kitchen paper before serving. Always dish fried fish on a d'oyley or dish-paper. The fat must not be left on the fire when finished with, but should be strained through a piece of muslin into a tin basin, and put aside for further use. If care is taken of it in this way it will keep for a long time, and will not be found an extravagance.

Dry Frying.—This is suitable for larger pieces of fish, such as cod or salmon steaks, and whole whiting or haddocks, which require a longer time to cook than French frying allows for. Dry frying means frying in a sauté or frying-pan with a small quantity of fat. The fat must be made smoking hot before the fish is placed in it, so that the outside is sealed up, and the juice and flavour retained. Brown the fish first on one side, then turn over with a knife or fish slice, and brown on the other. When cooked, lift out and drain on paper. Serve on a hot dish with a fish-paper or d'oyley on it.

Broiling.—This is cooking fish on a grill either in front of or over a nice clear fire. Herring, mackerel, trout, haddock, red mullet, &c., may all be cooked in this manner. They may be prepared in either of the following ways :—

1. Wash and clean the fish, cutting off the heads and fins, and dry them lightly in a cloth. Then score the skin across three times on each side to prevent it cracking during the process of cooking. Season the fish with pepper and salt, and brush it over with oil or melted butter, or allow it to soak for an hour in a mixture of oil and vinegar with a little chopped parsley and shallot ; or

2. The fish may be split open, the bone removed and then lightly coated with flour or fine oatmeal. The latter is most suitable for herring, mackerel, or trout. A coating of egg and bread-crumbs may also be used if liked.

Thoroughly heat the gridiron, grease it well, and lay the fish on it. Keep the fish rather near the fire while cooking or it will become flabby. Cook it from seven to ten minutes according to the thickness of the fish, and turn it once at least during the process. When finished it should be nicely browned on both sides and show the marks of the grill. Serve at once with cut lemon and small pats of Maitre d'Hôtel Butter. If there are any roes belonging to the fish these may be cooked on a tin in the oven and used as a garnish.

Note.—Fillets of fish, such as salmon, turbot, or sole, are sometimes wrapped in a heart-shaped piece of greased paper with a spoonful of any good sauce and grilled thus. They may also be soaked or marinaded in a mixture of oil, &c., as above, previous to being wrapped up. They should be served in the paper (*en papillottes*).

To Skin and Fillet Fish

A Haddock.—First wash the haddock in cold water, and cut off all the fins.

Make a slit in the skin up both sides, so that it can easily be removed.

Make a cut across the skin just below the head, and commence at the flap part.

Loosen the skin there, keeping down the flesh with the knife, and beginning very carefully ; then pull downwards towards the tail.

Turn, and do the other side in the same way.

To fillet it, remove the flesh cleanly from the bones on both sides of the fish.

Commence at the open side of the fish, slipping the knife along close to the bone, and laying the flesh backwards, but do not separate it from the other side.

Turn, and do the other side in the same way.

A filleted haddock should be in one piece.

A Sole or Plaice.—First wash the fish, and cut off all the fins.

Lay on a board with the tail end nearest to you.

Make a cut across the skin just above the tail, slip a knife under it, and commence raising the skin from the flesh.

Then with the right thumb loosen the skin all the way up the right-hand side.

Loosen up the other side in the same way, this time using the thumb of the left hand.

Hold the tail of the fish firmly down on the board ; take hold of the loosened skin with a cloth, and pull it off quickly, drawing it upwards towards the head.

The white skin may be removed in the same way, but this is frequently left on.

To fillet the fish, make a cut straight down the middle of the back to the backbone.

Then remove the flesh, first from one side and then from the other.

Two fillets are taken from each side.

It will be found easiest to raise the first fillet from the left-hand side of the fish, working from the head towards the tail; and then to turn the fish round, and to raise the second fillet, working from the tail towards the head.

Turn the fish right over, and do the other side in the same way.

Note.—Filleting is really best learnt by watching a fishmonger or other competent person at work.

Cold Fish Re-dressed

It is wonderful the variety of little dishes which can be made out of the scraps of cold cooked fish. Either smoked or fresh fish may be utilised in this way and made to appear again in an appetising form. The smallest pieces should not be thrown away, even two or three table-spoonfuls will suffice to make a fish omelet, or, with the addition of some potatoes or rice, enough fish-cakes for two or three persons.

Whenever possible, the skin and bone should be removed from the fish while it is still warm, as when cold the gelatine in the fish hardens and it becomes more adhesive. Cooked fish very soon becomes dry and then hard, so it is better to keep it covered with a plate or basin and to use it as soon as possible.

The removing of the bones must be done with the greatest care, as it is just the very small bones which are so difficult to see which sometimes get into the throat and cause trouble. It is often an improvement to use a little smoked or salt fish along with the fresh; it gives more flavour to the dish.

Fillets of Cod au Gratin

(*Fr.* Cabillaud au Gratin)

Ingredients—

1½ lbs. of Cod.	5 or 6 Button Mushrooms.
2 oz. Butter.	2 table-spoonfuls Bread-crumbs.
1 Shallot.	½ Lemon.
1 tea-spoonful chopped Parsley.	Pepper and Salt.

Method.—A piece from the tail end of the cod is best, for it is the most tender. Remove the skin and the bone, and cut the fish into neat fillets. Mix together the bread-crumbs, the shallot, parsley, and mushrooms finely chopped, a little grated lemon rind, pepper and salt, and melt the butter in a small pan. Grease a dish which can stand the heat of the oven, sprinkle over it some of the mixture, then place on the dish a few fillets of cod with a little lemon juice, melted butter and more mixture, then more fish, and so on until all is used. Stand the dish in a tin containing water, and bake in a moderate oven for half-an-hour, basting the fish occasionally with the butter on the dish. Serve hot. A little white wine may be added.

Note.—Other kinds of fish, such as halibut, haddock, whiting, or even smelts, may be prepared in the same way.

Cod Baked in Batter

Ingredients—

1 lb. Cod.	1 tea-spoonful chopped Parsley.
2 oz. Flour.	Pepper and Salt.
1½ gills Milk.	1 oz. Butter or Dripping.
1 Egg.	

Method.—Wash the cod, dry it, and cut into small neat pieces, free from skin and bone. Place these at the foot of a greased pie-dish, and sprinkle them with a little white pepper and salt. Then make the batter according to directions given on p. 192. If time permits, let this batter stand for a short time. It gives the flour time to swell, and makes it lighter. Then pour it over the fish, and wipe round the edges of the pie-dish. Bake in a moderate oven from twenty to thirty minutes until the batter is well risen and nicely brown, and the fish feels tender. Serve as soon after it is taken from the oven as possible.

Notes.—Any white fish may be used instead of cod, or the remains of cold cooked fish may be utilised.

Half a tea-spoonful of finely powdered mixed herbs may be used in addition to or instead of the parsley.

The dish may be made richer by adding a few oysters, shrimps, or slices of hard-boiled egg.

Cod's Roe (To Boil)

(*Fr.* Laitance de Cabillaud)

Required—

Cod's Roe.	Vinegar.
Boiling Water.	White or Parsley Sauce.
Salt.	

Wash the roe well in cold water, but do not let it soak, then tie it up in a piece of muslin or a pudding cloth, to prevent it breaking. Put it into a saucepan or fish-kettle of slowly boiling water, salted in the proportion of one table-spoonful to one quart of water, and add a few drops of vinegar. The water should just cover the roe. Simmer slowly from fifteen to twenty minutes according to size. When ready, lift the roe out, and let the water drain well from it. Serve on a hot dish with white or parsley sauce poured over it, or on a folded serviette, and hand the sauce separately.

Cod's Roe (Fried)

(*Fr.* Laitance de Cabillaud)

Cut cooked cod's roe in half-inch slices, coat them with a little flour, and fry in a small quantity of butter or clarified fat. Serve garnished with parsley.

Note.—If wished the slices may be egged and bread-crumbed before frying.

Salt Cod with Parsnip Purée

(*Fr.* Morue à la Purée de Panais)

Ingredients—

1 lb. Salt Cod.	2 or 3 table-spoonfuls thick Cream.
3 or 4 Parsnips.	Pepper and Salt.
1 oz. Butter.	

Method.—Soak the fish overnight in cold water, then take it out and wash it well in clean cold water. Put it into a saucepan with cold water to cover it, and let it boil slowly until it is quite tender, about one hour. Then drain it, remove the skin and large bones, put it on to a dish, and keep it warm while the purée is being prepared.

Boil the parsnips until quite tender, then drain and rub them through a fine wire or hair sieve. Reheat this purée with the butter, pepper, salt, and a little cream. Pour it over the fish, and garnish with a little very finely chopped parsley.

Note.—Instead of the parsnip purée a good egg sauce may be poured over the fish.

Dressed Crab (Cold)

Ingredients—

1 Crab (boiled).	1 tea-spoonful made Mustard.
2 table-spoonfuls Cream or Salad Oil.	1 tea-sp. chopped Parsley.
1 table-sp. White Vinegar.	2 table-spoonfuls white Bread-crumbs.
1 tea-spoonful Tarragon Vinegar.	Pepper and Salt.
	A pinch of Cayenne.

Method.—Pick the meat from the crab, keeping back the unwholesome part near the head. Scrub the shells thoroughly to receive the mixture, dry and grease it with a little oil or butter. Chop the meat from the crab very finely, being very careful to remove any small pieces of shell. Mix all the ingredients together in a basin, and season rather highly with pepper, salt, and cayenne. Return this to the prepared shell, and garnish with sprigs of parsley, thin slices of lemon, and the small claws. Serve on a folded d'oyley or dish-paper.

Note.—Dressed crab may be served in a fancy china dish instead of the crab shell.

Dressed Crab (Hot)

(*Fr.* Crabe au Gratin)

Ingredients—

1 Crab (boiled).	1 tea-spoonful chopped Parsley.
2 oz. Bread-crumbs.	A little grated Lemon Rind.
2 table-sp. Melted Butter, Cream, or Salad Oil.	1 tea-spoonful Anchovy Essence.
A pinch of Nutmeg.	A few browned Bread-crumbs.
A pinch of Cayenne.	½ oz. Butter.
Pepper and Salt.	
1 tea-spoonful Vinegar or Lemon Juice.	

Method.—Chop the meat finely, removing any small pieces of shell. Put this into a saucepan with all the other ingredients except the browned bread-crumbs and half ounce of butter. Season rather highly with pepper, salt, and cayenne. Make the mixture thoroughly hot over the fire, and return it to the shell prepared as above. Sprinkle the browned bread-crumbs over the top, and put the butter on in small pieces. Bake in the oven or in front of the fire for about fifteen minutes. Serve on a d'oyley or dish-paper, and garnish with parsley and small slices of lemon.

Note.—If liked, two table-spoonfuls of tomato purée may be added.

Fish Cakes

(*Fr.* Croquettes de Poisson)

Ingredients—

½ lb. cooked Fish.	1 tea-spoonful Anchovy Essence.
½ lb. cooked Potatoes.	Pepper and Salt.
1 oz. Butter.	A little Flour, Egg, and Bread-crumbs.
1 yolk of Egg.	
1 tea-sp. chopped Parsley.	

Method.—The remains of any cold cooked fish may be used for making fish-cakes. Free the fish from all skin and bone, then weigh it. Chop it finely, being most careful to remove any small bones, which might be most dangerous if left in. Sieve the potatoes, or put them through a vegetable presser, and chop the parsley very finely. Melt the butter in a saucepan, then add to it the fish, potatoes, parsley, yolk of egg, and seasonings, and mix well together over the fire. Turn out on to a plate, smooth over with a knife, and set aside to cool. When the mixture feels firm, divide it into ten or twelve small pieces. Flour the hands, take one piece at a time, and roll it into a ball, laying them as they are formed on a slightly floured board. Then with a knife, also floured, flatten them slightly, and shape them into neat round cakes. Egg and bread-crumb them, and fry in boiling fat to a nice brown colour. Drain well, and serve piled high on a hot dish with a dish-paper under them, and garnish with parsley.

Note.—Well-boiled and dried rice may be used instead of potatoes.

Fish Cream

(*Fr.* Crème de Poisson)

Ingredients—

½ lb. uncooked Fish.	1 gill Double Cream.
1 oz. Butter.	1 white of Egg.
1 oz. Bread-crumbs.	A pinch of Nutmeg.
1 gill of Milk.	A squeeze of Lemon Juice.
White Sauce.	Pepper and Salt.

Method.—Weigh the fish, free from skin and bone, and shred it down finely with a knife. Put it into a mortar, and pound it well. Rinse out a small saucepan with cold water, to prevent the mixture sticking to it. Put into it the butter and the milk, and bring them to the boil over the fire. Then add the bread-crumbs, and stir with a wooden spoon over the fire until the bread-crumbs swell and the mixture thickens. Add this mixture to the fish in the mortar, pound well together, and rub through a wire sieve, scraping the sieve underneath.

Put the mixture into a basin, and season to taste. Beat up the white of egg with a knife on a plate until stiff, and whip the cream in a basin with a wire whisk until thick. Add both these to the fish mixture, and stir them in as lightly as possible with an iron spoon. Pour the mixture into a well-greased mould. The mould must not be more than half-filled. Twist a piece of greased paper over the top of it, and steam slowly for half-an-hour, or until firm to the touch. Turn out carefully on to a hot dish, and pour anchovy or white sauce round it.

Note.—This may be steamed in a border mould, and the inside afterwards filled with green peas, or oysters mixed with a little of the sauce.

Fish Curry

Ingredients—

½ lb. cooked Fish.	½ tea-spoonful Chutney.
1 oz. Butter.	1 gill Fish Stock.
1 small Apple, or	1 tea-spoonful Rice Flour.
1 stick of Rhubarb.	Pepper and Salt.
1 small Onion.	A squeeze of Lemon Juice.
1 tea-spoonful Curry Powder.	

Method.—Melt the butter in a saucepan and add the onion and apple or rhubarb cut in small pieces. Cook until a nice brown colour, and add the chutney, curry powder, rice flour, pepper and salt. Stir until boiling and then simmer slowly for twenty minutes. Rub the sauce through a sieve and return it to the saucepan to re-heat. Add the fish, broken in flakes and free from skin and bone. Allow it to get thoroughly hot, and add the lemon juice at the last. A little cream is an improvement. Serve boiled rice separately.

Fish Custard Puddings

Ingredients—

½ lb. cooked Fish.	2 whites of Eggs.
½ pint Milk.	1 dessert-spoonful chopped Parsley.
4 yolks of Eggs.	A little Coralline Pepper.
1 tea-spoonful Anchovy Essence.	Pepper and Salt.

Method.—Grease very carefully about six dariol moulds or tiny basins, and decorate each one at the foot with a little finely-chopped parsley or coralline pepper. Free the fish from all skin and bone, and then weigh it. Chop it rather finely, and about half-fill the moulds. Make a custard with the eggs and milk. Beat up the eggs, yolks and whites, in a basin, and add the milk. Season with white pepper, salt, and anchovy essence. Strain and pour over the fish. Place the moulds in a tin with boiling water to reach half-way up the sides, cover with greased paper, and poach in the oven or on the top of the stove until the custards are set, about fifteen minutes. Turn out and serve hot.

Note.—These are excellent made with cold salmon.

Fish Cutlets

(*Fr.* Côtelettes de Poisson)

Ingredients—

½ lb. cooked Fish.	1 tea-sp. chopped Parsley.
1 oz. Butter.	1 tea-sp. Anchovy Essence.
1 oz. Flour.	Pepper and Salt.
1 gill Milk or Fish Stock.	Egg and Bread-crumbs.
1 yolk of Egg.	

Method.—Free the fish carefully from all skin and bone, then weigh and chop it finely. Melt the butter in a saucepan, add the flour, and mix with a wooden spoon until smooth; then pour in the milk or fish stock, and stir until the mixture boils and draws away from the sides of the saucepan. Remove the pan from the fire, add the fish, yolk of egg, and seasonings, and mix well together. Turn the mixture out on to a plate, smooth over with a knife, and set aside in a cool place until firm. Divide into eight equal-sized pieces, and finish in the same way as lobster cutlets (p. 137).

Fish Omelet

(*Fr.* Omelette au Poisson)

Ingredients—

2 oz. cooked Fish.	2 Eggs.
1 tea-sp. chopped Parsley.	Pepper and Salt.
1 oz. Butter.	

Method.—Free the fish from skin and bone, and chop it finely. Separate the yolks and whites of the eggs. Put the yolks into a medium-sized basin, and the whites on to a plate. Add to the yolks the chopped fish, parsley, pepper and salt, and work these well together with a wooden spoon until of a creamy consistency. Beat up the whites of the eggs on the plate with a broad-bladed knife until so stiff that you could turn the plate upside down without the whites falling off. Remove the wooden spoon from the basin, and with an iron one stir into it the beaten whites lightly and thoroughly. Melt the butter in an omelet pan, and pour the mixture into it, scraping out the basin as quickly as possible. Stir the mixture round with an iron spoon until it begins to set, stirring mostly on the surface, and not scraping the foot of the pan. Then hold it a little longer over the fire until the omelet is nicely browned on the under-side. Slip a knife under it, and double over first from one side and then from the other towards the centre. If not quite cooked on the top, hold it in front of the fire for a minute or two. Then turn it on to a hot dish with a fish-paper on it, and serve as quickly as possible.

Note.—One or two table-spoonfuls of cream added to the mixture is an improvement.

Fish Pie with Potatoes

Ingredients—

½ lb. cooked Fish.	½ lb. cooked Potatoes.
1 gill White Sauce.	1 oz. Butter or Dripping.
1 hard-boiled Egg.	A little Milk.
Pepper and Salt.	

Method.—Break the fish into flakes, free from skin and bone, and put it into a greased pie-dish. Sprinkle with white pepper, salt, and a little lemon juice, and put the egg cut in slices on the top. Make the sauce by melting ½ oz. butter in a small pan, add ½ oz. flour and mix until smooth, pour in 1 gill of milk or fish stock, and stir until boiling and thick. Season to taste, and pour this sauce over the fish and egg.

Melt the butter or dripping in a saucepan, have the potatoes sieved, and add them to it; season with white pepper and salt, and moisten with a little milk. Pile this on the top of the fish, &c., and smooth over with a knife. Mark up the sides with a fork or the point of a knife, and brush over with milk or beaten egg. Bake in a moderate oven until nicely browned, and serve hot.

Gâteau of Fish and Rice

Ingredients—

¼ lb. Carolina Rice.	Grated rind of ½ Lemon.
½ pint Fish Stock or Milk.	Pepper and Salt.
2 Eggs.	1 tea-spoonful chopped Parsley.
½ lb. Fish (cooked).	A little Coralline Pepper.
1 oz. Butter.	

Method.—Wash the rice, and put it into a saucepan with the milk or stock. Allow it to cook slowly until quite soft, adding more liquid if necessary. Then add to it the fish chopped, the butter, pepper, salt, and grated lemon rind. Beat up the eggs and add them, mixing well. Then grease a plain mould or basin, and decorate it with chopped parsley and a little coralline pepper; pour the mixture into this; cover with greased paper, and steam slowly from one to one and a half hours, until firm to the touch. Turn out on a hot dish, and serve with or without sauce.

Fish Pie with Macaroni

(*Fr.* Poisson au Macaroni)

Ingredients—

½ lb. Fish, cooked or uncooked.	Lemon Juice.
¼ lb. Macaroni.	A little grated Lemon Rind.
½ pint White Sauce.	Pepper and Salt.
½ oz. Butter.	1 table-spoonful Bread-crumbs.

Method.—Put the macaroni into a saucepan of hot water and boil until quite soft, drain, and chop it rather small. Remove all skin and bone from the fish, and cut it into small pieces, or if cooked, break it into flakes. Grease a pie-dish, and put in half the fish, seasoning with pepper, salt, a little grated lemon rind, and lemon juice. Next put in half the macaroni and half the sauce, then the remainder of the fish, more seasoning, and the rest of the macaroni and sauce. Sprinkle the bread-crumbs over the top, and place the butter on in small pieces. Wipe round the edges of the pie-dish, and bake in a moderate oven for fifteen minutes if the fish is cooked, or half-an-hour if uncooked fish is used. Brown the pie nicely on the top, and serve hot, garnished with sprigs of parsley.

Note.—A few oysters, picked shrimps, or hard-boiled egg, cut in slices, may be added to this pie.

Another very good pie can be made by using cooked and sieved potatoes in place of the macaroni.

Steamed Fish Pudding

(*Fr.* Pouding de Poisson)

Ingredients—

½ lb. cooked Fish.	1 tea-sp. Anchovy Essence.
2 oz. Bread-crumbs.	1 tea-sp. chopped Parsley.
1 oz. Butter.	Pepper and Salt.
1 gill Milk.	Anchovy or Parsley Sauce.
1 Egg.	

Method.—First grease a plain mould or basin, or several small moulds, with clarified butter, and sprinkle the chopped parsley over the inside. Free the fish from all skin and bone, and chop it finely. Put it into a basin with the bread-crumbs, pepper, salt, and anchovy essence. Put the milk and butter into a small saucepan, bring them to the boil, and then pour over the ingredients in the basin. Let these soak for a few minutes, then add the egg well beaten. Mix together, and pour into the prepared mould or moulds. Cover with greased paper and steam from ten to fifteen minutes if in small moulds, and for half-an-hour if done in one large mould. When ready, the mixture should be firm to the touch. Turn out on to a hot dish, and serve with anchovy or parsley sauce poured round.

Potato and Fish Timbale

(*Fr.* Timbale de Poisson)

Ingredients—

½ lb. cooked Potato.	2 table-sp. white Bread-crumbs.
1 yolk of Egg.	¼ lb. cooked Fish.
1 oz. Butter.	2 table-sp. White Sauce.
2 table-spoonfuls grated Cheese.	1 tea-sp. chopped Parsley.
Seasoning.	Seasoning.

Method.—Sieve the potatoes, add to them the butter melted, the yolk of egg, cheese, and seasonings. Mix well together, and if not sufficiently moist add a very little milk. Butter a basin or plain mould, and sprinkle it with the bread-crumbs. Line the bottom and sides with the potato mixture, keeping back a little for the top. Then remove all skin and bone from the fish, mix it with the white sauce, and add parsley and seasoning to taste. Hard-boiled egg cut in pieces, oysters, anchovy, or mushrooms may be added. The mixture must not be too moist. Put it into the prepared mould, and cover with the rest of the potato mixture. Make the top very smooth with a knife. Bake in a moderate oven about forty minutes. Place a hot dish on the top, invert the mould, and let it stand a few minutes. Then carefully withdraw the mould. Serve plain or with white sauce.

Scalloped Fish

(*Fr.* Coquilles de Poisson)

Ingredients—

- ½ lb. cooked Fish.
- 1 gill White Sauce.
- A squeeze of Lemon Juice.
- White Pepper and Salt.
- 1 table-spoonful browned Crumbs.
- ½ oz. Butter.
- Some Scallop Shells.

Method.—Flake any nice white fish (herring or mackerel would be too rich) into neat pieces. Season the fish with white pepper, salt, and a few drops of lemon juice. Butter some clean scallop shells and sprinkle with a few bread-crumbs. Put in a spoonful of sauce with some of the prepared fish on the top, and continue putting in fish and sauce in layers until the shells are full. Cover the top with bread-crumbs and a few tiny pieces of butter. Bake in a moderate oven until nicely browned and serve very hot.

Notes.—A little grated parmesan or a few oysters or picked shrimps may be added to the sauce if wished, and a little cream is always an improvement.

A fireproof dish may be used instead of the scallop shells.

Stuffed Fillets of Haddock

(*Fr.* Filets d'Eglefin Farcis)

Ingredients—

- 2 small filleted Haddocks.
- Pepper and Salt.
- Lemon Juice.
- 2 table-spoonfuls browned Bread-crumbs.
- Maître d'Hôtel Butter.
- Anchovy or Parsley Sauce.

Stuffing—

- 2 table-sp. Bread-crumbs.
- 1 tea-sp. chopped Parsley.
- 1 dessert-spoonful melted Butter.
- Grated Lemon Rind.
- Pepper and Salt
- A little Milk.

Method.—Wipe the fish with a clean cloth, and cut them in half lengthways. Lay them out on a board with the side which the skin was taken off uppermost, and season each piece with white pepper, salt, and a little lemon juice. Prepare the stuffing as directed on p. 169, lay a little on each fillet, and roll them up, commencing at the thick end, and rolling towards the tail. Stand them up on a greased tin, cover with a piece of greased paper, and bake in a moderate oven about fifteen minutes, or until the fish has lost its clear appearance, and looks quite white. When ready, roll the pieces in some fine browned bread-crumbs, coating them well. Place them on a hot dish, pour some anchovy or parsley sauce round, and put a small pat of maître d'hôtel butter on the top of each.

Smoked Haddock Balls

Ingredients—

- 6 oz. cooked Smoked Haddock.
- 6 oz. cooked or sieved Potatoes.
- 1 oz. Butter or Dripping.
- 1 hard-boiled Egg.
- 1 yolk of Egg.
- A little Milk.
- Pepper and Salt.
- A little Flour.
- Egg and Bread-crumbs.

Method.—Chop the fish finely, being most careful to remove all skin and small bones. Chop also the hard-boiled egg and sieve the potatoes. Melt the butter or dripping in a saucepan, and put in the potatoes, fish, and hard-boiled egg. Add the raw yolk of egg, and season to taste with pepper and salt. Mix all together over the fire, and if too dry add a little milk. Turn the mixture on to a plate, and then form into balls. Egg and bread-crumb, and fry in boiling fat.

Smoked or Finnan Haddock Stewed in Milk

Ingredients—

- 1 Smoked Haddock.
- ½ pint Milk.
- 1 oz. Butter.
- ½ oz. Flour.
- Pepper.
- Sippets of Toast.

Methods.—Dip the haddock into boiling water for a minute or two, then remove the skin and all fins. Cut the fish in neat-sized pieces, put them into a saucepan with the milk, and simmer slowly about fifteen minutes or until the fish is quite tender. Then lift out the pieces of fish, and keep them hot on a dish. Work the butter and flour together on a plate with a knife, and when thoroughly blended add them to the milk in the pan. Stir over the fire, and cook a few minutes. Add a pinch of pepper, and strain this sauce over the fish. Garnish with sippets of toast, and serve hot.

Halibut with Tomatoes

(*Fr.* Flétan aux Tomates)

Ingredients—

- 1½ lbs. Halibut.
- 3 or 4 Fresh Tomatoes.
- 1 table-spoonful Flour.
- Pepper and Salt.
- Juice of ½ a Lemon.
- 2 table-spoonfuls Bread-crumbs.
- ½ oz. Butter.

Method.—Wash the halibut, and cut it into small neat pieces free from skin and bone.

Put the flour on to a plate, and coat each piece of fish lightly with it. Let the tomatoes soak in boiling water for a few minutes, then lift them out, dry, and skin them. Put them on a plate and cut them in slices. Grease out a pie-dish with a little butter, lay in a few pieces of fish, and season with pepper, salt, and lemon juice. Over these put some of the tomatoes, then more fish and seasoning, and so on until all is in. Make the top layer tomatoes; sprinkle the bread-crumbs over last of all, and put the butter on in small pieces. Bake in a moderate oven from three-quarters to one hour, and brown nicely on the top. When ready remove from the oven and wipe round the edges of the pie-dish. Place the pie on a dish, and serve very hot.

Halibut (Mayonnaise of)

(*Fr.* Flétan à la Mayonnaise)

Required—

Halibut.
Mayonnaise Sauce.
Parsley, Lobster Coral or Salad to garnish.

Method.—Boil a nice middle cut of halibut, being careful not to overcook it, or it will lose its shape. Drain well, and remove the skin. When quite cold, lift on to a clean dish, and pour over enough Mayonnaise sauce to coat it nicely. Garnish with some finely chopped parsley or lobster coral sprinkled lightly over it, and round the dish arrange some sprigs of parsley or some nice leaves of lettuce or cress.

Cucumber or tomato salad would make a nice accompaniment to this dish.

Note.—Cold halibut can also be served quite simply without the sauce. It should be prettily garnished and accompanied with salad.

Fresh Herring au Gratin

(*Fr.* Harengs au Gratin)

Required—

4 fresh Herring.
1 dessert-spoonful chopped Parsley.
Mustard Sauce.
1 dessert-spoonful chopped Mushrooms.
1 oz. Butter.
Browned Crumbs.
Pepper and Salt.

Method.—Butter a gratin dish rather thickly with some of the butter, and sprinkle over the foot half the parsley and half the mushrooms. Have the herring nicely cleaned and trimmed, remove the heads, and score the skin across in several places. Lay the fish in the dish, season them well, and sprinkle with the remainder of the parsley and mushrooms. Cover with browned bread-crumbs, and put the rest of the butter in small pieces on the top. Bake in a moderate oven about twenty minutes, and serve with mustard sauce (if liked) in a sauce-boat.

Pickled Herring

(*Fr.* Harengs Marinés)

Required—

3 or 4 Herring.
1 table-spoonful Flour.
½ tea-spoonful powdered Mace.
Pepper and Salt.
4 or 5 Cloves.
12 Peppercorns.
Brown Vinegar and Water.

Method.—Wash and clean the herring, cutting off the heads and the fins, and scraping the skin well with a knife. Dry them in a cloth, and then split them open, and remove all the bones. Cut each herring in two lengthways. Put the flour, pepper, salt, and mace on to a plate, and mix them well together. Dip each piece of herring into this, and roll them up from the thick end towards the tail. Pack them into a greased pie-dish, putting them in two layers if necessary. Pour round them in equal quantities water and brown vinegar, enough to half fill the dish. Put in the cloves and peppercorns. A bay leaf may also be added. Place small pieces of dripping here and there over the top, and bake in a moderate oven for one hour. Set aside till cold. Serve as many pieces of fish as will be required at one time on a clean dish, pour a little of the liquid round them, and garnish with parsley. Herring done in this way will keep for several days. More vinegar should be added if required. Do not let the fish become too dry.

Note.—Mackerel may be prepared in the same way.

Lobster Cutlets

(*Fr.* Côtelettes de Homard)

Ingredients—

1 Hen Lobster.
1 oz. Butter. }
1½ oz. Flour. }
1 gill Water or Fish Stock. } Panada.
Pepper and Salt.
1 table-spoonful Cream.
A squeeze of Lemon Juice.
A pinch of Cayenne.
Spawn or Coral.
½ oz. Butter.
Egg and Bread-crumbs.

Method.—Remove all the flesh from a boiled lobster, and chop it very finely, carefully keeping back any little pieces of shell. Pound some spawn or coral in a mortar with the half ounce of butter, and rub it through a hair sieve. This is called lobster butter.

Make a panada by putting the butter and water or stock into a saucepan, and when they boil, stirring in the flour. Mix well with a wooden spoon until perfectly smooth and well cooked. Then add the lobster, the lobster butter, cream, and seasonings. Mix well together, and turn out on a plate to cool. When cold and firm, form the mixture into small cutlet-shaped pieces, using a little flour to enable you to shape them more easily. Then egg and bread-crumb them and fry in hot fat to a golden brown. Drain well on kitchen paper, and stick a small piece of the feeler or a piece of parsley stalk into the narrow end of each to represent a bone. Dish in a circle on a hot dish with a dish paper under them, and garnish with fried parsley.

Note.—**Crab Cutlets** may be made in the same way.

Mussels à la Poulette

(*Fr.* Moules à la Poulette)

Ingredients—

1 quart Mussels.	½ oz. Butter.
1 Onion.	½ oz. Flour.
A few sprigs of Parsley.	1 dessert-spoonful chopped Parsley.
Pepper and Salt.	1 yolk of Egg.
½ pint White Wine.	

Method.—Choose small mussels; they are the most delicate. Scrape the shells carefully with a knife, and wash well in cold water, changing the water several times until the mussels are quite free from grit. Put the mussels into a sauté pan or shallow stewpan, with the onion thinly sliced, sprigs of parsley, white wine, pepper and salt. Cover the pan, put it on the fire, and toss the mussels occasionally. When the shells open, the mussels are done. Drain them, and strain the liquor into a basin. Remove the shells from the mussels and carefully remove the piece which looks like a weed. Melt the butter in the pan, add the flour, and mix until smooth with a wooden spoon. Pour in the strained liquor, and stir until boiling. Add the yolk of egg and chopped parsley, and allow the sauce to thicken, but do not boil again. Put in the mussels to re-heat and serve at once.

Oyster Soufflés (Baked)

(*Fr.* Petits Soufflés d'Huîtres)

Ingredients—

1½ dozen Oysters.	1 oz. Butter.
1 Whiting.	1 oz. Bread-crumbs.
2 Eggs.	1 gill Oyster Liquor, Milk, or Fish Stock.
2 table-spoonfuls Cream.	A squeeze of Lemon Juice.
White Pepper and Salt.	A pinch of Nutmeg.
A pinch of Cayenne.	

Method.—Put the oysters into a saucepan with their liquor, bring to the boil and strain. Then remove the gristle, and break them into small pieces with a fork. Scrape the flesh from the whiting, free it from all skin and bone, and pound well in a mortar. Melt the butter in a small pan, add the oyster liquor and bread-crumbs, and stir over the fire until the mixture thickens. Add this panada to the whiting in the mortar, pound again for a few minutes, and then rub through a fine wire sieve. Put the sieved mixture into a basin, and add the oysters, yolks of eggs, seasoning, and cream. Mix well. Beat up the whites of eggs to a stiff froth on a plate, and stir them lightly into the mixture with an iron spoon. Pour into small greased soufflé cases, china or paper, and bake in a moderate oven for about fifteen minutes, until well risen and firm to the touch. When ready, garnish with sprigs of parsley, and serve quickly.

Perch (To Stew with Wine)

(*Fr.* Perche au Vin Blanc)

Ingredients—

3 or 4 Perch.	1 oz. Butter.
White Stock and Sherry.	1 oz. Flour.
2 Bay Leaves.	1 tea-spoonful Anchovy Essence.
A few Parsley Stalks.	Pepper and Salt.
1 small Onion.	
2 or 3 Cloves.	

Method.—Wash and clean the fish thoroughly, scrape well to remove the scales, and cut off the fins. Lay the perch in a stewpan with equal quantities of sherry and stock to cover them. Add the bay leaves, cloves, parsley stalks, and onion thinly sliced. Season with pepper and salt, put the lid on the pan, and stew slowly until tender, about twenty minutes. When ready, lift the fish carefully on to a hot dish, and strain the liquid into a basin. Put the butter into the pan, and let it melt over the fire. Add the flour, and mix with a wooden spoon until smooth. Then pour in the strained liquor, add the anchovy essence, and stir over the fire until boiling. The sauce must be of a consistency to coat the fish. If too thin, allow it to reduce for a few minutes; if too thick, add more stock or sherry. Pour this over the fish, and serve hot.

Note.—Perch may also be boiled or fried.

Red Mullets au Gratin

(*Fr.* Rougets au Gratin)

Ingredients—

2 Red Mullets.	1 tea-spoonful chopped Parsley.
½ glass of Sherry.	½ tea-sp. chopped Onion.
1 tea-spoonful Ketchup.	Grated rind of ½ a Lemon.
1 tea-spoonful Anchovy Essence.	1 table-spoonful browned Bread-crumbs.
3 or 4 Button Mushrooms.	Pepper and Salt.
1 oz. Butter.	

Method.—Wash and clean the mullets, cutting off the heads and fins, and dry them in a cloth. Grease a gratin dish with some of the butter, and sprinkle over it half the chopped parsley, mushrooms, and onion, and a little grated lemon rind. Score the fish across once or twice with a knife, and lay them on the top. Sprinkle with pepper and salt and the remainder of the chopped ingredients. Pour over the wine, ketchup, and anchovy sauce, and cover with browned bread-crumbs. Put the rest of the butter in small pieces on the top, and bake in a moderate oven about twenty minutes. Wipe the dish, and garnish with parsley before serving.

Russian Fish Pie

(*Fr.* Pâté de Poisson à la Russe)

Ingredients—

¾ lb. White Fish.	1 table-sp. White Sauce.
1 tea-spoonful chopped Parsley.	A little grated Lemon Rind and Lemon Juice.
1 hard-boiled Egg.	A pinch of Cayenne.
White Pepper and Salt.	Rough Puff Pastry.

Method.—The fish for this pie may either be cooked or uncooked according to the kind used. Cod, halibut, or turbot would require to be cooked first, but such fish as haddock, sole, or whiting may be used raw. Break or cut the fish into small neat pieces and put them on a plate. Season with pepper, salt, cayenne, grated lemon rind and lemon juice. Add the white sauce and hard-boiled egg cut in small pieces and mix all carefully together.

Make the proportion of pastry with ½ lb. of flour (see p. 164), and roll it out to a square shape and about one-eighth of an inch in thickness. Trim the edges with a sharp knife, reserving the scraps for decorating the pie. Put the fish mixture in the centre of the square, wet the corners of the pastry with cold water or beaten egg and fold them upwards, making them meet and overlap slightly in the centre like a handkerchief sachet. Press the joins well together and brush the pie over with beaten egg. Decorate the top with some leaves cut out of the scraps of pastry that were trimmed off. Brush over the leaves also with beaten egg and lift the pie very carefully on to a greased baking-tin. Bake in a good oven from three-quarters to one hour, until the pastry is thoroughly cooked and of a brown colour. Serve hot garnished with parsley.

Notes.—Cooked salmon may be used for this pie.

Sometimes a little cooked rice is mixed with the fish.

A few oysters or picked shrimps may be added.

Salmon (Mayonnaise of)

(*Fr.* Mayonnaise de Saumon)

Required—	*Decorations*—
A middle cut of Salmon.	Lobster, Coral, Truffle, Parsley, Lettuce, Endive, or Cucumber.
Mayonnaise Sauce.	
Aspic Jelly.	

Method.—Boil a nice cut of salmon, remove the skin, and let it become cold. Put it on to a clean dish, and coat with thick Mayonnaise sauce, to which liquid aspic has been added in the proportion of half gill to half pint of sauce. Use the sauce in a setting condition, covering the fish all over, and then set aside until firm. Garnish with anything suitable, such as lobster, coral, truffle, parsley, lettuce, endive, cucumber, &c. A border of chopped aspic will make a pretty finish to the dish.

Notes.—Remains of cold salmon may be used for this dish. The fish ought to be flaked, piled high on a dish, and then coated with sauce.

Potted Salmon

Ingredients—

¼ lb. cooked Salmon.	½ tea-spoonful Vinegar.
2 oz. Butter.	Pepper and Salt.
1 tea-spoonful Anchovy or Shrimp Essence.	A pinch of powdered Mace.
	A pinch of Cayenne.

Method.—Free the salmon from all skin and bone, and then weigh it. Put it into a mortar with most of the butter melted, and season to taste and rather highly. Pound well until smooth, and then rub through a sieve. Pack this smoothly into a small pot or jar, and run the rest of the butter over the top, which will preserve the mixture and prevent it from becoming dry. This makes delightful sandwiches, when a little thinly sliced cucumber or small cress would be an improvement.

Note.—Other fish, such as cod, halibut, brill, or mackerel, may be used in the same way.

Fried Scallops

(*Fr.* Coquilles Frits)

Required—

½ dozen Scallops.	A little Flour.
Pepper and Salt.	Egg and Bread-crumbs.

Method.—Wipe the scallops and cut them in two pieces. Dry them with a little flour and then coat with egg and bread-crumbs. Fry a nice brown colour in boiling fat, drain and serve garnished with cut lemon and parsley.

Scalloped Scallops

Required—

Scallops.	White Bread-crumbs.
Pepper and Salt.	A little chopped Parsley.
Lemon Juice.	Butter.

Method.—Choose perfectly fresh scallops, open and remove them from the shells. Cut off the beards and black part, and wash them thoroughly. Wash and scrub the deeper shells and dry them. Grease them with butter, and sprinkle a few white bread-crumbs over. Lay three scallops into each shell, and season them with pepper, salt, lemon juice, and a little chopped parsley. Cover with more bread-crumbs, and put some small pieces of butter on the top. Brown quickly in a hot oven or before the fire. Serve on a hot dish with a dish paper under them, and garnish with cut lemon and parsley.

Shrimp Patties

(*Fr.* Petits Pâtés de Crevettes)

Ingredients—

¼ lb. picked Shrimps.	Pepper and Salt.
2 table-sp. White Sauce.	A pinch of Cayenne.
1 tea-sp. Shrimp Essence.	A squeeze of Lemon Juice.
2 table-spoonfuls Cream.	Rough Puff or Puff Pastry.

Method.—Heat the sauce, add the shrimps and seasoning and mix well. Pour in the cream and make thoroughly hot before using.

To make the Patties.—Make the pastry cases according to directions given on p. 165 (first or second method), and fill them with the shrimp mixture. Put on the lids of pastry and garnish with sprigs of parsley. Serve on a hot dish with a d'oyley or dish-paper under them.

Note.—*Lobster or Oyster Patties* can be made in the same way, using small pieces of cooked lobster or oysters instead of the shrimps.

The white sauce should be made, if possible, with fish stock.

Sole a la Béchamel

(*Fr.* Sole à la Béchamel)

Ingredients—

1 Sole.	1 table-spoonful Cream.
½ oz. Butter.	Pepper and Salt.
½ oz. Flour.	A squeeze of Lemon Juice.
1¼ gills Fish Stock.	Decoration.

Method.—Prepare and cook in the same way as Sole au Parmesan (see below), omitting the cheese and adding a little cream to the sauce. Decorate with chopped parsley, chopped truffle, hard-boiled and sieved yolk of egg or lobster coral, or alternate strips of each.

Sole au Gratin

(*Fr.* Sole au Gratin)

Prepare and cook in the same way as red mullets au gratin.

Fillets of Sole au Parmesan

(*Fr.* Filets de Sole au Parmesan)

Ingredients—

1 Sole.	½ oz. Butter.
2 oz. grated Parmesan.	½ oz. Flour.
Pepper and Salt.	1¼ gills Fish Stock.
A pinch of Cayenne.	A little Lemon Juice.

Method.—Skin and fillet the fish. Wash the trimmings and bones, and put them into a saucepan with one gill of water and one gill of milk, a small piece of onion, a bay leaf, a blade of mace, and some parsley stalks. Simmer slowly for fifteen minutes, and strain this stock ready for use. Trim the fillets neatly, and lay them on a board with the side from which the skin was taken uppermost. Season with pepper, salt, and a squeeze of lemon juice. Double each fillet over lengthways, place them on a greased baking-tin, cover with greased paper, and bake from ten to fifteen minutes. Make a sauce with the butter, flour, and stock and season with pepper, salt, and cayenne. The sauce must be thick enough to coat the fish. Add most of the cheese to the sauce, but do not boil again. Dish the fillets on a hot dish, one leaning against the other; pour the sauce over, and sprinkle the rest of the cheese on the top. Brown in the oven and serve hot.

Note.—Fillets of any other white fish may be prepared in the same way.

Whitebait (to Fry)

(*Fr.* Blanchailles)

Required—

Whitebait.	Flour

Method.—These fish must be perfectly fresh, and should be carefully looked over and put into water with a lump of ice in it, and kept there until required. Have ready on the fire a saucepan of boiling fat or oil (see French Frying, p. 130). Put two or three table-spoonfuls of flour on the centre of a clean cloth, drain some of the whitebait free from water in a colander, and then shake them lightly in the flour. Empty the bait without delay into a frying basket, and shake well to let the loose flour drop out. Plunge it into hot fat and let the fish fry for a minute or two. Then lift out the basket of fish and let the fat re-heat; put in the fish a second time and fry till crisp and lightly browned. If there is a quantity of whitebait to be cooked it is a good plan to fry it all the first time and let it drain, and give it the second frying just when it is required. Serve garnished with quarters of lemon and fried parsley, and hand brown bread and butter separately.

Note.—Devilled Whitebait is prepared by sprinkling the fish with black or red pepper before the final frying.

SAUCES—SAVOURY AND SWEET

General Notes on Sauce-making.—Sauces are easily made if the rules for making them are closely followed and the various ingredients carefully measured to the exact quantities given in the recipes.

The basis of most sauces is butter and flour cooked together, which makes a thickening. This thickening is frequently called a "roux." If for a white sauce, the flour and butter are not coloured; if for a brown, the butter is first allowed to take colour and then the flour is cooked until brown. To this thickening is added the liquid and seasoning suitable to the dish with which the sauce has to be served. After the liquid is poured on to the thickening the sauce must be stirred constantly until boiling or it will be lumpy. Sauces frequently have a raw taste owing to the flour in them not being properly cooked. No sauce is ready as soon as it thickens; it must boil at least three minutes. The thickness of the sauce can be regulated according to the purpose for which it is to be used by adding more or less liquid.

When wine is required allow the sauce to boil for two or three minutes after it has been added in order to blend the flavour. If cream is added let it boil in the sauce for a minute or two. Before adding yolks of eggs to a sauce, draw the saucepan to the side of the fire and drop them in one at a time, stirring briskly, and do not boil again. When lemon juice is added to any sauce containing milk or cream, add it last of all, and do not boil again. Strain all sauces before using except those which have a chopped ingredient served in them such as caper, parsley, egg sauce, &c.

The best sauces are usually rubbed through a hair sieve or wrung through a tammy-cloth, to make them perfectly smooth and velvety in appearance. The washing of the tammy-cloth must be carefully attended to, or it is apt to give the sauce an unpleasant flavour.

To Keep Sauces Warm.—Stand the saucepan containing them inside another pan of hot water and cover the sauce with a lid to prevent a skin forming on the top. With very thick sauces a little water may be run over the top.

Sauce Allemande

Ingredients—

1 pint Velouté Sauce (p. 146).	3 yolks of Eggs.
	½ oz. Butter.

Method.—Put the velouté sauce into a saucepan, and let it boil until reduced one-fourth. Then draw the pan to the side of the fire, and add the yolks of eggs and butter. Stir briskly, and cook for a minute or two over a slow fire. Do not boil again, or the sauce will curdle. Strain through a fine strainer or tammy before using.

Anchovy Sauce

(*Fr.* Beurre d'Anchois)

Ingredients—

½ oz. Butter.	1 dessert-spoonful Anchovy Essence.
½ oz. Flour.	White Pepper and Salt to taste.
½ pint Fish Stock or 1 gill of Milk and 1 gill of Water.	

Method.—Melt the butter in a small lined saucepan, add the flour, and mix smoothly with a wooden spoon. Cook for a minute or two over the fire without discolouring, and then draw the pan to the side before adding the liquid. Fish stock will give the sauce a better flavour; but if that is not to be had, use milk and water. Add the liquid gradually, then return the pan to the fire, and keep stirring constantly until boiling. Add the anchovy essence, and season to taste with white pepper and salt.

Note.—Preserved anchovies may be used instead of the anchovy essence. Three or four will be required for the above quantity of sauce. Lift them out of the oil in which they are preserved, dip them for a minute into warm water, and then scrape off the silver skin. Pound them in a mortar, and rub through a wire or hair sieve. Scrape the sieve well underneath, and add this paste to the sauce.

Apple Sauce

(*Fr.* Sauce aux Pommes)

Ingredients—

3 or 4 Apples.	½ gill of Water.
½ oz. Butter.	1 table-spoonful Brown Sugar.
A pinch of Nutmeg.	

Method.—Wipe the apples with a cloth, then peel, core and slice them thinly. Put them into a lined saucepan with the water, sugar and nutmeg. Let them stew slowly until reduced to a pulp and stir frequently with a wooden spoon. Add the butter and mash them until smooth or rub through a hair sieve. Make thoroughly hot before serving.

Béchamel Sauce

(*Fr.* Sauce Béchamel)

Ingredients—

1½ oz. Butter.	White Pepper and Salt.
1½ oz. Flour.	A pinch of Cayenne.
1 pint Seasoned Milk.	A squeeze of Lemon Juice.
½ gill Cream.	

Method.—Melt the butter in a lined saucepan, add the flour, and mix smoothly with a wooden spoon. Cook for a minute or two over the fire, but do not brown. Draw the saucepan to one side of the fire, and add the milk all at once. Return to the fire, and stir constantly until boiling. Add the cream and seasoning, and cook for a minute or two longer. Remove the saucepan from the fire before adding the lemon juice, and strain before using.

Note.—Seasoned Milk—(1) Put as much milk as is required into a lined saucepan, with a small piece of carrot, turnip, onion, and celery, a bay leaf, one or two cloves, and a few parsley stalks. Let the saucepan stand by the side of the fire until the milk is well seasoned, then strain and cool before using.

(2) More or less milk may be added, according to the thickness of the sauce required. If considered too rich, the cream may be omitted.

(3) If used for masking meat, this sauce must have two or three leaves of gelatine or some aspic jelly added to it.

Black Butter

(*Fr.* Beurre Noir)

Ingredients—

2 oz. Butter.	1 dessert-sp. Minced Parsley.
1 table-spoonful Vinegar.	Pepper and Salt.

Method.—Melt the butter in a small saucepan, and stir it briskly until it becomes quite brown, but not burnt. Mince the parsley rather coarsely, throw it in, and add the vinegar and seasoning. Simmer a minute or two and the sauce will be ready for serving.

Black butter is frequently served with fish.

Bread Sauce

(*Fr.* Sauce au Pain)

Ingredients—

½ pint Milk.	½ oz. of Butter or
2 oz. Bread-crumbs.	1 table-spoonful Cream.
½ small Onion.	White Pepper and Salt.
3 or 4 Cloves.	A pinch of Cayenne.

Method.—Rinse out a small lined saucepan with cold water and put into it the milk and the piece of onion stuck with cloves. Set this by the side of the fire and simmer very gently until the milk is well flavoured. Then remove the onion and cloves and add the bread-crumbs, which must be finely made by being rubbed through a wire sieve. Stir over the fire and cook slowly until the bread-crumbs swell and thicken the sauce. Add the butter or cream and season to taste with white pepper, salt, and a pinch of cayenne.

Brown Sauce

(*Fr.* Sauce Espagnole)

Ingredients—

1 oz. Butter.	1 dessert-sp. Ketchup.
1 oz. Flour.	1 tea-sp. Harvey's Sauce.
1 pint Brown Stock.	A small sprig of Thyme, Parsley, and Marjoram.
1 small Onion.	1 Bay Leaf.
A small piece of Carrot and Turnip.	1 blade of Mace.
1 stick of Celery or ½ teasp. Celery Seed.	3 or 4 Cloves.
	Pepper and Salt.

Method.—Melt the butter in a small stewpan, and let it brown. Add the onion, skinned and cut, in thin slices, and stir until it is brown. Add the flour, and brown it also. Then draw the stewpan to one side, pour in the stock, and stir over the fire until boiling. Boil for a few minutes, and remove all scum with an iron spoon. Have the other vegetables prepared and cut small, and add them next with the seasonings. If celery seed is used, tie it in a piece of muslin. Simmer the sauce slowly for at least half-an-hour, stirring occasionally, and skimming when necessary. Strain through a fine strainer or tammy-cloth, and re-heat before using.

Note.—If the stock used is well flavoured, some of the seasonings and vegetables may be omitted.

A few chopped mushrooms and a sliced tomato may be added if wished, also a little wine.

This sauce is the foundation for many other brown sauces, as for instance :—

Sauce aux Olives.—Cook one dozen or more turned olives in a glass of sherry and add half pint brown sauce.

Sauce Madère.—Add one glass Madeira and one tea-spoonful lemon juice to half pint of brown sauce.

Sauce Piquante.—Cook one table-spoonful chopped capers, one tea-spoonful chopped shallot, one table-spoonful chopped gherkin, in half gill vinegar, add half pint of brown sauce and just before serving one dessert-spoonful chopped parsley.

Caper Sauce

(*Fr.* Sauce aux Câpres)

Ingredients—

¾ oz. Butter.	1 table-spoonful Capers.
¾ oz. Flour.	1 table-spoonful Vinegar.
½ pint Fish Stock or Meat Boilings.	White Pepper and Salt.

Method.—Melt the butter in a small lined saucepan, being careful it does not brown. Add the flour, and mix until smooth with a wooden spoon. Cook a minute or two, then draw the pan to the side of the fire, and pour in the liquid. Return to the fire, and stir constantly until boiling. Add the capers, roughly chopped, and season to taste with white pepper and salt. Boil two or three minutes longer, and add the vinegar last.

Celery Sauce

(*Fr.* Sauce Céléri)

Ingredients—

1 oz. Butter.	1 head of Celery.
1 oz. Flour.	White Pepper and Salt.
3 gills White Stock or Milk.	2 table-spoonfuls Cream.

Method.—Wash the celery, cut it in shreds, and stew it slowly in the stock or milk until tender. Then rub as much as possible through a hair or fine wire sieve. Melt the butter in a saucepan, add the flour and cook two or three minutes. Pour in the celery purée and stir until boiling. Add seasoning to taste and the cream at the last.

Chaudfroid Sauce

(*Fr.* Sauce Chaudfroid)

Ingredients—

½ pint Béchamel or Velouté Sauce (see Recipes).	2 or 3 table-spoonfuls liquid Aspic.

Method.—Add the aspic to the sauce, boil for a few minutes, and strain or tammy before using.

Note.—This sauce is used for coating large or small joints of meat, and care should be taken to get it of the right consistency. If too thin, it will not look well; and if too thick, it will have a lumpy appearance.

If aspic is not to be had, dissolve two sheets of gelatine in a little water or stock, and strain it into the sauce.

Brown Chaudfroid Sauce can be made in the same way, substituting brown sauce for the white and adding about a quarter of an ounce meat glaze.

Chestnut Sauce (White)

(*Fr.* Sauce aux Marrons)

Ingredients—

½ lb. Chestnuts.
3 gills White Stock.
2 table-spoonfuls Cream.
Rind of ½ Lemon.
Pepper and Salt.

Method.—Remove the brown outside skin from the chestnuts, and throw them into a saucepan of boiling water. Boil for a few minutes, then drain and peel off the inside skin. Put them back into the saucepan with the stock and thinly peeled rind of half lemon, and simmer slowly for one hour or longer until the chestnuts are quite soft and pulpy. Rub them and the stock through a hair sieve with a wooden spoon, and return again to the saucepan. Add the cream, season to taste, and stir until boiling. Serve very hot.

Note.—Brown chestnut sauce may be made by using half a pint of brown sauce and one gill of brown stock instead of the white stock and cream.

Cranberry Sauce

(*Fr.* Sauce aux Canneberges)

Ingredients—

1 lb. Cranberries.
¼ oz. Brown Sugar.
1 teacupful Water.

Method.—Pick and wash the cranberries and stew them slowly with the water until reduced to a pulp. Stir them frequently while cooking and add the sugar at the last. Sometimes a little port wine is added before serving.

Curry Sauce

(*Fr.* Sauce Cari)

Ingredients—

1 oz. Butter or Dripping.
¾ oz. Rice Flour.
3 gills of Stock.
1 Onion.
1 lump of Sugar.
1 tea-sp. Curry Powder.
1 tea-sp. Chutney.
1 small Apple.
Pepper and Salt.
A squeeze of Lemon Juice.

Method.—Peel and chop the apple, and skin and slice the onion very thinly. Melt the butter or dripping in a small stewpan, put in the apple and onion, and fry them for a few minutes. Next add the curry powder, rice flour, and chutney, and mix well together with an iron spoon. Add the stock, and stir until boiling. Season to taste with pepper and salt, and let the sauce simmer for half-an-hour, or until the apple and onion are quite soft. If a smooth sauce is wanted, rub through a sieve before using, and return to the saucepan to re-heat. Add the lemon juice and sugar just before serving, and a table-spoonful of cream would be a great improvement.

Note.—A stalk of rhubarb, or a few green gooseberries, may be used instead of the apple.

Devilled Sauce

(*Fr.* Sauce au Diable)

Ingredients—

½ pint Brown Stock.
½ oz. Butter.
½ oz. Flour.
½ tea-sp. Red-currant Jelly.
1 tea-spoonful Chili Vinegar.
1 table-sp. bottled Chutney.
1 tea-spoonful Mustard.
1 table-sp. Worcester Sauce.
1 table-spoonful Marsala.

Method.—Melt the butter in a stewpan and brown it slightly. Add the flour, and mix until smooth. Then draw the stewpan to the side of the fire and pour in the stock, stir again over the fire until boiling, when the other ingredients may be added. (The mustard should be mixed into a smooth paste with the Worcester sauce.) Cook all slowly from ten to fifteen minutes, and strain before using. Add salt if necessary.

Dutch Sauce

(*Fr.* Sauce Hollandaise)

Ingredients—

2 oz. Butter.
1 table-spoonful Vinegar.
2 table-spoonfuls Water.
2 yolks of Eggs.
A squeeze of Lemon Juice.
Salt and Pepper.
A pinch of Cayenne.

Method.—Put the water, vinegar, and yolks of eggs into a saucepan, place the pan in another saucepan of hot water, and stir over the fire constantly until the sauce thickens. Draw the pan to the side of the fire, and add the butter in small pieces, letting each piece melt before another is added. The sauce must not boil, or it will curdle. Add the lemon juice, and season to taste. Tarragon vinegar may be used instead of plain, and is preferred by many.

Egg Sauce

(*Fr.* Sauce aux Œufs)

Ingredients—

¾ oz. Butter.
3 gills Milk or Fish Stock.
¾ oz. Flour.
1 hard-boiled Egg.
White Pepper.
Salt.

Method.—Make a sauce with the butter, flour, and liquid. Chop the hard-boiled egg finely, and add it to the sauce, with white pepper and salt to taste. Boil two or three minutes longer, and the sauce is ready.

Note.—A plainer sauce may be made by using half water and half milk. Sometimes the white only of the egg is used, and the yolk rubbed through a sieve, and used to decorate whatever the sauce is poured over.

Gooseberry Sauce

(*Fr.* Sauce aux Groseilles)

Ingredients—

½ pint Green Gooseberries.
1 gill White Sauce.
1 dessert-spoonful Sugar.
1 oz. Butter.
Pepper and Salt.
A pinch of Nutmeg.
¼ gill of Water.

Method.—Top and tail the gooseberries, and wash them in cold water. Put them into a stewpan with half a gill of cold water, put the lid on the pan, and simmer slowly for half-an-hour, or until the gooseberries are quite soft, then rub through a hair sieve. Put the white sauce into a saucepan, add to it the gooseberry pulp, the butter and seasoning, mix well together, and stir over the fire until boiling.

Note.—Rhubarb sauce may be made in the same way.

Horse-Radish Sauce

(*Fr.* Sauce au Raifort)

Ingredients—

2 table-spoonfuls grated Horse-radish.	1 tea-sp. Castor Sugar.
2 table-spoonfuls Vinegar.	1 tea-sp. made Mustard.
	Pepper and Salt.

Method.—Wash and scrape the horse-radish until it is quite white, then grate it on a grater. Put it into a basin with the other ingredients, and mix well together. A little thick cream added is a great improvement. Serve in a sauce tureen.

Note.—If this sauce is to be served with hot fish or meat, heat by standing the basin containing it in a saucepan of hot water. Do not boil or it will curdle.

Maître d'Hôtel Butter

Required—

1 oz. Butter.	1 tea-spoonful Lemon Juice.
1 tea-sp. chopped Parsley.	

Method.—Put all on to a plate, and with a knife work them well together, to form a neat pat. Stand the plate slightly on end, that the lemon juice may run out of the butter again; and set in a cool place or on ice until wanted.

The parsley should be very green and very finely chopped to make this butter look well.

Mayonnaise Sauce

(*Fr.* Sauce Mayonnaise)

Ingredients—

2 yolks of Eggs.	White Pepper and Salt.
About 1 gill Salad Oil.	1 tea-sp. Chili Vinegar.
1 table-sp. White Vinegar.	½ tea-sp. made Mustard.
1 table-spoonful Tarragon Vinegar.	A pinch of Sugar.
	A pinch of Cayenne.

Method.—Take a basin large enough to hold 1½ pint (the size of the basin is important), and twist round the foot of it a cloth wrung out of very cold water to keep it steady and cool while mixing the sauce. Divide the yolks very carefully from the whites of the egg, and put them into the basin with the pepper, salt, mustard, and sugar. (The sugar may be omitted if not liked.) Mix these well together with a wooden spoon or small wire whisk. Cut a small wedge from the cork of the salad-oil bottle, large enough to allow the oil to come out, drop by drop, when it is held up. Keep stirring the yolks all the time with the right hand, and dropping in the oil from the bottle with the left, until the sauce is so thick that it is stirred with difficulty. One gill is about the usual quantity required for two yolks, but there is no necessity to measure it. Next add the vinegars gradually, and mix well.

Notes.—If this sauce is not kept cool, or the oil mixed in too quickly, it will curdle. It cannot be made in a hurry. If it should curdle, the fault *may* be remedied by putting a fresh yolk into another basin and adding the sauce very slowly to it, stirring all the time. A whiter sauce can be made by using lemon juice instead of vinegar.

More or less vinegar may be added to the sauce according to taste, and according to the purpose for which it is to be used.

If used for dressing a salad, it should be thinned down considerably with vinegar. If used for coating joints of meat, a little liquid aspic is usually added to make it stiffen.

If this sauce has to be kept for several hours before using, cover the basin containing it with a cloth wrung out of very cold water. This will prevent a skin forming on the top. If bottled and kept in a cool dark place, it will be good for a week or longer.

Be particular to use good oil. If the taste of the oil is not liked, two table-spoonfuls of thick whipped cream may be stirred into the sauce at the last, which will tone down the taste. Or cream may be used instead of the oil.

Melted Butter

(*Fr.* Beurre Fondu)

Ingredients—

2 oz. Fresh Butter.	A squeeze of Lemon Juice.
Pepper and Salt.	

Method.—Put the butter into a lined saucepan, and melt it gently over a slow fire. It should not lose its creamy appearance. Add the lemon juice and a little pepper and salt. Serve in a hot tureen.

Mint Sauce

(*Fr.* Sauce Menthe)

Ingredients—

2 table-sp. finely chopped Mint.	2 table-spoonfuls boiling Water.
1 table-sp. Brown Sugar.	1 gill Brown Vinegar.

Method.—Put the sugar into a basin or sauce tureen, pour over it the boiling water and stand until dissolved. Wash the mint, which should be young and fresh, pick it from the stalks and chop finely. Mix all the ingredients together and stand two or three hours before serving.

Mushroom Sauce

(*Fr.* Sauce aux Champignons)

Ingredients—

½ pint Brown or Madeira Sauce.	1 gill tinned Mushrooms..
	1 tea-spoonful Lemon Juice.

Method.—Cut the button mushroom in halves, and let them boil quickly in a little water for seven or ten minutes. Then strain and put them into half a pint Brown or Madeira sauce. Let them continue to simmer in the sauce for ten minutes, and add the lemon juice at the last.

Note.—If fresh mushrooms are used they should be picked, washed, cut in small pieces, and then stewed for a short time in brown stock before the sauce is added to them.

White Mushroom Sauce may be made in the same way as above, using white sauce instead of the brown.

Mustard Sauce

(*Fr.* Sauce Moutarde)

Ingredients—

1 oz. Butter.
1 tea-spoonful Flour.
1 tea-spoonful dry Mustard.
1 tea-sp. Chili Vinegar.
1 gill Water.
Salt.

Method.—Melt the butter in a small saucepan without discolouring it, add the flour and mustard, and mix until smooth with a wooden spoon. Pour in the water, stir until boiling, and cook three minutes. Add the vinegar and salt, and serve hot.

Onion Sauce

(*Fr.* Sauce Soubise)

Ingredients—

½ pint White or Béchamel Sauce.
3 or 4 large Onions.
White Pepper and Salt.
A pinch of Cayenne.

Method.—Skin the onions, put them into a saucepan with boiling water and a little salt, and boil quickly for one hour, or until tender. Then drain *well* and chop them finely. Put this onion purée into a saucepan with the sauce, bring to the boil, and reduce if necessary. Season to taste with white pepper, salt, and a pinch of cayenne.

Note.—A smoother sauce may be made by rubbing the onions through a sieve after chopping. One or two table-spoonfuls of cream are an improvement.

Oyster Sauce

(*Fr.* Sauce aux Huitres)

Ingredients—

1 oz. Butter.
1 oz. Flour.
½ pint Milk or Fish Stock.
A squeeze of Lemon Juice.
1 dozen Oysters and their Liquor.
½ gill Cream.
White Pepper and Salt.
A pinch of Cayenne.

Method.—Remove the beard and gristle from the oysters. Cut each oyster in two, and scald them in their own liquor—that is, bring them to the boil and strain. (Keep the liquor for flavouring the sauce.) Put the beards and trimmings of the oysters into a saucepan with the milk, and simmer for a few minutes to extract the flavour. Then strain the milk and oyster liquor through muslin, and keep them for making the sauce. The trimmings of the oysters may now be thrown away. Then make a sauce with the butter, flour, and strained liquid. Season to taste and put in the cream, add the oysters and lemon juice last.

Parsley Sauce

(*Fr.* Sauce Maître d'Hôtel)

Ingredients—

½ oz. Butter.
½ oz. Flour.
½ pint Fish Stock or Meat Boilings.
1 des.-sp. chopped Parsley.
White Pepper and Salt.
A squeeze of Lemon Juice.

Method.—Make a sauce with the butter, flour, and liquid. Add the parsley, pepper, and salt, and boil two or three minutes. Squeeze in the lemon juice just before serving.

Poulette Sauce

(*Fr.* Sauce Poulette)

Ingredients—

1 pint Velouté Sauce.
3 or 4 Mushrooms.
1 des.-sp. chopped Parsley.
2 or 3 yolks of Eggs.

Method.—Chop the mushrooms, and simmer them in the sauce for about fifteen minutes. Then draw the saucepan to the side of the fire, and add the yolks of eggs and parsley. Cook for a minute or two, but do not boil again.

Shrimp Sauce

(*Fr.* Sauce aux Crevettes)

Ingredients—

¾ oz. Butter.
¾ oz. Flour.
½ pint Milk or Fish Stock.
1 gill of picked Shrimps.
A squeeze of Lemon Juice.
Pepper and Salt.

Method.—Make a sauce with the butter, flour, and fish stock. Pick the shrimps, and add them, with white pepper and salt to taste. Squeeze in the lemon juice before serving.

Tartare Sauce

(*Fr.* Sauce Tartare)

Ingredients—

½ pint Mayonnaise Sauce.
1 table-sp. chopped Parsley.
1 table-sp. chopped Capers.
1 table-spoonful chopped Gherkins.

Method.—Make the Mayonnaise according to directions given for that sauce, and add to it the above ingredients.

Tomato Sauce

(*Fr.* Sauce aux Tomates)

Ingredients—

¾ oz. Butter.
¾ oz. Rice Flour.
5 or 6 Tomatoes.
1 oz. lean Ham.
½ pint Stock.
Pepper and Salt.
A small piece of Carrot, Celery, Turnip, Onion.
A sprig of Thyme, Marjoram, and Parsley.
A squeeze of Lemon Juice.
1 lump of Sugar.

Method.—Melt the butter in a small stewpan, put into it the ham and vegetables cut in small pieces, and fry them a few minutes. Wipe the tomatoes, and cut them in slices on a plate. Add them next to the saucepan with the rice flour, and mix well. Pour in the stock, and stir until boiling. Season to taste with pepper and salt, and simmer slowly for at least half-an-hour, stirring occasionally. If the sauce becomes too thick, add more stock. Strain through a fine strainer, hair sieve, or tammy, re-heat, and add a squeeze of lemon juice and a lump of sugar.

Note.—Tinned tomatoes may be used instead of fresh, and these will not require slicing. If the stock is well flavoured, the vegetables may be omitted.

Velouté Sauce

(*Fr.* Sauce Velouté)

Ingredients—

1 oz. Butter.	A few drops of Lemon Juice.
¾ oz. Flour.	White Pepper and Salt.
½ pint White Stock.	A pinch of Cayenne.

Method.—Make in the same way as white sauce, using the stock instead of milk.

White Sauce

(*Fr.* Sauce Blanche)

Ingredients—

¾ oz. Butter.	White Pepper.
¾ oz. Flour.	Salt.
½ pint Milk.	A squeeze of Lemon Juice.

Method.—Melt the butter in a small lined saucepan, add the flour, and mix smoothly with a wooden spoon. Cook for a minute or two over the fire without discolouring, then draw the pan to the side and pour in the milk. Return to the fire, and keep stirring constantly until boiling. Boil for two or three minutes so as to thoroughly cook the flour, and season to taste with white pepper and salt. Remove the pan from the fire before adding the lemon juice.

Note.—A plainer sauce can be made by using half milk and half water. If required for fish, fish stock may be used instead of milk.

Cornflour is sometimes used instead of flour.

SWEET SAUCES

Apricot Sauce

(*Fr.* Sauce à l'Abricot)

Ingredients—

1¼ gills Apricot Purée.	1 dessert-spoonful Sugar.
¼ oz. Arrowroot.	2 or 3 drops of Carmine.
¼ gill Water.	

Method.—Make the purée from tinned apricots by rubbing four or five pieces through a hair sieve and making up the quantity with the syrup. Put this purée into a small lined saucepan, add to it the arrowroot broken with the cold water, and stir over the fire until it boils and thickens. Add the sugar, flavouring, and enough carmine to make it a pretty pink colour. Cook two or three minutes longer, and serve.

Brandy Sauce (1)

(*Fr.* Sauce au Cognac)

Ingredients—

1 oz. Butter.	1¼ gills Water.
½ oz. Flour.	½ glass Brandy.
1 oz. Sugar.	

Method.—Melt the butter in a small lined saucepan, add the flour, and mix with a wooden spoon until smooth. Draw the pan to one side, and pour in the water; then return to the fire and stir constantly until boiling. Add the brandy and sugar, and boil a few minutes longer.

Brandy Sauce (2)

Ingredients—

2 yolks of Eggs.	½ glass of Brandy.
½ gill Cream.	1 oz. Sugar.
½ gill Water.	

Method.—Put all the ingredients into a basin, and stand the basin in a saucepan of slowly simmering water. Whisk the contents with a fork or small wire whisk from six to eight minutes until thick and frothy, when the sauce will be ready. Do not boil, or it will curdle.

Chocolate Sauce

(*Fr.* Sauce au Chocolat)

Ingredients—

1 gill Milk.	1 yolk of Egg.
1 oz. Chocolate.	4 or 5 drops of Vanilla Essence.
1 tea-spoonful Sugar.	

Method.—Rinse out a small lined saucepan with cold water, and put into it the milk and chocolate, either grated or shred down finely with a knife. Simmer until quite dissolved. Mix the yolk of egg and sugar together in a basin, and pour the chocolate gradually on to them. Return to the saucepan, and stir over the fire until *almost* boiling. Remove at once, and add the flavouring.

Custard Sauce

(*Fr.* Crème Cuite)

Ingredients—

2 yolks of Eggs.	1 dessert-spoonful Sugar.
1 white of Egg.	A few drops of Flavouring.
½ pint of Milk.	

Method.—Rinse out a small lined saucepan with cold water, put the milk into it, and let it heat over the fire. Put the yolks and white of egg into a basin with the sugar, and mix them well together with a wooden spoon. Then pour the hot milk gradually on to them, stirring all the time, and mix thoroughly. Return all to the saucepan, and stir very carefully over the fire until the sauce thickens. On no account must it be allowed to boil, or it will curdle. Have ready at hand a clean basin and a strainer. As soon as the sauce shows signs of thickening, and it is *almost* boiling, remove the pan from the fire, continue stirring for a second or two, then strain into the basin. Add flavouring to taste. To keep the sauce warm, stand the basin containing it in a saucepan of hot, not boiling water.

Note.—The sauce may be made richer by using more yolks of eggs and no whites.

Hard Sauce

Ingredients—

2 oz. Fresh Butter.
4 oz. Castor Sugar.
2 whites of Eggs.
A few drops of Vanilla or 1 dessert-spoonful Brandy, Sherry, or Liqueur.

Method.—Warm the butter very slightly in a basin, but be careful not to oil it. Sieve the sugar over it, and beat these two together with a wooden spoon until they are very white and light. Then add the whites of egg whipped to a stiff froth, and beat again for a few minutes. Flavour to taste, and set the sauce in a cool place or on ice to harden. Serve as cold as possible.

Jam Sauce

(*Fr.* Sauce au Confiture)

Ingredients—

2 table-spoonfuls Red Jam.
1 gill of Water.
1 oz. Loaf Sugar.
A squeeze of Lemon Juice.
2 or 3 drops of Carmine.

Method.—Put the water, sugar, and jam into a small lined saucepan, and let them boil quickly for a few minutes, skimming if necessary. Add the lemon juice and two or three drops of carmine. Strain before using.

Note.—Raspberry or strawberry jam is to be preferred for making this sauce.

A little wine may be added.

Lemon Sauce

(*Fr.* Sauce Citron)

Ingredients—

½ oz. Arrowroot.
Rind and juice of ½ Lemon.
1 oz. Sugar.
1½ gills Water.
½ oz. Butter.

Method.—Wipe the lemon with a damp cloth and grate off half the rind on to the top of the sugar. Grate very lightly, being most particular not to take any of the white, as it is bitter. Work the lemon rind and sugar together until they are well blended. Break the arrowroot with a little of the water, then add the rest of the water, and pour into a saucepan. Stir over the fire until boiling, add the lemon sugar, and the lemon juice strained, and cook for a few minutes. Break the butter in small pieces, and put it in just before serving.

Orange Sauce

(*Fr.* Sauce à l'Orange)

Ingredients—

½ oz. Arrowroot.
1 oz. Sugar.
Juice of 1 Orange.
2 table-spoonfuls Water.

Method.—Squeeze and strain the orange juice into a saucepan. Break the arrowroot with the water, and add it to the orange juice. Stir these over the fire until boiling, then boil for a few minutes and add the sugar. If too thick, a little more orange juice may be added. Strain before using.

Pineapple Sauce

(*Fr.* Sauce à l'Ananas)

Ingredients—

½ gill Pineapple Syrup.
2 oz. Pineapple.
½ oz. Sugar.
A few drops of Carmine.
2 table-spoonfuls Water or Wine.
A squeeze of Lemon Juice.

Method.—Strain the pineapple syrup into a small saucepan, and add all the other ingredients. Boil for a few minutes, and remove any scum that rises.

Sweet White Sauce

Ingredients—

1 oz. Butter.
½ oz. Flour.
½ pint Milk.
1 dessert-spoonful of Sugar.
A little Flavouring.

Method.—Make in the same way as white sauce (p. 146), adding sugar instead of pepper and salt.

Wine Sauce

Make in the same way as Brandy Sauce, using one wine-glassful of sherry instead of brandy.

VEGETABLES AND SALADS

General Notes on Vegetables

To have vegetables in perfection they should be cooked very soon after they are taken from the ground. If freshly gathered out of the garden they should be washed just before they are cooked, but when bought in the shops, it is often necessary to soak them in water for some time that they may regain some of their original freshness.

To secure a good colour and flavour in vegetables when cooked, careful dressing and preparation beforehand are essential. Earthy roots, such as potatoes, turnips, carrots, &c., must be both well scrubbed and thoroughly rinsed in cold water before peeling.

All vegetables, such as cauliflower, cabbage, sprouts, &c., which may contain slugs, must be soaked in cold water with vinegar in it for some time before cooking.

Coarse or discoloured leaves and any dark or decayed spots should be removed from all vegetables before cooking.

Throw all vegetables as they are prepared into cold water.

To Prepare Vegetables

A Carrot.—Wash in cold water, brushing well with a vegetable brush. Then cut off the top and any green part, and with a knife scrape the outside lightly until the carrot is quite clean. Scrape from the thick end downwards, and do not take off any more than is necessary, as the best part of the carrot lies on the outside. Throw into clean water until required.

A Turnip.—Wash in cold water and brush well with a vegetable brush. Then with a knife cut off the top, and peel rather thickly, as far as a yellow line which will be seen a little way in from the skin. The outside of the turnip is hard, indigestible, and bitter in flavour. Throw into clean water until wanted.

An Onion.—Cut off the root and top, and remove all the brown outside skin. If the strong flavour is objected to, put the onion into a small basin with a pinch of salt, or small piece of washing soda. Cover it with boiling water, and let it stand for at least five minutes. The water in which it soaks turns quite green in colour.

Note.—The preparation of other vegetables will be described under their special headings.

The Cooking and Serving of Vegetables

As a rule the ordinary cook pays far too little attention to this branch of cookery, although, thanks to the growing popularity of vegetarianism, more efficiency in this department of the culinary art is now demanded.

Vegetables boiled in water (*cuit à l'eau*), as often as not without salt, and served, or rather tumbled, into a vegetable dish without further attention would be looked down upon with scorn by the French housewife and regarded as something almost savage.

Take, for example, the potato, which is one of our most useful vegetables and without which no dinner is thought to be complete—why is it that in nine cases out of ten it is the *boiled* potato we see? Simply because our cooks do not exercise a little ingenuity and seldom care to bestow a little extra trouble on so simple a dish. In fact the *throwing away* of cold cooked potatoes is one of the commonest forms of waste in the kitchens both of the rich and of the poor; and yet the variety of ways in which a potato can be cooked and a cold one re-cooked are almost legion.

The cooking of vegetables requires as much care as the cooking of meat or the turning out of a pudding, and the simplicity of the operation should not be an excuse for slovenliness; a vegetable must be tastefully seasoned, well served, and temptingly arranged, with an eye to colour. These little attentions will give a special air of finish to the simplest cuisine, and a well-prepared vegetable, instead of forming a mere adjunct to another dish, can often be served as a separate course, thus saving a joint or avoiding the necessity for another meat dish.

Steaming of Vegetables

This is one of the best and most successful ways of cooking vegetables. The old-fashioned method of boiling them in a quantity of water and then throwing that water away has much to condemn it, as so many of the valuable properties are lost in the water.

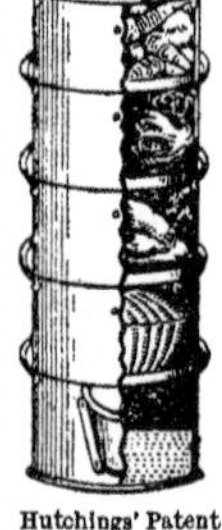
Hutchings' Patent Cooker.

A steam cooker is a most valuable addition to any kitchen—there are several different makes, and the prices range from 5s. upwards, according to the number of steamers. They are particularly useful and economical on a gas stove, where one light will serve to cook meat, fish, one or two vegetables, and a pudding if necessary. The time for steaming will depend upon the kind of vegetable and also upon its freshness. Full instructions for use are generally given with each kind of steamer. See also under separate recipes.

Vegetables Cooked "En Casserole"

This is another excellent method for cooking the lighter vegetables, and various recipes are

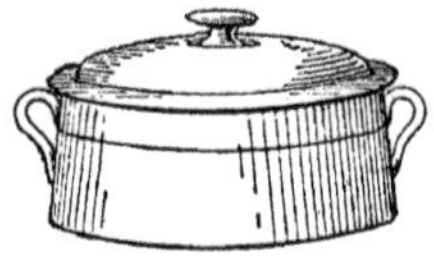
Fireproof Pot.

given to show how a vegetable may be both cooked and served up in this clean and useful fireproof cooking-pot.

Vegetarianism

It is impossible to deal with vegetarianism fully in a book of this kind. The subject is one which opens out so many important questions that it would require a book itself in order to do it justice. Suffice it to say, however, that it does not do to give up a meat diet suddenly and live on vegetables such as one finds in the ordinary English cuisine. There must be something to take the place of meat if the body is to be built up as it ought to be, and any one wishing to follow this régime could not do better than write to some specialist such as Eustace Miles, Chandos Street, London, who will supply pamphlets and give all particulars about a non-meat diet, or to the Reform Food Co., 4 Furnival Street, Holborn, London, who will also give valuable information about a special vegetarian diet.

Globe Artichokes (to Boil)

(*Fr.* Artichauts au Naturel)

Cut the stem off even with the leaves, remove the hardest bottom leaves, and cut about an inch off the others at the top, thus making an opening in the centre of the artichoke. Wash the artichokes thoroughly, and soak them in cold water with a few drops of vinegar in it for half-an-hour, to draw out any insects. Lift them out, rinse in cold water, and place upside down in a colander or sieve to drain. Have ready on the fire a deep saucepan three parts full of boiling water salted in the proportion of one dessert-spoonful of salt to one quart of water. Put the artichokes into this, and boil quickly for half-an-hour or longer. To ascertain when they are ready, pierce with a skewer or trussing needle, which should enter easily, or try if the leaves can easily be removed. Drain well, cut them in halves or quarters with a sharp knife, remove the hard inside or "choke" with a spoon, and dish on a folded napkin.

Different sauces may be served separately, the dish taking its name from the sauce, thus:—

Served with— *French*

Melted Butter—Artichauts au Beurre.
Bechamel Sauce—Artichauts à la Béchamel.
Dutch Sauce—Artichauts à la Hollandaise.
Or cold with Oil and Vinegar—Artichauts à l'Huile.

Note.—Only the bottom of the artichoke and base of the leaves are eatable.

Jerusalem Artichokes with White Sauce

(*Fr.* Topinambours à la Sauce Blanche)

Ingredients—

1 to 1½ lbs. Jerusalem Artichokes. | ½ pint White Sauce.

Method.—First wash and brush the artichokes thoroughly, and throw them into clean cold water. Then peel them carefully with a small knife, and as each one is done, throw it into another basin of fresh cold water with a few drops of vinegar or lemon juice to preserve the colour. Do not allow the water in which the artichokes are being peeled to become too dirty; change it if necessary. Have ready on the fire a lined or earthenware saucepan with just sufficient boiling water to cover the artichokes, and salted in the proportion of one tea-spoonful to one pint of water. Drain the artichokes and throw them into this, and cook them gently with the lid on the saucepan from fifteen to twenty minutes, or until they can be pierced fairly easily with a skewer. Or put them into a double cooker and steam them for half-an-hour. Strain off the water, pour in the white sauce, and finish the cooking over a slow fire. A little finely-chopped parsley may be added at the last, or one or more tablespoonfuls of grated Parmesan.

Note.—They can also be served with brown, tomato, or Hollandaise sauce.

Asparagus

(*Fr.* Asperges)

Choose the asparagus with fresh purple points and white stalks. If the cut end is brown and dry and the heads droop, the asparagus is stale. It may be kept for a day or two by standing the stalks in a jug of cold water, but is better used fresh. Cut the asparagus all one length, scrape the white part lightly with a knife, and wash in cold water. Tie with tape into bundles of eight or ten, keeping the heads all one way,

Asparagus Cooker.

and cook in a steamer over boiling salted water until the vegetable is tender, from thirty to forty minutes. Or what is better still, cook it in an asparagus cooker which has an arrangement whereby the stalks only are in the water while the points are cooked by steam. When asparagus is done, which is ascertained by pressing the points with the fingers, it should be taken up at once, else it will become flabby and spongy. Drain well and send it to table on a folded napkin or in an asparagus dish.

Asparagus may be served with many different sauces.

Served with— *French*

Melted or oiled Butter—Asperges au Beurre.
White Sauce—Asperges à la Sauce Blanche.
Dutch Sauce—Asperges à la Hollandaise.
Or cold with Oil and Vinegar—Asperges à l'Huile.

Beetroot (to Boil)

(*Fr.* Betteraves au Naturel)

Required—

Beetroots.	Salt.
Boiling Water.	

Method.—Wash the beetroots very gently and carefully. On no account must the skin be broken, or the juice will run out, and the colour of the beetroots be spoilt. Put them into a saucepan of boiling water large enough to hold them without breaking. Add salt in the proportion of one dessert-spoonful to one quart, and boil gently with the lid on the pan. They will take from two to three hours to cook, according to age and size. To test them, lift them out of the water, and press them with the finger; they should feel rather soft. Never pierce a beetroot with a fork. When ready, drain, and put them on a plate. If to be served hot, peel them quickly, cut in thin slices, and arrange these in a hot vegetable dish, and pour white or any other suitable sauce over. Small beetroots may be served whole.

Broad or Windsor Beans (to Boil)

(*Fr.* Fèves)

Beans to be nice must be young and freshly gathered. They should not be shelled until about to be cooked. After shelling, wash and drain them. If old, the skins should also be removed before cooking. To do this, put the beans into a basin with boiling water to cover them, stand for a few minutes, then drain, and remove the skins. Throw into a saucepan of fast-boiling water, salted in the proportion of one dessert-spoonful to a quart, and boil rapidly until tender. They will take from fifteen minutes to half-an-hour, according to age and size. Any scum rising on the water must be removed. When ready, drain in a colander, return the beans to the pan with a small piece of butter, season with pepper and salt, and shake over the fire for a few minutes. Beans are frequently served as an accompaniment to boiled bacon, but should always be cooked separately.

Broad Beans à la Poulette

(*Fr.* Fèves à la Poulette)

Ingredients—

1 pint Shelled Beans.	½ oz. Flour.
1 gill White Stock.	½ gill of Cream.
Pepper and Salt.	1 yolk of Egg.
A pinch of Sugar.	½ tea-spoonful Mixed Herbs.
½ oz. Butter.	

Method.—Prepare the beans (removing the skins), boil until tender and drain well in a colander. Melt the butter in a small stewpan, add the flour, and stir over the fire for two or three minutes; then pour in the stock, and stir until boiling. Put in the beans, season with pepper, salt, and the herbs very finely powdered. Simmer five or ten minutes, then draw the pan to the side of the fire; add the yolk of egg and cream, stir and make thoroughly hot, but do not boil again. Serve at once in a hot vegetable dish.

Brussels Sprouts

(*Fr.* Choux de Bruxelles au Beurre)

Ingredients—

1 lb. Brussels Sprouts.	Pepper and Salt
Boiling Water.	1 oz. Butter.

Method.—Wash the Brussels sprouts carefully, and trim them, cutting away any outside discoloured leaves. Make a slit across the stalk of each to allow them to cook more easily, and as they are prepared, throw them into a basin of clean cold water with one tea-spoonful of vinegar added, to draw out any insects. Let them soak in this from twenty to thirty minutes, then rinse and drain in a colander. Cook them in a perforated steamer (see p. 148) until quite tender, about half-an-hour. Test them by trying if they can easily be pierced with a fork, and do not overcook them. When ready, drain well. Melt the butter in the pan, toss the sprouts in this, sprinkling them with pepper and salt, and serve very hot. Sometimes a little cream is added.

Carrots à la Flamande

(*Fr.* Carottes à la Flamande)

Ingredients—

6 or 8 young Carrots.	½ gill Cream.
Boiling Water.	1 yolk of Egg.
Salt.	½ tea-spoonful chopped Parsley.
½ gill Water.	
2 oz. Butter.	Pepper and Salt.

Method.—Wash and scrape the carrots very lightly, cutting off the green tops. Put them into an earthenware casserole with boiling water to cover them and salted in the proportion of one dessert-spoonful to one quart; boil ten minutes, and strain. Then cut the carrots into thin slices, and return them to the casserole with the butter, half gill of water, pepper, and salt. Put on the lid, and simmer for twenty minutes. When the carrots are tender, add the yolk of egg and cream, beaten together, and the chopped parsley; stir carefully over the fire until thick, but do not boil. Serve hot *en casserole*.

Cabbages with Butter

(*Fr.* Choux au Beurre)

Take one or two young cabbages and trim them carefully, removing the outside leaves and any discoloured parts. Cut in three or four pieces according to size and wash in plenty of cold water. Then soak in cold water with a few drops of vinegar to draw out any slugs, and rinse again in fresh cold water. Place the prepared cabbage in a steamer, sprinkle with salt and steam from three-quarters to one hour, or until tender. Score across with a knife and serve in a hot dish with a good pat of salt butter on the top.

Cauliflower with White Sauce

(*Fr.* Choufleur à la Sauce Blanche)

Required—

1 Cauliflower.	Salt.
Boiling Water.	White Sauce.

Method.—Select a fresh cauliflower with firm, close head. Trim off the thick part of the stalk, and nearly all the leaves, only leaving on a few of the smaller ones to protect the flower. Make a cut across the stalk in both directions so that it may cook more easily. Wash the cauliflower in plenty of cold water, and then let it lie for half-an-hour in fresh cold water, to which one tea-spoonful of vinegar has been added, to draw out any insects. Cook it in a steamer until the flower feels tender but not broken from thirty to forty minutes. When ready, lift it out, drain for a minute or two, and serve in a hot vegetable dish with white or any other suitable sauce poured over it.

Cauliflower with Cheese

(*Fr.* Choufleur au Fromage)

Ingredients—

1 Cauliflower.	1 gill of Water.
1 oz. Butter.	2 table-spoonfuls Cream.
1 oz. Flour.	2 oz. grated Parmesan Cheese.
A pinch of Cayenne.	

Method.—Prepare and cook the cauliflower as above, drain and break it up into small, neat pieces. Make a sauce with the butter, flour and water, adding the cream, seasoning and rather more than half the cheese. Butter a fireproof fancy dish, and arrange in it the cauliflower and sauce in alternate layers. Sprinkle the remainder of the cheese over the top, pour a little melted butter over and place the dish in the oven to brown.

Note.—The remains of cold cooked cauliflower may be used up in this way.

Chestnuts

(*Fr.* Marrons)

These may be prepared in different ways and make a good winter vegetable. Wash the nuts and make a slit in the skin at the stalk end. Put them into boiling salted water and cook them until tender from twenty to thirty minutes. Then drain, remove the skins, and serve them quickly with a little melted butter, salt, and white pepper. Or they may be served in a good brown or tomato sauce.

A Chestnut Purée too is very good as an accompaniment to roast fowl or beef. Cook the nuts as above and rub them through a sieve. Re-heat with a little butter, seasoning, and enough brown sauce to bind all together and make the mixture of a right consistency.

Celery with Cream (to Stew)

(*Fr.* Céléri à la Crême)

Required—

1 head of Celery.	½ gill Cream.
½ pint White Stock or Broth.	½ oz. Butter.
	½ oz. Flour.
Pepper and Salt.	A pinch of Nutmeg.

Method.—Wash the celery and cut it in convenient-sized pieces. Put the stock or broth into a saucepan, and when hot put in the celery and parboil it. Then strain, and make a sauce with the butter, flour, and stock. Add the cream, season to taste. Return the celery to the saucepan and allow it to simmer slowly in the sauce until it is quite tender. A few sippits of toast or a little chopped parsley may be used as a garnish. Or the celery may be cooked and served *en casserole.*

Celery (to Fry)

(*Fr.* Céléri Frit)

Required—

Celery.	Egg and Bread-crumbs.
A little Flour.	Frying Fat.

Method.—Prepare the celery, cut it in short lengths, and cook in salted water until fairly tender. Drain it well, and spread the pieces out on a cloth to dry. Dip the pieces first into a little flour, coating them lightly; then egg and bread-crumb them and fry in boiling fat until a nice brown colour, and drain well on kitchen paper. Dish them up, cross bars, on a hot dish, with a d'oyley or dish paper under them, sprinkle liberally with grated Parmesan, and garnish with parsley.

Note.—Frying batter may be used instead of egg and bread-crumbs.

Cucumber

(*Fr.* Concombre)

Cook in the same way as vegetable marrow (see p. 159).

Curried Vegetables

(*Fr.* Légumes en Cari)

Ingredients—

Curry Sauce (see p. 143).
Any kind of cooked Vegetable.
Boiled Rice.

Method.—Any cooked vegetable may be used for a curry, such as turnip, carrot, cauliflower, vegetable marrow, beans, &c., or a mixture of vegetables. If large, cut them in small neat pieces. Make the curry sauce rather thick. When made, put the cooked vegetables into it, and let them simmer for a few minutes, so as to get thoroughly heated and flavoured with the sauce. Serve on a hot dish with a border of boiled rice (see p. 157) round, or the rice may be served in a separate dish.

Egg-Plant (to Fry)

(*Fr.* Aubergine Frit)

Required—

Egg-plant.	Frying Fat.
Egg and Bread-crumbs.	

Method.—Cut the egg-plant in slices about a quarter of an inch thick. Peel the slices, and let them soak in strong salt and water, proportion one table-spoonful to one pint, for two hours to remove the bitterness. Drain and wipe each slice dry in a towel. Egg and bread-crumb the slices, and fry in boiling fat until nicely browned. Drain on kitchen paper, and serve piled up on a hot dish with a d'oyley or dish paper under them. Garnish with parsley.

Note.—Egg-plants should be fresh and glossy looking when purchased, or the cooking of them will not be successful.

They may also be split and baked simply with a little butter.

Egg-Plant (Stuffed)

(*Fr.* Aubergines Farcies)

Required—

2 Egg-plants.	1 tea-sp. chopped Parsley.
2 table-spoonfuls Bread-crumbs.	1 oz. Butter.
1 table-spoonful chopped Ham or Tongue.	1 dessert-spoonful chopped Mushrooms.
1 tea-spoonful chopped Onion.	Pepper and Salt.
	Some beaten Egg.
	A little grated Lemon Rind.

Method.—Wipe the egg-plants, and cut them in half lengthways. Scoop out the meat, leaving the rind about half an inch thick, that the shape may be firm. Melt the butter in a small saucepan, add the chopped onion, and cook a few minutes. Then add the bread-crumbs, ham or tongue, mushrooms, parsley, and the pulp from egg-plants chopped finely. Season with pepper, salt, and a little grated lemon rind, and add sufficient beaten egg to bind all together. Sprinkle the inside of the egg-plants with bread-crumbs, pepper and salt, and fill up with the mixture. Spread a few more crumbs on the surface of the mixture, and place the pieces on a greased tin or sauté pan. Cover with greased paper, and bake in a moderate oven for one hour. Serve hot on a folded d'oyley.

Endive (Dressed)

(*Fr.* Chicorée)

Required—

2 or 3 Endives.	1 table-spoonful Cream.
Boiling Water.	Lemon Juice.
Salt.	Pepper and Salt.
1 oz. Butter.	

Method.—Wash the endives carefully, separating the leaves and removing any decayed parts. Let them soak for half-an-hour in clean cold water, to which one tea-spoonful of vinegar has been added to draw out any insects. Then drain and steam according to directions given on p. 150, until the leaves feel quite tender, from twenty-five to thirty-five minutes. Next chop the endives finely, or rub through a wire sieve; the latter mode is preferable. Make hot again in the pan with the butter and cream, and season to taste with pepper, salt, and a squeeze of lemon juice. Dish in the shape of a pyramid in a hot vegetable dish, scoring up the sides with a fork, and decorate with sippets of toast or slices of hard-boiled egg.

Note.—Lettuce may be cooked in the same way.

Flageolets

Wash the flageolets, and let them soak in cold water overnight. Next day drain, and put them in a saucepan with fresh cold water, and boil slowly until tender (about two hours). Then serve in the same way as green peas (see p. 153).

Note.—They are good also as a purée made in the same way as purée of green peas.

French Beans

(*Fr.* Haricots Verts au Naturel)

Choose young fresh beans; when old they are tough and stringy when cooked. First wash them well in cold water, then cut off the heads and tails, and a thin strip on each side of the bean to remove the strings. Lay several together, and cut them into thin strips lengthways or across in a slanting direction into lozenge-shaped pieces. As they are cut drop them into cold water, with a small quantity of salt in it. Have ready on the fire a saucepan of boiling water, salted in the proportion of one dessert-spoonful to one quart; drain the beans well, and throw them into this. Boil quickly from twenty to thirty minutes with the lid off the saucepan, removing any scum as it rises. When the beans are ready they will sink to the bottom of the pan, and must be taken off the fire at once. Drain well in a colander, return them to the pan, and shake over the fire to dry up the moisture from the beans; add a small piece of butter, pepper and salt, and keep moving the pan until the butter is melted, and the beans thoroughly hot. Do not stir the beans with a spoon, as it is apt to break them. Serve them up as quickly as possible. Very young beans are sometimes cooked whole. Scarlet runners may be cooked in the same way.

Sometimes a little lemon juice and some finely chopped parsley are added to the beans; they are then called French Beans à la Maitre d'Hôtel (*Fr.* Haricots Verts à la Maitre d'Hôtel).

Green Peas

(*Fr.* Petits Pois au Naturel)

Required—

½ peck Peas.	White Pepper and Salt.
1 oz. Butter.	1 tea-spoonful Demerara
1 or 2 sprigs of Mint.	Sugar.

Method.—Shell the peas a very short time before they are to be cooked, otherwise they become hard. Wash them in cold water and drain well. Put them into a lined or earthenware saucepan with just sufficient boiling water to cover them, add the mint, salt, and sugar, and simmer slowly with the lid off the saucepan until the peas are nearly tender, from twenty to thirty minutes. Add the butter, sprinkle with pepper, and allow them to finish cooking, shaking the pan occasionally. Lift out the mint and serve the peas very hot. A little chopped parsley may be added.

Green Peas with Lettuces

(*Fr.* Petits pois aux Laitues)

Cook the peas as above, adding one or two young lettuces cut in shreds. If desired a thickening may be added made of two yolks of eggs beaten up with two table-spoonfuls of milk or cream. The mixture should not boil after these are added, but must be gently stirred to cook the eggs.

Green Pea Purée

(*Fr.* Purée de Petits Pois)

When the peas become too old for serving whole, they can very well be made into a purée. Boil them in salted water until tender, then drain and pass them through a sieve. Return them to the saucepan with a good piece of butter and enough hot milk or cream to moisten. Add seasoning and a very little sugar. This may either be served separately along with meat, or kept fairly thick and pressed through a forcing bag as a garnish for the centre of an entrée or as a fancy border.

Note.—Dried green peas may be used, but they require soaking and long boiling to make them tender.

Haricot Beans à la Maître d'Hôtel

(*Fr.* Haricots Blancs à la Maître d'Hôtel)

Ingredients—

½ lb. Haricot Beans.	½ oz. Butter.
1 small Onion.	1 tea-sp. chopped Parsley.
Cold Water.	White Pepper and Salt.

Method.—Wash the haricot beans, and let them soak in cold water overnight to soften them. Next day put them into a saucepan with plenty of cold water, and the onion skinned and cut in four. Let them boil from two to two and a half hours, or until they feel quite soft. The time will vary according to the age and size of the beans used. If the water boils away while they are cooking, add more cold water. Keep the lid on the pan, and let the water boil steadily all the time. When ready, drain in a colander, and lift out the pieces of onion. Return the beans to the pan, and let them stand by the side of the fire with the lid partially off, to allow them to dry; then add the butter, parsley, pepper, and salt. Shake the beans over the fire for a minute or two, and serve them hot. Do not stir with a spoon, as it is apt to break them. A squeeze of lemon juice is sometimes added, or they may be served with parsley sauce poured over them.

Note.—The water in which the beans have been cooked should be reserved for making a sauce or put into the stock-pot.

Haricot Bean Rissoles

Ingredients—

½ lb. cooked Haricot Beans.	1 Egg.
1 oz. Dripping.	A little Flour.
1 Onion.	Pepper and Salt.
1 oz. Butter.	Bread-crumbs.

Method.—Rub the beans through a wire sieve, and add to them the butter, seasoning, and enough beaten egg to bind all together. Allow the mixture to cool, then form it into balls with the aid of a little flour. Egg and bread-crumb these, and fry them in boiling fat to a nice brown colour. Drain on kitchen paper, and serve the fritters hot garnished with parsley.

Japanese Crones

(*Fr.* Crônes Japonaises)

Required—

½ lb. Crones.	1 table-spoonful Cream.
1 oz. Butter.	Salt and Pepper.

Method.—This is a vegetable which has not yet become very popular, but it is very light, and well worth eating. Crones have a slight resemblance to Jerusalem artichokes, only they are very much smaller. Trim the ends of the crones, and wash and brush them well in cold water. Warm the butter in an earthenware saucepan, put in the crones, and cook them in the oven from twenty to thirty minutes, shaking them from time to time. Add the cream and seasoning a few minutes before serving.

Note.—They must not be overcooked or the flavour will be spoilt.

A good white sauce with cream may be added at the last, or the crones may be served in small scallop shells with the sauce over and a little grated Parmesan on the top.

Stewed Leeks

(*Fr.* Poireaux au Jus)

Required—

6 Leeks.	Some light Stock.
½ oz. Butter.	Pepper and Salt.

Method.—Trim off the root, the green ends, and the outer leaves of the leeks. Split them down the middle, wash thoroughly, and let them lie in cold water with a little vinegar for half-an-hour. Then drain, cut in convenient-sized pieces, and wash again in fresh cold water. Put the leeks into a lined or earthenware saucepan with enough stock to cover them, and stew slowly until they are quite tender, from thirty to forty minutes. Allow the stock to reduce until there is just sufficient to serve as gravy. Season with salt and pepper, and add a small piece of butter just before serving.

Lentils à la Bretonne

(*Fr.* Lentilles à la Bretonne)

Ingredients—

1½ tea-cupfuls of Lentils.	3 tea-cupfuls of Cold Water.
2 oz. Ham Fat.	1 tea-sp. chopped Parsley.
Pepper and Salt.	1 Shallot (finely chopped).

Method.—Wash the lentils in several waters. Put them into a basin with three cupfuls of cold water. Cover over and soak all night. Next day put them into a saucepan with the water in which they have been soaked, the ham fat (cooked or uncooked) cut in very small pieces, the shalot, a pinch of pepper, and a very little salt. Simmer slowly for two hours until you have a smooth thick purée. It will be necessary to stir from time to time, and if the mixture becomes too dry, to add more water. Add the parsley at the last, and serve very hot.

Macaroni and Walnut Scallops

Ingredients—

2 oz. Macaroni.	1 oz. Butter.
3 oz. shelled Walnuts.	1 table-spoonful Brown or Tomato Sauce.
1 tea-sp. Chopped Parsley.	Salt and Pepper.
Bread-crumbs.	

Method.—Cook the macaroni and cut it into half-inch lengths. Roast the walnuts for a few minutes and chop them moderately fine. Mix these two together with the sauce, parsley, and seasoning. Then grease out a few scallop shells and sprinkle them with bread-crumbs. Fill them with the mixture, sprinkle with more bread-crumbs, and put the butter in small pieces on the top.

Scallop Shell.

Mushrooms (to Stew)

(*Fr.* Champignons au Jus)

Ingredients—

½ lb. Mushrooms.	1 table-spoonful Cream.
½ oz. Butter.	Pepper and Salt.
1 gill of Stock.	A slice of Toast.
1 tea-spoonful Flour.	Lemon Juice.

Method.—Peel the mushrooms, and cut off the ends of the stalks. Wash them in cold water with a little salt in it, and then dry in a cloth. If small, they may be left whole; but if large, cut in pieces, it will make a neater dish. Put them into an earthenware casserole, and sprinkle with pepper, salt, and a good squeeze of lemon juice. Put the lid on the pan, and stew very slowly for ten minutes. Add the stock very gradually to the flour in a basin, mixing with a spoon until quite smooth; pour this in beside the mushrooms, and stir until boiling. Stew ten or fifteen minutes longer, add the cream at the last, and serve very hot.

Mushrooms (Stuffed)

(*Fr.* Champignons Farcis)

Ingredients—

6 or 8 medium-sized Mushrooms.
6 or 8 croûtons of Fried or Toasted Bread.

Stuffing—

½ oz. Butter.	1 table-sp. Bread-crumbs.
1 tea-sp. chopped Onion.	1 table-sp. Stock or Gravy.
Trimmings of Mushrooms.	1 dessert-spoonful chopped Ham or Tongue.
Pepper and Salt.	

Method.—Peel the mushrooms and cut off the stalks. Throw them into a basin of cold water and salt, and let them soak a few minutes. Then remove and dry them. Trim them all one size, keeping these trimmings to add to the stuffing. Place the mushrooms, with the black side uppermost, on a greased baking-tin, and then make the stuffing. Chop the onion, mushroom trimmings, and ham, all very finely. Melt the butter in a small pan, add to it the chopped ingredients, and cook for a few minutes. Then add the bread-crumbs, seasoning, and stock, and cook a few minutes longer. Put a little of this stuffing into each mushroom, cover them over with greased paper, and bake in a moderate oven for ten minutes. Put a dish paper on to a hot dish, arrange the fried croûtons of bread on this, and then stand a mushroom on the top of each. Garnish with parsley, and serve as a vegetable entremet or savoury.

Nuts and Nut Foods

Nuts of various kinds are now becoming quite a popular food, and instead of being used as a mere adjunct to our dessert course they can be made to take an important part in our diet.

They are among the most nourishing of our vegetable foods, and potatoes and nuts are said to have been the principal diet of the monks in many of the old monasteries.

Nuts are frequently found difficult of digestion, but this is partly owing to their being taken at the end of an already substantial meal, or because they have not been properly prepared nor masticated.

They form a very good substitute for meat for those who choose to adopt a non-flesh diet, as they contain a large amount of proteid matter which is valuable for building up the tissues and enriching the blood. They are also rich in oil, which supplies us with heat for the body.

There are quite a variety of nuts now on the market, both shelled and unshelled, such as the hazel, cashew, Brazil, peanut, walnut, almond, pignolia, chestnut, filbert, &c. Mixed nuts are also sold for about Is. 2d. the pound.

There are also various nut foods to be had from the different nut food specialists, along with special recipes for their use and several kinds of nut butter, which form very good frying media.

For those who go in for nut cookery to any extent, a nut mill will be found invaluable. The price of this little machine is from about Is. 6d. upwards, and if the nuts are first slightly roasted and then ground they are more likely to have a good flavour than those bought in the ground form.

Nut Omelet

Ingredients—

3 Eggs.	A pinch of Nutmeg.
¼ lb. shelled Brazil Nuts.	Pepper and Salt.

Method.—Make in the same way as savoury omelet (see p. 186), adding the nuts finely grated to the eggs. When the omelet is cooked, sprinkle a few ground nuts over the top and brown slightly.

Nut and Potato Rissoles

Ingredients—

½ lb. Cooked Potatoes.	2 table-spoonfuls Milk or White Sauce.
¼ lb. Mixed Nuts.	1 table-sp. grated Parmesan.
1 oz. Butter.	Egg and Bread-crumbs.
Pepper and Salt.	

A little Flour.

Method.—Roast the nuts slightly and put them through the mill. Melt the butter in a small saucepan, sieve the potatoes and add them to it with the prepared nuts, milk, and seasoning. Mix thoroughly, and turn on to a plate to cool. Form into balls with the help of a little flour; egg and bread-crumb and fry in boiling fat. (See Potato Balls, p. 156.)

Onions "en Casserole"

(*Fr.* Oignions en Casserole)

Required—

3 Spanish Onions.	Pepper and Salt.
1½ oz. Butter or good Beef Dripping.	A pinch of Nutmeg.

Method.—Skin and scald the onions. Then remove *some* of the outer part, mince this rather finely, and place it in the casserole with the fat and seasoning. When hot place in the whole onions, put on the lid, and cook slowly from one and a half to two hours until tender.

Parsley (to Fry)

(*Fr.* Persil Frit)

Required—

Parsley.	Boiling Fat or Oil.

Method.—Wash the parsley and pick it, leaving the stalks about an inch long. Let it lie between the folds of a cloth until dry, and then put it into a wire frying basket. Have ready on the fire a saucepan of deep fat or oil (see French Frying, p. 131), deep enough to cover the parsley. Plunge the parsley into this for a second or two, and lift it out. The moisture in the parsley will make the fat bubble up, and if kept in too long will make the fat come over the sides of the pan. When the fat becomes quite still, plunge the parsley in again for a second or two, and it will be ready. It ought to be quite green and crisp. Turn on to kitchen paper and drain well.

Note.—This is used as a garnish for fried dishes, such as fried fish, rissoles, croquettes, &c.

Pease Pudding

Ingredients—

½ lb. Split Peas.	Pepper and Salt.
1 oz. Butter.	A pinch of Sugar.
1 Egg.	

Method.—Wash the peas well, remove any discoloured ones, and soak overnight in cold water. Tie them loosely in a cloth, leaving room for them to swell, and put them into a saucepan with a good pinch of salt and enough boiling water to cover them. Boil quickly from two to two and a half hours, or until the peas are quite soft. Keep them well covered with water all the time. When ready, take them up and drain. Turn the peas out of the cloth, and rub them through a wire sieve or colander. Add the butter, egg, well beaten, pepper, salt, and a pinch of sugar. Beat all well together for a few minutes until the ingredients are thoroughly mixed, then tie up tightly in a floured cloth. Boil the pudding for another half-hour, turn on to a hot dish, and serve as an accompaniment to salt beef or pork.

Potatoes (to Steam)

Required—

Potatoes.	Salt.
Boiling Water.	

Method.—Steaming is one of the simplest and best ways of cooking potatoes. First wash and brush the potatoes well in cold water, to get rid of all the earth, and throw them into a basin of clean cold water, ready for peeling. With a potato-knife peel them as thinly as possible, and with the point of the knife remove all the "eyes" or black specks, and keep the potatoes in water until they are wanted. Have them all of one size. If some are larger than others, cut them in two or three to make them equal. Put them in a steamer and sprinkle with salt. Place the steamer on the top of a saucepan of boiling water, and put the lid on. Keep the water in the saucepan underneath the potatoes quickly boiling the whole time. If the potatoes are steamed in their skins, peel them before they are quite ready, and then return them to the steamer to finish cooking. They will require from thirty to forty minutes, according to their size and kind. When they can be pierced easily with a skewer, cover them with a clean cloth, remove the steamer from the water and stand it in a warm place until the potatoes are dry and mealy. Ten minutes should be sufficient.

Mashed Potatoes

Ingredients—

½ lb. cooked Potatoes.	2 or 3 table-spoonfuls Milk.
1 oz. Butter or Dripping.	White Pepper and Salt.

Method.—The potatoes should be well cooked, dry and floury. Rub them quickly through a wire sieve or put them through a vegetable presser. Melt the butter or dripping in a sauce-pan and add the potatoes to it. Season to taste with white pepper and salt, and add the milk. Mix well together and pile up in the form of a pyramid on a greased tin or plate that will stand the heat of the oven. Smooth over and mark with a knife or fork, and brush over with milk or beaten egg. Bake in the oven until nicely browned, and then with a fish slice or broad knife slip the pudding on to a hot vegetable dish.

Note.—The yolk of an egg may be added to the mixture, or cream may be used instead of milk.

Potato Rice

(*Fr.* Pommes de Terre au Neige)

This dish is made by putting freshly boiled potatoes through a vegetable presser or wire sieve, and letting them fall on to a hot vegetable dish. The potato grains resemble rice and make a good accompaniment to stewed or roast meat.

Potato Balls

(*Fr.* Croquettes de Pommes de Terre)

Ingredients—

½ lb. cooked Potatoes.	Frying Fat.
1 oz. Butter or Dripping.	1 yolk or ½ a whole Egg.
White Pepper and Salt.	Egg and Bread-crumbs.

Method.—Rub the potatoes through a wire sieve, or press them through a vegetable presser. Melt the butter or dripping in a saucepan, and put the sieved potato into it. Season with white pepper and salt, and add one yolk of egg or half a whole egg well beaten (the other half may be used for egging and bread-crumbing). Mix all well together, and turn the mixture on to a plate to cool. Then flour the hands slightly and roll the mixture into small balls of equal size and free from cracks. Egg and bread-crumb these balls, and fry them until nicely browned in boiling fat. Do not put too many into the fat at one time, or they will cool the fat so much that it will soak into them and cause them to burst. After frying, drain well on kitchen paper, and serve on a hot dish with a dish paper under them, and garnish with parsley.

Note.—This mixture may be made into different shapes, such as cutlets, cones, or small rolls. A little chopped parsley, chopped ham or tongue, or grated cheese may be added to the mixture.

Potato Fritters

(*Fr.* Beignets de Pommes de Terre)

Ingredients—

½ lb. cooked Potatoes.	1 yolk and 2 whites of Egg.
1 oz. Butter.	Frying Fat.
Pepper and Salt.	

Method.—Prepare the potato mixture as above, adding the whites of eggs beaten to a stiff froth at the last and mixing them in very lightly. Drop the mixture in pieces about the size of a walnut into boiling fat, and fry until nicely browned. Lift out with a perforated spoon on to kitchen paper; drain well, dish on a dish paper or folded napkin, and garnish with parsley.

Potatoes (to Fry)

(*Fr.* Pommes de Terre Frites)

Required—

Potatoes.	Frying Fat or Oil.
Salt.	

Method.—Wash and peel the potatoes. Cut them into *thin* slices as nearly the same size as possible. Make them quite dry in a cloth, and put them into a frying basket. Have ready some deep fat and make it moderately hot, but not boiling. Plunge the potatoes in and cook them at a moderate rate until tender and slightly coloured. Then lift them out, drain them, and let them get partly cold. Replace the fat on the fire, and when it steams return the potatoes to it and shake them about until they are crisp and nicely browned. Drain quickly and sprinkle with salt. These potatoes are usually served with grilled chops or steaks.

Potato Chips and Ribbons.—Choose large, smoothly shaped potatoes. Dry them well after they have been washed and peeled.

For Ribbons cut the potatoes first in slices half an inch in thickness. Then take one slice at a time and with a small knife peel slowly round and round it, cutting the ribbons so thin that you can see the knife through them, and making them as long as possible. Do not throw them back into the water; keep them lying on the cloth until it is time to cook them. Some of them may be tied into bows or knots. The drier they are the more easily they will fry.

For Chips cut the potatoes first into thin slices, then across into strips or chips. Cook both these in the same way as above.

New Potatoes

Required—

1 lb. Potatoes.	1 or 2 oz. Butter.
1 gill light Stock.	1 tea-spoonful chopped Parsley.
Salt.	

Method.—Wash and peel the potatoes very

thinly (unless this is done they will not absorb the butter). Put them into a stewpan or earthenware dish with the stock and a little salt if necessary. Cover with the lid and cook in a moderate oven for twenty or thirty minutes, or until sufficiently cooked. Strain off any stock that may be left, add the butter and parsley, and toss over the fire for a few minutes. Serve very hot.

Rice (to Boil for Curries)

Required—

Patna Rice.	Boiling Water.
Salt.	

Method.—Patna rice is the best to use for curries. It is a long, slender grain, pointed at the ends. Well wash it in several waters until the last water that is poured off looks quite clean. Have ready on the fire a saucepan, three parts full of freshly boiling water, add salt to it in the proportion of one dessert-spoonful to a quart, and throw the rice into this. Boil quickly with the lid off, stirring it frequently with a fork to prevent the rice sticking to the pan, and also that it may be well tossed about with the water. Cook from twelve to fifteen minutes, or until the grains will rub down easily, when one is tested between the finger and thumb. Then strain through a sieve or strainer, and finish cooking and drying it, either by putting it back into the saucepan by the side of the fire, or leaving it on the sieve, which may be placed on the rack above the fire, or on a plate in a moderate oven. While drying stir lightly with a fork every now and then to keep the grains separate.

Neapolitan Rice

(*Fr.* Riz à la Napolitaine)

Ingredients—

¼ lb. cooked Rice.	1 oz. Butter.
2 Tomatoes.	Pepper and Salt.
2 oz. grated Cheese.	

Method.—Have the rice well cooked, the tomatoes rubbed through a hair sieve and the cheese grated. Melt the butter in a fireproof dish, add the other ingredients, and stir together over the fire. Season to taste and serve very hot in the casserole.

Salsify (to Fry)

(*Fr.* Salsifis Frit)

Required—

Salsify.	Frying Fat.
Flour.	Pepper and Salt.
Egg and Bread-crumbs.	

Method.—Wash the salsify and scrape the roots gently to rid them of their outside coating. Throw them into cold water to which a little lemon juice or vinegar has been added to preserve the colour. Then boil them in salted water until just tender, and drain carefully so as not to break them. Finish in the same way as fried celery (p. 151).

Note.—Salsify may also be served in any suitable sauce according to directions given for Jerusalem Artichokes (p. 149).

Sea-Kale

(*Fr.* Chou Marin)

Cook in the same way as celery (see p. 151).

Sorrel

(*Fr.* Oseille)

This must be very fresh to be good. It can be cooked according to directions given for cooking spinach. Sometimes it is mixed with equal quantities of spinach, or with a few leaves of lettuce.

Spinach (to Boil)

(*Fr.* Epinards au Naturel)

Required—

1 lb. Spinach.	Lemon Juice.
½ oz. Butter.	Sippets of Toast or Fried Bread.
Pepper and Salt.	

Method.—Spinach reduces so enormously in cooking that one pound will make a very small dish. Double the leaves lengthways and strip off the stalks. Then wash the spinach thoroughly in several waters until quite free from grit. It is a vegetable which requires most particular washing, growing as it does so near the ground. It is very earthy, and takes a great deal of water to make it clean. Handle it as lightly as possible, as touching it too much with the hands causes the leaves to lose all their crispness. Put it into a saucepan, without any water except that which adheres to the leaves, sprinkle it with salt, and put the lid on the pan. Spinach is the only green vegetable which is cooked with the lid on the pan; but, as no water is used, were the lid left off, evaporation would be so great that the spinach would soon burn. The green of it is so intense that there is no fear of its discolouring unless it is cooked too long. Cook until it is quite tender, from twenty to thirty minutes, stirring frequently with a spoon. When ready, drain well on a fine wire sieve with a basin below it, and press out as much water as possible with the back of a wooden spoon. Then remove the basin, put a clean dry plate underneath the sieve, rub the spinach through on to this, and scrape the sieve well underneath. Return the spinach to a saucepan, with the butter, pepper and salt if necessary. Stir over the fire until thoroughly hot, and add a squeeze of lemon juice. Arrange it in a neat pyramid on a hot dish, marking it up the sides with the back of a fork, and garnish round the base with sippets of toast or fried bread, a few slices of hard-boiled egg, or some cooked beetroot cut in fancy shapes, unless served as a garnish to meat, when the croûtons should be omitted.

Spinach with Cream

(*Fr.* Epinards à la Crème)

Prepare in the same way as above, adding two or three table-spoonfuls of cream at the last.

Note.—A garnish of poached eggs or some thin slices of nicely fried ham or bacon is a very nice accompaniment to this dish.

Stewed Spaghetti

Ingredients—

¼ lb. Spaghetti.	1 oz. Butter.
½ pt. Veal or Chicken Broth.	Pepper and Salt.

Method.—Spaghetti is a very fine form of Italian paste, and it is considered more delicate than macaroni. Break the spaghetti into small pieces, and put it into a small saucepan with the broth or any good light stock. Allow it to simmer slowly from fifteen to twenty minutes until soft and the liquid is all absorbed. Then add the butter, and season to taste. The sieved pulp of one or two tomatoes may be added for a variety, or poached eggs may be served on the top of the spaghetti. A little grated cheese too may be added.

Sweet Potatoes

This vegetable is not as yet very well known in this country. It resembles the common potato in size and appearance, and can be cooked in the same way. Or, the following two recipes are very good.

Sweet Potato Pie

Ingredients—

1 lb. cooked Sweet Potatoes.	½ pint well-seasoned White Sauce.
2 table-spoonfuls Browned Crumbs.	1 oz. Butter.

Method.—Cut the potatoes in slices and arrange them in a greased pie-dish in layers with the white sauce. Sprinkle the crumbs over and place the butter in small pieces on the top. Bake in a moderate oven for twenty minutes.

Sweet Potatoes with Cream

Ingredients—

1 lb. cooked Sweet Potatoes.	½ oz. Flour.
2 oz. Butter.	1 table-spoonful chopped Parsley.
1 gill Cream.	

Method.—Stir the butter and flour in an earthenware dish until they form a paste. Add the parsley and cream and then the potatoes cut in slices. Season to taste and serve very hot *en casserole.*

Tomatoes à l'Americaine

Ingredients—

6 small Tomatoes.	2 table-sp. Bread-crumbs.
1 gill Tomato Sauce.	2 table-sp. grated Cheese.
1 tea-sp. Curry Powder.	½ oz. Butter.
1 tea-spoonful Red Currant Jelly.	Pepper and Salt.

Method.—Choose small firm tomatoes, not over-ripe. Put them into boiling water for a minute or two, then lift them out, dry and peel them. Then grease a fireproof dish, and place the tomatoes in it. Sprinkle them with half the crumbs and cheese, and a little pepper and salt. Add the curry powder and red-currant jelly to the tomato sauce (see p. 145), and pour this over the tomatoes. Put the remainder of crumbs and cheese on the top, then the butter in small pieces, and bake in a moderate oven about twenty minutes. Serve hot. This dish may be garnished with rolls of bacon.

Tomatoes au Gratin

(*Fr.* Tomates au Gratin)

Ingredients—

½ lb. Tomatoes.	1 oz. Butter.
2 oz. Bread-crumbs.	Pepper and Salt.

Method.—Put the tomatoes into a basin, cover them with boiling water, and let them stand for a few minutes. Then take them out, dry them, and remove the skins. Cut them in slices, keeping them on a plate, so as not to lose any of the juice. Grease a small pie-dish or gratin dish, and put half the tomatoes at the foot of it. Sprinkle with pepper and salt, and put in half the bread-crumbs, and half the butter in small pieces. Then lay in the rest of the tomatoes, season them, and put the remainder of the bread-crumbs and butter on the top. Wipe round the edge of the dish, and bake in a quick oven from fifteen to twenty minutes. Serve in the dish in which it is cooked.

Tomatoes (Stuffed)

(*Fr.* Tomates Farcies)

Ingredients—

5 medium-sized Tomatoes.	A little Stock.
Pepper and Salt.	1 tea-sp. chopped Parsley.
1 oz. Butter.	A few browned Bread-crumbs.
3 table-sp. Minced Meat.	5 croûtons of Fried Bread.
2 table-sp. Bread-crumbs.	
1 Shallot.	

Method.—Wipe the tomatoes first with a cloth, then remove the stalk, and make a small round hole at that end. With the end of a teaspoon, scoop out the soft part from the inside, and put it into a basin. Be very careful whilst doing this not to break through the skin of the tomatoes, and do not make the sides too thin. Season the inside with pepper and salt, and turn them upside down on a plate to drain. The soft part from the inside must be strained or rubbed through a sieve, and kept for moistening the stuffing. The best meat to use for stuffing the tomatoes is ham, tongue, or chicken, but any nicely cooked meat will do. Melt the butter in a small saucepan, add to it the shallot, very finely chopped, and cook it slowly over the fire for a few minutes. Then add to it the meat, white bread-crumbs, and parsley mixed well together, season to taste, and moisten with the liquid from the tomatoes, and a little stock if necessary. Cook over the fire to swell the bread-crumbs, and then fill up the tomatoes with this stuffing. Do not fill them too full or they will burst whilst cooking. Sprinkle a few browned bread-crumbs over the top, and place them side by side on a greased baking-tin. Cover with greased paper, and bake in a moderate oven until they feel tender, from fifteen to twenty minutes. Put the fried croûtons of bread on to a hot dish with a dish paper on it, lift the tomatoes carefully on to this, and garnish with parsley.

Note.—If liked, sauce, brown or tomato, may be served round the tomatoes or separately.

A little grated Parmesan cheese or chopped mushrooms may be added to the stuffing.

Small stuffed tomatoes are sometimes used as a garnish for meat dishes.

Young Turnips in Butter

(*Fr.* Navets au Caramel)

Required—

6 or 8 young Turnips.	Butter.
Salt.	A pinch of Sugar.
A pinch of Cinnamon.	

Method.—Prepare the turnips and steam them until half cooked. Then take them up and put them into a casserole with a little butter, sprinkle with salt, and add the sugar and cinnamon. Put on the lid and cook slowly until the turnips are tender. They should be turned gently from time to time to be a nice golden brown colour when ready.

Mashed Turnips

Required—

Turnips.	Butter.
Pepper and Salt.	

Method.—Prepare as many turnips as required and cut them into medium-sized pieces. Cook them in a perforated steamer, or, if old, boil in salted water until thoroughly tender. The time will depend upon the age and freshness of the turnips, from ¾ of an hour to 1½ hours. When quite tender drain them thoroughly and return to a dry saucepan. Mash them with a fork or potato-beater until free from lumps, and add butter in the proportion of ½ oz. to each cupful. Season to taste and serve in a hot vegetable dish in the form of a pyramid, marking up the sides with the back of a fork.

Vegetable Marrow with White Sauce

(*Fr.* Courge à la Sauce Blanche)

Required—

1 Vegetable Marrow.	White Sauce (see p. 146).
Boiling Water.	Salt.

Method.—Wash the marrow, cut it in quarters, remove the seeds, and peel it very thinly. If large, cut it into neat-sized pieces, and throw them into cold water until wanted. Then place the pieces in a steamer and cook them until tender from ½ to ¾ of an hour. Serve in a hot vegetable dish with white sauce or any other suitable sauce poured over it.

Note.—The marrow may be boiled in milk, and the milk afterwards used for making the sauce.

Vegetable Marrow with Cheese

(*Fr.* Courge au Fromage)

Method.—Cook the marrow as above and finish according to directions given for cauliflower with cheese (p. 151).

GENERAL NOTES ON SALAD-MAKING

Nearly all vegetables and meats may be used as salads.

Cooked vegetables must not be pulpy but firm, in order that they may be cut in slices or fancy shapes.

All green vegetables should be young and crisp, and must be carefully washed in cold water to free them from dust and insects.

The main thing to observe in the washing of green vegetables, such as lettuce, endive, cress, &c., is to handle them very lightly; if too much touched their crispness is destroyed.

It is also important to have the vegetables well dried after washing; if any water is left on them the dressing will not adhere, but will run to the bottom of the dish, and both salad and dressing will be poor. Green salad vegetables should be shaken in a sieve or wire basket first and then tossed lightly in a cloth.

Salad Basket.

There are few vegetables which cannot be used as a salad. Among the most appropriate may be named lettuce, endive, mustard and cress, water-cress, tomatoes, celery, cucumber, spring onions, radishes, &c., various cooked vegetables, such as beetroot, cauliflower, French or haricot beans, asparagus, carrot, turnip, potatoes, Spanish onions, &c.

Poultry and game of any kind, ham, tongue, or, in fact, any tender, well-flavoured meat cut in small pieces may be used.

Fish too, such as salmon, turbot, halibut, sole, cod, lobster, crab, oysters, &c.

A few hints on the preparation of the various salad vegetables may be useful.

Lettuce.—Cut off the root and remove any coarse and discoloured outside leaves, and trim away any decayed parts from the inside ones. Separate the rest of the leaves one from the other, trim off the hard pieces of stalk, and throw them into a basin of fresh cold water. Wash lightly in this, and then take a second clean cold water, and wash again. If rather limp let the lettuce soak for half-an-hour or so in cold water, then shake as dry as possible in a sieve or wire basket, and toss lightly in a towel. The larger leaves of the lettuce may be cut across in fine shreds with a knife, and the smaller ones used as a garnish. Many people object to use a knife and prefer to tear the leaves in pieces with the fingers, but if a sharp knife is used, and it is quickly and lightly done, it really does no harm, and the lettuce looks much better.

Endive.—Prepare in the same way as lettuce.

Mustard and Cress.—Wash in several waters, removing all black seeds. If rather limp, soak for half-an-hour in cold water. Shake in a wire sieve or basket, and then in a cloth until dry.

Water-cress.—From the nature of its growth, it requires most careful cleansing, or it may prove most harmful. Remove all fibres and decayed leaves from the stalks. Then wash carefully in several waters, and shake dry.

Radishes.—Cut off the tops and wash well in cold water, rubbing off all black with the fingers. If large, they may be scrubbed with a brush. Dry in a towel. These may either be served whole in a salad or cut in thin slices.

Carrot and Turnip must be cooked, but not too soft, well drained, and cut in dice or fancy shapes.

Spring Onions.—Cut off the roots, part of the green tops, and the outside skin. Wash well, letting the water run between the leaves. Dry in a cloth, and serve whole or cut in thin slices.

Celery.—Use the white inside part for salads. Divide the stalks, and brush each part in cold water with a vegetable brush. With a knife remove any brown or discoloured parts, and, if limp, soak for a short time in cold water. Then dry and serve in a celery glass or cut in shreds in a salad.

For preparing the other vegetables see under the special salads.

TO SERVE A SALAD

A salad should be served as cold as possible, and the dressing should not be mixed with it long before it has to be eaten.

A special spoon ought to be used for mixing the dressing in horn, wood, or ivory, Silver is apt to promote verdigris.

The dressing itself may be made hours before, and even sufficient for two or three days made at one time and bottled ready for use.

Although exact quantities have been given for the various salad dressings, diversity of taste must be considered. There are two typical dressings, *i.e.*, Vinaigrette sauce or French dressing, made of oil and vinegar, and Mayonnaise. The former is the simpler and more wholesome of the two, and that most frequently used on the Continent. Mayonnaise is as a rule more appreciated by the English people.

When a salad is served along with other dishes the French dressing is the more suitable, but for such salads as chicken, lobster, game, &c., Mayonnaise is generally used, as these are as a rule served as a separate course.

Never use any but the best oil, and if not using it frequently buy it in small quantities, as it is apt to become rancid. Keep it in a cool dark place. Cream may always take the place of salad oil.

The variety of ways in which a salad may be garnished is endless, and although special garnishes are specified in the following recipes, they can of course be altered according to the season of the year and to suit individual taste.

A salad may either be served in a salad bowl, a glass dish, or in one of the various fancy china dishes which can now be bought for a very small sum. It is also customary to serve salads in small dishes, allowing one to each person.

SALAD DRESSINGS

French Dressing or Vinaigrette Sauce

Ingredients—

2 table-spoonfuls Salad Oil.	Salt
1 table-spoonful Vinegar.	½ tea-sp. made Mustard.
White Pepper.	

Method.—This dressing is frequently made at table in or over the salad bowl. If it is prepared beforehand it should not be poured over the salad until the time of serving. Mix the salt, pepper, and mustard together, and add the oil gradually. When these are well blended and the salt dissolved add the vinegar. A pinch of cayenne and a little sugar may be added. Sometimes a tea-spoonful of Tarragon vinegar is put in, and by some people more oil is preferred.

Salad Dressing

Ingredients—

2 hard-boiled Yolks.	3 tea-spoonfuls Salad Oil or Cream.
½ tea-sp. made Mustard.	2 table-spoonfuls Vinegar.
White Pepper and Salt.	1 dessert-spoonful Tarragon Vinegar.
A pinch of Cayenne.	
A pinch of Sugar.	

Method.—Rub the hard-boiled yolks through a sieve, and put them into a basin with the seasoning. Mix well together, and add the oil gradually, stirring all the time. Then add the vinegar, a little at a time, and mix well. The sauce should be of the consistency of cream.

Note—If the dressing is to be used for fish

or lobster salad, a tea-spoonful of anchovy or shrimp sauce is an improvement. The hard-boiled whites of eggs may be shred and used as a garnish for the salad.

Potato Dressing

Ingredients—

2 table-spoonfuls boiled and sieved Potatoes.	1 table-spoonful Vinegar.
3 table-spoonfuls Salad Oil.	½ tea-sp. made Mustard.
White Pepper and Salt.	A pinch of Sugar.

Method.—Put the potato into a basin with the seasoning, and mix well together. Add the oil gradually, stirring all the time, and then pour in the vinegar. A little Tarragon vinegar may be added. Cream may be substituted for the oil.

Celery Salad

(*Fr.* Salade de Céléri)

Required—

1 head of Celery, Salad dressing.

Garnish—

Parsley, Beetroot, or Small Cress.

Method.—Remove the outside stalks from the celery, reserving these for flavouring stocks or soups, and use the white inside part for the salad. Separate the stalks, and wash and brush them well in cold water. If time permits, let these lie for half-an-hour in cold water, then lift out and dry in a cloth. With a sharp knife cut the celery across in shreds, and also shred the white of egg left from the salad dressing. Mix these lightly together, put them in a salad dish, and pour the dressing over.

Garnish with a little finely-chopped parsley, small sprigs of parsley, the green tops of the celery, small cress, or beetroot cut in fancy shapes. Curled celery may also be used as a garnish.

To Curl Celery.—Cut a few firm sticks of celery into pieces about four inches in length. Then with a sharp knife cut these in fine strips, like a fringe, about three inches from the top, and leaving about one inch at the foot as foundation. Let these lie in cold water for half-an-hour, or until they have a curled appearance, and use as a garnish.

Chicken Salad

(*Fr.* Salade de Volaille)

Required—

Some cooked Chicken.	Some small Cress.
1 Lettuce.	A few Radishes.
1 or 2 sticks of Celery.	Mayonnaise Sauce (p. 144).

Method.—Cut the chicken in dice, removing the skin. Wash the lettuce and celery. Dry well and cut them in shreds. Mix these with the chicken, half the cress, and a little Mayonnaise. Pile high on a salad dish, and pour some more Mayonnaise over the top. Garnish with the small leaves of lettuce, radishes, and the remainder of the cress.

Note.—Endive may also be used as a garnish, and cucumber used instead of celery. A hard-boiled egg cut in pieces may be added.

Crab Salad

(*Fr.* Salade de Crabe)

Required—

1 Crab (boiled).	1 hard-boiled Egg.
1 Lettuce.	1 Tomato.
1 bunch of Water-cress.	French Dressing (p. 160).

Method.—Pick all the meat from the crab and shred it finely, carefully removing all pieces of shell. Wash and dry the lettuce and cress, and shred them finely. Mix these in a basin with the crab and salad dressing, and season rather highly with pepper and salt. Pile this mixture in a salad dish, and garnish with the tomato and hard-boiled egg cut in pieces.

Note.—Mayonnaise sauce may also be used for this.

Fish Salad

(*Fr.* Salade de Poisson)

Make in the same way as crab salad, using neat little flakes of cooked fish instead of the crab. A little cucumber or a few radishes may be used as a garnish.

Cucumber Salad

(*Fr.* Salade de Concombre)

Required—

1 Cucumber.	3 or 4 Spring Onions.
White Pepper and Salt.	French Dressing (p. 160).

Method.—Peel and shoe the cucumber as thin as a sheet of note-paper. When doing this always commence at the thick end and slice towards the stalk; if done the opposite way, the cucumber will have an exceedingly bitter taste. Lay these shoes on a plate with the onions washed and thinly sliced, and sprinkle them rather liberally with salt. Cover with another plate, stand for half-an-hour, and then pour off the water that has exuded from them. This tends to make the salad more digestible. Arrange the slices neatly in a salad dish and pour the dressing over.

Note.—The oil may be omitted and vinegar only used, and water-cress may take the place of the onions.

French Bean Salad

(*Fr.* Salade de Haricots Verts)

Required—

1 breakfast-cupful of cooked French Beans.	½ tea-spoonful finely powdered Herbs.
1 tea-spoonful finely chopped Parsley.	French Dressing (p. 160).

Method.—Have the beans cut in shreds and as dry as possible. Mix them with the parsley and mixed herbs finely powdered. Arrange neatly in a salad dish, and pour the dressing over.

Game Salad

(*Fr.* Salade de Gibier)

Make in the same way as chicken salad, and use Tartare sauce instead of Mayonnaise.

Haricot Bean Salad

(*Fr.* Salade de Haricots Blancs)

Prepare in the same way as French bean salad (p. 161), using small cooked haricot beans instead of French beans. Garnish with tiny sprigs of parsley or some curled celery.

Lobster Salad

(*Fr.* Salade de Homard)

Prepare in the same way as oyster salad (see below), using some nice pieces of cooked lobster in place of the oysters. It may be garnished with slices of hard-boiled egg and bunches of sliced cucumber and radish.

Mixed Salad

For this take as great a variety of salad vegetables as you can get, according to the season of the year, and a suitable proportion of each.

Such vegetables as finely shred lettuce and endive, spring onions thinly sliced, tomatoes peeled and cut in pieces, sliced beetroot, sliced cucumber, shred celery, mustard and cress, radishes, small pieces of cooked carrot and turnip, &c., &c., are suitable. Mix well with any of the salad dressings, and garnish according to taste.

Oyster Salad

(*Fr.* Salade aux Huitres)

Required—

1 dozen Oysters.
Cayenne Pepper.
Salt.
Mayonnaise Sauce.
1 Lettuce.
A little Cress.
Small slices of Lemon.

Method.—Wash, drain, and shred the lettuce very finely, and arrange a bed of this on six little china dishes. Put two oysters in each, and sprinkle with cayenne pepper and salt. Then coat the oysters with some thick Mayonnaise, and garnish with small cress and a small slice of lemon. This salad is sufficient for six persons. The quantities can of course be increased or reduced at pleasure.

Note.—This may also be served on one larger dish.

Potato and Beetroot Salad

(*Fr.* Salade de Pommes de Terre et Betterave)

Required—

4 or 5 cooked Potatoes.
1 cooked Beetroot.
1 tea-spoonful finely chopped Parsley.
1 tea-spoonful finely chopped Shallot.
Potato Dressing (p. 161).

Method.—Potatoes for a salad should be rather waxy, not mealy—new potatoes are best. Cut them into neat slices, and trim the slices with a round cutter. Peel and slice the beetroot, and arrange it in a salad dish in alternate rows or circles with the potato. Sprinkle with finely chopped parsley and shallot, and pour the dressing over.

Note.—A little grated horse-radish may be mixed with the dressing, and some water-cress used as a garnish.

Tomato Salad

(*Fr.* Salade de Tomates)

Required—

3 or 4 Tomatoes.
1 tea-sp. chopped Parsley.
1 tea-sp. chopped Shallot.
French Dressing (p. 160).

Method.—First peel the tomatoes. To do this either soak them in a basin of very hot water for two or three minutes, or put them in a wire basket and plunge them into boiling water for a minute. The latter method is better; it does not soften the tomatoes so much. Remove the skins very carefully with a small knife, and if time permits allow the tomatoes to become quite cold before cutting them up. Then slice them rather thinly and, if large, cut the slices in two. Place these slices very neatly on a salad dish, sprinkling them with chopped parsley and shallot. Pour the dressing over.

Note.—Mayonnaise sauce may be used instead of the plain salad dressing, and the shallot may be omitted.

PASTRY AND PASTRY-MAKING

General Notes on Pastry-making.—The making of pastry requires a considerable amount of practice, and failure at first must not discourage the beginner. The following rules must be carefully attended to:—

Use only the best materials, and if an economical pastry is wanted use good dripping or lard in preference to inferior butter.

See that all the utensils used, such as board, rolling-pin, and basin are particularly clean and cool. Clean hands are also imperative. If the hands are inclined to be very warm wash them some little time before beginning the pastry in very warm water. Make the pastry in as cool a place as possible; the colder it is kept during the making the lighter it will be. Roll the pastry lightly and press equally lightly with both hands.

Never rub little pieces off the fingers on to the pastry, as, when cooked, they will form hard lumps; but clean the hands back into the basin with a little dry flour.

Never allow pastry to stick to the board, but lift it occasionally on the rolling-pin and dust some flour underneath. If anything has stuck to the board, scrape it off carefully with a knife before beginning again. Always sprinkle flour over the board and pastry through a flour-dredger; it makes it finer and lighter.

If the rolling-pin sticks to the pastry dust a little flour over it, and brush it off again lightly with a small brush kept for the purpose. Never roll a quantity of dry flour into pastry as it gives it a white pasty appearance.

The exact amount of water to use is not given in the recipes, as so much depends upon the consistency of the butter and also upon the flour used. The finer the flour the more water it will take up.

However well pastry is made it will not be a success unless the baking is carefully attended to and the oven properly heated. If the oven is not hot enough the butter will melt and run out of the pastry before the starch grains in the flour have time to burst and absorb it. This makes the pastry heavy.

When the pastry is well thrown up and nicely browned, cover it over with kitchen paper and remove it to a cooler part of the oven until sufficiently cooked. Before baking pastry in any oven you should thoroughly understand the heating of it, as the hottest part of one may be the coolest part of another. Never slam an oven door, but open and close it gently and not oftener than necessary.

Flaky Pastry

Proportions—

10 oz. Flour.	A pinch of Salt.
7 oz. Butter.	Cold Water.
A squeeze of Lemon Juice.	

Method.—Weigh the butter, and let it lie for some time in cold water before using it. Sieve the flour and salt into a clean dry basin, and add the lemon juice. Lift the butter out of the water, and squeeze it dry in a clean floured cloth. Divide it into four equal pieces. Take one of these pieces and rub it into the flour with the tips of the fingers and thumbs until quite free from lumps. Then add sufficient cold water to form all into one lump. Mix with the hand as lightly as possible, and turn out on to a floured board. Knead lightly until free from cracks, and then roll out into a long narrow strip. Take one of the remaining portions of butter, and with the point of a knife spread it in small pieces and in even rows all over the pastry. Now flour the surface lightly, and fold the paste exactly in three. Turn the pastry half round, bringing the joins to the right-hand side. Press down the folds sharply with the rolling-pin, so as to enclose some air. Roll out the pastry again into a long narrow strip, and proceed as before until the two remaining portions of butter have thus been used. If the butter becomes soft during the rolling, lay the pastry aside, for a short time, before completing the process. The last time roll out the pastry to the desired thickness, and if it requires widening, turn it across the board and roll across. Never roll in a slanting direction, or the lightness of the pastry will suffer.

This pastry is not quite so rich as puff pastry. It may be kept for several days in cold weather if wrapped in greased paper or in a damp cloth.

Puff Pastry

(*Fr.* Feuilletage

Proportions—

½ lb. Flour.	A squeeze of Lemon Juice.
½ lb. Butter.	Cold Water.
A pinch of Salt.	

Method.—Weigh the butter, and let it lie in a basin of cold water for some time before using it. Sieve the flour and salt into a clean dry basin, and add the lemon juice to them. Lift the butter out of the cold water and dry it lightly in a floured cloth. Take a quarter of this and rub it into the flour with the tips of the fingers and thumbs until there are no lumps left, then mix with cold water into a stiffish dough. Turn this on to a floured board and work it well with the hands until it will no longer stick to the fingers and forms a perfectly smooth dough. Then roll it rather thinly into a square or round shape. The butter to be used should be as nearly as possible of the same consistency as the paste. Form it into a neat flat cake, and place it in the centre of the pastry. Fold it up rather loosely, and flatten the folds with a rolling-pin. Then roll out the pastry into a long narrow strip, being careful that the butter does not break through. Fold it exactly in three, press down the folds, and lay the pastry aside in a cool place for a quarter of an hour at least. This is called giving the pastry one " turn " and seven of these is the number usually required for puff pastry. The next time the pastry is rolled, place it with the joins at your right-hand side, and the open ends towards you. Give it two " turns " this time, and again set it aside in a cool place for at least fifteen minutes. Repeat this until the pastry has had seven rolls in all, one roll or turn the first time and after that two each time with an interval between. The object of this cooling between the rolls is to keep the butter and flour in distinct and separate layers, in which it is the function of the rolling-pin and folding to arrange them, and on which the lightness of the pastry depends. After it has received its last roll, it is better to be laid aside for some time before using it, then roll to the thickness required. This pastry will keep for several days in cold weather if wrapped in a piece of well-greased paper.

Rough-Puff Pastry

Proportions-

½ lb. Flour.	A squeeze of Lemon Juice.
¼ lb. Butter or Lard.	Cold Water.
A pinch of Salt.	

Method.—Prepare the butter as above, and sieve the flour and salt into a clean dry basin, and add the lemon juice to it. Put the butter into the basin, cover it well over with the flour, and then break it into pieces the size of a hazel-nut. Have some very cold water in a jug ready for mixing with, and make a well in the centre of the flour and butter. Mix very lightly with the right hand or with a knife, pouring the water in gradually with the left until you have added sufficient to bind all together. Flour the baking-board and turn the dough out on to it. Flour the rolling-pin and roll the dough out very carefully into a strip about three-quarters of a yard in length and from seven to eight inches wide. Lift occasionally while rolling, and dust some flour underneath the pastry to prevent it from sticking to the board. Roll the pastry on the one side only, do not turn it over, and roll in short quick strokes always from you. When rolled to the required length, fold it in three, and press down with the rolling-pin. Turn the pastry half round, bringing the joins to the right-hand side, and roll again in the same way as before. Fold again in three, half turn and roll again, repeating this until the pastry has had three rolls and three folds. The fourth time of rolling out, roll to the size and shape required for use.

Note.—If the pastry becomes very soft while rolling, it should be laid away in a cool place before completing the process. It is improved by being kept for a few hours before using. In cold weather it will keep for several days if wrapped in a piece of greased paper. This pastry may be made richer by using 6 oz. of butter instead of 4 oz. to ½ lb. flour. An egg well beaten may be used for mixing with along with a little water.

Short Crust

Proportions—

½ lb. Flour.	A squeeze of Lemon Juice.
1 tea-spoonful Castor Sugar.	Cold Water.
¼ lb. Butter.	

Method.—Rub the flour and sugar through a wire sieve into a clean dry basin. Add a squeeze of lemon juice, and if fresh butter is being used, a pinch of salt also. Put in the butter, cover it well over with the flour, and break it in pieces. Then rub together lightly with the tips of the fingers and thumbs until as fine as bread-crumbs. Next make a well in the centre of these dry ingredients, and add cold water very gradually with the left hand whilst mixing with the right. Mix with the hand or with a knife. Use very little water in the mixing of this paste, or it will be tough instead of short. Flour the pastry-board slightly, lay the dough on it, and work lightly with the hands until free from cracks. Then flour a rolling-pin, press down the pastry first, then with sharp quick strokes roll it out to the thickness required. This pastry only requires one roll. Roll it on the one side only, and be careful it does not stick to the board.

Notes.—The above is a fairly rich paste, and if a plainer one is wished, use only 3 oz. of butter, or substitute lard or dripping for the butter.

The pastry may be made richer by using rather more butter, 6 oz. to ½ lb. flour, and the yolk of an egg beaten up with a little water for mixing.

The quantities given will make a pastry quite suitable for all ordinary purposes.

This is one of the most wholesome kinds of pastry. The butter is so thoroughly mixed with the flour, that the latter is more thoroughly cooked and is more digestible than in some of the flaky pastries.

Plain Short Crust

Proportions—

½ lb. Flour.	½ tea-sp. Baking Powder.
4 oz. Lard or Dripping.	Cold Water.
A pinch of Salt.	

Method.—Make in the same as above. A little castor sugar should be added if the pastry is to be used for a sweet dish.

Suet Pastry

Proportions—

½ lb. Flour.	½ tea-sp. Baking Powder.
¼ lb. Suet.	Cold Water.
½ tea-spoonful Salt.	

Method.—Weigh the flour carefully, add the salt and baking powder to it, and rub these through a wire sieve into a clean dry basin. Remove the skin from the suet, shred it very finely with a sharp knife, and then weigh it. Put it on a chopping-board, and sprinkle it with some of the flour already weighed out. Then chop it very finely, using enough flour to prevent it sticking to the board and knife. The finer it is chopped, the better the pastry will be. When ready, mix it thoroughly with the flour in the basin, rubbing all the ingredients lightly together with the tips of the fingers. Then make a well in the centre of these dry ingredients, and add enough cold water to form into a smooth soft dough. Turn out on to a floured board, leaving the basin [illegible]e clean. Work lightly with the hand[illegible] from cracks, then flour a rolling-pi[illegible] making [illegible]t to the thickness required.

Note.—Buttermilk or sweet milk may be used instead of water for mixing.

Half the quantity of flour may be omitted, and ½ lb. bread-crumbs used in its place.

To Make Patty Cases

First Method.—Take ½ lb. of puff pastry that has had seven rolls, and roll it out to ¼ inch in thickness. Let it rest for fully five minutes before cutting, to allow for shrinking, or the patties will be oval instead of round in shape. Then take a cutter 2½ inches in diameter, and stamp out as many rounds as possible from the pastry. Do not cut too near to the edge of the pastry, as it is usually of rather uneven thickness there. Mark the middle of these rounds to about half their depth with a cutter 1½ inch in diameter, a border being thus left outside the centre cut of about ½ inch in width. The pastry should be icy cold when cut, or it will not rise evenly. Lay the rounds on a baking-tin, keeping them as much to the middle of this as possible, a precaution which also promotes their rising evenly. Brush over the tops with beaten egg, being careful not to touch the edges, as the egg would harden the pastry and prevent it rising.

Bake in a hot oven for twenty minutes, or until the pastry is well risen and nicely browned. If on taking the patties out of the even one side is found to be higher than the other, press the tops gently into place at once before they have time to stiffen, using if necessary a little beaten egg on a brush to make them stick. When the patties are ready, lift off the inner circle of pastry and remove the uncooked paste from the interior to make room for the filling. If lids are wanted for the cases, roll out the remainder of the pastry to about ¼ inch in thickness, and stamp out rounds for covers with the smaller of the two cutters used for the patties. Bake these on a separate tin, as they will take a shorter time to cook. About ten minutes should be sufficient.

Second Method.—Use either rough puff or flaky pastry, rolling it out to rather more than ¼ inch in thickness. Let it rest for a few minutes to allow for shrinking, and cut into rounds with a plain or fluted cutter 2½ inches in diameter. From half of these rounds cut a hole in the centre 1½ inch in diameter. Moisten the edges of the whole rounds with egg or water, and lay the rings on the top. Place the patties on a baking-tin, and prick the centres with a fork to prevent them rising. Brush over with beaten egg, and bake in a hot oven for twenty minutes. On another tin put the small rounds cut from the centre of the rings, brush them over with beaten egg, and bake about ten minutes. These will serve as covers. When the patties are ready, fill up the hollows in the centre with any mixture, and put on the lids.

MEAT AND MEAT DISHES

SIMPLE METHOD OF COOKING MEAT

BAKING AND ROASTING

Roasting, properly speaking, is cooking in front of an open fire, but owing to the limited accommodation and the construction of the stoves in modern houses, this method of cooking has become almost a thing of the past, and baking, or roasting in the oven, has almost entirely taken its place.

The rules for both are practically the same. The meat to be roasted should be weighed and well wiped with a damp cloth, but never washed. If frozen meat is being used the joint should be allowed to thaw slowly in a warm kitchen for some hours before it is cooked.

The tin used for roasting should, if possible, be a double one, the under one being large enough to hold a little water, which will prevent the dripping in the upper portion from becoming too hot and acquiring a burnt taste. The meat should be placed on a small stand or trivet in the baking-tin to prevent it soaking in the dripping and becoming sodden. The tin should be large enough to hold the meat comfortably without projecting over the edges.

The first point in baking or roasting is to expose the meat to a high temperature for ten minutes in order to harden the outside and form

Double Roasting-Tin.

a coating, as it were, to prevent the escape of the juice. Then the heat must be reduced and the cooking continued until the joint is sufficiently roasted.

During the process of cooking the meat ought to be basted with dripping or butter at intervals of 15 to 20 minutes to prevent its becoming dried up. If the meat is not sufficiently fat in itself a little extra dripping or butter should be added or kept in a jar on the top of the stove. The spoon used for basting ought to be laid on a plate to prevent the drops of grease soiling the stove.

There are one or two patent roasting-tins now on the market which save the trouble of basting; one which bastes the meat automatically without any trouble, and another where no attention is required for either turning or basting.

It is very important that the oven should be clean and well ventilated, otherwise the operation of roasting will cause a most unpleasant smell.

It is impossible to lay down any exact rule regarding the time for roasting meat, as the form and thickness of the joint must always be taken into consideration. A thin long piece of meat would naturally take a shorter time to cook than a thick solid piece of equal weight. The approximate time for cooking beef and mutton is 15 minutes to the pound and 15 minutes over, and for pork, lamb and veal, 20 minutes to the pound and 20 minutes over; but common-sense and experience will be found to be the best guides. Beef and mutton may be left rather underdone if fancy dictates, but white meats are unwholesome unless thoroughly cooked. If the joint is large and thick it should be turned upside down during part of the time to ensure the under part being sufficiently cooked.

When the meat is ready lift it on to a hot dish and keep it hot while the gravy is being made. Pour the dripping from the tin into a jar and add a small quantity of boiling water. Then with an iron spoon scrape down any glaze or meat juice which adheres to the side of the tin and add salt to taste. Never add colouring. If a large quantity of gravy is required, a little stock may be necessary, but any with a strong pronounced flavour of vegetables should be avoided. The pure juice of the meat is the best gravy. Remove any grease from the surface of the gravy with a piece of kitchen paper. Strain some of it round the joint, and serve the surplus in a sauce-boat, as it is awkward for the carver if the dish is made too full.

BOILING

Although this is one of the simplest methods of cooking meat, it is one which frequently meets with failure. Instead of having a tender joint full of juice, a piece of meat both tough and tasteless will be served up. Boiling is best suited to large joints; in fact, nothing under three or four pounds should be attempted.

If it is fresh meat, wipe and weigh the joint the same as for roasting and then plunge it into a saucepan with sufficient boiling water to cover it. Boil quickly for 5 minutes to form a casing on the outside of the meat, then draw the saucepan to one side and allow it to simmer only until sufficiently cooked. There should be just a gentle bubbling on the surface of the water; if boiled hard the meat will be leathery and tasteless.

Salt in the proportion of one table-spoonful to a gallon of water should be added to the water, and any scum that rises should be carefully removed. Suitable vegetables, such as carrots, turnips, or parsnips, should be cooked along with the meat.

Salt meat should be put into cold or tepid water to begin with in order to soften it and draw out some of the salt. In fact, if it is very salt it is a good plan to soak it in cold water for some time before cooking. The time for boiling will vary from 20 to 30 minutes to the pound and 20 or 30 minutes over according to the kind and shape of the meat. It must be borne in mind that boiled meat should never be underdone, and it is better to err on the safe side and give it too much time than to undercook it.

If the meat is to be served cold, it should be allowed to cool in the water in which it was cooked.

The usual gravy for boiled joints is some of the liquor in which they are cooked A tasty sauce can also be served separately, such as caper sauce, or onion sauce with boiled mutton, béchamel sauce with boiled lamb, horse-radish sauce or tomato sauce with boiled beef, &c.

The remainder of the liquor in which the meat has been cooked should be reserved for making soup.

BRAISING

Take a stewpan with a tight-fitting lid and place a few slices of fat bacon at the foot. On the top of this put a layer of carrot, turnip, onion, and celery cut in dice and in equal proportions. Season with pepper, salt, and a small bunch of herbs. Pour in enough stock or water to reach the top of these ingredients and bring to the boil. Place the meat to be braised on the top and cover with greased paper so as to keep down the steam, and cook slowly at the side of the fire or in the oven. This method of cooking makes tough meat tender and of good flavour. The time will depend upon the size and kind of meat.

FRYING

Dry Frying or, properly speaking, **Sautéing**, is cooking in a shallow pan with a small quantity of fat. The fat should be made quite hot and then the meat placed in and cooked on both sides. Chops and steaks can be cooked in this way, but they will not be so digestible as when grilled.

Deep Frying or Frying Proper.—Proceed in the same way as for fish by this method (p. 131).

STEAMING

Both meat and poultry can be steamed by placing them in a double cooker or patent steamer, or even in a jar placed in a saucepan of boiling water. It is a slow method of cooking and most suitable for tender pieces of meat.

There must be plenty of steam or the process will not be a success.

STEWING

Stewing means cooking in a small quantity of liquid at a low temperature. It is one of the most economical ways of cooking, firstly because there is nothing lost, any juice that is drawn from the meat being served in the gravy. Secondly, because the coarser and cheaper pieces of meat may be used as the long slow cooking makes them tender; and, thirdly, very little fuel is required and very little attention when once the stew has been set going.

A stew is generally a mixture of meat and vegetables, and success depends very much upon the careful seasoning and blending of flavours. Examples of several different kinds of stews will be found in the following recipes.

A stew may be cooked in a stewpan or in a jar in the oven. A double saucepan is also very useful for this mode of cooking or the saucepan containing the stew may be placed in a larger one containing hot water. The lid should be removed as seldom as possible, and it should fit the saucepan or jar tightly so as to avoid all waste through evaporation.

The time for stewing will depend upon the kind of meat used and the size of the pieces.

Stewing in Earthenware.—This method of cooking is becoming very popular, and the simple clay casseroles which can now be bought in so many different shapes and sizes are admirably adapted to the purpose. They have much to recommend them from the point of view of cleanliness; they are easily cleaned and there is no danger of rust. They are also economical as far as fuel is concerned, as their heat-retaining power being so great they will simmer for hours over a gentle heat without burning the food. They are not expensive to buy, and if proper care is taken of them they will last a long time.

Food cooked in them is usually served in the pot, hence the term "En Casserole," and therein lies part of the novelty. A folded serviette may, if liked, be pinned round the outside, but some of the pots are so quaint and ornamental, this rather spoils the effect.

There are different kinds of ware for cooking purposes now on the market; besides the all brown clay-pot there is the brown and green fire-proof ware with white or yellow linings and the all white fire-proof china.

Little rechauffés of meat, fish, and poultry can all be served up "en casserole," and it is also an excellent method of stewing fruit.

BROILING OR GRILLING

This is cooking on a hot gridiron either over or under a bright clear fire. The process can only be applied to small thin pieces of meat, which will cook quickly, such as chops, steak, kidneys, joints of game and poultry, &c.

The meat chosen must always be of the best quality, otherwise it will be tough and uneatable. It is impossible to obtain that red juicy appearance which is essential to a good steak or chop with inferior meat.

The state of the fire is one of the next points of consideration. It ought to consist of glowing red embers, without any smoke or flame. A handful of salt sprinkled over it sometimes helps to disperse any smoke.

Place the gridiron, which must be very clean, over the fire and allow it to become hot, then grease it with a piece of fat or suet held on the end of a fork. The gridiron must be placed or held in a slanting position and from three to six inches above the coals, according to the intensity of the heat. Lay the meat on it and let one side cook while you count ten at about the same rate as the ticking of a clock, then turn with the steak tongs or the blades of two knives and cook the same length of time on the other side, and repeat the process until the meat is sufficiently cooked. The regular turning is very important, as it means slower cooking and prevents the surface from being burned.

The time must be regulated by the thickness rather than by the weight of the meat, and experience alone can teach when the chop or steak is done to a nicety. Touch is the best guide. If, when pressed with the back of a fork, the meat feels spongy and very elastic it is still in a raw state; if, on the other hand, it is hard and without resistance it is overcooked. The aim must be to hit the happy medium and serve the meat well browned on both sides before that puffed appearance has disappeared and all the steam of the juices has escaped through the crust.

Broiling can also be done in a hanging gridiron in front of a clear fire, but the result is not so satisfactory.

When a gas stove is used the grilling is done underneath the light instead of on the top (see p. 96). A little water put in the dripping tin will prevent the fat catching fire.

BEEF AND MUTTON

Boiled Salt Beef

Choose a nice piece of salt beef, aitchbone, round or brisket, and bind it up firmly with a piece of tape to prevent it having a ragged appearance when cooked. (For Boiling Salt Meat, see p. 166.)

It is usual to cook vegetables along with this meat. Prepare a supply of carrots, turnips, and onions in proportion to the size of the meat; keep the onions whole, cut the carrots into three or four pieces lengthwise, and the turnips in thick slices. When the meat has come to the boil add the vegetables, or if the meat is very large put them in rather later so that they do not become too much cooked. Small dumplings are also a favourite accompaniment to this dish.

For serving lift the meat on to a hot dish and remove the tape. A silver skewer may be put in to keep the meat together. Garnish with the vegetables and dumplings placed alternately round the dish. Strain a little of the liquid round and serve an extra supply in a sauce-boat.

A dish of green vegetables may be served separately.

Dumplings to Serve with Meat

Ingredients—

6 oz. Flour.	¼ tea-sp. Baking Powder.
2 oz. Suet.	A little Water or Milk.
1 tea-spoonful Salt.	

Method.—Chop the suet and mix it lightly with the flour, salt, and baking powder. Bind all together with water or milk and knead lightly. The dough must be soft without being sticky. Make it up into small balls and cook them from ten to fifteen minutes beside the meat. The water must be kept simmering all the time they are in. Serve at once, or they will be heavy.

Roast Beef

(*Fr.* Bœuf Rôti)

The best joints for roasting are the sirloin and the ribs. The round and aitchbone can also be cooked in this way, but to be successful the meat requires to be very tender. If a large sirloin has to be roasted it is a good plan to cut a piece off the thin end and either stew or cook it in some other way, as if roasted with the rest of the joint it is apt to become overcooked before the other part is ready.

Ribs of beef are often better boned and rolled before roasting; it makes a neater joint and is more economical, as the bones with all their goodness can be used for soup. (For Roasting and Making the Gravy, see p. 165.)

A little shredded horse-radish may be used as a garnish, or horse-radish sauce may be served separately. Yorkshire pudding (p. 193) and roast or baked potatoes are the usual accompaniments.

Grilled Steak

The steak must be cut from a well-hung juicy piece of meat. The best are from the rump or fillet or from the tender part of the round. The steak should be cut from 1¼ to 1½ inches in thickness. Wipe it with a damp cloth and trim off any superfluous fat. Beat the meat slightly with a cutlet bat and then make it as shapely as possible. If small round steaks are required, it is best to use the fillet cut in slices. Moisten both sides of the meat with a little salad oil or melted butter, place it on a well-heated gridiron and cook according to directions given for broiling. The time will vary from twelve to fifteen minutes according to the thickness of the meat, and also upon whether it is liked very underdone or well cooked. Serve at once on a very hot dish and put a pat of maître d'hôtel butter on the top. The heat of the meat should melt the butter and the parsley should look fresh and green.

A little water-cress may be used as a garnish, or a few small baked tomatoes may be put round the dish. Potato chips or balls should be served separately.

Braised Round of Beef

(*Fr.* Bœuf à la Casserole)

Ingredients—

3 lbs. Round of Beef.	1 Onion.
2 oz. good Dripping.	Bunch of Herbs.
Trimmings of Ham or Bacon.	1 pint Stock.
1 Carrot.	Seasoning.

Method.—Put the dripping and some trimmings of ham and bacon into a stewpan, and, when melted, put in the vegetables cut in pieces and the seasonings. Tie the meat into a neat shape with a piece of tape, and when the contents of the saucepan are hot place it on the top with any bones or scraps round the sides. Put on the lid and cook slowly for twenty minutes until the meat has taken colour. Add the stock and, if liked, a glass of white wine. Cook slowly from three to four hours until the meat is thoroughly tender. Lift it on to a hot dish, remove the tape, and keep it warm while the gravy is prepared. If the liquid in the saucepan has reduced very much add a little stock, and strain into another saucepan. Boil for a few minutes, remove any grease from the top, pour some of this gravy round the meat, and serve the remainder separately.

A purée of potato is a good accompaniment with this dish.

Scotch Collops

Ingredients—

1 lb. lean juicy Beef.	½ pint Stock.
2 table-sp. Bread-crumbs.	Pepper and Salt.
1 oz. Beef Dripping, Butter, or Bacon Fat.	1 tea-sp. Flavouring Sauce.
1 Onion.	1 Slice of Toast.

Method.—Have the meat minced along with a small proportion of fat. Melt the one ounce of fat into a stewpan, and, when hot, put in the onion finely chopped and the meat. Pound well with a wooden spoon until nicely browned. Add the stock and seasoning and simmer slowly for half-an-hour. Add the bread-crumbs about ten minutes before it is ready, so as to absorb the grease. Serve garnished with small croûtons of toast.

Haricot of Ox-Tail

(*Fr.* Queue de Bœuf en Haricot)

Ingredients—

1 Ox-tail.
1 pint Brown Stock.
1 Carrot, 1 Turnip, and 1 Onion.
A sprig of Parsley, Thyme, and Marjoram.
1 Bay Leaf.
1 stick of Celery.
2 oz. Butter.
2 oz. Flour.
Pepper and Salt.
1 glass of Claret.

Garnish.

Fancy shapes of Carrot and Turnip or Glazed Onions.

Method.—Wash the tail, and cut it in pieces, removing any superfluous fat. Put them into cold water, and bring to the boil. Boil for ten minutes, then strain and rinse the pieces of tail. Dry them well, and coat them with the flour. Melt the butter in a saucepan; when smoking hot put in the tail, and fry a nice brown colour. Add some small pieces of vegetable, the herbs, stock, and seasoning. Cover the pan, and simmer slowly from three to four hours, skimming when necessary. When the tail is tender lift the pieces on to a hot dish. Skim the sauce, add the wine, and strain through a fine strainer over and round the tail. Garnish with fancy shapes of carrot and turnip which have been cooked separately.

Beef Creams

(*Fr.* Crèmes de Bœuf)

Ingredients—

¾ lb. lean juicy Beef.
Pepper and Salt.
Purée of Spinach or Potato.
1 table-sp. Brown Sauce.
1 Egg.
2 table-sp. whipped Cream.
1 des.-sp. chopped Parsley.
1 des.-sp. chopped Mushrooms.
Brown or Piquante Sauce.

Panada

1 gill Stock.
½ oz. Butter.
2 oz. Flour.

Method.—Grease six or seven small entrée moulds, and decorate them at the foot with chopped parsley and mushrooms.

To Prepare the Cream.—Remove all skin and fat from the meat, and pass it through the mincing machine. Make a panada with the stock, butter, and flour; put the stock and butter into a saucepan, bring them to the boil, and sprinkle in the flour. Then mix until perfectly smooth, and cook thoroughly. Put this panada into a mortar with the meat, brown sauce, egg, and seasoning. Pound well, and rub all through a wire sieve. Add the cream and the remainder of the parsley and mushrooms. Mix lightly, and fill up the prepared moulds. Place these in a shallow pan or tin with a double fold of paper at the foot. Pour in enough boiling water to come half-way up the sides of the moulds, and cover with greased paper. Steam slowly for fifteen minutes, or until the creams feel firm to the touch. Lift them out, and allow them to stand for a minute or two. Then unmould them carefully, and dish on a purée of potato or spinach and pour brown sauce or piquante sauce round.

Beef Olives

Required—

1½ lb. Beef (cut thin).
1 oz. Butter or Dripping.
1 oz. Flour.
½ pint Stock.
1 dessert-spoonful Ketchup.
Pepper and Salt.
3 table-sp. Bread-crumbs.

Force-meat

1 table-sp. chopped Suet or melted Butter.
1 tea-sp. chopped Parsley.
¼ tea-sp. mixed Herbs.
Pepper and Salt.
Egg or Milk to bind.

Method.—First prepare the force-meat. Put the bread-crumbs into a basin, and add to them the parsley, herbs, suet or butter, pepper and salt. Mix all together, and add enough milk or beaten egg to bind, but do not make the mixture too moist.

Wipe the meat with a damp cloth and cut it into oblong-shaped pieces, suitable for rolling up, and as much one size and shape as possible. Any nice pieces of meat that are too small or ragged to make into rolls may be cut up and rolled inside the other pieces, also some small pieces of hard fat. Spread out all the strips of meat on a board, put some of the force-meat into the centre of each, and roll them up. Tie round with a piece of coarse thread or fine twine, and roll them in the flour. Melt the dripping or butter in a stewpan, and when smoking hot put in the rolls of meat and keep turning them over with a spoon until they are browned on all sides. Lift them out on to a plate as they are ready, and when all are done, pour away the fat from the pan and add the stock. Add also the seasonings, bring to the boil, and skim well. Return the rolls of meat, put the lid on the pan, and simmer very slowly from one and a half to two hours, or until the meat feels quite tender.

To Serve.—Lift out the beef olives on to a hot dish, remove the strings, and arrange them neatly down the centre of the dish. Strain the gravy over and round. Garnish with a little very finely chopped parsley, green peas, or carrot and turnip cut in fancy shapes.

Note.—Some finely chopped ham or tongue may be added to the stuffing, also a little chopped onion if desired. Or a turned olive, an oyster, or some chopped mushrooms may be put inside. Sometimes sausage meat is used instead of the above force-meat. The beef olives may, if liked, be dished on a border of potatoes or spinach.

Instead of cutting the meat in pieces it may be made in one large roll. Veal olives can be done in the same way.

Russian Steaks

(*Fr.* Biftecks à la Russe)

Ingredients—

½ lb. tender Steak.
½ lb. Fillet of Veal.
1 small Shallot finely chopped.
1 Egg.
1 tea-sp. chopped Parsley.
Pepper and Salt.
Egg and Bread-crumbs.
2 oz. clarified Fat.
Tomato Sauce.

Method.—Remove all skin from the meat, cut it in pieces, and pass it twice through the mincing machine. Then put it into a basin, and add the shallot, parsley, and seasoning. Moisten with the egg well beaten, and mix well. Spread the mixture on a plate, and allow it to set for half-an-hour. Then divide it into eight or ten equal-sized pieces. Form each piece into a round flattish cake, using flour to prevent the mixture from sticking to the board, and egg and bread-crumb them. Then flatten the steaks with a knife and re-shape them. Melt the fat in a frying-pan. When smoking hot, put in the steaks, and fry them first on one side and then on the other until nicely browned. They will require fully ten minutes to cook. Drain them well, and serve in a circle on a hot dish. Pour tomato sauce round.

Note.—These steaks may, if liked, be dished on a border of potatoes (p. 156), and green peas used as a garnish.

Tripe with Tomatoes

(*Fr.* Tripes à l'Italienne)

Ingredients—

1½ lbs. dressed Tripe.
1½ oz. Butter.
1 cupful Tomato Sauce.
2 table-sp. Grated Cheese.
½ lb. Mushrooms.
Stock.
2 table-sp. Bread-crumbs.
Seasoning.

Method.—Wash the tripe in warm water and cut it in thin strips. Put it into a stewpan with the mushrooms peeled and sliced, the butter, seasoning, and enough light stock to cover. Stew slowly until the tripe is tender, add the tomato sauce and cook a few minutes longer. Arrange the stew in a fire-proof dish, sprinkle the bread-crumbs and cheese over the top, and brown in the oven.

Boiled Tongue with Caper Sauce

(*Fr.* Langue de Bœuf—Sauce aux Câpres)

Required—

1 Fresh Tongue.
1 Carrot.
Turnip.
1 Onion stuck with Cloves.
A bunch of Herbs.
Salt.
Caper Sauce.

Method.—Trim the tongue, removing any untidy-looking pieces from the root end. Put it into a saucepan with cold water to cover, bring to the boil and boil for ten minutes. Strain and rinse away any scum with fresh water. Cover the tongue again with warm water, add the trimmings, and, when boiling, add the vegetables cut in pieces and the other seasonings. Cook slowly for four hours or until the tongue is quite tender, then lift it up on a hot dish; remove the skin and cut it in halves without quite severing the pieces. Make some caper sauce (see p. 142), adding to it two yolks of eggs and mask the tongue with this.

Stuffed and Roast Shoulder of Mutton

Required—

A shoulder of Mutton.
4 oz. Bread-crumbs.
1½ oz. chopped Suet.
A little grated Lemon Rind.
1 table-sp. chopped Parsley.
A little Milk, or 1 Egg.
A pinch of Nutmeg.

Method.—Remove the bone from the mutton, wipe it well with a damp cloth, and season with pepper and salt. Then prepare the stuffing:—Put all the dry ingredients into a basin, and season to taste. A little finely chopped ham or tongue may be added or some finely powdered herbs. Add enough beaten egg or milk to bind all together into a stiffish paste. Place this in the centre of the mutton and either sew it in or strap it into shape with a piece of tape. Weigh the joint and then roast according to directions given on p. 165.

Remove the tape or sewing-cotton before serving and keep in shape with a silver skewer. Pour a plain gravy round and garnish with small baked tomatoes.

Hot Pot

Ingredients—

1½ lbs. of Mutton.
1 lb. Potatoes.
3 Onions.
A little Parsley.
2 Sheep's Kidneys.
1 oz. Butter or Dripping.
½ pint Stock.
Pepper and Salt.

Method.—This dish should be cooked and served in an earthenware pot. Trim the meat and kidneys and cut them into small neat pieces. Slice the onions thinly and scald them in boiling water a few minutes. Peel the potatoes, cut a few of them in halves or quarters, and slice the remainder rather thickly. Arrange the ingredients in layers in the dish, seasoning each with a little pepper and salt. The last layer should be the pieces of potato. Pour in the stock and put the butter or dripping in pieces on the top. Cover with the lid or twist a piece of strong paper over the top, and cook in the oven from one and a half to two hours. About half-an-hour before serving remove the cover and allow the top to become a nice brown colour. Sprinkle with finely chopped parsley and serve in the dish.

Note.—Beef or veal may be used instead of mutton. A few mushrooms may be added if liked.

Dutch Stew

Ingredients—

1½ lbs. Mutton.	4 or 5 Potatoes.
1 tender Cabbage.	1 Spanish Onion.
1 gill warm Water.	Pepper and Salt.

Method.—Wipe the meat and cut it in convenient-sized pieces. Put it into an earthenware stewpan, add water and seasoning, and simmer for half-an-hour. Then add potatoes sliced and cabbage carefully prepared and cut in six or eight pieces. Replace the lid and stew from three-quarters to one hour longer. Add more seasoning if necessary and serve in the casserole.

Note.—Any bones should be stewed with the meat and lifted out before serving.

Mutton Cutlets

(*Fr.* Côtelettes de Mouton)

Required—

1½ lb. best end of the Neck of Mutton.	Frying Fat.
Pepper and Salt.	A Potato Border.
Egg and Bread-crumbs.	Brown, Tomato, or Piquante Sauce.

Method.—For mutton cutlets the meat should be very small, and the butcher should be instructed to saw off the chine bone, since when this is done the cutlets can be easily divided without the aid of a saw or chopper. Wipe the meat first with a damp cloth, then cut it with a very sharp knife, allowing a bone to each cutlet. (This quantity should make five.) Trim off the fat, leaving only a narrow rim, and scrape one inch of the bone at the end quite clean to allow of a cutlet frill being put on afterwards. Scrape also the bone on the inner side, and if too long and unsightly, chop a piece off from each, but make all the cutlets as nearly as possible the same shape and size.

Season them with pepper and salt, brush over with well-beaten egg, and coat with finely made bread-crumbs. Put the cutlets on a board and re-shape them with a clean dry knife, and remove all crumbs from the inside bone. Then lay them on a dish or tin with a double paper under them, and they are ready for cooking.

To Cook the Cutlets.—Melt about two ounce of clarified fat in a frying-pan, and allow it to become smoking hot over the fire. Then lay in the cutlets, and fry them rather slowly, first on one side and then on the other, until they are nicely browned. They will require from eight to ten minutes to cook. Drain them well on the kitchen-paper before dishing.

To Serve the Cutlets.—Arrange a border of mashed potatoes on a hot dish and arrange the cutlets on the top of this, one leaning against the other, and with all the bones to the inside. The ends of the bones may be garnished with small cutlet frills. Pour brown, tomato, piquante, or any other suitable sauce round. (See Sauces.)

Notes.—The cutlets may be dished in a straight row down the dish instead of in a circle. Spinach may be used in place of potato, or the cutlets may be dished without either.

Green peas, small baked tomatoes, or a macedoine of vegetable may be put in the centre as a garnish.

Curry of Kidneys

Ingredients—

4 or 5 Sheep's Kidneys.	1 small Apple.
½ oz. Butter.	½ pint Stock
1 dessert-sp. Rice Flour.	A little Chutney.
1 tea-sp. Curry Powder.	Pepper and Salt.
1 table-spoonful Cream.	Boiled Rice.
1 small Onion.	

Method.—Melt the butter in a stewpan or earthenware casserole, put in the kidneys, split and skinned, and cook them for a few minutes. Skin and slice the onion very thinly, peel and chop the apple, and put these two into the pan with the kidneys. Fry for a few minutes, then add the rice flour, curry powder, chutney, pepper, and salt. Mix well, and pour in the stock. Allow the kidneys to stew slowly in this sauce until they are quite tender, from half to three-quarters of an hour. Add a little cream at the last, and serve with boiled rice.

Note.—Veal kidney may be used instead of sheep's, but it will take rather a longer time to cook.

Grilled Sheep's Kidneys

(*Fr.* Rognons de Mouton Grillés)

Ingredients—

6 Sheep's Kidneys.	Croûtons of Fried Bread or Buttered Toast.
1½ oz. Butter.	
Pepper and Salt.	

Method.—The kidneys must be very fresh. Take off the thin skin which covers them, and split them open without separating the two parts. Remove the white tube or duct, and cut away the fat from the middle. Hold the kidneys open and pierce them from one side to the other with small wooden or silver skewers. Melt the butter and brush the kidneys over with it, season them with pepper and salt, and sprinkle them with a few bread-crumbs. Warm a grid-iron, grease the bars, place the kidneys on it with the cut-side downwards, and grill over a clear fire for about eight minutes. Turn the kidneys frequently whilst they are cooking. When done, place them on a hot dish, with a croûton under each, and remove the skewers if they are wooden ones. The hollows in the kidneys may be filled with maître d'hôtel butter and devil sauce may be served separately.

Sheep's Tongues à la Madère

(*Fr.* Langues de Mouton à l'Italienne)

Ingredients—

4 Sheep's Tongues.	1 pint Madeira Sauce.
1½ pint Stock.	

Method.—Sheep's tongues may be bought either fresh or partially boiled. If fresh, soak them in salt and water for two or three hours, and then rinse them. Put them into a stewpan with enough well-flavoured stock to cover them, and simmer slowly about two hours or until tender. If partially cooked, the tongues will not require soaking, and from half to three-quarters of an hour will be sufficient to cook them. When ready take them up, remove the skin, trim the roots, and cut each tongue in three lengthways. Put them into a stewpan with the sauce, and simmer for ten minutes. Then dish the pieces of tongue neatly, and pour the sauce over.

Lamb Cutlets with Chestnuts

(*Fr.* Côtelettes d'Agneau à la Purée de Marrons)

Ingredients—

8 or 9 Lamb Cutlets	1 oz. Butter.
Pepper and Salt.	A pinch of Salt.
2 oz. Butter.	A pinch of Sugar.
Brown Sauce.	Water.
1 lb. Chestnuts.	A little Stock or Milk.

Method.—Prepare the purée of chestnuts (p. 126), and keep it warm.

Trim and cook the cutlets in the same way as mutton cutlets (p. 171), and arrange them in a crown on a hot dish with the purée of chestnuts in the centre. Pour a good brown sauce (not too thick) round the dish.

Ragoût of Lamb with Green Peas

(*Fr.* Ragoût d'Agneau aux Petits Pois)

Ingredients—

2 lbs. Breast or Neck of Lamb.	1 Lump Sugar.
2 oz. Butter.	Seasoning.
1 table-spoonful Flour.	Some light Stock.
1 pint Shelled Peas.	A sprig of Mint.
	A small bunch of Herbs.

Method.—Cut the meat in neat pieces and sprinkle it with the flour. Melt the butter in a stewpan, put in the meat and brown it slightly. Add the seasonings, peas, and enough light stock or meat boilings to cover. Stew slowly for one and a quarter hours or until the lamb is quite tender. Lift out the mint and herbs before serving. One or two table-spoonfuls of cream added to it at the last will be an improvement.

Note.—Veal or mutton may be cooked in the same way.

Lamb's Fry

(*Fr.* Foie et Fressure d'Agneau)

Ingredients—

Lamb's Fry.	1 Onion.
Parsley.	2 oz. Butter.
Lemon Juice.	

Method.—Wash and dry the fry, then cut the liver in slices and the heart and lungs in small pieces. Melt the butter in a stewpan, add the onion finely chopped, and fry it a light brown colour. Then put in the heart and lungs and stir them over the fire for seven or eight minutes. Add the liver and seasoning and cook for ten minutes longer or until all is well browned. Sprinkle with parsley, add the lemon juice, and serve very hot. This dish is suitable to serve *en casserole*.

PORK AND VEAL

Pork Cutlets

(*Fr.* Côtelettes de Porc)

Ingredients—

5 or 6 Pork Cutlets.	1 table-spoonful Flour.
Seasoning.	Fried Apples.

Method.—The cutlets should be taken from the loin or best end of the neck and must not be more than half an inch in thickness. Trim them neatly, removing most of the fat, and try to make them of uniform shape. Season with pepper and salt and coat lightly with flour. Melt some of the fat trimmings in a frying-pan, and fry the cutlets in this. Cook slowly, turning them three or four times. Serve them on a very hot dish and garnish with fried apples.

Fried Apples.—Cut some rather acid apples in quarters. Remove the core, but not the skin. Then fry the pieces in butter until tender but not broken.

Note.—Apple sauce may be served instead of the fried apples.

To Boil a Ham

(*Fr.* Jambon Bouilli)

Soak in lukewarm water at least twelve hours before cooking, then scrape it and weigh it. Put it into a saucepan with sufficient lukewarm water to cover it (if the ham is very salt, cold water will be better), bring to the boil, and skin well. Then simmer slowly until the ham is cooked. Allow from twenty-five to thirty minutes to the pound according to the kind and thickness of the ham. It is ready when the skin peels off easily. A few vegetables may be cooked with the ham if liked, or sometimes a pint of ale or a gill of brown vinegar is added to give the ham a more mellow flavour. If the ham is to be served cold, allow it to cool in the water in which it was boiled. Then remove the rind and trim the fat. Sprinkle with brown bread-crumbs and brown sugar, and, if liked, stick in a few cloves. Place in the oven for a few minutes to brown. Fasten a paper frill round the knuckle.

If the ham is to be served hot, lift it from the water when cooked, and remove the skin. Then place it in the oven for a few minutes, and brush it over with liquid glaze. Serve with greens, Brussels sprouts, spinach, green peas, &c.

Brawn

Ingredients—

½ Pig's Head (salted).	A sprig of Parsley, Thyme and Marjoram.
2 Onions.	1 Carrot.
6 Cloves.	1 Turnip.
1 dozen Peppercorns.	Cold Water.
1 blade of Mace.	

Method.—Wash the head thoroughly in tepid water, and remove all gristle and soft parts from the nostrils. Rinse well in cold water. Then put the head into a large saucepan with sufficient cold water to cover it, and bring slowly to the boil. Skim well, and add the vegetables cut in pieces and the herbs tied in a piece of muslin. Simmer slowly from three to four hours until the flesh will leave the bones easily, and skim when necessary. Then strain the liquid into a large basin and put the head on a dish. Next day cut the tongue and the meat from the head into small pieces, removing gristle and any superfluous fat.

Skim all fat carefully off the stock, and return it to a saucepan with the bones from the head. Boil quickly until reduced to about half the quantity, and then strain over the meat. Let this stand until slightly cooled, add more seasoning if necessary, and then pour into wetted moulds. Set aside until cold, and when firm, turn out on a dish and garnish with parsley.

Notes.—If liked, the moulds may first be decorated with slices of hard-boiled eggs.

The feet may be cooked along with the head if wished.

Breast of Veal Stuffed and Roasted

Ingredients—

3 or 4 lbs. Breast of Veal.	Seasoning.
6 oz. Bread-crumbs.	1 des.-sp. chopped Parsley.
3 oz. chopped Suet.	1 Egg.
½ Lemon Rind Grated.	A little Milk.
2 oz. Cooked Ham.	

Method.—Remove all the bones from the veal (these must be kept for making stock of soup). Then trim and season the meat and lay it out on a board with the skin side underneath. Prepare the stuffing as for roast shoulder of mutton (p. 170), adding to it the ham chopped finely. Spread the stuffing over the veal, roll up and fasten securely with a needle and fine string. Then flour the meat and roast it carefully, basting well. When ready lift the roll on to a hot dish, remove the sewing, and pour thin tomato or brown sauce round. Garnish with rolls of bacon (p. 174).

Steamed Veal with Celery

Ingredients—

2 lbs. Fleshy Veal.	1 Head Celery.
½ lb. Bacon.	Seasoning.
A few Parsley Stalks.	Parsley Sauce.
1 Onion.	

Method.—Trim the veal and bind it up with a piece of tape. Put it into a double cooker with the bacon cut in strips, the parsley stalks, and seasoning. Use the white part only of the celery, cut it in small pieces and the onion in quarters. Add these to the veal and steam slowly for two hours or until the veal is tender. Lift it on to a hot dish, remove the tape, place the vegetables, &c., round and smother in parsley sauce made with white stock.

Jellied Veal

Ingredients—

1 lb. Fillet of Veal.	1 tea-sp. chopped Parsley.
½ lb. fat Bacon.	Grated Rind of half Lemon.
1 gill Jelly Stock.	Pepper and Salt.
2 hard-boiled Eggs.	

Method.—Take a plain tin mould and decorate the foot of it with a few slices of hard-boiled egg and a little chopped parsley. Wipe the veal with a damp cloth, remove all skin and bone, and cut it into small neat pieces. Remove all skin and gristle from the bacon, and cut it into narrow strips. Mix the veal and bacon together on a plate with the remainder of the eggs cut in pieces and the seasonings. Pack this mixture loosely into the prepared mould, melt the stock, and pour it over. Should the stock not be sufficiently stiff, dissolve a little gelatine in it first, and if no stock is at hand, boil the bones from the veal for about half-an-hour with a little water and small pieces of flavouring vegetables, then strain. Fill up the mould with the stock, cover over with greased paper, and bake in a slow oven for two hours. When ready, the veal should feel quite tender when it is tested with a fork. If necessary, fill up the mould with a little more stock, and set aside to cool. When wanted, turn out on a dish, and garnish with parsley or some fresh salad.

Note.—Rabbit may be prepared in the same way.

Veal Olives

Prepare and cook in the same way as beef olives, adding a little chopped ham and grated lemon rind to the stuffing.

Veal Cream

(*Fr.* Crème de Veau)

Ingredients—

¾ lb. Fillet of Veal.	2 Eggs.
1 oz. raw Ham.	Pepper and Salt.
1 gill thick Cream.	A pinch of Cayenne.
1 gill Béchamel or Velouté Sauce.	A pinch of Nutmeg.
	Grated rind of ½ Lemon.

Velouté or Béchamel Sauce, Green Peas.

Method.—Wipe the veal, cut it in small pieces, and put it twice through a mincing machine with the ham. Put this minced meat into a mortar, add the eggs, sauce, and seasonings. Pound all well together, and rub through a fine wire sieve. Put this purée into a basin. Whip the cream lightly and mix it with the purée of meat. Pour all into a well-greased mould or moulds. The moulds must not be more than three-quarters filled. Place them in a saucepan resting on a double fold of kitchen-paper. Pour in enough hot water to come half-way up the sides, cover with greased paper, and steam very slowly until the cream feels firm to the touch. About three-quarters of an hour if a large mould, from fifteen to twenty minutes if the moulds are small.

Turn out carefully, and coat with béchamel or velouté sauce, and garnish with green peas.

Note.—This may be made richer and of a more delicate texture by using 1½ pint of cream with the purée of meat, and no sauce and no eggs. Or, plainer, by using ½ pint sauce, one or two eggs, and no cream. The mixture, especially when containing much cream, must be steamed very gently.

Veal and Ham Cutlets

(*Fr.* Côtelettes de Veau)

Ingredients—

¾ lb. Fillet of Veal.	Bread-crumbs.
3 or 4 oz. of Bacon.	Fat for frying.
1 tea-sp. chopped Parsley.	A Border of Potatoes or Spinach.
1 Egg.	Brown or Tomato Sauce.
A little grated Lemon Rind and Lemon Juice.	Slices of Lemon.
1 tea-sp. melted Butter.	

Method.—Have the veal cut in a slice about ¾ inch thick. Wipe it with a damp cloth, and beat it slightly with a wetted cutlet bat or rolling-pin. Trim it into nice oblong-shaped pieces, free from skin and bone, and squeeze a very little lemon juice over each. Beat up the egg on a plate, and add to it pepper, salt, the chopped parsley, grated lemon rind, and melted butter. (The butter is added to soften the veal.) Brush over each of the cutlets with this, and then bread-crumb them. Press the bread-crumbs well on with a knife, re-shape the cutlets neatly, and lay them on a tin or dish with double paper under them ready for frying.

Have the bacon cut in thin slices, remove all rind and rust from it, and roll it up into neat little rolls. Place these on a skewer, and cook them on a tin in the oven for about ten minutes while the cutlets are being fried.

To Cook the Cutlets.—Fry in a small quantity of fat in a frying-pan (see p. 166). They will take from ten to twelve minutes to cook and should be well done. Drain on paper.

To Serve the Cutlets.—Make ready a border of spinach or potatoes on a hot dish, and dish the cutlets along the top, one leaning against the other. Pour some brown or tomato sauce round, and place the rolls of bacon in the centre or round the sides. Cut one or two thin slices of lemon, quarter these slices, and place a piece of lemon between each cutlet.

Note.—The cutlets may be served without the border of potatoes or spinach, and green peas or any other suitable vegetable used as a garnish.

Stewed Veal Kidney

(*Fr.* Rognons de Veau Sautés)

Ingredients—

3 Veal Kidneys.	1 cupful of good Stock or Gravy.
2 oz. Butter.	A few Mushrooms.
1 small Onion.	Juice of ½ Lemon.
Pepper and Salt.	1 des.-sp. chopped Parsley.
1 oz. Flour.	

Method.—Remove the skin from the kidneys, and cut them in halves lengthwise. Take out the white nerve from the centre, and cut each half into thin slices. Melt the butter in a small stewpan, add the onion finely chopped, and brown it slightly. Then put in the kidneys, pepper and salt, and stir briskly over the fire until the pieces are all equally coloured. Sprinkle with the flour and mix well. Add the stock and wine, and stir until boiling. A few mushrooms, sliced and cooked with the kidney, will be an improvement. Cook slowly from fifteen to twenty minutes, and add the lemon juice and parsley at the last.

Calf's Liver Sauté

(*Fr.* Foie de Veau Sauté)

Ingredients—

1½ lbs. Calf's Liver.	1 oz. Butter.
1 table-spoonful Flour.	1 gill Button Mushrooms.
1 teacupful Stock or Gravy.	1 tea-spoonful Ketchup.
Pepper and Salt.	1 table-spoonful Sherry.
A little finely chopped Parsley.	

Method.—Wash the liver well in several waters and dry it in a cloth. Then cut it in slices ½ inch in thickness, and coat these very lightly with flour. Melt the butter in a frying or sauté pan. When quite hot, put in the liver, and fry gently for twenty minutes, until the liver is a nice brown colour and thoroughly cooked. Lift the pieces on to a plate, and pour away all fat from the pan. Pour in the gravy, add the mushrooms cut in halves and the seasonings, and stir for a few minutes. Then return the liver, and cook it for five minutes in the sauce. Dish neatly with the gravy poured over and round, and sprinkle with a little finely chopped parsley.

Note.—The mushrooms may be omitted.

Calves' Brains in Sauce

(*Fr.* Cervelles de Veau en Sauce)

Ingredients—

2 or 3 sets Calves' Brains.	Pepper and Salt.
White Stock.	2 yolks of Eggs.
½ oz. Butter.	A squeeze of Lemon Juice.
½ oz. Flour.	6 rounds of Fried Bread.

Method.—The brains must be very fresh. Blanch them and remove any clots of blood and fibre. Put them into a saucepan with white stock to cover and simmer gently for twenty minutes; then strain. Make a sauce with the butter, flour, and about half a pint stock from the brains. When well cooked, add the yolks of eggs, seasoning, and lemon juice. Reheat the brains in this, but do not boil again. Serve on small rounds of fried or toasted bread and garnish with chopped parsley.

Note.—Sheep's brains may be cooked in the same way.

Calf's Feet with Poulette Sauce

(*Fr.* Pieds de Veau à la Poulette)

Ingredients—

2 Calf's Feet.
2 pints White Stock.
1 pint Poulette Sauce.

Method.—Put the feet into a saucepan with cold water to cover them, bring to boiling point, and throw the water away. Rinse well and return the feet to the saucepan with enough light stock or meat boilings to cover them, and simmer gently for four hours. Then remove the bones, and press the feet between two dishes with a weight on the top until they are cold. Cut them into small neat pieces and simmer for five minutes in the sauce. Serve garnished with croûtons of toast.

Braised Sweetbreads

(*Fr.* Ris de Veau, braisée)

Ingredients—

1 pair Calf's Sweetbreads.
1 Carrot.
1 Turnip.
1 Onion.
½ pint Brown Sauce.
A Croûton of Bread.
Chopped Parsley.
½ pint Stock.

Method—To Prepare the Sweetbreads.—Wash them well and then soak in salt and water for at least half-an-hour. Then rinse and put it into a saucepan with enough cold water to cover. Bring to the boil and pour the water away. Throw the sweetbread again into cold water, and trim off all fat with the fingers. Then press between two plates until cold.

To Braise the Sweetbreads.—Prepare the vegetables, cut them in rough pieces, and put them into a stewpan. Pour the stock over and warm slightly. Then lay the sweetbread on the top, cover with greased paper, and braise carefully from thirty to forty minutes. When the sweetbread is tender, lift it out and place it on a croûton of fried bread in an entrée dish. Brush it over with liquid glaze, and pour the sauce round. Garnish with button mushrooms which have been cut in halves and warmed in a little stock. Sprinkle some very finely chopped parsley over.

Sweetbreads "en Casserole"

(*Fr.* Ris de Veau en Casserole)

Ingredients—

1 pair Calf's Sweetbreads.
White Stock.
A Bunch of Herbs.
1 Onion.
1 oz. Butter.
½ oz. Flour.
A little Cream.
Seasoning.

Method.—Prepare the sweetbreads as in last recipe, and, after pressing, cut them in neat pieces. Put them into an earthenware saucepan with white stock to cover them, an onion cut in pieces, and a small bunch of herbs. Simmer for three-quarters of an hour or until tender; then strain and make a sauce with the butter, flour, and stock. Return the sweetbread without the herbs, &c., and stew a few minutes longer. Season to taste and add cream at the last. Serve in the saucepan.

Galantine of Veal

(*Fr.* Galantine de Veau)

Ingredients—

3 or 4 lbs. Breast of Veal.
1 lb. Sausage Meat.
Seasoning.
Glaze.
lb. Ham or Tongue.
2 hard-boiled Eggs.
Truffles.
Aspic Jelly.

Method.—Prepare the meat as in breast of veal stuffed and roasted. Season the sausage meat rather highly and spread it on the top. Cut the hard-boiled eggs in pieces lengthwise and the tongue or ham in strips, and place these in rows on the top of the sausage meat. Two or three truffles and a few pistachio nuts may also be put in if wished. Roll and sew up the meat, then tie it in a cloth very firmly and in the shape of a bolster.

Put the bones from the veal into a saucepan with stock or water to cover them and a few pieces of flavouring vegetable. Bring this to the boil, put in the roll of veal, and cook slowly from two and a half to three hours.

When done, lift it out, and if, owing to the shrinking of the meat, the cloth looks wrinkled, take it off and re-roll it, and press till cold between two boards or dishes with a three or four pound weight on the top.

When cold, take the galantine out of its cloth, and trim the ends. Brush over the surface with a little melted glaze, and apply two coatings if necessary.

Serve garnished with aspic jelly or some nice salad.

GAME AND POULTRY

To Roast a Fowl

(*Fr.* Poulet Rôti)

Have the fowl trussed for roasting, which may be done either before the fire or in the oven. In either case the breast of the fowl should be covered over with a piece of greased paper or some slices of bacon, to prevent it from taking too high a colour. Keep the fowl well basted with butter, dripping, or bacon gravy. The time will depend upon the age and size of the fowl; a chicken will take three-quarters of an hour, a fowl from one to one and a half hours to cook.

When the fowl is ready lift it on to a hot dish, remove any trussing string or paper and pour away any grease that may run on the dish. Garnish with water-cress seasoned with lemon juice and salt.

A nice gravy should always be served with the fowl. Pour away the fat from the tin in which it was roasted and add one cupful of stock or water. Stir over the fire until boiling, rubbing down any browning from the tin. Season nicely and serve in a sauce-boat. Bread sauce may also be served with the fowl.

The best accompaniment to roast poultry is a well-made salad, although many people still prefer hot vegetables.

Note.—Instead of the above sauce, chestnut or mushroom sauce may be used.

It is no longer the fashion to stuff a fowl with veal force-meat, but it may be filled with shelled chestnuts before cooking.

To Steam a Fowl

First rub the fowl over with a piece of cut lemon to keep it white, sprinkle it with salt and wrap it in a sheet of buttered paper. Put it into a double saucepan or steamer (see p. 148) and cook from one and a half to two and a half hours according to age and size.

When sufficiently tender lift it on to a hot dish and remove the paper and string. Mask it with parsley, oyster, béchamel, egg, or celery sauce and garnish with little rolls of bacon or hard-boiled egg. There should be sufficient sauce to coat the fowl and to cover the flat part of the dish.

Fricassée of Fowl

(*Fr.* Fricassée de Poulet)

Ingredients—

1 tender fowl.	A bunch of Herbs.
Cold Water.	6 Button Onions.
2 oz. Butter.	3 or 4 Cloves.
Pepper and Salt.	2 yolks of Eggs.
1 table-spoonful Flour.	A squeeze of Lemon Juice.
1 pint White Stock	1 oz. Fresh Butter.
1 glass White Wine.	1 tea-sp. chopped Parsley.

Method.—The colour of the fowl for this dish should be very white, therefore it is sometimes blanched before cooking it, although this cannot be said to improve the flavour. Cut the fowl into neat joints, removing as much of the skin as possible. Warm two ounces of butter in a stewpan. Add the fowl, salt, and pepper. Colour for a few minutes over the fire, but do not let it take a deep tint. Add the flour, and one pint of hot white stock. Stir until boiling to prevent lumps; add the herbs, onions, one of them pierced with cloves, and the wine. Put on the lid, and simmer gently for one hour at least, or until the fowl is tender. The sauce should have reduced one-half. Then strain and return sauce to saucepan. Add the yolks of eggs, lemon juice, fresh butter, and parsley, but do not boil again. Serve garnished with croûtons of fried bread.

Notes.—This may be cooked in an earthenware pot and served *en casserole.*

Rice cooked in stock may be served separately.

Chaudfroid of Chicken

(*Fr.* Chaudfroid de Volaille)

Ingredients—

Cooked Chicken.	Cucumber, Radishes, or Tomatoes.
White Chaudfroid Sauce.	Aspic Jelly.
Mayonnaise Sauce.	
Some Green Salad.	

Decorations (see below).

Method.—Cut the chicken into neat joints, removing as much of the skin as possible. Place the joints on a draining tray or on a dish turned upside down, and coat them all carefully with white chaudfroid sauce (see p. 142). Give them two coatings of the sauce if necessary. Then decorate the joints lightly and tastefully. For this may be used small fancy shapes of tongue or truffle, finely chopped truffle or ham, tiny sprigs of chervil, chopped parsley or yolk of egg, fancy shapes of the red part of radishes, tiny pieces of tomato, &c. Do not overload the joints with decoration, and use colours that will blend well together. After decorating, run a little aspic jelly over each joint, so as to give them a glossy appearance, then let them set.

Shred some green salad, mix it with any remains of decoration and a little chopped chicken (any trimmings will do for this), and moisten with mayonnaise sauce. Pile this in the centre of an entrée dish, and arrange the joints of chicken round it. Decorate with chopped aspic jelly, more salad, and thin slices of radish or cucumber.

Mayonnaise of Chicken

(*Fr.* Mayonnaise de Poulet)

Prepare in the same way as chaudfroid of chicken, using mayonnaise sauce instead of chaudfroid sauce.

Aspic Jelly

(*Fr.* Aspic)

Ingredients—

1½ pints Water or Meat Stock.	1 tea-spoonful Salt.
1 gill Sherry.	A sprig of Thyme.
1 gill assorted Vinegars.	A sprig of Marjoram.
2 oz. Sheet Gelatine.	A few Parsley Stalks.
Rind of 1 Lemon.	2 or 3 Bay Leaves.
Juice of 2 Lemons.	1 blade of Mace.
A small piece of Carrot.	The whites and shells of 2 Eggs.
A small piece of Turnip.	20 White Peppercorns.
1 stick of Celery or tea-sp. Celery Seed.	6 Cloves.

Method.—Take a clean lined saucepan and rinse it out with hot water. Put into it the water or stock (which must be quite free from grease) and the gelatine cut in small pieces. If the stock is a jelly, less gelatine may be used. Add the vegetables, prepared and cut in pieces, the herbs tied together with fine string or thread, and the smaller seasonings tied in a piece of muslin. Add also the sherry, whites of eggs, and the shells washed and crushed. To measure the vinegars, take half a gill brown malt vinegar, nearly half a gill of Tarragon vinegar, and make up the remainder with Chili vinegar. Or less brown vinegar may be used and some spiced vinegar added. Add the vinegars to the other ingredients, with the salt, lemon rind peeled off very thinly, and the juice strained. Whisk all together over the fire until a good froth rises and the jelly is almost boiling. Allow it to boil up as high as it will without boiling over, then draw the saucepan gently to one side of the fire, when the jelly will keep warm without simmering, and cover it with a lid or plate. Allow it to stand for ten minutes, and then strain.

Any kind of cloth will do for straining the jelly, as long as it is not too close in texture and is kept for the purpose. Tie the cloth to a jelly-stand, or to the four legs of a kitchen-chair turned upside down, letting it sink in the middle so as to form a bag. Have ready two basins and some boiling water. Pour the water through the cloth into one of the basins, so as to heat it thoroughly; then put the dry basin underneath and pour away the water. Remove the lid from the pan, lift it carefully over without shaking it, and pour all the contents into the cloth. The jelly will not be clear the first time, as it is shaken up in pouring through, so change the basin, and pour what has run through back again into the cloth. Repeat this several times, until the jelly runs through perfectly clear. Cover the stand over with a piece of flannel or blanket, and let it remain until all the jelly has run through.

Chicken à la Cardinal

(*Fr.* Poulet à la Cardinal)

Ingredients—

1 Chicken.	½ pint thick Tomato Sauce (p. 145).
Some White Stock.	1 dozen Cherry Tomatoes.
1 gill Button Mushrooms.	

Pepper and Salt.

Method.—Cut the chicken into neat joints, and put it into a stewpan with sufficient white stock to cover it. Simmer gently from one to one and a half hours until the chicken is quite tender. Add the tomato sauce, which must be very thick, and cook a few minutes longer. Then lift out the pieces of chicken, and arrange them neatly on a hot dish. Reduce the sauce, if necessary, until it is thick enough to coat the pieces of chicken, and then strain it over the joints. Garnish the dish with small cherry tomatoes which have been cooked in the oven but not broken, and button mushrooms sautéd in a little butter.

Curried Fowl

(*Fr.* Poulet en Cari)

Ingredients—

1 tender Fowl.	1 pint Stock.
1½ oz. Butter.	1 gill Cream.
1 Onion.	Juice of ½ Lemon
1 tea-sp. Curry Powder	Boiled Rice.
A pinch of Salt.	

Method.—Cut the fowl into neat joints, removing as much of the skin as possible. Melt the butter in an earthenware stewpan, and colour in it the onion, sliced or chopped. Add the fowl, curry powder, and salt, and colour gently over a moderate fire, turning the pieces frequently. Then add the stock, and cook for one hour at least, until the fowl is tender and the liquid is reduced to one-third. Add the cream, simmer a few minutes longer, and add the lemon juice last. Serve *en casserole* and hand boiled rice separately.

Roast Duck

(*Fr.* Caneton Rôti)

Fill the duck with apples peeled and cut in quarters and a few French plums which have been soaked and stoned. Roast in the same way as a fowl. It will take from three-quarters of an hour to one hour.

Serve with brown gravy and salad.

Note.—Sage and onion stuffing the same as for roast goose may be used instead of the above.

Roast Goose

(*Fr.* Oie Rôtie)

Roast in the same way as a fowl. The time required will be from two to two and a half hours. The following stuffing may be put inside:—

Sage and Onion Stuffing

4 Spanish onions.	½ lb. Bread-crumbs.
8 or 10 Sage Leaves.	Liver from the Goose.
1 Egg.	Seasoning.

Parboil and chop the onions, add the bread-crumbs, sage leaves finely powdered, and liver boiled and chopped. Mix all together, season well, and add the egg slightly beaten.

Apple sauce and brown gravy should be served separately.

Note.—The goose may be stuffed with apples instead of the above stuffing. (See Roast Duck.) Apple sauce would not then be required.

Partridge Braised with Cabbage

(*Fr.* Perdrix aux Choux)

Ingredients—

1 Partridge.	2 Small Cabbages.
Slices of Fat Bacon.	1 Carrot.
A bunch of Herbs.	1 Onion.
Seasoning.	Gravy of Stock.

Method.—Wash and parboil the cabbages,

then drain them well and cut into quarters. Place some slices of bacon over the breast of the partridge and tie it up. Lay some more bacon at the foot of a stewpan, the carrot and onion cut in slices, and a bunch of herbs. Place the bird on the top of this, and put the pieces of cabbage round. Season well and add enough stock or gravy to half cover the contents. Put on the lid and stew slowly for at least one hour or until the partridge is tender. Then lift it out, cut it in quarters, and keep it warm. Strain the cabbage and place it in the centre of a hot dish. Arrange the joints of partridge on the top and garnish with the carrot and pieces of bacon. Remove the stock and pour it round the dish.

Note.—Small slices of cooked sausage are sometimes added to this dish.

Broiled Partridge

Ingredients—

2 or more young Partridges.	Butter.
Chopped Parsley.	Browned Bread-crumbs.
Chopped Mushrooms.	Potato Chips.
Chopped Shallot.	Some good Gravy.
Pepper and Salt.	

Method.—Pick and clean the partridges, cutting them in halves. Leave on the legs, but cut off the toes. Press the legs well back towards the wings, and make the joint as much in the shape of a cutlet as possible. Mix together some chopped parsley, mushrooms, and shallot with pepper and salt, and sprinkle the pieces of partridge with this mixture, and baste them with warm butter. Then sprinkle them with browned bread-crumbs, and broil over a clear fire for fifteen minutes. Baste again with warm butter, and serve very hot garnished with potato chips. Serve good gravy or some thin brown sauce separately.

Roast Turkey

(*Fr.* Dinde Rôtie)

This can be cooked in the same way as roast fowl. The time will depend upon the size of the bird; a small turkey will require one and a half to two hours and a large bird from two and a half to three hours. A turkey is usually stuffed before being roasted, and the following makes a nice force-meat:—

Take one pound sausage meat (pork preferred) and add to it six ounces cooked and sieved chestnuts and the liver of the turkey parboiled and chopped. Season rather highly, and put this into the crop of the turkey before trussing. The above is sufficient for a medium-sized bird.

Brown gravy and bread sauce should be served with the turkey.

If the turkey is to be served cold, brush it over with liquid glaze after roasting. A little chopped aspic and some fresh salad may be used to decorate it.

Salmi of Game

Ingredients—

Remains of Game.	The Rind of 1 Orange.
½ pint Gravy or Stock.	The juice of ½ Lemon.
1 glass Port Wine.	A pinch of Cayenne.
2 or 3 Shallots.	A sprig of Thyme.
1 oz. Butter.	Croûtons of Fried Bread.
1 oz. Flour.	

Method.—Cut the game into neat pieces, and put the bones and trimmings into a saucepan. Add the gravy or stock to the bones in the pan, also the shallots, orange rind peeled very thinly, and thyme. Simmer this for at least half-an-hour, and then strain. Melt the butter in a saucepan, and when it is slightly brown stir in the flour, add the strained stock, and stir again until boiling. Add the wine, lemon juice, and seasoning to taste. Warm the pieces of game thoroughly in this, and skim well. Serve garnished with some pretty croûtons of fried bread.

Stewed Rabbit with Brown Sauce

Ingredients—

1 Rabbit.	2 Onions.
2 oz. Ham.	1 pint Stock or Water.
1 oz. Butter or Dripping.	½ table-spoonful Ketchup.
1 oz. Flour.	Pepper and Salt.

Method.—Clean and wash the rabbit well. Dry and cut it into neat joints. Melt the dripping or butter in a saucepan. Coat the pieces of rabbit with flour, and brown them in the fat. Then add the ham cut in small pieces and the onions in slices, sprinkle with pepper and salt, put the lid on the pan, and cook slowly for ten minutes. Then add the stock and ketchup, mix well and cover again with the lid. Allow the stew to simmer slowly from one and a half to two hours, or until the rabbit is quite tender. Remove any grease before serving, and dish very neatly on a hot dish.

Stewed Rabbit with Onion Sauce

Ingredients—

1 Rabbit.	1½ oz. Butter.
3 Spanish Onions.	1 oz. Flour.
2 oz. Ham.	A small bunch of Herbs.
Seasoning.	Croûtons of Fried Bread.

Method.—Prepare the rabbit as in last recipe and put it into a saucepan with cold water to cover it. Bring to the boil, pour the water away, and rinse both rabbit and saucepan. This is to whiten the rabbit. Cover again with warm water or white stock, add the seasoning, herbs, ham cut in small pieces, and onions scalded and cut in quarters. Put the lid on the pan and cook slowly for one and a half hours or longer if necessary. Strain and keep the gravy and ham. Place the pieces of rabbit on a dish and keep them warm. Make a sauce with the butter, flour, and gravy from rabbit. Add the onions finely chopped, season nicely, and pour this over the rabbit. Decorate with small croûtons of fried bread.

Jugged Hare

(*Fr.* Civet de Lièvre)

Ingredients—

1 Hare.
½ lb. fat Bacon.
1 Onion stuck with 6 Cloves.
Bunch of Sweet Herbs.
2 glasses of Port Wine.
1 inch Stick Cinnamon.
2 Bay Leaves.
Juice of ½ Lemon.
1 dessert-sp. Arrowroot.
1 pint good Stock or Gravy.
1 table-spoonful Red-Currant Jelly.
Pepper and Salt.
Force-meat Balls.

Method.—Cut the hare into neat pieces, not larger than the size of an egg, and wipe the pieces with a cloth. Cut the bacon into small pieces, and put it into a saucepan. Fry it for a few minutes, and then add the hare, onion, herbs, pepper, salt, cinnamon, and bay leaves. Put the lid on the saucepan, and cook slowly for twenty minutes, shaking the pan occasionally. Mix the arrowroot smoothly with the stock, and add to it the hare with the lemon juice and one glass of port wine. Stir over the fire until boiling, and then turn the contents of the saucepan into a strong jar. Cover the jar closely, and cook in a moderate oven from three to four hours. It is safer to place the jar in a shallow tin, and to keep a little boiling water round it. The time will depend very much upon the kind of hare used, but the cooking must be continued until the meat is quite tender. A few minutes before serving, add the other glass of port wine and the red-currant jelly. Dish the pieces of hare neatly, and strain the gravy over. Garnish with force-meat balls (see below).

Force-meat Balls

Ingredients—

3 oz. Bread-crumbs.
The grated rind of ½ Lemon.
1 tea-sp. chopped Parsley.
1 tea-sp. Thyme and Marjoram.
Pepper and Salt.
A pinch of Cayenne.
A pinch of Nutmeg.
2 oz. Butter or chopped Suet.
1 whole Egg or 2 yolks.

Method.—If the liver from the hare is good, it may be added to above ingredients. Cook it until it is firm, and then grate or chop it finely. Put it into a basin with all the dry ingredients and season nicely. Rub in the butter, and then bind into a paste with the egg. Form this mixture into small balls and flour them well. Fry them in boiling fat until a nice brown colour.

RECHAUFFÉS OF MEAT

Cold Meat Shape

Ingredients—

½ lb. cooked Meat.
1 tea-sp. chopped Parsley.
1 hard-boiled Egg.
½ pint light Stock.
½ oz. sheet Gelatine.
Pepper and Salt.

Method.—The meat used for this must be very tender, as it gets no further cooking. A mixture of meats such as veal and ham, mutton and tongue, &c., is best. Trim away all skin and gristle, and cut the meat in small neat pieces. Chop the parsley very finely, and cut the hard-boiled egg in slices. Then rinse out a mould with cold water, and decorate it at the foot with some of the egg and parsley. Place in very lightly a little of the meat with seasoning and more egg, then more meat, &c., and so on until all is in. Do not press it down. Dissolve the gelatine in the stock, and strain it over the meat. Set aside in a cool place until cold and firm. When wanted, turn out and garnish with parsley or salad.

Darioles of Beef

Ingredients—

6 oz. cooked Beef.
2 oz. cooked Potatoes.
1 tea-sp. chopped Parsley.
1 Egg.
½ oz. Bread-crumbs.
½ oz. Butter.
A little Stock.
Seasoning.
Browned Bread-crumbs.

Method.—Grease half-a-dozen dariol moulds or small basins and coat the sides with fine browned bread-crumbs. Melt the half-ounce of butter in a small saucepan, add the meat finely chopped, the potato sieved, and enough stock to moisten. Mix well, season rather highly and according to taste, and the egg slightly beaten. Fill the prepared moulds with this mixture, sprinkle a few more browned crumbs on the top and bake in a moderate oven from fifteen to twenty minutes. Turn out the darioles on a hot dish and pour some brown gravy or thin tomato sauce round.

Note.—Any kind of meat may be used, and a little ham or tongue used along with the other meat is always an improvement.

The mixture must not be made too wet or the darioles will not keep their shape.

Glazed Beef Roll

Ingredients—

½ lb. cold Roast Beef.
2 or 3 oz. cooked Ham or Tongue.
1 dessert-spoonful Ketchup.
A little Stock.
1 Egg.
4 oz. Bread-crumbs.
1 tea-sp. chopped Parsley.
1 des.-sp. chopped Pickles.
½ tea-sp. Mixed Spice.
Pepper and Salt.
Some Meat Glaze.

Method.—Mince the beef and ham finely, being careful to remove all skin and gristle. Put them into a basin, and add the bread-crumbs, pickles, parsley, spice, pepper, and salt. Mix well, and bind with the egg well beaten, the ketchup, and, if necessary, a little stock or gravy.

Form into a roll, and tie into a pudding cloth like a rely-poly. Boil this roll in the stock-pot for half-an-hour, then lift out and press between two dishes with a weight on the top until cold. Remove the cloth and brush over with a little melted glaze. Serve cold garnished with parsley or salad.

Note.—This roll may also be made with fresh uncooked meat. It will then require longer time for cooking, from one and a half to two hours.

Meat Scallops

(*Fr.* Coquilles de Viande au Gratin)

Ingredients—

½ lb. cooked Beef or Veal.	2 table-spoonfuls browned Bread-crumbs.
1 gill Brown Sauce.	1 table-sp. grated Cheese.
1 table-spoonful Sherry.	

1 oz. Butter.

Method.—Cut the remains of beef or veal into small squares, and heat them in the above proportion of good brown sauce. Season highly, and add the sherry. Grease six or seven china shells, and fill them with the mixture, piling it higher in the centre than at the sides. Sprinkle over them some browned bread-crumbs and grated cheese, and place a small piece of butter on the top. Place them in a hot oven about ten minutes. Garnish each with a sprig of parsley and a small slice of lemon.

Potted Chicken or Game

Ingredients—

½ lb. cooked Chicken or Game.	2 oz. Butter.
2 oz. cooked Ham or Tongue.	Pepper and Salt.
A little powdered Mace.	A pinch of Nutmeg.

Method.—Take all the meat from the remains of cold fowl or game, remove all skin and gristle, and allow butter and ham or tongue in the above proportion.

Put the meat twice through a mincing machine and then pound it in a mortar with most of the butter (previously melted) and season to taste. Rub the mixture through a fine wire sieve, pack into little pots, and run the remainder of the butter over the top.

Note.—Almost any meat can be potted in the same way. Two different meats used together are always tastier than one, and a little ham or other salted meat is always an improvement. If the ham is very fat, some of the butter may be omitted.

The above seasonings are very simple, and different condiments may be added to suit individual taste.

Chicken and Spaghetti

Ingredients—

6 oz. cooked Chicken.	½ lb. Spaghetti.
1 pint White Sauce.	A pinch of Nutmeg.
2 or 3 oz. cooked Ham.	1 tea-sp. chopped Parsley.
A little grated Lemon Rind.	Pepper and Salt.
1 oz. Butter.	A few Bread-crumbs.

Method.—Chop the chicken and ham finely, removing all skin and gristle. Cook the spaghetti in boiling water and salt for half-an-hour or until quite soft, then drain and cut in small pieces. Make a sauce with one ounce of flour, one ounce butter, and half a pint milk or chicken stock, and season with white pepper and salt. Mix the chicken and ham in a basin with the sauce, adding the nutmeg, lemon, and parsley. Then grease a pie-dish, and put into it alternate layers of the chicken mixture and the spaghetti. Sprinkle the top with bread-crumbs, put the butter on in small pieces, and bake in a moderate oven from twenty to thirty minutes.

Rissoles

Ingredients—

½ lb. cold cooked Meat.	1 tea-sp. chopped Parsley.
1 oz. Butter.	A pinch of Nutmeg.
1 oz. Flour.	Pepper and Salt.
1 gill of Stock.	A little Flour.
1 tea-sp. chopped Onion.	Egg and Bread-crumbs.

Method—Remove all skin and gristle from the meat, chop it very finely and then weigh it. Melt the butter in a small saucepan, add the onion, and cook for a few minutes over the fire. Then add the flour, and stir until slightly browned. Pour in the stock, and stir until the mixture begins to draw away from the sides of the saucepan. Add the meat and the seasonings and mix well together. Turn the mixture on to a plate, smooth it over with a knife, and set aside to cool. When cold, it will be firm and easily shaped. Portion it out into about twelve equal-sized pieces. Take the pieces one at a time, and shape them on a board with the aid of a knife and a little flour. They may be made into any shape that is liked, such as cutlet shapes, balls, small rolls, round cakes, or cone shapes. The dish will look neater if only one or two shapes are used. Use as little flour as possible in the shaping, just sufficient to keep the mixture from sticking to the board. Then egg and bread-crumb them, and fry in boiling fat until they are a nice brown colour. Drain well, and serve hot with a dish-paper under them. Garnish with parsley.

Note.—Any kind of meat may be used for making rissoles or a mixture of meats. A little ham or tongue used along with fresh meat is a great improvement.

Scrambled Mutton and Tomatoes

Ingredients—

½ lb. cold Mutton.	1 tea-sp. chopped Parsley.
2 Eggs.	1 or 2 slices of Toast.
1 cupful Tomato purée.	Pepper and Salt.
1 oz. Butter or Dripping.	

Method.—Remove all skin and gristle from the mutton, then weigh it and mince it finely. Either fresh or tinned tomatoes may be used; rub them through a hair or wire sieve in order to get a purée. Melt the butter or dripping in a saucepan, add the purée, meat, eggs well beaten, pepper and salt. Mix quickly over the fire until thoroughly hot and thick, and taste to see if sufficiently seasoned. Serve on neat pieces of toast or fried bread, and sprinkle each with a little very finely chopped parsley. Send to table very hot.

MEAT DISHES WITH PASTRY

Beef Steak and Kidney Pie

(*Fr.* Pâté de Bifteck et Rognons)

Ingredients—

1 lb. Beef (cut thin).	Pepper and Salt.
2 Sheep's Kidneys.	4 table-sp. Stock or Water.
1 hard-boiled Egg.	½ tea-sp. Jamaica Pepper.
1 tea-spoonful Ketchup.	Flaky, Rough-Puff or Dripping Pastry.
1 dessert-spoonful Flour.	
1 tea-sp. chopped Parsley.	

Method.—Wipe the meat with a damp cloth and trim away all skin and any superfluous fat. Cut it into narrow strips suitable for rolling up. Split the kidneys, removing the skin and inside fat, and cut them into small pieces. Mix the flour, salt and pepper together in a plate. (The usual proportions of seasoning to allow are one tea-spoonful of salt and half a tea-spoonful of pepper to each pound of meat, but this must vary according to taste. The flour is used to thicken the gravy, and this should be omitted in a pie which is to be served cold.) Dip the pieces of meat and kidney into this mixture, coating them well. Roll up the strips of steak with some of the kidney and a small piece of fat inside each. Place these rolls loosely in a pie-dish, heaping them rather high in the middle of the dish to support the crust, and sprinkling them with the chopped parsley. Remove the shell from the hard-boiled egg, and cut it into six or eight pieces. Arrange these pieces round the meat and pour in the ketchup and half the stock.

Notes.—The best steak should be used for pies, any other is likely to be tough. It is not a good plan to partly stew the meat beforehand, the pie will not have such a good flavour. The addition of a little potato and onion, partly cooked and thinly sliced, is considered by some people an improvement. The egg might then be omitted.

To Cover the Pie.—For a plain pie, to be eaten hot, dripping crust (p. 164) does very well; but for a superior pie, either rough-puff or flaky pastry is more suitable. The quantity made with half a pound of flour will be about the requisite amount for the above proportion of meat.

Roll out the pastry into an oblong shape and from one-quarter to three-eighths of an inch thick. From this cut a strip about one and a half inches in width or rather wider than the rim of the pie-dish. Then wet the rim of the dish with cold water, and lay this neatly on. Where a join is made wet one of the edges to make them stick. Do not overlap the pieces or one part of the edge will be thicker than the other. Wet this strip of pastry with cold water and lay on the larger piece of pastry to cover the top of the pie. Press this piece of pastry well on, easing it in slightly and not dragging it over the dish. With a sharp knife cut off the larger pieces of pastry hanging round the dish, then hold the dish up in the left hand and with the right trim neatly round the edges. When trimming take short quick strokes, always cutting away from you, inclining the knife in such a way that the edges of the crust will have a considerable outward slope. Then flour the first finger of the left hand and keep pressing the back of it down on the rim of the pastry, while with the back of a floured knife you tap the edges smartly all round, making them look like the leaves of a book. To scallop them, draw the back of the knife sharply across them at intervals of about half an inch, drawing the knife upwards and inwards, while with the thumb of the left hand you keep pressing the pastry just in front of the knife downwards and outwards. Make a hole in the centre of the pie with a knife and brush over with beaten egg, omitting the edges. Roll out the trimmings of the pastry and cut out leaves for decorating. To do this in a simple way, cut the pastry into strips about one and a half inches wide. Then divide these obliquely into diamond-shaped pieces. Mark each with the back of a knife to imitate the veins of a leaf. From seven to nine of these leaves will be required for a centre ornament. Radiate the leaves from the hole in the centre of the pie, towards the edges of the dish, brush them over with beaten egg and the pie is ready to bake. Place it on a baking-tin and put it in a hot oven for the first half-hour or until the crust is risen and set and of a brown colour. Then move it to a cooler part, so that the meat may cook more slowly. As soon as the crust is dark enough, it should be kept covered with a double piece of paper until the pie is cooked. The time required will be from one to one and a half hours or longer if the meat seems tough or the pie is a large one. It may be tested by running in a skewer through the hole in the top. As soon as the pie is done remove it from the oven. Wipe the dish with a wet cloth and garnish with parsley before serving.

Note.—A few chopped mushrooms or an oyster may be rolled up inside the meat instead of the kidney. A little finely chopped shallot may be added if desired.

Beef Steak and Kidney Pudding

Ingredients—

1 lb. Beef (cut thin).	Pepper and Salt.
2 Sheep's Kidneys.	3 table-sp. Stock or Water.
1 dessert-spoonful Flour.	1 tea-spoonful Ketchup.

Method.—Prepare the meat according to directions given in previous recipe. Take a pint basin and line it with suet crust according to directions given on p. 164. Fill up with the prepared meat and pour in the ketchup and stock. The contents should be rather heaped in the middle, as they shrink in cooking. Roll out the trimmings of pastry into a round shape to form a cover. Double down the edge of the pastry which lines the basin over the meat and wet it with cold water. Place the round piece on the top and press the edges well together. Cover with a scalded and floured pudding cloth. Plunge the pudding into a basin of fast-boiling water and boil quickly for at least two and a half hours or steam for three hours. When ready, lift out and let it stand for a minute or two. Then remove the cloth and turn the pudding carefully out on to a hot dish. Make a slit in the pastry at the side to let the gravy run over the dish.

Note.—Larger puddings may be served in the basin in which they are made. Heat a table-napkin, fold it neatly and pin it round the basin. Chopped mushrooms or onions may be used for flavouring. The pudding may be baked instead of boiled.

Chicken and Ham Pie (Cold)

(*Fr.* Pâté Froid de Volaille)

Ingredients—

1 tender Chicken.	A little grated Lemon Rind and Lemon Juice.
2 Hard-boiled Eggs.	Pepper and Salt.
2 oz. Ham or Bacon.	Some Jelly Stock.
A pinch of ground Mace.	Rough-Puff or Flaky Pastry.
1 tea-sp. chopped Parsley.	

Method.—Cut the chicken into neat pieces free from bone and with as little skin as possible. Season it with pepper, salt, and parsley, and add the ham cut in small pieces. Take a pie-dish just large enough to hold the meat, rinse it out with cold water and leave it wet. Then decorate the foot with sections of hard-boiled egg and chopped parsley. Fill up with the chicken and ham, &c., and press the meat well down, making it level with the top of the dish. Pour in half a gill of white stock, or just enough to moisten the meat. Cover the pie according to directions given on p. 181, but put on no decorations. Bake in the oven from one to one and a half hours, or until the chicken feels tender when it is tested with a skewer. When ready remove the pie from the oven and pour in as much stock (that will jelly when cold) as the pie will hold. If the stock is not stiff enough a little gelatine must first be dissolved in it. Then set the pie away until it is quite cold. *To serve*—remove the pastry from the top and place it upside down on a clean dish, and turn the meat part carefully out on the top of this. If it is inclined to stick, dip the dish into hot water for a moment, and then loosen round the edges. Garnish round the sides of the pie with some nice salad and serve cold.

Note.—This makes a nice supper or luncheon dish.

Pigeon Pie

(*Fr.* Pâté de Pigeons)

Ingredients—

2 Pigeons.	1 tea-sp. chopped Parsley.
½ lb. best Steak.	1 oz. Butter.
1 tea-spoonful Ketchup.	1 dessert-spoonful Flour.
1 gill of Stock.	Pepper and Salt.
1 hard-boiled Egg.	Rough-Puff or Flaky Pastry.

Method.—Draw and singe the pigeons, then cut them in quarters and wipe or wash the pieces. Reserve the feet for decorating the pie. Remove as much of the skin from the joints as possible, and trim away any parts which do not look eatable. Wipe the beef with a damp cloth, trim off the skin, and cut it into small neat pieces. Put the flour on a plate and dip the pieces of pigeon and beef into it, coating them well. Melt the butter or dripping in a frying-pan; when smoking hot put in the beef and pigeons and fry them until nicely browned. Lift out and arrange in a pie-dish, sprinkling with pepper, salt, and the chopped parsley. Pile the meat high in the centre and put the egg cut in small pieces round the sides. Pour in the ketchup and half the stock and cover the pie according to directions given for beef-steak and kidney pie (p. 181). Brush the pie over with beaten egg and place it on a baking-tin. Bake in a good oven for two hours or until the contents feel tender when tested with a skewer. When ready, lift from the oven and pour in the rest of the stock through the hole in the top by means of a filler. Wipe the dish with a damp cloth. Scald the pigeon feet in some boiling water and scrape off the outside skin. Stand these up in the hole at the top of the pie and garnish with some sprigs of parsley.

Note.—Be particular to choose very tender pigeons for making pies. A little bacon is sometimes put in to give flavour. Partridge pie can be made in the same way.

Roman Pie

Ingredients—

6 oz. cooked Meat.	Pepper and Salt.
3 oz. cooked Macaroni.	1 table-spoonful crushed Vermicelli.
3 oz. grated Cheese.	1 gill Brown or Tomato Sauce.
1 gill Stock or Cream.	Dripping Crust.
1 parboiled Onion.	
1 tea-sp. made Mustard.	

Method.—White meat, such as rabbit, mutton, chicken, or veal is the best to use for this pie. Remove from it all skin, bone, and gristle and chop it finely. Put it into a basin with the macaroni, cut in small pieces, and add the onion finely chopped and grated cheese. Season with pepper, salt, and mustard, pour in the cream or stock and mix well together.

To Make the Pie.—Take a pint basin and grease it with butter or dripping. Put in the crushed vermicelli and coat the sides of the basin with this. Line the basin with some dripping crust rolled out thinly. Fill up with the meat mixture and put a cover of pastry on the top. Make a small hole in the top of the pie and place it on a baking-sheet. Bake in a good oven for one hour. When ready, remove from the oven and turn out on a hot dish. Heat some brown or tomato sauce and pour it round.

Note. — Bread-crumbs may be used instead of vermicelli. The onion may be omitted.

Sweetbread Patties

(*Fr.* Petits Pâtés de Ris de Veau)

Ingredients—

3 oz. cooked Sweetbread.	A squeeze of Lemon Juice.
1 oz. cooked Ham or Tongue.	A pinch of Nutmeg.
1 table-spoonful good White Sauce.	2 table-spoonfuls Cream.
A little grated Lemon Rind.	Pepper and Salt.
	Rough-Puff or Puff Pastry.

Method.—To Make the Mixture.—Chop the sweetbread and ham or tongue very finely. Put them into a small saucepan with the sauce and stir over the fire until well mixed. Season to taste with pepper, salt, grated lemon rind, lemon juice, and a pinch of nutmeg. Pour in the cream and make the mixture thoroughly hot before using.

To Make the Patties.—Make the patty cases according to direction given on p. 165, first or second method, and when baked fill them with the mixture. Put on the lids of pastry, and garnish with sprigs of parsley. Serve on a hot dish with a d'oyley or dish-paper under them.

Note.—Chicken and ham patties may be made in the same way, and tongue may be used instead of ham. The cream may be omitted and white stock added to make the mixture sufficiently moist.

Chicken and Ham Croquettes

(*Fr.* Croquettes de Volaille)

Ingredients—

3 oz. cooked Chicken.	A little grated Lemon Rind.
1 oz. cooked Ham.	A pinch of Nutmeg.
1 table-spoonful thick good White Sauce.	1 Truffle chopped.
1 tea-spoonful finely chopped Parsley.	Pepper and Salt.
Scraps of Pastry.	Egg and Bread-crumbs or Vermicelli.
	Frying Fat.

Method.—First prepare the mixture to put inside the pastry. Remove all skin and gristle from the meat, and then weigh it. Chop it very finely with a knife or put it through a mincing machine. Then mix in a saucepan with the white sauce, which ought to be fairly thick, and add the seasoning. Turn the mixture on to a plate to cool.

To Make the Croquettes.—Roll out some scraps of pastry very thinly. The thinness of the pastry is very important. If left too thick it will not be properly cooked, and will be most unwholesome and unpleasant. Stamp the pastry out into rounds with a plain or fluted cutter three to four inches in diameter, and with a small brush wet round the edges with a little water or beaten egg. Put a small portion of the mixture into the centre of each piece of pastry, and double over, pressing the edges well together. Any other suitable shape may be used instead of rounds if preferred. Next egg and bread-crumb the croquettes, or, instead of bread-crumbs, use crushed vermicelli. Fry them a nice brown colour, but not too quickly, in boiling fat, and drain well on kitchen-paper. Pile them on a hot dish with a d'oyley or dish-paper under them, and garnish with parsley.

Note.—Cooked game, sweetbread or tender veal may be used instead of the chicken.

These can be baked instead of fried.

EGG AND CHEESE DISHES, SANDWICHES, ETC.

Eggs in Bread Sauce

Ingredients—

4 Eggs.	2 table-sp. grated Cheese.
½ pint Bread Sauce.	Pepper and Salt.

Method.—Heat the bread sauce and pour it into a fire-proof dish. Slip into it the four eggs without breaking them, sprinkle the grated cheese over the top, and bake in the oven about ten minutes. Allow time to cook the eggs and to brown the cheese.

Note.—The cheese may be omitted and browned bread-crumbs used in its place.

Eggs à la Chartres

(*Fr.* Œufs à la Chartres)

Ingredients—

5 Eggs.	2 oz. Butter.
5 round croûtons of Bread.	3 or 4 table-spoonfuls Stock.
5 rounds of Tongue or Ham.	1 tea-spoonful Meat Glaze.
White Pepper.	Salt.

Method.—Cut the rounds of bread about three and a half inches in diameter, and the rounds of ham or tongue of the same size. Take an egg-poacher (this is necessary in order to keep the eggs a good shape), and first pour a little of the butter (melted) into the cups, then break the eggs carefully and drop them in; the yolks must on no account be broken. Sprinkle lightly with white pepper and salt. Put the poacher in hot water, and cook the eggs for four minutes, or until set without being hard. Meanwhile fry the croûtons a nice brown colour in the rest of the butter, and warm the slices of tongue or ham in the stock. Place the croûtons on a hot dish, the slices of tongue or ham on the top, and then the eggs. Melt the glaze in the stock and pour it round.

Eggs en Cocottes

(*Fr.* Œufs en Cocottes)

Ingredients—

Eggs.	A little Cream.
Butter.	Pepper and Salt.

Method.—Butter as many small fire-proof dishes as you wish. Break an egg into each, sprinkle with pepper and salt, and pour one tea-spoonful of cream over each egg. Stand the cases in a tin with enough hot water to come half-way up the sides, and cook in the oven about seven minutes, or until the eggs are set.

Note.—This dish may be varied very much by putting one teaspoonful of chopped ham, tongue, mushroom, &c., at the foot of the little case, then the egg with the cream on the top. Or grated cheese may be sprinkled both above and below the egg, and this makes a nice dinner savoury.

Eggs with Green Peas

Ingredients—

4 Eggs.	A pinch of Sugar.
½ pint cooked Green Peas.	Sippets of Toast or Fried Bread.
1 gill light Sauce.	
2 table-sp. Milk or Cream.	Pepper and Salt.

Method.—Heat a little light-coloured sauce and add the peas and seasoning. Cook for a few minutes, and add the milk or cream at the last. Turn the peas with their sauce on to a hot dish, and place on the surface four nicely poached eggs. Garnish with sippets of toast or fried bread.

Eggs à la Maître d'Hôtel

(*Fr.* Œufs à la Maitre d'Hôtel)

Ingredients—

6 Eggs.	6 pieces of hot buttered Toast.
Maitre d'Hôtel Butter.	

Method.—Arrange the eggs, nicely poached, on the top of the pieces of toast. Put a pat of maitre d'hôtel butter about the size of a shilling on the top of each egg, and send them to table while the butter is just melting. (For Maître d'Hôtel Butter, see p. 144.)

Eggs à la Reine

(*Fr.* Œufs à la Reine)

Ingredients—

4 Eggs.	A little chopped Parsley.
4 rounds of hot buttered Toast.	2 oz. cooked Ham or Tongue.
¼ lb. cooked Chicken or Veal.	2 table-sp. light Sauce or Gravy.
	Seasoning.

Method.—Mince the meat and ham or tongue very finely, and heat it in a small saucepan with the sauce to moisten it. Season to taste, and spread this neatly on the rounds of hot buttered toast. Place a poached egg on the top of each, and sprinkle with a little finely chopped parsley. Serve at once and very hot.

Eggs with Shrimp Sauce

Ingredients—

6 Eggs.	1 cupful White Sauce.
6 rounds of hot buttered Toast.	Fresh or potted Shrimps.
	Pepper and Salt.

Method.—Heat the sauce in a small saucepan and add enough potted or shelled fresh shrimps to thicken the sauce well. Poach the eggs, and lay them on six rounds or squares of hot buttered toast. Season the sauce with pepper and salt, and pour it over the eggs. Serve very hot.

Eggs sur le Plat

(*Fr.* Œufs sur le Plat)

Ingredients—

3 Eggs.	1 oz. Butter.
Salt and Pepper.	

Method.—Lightly butter a flat fire-proof dish, and break the eggs into it without breaking the yolks. Season with pepper and salt, and put the rest of the butter in small pieces on the top. Set the dish in a moderate oven, and let it remain until the whites become set, but by no means hard. They will require about ten minutes. Serve hot.

Note.—A little cream may be poured over the eggs before putting them in the oven.

Eggs with Tomatoes

Ingredients—

2 Tomatoes.	2 Eggs.
1 oz. Butter.	1 or 2 slices of Toast.
1 tea-sp. chopped Onion.	Parsley.
1 oz. Ham (chopped).	Pepper and Salt.

Method.—Put the tomatoes into boiling water for a minute, lift them out, dry and peel them; then cut them in small pieces. Melt the butter in a small saucepan, add the tomatoes, onion, and ham, cook for about ten minutes, and season to taste. Remove the pan from the fire, and add the eggs well beaten. Stir again over the fire until the mixture becomes thick, but on no account must it be hard. Cut the toast into neat fingers or fancy-shaped pieces, put a little of the mixture on each, garnish with parsley, and serve very hot.

Eggs Stuffed with Sardines

Ingredients—

5 hard-boiled Eggs.	1 dessert-sp. Sardine Paste.
2 oz. Butter.	Cayenne Pepper.
2 or 3 drops Vinegar.	Salad and Small Biscuits.

Method.—Cut the eggs in halves across, remove the yolks, and cut a small piece off the white so that the pieces stand like little cups. Put the yolks into a mortar or strong basin with the butter, sardine paste, and seasoning, pound well and then rub through a sieve. Spread the biscuits with some of the mixture, and fill up the egg-cups with the remainder, piling it high in the centre. Serve very cold, garnish with cress or other small salad.

Note.—This dish will look better if the mixture is put into a forcing bag and forced into the eggs; a little being used to garnish round the sides of the biscuits.

There are many varieties of this dish, as any savoury paste may be used instead of sardine flavouring. The decoration may also be varied—small pieces of pickle, ham, beetroot, or truffle cut in fancy shapes will help to give a little colour, while chopped aspic instead of the little biscuits may serve as a bed upon which to dish the eggs.

Poached Eggs with Cheese

(*Fr.* Œufs pochés au Fromage)

Ingredients—

4 or 5 Eggs.	3 table-sp. Bread-crumbs.
1 gill White Sauce.	Pepper and Salt.
3 table-sp. grated Cheese.	A little Butter.

Method.—Butter a flat dish, and sprinkle it with half the bread-crumbs and cheese. Poach the eggs, and place them on the top. Then pour over the sauce, and put the rest of the cheese and bread-crumbs on the top. Lay on a few small pieces of butter, and place in a hot oven to melt the cheese and lightly brown the top.

Savoury Egg Cutlets

Ingredients—

3 hard-boiled Eggs.	½ tea-sp. Anchovy or Shrimp Essence.
½ oz. Butter.	6 or 8 Button Mushrooms.
½ oz. Flour.	Egg and Bread-crumbs.
½ gill Milk.	A little Flour.
2 table-sp. Bread-crumbs.	

Seasoning.

Method.—Boil the eggs very hard; let them lie in cold water for a few minutes, then remove the shells and chop them rather finely. Melt the butter in a small saucepan, add the flour, and mix until smooth. Then draw the saucepan to one side, add the milk, and cook again over the fire, stirring all the time until smooth and thick. Add now the chopped eggs, the mushrooms finely chopped, the bread-crumbs, and seasoning. Mix well together, and spread the mixture on to a plate to cool. Finish in the same way as lobster cutlets (p. 137).

Scrambled Eggs

(*Fr.* Œufs Brouillés)

Ingredients—

4 Eggs.	1 oz. Butter.
1 table-sp. Milk or Cream.	Seasoning.
1 table-sp. Stock or Gravy.	1 slice hot buttered Toast.

Method.—Melt the butter in an enamelled or earthenware saucepan—add the eggs slightly beaten and the milk and stock, and season to taste. Stir over a moderate fire until the eggs begin to set and the mixture is of a nice creamy consistency. It must not be overcooked or the eggs will be tough. Place the toast on a hot dish, cut it in three or four pieces, and pour the scrambled eggs over. Garnish with small sprigs of parsley.

Note.—This dish may be varied by adding different ingredients to the eggs, &c., thus :—

With Ham.—Fry one or two ounces of chopped lean ham in the butter before adding the other ingredients. Tongue can be used in the same way.

With Peas or Asparagus Points.—Add two or three table-spoonfuls cooked green peas or asparagus points to the eggs before they begin to thicken.

With Anchovies.—Add one tea-spoonful anchovy essence to the mixture, and serve garnished with fine strips of anchovy which have been warmed on a plate over hot water.

Plain Omelet

(*Fr.* Omelette Naturel)

Ingredients—

3 Eggs.	Flavouring according to taste.
1 oz. Butter.	

Pepper and Salt.

Method.—An omelet is the most difficult to prepare of any egg-dish. It requires some practice to give it the right shape, to have it soft inside and to give it a smooth slightly browned surface. The first essential is to have a perfectly clean and smooth pan—and one which is kept for this special purpose.

Beat the eggs just enough to break them, and at the last moment, or they will become watery. The rule is twelve beats. Add pepper, salt, and minced onion, parsley, herbs, mushrooms, or whatever fancy may dictate. A dessert-spoonful of milk or cream may be used or not. Have the pan evenly heated, but not scorching. Put in the butter, and let it run evenly over the pan, but not brown, and then add the eggs, &c. With a fork break the cooked surface in several places quickly, so that the egg from the top may run to the bottom and cook, or loosen the omelet from the sides of the pan, letting the uncooked part run under. This must be done in the beginning, so as not to make the surface uneven. When the egg is cooked, but yet quite soft on the top, lift the pan on one side, slip a knife-blade under one half of the omelet, and carefully roll the egg to the centre. Let it cook a moment to set any egg that has run out. Place a hot dish over the pan and turn them together so that the omelet will fall in the right place. The outside of the omelet should be firm and lightly browned, the inside soft and creamy. Garnish with parsley, and serve at once. Have everything ready before beginning to cook an omelet, as it will not improve being kept while the dish is heated and the garnishing found.

Note.—The size of the pan must always be considered. Unless it is proportioned to the number of eggs, it will be unmanageably thick or thin.

More eggs may be used if a larger omelet is required, but never more than eight.

Savoury Omelet

(*Fr.* Omelette aux Fines Herbes)

Ingredients—

1 tea-sp. chopped Parsley.
½ tea-sp. mixed Herbs.
2 Eggs.
½ tea-spoonful chopped Onion or Shallot.
1 oz. Butter.
Pepper and Salt.

Method.—Separate the yolks from the whites of the eggs. Put the yolks into a medium-sized basin and the whites on to a plate. Add to the yolks the parsley, onion, herbs, pepper, and salt, and work these well together with a wooden spoon until of a creamy consistency. Beat up the whites of the eggs with a broad-bladed knife until so stiff that you could turn the plate upside down without the whites falling off. Remove the wooden spoon from the basin, and with an iron one stir the whites lightly into the other mixture. Melt the butter in an omelet pan, and pour the mixture into it, scraping out the basin as quickly as possible. Stir the mixture round with an iron spoon until it begins to set, stirring mostly on the surface, and not scraping the foot of the pan. Then hold it a little longer over the fire until the omelet is nicely browned on the under-side. Slip a knife under it, and double over first from one side and then from the other towards the centre. If it is not quite cooked on the top, hold it in front of the fire for a minute or two. Then turn it on to a hot dish, and serve as quickly as possible.

Cheese Omelet

(*Fr.* Omelette au Parmesan)

Ingredients—

4 Eggs.
2 oz. Butter.
3 table-sp. grated Cheese.
Pepper and Salt.

Method.—Make in the same way as Savoury Omelet, adding the grated cheese to the eggs.

Ham Omelet

(*Fr.* Omelette au Jambon)

Ingredients—

2 oz. cooked Ham.
2 Eggs.
1 oz. Butter.
1 tea-sp. chopped Parsley.
A little made Mustard.
Pepper and Salt.

Method.—Make in the same way as Savoury Omelet, adding the ham (finely chopped) and mustard to the yolks of eggs.

Mushroom Omelet

(*Fr.* Omelette au Champignons)

Ingredients—

6 or 8 fresh Mushrooms.
1 Shallot.
1 tea-sp. chopped Parsley.
Pepper and Salt.
½ oz. Butter.
A Savoury or Plain Omelet.

Method.—Remove the skins and stalks from the mushrooms, and let them lie in salt and water for five minutes. Then dry them thoroughly and cut them small. Melt the butter in a small saucepan, and put in the mushrooms, shallot finely chopped, parsley, pepper and salt. Cook these together for about ten minutes. Make a plain omelet, and before folding it over lay the cooked mushrooms on one half.

Shrimp Omelet

(*Fr.* Omelette aux Crevettes)

Ingredients—

3 Eggs.
1 oz. Butter.
1 tea-sp. Anchovy Essence.
Pepper and Salt.

Mixture—

1 cupful picked Shrimps.
1 gill White Sauce.
Seasoning.

Method.—Put the shrimps into a small saucepan with the sauce, season to taste, and make thoroughly hot over the fire.

Make a Plain Omelet, and before folding it over put the shrimp mixture in the centre.

Cheese Custard

Ingredients—

1 pint Milk.
2 Eggs.
½ tea-spoonful Mustard.
3 oz. Cheddar or Gruyère Cheese.
Cayenne Pepper and Salt.

Method.—Beat up the eggs with the mustard, pepper and salt. Heat the milk and pour it on to them. Add the cheese and pour all into a greased pie-dish, sprinkle a little more cheese over the top and bake in a moderate oven for half-an-hour. Serve hot with plain biscuits.

Cheese Fondue

(*Fr.* Fondue au Fromage)

Ingredients—

1 oz. Butter.	1 gill of Milk.
3 oz. grated Parmesan Cheese.	2 Eggs.
1½ oz. Bread-crumbs.	Pepper and Salt.
A little made Mustard.	A pinch of Cayenne.

Method.—Put the bread-crumbs and butter into a basin, boil the milk, and pour it over them. Add the cheese (keeping back about one dessert-spoonful), yolks of eggs, and seasonings, and mix well. Beat up the whites of eggs to a stiff froth, and mix them in lightly at the last. Pour the mixture into a greased pie-dish or fire-proof dish, sprinkle the remainder of the cheese over the top, and bake in a good oven about twenty minutes, or until nicely browned and well risen.

Note.—Instead of baking this in one large dish, the mixture may be poured into small china dishes or paper cases, and baked from ten to fifteen minutes in a good oven. Those would be called **Cheese Ramequins.**

Cheese Soufflé

(*Fr.* Soufflé au Parmesan)

Ingredients—

1 oz. Butter.	2 yolks of Eggs.
½ oz. Flour.	3 whites of Eggs.
1½ oz. Cheddar Cheese.	Pepper and Salt.
1½ oz. Parmesan Cheese.	A pinch of Cayenne.
1 gill of Milk.	

Method.—Melt the butter in a small stewpan, add the flour, and mix these two well together with a wooden spoon. Pour in the milk, and stir quickly over the fire until the mixture draws away from the sides of the saucepan. Then remove the pan from the fire, and add the grated cheese and the seasonings. Next add the yolks, one at a time, and beat well together. Have the whites beaten to a very stiff froth with a wire whisk, and stir them lightly in with an iron spoon. Pour the mixture into a greased fire-proof soufflé dish, and do not fill it more than three-quarters full. Bake in a good oven from twenty to thirty minutes, or until the soufflé is well risen, is nicely browned, and feels firm to the touch. Serve in the dish in which it is baked, and as quickly as possible.

Note.—This may be baked in small china or paper soufflé cases instead of in one large one.

Parmesan Balls

Ingredients—

2 oz. grated Parmesan Cheese.	Salt.
2 whites of Eggs.	Cayenne Pepper.

Method.—Beat the whites of eggs to a perfectly stiff froth with a pinch of salt and a dust of cayenne. Then stir in quickly and lightly 2 oz. of freshly grated Parmesan cheese. Drop small tea-spoonfuls of the mixture into a saucepan of boiling fat, and cook them until a pretty brown colour (about five minutes). Drain well and serve on a d'oyley or dish-paper, sprinkled with Paprika pepper and grated cheese.

Potato and Cheese Mould

Ingredients—

½ lb. cooked Potatoes.	2 Eggs.
2 oz. grated Cheese.	A few browned Bread-crumbs.
2 table-sp. Milk or Cream.	Pepper and Salt.
1 oz. Butter.	

Method.—Sieve the potatoes, and add to them the butter melted, the yolks of eggs, cheese, seasoning, and the milk or cream. Mix well together. Whip the whites to a stiff froth, and stir them in lightly to the other mixture. Grease a plain mould or basin, and line it with browned bread-crumbs. Three parts fill it with the mixture, and bake in a moderate oven about thirty minutes. Turn out on a hot dish, and serve at once.

Swiss Fondue

Ingredients—

4 Eggs.	A little made Mustard.
2 oz. Gruyère Cheese.	Plain Biscuits or thin Toast.
1 oz. Butter.	Pepper and Salt.

Method.—Beat the eggs in a saucepan, add the cheese grated and the butter. Season highly, and stir over the fire until the mixture is soft and creamy. Serve very hot on toasted biscuits or fingers of thin toast.

Note.—White wine should be served with this savoury.

SANDWICHES

This term has now a much wider meaning than formerly; it includes not only the plain sandwich consisting of slices of meat placed between two pieces of bread-and-butter, cut in varying degrees of thickness, but also many dainty trifles suitable for afternoon teas and other light refreshments.

The variety of these little sandwiches is endless, and the following hints and recipes are merely suggestive. Clever fingers and a little ingenuity will soon invent many others.

Sandwiches may be made of white or brown bread, small rolls, various kinds of biscuits, toast, or pastry, filled with meat, salad, eggs, fish, flavoured butter, nuts, &c., and made up in a variety of ways.

When *Bread* is used it should be a day old and fine in texture. New bread that is full of holes and crumbly will not cut well. A sandwich loaf is the best for white bread, and Hovis, Bermaline, or other fine makes for brown.

If rolls are preferred they must be quite fresh and small, and with a soft crust. The little finger-shaped ones are neatest and are very easy to arrange.

There are many kinds of plain *Biscuits* which can be utilised for making sandwiches, and they make a nice change from the usual bread-and-butter species. The plain water, milk, wheaten, and parmesan are all suitable; in fact, any kind which is unsweetened and not too crumbly.

Toast when it is served for this purpose must be thin, well made, and not too crisp.

Slices of *Pastry* can also be employed, and are especially suitable for evening refreshments. Any good pastry may be cut in strips or rounds, baked in the oven, then allowed to cool and split open to receive the sandwich mixture.

The *Butter* used for sandwiches must be very good and of a consistency that will spread easily on the bread without crumbling it to pieces. If hard it should be creamed first, or worked on a plate with a knife until it is soft enough to use. The knife may be dipped in boiling water occasionally so as to make the butter less hard.

The *Meat* used must be free from all skin, gristle and a superabundance of fat. In most cases it is better to mince the meat and mix it with its special seasonings before placing it on the bread, unless a more substantial sandwich is wanted for travellers or sportsmen.

Fish too is better either chopped or pounded to a paste, and *Salads* should be cut in small pieces.

As will be seen in the following recipes a little well-flavoured sauce or a little cream is sometimes mixed with the meat or fish, especially when it is dry, in order to bind all together.

The various kinds of potted meat now on the market are all most useful for sandwich-making, and these can either be combined with the butter or put on as a separate layer.

Sandwiches may be cut in various shapes—square, triangular, oblong or diamond, while different fancy shapes may be stamped out with a cutter, although the latter method is apt to be wasteful unless the scraps can be otherwise used up.

Very dainty little sandwiches can also be made by spreading a tasty mixture on thin bread and then rolling it up, instead of putting a second piece of bread on the top.

The thickness and size of the sandwiches will depend upon the purpose for which they are to be used. For afternoon tea they must be cut very thin, and nothing of a substantial nature must be offered, as it would take away the appetite for dinner which follows so shortly after. For evening refreshments they may be made more substantial, and still more so if they are to serve as a substitute for meat.

Sandwiches should be served on a pretty serviette or lace-edged paper and may be decorated with a little parsley, small cress, tomato, &c., according to their kind.

Beef and Chutney Sandwiches

Ingredients—

3 oz. cold Roast Beef.
1 dessert-spoonful Chutney.
A little Mustard.
1 dessert-spoonful Sauce.
White Bread and Butter.
Seasoning.

Method.—Mince the beef finely, add to it the chutney (cut very small) and seasoning, and moisten with a little well-flavoured sauce. Put a layer of this between slices of bread and butter, trim and cut into shapes.

Note.—Different kinds of meat may be used in the same way, varying the flavouring according to the kind of meat used. Or, two different kinds of meat may be used together, such as ham and chicken, veal and tongue, &c., mayonnaise, tomato, brown curry or any savoury sauce can be used to moisten the mixture.

Egg and Shrimp Sandwiches

Ingredients—

2 hard-boiled Eggs.
A few picked Shrimps.
1 oz. Butter, or
1 table-spoonful Cream.
Cayenne Pepper.
A squeeze of Lemon Juice.
Small Rolls.

Method.—Chop the eggs and add the shrimps cut in small pieces, season to taste, and add the butter melted or the cream. Mix well together. Split some finger-shaped rolls, put a good tea-spoonful of the mixture into each, and close them up.

Note.—A little mayonnaise sauce may be used instead of the cream or butter, and chopped salmon or sardines may take the place of the shrimps.

Sardine and Cucumber Sandwiches

Ingredients—

Sardine Paste.
Butter.
Cucumber.
Brown Bread.
Seasoning.

Method.—Mix equal quantities of butter and sardine paste together, adding seasoning if necessary. Spread this on thin slices of brown bread. Put some pieces of prepared cucumber on half the number of pieces, cover with the others, trim and cut in shape.

To prepare the Cucumber.—Peel a small piece of cucumber and cut it in thin slices. Lay these on a plate, sprinkle with salt, and let them remain at least half-an-hour. Then pour off the water and season the cucumber with pepper, salt, and a few drops of oil and lemon juice. Turn over and over so as to mix thoroughly.

Note.—Any other potted meat may be used instead of the sardine paste, and white bread instead of brown.

Tomato Sandwiches

Ingredients—

1 or 2 ripe Tomatoes. | Seasoning.
1 Gherkin. | Bread and Butter.

Method.—To prepare the Tomatoes.—Allow them to soak in boiling water two or three minutes, then remove the skin and cut them in very thin slices. Put the slices on a plate and season with pepper, salt, cayenne, and a few drops of oil and lemon juice. Arrange the tomato on the top of some thin bread and butter, sprinkle a little chopped gherkin or pickle over, and put another piece of bread and butter on the top. Trim and cut in shape.

Cheese Sandwiches

Ingredients—

Cheese. | Seasoning.
Butter. | Plain Biscuits.

1*st Method.*—Season butter with cayenne pepper and mustard and spread it on some plain biscuits. Put a thin slice of Gruyère, Cheddar, or Dutch cheese on the top and cover with another biscuit.

2*nd Method.*—Season the butter as above and mix into it an equal quantity of grated cheese and spread a layer of this between two biscuits. A little thick cream may be added to the mixture.

Note.—Almost any kind of cheese may be used for making sandwiches, and the various kinds of cream cheeses are also very suitable. It is a nice way of using up small remains. A little salad may be served with these sandwiches.

Nut Sandwiches

Ingredients—

Shelled Nuts. | Slices of Pastry.
Cream. | Seasoning.

Method.—Any kind of shelled nuts can be used. Toast them for a few minutes in the oven or in front of the fire and then chop them rather small. Mix with clotted or whipped cream and season to taste. The mixture may be made either sweet or savoury. Put a thick layer of this inside a finger-shaped piece of pastry.

Note.—Honey may be used instead of cream for sweet sandwiches. Gingerbread or any plain cake may be used instead of pastry.

Chicken and Celery Sandwiches

Ingredients—

Cooked Chicken. | Mayonnaise Sauce or Cream.
Celery. | Bread and Butter.

Method.—Take equal quantities of tender chicken and the heart of celery and chop them together. Moisten with a little mayonnaise sauce or thick cream and season to taste. Spread between bread and butter or small sandwich rolls.

Rolled Sandwiches

Ingredients—

Potted Meat. | Butter
Bread and Butter.

Method.—Cream the butter on a plate with an equal quantity of some tasty potted meat. If a highly flavoured paste is used, such as anchovy, a smaller proportion will be sufficient. The mixture must be delicate in flavour and of a nice smooth consistency. Spread this on thin slices of brown bread from which the crust has been removed and then roll up the pieces.

If white bread is preferred the round sandwich loaf makes a very pretty shape.

Spiced Beef Sandwiches

Ingredients—

Spiced Beef. | White Bread.
Curry Powder. | Seasoning.
Butter.

Method.—Flavour the butter with curry powder and season with mustard and cayenne pepper, working all together on a plate. Spread slices of white bread with the mixture and put small thin slices of sliced beef between each two. Trim and cut in shape.

HOT AND COLD SWEETS

General Notes.—The number and variety of culinary preparations to which the term "pudding" may be applied is very varied, comprising milk puddings, suet and custard puddings, batter pudding mixtures, cake-like mixtures, soufflés, and pastry of different kinds.

For a baked pudding, see that the oven is at the right degree of heat. Milk puddings require a moderate oven, whilst for pastry and any pudding of the nature of a soufflé a hot oven is required. Custard puddings and all those containing custard must be cooked slowly. It is a good plan when cooking a custard pudding to stand the dish in a tin of water. This will prevent the custard becoming watery.

A pudding to be steamed must be put into a well-greased mould or basin and covered over with a piece of buttered paper. If a steamer is not available for the purpose, put the pudding into a stewpan with just sufficient water to come half-way up the mould, put the lid on the pan, and keep the water at simmering point until the pudding is cooked. Any pudding of the nature of a custard must be very carefully steamed, as extreme heat would curdle the eggs and make the pudding watery. More solid puddings may be steamed more quickly. The basin should not be more than three-quarters full.

A pudding which is to be boiled must be tied over firmly with a cloth which has been wrung out of boiling water and sprinkled with flour. Have sufficient boiling water in the pan to cover the pudding, and keep it boiling steadily the whole time the pudding is in it. A kettle of boiling water should be kept at hand to fill up the saucepan when necessary. Fill the basin to the brim for a boiled pudding.

Pudding cloths should be quickly washed after using and hung in the air to dry.

When suet is used in a pudding it should be hard and dry. Remove all skin and fibre from it and shred it as finely as possible. Dust it over generously with sieved flour, and then chop it finely with a long pointed knife. Hold down the point of the knife on the board with one hand, and with the other work handle end up and down. Any suet, if good, can be used, although beef suet is generally preferred. Mutton suet, however, makes the lightest puddings, while veal suet is the most delicate.

To prepare fruit (currants, peel, and sultanas), see p. 191.

Use moist sugar for all general sweetening purposes, but caster sugar for all light puddings.

To turn a pudding out of a mould or basin, lift it from the pan, and allow it to stand a minute or two. If too great haste is used, the first steam escaping from the pudding will crack it. Remove the cloth or paper from the top, then take hold of the basin with a cloth, and shake it gently to ascertain that it is coming away freely from the sides, then reverse it on a dish, and remove the mould carefully. When the pudding is in a cloth untie the strings, and draw the cloth a little from the sides of the pudding, then reverse it on a hot dish, and draw the cloth carefully away.

HOT PUDDINGS

Amber Pudding

Ingredients—

6 oz. Bread-crumbs.	2 table-spoonfuls Golden Syrup.
4 oz. minced Apple.	2 Eggs.
2 oz. Sugar.	A pinch of Nutmeg.
2 oz. Flour.	A pinch of Salt.
4 oz. chopped Suet.	A little grated Lemon Rind.
1 tea sp. Baking Powder.	

Method.—Mix all the dry ingredients together in a basin, and make a well in the centre. Add the syrup slightly warmed and the two eggs well beaten, and mix together, adding a little milk if necessary. Pour the mixture into a well-greased mould or basin, cover with a scalded and floured cloth, and boil quickly for two hours. Serve with lemon or orange sauce.

Boiled Batter with Fruit

Ingredients—

¼ lb. Flour.	1 tea-sp. Baking Powder.
½ pint Milk.	2 Eggs.
Fruit.	A pinch of Salt.

Method.—Sieve the flour into a basin with the salt and the baking powder. Make a well in the centre, and add the two eggs without beating them. Mix the flour gradually into these, and then add the milk by degrees. Beat the batter well, and then add as much fruit as it will hold. Apples, cherries, raspberries, or strawberries are about the best fruits to use. Apples would require to be peeled, cored, and sliced, cherries stoned, and raspberries or strawberries carefully picked. Pour the mixture into a well-greased mould, and boil quickly for one hour. Serve with fruit syrup or any nice sweet sauce.

Cabinet Pudding with Pineapple

Ingredients—

3 or 4 slices of Bread.	2 Eggs.
½ lb. tinned Pineapple.	1 table-spoonful Sugar.
½ pint Milk.	

Method.—Grease a plain round mould, and cut the bread in rounds to fit it. Drain the pineapple, and cut it into small pieces. Fill the mould with alternate layers of bread and pineapple. Beat up the eggs with the sugar, and add the milk. Strain this custard into the mould, cover with greased paper, and allow the pudding to stand for half-an-hour before cooking, so that the bread may become thoroughly soaked. Then place the mould in a tin with hot water to come half-way up the sides, and cook in a slow oven from a half to three-quarters of an hour, or until the custard is set. Let it stand in the mould for a few minutes after it is cooked. When ready to serve, turn carefully out and serve with pineapple sauce.

Note.—Sponge-cake cut in slices may be used in place of bread, and a little liqueur added for flavouring is an improvement.

Chester Pudding

Ingredients—

1 teacupful Flour.	1 teacupful Blackcurrant Jam.
1 teacupful Sugar.	½ tea-spoonful Carbonate of Soda.
1 teacupful Bread-crumbs.	A pinch of Salt.
1 teacupful chopped Suet.	
1 teacupful Milk.	

Method.—Chop the suet finely, and put it into a basin with the bread-crumbs, flour, sugar, and salt. Mix these dry ingredients together, make a well in the centre, and put in the jam. Heat the milk slightly in a small saucepan, add the soda free from lumps, and mix quickly. Pour this while still frothy on to the top of the jam, and mix all together. Put the mixture into a greased mould or basin, cover with a scalded and floured cloth, and boil for three hours. Serve with jam sauce.

Chocolate Pudding

(*Fr.* Pouding au Chocolat)

2 or 3 oz. Chocolate.	1 gill of Milk.
5 oz. Bread-crumbs.	2 Eggs.
3 oz. Butter.	A few drops of Vanilla.
3 oz. Castor Sugar.	A pinch of Cinnamon.

Method.—Cut the chocolate into small pieces, and dissolve it slowly in the milk. Cream the butter and sugar together in a basin, add the yolks of eggs and a few of the bread-crumbs, and mix well; then the dissolved chocolate, vanilla, and the rest of the crumbs, and mix again. Whip the whites of eggs to a stiff froth and mix them in lightly at the last. Pour the mixture into a well-greased mould, and steam slowly for one and a half hours, until the pudding is well risen, and feels firm to the touch. Serve with chocolate, custard, or wine sauce.

Christmas Plum Pudding

(*Fr.* Pouding de Noël)

Ingredients—

2 lbs. Valencia Raisins.	½ lb. Sweet Almonds.
2 lbs. Currants.	2 Bitter Almonds.
2 lbs. Sultanas.	1 table-spoonful Mixed Spice.
2½ lbs. Sugar.	½ tea-spoonful Salt.
2 lbs. Suet.	Rind and juice of 3 Lemons.
1 lb. Flour.	1 glass of Brandy.
½ lb. Apples.	1 glass of Rum.
1½ lbs. Bread-crumbs.	12 Eggs.
½ lb. mixed Peel.	Milk if necessary.

Method.—First prepare the fruit. Stone the raisins and chop them slightly. Pick and clean the currants and sultanas. Shred the peel and blanch and chop the almonds. Peel and chop the apples, and grate the rind very thinly from the lemons. Put all the fruit into a large basin or crock, add the other dry ingredients and mix thoroughly. Then beat the eggs, and add them with the wine, lemon juice, and enough milk to bind all together. Mix again with a long spoon, cover the mixture, and let it stand for twenty-four hours before cooking. Then fill up greased moulds or basins with the mixture, tie over them a scalded and floured cloth, and boil from six to eight hours according to size. Keep the puddings in a cool place for several weeks before using them, and reboil for several hours as required. Before serving the pudding, pour a wine-glassful of brandy round the base, and set a light to it just before putting to on the table. The dish must be hot and perfectly dry, or the brandy will not burn well.

Notes.—A little grated orange rind and juice may be added to the above mixture.

Remains of cold plum pudding are very good cut in slices and fried.

Date Pudding

(*Fr.* Pouding aux Dattes)

Ingredients—

½ lb. Dates.	½ tea-spoonful mixed Spice.
2 oz. Sugar.	¼ tea-sp. Baking Powder.
3 oz. Suet.	A little Milk.
2 oz. Bread-crumbs.	A pinch of Salt.
2 oz. Flour.	1 table-spoonful Treacle.
1 Egg.	

Method.—Stone the dates and cut them in small pieces, and chop the suet. Mix all the dry ingredients together in a basin, and make a well in the centre. Add the eggs well beaten, the treacle slightly warmed, and enough milk to make all of a softish consistency. Pour the mixture into a well-greased mould, and steam steadily for at least two hours. Turn out on a hot dish, and serve with lemon or any other suitable sauce.

Fig Pudding

(*Fr.* Pouding aux Figues)

Ingredients—

½ lb. Figs.	2 Eggs.
6 oz. Suet.	1 tea-spoonful Mixed Spice.
¼ lb. Bread-crumbs.	A pinch of Salt.
¼ lb. Flour.	½ tea-sp. Baking Powder.
¼ lb. Sugar.	½ pint Milk.

Method.—Soak the figs in boiling water for ten minutes, then dry them and cut them in small pieces, removing the stalks. Sieve the flour into a basin, add the suet finely chopped, the sugar, bread-crumbs, spices, baking powder, and salt, and mix all lightly together with the fingers. Then add the figs, mix again, and make a well in the centre. Beat the eggs in another basin, and pour them into the centre of the dry ingredients. Add also the milk, and stir well together. Pour the mixture into a greased mould or basin, and steam steadily for at least four hours. Serve with custard or wine sauce.

Note.—This pudding may be made richer by adding two ounces of candied peel and two ounces of sweel almonds. A little wine may also be added and less milk.

Little Russian Puddings

Ingredients—

2 Eggs, their weight in Butter, Flour, and Castor Sugar.	2 or 3 drops of Essence of Lemon.
½ tea-sp. Baking Powder.	1 dessert-spoonful grated Chocolate.
2 or 3 drops of Vanilla.	2 or 3 drops of Carmine.

Method.—Cream the butter and sugar and add the eggs and flour by degrees (see p. 212).

When the mixture looks light and shows air-bubbles, add the baking powder, and then divide it into three equal portions. To one portion add the chocolate, to another a few drops of carmine to make it a pretty pink colour, and two or three drops of essence of almonds to flavour, and leave the third portion its natural colour, flavouring with vanilla. Have about nine small moulds or dariols well greased, and put into them alternate spoonfuls of the different mixtures. Fill them rather irregularly, and then shake the mixture down. They should not be more than three-quarters full. Put them into a saucepan with a double fold of paper at the foot, pour in enough hot water to come half-way up the sides, and cover with greased paper. Put the lid on the pan, and steam the puddings slowly for half-an-hour. Then turn them out and serve with custard sauce.

Orange Pudding

(*Fr.* Pouding à l'Orange)

Ingredients—

¼ lb. Bread-crumbs.	The grated rind of 2 Oranges and the juice of 1.
2 oz. Flour.	¼ lb. chopped Suet.
2 oz. Rice Flour.	A little Milk.
3 oz. Castor Sugar.	A pinch of Salt.
½ tea-sp. Baking Powder.	

Method.—Wipe the oranges with a damp cloth, and grate the rind off them on to the top of the sugar. Work the sugar and orange rind together with a broad-bladed knife until they are thoroughly blended. Then chop the suet finely, using some of the flour to prevent it sticking to the board and knife. Mix all the dry ingredients together in a basin, and make a well in the centre. Add the orange juice strained, the eggs well beaten, and enough milk to make all of a softish consistency. Pour the mixture into a greased mould or basin, and steam or boil for at least two hours. Serve with orange sauce.

Note.—Lemon Pudding may be made in the same way, substituting lemon for orange, and using rather a smaller quantity of rind.

Pancakes

Ingredients—

½ lb. Flour.	A little Lard for frying.
1 pint Milk.	Castor Sugar.
2 Eggs.	Lemon or Orange Juice.
A pinch of Salt.	

Method.—There are several kinds of batter for making pancakes. The above is one of the simplest.

Sieve the flour and salt into a basin, and make a well in the centre. Drop in the two yolks of eggs, and with a wooden spoon mix a little of the flour gradually into them. Then add about half the milk very gradually, mixing in the flour by degrees from the sides of the basin. Keep the batter thick enough to allow of all lumps being rubbed smooth, then beat well until it is full of air-bubbles. Add the rest of the milk, and, if possible, allow the batter to stand for an hour at least before using it. Just at the last stir in quickly and lightly the whites of the eggs beaten to a stiff froth.

Melt some lard in a saucepan, and let it stand by the side of the fire to keep warm. Put a little into a small frying or omelet pan, and make it smoking hot. Then pour quickly into the centre of the pan half a gill or so of batter. If the fat is hot enough, the batter will run all over the pan at once, whereas if it has not quite reached the required heat, the pan may have to be tilted a little to get the batter to cover it properly. Allow it to rest for a minute or two until set or nicely browned on the under side, then slip a broad-bladed knife round the edges, and then either toss the pancake over or turn it with the knife. Brown on the other side, then slip the pancake on to sugared paper, strew sugar over it, sprinkle with lemon or orange juice, and roll up. Keep this pancake hot on a plate placed over hot water until the rest are cooked. Each pancake will require a little fresh fat added to the pan. Serve them very hot and as quickly as possible, and send cut lemon or orange to table with them.

Preserved Ginger Pudding

Ingredients—

2 Eggs.	¼ lb. preserved Ginger.
3 oz. Butter.	1 table-sp. Ginger Syrup.
3 oz. Castor Sugar.	½ tea-sp. Baking Powder.
2 oz. Flour.	½ tea-sp. ground Ginger.
2 oz. Rice Flour.	

Method.—Put the butter into a basin, and sieve the sugar on the top of it. Beat these two together with a wooden spoon until of a creamy consistency. Then add the eggs and the two flours by degrees. Beat well for a few minutes. Cut the ginger into small pieces, and mix it in lightly at the last with the baking powder, ginger syrup, and ground ginger. Pour the mixture into a well-greased mould, cover with greased paper, and steam slowly for one and a half hours. Turn out on a hot dish, and pour custard sauce round.

Rice and Orange-Marmalade Pudding

Ingredients—

¼ lb. Rice.	1 oz. Butter.
½ pint Water.	3 Eggs.
1 quart Milk.	2 table-sp. Marmalade.
4 oz. Sugar.	A pinch of Salt.

Method.—Wash the rice in several waters until quite clean, and then put it into a lined saucepan with half-pint fresh cold water. Bring to the boil, and pour the water off. Add the milk and butter, and simmer slowly until the rice is quite soft and thick. Stir well from time to time, or cook in a double saucepan. When

ready add the yolks of eggs and half the sugar. Pour the mixture into a greased pie-dish, and bake about fifteen minutes in a moderate oven. Then spread the top of the pudding rather thickly with marmalade. Add a pinch of salt to the whites of eggs, and beat them up to a stiff froth. Sieve the remainder of the sugar over them, and pile this meringue over the marmalade. Return the pudding to a moderate oven until the meringue is nicely browned and set, and sprinkle with sugar before serving.

Caramel Semolina Pudding

(*Fr.* Caramel au Semoule)

Ingredients—

2 oz. Semolina.	2 Eggs.
1 oz. Sugar.	Flavouring.
1 pint Milk.	

CARAMEL

2 oz. Loaf Sugar.	A squeeze of Lemon Juice.
¼ gill Water.	

Method.—Rinse out a small saucepan with cold water, and put into it the semolina and the milk. Stir these over the fire until boiling, then simmer from ten to fifteen minutes until the semolina is quite cooked and the mixture thick. Remove the pan from the fire, and add the sugar flavouring to taste, and the two eggs well beaten. Mix well. To make the caramel, put the sugar, water, and lemon juice into a small iron saucepan or sugar-boiler, and let them boil until they become a golden brown colour. Watch it carefully as it quickly browns. Then pour the caramel into a plain mould, one and a half pint size; take hold of the mould with a cloth, as it will be very hot, and run the caramel over the bottom and sides, coating them well. Allow this to cool for a few minutes, then pour in the semolina mixture, and cover over with greased paper. Steam slowly for three-quarters of an hour, or bake in a moderate oven for half-an-hour. This may be served either hot or cold. Turn out carefully when wanted.

Note.—Rice may be used instead of semolina.

Yorkshire Pudding

Make batter the same as for pancakes (p. 192), pour it into a baking-tin that has been well greased with dripping from roast-beef, and bake in a good oven for half-an-hour. Serve at once cut in small pieces.

SOUFFLÉS AND FRITTERS

Notes on Soufflé-making.—This is a class of puddings known only by its French name, which is so generally understood that it has become almost an anglicized word.

A soufflé is a pudding which is made very light by having stiffly beaten whites of eggs added to it, or sometimes whipped cream, and of which the basis is a cooked batter, with raw yolks of eggs and some distinctive flavouring, or other ingredient which requires little cooking, added to it.

The preparation of a soufflé is exceedingly simple if exact measures are taken, and if the directions given for making it are carefully followed. The only difficulty is in serving it soon enough, as it falls so quickly when taken from the heat. Have everything ready before beginning to make the sonfflé. If it is a steamed one prepare the tin, and put on the saucepan with the water in which it is to be cooked. If, on the other hand, it is a baked soufflé, see that the oven is at a right heat for cooking, and grease the tin or dish to be used.

A soufflé tin is a plain round one with high sides. (A fancy mould is not suitable.) First grease the mould very carefully and thickly with clarified butter. If for a steamed soufflé, cut a double band of paper wide enough to stand three or four inches above the top of the tin and to reach down to the middle of it. Grease this band, and tie it round the outside of the tin, putting the single edges to the top and the double fold below. Also grease a round or square of paper to cover the top.

Prepared Soufflé Tin.

The whites of eggs for all soufflés must be beaten up very stiffly in a basin with a wire whisk, and folded rather than mixed in to the other ingredients, care being taken not to break them down by too much mixing.

As the mixture rises considerably when cooking, the mould should not be more than half filled. In a steamed soufflé the band of paper forms a protection to prevent the mixture falling over the sides; in a baked soufflé this is not so necessary, as the mixture hardens as it rises.

When steaming a soufflé, cook it very slowly and steadily; the water must only reach half-way up the side of the mould, and merely simmer slowly all the time. If cooked too quickly, the soufflé will rise rapidly without becoming firm, and will then sink in the middle when turned out, and look like a crushed hat. A sonfflé is ready when it feels firm to the touch.

Steamed soufflés are always turned out of the moulds in which they are cooked, and a suitable sauce poured round, never over them.

A soufflé that has to be baked should be scored across two or three times on the top to divide the mixture before putting it in the oven, otherwise the first stroke of the spoon when serving it would lift off all the surface skin. The oven for baking them should be moderate and steady.

Baked soufflés are sent to table in the tins in which they are baked, and these are either slipped inside a hot silver case, or a warm serviette is folded round them. China fireproof dishes may be used instead of the tins.

Apricot Soufflé

(*Fr.* Soufflé aux Abricots)

Ingredients—

1 oz. Butter.	2 or 3 drops of Carmine or Cochineal.
1 oz. Flour.	4 whites of Eggs.
1 oz. Castor Sugar.	A pinch of Salt.
1 gill Apricot Purée.	A squeeze of Lemon Juice.
3 yolks of Eggs.	

Method.—First prepare the purée by rubbing some tinned apricots through a hair sieve. Use some of the syrup from the tin along with the apricots so as not to have the purée too thick. Fresh apricots may be used in place of the tinned, but these would require to be stewed first with a little water and sugar.

In making the soufflé, proceed exactly according to directions given for lemon soufflé using the gill of apricot purée instead of the gill of milk. Before mixing in the whites, add a squeeze of lemon juice, and just enough carmine or cochineal to make the mixture of a peachy colour. Pour the mixture into a greased soufflé tin and steam slowly and steadily from half to three-quarters of an hour, or until the soufflé is well risen and feels firm to the touch. Turn out carefully, and serve at once with apricot, custard, or wine sauce poured round it.

Note.—Peach soufflé may be made in the same way.

Apple Soufflé (Baked)

(*Fr.* Soufflé aux Pommes)

Ingredients—

3 large Apples.	½ oz. Butter.
2 Eggs.	Grated rind of ½ Lemon.
2 oz. Castor Sugar.	

Method.—Bake the apples in the oven until they are thoroughly cooked. Then scoop out all the soft inside and rub this pulp through a hair sieve. Put the sugar, lemon rind, and yolks of eggs into a medium-sized basin, and beat them together with a wooden spoon until of a creamy consistency; then add the apple pulp, and mix all together. Beat the whites of the eggs to a stiff froth, and stir them lightly in at the last. Pour the mixture into a greased china soufflé dish or pie-dish, and bake in a moderate oven for about twenty minutes, or until well risen and firm to the touch. When ready sprinkle with sugar and serve as quickly as possible.

Chocolate Soufflé

(*Fr.* Soufflé au Chocolat)

Ingredients—

2 or 3 oz. Chocolate.	3 yolks of Eggs.
1 gill Milk.	4 whites of Eggs.
½ oz. Potato Flour.	A few drops of Vanilla.
1 table-spoonful Cream.	2 oz. Castor Sugar.

Method.—Break the chocolate into small pieces, and put it into an enamelled saucepan with half the milk and potato flour. Cook gently over the fire, stirring from time to time, until the chocolate is melted and quite free from lumps. Put the sugar, yolks of eggs, and vanilla into a basin, and work them together with a wooden spoon until they are of a creamy consistency. Add the rest of the milk to this, then the chocolate by degrees. Return all to the saucepan, and cook together over the fire until almost boiling. Then remove from the fire, add the cream, and stir occasionally for a few minutes. Beat up the whites of the eggs to a stiff froth, and mix them by degrees with the other mixture, stirring them in as lightly as possible. Pour into a greased soufflé dish, and cook from fifteen to twenty minutes in a good oven. Should the soufflé become too brown, put a piece of paper on the top, but do not open the oven door too often. Sprinkle with a little sugar just before serving, and send to table directly.

Lemon Soufflé

(*Fr.* Soufflé au Citron)

Ingredients—

1 oz. Butter.	A squeeze of Lemon Juice.
1 oz. Flour.	3 yolks of Eggs.
1 oz. Castor Sugar.	4 whites of Eggs.
Grated rind of 1 Lemon.	A pinch of Salt.
1 gill of Milk.	

Method.—Melt the butter in a small stewpan, add the flour, and mix well together with a wooden spoon. Pour in the milk, and stir quickly over the fire until the mixture boils and thickens. Wipe the lemon with a damp cloth, and grate off the rind very thinly on to the top of the sugar. Rub the sugar and lemon rind together with the tips of the fingers until the sugar looks quite yellow. Remove the pan from the fire, and add this sugar and a squeeze of lemon juice, then the yolks one at a time, beating well between each. Add a pinch of salt to the whites, and whisk them to a very stiff froth, then with an iron spoon stir them lightly but thoroughly into the other mixture. Pour all into a prepared soufflé tin and steam slowly from thirty to forty minutes, or until firm to the touch. Turn out carefully on to a hot dish, and serve with custard, lemon, or wine sauce poured round it.

Note.—Vanilla or orange soufflé can be made in the same way, substituting vanilla or orange for the lemon.

Omelet Soufflé

(*Fr.* Omelette Soufflé)

Ingredients—

3 Eggs.	Grated rind of ½ Lemon.
1½ oz. Sugar.	A little Jam.

Method.—Put the yolks into a basin with the sugar and grated lemon rind or other flavouring, and mix well with a wooden spoon until of a pale creamy consistency. Whip the whites, with a pinch of salt added to them, to a very stiff froth, and fold them very lightly into the yolks. Do not stir more than is necessary. Pour the mixture into a well-greased omelet pan, and put in a brisk oven from seven to ten minutes until of a pale brown colour. When firm to the touch, turn the omelet out of the pan on to sugared paper, put a table-spoonful of warm jam in the centre, and fold over. Lift the omelet on to a hot dish with a dish-paper, and serve at once.

Notes.—A little stewed fruit may be used instead of jam, or the omelet may be served plain.

A plain iron or copper pan is the best. If there is any danger of the omelet sticking to the pan, the foot may be lined first with a round of greased paper.

(*Another Way*)

If preferred, turn part of the mixture on to a flat dish, and with a knife shape it into a round with a depression in the centre. Put the rest into a forcing-bag, and press it out through a large pipe into lines or dots over the mound. Sprinkle with sugar, and bake in a good oven from ten to twelve minutes. Serve at once on the dish on which it is baked.

Note.—A little jam may be put in the centre before using the bag and pipe.

Rum Omelet

(*Fr.* Omelette au Rhum)

Make a plain omelet according to directions given above. When ready to place on the table pour over the omelet a few spoonfuls of rum and set fire to it.

Semolina Soufflé

(*Fr.* Soufflé de Semoule)

Ingredients—

1 oz. Semolina.	4 whites of Eggs.
1 pint Milk.	A pinch of Salt.
2 oz. Castor Sugar.	Flavouring.
3 yolks of Eggs.	

Method.—Rinse out a small stewpan with cold water, and put the semolina and milk into it. Stir over the fire with a wooden spoon until boiling, and then allow the semolina to simmer slowly for about ten minutes well between each. Put the whites into a large basin or beating-bowl, add a pinch of salt to them, and with a wire whisk beat them up to a very stiff froth. Remove the wooden spoon from the mixture, and with an iron one stir the beaten whites lightly but thoroughly in. Pour this into a prepared soufflé tin one and a half pint size, cover with greased paper, and steam slowly and steadily from half to three-quarters of an hour, or until the soufflé is well risen and feels firm to tho touch. Turn out carefully on to a hot dish, and serve *at once* with jam, custard, chocolate, or wine sauce poured round it.

Note.—A ground-rice soufflé may be made in the same way, using ground rice in place of semolina. These soufflés may be baked in a fireproof dish instead of being steamed.

Batter for Fritters

Ingredients—

½ lb. Flour.	1 table-spoonful Salad Oil or melted Butter.
1 gill tepid Water.	A pinch of Salt.
2 or 3 whites of Eggs.	

Method.—Sieve the flour and salt into a basin, and make a well in the centre. Add the water by degrees, and beat well with a wooden spoon to make a smooth paste free from lumps. Then add the oil or butter, and beat again for a few minutes. Whisk the whites of eggs to a stiff froth, and stir them in very lightly at the last.

Notes.—This batter may be used for all kinds of fritters.

Sugar should not be added, as it is apt to make it heavy.

It is better if allowed to stand for some time before using, and before the whites of eggs are added.

A little rum or liqueur may be added if desired.

The batter should be very thick, and of the consistency to coat completely the article it is intended to cover.

Apple Fritters

(*Fr.* Beignets de Pommes)

Ingredients—

Frying Batter.	Sugar.
Apples.	Flavouring.

Method.—Choose firm ripe apples; rennets are best. Peel three or four, and cut them in slices an eighth of an inch in thickness. Then with a small round cutter stamp out the cores. Put the apple rings on a plate, and sprinkle them with orange or lemon sugar (see under Lemon Soufflé), and, if liked, a few drops of rum or brandy. Let them soak for a few minutes, then steep a round of apple in the batter. Coat it well, lift it out with a skewer, and drop it into a saucepan of boiling fat. Repeat this with the other rounds of apple, but do not put more than six or seven pieces into the fat at one time, as they swell considerably in the cooking. Turn them over while in the fat, and let them fry a nice amber colour. Lift them out with a skimmer or perforated spoon, and dry on sugared paper in a moderate oven until all are fried. Then serve them on a folded serviette or dish-paper, the slices over-lapping.

Banana Fritters

(*Fr.* Beignets de Bananes)

Ingredients—

3 or 4 Bananas.	Frying Batter.
Castor Sugar.	Wine or Lemon Juice.

Method.—Peel the bananas, cut them in two lengthways and then once across, making four pieces in all. Lay these pieces on a plate, sweeten and flavour, and let them lie for a few minutes. Finish off in the same way as Apple Fritters.

Peach or Apricot Fritters

(*Fr.* Beignets d'Abricots ou de Pêches)

Ingredients—

Peaches or Apricots.	Maraschino or other flavouring.
Macaroon or Biscuit-crumbs.	Frying Batter.
Castor Sugar.	

Method.—Cut the fruit in halves or quarters, and remove the stones. Sprinkle the pieces with sugar and a few drops of maraschino, and roll them in macaroon or other biscuit-crumbs before dipping them in the batter. Finish in the same manner as Apple Fritters.

Note.—Tinned fruit does very well for these if it is drained.

Soufflé Fritters

(*Fr.* Beignets Soufflés)

Ingredients—

5 oz. Flour.	½ pint Water.
2 oz. Butter.	Flavouring.
1 oz. Castor Sugar.	A pinch of Salt.
3 Eggs.	

Method.—Put the water, butter, sugar, and salt into a stewpan, and bring them to the boil over the fire. Then draw the pan to the side of the fire, and add the flour which has been previously passed through a sieve. Mix all briskly with a spoon until it becomes a perfectly smooth paste. Stir this paste for a minute or two over a moderate fire, then remove the pan from the fire, and add the flavouring and one egg. Work the paste well until the egg is completely mixed in, then add the other two eggs one at a time, beating well between each. Let it stand till cold. When ready to serve, drop a spoonful at a time into hot fat, and fry to an amber colour. Fry only a few at a time, as more cools the fat too much, and also they require room to swell. The paste will puff into hollow balls, and increase three times in size. When ready, drain well on sugared paper, and arrange in a pyramid on a dish. Serve with lemon or orange sauce.

PIES, TARTS, AND SWEETS WITH PASTRY

Small Apple Dumplings

Ingredients—

Short Crust (p. 164).	1 oz. Butter.
6 Apples.	Grated rind of ½ Lemon.
1½ oz. Demerara Sugar.	

Method.—Roll out some short crust rather thinly, and cut out six rounds about six inches in diameter with a cutter or saucepan lid. Wet round the edge of these rounds with cold water, and place an apple peeled and cored whole in the centre of each. Put the butter, sugar, and grated lemon rind on to a plate, and mix them together with a knife. Fill up the holes in the apples with this mixture. Draw up the edges of the pastry so that they meet on the top of the apple, and roll the apple in the hands to make it a good shape. Place the apple balls as they are ready on a wetted baking-tin with the join downwards, brush them over with water or slightly beaten white of egg, and dredge with sugar. Bake in a moderate oven from twenty to thirty minutes. When ready, the apples should be soft, and the pastry nicely browned. Serve hot or cold on a dish with a dish-paper on it, and dredge again with sugar.

Note.—Ground cloves, ginger, or cinnamon may be used for flavouring the butter and sugar instead of lemon rind.

Apple Pudding

Ingredients—

Suet Crust (p. 164).	¼ lb. Sugar.
1 lb. Apples.	A little grated Lemon Rind or 2 or 3 Cloves.
2 table-sp. Cold Water.	

Method.—Wipe the apples with a damp cloth and peel them thinly. Then cut them in quarters, remove the cores, and slice them thinly. Roll out the pastry to about quarter of an inch in thickness, grease a basin, and line it with it. Press the pastry well on to the sides of the basin, and try to keep it of a uniform thickness. Cut off the trimmings, and roll them out in a round shape, large enough to cover the pudding. Fill up the basin with the apples, sugar, and flavouring, pressing them well down, as the fruit sinks considerably when cooking. Wet the edge of the pastry which lines the basin, put on the cover, and press the two edges well together. Dip the centre of a pudding-cloth in boiling water, and dredge it with flour. Tie this over the top of the pudding, and plunge it into a saucepan of fast-boiling water. Boil quickly for two hours at least. More boiling water must be added as required. When ready, turn out on a hot dish, and serve at once.

Notes.—(1) Any other fruit may be used instead of apples, and the amount of sugar will vary according to the acidity of the fruit. Gooseberries must be topped and tailed and washed in cold water; plums washed in cold water, and, if time permits, stoned; rhubarb wiped and cut in small pieces. All fruit must be carefully prepared before being put in.

(2) The pudding may be baked instead of boiled; a piece of greased paper should then be twisted over the top of the basin.

(3) Short crust may be used instead of suet crust if the pudding is baked.

Apple Tart with Meringue

SHORT CRUST

Ingredients—

¼ lb. Butter.	1 yolk of Egg.
6 oz. Flour.	½ tea-sp. Baking Powder.
2 oz. Corn-flour.	A squeeze of Lemon Juice.
1 oz. Sugar.	Cold Water.

APPLE MIXTURE

1 lb. Apples (weighed after peeling).	¼ lb. Sugar.
The Rind of ½ Lemon.	2 or 3 table-spoonfuls Water.
	2 yolks of Eggs.

MERINGUE

3 whites of Eggs.	3 oz. Castor Sugar.

Method.—First make some short crust with the ingredients given above, and according to directions given on p. 164. Wet a dish with cold water, and cover it with the pastry rolled out rather thinly. Trim round the edges, and prick all over the foot with a fork. Then roll out the scraps of pastry and cut from it bands about two inches in width. Wet round the pastry covering the edge of the dish, and lay the band round. Where there is a join wet one edge with cold water, and fix the two pieces as neatly as possible. Then decorate round the edges according to taste, and bake the pastry in a moderate oven for about half-an-hour, until brown and crisp. Meanwhile prepare the apple mixture. Peel the apples, and then weigh them. Slice them thinly, and put them into a stewpan with the sugar, lemon rind, and a very little water. Allow them to stew slowly until quite soft and pulpy, and rub them through a hair or wire sieve. Add to them the two yolks of eggs, and put the mixture into the covered dish. Whip the whites of eggs to a stiff froth, add the sugar sifted to them, and pile this roughly on the top of the apples. Dredge a little sugar over, and return the tart to a slow oven to dry and brown the meringue. About fifteen minutes will be required. This tart may be served hot or cold.

Almond Cheese Cakes

(*Fr.* Tartelettes aux Amandes)

Ingredients—

6 oz. Castor Sugar.	A little Jam.
3 oz. Sweet Almonds (ground).	A squeeze of Lemon Juice or 1 tea-spoonful Orange-flower Water.
3 to 4 whites of Eggs.	
Short Crust or Puff Pastry.	

Method.—Sieve the sugar into a basin, and add the ground almonds to it, with a good squeeze of lemon or the orange-flower water. Then add three or four whites of eggs, according to size, and beat all with a wooden spoon or spatula. The mixture must be of a creamy consistency. Line some patty tins with any good pastry, and put a little jam at the foot of each. Then fill them up with the almond mixture. Lay two thin strips of pastry across the top, and dredge the tartlets with sugar, which will give them a cracked appearance when baked. Bake in a rather slow oven about three-quarters of an hour. If baked too quickly, they will rise and then fall again. When ready, they should be nicely browned, and feel firm to the touch. This amount of mixture should fill twelve cases.

Chocolate Tartlets

(*Fr.* Tartelettes au Chocolat)

Ingredients—

3 Macaroons.	1 dessert-spoonful Castor Sugar.
1 table-sp. grated Chocolate.	A few drops of Vanilla.
½ pint Milk.	Short Crust or Puff Pastry.
2 yolks of Eggs.	

Method.—Line some dozen small tartlet tins with any good pastry, but do not bake them. Put the chocolate into a saucepan with the milk, and let them simmer for about ten minutes over the fire, then add the macaroons crushed to a powder, and simmer a few minutes longer. Remove the pan from the fire, and add the sugar, flavouring, and yolks of eggs. Mix well, and fill the lined tins with this mixture. Lay some narrow strips of pastry in a trellis-work pattern over the top, wetting one edge of pastry wherever a join is made. Bake in a good oven for about twenty minutes; then brush the tartlets over with slightly beaten white of egg, and sprinkle them with sugar.

Lemon Curd Cheese Cakes

(*Fr.* Tartelettes au Citron)

Ingredients—

½ lb. Castor Sugar.	3 yolks of Eggs.
3 oz. Butter.	2 whites of Eggs.
2 Lemons.	Tartlet Cases (p. 199).
2 Finger Biscuits.	

Method.—Sieve the sugar on to a plate, grate the lemon rind on the top of it, and work the two together with a knife until of a uniform yellow colour. Then put this sugar into a saucepan with the butter and eggs slightly beaten and the finger biscuits made into crumbs. Stir all gently over a slow fire until the mixture thickens and becomes like honey. Then pour into jars, and cover tightly with parchment paper. If stored in a cool place, this will keep for some time.

When tartlets are wanted, fill pastry cases with the mixture, and warm in the oven, or they may be served cold.

Or this lemon mixture may be used instead of jam for an open tart.

Gooseberry Tart

(*Fr.* Tourte aux Groseilles Vertes)

Ingredients—

Short Crust.	2 table-spoonfuls Water.
1 lb. Gooseberries.	¼ lb. Sugar.

Method.—Top and tail the gooseberries and wash them in cold water. Put them into a pie-dish in alternate layers with the sugar, making the last layer gooseberries. Have the fruit piled high and well away from the sides of the dish. Make some short crust (p. 164) and roll it out rather thinly. Wet round the edges of the pie-dish with cold water. Cut a strip an inch wide off the pastry, and lay it round the dish. Press it well on, and where there is a join wet one of the edges with cold water and press the two together. Then wet round again with cold water, and lay on a piece of pastry large enough to cover the top. Ease this on slightly, and press the two edges well together. With a sharp knife cut off the larger pieces of pastry hanging round the dish, then hold up the dish in the right hand, and with the left trim neatly round the edges. When cutting, take sharp quick strokes, cutting always from you, and slanting the knife outwards from the dish to avoid cutting the pastry too close. Then with the back of the knife mark round the edges of the pastry. Make the marks quite close together, and as neat as possible. Next flute round the edges by drawing the knife quickly upwards and towards you, and being careful to make the flutes an equal distance apart.

Brush the pie over with beaten white of egg or a little cold water, and dredge well with sugar. This is to glaze it, and should be done just before the pie is put in the oven. Then with a skewer make four small holes at the sides of the pie, to allow the steam to escape while cooking. Bake in a moderate oven about one hour, or until the gooseberries are cooked and the pastry is nicely browned. When ready, lift out of the oven and wipe the dish well with a damp cloth. Sprinkle the tart with castor sugar, and serve either hot or cold.

Note.—Any other fruit tart may be made in the same way. All fruit must be carefully prepared before being used, and sugar added according to the acidity of the fruit. A mixture of fruits may also be used.

Marigold Tartlets

Ingredients—

Puff or Flaky Pastry.	Sweet Almonds.
Apricot Jam.	Angelica.

Method.—Roll out some puff or flaky pastry rather thinly, and stamp it in rounds with a cutter about 2½ inches in diameter. Place these rounds on a baking-tin, prick them with a fork, and bake in a good oven from ten to fifteen minutes. When ready, lift them on to a sieve and let them cool. To finish put a small tea-spoonful of apricot jam on the centre of each round of pastry. Stick thin shreds of blanched almonds round this to imitate the petals of a marigold, and then garnish with a few small leaves of angelica.

Mincemeat

Ingredients—

½ lb. Suet.	3 oz. Citron Peel.
½ lb. Valencia Raisins.	3 oz. Lemon Peel.
½ lb. Sultana Raisins.	3 oz. Orange Peel.
½ lb. Currants.	6 oz. Sweet Almonds.
¼ lb. Figs.	1 dessert-sp. Mixed Spices.
½ lb. Apples.	Rind and juice of 2 Lemons.
1 lb. Sugar.	2 glasses of Brandy.
2 table-sp. Marmalade.	1 glass of Rum.

Method.—First prepare the fruit, and as each article is ready put it into a large crock or basin. Pick and clean the currants and sultanas. Stone the raisins, peel and core the apples, and chop these two together with a long sharp knife. Shred the peel finely, and blanch and chop the almonds. Remove the stalks from the figs, wash them in very hot water, and then dry and cut them in small pieces. Add the spice to the fruit, also the suet finely chopped, and the lemon rind grated, and mix thoroughly with the hands. Then add the marmalade, lemon juice, rum, and brandy, and mix again. Cover and stand in a cool place for twenty-four hours. Then mix once more, and pack into pots or jars. Tie a piece of parchment over the top of the pots to make them perfectly air-tight, and keep the mincemeat in a cool place. Do not use for several weeks.

Note.—This mincemeat will keep quite good for a year at least. If it should become rather dry, more wine or spirit may be added.

Mince Pies

Required—

Puff Pastry.	Mincemeat.

Method.—Roll out puff pastry to one-eighth of an inch in thickness, and stamp out rounds with a cutter three to four inches in diameter. Fold up the scraps of pastry and roll them out again, cutting out more rounds as before. (The first rounds that are cut out are always the best, so keep these more especially for the top of the pies.) Wet round the edge of half the number of rounds with a little cold water, and put a good tea-spoonful of mincemeat in the centre of each. Cover with the other rounds of pastry, and press the two edges well together. Make a small hole with a skewer on the top of each pie, brush them over with slightly beaten white of egg, and dredge them with sugar. Place the pies on a wetted baking-sheet, and bake in a good oven for twenty minutes until the pastry is well risen and nicely browned. When ready, sprinkle again with sugar and serve hot.

Orange Pudding (Baked)

Ingredients—

2 oz. Cake-crumbs.	1 gill Milk.
2 oz. Castor Sugar.	2 Oranges.
1 oz. Butter.	A little Pastry.
2 Eggs.	

Method.—Line a medium-sized pie-dish with

any good pastry, and then prepare the mixture. Wipe the oranges with a damp cloth, and grate off the rind on the top of the sugar. Work the rind into the sugar with a broad-bladed knife until they are of a uniform yellow colour. Then put this into a basin, and add the cake-crumbs sieved and the butter broken in pieces. Heat the milk in a small saucepan, and pour it over the crumbs, &c. Stir until the butter is melted, add the yolks of eggs, the strained juice of oranges, and lastly the whites of eggs beaten to a stiff froth. Mix lightly, and pour all into the prepared dish. Bake in a moderate oven until set and of a light brown colour. It will take about three-quarters of an hour. Sprinkle with sugar and serve hot.

Note.—Lemon Pudding may be made in the same way, substituting one lemon instead of the two oranges.

Tartlet Cases

In families where there are unexpected visitors, it is a good plan to keep some tartlet cases ready at hand. With some fresh fruit or preserve they make a nice sweet for an emergency. Grease any small patty tins or quenelle-shaped moulds, and line them with rounds of short crust rolled out rather thinly. (The rounds of pastry should be cut rather larger than the diameter of the tins, to allow of some being taken up in the depth.) Press the pastry well into the moulds so that it may take the exact shape, and prick it all over the foot to prevent it blistering while baking. Lay a small round of paper into each, and fill with rice or small beans. Bake in a moderate oven until the pastry is dry and nicely browned. Then remove the tartlets from the tins, empty them of the rice or beans, and store them in an air-tight tin until wanted. The pastry for these should be rather stiff and not too rich.

The cases may be filled with a little jam or fresh fruit (see below), and some whipped and sweetened cream may be piled on the top.

Strawberry, Raspberry, or Red Currant Tartlets

Required—

½ pint Fruit.	¼ lb. Sugar.
A little Liqueur or any Fruit Syrup.	1 dozen Tartlet Cases.
	½ gill of Water.

Method.—Choose nice ripe fruit, pick it, and put it into a basin. Put the sugar and water into a saucepan, and boil them to a syrup, but do not let them colour. Add a little liqueur or some fruit syrup or essence to flavour. Pour this syrup over the fruit, and stand in a warm place for half-an-hour. Then lift out the fruit carefully, place it in the tartlet cases, and pour one or two tea-spoonfuls of the syrup over. Serve either hot or cold.

Note.—A little whipped cream sweetened and flavoured may be piled on the top.

West Riding Pudding

Ingredients—

2 Eggs.	½ tea-sp. Baking Powder.
The weight of the Eggs in Butter, Flour, and Sugar.	A little Flavouring.
Some scraps of Pastry.	2 table-spoonfuls Jam.

Method.—Roll out scraps of any suitable pastry into a strip four or five inches in width, and line the sides and edges of a wetted pie-dish with it. Join the ends neatly, and press the pastry well on to the rim of the dish and slightly over the outer edge; then trim round with a knife. Wet the rim of pastry with a little cold water, and decorate all round the edge with small fancy-shaped pieces of pastry. Press these well on. Put the jam at the foot of the pie-dish, and then prepare the mixture. Sieve the sugar into a basin, add the butter, and beat these two together with a wooden spoon until they are of a creamy consistency. Then add one egg and half the flour sieved, beat well, then the second egg and the rest of the flour, and beat again. Flavour to taste, and add the baking powder at the last. Half fill the pie-dish with this mixture, and bake in a good oven for one hour, or until the mixture is quite set and of a nice brown colour. Sprinkle with sugar before serving.

COLD PUDDINGS

Jellies

The Setting of Jellies.—The moulds in which jellies are to be set should have been well washed with hot water to render them perfectly free from grease, and then soaked in hot water, or left filled with cold water up to the time of using.

The best moulds for jellies are those which are made of copper and tinned inside.

The temperature at which jelly is moulded ought to be such that, while still perfectly liquid, it is not sensibly warm. If poured into the mould hot it is apt to become cloudy, and there is likely to be difficulty in turning it out.

When putting the jelly aside to cool, see that the mould stands perfectly even, in order that the jelly may stand straight and firm when unmoulded.

The great secret in making jelly that looks bright is to take pains with the clearing of it. The right preportions must also be taken, so that the jelly may hold its shape without being firm and solid. It is much easier to turn a stiff jelly out of a mould than one that is just of sufficient consistency to stand, but a stiff jelly is never good.

As a rule, a jelly is ornamental in itself, provided it is bright and is served in an equally bright crystal or silver dish; but with different flavours, colours, and combinations, a great variety of more fanciful-looking sweets may be obtained. Ornamentation, however, requires care and taste; unless the decoration is nicely done, the dish will have a slovenly appearance, corresponding very much to tawdry finery in dress.

To Unmould a Jelly.—Take a basin of hot water, hotter than the hand can comfortably bear, and dip the mould quickly into it, letting the water cover it for a second (if a china mould is used a little longer immersion in the water will be necessary). Then wipe the moisture off the mould with a cloth, and loosen the jelly away from the sides with the tips of the fingers. Shake the jelly gently until it seems to be loose in the mould, place the dish on which it is to be served on the top, and reverse both together. Give another slight shake, and draw the mould slowly off.

Jellies are improved by having whipped cream, custard, or a purée of fruit served with them. This may either be put round the dish or served separately.

Apple Jelly

(*Fr.* Gelée de Pommes)

Ingredients—

1 lb. Apples (weighed after peeling).
3 oz. Sugar.
3 gills of Water.
The rind of 1 Lemon.
1 oz. Gelatine.
A few drops of Carmine.
½ pint Double Cream.
A little Sugar.
A few Pistachio Nuts.

Method.—Peel, core, and slice the apples, and then weigh them. Put them into a lined stewpan with two gills of water, the thinly peeled rind of a lemon, and the sugar. Stew until reduced to a pulp, and then rub through a hair sieve. Melt the gelatine in the remainder of the water and strain it into the apple pulp. Colour part of this apple jelly pink with a few drops of carmine, and fill a border mould with alternate layers of yellow and pink, always allowing one layer to set before pouring in another. When quite full, set in a cool place until firm. Turn out when wanted, and fill the centre with the cream, whipped and sweetened.

Decorate with a few chopped pistachio nuts or other suitable decoration.

Bananas in Jelly

(*Fr.* Gelée aux Bananes)

Ingredients—

Bananas.
Lemon or Wine Jelly.
Pistachio Nuts.

Method.—Pour into a plain mould enough sweet jelly to cover it to the depth of quarter of an inch. Peel the bananas, and cut them in slices with a silver knife. Place them on the jelly when it is firm, arranging them in a circle, one resting on the other. Make a small circle also in the middle of the mould if it is large enough. Pour a very little jelly over to keep the fruit in position, and let it set. Then cover with more jelly, and when that is firm put in more banana, and proceed in this way until the mould is full. Some blanched and shredded pistachio nuts may be used with the bananas, or the jelly may be coloured slightly pink with a few drops of carmine.

Note.—Other fruits such as grapes, strawberries, raspberries, red or white currants, sections of orange, &c., may be set in jelly in the same way. A mixture of fruits (Macedoine de Fruit) also looks pretty.

Coffee Jelly

(*Fr.* Gelée au Café)

Ingredients—

½ pint strong Coffee.
¼ oz. Gelatine.
1 oz. Sugar.
3 or 4 drops of Vanilla.

For the Centre.

1 gill double Cream.
Sugar and Flavouring.
A few pieces of preserved Cherry and Angelica.

Method.—The coffee must be strong and clear. Put it into a lined saucepan with the sugar and gelatine, and dissolve slowly over the fire. Then strain into a basin, add the vanilla, and cool slightly. Rinse out a border mould with cold water, and fill it with the coffee jelly. Set aside until firm, and turn out when wanted. For the centre, whip the cream with a fork until thick, and sweeten and flavour to taste. Pile this in the centre of the coffee jelly, and decorate with a few pieces of preserved fruits.

Lemon Jelly

(*Fr.* Gelée au Citron)

Ingredients—

½ pint Lemon Juice.
1½ pints Cold Water.
6 oz. Loaf Sugar.
1 inch of Cinnamon Stick.
4 Cloves.
2 oz. Leaf Gelatine.
The rind of 2 Lemons.
2 whites and shells of Eggs.

Method.—Take a clean lined saucepan, and put into it the water, gelatine, sugar, cinnamon stick, and cloves. Wipe the lemons with a damp cloth, and peel the rind very thinly off two of them. Do not peel off any of the white part, as this would give the jelly a bitter taste. Then roll the lemons on the table to soften them, cut them in halves, and squeeze out the juice until there is half a pint. Strain this into the saucepan, and add the lemon rind and the whites and shells of eggs. The latter should be washed and crushed. The pan should not be more than half full, as the jelly is very apt to boil over. Take a wire whisk, and whisk the jelly over the fire until a good froth rises on it and it is just beginning to boil. Watch the jelly carefully, and let it boil up as high as it will without boiling over. Then draw the pan gently to one side of the fire, where it will keep warm without simmering, and cover it over with a lid or plate. Let it stand for ten minutes, and then strain in the same way as Clear Soup (p. 120). Cover the stand over with a piece of flannel or blanket, and let it remain until all the jelly has run through.

Pour the jelly into a mould that has been rinsed out with cold water, and put it in a cool place to set. Turn out on a glass or silver dish when wanted.

The jelly should be strained in a warm place and out of a draught. Should it stiffen in the cloth before all has run through, place a small basin or cup in the centre and fill it with boiling water.

Orange Jelly

(*Fr.* Gelée d'Orange)

Ingredients—

½ pint Orange Juice (4 or 5 Oranges).	1 oz. Sheet Gelatine.
The rind of two Oranges.	½ pint Water.
¼ lb. Loaf Sugar.	The rind and juice of 1 Lemon.

Method.—Wipe the oranges and lemon with a damp cloth, and then peel off very thinly as much rind as is required. Put the rinds into a small lined saucepan with the gelatine cut in small pieces, the loaf sugar, and water. Stir these over the fire until the gelatine is quite dissolved, and then simmer for ten minutes. Skim and strain into a basin. Roll the oranges and lemon on the table to soften them slightly, cut them in halves, and squeeze out the juice. Strain and measure this, and add it to the other ingredients in the basin. Stir occasionally, and do not mould until cool. Pour into a wetted mould or moulds, and set in a cool place until firm. Turn out when required, and serve with cream. Or the jelly may be set in a border mould, and when turned out the centre filled with whipped and sweetened cream. Decorate the cream with chopped pistachio nuts or small pieces of cherry.

Note.—This jelly may be cleared with the white of an egg in the same way as Lemon Jelly (see above).

Port Wine or Claret Jelly

(*Fr.* Gelée au Vin Rouge)

Ingredients—

½ pint Port or Claret.	1 table-sp. Red Currant Jelly.
½ pint Water.	1 inch Cinnamon Stick.
The rind and juice of 1 Lemon.	3 Cloves.
	1 oz. Sheet Gelatine.
¼ lb. Loaf Sugar.	2 or 3 drops of Carmine.

Method.—Put into a small lined stewpan the water, sugar, red currant jelly, cinnamon, and cloves. Cut the gelatine into small pieces, and add it with the lemon rind peeled off very thinly and the strained juice. Stir over the fire until the gelatine is quite dissolved. Simmer for a few minutes, and add the wine. Do not boil again. Strain through a piece of muslin, and if necessary, add a few drops of cochineal or carmine. When nearly cold, pour into one large or several small moulds that have been rinsed out with cold water. Set aside in a cool place until cold and firm. Turn out when required, and if wished, decorate with whipped and sweetened cream.

Prune Jelly

(*Fr.* Gelée aux Prunes)

Ingredients—

½ lb. Prunes.	½ pint Water.
2 oz. White Sugar.	1 oz. Sweet Almonds.
Rind of ½ Lemon.	1 glass Claret.
1 oz. Gelatine.	1 gill whipped Cream.
1 inch Cinnamon Stick.	Sugar and Flavouring.

Method.—Wash the prunes, and allow them to soak at least half-an-hour in the cold water. Then put both into a clean lined saucepan, and add the lemon rind thinly peeled, the cinnamon stick, and sugar. Stew until quite tender, then strain off the liquid, and rub the prunes through a sieve. Crack the stones, blanch the kernels, and add them to the pulp. Put the liquid from the prunes into a saucepan, add to it the claret and gelatine, and dissolve carefully over the fire. Strain this into the pulp, and stir occasionally until nearly cold. Rinse out a border mould with cold water, and decorate it with some sweet almonds, blanched and shred, fill up with the prune mixture, and set aside in a cool place until firm. Then turn out, and serve with whipped and flavoured cream in the centre. Decorate with some chopped pistachio nuts or with a few glacé cherries cut in small pieces.

Wine Jelly

(*Fr.* Gelée au Vin)

Ingredients—

½ pint Sherry.	2 Cloves.
1 gill Lemon Juice.	The rind of 2 Lemons.
5 gills Water.	2 oz. Sheet Gelatine.
½ lb. Loaf Sugar.	2 whites and shells of Eggs.
1 inch Cinnamon Stick.	

Method.—Prepare the ingredients and make the jelly according to directions given for lemon jelly (p. 200). Set in one large or several small moulds, and turn out when wanted.

CREAMS

Apricot Cream

(*Fr.* Crème d'Abricots)

Ingredients—

½ pint Apricot Purée.	Squeeze of Lemon Juice.
½ pint Double Cream.	A few drops of Carmine.
½ oz. Sheet Gelatine.	*Decorations.*
2 table-sp. Water or Syrup from the Apricots.	Sweet Jelly. Pieces of Apricot and Pistachio Nuts or Glacé Cherries.
2 oz. Castor Sugar.	

Method.—Rinse out a mould with cold water and leave it wet. Then decorate the top of it with some lemon or wine jelly, and small pieces of apricot and chopped pistachio nuts, or any other suitable decoration. Set this aside until the jelly stiffens. Make the purée by rubbing tinned apricots through a hair sieve. Use a little of the syrup from the tin, so that the purée is not too thick, and weigh the half pint after sieving. Put the purée into a basin, and stand the basin over a saucepan of hot water until the contents are slightly warm. If quite cold, the gelatine would not mix well with it. Cut the gelatine into pieces with a pair of scissors, and put it into a small saucepan with two table-spoonfuls of water or apricot syrup. Stir it over the fire until quite dissolved, strain it into the apricot purée, and mix well. Add the sugar and a squeeze of lemon juice. The quantity of sugar may be regulated according to taste. Whip the cream in a separate basin until quite thick, and then mix it lightly to the other ingredients. Add enough carmine to make the cream of a peachy colour, not too pink, and stir occasionally until beginning to set. Then pour it into the prepared mould, and place in a cool place or on ice until set.

When required, turn out on a glass or silver dish, and put a border of chopped jelly round.

Note.—If fresh apricots are used, they must be stewed first with a little water and sugar.

A Peach Cream (*Fr.* Crème aux Pêches) may be made in the same way.

Coffee Cream

(*Fr.* Crème au Café)

Ingredients—

½ pint Double Cream.	1 gill strong Coffee.
½ pint Coffee Custard.	1 gill Milk.
¾ oz. Sheet Gelatine.	3 yolks of Eggs.
2 table-spoonfuls Coffee.	1 white of Egg.
A few drops of Vanilla.	2 oz. Sugar.

Decorations—Sweet Jelly and a few pieces of Preserved Fruits.

Method.—Decorate the foot of a wetted mould with some sweet jelly and some pieces of preserved fruit.

Have ready some very strong and clear coffee, and put one gill of this and one gill of milk into a small saucepan to heat. Beat up the yolks and white of egg with the sugar in a basin, and pour the hot milk and coffee slowly on to them, stirring all the time with a wooden spoon. Return this to the saucepan, and stir carefully over the fire until the custard thickens without allowing it to boil. Remove at once from the fire and strain into a basin. Cut the gelatine in pieces, and dissolve it in a saucepan with two table-spoonfuls of coffee, and then strain it into the custard. Add two or three drops of vanilla and more sugar if wished. Whip the cream and add it to the custard mixture. Stir occasionally until the mixture shows signs of setting, and then pour it into the prepared mould. Set aside in a cool place until firm. When required, turn out on a pretty dish, and decorate with preserved fruits or chopped jelly.

Note.—The decoration may be varied according to taste.

Chestnuts in Cream

(*Fr.* Nid de Marrons à la Crème)

Ingredients—

1 lb. Chestnuts.	¼ lb. Castor Sugar.
Milk.	1 pint Double Cream.
A small piece of Vanilla.	Sugar and Flavouring.

Decorations—Crystallised Violets.

Method.—To peel the chestnuts, cut them round lightly with a knife; put them into a stewpan just covered with cold water, and boil for five minutes over the fire. Then strain and peel off both the shell and the inner skin. Put the chestnuts thus prepared into a saucepan, cover them with milk, and add a small piece of vanilla. Put the lid on the saucepan, and cook slowly until the chestnuts are quite tender and the milk reduced. Crush them in the stewpan with a wooden spoon, add the sugar, and pass all through a fine sieve. Put the purée into a basin, and stir it for a minute or two to render it smooth; if it is too thick, add a little milk to it, but it is necessary for it to be of a good consistency.

Form a border round a dish with this chestnut purée forced through a syringe made for the purpose, when it takes the form of vermicelli, or if there is no syringe at hand, simply place a fine sieve upon a round dish, and pass the chestnut purée through it, forming a border round the dish. Whip and flavour the cream and pile it in the centre. Decorate with a few crystallised violets and nuts.

Italian Cream

(*Fr.* Crème à l'Italienne)

Ingredients—

1 pint Milk.	¾ oz. Gelatine.
3 Eggs.	2 table-spoonfuls Water.
2 table-spoonfuls Sugar.	Flavouring.
A pinch of Salt.	

Method.—Make a custard with the yolks of eggs, sugar, and milk. Pour it into a basin, and add the flavouring and salt. Dissolve the gelatine in a little water, and pour it into the custard. Mix well together, and strain all into another basin. When the custard begins to stiffen, stir in very lightly the whites of the eggs beaten to a stiff froth. Turn all into a wetted mould, and set aside until firm. When wanted, turn out on a glass or silver dish.

Meringues with Cream

(*Fr.* Meringues à la Crème)

Ingredients—

3 whites of Eggs.	½ pint Double Cream.
A pinch of Salt.	1 table-spoonful Sugar.
9 oz. Castor Sugar.	A few drops of Vanilla.

Method.—Put the whites into a large basin, add a pinch of salt, and with a wire whisk beat them to a very stiff froth. Sieve the sugar, and mix it in gently and lightly with an iron or silver spoon. Place a sheet of white paper all over a wooden board or baking-sheet of iron, and place the meringues on it.

To Shape the Meringues.—You will require two dessert-spoons, a palette knife, and a jug or basin of cold water. Take up a spoonful of the meringue mixture in a wetted spoon, and with a palette knife also wet, smooth it quickly over, piling it high in the centre and pointed at the two ends. With the second spoon, scoop the meringue out, and place it on the prepared tin or board. Or the meringue mixture may be put into a forcing-bag, and the shapes forced out on the tin. Leave a space of half an inch between each meringue, and sprinkle them with fine sugar. Place them in a very gentle oven until they are crisp and delicately tinted golden. Turn the paper on which the meringues have been baked upside down upon the table; moisten the paper on the back with a brush dipped in cold water; five minutes after the meringues will come off easily. Make each meringue hollow by pressing with the finger on the centre of it. place them back on the tin, and put them again in the oven for a few minutes to dry.

Whip the cream until thick, sweeten and flavour it. Fill the meringues with this, putting two pieces together, and pile them on a glass or silver dish.

Notes.—In making meringues the stiff beating of the whites of eggs is essential, but it is equally essential that this beating should cease directly the right consistency is attained, or a broken curdled appearance will be the result, and the mixture will be close and heavy. As soon as the egg froth stands up in solid points on the withdrawal of the whisk, or will allow itself to be divided with a knife into two separate halves, stop beating.

The oven will be suitable for cooking meringues when it has cooled down after other uses, or when the fire is allowed to get quite low. One of the main points in making meringues is their prolonged and thorough drying in a cool oven.

Instead of baking them on paper, warm an ordinary baking-tin, rub the bottom of it all over with white wax, and cook the meringues on that.

Meringues may be stored in a tin and kept for use at any time.

For the filling, any flavouring or liqueur may be added to the cream, or small pieces of fresh fruit may be mixed in. The cream may also be coloured pink with a little carmine.

Rice Cream

(*Fr.* Riz à l'Impératrice)

Ingredients—

1½ pint Milk.	½ oz. Gelatine.
The rind of 1 Lemon.	2 table-spoonfuls Water.
¼ lb. Carolina Rice.	½ pint Double Cream.
A pinch of Salt.	2 or 3 oz. Sugar.

Method.—Put the rice and milk into a saucepan with the thinly peeled rind of one lemon and a pinch of salt. Cook until the rice is perfectly tender. (A double saucepan is best for this.) The milk should be nearly boiled away, leaving the rice very moist. Then add the gelatine dissolved in a little water, the sugar, and more flavouring if wished. A little liqueur or wine added is a great improvement. Mix well, and when beginning to set, stir in the cream whipped stiffly. Pour the mixture into a wetted mould, and allow it to set. Turn out when wanted on to a glass or silver dish.

Notes.—This is a very white dish, and makes a delicious dessert. It may be served alone or with a purée of apricots poured round it as a sauce. A compôte of fruits may be served separately, or small pieces of ripe fruits previously soaked in wine or liqueur may be mixed with the rice mixture before moulding, or, if liked, the mould used may be first decorated with some sweet jelly and pieces of fruit.

Strawberry Cream

(*Fr.* Crème aux Fraises)

Ingredients—

1 lb. Strawberries.	¾ oz. pink Gelatine.
½ pint Double Cream.	2 table-spoonfuls Water.
3 oz. Castor Sugar.	Squeeze of Lemon Juice.

Decorations—Some Sweet Jelly, Strawberries, and Pistachio Nuts.

Method.—Rinse out a mould with cold water and leave it wet. Then decorate the top of it with some sweet jelly (in a liquid state), some nice pieces of strawberry, and a few chopped pistachio nuts. Let this decoration set before pouring in the cream.

Pick the strawberries, and rub sufficient of them through a fine hair or silk sieve to make half a pint of purée. Put this purée into a basin, and stand the basin over a saucepan of hot water until the contents are slightly warm. Unless this is done the gelatine will not mix properly with it. Cut the gelatine into pieces, and dissolve it in a small saucepan with the water. Keep stirring it constantly with a wooden spoon to prevent it sticking to the foot of the pan, then strain it into the purée, being careful not to lose any. Mix well. If white gelatine is used, a few drops of carmine will require to be with some lemon or wine jel'y, and small pieces of apricot and chopped pistachio nuts, or any other suitable decoration. Set this aside until the jelly stiffens. Make the purée by rubbing tinned apricots through a hair sieve. Use a little of the syrup from the tin, so that the purée is not too thick, and weigh the half pint after sieving. Put the purée into a basin, and stand the basin over a saucepan of hot water until the contents are slightly warm. If quite cold, the gelatine would not mix well with it. Cut the gelatine into pieces with a pair of scissors, and put it into a small saucepan with two table-spoonfuls of water or apricot syrup. Stir it over the fire until quite dissolved, strain it into the apricot purée, and mix well. Add the sugar and a squeeze of lemon juice. The quantity of sugar may be regulated according to taste. Whip the cream in a separate basin until quite thick, and then mix it lightly to the other ingredients. Add enough carmine to make the cream of a peachy colour, not too pink, and stir occasionally until beginning to set. Then pour it into the prepared mould, and place in a cool place or on ice until set.

When required, turn out on a glass or silver dish, and put a border of chopped jelly round.

Note.—If fresh apricots are used, they must be stewed first with a little water and sugar.

A Peach Cream (*Fr.* Crème aux Pêches) may be made in the same way.

Coffee Cream

(*Fr.* Crème au Café)

Ingredients—

½ pint Double Cream.	1 gill strong Coffee.
½ pint Coffee Custard.	1 gill Milk.
¾ oz. Sheet Gelatine.	3 yolks of Eggs.
2 table-spoonfuls Coffee.	1 white of Egg.
A few drops of Vanilla.	2 oz. Sugar.

Decorations—Sweet Jelly and a few pieces of Preserved Fruits.

Method.—Decorate the foot of a wetted mould with some sweet jelly and some pieces of preserved fruit.

Have ready some very strong and clear coffee, and put one gill of this and one gill of milk into a small saucepan to heat. Beat up the yolks and white of egg with the sugar in a basin, and pour the hot milk and coffee slowly on to them, stirring all the time with a wooden spoon. Return this to the saucepan, and stir carefully over the fire until the custard thickens without allowing it to boil. Remove at once from the fire and strain into a basin. Cut the gelatine in pieces, and dissolve it in a saucepan with two table-spoonfuls of coffee, and then strain it into the custard. Add two or three drops of vanilla and more sugar if wished. Whip the cream and add it to the custard mixture. Stir occasionally until the mixture shows signs of setting, and then pour it into the prepared mould. Set aside in a cool place until firm. When required, turn out on a pretty dish, and decorate with preserved fruits or chopped jelly.

Note.—The decoration may be varied according to taste.

Chestnuts in Cream

(*Fr.* Nid de Marrons à la Crème)

Ingredients—

1 lb. Chestnuts.	¼ lb. Castor Sugar.
Milk.	1 pint Double Cream.
A small piece of Vanilla.	Sugar and Flavouring.

Decorations—Crystallised Violets.

Method.—To peel the chestnuts, cut them round lightly with a knife; put them into a stewpan just covered with cold water, and boil for five minutes over the fire. Then strain and peel off both the shell and the inner skin. Put the chestnuts thus prepared into a saucepan, cover them with milk, and add a small piece of vanilla. Put the lid on the saucepan, and cook slowly until the chestnuts are quite tender and the milk reduced. Crush them in the stewpan with a wooden spoon, add the sugar, and pass all through a fine sieve. Put the purée into a basin, and stir it for a minute or two to render it smooth; if it is too thick, add a little milk to it, but it is necessary for it to be of a good consistency.

Form a border round a dish with this chestnut purée forced through a syringe made for the purpose, when it takes the form of vermicelli, or if there is no syringe at hand, simply place a fine sieve upon a round dish, and pass the chestnut purée through it, forming a border round the dish. Whip and flavour the cream and pile it in the centre. Decorate with a few crystallised violets and nuts.

Italian Cream

(*Fr.* Crème à l'Italienne)

Ingredients—

1 pint Milk.	½ oz. Gelatine.
3 Eggs.	2 table-spoonfuls Water.
2 table-spoonfuls Sugar.	Flavouring.
A pinch of Salt.	

Method.—Make a custard [illegible]
eggs, sugar, and mil[illegible]
and ad[illegible]
gelat[illegible]
cus[illegible]
an[illegible]
st[illegible]
b[illegible]
r[illegible]
t[illegible]

Meringues with Cream

(*Fr.* Meringues à la Crème)

Ingredients—

3 whites of Eggs.	½ pint Double Cream.
A pinch of Salt.	1 table-spoonful Sugar.
9 oz. Castor Sugar.	A few drops of Vanilla.

Method.—Put the whites into a large basin, add a pinch of salt, and with a wire whisk beat them to a very stiff froth. Sieve the sugar, and mix it in gently and lightly with an iron or silver spoon. Place a sheet of white paper over a wooden board or baking-sheet of iron, and place the meringues on it.

To Shape the Meringues.—You will require two dessert-spoons, a palette knife, and a jug or basin of cold water. Take up a spoonful of the meringue mixture in a wetted spoon, and with a palette knife also wet, smooth it quickly over, piling it high in the centre and pointed at the two ends. With the second spoon, scoop the meringue out, and place it on the prepared tin or board. Or the meringue mixture may be put into a forcing-bag, and the shape forced out on the tin. Leave a space of half an inch between each meringue, and sprinkle them with fine sugar. Place them in a very gentle oven until they are crisp and delicately tinted golden. Turn the paper on which the meringues have been baked upside down upon the table; moisten the paper on the back with a brush dipped in cold water; five minutes after the meringues will come off easily. Make each meringue hollow by pressing with the finger on the centre of it, place them back on the tin, and put them again in the oven for a few minutes to dry.

Whip the cream until thick, sweeten and flavour it. Fill the meringues with this, putting two pieces together, and pile them on a glass or silver dish.

Notes.—In making meringues the stiff beating of the whites of eggs is essential, but it is equally essential that this beating should cease directly the right consistency is attained, or a broken curdled appearance will be the result, and the mixture will be close and heavy. As soon as the egg froth stands up in solid points on the withdrawal of the whisk, or will allow itself to be divided with a knife into two separate halves, stop beating.

The oven will be suitable for [illegible] when it has cooled dow[illegible] when the fire is allo[illegible] of the main poi[illegible] prolonged [illegible]

be added to the cream, or small pieces of fresh fruit may be mixed in. The cream may also be coloured pink with a little carmine.

Rice Cream

(*Fr.* Riz à l'Impératrice)

Ingredients—

1½ pint Milk.	½ oz. Gelatine.
The rind of 1 Lemon.	2 table-spoonfuls Water.
¼ lb. Carolina Rice.	½ pint Double Cream.
A pinch of Salt.	2 or 3 oz. Sugar.

Method.—Put the rice and milk into a saucepan with the thinly peeled rind of one lemon and a pinch of salt. Cook until the rice is perfectly tender. (A double saucepan is best for this.) The milk should be nearly boiled away, leaving the rice very moist. Then add the gelatine dissolved in a little water, the sugar, and more flavouring if wished. A little liqueur or wine added is a great improvement. Mix well, and when beginning to set, stir in the cream whipped stiffly. Pour the mixture into a wetted mould, and allow it to set. Turn out when wanted on to a glass or silver dish.

Notes.—This is a very white dish, and makes a delicious dessert. It may be served alone or with a purée of apricots poured round it as a sauce. A compôte of fruits may be served separately, or small pieces of ripe fruits previously soaked in wine or liqueur may be mixed with the rice mixture before moulding, or, if liked, the mould used may be first decorated with some sweet jelly and pieces of fruit.

Strawberry Cream

(*Fr.* Crème aux Fraises)

Ingredients—

1 lb. Strawberries.	¾ oz. pink Gelatine.
½ pint Double Cream.	2 table-spoonfuls Water.
3 oz. Castor Sugar.	Squeeze of Lemon Juice.

Decorations—Some Sweet Jelly, Strawberries, and Pistachio Nuts.

Method.—Rinse out a mould with cold water and leave it wet. Then decorate the top of it with some sweet jelly (in a liquid state), some nice pieces of strawberry, and a few chopped pistachio nuts. Let this decoration set before pouring in the cream.

Pick the strawberries, and rub sufficient of them through a fine hair or silk sieve to make [illegible] purée into a basin.

[illegible] machines, and is [illegible] Bradford & Co., [illegible] for different kinds of

added. Put the cream into a large basin, and with a wire whisk switch it until quite thick. Mix this lightly but thoroughly beside the purée, and add sugar and a squeeze of lemon juice. Stir this mixture occasionally until it is almost setting, and then pour it carefully into the prepared mould. Let it stand in a cool place or on ice until it is quite firm. When wanted, turn out the cream on to a silver or glass dish with a lace-edged paper on it, and decorate round with strawberry or fern leaves and a few fresh strawberries.

Note.—Do not allow a strawberry cream to remain too long in the mould, as it is apt to discolour.

Several small moulds may be used instead of one large.

Raspberry Cream (*Fr.* Crème aux Framboises) may be made in the same way, using raspberries instead of strawberries. A few red currants may also be added.

Vanilla Cream

(*Fr.* Crème à la Vanille)

Ingredients—

	Custard.
½ pint Double Cream.	3 yolks of Eggs.
½ pint Custard.	1 white of Egg.
Vanilla Flavouring.	½ pint of Milk.
¾ oz. Sheet Gelatine.	1 oz. of Sugar.
2 table-spoonfuls Water.	

Decorations—A little Lemon Jelly, a few Cherries, and Pistachio Nuts.

Method.—First rinse out a mould with cold water and leave it wet. Then decorate it at the foot with some liquid jelly, pieces of cherry and chopped pistachio nuts. (Any preserved fruit may be used for decorating that will make a pretty contrast to the pale colour of the cream, or the jelly may be coloured pink with a little carmine or cochineal.) Let the jelly at the foot of the mould set before pouring in the cream mixture.

To Prepare the Cream.—Make the custard according to directions given on p. 146. Flavour the custard with vanilla essence, or it may be flavoured with vanilla pod by stewing the pod in the milk for a short time before making the custard.

Cut the gelatine into pieces with a pair of scissors, put it into a small saucepan with the water, and stir over the fire, letting it dissolve slowly. Then strain into the custard, being careful not to lose any, and mix well.

Put the cream into a separate basin, and switch it until thick. Add this to the custard mixture, and stir occasionally until the cream shows signs of setting. Then pour into the prepared mould, and set aside in a cool place or on ice until cold and firm. When wanted, turn out on a glass or china dish, and decorate with preserved fruits or chopped jelly. A lace-edged paper may, if liked, be put on the dish first.

Walnut Cream

(*Fr.* Crème aux Noix)

Ingredients—

	Custard.
¼ lb. shelled Walnuts.	½ pint Milk.
½ pint Custard.	3 yolks of Eggs.
½ pint Double Cream.	1 white of Egg.
¾ oz. Sheet Gelatine.	2 oz. Sugar.
2 table-spoonfuls Water.	
Vanilla or other Flavouring.	

Decorations—Sweet Jelly, Pistachio Nuts, Violets or Rose Leaves crystallised.

Method.—Rinse out a mould with cold water and leave it wet. Decorate the foot with a little sweet jelly, pistachio nuts, and crystallised violets or rose-leaves, and allow the jelly to set.

Make the custard as directed on p. 146. Melt the gelatine in a small saucepan with the water, and strain it into the custard, being careful to scrape it well out of the pan. Put the walnuts on a tin and roast them in the oven for a few minutes, so as to draw out the flavour. Then pound them in a mortar or crush them with a rolling-pin. Add them to the custard with a little flavouring. Whisk the cream until thick, and mix it lightly in beside the other ingredients. Stir the cream occasionally until it is almost setting, and then pour it into the prepared mould. Place the mould in a cool place or on ice until the cream is firm. When required, turn out on to a glass or silver dish, and decorate round the edges with a little chopped jelly and a few crystallised violets.

SIMPLE COLD PUDDINGS

Caramel Custard

(*Fr.* Crème Renversée à la Vanille)

Ingredients—

Caramel.	*Custard.*
3 oz. Loaf Sugar.	2 yolks of Eggs and
½ gill Cold Water.	2 whole Eggs.
A squeeze of Lemon Juice.	½ pint Milk.
	1 dessert-spoonful Sugar.
	Vanilla Flavouring.
	A pinch of Salt.

Method.—Make the caramel according to directions given on p. 193, and coat a plain soufflé tin with it. Allow this to become cold whilst making the custard. Put the eggs into a basin with the sugar, flavouring, and a pinch of salt, and mix them to a cream with a wooden spoon. Heat the milk and pour it slowly on to the egg mixture, stirring all the time. Strain the custard into the prepared mould and cover with greased paper. Steam very slowly for one hour, or until the custard feels firm in the centre; or bake in a moderate oven with some warm water round the mould. When the custard is cold, turn it out on a glass dish. It will have a glaze of caramel over the top, and some will run round the sides and serve as a sauce.

Note.—The custard may, if liked, be flavoured with some coffee essence (Coffee Caramel Custard).

Chocolate Custard

(*Fr.* Crème Tournée au Chocolat)

Ingredients—

3 tablets of Chocolate or 2 oz.	5 yolks of Eggs.
1 gill of Hot Water.	4½ oz. fine Sugar.
1 pint Milk.	4 whites of Eggs.

Method.—Dissolve the chocolate in a saucepan with the hot water, add the milk, and let it boil up. Put the yolks of eggs into a basin with the sugar, and cream them well together with a wooden spoon. Add the chocolate little by little to the eggs, then return all to the saucepan, and stir over the fire until it thickens. At this point remove the stewpan from the fire and add to the custard the whites of eggs beaten to a stiff froth. Stir for a minute or two longer over the fire, but it must not boil. Serve in a glass dish or bowl.

Chocolate Mould

(*Fr.* Moule au Chocolat)

Ingredients—

2 oz. Chocolate.	½ oz. Gelatine.
3 gills of Milk.	1 or 2 oz. Sugar.
2 yolks of Eggs.	A few drops of Vanilla.

Method.—Break the chocolate in small pieces and put it into a lined saucepan with one gill of milk. Dissolve slowly over the fire and cook until . smooth. Then remove the saucepan from the fire and add the remainder of the milk, the gelatine, sugar, and yolks of eggs. Stir again over the fire until almost boiling and until the gelatine is dissolved. Strain into a basin, add a few drops of vanilla, and cool slightly. Then pour into a wetted mould and set aside until firm. Turn out when wanted, and serve plain or with whipped cream.

This pudding may be made less rich by omitting the yolks of eggs.

Coffee Blanc-Mange

(*Fr.* Moule au Café)

Ingredients—

½ pint Milk.	2 oz. Sugar.
½ pint strong clear Coffee.	A few drops of Vanilla.
2 oz. Corn-flour.	1 oz. Butter.

Method.—Put the coffee and half the milk into a saucepan to heat. Mix the corn-flour smoothly with the remainder of the milk and add it to the hot liquid in the saucepan. Stir over the fire until boiling, and boil slowly about ten minutes. Add the sugar, butter, and vanilla, and mix well. Pour all into a wetted mould, and set aside until cold.

Note.—A little cream added to this is an improvement. The coffee used should be very strong and clear.

Devonshire Junket

Ingredients—

1 pint new Milk.	1 table-sp. Castor Sugar.
1 tea-sp. Essence of Rennet.	½ tea-sp. ground Cinnamon.
½ glass of Brandy.	Clotted Cream.

Method.—Mix together in a glass bowl or deep dish the brandy, cinnamon, and sugar. Pour on to these one pint of new milk, or fresh milk heated to the temperature of new milk, and add the rennet. Stir it well, and let it remain until it is set. Then spread some clotted cream over the top, and sprinkle with castor sugar.

When well made, junket should cut into smooth shiny slices like jelly. Unlike jelly, it will set better and more quickly in a room of ordinary temperature than in a cold larder.

Gâteau of Cherries with Cream

(*Fr.* Gâteau de Cerises à la Crème)

Ingredients—

1 lb. Cherries.	½ lb. Sugar.
3 gills of Water.	A few drops of Carmine.
¾ oz. Leaf Gelatine.	1 gill of Double Cream.
The juice of ½ Lemon.	Sugar and Flavouring.

Method.—Wash and pick the cherries, then cut them in two and remove the stones. Put them into a lined saucepan with the sugar, lemon juice, and water, and stew them gently until quite tender. Then strain the juice from the cherries and measure it; if not three gills, make up the quantity with water. Return this juice to the saucepan, and add to it the gelatine cut in small pieces, and a little carmine. Stir over the fire until the gelatine is quite dissolved. Put the cherries into a border mould that has been rinsed out with cold water, and strain the liquid over them. Set aside until firm, then turn out and pile whipped and flavoured cream in the centre.

Note.—The stones of the cherries may be broken, and the kernels blanched and added to the mixture.

The gâteau may be further decorated by putting some fresh cherries and leaves of angelica round the cream.

Cold Gooseberry Soufflé

Ingredients—

1 lb. Gooseberries.	A little Carmine or Cochineal.
1 gill Custard.	
6 oz. Sugar.	

Method.—Top and tail the gooseberries and wash them well. Put them into a lined stewpan with the sugar, and stew them until reduced to a pulp, then rub them through a coarse sieve. Put this fruit purée into a glass dish and pour the custard over. Whip up the whites of the eggs to a stiff froth, add sugar to taste, and colour one half pink with a few drops of carmine or cochineal. Pile this on the top of the custard and sprinkle with a little chopped pistachio nut or pink sugar.

Orange Custard

(*Fr.* Crème Renversée à l'Orange)

Ingredients—

2 whites of Eggs.
4 yolks of Eggs.
½ pint Milk.
2 large Oranges.
2 oz. Castor Sugar.
½ oz. Gelatine.
1 table-spoonful Water.

Method.—Sieve the sugar on to a plate, and grate the rind from the oranges on the top of it. Rub those two together with the fingers until thoroughly blended, and then put this orange sugar into a basin. Add to it the yolks and whites of eggs, and beat together for a few minutes. Heat the milk, and pour it gradually into the basin, stirring all the time. Then return all to the saucepan, and stir carefully over the fire until the custard thickens, but do not let it boil. Remove quickly from the fire, and strain into a basin. Dissolve the gelatine in a very little water, and strain it into the custard, also the orange juice. Stir occasionally until lukewarm, then pour into a wetted mould, and set in a cool place until firm. Turn out on a glass or silver dish.

Note.—The mould may, if liked, be decorated at the top with a little clear jelly set with a few small sections of orange.

Raspberry Sponge

Ingredients—

Rind and juice of 1 Lemon.
1 oz. Sugar.
2 whites of Eggs.
1 gill of Water.
½ oz. Gelatine.
4 or 6 table-spoonfuls Purée from fresh Raspberries.
2 or 3 drops of Carmine.

Method.—Wipe the lemon, and peel off the rind as thinly as possible. Put the rind into a saucepan with the gelatine, sugar, and water, and dissolve slowly over the fire. Then strain into a basin, and cool slightly. Add the whites of eggs, carmine, lemon juice, and raspberry syrup or purée, and whisk all together until thick and frothy. Pile up in a rocky manner on a glass dish, and sprinkle with a little grated cocoanut or chopped pistachio nuts.

Note.—Strawberry sponge may be made in the same way, using strawberry instead of raspberry purée.

Rhubarb Mould

Ingredients—

1 bunch of Rhubarb.
Gelatine.
Sugar.
Carmine or Cochineal.
Water.
1 gill Double Cream.

Method.—Wipe the rhubarb, but do not peel it. Cut it into short lengths, and put into a lined saucepan with enough water to cover it, and sugar to taste. Stew slowly until the rhubarb is reduced to a pulp, then strain through a fine strainer or hair sieve, pressing well with a wooden spoon in order to obtain all the juice. Measure this juice, and return it to the saucepan, adding French leaf gelatine in the proportion of 1 oz. to each pint of liquid. Stir carefully over the fire until the gelatine is dissolved; add a few drops of carmine or cochineal, and taste if sufficiently sweetened. When slightly cooled, pour into a wetted mould and set aside until firm. Then turn out and serve with whipped and sweetened cream.

COMPÔTES AND FRUIT SALADS

Compôte of Apples

(*Fr.* Compôte de Pommes)

Ingredients—

1 lb. Apples.
¼ lb. Loaf Sugar.
½ pint Water.
The juice of ½ Lemon.
A few drops of Carmine or Cochineal.

Method.—Put the sugar, water, and lemon juice into a clean lined saucepan, and let them boil quickly for ten minutes. Meanwhile peel the apples, cut them in quarters, and remove the cores. Throw the pieces into the boiling syrup, and let them cook slowly until clear and tender, but not broken. Then remove the quarters of apple carefully, reduce the syrup a little, and colour it pink with a few drops of carmine or cochineal.

Arrange the apples on a glass dish and pour the syrup over.

Notes.—If the apples are small, they may be cored and cooked whole.

A little wine may, if liked, be added to the syrup.

A little cream or custard served with the compôte is a great improvement.

Compôte of Cherries

(*Fr.* Compôte de Cerises)

Ingredients—

1 lb. Cherries.
¼ lb. Sugar.
Juice of 1 Lemon.

Method.—Wipe the cherries carefully, and separate them one from the other. Trim the stalks with a pair of scissors, leaving only from an inch to an inch and a half on each. Put the cherries into a lined saucepan with the sugar, and strain in the lemon juice. Put the lid on the pan and stew gently for ten minutes, or until the cherries are cooked without being broken. Lift them carefully on to a glass dish, and pour back into the saucepan any juice which may be round them. Boil this juice a few minutes longer, and then pour it over the cherries.

Compôte of Pears

(*Fr.* Compôte de Poires)

Ingredients—

1½ lb. Pears.	2 table-spoonfuls Port Wine.
½ lb. Loaf Sugar.	½ pint Cold Water.
A few drops of Carmine.	Juice of ½ Lemon.
1 inch Cinnamon Stick.	2 or 3 Cloves.

Method.—Put into a lined saucepan the sugar, water, lemon juice, cloves, and cinnamon stick, and allow these to boil for ten minutes. Peel the pears, cut them in halves or quarters, according to size, remove the cores, and stew them slowly in the syrup until tender, from half to one and a half hours. When nearly ready, add the wine and carmine.

Serve the pears in a glass or silver dish, allow the syrup to cool slightly, and then strain it over.

Compôte of Strawberries

Pick the strawberries and pile them on to a glass dish. Make a syrup. Put into a saucepan ¾ lb. of loaf sugar and ½ pint cold water; let this boil until reduced to half the quantity, flavour with lemon juice, brandy, or liqueur, and colour pink with a few drops of carmine. Allow the syrup to cool slightly, then pour it over the strawberries. Keep the compôte in a cold place or on ice for one hour before using it, and serve whipped cream separately.

Fruit Salads

(*Fr.* Salades de Fruits)

Almost any fruit may be employed in the making of a salad, such as strawberries, raspberries, white, red, or black currants, grapes, oranges, bananas, pears, peaches, apricots, &c. The fruits must all be dry and perfectly ripe. Hard or unripe morsels will spoil any salad. The salad may be composed of several kinds of fruit according to the season of the year, or merely of one or two fruits. Sometimes a small quantity of nuts, grated cocoanut, pounded almonds, or pounded walnuts is mixed with the fruit.

Oranges should be skinned, every particle of white pith removed from them, cut in slices, or divided in sections, and the pips taken out. Plums peeled, cut in halves or quarters, and stoned. Grapes cut in two and the seeds removed. Bananas, apples, pears, peaches, &c., peeled and cut in small pieces or dice. All the cutting of the fruit must be done with a silver knife. A crystal salad bowl, or, failing that, a deep compôte dish is the best to use for the purpose.

Pure white sugar and wine suited to the fruit form the dressing. For 1 lb. of fruit allow ¼ lb. sugar and about ½ pint wine. Turn the fruit over occasionally after the fruit has been added, that it may all be thoroughly saturated.

The kind of wine to use for the dressing is pretty much a matter of taste.

For a salad composed principally of light-coloured fruits, such as apricots, peaches, pineapple, pears, &c., use a light sweet wine such as Madeira or sherry.

For strawberries and raspberries claret or port is preferable, while with oranges or bananas a white wine should be used. A table-spoonful of liqueur or brandy is an improvement to any salad.

ICES

Our American cousins have always been experts at the art of making ices of every kind and variety. It may be said, indeed, that ice in some form or other is never absent from the American dinner-table, if it is only represented by iced water, or some of those delicious iced drinks for the concoction of which the Americans are so famous.

Of late years the cult of the "ice" has become somewhat pronounced in England also. No dinner-party with any pretence to that name is considered complete without an ice pudding or ice-creams to give the finishing touch to the menu, whilst young people invited to join in even the smallest of "small and early" dances would feel distinctly aggrieved if the delectable "ice-cream" failed to be included in the refreshments provided.

When ordered from the caterers, however, ices are apt to be somewhat expensive luxuries, and for that reason, however festive the occasion, they but seldom figure in the menu of families where ways and means form an important consideration. There is no reason, however, why people of the most slender means should have to restrict their menu in this direction, for ices can be easily made at home, and at a very small cost.

There are many inexpensive machines now on the market, and quite a good practical one for family use (2 quarts) can be bought for 8s. or 10s. The working of the different machines varies somewhat; with some a freezing mixture is used, and with others a mixture of ice and coarse salt. Full directions for use are issued with each special make of freezer.

The accompanying diagram shows one of the

Freezing-Pail.

simplest forms of freezing machines, and is manufactured by Thomas Bradford & Co., High Holborn, London.

Before giving recipes for different kinds of

ices it will be as well to give a few general directions for freezing.

First of all be most particular to have every part of the freezer scrupulously clean, and then see that it is properly charged with ice and salt. Ice alone cannot produce a sufficient degree of cold, therefore salt is used in the proportion of one part salt to three parts ice. The salt should be broken up into small pieces about the size of a marble. This may be done by means of an ice-pricker or with a large hat-pin. Pack the

Ice-Pricker.

sides of the pail with three inches of ice and one inch of salt in alternate layers until within an inch from the top of the pot, and keep pressing the mixture down with an ice-spaddle or strong wooden spoon in order to make it close and compact. When ready, remove the lid from

Ice-Spaddle.

the pot, pour in the mixture to be frozen, and re-cover quickly. The pot should not be more than three parts full, and the greatest care must be taken in opening and shutting that no salt is allowed to enter, or the mixture would be entirely spoilt. Now turn the handle at the side of the machine with a slow and regular motion until the mixture is sufficiently frozen. As the freezing process proceeds the turning of the handle will become gradually harder. The dasher inside the pot is continually scraping the frozen mixture from the sides and mixing it thoroughly, so that there is no occasion to open the can until the freezing is sufficiently advanced.

The time required for freezing will vary somewhat according to the make of the machine used and the kind of mixture being frozen. It is always better if an ice can be made some time before it is required, as the flavour becomes blended with standing. The pail must be kept well packed and more ice and salt added as required. The water, too, should be run off from time to time by the hole to be found in the side of the pail.

If the iced mixture has to be kept some time remove the dash-wheel from the pot and plug up the hole in the lid with a cork. Pack up with plenty of ice and salt, and cover the pail with a piece of thick flannel or felt. The ice will then remain in a frozen condition for several hours, or even longer if more ice and salt is added when required.

Water Ices

Water ices may be divided into several different classes according to whether they are made with fruit juice, fruit purée, or liqueur or perfume. The last-named are seldom used alone, but generally as an accompaniment or filling to another ice. The following recipes will serve as a guide from which many other varieties may be made.

In the making of all water ices a syrup of sugar and water is required as below.

Syrup for Water Ices

Proportions—

1 pint Water.	The juice of ½ a Lemon.
½ lb. Loaf Sugar.	

Method.—Put the sugar and water into a lined saucepan, bring to the boil and boil for ten minutes, removing any scum that rises. Add the lemon juice and strain through fine muslin.

Class I

Make with fruit juice and syrup.

Orange and Lemon Water Ice

(*Fr.* Glacé de Citron et d'Orange)

Proportions—

½ pint Orange Juice.	1 pint Syrup as above.
½ pint Lemon Juice.	2 whites of Eggs.

Method.—Pour the syrup while still hot over the thinly peeled rind of two oranges and two lemons. When cold add the fruit juice and strain all through muslin. Put this mixture into the freezing-pot, and when half frozen mix in the whites of eggs beaten to a stiff froth. Continue the freezing process until the ice is sufficiently stiff for serving.

Note.—Either orange or lemon juice may be used separately, but the above makes a nice combination.

Red Currant Water Ice

(*Fr.* Glacé de Groseilles)

Proportions—

1 pint Red Currant Juice.	2 Whites of Eggs.
1 pint Syrup for Ices.	

Method.—Extract the juice from the red currants in the same way as for red-currant jelly (p. 230), and then proceed in the same way as for orange and lemon water ice.

Note.—Black Currant Water ice can be made in the same way. A few drops of carmine should be added.

Class II

Made with fruit purée and syrup.

Strawberry Water Ice

(*Fr.* Glacé de Fraises)

Proportions—

1 pint Strawberry Pureé.	The Juice of 1 Lemon.
1 Pint Syrup for Ices.	A few drops of Carmine.

Method.—Prepare the purée by rubbing some fresh strawberries through a hair sieve (or bottled strawberries may be used). Add the lemon juice, and deepen the colour if necessary by adding a few drops of liquid carmine. Freeze as directed on p. 208.

Note.—The following ices can be made in the same way by using the different purées of fruit: apple, apricot, banana, pineapple, and raspberry. With the more acid fruits the lemon juice must be reduced in quantity or omitted altogether. The harder fruits will require to be stewed before the purée is made. A little liqueur is sometimes added.

Tutti-Frutti (Mixed Fruit Ice)

(*Fr.* Tutti-Frutti Glacés)

Proportions—

1 pint Lemon or Orange Water Ice.
¼ lb. Mixed Fruits.
1 table-spoonful Liqueur.

Method.—Take any kind of fruit, fresh, tinned, or glacé, and cut them up into dice. Sprinkle them with some liqueur and then stir into half-frozen water ice. Continue the freezing and serve in small cups.

Class III

Made with syrup and either perfume, such as orange flower water or rose water, or a liqueur of some kind such as maraschino or noyeau.

Orange Flower Water Ice

(*Fr.* Glacé à la Fleur d'Orange)

Proportions—

1 gill Orange Flower Water.
½ pint Syrup for Ices.
2 drops Essence of Almond.

Method.—The very best French make of orange flower water must be used for this. Mix all the ingredients together and freeze.

Cream Ices

Cream ices may also be divided into the following different classes:—

Class I

Made with cream and custard with some special flavour.

Vanilla Cream Ice

(*Fr.* Glacé à la Crème de Vanille)

Proportions—

1 pint Double Cream.
1 pint Custard.
Vanilla Pod or Essence.
Sugar.

Method.—Make the custard according to directions given on p. 146, flavour with vanilla and sweeten to taste. Allow this to cool and add the cream lightly whipped. Mix both together and freeze until of a proper consistency.

Note.—A cheaper ice may be made by using a simple corn-flour custard and adding less cream.

Chocolate Ice Cream

(*Fr.* Glacé au Chocolat)

Proportions—

1 pint Custard.
1 pint Double Cream.
2 or 3 oz. Chocolate.
A little Water.
Vanilla.

Method.—Dissolve the chocolate in a little water and add it to the custard. Flavour with vanilla and then continue as in preceding recipe.

Coffee or Tea Ice Cream

(*Fr.* Crème au Thé ou Crème au Café Glacé)

Make in the same way as vanilla ice cream, making the custard with equal quantities of strong tea or coffee and milk.

Walnut Ice Cream

Make in the same way as vanilla ice cream, adding 6 oz. roasted and ground walnuts to the custard.

Ginger Ice Cream

(*Fr.* Glacé à la Crème de Gingembre)

Add 6 oz. preserved ginger cut in small pieces and a little of the syrup to the custard.

Lemon Cream Ice (Cheap)

(*Fr.* Glacé à la Crème de Citron)

Proportions—

1 pint Custard.
2 Lemons.
3 oz. Castor Sugar.
A little yellow colouring.

Method.—Grate the rind very lightly off the two lemons, rub it into the castor sugar, and use this for sweetening the custard. Add the strained juice of one lemon and a little yellow colouring. Mix well and freeze.

Orange Cream Ice

(*Fr.* Glacé à la Crème d'Orange)

Make in same way as above, using the juice of two oranges. Add one or two drops of carmine as well as the yellow to produce an orange colouring.

Class II

Made with equal quantities of cream and purée of fruit.

Apricot Ice Cream

(*Fr.* Glacé à la Crème d'Abricots)

Proportions—

½ pint Apricot Purée.
½ pint Cream.
A squeeze of Lemon Juice.
2 or 3 drops of Carmine.

Method.—Use tinned apricots and rub sufficient through a hair sieve to make ½ pint. Some of the syrup must be used along with the fruit, as the purée should not be too thick. Mix the cream lightly whipped with the purée and add the lemon juice and enough carmine to make an apricot colour. Add also a little sugar if necessary. Freeze as directed on p. 208.

Note.—Sometimes a little liqueur is added to this ice.

Strawberry or Raspberry Cream Ice

(*Fr.* Glacé à la Crème de Fraises ou de Framboises)

Prepare in the same way as above, adding sugar to taste and enough carmine to make the ice a pretty pink colour.

The following ices can also be made in the same way: peach, pineapple, banana, pear, &c.

Note.—The ices in this class may be made more cheaply by using partly custard and milk instead of so much cream.

Cream Ices with Fruit Purée

Very delicious ices can be made by combining an iced-cream mixture with some purée of fresh fruit. For instance, put some lemon cream ice into some pretty glass cups, and then a spoonful of raspberry purée, which has been iced and flavoured with a little liqueur. Pile a little whipped and iced cream on the top and put the ices in an ice safe or on ice until required. Or, again, a raspberry ice cream may be used with a purée of raspberries or strawberries, or a walnut or coffee cream with apricot or pineapple, and so on. These ices may be varied according to individual taste and the materials at hand.

Iced Coffee (White)

(*Fr.* Café Frappé)

Proportions—

1 pint strong Coffee.
2 or 3 oz. Sugar.
½ pint Cream.

Method.—The coffee used for this must be first-rate in quality, freshly roasted and freshly ground. It should be made rather stronger than for ordinary use, and must be perfectly clear. Mix the different ingredients together and stand until cold. Then freeze until it can be poured with difficulty. Keep on ice until wanted. Half milk and half cream may be used if the above proportions are too rich.

Iced Coffee (Black)

(*Fr.* Café Frappé)

Proportions—

1 pint strong clear Coffee.
1 table-spoonful Brandy.
2 oz. Sugar.

Method.—Mix the ingredients together in a jug and set deep in ice until wanted. Before serving add a lump of ice, and hand-whipped and iced cream separately.

To Serve Ices

The simplest way of serving ices is to put portions sufficient for one person in fancy paper cases, in pretty glass cups, or on ice plates. The top may be daintily decorated with a few crystallised flower petals, such as rose-leaves, violets, or orange blossom, or even a light sprinkling of chopped pistachio nut, but the decoration must on no account be overdone. Wafer biscuits should always be served with ices.

To Mould Ices

If something more elaborate is wanted the ice may be moulded and turned out in a shape. The mixture in this case should not be frozen too hard, or it will not mould prettily. Take an ice pudding mould and let it be in cold water some little time before it is required. Then pack it tightly with the frozen mixture, cover with a piece of wet white paper and put on the lid. Seal round the join with a little lard, which, when hard, will make the mould perfectly water-tight. Imbed the mould in a mixture of ice and salt and allow it to remain from one to three hours.

If an ice safe is used the lard will not be necessary; in fact, the mixture might then be put into any fancy pudding mould, which are not so expensive as the proper ice moulds. A mould of some simple pattern is best.

A little ice safe or refrigerator is not the expensive article it used to be when £3 had to be given for one of a very small size; 32s. 6d. will now buy one that is quite sufficient for all ordinary purposes.

When iced puddings or other moulded ices are frequently required an ice safe would be found a great boon, and would simplify their manufacture to a great extent. Apart from ice-making, too, they are most useful in hot weather for keeping all viands cool and fresh.

To Unmould an Ice

If the mould has been buried in ice, scrape off the lard and wipe the outside carefully. Then remove the lid and dip the mould in cold or slightly tepid water. Wipe it dry and invert it on a dish which has a pretty lace-edged paper on it and draw the mould slowly off. If it does not come away at once, let it stand for a minute or two. This unmoulding must be done with care, and a little practice will be required to do it nicely. If the outside is allowed to become too soft some of the mixture will run down on the dish, and the appearance of the pudding will be altogether spoilt.

Iced Puddings

Almost any good ice mixture may be made into a pudding, or a mixture of two or three kinds may be used together. A mixture of fruits cut in small pieces is often added, and liqueur of some kind is a favourite flavouring.

When two kinds of cream are to be used in the mould, set the mould on ice and line it about an inch thick with the heavier of the two mixtures, and then fill up the centre with another mixture of a different flavour.

If a cream ice and water ice are being used together, the cream mixture should be used to line the mould and the water ice for filling the centre. Then, again, if the mixtures are being set in layers, the lightest should be put in first and the most solid last, as there will then be a firm foundation for the pudding to rest on when it is turned out.

Very pretty combinations may be made by setting the iced mixture in a border mould and filling the centre with fruit or whipped cream when it is turned out. For instance, a pink ice-cream with white whipped cream in the centre and a few crystallised rose petals to decorate it, or a lemon-coloured ice-cream with small pieces of pineapple and whipped cream in the centre and a decoration of maidenhair fern, or, again, a white cream with small strawberries or raspberries in the centre flavoured with a liqueur, and so on; the variety is almost endless and leaves room for individual taste and ingenuity.

Small ices set in separate moulds are often used as a decoration for larger puddings; they are often made in the form of fruit or flowers. A little colouring is generally used to make the resemblance more natural. These little moulds are, however, somewhat expensive, and as they are not particularly easy to use the amateur should scarcely attempt them, as so many pretty dishes can be made with less trouble.

Sorbets

A sorbet is a half-frozen water ice, which is served directly before the roast at a dinner. It is also fashionable at present to serve a delicately flavoured sorbet at an afternoon tea or tennis party. Its preparation is quite simple and may easily be undertaken by the unprofessed cook.

The foundation of a sorbet is always a water ice of some kind with the addition of one or more kinds of liqueur and generally some fruit. It should be served in pretty glass cups.

Red Currant and Raspberry Sorbet

(*Fr.* Sorbet aux Groseilles et Framboises)

Proportions—

1 pint Red Currant Water Ice.	1 gill Curaçoa.
	A few ripe Raspberries.

Method.—Freeze the ice until smooth, but not too hard. Stir in the Curaçoa and serve garnished with raspberries which have been sprinkled with sugar and placed on ice until cold.

Lemon Sorbet

(*Fr.* Sorbet au Citron)

Proportions—

1 pint Lemon Water.	½ wine-glassful Rum.
1 wine-glassful Maraschino.	2 table-sp. Mixed Fruits.

Method.—Cut the fruit in small pieces and marinade it in the liqueur and rum. Half freeze the lemon water ice and stir in the fruits, &c.; freeze a little longer, but do not make the mixture hard.

Note.—There are several other kinds of ices, such as soufflés, parfaits, mousses, moscovites, &c., but as these are all more troublesome to make, we feel that it is beyond the scope of this book to enter into their manufacture.

BREAD, SCONES AND CAKES

PREPARATION OF MATERIALS

Flour.—Ordinary household flour should be used in all the recipes except where otherwise stated, as in the case of some of the very light cakes, where Vienna or Hungarian flour is preferable. It is very important to have the flour dry, as damp flour would render any cake heavy. If there is any doubt about the dryness it will be safer to warm the flour in a cool oven or on the rack above the stove before weighing and using it. Flour should be sieved for all cakes, as this not only renders it lighter, but keeps back any hard lumps it may contain. For sieving, use either a very fine wire sieve, or a patent flour-sifter, which can be bought for about 1s. 8d.

Butter or Dripping.—Inferior or tainted butter should never be used for cakes; if butter is used at all, it must be good. In cases where the butter is rubbed into the flour, the butter should be as cool and firm as possible; where it is to be creamed with the sugar it may be rather softer, but not on any account oily. If the butter is very salt it will be better to wash it in cold water and dry it in a floured cloth before using. If the butter contains a large proportion of water it should be dried and squeezed in a floured cloth before using. For many of the plainer cakes good beef dripping may be used instead of butter. The dripping should be clarified and free from any meat juice, and any brown sediment should be scraped from the foot of it before using. For nursery cakes beef dripping is always to be recommended in the place of butter.

Sugar.—Take castor or sifted sugar for all the recipes except where otherwise stated, and always sieve it before use.

Candied Peel.—Remove the hard sugar from the inside, and with a sharp knife shred the peel very finely. The strip may be left any length desired, but as candied peel at the best is an indigestible article it should never be cut in thick chunks. If the peel is too hard to shred easily, it may be soaked for a few minutes in boiling water.

Currants.—Rub these on the top of a sieve with a little dry flour to clean them and remove the stalks. Then drop them on a plate a few at a time to make sure there are no stones amongst them. If the currants are dirty they may be washed first in hot water, then dried in a cloth or a cool oven, and rolled in flour. This should be done some little time before the currants are required, as they should be quite dry and cold before being added to the cake, otherwise they will spoil the mixture.

Sultana Raisins.—Rub these on the top of a sieve with a little dry flour, and carefully remove all stalks.

Valencia Raisins.—Remove the stalks, split them open with a small knife, and take out the stones, using a little warm water to prevent them sticking to the fingers. These raisins are usually cut in small pieces or chopped roughly.

Almonds.—Blanch these by putting them in a saucepan of cold water and bringing them to the boil; then strain and run some cold water over them. Remove the brown skins and dry the almonds in a cloth. They are usually shred or chopped before being used, and it is better to prepare them some little time before they are required to ensure their being dry. For decorative purposes they are sometimes split in halves broadways.

Glacé Fruits, such as cherries, apricots, ginger, or pineapple, should have the hard sugar removed from them first by soaking them for a minute in hot water. Then dry the pieces lightly, cut them to the size required, and roll them in flour.

Note.—All fruit should be mixed with a little dry flour (taken from the quantity given in the recipe) before being added to the cake mixture.

EXPLANATION OF TERMS

To Beat Eggs (yolk and white together).—If more than one egg is used, break them separately first into a small cup or basin to make sure that each one is fresh. Remove the tread, or the hard speck in the egg, and mix them all together. Then with a fork or egg whisk beat them lightly with an upward motion until they are light and frothy, and the whites and yolks thoroughly mixed together. Do not over-beat the eggs or they will not be so light. Eggs used for cake-making must be fresh, although not necessarily new laid.

To Whip the Whites of Eggs.—When only one or two are used put them on a flat dinner-plate, being careful that not a particle of yolk gets in. Add a pinch of salt, and with a broad-bladed knife or spatula whip them with an upward motion to a stiff dry froth, or until so firm that when the plate is reversed they will not fall off. When more than two whites are used put them into a dry basin, add a pinch of salt, and beat them with a wire whisk until stiff enough to stand on the end of the whisk without dropping. The whites of eggs ought to be beaten in a cool place, and if the eggs are fresh and cool, the beating will only take a few minutes.

To Cream Yolks of Eggs and Sugar.—Sieve the sugar into a basin, drop the yolks of eggs on the top, and work the two together with a wooden spoon or wire whisk until they are of a pale lemon colour and light and frothy-looking.

To Cream Butter and Sugar.—Sieve the sugar into a basin, add the butter, and beat the two together until of a light creamy consistency. Either a large wooden spoon or the hand may be used for this. If over half a pound of butter is being used, it is quicker to take the hand. If the butter is very hard, the basin may be warmed slightly before commencing, but the butter must on no account be oiled, or it will make the cake heavy. This process requires some time, and unless it is well carried out the cake will be heavy. The time will depend upon the quantity of butter and sugar that are used.

To Clarify Butter.—Put the butter into a lined saucepan, and bring it slowly to the boil. Let it simmer for a few minutes, then draw the saucepan to the side of the fire, and let it stand until the butter has ceased to bubble. Then, with an iron spoon, remove all the froth from the top, and pour the clear oil into a dish ready for use, leaving the sediment at the foot of the saucepan.

To Rub Butter into Flour.—Sieve the flour into a dry basin. Place the butter on the top of the flour, cover it over, and break it in small pieces. Then rub together lightly with the tips of the fingers and thumbs until as fine as breadcrumbs. While rubbing, keep lifting the flour well up in the basin, so that air may mix with it, and the butter is not made too soft. Unless this operation is well carried out, the cake will look streaky.

PREPARATION OF CAKE TINS

This should be seen to before the mixing of the cake is commenced, as some cakes will spoil if the mixture is allowed to stand and wait because the tins are not ready.

To Line a Round Cake Tin with Paper.—Cut a double band of paper two or three inches deeper than the cake tin and rather longer than the circumference. Fold up an inch of this band on the double fold and make a mark. Open out and make cuts along the marked-off inch of the paper an inch or two apart. Arrange this band inside the cake tin, making the notched part of the paper to lie flat *on* the bottom of the tin. Then cut a double round of paper *exactly* the size to fit inside the tin, and lay it smoothly on the foot. The paper must lie perfectly flat: there must be no wrinkles. If the tin used is very large, three or four folds of paper may be used. *No grease is required;* it would only make the cake more liable to burn.

To Line a Flat Tin with Paper.—If the tin is very shallow the paper will not require to be shaped, but just pressed in smoothly and snipped at the corners if necessary.

For Scones or Small Rock Cakes.—A flat baking-sheet should be greased and sprinkled with flour; then knock the edges of the tin on the table so that the flour coats it all lightly, and then shake off any that is superfluous.

For Sponge Cakes.—Tie a double band of paper round the outside of the tin and so as to project two or three inches over the edge at the top. Then coat the inside of the mould and the paper with melted clarified butter. This should be put on with a brush, and the butter should not be too liquid or the coating is apt to be too thin. Then pass through a sieve together one tablespoonful of flour and one tablespoonful of castor sugar, and dust over the inside of the mould and paper with this mixture. Turn the mould round and round until every part is coated, and then empty out what does not adhere. It is this preparation which gives the light dry coating to a sponge cake.

Small Cake Tins.—Prepare these in the same way as a tin for a sponge cake by greasing them with clarified butter and dusting them out with a mixture of flour or potato flour and sugar.

If two ounces each of flour and sugar are sieved together, the mixture may be kept in a tin, and will always be in readiness for the preparation of cake tins.

When tins are greased only clarified butter or fresh butter must be used. Any salt in the butter would be apt to make the cake stick to the tin and burn. For the plainer cakes good clarified dripping may be used.

THE BAKING OF CAKES

This is one of the most difficult parts of cake-making. No matter how carefully the mixture has been prepared, the success or failure of the cake will very much depend upon the proper regulation of the heat of the oven. This requires very close observance, and it is only by experience and careful watching that the capabilities and faults of individual ovens can be learned.

There are one or two popular tests which may be applied by novices, such as the following:—Sprinkle a little dry flour on a tin and place it in the oven. If there is sufficient heat to bake a cake, this will be brown in about five minutes. Or, put a piece of white paper in the oven, and if at the end of five minutes it is a good yellow colour, the heat is moderate and suitable for most cakes. Small thermometers can also be bought to tell the heat of the oven, but as these are somewhat fragile articles they are not always satisfactory. Still, if used with care, they act as a guide. The degrees of heat would be nearly the following:—

From 350°–400° Fahr. . . .	a hot oven.
300° Fahr.	a moderate oven.
250°–275° Fahr.	a slow oven.

After a very little experience the heat of the oven can easily be discriminated by simply feeling it with the hand.

It is very important that the fire should be made up some little time before the cake is to be put in the oven, and in such a way that it will last, if possible, during the baking, or will not at least require fresh coal during the first hour of baking, when the cake is in process of rising, and when it is most essential for it to have steady heat. If a large cake requiring several hours' cooking is in the oven, the fire should never be allowed to get too low, except perhaps the last half-hour when the cake is just "soaking," but a little coal should be added from time to time in order to keep up a uniform heat.

The heat of the oven can generally be regulated by opening or shutting the damper. If shutting the damper is not sufficient to reduce the heat, the lid of the range over the oven may be opened a little way. If the oven does not get hot enough in spite of a good fire, the trouble probably is that it has not been properly cleaned of the cinders and soot which collect underneath and above the oven, and prevent the heat reaching these parts. This is a point which should be attended to before cake-making is thought of.

For all cakes, except where otherwise stated, a moderate oven is best; if anything, it should be rather hotter for small and light cakes than for the thicker fruit cakes.

A cake to be baked to perfection should rise evenly and be smooth on the top, and by the time it has been in the oven half its time a light brown crust should be formed. Owing to the variation in the heat of an ordinary oven, it is not always possible to arrive at this point of perfection; still, by careful manipulation, it may be aimed at. When a cake rises in a cone in the centre, it shows that the oven has been too hot at the commencement, with the result that the sides of the cake became hardened with a crust before the mixture had had time to rise. If the cake seems inclined to rise at one side, it shows that the oven is hotter on one side than the other, and this fault may be obviated to a certain extent by turning the cake carefully during the baking. If the bottom of the oven is found to be the hottest part, it is a good plan to place an asbestos mat below the cake to prevent it burning at the foot, or stand the cake in another tin containing a bed of sand.

When a cake shows signs of becoming sufficiently brown before it is ready, it should be covered with a double fold of kitchen paper.

The oven door should not be opened for at least five minutes after the cake has been put in, and then only with the greatest care. If by slamming the oven door a draught of cold air is allowed to enter, it will be fatal to the successful rising of the cake. Any moving or turning of the cake must be done very cautiously; it cannot have too careful handling. Moving or shaking the cake during the process of rising is almost sure to cause it to fall.

Be sure the cake is sufficiently cooked before removing it from the oven. Small cakes are ready if they feel firm when gently touched with the finger. Larger cakes should be tested by running a bright and heated skewer into the centre of them. If the skewer comes out sticky the cake is not cooked enough, but if it is dry and undimmed the baking is finished. A cold knife should never be run into a cake, as it would make it "sad." Cakes should be allowed to stand for a minute or two before removing them from the tin; they will then come out more easily. (For baking in gas oven, see p. 96.)

The time given for baking in the following recipes is only approximate; it is impossible to lay down any hard-and-fast rules, as the time is bound to vary slightly owing to various causes.

Baking Powder

Ingredients—

3 oz. Cream of Tartar.
3 oz. Carbonate of Soda.
3 oz. Ground Rice.

Method.—Pass all these ingredients twice through a fine wire sieve. Then put the mixture in a dry tin and store in a dry place.

BREAD AND SCONES

Household Bread

Ingredients—

3½ lbs. Flour (a quarter Stone).
1 oz. German Yeast.
1 tea-spoonful Sugar.
2 tea-spoonfuls Salt.
About 2 pints lukewarm Water.

Method—Sieve the flour and salt into a large basin, and place it in a cool oven, or some other warm place, to get warmed through, as this will assist the rising of the bread. Put the yeast into a smaller basin with the sugar, and mix these two together until they become smooth and liquid. (This is called creaming the yeast, and may be accomplished with either salt or sugar.) Add half the water to the creamed yeast, and mix well together. Make a well in the centre of the warm flour, and strain in the milk and water. Stir in gradually from the sides enough flour to form a thick and smooth batter, still leaving a wall of flour round the edges. Cover the basin with a cloth, and set it in a warm place until the sponge (mixture of flour, yeast, and water) is well risen. If the yeast is good, fifteen or twenty minutes will be sufficient; the batter should then be covered with large bubbles. Mix in the rest of the flour by degrees, adding the rest of the lukewarm water, or enough to form rather a soft dough, as it will become firmer with kneading. Turn the dough on to a floured board, and knead well for fifteen minutes, or until it ceases to cling to the hands. Then flour the basin, and put the dough back into it, making a deep cross cut on the top from side to side with a sharp knife. Cover the basin, and let it stand in a warm place again for about one hour, or until the dough is well risen. It should be about twice its original size, and the cut on the top almost invisible. Turn out again on the board, re-knead lightly, and make up into loaves the size and shape desired. For a cottage loaf make one large ball with a smaller one on the top. Press a floured finger through the middle of both, and make four or five cuts at regular intervals round the sides. For a Coburg loaf form the dough into an oval shape, and make several deep cuts across the top. If the loaves are to be baked in tins, grease the tins first, and do not more than half fill them. After shaping the loaves, place them on a baking-sheet (greased and floured for the loaves that are not in tins), and set them to prove for fifteen or twenty minutes. That is, place them again in a warm place to rise—on the rack above the fire is a very good place. The bread should be covered with a cloth or piece of paper, to prevent any smuts from falling on it. To bake the bread, place it in a hot oven to begin with until the loaves are well risen and slightly browned, then in a more moderate oven until they are cooked through to the middle. The time will depend upon the size of the loaf. When ready, the bread should give a hollow sound when tapped on the bottom.

Brown Bread

Ingredients—

1¾ lb. Brown Meal.
3 gills Tepid Water.
2 tea-spoonfuls Salt.
½ oz. Yeast.

Method.—Either fine, coarse, or medium whole-meal may be used, or half quantity whole-meal and the other half household flour. Put this into a basin and make a well in the centre. Mix the yeast with the salt, add the tepid water and pour into the middle of the meal. Mix the meal in gradually, making a smooth but rather soft dough—more water must be added if required. Knead for a few minutes, and then put in greased and floured tins. Allow the dough to rise in a warm place for one hour or longer, then bake in a moderate oven.

Vienna Bread

Ingredients—

- 1 lb. Vienna Flour.
- 1 tea-spoonful Sugar.
- ½ oz. German Yeast.
- 1 oz. Butter.
- Milk.
- 1 tea-spoonful Salt.

Method.—Sieve the flour and salt into a warm basin, rub in the butter until free from lumps, and make a well in the centre. Cream the yeast in a smaller basin with the sugar, heat the milk to a lukewarm temperature, and pour it on to it. Strain this into the middle of the flour, and mix lightly. Beat all together for a few minutes, then cover the basin, and put the dough to rise for about two hours. When the dough is well risen, turn it out on a floured board, and make it up into small rolls or a variety of fancy shapes. One of the prettiest shapes is the horseshoe twist, which is made as follows: Roll out some of the dough to about a quarter of an inch in thickness, and cut it into triangular-shaped pieces. Then take the two corners at the base of the triangle, and roll up each piece so that the other point turns over on the outside. Another shape is to make small round rolls, and then to cut two slits across the top with a very sharp knife. Place the rolls on a greased and floured tin, and set them in a warm place to prove for about twelve minutes. Then bake in a rather quick oven from fifteen to twenty minutes, according to the size of the rolls. Just before removing the rolls from the oven, brush them over with milk, or egg and milk, to make them shiny.

Note.—Sometimes an egg is added to the above dough.

Cream Scones

Ingredients—

- ½ lb. Flour.
- 1 Egg.
- 1 oz. Butter.
- 1 gill Sour Cream.
- 1 tea-sp. Baking Powder.
- A pinch of Salt.

Method.—Sieve the flour, salt, and baking powder into a basin, and rub in the butter with the tips of the fingers until free from lumps. Then make a well in the centre, and pour in the egg and cream beaten together. Mix from the centre outwards, gathering in the flour gradually until all is formed into one lump. Turn out the dough on a floured board, and knead lightly until free from cracks. Roll out to about half an inch in thickness, cut in rounds, and bake on a greased tin in the oven from ten to fifteen minutes, or on a greased girdle. If the latter, brown the scones, first on one side and then on the other, until they are cooked through.

Crumpets

Ingredients—

- ¾ lb. Vienna Flour.
- ½ tea-spoonful Salt.
- ¾ oz. Baking Powder.
- 1 Egg.
- Milk.
- 1 oz. Butter.

Method.—Sieve the flour, salt, and baking powder into a basin, and make a well in the centre. Add the butter melted and the egg well beaten, then gradually enough milk to make a thinnish batter. Grease some muffin rings, and lay them on a hot and greased girdle. Pour a little batter into each, and watch until air-bubbles begin to rise. Then remove the rings, turn the crumpets, and brown on the second side. Repeat this until all are finished. Toast the crumpets lightly, spread them with butter, and pile them one on the top of the other. Cut in four, and serve hot.

Dropped Scones

Ingredients—

- 1 breakfastcupful Flour.
- 1 table-sp. Castor Sugar.
- ½ tea-spoonful Cream of Tartar.
- ½ tea-spoonful Carbonate of Soda.
- 1 Egg.
- ¾ breakfastcupful Milk.

Method.—Sieve all the dry ingredients into a basin, and make a well in the centre. Add the egg well beaten, and then the milk gradually, beating all well together with the back of a wooden spoon. When the batter looks light and full of air-bubbles pour it into a jug. Heat a girdle and grease it well. Pour the batter on to it, about a table-spoonful at a time, being careful to keep the scones a nice shape and a little distance apart. When the top surface looks covered with bubbles, slip a broad-bladed knife under the scones and turn them over. When both sides are nicely browned the scones are ready. They should be served quickly and hot buttered.

Elcho Scones

Ingredients—

- ½ lb. Flour.
- 2 oz. Butter.
- ½ tea-sp. Cream of Tartar.
- ½ tea-sp. Carbonate of Soda.
- 1 Egg.
- A pinch of Salt.
- Some Buttermilk or Sour Milk.

Method.—Sieve the flour, soda, cream of tartar, and salt into a clean, dry basin, and rub in the butter with the tips of the fingers until free from lumps. Then make a well in the centre, add the egg, well beaten, and enough buttermilk to form all into one lump. The mixing should be done very quickly and lightly with the hand or with a broad-bladed knife. Turn the dough on to a slightly floured board, and knead lightly with the hands until free from cracks. Form into a round (do not roll) about one inch in thickness, and place the scone on a greased and floured baking-tin. Prick all over with a fork, and mark in four with the back of a knife.

Bake in a good oven about twenty minutes. Two or three minutes before removing the scone from the oven break it in four, and brush it over with a little milk or egg and milk.

Tea Cakes

Ingredients—

¾ lb. Flour.	1 Egg.
½ oz. German Yeast.	½ pint Milk.
2 oz. Butter.	A pinch of Salt.
1 tea-spoonful Sugar.	

Method.—Sieve the flour and salt into a warm basin, and make a well in the centre. Put the yeast into a smaller basin with the sugar, and mix them together until smooth and creamy. Melt the butter in a small saucepan, and add the milk. When lukewarm, pour on to the yeast and mix well. Strain this into the centre of the flour, and add the egg well beaten. Mix from the centre outwards, and then beat with the hands for a few minutes. Cover the basin with a cloth, and allow the dough to rise in a warm place from three-quarters to one hour. Turn out the dough on to a slightly floured board, and knead lightly with the hands until smooth and free from cracks. Form into two or three round cakes, and place them on a greased and floured tin. Set the cakes again to rise on the rack above the fire for ten or fifteen minutes, until they look light and puffy. Then bake them in a good oven from fifteen to twenty minutes. A few minutes before removing the cakes from the oven, brush them over with sugar and milk to give them a gloss. These cakes should be split and buttered hot.

A few currants or some very finely chopped candied peel may be added to the mixture if wished.

Wheaten Meal Scones

Ingredients—

¾ lb. Wheaten Meal.	½ tea-sp. Carbonate of Soda.
¼ lb. Flour.	½ tea-spoonful Salt.
¾ tea-sp. Cream of Tartar.	Some Buttermilk or Sour Milk.
1 or 2 oz. Butter.	

Method.—Make in the same way as Elcho Scones (p. 215).

BUNS AND SMALL CAKES

Almond Rock Cakes

Ingredients—

½ lb. Flour.	2 or 3 drops of Essence of Almonds.
2 oz. Butter.	1 Egg.
2 oz. Sugar.	1 tea-sp. Baking Powder.
2 oz. Sweet Almonds.	A little Milk.
A pinch of Salt.	

Method.—First blanch and chop the almonds finely, and put them to dry, but not brown, on a tin in the oven. Then sieve the flour, sugar, and baking powder into a basin, and rub in the butter until free from lumps. Add the prepared almonds, and make a well in the centre of the dry ingredients. Add the egg well beaten, the flavouring, and enough sweet milk to bind all together. The mixture must be kept stiff enough for the spoon to stand upright in it. Have ready a baking-tin, greased and sprinkled with flour, and arrange the mixture on it in small heaps (one tea-spoonful of the mixture in each) and at some little distance apart. Sprinkle the cakes with sugar or with ground almonds and sugar mixed, and bake in a quick oven from ten to fifteen minutes.

Note.—Cocoanut or Currant Rock Cakes can be made in the same way, using 2 oz. desiccated cocoanut or 2 oz. cleaned currants instead of the almonds.

Almond Slices

Ingredients—

¼ lb. Butter.	½ tea-sp. Baking Powder.
¼ lb. Castor Sugar.	3 Eggs.
¼ lb. Sweet Almonds.	A few drops of Essence of Almonds.
7 oz. Flour.	

Method.—Cream the butter and sugar. Dry and sieve the flour, and add it by degrees with the eggs. Then beat for ten minutes until the mixture looks light and full of air-bubbles. Add most of the almonds, blanched and finely shred, the baking powder, and flavouring, and pour out on a shallow tin that has been lined with paper. Sprinkle the remainder of the almonds on the top, and bake in a moderate oven for twenty minutes. When the cake is nicely browned and feels firm to the touch, turn it out on a sheet of sugared paper, and, when cold, cut it in neat slices with a very sharp knife.

Chocolate Cakes

Ingredients—

4 oz. Chocolate.	3 Eggs.
3 oz. Butter.	3 oz. Flour.
4 oz. Castor Sugar.	½ tea-sp. Baking Powder.

Method.—Grate the chocolate and place it in a jar in the oven or in a saucepan of hot water, allowing it to melt slowly. Cream the butter and sugar, then add the yolks of eggs and chocolate, and beat for a few minutes. Whip the whites of the eggs to a stiff froth, and sieve the flour with the baking powder. Add a little flour and a little white of egg alternately to the other mixture until all is lightly blended together. Half fill small prepared tins (p. 213) with the mixture, and bake in a moderate oven about fifteen minutes.

Coburg Cakes

Ingredients—

½ lb. Flour.	1 tea-sp. Ground Ginger.
½ tea-sp. Carbonate of Soda.	½ tea-sp. Ground Cinnamon.
¼ lb. Syrup.	½ tea-sp. Allspice.
2 Eggs.	1½ oz. Butter.
¼ lb. Sugar.	A few Sweet Almonds.

Method.—Sieve all the dry ingredients except the almonds into a basin, and make a well in the centre. Melt the butter and syrup in a small saucepan, and pour them into the middle of the dry ingredients. Add the eggs well beaten, and mix all together. Have ready some small patty tins well greased, and with a half-blanched almond at the foot of each. Half fill the tins with the mixture, and bake them in a moderate oven three-quarters of an hour.

Cocoanut Slices

Ingredients—

3 oz. Butter.	3 Eggs.
3 oz. Castor Sugar.	½ tea-sp. Baking Powder.
3 oz. Desiccated Cocoanut.	A few drops of Vanilla.
2 oz. Flour.	

Icing—½ lb. Icing Sugar, the juice of half a Lemon, and a little Water.

Decorations—1 oz. Cocoanut and a few Pistachio Nuts.

Method.—Cream the butter and sugar, then add the eggs and flour by degrees, beating well. When the mixture looks light and full of air-bubbles, add the cocoanut, vanilla, and baking powder, and mix these in. Pour the mixture into a shallow tin that has been lined with paper, and bake in a moderate oven until lightly browned and cooked through; from fifteen to twenty minutes should be sufficient. When the cake is ready, turn it out on to a sheet of sugared paper and allow it to cool.

Then prepare the icing. Sieve the sugar and put it into a small lined saucepan. Strain in the lemon juice and warm slightly over the fire, adding a little water if necessary. Care must be taken not to make the icing too liquid, but just sufficiently so to pour over the cake. Coat the cake nicely with the icing by means of a spoon, and sprinkle with the one ounce of cocoanut and a few chopped pistachio nuts. Cut in neat slices whilst the icing is still soft.

Crullers

Ingredients—

½ lb. Flour.	1 tea-sp. Baking Powder.
2 oz. Butter.	A pinch of Nutmeg.
1 oz. Sugar.	The grated rind of half a Lemon.
2 Eggs.	

Method.—Sieve the dry ingredients into a basin, and rub in the butter. Add the grated lemon rind or any other flavouring preferred, and bind the mixture with two eggs well beaten. Turn the dough on to a floured board, and work with the hands until free from cracks. Roll out to about half an inch in thickness, and cut into fancy shapes, or make into twists. Have ready on the fire a saucepan of boiling fat, drop the crullers into this, a few at a time, and cook slowly from ten to twelve minutes until they are a nice brown colour, and have swelled to double their original size. When the crullers are ready, lift them out of the fat with a perforated spoon, drain them on kitchen paper, and dredge well with sugar. These should be used while fresh.

Dough Nuts

Ingredients—

½ lb. Flour.	1 Egg.
2 oz. Butter.	A little Milk.
1 tea-sp. Baking Powder.	Some Jam.
1 oz. Castor Sugar.	

Method.—Prepare the mixture in the same way as for crullers recipe. Turn out on a floured board, and roll out to a quarter of an inch in thickness. Stamp out rounds with a cutter about three inches in diameter. Put a small tea-spoonful of red jam in the centre of half of these, and brush over the others with beaten egg. Place two together, one with jam and the other without, and press the edges well where they join. Fry as in last recipe.

Genoise Pastry

Ingredients—

6 oz. Flour (Vienna).	7 Eggs.
6 oz. Butter.	A few drops of Flavouring.
8 oz. Castor Sugar.	

Method.—First clarify the butter (see p. 212), and pour into a basin ready for use. Sieve the flour and put it into a warm place to get thoroughly dry. Break the eggs into a large basin and sieve the sugar over them. Stand this basin over a saucepan of hot water and beat well with a wire whisk from fifteen to twenty minutes, or until the mixture looks light and frothy. The water in the saucepan underneath ought to be kept slowly simmering. When ready, remove the basin to the table and continue the beating a few minutes longer. Stir in the flour and butter very lightly, a little at a time, and do not mix more than is necessary. Add a few drops of any flavouring that is liked. Pour the mixture out on a shallow tin lined with paper, but not greased. The shape of the tin must depend upon what the pastry is to be used for. Bake in a quick oven for about twenty minutes until lightly browned and firm to the touch. When ready, turn out on a sheet of sugared paper and place on a wire stand to cool.

Brown Genoise Pastry.—Melt 2 oz. of unsweetened chocolate in a table-spoonful of water and add it to the above mixtures before beating up the eggs.

Pink Genoise Pastry.—Add a few drops of carmine to the above mixtures just before baking.

Note.—Genoise pastry is used for various kinds of fancy cakes. (For Icing and Decoration, see p. 227.)

Girdle Cakes

Make some pastry (flaky or rough puff will do) and roll it out to a quarter of an inch in thickness. Cut out into squares or oblong-shaped pieces, and place these on a hot girdle. Brown first on the one side and then on the other until the pastry is thoroughly cooked. Then split, butter, and serve hot.

Note.—A few currants may be rolled into the pastry before cooking.

Ginger Cakes (Small)

Ingredients—

4 oz. Flour.
4 oz. Butter.
4 oz. Sugar.
½ tea-sp. Ground Ginger.
2 Eggs.
A few drops of Ginger Essence.
½ tea-sp. Baking Powder.
1 oz. candied Lemon Peel.

Method.—Cream the butter and sugar together, and add to them the ground ginger, essence of ginger, and the lemon peel chopped finely. Then add one egg and half the flour and beat well, then the other egg and the remainder of the flour and beat again. When the mixture is light and frothy-looking mix in the baking powder, and half fill small tins that have been greased and dusted out with flour and sugar (see p. 213). Place the tins on a baking-sheet, and bake the cakes in a moderate oven from fifteen to twenty minutes, or until they feel firm to the touch.

Honey Cakes

Ingredients—

1 lb. Honey.
½ lb. Butter.
1 lb. Flour.
A pinch of Salt.
½ lb. Ground Almonds.
A pinch of Ground Cloves.
Grated Rind of half a Lemon.
½ oz. Carbonate of Soda.

Method.—Sieve the flour, salt, carbonate of soda, and ground cloves into a basin, add the almonds and grated lemon rind, and make a well in the centre. Melt the butter and honey in a lined saucepan, and pour them into the centre of the dry ingredients. Mix together until all is thoroughly blended, then cover the basin and allow the mixture to stand all night. Next day sprinkle the paste with a little flour and turn it out on a baking-board. Flour a rolling-pin and roll out the paste to half an inch in thickness. Cut in small square pieces or round cakes, and place them on a greased and floured tin. Brush over the top of the cake with slightly beaten white of egg, and sprinkle with some chopped almonds. Bake in a moderate oven about fifteen minutes, or until the cakes feel firm to the touch and are of a pale brown colour.

Queen Cakes

Ingredients—

4 oz. Flour.
4 oz. Butter.
4 oz. Sugar.
A pinch of Salt.
2 Eggs.
½ tea-sp. Baking Powder.
A little grated Lemon Rind.
A few Currants.

Method.—Grease nine or ten small tins, and dust them out with flour and sugar mixed (see p. 213). Place a few cleaned currants at the foot of each, and then proceed to make the mixture. Cream the butter and sugar together in a basin, and add the salt and grated lemon rind. Sieve the flour, and add half of it to the creamed butter and sugar with one of the eggs. Mix slowly, and then beat well for a few minutes. Add the second egg and the remainder of the flour, and beat again. Sprinkle in the baking powder at the last, and half fill the prepared tins with the mixture. Bake the cakes in a moderate oven from fifteen to twenty minutes, and, when ready, allow them to cool on a sieve or wire stand.

Rice Buns

Ingredients—

2 oz. Ground Rice.
3 oz. Flour.
3 oz. Sugar.
2 oz. Butter.
2 Eggs.
½ tea-sp. Baking Powder.
A little Flavouring.

Method.—Make in the same way as Queen Cakes.

Note.—This mixture may, if liked, be made in one large cake. It will take about one hour to bake.

Walnut Buns

Ingredients—

2 oz. Flour.
1 oz. Rice-flour.
3 oz. Castor Sugar
3 oz. Butter.
3 oz. shelled Walnuts.
2 Eggs.
A pinch of Nutmeg.
1 table-spoonful Cream.
½ tea-sp. Baking Powder.
Some Red Currant Jelly.

Method.—Cream the butter and sugar. Toast the walnuts for a few minutes in a moderate oven, then pound or chop them rather finely. Reserve one table-spoonful of these, and add the rest to the creamed butter and sugar with one egg and the rice-flour. Mix well for a few minutes, then add the other egg, flour, cream, nutmeg, and baking powder. Beat well for a few minutes longer, and half fill small tins which have been greased and dusted out with equal parts of flour and castor sugar mixed. Bake in a good oven about fifteen minutes. Turn out and cool slightly. Then coat the top of the buns with red currant jelly and sprinkle them with the remainder of the walnuts.

PLAIN AND FANCY BISCUITS FOR DESSERT AND AFTERNOON TEA

Ayrshire Shortbread

Ingredients—

½ lb. Flour.
½ lb. Rice-flour.
½ lb. Butter.
4 oz. Castor Sugar.
1 Egg.
1 or 2 table-spoonfuls Cream.

Method.—Sieve the two kinds of flour into a basin, and rub the butter into them. Sieve in the sugar, and add the flavouring. Beat up the egg in a small basin, and add a little cream to it; pour this into the centre of the dry ingredients, and mix all into a paste with the hand, using more cream if necessary. Turn out on a floured board, and knead lightly until free from cracks. Flour a rolling-pin, and roll out the paste to about ¼ inch in thickness. Stamp it out in small rounds with a cutter, and place the biscuits on a greased and floured tin. Roll the scraps again, and cut out more biscuits until all is used, then bake the biscuits in a moderate oven from ten to fifteen minutes. Sprinkle them well with sugar while they are still hot, and lift them on to a sieve or wire stand to cool.

Note.—These biscuits will keep crisp if placed in a tin box with paper.

Bachelors' Buttons

Ingredients—

5 oz. Flour.
3 oz. Castor Sugar.
2 oz. Butter.
1 Egg.
A little Flavouring.

Method.—Cream the butter and sugar together, and add a little flavouring. Beat the egg, and add it gradually with the flour until a stiffish paste is formed. Do not add all the egg unless necessary. Take small portions of the mixture and roll them into balls the size of a hazel nut, using a little flour to prevent them sticking to the hands. Place them on a greased and floured tin, and when all are ready sprinkle them with sugar. Bake in a good oven about twelve minutes or until the biscuits are lightly browned, then lift them on to a sieve to cool.

Cheese Straws

Ingredients—

3 oz. Flour.
2 oz. Butter.
2 oz. grated Parmesan Cheese.
½ yolk of Egg.
A pinch of Cayenne.
A pinch of Salt.
A little Water.

Method.—Rub the butter lightly into the flour. Add the grated cheese and seasoning, and mix into a paste with half the yolk of an egg beaten with a little water. Make the pastry rather stiff, and work with the hands until free from cracks. Then roll it out on a floured board into a strip about four inches wide. Trim evenly at the edges, and cut most of the pastry into straws about quarter an inch wide. Place these on a greased tin, and out of the remainder of the pastry cut six or eight rings. Bake all together in a good oven for about ten minutes. Watch them most carefully, as they burn very quickly. Serve them with a bundle of straws placed in each ring.

Cinnamon Biscuits

Ingredients—

½ lb. Flour.
¼ lb. Castor Sugar.
1 yolk of Egg.
1 tea-sp. Ground Ginger.
Milk if necessary.
¼ lb. Butter.

Method.—Sieve all the dry ingredients into a basin and rub in the butter with the tips of the fingers until free from lumps. Then bind together with the yolk of an egg, and a little milk if necessary. The dough must not be made too soft, but of the consistency of pastry. Knead with the hand until free from cracks, and turn out on a slightly floured board. Flour a rolling-pin and roll out the dough to one-eighth of an inch in thickness. Finish in the same way as Ayrshire Shortbread (p. 218).

Cinnamon Macaroons

Ingredients—

½ lb. Ground Almonds.
½ lb. Icing Sugar.
1 oz. Flour.
½ tea-spoonful Ground Cinnamon.
Some White of Egg.

Icing—3 table-spoonfuls Icing Sugar, 1 tea-spoonful Flour, White of Egg.

Method.—Sieve the flour, icing sugar, and cinnamon on to the baking-board, and mix with the ground almonds. Then add gradually enough white of egg to form a very stiff paste. Work with the hands until perfectly smooth and elastic, and form into a long roll quite free from cracks. Flour the rolling-pin and press out the roll into an even strip, keeping it perfectly straight at the edges so as to avoid any waste. Then prepare the icing. Mix the flour and icing sugar together, and bind with a very little white of egg. Spread this smoothly over the almond paste with a wetted knife, and then cut in neat fingers. Place these on a greased and floured tin, and bake in a moderate oven until a light brown colour, and firm and crisp to the touch.

Cocoanut Biscuits

Ingredients—

2 oz. Desiccated Cocoanut.
2 oz. Castor Sugar.
1 tea-spoonful Flour.
1 white of Egg.
Wafer Paper.

Method.—Chop the cocoanut a little more finely if necessary, and mix it in a basin with the other dry ingredients. Whip the white of egg to a stiff froth, and bind all together with this. Put small squares of wafer paper on a dry baking-tin, arrange a tea-spoonful of the mixture on each, and bake in a slow oven for half-an-hour, or until the biscuits are firm and of a pale brown colour. Cool them on a sieve, breaking off the wafer paper which projects beyond the edges.

These biscuits should be kept in paper in an air-tight tin box.

Ginger Biscuits

Ingredients—

½ lb. Flour.
4 oz. Castor Sugar.
A little Sherry.
¼ lb. Butter.
1 oz. Ground Ginger.

Method.—Sieve the flour, sugar, and ginger into a basin, and rub in the butter until free from lumps. Then form into a stiff paste with sherry, turn on to a floured board, and knead with the hands until free from cracks. Flour a rolling-pin, and roll the paste out very thinly.

Cut it into small round or fancy-shaped pieces with a cutter, lay them on a greased tin, and bake in a moderate oven from ten to fifteen minutes.

Macaroons

Ingredients—

½ lb. Ground Almonds.	A squeeze of Lemon Juice.
½ lb. Castor Sugar.	Wafer Paper.
3 or 4 Whites of Eggs.	

Method.—Put the almonds and sugar into a basin, and add the lemon juice and the white of eggs very gradually, beating well with a wooden spoon or spatula. Beat thoroughly and make the mixture just moist enough to drop from a spoon. Put it into a forcing-bag with a plain pipe at the end, and force out small portions on rounds or squares of wafer paper. This quantity should make twelve. Dust over with icing sugar, which will make the macaroons crack on the top, and place a half-blanched and split almond on the top of each. Bake in a very moderate oven until nicely browned, dry, and well risen. Lift on to a sieve to cool, and break off any scraps of wafer paper that extend beyond the edges.

Milk Biscuits

Ingredients—

½ lb. Flour.	1 gill of Milk.
1 tea-sp. Baking Powder.	1 oz. Butter.
A pinch of Salt.	

Method.—Sieve the flour, salt, and baking powder into a basin, and make a well in the centre. Melt the butter in a small saucepan, add the milk, and make it just lukewarm. Pour this into the centre of the flour and mix all together. Flour a baking-board, turn the paste on to it, and knead with the hands until free from cracks. Then roll out as thin as possible, and prick all over with a fork or biscuit-pricker. Stamp out in rounds with a cutter about three inches in diameter, place the biscuits on a greased tin, and bake them in a moderate oven for about twenty minutes. The oven must not be too hot, but regular. When the biscuits are ready, remove them from the tins and put them on a sieve or wire stand to cool.

Norwegian Biscuits

Ingredients—

4 oz. Flour.	2 oz. Castor Sugar.
4 oz. Rice-flour.	2 table-spoonfuls Cream.
1 oz. Butter.	1 oz. Ground Almonds.

Method.—Make in the same way as Ayrshire Shortbread (p. 218), sprinkling the ground almonds over the biscuits before baking.

Oatmeal Biscuits

Ingredients—

3 oz. Flour.	1½ oz. Butter.
3 oz. Oatmeal.	A pinch of Baking Powder.
1 oz. Sugar, or ¼ tea-sp. Salt.	A little Water or Milk.

Method.—Put all the dry ingredients into a basin, and rub in the butter with the tips of the fingers until free from lumps. Beat up the egg in a small basin, add half of it to the mixture, and then enough water or milk to form all into one lump. Knead with the hands until free from cracks, and turn the dough on to a floured board. Finish in the same way as Ayrshire Shortbread (p. 218).

Note.—Wheaten meal may be used instead of oatmeal.

Raspberry Biscuits

Take any sweet biscuits, such as Milan or Ayrshire shortbread, and place two together with a little raspberry jam between. Coat them with raspberry glacé icing (p. 226) and decorate them with a few chopped pistachio nuts or small pieces of preserved fruit.

LARGE CAKES

Angel Cake

Ingredients—

2 oz. Vienna Flour.	1 tea-spoonful Orange Flower Water.
1 tea-spoonful Cream of Tartar.	6 whites of Eggs.
A pinch of Salt.	3 oz. Castor Sugar.

Method.—Dry and sieve the flour with the cream of tartar. Add a pinch of salt to the whites of eggs, and beat them to the stiffest possible froth. Well sieve the sugar, and mix it very lightly in. Then the flour and cream of tartar in the same way, and lastly the flavouring. Do not stop beating after the mixing is begun, and keep the mixture as light as possible. Bake in a perfectly clean and ungreased tin, and from twenty to thirty minutes in a moderate oven. Test the cake with a fine skewer before removing it from the oven, and do not allow it to become too brown. When ready turn the cake upside down on a sheet of paper and leave it until the tin can be slipped off quite easily. The cake may be iced with fondant or glacé icing if desired.

Cherry Cake

Ingredients—

½ lb. Flour.	½ tea-sp. Baking Powder.
3 Eggs.	2 or 3 oz. Glacé Cherries.
5 oz. Castor Sugar.	A pinch of Nutmeg.
4 oz. Butter.	

Method.—Cream the butter and sugar. Sieve the flour, and add it to the butter and sugar by degrees with the eggs, beating well after the addition of each egg. Lift the mixture well up in the basin while mixing, and make it very light. Add the cherries cut in small pieces, baking powder and nutmeg at the last, mix them gently in, but do not beat again. Pour the mixture into a small lined cake tin, and bake in a good oven about three-quarters of an hour.

Chocolate Tea Cake

Ingredients—

- 4 oz. Butter.
- 3 oz. Castor Sugar.
- 3 oz. Grated Chocolate.
- 1 oz. Ground Almonds.
- Grated Rind of half a Lemon.
- 4 oz. Vienna Flour.
- 1 dessert-spoonful Orange Flower Water.
- 1 tea-sp. Baking Powder.
- A pinch of Ground Cinnamon.
- A pinch of Nutmeg
- 3 small Eggs.

Method.—Sieve the sugar, cinnamon, chocolate, and nutmeg into a basin. Add the butter and beat together with a wooden spoon until of a soft creamy consistency. Then add the eggs and flour by degrees, beating and mixing well between the addition of each egg. Flavour to taste, and add the baking powder at the last. Pour into a tin that has been greased and dusted out with flour and sugar mixed, and bake the cake in a moderate oven about one hour, until well risen and until it feels dry when tested with a skewer.

Note.—When cold, this cake may be iced with chocolate glacé icing (p. 225), and then decorated with crystallised violets and leaves cut out of angelica or any other suitable decoration that will form a nice contrast to the brown icing.

Christmas Cake

Ingredients—

- 1 lb. Butter.
- 1 lb. Castor Sugar.
- 2 lbs. Flour.
- 3 lbs. Currants.
- 1 lb. Candied Peel.
- ½ lb. Sweet Almonds.
- 1 tea-spoonful Ground Cinnamon.
- 1 tea-spoonful Mixed Spice.
- 12 Eggs.
- 2 glasses Brandy.

Method.—Put the butter and sugar into a large warm basin, and beat them together to a cream. Add the yolks of eggs and spices, and beat for a few minutes. Have the whites of eggs beaten to a stiff froth, and add them next alternately with the flour. Beat again for twenty minutes. Add the fruit, carefully prepared, and the brandy at the last. Pour the mixture into one or two well-lined cake tins, and bake in a moderate and steady oven from two to four hours according to size. This cake ought to be kept at least three months before it is cut. It should be wrapped in a clean cloth or paper, and stored in a tin box. It may be iced in the same way as a wedding-cake (p. 226).

Easter Cake

Make in the same way as Simnel Cake (p. 224). Arrange the almond paste on the top of the cake in the form of a bird's nest. Score roughly with a fork and brown lightly in the oven or under the grill of the gas stove. Finish off by putting a few sweets to imitate birds' eggs in the hollow.

German Pound Cake

Ingredients—

- 6 oz. Butter.
- 6 oz. Castor Sugar.
- 10 oz. Flour.
- The grated rind of half a Lemon.
- ½ lb. Sultanas.
- ¼ lb. Candied Peel.
- 5 Eggs.
- ½ tea-sp. Baking Powder.

Method.—First clean and pick the sultanas, and shred the candied peel very finely. Then put the butter and sugar into a basin, and beat them to a cream. Add the grated lemon rind, one egg, and a little of the flour sieved, and mix well for a few minutes. Add the second egg and a little more flour, and so on, repeating this process until all the eggs and flour have been added. Beat all together for about ten minutes, lifting the mixture well up in the spoon so as to introduce some air. Mix in the fruit and baking powder at the last, but do not beat again, or the fruit will be inclined to fall in the baking. Pour the mixture into a lined cake tin, and bake in a moderate oven for two hours, or until thoroughly cooked and nicely browned. When ready, remove the cake from the oven, allow it to stand a few minutes, then turn on to a wire stand to cool.

Gingerbread

Ingredients—

- 1 lb. Flour.
- ¼ lb. Sugar.
- ¼ lb. Butter, Lard, or Dripping.
- ½ lb. Syrup or Treacle.
- 2 oz. Sweet Almonds.
- 1 gill Buttermilk or Water.
- 2 Eggs.
- ¼ lb. Candied Peel.
- 1 dessert-spoonful Ground Ginger.
- 1 tea-sp. Ground Cinnamon.
- 1 tea-sp. Baking Soda.
- A pinch of Cayenne.

Method.—Sieve the flour, spices, and soda into a large basin, and rub in the fat until free from lumps. Add the sugar, peel finely shred, and the almonds blanched and shred, and mix well. Make a well in the centre, pour in the treacle or syrup slightly warmed, the eggs well beaten, and the buttermilk or water. Mix in the dry ingredients from the sides of the basin, and beat all well for a few minutes. Pour the mixture into a greased shallow tin, and bake in a moderate oven for at least one hour, or until firm to the touch.

Note.—The fruit may be omitted from this recipe, or sultanas or currants added as desired.

Holiday Cake

Ingredients—

- 1 lb. Flour.
- ½ lb. Butter.
- ½ lb. Currants.
- ¼ lb. Mixed Peel.
- ½ lb. Sultanas.
- ¾ lb. Demerara Sugar.
- 2 tea-spoonfuls Mixed Spice.
- ½ pint Stout.
- Rind of 1 Lemon.
- 1 tea-sp. Carbonate of Soda.
- 4 Eggs.

Method.—First prepare the fruit (see p. 212),

and mix it with a little of the flour. Then put the rest of the flour into a large basin, and rub in the butter until free from lumps. Add the fruit and other dry ingredients except the soda, mix all together, and make a well in the centre. Heat the stout in a small saucepan and add the soda to it. Mix quickly, and while still frothy pour it into the centre of the dry ingredients. Add also the eggs well beaten, and beat all together for fifteen minutes. Pour the mixture into a lined cake tin, and bake in a slow oven for three hours.

Invalid Cake

Ingredients—

3 oz. Flour.
2 Eggs.
2 oz. Castor Sugar.
½ tea-sp. Baking Powder.
2 oz. Butter.
Half Lemon Rind grated.

Method.—Make in the same way as cherry cake (p. 220). Or the mixture may be baked in small patty pans that have been greased and dusted out with flour and sugar; ten or fifteen minutes will be sufficient to cook them.

Jam Sandwich

Ingredients—

3 Eggs, their weight in Butter, Flour, and Sugar.
A few drops of Vanilla or other flavouring.
2 or 3 table-spoonfuls Jam.

Method.—Make the cake mixture according to directions given for cherry cake (p. 220), beat it well. Pour the mixture into two sandwich cake tins that have been lined with paper, and bake in a good oven from fifteen to twenty minutes. When the cakes are nicely browned and cooked through, turn them out on a sheet of sugared paper, and, when cool, spread one with jam, and place the other on the top.

Jubilee Cake

Ingredients—

10 oz. Butter.
10 oz. Sugar.
14 oz. Flour.
¼ lb. Candied Peel.
¼ lb. Glacé Cherries.
A few drops of Vanilla Essence.
¼ lb. Sultanas.
2 oz. Sweet Almonds.
6 Eggs.

Almond Paste—½ lb. Ground Almonds, ¼ lb. Castor Sugar, ¼ lb. Icing Sugar, 1 table-spoonful Brandy, and 1 or 2 whites of Egg.

White Glacé Icing—Page 225.

Decorations—2 oz. Shred and Browned Almonds, some Red Jam, and a few Pistachio Nuts.

Method.—Make the cake in the same way as German pound (p. 221) and bake in a moderate oven from two to three hours until well risen and firm to the touch. When ready, lift the cake on to a sieve, and let it cool. Prepare the almond paste as on p. 225, and put a nice smooth layer on the top of the cake, and set it aside for several hours to become quite dry. Then coat the top with a little white glacé icing. Coat the sides of the cake with some red jam, and then with a layer of shredded almonds and pistachio nuts, or with browned cocoanut and some cocoanut coloured pink with cochineal. The top of the cake may be further decorated with some pieces of preserve fruits or with some of the icing put through a forcing-bag, and little silver balls.

Luncheon Cake

Ingredients—

¾ lb. Flour.
¼ lb. Rice-flour.
6 oz. Castor Sugar.
¼ lb. Butter.
3 large Eggs.
½ lb. Currants.
2 oz. Candied Peel.
A pinch of Nutmeg.
1 tea-sp. Carbonate of Soda.
The grated Rind of half a Lemon.
1 gill of Milk.

Method.—Sieve the flour, rice-flour, and sugar into a basin, and rub in the butter until free from lumps. Then add the nutmeg, lemon rind, sugar, and fruit, carefully prepared. Mix together, and make a well in the centre. Heat the milk in a small saucepan, add the soda to it, and, while still frothy, pour it into the midst of the dry ingredients. Add also the eggs, the yolks and whites beaten separately, and mix all together. Beat the mixture well for a few minutes, and then pour it into a cake tin that has been lined with paper (see p. 212). Bake the cake in a moderate oven for about two hours.

Madeira Cake

Ingredients—

6 oz. Butter.
6 oz. Castor Sugar.
9 oz. Flour.
4 large Eggs.
½ tea-sp. Baking Powder.
Grated Rind of half a Lemon, or 3 or 4 drops of Vanilla Essence.
1 or 2 Strips of Citron Peel.

Method.—Cream the butter and sugar. Beat the eggs in a separate basin until they are light and frothy, and add them to the creamed butter and sugar. Mix well for a few minutes. Sieve the flour and baking powder, and mix these lightly but thoroughly into the other mixture. Have ready a cake tin lined with paper, pour in the mixture, not more than half filling it, and bake in a moderate oven from one and a half to two hours, or until the cake is well risen and feels firm to the touch. When the cake has been in the oven about twenty minutes place the strips of citron peel on the top.

Mocha Cake

Ingredients—

¼ lb. Castor Sugar.
¼ lb. Vienna Flour.
A few drops of Vanilla Essence.
4 Eggs.
1 tea-sp. Baking Powder.
Mocha Icing.

Method.—First prepare a plain round cake tin in the same manner as for a sponge cake (p. 213), then proceed to make the cake.

Separate the yolks from the whites of the eggs, putting each into a medium-sized basin. Sieve the flour with the baking powder, and put it in a warm place until required. Add the sugar and vanilla to the yolks of eggs, and cream these together with a wire whisk from ten to fifteen minutes, or until they look very light in colour and consistency. Then whip the whites to a stiff froth and stir them very lightly in, and alternately with a little flour, turning the mixture over and over and as delicately as possible. When all is blended, pour the mixture into the prepared tin, place it on a bed of salt or sand on a baking-tin, and bake in a good oven for half-an-hour, or until well risen and firm to the touch. As soon as the top is brown, the cake ought to be covered with paper to prevent it taking too deep a colour. Allow the cake to stand for five minutes after removing it from the oven, then turn it out on a sieve and let it cool gradually. Then ice the cake as below :—

To Ice the Cake.—Prepare some Mocha icing as on p. 227, and keep it on ice or in a very cool place until it is required. Split the cake once or twice according to height, spread each piece with a layer of the icing, and put the cake back into shape. Then with a spatula or broad-bladed knife spread the top, and, if wished, the sides of the cake with the icing. Put the remainder into a forcing-bag with a rather large fancy-shaped pipe at the end of it, and force out pretty patterns on the top of the cake. A few crystallised violets or pistachio nuts may be used as an ornamentation, or any sweet that will make a pretty contrast in colour to the brown icing. Allow the cake to stand in a cool place for an hour or two before cutting, so as to harden the icing.

Orange Cake

Ingredients—

6 oz. Vienna Flour.
The grated Rind of 1 Orange.
3 Eggs.
1 tea-sp. Baking Powder.
5 oz. Castor Sugar.

Method.—Sieve the sugar into a basin, grate the orange rind on the top of it, and rub the two together with the tips of the fingers until they are thoroughly blended. Add the eggs to the orange sugar, and beat with a wire whisk about fifteen minutes until smooth and creamy. Then add the flour dried and sifted, and also the baking powder. Mix these in very lightly, and pour the mixture into a tin that has been greased and dusted out with a mixture of flour and sugar. Bake in a quick oven from twenty to thirty minutes, and, when ready, turn carefully on to a sieve to cool.

Coat the cake with icing and decorate with chopped pistachio nuts, crystallised violets, or small sections of crystallised orange.

Note.—Instead of icing this cake, it may be split when cold, and spread with the following cream mixture :—Whip one gill of double cream until quite thick, sweeten to taste, and flavour with orange flavouring.

Pitcaithly Bannock

Ingredients—

½ lb. Butter.
¾ lb. Flour.
¼ lb. Rice-flour.
2 oz. Sweet Almonds.
2 oz. Candied Orange Peel.
¼ oz. Castor Sugar.
A little Flavouring.

Method.—Warm the butter slightly and then beat it to a cream. Blanch and chop the almonds, and shred the peel very finely. Mix all the other ingredients with the creamed butter, and knead into one lump with the hands. This may take some little time, but no liquid must be used. Form into a round flat cake about one and a half inches thick, and prick all over with a fork. Place the cake on a baking-tin and tie a band of double paper round it. Bake in a moderate oven from one to one and a half hours, or until the cake feels firm and is a nice brown colour. Allow it to cool on the tin before removing it, and take off the band of paper.

Note.—This cake should be rolled in paper and kept in an air-tight tin box, and then broken in pieces when required.

Scotch Seed Cake

Ingredients—

½ lb. Butter.
½ lb. Castor Sugar.
14 oz. Flour.
6 Eggs.
½ lb. Candied Peel.
¼ lb. Sweet Almonds.
1 tea-sp. Baking Powder.
A little grated Lemon Rind.
Some Sugar Carraways.

Method.—Shred the candied peel finely, and blanch and chop the almonds. Mix them with about one table-spoonful of the flour, or just sufficient to prevent them clotting together, and then make the cake mixture according to directions given for German pound cake (p. 221). Pour into a papered cake tin and put some sugar carraways on the top. Bake in a moderate oven from two to two and a half hours.

Shortbread

Ingredients—

4 oz. Flour.
2 oz. Rice-flour.
4 oz. Butter.
2 oz. Castor Sugar.
A few drops of Flavouring.

Method.—Sieve all the dry ingredients into a basin, and rub in the butter. Add the flavouring and then knead all into one lump without using any liquid. Turn out on a board sprinkled with rice-flour, and form into a smooth round. If a shortbread mould is obtainable, shape the cake in that; if not, pinch it round the edges with the fingers, or mark it with a knife. Then place the shortbread on a greased baking-tin, and prick it all over with a fork. A strip of candied peel may be put on the top if wished, or any other decoration that is desired. Bake in a moderate oven from twenty to thirty minutes or until the shortbread is of a uniform brown colour, and feels firm to the touch. Allow it to cool before removing it from the tin.

Note.—If the dough becomes rather soft in the making, it will be well to allow the shortbread to stand until quite cool before baking, otherwise it is apt to lose its form.

Simnel Cake

Ingredients—

1 lb. Flour.	¼ lb. Candied Peel.
½ lb. Butter.	½ lb. Valencia Raisins.
½ lb. Castor Sugar.	¾ lb. Currants.
5 Eggs.	1 gill Brandy.
The grated Rind of 1 Lemon.	¼ tea-sp. Ground Ginger.
The grated Rind of 1 Orange.	¼ tea-sp. Ground Cinnamon.
1 tea-sp. Baking Powder.	¼ tea-sp. Grated Nutmeg.
½ lb. Sultanas.	

Almond Icing (see p. 225).

Method.—First prepare the fruit (see p. 212), and mix it with one table-spoonful of the dry flour. Then take a strong cake tin and line it with at least two folds of thick white paper. When these are ready, proceed to make the cake. Cream the butter and sugar. Add the spices, grated orange and lemon rinds, yolks of eggs, and brandy. Beat for a few minutes, and add the flour sieved and the whites of the eggs beaten to a stiff froth. Mix very lightly, and stir in the prepared fruit and baking powder last of all. Do not beat after the fruit is added. Pour the mixture into the prepared cake tin, smooth it over the top, and bake in a steady oven from two to three hours.

This cake improves with keeping, and should not be cut for three or four weeks after making.

A Simnel Cake is usually coated with almond paste, and this should be put on two or three days before the cake is to be used.

To Coat with Almond Paste.—Take the quantity of almond paste, given on p. 225, and spread it smoothly on the cake. Then take a fork and score the paste across first one way and then the other, and coat lightly with beaten yolk of egg. Place the cake in a moderate oven, or place it beneath the grill light on a gas stove until the almond paste is nicely browned.

Note.—Sometimes a layer of almond paste is put in the middle of this cake. When this is desired, half the above quantity of the paste should be made before the cake is baked, and this should be made in a round the size of the cake tin and laid in the middle of the mixture before baking.

Sponge Cake

Ingredients—

5 oz. Loaf Sugar.	2 whole Eggs and 1 Yolk.
1 wine-glassful Water.	A little grated Lemon Rind.
¼ lb. Flour (Vienna).	

Method.—Put the sugar and water into a small lined saucepan, bring them to the boil, and simmer slowly for five minutes. Beat the eggs slightly in a basin with a wire whisk, and pour the syrup of sugar and water on to them, stirring all the time. Then whisk steadily for half-an-hour, until the mixture looks light and frothy and is well risen in the basin. Dry and sieve the flour, and mix it in lightly at the last, with a little grated lemon rind or any other flavouring preferred. Pour the mixture into a cake tin prepared according to directions given on p. 213, and do not more than half fill the tin. Bake the cake in a very steady oven for about three-quarters of an hour, or until it is well risen and feels firm to the touch. If the heat from the oven is great, stand the cake on a bed of sand placed on a baking-tin, or put a tile or brick under the tin.

Wedding Cake

Ingredients—

1½ lb. Fresh Butter.	4 lbs. Currants.
½ lb. dark Treacle.	½ lb. Sweet Almonds.
1½ lb. raw Sugar.	2 or 3 Bitter Almonds.
½ pint warm Milk.	½ lb. Citron Peel.
½ pint Brandy.	½ lb. Orange and Lemon Peel.
1 tea-spoonful Salt.	2 lbs. Flour.
12 Eggs.	Almond and Royal Icing.

Method.—Put the butter into a large and warm basin, and beat it to a cream with the hand or with a large wooden spoon. Add the sugar and treacle slightly warmed, and beat again for a few minutes. Then add the eggs two at a time, beating the mixture well after each addition. (It will be safer to break the eggs into a small basin previous to adding them to the mixture, to ensure their being fresh.) Have the fruit carefully prepared (p. 212), and mixed with one or two table-spoonfuls of the flour, and add it next with the milk, brandy, and salt. Dry and sieve the flour, and add it last of all. The mixture must not be beaten after the flour is added. When all is thoroughly blended pour the mixture into two lined cake tins, one of which is three or four sizes smaller than the other, and bake in a moderate and steady oven. The larger cake will probably require from four to five hours to bake, and a smaller one less in proportion. When the cakes begin to brown they should be covered with a double fold of white paper to prevent them burning on the top. The success of the cake will depend very much upon the long steady baking. When the cakes are baked and cold, they should be wrapped in a thick sheet of white paper or a cloth, and kept in a tin box for two or three months before being iced or used.

Note.—For icing and decoration of cakes, see pp. 225 and 226.

ICING AND DECORATION OF CAKES

The following are a few of the materials which may be used for decorating purposes :—

Coloured Sugars.—Put some coarse granulated sugar on to a stiff sheet of white paper, and pour a few drops of liquid colouring on the top. Work this in with the point of a knife until an even tint is obtained, and then leave the sugar to dry. Pink, green, yellow, &c.,

sugar may be made in this way, and these sugars will keep if put in corked bottles.

Pistachio Kernels.—Put these into cold water, and bring them quickly to the boil. Then drain and pour plenty of cold water over them. Rub off the skins, and dry the pistachios in a cloth. Shred or chop before using.

Browned or Coloured Almonds.—First blanch the almonds (see p. 212), and dry them thoroughly. Shred them finely, or chop them rather roughly. To brown the almonds, put them on a tin in a very moderate oven, and keep turning them over and over until very evenly and lightly browned. To colour them, sprinkle a few drops of colouring on the top, and rub it into the almonds. Pistachio nuts (which are much more expensive than almonds) may be imitated by colouring the almonds pale green.

Cocoanut.—This may also be browned or coloured in the same way as almonds, and used for decorating purposes.

Candied Cherries and other Fruits.—These are very pretty and useful for decorating cakes, and as they will keep almost indefinitely in an air-tight tin box, they are not expensive. They are generally cut in pieces unless they are very small.

Angelica.—This is also a very effective decoration. If it is hard and sugary, soak it in warm water for a minute or two, then dry. Cut it first into thin strips, then into diamond-shaped pieces to represent leaves, stars, rounds, &c. A combination of angelica and cherries is very pretty.

Nuts, such as walnuts, filberts, Barcelona nuts, &c., either plain, or iced, or caramelised, may also be used.

Bonbons.—These may be had in many forms, and if tastefully used they make a very simple and easy decoration. Silver and gold dragees are among the most useful.

Crystallised Flowers.—These can be bought ready, such as rose petals, violets, orange flowers, lilac; and leaves to suit can be cut from angelica, or even from citron peel.

VARIOUS ICINGS

Almond Paste or Icing

Proportions—

1 lb. Ground Almonds.	Juice of half a Lemon.
½ lb. Icing Sugar.	1 or 2 table-sp. Brandy.
½ lb. Castor Sugar.	Yolks or Whites of Eggs.

Method.—Be particular to choose good ground almonds; unless they are well preserved they are liable to have a bitter or mouldy taste, or perhaps no taste at all. Put the ground almonds into a strong basin, and sieve the two sugars on the top of them. Add the flavouring, lemon juice, and brandy. The brandy may, of course, be omitted if it is objected to, but it renders the almond paste more wholesome, and it will keep better. Then add enough egg to bind all together. Knead well with the hand, adding the moisture very gradually. Either yolks or whites of eggs may be used; the yolks will make the paste richer and yellower, the whites drier and of a paler colour. Or both yolks and whites may be used if it is more convenient. The paste ought to be very smooth when finished, and just moist enough to be bound together.

Sometimes, for fancy purposes, the almond paste is coloured pink, green, &c., and different flavourings used.

To Use the Almond Paste.—This is generally used for coating rich fruit cakes, such as wedding, Christmas, or Simnel cakes. Cut the cake to be iced flat on the top, or coat the foot of it. Lay on a nice thick layer of the paste and shape it first with the hands. Then take a wetted knife, and make the top and sides perfectly smooth and level, and a sharp straight ridge round the edges. If the cake is to be iced with a white icing as well, allow the almond paste to become quite dry and hard before putting on the second icing. Sometimes, as in the case of a Simnel or Easter cake, no white icing is put on the top. In this case the almond paste should be scored across with a fork, or marked in checks with a fluted roller, brushed over with yolk of egg, and browned under a gas grill or in a quick oven.

Glacé Icing

Proportions—

½ lb. Icing Sugar.
About 3 table-spoonfuls Water or other Liquid.

Method.—This is a simple soft icing, and one that is very quickly made. Sieve the sugar and put it into an enamelled saucepan or sugar-boiler. Add the liquid (see below) very gradually and stir over the fire until warm. The icing must not be made too hot or it will become lumpy and have a dull appearance. Whilst adding the liquid it must be borne in mind that, as the sugar melts, the icing will become softer. The icing must be just soft enough to pour over the cake and perfectly smooth. The following are a few of the colourings and flavourings in which this icing may be made:—

Chocolate Glacé.—Dissolve 1½ or 2 oz. unsweetened chocolate in a *very* little water until it is perfectly smooth. Prepare the above icing with water and a few drops of vanilla, and add it to the chocolate. Mix the two together and use.

Coffee Glacé Icing.—Use strong coffee or essence of coffee and a little water to moisten the icing. One or two drops of vanilla may be added if liked.

Tea Glacé Icing.—Make in the same way, using tea instead of coffee.

Lemon or Orange Glacé Icing.—Use strained

orange or lemon juice to moisten the icing, adding water if necessary. A little yellow colouring may also be added, the same as in fondant icing.

Raspberry or Strawberry Glacé Icing.—Use raspberry or strawberry syrup to moisten the icing.

If by any chance this icing should become too soft in the making it may be stiffened by adding more sieved icing sugar, but it is always better if this has not to be done.

To Use the Icing.—This icing may either be poured over the cakes, or the cakes may be dipped into it. If a large cake is to be iced, put it on a wire stand placed on a sheet of white paper, and pour over enough icing to cover the top only, or the top and sides as desired. Any icing that runs over may be gathered up and used again. Small cakes may be iced in the same way, or they may be held on the point of a palette knife over the pan of icing, and the icing poured over them, or they may be dipped right into the icing.

Royal Icing

Proportions—

½ table-sp. Lemon Juice, or 6 drops of Acetic Acid.	6 or 7 Whites of Eggs
A little Blue Colouring.	2 lbs. Icing Sugar.

Method.—This is a hard white icing used principally for the icing of wedding, birthday, or Christmas cakes. Sieve the sugar, and put most of it into a basin, reserving a small proportion in case the icing should be made too moist, when this may be used. Add a *very* little blue colouring, either a drop of liquid blue or a tiny dust of stone washing blue, and just enough to take off the yellow shade from the sugar, and to make the icing a finer white. Then put in some acid, lemon juice, or acetic acid, as without this the icing would not harden on the cake. Now add the whites of eggs by degrees, mixing the icing with a wooden spoon or spatula. It is very important that both basin and spoon should be dry and free from grease before commencing, or otherwise the icing might be spoiled. Beat the icing as quickly as possible until it is perfectly smooth and of the right consistency; from five to ten minutes may be sufficient, but it requires some hard beating to make it workable. To be of the right consistency, the wooden spoon should be able to stand vertically in it without falling. The icing is now ready for use, but in order to prevent a skin forming on the top it must be kept covered with a damp cloth. Place a piece of stick or wire across the basin to prevent the cloth falling down on the icing. This icing will keep for several days if it is attended to, but the cloth on the top must be kept damp, and the icing itself beaten up occasionally. If once a skin is allowed to form on the top through exposure to the air, the icing will be spoilt for all fine purposes, and especially for piping, as the little hard particles would choke up the tube. Keep the icing in a cool place.

To Ice a Cake.—It is a comparatively easy matter to put a plain coating of icing on a cake; it is when something more elaborate—designs and ornaments—are required that much patience and practice are necessary. To begin with, the cake must be perfectly flat; if there is not a coating of almond paste to make it so, it will be better to trim the cake so as to make it stand evenly, and then to turn it upside down and ice the bottom. If cake icing is frequently done in a house, a rotation-stand or cake-drum should be bought, as this will simplify the process very considerably. Fix the cake on to the stand by means of a little icing, and then have it raised to a convenient height for the hand. Failing a proper cake-stand, fix the cake on to the bottom of a cake tin turned upside down, always choosing the tin a size smaller than the cake itself, in order that the knife may pass freely round it whilst icing. Then pile on the top of the cake sufficient icing to cover it and spread it over, quite roughly at first, with a good-sized table-knife. Now place the point of the knife to the centre of the cake, holding it horizontally and steadily with the right hand and with the left; move the rotation-stand round until a complete circle has been made, when the knife may be slipped off. It will require some practice to leave the surface smooth after one turn of the stand, a little touching up may be necessary, but skill will be acquired by degrees. If the cake is being iced without a rotation-stand, the knife must just be brought smoothly across it in one direction. If the top only of the cake is to be iced, allow it to dry, then decorate to taste and cover the sides with a silver or gilt paper band or with a coloured paper frill, and perhaps a band of ribbon.

To Ice the Sides of a Cake.—Place some more icing on the bare parts and spread it roughly round with a knife. Then hold the knife vertically and in a slanting position against the cake, seeing that it touches the complete width, and turn the stand round with the left hand. Any superfluous icing should be carried off with a sweep of the knife when the circle is finished. If not smooth after the first attempt, repeat the process. Touch up the edges with the point of the knife and allow the cake to dry. For a wedding cake, two or even three coats of this icing are generally put on, but one coat must always be dry before another is added; in fact, if more convenient, the cake may rest for several days between the coatings.

The next step is to **decorate the cake.** The simplest method of decorating a Christmas or birthday cake is to use bon-bons or preserved fruits, and these can easily be fixed in place with a little icing. The other style of decoration, known as "piping," is more elaborate and requires a considerable amount of practice. A few lessons from an experienced teacher would be an immense help to a beginner. For piping purposes bags and fancy forcing-pipes are necessary. The pipes or tubes are made with various-shaped openings to give different forms to the icing pressed through them. Put some icing into this bag and fold down the top to keep it in. Now force out this icing as fancy dictates, experimenting first on the back of a plate or even a piece of paper until you get a definite and regular pattern. Dots, stars, or rosettes are easier than a long flowing pattern, and they can be arranged very effectively. Points may be pricked at regular intervals on the cake to act as a guide in forming any pattern. Then press the icing slowly through the tube, following any device you may have in view. Of course, this piping is an art which cannot be learned in a day, but if it is commenced at the simple stages and gradually worked up to something more difficult it will be found a most fascinating employment. A little colouring may also be added to the icing when desired.

When a cake is to be in two or three tiers, as in the case of a wedding cake, the cakes must be in graduated sizes, the plain coatings of icing put on separately, and then the cakes stuck together by means of a little icing before the decorating or piping is commenced.

Vienna or Butter Icing

Ingredients—

6 oz. Fresh Butter. | ¾ lb. Icing Sugar.

Method.—If salt butter must be used, wash and work it in several cold waters, and finally press out the water in a cloth before using it. Put the butter into a basin and sieve the sugar on the top of it. Cream these two together with a wooden spoon in the same way as for a cake. Then add the desired flavouring and colouring as below.

1. **Coffee or Mocha Icing.**—Add two tablespoonfuls of strong coffee to the above, mixing it in a little at a time.

2. **Chocolate Icing.**—Add two or three ounces of unsweetened chocolate dissolved in one tablespoonful of water to the above mixture.

3. **Strawberry or Raspberry Icing.**—Add a few drops of essence of strawberry or raspberry to flavour, and colour pink with carmine.

4. **Orange or Lemon Icing.**—Grate the rind off an orange or a lemon, and rub it into two ounces of the sugar to be used for the icing. Proceed to make the icing as above, and colour with a little yellow colouring.

The colouring and flavouring of this icing may be varied according to taste. Spirit or liqueur is frequently added, such as rum, maraschino, Curaçoa, &c.

Any of the above icings may be made in half or quarter quantities, or if a number of little fancy cakes are to be iced, the plain butter and sugar may be worked together first, and then the quantity divided and different flavourings and colours added.

To use the Icing.—The icing must be allowed to become quite cold and hard before using. In hot weather the basin containing the icing should be placed on ice or put in a very cold place. If a large plain cake is to be iced, it is usual to split it once or twice, and put a layer of the icing between. Sometimes for this purpose a little thick cream is worked into the icing just before using. Spread a thin coating of the icing on the top and sides of the cake, and put more of the icing in a forcing-bag, with rather a large pipe on the end of it. Force out the icing on the cake in stars or scrolls, and do it as quickly as possible, before the heat of the hand has time to soften the icing. If liked, two different colours of icing may be used, such as yellow and pink, yellow and brown, pink and white, &c. Do not put too much of this icing on any cake, as it is decidedly rich. Some other light and suitable decoration may be used as well, such as a little finely chopped pistachio nut, a few rose-leaves or violets, small pieces of angelica, &c.

GENERAL HINTS ON DECORATING

Cakes, as well as other eatables, should be made to look pretty as well as to taste good. Of course, many cakes are better left in their simple state without any decoration at all, and when this is the case particular care should be taken with the baking to avoid overcooking or burning, and consequently an unsightly appearance.

Under no circumstances should a cake be over-decorated, and there are many simple and harmless forms of decoration which may be employed.

One of the simplest forms of decoration is a sprinkling of sugar, or the cake may be brushed over with white of egg and sprinkled with sugar in two colours, or even chopped nuts.

Another simple decoration is to spread a thin coating of jam or jelly over the cake, and then to sprinkle with browned or coloured almonds, cocoanut, pistachio nuts, &c., or a mixture of these. This is very suitable for the sides of cakes where the top only is iced.

When a more elaborate decoration is wanted, one of the various icings may be used. With a large cake it is very usual to ice the top only and then to decorate with preserved fruits, bon-bons, or icing in two colours put through a forcing-bag. Any decoration may be fixed in place with a little soft icing.

Pleasing effects in colour must always be studied. Light and delicate colours are preferable to the darker shades, which are apt to suggest "something painted."

In the decorating of little fancy cakes there is a wide range for individual taste and arrangement. With the help of the icings and decorations above described, or even odds and ends of icings, the variety of pretty cakes which can be made is endless, and it is just these pretty *little* cakes which cost so much to buy, and which add so immensely to the attractiveness of an afternoon tea-table.

The making and decorating of these cakes require the same amount of taste and ingenuity as any other fancy or artistic work, but it is wonderful how many new kinds of cakes in novel designs can be made with a little careful handling and some good-will.

Most of the small fancy cakes are made up from Genoese pastry, sponge cake, Madeira cake, chocolate cake, orange cake, or any other plain cake mixture. These are sliced and cut in small fingers, diamonds, rounds, heart-shapes, &c., and iced or made into sandwiches. Two different cake mixtures may be put together, such as pink and white, chocolate and white, chocolate and pink, orange and pink, and so on; and for spreading purposes jam, marmalade, soft almond paste, thick flavoured custard, clotted or whipped cream mixed with chopped nuts, sieved jam or pieces of fruit, Vienna icing, fondant icing, and so on may be used. Then a coating of icing or a little piping in icing put on the top with some other form of decoration. The following are a few examples of what may be done :—

1. Genoese pastry made into a sandwich with raspberry jam and cut into fancy shapes. Coated with chocolate or white icing, and decorated with leaves of angelica and crystallised violets.

2. Sandwich of orange cake spread with marmalade, iced with yellow glacé, and decorated with crystallised sections of orange, and a little chocolate icing to mark the seeds.

3. Sandwiches of chocolate cake spread with pink Vienna icing, a piping of Vienna icing on the top, and a few silver dragees.

4. Sandwiches of Madeira cake spread with soft almond paste. Spread the top with almond paste, brush over with white of egg, and decorate with chopped pistachio nuts or browned almonds.

5. Sandwiches of Genoese pastry spread with clotted cream. Coat with pale yellow fondant or glacé, and decorate with leaves of angelica and red berries (bon-bons).

These hints may be varied indefinitely, and according to what there is at hand to make the cakes of, but they will perhaps serve as a guide to the beginner, who, after a little practice, will soon launch out on her own account, and be able to make dainty morsels without any trouble or difficulty.

THE PRESERVING AND BOTTLING OF FRUIT

JAMS AND JELLIES

HINTS ON JAM-MAKING

UNLESS we have a garden of our own which supplies us with fruit, home-made jam is almost of necessity more expensive than that which is bought, although, when well made, it is beyond doubt superior in quality.

Fruit for preserving should be uniformly ripe, sound, and fresh, and it should be picked, if possible, on a dry, sunny morning, and not with the dew upon it. If the fruit be damp, or even if the weather be foggy when it is gathered, there is nothing more likely than this to prevent the jam from keeping.

The fruit should be made into jam as soon as possible after picking, and this is one point where housewives have the advantage over manufacturers.

We must first see that the fruit is free from dust and dirt, after which it must be picked and all stalks removed. The harder fruits, such as apples, plums, and gooseberries, may be washed before being preserved.

There are many different methods of making jam, and opinions vary as to which is the best. One method is to boil the sugar and water first, and thus make a syrup to which the fruit is added; another is to boil the fruit by itself and then to add the sugar in a crushed or half-melted condition; and a third way is to boil both sugar and fruit together.

The sugar used for preserving should always be of the finest—pure cane sugar—and crushed or crystallised, not powdered. Inferior sugar is expensive in the end, as it causes so much waste by the extra amount of scum it produces; and if beetroot sugar is used the jam will neither have such a good colour nor will it keep so long. The quantity of sugar required will vary slightly according to the nature of the fruit used, the usual proportion being from three-quarters to one pound sugar to one pound of fruit. If too little sugar is used the jam will not keep, if too much it will candy and the flavour will not be so good.

It is possible, but not easy, to make jam without a proper preserving-pan; an iron one would discolour the fruit, while a tin one is so thin that the jam would be liable to burn. Copper, brass, and aluminium pans are the best for the purpose. Enamelled iron ones are also sold and are less expensive, but jam made in them is much more likely to burn unless it has very careful attention. If much preserving is to be done it will be found a wise investment to buy a thoroughly good preserving-pan, a brass one for preference. The greatest care must be taken to keep the pan in good condition, and it must always be scrupulously clean and dry before the fruit is put in.

An iron spoon must never be used, but stir always with a wooden or silver one. The skimming should not be commenced too early in the process. It is only a froth which rises at first; the scum itself is very thick.

During the time the fruit and sugar are being boiled together they must be stirred carefully and almost constantly. Be careful, too, that the pan is raised a little from the fire and not directly over it, or it will be liable to burn; on the hot-plate of a close range is really the best place for cooking it. It is the amount of sugar employed in the making of jam which makes it so liable to catch.

The time for cooking will depend very much upon the method employed, the kind of fruit used, and also upon the rate of boiling. It does not do to let the fruit boil too slowly. As a matter of fact, it is impossible to lay down any hard-and-fast rule as regards time; experience is the best guide, as not only will the time vary according as to whether the fruit is quickly or slowly boiled, but the same kinds of fruits will be found to differ, some being more watery than others, and the more watery the fruit the longer boiling will it require. If boiled too short a time the jam will neither set firmly nor keep well, while, on the other hand, if it is boiled too long the flavour will be spoilt and the jam become sticky. When a little of the jam, poured upon a cold plate, sets in a few minutes, it is ready and should be put at once into pots. It ought to be ladled out of the pan with a silver soup-ladle or with a cup or small jug.

The pots must be thoroughly dried beforehand, and then filled to within quarter of an inch from the top. If any drops are spilt on the sides of the pots they should be immediately wiped off with a cloth wrung out of hot water.

To cover the jam, cut rounds of thin white paper the proper size of the pots, dip these in brandy, whisky, or vinegar, and lay them on the surface, then tie over each pot a piece of wetted vegetable parchment or a gummed paper cover sold for the purpose. Label the pots on the sides with a written or printed label, stating the name of the jam and the date when made. (For Storing, see p. 104.)

It is impossible to give a large number of recipes for jam and jelly-making in a book of this kind, but it is hoped that the following will give a good idea of the ordinary methods.

Apple Ginger

Proportions—

3 lbs. Apples.	6 oz. Whole Ginger.
3 lbs. Preserving Sugar.	Water.

Method.—Put the ginger into a jug or lined saucepan with boiling water and let it infuse by the side of the fire for several hours, keeping it well covered. Peel the apples, cut them into neat pieces, removing the core, and throw them into cold water to preserve the colour. Drain the water from the ginger and make up the quantity to one and a half pints. Put this into a preserving-pan with the sugar, bring to the boil and boil from eight to ten minutes. Drain the pieces of apple, throw them gently into this syrup, and let them boil until transparent but not broken. Then lift them out carefully, put them into jars, and pour the syrup over.

Apple Jelly

Proportions.—To each pint of apple juice allow one pound of preserving sugar and the rind and juice of one lemon.

Method.—Wash the apples and cut them in four or six pieces, according to size, without removing the peel and cores. Put these into a preserving-pan with just sufficient cold water to cover them. Bring to the boil and boil gently for one hour or longer, stirring occasionally with a wooden spoon. When reduced to a pulp pour all into a jelly-bag or cloth (see below) and allow the juice to drip all night. The juice ought to be of a thickish consistency when cold; if very watery either too much water has been added or the pulp has not been sufficiently cooked.

Next day measure the juice carefully and put it into a preserving-pan with the lemon rind peeled off thinly and tied in muslin and the lemon juice, if liked. Bring to the boil and add the proper proportion of sugar. Stir carefully until the sugar is melted, and then boil quickly from twenty to thirty minutes or until the jelly will set when tested on a plate. The time depends very much upon the kind of fruit used. Remove any scum from the top before potting.

Note.—This jelly may be flavoured with whole ginger instead of lemons, or orange juice and rind may be used instead of lemon juice and rind.

The apple pulp may be sieved, mixed with sugar and boiled carefully for half-an-hour, and can be used for making puffs or an open tart. It will not keep long.

The Jelly-Bag or Cloth

The best strainer for jelly is a piece of huckaback or strong cheese-cloth. This is more easily kept in order than the old-fashioned flannel bag, and serves the purpose equally well. The material may be either in the form of a towel tied on the four legs of a chair (see p. 120), or a conical-shaped bag may be made with loops through which a stick may be put in order to suspend it between two chairs with a basin underneath. The jelly-bag should be well scalded with boiling water before it is used. After the fruit has been emptied into it no pressure must be used or the juice will not be clear. The straining must be done in a warm place and out of a draught, and sufficient time must be allowed to let every possible drop of juice run through. The best plan is to let it drain over-night. Some people use a hair sieve instead of a cloth, but this is not so roomy and not such a convenient plan on the whole.

Apricot Jam

Proportions.—To each pound of apricots weighed after stoning allow three-quarters of a pound preserving sugar.

Method.—Wipe the apricots, and, if time permits, remove the skins. Cut them in halves with a silver knife and take out the stones. Spread out the apricots on large dishes and strew over them their proper proportion of sugar. Let them stand thus for at least twelve hours. Meanwhile break the stones, or at least some of them, blanch the kernels, and add them to the apricots. Next day turn all into a preserving-pan and simmer very gently until the apricots are clear and the jam will set. It must be stirred very carefully, and the time required will be from three-quarters to one hour.

Note.—*Greengage Jam* may be made in the same way.

Blackberry and Apple Marmalade

Proportions.—Equal quantities of apples and blackberries and one pound of sugar to one pound pulp.

Method.—Wash the apples and cut them in slices without removing skins and cores. Pick the blackberries carefully, discarding any that are unsound. Put both kinds of fruit into a preserving-pan with just enough water to keep them from burning. Cook until reduced to a pulp, stirring frequently. Then rub through a hair sieve, leaving only the skins and seeds. Return the sieved pulp to a clean preserving-pan with sugar in the above proportion, and stir almost constantly for twenty minutes or until it is firm. If this is put in small pots it can be turned out in shape when wanted, and is very good served with blancmange or with cream.

Black Currant Jam

Proportions.—To three pounds black currants allow one pint rhubarb juice and four pounds preserving sugar.

Method.—The black currants should be as ripe as possible. Strip them from the stalks and wash them if they are very smoked and dirty. Put them into a preserving-pan with the proper portion of rhubarb juice (see p. 231), bring to the boil, and allow the berries to simmer slowly for fifteen minutes. Warm the sugar without allowing it to brown and add it next. Boil with the sugar from twenty to thirty minutes, or until the jam will set. It must be stirred almost constantly.

Note.—Raspberry or red currant juice may be used instead of rhubarb, but either of these will give a distinct flavour.

Black Currant Jelly

Proportions.—To one pint of black currant juice allow one pound of sugar.

Method.—Pick the currants from the stalks and wash them if necessary. Put them into a double saucepan or into a jar placed in a saucepan of boiling water with one gill of water or rhubarb juice (see p. 231) to each pound of fruit, and cook for two hours at least, or until all the juice is drawn out. Then strain them through a jelly-cloth or large sieve, allowing them to drip all night. Next day measure the juice and put it into a preserving-pan with the above proportion of sugar. Stir carefully until the sugar is dissolved, and then boil for half-an-hour, or until the jelly will set.

Note.—A few red currants may be mixed with the black.

Red currant or *Cranberry jelly* can be made in the same way.

Damson and Apple Jam

Proportions—

8 lbs. Damsons.	10 lbs. Sugar.
2 pints Apple Juice.	

Method.—Pick the fruit carefully, rejecting any that is not sound. Then wash if necessary or rub it between the folds of a coarse towel. Prepare the apple juice in the same way as for apple jelly (see p. 229). Put the damsons into the preserving-pan with their proper proportions of sugar and apple juice and stir carefully until they come to the boil. Take out as many stones as possible and boil the jam for twenty minutes, or until it will stiffen.

Note.—This jam will be nicer if the stones can be removed from the damsons before they are used. A few of them can then be cracked and the kernels blanched and used for flavouring. They should be tied in muslin and removed before the jam is potted, as they are too bitter to eat.

Gooseberry and Red Currant Jam

Proportions.—To three pounds gooseberries allow one gill red currant juice and three and a half pounds sugar.

Method.—Top and tail the gooseberries and remove any that are unsound. Wash them thoroughly and dry in a coarse cloth. Put them into a preserving-pan with red currant juice (see below) in the above proportion. Heat the contents slowly over the fire and then boil for fifteen minutes. Add the sugar gradually, and boil again until the jam will set. Skim when necessary.

Orange Jelly

Proportions—

4 lbs. Marmalade Oranges.	4 pints Water.
2 Lemons.	Preserving Sugar.

Method.—Wipe the oranges and lemons with a damp cloth, and grate off the yellow rind only. Then remove all the white skin, which is not used in the making of the jelly. Cut the inner part of the oranges and lemons into small pieces, and put it into a preserving-pan with the water. Boil for half-an-hour, stirring frequently, then strain through a hair sieve or jelly-bag, and allow the juice to drop without pressure.

Measure this liquid and put it into a clean preserving-pan, with the grated rinds and one pound preserving sugar to each pint of juice. Bring to the boil, and boil from ten to fifteen minutes, or until it will jelly. Skim well, pour into jars, and cover while hot.

Orange Marmalade

Proportions—

3½ lbs. Marmalade Oranges.	½ pint boiling Water.
3 Lemons.	Sugar (see below).
13½ pints cold Water.	

Method.—Wipe the oranges and lemons with a damp cloth, and cut them in halves. Squeeze out the juice on a lemon-squeezer, and strain it into a basin. Put the pips into a smaller basin with the boiling water, and let them stand to extract the flavour. Cut the skins of both oranges and lemons into very thin strips, put them into a large basin or crock with the cold water, and let them soak twenty-four hours. Then pour into a preserving-pan, and boil until the pieces of peel are quite tender. Put the seeds with their water into a smaller saucepan, and boil for fifteen minutes; then strain the water from them into the preserving-pan beside the rest. Pour again into the basin or crock, add the orange and lemon juice, and stand for at least twelve hours longer. Next day measure and allow one pound of preserving sugar to each pint of liquid. Boil together in the preserving-pan about twenty minutes, or until the marmalade will jelly. Then pour into pots, and cover while hot.

Quince Jelly

Proportions.—One pound sugar to one pint quince juice.

Method.—Peel, quarter and core the quinces. Then weigh the pieces and put them into a preserving-pan with two teacupfuls of water to each pound of fruit. Simmer slowly until the fruit is quite soft, but not too pulpy or the jelly will not be clear. Strain though a hair sieve or jelly-cloth without pressing the pulp. Measure the juice and put it into a preserving-pan with the above proportion of sugar. Bring to the boil and boil quickly from fifteen to twenty minutes.

Note.—To use the pulp that is left see under Apple Jelly (p. 229).

Raspberry and Red Currant Jam

Proportions.—To every pound of raspberries allow one gill of red currant juice and one and a quarter pounds of sugar.

Method.—Stalk the currants and put them into a double saucepan, or into a jar placed in a saucepan of boiling water, and let them cook until all the juice is drawn out; then strain either through a flannel jelly-bag or though a cloth, allowing the juice to drip all night.

Pick the raspberries, removing the stalks, then weigh them, and put them into a preserving-pan with the proportion of red currant juice. Bring to the boil and boil for ten minutes, then add the sugar by degrees, and boil until the jam will set, stirring almost constantly, and skimming when necessary.

Rhubarb Jam

Proportions—

6 lbs. Rhubarb.	3 Lemons.
6 lbs. Preserving Sugar.	

Method. — Choose some nice red-stalked rhubarb. Wipe it and, unless young and tender, take off the peel. Cut it into small pieces and then weigh it. Put it into a large crock or basin in layers with the sugar, sprinkling over with the grated rind of the lemons. Strain the lemon juice over, cover the basin, and stand for twenty-four hours.

Next day pour off the liquid and as much of the melted sugar as possible into a preserving-pan and boil for ten minutes. Put in the rhubarb and boil all together from half to three-quarters of an hour or until the jam will set. It must be stirred very frequently and skimmed when necessary.

Note.—This jam may be flavoured with ginger if preferred, or oranges may be used instead of lemons. A few blanched and shredded almonds may be added.

Rhubarb Juice

Rhubarb juice may be used instead of water in the making of many jams, especially in the preserving of the less juicy fruits. Its flavour is so delicate that it does not overpower the special fruit with which it is used. Wash the rhubarb, but do not peel it unless the skin is very coarse, as this helps to give a pink colour. Cut it up in small pieces and put it into a large jar with just enough water to moisten the base. Cover the jar and steam in a saucepan of water, or cook in the oven until the juice is drawn out of the rhubarb. Then strain through a jelly-cloth or clean hair sieve.

Rowan Jelly

Proportions.—To each pint of rowan juice allow one pound sugar.

Method.—Pick and wash the rowans and put them into a preserving-pan with just enough water to prevent them burning. Cook slowly until the berries are reduced to a pulp; then strain in order to get the clear liquid. Measure this and return it to a clean pan. Bring to the boil and add the proper proportion of sugar. Then boil quickly for twenty minutes or until the jelly will set, skimming when necessary.

Strawberry Jam

Proportions.—Allow three-quarters of a pound preserving sugar to each pound of strawberries.

Method.—Choose small or medium-sized red strawberries, and remove the husks and any decayed ones before weighing. Put them into a preserving-pan and boil them for half-an-hour, stirring almost constantly. During this time allow the proper proportion of sugar to warm in the oven without taking colour. Add it to the strawberries and boil the two together, stirring all the time for another half-hour or until the jam will set.

Note.—The addition of one gill of red currant juice to each pound of strawberries will much improve the flavour of this jam. It should be added with the sugar.

Tomato Jam

Proportions—

4 lbs. Tomatoes.
4 lbs. Sugar.
1 pint Water.

Method.—The red home-grown tomatoes are the best. Wipe them and put into a basin with boiling water to cover them. Allow them to remain for a few minutes, then lift them out and peel them. Next cut them into quarters and remove the hard pieces from the end and some of the seeds. Put the seeds, skins, and one pint of the water in which the tomatoes were soaked into a saucepan, boil for half-an-hour and strain. Then put the sugar and this strained liquid into a preserving-pan and bring them to the boil. Add the tomatoes and boil until the jam will set, stirring almost constantly.

Note.—A little lemon juice or ginger may be added if liked.

Vegetable Marrow Jam

Proportions.—To each pound of prepared marrow allow one pound sugar, half a lemon, and half ounce whole ginger, water.

Method.—The vegetable marrows should be medium-sized and fresh. Wash, dry, and peel them. Then cut in slices an inch thick. Stamp out the seeds with a round cutter and cut the rings in blocks an inch in width. Weigh the marrow and put it into a large basin with the proper proportion of sugar, the grated rind and juice of lemon and the ginger broken in small pieces. Put the skins and seeds into a saucepan with water to cover them and boil half-an-hour. Then strain, and allow one gill of this liquid to each pound of marrow. Pour this into the basin, cover, and stand for twenty-four hours.

Next day boil all together, stirring almost constantly until the pieces of marrow look transparent, and the liquid will jelly when tested on a plate. From three-quarters to one hour will be required.

THE ART OF BOTTLING FRUIT

The valuable notes following have been quoted by kind permission from "The Book of Fruit-Bottling," by Edith Bradley and May Crooke, published by John Lane.

Until the last few years, when there has been a decided renewal in the industry, fruit-bottling had become almost a lost art. Perhaps it requires more of that leisure and composure which we of to-day so sorely lack. And yet fruit-bottling is essentially a work for ladies, whether it be for the replenishment of their own store-rooms or as a pleasant and convenient means of adding a trifle to a straitened income.

It is by no means laborious, but interesting, pleasant and healthy, though at the same time it demands the utmost nicety, cleanliness, and attention to details; and it is just in this minute attention to detail that an uneducated cook so often fails. All fruits may be—nay, should be—bottled. The method is admirably suited to those particular fruits which are least in flavour when fresh gathered, as black currants and damsons. These, when bottled and kept six or eighteen months (or even longer), are vastly improved. They lose that element of roughness, almost acridity, which in the fresh fruit sometimes runs round the mouth and makes one shudder.

First of all the fruit must be sterilised, and for this a special steriliser must be used.

The following simple directions for using the Mercia Steriliser (and in general terms the same will hold good for other kinds) may be of use to those who are tempted to take up this fascinating occupation.

It will be easier, however, to describe the steriliser after explaining the process of sterilisation. Sterilisation is briefly this—to make sterile or deprive of vitality the bacteriological germs which cause decay and putrefaction in fruit and vegetables, as well as in other forms of food. If these germs are destroyed and kept from approaching the sterilised object again, it will keep perfectly sound and good for a considerable time, possibly an unlimited time. This result is brought about by the following process. The article (fruit or vegetable) to be sterilised is packed into a glass jar or bottle, which is then filled with cold water and closed either by a metal or glass cap fastened by a clip or a screw; the bottles are placed in a vessel containing cold water; heat is applied in one form or another, and the temperature of the water bath is slowly raised until it is sufficiently high inside the glass jars to kill the bacteriological germs. The exact degree of heat required to destroy the germs varies considerably according to the object which is being sterilised; in fact, some fruits and some vegetables require three or four successive sterilisations (by which first one bacteriological family and then another are destroyed) to bring about the required conditions.

The hot air and steam by which the bottles in the steriliser or other vessel are now surrounded causes the water or juice inside the bottles to get hot and expand until it reaches the air-tight capsule or cover. The requisite temperature is sustained for some time at an equal height until the process is complete (this can be determined to a nicety by the fixed thermometer), and the bottles are either lifted out and put into a cool place, or else cold water is turned into the machine whilst the bottles are in it (the hot water having been previously drawn off). With the decreasing temperature the vacuum is created, and unless the caps or tops are imperfect or imperfectly adjusted, and so admit the air, the contents of the jar, as before stated, will keep for any length of time, because germs do not incubate in a vacuum. This, then, is the theory carried out by the process of sterilisation. If sufficiently complete, and, as before stated, the requisite temperatures for the different fruits and vegetables have been proved, and these temperatures have been registered by a thermometer, the vacuum is attained and the germs made sterile. It may chance, however, that the rubber bands or the caps are not placed on the bottles quite evenly, or, if the cap is screwed, that the screw ring is not quite perfect; then if from one cause or another air is admitted, as a certain consequence the vacuum is destroyed, the germs come into life, and immediately begin to cause decay and decomposition or fermentation. If this is not at once noted, and the batch of bottled fruit re-sterilised and re-capped, it will all go bad.

In the Mercia Patent Steriliser every attempt has been made to put upon the market a steriliser which is the outcome of practical experience, presented in a portable, tangible, practical, and workmanlike form, and at a price which brings it within the reach of all who are taking the bottling of fruit year by year seriously.

It is made in three sizes of the best steeled tin. The largest, A, takes twenty-five bottles, holding

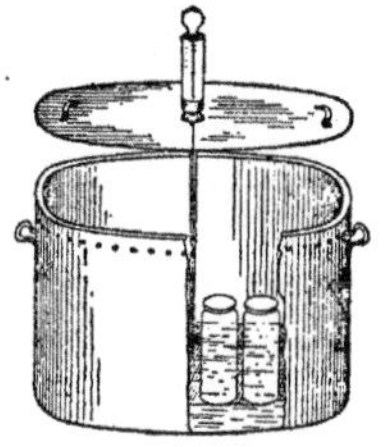

Mercia Steriliser.

two pounds each, *i.e.* fifty pound of fruit—price £4. The second size, B, takes twelve bottles, containing two pound each—price £3, 3s. The third size, C, which is for household use, holds six bottles, containing two pounds each, or nine smaller ones—price 18s.

Upon the copper bottom of the vessel stands a low tin shelf pierced with holes. The bottles, when filled, stand on this shelf, and it prevents them from cracking, as they are liable to do, by coming into too close contact with the heating underneath. In the lid is an aperture in which is inserted a socket; into this socket is screwed (when it is required) a specially constructed thermometer, consisting of a long tube, the bulb of which reaches about midway down the bottles which contain the fruit for sterilising (see illustration). As will be readily understood, when the water in which the bottles is immersed is heated and turned into steam, the temperature at which the process is actually going on is registered on the porcelain scale above the lid, and it is thus possible to adjust the temperature to a degree. The necessary heat for the Mercia steriliser can be supplied either by using a small oil stove or gas-burner and raising the steriliser on a strong stand above it, or the ordinary kitchen range upon which the steriliser may stand.

Special bottles must be used with lip and clip or screw-top lid, and the cost of these generally amounts to 3d. or 4d. each. The bottles will do again year after year, only the caps and rings will require renewal each season. They are to be obtained by the dozen from the Mercia Agricultural Store, Bredon's Norton, near Tewkesbury.

The best fruits for bottling are gooseberries, cherries, raspberries, apricots, plums, damsons, blackberries, tomatoes, apples, and pears. Strawberries can also be successfully bottled, but they require more care and trouble than other fruits, because they are so much softer.

Gooseberries.—Gooseberries are the easiest of all fruits to bottle, and as a rule give the most satisfactory results. The following directions should be carefully followed. Have the bottles ready, making sure that they are perfectly clean and quite dry. The gooseberries should be picked when green and hard, and before they get too large. For bottling they ought always to be picked in the same condition as that in which they are used for green gooseberry tart. Before putting the fruit into the bottles it should be topped and tailed, and to ensure a good appearance when finished it is always best to grade the fruit and only put berries in which are the same size, rejecting any that are too large and not sound, or are disfigured in any way. These can always be used up in the preserving-pan. Pack the fruit closely into the jars without bruising to within an inch of the top, and fill up with cold water or syrup to the very top of the bottle. Do not put on the cap at once, as the water often sinks when it has worked its way down among the fruit. If this happens the bottles should be filled up again, as the fruit ought always to be well covered.

Capping the Bottles.—The bottles are now ready for capping, and much of the success depends upon the care taken in capping. The india-rubber rings are next put on. Have ready a basin of hot water, and before laying the ring on the mouth of the bottle dip it into hot water for a second or two. This makes the rubber more flexible and more likely to lie flat, which is an important point. When the ring is in its place put on the metal cap. Care must be taken to place it on the bottle perfectly straight. The spring clip is then put on, and the bottle is ready to go into the steriliser. Imperfect capping is often due to the ring or the cap being carelessly put on. This allows the air to get in, and prevents the bottle becoming hermetically sealed, as it should be.

Sterilising the Fruit.—The bottles are now placed in the steriliser. They should stand just clear of each other. A sufficient quantity of cold water is put in to cover the bottle three parts of the way up. The lid is then put on and the thermometer screwed into its socket. The temperature generally registered at this stage is about 60°. It is very gradually allowed to rise until it reaches 155°. An increase of two degrees a minute is enough. If the temperature is allowed to go up with a rush the skin of the fruit in the bottles will be cracked. It nearly always takes an hour, if not more, before the required temperature is reached. The bottles should be kept at 155° for forty-five minutes. If gas or oil is used for the heating this is easily done by regulating the flame. At the end of forty-five minutes the bottles are taken out and put to cool. If a screw-topped bottle is used the loose rim is now tightly screwed down. Where the spring clip is used it is left on till the bottles are quite cold. When this stage has been reached (probably the next day) each bottle should be examined to see if the cap is perfectly tight; if so it has become hermetically sealed, and will only move by pressure from without, such as the insertion of a knife between cap and rubber ring to raise it. This will be a proof of the fruit keeping. If any are found imperfectly capped they should be re-sterilised; but a careful examination should be made of the cap to see if it fits properly or not, as a certain percentage of those sent out are sure to be faulty.

Cherries.—The Kentish cherry is excellent for preserving in this way. Pick the cherries off their stalks and pack in the bottles. The fruit should be firm but nearly ripe. When packing shake the bottle gently up and down so that the fruit may fit in closely. If the fruit is pricked at one end with a needle it prevents bursting. Fill up the bottles with syrup or water. Proceed as indicated in the foregoing recipe and sterilise at 150°. Another method is to split the cherries in half with a sharp knife, take out the stones, crack some, and return the kernels to the bottles when packing. This latter method keeps the fruit a beautiful colour, but it would be well to use syrup instead of water, because, preserved in this way, they are richer in flavour and appearance.

Raspberries and Red Currants.—Raspberries and currants together make one of the very best fruits for winter use. They are always liked, and as they keep their colour well when bottled they look appetising. Discrimination should be used in the weather for bottling, and a specially dry day should be chosen for doing soft fruits, for if saturated with rain they lose their flavour, and do not keep as well as when picked on a warm dry day. The currants should be carefully picked off their stalks and also the raspberries. Place a layer of raspberries about one inch thick first in the bottle, and shake gently down; then place a layer of red currants. Proceed in this manner till the bottles are filled to within an inch of the top. Fill up and proceed as in the foregoing recipes. Sterilise at 155°.

Syrup for Bottled Fruits.—Sometimes it is desirable to bottle the fruit in syrup instead of water only. The following is a good recipe: To every quart of water allow half a pound of the best cane sugar. Bring to the boil and continue to boil at 212° for half-an-hour, taking care to skim when necessary. Pour the syrup into a vessel and keep till quite cold before pouring over the fruits.

The foregoing directions can be applied, broadly speaking, to all soft fruits enumerated at the commencement of the chapter. The temperature must also depend upon the quality of the fruit. If young and tender 155°–160° is a usual standard. The time occupied in sterilising varies with the fruit; larger fruit, such as plums, require twenty-five minutes, pears one hour, apricots forty-five minutes, peaches forty-five minutes, tomatoes thirty minutes, rhubarb twenty minutes.

Plums.—Plums should be quite freshly gathered for bottling, and only those of a fairly good size should be used. The smaller plums can always be turned into jam. The fruit should be quite firm and not quite ripe. For all the stone fruits it is better to use the larger bottles, as with the smaller bottles the mouths are not large enough to allow the insertion of any very fine fruit. The packing of plums in the bottles is an important item, because if the fruit is not properly packed the bottles present a very ugly appearance when finished. To pack properly the fruit must be graded, and plums chosen as near of a size as possible. It is always best to make a good beginning by getting three even fruits if possible into the bottom of a bottle. When the lowest round is started properly the rest of the packing is fairly simple. The bottles should be gently shaken from side to side, and a round piece of wood with a blunt end should be used to help to slide the fruit gently into place. Great care must be taken not on any account to break the skin. Some people prick their fruit with a steel knitting-needle at the stalk end to prevent the skin breaking, but we have serious doubts whether anything is gained by so doing. The bottles, after packing, are filled up with syrup or water. When very large plums are used, they may be cut in half with a dessert-knife, and the stones extracted and cracked. The kernels may then be distributed among the fruit in the bottles.

Sterilising Plums.—When placed in the steriliser the temperature should be brought up very gradually till it reaches 160°. If the Plums are in good condition the temperature should rise to this point without the skin cracking, but if the fruit is at all soft 155° will be sufficient. Victorias, Czars, and Monachs are the best varieties for preserving. The well-known Pershore plum must not be forgotten, as it bottles admirably. Damsons can be bottled in the same way.

Apricots, Peaches, and Nectarines.—These fruits, unless quite small, should be cut in halves, always remembering to use a dessert-knife, as a steel knife will not only make the fruit taste but mark it and turn it brown or black. The stones should be cracked and some of the kernels placed amongst the fruit when packing. The packing of the fruit is a slightly difficult operation. The halves should overlap each other evenly up the sides of the bottle, no space being left. Before trying packing of this sort it would be well to purchase a properly packed bottle and use it as a model. Care must be taken that all the juice which the fruit loses when it is being cut is saved and put into the bottles with the kernels. This can be done by halving the fruit on a plate. As these are choice fruits, syrup may be used in the bottling instead of water. When used the fruit must not be ripe, but quite firm. Care must be taken not to bruise it when placing in the bottles. Bring them gradually up to a temperature of 155°, following in all cases the general directions for bottling.

Apples and Pears must be carefully and evenly peeled before bottling. They should be cut down the middle as already advised for peaches, &c., removing the cores. Have ready a basin of water into which some lemon juice has been squeezed; drop the fruit into this, and then fill the bottles with the fruit so prepared, and at once add the water or syrup. If there is any delay the fruit will turn brown, and it is to prevent this happening that it is dropped into the basin of water, the lemon juice keeping it white.

Tomatoes may be taken either as fruit or vegetable. Generally they come under the head of the latter, but as either they are most excellent bottled. They require a little more trouble than most other fruits to bottle successfully. They should be used small, and just coloured, as they have to be done at a high temperature, in order to ensure complete sterilisation. In places where tomatoes are grown in quantities the small ones are often reserved for bottling. Pack in bottles as directed for plums, and cover with water. Bring the temperature up to 170°. Take out of the steriliser after an hour at this temperature, and leave for twenty-four hours; then repeat sterilisation at 170°. Again leave for two or three days, and again sterilise at the same temperature. By doing them thus three times they will remain like fresh fruit, and can be kept for any length of time.

THE TABLE

A good housewife will not rest content with the fact that the meals in her house are well cooked. She will also see to it that they are well served, knowing that dainty table equipment and skilful service does much to enhance the enjoyment of the fare provided.

This article deals with all the many important subjects bearing upon table service, including the fittings and arrangement of the pantry and its contents; the choice of silver, china, cutlery, and glass, the arrangement of a menu, with order of courses; valuable hints are also given in regard to the choice of wines, and the rules which govern waiting at table in every refined and well-ordered house.

THE PANTRY

Where more than one servant is kept a small pantry is a very necessary apartment in a house, as it enables the maid who has charge of the table arrangements to do all her washing up without interfering with the work of the cook or getting in her way.

In large establishments the pantry would be the special sanctum of the butler. In it he would keep all the silver, glass, and china that came under his care, as well as the supply of wine that was required for immediate use. There would also be a small table or desk at which he could write his orders and make up his books.

In smaller houses the pantry need not be a spacious apartment, but even a small place conveniently fitted up will be found a great convenience, not only to the table-maid but also to the ladies of the house, as it is a place where they can do any washing of tea dishes or fine china, preparing of dessert, cutting bread and butter for afternoon tea, and the arranging of flowers, &c., without having to enter the cook's domain.

A pantry should be fitted with a small sink with hot and cold water-supply. At the side of the sink there should be a good-sized draining-board on which wet dishes can be placed, above the sink a plate-rack in which to drain plates, while a small cupboard fitted underneath would be a useful receptacle for plate powder, silver brushes, furniture polish, ammonia, soap powder, and other indispensable articles for cleaning purposes. Another necessary fitting is a dresser. It should be provided with two or three drawers in which glass cloths, dusters, leathers, and furniture sheets could be kept, one drawer being reserved for the maid's private use. The lower part of the dresser should be fitted with cupboards divided off into separate portions. One part might be reserved for cleaning utensils, another for larger dishes, and a third as a small store for sugar, jam, butter, &c. Then above the dresser there should be a nice high narrow cupboard, with sliding glass doors if possible, for holding china, glass, cruets, sugar basins, jam dishes, &c. If this is large enough one portion of it might hold a reserve supply of china and glass and be kept locked.

Other useful fittings would be a small pulley or rail for drying towels and a rack for holding two or three brushes.

If room permits there might be a good solid table in the pantry and also a chair on which the maid could sit down while doing her silver cleaning and other work of the kind.

The floor should be covered with cork carpet or linoleum and the walls papered with a good washing paper or coated with a light-coloured ripolin or distemper, which could easily be renewed when dirty.

The pantry should contain all that the table-maid requires for cleaning purposes, and the sink must be supplied with one or two tubs and other necessary appliances for washing up.

It is a good plan also to hang up somewhere in the pantry a list of all glass, china, &c.; this list should be checked periodically by the mistress and servant together.

Cleanliness and order in the pantry are very important. Each time the sink is used it should be scrubbed out with hot water and then thoroughly rinsed with cold. The dresser and table should be scrubbed once a week and the floor washed when necessary. No dirty towels or dish cloths should be seen lying about, and a pride should be taken in the neat arrangement of the cupboards. (For "Washing Up," see p. 76.)

SILVER AND CUTLERY

Choice of Silver.—There are few families, except perhaps the very wealthy, who care to use solid table silver every day, for even if they are fortunate enough to possess a set it is carefully guarded under lock and key and only brought out on special occasions, and with the exception perhaps of a few small articles, such as salt and mustard spoons, pepperettes, butter-knives, sugar-tongs, electro-plate is made to do duty for ordinary use.

Although silver costs about three times as much as electro-plate, it must be remembered that it will last for years without requiring any repair, and can even be handed down from generation to generation.

Solid silver is sold by weight and fluctuates a little in price, but the current price for table silver is about the following :—table-spoons and forks from £4, 12s. per dozen, dessert-spoons and forks from £2, 15s. per dozen, and tea-spoons from 30s. per dozen.

Solid silver is one of the things which can often be bought very well second-hand, and in most large towns reliable shops are to be found where it can be obtained at fairly moderate prices.

Electro-Plate.—A good quality should always be bought, as the plating soon wears off the cheaper makes. Good electro-plate ought to last from twenty to thirty years without requiring any renewing. For those who have only a small amount to spend on silver and who are not fortunate enough to have it given to them as a present when they start housekeeping, it is better to purchase a little of a good quality rather than full sets of an inferior kind. There are several regulation patterns such as Old English, King's, Bead or Thread, and Rat Tail, so that additions can always be made by degrees, as the best plated goods are sold by the single article when required. The above patterns are all simple and will easily be kept in order; in fact, heavily ornamented patterns are rarely seen nowadays.

The price of electro-plate varies, but, roughly speaking, good electro-plate of a quality that will last for years can be had at the following prices :—table-spoons and forks from 25s. per dozen, dessert-spoons and forks from 19s. 6d. per dozen, and tea-spoons from 9s. per dozen.

When electro-plate begins to look shabby it can be replated for about the following charges:—table-spoons and forks from 17s. 6d. per dozen; dessert-spoons and forks from 13s. per dozen, and tea-spoons from 7s. per dozen. (For the Cleaning of Silver, see p. 74.)

Choice of Cutlery.—As in the case of electro-plate, so with cutlery, a low-priced article is the

Knife with Through-Tang Rivet.

reverse of economical; not only will the handles of cheap knives be badly fixed, but the blades will be made of a soft steel which never takes a proper edge. It is a wise policy, therefore, to buy knives the blades of which are made of the best Sheffield steel, and to see that they are fixed to the handles with what is called the through-tang rivet, which never comes undone.

There is a choice of materials for the handles, the cheapest of which are bone and horn; then comes ivorine and ivoride, which is the nearest appoach to real ivory that can possibly be made; and, lastly, fine African ivory and sterling silver-plated handles.

Real ivory and sterling silver are rather expensive articles, and most people have to content themselves with one of the cheaper materials. The following will be a fair price to pay for really good articles :—

Best white Bone Handles with Through-Tang :—Table-knives from 13s. 6d. per dozen, dessert-knives from 12s. per dozen, joint or game carvers from 5s. per pair, steel 1s. 9d.

Imitation Ivory Handles :—Table-knives from 17s. 6d. per dozen, dessert-knives from 14s. per dozen, joint or game carvers from 6s. per pair, steel 2s. 4d.

African Ivory Handles :—Table-knives from 38s. per dozen, dessert-knives from 30s. per dozen, joint or game carvers from 12s. 6d. per pair, steel 4s. 3d.

Knives will cost about 2s. 6d. per dozen less without the tang fastening. New blades can always be fitted to good ivory handles at a reasonable charge. (For the Care and Cleaning of Knives, see p. 76.)

CHINA AND GLASS

Choice of China.—Now that both china and glass can be bought at such moderate prices and in such artistic shapes and pretty colours, there is no excuse for any one to have what is chipped and ugly on their tables. Although some of the china dealers of to-day make specialities of tea and dinner services of the most gaudy colouring and in the most impossible patterns, and ornament them with a liberal supply of gilt, there are other manufacturers who reproduce the most tasteful designs of Wedgwood, Spode, and the famous old Crown Derby Wares.

The choice of china is very much a matter of taste and circumstances, and space will not permit of giving many details regarding designs and price, as these are so numerous and varied. Before selecting it is advisable to send for the catalogues of some of the largest firms and to visit their show-rooms. Many valuable ideas may be gleaned in this way.

The frugal housewife whose means are limited and who will in all probability have to leave her china in the hands of inexperienced servants, will do well to buy the strong make of stone-ware or semi-porcelain for every-day use and to choose a style which can be renewed when pieces are broken.

Such patterns as the willow, delf, rose-bud,

white fluted, and white with a gilt or coloured band are always stocked. Strong colouring should always be avoided whether for tea, breakfast, or dinner services, and it must be remembered that the price will be influenced very much by the amount of good gilt and also upon the novelty of the design and shape.

A Dinner Service.—When choosing a dinner service it is better to select one in which the centre of the dishes and plates is white, as food always looks more appetising when served on a light surface. Choose also a porcelain that will wear well and that will not chip and crack with the heat. China can either be bought in large or small sets for six or twelve persons, or single pieces can be bought in quite a number of different patterns by paying at a little higher rate. A nice set of what is called the "cottage" size can be bought from a guinea upwards consisting of the following pieces, while a medium set will cost from about £1, 14s. 6d. upwards—

Cottage Set (52 *pieces*):—Twelve meat plates, twelve pudding or pie plates, twelve cheese plates, two covered dishes, six meat dishes, two sauce tureens.

Medium Set (81 *pieces*):—Twenty-four meat plates, twenty-four pie plates, twelve soup plates, seven dishes, two covered dishes, two sauce tureens, one soup tureen, one fish drainer.

It must be remembered that in houses where there are a number of people or where small dinner-parties are given, the number of plates must not be too limited.

Tea and Breakfast Sets.—A small tea and breakfast service in plain ware can be bought for 6s. or 7s. and upwards, and in china from 16s. to 17s. and upwards. They would consist of the following pieces:—

Tea Set (40 *pieces*):—Twelve tea-cups and saucers, twelve tea plates, two cake plates, one slop basin, one cream jug.

Breakfast Set for Six (29 *pieces*):—Six cups and saucers, six plates, two cake plates, one slop basin, one sugar basin, one milk jug, six egg cups.

Choice of Glass.—Not a little of the handsome appearance of a well-set dinner-table may be ascribed to its array of shining well-kept and well-polished glass. The table glass should always be of as good a quality as possible, and the design should be characterised by its refined simplicity. Too much design and ornamentation is a mistake, as it tends to rob the glass of that bright transparency which forms the great charm of its appearance. But here, again, unless the glass is always under the care of a reliable servant, it is best to buy it of not too fine a quality and of a design that can be easily replaced. Very thin glass is no doubt appreciated by those who like dainty articles, but it requires the utmost care in the washing and drying. When cut glass cannot be afforded, plain thinnish glass or plain glass with a little engraving looks the best. Very good plain tumblers can be had from 4d. each or with a little engraving from 6s. 6d. per dozen, while a cut glass tumbler will cost from about 1s. upwards.

Wine-glasses are made in various sizes to suit the different wines for which they are used; the form changes with fashion, but they should always match the tumblers in quality and design.

Coloured wine-glasses were at one time much in vogue, but people of taste now appreciate the fact that the white wine-glasses of tasteful design are infinitely preferable.

Decanters also should be carefully chosen with due regard to their design. More ornamentation in the way of cutting or engraving is allowable in the case of all kinds of decanters.

HOME DINNERS

No matter how simple a meal may be, it should be put neatly upon the table and made attractive to the eye. There are certain table refinements which are within the reach of the very humblest; they may not be essentials, but they are beyond doubt among the ameliorating influences of life which help to cultivate the mind and improve the manners. The every-day dinner should be as carefully prepared as the more formal meal when visitors are expected. The decoration of the table may be simpler, the number of courses fewer, and the dishes less expensive, but so far as the appointments are concerned they should receive the same attention.

Under these conditions if paterfamilias should take it into his head to bring in a friend to dinner without any previous notification of his intention of so doing, no disturbance will be caused by the arrival of the unexpected guest—rather will he be looked upon as a welcome addition to the family party.

The dinner-hour must be chosen with due regard to the needs and employments of the various members of the household, and, if possible, let it be at an hour when it does not require to be hurried over. It should be made a time of relaxation, when there can be pleasant and cheerful conversation, and worries and care are, for the moment at least, laid aside. It is a well-known fact that a cheerful frame of mind is a valuable aid to digestion.

Having fixed upon an hour see that the meal is punctually attended and punctually served. The very best cooking will be spoiled if the dinner has to be kept back owing to the unpunctuality of some member of the family, while, on the other hand, the cook who cannot send up a dinner to time should remember that a meal that has to be waited for often fails to be appreciated. Regularity is also good from a health point of view, and for those who are delicate it is all the more important.

The dishes given may be as simple and inexpensive as possible, but let them be well cooked and nicely served.

Then the arrangement is an important consideration—we do not all possess beautiful china and glass, and the choicest silver and damask, but it is possible to have even the simplest things spotlessly clean and bright and to have them arranged with order and taste.

And, again, no table should be considered properly laid unless decorated with some flowers or ferns. Some people may consider this an extravagance, but a small quantity is all that is required, and if flowers are scarce or too expensive, any plant which looks fresh and healthy or even some pretty foliage can take their place.

The dining-room itself ought to be in order and free from dust, and there should be a tidy fireplace and a bright fire burning in the grate if the weather is cold. Also pay attention to the ventilation of the room, as a stuffy atmosphere tends to spoil the appetite; so if the room has been occupied beforehand, let the windows be thrown open for a few minutes at least before the meal is served.

The clean cloth, the bright silver and glass, the tidy and pleasant room with the tasteful floral decoration will all add to the enjoyment of the meal. It may not be every one who bestows direct attention upon these details, but they affect the mind none the less. There is something elevating in beauty and order, whereas an untidy table is just as degrading as a slovenly dress. Let us make the home dinner as attractive as possible, and the simplest meal will then give satisfaction.

SETTING THE TABLE

The Informal Dinner.—Before the actual laying of the cloth there are certain preliminaries in the pantry, or in the kitchen if there is no pantry, which should be attended to. The cruets, for instance, will require attention. The salt-cellars should be filled with fine salt free from lumps, the surface made perfectly smooth, and a clean bright spoon laid across the top. The mustard-pots should be filled with well-made mustard. When fresh mustard is required, mix it first in a small cup and never in the pot itself. It must be mixed with a little water and beaten until perfectly smooth, and be of a consistency that will not run off the side of the plate. A pinch of salt should always be added. If French mustard is preferred, mix the dry mustard with vinegar instead of water, or half vinegar and half water. Tarragon Vinegar is best. The pepperettes should also be well filled with white pepper, black being unsuitable for table use. Large cruets are not used now as a rule, but if bottles of any kind are put on the table, they should be clean and bright and the stands themselves kept in good order.

Next consider the number of people to be laid for, and count out the glasses required and rub them up, and fill the water-bottles with fresh water. Collect the necessary knives and examine the steel parts to see that they are free from tarnish. The bread too that is required should be put on the platter or small pieces put in a bread-basket. All these articles should be put on a tray and carried to the dining-room as soon as the table-cloth and sideboard-cloth have been laid.

Then in the dining-room itself see that the room is in order and well ventilated and the fireplace tidy before beginning to lay the cloth.

A dining-room table is usually made with leaves which can be taken out and put in as required according to the number of persons to be seated. An oval or round table is considered more sociable than a square or oblong one and will accommodate more people, but the shape is of little importance as long as the table is of a suitable height and size for individual needs.

An under-covering or "silence cloth" should first be laid on the table to prevent hot dishes spoiling the polish of the wood, to give the table-cloth a smoother and better appearance, and also to deaden the sound when silver, dishes, &c., are laid down. This can either be an old woollen table-cloth of some light colour, a piece of blanket or serge, or a piece of cotton felting or interlining sold for the purpose. This silence cloth should be about six inches larger than the table all round, and to keep it in position it may either be tied to the four legs by means of tapes, or hemmed and drawn up beneath the edges with a running string.

The table-cloth itself must be laid on perfectly even and as smoothly as possible, the centre of the cloth in the centre of the table, and the sides hanging gracefully with the creases in a straight line. As the appearance of the table will depend very much on the kind of table-cloth used, an effort should be made to have this as clean and unruffled as possible.

Next lay a carving-cloth at one or both ends of the table or wherever there is carving or serving to be done. This cloth may either be square or oblong—very pretty cloths with hem-stitched or fringed edges are sold for the purpose, but, failing these, an ordinary serviette of a large size will do very well.

Spread the sideboard also with a cloth and the dinner-waggon or butler's tray if required. In small houses and flats it is sometimes more convenient to have the latter placed just outside the dining-room door.

Now put the flowers or any other decoration on the table (see p. 253), as this is more easily arranged before the glasses, &c., are placed on the table.

In the allowance of space a good rule to go by is to allow twenty inches at least for each person's accommodation, but if the table is large a little more room does not matter. It is a good plan to place round the serviettes before laying the rest of the cover, as this will give an idea of the amount of space available. The fancy and artistic folding of serviettes is quite out of fashion for the moment and is only to be seen in hotels and restaurants. When clean they should be simply folded, and after they have been used put into rings.

The silver required must next be taken from the sideboard and everything must be carried to the table on a tray and not in the hands. Put a table-knife at the right-hand side and a fork at the left for each person, leaving room for a plate to be placed between, and place a small dessert-spoon and fork horizontally across the top, the handle of the spoon to the right-hand side and that of the fork to the left. If fish is to be served, place a fish-knife and fork outside the other knife and fork, as they will be required first; if soup, a table-spoon on the right-hand side, and if cheese, a small knife at the right-hand side next the plate. Everything must be placed evenly and about an inch up from the edge of the table.

Next put down the spoons and carving-knives and forks that are required for serving the different dishes, and small cruets and water-bottles at a convenient distance down the table. It is no longer the custom to put dinner-mats on the table, but those made of asbestos may be placed under the cloth when there is danger of very hot dishes spoiling the table.

The glasses and bottles of water should be placed on the table almost last—a tumbler at the right-hand side of each person and a wine-glass for each kind of wine that is to be served. The bread may either be put round, a piece to each person, or left in the bread-basket to be handed.

The sideboard should be arranged as carefully as the table, and everything that is required for after use placed upon it, such as a few extra knives, forks, and spoons, extra bread, a basket for receiving dirty knives and silver, and a crumb brush and tray. See also that the chairs are put in their places before bringing in the first course and announcing that the meal is ready.

A Dinner-Party.—*Service à la Russe.*—A dinner-party ranks highest among entertainments, and time and thought are required if it is to be made a success. There are prescribed rules for the sending out of the invitations, the arranging of the guests, and the manner of serving the dinner (see Etiquette). The most popular way of serving a dinner at present is *à la Russe.* By this mode all the carving and serving is done from the side-table and none of the dishes are placed on the dining-table itself. It is certainly a much more luxurious and pleasant method than the old-fashioned style of having all the helping done by the host and hostess, who by this means are left free to attend to their guests and enter more fully into the conversation. It means, however, a more elaborate service as far as waiting is concerned and one which cannot be carried out where there is only one table-maid. On the other hand, a dinner of this kind is more economical as regards food. When served from the side the quantity can be more exactly calculated and smaller joints can be supplied, whereas if the dishes are put on the table they must be handsome ones and there must be more than sufficient to go round. When dinner *à la Russe* is found too troublesome, a compromise between the two styles is very often adopted, some of the dishes, such as soup and joints, being served from the table and entremets handed round in the same manner as the entrées.

A dinner-party is looked upon by many people as a very difficult form of entertainment, and they will hesitate to give one for fear of its not being a success.

Certainly when one possesses a handsome dinner service, good silver and glass and well-trained servants it is a comparatively easy matter, but these are conditions which cannot always be fulfilled. But still this should not debar the housewife of more modest means from the pleasure of giving a little dinner-party to her friends, as a simple dinner well planned is very often more enjoyable than a very formal affair. There is no occasion to have things elaborate and costly, and if we as a nation were a little less pretentious in our tastes, pleasant social intercourse would be less rare. An invitation to a dinner is always considered a greater compliment than one to an "At Home." It is an indication of a wish for greater intimacy, for dinner-parties serve to place us in closer touch with our friends than is the case with almost any other social gathering.

If dinner *à la Russe* is decided on preparations should be commenced in good time so that there need be no cause for a hurry and bustle at the last minute. If special dishes, glass and silver are to be used for the occasion they should be looked out early in the day and made clean and ready for the table.

The setting of the table is very much the same as for the more simple meal, only no carving-cloths will be required and no spoons and forks for serving the different dishes.

Some possessors of polished oak and mahogany tables have adopted the fashion of replacing the large table-cloth with small mats of fine damask and rich lace laid before each guest and below the various dishes, but this is by no means a prevailing fashion. Another custom is to have small tables at which four or six persons can be seated instead of one large table, as this is considered a little more sociable and conducive of conversation.

As regards decoration the tendency is to have it as light as possible, but to have the damask of the whitest and finest that can be afforded. (For Table Decoration, see p. 253.)

The covers must not consist of too many

knives and forks—it is always better to put down others as the meal proceeds than to crowd the table in any way—but they must always be arranged so that the diner commences with those on the outside. The necessary glasses must be put at the right-hand side, with the highest one placed farthest away to avoid its being knocked over. The number of glasses will depend upon the wines to be served—three (sherry, claret, and champagne) is a very usual number, and small tumblers should be provided for non-wine-drinkers. The serviettes should be simply doubled and a small roll or some bread sticks laid to each guest. When name cards are used they must be clearly written and placed beside each cover in such a way as to avoid all confusion later. A menu card should be allowed for each two or three people. The fruit may or may not be placed on the table from the beginning; this is entirely a matter of taste, but small bon-bon dishes containing salted almonds or sweets are generally placed at intervals down the table or arranged amongst the decorations.

A good deal will depend on the lighting of the room, and as the table will be the chief attraction for the time being, the light ought to be centred on that while the rest of the room may be in shadow. If there is a large centre-light it should have a shade corresponding in colour to the flowers used or else forming a pleasing contrast. The pleasantest light is perhaps from shaded candles or small electric lights placed at intervals down the table. If candles are used they should be lighted at least fifteen minutes before dinner commences in order to ensure steady burning.

The sideboard will also require careful preparation. All wine decanters and extra glasses should be placed well to the back, and the dessert plates, finger bowls and doyleys, extra knives and forks and the like laid neatly in the front. When the fruit is not placed on the table that also must find a place on the sideboard until required. Champagne, hook, and other wines that are not decanted should be placed underneath on the floor.

The carving-table is another important item in the *dîner à la Russe*. It must be furnished with a good light, and everything in the way of knives, forks, and spoons must be placed in readiness for the carver during the different courses of the dinner.

The temperature of the room must also be thought of; it must be well aired and still warm and comfortable. It must be remembered that the ladies will be in light attire and the room must not strike chilly. Many a good dinner has been spoilt by inattention to this point. If windows have to be opened a little way it is generally possible by a careful adjustment of screens to prevent the draught from beating down upon the persons seated.

Chairs must be put in position, and the first course, hors d'œuvres or soup, brought to the room before the meal is announced.

A word might be said here about the drawing-room fire; it ought to be one of the maid's duties to attend to this and to see that it is not allowed to burn too low. A bright fire ought to await the guests when they return from dinner.

WAITING AT TABLE

General Directions for Waiting at Dinner.—If a dinner is to be a success the waiting must be above reproach. Perhaps nothing tends so much to spoil the good effect of a meal as inferior service; then, no matter how excellent the cooking, nor how pretty and dainty the table, the result will not be satisfactory. If there are long pauses between the courses, if the waitress is clumsy and noisy in her movements and inattentive to the needs of the company, the finest dinner will be marred.

Even if the meal be but a simple homely one with one maid in attendance a mistress should make a point of having the service as perfect as it is possible, as intelligent and proficient waiting at once stamps the orderly and well-regulated household.

The maid who waits at table should be neatly dressed in a well-brushed black frock and spotless apron, collar and cuffs, and neat cap; or a clean and tidy print gown may take the place of the stuff dress at an early dinner or luncheon in small households when the maid has housework to do after the meal is served. Her hair must be neatly done without any untidy ends flying about, and she ought to pay particular attention to her hands and nails to keep them clean and in good order. If the lighting of fires and cleaning of stoves is part of her work she ought to be careful to wear gloves for the purpose, as it is almost impossible to remove black-lead from the hands when once it has sunk into the skin. She ought also to keep the skins of lemons to rub on her hands, as this helps to remove any stains.

A good waitress must be quick and light in her movements and at the same time quiet and gentle. Although it is of paramount importance to have the courses served quickly one after the other there must be no appearance of hurry; there is a happy medium between long waits and rushing people through, scarcely leaving them time to finish what is on their plates. The service should be carried on as noiselessly as possible; there must be no clatter of dishes nor rattling of knives and forks. The waitress must have all her wits about her and be ever on the alert to see what is wanted, and ready to give her whole attention to the work in hand. Forethought is another very necessary quality—she ought to consider beforehand what will be required for the meal so that there need be no unnecessary moving about or leaving the room when once the meal is served.

She must try to cultivate a pleasant and gracious manner, being thoughtful for the comfort of those she is serving and ready to forestall their wants. She must not take notice of any conversation that is going on, nor let a joke or funny story distract her thoughts. Should any of the company happen to be a little peculiar in manner and perhaps depart from the orderly rules of behaviour, the waitress must not appear to observe it, and if at any time an accident should occur, such as the spilling of a glass of wine or water, she must be ready to put the matter right without showing any signs of annoyance.

When the meal is ready, the chairs in their places and everything in order, the maid ought to see that doors leading into all kitchen and back premises are shut; then when the first course is placed upon the table the dinner may be announced. This may be done either by sounding a gong, ringing a bell, or by going to the drawing-room and saying in a clear voice, "Dinner is served" or "Dinner is on the table, Madam." The drawing-room door should then be left open, and the maid, returning to the dining-room, should take up her position there.

When the courses are served from the table, as is frequently the case at the ordinary family dinner, the waitress should stand on the left-hand side of the one who serves and commence by removing the cover if one is in use. At present the tendency is to abolish dish covers, although in many houses, especially where old-fashioned customs prevail, they are still to be seen. A cover must be taken off and turned up quickly to prevent any drops of steam from falling on the table-cloth.

A waitress should accustom herself to carry two things at a time, one in each hand, as for instance a plate of soup in one hand and a plate of croûtons in the other, a plate of meat in the right hand and a vegetable or sauce in the left, or a plate of meat in each hand. Vegetable and sauces are not placed upon the table when a maid is in constant attendance; they are kept on the sideboard and handed—an attentive servant will see at once when they are required. If the maid leaves the room, she usually puts them down on the table after she has passed them round.

When a dish is handed round it must be held steadily and firmly on a finger napkin and at a convenient height, so that the person seated may find no difficulty in helping himself. A table-spoon or fork and spoon, according to what is required, must be placed in the dish in readiness.

Except at the formal dinner it is customary also to ask if a little more meat or pudding, &c., is desired before the plate is removed.

Do not remove a soup tureen nor any dish being served until every one at the table has finished that particular course.

Soiled plates must be removed at once when finished with; they should never be allowed to remain in front of the person who has used them. They must be removed quietly, and care must be taken not to drop the knife or silver. A plate may be taken in each hand and they should be carried at once to the sideboard, the knives and silver placed in the box or basket placed there for the purpose, and the plates piled without noise one on the top of the other or put into a plate-carrier. A tray or basket must never be carried round the table to receive the knives and silver from the plates, although the reverse is the case with the dishes from which meat, &c., has been served. A carving-knife and fork should never be removed on the dish, as being large and heavy they would be very liable to fall, but a small tray for the purpose should be brought to the table to receive them. The dishes themselves must be removed carefully in order that no grease or gravy be spilt.

Before sweets and dessert, remove on a small tray all cruets and salt-cellars and any knives, forks, spoons, and glasses that will not be required. Also take away the carving cloth if one has been used. All crumbs should then be very carefully removed from the left-hand side of each person seated with a brush or crumb scoop on to a small tray or silver waiter.

A waitress must never reach across a person seated to put down or remove anything from the table, but should walk quietly to the right or left-hand side as required.

If any extra knives or silver are required they should be put down on the table in their proper place with the empty plate before the serving of a course—they must never be offered on a tray.

If more bread is asked for small pieces should be handed in a bread-basket or on a plate. If any small condiment is wanted it should be handed on a small tray or silver salver.

When dinner is served in the old-fashioned way it is quite possible for one maid who is quick and clever to wait upon six or even eight people, although of course the service can be better performed when there are two in attendance, or if some assistance can be given by dishes being brought from the kitchen to the dining-room door and soiled plates carried away.

If two maids are in attendance, the head servant passes round the fish and the second follows with the sauce and other accompaniments; the head passes the meat and the second the vegetables, and so on. The principal servant should never leave the room; the younger maid should inform the cook as soon as a course has been served and prepare her to send up the next at once. The younger maid should also do the carrying of the dishes to and from the room. When a maid is single-handed and is obliged to be absent for a short time a member of the family usually rings the bell at the end of each course.

Novices in the art of waiting have sometimes

a little difficulty in knowing at what side a dish or plate, &c., should be handed or removed. To these the following hints may be useful :—

(1) When there is no choice to be made, the plate with its contents should be put down at the right-hand side of the person seated.

(2) When there is a choice, as for instance two different sweets or two different kinds of fish, hand these at the left-hand side.

(3) When a dish has to be offered, as in the ease of a side dish or vegetable, carry it to the left-hand side. It is a good rule to remember that everything that is offered (except wine) must be carried to the left-hand side.

(4) Soiled plates should be removed from the right-hand side.

(5) Clean and empty plates are put down at the right-hand side.

(6) Wine is offered from the right-hand side as the glasses are naturally standing in that position.

Precedence in Serving.—At a family dinner the lady of the house should be served first unless she is carving, then the daughters of the house according to age, and the governess, if there is one present, and lastly the master of the house and the sons according to age.

If only one or two guests are present serve them first, commencing with the ladies and the principal guest. At a formal dinner-party, where there are a number of guests, commence with the lady on the right-hand side of the host (the principal guest) and continue straight round the table irrespective of sex. It is not then the custom to serve the ladies before the gentlemen. If there are several maids in attendance the two sides of the table may be served simultaneously, commencing with the lady seated next the host on each side. In the case of small tables, the one where the principal guests are seated should be served first.

Hired Cooks and Waitresses.—When the staff of servants is not sufficiently experienced and a large and important party is to be given it is sometimes necessary to hire outside assistance. Both cooks and waitresses can be hired at the principal catering establishments ; or very often they can be heard of through private recommendation, which is even better. The usual fee for such assistance is from 5s. an evening for a waitress, and from 10s. 6d. a dinner for a cook.

DRAWING UP A MENU

It requires some skill and experience to make a good bill of fare; any miscellaneous collection of good dishes does not necessarily produce a first-class menu.

There are several points to bear in mind when arranging the dishes for a dinner :—

(1) Dishes that are in season should be chosen. Although many articles, such as vegetables, fruit, and fish, can be had out of their proper season, it must be remembered that an exorbitant price will likely be asked for them, and even at that they will in all probability be wanting in flavour.

(2) There must be variety in flavour, and the dishes must follow each other in such a way as will please the palate. An insipid dish must not directly follow one that is very tasty, and if two or three different entrées are served the most savoury one should come last. The same flavouring must not be repeated in two consecutive dishes.

(3) There must be variety in the method of cooking and in the character of the different dishes. It would not do for fried cutlets to follow fried fish, nor for two braised dishes or two grills to come together, and so on. A simple dish should be followed by one a little more elaborate or *vice versâ*.

(4) There must be variety in colour and decoration. The dishes must be pleasing to the eye as well as to the palate, there should be no sameness, and an element of refinement rather than ostentation.

(5) The names of the dishes should be written on the menu cards either in French or in English, French is perhaps the more fashionable, but this is entirely a question of choice. The names of standard dishes should never be altered, although more liberty may be taken with the names of made-up dishes.

(6) And, lastly, the powers of the cook and the capabilities of the kitchen-range must be borne in mind. If the cook is single-handed do not attempt too much and do not give her a number of dishes that cannot be finished off until the last minute. Of course it will always be possible to have a certain number of dishes sent in from a caterer, but this will add considerably to the expense, and in the end there is nothing better than good cooking well done at home. An important point is to give the cook plenty of notice and explicit directions as to what will be required.

The different courses of a complete menu will comprise the following :—hors d'œuvres, potage, poisson, entrées, relevé, sorbet, rôti, entremets, dessert, café.

Hors d'Œuvres.—These consist of small appetising morsels usually served cold, such as oysters, olives, anchovies, caviare, smoked salmon, small salads, thin slices of sausage, &c. They may either be served plain or made up in some more elaborate style. Small plain biscuits or thin brown bread and butter may accompany the plain hors d'œuvres.

Potage (Soup).—Either one or two soups may be served. If only one it is preferable to have it clear or of a very light character, especially if there are a number of courses to follow. If there are two soups one may be thick and the other clear.

Poisson (Fish).—This may either be plainly boiled with a sauce or dressed in a more elaborate fashion, or there may be one dish of each.

Entrées.—These may come either before or after the relevé; in fact, they can be served between any of the courses or omitted altogether. They consist of various kinds of made dishes and ought to be served very daintily. If more than one is served one might be brown and the other white, or one might be hot and the other cold.

Relevé (or Remove).—This consists of a solid joint either roasted, boiled, or braised, and a garnish generally gives the characteristic name. One vegetable besides potatoes is usually served with the remove.

Sorbet.—A half-frozen water ice which is served in cups immediately after the roast.

Rôti.—Roast game or poultry usually served with salad and chip potatoes.

Entremets.—These may be divided into three classes—(1) *dressed vegetables* (légumes); (2) *sweet entremets*, both hot and cold; (3) *savouries*, which precede the dessert and are usually hot.

Dessert.—Fruits of various kinds and *petits fours* or other fancy biscuits.

Coffee.—This must be black—cream being served separately.

In a small dinner some of these courses would be omitted. The number of dishes depends entirely upon the style of the dinner; it may consist of three or four or of eleven or twelve. For instance, the hors d'œuvres and sorbet are seldom given at a small dinner, and either the relevé or the rôti would be omitted. One sweet might follow the last meat course to be followed by a cheese dish or other savoury. Ices may either be served in place of a cold sweet, or they may form a separate course after the savoury.

HINTS ON SERVING THE DIFFERENT COURSES

Hors d'Œuvres.—These are frequently placed on the plate before dinner is announced—especially in the case of oysters—or a choice of several kinds is offered on a small tray.

Soup.—If the soup is served from the side and the dinner consists of numerous courses, three-quarters of a ladleful will be sufficient to give as a helping. If there are two different soups, the waitress should take a plate of each and offer a choice; if only one she should take a plate of soup in one hand and a plate of croûtons or pulled bread in the other. Parmesan cheese may also be served with clear soup.

Fish.—The waitress should take a portion of fish in the right hand and the sauce or other accompaniment in the left. If there is a choice she should take a portion of each kind and the accompaniments would be offered by a second waitress.

Entrées.—A hot or cold plate as required must first be put down to each person, and it must be seen that they have the necessary knives and forks. The entrée must then be handed with a spoon and fork in readiness in the dish. Entrées are always handed, no matter how simple the dinner.

Joints and Game.—Unless these have been carved beforehand, the head waitress must be able to help them neatly from the side and serve them out in small portions, which must be handed round followed by their various accompaniments.

Salad.—A small salad plate should be put to the left of each guest before the salad is carried round. The salad itself should be mixed at the side or in the kitchen and handed in the bowl with the salad spoon and fork in readiness. If not partaken of the special plate should be removed.

Sweets and other Entremets are usually handed in the same way as entrées, a hot or cold plate with necessary fork or spoon and fork being put before each guest previously. In the case of any sweet requiring cutting, such as tart, this would be served out in portions from the side.

Cheese.—It is not customary to serve plain cheese at a formal dinner, but when it is wished it is usually handed in a dish with different divisions containing cheese in small pieces, butter, and one or two different kinds of biscuits. A small plate and knife would be put down to each guest before the dish is handed.

Dessert.—The table should be cleared of crumbs and all unnecessary glasses, &c., before dessert is served. Unless the fruit has not been on the table during the dinner it should now be put down, and a dessert plate with a doyley and finger bowl, along with a fruit knife and fork, should be placed before each guest. If ices are served in this course they should be served first and the ice plates removed before the fruit is handed. Each kind of fruit must be offered in turn and then replaced on the table.

It is not usual to offer a second helping of any of the courses at a formal dinner. (For the Serving of Wine, see p. 248.)

CARVING AND SERVING

Although at the present time the formal dinner is always served *à la Russe*, when all carving and serving is done at the side-table or in the kitchen, the art of carving is still required at family repasts.

Every lady ought to know how to carve; in fact, it would be a good thing if even the young people in the house took turns in performing this duty; they would not then feel at a loss when they came to have homes of their own or when called upon to take the place of their parents.

The art of carving can only be learnt by practice; some instruction may no doubt be given in a book, and a beginner may also learn from watching an expert carver, but proficiency can only come by actually doing the work oneself.

To begin with there must be some knowledge of the anatomy of the various joints, of the relative position of bones, joints, muscles, and fat, and also which are the choicest portions. The most satisfactory way of learning this is to take the chance when opportunity occurs of studying the various pieces of meat off the table. In the case of game or poultry, for instance, the bird might be cut up in its raw state for a *fricassée* or stew and a point made of examining the different joints.

Carving does not require much physical strength; in fact, any undue effort or exhibition of exertion only shows want of skill or bad implements: the really clever carver is able to cut up the most difficult joints with perfect ease.

One must first of all learn to carve neatly without splashing the gravy over the cloth or pieces of meat beyond the dish, and then to cut straight and uniform slices so that the joint may not be made to look untidy and jagged, but inviting enough to tempt one to desire another helping, or, if large enough to appear at another meal, it may do so wearing a presentable appearance. A number of cut surfaces only allow the escape of juice and tend to make the joint flavourless. Bad carving is always wasteful, but the good carver will cut in such a way as to make every portion inviting and full of flavour.

Both the butcher and the cook can do much to facilitate the work of the carver—in the case of a loin of mutton or veal, for instance, neat carving would be impossible unless the butcher had performed his part of well jointing between the ribs. The cook, too, should see that all skewers, pieces of string, &c., are removed. The size of the dish on which the joint is served is also important. It must be large enough not only to hold the joint when whole, but also to allow room for several cut portions when they are detached. Some people prefer to have a separate dish for the cut portions, and these can, if liked, be handed round. It is a mistake to put a garnish on any meat which requires carving at table, and the less gravy there is the easier it will be for the one who is serving. An extra supply can always be served separately in a sauce-boat. The dish must always be placed near enough the carver to allow of her reaching it without any difficulty, and the chair on which she is seated ought to be high enough to allow her to have perfect control over her work without the necessity of standing. Some will find it easier to be raised on a firm cushion.

The sharpness of the knife is another very important matter. It must always be sharpened before dinner and never at the table, where the performance is most trying to people's nerves. It should have a handle that can be grasped easily and a long thin blade of a size adapted to the article to be served. A carving-knife should never be used for anything but its one legitimate purpose. There are different kinds of knives sold for the purpose, as, for instance, a meat carver, a slicer, a breakfast carver, a game knife, and game scissors; but if means are limited and only one general carver can be afforded, choose one made of the best steel one and a half inches wide at its broadest part and from eight to ten inches long.

The carving fork should have two long prongs and a good guard to protect the fingers. The hand should be held over the handle of the fork with the palm downwards and the first finger extended. Insert the fork deep enough into the meat to enable you to hold it firmly in position. The knife also should generally be held firmly and then applied lightly. There will be less gravy squeezed out if the pressure on the meat is not too heavy. Both knife and fork must be held in a natural manner and not grasped as if they were weapons; the cutting must be sharp and clean, never jagged like a saw. All meat should be cut across the grain with the exception of saddle of mutton.

The carver must try to make a fair distribution of the different cuts and bear in mind individual likes and dislikes. As a rule, one small slice is sufficient to serve to a lady and two small or one large to a gentleman, but the quantity must be regulated somewhat by the number of courses in the dinner. If there is only one joint on the table and there are ladies and gentlemen present, she should try to regulate the helpings so that a smaller portion is served to the ladies. If there is more than one dish to choose from the portions should be made equal and rather small in size.

Never ask a guest before beginning to carve to make a choice between two different dishes, but help the dishes first and then make the inquiry, otherwise they might feel that it was being cut into solely for them.

The following notes on the carving of some of the principal joints indicate the *general* method adopted, but these rules need not be hard and fast, and clever carvers very soon acquire their own style.

BEEF

Sirloin of Beef.—This joint should be placed with the back bone or thickest end at the left-hand side of the dish. Although it is usual to carve the undercut first, as this is one of the primest cuts when hot, the joint is served with this piece underneath and the carver raises it and turns it over. The undercut should be cut across in fairly thick slices C to D and a small portion of fat served with each. The upper part should be cut in long slices parallel with the ribs A to B. The slices should be as thin as possible

Sirloin of Beef.

without being ragged, and the point of the knife should be inserted to loosen the slices from the bone.

Ribs of Beef.—This joint should be carved in the same way as the upper part of the sirloin. There is no undercut.

Round of Beef or Rolled Ribs.—A thin-bladed and very sharp knife is required for this. First cut rather a thick slice off the outside to make the top surface even and then continue cutting thin slices right across the joint.

Ox Tongue.—As the centre is the choicest portion, the tongue should be cut through three or four inches from the top and thin slices cut from both ends. A small piece of the fat which lies near the root might be served with each portion.

MUTTON AND LAMB

Leg of Mutton.—Place this joint on the dish with the thickest part lying towards the outside of the dish and the small end to the left. The carving is not difficult and it is always done in the same way. Insert the fork in the thickest part and raise the joint slightly towards you. Then cut several slices of medium thickness through the thickest part and right down to the bone B to A. Next slip the knife along underneath

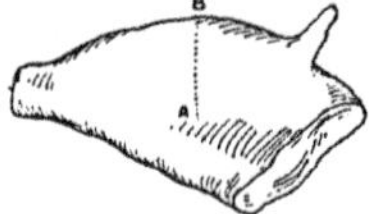

Leg of Mutton.

the slices and detach them from the rest. Some prefer a piece from the upper end and others one nearer the knuckle, as the meat is usually better done towards the thin end, and one of the tastiest morsels lies quite close to the knuckle or lower joint. A small piece of fat which lies underneath the thick end should be served with each portion. When the thick side of the meat is finished, slices should be cut from the other side in the same way.

Loin of Mutton and Lamb.—This cut must be thoroughly well jointed by the butcher or it will be found most difficult to carve. It will be well also to examine it before cooking, and, if necessary, joint any part that has been forgotten. Place the joint on the dish with the thick part towards the outside. Insert the

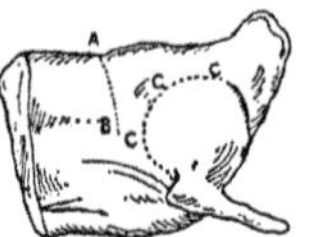

Forequarter of Lamb.

knife between the bones and cut right through, separating all the cutlets in the same manner. If there is a kidney a piece of it should be served with each portion.

Saddle of Mutton should be placed on the dish with the tail end to the left. Insert the fork firmly in the middle and carve across the ribs in long slices running parallel with the backbone. Then slip the knife under and detach the slices from the ribs. If too long they may be cut across in two or three pieces. A small piece of crisp fat from the lower part of the ribs may be served with each portion.

Shoulder of Mutton.—This is one of the most difficult joints to carve. Serve with the skin side uppermost on the dish. Insert the fork in the fleshy part and raise the joint slightly from the dish. Take as many slices as possible from

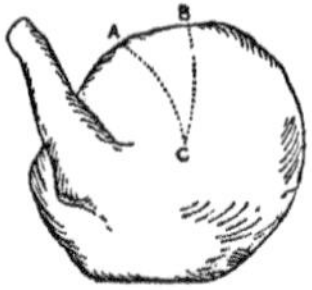

Shoulder of Mutton.

the side A and B to C, cutting in each case right through to the bone. The meat lying on each side of the blade-bone on the upper side of the joint should next be cut, carving the whole length of the meat from the knuckle end.

Then turn the joint and take slices off the under-side. The under-part is the juiciest and most delicate part, and is frequently cut before the upper portion.

Forequarter of Lamb.—This is another somewhat troublesome joint to carve. The first point to attend to is to raise the shoulder from the ribs and breast. Insert the fork in the most fleshy part of the shoulder and with the knife cut round as shown by dotted line C. Raise up the shoulder on the fork and cut it away without removing too much of the meat from underneath. The shoulder portion should be carved in the same manner as a shoulder of mutton, but unless the whole joint is required for one meal it is usual to have this put aside on

Loin of Pork.

a separate dish and served cold. Cut the under portion across, separating the ribs from the breast. Divide the ribs one from the other, A to B, and cut the breast in slices. A small portion of each may be served to each person.

VEAL

Fillet of Veal.—This should be carved in thin even slices in the same way as a round of beef. If there is stuffing a small quantity should be served with each portion.

Loin of Veal.—Carve in the same way as loin of mutton unless the cutlets are very large, when they may be cut in slices like ribs of beef.

Knuckle of Veal.—Carve in the same way as a leg of mutton.

PORK

Leg of Pork.—Carve in the same way as a leg of mutton, serving a piece of the crisp fat and a small quantity of stuffing, if there is any, to each person.

Loin of Pork.—Carve in slices from A to B, separating the cutlets between the bones in the same way as the loin of mutton.

Sucking Pig.—This is generally sent to table cut in half down the centre and with the head cut off with one piece laid at each side. First cut off the four legs from the carcase and then separate the ribs into small cutlets. It is all good, and it is just a matter of choice which part is served.

Ham.—If the ham is sent to table whole, the thickest part should be placed towards the outer side of the dish. Take a very sharp knife and make an incision through the thickest part and right down to the bone. Continue cutting in very thin slices towards both ends of the ham and serve a fair amount of fat with each portion.

A more economical way of carving a ham is to commence at the knuckle end and cut off thin slices working towards the thicker part. When the bone begins to look unsightly it can be sawn off.

GAME AND POULTRY

Fowl (Roast or Boiled).—The fowl should be placed on the dish with the legs to the left-hand side. Insert the fork deeply across the breast-bone so that it takes a firm hold. First remove the wing on the side nearest you by cutting through the skin and shaving off a thin slice of the breast towards the wing joint. Then with the point of the knife sever the joint from the carcase. Next remove the leg on the same side by making a downward cut between the thigh and the body. Bend the leg over and sever the joint with the point of the knife. Now cut the meat from the breast in thin slices and the whole length of the bird B to A. The fork should never be moved from its original position, and the necessary carving should be finished before beginning to serve.

If the family is small and the whole fowl is not required the second side may be left, and if the bare piece of carcase is cut away and the half fowl served bone downwards on a dish with a nice garnish of parsley or salad, it will make quite a nice-looking dish. If, however, the whole fowl is required, remove the wish-bone from the neck in front of the breast-bone by inserting the point of the knife at the end. Then turn the bird round and carve the second side in exactly the same way as the first, and

Roast Fowl.

finally turn the carcase over and remove the oyster, a small dark portion which lies near the centre of the side bones. The wing and the breast are considered the finest parts.

Turkey.—This is carved in very much the same way as a fowl, only if it is large and the whole is not required it is usual to commence with the breast and to cut slices from that before removing the legs and wings. When the legs are cut off they should be divided in two at the joint and then cut in slices, as they make too large portions by themselves. If the bird is stuffed a small quantity of the force-meat should be served with each portion.

Goose.—Serve the bird with the neck at the left-hand side of the dish. As the breast is the best part it is usual to carve this first and not to use the legs and wings the first day unless they are required. Insert the fork in the centre over the ridge of the breast-bone and cut the breast in thin parallel slices, commencing at the wing and continuing until the breast-bone is reached. Then slip the knife under and detach them from the bone. Remove the legs and wings in the same way as from a fowl. If there is sage and onion farce inquire of each one if a small helping is agreeable, or hand it round separately.

Roast Duck.—Carve in the same way as roast goose.

Pigeon.—The usual plan to adopt is to cut the bird right through the middle into two equal parts. If these are too large they may be cut through again into quarters.

Partridge and Grouse should be carved in the same way as pigeon, a piece of toast being served with each portion.

Small birds, such as snipe, landrail, ortolan, are usually served whole or may be cut in two for ladies.

FISH

A silver or plated fish knife and fork or fish carvers ought to be used for serving fish. A steel knife should never be used or the flavour of the fish will be spoiled. Care should be taken not to break the flakes more than is necessary and to serve as little bone as possible.

Cod or Salmon.—The fish should be placed on the dish with the thick part of the back towards the further side. Carve in fairly thick slices right through to the centre bone, then slip the knife underneath and detach them. When the top part is finished remove the bone and cut through the lower portion in the same manner.

Turbot and Brill are both served in the same way. First cut through the thickest part of the fish right down to the back bone. Commence at the head end and continue to the tail. Then cut slices across from the centre towards the sides of the fish and detach them from the bone. Part of the fins and a little of the gelatinous skin should be served with each portion.

Sole.—Cut through the whole length of the thick part and then raise the fillet from each side. Then remove the bone and separate the other side into two fillets.

Plaice.—If large carve in the same way as a turbot; if small according to directions given for sole.

Small fish are either served whole or cut in two pieces.

SERVING OF WINES

In former times it was considered the correct thing to serve a different kind of wine with each course, and the choice was very complicated, but nowadays the number has been much reduced, and it is quite usual to serve only one or two kinds throughout the whole meal.

When wine is offered it must be good of its kind; poor cooking is bad enough, but cheap wine is even worse, being at times almost poisonous. People with limited means should not give champagne or sparkling hock, which in a cheap form are very deleterious, but let them rather be content in offering some other wine less expensive and yet good of its kind, such as claret, sherry, or some light white wine.

When one is in doubt as to what wine to buy or what brand to get, the best plan is to consult a reliable wine-dealer, as it is impossible for an amateur to know all the different brands and their distinctive qualities.

For a simple informal dinner it is very customary to give a good claret or burgundy and a good sherry or some light white wine. For a formal dinner champagne or hock is usually given either alone or with other wines.

If a variety of wines is given the following is the usual order in which they are served:—

Sherry with soup, champagne with the first entrée and throughout the meal; sherry and claret at dessert, and liqueurs with the ices and after coffee. Sometimes a white Rhine wine, chablis, or sauterne is offered with fish or with oysters when they commence the meal.

At luncheon one wine is usually sufficient, such as claret, burgundy, or hock. Champagne is rarely given. Whisky and soda may be offered if gentlemen are present.

At supper sherry, claret and hock, or champagne may be offered, or one wine only.

Claret should always be decanted when used for dessert—at other times it is a question of taste. Both claret and burgundy should be warmed to the temperature of the room. The best way to do this is to allow them to stand in a warm dining-room some hours before they are required; or if wanted in a hurry to stand the bottle in a pail of warm water for a short time. These wines will not keep long after the bottle has been opened.

Sherry and port should always be decanted, and this should be done carefully and some time before the wine is required, so as to allow any sediment to sink to the foot of the decanter.

Port and Madeira are little used, especially at large dinners, although they may be served with dessert or with a cheese course at the end of a dinner. A fine Madeira sometimes takes the place of sherry at the soup course.

Champagne is generally served from the bottle. A serviette should be wrapped round the bottle, or held beneath the neck after the wine has been poured out to prevent the drops falling on the cloth. It ought to be very cold, and in hot weather it is customary to stand the bottles in ice for two hours before using. Metal pails are sold for the purpose, and these are filled with a mixture of broken ice and salt. A dry champagne is the favourite, the sweet brands being little used, except sometimes for ladies. Hock and Moselle are not decanted; they should be drunk at a temperature of about 40° Fahr.

Decanters of wine are not put on the table at a formal dinner until dessert is served, when claret and sherry can be placed in front of the host.

To open champagne or other sparkling wines, first cut the wire with a pair of champagne nippers and then cut the strings. Hold the bottle in a slanting position and remove the cork slowly and carefully. The bottle must be held on the slant until the wine has been poured out. When drawing ordinary bottles care must be taken not to break the cork; the corkscrew should be screwed into the middle of the cork as straight as possible. A lever corkscrew is best.

Wine should always be poured out at the right-hand side of the person seated, and poured out very carefully. When handing champagne at a dinner it is usual to ask in the first instance if it is desired, but when handing it later the glass should be refilled without any comment.

Liqueurs are always served in small liqueur glasses on a silver tray or liqueur stand and handed at the left-hand side.

Mineral waters and lemonade should be at hand at all meals, as so many do not take wine. Barley water too is a favourite and fashionable drink, especially among ladies, and is often served at luncheon.

Brandy or whisky and soda may be in readiness at informal meals where men are present. These spirits should always be decanted.

When stout or ale is taken the bottle should be opened at the sideboard and then poured out carefully and slowly, holding the bottle at an angle so that the glass may be filled with ale and not froth. It should then be handed on a silver waiter. If it is draught ale it should be poured out briskly and then slowly from a jug in order to give it a head.

BREAKFAST

The service of the breakfast-table does not alter much, and whether the meal be simple or elaborate the mode of laying the table remains very much the same. Although there are no hard-and-fast rules as in the case of the formal dinner, as much daintiness should be observed in the setting of the breakfast-table.

In large houses this meal is usually set in the morning-room and not in the dining-room and at an hour to suit the habits of the household. In all cases it must be served early enough to permit of those who have special work to perform to take their meal quietly and without hurry. This is especially necessary in the case of children having to go off to school. The seeds of indigestion have often been sewn even in childhood by having to swallow this meal in a hurry.

Both table and sideboard must be covered with a cloth, sometimes a plainer one than that used for dinner; any decoration must be of the very simplest—a pretty plant or fern, or a few flowers in vases will be all that are required.

The usual plan is to place the tea or coffee or both at one end of the table in front of the hostess along with the necessary accompaniments of sugar and milk, the required number of cups and saucers and a jug or kettle of hot water. Everything must be within easy reach for serving, and hot articles should be placed on silver or china stands.

At the other end would be placed any dishes that were being served and the necessary plates. If there is a choice of dishes cold dishes such as ham, tongue, or cold pie are usually placed on the sideboard and served from there. When boiled eggs are served they are put on an egg-stand or in a folded serviette or lined basket to keep them warm. Butter and jam or marmalade should also find a place on the breakfast-table, the former neatly rolled or made up in pats in the butter dishes, and the latter tidily served in jam dishes or fancy pots.

Different kinds of bread would also be served according to taste, such as rolls and scones (white or brown), toast, oatcakes, cut white and brown bread, &c. These must be served on bread plates with doyleys underneath. If a loaf of bread is required as well it is usually placed on the bread platter on the sideboard and cut as required.

Fruit either stewed or raw is also becoming a recognised addition to the breakfast-table, the kind varying according to the season of the year.

When cereal foods, such as porridge, grape-nuts, quaker oats, bread and milk, &c., are wanted, they must be daintily served—some of the pretty bowls or fire-proof dishes now sold are very suitable for the purpose.

The other appointments of the table will depend on the number of persons and the special dishes being served. A small plate and knife and serviette must be put to each place and the necessary knives, forks, and spoons for the different dishes. Provision must also be made for any dish that is to be served, not forgetting such things as cruets, butter knives, jam spoons, &c.

A table-heater is a most useful article to have for the breakfast-table, especially in houses where the meal is a prolonged one. By this means dishes can be kept warm, and if the heater has a sliding top, as in the "Heatorboil," as shown in illustration, it can be utilised for boiling eggs or a little water as well.

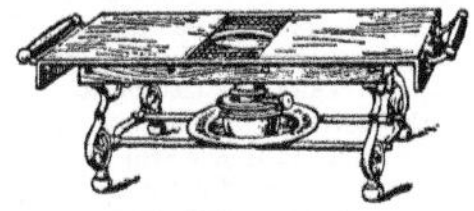

The "Heatorboil."

As a rule, there is no waiting done at breakfast, so that it is all the more important that the table be set carefully and that nothing is forgotten.

Variety of Food.—Perhaps there is no meal at which variety is more necessary than at breakfast, but in many middle-class houses it is made a most monotonous and uninteresting repast. This may be due partly to the early hour at which the meal is served, but it is also the result of want of thought or resourcefulness on the part of the cook or housewife. Elaborate dishes are not required; in fact, they would be out of place; what is wanted is simple tasty dishes nicely served—always remembering that what pleases the eye helps also to please the palate. It is well as far as possible to choose for breakfast such dishes as can either be prepared the night before or will take little time to get ready in the morning.

Besides such well-known favourites as ham, eggs, bacon, fried fish, fried sausages, &c., the dishes detailed below, recipes for which will be found in the Guide to Cookery (pp. 116 to 235), might be quoted:—

Cod's roe, fish cakes, fish curry, fish cutlets, steamed fish pudding, scalloped fish, smoked haddock balls, herring au gratin, pickled herring, fish pies (various), tripe with tomatoes, grilled kidneys, sheep's tongues, brawn, jellied veal, calf's liver, calves' brains, calves' feet, galantine of veal, cold meat shape, meat scallops, glazed beef roll, chicken and spaghetti, potted fish and meat, rissoles and croquettes, cold pie, various egg dishes and omelets, stewed mushrooms, nut rissoles.

If more suggestions as to what to give are required, the housewife would do well to supply herself with the little volume entitled "Breakfast Dishes," published by T. C. and E. C. Jack.

Tea and Coffee.—It is very important that the tea and coffee for breakfast should be well made and served very hot, and the few hints given below for the use of the novice in the art of tea and coffee-making may not be out of place.

Tea.—Half fill the teapot with boiling water, let it stand a minute or two until thoroughly hot, then empty it. Put in the requisite quantity of tea (the old rule of a level teaspoon for each person and one over is a good one, but for a number a smaller proportion may be allowed), and pour on, gently enough, boiling water to half fill the teapot. Take the teapot to the kettle, and never the kettle to the teapot. Cover with a cosy or let it stand in a warm place to infuse for three minutes, then fill up the teapot and pour out the tea. Tea is never good if allowed to stand too long, and the use of a tea-cosy is to be deprecated if it is employed to keep tea hot for a long time until it becomes black and bitter. If the tea has to be kept hot for any length of time, it should be poured off the leaves into another teapot, or some teapots are fitted with an inner case which contains the leaves, and which can be removed when the tea has infused sufficiently.

When sugar and milk or cream are used, they should be put into the teacup before the tea. The addition of milk makes the tea more wholesome, that of sugar less so.

Coffee.—To get good coffee is often one of the difficulties of the housekeeper, and yet it need not be so. The making of it is very simple. It just requires some nicety and care.

Coffee to be good should be freshly roasted and freshly ground. When this cannot be done at home, it should be bought in very small quantities and kept in a tin box with a tight-fitting lid.

If pure coffee is wanted chicory must not be used. Chicory imparts a slight bitterness to the coffee and darkens the colour, and some people prefer coffee with it. The usual proportions are two ounces chicory to one pound coffee. The water, as for tea, must be freshly boiled. It is also important to have the coffee-pot very clean.

There are many different kinds of cafetières, and some of them are more complicated than others, but for ordinary purposes the simple tin or china cafetière with percolator answers very well and requires no spirit-lamp.

First fill the cafetière with boiling water, let it stand until thoroughly heated, and pour the water away. Then put in the required amount of coffee—the quantity will vary according to the taste of the consumer; but a very good proportion is one table-spoonful coffee to each half-pint of boiling water. Pour the boiling water gently and gradually over the coffee, and let it filter slowly through. Keep the pot standing in a warm place, and serve as hot as possible. Coffee to be good must be hot. If there is no percolator attached to the coffee-pot, it is a good plan to have an iron ring made to fit the top of the coffee-pot inside. To this ring sew a muslin bag, and fit the bag into the pot. Pour some boiling water through it, and when it is well warmed pour the water away. Put the coffee into the bag and proceed as before.

Coffee can also be made in a jug. Heat the jug thoroughly with boiling water and pour the water away. Put the coffee into the jug, and stand it on the top of the stove for a few minutes until the coffee is hot. Then pour the proper quantity of boiling water over it and stir with a spoon. Cover the jug with a lid or thickly folded cloth, and let it stand by the side of the stove for fifteen minutes. Have the jug or pot in which the coffee has to be served made very hot. Stretch a piece of muslin over it and strain the coffee through.

When milk is served with coffee it should be scalded but not quite boiled. The proportions are equal quantities of strong coffee and milk, or two-thirds milk to one-third of coffee. A little cream may be added.

LUNCHEONS

There are several different kinds of luncheons, and the manner of serving them is more varied and less formal than that of the late dinner.

First there is the simple meal of two or three courses, which serves as the dinner of the children of the family and also that of the servants.

Then there is the still simpler meal partaken of by those who look forward to a more substantial meal in the evening and consisting of some egg or vegetable dish, or perhaps some made-up meat dish, cold meat, or the remains of dinner of the night before, along with a little fruit, cheese, and perhaps a cup of coffee.

And, lastly, there is the rather more formal luncheon, very similar to the late dinner, but with fewer courses and simpler ceremony.

The mid-day dinner has already been described under "Home Dinners," and requires no further comment.

The luncheon proper is a more or less informal meal according to the style of the house and customs of the family. As a rule all the dishes are served from the table, the waitress only passing the plates and handing any vegetable. The plates would also be changed by the maid in attendance, but any other service is generally performed by members of the family themselves, unless there is a good staff of servants.

A more formal luncheon would be served *à la Russe*, but this is only suited to large establishments, as one or two maids would require to be in constant attendance. The decorations should be very simple and menu and name cards are not necessary. Long luncheons consisting of many courses are not liked, and the dishes should be lighter than for a dinner.

When soup is on the menu it is frequently served in cups instead of soup plates, and small racks of toast should be supplied as well as bread.

Entrées of different kinds frequently take the place of more substantial joints which require carving, and the sweets should be simple in character, or some novelty in the way of pastry or French gâteaux might be offered. Dessert may be omitted if it makes the service too long, but a few little dishes of bon-bons or salted almonds may be placed on the table as at dinner.

The table is not cleared at dessert, and fruit plates are used without finger glasses. Black coffee is usually handed at the table after the last course has been served.

AFTERNOON TEA

This can scarcely be called a meal, but rather a light refreshment taken in the afternoon to break the fast between luncheon and late dinner. It is usually served in the drawing-room between four and five o'clock, and although unceremonious in character, it is one of the most social and popular events of the day, and the taste and refinement of the hostess are readily recognised in the manner in which it is served. Everything should be as dainty and attractive as possible.

The tea itself should be of the best that can be afforded and must be well made (see p. 250). The question as to what special tea to use is entirely a matter of taste—China tea is much appreciated by many people, and it is light and refreshing, but it is an acquired taste and not liked by every one, so that when tea is to be offered to a mixed company whose individual tastes are not known, it is safer to use a good blended tea with no pronounced flavour.

The beauty and delicacy of the china is also important, and it is usual to have small thin cups and saucers of some dainty design with teaspoons of a suitable size. All the silver must be very bright. Plates are not as a rule required, unless cream cakes or other similar dainties are being offered—when used they must be quite small in size.

The hostess should try to study novelty and variety in the cakes or bread offered, and nothing of a large or clumsy nature must be seen. Plain bread, either brown or white, should be buttered and sliced very thinly and cut in any shape desired, or, for a change, it may be made up in little rolls. Scones and tea-cakes are best hot buttered and served in a muffin dish or in a folded doyley. Different kinds of small sandwiches might also be served (see p. 187), and there must always be a nice choice of cakes. Petits-fours and other fancy biscuits of various sorts are also favourites, as they are dry and not likely to soil the gloves.

All the bread plates should be covered with pretty doyleys or lace-edged papers; the latter is better for placing under any cake that has to be cut. The tea should be prepared in the pantry or kitchen. If the tray is not of silver cover it with a dainty white tray-cloth, then arrange the cups and saucers, sugar basin, slop-basin and cream jug on it, and have the plates of bread and butter and cake in readiness. When all is ready and a good kettle of water boiling, prepare the table in the drawing-room—this may or may not be covered with a cloth according to its kind, but if one is used it must be as dainty as possible—there is nothing prettier than the all-white cloth, embroidered or trimmed with lace, but if colour is introduced it must tone with the colour of the teacups. Small serviettes to match are sometimes used, but this is not a universal custom.

The table is generally low and should be placed beside the hostess. The plates of cake may be placed on a cake-stand or on another small table close at hand. Infuse the tea and fill up the hot-water jug or kettle last of all and carry all to the drawing-room at the hour appointed. Tea-cosies are no longer fashionable, although many people still prefer to use them.

When guests are expected the table is sometimes prepared beforehand, leaving only the tea and water to be carried in when it is required. If more visitors should arrive after the tea has been served, the waitress must see that there is a sufficient number of cups and bring more if necessary without requiring to be told. Fresh tea should also be made and more bread cut if needed.

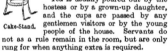

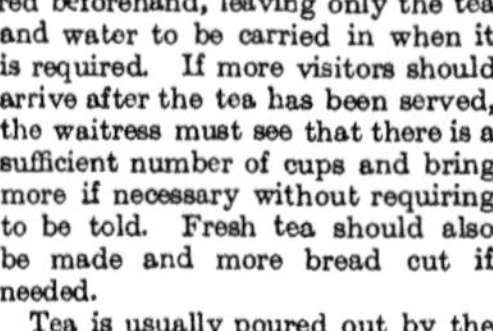
Cake-Stand.

Tea is usually poured out by the hostess or by a grown-up daughter, and the cups are passed by any gentlemen visitors or by the young people of the house. Servants do not as a rule remain in the room, but are only rung for when anything extra is required.

AFTERNOON "AT HOMES"

When a number of guests are expected the tea itself is sometimes served in a back drawing-room. A good-sized table spread with a pretty cloth should be placed in one corner, and upon it should be arranged the tea things with plates of bread and butter cakes and other dainties. The tea in this case should be poured out by one of the daughters of the house or by a lady friend, leaving the hostess free to receive and entertain her guests in the drawing-room proper.

At very large "At Homes" tea is frequently served in the dining-room, but this is a more formal affair. Visitors are shown into the room on arrival and waited on by servants before they enter the drawing-room. Gentlemen visitors often assist in handing round the refreshments. The table should be made into a sort of buffet, and, if space is limited, it should be moved to one end of the room. It must be covered with a fine damask cloth and the serving should be done from the back. Both tea and coffee are frequently served on these occasions and rows of cups and saucers should be in readiness. The jugs of cream and milk and bowls of sugar might be placed on the side of the table next the guests, allowing them to help themselves. There should be an abundant supply of all kinds of dainties, and one or two large cakes on high stands would help to give an ornamental appearance. The table must be prettily decorated with a few flowers or plants and everything made as attractive as possible.

In summer it is very usual to offer fruit, strawberries especially, and these are best served in small quantities on little plates. Ices too are sometimes served.

If there is sufficient space in the dining-room there might be two or three little tables and some chairs dotted about the room for the convenience of those who do not care to take their refreshment standing.

SUPPER

The Family Supper.—In houses where early dinner is the rule, supper of a more or less substantial kind is the concluding meal of the day. This is generally quite an informal meal, and the arrangement of it depends entirely upon individual requirements. As a rule, all the dishes are placed on the table and there is little or no waiting. The table is laid in very much the same way as for luncheon, and as the articles required depend entirely upon the kind of food provided, it is impossible to give any definite rules. If coffee is served, it is either placed at one end of the table and served by the hostess as at breakfast, or it is served by one of the daughters of the house.

The Formal Supper.—This may be served in several ways, and the arrangement chosen depends very much upon the wishes of the hostess. Many people consider it inhospitable not to provide a substantial meal to which their guests can sit down and be waited on by the servants of the house. In this case one large or several small tables are laid and the service is very much the same as for *Dîner à la Russe.*

As a rule the dishes are cold, although hot soup and perhaps one hot entrée are frequently served. Such dishes as the following would all be suitable for the bill of fare :—

Cold meats of different kinds, such as game, poultry, ham, tongue, galantine and meat pies, dishes with aspic and mayonnaise, and various salads—jellies, creams, and all kinds of fancy sweets and plenty of fruit in season.

Buffet Supper.—When there are a number of guests and space is limited, a "stand up" supper is very often given. The different dishes are placed on the table, the ladies sit round the room, and the gentlemen wait on them and help themselves. Waitresses may also be in attendance. Only such dishes as can be easily eaten must be served, such as sandwiches, patties, aspic and mayonnaise dishes, and perhaps cold meats neatly sliced, followed by jellies, creams, various other sweets, and perhaps ices. Cooling drinks and light wines should also be offered.

This is a less expensive mode of serving the meal and one most frequently adopted by the housewife of moderate means.

Another way is to arrange a sort of buffet and to serve refreshments at any time throughout the evening without having a fixed hour for the meal. It will be the duty of the host and hostess to let this be understood by their guests and to see that every one is taken into supper in the course of the evening.

When only cold and light refreshments are given at an evening party it is very usual to offer a cup of hot soup or coffee to the guests just before they leave.

TABLE DECORATIONS

The floral decoration of the table is now a universal custom. Large sums of money are often spent upon the flowers and vases for a smart dinner-party, and hostesses will vie with each other as to whose table will present the most novel and effective appearance. But unless means are unlimited it is impossible to follow every passing fashion, and it is a good thing for most of us that floral decoration does not depend upon costly vases and expensive flowers; in fact, in most cases the simpler the arrangement the more charming the result.

Even although we are not all the happy possessors of a garden, flowers are brought into our towns in such lavish quantities nowadays, not to speak of those from our own market-gardens, that they have been brought within the means of the poorest. It is seldom one cannot get a bunch of some sort of bloom for a few coppers or even the modest penny, and when we consider the joy and comfort they bring we are amply compensated for the outlay. The delight a few flowers can give is unlimited.

What a difference between a table that is tastefully decorated with a few flowers and one on which a huge cruet-stand takes the central position. A table without a plant or flower is a desolate affair. There is no occasion to have a great display; more taste can often be shown in the arrangement of a few blooms than in an exuberant show. Flowers should not be crowded; they should have room to stand out individually. The Japanese, who are so artistic, consider one choice bloom quite sufficient to put in a vase. The main thing is to make the table pretty and attractive, and at the same time to think of something novel.

The foliage sprays should be inserted first, and the flowers then placed in carefully, so as to face whatever direction is required. If some flowers have a tendency to twist about, this can be remedied by pushing a piece of thin wire up the inside of the stem and allowing it to project half an inch. This projection can usually be inserted into a piece of foliage or stem, and the flower thus retained in the desired position.

Needless to say, the flowers must be fresh and the water should be changed every day.

The arrangement of flowers is very much a matter of skill and taste and the following paragraphs are only suggestive. The tendency at present is to keep the floral decoration low, tall-growing flowers, when they are used, being put in slender glasses or arranged in such a way that they do not obstruct the view. From the conversational point of view this is a great advantage, as it is never pleasant to be forced to look around ornaments in order to talk to some one on the opposite side of the table. Harmony of colour with the surroundings and a sense of proportion as to height, size, and shape of vases —a lightness of touch in the grouping together, with a quick eye for possibilities in the blending of shades, are all necessary to ensure success.

The quantity must depend upon the size of the table; a large table will stand some display of abundance, but now that small tables are fashionable, even for private houses, a very light form of decoration is all that is necessary.

Choice and Colour of the Flowers.—Flowers are now to be had in such variety and at every season of the year that their choice is very much a matter of individual taste, limited only by the resources at one's command. Flowers typical of the season are as a rule more pleasing than exotics and forced productions. Those with a strong scent should be avoided, especially if they are to be used in large quantities and in a heated room. When selecting a little thought must be given to the general tone of decoration. The colour of the room must be taken into consideration, unless the walls are cream or of some pale shade which will not clash with any of the brighter colours. Pleasing effects of colour are the first consideration. A mixture of colours rarely looks well; one or at most two colours with green is quite sufficient, although there may of course be graduations in shade of the prevailing colour.

Colour schemes are now the fashion, the flowers, candle shades, dinner ware, bon-bons, &c., being of corresponding hues. Some hostesses even aim at having the flowers, &c., to match the gown they are going to wear.

Foliage and Plants.—Plenty of foliage should be used, that of the flower itself wherever possible, and the teaching of nature followed if perfection is to be attained. The leaves themselves should not lie in the water, but should be stripped off the stalk, as they only crowd the vase and prevent the flowers getting sufficient water.

Asparagus, springeri, maidenhair, and smilax are among the choicest and best-known foliage plants, but there are many people, especially in the country, who may find these too costly for ordinary use or difficult to procure; to these it may be suggested that there are many trailing plants to be had for little or nothing, which could be employed in a similar way, such as the small-leaved gold or silver ivy, creeping jenny, canary creeper, periwinkle, and traveller's joy. To keep them from drooping the ends can be inserted in button-holders filled with wet sand and hidden among the leaves. Trailing plants can have silver wire inserted among the stems if it is wished to keep them in a special position. The tops of asparagus can often take the place of the more expensive fern; while more use might be made of carrot-leaves and those of the wild geranium, the latter sometimes being found in delightful shades of a red-brown colour. Convolvulus trails, with thick clusters of scarlet berries lasting for months after the leaves have withered, are a splendid addition to our winter decorations.

Vases.—Almost any kind of vase can be used as long as it suits the style of flower and does not clash in colour. As a rule, white and green crystal ones are the most adaptable. Tall-stalked flowers, such as chrysanthemums, lilies, lilac, daffodils, &c., look best in high glass, whilst short-stemmed flowers, such as violets, primroses, snowdrops, forget-me-nots, &c., should be arranged in low vases. Roses look especially well grouped in a bowl or single blooms set in slender glasses. Most people pick up quaint vases at different times, especially on a holiday, when they can often be found both pretty and cheap. It is astonishing, too, what can be done in case of necessity; an old meat or fruit tin packed with wet silver sand and hidden by moss can be made to do duty inside a basket quite as effectively as a proper zinc lining, while small baskets with the little china or glass drinking vessels used for birds or even a penny mustard tin are equally useful; similarly, all sorts of glass jars for potted pastes come in handy, so do cups without handles, especially the Japanese blue ones, also small china ash trays and saucers; indeed, any one at all resourceful need never be at a loss. If high glasses are used they should be slender and so arranged that they leave the line of vision clear. For corners all kinds of specimen glasses, upright or globular, cups, saucers, or pots filled with ferns, miniature trees or shrubs may be employed; a variation of the latter can be obtained by planting in tiny tubs (doll's washing-tubs painted dark brown serve the purpose), pips of oranges, lemons, grape fruit, apples, &c., which make excellent little trees; while rambles in woods and lanes will reward a search by giving us tiny oak, holly, and other trees to adorn our tables: these are especially desirable now that Japanese dwarf trees are the fashion.

Wild Flowers.—These who live in the country often overlook or despise the decorative possibilities of the flowers around them; yet what can be more lovely than a large vase of golden buttercups loosely arranged. It is true the petals soon drop, but then how easy to renew them. Then, again, what a delightful effect is produced by a bowl filled with half-open buds of the deep pink wild-rose with pieces of sweet-briar among it. We do not half appreciate the artistic possibilities of the wild anemone with its delicate green leaf, or of the snowdrop, crab-apple blossom, wild hyacinth, the meadow crane's-bill with its charming lavender shade, meadow-sweet, poppies, corn-flower, and a host of others too numerous to mention, along with grasses and leaves of all kinds.

Table Decorations in Spring.—For spring there is nothing more easy to grow than bulbs of all kinds; they can be grown in bowls of cocoa-nut fibre in sitting-rooms; the lovely blooms are in this way always available for decoration and they last long. Daffodils, pheasant's eye, narcissus, tulips, and hyacinths of all colours following one another give a glorious variety with the added interest of being grown by oneself. A pretty picture is made of a low dark-green bowl filled with crocuses ranging from white through the shades of mauve to dark purple, or massed with the golden kind the bowl is particularly striking. Lily of the valley can also be grown in the same manner; but in growing bulbs it should always be borne in mind that a hot room is fatal for good results. As the season advances we get a bewildering choice of flowers, among which violets take a first place for their sweetness; a favourite combination is that of dark violets with the lavender-coloured parma-violets. Pansies and violas associate well with almost any light green foliage, but nothing is so suitable as their own foliage when that can be procured bright and fresh and of good colour. Violets, however, do not make a good show at night. A well-grown bowl of lily of the valley with smaller ones of violets looks charming. Violets can also be used with the lavender shades of iris. Another sweet spring decoration is that of lilac in blending shades, but the stalks of this flower and other woody kinds must be split up to allow them to get plenty of water, otherwise they soon droop. A large bowl of crimson peonies makes a very handsome centre-piece, and, being so showy, does not require more than ferns round it.

What an important niche is filled in our decorations by the little salmon pink anemone which appears in the late spring. Sold in small bundles of unopened flowers, it looks insignificant to those who do not know its value, but if kept for a few days a lovely show is made by the gradual unfolding of the buds to their full size, its colour alone making it valuable, coming as it does at a time when most of our flowers are white or yellow; as the blooms last well, its purchase is always a safe investment. The larger kind, though more showy, do not blend so well with other colours.

Table Decorations in Summer.—Summer brings us the rose, the queen of flowers, in all its many forms and shades, but as a queen it must reign alone, no other flower being permissible near it. You may have all one colour, or various shades as from pink to crimson, but do not mix all colours together; it is a fatal mistake. What is more perfect than an old silver or china bowl filled with rich crimson roses; or a few long-stalked pink ones in branched glass or other vases, small corner bowls holding each a rose with perfect foliage, the stems kept in place by leaden clips covered with moss? Rambler roses are more difficult to deal with, but if the dusters of bloom are not too heavy, and you get the right kind of vase to suit them, they make a perfect picture. All the larger lilies make a splendid show in tall vases, but many people find the scent too powerful in a room. Carnations rank next the rose, combining as they do both beauty of colour and fragrance. A simple but effective decoration can be made by arranging short trails of the dwarf nasturtium in a slender but broad-rimmed vase and allowing the ends to fall over, a few leaves and half-opening flowers being arranged in small bowls or saucers.

Sweet peas are both beautiful and plentiful; also particularly useful in schemes of colour with their many shades of pink and mauve, but theirs is a fragile loveliness, for should the weather be hot they droop almost as soon as picked; they look best in slender vases loosely arranged. The dainty colourings of gladioli are very charming, though the form is somewhat stiff; the defect can in this and many other cases be lightened by sprays of gypsophila. Pink or mauve ivy geraniums go well with some shades of gladioli as a combination. A delightful table decoration for a hot day is formed by large marguerites, blue Canterbury bells, and wild oats; the sense of coolness imparted by these in a white-papered room must be felt to be understood Harebells and dog daisies give the same effect.

The soft yet brilliant shades of the Shirley poppies make another welcome addition to our list of summer favourites; arranged in a tall tapering glass with sprays of the feathery white statice or gypsophila they look charmingly graceful, the various shades of white, yellow and orange or reds and pinks, blending beautifully together. Many people think they drop quickly, but they should be chosen as much in bud as possible, as every bud opens and then they will be found to last nearly a week.

Charming combinations can be worked in cream and lavender, in white and dark violet, in yellow and cream, and in mauve and white. Large fine blooms of fancy pansies are always admired on a table, and when well arranged no combination can be more attractive.

Table Decorations in Autumn and Winter.—As the autumn comes along we get the asters and dahlias in all their varied colourings; the single dahlias are the best for table ornamentation, though a bowl of the crimson or yellow double ones makes a rich feast of colour. The loose petalled asters are the most effective, and pink and white or mauve and white combine well together. The Michaelmas daisies have been much improved of recent years, and many varieties can now be obtained. There are two kinds of white Michaelmas daisies which are invaluable for putting among flowers; the blooms are very small and feathery. Now we get the lovely tones of the Virginian creeper, so charming for adorning our tables, but it is necessary to wire it, as the leaves so soon drop off; a few trails should hang from vases as well as be used in draping.

In the country many richly-shaded leaves of all sorts, also berries, can now be gathered, the leaves pressed and put aside for winter use. Hips and haws are well known, as are also the rowan berries. Trails of Virginian creeper, a vase of bronze, yellow chrysanthemums, and smaller vases (of copper, if possible) filled with yellow marguerites make a charming picture, especially if the surroundings are of a brown tone.

For those who live in the country there is the possibility of making use of the rich hues of the crab-apple. A few discreetly selected small branches well laden with fruit, the stems clipped together with the soft leaden supports so cheap to buy, placed in a large green pot as if growing, the pot being half filled with moss, would make a novel decoration, while tiny specimen baskets, each containing one or two of the brilliantly coloured Quarantine apples, and the basket handles tied with a bow of green ribbon, might be placed round. This decoration would be suitable for a harvest home.

Winter gives us the ever-popular chrysanthemum, now grown in such quantities that it is brought within the reach of the most modest purse. Chrysanthemums always look best in tall jars or vases and require plenty of water; in fact, they should be left in a pail of water up to their heads every night. These flowers bring us to Christmas when holly reigns supreme, helped out by Christmas roses and forced scarlet tulips, the fragile-looking white of the Christmas roses making a delicate contrast to the prickly and brilliant holly.

Decorations for Special Occasions.—A few suggestions may be given for special occasions.

For Christmas the centre vase might be filled with large white or yellow chrysanthemums; round the base should be placed the small-leaved golden variegated holly, a well-berried piece of dark holly put at intervals; at the four corners horseshoes made of the leaves of the variegated sort, "A Merry Xmas," or similar motto formed of the berries running round or across as preferred, one corner of the horseshoe being tied with a bow of crimson ribbon. Fancy pots or baskets filled with ferns and scarlet tulips and tied with green ribbon could be used, or bowls of Christmas roses could take their place. The menu cards might have a robin or other seasonable device painted on them.

For Primrose Day.—Fill three round or long vessels with wet silver sand, put in the flowers one by one, separate the vessels with pots of light maidenhair, put the whole on a tin or zinc tray and bank up with moss. Smilax should be arranged round and draped along the sides, with small pots of maidenhair at the corners tied with bows of red ribbon, and a primrose button-hole put to each guest.

For a Wedding.—The place of honour being occupied by the wedding cake, pink and white roses, carnations, sweet peas, lily of the valley, and white heather are the most usual decorations. A pretty touch can be given by having tiny horseshoes for each guest; these can be made of lily of the valley or forget-me-nots, with a small bunch of white heather at the side tied with pink or white ribbon.

SERVING OF FRUIT

Fresh fruit should find a place on every table; it is always wholesome and beautiful, and much taste can be shown in the manner in which it is arranged. When fruit is served at a dinner-party it may either be placed on the table at the beginning and remain throughout the meal, or it may be put down when the guests are ready to partake of it. The first method is to be recommended as far as the decorative appearance of the table is concerned, although the fruit itself suffers from being exposed to the heat of the room for so long. The softer fruits especially suffer from the hot atmosphere and the odours of savoury dishes. Perhaps the best plan to adopt is to put down the harder and drier fruits, such as nuts, oranges, and apples, and to reserve the daintier and finer ones to be brought in fresh and cool when they are required, either in their natural state or *en salade.*

When arranging fruit it must be carefully looked over and any that is blemished put aside. Oranges and apples, pears and other fruit of the kind should be wiped with a damp cloth and polished. Grapes should be lightly brushed with a soft brush, peaches and plums very lightly rubbed, and all berries carefully picked and washed if necessary.

Fruit may be arranged in a variety of ways. Each dish may contain either a different kind of fruit, or else a miscellaneous assortment artistically grouped. If the table is large, a handsome centre-piece of mixed fruits sometimes looks well. Many pretty designs for fruit dishes are now sold, and these may either match the fruit plates or form a pleasing contrast. Rustic baskets of different shapes can also be made to look very pretty and artistic. Green leaves should always cover the dishes on which the fruit is served. For the larger fruits vine-leaves are the most suitable, while currant-leaves can be used for the smaller kinds. In winter when fresh leaves are scarce gold and silver paper leaves can often be employed with good effect, especially for dried fruits, dates, figs, Carlsbad plums, crystallised fruits, and such-like.

One important point to remember is that when arranging a dish of mixed fruits the lighter kinds must always be put on the top. Apart from this, there are no fixed rules for the arrangement of fruit, but an eye for colour and artistic taste are as necessary here as in floral decorations.

The following is a specimen of a Dinner Menu, written in both French and English:—

MENU	MENU
Melon Glacé	Iced Melon
Consommé aux Quenelles	Clear Soup with Quenelles
Turbot. Sauce aux Crevettes	Turbot with Shrimp Sauce
Crèmes de Bœuf aux Champignons	Beef Creams with Mushrooms
Gigot d'Agneau. Sauce Menthe	Lamb with Mint Sauce
Sorbet au Rhum	Rum Sorbet
Faisans Rôtis. Salade d'Orange	Roast Pheasants with Orange Salad
Nid de Marrons à la Crème	Nest of Chestnuts with Cream
Gelée au Vin Rouge	Port Wine Jelly
Pailles au Parmesan	Cheese Straws
Glacés aux Fraises	Strawberry Ices
Dessert.	Dessert.

HOUSEHOLD LINEN

A GOOD housewife will take great care of her household linen, and it will be her pleasure to see that it is kept in beautiful order.

In beginning housekeeping the quantity and quality of the linen that is bought must depend upon individual taste and means, the size of the household to be provided for, and the room there is for keeping it.

As a rule, it is a wise plan to buy just what is necessary to start with and to add to the stock as time goes on and the necessity for more arises. The space in modern houses is often somewhat limited, and if surplus linen has to be stored away in boxes in a cellar, it will probably be attacked by mildew and become unfit for use. Whatever is bought should be good of its kind, not necessarily of the finest quality, as this would be unsuitable in many cases, and the price paid will naturally depend upon the means at disposal; but an inferior quality should never be bought. Even a little extra outlay at the beginning in order to obtain first-rate material will be amply repaid in the ultimate satisfaction afforded. Cheap linen may look very well when new, when it has dressing in it and a certain amount of gloss, but after the first washing it will be found limp and thin and without any body.

The material for household linen can always be bought by the yard and made up at home, but now that good ready-made articles can be had at such moderate prices, there is really nothing to be gained by taking this extra trouble. If hand work is still preferred to machine work, it can always be ordered or asked for specially. Of course, it is important to go to a first-class shop where the goods can be trusted. In this chapter useful information is given in regard to standard qualities and prices.

BED LINEN

Sheets.—*Material.*—Until within recent years linen was always considered the correct material for sheeting, and it would have been thought a breach of etiquette to provide a guest with anything but the finest and whitest of linen sheets. But now, owing to the many improvements made in its manufacture, cotton has to a large extent taken the place of linen. Linen is, however, still preferred by many people; it is so fine and smooth to the touch, and delightfully cool in summer. One must of course be prepared to pay a good price for linen; but it will be found very durable, and it keeps its colour better than cotton. Good linen is fine and even in texture. It should be bought fairly heavy, otherwise it will curl up and soon look shabby and crushed.

It is not wise to let delicate and rheumatic people sleep in linen sheets, as linen carries off the heat of the body and is very apt to give cold.

Cotton, on the other hand, is much warmer than linen, and for this reason it is often liked better. Besides, it is possible now to buy it of such fine quality and with such a nice soft finish, that even the most fastidious can scarcely object to it. The difference in price, too, is a consideration with people of moderate means.

Cotton sheets can be had in two kinds, twilled and plain. At the present time the plain calico seems to be the favourite and the kind most generally asked for, but this of course is a matter of taste, and the price of both is very much the same.

Both linen and cotton sheets can be had with either plain or hem-stitched hems at the ends; the latter add very little, if anything, to the price, and they certainly add to the dainty appearance of the bed.

It is always well to have the top hem a little wider than the one at the bottom, or to have some other distinction, in order to prevent the foot of the sheet being placed near the face.

For servants' use a well-woven twilled calico is best. The unbleached material used to be bought for the purpose, but it is now seldom asked for, and the white certainly looks nicer.

A very usual plan when providing sheets for a household is to buy linen for the best beds, fine cotton for ordinary use, and a heavier twill for the servants. As some people object to linen sheets, it is well to keep one or two pairs of fine cotton in reserve for the use of guests.

Size and Price.—Sheets must always be bought of a right size for the bed for which they are intended. They must be long enough and wide enough to permit of their being tucked in all round the mattress. An extra length, about three-quarters of a yard, must be allowed if the under-sheet has to cover the bolster as well. In breadth a sheet should at least be 72 inches wide for a single bed, and 90 inches for a double bed, and from 2 to 3½ yards long.

As regards quality taste varies so much that individual preference and the means at command can alone decide the choice. The following prices may, however, be a guide to those who have little knowledge of what ought to be paid. Only thoroughly recommended prices are quoted.

Cotton Hem-stitched Sheets.

Single-bed size—8s. 6d. to 15s 6d. per pair.
Double-bed size—12s. to 23s. 6d. per pair.

The difference in price depends upon the fineness of the material, and also upon the length.

Hem-stitched Linen Sheets (Irish).

Single-bed sheets—18s. 9d., 23s. 6d. to £3, 3s. per pair.

Double-bed sheets—25s. 9d., 30s. to £4, 4s. per pair.

For servants' use a very good twilled calico sheet with plain hem can be bought at 6s. 6d. per pair, and a rather better quality at 8s. per pair.

The more expensive sheets have very often a pretty embroidered piece for turning over at the top.

The Jaeger or Sanitary Sheet.—This is a special kind of sheet made of pure wool, and of a thin texture that can easily be washed. The Jaeger sheets are used principally for children and delicate people, and especially for those troubled with rheumatism. The price varies from 19s. 6d. to 30s. for a single-bed sheet, and from 33s. 6d. to 60s. for a double-bed sheet. They can be had either of a fine white cashmere or in the natural wool or camel-hair shade. Pillow-cases can also be obtained in the same material.

Sheet-Shams.—These are fancy articles, and not by any means a necessity for any one starting housekeeping. They are strips of linen hem-stitched, and generally very prettily embroidered, which are slipped in under the bed-clothes and turned back over the cover to resemble a sheet, and they give to a bed a dainty appearance during the day.

Mattress Covers.—Every mattress should be covered with a cotton slip to keep it clean, and this need only be removed once or twice a year to be washed. Unbleached calico or thin holland is usually sold for the purpose.

Pillow and Bolster-Slips.—*Material.*—These can be either of cotton or of linen, to match the sheets with which they are used, although linen pillow-slips are very often used with cotton sheets. Lovers of ease always prefer linen pillow-slips to cotton ones, as they are cooler for the head and smoother and softer to lie on. Any one troubled with headaches or sleeplessness should always use them, as they check the flow of blood to the head, and almost act as a cold-water bandage.

Pillow-slips can be bought ready made in different sizes. They look very pretty hem-stitched, and they can also be had with dainty frills; but it must be borne in mind that these latter are not so durable, and that the washing of them will cost more than that of the plainer kinds. They can be had either fitted with tapes or with buttons and button-holes. Upon the whole, the latter method of fastening is to be preferred, as it is more conducive to neatness.

The newest method of fastening is with a double set of button-holes and small bone studs, which can easily be slipped out when the pillow-slips are sent to the washing. It is a good plan to sew these studs on to a length of tape—the proper distance apart—and this will prevent them from getting lost.

Bolster-slips are not always used, the under-sheet being rolled round the bolster and made to act as a cover. However, some people prefer the separate cover, and it is certainly the more comfortable arrangement, especially for indifferent sleepers, as the cushions can be moved about at will and arranged to suit one's special comfort.

Bolster-slips can also be bought ready made, but it is almost better to have them prepared to order, and to suit the special shape of bolster. They look better when they are drawn in at the ends and not button-holed, or sometimes they are made with a shaped piece at each end, which gives the bolster a more handsome appearance.

The newest shape of bolster-slip is made about half a yard longer than the bolster on each side. The ends, which are left open, are either hem-stitched or embroidered, and the extra length is allowed to hang over the sides of the bed.

Both bolsters and pillows should also have an under-cover of calico to preserve the tick, and also to prevent the stripes of the latter showing through the outer case. An old pillow-slip or bolster-slip will answer the purpose very well, and they should be removed once or twice a year to be washed. These inner slips are usually sewn on, but if fastened with tapes or buttons, the open end should be put into the outer case first, to prevent both fastenings coming together.

Size and Price.—Pillow-slips must be bought to fit the pillows for which they are intended, and as these vary somewhat in size, it is important to take careful measurements. If too tight the softness of the pillow is destroyed, and on the other hand if they are too large they look clumsy.

Very good hem-stitched pillow-cases can be bought for 2s. 6d.—fastened neatly at the ends with hand-made button-holes and well finished—and upwards to 8s. each, and even more. With frills they will cost from 3s. 6d. upwards. Plain white calico slips can be had from 8d. to 2s. each, and with frills from 2s. 6d. upwards.

Pillow-Shams.—These are dainty ornamental covers, which are laid over the pillows during the day and removed at night. They are generally made of fine linen or muslin, embroidered prettily with initials and some other design, and finished round the edges with lace or cambric frills. Sometimes a large bow of ribbon will ornament the centre. They help to make a bed look pretty, and when carefully folded at night they will keep clean for quite a long time.

Quantity Required.—*Allowances.*—The careful housewife should see that the linen cupboard is always kept well stocked with sufficient linen to meet all emergencies. If each bed has its own special linen, then three pairs of sheets, six pillow-slips, and two or three bolster-slips will be a very moderate supply for each, in order that the linen cupboard may never be left without a pair of sheets to fall back upon. If, however, the linen is used generally, and the cost of washing has to be considered, six pairs of sheets, twelve pillow-cases, and half-a-dozen bolster-slips might do service for three beds. This, however, is a minimum supply, and if frequent change is indulged in, double the number would not be too many.

Ideas vary much as to how often bed-linen ought to be changed, and to have a liberal allowance is certainly a luxury. When the expense and trouble of washing has not to be thought of, sheets may be changed as often as three times a week, and pillow-slips every day; but this amount is beyond the means of the ordinary household, both as regards the supply of linen required and the somewhat heavy washing bill entailed. Once a week is considered a very good allowance, while once a fortnight should be the minimum of change. To keep sheets in use longer than this is not healthy. Some people prefer to change one sheet each week, always putting the top sheet down, while others prefer to have all clean at once. One pillow-slip a week at least should be allowed for each person, and a bolster-slip if used should be changed once a fortnight.

If the supply of bed-linen is limited, housekeepers should arrange that all the beds are not changed the same week, but in rotation. If there is a number of beds, it will be as well to make a note in a small book of the dates when each have been changed.

Servants too should be allowed one clean sheet a week, or a pair a fortnight, and one clean pillow-slip each week.

BED-COVERS OR COUNTERPANES

Dainty bed-covers add not a little to the attractive appearance of a bedroom, and they should always be kept as fresh and clean as possible. A little care expended in selecting new bed-covers will be amply rewarded in the additional wear to be had out of a well-selected article, which as a rule will combine the qualities of both decorativeness and durability.

Bed-covers are to be had in various styles, but the all-white coverlet is always a good investment, as it washes easily and looks well on any bed.

The tendency now is to have them of a very light make, and some of the newest styles are in white cotton or linen embroidered and hem-stitched, or a pretty white embroidered muslin. The finer and open-work ones are usually mounted on a sateen slip of a colour to match the bedroom, and these slips are fastened to the cover by means of small buttons and button-holes, which are easily undone when the upper part requires washing.

A very pretty embroidered cotton quilt can be bought for 12s. 6d. for a small bed, and 18s 6d. for a double-bed size and upwards. An embroidered and hem-stitched linen cover will cost from 23s. 6d. for a small, and 31s. 6d. for a double-bed size, while several pounds may be paid for one with a very elaborate design of drawn-thread work and lace.

A white embroidered muslin cover, which is very dainty and particularly suitable for summer use, can be obtained for 16s. 6d. small size, and 18s. 9d. large size, and upwards. An under-slip of sateen for these covers costs 10s. 6d. or 12s. 6d., according to size, and any colour can be chosen.

Coloured bed-spreads are also greatly used, made of printed cotton or taffeta. To obtain one of a good quality, it will be necessary to pay from 12s. 9d. upwards. They should be chosen to suit the curtains, or the prevailing colour in the room for which they are intended. For winter use, and especially if fires are burned in the bedroom, these coloured quilts are perhaps more practical than the all white, and especially where washing is a consideration.

Stronger counterpanes in colour suitable for servants' use are sold for 4s. or 5s., and it is quite possible too to get these with a nice design and of a pretty shade. There is no occasion to have something ugly because it is cheaper than the finer qualities, and a maid is more likely to take a pride in keeping her room in order if some encouragement is given to her to make it pretty.

Although somewhat out of date, the thick white Marcella and honeycomb quilts will always be useful for hard wear, as they stand frequent washing without any harm, and with care will last for years.

The bed-spread or cover must be large enough to cover the bed and hang well over the sides. If no valance is used, a little extra width will be required.

One bed-cover at least will be required for

each bed, and two or three extra ones to allow for washing. It is a good plan to have a change of quilts in summer and winter.

TOILET COVERS AND DUCHESSE SETS

No toilet table is complete without its toilet cover and doyleys, and the bedroom would indeed have a neglected appearance where their use was dispensed with. A daintily dressed toilet-table adds materially to the cleanly and cheerful aspect of a room, and besides nothing is more calculated to show off a good piece of furniture than this time-honoured essential to the toilet-table equipment, whilst on the other hand the appearance of shabby furniture can be considerably improved upon by the use of clean and dainty toilet sets. The variety in these is almost endless, and choice must depend upon individual taste.

The all-white covers, such as the Marcella and Honeycomb, can be bought ready made in various sizes from 1s. and 1s. 9d. each, and upwards. They will stand any amount of hard wear and frequent washing; in fact, the material will scarcely wear out. When the fringes become shabby, they should be cut off, and the ends of the cover hemmed and trimmed with a little edging if desired. The same material is also to be had by the yard, known as "Toileting." The required length can then be bought, neatly hemmed at the ends and trimmed with crochet edging or other suitable embroidery.

Of course, from an artistic point of view, the above covers are not pretty; they are strong and clean-looking, but there is nothing distinctive about them. The daintiest covers are those made to suit the room. A pretty cretonne edged with lace and insertion, or a dainty muslin with a frill of the same material, and coloured sateen underneath, or again, a nicely embroidered linen or some fancy material worked in colours, can all be made to look very nice and give a homelike appearance to the room.

Instead of the all-over toilet cover, a Duchesse set of mats is frequently used, and this permits of some of the wood of the toilet-table being seen. Needless to say, these should only be used where the table or chest has a good surface. If the wood is shabby, it is much better to have it entirely covered.

Duchesse sets can also be had in strong white Marcella material, and will cost from 1s. per set and upwards. The prettiest ones, however, are in fine linen or damask and lace, or drawn-thread work. The price of these will vary according to the amount of work in them and the quality of the lace. A simple hem-stitched set can be procured for 1s. 6d., while linen and lace will cost from 2s. 6d. and upwards to almost any price. But these are things which are frequently made at home, as small odds and ends of linen, muslin, lace, &c., can be so easily utilised for the purpose.

For the changing of toilet covers no regular rule can be laid down; if the table is standing near the open window and in a dusty situation, the cover may look dirty at the end of a week, whereas in a clean place it may retain its fresh appearance for a month and even longer—therefore the only rule to go by is to change when necessary.

Two toilet covers or sets will be required for each room, unless they are used generally for the different bedrooms, when one each and two or three over to allow for washing will be sufficient.

TOWELS

Bedroom Towels.—*General Remarks and Material.*—For ordinary use the linen huckaback are the most suitable, while linen, damask or diaper will serve the purpose when a fine towel is required. The latter make very nice face towels, as they are so fine and soft. Towels can be bought ready made, either hemmed, hem-stitched, or with fringes. Those with fringes are scarcely to be recommended, as they so soon become shabby and untidy-looking. If they are chosen, it is wise to overcast the ends before putting the towels in use, as this will prevent any fraying out, unless this has already been done, which is sometimes the case with the more expensive towels. When the fringes become shabby they should be cut off, and the ends of the towels neatly hemmed.

Towelling can also be bought by the yard, fifteen yards being of fair allowance for twelve towels. But there is really little to be gained by doing this, as the ready-made towels have generally some kind of border, and the others would not have the same finished appearance.

The ends of towels are sometimes made ornamental by having a border worked across them, very often in Russian cross-stitch, in blue and white, red and white, or simply all white; or a monogram or initials may be worked in one corner, or any other effective design. The ends, too, are sometimes trimmed with hand-made lace—that of a strong make, such as a crochet or knitted edging, being the most appropriate. These little additions are considered by some people to greatly improve the appearance of a towel, and to make a pretty finish for those destined for the guest-room; but for practical purposes the perfectly plain towel is to be preferred.

Turkish towels are generally used for the bath. They are made of cotton, with a raised fluffy surface, and are very soft in texture. They can be had either all white or a mixture of red and white. Those of a large size are called bath sheets. When a very rough towel is wanted to produce friction after a bath, the brown linen towelling should be asked for.

Unbleached huckaback towels of a stouter make should be bought for servants' use, and these can generally be had with a coloured border, which would serve as a distinguishing mark where there are several maids. If something cheaper is desired, then the cotton honeycomb towels should be bought, and these too are made with some colour introduced.

Size and Price.—Very good pure linen huckaback towels, grass bleached and of a soft finish, can be bought for 14s. per dozen, and with a damask border in a heavier make for 21s. per dozen.

Damask and diaper towels will cost from 15s. to 35s. per dozen.

Turkish bath towels (Christie's) are also sold at from 15s. to 35s. per dozen, according to size and quality, while a bath sheet can be obtained for 3s. 9d., 5s., 6s. 6d. or 8s. 6d.

The rough crown linen towels are 2s. each and upwards.

The unbleached huckaback for servants' use will be about 8s. 6d. or 12s. per dozen, while the white honeycomb are only 6d. each and upwards. A very suitable bath towel is also to be had for 10d. or 1s.

When buying towels it is well to compare the sizes, as often by paying a shilling or two more per dozen a few extra inches in length can be obtained, and as the larger towel will not cost more in the washing, this is a point worth considering.

An ordinary towel should be at least 40 inches long and 24 inches wide; anything less than this is very inadequate for the purpose, while an inch or two larger would be a distinct advantage. Bath towels especially are better if of a larger size, while for a bath sheet double the above proportions would not be too much.

Quantity Required—Allowances.—At least half-a-dozen bedroom towels and three bath towels should be allowed for each person. This will allow of two face towels and one bath towel being given out each week, the same number would be at the washing, and the other three would be in reserve. This is of course a very limited supply; as many people like to have their towels changed more than once a week, the supply would then have to be increased accordingly.

Bath sheets may be had in addition to the above; these need not be changed so frequently as the bath towels.

The usual allowance for servants is one face towel a week and a bath towel once a fortnight. Three face towels and two bath towels would be enough to allow for each maid.

BLANKETS

Choice.—In choosing blankets for the household it is advisable to select those of a first-rate and reliable quality. Good blankets will not only last longer than inferior ones, but they are warmer and lighter in make. Touch is the best guide to choice; they should have a soft and silky feeling, with a nice woolly surface.

In England the Witney blankets have the finest finish, but the Yorkshire and Welsh are very good for hard wear.

The Scotch blankets are also famous, and one special feature of their manufacture is that they are generally all wool. They have a raised surface, although not so much so as a Witney blanket.

A blanket should be large enough to tuck in at both sides and at the bottom of the bed, but must not be so wide that it touches the floor. Where economy has to be considered, one pair might be chosen smaller, if the upper one is large enough to tuck in and keep all in position.

Before buying blankets it is very important to know the exact size of the beds for which they are required.

Quantity Required and Price.—Two pairs of upper blankets and one under-blanket is a very fair allowance for each bed. When an eider-down quilt is used one upper blanket may be sufficient, but this is very much a question of individual needs, and it is always well to have one or two pairs of blankets in reserve.

A pair of very good single-bed blankets, guaranteed all pure wool, can be bought for 16s. per pair, while as much as 45s. can be paid for the same size in the finest and softest wool, with a pretty silk binding in sky-blue, rose-pink, or cream. For a double-bed blanket the price will range from 21s. to 75s. per pair. They can be supplied either all white or with blue or red lines, button-holed in the same colour.

For servants' use union blankets are generally bought. These are rather harder to the touch, as they are not all wool, but are woven with a certain amount of cotton. They are not so light in weight as an all-wool blanket, but are very suitable for hard wear. The price of these blankets will range from 8s. to 12s. 6d. per pair.

The under-blanket is generally a single blanket which can be bought new for 4s. and upwards, but except in the case of a new ménage, a worn or thin upper blanket can generally be used for the purpose.

Scarlet blankets when they are preferred can be bought for the same price as the white. Grey blankets are now little used, except those of a very hard make, which are sold for charity purposes.

The Scotch blankets are generally sold by weight. For instance, the well-known make called "Scotch Teviot" are made in weights from 5 lbs. to 10 lbs. 6 lbs. is a good single-bed size, and measures about 68 by 76 inches. 9 lbs. is a good double-bed size, and measures about 78 by 90 inches. An extra large size weighs 10 lbs., and measures 80 by 94 inches.

This range is sold according to quality—6 lbs. weight from 17s. 9d. to 25s. retail; 9 lbs. weight from 21s. 9d. to 42s. retail.

The twilled blanket is also much used as binders or under-blankets. They resemble very much a serge material, but are very warm and durable. The prices are from 10s. to 18s. a pair (retail).

Note.—The above particulars and prices regarding Scotch blankets have been kindly supplied by Messrs. Charles Jenner & Co., Princes Street, Edinburgh.

Of course, it will be quite possible to buy blankets at a much lower price than the above, but nothing cheaper can be really recommended for comfort and good wear, unless it may be a lot slightly soiled which can sometimes be picked up at a sale.

Marking Blankets.—Blankets should always be carefully marked. This is best done in wool, worked in cross-stitch from a sample (see p. 406). The lettering should match in colour the button-holing on the blanket or any colour introduced in the weaving. If the blanket is all white, then the sewing might be done in some pretty contrasting colour. Cash's woven lettering can also be used for the purpose, or the name be written in ink on a piece of tape and sewn on to the blanket, but the first method looks best.

Care and Cleaning of Blankets.—Blankets that are not in use should be stored away in a blanket chest or on the shelves of the linen cupboard. If they are to be left for some time, precautions must be taken to prevent their being attacked by moths. Put camphor, naphtha balls, or Russia leather parings between the folds, and then sew the blankets into a piece of old sheeting or other cotton material, taking care that no holes are left where the moths could enter.

The washing or cleaning of blankets is another very important point. Some people consider that if they are cleaned once a year, generally at the annual spring cleaning, this should be sufficient; but one must be guided somewhat by circumstances. If the blankets are used in a room where a fire is frequently lighted, or in a smoky and foggy neighbourhood, twice a year will not be too often to have them attended to. Then again after a case of illness the blankets used on the bed should always be cleaned, and, if necessary, disinfected as well. Of course, unnecessary washing must be avoided, as it impoverishes the material, and there is always the danger of a certain amount of shrinking.

If washing is the mode of cleaning to be adopted, then great care must be taken in the choice of the laundry to which they are sent. Preference should be given to one where they are dried in the open air. If there is the slightest doubt as to their being well done at a laundry, then it is a much wiser plan to send blankets to a professional cleaner. The price for cleaning will vary from 1s. to 2s. per pair, according to size, which may mean a little extra expense as compared with washing, but it is cheap when one considers that the so-called washing often spells "ruin" to a beautiful blanket. In the case of new blankets, it is always better to have them cleaned instead of washed, as the first time of washing is always more difficult. It must be remembered, too, that once a blanket becomes clotted and non-porous through bad washing, it ceases to be so healthy.

The length of time blankets keep clean depends upon the care that is taken of them. They should be protected by night as well as by day with a cover of some sort. So if the bed-cover is removed at night, which is the correct thing to do, there should be a thin cover underneath or an ordinary sheet to cover the blankets. Then again, when a bed is being turned down or made, the blankets must not be allowed to sweep the floor, but be laid over the backs of two chairs, and then handled carefully. It is a good plan to have the blankets well brushed from time to time, and hung in the open air for a few hours.

Upper blankets are always sold in pairs, but some people prefer to have them neatly cut in two, and the raw edges button-holed in wool to match the other end of the blanket.

Mending of Blankets.—When blankets begin to show signs of wear, they should be carefully darned with wool of the same colour, and when a hole appears it should be neatly patched with a piece of blanketing of a suitable texture. (For details, see under Needlework, p. 415.)

What to do with Old Blankets.—Old blankets can be utilised in many different ways. Large blankets can be cut down to make blankets for beds of a smaller size, or if not sufficiently good for the purpose they may be used as under-blankets. If very thin, the material might be doubled and button-holed together at the edges, and this would make a capital under-blanket. Then in houses where there are children small pieces of blankets will be found invaluable, either to cover them when they are asleep or for them to sit on. In cases of sickness, too, scraps of blanket are frequently required for fomentations and other purposes. Small pieces will also be required for patching other blankets; and very old pieces will always be found useful as floor-cloths or for cleaning purposes, such as the washing of paint, &c.

TABLE LINEN

It has often been said that the refinement of a household may be judged to some extent by its table appointments, and more particularly by the dainty freshness of the table napery. The soiled and crumpled table-cloth replete with holes is characteristic of the third-rate lodging-house and not of the well-ordered household.

If when buying table-cloths a little care is expended upon their selection, to keep them in good condition should be a comparatively simple matter; always providing, of course, that they are entrusted when soiled to a fairly capable laundress, and that the proverb "A stitch in time saves nine" is borne well in mind.

Double damask, bleached or unbleached, is the best material to buy. It wears well, and keeps its appearance to the end. There is nothing to be gained by buying inferior table linen; it may have a very fine glossy surface when new, but the first washing removes all this dressing and leaves only a poor limp material which wrinkles up and soils very readily.

The design to be chosen is entirely a matter of taste, and each season shows something new. It must be borne in mind, however, that the newest designs generally cost a little more money, so, where economy has to be considered, it is as well to ask for something of an earlier date, which may at the same time be just as pretty and effective. As a rule, a table-cloth with a small all-over pattern, such as spots, stars, diamonds or small sprigs, is cheaper than one with a large central design and border.

Table-cloths with some colour introduced, generally red or blue, are used by some people as luncheon or breakfast cloths, but the fashion is more German than English, and at present is not much in favour.

Then there is a fashion at present for using dinner sets—a centre and mats in place of a cloth; but this can only be adopted by those who have a very finely polished table or a beautiful oak surface to show, and is not likely to become general.

For kitchen use the unbleached damask cloths answer the purpose very well, as they will not soil so quickly as the pure white cloths. They ought to be bought strong and good, although the quality need not be so fine as the other household cloths.

Table napkins, or serviettes, to be correct, should match the table-cloth with which they are to be used in quality and design. This, however, entails additional expenditure, as a much larger number will be required than when they are used generally with any cloth. For this reason it is a good plan to buy two table-cloths of one pattern, as it will then be found easier to regulate the supply of serviettes. In fact, in small households of moderate means it is just as well for everyday use to buy all the serviettes alike, and to choose a small unobtrusive pattern that can be used with any cloth. Then for special occasions there can be a set kept in reserve which matches the best table-cloth in pattern and quality.

Size and Price.—The size of the table-cloth is very important, as it will not look well unless it hangs at least half a yard over each end of the table and twelve inches at the sides. Careful measurements should therefore be taken of the tables for which the cloths are required before buying is thought of.

A very good double damask table-cloth in a small spot design can be bought at the following prices:—2 by 2 yards, 10s.; 2 by 2½ yards, 12s.; and 2 by 3 yards, 14s.; and these are particularly suitable for breakfast or luncheon cloths. Those of a more elaborate design will cost from 14s. 6d. to 27s. 6d., 18s. to 35s. 6d., and 21s. 6d. to 42s. and upwards for the same sizes respectively, while larger sizes will cost still more in proportion. A large cloth of very fine quality cannot be bought under £4 or £5.

Other designs in fine quality damask, with hand-made lace insertion and hem-stitched borders, will cost from 50s. to £18 and upwards, according to size and the quality of the work.

Serviettes are made in different sizes—*i.e.* 22, 27, and 31 inches square; the medium size is the most usual, although the smallest ones are frequently used for breakfast. Very good serviettes can be bought for 16s. 6d. per dozen for the medium size and 12s. 9d. for the small size, while as much as 45s. and 68s. can be given for the same size in an extra fine quality.

There are a number of small articles in the way of table linen, such as tray-cloths, afternoon tea-cloths, doyleys, carving-cloths, sideboard-cloths, table-cloths, &c., which will also be required in a household, but a list of these is scarcely necessary, as they must be bought to supply individual needs. These are the little things which are frequently given as presents to those starting house for the first time, while in an old-established ménage scraps of damask, linen, &c., can often be utilised for the purpose. In any case, they should never be bought in large quantities, as they can so often be picked up at a very moderate rate and at odd times as the use for them arises. Fashions too change so quickly, that it is better to have a small stock and renew it when necessary.

Quantity required.—*Allowances.*—This, again, depends very much upon the means of the household, and must be regulated according to individual circumstances and the special arrangement of meals. In houses where a large amount of entertaining is done the quantity will necessarily be increased.

A very moderate supply would be four table-cloths of average size for each meal, and three dozen serviettes, two cloths of extra quality and extra size, if necessary, for each meal, and two dozen serviettes to match.

It is always better to keep a cloth specially for dinner, and a different one for breakfast and luncheon or supper. In this case perhaps it will be sufficient to give out one of each kind in a week, although in many houses the dinner cloth will be changed as often as three times a week.

Serviettes should be changed at least twice a week, or fresh ones for dinner every day where it can be afforded. One table-cloth a week is the usual allowance for servants' use.

The table linen has so much to do with the success of a meal that it should never be allowed to become too dirty or crushed. If a table-cloth has to do duty for several days and look well all the time, great care must be taken of it. It should be folded carefully and always in the original creases, and each fold should be smoothed out with the hands. If it is kept in a drawer, it must be laid perfectly flat, but what is better still is to put it into a linen press, as shown in the accompanying diagram. When the cloth has been laid in between the boards, the tension should be screwed down as tightly as it will go without destroying the material, and if the table-cloth is allowed to remain several hours, it will come out looking as if it had been newly "done up." The screw of the press should be loosened when not in use. Failing a press, the cloth may be slowly mangled if it has become very much crushed.

Linen Press.

Another point about table-cloths is that they should never be put directly on the bare table. An old table-cloth or piece of felt should always be laid under it. This not only acts as a silence cloth, but it enables one to lay the cloth more smoothly. If a piece of felt has to be bought for the purpose, then white should be chosen, as then there will be no fear of staining should water or any other liquid be spilt.

Kitchen and Household Towels.—Besides the towels required for bedroom use, there is also a stock indispensable to kitchen and household purposes, such as :—

Roller Towels.	Lavatory Towels.
Glass Towels.	Pudding Cloths.
Tea Cloths.	Hearth Cloths.
Kitchen Towels.	Dusters.
Slop Cloths.	Oven Cloths.

&c.

All household cloths should be hemmed and marked with the name and purpose for which they are intended. If there are several servants in a house, it is a good plan to let each one have her own special set for which she is held responsible, and they ought to be instructed as to the legitimate use of each kind. In some household towels the name of its kind is woven into each one, such as "Glass Towel," "Tea Cloth," "Kitchen," &c., then to distinguish one maid's towels from another's they can be bought in various styles and colours, with a blue and white or red and white check, a blue or red border, or all white, and so on. If just a little difference is made, confusion will be avoided, and the blame of lost towels will not be likely to fall upon the wrong person.

Towels and dusters should be given out regularly once a week, and the last week's lot should always be accounted for. The number required depends entirely upon the amount of work to be done. It is a mistake to be niggardly in giving out supplies—it should be remembered that people have different ways of working, and as a rule it is not wise to limit a good worker, but to give what is asked for within reason.

The only point that must be insisted upon is that the towels and dusters are kept clean, taken care of, and never bundled away damp in dark corners.

Except in the case of a young ménage, it should not be necessary to buy all these towels new. The duster supply especially can generally be provided for by using up pieces of old soft material; thin bedroom towels can be cut down to make lavatory towels or basin cloths, and old bath towels for drying floors and so on. (See also "What to do with Old Linen," p. 267.)

If new dusters must be bought, they can be procured ready made from 3d. each, or if the material alone is bought, there is nothing better than a cheap sateen. This can be cut up in convenient pieces, and a hem laid and machined round in a very short time. These will be found excellent for furniture, and they become softer each time they are washed.

Dish cloths again can be made of any old soft material, such as remnants of Turkish or other old towelling. It is a mistake to have them very close in texture, or they will too readily absorb grease. There is really nothing better than the knitted kind, made of strong unbleached knitting cotton worked with rather coarse needles. These wear well and can be washed and boiled over and over again.

Cloths known as "swabs" are very useful for house cleaning. They are made of a coarse open material, and are better and stronger than flannel for washing floors, tiles, and doorsteps, and they have the further advantage of leaving no fluff behind. The price is about 2d. each.

Dust Sheets.—Old sheets or bed-covers can generally be used, but where these are not available, thin unbleached calico or holland should be bought and sewn up into suitable sizes. It will cost from 4½d. to 6d. per yard. The number of dust-sheets required will depend entirely upon the amount of furniture to be covered.

House Flannel.—A linen cupboard should always contain a supply of this, but it must be given out with care. The remains of old blankets can often be utilised.

THE LINEN CUPBOARD

The durability of linen depends very much upon its being well kept. If it is treated with care, it will not only look better, but it will last longer. To keep it nicely, a linen cupboard or its equivalent is a necessity. In houses with good cupboard accommodation, and especially in the old-fashioned ones, a place specially fitted up for linen is generally provided. Sometimes even a small room can be reserved for the purpose, where, in addition to the linen proper, spare blankets, curtains, and other upholstery which is not in use can be comfortably stored away. The linen cupboard should be in a

Linen Cupboard.

dry and airy situation, and not against an outside wall, which is not always free from moisture. If linen is allowed to become damp it mildews and rots very quickly. It can frequently be arranged that the hot-water pipes going to the bath-room pass through the linen cupboard, and the inner wall is warmed by a kitchen flue, or that the shelving is fitted in close proximity to a hot-water tank. In this way the linen is kept well aired.

If no special cupboard is provided, and in modern houses, and especially in flats, this is frequently the case, then perhaps an ordinary cupboard can be utilised, or an old-fashioned wardrobe with shelves and drawers underneath. Failing this, it is sometimes possible to have shelving fitted up in some recess, and then a light wooden door made to keep it free from dust; or merely a door frame, the panels being filled in with some pretty cretonne or tapestry.

A linen cupboard should be well provided with shelves, and these should be wide enough to hold folded bed and table linen comfortably, with a little room to spare. The shelves are frequently made of simple spars of wood with spaces between, and this plan allows the air to circulate round the linen better than it would in the case of solid wood.

Arrangement.—The shelves of the linen cupboard should be covered with thin calico or with strong white paper, which can be renewed from time to time. Each kind of linen should have a shelf or a portion of a shelf devoted to itself; thus bed linen should be arranged in one place, table linen in another, towels in another, and so on. Linen sheets should be kept separate from cotton sheets, large sheets from small sheets, different sets of table-linen by themselves, each class of towel by itself, &c., and all of one kind together. Arrange the linen methodically in neat piles, and in an order most convenient to yourself. Finer and better things which are not in common use should be wrapped up in muslin or pieces of old sheeting and labelled; otherwise they are liable to be pulled out by mistake and used in a hurry. The shelves of the linen cupboard must be kept carefully covered to prevent the dust falling on the linen. Some people have small rods fixed to the edges of the shelves, by which covers can be attached by means of rings or a casing, and these can then be folded back over the linen, or loose covers of thin holland fastened to the edges of the shelves with large drawing-pins will answer the purpose very well. The covers must be large enough to cover the linen well and to tuck in all round. Needless to say, they must be kept very clean and washed at regular intervals. The door of the linen cupboard must always be kept locked, or at least tightly closed.

Scenting the Linen.—The old-fashioned plan of putting lavender among the bed linen is a very dainty one. The dried lavender can either be bound up in bundles, or the flowers put into a muslin or thin silk bag, and laid between the folds of the sheets and pillow-cases. Instead of lavender, dried rose-leaves, heliotrope, verbena, or powdered oris-root can all be used. Any of these will give a delicate scent to the bed-linen.

Marking.—It is very important to have every article in the linen cupboard carefully and distinctly marked. Shopkeepers who supply the linen are generally very willing to do this in ink, free of charge. There are different methods of marking, and, of course, the most artistic is to have the name or monogram of the owner embroidered on the material. Linen drapers will generally undertake to do this on payment of the required fee—the simple initials will only cost a few pence, while more elaborate designs will, of course, be more costly. A pretty monogram may cost as much as 5s. or 7s. Those who have time and clever fingers will like to do it at home, and the process is not a difficult one.

Cash's lettering is another way of marking. A combination of any two letter combinations can be bought ready for 10d. per box of one gross, or any length name made to order in ten days, in Script, Old English, or Block style type, for 4s. 6d. per gross, 2s. 9d. per half gross. These can be embroidered in red, navy, black, blue, yellow, green or white, on fine tape, and are easily sewn on to the linen. They do very well, for such things as sheets, blankets and towels, but would not look well on table linen. There is always the danger, too, of their being picked off if the linen passes through the hands of dishonest people. If the washing of the linen is to be done in a public laundry, the simple ink marking is as good as any. The mark should be put in the top left-hand corner, as it is most convenient for folding. In addition to the name, it is a good plan when marking to put the number of articles in each set, and the date of purchase as well, thus—supposing the name to be Grant, and the number of articles six, one would put

6—Grant, 1910.

In the case of bed-linen some people put a mark to show for which room it is intended as well, and with table-linen when separate table-cloths are used, for luncheon and dinner, the word luncheon or dinner could be marked in accordingly. If the marking is to be done in ink at home, be careful to choose one of a reliable quality, as inferior kinds turn a bad colour, and sometimes burn a hole in the fabric. If there is any uncertainty as to the ink being satisfactory, it will be wise to test it first on a piece of rag; then submit the rag to all the processes of washing, boiling, and ironing, and see how the ink stands the treatment. If good, it should come out clear and black. A metal pen should never be used for marking, as the steel of the pen combined with the ink often forms an acid, which spoils the linen. A proper quill pen for the purpose is usually sold with each bottle of ink.

Small india-rubber stamps can be bought for marking linen, but the result is not elegant. These are more suitable for large institutions than for home use.

Kitchen towels and dusters must be marked as methodically as bed linen.

Inventory.—It is very important, too, that a list be made of every article the linen cupboard contains. This should be entered in a small book kept for the purpose, and space should be left for any notes or alterations. It is a good plan to put a note of the price and the date of purchase against each article, as this is useful for future reference. When new linen is bought, it must at once be added to the list, and any that is discarded should be struck off. The list will require revision from time to time, and the stock should be counted carefully and compared with the numbers in the book. If the linen is in charge of one of the maids of the household, the mistress should go over the list with her and check every item. A simple copy of the list, without any notes and comments, might also be fastened to the door of the linen cupboard by means of drawing-pins, as this can be easily referred to at a glance. Of course, some of these details may be simplified in very small houses, although at all times it is wiser to have housekeeping done in a methodical and business-like manner, and it really saves time and expense in the end.

Care of Soiled Linen.—To allow soiled linen to accumulate is a habit to be condemned. Both personal and bed linen is liable to have an unpleasant odour, and the sooner it can be washed the more sanitary and hygienic it will be for every one concerned. A weekly washing is strongly to be recommended, and under no circumstances should soiled linen remain unwashed longer than a fortnight. Meanwhile, it must be kept in a ventilated receptacle. A light basket is the usual thing, and nothing could be better. If possible, the soiled linen should be kept in a small room or closet that is not used for sleeping purposes—it is not a healthy custom to store it in a bedroom, but where this is unavoidable, there is all the more necessity to have it turned out and washed as soon as possible.

Sending out the Washing.—Before sending out a washing, great care must be taken to make an accurate list of all the articles. The list should be written in a book, and not on slips of paper, which are readily lost. In large households it is a good plan to make the list in duplicate, sending one copy to the laundry and reserving the other for reference on return of the washing. Some laundries supply their own books with a printed list of the different items, and all that is necessary is to date it and fill in the number of the different articles. Or special laundry books, such as Lett's, can be bought for a few pence. Everything that requires washing should first be collected together in a given place, and if there are different maids in the house each one should be responsible for the collecting of her own towels, &c. Then have the things divided into lots, according to their kind, and carefully counted. If the washing is a large one, it will be much easier if two can be engaged at the work; then one can do the counting, while the other enters the numbers in the book. It is always safer to count everything twice in case of any mistakes. It is always well too, in making the list, to put some notification of the kind of article sent—such as *linen* sheets, *cotton* sheets, *large* table-cloths, *kitchen* table-cloths, and not merely to classify them under the heading of *sheets* or table-cloths respectively.

The soiled linen must then be put into bags or packed in a basket ready to be sent away, and the written list must in all cases accompany it.

For directions for home washing, see "Guide to Laundry Work," p. 271.

Return of the Washing.—When the linen is returned from the washing, it must be most carefully checked, first as regards numbers, and then as regards the kind of washing it has received, and the mending that may be required. If there is any article missing, it should have a mark put against it in the book, and inquiry must at once be made about it, and when received a note must be made of the fact in the book. It is also important when checking to examine the linen to see that all has been well washed, and if there is anything faulty, it should be returned to the laundry with a note asking that it should be redone and returned in better condition. It is a good plan to keep a list of the laundry prices at hand, so as to compare them with those marked in the book. Anything requiring mending must be put aside until it can have attention, and the remainder aired if necessary, and then put away in its proper place on the shelves. The freshly washed articles should always be put at the foot of the pile already there, as this will ensure equal wear, everything being used in rotation. Regular use is also a protection from mildew.

Airing of Linen.—It is most important that all linen should be thoroughly dry before it is laid away. In many cases it is not necessary to air it when it comes from the laundry, as it arrives almost warm from the hot air closets, but where the least dampness is suspected it should have attention, or it will be liable to gather mildew. And then again, just before bed linen is used, it should be well aired, unless the linen cupboard happens to be a heated one. The sheets should be hung in front of a good hot fire, and turned and re-turned until they are warmed through and through. If linen is stored in a cold cupboard, it readily absorbs moisture, whilst a spell of wet weather, especially after frost, will render it quite damp, and when we consider what serious results may follow the sleeping in damp sheets, the slight extra trouble of airing the linen will not be objected to.

Mending of House Linen.—After the first few weeks of wear linen will require examination for repairs. Buttons and tapes soon begin to disappear, the ends of hems and seams come undone, and other stitches here and there will be required. Then later on more serious mending will be necessary—patching, darning, and adapting. The housewife need never be ashamed of linen that is well mended; on the contrary she should be proud of it, for it will serve to give eloquent testimony of her patience and thrift.

The proper time for patching and darning house linen is before sending it to the washing, and slight rents must have instant attention. If it is not convenient to mend bed linen and towels before washing, any holes or tears must at least be drawn together or roughly mended with a needle and cotton, or the hard treatment to which they will probably be subjected in the laundry will only tend to increase them tenfold. Table linen, however, must always be mended before it is done up, as it would be impossible to do it when starched and ironed without crushing it considerably. If a large patch or darn is required, it is even better to have the damask washed and rough dried in order to remove all the dressing before attempting the mending.

When sheets show signs of wear in the middle, it is a good plan to cut them in two lengthways, and to join the two outer edges together. The cut edges will then require to be hemmed. Or if a large sheet begins to wear in other parts, perhaps the best pieces can be taken to make a sheet for a smaller bed or cot. Always try to get as much as you can out of a sheet before putting it aside as old linen.

Note.—For directions for mending, see Needlework Section, p. 411.

What to do with old Linen.—No matter how much care is taken of house linen it will eventually wear out.

Old cotton sheets can always be used as dust-sheets, or if these are not required, the best pieces can be cut out and made into cloths for various household purposes, covers for the linen cupboard, covers for drawers, or for wrapping up fine linen or blankets, &c.

An old linen sheet is more valuable, and the remains should be put to some better use. The top and bottom which has not had very hard wear will likely be in good condition, and a strip can no doubt be cut off which, with a little hem-stitching and embroidery, will make quite dainty sheet-shams. Or small good portions might be made into pillow-shams, and smaller pieces still could be cut up into centres for doyleys and tray cloths, or the cover for a cosy, or perhaps even a complete toilet set for a bedroom. Any one with clever fingers and a little ingenuity can, with some embroidery and the addition of pretty lace and insertion, make many a dainty article out of small pieces of linen. Pieces of linen which are too worn to be worth any sewing should be carefully rolled up and laid aside, as they will no doubt be found invaluable in the case of sickness.

Old table-cloths, when they can no longer be darned or patched, can be cut down into tray cloths, sideboard cloths, carving cloths, &c., and also it is always well to keep a few old pieces of damask at hand for patching and mending.

Old towels can always be used up as household cloths; in fact, the more thin and worn they are the more useful and valuable they will be for some purposes. A collection should always be made in view of any spring or special cleaning; they will come in very handy for the drying of paint and woodwork, &c., and a plentiful supply will be a great boom.

Old pillow-cases make useful bags for keeping various patching materials, &c.

Old Blankets. (See p. 262.)

Replenishing the Linen Cupboard.—It is not wise to allow the linen supply to fall too low, as this will mean paying out a big sum sooner or later to bring it back to its normal condition. It is much better, when it can be managed, to add something new every year, even although it may only be a pair of good sheets, half-a-dozen towels, a fine table-cloth, or a few serviettes. In this way the supply is kept up at very little expense. It might just be mentioned here that household linen is one of the things that can often be very profitably bought at a sale. The large linen warehouses sell off their old stock, either because the patterns are not of the latest or because the materials are shop soiled, and as this in nowise detracts from the value of the article a great saving can be realised by buying what is necessary at these times.

The following lists with estimates have been compiled from information kindly supplied by Messrs. Waring & Gillow, Oxford Street, London, and will perhaps be a guide to those who have to stock their linen cupboard for the first time.

The quantities can, of course, be increased or decreased according to special requirements.

Estimate No. 1—£17 18s. 5d.

Description.	Price.		Amount.		
	s.	*d.*	£	*s.*	*d.*
3 double damask cloths, 2 by 2½ yards . . .	10	6	1	11	6
2 double damask cloths, 2 by 3 yards	12	9	1	5	6
1 dozen double damask dinner napkins . .	15	0		15	0
3 damask tray cloths . .	2	0		6	0
2 damask sideboard cloths	2	9		5	6
2 kitchen table cloths .	3	6		7	0
3 pair cotton sheets, 2¾ by 3½ yards	12	6	1	17	6
2 pair cotton sheets, 2 by 3½ yards	8	6		17	0
12 cotton pillow-cases .		10½		10	6
4 pair servants' cotton sheets, 2 by 3 yards	6	0	1	4	0
4 servants' pillow-cases .		8½		2	10
1 dozen linen bedroom towels	11	9		11	9
6 servants' towels . . .		8½		4	3
6 white Turkish bath towels	1	4½		8	3
½ dozen glass cloths . .	5	0		2	6
½ dozen tea and china cloths	5	0		2	6
½ dozen strong kitchen rubbers	6	6		3	3
½ dozen housemaids' cloths	6	6		3	3
1 dozen check dusters .	4	6		4	6
4 linen roller towels . .	1	4		5	4
2 pudding cloths . . .		4½			9
4 knife cloths		4½		1	6
2 pair double-bed blankets	18	6	1	17	0
2 under blankets . . .	3	9		7	6
1 pair single-bed blankets				12	0
1 under blanket . . .				2	9
2 large white toilet quilts	10	0	1	0	0
1 single-bed white toilet quilt	7	6		7	6
2 pair servants' blankets .	10	0	1	0	0
2 under blankets . . .	2	9		5	6
2 servants' coloured quilts	4	6		9	0
4 white toilet covers . .	1	3		5	0
2 servants' toilet covers .	1	0		2	0
			£17	18	5

Estimate No. 2—£31 16s. 2d.

Description.	Price.		Amount.		
	s.	*d.*	£	*s.*	*d.*
4 superior double damask cloths, 2 by 2½ yards (hand woven) . . .	15	0	3	0	0
2 superior double damask cloths, 2½ by 3 yards (hand woven) . . .	23	0	2	6	0
1½ dozen superior double damask napkins, 27 inches square (hand woven).	24	0	1	16	0
½ dozen damask fish napkins	6	0		3	0
4 damask carving napkins or tray cloths . . .	2	0		8	0
2 damask (or hem-stitched linen) sideboard cloths	3	6		7	0
2 kitchen table cloths, 2 by 2 yards	4	6		9	0
3 pair double-bed linen sheets, 2¾ by 3½ yards	27	6	4	2	6
3 pair single-bed linen sheets, 2 by 3½ yards	21	0	3	3	0
12 linen pillow-cases (hem-stitched)	2	0	1	4	0
4 pair servants' cotton sheets, 2 by 3 yards .	7	0	1	8	0
4 servants' cotton pillow-cases	1	0		4	0
1 dozen linen huckaback bedroom towels . .	14	0		14	0
1 dozen linen diaper bedroom towels (hem-stitched)	15	0		15	0
½ dozen servants' linen bedroom towels . .	10	0		5	0
6 large white Turkish bath towels	2	0		12	0
1 dozen glass cloths . .	6	6		6	6
1 dozen tea cloths . . .	6	6		6	6
1 dozen strong kitchen rubbers	8	0		8	0
½ dozen housemaids' cloths	6	6		3	3
1 dozen check dusters . .	4	6		4	6
1 dozen soft polishing dusters	3	6		3	6
6 linen roller towels . . .	1	6		9	0
3 pudding cloths		6		1	6
½ dozen knife cloths . .	4	6		2	3
1 hearth-rug cover . . .	2	11		2	11
1 dozen sponge cloths, for lamps, &c.	2	0		2	0
2 pair double-bed fine wool blankets	25	0	2	10	0
2 under blankets	5	0		10	0
1 pair single-bed fine wool blankets	16	6		16	6
1 under blanket				3	3
2 pair servants' blankets .	12	0	1	4	0
2 under blankets	2	9		5	6

Estimate No. 2—continued.

Description	s.	d.	£	s.	d.
2 fine white toilet quilts, for double beds . .	15	0	1	10	0
1 fine white toilet quilt, for single beds . . .	10	6		10	6
2 servants' coloured quilts .	5	6		11	0
4 white toilet covers . .	1	9		7	0
2 servants' toilet covers .	1	0		2	0
			£31	16	2

Estimate No. 3—£67 5s. 10d.

Description.	Price. s.	d.	Amount. £	s.	d.
4 fine double damask table cloths, 2½ by 2½ yards	25	0	5	0	0
3 fine double damask table-cloths, 2½ by 3 yards .	30	0	4	10	0
1 fine double damask table cloth, 2½ by 4 yards .	42	0	2	2	0
4 dozen fine double damask napkins, 27 by 27 ins.	30	0	6	0	0
1 dozen damask fish napkins	7	6		7	6
1 dozen damask pastry napkins	7	6		7	6
6 damask tray or carving napkins, 31 by 36 ins.	3	6	1	1	0
2 damask (or hem-stitched linen) sideboard cloths	7	6		15	0
3 kitchen table cloths, 2 by 2½ yards	5	6		16	6
2 dishing-up cloths, 1½ by 1½ yards	2	6		5	0
4 pair fine linen sheets for double beds, 3 by 3½ yards (hem-stitched) .	42	0	8	8	0
4 pair fine linen sheets for single beds, 2 by 3½ yards (hem-stitched) .	30	0	6	0	0
18 fine linen hem-stitched pillow-covers (square or oblong)	3	6	3	3	0
6 pair servants' superior cotton sheets, 2 by 3 yards	8	6	2	11	0
6 servants' superior cotton pillow-covers . . .	1	0		6	0
1 dozen strong linen buckaback towels . . .	15	9		15	9
1 dozen fine linen buckaback towels (hem-stitched)	19	6		19	6
1 dozen fine soft linen diaper towels (hem-stitched)	21	0	1	1	0
1 dozen servants' strong linen huckaback towels	12	6		12	6

Estimate No. 3—continued.

Description	s.	d.	£	s.	d.
6 large white Turkish bath towels	3	0		18	0
6 extra large Turkish bath towels	3	6	1	1	0
2 white Turkish bath sheets	5	0		10	0
1 dozen glass cloths, fine quality	7	6		7	6
1 dozen tea or china cloths, fine quality	7	6		7	6
1 dozen linen dusters . .	5	6		5	6
1 dozen soft polishing cloths or dusters	4	6		4	6
1 dozen housemaids' cloths (basin)	6	6		6	6
1 dozen strong large kitchen rubbers	8	6		8	6
1 dozen soft large kitchen rubbers	8	6		8	6
8 linen roller towels . . .	2	0		16	0
½ dozen pudding cloths. .	6	0		3	0
1 dozen knife cloths . .	4	6		4	6
2 hearth-rug covers . . .	2	11		5	10
1 dozen sponge cloths, for lamps, &c.	2	0		2	0
2 pair large double-bed blankets	30	0		0	0
2 under blankets	6	0		12	0
2 pair single-bed blankets .	18	6		17	0
2 under blankets . . .	4	3		8	6
3 pair servants' strong heavy blankets . . .	12	6	1	17	6
3 under blankets	3	3		9	9
3 fine white toilet quilts for double beds	21	0	3	3	0
3 fine white toilet quilts for single beds	15	0	2	5	0
4 servants' coloured quilts	5	6	1	2	0
6 fine white toilet covers .	2	6		15	0
4 servants' toilet covers .	1	6		6	0
			£67	5	10

Estimate No. 4—£177 3s. 1d.

Description.	Price. s.	d.	Amount. £	s.	d.
6 extra fine double damask table cloths, 2½ by 2½ yards	37	6	11	5	0
4 extra fine double damask table cloths, 2½ by 3 yards	45	0	9	0	0
4 extra fine double damask table cloths, 2½ by 4 yards	63	0	12	12	0
2 extra fine double damask table cloths, 2½ by 5 yards	84	0	8	8	0

Estimate No. 4—continued.

	s.	d.	£	s.	d.
1 extra fine double damask table cloth, 2½ by 6 yards	105	0	5	5	0
6 dozen extra fine double damask napkins, 27 by 27 inches	45	0	13	10	0
2 dozen extra fine double damask breakfast napkins, 22 by 22 inches	30	0	3	0	0
dozen extra fine double damask tray or carving napkins, 31 by 36 ins.	63	0	3	3	0
2 dozen damask fish napkins (large and small)	7	6		15	0
2 dozen bread and pastry napkins	5	0		10	0
4 damask (or hem-stitched linen) sideboard cloths	10		2	2	0
3 afternoon tea cloths	15	6	2	5	0
4 strong damask cloths, for upper servants, 2 by 2 yards	6	6	1	6	0
4 kitchen table cloths, 2 by 2½ yards	7	6	1	10	0
4 extra strong dishing-up cloths, 1½ by 2 yards	4	0		16	0
6 pair fine linen hem-stitched sheets, for double beds, 3 by 3½ yards	57	6	17	5	0
8 pair fine linen hem-stitched sheets, for single beds, 2 by 3½ yards	42	0	16	16	0
30 fine linen hem-stitched pillow-covers (square or oblong)	5	6	8	5	0
6 duchesse toilet covers	5	0	1	10	0
8 pair strong cotton sheets, for servants, 2 by 3½ yards	10	6	4	4	0
12 strong linen pillow-covers, for servants	2	0	1	4	0
2 dozen extra strong hem-stitched huckaback towels	21	0	2	2	0
2 dozen fine hem-stitched huckaback towels	25	0	2	10	0
2 dozen fine soft diaper bedroom towels, for ladies' use	25	0	2	10	0

Estimate No. 4—continued.

	s.	d.	£	s.	d.
2 dozen linen huckaback towels, for servants	14	0	1	8	0
1 dozen medium-size white Turkish bath towels	30	0	1	10	0
½ dozen large-size white Turkish bath towels	42	0	1	1	0
6 brown Turkish bath towels	2	6		15	0
6 large white Turkish bath sheets	7	6	2	5	0
1 dozen Turkish towels, for servants	12	6		12	6
2 dozen glass cloths	8	6		17	0
2 dozen tea or china cloths (pantry)	10	0	1	0	0
1 dozen linen dusters (strong and fine)	5	6		5	6
1 dozen linen dusters (strong and fine),	8	0		8	0
1 dozen soft polishing cloths or dusters	4	6		4	6
1 dozen housemaids' cloths (basin)	8	6		8	6
2 dozen kitchen and scullery cloths, 1 yard square	10	6	1	1	0
1 dozen kitchen china cloths, 1 yard square	10	0		10	0
1 dozen linen roller towels	30	0	1	10	0
½ dozen pudding cloths	6	6		3	3
1 dozen knife cloths	4	6		4	6
2 hearth-rug covers	2	11		5	10
4 butlers' aprons	2	0		8	0
3 pair large double-bed superior Witney blankets	42	0	6	6	0
3 under blankets	6	6		19	6
4 pair single-bed superior Witney blankets	30	0	6	0	0
4 under blankets	5	3	1	1	0
4 pair strong blankets, for servants	15	0	3	0	0
4 under blankets	2	9		11	0
4 fine white toilet quilts, for double beds	27	6	5	10	0
5 fine white toilet quilts, for single beds	21	0	5	5	0
5 coloured or white quilts, for servants	6	6	1	12	6
6 toilet covers, for servants	1	3		7	6
			£177	3	1

GUIDE TO LAUNDRY WORK

THE proper washing and "getting up" of linen is an art which remains practically unsolved by the average housewife, who, when she is obliged to do even the simplest laundry work at home, is content to get through her task in a most rough-and-ready fashion.

"What is worth doing at all is worth doing well" is a maxim which might be followed with advantage by the home laundress, who should make a point of acquiring a real practical knowledge of her work. The information contained in this chapter has been compiled as a result of many years' practical experience of laundry work in all its branches, and the amateur laundress should derive much help from a careful study of these pages.

Home-Washing.—Whether the washing should be done at home or not is a question which every housekeeper must decide for herself. There is a great diversity of opinion on the subject, and much to be said on both sides.

Given the necessary accommodation, a wash-house fitted with tubs, a plentiful supply of hot water, a good drying-green and convenient room for ironing, there is no doubt that home washing is more satisfactory and more economical than having the work sent out. It is more economical, not only from the money point of view, but in the wear and tear of the clothes the saving is unquestionable. Besides, there is the pleasure of wearing and using linen which we know has been washed and rinsed in clean water, and that has not come in contact with all and sundry garments. There is also the feeling that one can be a little more lavish with the supply when it is not necessary to reckon up the cost for the washing of each separate article. This is a very important point, when we consider that cleanliness in our garments and surroundings is one of the first laws of health, and a law which it would be false economy to break.

On the other hand, a housekeeper must consider whether there is the adequate convenience for doing such a large piece of work as the family washing, and also if there is sufficient help available for the labour to be undertaken satisfactorily.

In many houses, especially town houses, where space is valuable it would be impossible to carry out the work successfully, and certainly not without a great deal of discomfort. There are other economies to consider besides the saving of money; there is the economy of time, the economy of labour, and the economy of patience and temper as well.

The probable discomfort of a washing day deters many people from entertaining the idea of doing their washing at home, and it certainly requires some planning and knowledge of the necessary details to have the extra work going on, and to keep the wheels of the house running smoothly at the same time. If, however, the work is to be done at the expense of every one's comfort, then by all means leave it alone; any advantages to be gained would be dearly bought at such a price.

Now that public laundries are springing up all around us, and their methods for treating the clothes are improving year by year, there is no longer the *absolute* necessity for home washing.

Sometimes, although it is found impossible to do the whole washing at home, a part can be done quite easily, the heavier and more complicated articles being sent out. There is always more difficulty in undertaking the dressing of starched linen, especially such things as gentlemen's shirts, collars and cuffs, white petticoats, dresses, &c., and heavy articles like sheets and table-cloths. If these are sent away to be done, perhaps the rest will cause no difficulty.

If the decision is in favour of home washing, then it is very important that the process be planned with care, and then carried out methodically.

A REGULAR TIME FOR WASHING

In arranging your washing-day, of course take into consideration the circumstances of the household, but have it as early in the week as possible, and at a fixed hour. As a general rule Tuesday is the most suitable day, as this lets you have all necessary preparations made on Monday. Never let soiled clothes remain unwashed longer than a fortnight, and you must judge from the amount of work to be done if a weekly washing is advisable. Begin operations early in the day, as clothes dried in the morning air are always whitest and freshest.

LAUNDRY UTENSILS, THEIR CHOICE AND CARE

As all the utensils used in laundry work are subjected to a considerable amount of wear and tear, it is of the utmost importance to have them good and durable. A little additional outlay at the commencement in order to obtain first-class articles will be money well spent, the replacing of faulty goods will not be necessary, and much needless worry will be saved.

At its best laundry work is a somewhat arduous occupation, and although it is possible to produce excellent results with the most primitive implements, this requires the skilled worker. Under ordinary circumstances, in order to have the work well done and time and labour economised, the necessary implements must be provided.

The number of utensils required will depend very much upon individual circumstances. A large household with good laundry accommodation, and all the washing done at home, will naturally require more than a small household where the work has to be done in a kitchen and scullery, and perhaps only part of the washing undertaken. In the latter case the number of utensils should be reduced to a minimum through lack of space to accommodate them. Whereever possible, laundry utensils should be kept apart from those used for cooking purposes. In all cases it is better to buy just what is absolutely necessary to begin with, and to add as the need arises.

The following utensils will be required to do a complete washing conveniently :—

Tubs.—Two or three fitted tubs with hot and cold water, and one or two smaller movable tubs or zinc baths for small articles, are the most convenient for washing purposes. If fitted tubs are not provided, then larger zinc or wooden tubs will be necessary, and a stand or bench to place them on. It is very important to have the tub placed at the right height for the worker. All tubs must be kept very clean, and dirty soapy water must on no account be allowed to remain in them. They must be well scrubbed out after use to remove any dirty scum that may have collected on the sides. Then zinc or porcelain ones may be dried, but wooden ones should have a little cold water left in them to prevent them shrinking.

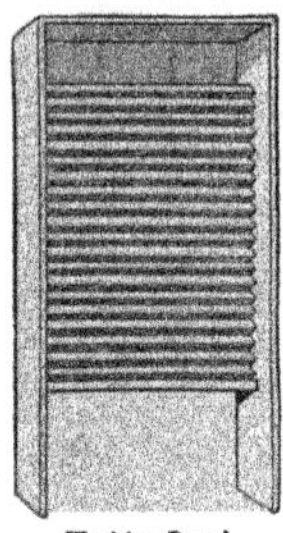
Washing-Board.

Washing-Board and Brush.—Both these will be found of great assistance. The board is useful in the washing of heavy articles, such as sheets, table-cloths, counterpanes, &c., and anything strong and dirty that will stand a fair amount of rubbing. A wooden board is preferable to one made of zinc. It should be well washed on both sides after use, and set up on end to dry. A brush with good bristles and not too hard is also useful in the washing of collars, cuffs, bands, or any very soiled parts which require extra attention. The brush should be well rinsed and set up to dry after use, and never used for any other purpose.

A Boiler.—This is generally a fitted arrangement with a small fireplace underneath. It must be kept very clean, and well washed and dried after use. If a greasy scum collects on the sides, a mixture of soft soap and shredded Brooke's soap should be applied with a wet flannel, or a little paraffin may be added to this mixture if something stronger is required. Clean cold water must always be put into the boiler before the fire is lighted, and the fire should be out before the boiler is emptied. Cinders from other fires do very well for burning in a boiler fire, or coke is very often substituted for coal. If no fitted boiler is provided, a large saucepan can be used and boiled on an ordinary fire or gas stove. A tin or enamelled one is best, and, if possible, it should be kept for laundry purposes only.

Mangle and Wringer.—A mangle is a large machine, with heavy wooden rollers used for smoothing household linen and the heavier articles of clothing. When in use the tension must be tight enough to press the clothes sufficiently, and loosened again when finished with. The rollers must be kept very clean and free from dust, and the working parts should be oiled occasionally. A *wringer* is a most useful machine and almost indispensable if any heavy washing is to be done. It is generally attached to a washing-tub, and the clothes are put through it while wet. The rollers are of india-rubber, and should be kept clean with soap and water, or if stained with any dyed material a little turpentine should be applied with a soft rag. As with the mangle, the tension must be tightened when in use and afterwards loosened. Nothing that is boiling hot should be passed through the wringer or the surface of the india-rubber will become roughened. With care the india-rubber ought to last a long time, and when it does wear out, the coating can be replaced and the wringer made as good as new. For small washings the wringer can almost take the place of the heavier and larger mangle.

Washing Machines.—Various machines are now made for home washing, and where there is a large number of things to be done they are certainly a great aid. A good machine carefully used will really wear the clothes less than the ordinary washing and rubbing in a tub. One of simple construction should be chosen, and the directions, which vary slightly with the different machines, will be given with each. Very often a wringer or small mangle is attached to the machine, and in this case the extra machinery would be unnecessary.

The "Sunrise" Patent Washing Machine can be thoroughly recommended. It is very simple

"Sunrise" Washing Machine.

in construction, absolutely efficient, and occupies very little space. The price too is only 35s., or with a rubber roller attached, 25s. extra.

Clothes-Ropes, Pins and Poles.—These are used when drying is done out of doors, and it is most important that they should be kept perfectly clean. Clothes are frequently seen with the mark of a dirty pin or rope upon them, and this happens through carelessness. The clothes-ropes should never be left outside when not in use. They not only get dirty, but will rot if exposed to the atmosphere. They should be rubbed over with a cloth, rolled up and put into a bag or basket where they will be under cover. The same care must be taken with the pins which fasten the clothes to the line. Do not let them lie on the ground, but see that they are quite clean, and put them away with the ropes. New clothes-ropes and pins should be soaked first in hot and then in cold water before use, as they are liable to mark the clothes. Clothes-poles, which are used for propping up the ropes, must be brought indoors when not in use, and kept in a clean place.

Clothes-Horse and Pulley.—These are necessary for drying and airing indoors. The horse, which is like a screen with bars, is placed round or near a fire, and the pulley is generally fixed to the roof of the kitchen or laundry, and can be pulled up and down as required.

The Ironing Table.—This must be of a good size, strong, and steady, and of a convenient height for working at. It should be covered first with felt or a double fold of thick blanket. The kind known as "charity" blankets, of a grey colour and rather a hard make, are very suitable for the purpose. The blanket should be large enough to come at least a few inches over the table all round. A clean sheet will then be required to place on the top of this, which should either be pinned at the four corners or fastened to the table legs by means of tapes. Patches and seams should be avoided as far as possible, or put where they will not come in the way of the ironing. The heat of the iron must never be tested on the ironing sheet, as if once scorched it is almost sure to wear into holes when washed.

Never lay ironing blankets and sheets away damp, or they will probably mildew; and never let them remain on the table longer than is necessary, as they get dusty. Shake them well, and fold evenly before laying away.

In addition to the ironing table, a smaller one for placing the work on will be found a great convenience if space permits.

Irons.—Those most generally used are called flat irons, and for all ordinary purposes they produce as good work as any other. They should be of different sizes and have comfortable handles. Numbers 5, 6, and 7 are useful sizes, and two, or better three, will be required for each worker. If any fine intricate work is to be done, one or two very small irons will be necessary. Flat irons are best heated on an ironing stove or on the top of a close range. Ironing stoves can be had in different sizes, they take up very little room, and where there is a large amount of work to be done, and consequently many irons to be heated, a proper stove will be found more economical than keeping up a large kitchen fire for the sole purpose of heating irons. If a cooking stove is used for heating, the fire must be well made up, the hearth swept, and the top of the range wiped free from grease before the irons are put down. It is not such a good plan to heat irons in front of an open fire, as their surfaces are liable to get roughened and smoky. If it must be done, have the fire bright and free from smoke before placing the irons, and when fresh coal has to be added let it be put at the back of the fire, drawing forward the red cinders. A smoked iron is fatal to good ironing. Never put irons into a fire to heat or the surface will be roughened and the iron ruined for any fine work. Gas stoves are very convenient for heating one or two irons, but where a number are required it will be found an expensive method.

Flat Iron.

An iron must be well cleaned each time before using. Have a wooden box, and put at the foot of it some sand-paper, or ordinary thick brown paper with fine sand or bath-brick dust sprinkled on it. Rub the iron well on this first, and the slight roughness of the sand, &c., will clean it. Then have a piece of coarse cloth or sacking with a little grease on it. A piece of bees'-wax or candle-end shred down and put between the folds of the cloth will do. Rub the iron next on this to make it run smoothly, then finish off by dusting it with a duster to make it quite free from sand or brick-dust. Occasionally it is well to wash the irons thoroughly with hot water, soda, soap, and a brush, and then thoroughly dry. On no account must irons be black-leaded. Never allow them to cool flat on a stove when the fire is going out, as damp collects and rusts them, but either stand them up on end at the side of the stove or on the hearth-stone. Irons must be kept in a perfectly dry place. If you once allow them to get rusty, the rust eats into them, and their surface is never so smooth again. If they are to be laid away for some time, see that they are thoroughly dry, then grease them well, and wrap them in brown paper.

It is almost impossible to iron with perfectly new irons; they must be seasoned first. To do this heat them on a stove for several hours, then clean in the ordinary way, and let them cool. Repeat this process for several days, and the irons will be ready for use.

A very good invention is the new patent "Slip-On" Ironing Shield, which can be put on to any flat iron, No. 4 to 7, after it has been well heated. This saves the trouble of so much cleaning, and the nickel-plated surface of the shield will iron the clothes without a mark, and produce a high gloss on the linen. The price is 1s.

Iron Shield.

Various special irons can now be had to replace the flat iron, such as box irons. These, as their name implies, are like a box, and are heated by means of a hot bolt placed inside. Charcoal or Dalli irons, which are heated with hot charcoal inside the iron. Gas irons, heated with gas, by means of an india-rubber tube attached to a gas jet. Asbestos irons, electric irons—heated by electricity, and also the spirit iron, which is heated with methylated spirits, and is most useful where no fire is obtainable, or for a lady's private use, and for travelling.

Polishing and Goffering Irons.—The polishing iron is like an ordinary iron with an oval surface of polished steel. It is used for polishing cuffs and collars or anything that requires a high gloss. Goffering irons are used for goffering

Polishing Iron.

Goffering Iron.

frills, and it is well to have them in different sizes if both wide and narrow frills are to be done. They should be heated in a gas jet, with methylated spirits, or be placed under a flat iron on an ordinary stove. They must never be put into a fire.

Iron-Stand and Holder.—Each ironer must be provided with an iron-stand, on which to rest the iron, and an iron-holder. Iron-stands are of different kinds, the simplest being a plain ring of iron, and others are of more elaborate design; but in any case they should stand high enough above the table to prevent the heat of the iron from scorching the ironing-sheet.

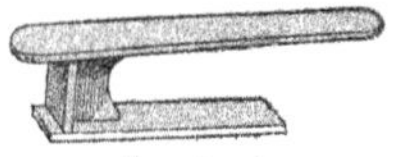

Sleeve Board.

Iron-holders should be made like kettle-holders, only more substantial. They should have several thick folds of flannel or two of felt inside, sewn together, and covered over with a clean cotton cover. A piece of kid put between the folds will help to keep the heat from the hands. The top cover must be strong. A piece of strong linen or ticking is suitable, but it must not be anything from which a dye will come off. For collars, cuffs, and shirts it is better to have the holder covered with white cotton. The holders must be made long enough to cover the length of the handle, and broad enough to come well round. When resting the iron, always take the holder off it. This not only keeps it cooler for the hand, but very often prevents it getting burnt when the iron is too hot to use. Iron-holders should be kept in a box or drawer where they will not get dusty.

Special irons which are provided with wooden handles will not require a holder.

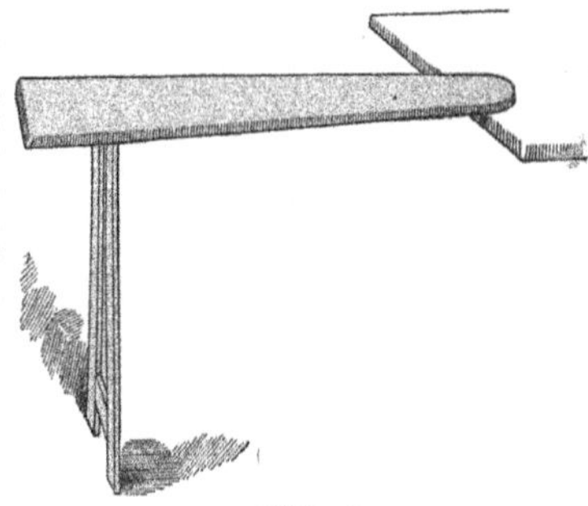

Skirt Board.

Shirt, Skirt, and Sleeve Boards.—These are all required in fitting out a laundry. The *shirt* board is used when ironing the fronts of shirts. One side at least must be covered with a double fold of white flannel, blanket, or felt stretched tightly over it, and either sewn or tacked on

Above this place a cotton or linen cover, which can be made like a slip, to be easily removed when dirty and replaced by a clean one.

Sleeve boards, used when ironing the sleeves of dresses, &c., must be covered in the same way. Keep both shirt and sleeve boards covered up when not in use, to prevent their becoming soiled.

Skirt boards are used when ironing petticoats, dress skirts, children's frocks, &c. These being larger will do quite well if covered with grey blanket like the tables, only it should be tacked on, and then covered with a small sheet pinned firmly underneath. It is better to have a sheet that can be taken off after use, as it will keep cleaner.

Polishing Boards are like skirt boards, only they are left uncovered. They are used for polishing collars and cuffs.

Basins.—Tin enamelled basins are the most satisfactory for laundry purposes, and it will be found useful to have several and of different sizes. These serve for the making of starch, for holding water when sprinkling the clothes, and for the soaking and even washing of small articles, such as lace, handkerchiefs, &c.

Bags.—One or two bags for boiling clothes in will be found useful. They can be made of strong net or of cotton with a slit in the side to allow the water to enter, otherwise they will blow up like a balloon and float on the surface of the water.

Sundries.—A soap dish, a small enamelled saucepan and knife for making soap jelly, a wooden fork or stick for lifting clothes from the boiler, a clothes-basket, a can for water, a steel comb and small brush for fringes, one or two tea-spoons, one wooden spoon, one gill measure, three or four towels, and some soft rag for rubbers, one or two pieces of white felt for the ironing of lace and embroidery, and three or four jars for keeping stores will complete the oufit of a laundry, and the following will give an idea of the approximate cost.

PRICE LIST OF LAUNDRY UTENSILS

Flat irons, from 8d. to 2s. according to side.
Box iron with pair of heaters, 2s. to 3s. each.
Dalli iron (charcoal), 6s. each.
Spirit-heated ladies' iron, 6s. or 7s. each.
Gas iron, 3s. 9d. to 6s. each.
Polishing iron, 1s. 6d. to 2s. each.
Electric iron, from 17s.
Tubs—wooden with galvanised hoops, 2s. to 6s. according to size.
Tubs—galvanised zinc, 1s. 6d to 3s according to size.
Shirt board, 3s. to 5s.
Skirt board, 4s. 6d. to 6s.
Sleeve board, 1s. 6d. to 4s.
Washing board, 1s. 3d.
Large tin boiler, 3s. 6d.
Tin enamelled basins, 1s. 2d. to 2s.
Mangle, from £2.
Wringer, from 18s.
Washing machine, various prices according to make.
Clothes-ropes, 16 yards for 1s.
Clothes-poles or props, 8d. to 1s.
Clothes-horse, 3s. 6d. to 6s.
Goffering irons, 8d. to 11d. per pair.
Iron-stand, 4d. to 6d.
Soap-dish, 4d. to 8d.
Clothes-basket, 1s. 6d. to 3s.
Can for water, 2s. 6d. to 3s.
Steel comb, 4d.
White felt, about 1s. 2d. per yard, double width.
Laundry blankets (grey charity), 4s. or 5s.
Laundry sheeting, about 1s. 3d. per yard.

MATERIALS REQUIRED AND THEIR USE

Water.—For washing purposes it is necessary to have an abundant supply of pure and soft water. Cleaning is almost an impossibility when the water is of an earthy colour, and contains a quantity of mineral matter. Rain water, when it can be obtained free from impurities, is preferable to river or spring water, which is generally hardened by a certain amount of lime acquired in running through the ground. There are many chemical tests by which one can tell soft water from hard water, but for laundry purposes it is sufficient to know that the harder the water the greater is the quantity of soap needed to produce a lather. When hard water must unavoidably be used for washing, some softening substance, such as soda or borax, must be added.

Soap.—Good yellow soap is best. Cheap soaps are no economy, as they contain a large percentage of water and waste quickly. Many of them also contain soda to an extent hurtful to the clothes. Soap must never be allowed to lie in the water, and all ends, which are too small for washing with, should be saved to make soap jelly, or else shred down and put into the boiler when boiling the clothes.

Soda.—This has a softening effect upon water, and absorbs and removes grease, but if used in too large quantities it will be found destructive to clothes, and will give them a grey appearance. It will also make the hands rough and sore. Before soda is used it must be completely dissolved in boiling or very hot water, for were it to touch the linen undissolved, yellow marks would be left, in reality burns, and these would eventually wear into holes. Soda must not be used for coloured clothes nor for flannels, and for fine articles borax will be found safer as a water-softener. When washing and boiling the coarser clothes, one ounce of soda will be sufficient to soften one gallon of water.

Borax.—This also softens water, but not so powerfully as soda, and as it is perfectly harmless it may be used even for woollen and dyed articles. Boron, a substance found in borax, acts as a disinfectant. Allow one table-spoonful of prepared borax to one gallon of water. Borax is also used for stiffening and glossing linen, such as collars and cuffs. It may be bought either as a powder or in lump form; the former is the more convenient of the two.

Blue.—This is added to the water in which white clothes are rinsed to give them a good colour. There are a number of different blues both in solid and liquid form—indigo, ultramarine, Prussian, and aniline; but the solid blues will, as a rule, be found handier, and the required quantity will be more easily judged. Having chosen the brand, keep to it, and then the question of quantity will be no difficulty. Blue which dissolves most readily and leaves least sediment after the water has stood some time is the best. Stone or solid blues should be firm and not gritty, and they ought to be kept in a dry place, as they readily absorb moisture. When a cake is required it should have the paper removed and be tied in a small bag or piece of flannel, when it will be ready to squeeze into the water. (See p. 278.)

Starch.—The stiffening and other qualities of starch vary according to the substance from which it is derived, so that it is a matter of great importance to choose a good kind.

Wheat and rice starches are those most commonly used. Rice starch is used as a substitute for wheat starch for all finer purposes.

Ammonia.—This is also used for the softening of water and will be found invaluable in the washing of flannel and knitted articles. It dissolves the grease and dirt in a wonderful way, and thus saves unnecessary rubbing. It must not, however, be used too freely, or it will impoverish the woolly fibre. Ammonia should be kept in a tightly corked bottle, as it is very volatile.

Turpentine.—Used in the making of cold-water starch, and also for the removal of certain stains. It should be kept in a tightly corked bottle.

Bees'-wax and White Wax.—The former is useful for the greasing of irons when candle-ends are not available, and the latter is sometimes put into hot-water starch.

Salts of Lemon—Salts of Sorrel.—These are useful for the removal of certain stains. As they are poisonous substances they ought to be labelled so, and kept in a safe place.

Chloride of Lime.—This is used for bleaching purposes, and also for the removal of very obstinate stains. It must be specially prepared. (See p. 277.)

Gum-Arabic.—This will take the place of starch in the stiffening of lace and silk.

Common Salt and Vinegar.—These are sometimes required for the rinsing of coloured articles.

Methylated Spirits.—This is used in small quantities in the washing of silks.

PREPARATION FOR A WASHING

Sorting.—Without order and method much time will be wasted. After having collected all the clothes to be washed, arrange them in different lots according to the kind of article and the tubs available for steeping.

1. Table linen.
2. Bed and other household linen.
3. Body linen.
4. Laces, muslins, and finer articles.
5. Flannels and other woollen or knitted goods.
6. Pocket-handkerchiefs.
7. Coloured prints, muslins, and sateens.
8. Kitchen towels and very dirty articles.

When there is a scarcity of tubs one may be used for bed and body linen.

Pocket-handkerchiefs should always be kept apart from other articles until after the first washing.

As table linen might be discoloured by contact with greasy clothes, keep it also separate until after washing.

Mending.—Before washing, all holes or tears must at least be drawn together if not actually mended, as the friction of washing would tend to enlarge them.

All strings should be untied and undrawn, and any buttons unfastened.

Removal of Stains.—This is generally looked upon as very troublesome, but it will be found that the results fully repay the time and labour involved, indeed, it is absolutely necessary for the production of good work. The sooner stains are removed the better. Most stains can be easily eradicated when fresh, while they harden if allowed to remain. As soap combined with hot water makes most stains permanent, the removing process must take place before the actual washing begins. Different chemicals are employed for this, all more or less injurious to the fabric, so that after the application of any of them, the article must be immediately rinsed in clean warm water.

Rust or Iron-Mould.—Take a small basin of boiling water, dip the stained part into it, and then stretch tightly over the basin. Sprinkle with salts of sorrel, and rub it well into the stain; use a piece of rag or smooth stick to do this, as salts of sorrel is most poisonous and might be injurious to the fingers. Allow it to steam for a short time with the salts on it, when the stain should entirely disappear.

A solution of oxalic acid may be used in the same way. Rinse at once.

Ink.—When ink stains are fresh they may be removed by dipping the stained part in hot milk and letting them soak for some time, then wash out thoroughly. If the stain has been in for some time it will be more persistent, and the same method as for rust stains should be adopted. A black ink stain can also be removed by pouring some red ink over it, allowing it to dry, and then washing it out.

Wine and Fruit.—Spread the stained part over a basin, rub well with common salt, and pour boiling water through to avoid spreading the mark. If the stain is still persistent, try salts of sorrel.

If a fruit stain is left in for any length of time, it is most difficult to remove. It is sometimes better to let it wear out gradually; but if it must be removed, use oxalic acid well rubbed into the part or chloride of lime.

Tea and Coffee.—Spread the stained part over a basin, rub well with powdered borax, and pour boiling water through. If still persistent, use a weak solution of chloride of lime.

Paint.—When fresh, remove with turpentine well rubbed in. If it has become dry, mix a little ammonia with the turpentine. When the stain is on a fabric of which the colour is apt to be destroyed, moisten first with a little oil, and then remove with turpentine or ether.

Mildew.—This is a species of fungus of which there are several varieties. It often attacks and stains linen or cotton, and is caused by the material being laid away damp. It is one of the most obstinate stains to remove, and often impossible without injury to the fabric. Stretch the stained part over a hard firm surface, and rub off as much as will come with a piece of soft dry rag. Rub in a little salt, and try if the juice of a lemon will take it out. Failing this, make a paste of French chalk and water, spread it on the stained part, and let it dry slowly, if possible in the sun. Repeat the process if necessary, and then rinse well.

Use of Chloride of Lime and Sanitas.—Put ¼ lb. chloride of lime into a basin, and break it to a smooth paste with a little cold water, then add as much cold water as will fill a quart bottle, about 1½ pints; stir the lime well up, and let it stand covered over for a day or two, stirring it occasionally. Then let it settle; skim it well, and pour the clear liquid off the top. Strain this into a quart bottle, and keep it tightly corked.

To remove stains wet a rag with this solution and apply it to the part. When anything is very much stained all over, it is best to soak it in cold water with some of this preparation of chloride of lime added to it. Make the water smell just slightly with the lime. This will also serve for bleaching things when they have become a bad colour.

Sanitas is now frequently used for removing ink, fruit, and wine stains on white cotton goods.

When removing stains the simplest method should always be tried first before any of the stronger chemicals are resorted to.

Care of the Chemicals.—Most of the chemicals used for removing stains are poisonous, therefore they ought to be labelled as such and kept in a safe place.

Soaking.—Soak everything except flannels, woollen goods, and most coloured articles. Place each assortment in a tub, using large basins if more convenient for the smaller things, and cover all with cold or tepid water. Never use hot water for soaking purposes, as it tends to make dirt adhere to linen, whilst cold or tepid water loosens it, and so simplifies the process of washing. If the water is hard, either borax or soda may be added before the clothes are put in. For the coarser and dirtier things use soda in the proportion of one ounce of soda to a gallon of water. This must be previously dissolved in a little boiling water. (See p. 275.) For the finer articles use borax instead of soda in the proportion of one table-spoonful to one gallon of water. It is perfectly harmless, even colours not being affected by its use, but it has a marvellous power of softening water and of drawing out dirt. A little soap may be rubbed on the more soiled part of the clothes, or some melted soap added to the water.

Very dusty articles, such as window-blinds and curtains, should be soaked in plain cold water until some of the dust is got rid of, and the water should be changed several times.

Pocket-handkerchiefs should have a handful of salt added to the water in which they soak; it will make the washing of them easier.

Let the clothes soak for one night at least. If Monday is your washing day, they may be soaked from Saturday without harm.

Disinfecting.—This is not always necessary, but where there has been infectious illness, or even bad colds, it will be wise to put the infected clothing through some process which will destroy the disease germs. There are various methods of disinfecting, such as the use of soaking fluids, exposure to hot air, exposure to steam, and others, but for home purposes there is nothing safer nor more effective than Izol. It is non-poisonous, and is undoubtedly very powerful as a germ destroyer. Use it in the proportion of 2 ounces of Izol to 1 gallon of water. In this solution the clothes should be allowed to soak for at least twelve hours. After this the clothes may be treated in the ordinary way.

Sundry Preliminaries.—The boiler fire should be laid the night before the washing day, and the boiler itself dusted out and filled with clean cold water. It will then be ready for lighting the first thing in the morning. Cold-water starch, as it requires soaking, and soap jelly should also be prepared beforehand. (See pp. 281 and 287.) It should also be seen that all utensils are clean and ready for use the following day, and that all necessary materials are at hand. Early in the morning the fire should be lighted, and as soon as there is hot water the washing commenced.

THE WASHING OF LINEN AND WHITE CLOTHES

The linen having been soaked and all stains removed as far as possible, it is now ready for washing. The object in washing is to get rid of the dirt with as little wear and tear to the clothes as possible, and to keep them a good colour. This may be done either by hand or by machine, but whichever method is adopted the principles are the same, and it is as well to know how to wash by hand. Commence with the finest and cleanest articles, generally table linen, then proceed to the bed and body linen. Fine towels and sheets must be washed before the ordinary household linen, and all coarse and kitchen articles left to the last. First rub the clothes and wring them out of the steeping water. Rinse out the tub and half fill it with water as hot as the hand can bear, adding, if necessary, a little borax or ammonia to soften it, or soda when it is to be used for the coarser clothes. Do not put too many articles into the tub at one time, and press them well down under the water. Then soap as much of the article as can conveniently be rubbed, and wash one part of the material against the other, and not against the wrist or hand. The pressure of rubbing should come on the lower and fleshy part of the thumb. Work methodically over every part, paying particular attention to those that are most soiled, and dip the article from time to time into the water so as to get rid of the soap and the dirt. A washing-board, preferably a wooden one, will be found of great assistance in the washing of the heavier and coarser things, and such articles as collars and cuffs will be cleaned most easily by being brushed on the washing-board with a softish brush. The brush is also valuable for the washing of very soiled articles, such as kitchen towels and aprons. Large articles, such as sheets and table-cloths, should be folded for washing and then rubbed by the selvedge from end to end until the middle is reached, when it will be advisable to turn and begin at the other end. If the clothes are not clean after the first washing, take fresh hot water and repeat the process. Soap and rub in the same way in the second water as in the first, turning any article that is turnable on to the wrong side.

If the washing is to be done by a machine, it will be better to follow the directions given with each special make, as they vary somewhat in structure. Most of them are simple enough, and will be found invaluable in houses where a large washing has to be undertaken.

The above directions only apply to the washing of ordinary white clothes; special articles, such as muslins, lace, coloured articles, &c., will be treated under special headings.

Boiling.—The clothes should be well wrung out of the water in which they have been washed and left twisted, as this will prevent their floating in the boiler. Soap should then be rubbed on them, or added to the water in the boiler in the proportion of one pound of soap to four gallons of water. A little soda, borax, or ammonia may also he added if the water is hard and the clothes a bad colour. Tie together or put into bags all small articles, such as cuffs, collars and pocket-handkerchiefs; in fact, a careful laundress will put everything into bags; this prevents any soapy scum from settling on the clothes, and avoids the necessity of lifting each article separately from the boiler.

As the clothes must have sufficient room to toss about, do not put too many things into the boiler at one time. Bring the water slowly to the boil, and boil from fifteen to twenty minutes, pressing the things down occasionally with a stick to keep them under water. Do not allow the clothes to boil too long, or they will become a yellow colour, and they must on no account be boiled before washing. When the clothes have boiled sufficiently, lift them out into a tub, and, if time permits, cover them with the water in which they have been boiled, letting them cool in it. This whitens the clothes, and is almost as good as bleaching, but it cannot of course be done where washing and drying have to be accomplished in one day.

The water in the copper must never be allowed to become dirty, and more water and more soap must be added for each lot of clothes.

Bleaching.—When the clothes become a very bad colour, bleaching will very much improve them. Take the clothes from the boiler, let them cool slightly, and, with the soap still in them, spread them on a green for some hours, sprinkling them with water from a watering-can if they become dry. If the clothes are spread out boiling hot, they will scorch and discolour the grass.

Rinsing.—This is one of the most important operations in laundry work. The reason of clothes having a streaked appearance and bad colour is very often that the soap has not been rinsed out of them. Ironing reveals the faulty work, making unrinsed clothes look absolutely dirty and giving them an unpleasant smell. Use plenty of water for rinsing—first tepid, then cold. To use cold water to begin with would be to harden the soap into the tissues of the material, so that to remove it would be almost impossible. First remove the soap with tepid water, and then use a plentiful supply of cold until every trace of it is removed. Too much stress cannot be laid upon this point.

Blueing.—This improves the appearance of the clothes by bringing back some of the clear colour which they lose through wear and age, and counteracting the slightly yellow tinge they acquire in boiling. In preparing blue water see that the tub in which the water is placed is perfectly clean and free from dust and soap suds, and add sufficient blue to make it a sky-blue tint. It is impossible to lay down absolute rules as to quantity, as it depends both upon the kind of blue used and the texture of the articles undergoing operation. As a rule, body linen requires more blue than other articles, and table linen less. If there is any uncertainty as to the right shade, the water should be tested first on some small article or piece of rag. The aim must be to get the clothes of a clear uniform tint and not too blue. Do not prepare the blue water long before it is wanted, as a sediment will fall, and stir it well before immersing the clothes.

Wring the clothes out of the last rinsing water, open them out, and put a few at a time into the blue water, those requiring most blue first. Work them so as to let the water well through, then wring out as dry as possible. The solution will get weaker as it is used, so that more blue must be added when required, and this always when there are no clothes in the water.

Wringing.—Wringing is getting rid of the superfluous water in the clothes. This you may do either by hand or machine, but certain precautions are necessary, or the process will be destructive. In wringing by hand, twist the articles selvedge-wise, and be careful not to wrench them unduly, but to wring with a sustained pressure. The use of a machine causes less wear and tear and also saves time. Shake out the clothes and fold them evenly before putting them through the wringer, then work the machine slowly and carefully. If worked hurriedly the moisture will not be properly extracted. Pass the clothes through the machine once or twice that they may be wrung as dry as possible. Do not screw the wringer too tight; it both spoils the machine and is too great a strain on the linen. Hide away buttons in the folds of the fabric in order to protect them as well as the rollers; tapes should also be concealed, to prevent their being wrenched off.

After wringing, the clothes must be sorted, those requiring starching put to one side, and the others hung up to dry.

Drying.—Clothes are always fresher and whiter if they can be dried in the open air, morning air being best of all. But in towns this is not always possible, owing to the presence of smoke and other obstacles, and the absence of space. Still a fine bright day with a little wind blowing, a good green, and clean lines and pegs are luxuries for any laundress who has the success of her work at heart. The clothes-line must first be rubbed over with a clean duster, and the clothes pinned or pegged on to it with the wrong side out, if there is one. The direction of the wind should be considered, and the clothes hung so as to catch the breeze. Hang the articles well over the line to prevent straining, and so that they may not slip off and get soiled on the ground. Do not hang sheets and table-cloths by the corners, or they will be apt to tear. Neither should they be hung next the post nor near a wall or tree; a towel or something small can be put in these spaces. Nightdresses, shirts, and the like should be hung up by the bottom or by the shoulders. If by the former, only one side should be fastened to the line, and the other side left open to face the wind, which will blow through and freshen every part. Small articles, such as collars and cuffs, may be strung together on a piece of tape, and if there is any chance of smuts falling, it is a good plan to cover them with a piece of muslin or cambric. On no account must anything be fastened up by the tapes, as this is most liable to strain and injure the garment. Raise the rope well above the ground by means of a prop or pole, and allow the clothes to remain until sufficiently dry. When clothes are dried indoors they must either be hung on a clothes-horse near a fire, on pulleys swung to the ceiling in a heated atmosphere, or in steam closets fitted up for the purpose. If the drying is done before a fire, the clothes will require turning or moving from time to time, as the heat is not regular. Care must be taken not to place them too near the fire, as the linen will not only become discoloured by too close contact with the heat, but become so dry as to burst into a flame.

Damping and Folding.—Anything that has to be mangled or ironed must be damped and folded evenly first. It is a saving of time and trouble if these things can be taken down from drying while still slightly wet, for if allowed to become quite dry they must be sprinkled with water either by hand or with a small watering-can. Every part of the article must be evenly sprinkled, and at the same time not made too wet. When sprinkling by hand, hold the basin of water in the left hand, take up as much in the right as it will hold, and sprinkle it lightly over the material, letting the drops be as small as possible, and going over every part. Smooth out the things well, fold evenly, seeing that the selvedges in such things as towels, counterpanes, sheets, &c., meet exactly.

Avoid all unnecessary creases, but fold the clothes to a convenient size for passing through the mangle, and of an equal thickness, so that the pressure of the mangle may come on every part. Pack the clothes into a basket, placing all of one kind together; those requiring ironing underneath, and those requiring mangling only on the top. Cover them over, and let them lie for some time, over-night if possible, before ironing or mangling them.

Mangling.—Mangling is a process of smoothing clothes by passing them between heavy rollers, which are sometimes heated. All household linen, such as towels, sheets, pillow-cases, table-cloths, table-napkins, &c., and most body linen may be mangled. Mangling requires great care and attention in order not to stretch the articles nor strain them unduly. Take the damp and folded things and place them in the mangle perfectly straight. Do not put too many things in at one time, and keep smoothing them out as they are put in to prevent pleats and creases. Work the mangle steadily, not too quickly, and not by fits and starts.

It is better if two people can work together; then one can smooth and hold the linen as it passes through, and the other can turn the handle. Pass the linen through once or twice, and keep the tension tight enough to press the material sufficiently without straining the mangle unduly. Then fold up and lay to one side such articles as require ironing, and hang up to air those that are finished, such as sheets and some towels.

Airing.—Everything must be thoroughly aired either after ironing or mangling, and before it is laid away. The greatest care must be taken that no dampness is left in them before they are folded and laid away. Carelessness in this respect may lead to very grave results.

GENERAL DIRECTIONS FOR IRONING

There is no process in laundry work which requires greater or neater handling than that of ironing, and the proverb, "Practice makes Perfect," can perhaps be better applied to this than to any other branch of household work. Until it can be done with speed it cannot be done well. An iron cools so quickly that, unless it can be expeditiously handled, very little can be done with one, and constant changing not only makes it a very tiring process, but the clothes become so dry before they are finished that they never look well. A novice at the work is almost sure to meet with disappointment until a certain amount of experience has been gained.

The ironing table must be placed in a good light. Daylight is best, and the worker should stand in such a position that the light will strike upon the work. Cover the table according to directions given on p. 273, and have everything at hand that will be required before commencing to iron. Have on the table a basin of clean cold water, set on a plate to prevent its upsetting, and one or two pieces of clean rag or old handkerchief to use for rubbing or damping down the clothes. Place the iron-stand and holder at the right-hand side and the articles to be ironed at the left.

The clothes to be ironed must be slightly damp, but not too wet. Knowledge of the correct heat of an iron can only be learnt with practice, no written rules can be of much assistance. If too hot, it will scorch, and if not hot enough it will fail to give the necessary gloss, and may even soil the work. A learner should test the heat of an iron on a piece of rag kept on the table for the purpose. The heat of the iron will be regulated by the kind of material to be ironed, and also by the speed of the worker.

Where there is a large plain surface to be ironed, as in table linen, a hot and heavy iron can be used, but when it is something more intricate and the work cannot be done so quickly, a cooler iron must be taken. When ironing, lift the iron as little as possible, and do not thump it down. Ironing should not be a noisy proceeding. Iron quickly and at the same time press well. Prepare and smooth out the work with the left hand whilst ironing with the right. When any wrinkle is made in ironing, damp it over with a wet rag and iron again. Handle the things so as not to crush the parts already ironed. There is quite an art in the way the clothes are lifted and moved about. Iron until the material is quite dry, and air everything before it is laid away.

THE MAKING OF STARCH AND GENERAL DIRECTIONS FOR ITS USE

Clear or Hot-Water Starch.—It is somewhat difficult to give exact proportions for the making of this starch, so much depends upon the number of articles to be starched and the stiffness required. Individual taste must also be taken into consideration, some preferring the articles very stiff, and others the merest suspicion of starch.

For a moderate quantity, take say two tablespoonfuls of dry starch, put it into a clean basin, and add to it enough cold water to make a thick paste. Work this with the back of a wooden spoon until quite smooth and free from lumps. Have a kettle of fast-boiling water on the fire, take the basin of starch to it, and let a second person pour the boiling water slowly in. Keep stirring all the time until the starch turns clear and transparent, when it is said to be made. The kettle should not be taken from the fire, but kept fast boiling all the time. The water used ought to be soft and colourless. Should the starch not become clear, it will show that either the water in the kettle has not been boiling, or too much cold water has been used in the first mixing. The mistake can, however, be remedied by turning the starch into a clean lined saucepan, and stirring it over the fire until it boils and turns clear. In fact, some people prefer always to boil the starch, and say that it brings out its stiffening qualities to the best advantage.

If the starch is of a yellow hue, a little blue may be added to it. A little wax is frequently added to hot starch to make the articles starched iron more smoothly, but if the iron itself is waxed as before described (see p. 273) this is not necessary.

The starch should be stirred for a short time after mixing to prevent a skin forming on the top of it, and should be kept covered when not in use.

It may be used in its present condition for making articles very stiff, or can be diluted to suit laces and muslins. For diluting purposes the water need not necessarily be boiling. It is sometimes more convenient to use it cold, as it makes the starch of a more comfortable heat to use. Do not make more of this starch than will be required at one time. It will keep for a day or two, but is better when used fresh.

This starch is used for the stiffening of table linen, prints, muslins, embroidery, petticoats, dresses, &c.

Coloured starches are made in the same way as the above. As a rule they require mixing with some white starch. Used alone, the colour is too deep for ordinary purposes. For instance, for a pale yellow colour, mix in the proportion of ¼ of cream starch to ¾ of white, or for a deeper tint use half of each. The quantity must be regulated according to the shade required. Special care must be taken when breaking these coloured starches with cold water, as if any lumps are left before the boiling water is poured on they will show up afterwards as dark coloured spots.

If there is any fear of the starch not being perfectly smooth, it is safer to strain it.

There are other ingredients which may be used for tinting starch, as for example :—

For an écru shade, colour the starch with coffee. Have some very strong clear coffee, and use this for mixing the starch with instead of water, then pour on boiling water until it turns clear.

A duller shade, such as is seen in old laces, can be produced by using tea instead of coffee. If a delicate pink hue is wished, use a decoction of logwood.

Cold-Water Starch.—The usual proportions are :—

2 oz. cold-water starch (rice starch preferred).
3 gills of cold water.
1 tea-spoonful turpentine.
½ tea-spoonful powdered borax, or a piece the size of a small nut of rock borax.

These proportions may vary slightly according to the starch used.

Mix the starch with the cold water, using the fingers to work out the lumps. Cover the basin over, and let the starch soak over-night at least. It is much better if it can soak for several days; even although it may turn slightly sour, it will be none the worse, in fact, almost better. The longer it can soak, the less apt it is to cake on to the linen.

Care must be taken to keep it very clean and free from dust.

When about to use it, mix it up again, add the turpentine, dissolve the borax in a little boiling water; if it is rock borax, dissolve it in a saucepan over the fire and add it. If the borax is left undissolved, it will appear afterwards in shiny patches on the linen. Use the best quality of turpentine, or it will smell strongly. The turpentine and borax are added to give a gloss and to make the iron run more smoothly.

The starch is then ready for use, but must be well mixed up from the foot of the basin. There is no harm in making more of this starch than is required, as it will keep from one week to another. It must be covered over, and when about to use it again, if the water on the top looks dirty, pour it off. The starch itself, which will have sunk to the foot of the basin, wipe free from dust, and add the same amount of clean water as before. Add also a little more borax and turpentine, about half as much as before.

This starch is used principally for the stiffening of collars, cuffs, shirts, and anything that is required particularly stiff.

BED, TABLE AND OTHER HOUSEHOLD LINEN

All bed and table linen should be washed according to general directions already given on pp. 278–80.

Bed Linen.—*Sheets* should be stretched well by two people while damp, folded very evenly in four, and then mangled. It is not necessary to iron them, but be particular to air them thoroughly, turning them occasionally so that they get dried right through. If there is any embroidery on the sheets, that must be ironed, pressing it out well on the wrong side; or, if they are hem-stitched, iron the hems to give them a finished appearance.

Pillow and Bolster-cases may either be mangled and the tapes only ironed, or they may be ironed all over as well as being mangled. The latter method will of course make them smoother, and it really requires very little time to run over them quickly on both sides with a hot iron. This is specially necessary for fine linen pillow-cases.

Embroidered Pillow-cases or pillow-shams will look better if they are put through some very thin hot-water starch, put several times through the wringer, and then rolled up for some time in a towel before ironing. If there are frills, these should be ironed first, ironing them on the right side so as to give them a gloss, and go well into the gathers without making any wrinkles. Next iron the centre on the right side. If there is embroidery, keep off it as much as possible, just ironing well round it—ironing it on the right side would press it down. If a pillow-case, put your hand inside and separate the two sides, as the starch always makes them stick a little, then turn over and iron the second side. Iron both sides free from wrinkles, and try to get a good gloss on the linen. Press out the embroidery well on the wrong side, and lastly crimp or goffer the frills (see pp. 284–85.) Air well, and it is finished.

Bed-Covers.—Thick heavy bed-covers only require to be stretched and folded evenly while damp, well mangled, and then thoroughly aired. Those of a lighter make are better to be put through some thin starch, or some ready-made starch may be added to the water in which they are rinsed. This will give them a slight stiffness, which will make them look better and keep their clean appearance longer. If a polish is wanted, they must be ironed as well as mangled. Any lace or embroidery must always be ironed, and fringes combed and brushed out.

Table Linen, Starching of.—Table linen will look better and keep its clean appearance longer if slightly starched. The amount of starch used depends upon individual taste and the quality of the damask. Many people object to the use of starch entirely on the ground that it rots the linen. If one had always the very best double damask to deal with the extra stiffening might certainly be dispensed with, as the material has sufficient body in itself to keep its appearance; but when the ordinary thin damask is under treatment a little starch does no harm, in fact, it saves in the end, as a table-cloth that is made slightly stiff will keep clean double the time a perfectly limp one would do. Starch also preserves from stains, and it is only when it is made too thick, rendering the articles so stiff as to make them not only lose all their natural beauty, but also disagreeable to use, that it can be said to be hurtful.

Table linen should be starched while wet; it would be too stiff if starched dry, and the starch would not penetrate through it so evenly. If there is a large quantity to starch, it will save time and much wringing if some very thick hot-water starch is made (p. 280) and added to the blue rinsing water; or if there are only a few things, after wringing them, put them through some thin hot-water starch. Wring well after starching, putting the things through the wringer as smoothly as possible; if wrung twisted they will have a streaky appearance when ironed. Table napkins and doyleys should be put through the starch before table-cloths, as they are required slightly stiffer.

Table-cloths.—After starching dry slightly, and then each one must be stretched by two people. Stretch it first one way and then the other, and shake it out well to get it a good shape and even at the sides. Fold it by doubling it, selvedge to selvedge, with the right side out. Let the single sides drop, and then pick them up, one on each side, to the double fold. The table-cloth will then be folded in four, and the right side will be inside. Spread the table-cloth out on a table and arrange it quite smoothly, making the folds and the hems at the ends quite even. Double it and mangle. Let it lie for some time rolled up in a cloth before ironing, or if there is difficulty in getting very hot irons, it will be as well to let it dry a little first, but be careful it does not get too dry, or it will not look well.

To iron a table-cloth spread it out smoothly on a table in the folds and with the two selvedges nearest the edge of the table. Keep it in the folds as much as possible. Iron first the upper part, turn that back, iron the next two parts, turn back again and iron the next two, and so on until the whole of the table-cloth has been ironed on both sides, then double the table-cloth and mark the fold down with the iron. Air well, and then either roll or fold. To get a good gloss on table linen, the hotter and heavier the irons are the better. Keep them well greased, and press heavily, ironing until almost dry. If the table-cloth is very large, it is better if two people can iron it at one time, otherwise it would get dry before it was all finished.

Table-Napkins.—Fold them double, selvedge to selvedge, perfectly evenly, and mangle several at one time, then let them lie rolled up in a towel for some time before ironing.

To iron them, take one at a time, shake out and stretch evenly, lay out very smoothly on the table with the right side uppermost and as square as possible. Iron the right side first, then the wrong, and back again on the right. Be careful not to stretch the edges out of shape, and iron until quite dry. They are ironed on both sides to avoid having one side rough and the other smooth, as sometimes happens. Give the hems an extra iron to dry them well.

Table-napkins can be folded either in three or in four, according to taste. To fold in four, fold in the same way as a table-cloth, only on the opposite side, bringing the right side outside instead of the wrong. Get the ends very even, press the folds well with an iron, and fold in four across, making a square again. Air well before laying them away. To fold in three, measure the sides (hems) first, and get them divided into three equal parts, press them down with an iron to keep them in place, then make the folds right across and iron them down, fold in three across to make a square again, and press with the iron once more. If there is a name, it must be on the outside when the table-napkin is folded; if a monogram or raised initials, iron well on the wrong side to make the embroidery stand out.

Doyleys.—Starch in the same way as table-napkins, and let them lie rolled up for some time. If they have fringes, shake them well out against the edge of the table before beginning to iron. This opens out the fringes. To iron, spread out on the table, and brush out the fringe all round with a small brush, and comb it with a fine comb until it lies quite straight, then iron the centre of the doyley and the fringes on both sides, and brush and comb the fringe again until it is quite soft and free. The brushing and combing must be done carefully, so as not to draw out the threads, and always before the fringe is dried with the iron. Finish by trimming off any untidy ends with a pair of scissors. If liked, the fringes may be curled, using a blunt knife or a paper-knife, and curling them in the same way as an ostrich feather.

Doyleys with netted or tatted edges should be pinned out on a covered board or table, stretching each point well and putting in pins where required. Then iron the centres only (ironing would spoil the edges), and leave them pinned out until dry. After unpinning them, if the edges feel rather stiff and hard, pull them out with the fingers.

Doyleys with a full lace edge should have the lace ironed first, then the centre, and, lastly, the lace goffered round very evenly. (See p. 284.)

Tray Cloths and Sideboard Cloths.—These should be treated in the same way as other table linen. If they have fringes these should be brushed and combed out before they become dry. If they can be ironed on both sides, then do so; but if they have a distinct right side, iron on the right side only, just pressing out any embroidery on the wrong side, and iron round the hems. If there is lace round the edges, iron it first before the centre, and do any goffering that is required last of all. There is no particular way of folding tray cloths and sideboard cloths; just fold them to the size which is most suitable for laying away. Long sideboard cloths are better rolled than folded.

Other Household Linen

Bedroom Towels.—These should be folded evenly while damp and well mangled. Then run over them quickly with a hot iron on both sides, fold them in four lengthways, and air well. If there are fringes, these should be brushed and combed out before ironing; and after ironing, combed out again to make them free and soft. If there are embroidered initials or monograms on the towels, press them out well on the wrong side.

Coarse Bath Towels and Turkish Towels.—These should neither be mangled nor ironed; the rougher they are the better. Stretch them well, iron the plain piece at the ends, comb the fringes, and fold them evenly. Air them well.

Toilet Covers.—These should be put through thin starch when wet, wrung out, and hung up to dry slightly. Then fold them very evenly, double, and mangle well. Next iron on the right side to get a good gloss, and brush out any fringes. To fold them, double lengthways and press the fold down, and then either roll up or fold once or twice across. Do not make too many folds in a toilet cover, or it will not lie well.

Kitchen Towels, Dusters, &c.—These should just be folded evenly while damp, and then mangled. It is quite unnecessary to iron them, but air them well before laying away.

BODY LINEN

General Directions for the Doing Up of Body Linen.—All underclothing must be damp for ironing. Very thin cambric articles will be improved by being slightly starched, otherwise they will have a limp undressed appearance. If a little hot-water starch is put into the water in which they are blued it will be sufficient. All that is wanted is to give the cambric the slight stiffness of new material, and not enough to make it unpleasant to wear. Ordinary cotton will not require any starch; it will be sufficiently crisp if ironed with a hot iron and slightly damp. All frills and embroidery are improved by being dipped in very thin hot-water starch, even although the whole garment is not being done. This should be done when the clothes are being damped and rolled up. Gather up the frill in the hand, dip it into some very thin starch, and then wring out in the hands or between the folds of a towel. The slight stiffness this will give will prevent the frilling curling up and otherwise looking limp.

First iron all embroidery or frills. Embroidery must be ironed on the wrong side over a piece of felt or double flannel, in addition to the ironing blanket, well pressed so as to raise the pattern, and the points pulled out and ironed until quite dry. Plain frills or frills with just a narrow lace edging must be ironed on the right side so as to give them a gloss; care must be taken to iron well up into the gathers and without making wrinkles. All bands, hems, and double parts should be ironed on both sides to give them a more finished appearance. Always keep the neck or the top of the garment at your left-hand side, so that the iron may be more easily run well up into the gathers. If the cotton should get dry before it is all ironed, damp it down with a wet rubber. It will never look glossy if ironed too dry, but will have a rough appearance. Iron out all tapes. Never leave them twisted and curled up. Iron round buttons, not over them, or it will be apt to mark them. Sometimes seams and tucks are inclined to drag the articles and cause creases, especially when the clothes are new. They should then be well stretched out before applying the iron. New cotton is always more difficult to iron and make glossy than that which has been washed several times.

Crimping.—As a rule this is done on plain frills, or on plain frills with a narrow lace edging; but embroidery can also be crimped, especially when it is put on only slightly full and not starched, in which case it would be unsuitable for goffering. Crimping can be done with an ordinary iron, using the back, side, or point according to the width of the frill. For a very narrow frill use the point; for a wider one the back or side, as is found easiest. When the frill is very wide, it is sometimes easier to crimp half of it at one time, crimping first down near the drawings with the side of the iron, keeping the point close to the gathers, and then the upper part with the back of the iron. The iron must be cool enough for you to hold the fingers on it.

To crimp, keep the gathering of the frill at your left-hand side, and the frill itself lying straight across the table. Commence with the part nearest the edge of the table, drawing the frill towards you as it is crimped. Hold the iron with the right hand, run up part of the frill with the part of the iron with which you are going to crimp, put two or three fingers of the left hand under the frill and close to the iron, draw the iron quickly back, following with the fingers of the left hand, and crimping the frill underneath it. Only a small piece, an inch or an inch and a half, can be crimped at one time.

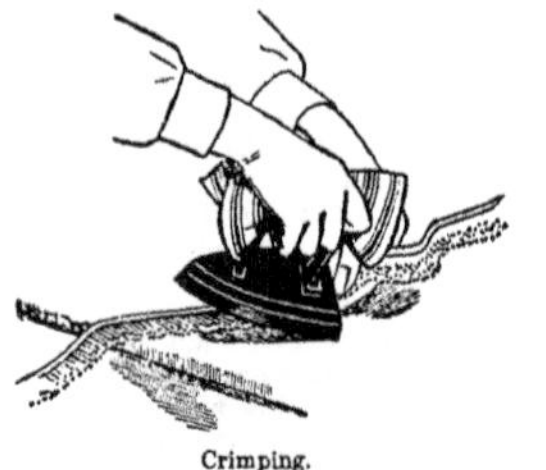

Crimping.

It requires a good deal of practice to do crimping quickly, and at the same time finely and evenly. The thicker the material, the firmer pull back must be given to the iron.

Special machines can now be had for crimping.

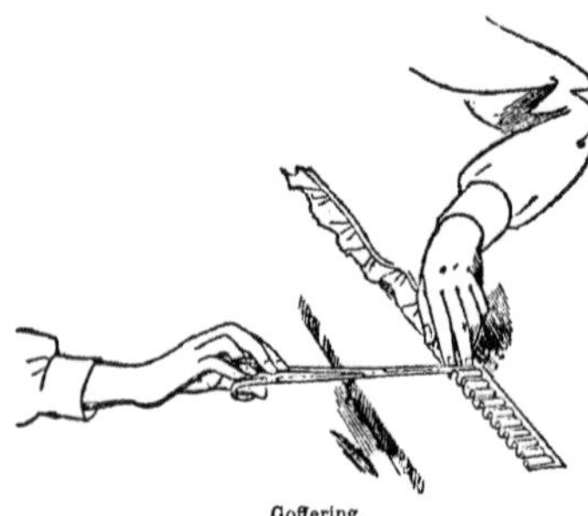

Goffering.

Goffering.—This is done with heated goffering tongs. A frill requires to be pretty full, and to be starched, in order to goffer well. For wide and full frills, use the large size of tongs; and for narrow ones, the smaller pair. Have two pairs of tongs of exactly the same size in use at one time, so that one pair can be heating whilst you are using the other. Always test them on a piece of rag or paper first, and see that they are thoroughly clean and not too hot before you apply them to the frill.

Place the frill to be goffered lengthways on the table, with the drawings from you. Pin out straight as much of the frill as possible at one time, to keep it steady. Commence at the right-hand end of the frill and work towards the left. Hold the tongs in the right hand, putting the thumb in the lower hole, and the second or third finger in the upper; put the tongs right up to the drawings of the frill, and then turn them half round, so that the hole with the thumb in it comes uppermost; keep two or three fingers of the left hand close to the tongs to keep the goffering in position, and let them remain there until the tongs are loosened slightly and drawn gently out. Then go a little distance further back and do the same again, working from right to left, and being careful not to pull out what has been already done. In drawing out the tongs be careful to keep them as flat to the table as possible, and do not give them an upward jerk.

The distance the goffers are apart depends on the fulness of the frill. The fuller the frill the closer the goffers can be. Sometimes when a frill is only slightly drawn merely the mark of the tongs can be shown.

Always keep the goffering tongs on the straight of the frill, or with the thread of the material. Goffering should be regular, and an equal distance apart. This is sometimes rather difficult if the frill is not drawn evenly. If there are two frills to be goffered, do the upper first, then the under.

With practice, goffering can be done quite quickly. The more quickly it is done, the hotter the tongs can be used.

Folding and Airing.—Folding depends very much upon individual taste, and upon the shape of the garment to be folded. Shapes vary so much that it is difficult to lay down any hard-and-fast rules, only it is as well to have some general rules for guidance.

Always fold so as to crush the garment as little as possible, laying in pleats carefully where required. Iron down each fold or pleat as you make it to keep it in position. Fold garments so as to show as much of the embroidery as possible, always having the inside as tidy and smooth as the outside, and making each a convenient size. Keep all tapes to the inside.

All underclothing must be thoroughly aired before it is laid away. Although the things seem dry after ironing, there is always a certain amount of moisture which clings to them from the iron. The greatest care and attention should be paid to this, as want of thought may lead to the gravest results.

How to Iron and Fold a Chemise.—Have the chemise on the right side to begin with. First iron any trimming, frills, or embroidery, and also bands on both sides. Next fold the chemise down the centre of the back, keeping the neck at your left-hand side. Iron the back, first on

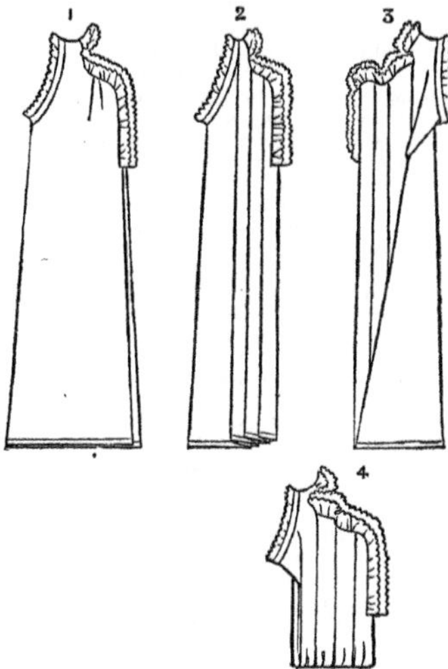

one side, and then turn over and iron on the other; iron the hem at the foot on the wrong side, and when ironing up near the gathers at the neck, lift up slightly, so that the iron may run well up into the gathers, being careful not to crease the under side. Then open the chemise out and lay it on the table, so that the whole of the back is uppermost; iron the front hem on the wrong side, and round the arm-holes and sleeves on the back. The back is then finished. Turn the chemise over and iron the front—first the bottom part straight across and the rest of it lengthways; iron well up into the gathers and round the arm-holes and sleeves, and the chemise is finished. Any goffering or crimping must be done before folding, laying it out on the table, or double it so as not to crush. If there is only a little fulness at the corners of the embroidery, this can be goffered after folding.

A chemise may be folded in two different ways—the side fold or the front fold. For a plain chemise the side fold is best; and for a more elaborately trimmed one the front fold. For the side fold, double the chemise, bringing the two side-seams and two shoulders together, with the back inside and the front out; lay it on the table with the neck at the left-hand side, and the band down the opening of the front, turned uppermost (Fig. 1). Take hold of the neck and the bottom of the chemise, and stretch it so that it falls in pleats. Arrange these pleats evenly, two or three according to the fulness at the band, and iron them well down (Fig. 2). Turn the chemise over, see that the pleats are even on the other side, fold the chemise again lengthways, making it the same width all the way down, and turning in an extra piece at the foot if it is too wide there; pleat the sleeves back a little so that the embroidery only shows over the sides (Fig. 3), and then fold from the bottom upwards in three or four, according to the size you wish it to be when finished (Fig. 4). Air well before laying it away.

For the front fold, first fold the chemise double so as to find the centre of the back, make a mark with the iron and open out again. Keep the back of the chemise uppermost on the table, and the neck at the left-hand side. Fold in two or three pleats from the side in towards the centre of the back and press them well down (Fig. 1). Then pleat the other side in towards the centre of the back in exactly the same way, making the chemise an equal width all the way down, and not too broad. Fold the sleeves so that the embroidery only shows over the sides (Fig. 2), and fold the chemise into three or four from the bottom upwards, press well, turn over and see that the front looks quite straight; air well, and it is finished (Fig. 3).

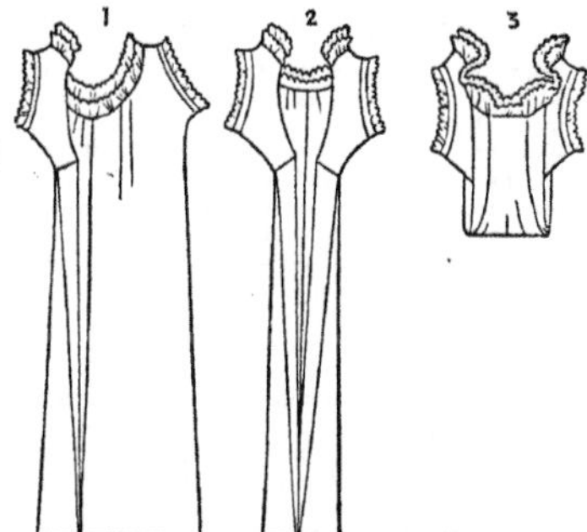

How to Iron and Fold a Pair of Drawers.—Iron any embroidery or trimming first, and the bands on both sides. When ironing the waistband, keep the band next you, and lying lengthways on the table, and iron the strings if there are any. Place the pair of drawers on the table front uppermost, with the waistband at the left-hand side. Commence with the leg nearest the edge of the table, smooth it out and iron straight across as far up and down as possible until the drawings interfere, then iron up into the draw-

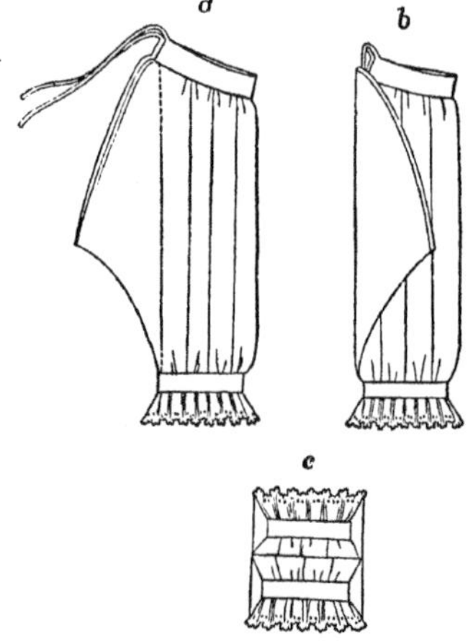

ings at the top, and if knickerbockers, iron down into the drawings at the foot, holding the iron with the left hand. Then iron the hem on the under part of the leg on the wrong side, and draw that leg over the table out of the way whilst the other leg is being ironed. Iron the second leg on the same side and in the same way. Next turn the pair of drawers over, still keeping the band at the left-hand side, and iron the other side of the legs in the same manner as the first, not forgetting to iron the hems of the front part on the wrong side. Goffer or crimp the frills if necessary, and the drawers are ready for folding.

To fold a pair of drawers, place the two legs evenly one on the top of the other, fold in the shaped piece so as to make them the same width all the way down, turn any strings inside to prevent their being pulled off, and fold the drawers from the top downwards in three or four. If there is any embroidery at the foot, separate the two pieces, doubling one leg back so far so as to show both pieces of embroidery. Crimp or goffer the trimming if necessary.

Knickerbockers require to be pleated to make them lie smoothly. Pleat one leg down, putting in two or three pleats according to the fulness between the bands, and not pleating the bands themselves, then iron the pleats well down. Place the other leg on the top of that one, and pleat it in the same way, keeping it exactly the same width, and having the same number of pleats (Fig. *a*). Finish off the same as a pair of drawers (Figs. *b*, *c*).

How to Iron and Fold a Pair of Combinations.—Iron all embroidery and bands first, then place the combinations on the table with the neck at the left-hand side, and iron the upper part down as far as the waist, smoothing out each piece. Then fold the legs evenly by the side-seams, and iron them in the same way as a pair of drawers, first on one side, and then on the other, and the sleeves on both sides. Iron the front hems on the wrong side, do any goffering or crimping that is required, and they are ready for folding. Combinations require very careful handling, one part is so liable to be crushed while another is being ironed.

To fold a pair of combinations, fold them double first, bringing the sides of the bodice, the sides of the legs, and the two shoulders together. As the back is usually longer than the front, see that it lies smoothly underneath. It generally requires a pleat put in it just at the waist. If the combinations are very wide and like knickerbockers, put pleats in them, two or three according to the fulness, and continue one or two of them up the front of the bodice (Fig. 1). Then place the combinations on the table with the button-hole side uppermost, double over the shaped part of the leg by dotted line (Fig. 1), so as to make them the same width all the way up, then double them from the bottom upwards, so as to make the trimming at the foot come just

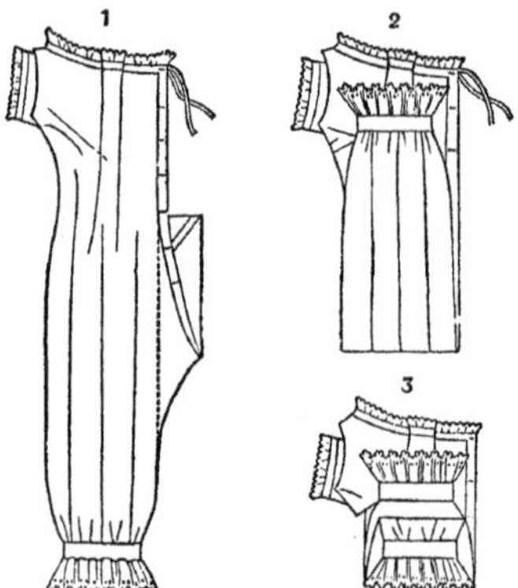

below the trimming at the neck (Fig. 2), turn over and double them again. Lastly, turn back and see that they look nicely arranged, doubling back the sleeves if necessary, and separating the legs so as to show both pieces of embroidery (Fig. 3).

How to Iron and Fold a Night-Dress.—A night-dress is ironed in very much the same way as a chemise. If there is a yoke, iron it after the embroidery and bands. Iron the skirt of the night-dress in the same way as a chemise, leaving the sleeves to the last. To iron the sleeves fold the night-dress double lengthways, keep the neck at the left-hand side and the sleeves towards the edge of the table, throw back the upper sleeve, and iron the under one on the top side; then fold it back underneath, draw the other one forward, and iron it on the same side. Next turn the night-dress so that the neck is at the right-hand side, and iron the other two sides of the sleeves in the same way. This way of ironing the sleeves prevents any crushing of the night-dress. Crimp or goffer any frills that require it, and the night-dress is ready for folding.

A night-dress may be folded in two ways, like a chemise, by the side fold or the front fold, and the two sleeves must be made to lie nicely over the front.

FLANNELS AND WOOLLEN ARTICLES

The term flannels, when used in the following paragraphs, applies to woollen goods of all kinds, whether knitted, crocheted, woven, or flannel proper.

The washing of flannels is one of the simplest branches of laundry work. The rules are few and easy, but none the less important. Given the necessary requisites, a tub of hot water, some liquid soap, a little ammonia and a wringer, there is no excuse for the flannels not being soft and elastic after washing, but if the rules are disregarded, the result will in all probability be hard shrunken garments resembling cheap tweed.

Soap Jelly.—As this is used instead of a piece of soap, it ought to be prepared first of all.

Take as much soap as will be required, and cut it down in shreds with a knife. Put it into a saucepan, and just cover it with cold or hot water. Allow the soap to melt slowly over the fire until it is quite clear and without lumps. Let it melt slowly, as boiling wastes it. Do not fill the saucepan too full, as soap is very liable to boil over. The soap may be put into a jar instead of a saucepan, and melted in the oven.

Any ends of soap may be used up in this way. It is better to make soap jelly freshly each week, as it loses its strength if kept many days.

Remember that soap will taste very strongly anything with which it comes in contact, so that the knife and board on which it is cut, also the saucepan in which it is melted, ought to be kept for that purpose only.

Any good soap will do; olive oil is excellent if it can be obtained, but, failing that, good yellow soap will serve the purpose.

Instead of soap jelly, Lux, or any other form of shredded soap, can be used, but care should be taken that it does not contain a quantity of soda.

General Directions.—The best plan is to wash flannels either before or after all the other clothes. The former is better if they can be dried outside, as they will then have the benefit of the morning air and sun. First shake the flannels, in order to get rid of any loose dust, and divide them into lots according to colour and kind—white articles and those that are least soiled by themselves, then other light-coloured articles, such as grey and drab. Stockings and socks should always form a lot by themselves, and also dark-coloured things, or those in which the colour is likely to run, as reds and crimsons. To wash the flannels prepare a tub half full of warm water, not too hot, but just comfortable for the hand to rest in. To be exact the temperature should be from 35° to 45° Centigrade. Then add enough ammonia to make the water smell slightly. The quantity will depend somewhat upon the strength of the ammonia; from one to two table-spoonfuls in a tub of water will generally be found ample. This will soften the water, dissolve the grease in the flannels, and thus save some of the friction of washing. Commence with the whitest and cleanest articles, leaving the most soiled and those in which the colour is likely to run until the last.

Avoid rubbing flannels except any particularly soiled parts, or those of a coarse make, as rubbing inclines to shrink them; but squeeze well and work up and down in the water, drawing them through the hands.

A little soap may be rubbed on any cotton bands. When the first garment is finished, squeeze it out in the hands, or, better still, put it through the wringer and proceed with the other articles in the same way. If not clean after the first washing, repeat the process, using less soap and ammonia in the second water. Garments that are turnable, as night-dresses, combinations, &c., should be washed on the right side in the first water and on the wrong side in the second, and then left on the wrong side until dry.

After the light-coloured flannels are done, the same lather may do for the darker ones; only, if the water is dirty or if the lather has disappeared, take entirely fresh water, and use the second lather of the light things as the first of the darker. Never wash in dirty water, and never rub soap on to flannels. Do not commence too many flannels at one time, as the sooner they are finished and hung up to dry the better. It is specially necessary to hurry through the process in washing coloured flannels.

Rinsing.—When the flannels are quite clean, rinse them in plenty of warm water, two or three times if necessary, until they feel soft to the touch. Should any soap be left in them, they will not only be hard and sticky, but have an unpleasant smell when dried. Never rinse in too hot or cold water, as either of these would cause them to shrink suddenly, and feel hard like pasteboard. A little blue may be added to the last water in which white flannels are rinsed. When thoroughly rinsed, wring the flannels as dry as possible. This is best done through the machine, as it does not twist them. Any rough twisting would break the fibres of the wool. Shake them well to raise the "nap" or soft woolly substance on the surface of the material, pull into a good shape, and they are ready for drying.

Drying.—Flannels must on no account be allowed to lie about wet. This shrinks them more than anything. Whenever it is possible, they should be dried in the open air in a good wind and not too bright a sun. Failing this, dry them in a warm atmosphere, where they will dry quickly; but at the same time they must not be put so close to an open fire or in such a hot place that they steam. This would be as bad as putting them into boiling water. Shake the flannels, and turn them once or twice while drying, pulling them into a good shape.

Mangling or Ironing.—For the coarser and thicker flannels it will be sufficient if they are mangled when nearly dry. Any bands or tapes must be ironed, and then the articles hung up again to finish drying. The finer kinds should be ironed when nearly dry with a rather cool iron. If they have become quite dry it will be necessary to spread a slightly damp cloth over them and iron over that, pressing heavily. Never iron flannels very wet or the hot iron will shrink them up, and on no account must the iron be too hot, especially in ironing coloured flannels. Should any scorching occur, dip the piece in warm water, squeeze it well, and rub gently, then wring out and re-dry, or rub with a silver coin and the scorch will disappear.

Reasons for Flannels Shrinking.—

1. Soap has been rubbed on them instead of soap jelly being used.
2. They have either been washed or rinsed in too hot or cold water.
3. They have been allowed to lie about wet, instead of being hung up to dry immediately.
4. They have been dried too slowly.
5. They have been dried so close to an open fire that they steamed.
6. They have been ironed while wet with a very hot iron.

Special Articles

New Flannels and Sanitary Underclothing.—These are better to be soaked for about half-an-hour before washing in warm water with ammonia in it, one table-spoonful to two gallons of water. Cover the tub over to prevent the heat escaping, and squeeze and wring them out of this before the water has time to get cold. This process draws out some of the sulphur which new flannels contain, and which would prevent the soap making a lather, and it also helps to remove the grease. Then wash in the same way as flannels.

Stockings and Socks.—The comfort of stockings and socks, as well as their durability, depends very much upon their being well washed. The soles, heels, and toes require special attention. These should always be rubbed, using the washing-board and a little soap if necessary. Wash them first on the right side, then turn and wash on the wrong, giving them two waters. Fold them evenly by the seam at the back of the leg before wringing and drying. When nearly dry either mangle them or iron them on the wrong side, and leave them wrong side out ready for mending.

Red or Crimson Flannel.—This is rather troublesome to wash, and however careful one may be it is almost impossible to prevent the colour running. Ammonia should be omitted from the water in which it is washed, and vinegar should be added to the rinsing water in the proportion of four table-spoonfuls to one gallon of water. This helps to brighten the colour.

Blankets.—Always choose a fine day for washing blankets, as it is a mistake to dry them indoors. First shake them well, and then prepare water with soap jelly, the same as for flannels, and in the largest tub you have. Put the blankets in, one or two at a time, move them up and down in this, squeezing and pressing them against the sides; then put them in a second tub of the same kind of water to repeat the process. In Scotland, instead of being washed with the hands, they are tramped with the bare feet. They may also be pounded with a dolly. Rinse well until free from soap, and then wring. If the wringer is used, let the rollers be as loose as possible. The colour of the blankets depends very much upon the cleanliness of the water they are washed in, so be particular to change it whenever necessary.

Shake the blankets well before hanging up to dry, and hang them quite straight and singly on the clothes-rope in a gentle wind. See that they are securely fastened and well raised above the ground. When dry, take them down, stretch them well, and rub all over with a piece of clean rough flannel so as to raise the pile, and then hang them near a fire for some time, as it is most important to have them thoroughly dry.

Shetland and other Shawls.—Wash in the same way as flannels, but handle more gently, especially the finer ones, squeezing them well, and being careful not to break the threads of wool. Rinse them in warm water, putting a little blue into the last rinsing water for white shawls, and for fine Shetland shawls a little hot-water starch, about one breakfast-cupful thick starch to half a gallon of water. Squeeze the water well out of the shawls, or put them through a wringer. Avoid twisting them in any way.

If there is no wringer, after squeezing out as much of the water as possible with the hands, beat well between the folds of a towel.

To dry a shawl, spread a sheet on the floor and pin it tightly at the corners; pin out the shawl on this, stretching it well but not over much, pin out each point, and be careful to keep the shawl a good shape. Leave it till quite dry, then unpin carefully, shake it out, and air if necessary.

The Sulphur Bath.—White shawls and flannels which have become yellow may be whitened by putting them in a sulphur bath. Take a deep barrel, break up about one oz. of rock sulphur, and put it on an old plate or tin dish at the foot of it; sprinkle over the sulphur a few drops of methylated spirits, and then set fire to it. When the methylated spirits has burnt out and the sulphur itself is burning, suspend the flannels or shawls across the fumes. This must be done just before they are dried. Twist them loosely round sticks, pinning them here and there to prevent their slipping down and catching fire, and place the sticks across the barrel; or a wire cage may be used, suspended on the top of the barrel. Cover over with a blanket or something thick enough to keep in the fumes, and let them remain about twenty minutes. Turn the things once during the time, so that every part of them gets whitened. Great care must be taken to have the things raised sufficiently high above the sulphur to avoid all danger of their catching fire.

A Chamois Leather.—This may be washed and made to look equal to new if the following directions are carried out. Prepare a lather with water and soap, the same as for flannels, put the leather into this, and squeeze it gently between the hands. Repeat the process if not clean after the first water, and until the last soapy water looks quite clean. Do not rinse, but wring straight out of the soapy water. Hang up to dry, rubbing and pulling it out occasionally with the hands in order to keep it soft. It may be smoothed out last of all with a cool iron.

Eiderdown Quilts.—To wash a large eiderdown quilt is rather hard work, and unless a good wringer is available and ample drying accommodation, it should scarcely be attempted. But with these conveniences an eiderdown of moderate dimensions can be very easily tackled, and the results will be most satisfactory if the few needful rules are attended to. Before starting the actual washing shake the quilt, to free it from all loose dust, and if there are any holes, either mend them or draw them together with a needle and cotton. Then wash according to directions given for flannel washing, or when large treat as blankets. If the colour runs, use the water just tepid. Rinse in an abundant supply of warm water, adding a little salt or ammonia to the last to brighten the colour. There must on no account be any soap left in the quilt. Wring it carefully through the machine, loosening the tension to the fullest extent if necessary. The drying requires special attention. Shake out the eiderdown; it is better if two people can do this—and hang it up, out of doors if possible, in a good wind and not too much sun, or, failing that, in a warm atmosphere in the house. Whilst drying the quilt must be taken down from time to time and rubbed and shaken, to loosen the down and prevent it forming into clots. When dry, it should be quite as soft as when new.

Swansdown.—Wash gently in warm water, making a lather with soap jelly, and rinse in tepid water. Then hold it a little distance from the fire and shake till quite dry and fluffy.

Flannelette.—Wash in the same way as flannel, only it will take no harm if rinsed in cold water. White flannelette may even be boiled along with cotton articles. Dry and finish off like flannels.

Delaine.—When carefully washed, delaine should look equal to new. Wash it in exactly the same way as flannels, and be careful with the rinsing. Add ammonia in the proportion of one table-spoonful to one gallon of water to the last warm water. This will help to brighten the colour. Iron while slightly damp, and not so dry as for flannel. If it is lined, iron the lining first.

Velveteen.—Cotton velvets, especially the light-coloured ones, can be washed and be made to look quite well. Wash in the same way as flannel with a lather of soap and warm water, and rinse first in warm and then in cold water. When nearly dry iron on the wrong side with a moderately hot iron.

White Coque Feather Boas.—(See p. 318.)

MUSLINS, LACE, CURTAINS, AND NET

The Washing of Muslin.—Muslin requires very careful treatment, and especially coloured muslin if it is being washed for the first time. It must be treated more carefully than ordinary cotton, and not be pulled out of shape nor stretched, or it will have a drawn appearance. Being thin and open in texture it is easy to wash without any rough treatment. First soak the muslin in cold or tepid water to take out the dressing or stiffening; then wring or squeeze out gently. Prepare a small tub or basin of warm water, and make a lather with melted soap in the same way as for flannels. Squeeze the muslin well in this, and work it up and down in the water. In the case of very soiled articles a little borax or ammonia may be added to soften the water and draw out the dirt. If not clean after the first washing, repeat the process in fresh soapy water, using rather less soap the second time. If washing is not sufficient to make the muslin a good colour, it should be boiled (see p. 278). Then rinse first in tepid and then in cold water, until every trace of soap has been removed. Pure white muslin may have a little blue added to the last rinsing water. If the muslin is *coloured*, and the colours are likely to run, soak it first in salt and water, allowing a handful of salt to a gallon of water. Let the water for the first washing be just tepid, and proceed as quickly as possible, putting salt again or a little ammonia in the final rinsing water. Coloured muslin must on no account be boiled.

Clear Starching and Ironing.—All muslin should be starched wet. If put into the starch dry, it never looks so clear. Prepare some clear starch (see p. 280), and thin it to the consistency required. This depends upon what the muslin is wanted for, and according to the degree of stiffness desired. It is impossible to give the exact quantities of starch necessary for clear starch, as different qualities and makes of starch require more water than others, but experience will soon teach this, and at first it will be just as well to test the stiffness of the starch on a small piece of muslin. Be sure to have the starch clear, put the muslins into it, putting in first those white articles which are wished stiffest. Let the starch soak well through, then wring well, putting them twice at least through the wringing machine. In starching coloured muslins do not let the starch be too hot, or it will destroy the colours; and never put things through the wringer straight out of boiling hot starch as it ruins the india-rubber rollers. In thinning the starch, after it has been made clear with boiling water, cold water may be used, and that will make the starch a more comfortable heat to use.

After wringing the muslins shake them well, smooth out, and let them lie for some time rolled up in a towel before ironing. Muslin must be ironed wet. If allowed to get dry, it will have a rough appearance when ironed. Iron on the right side to give it a gloss, and the way of the thread as much as possible. When ironing a large piece of muslin, keep as much of it covered over at one time as you conveniently can, to prevent it becoming dry. Should the muslin dry before it is ironed, damp it down very evenly with a wet rubber or towel, not missing a piece, or it will not look smooth. *Embroidered muslin* should be ironed on the wrong side, to raise the pattern. *Spotted muslin* should also be ironed on the wrong side, unless the spots are pretty far apart, when it may look better ironed first on the right side to give the muslin a gloss, and afterwards ironed over on the wrong to press out the spots. In ironing coloured muslins do not use the iron too hot, as it is apt to destroy the colours.

Muslin trimmed with lace should have the lace ironed first and then the muslin itself. If the muslin feels too stiff after ironing, the fault can be remedied by putting it through water and then ironing again. Air muslin well after ironing or it will become limp.

Washing of Lace.—To "do up" lace nicely is by no means difficult, in fact, it is one of the most interesting and least fatiguing branches of laundry work and amply repays the trouble expended upon it. Care and attention to details is all that is required. The lace should first be carefully mended if necessary, and any tacking or drawing threads removed.

If very much soiled, soak it for several hours in a lather of warm water and soap, and allow one tea-spoonful of powdered borax to one quart of water. Then squeeze it out of the soaking water, and wash it in two or three warm lathers of soap and water. Do not rub it, but squeeze between the hands and press it well. Any rubbing or twisting would break the threads of the lace, especially if it were of a fine make. When clean, rinse well in tepid water and then in cold, and if time permits allow it to lie for some time in the cold water to clear it. Pure white lace may have the last rinsing water slightly tinged with blue.

If after repeated washings the lace still has a soiled look, it may either be bleached in the sun or boiled. To boil lace put it into a jar or jam pot, with cold water to cover it, and a little soap jelly; stand the jar in a saucepan with boiling water to reach fully half-way up the jar, put the lid on the pan and boil for two or three hours. Care must be taken that the water in the pan does not boil away.

Stiffening of Lace.—There is great difference of opinion about the stiffening of lace, and many object to the use of starch on the ground that it makes the lace too stiff and tends to destroy it. As a rule, however, a little starch or other stiffening is an improvement to most laces, but the aim must be to get the lace of the same stiffness as when new and no stiffer. For the thicker and commoner laces use hot-water starch. (See p. 280.)

Take some clear starch and thin it down until it feels like slightly thickened water, or for heavy laces it may be a little thicker. Allow the lace to soak in this for some little time, and then squeeze out gently with the hands. Spread it out between the folds of a fine towel or old handkerchief, and either beat it between the hands to remove some of the starch or pass it carefully through the wringing machine. Avoid twisting the lace in any way.

Cream lace may be put through cream starch or through starch coloured with tea or coffee (see Coloured Starches, p. 281), instead of white starch.

In the case of very fine lace use gum water instead of starch. This can be used without any danger of its rotting the fabric, and the following are the directions for making it:—

Gum Water.—Take one ounce of gum-arabic and put it into a saucepan with one pint of boiling water. Dissolve slowly over the fire, stirring occasionally, then strain through muslin, and bottle ready for use. Allow one table-spoonful of this melted gum to half a pint of cold water. Soak the lace in it for half-an-hour, and proceed in the same way as with starched lace. To tint the lace use strained tea or coffee with the gum water instead of plain water.

After wringing pull the lace out gently with the fingers and roll it up with the wrong side inside. Wrap it in a towel and let it lie for an hour at least before ironing.

Ironing of Lace.—Take a piece of clean white felt or flannel of three or four thicknesses, and iron the lace over this on the wrong side and with a moderately hot iron. The points of the lace must be placed furthest from the edge of the table, and must be well ironed out. Do not unroll too much of the lace at one time, and iron until quite dry. If too stiff rub gently between the fingers to take out some of the starch, and iron again. Press well with the iron, and at the same time not too roughly, and use the point of the iron to raise the pattern of the lace. Keep the lace the same width all the way along, and air it well before laying it away. Very fine lace should be ironed with a piece of muslin over it, and never touched with the bare iron. Ironing too with regard to lace is frequently objected to, but if carefully done no trace of the iron should be seen, and the result should be most satisfactory.

White Silk Lace.—This may be washed in the same way as any other lace, but should never be boiled. After rinsing, steep for half-an-hour in half a pint of hot milk, to which one dessert-spoonful of gum water has been added. This will restore the colour. Then proceed as for other lace.

How to Iron a Muslin and Lace Handkerchief.—This must be put through the very thinnest starch or gum water, and wrung in the same careful way as lace.

Iron the lace first, pulling it out after ironing to keep it soft, and then iron it over again. Iron the centre part next. Turn over to the right side, and wet the muslin part over with a damp rubber (it is sure to have become dry while the lace was being ironed). Iron it with a rather cool iron until smooth and glossy. If necessary, press out the lace round the edges last of all, and the handkerchief is finished.

Black Lace.—First brush it well with a soft brush to get rid of as much dust as possible. If it is spotted or stained, wash it in tea with a very little soap jelly added, then rinse it in more tea, and finally let it soak for about half-an-hour in prepared tea. Add prepared gum (see p. 290) in the proportion of one table-spoonful to one pint of tea. If the lace is quite clean, and you merely wish to stiffen and renew its appearance, you may dispense with the washing, and simply soak it in the prepared tea. The gum-arabic in the tea gives the lace a slight stiffness. When doing up silk lace, add two tea-spoonfuls of methylated spirits to a half-pint of prepared tea to give a gloss to the silk in the lace.

After soaking, squeeze the lace out of the tea. Shake it well, and spread it out between the folds of a towel or cloth, and either beat it with the hands or pass it once or twice through the wringer, then pull it out with the fingers, and roll up in the same way as white lace.

To iron black lace take a sheet of kitchen paper, spread the lace out on the smoothest side of it with the points away from the edge of the table, cover over with more paper, and iron over that. Lift the upper pieces of paper occasionally to see that the lace lies smoothly underneath. Iron until quite dry, and hang up to air. Black lace must never be touched with the bare iron; there must always be something over it to prevent it getting glazed. Paper not only prevents the lace staining the ironing sheet, but it also imparts a slight stiffness to it.

Curtains.—First shake the curtains well, or hang them up and brush them down with a soft brush to get rid of the superfluous dust, then soak in warm water and borax—one table-spoonful to two gallons of water—for an hour or two. Squeeze them well in this, and then pass through the wringing machine.

Wash in warm water, making a lather with boiled soap. Work them up and down in this, squeezing and pulling them through the hands. If not clean after the first washing, repeat the process.

Rubbing of all kinds must be avoided, and it is always dangerous to wash curtains by machinery. Rinse them first in warm water, then in plenty of cold. Wring well and starch them. Pure white curtains may have a little blue either added to the rinsing water or mixed in with the starch. If two ounce of alum dissolved in one gallon of water be used for rinsing, it will prevent the curtains catching fire at any time. Starch curtains wet, and have the starch just a moderate degree of stiffness. For white curtains, use the ordinary white hot-water starch; for cream or écru, use starch coloured with tea or coffee, or cream starch. (See Coloured Starches, p. 281.)

Curtains ought to be dried quickly; they are always better to be stretched and pinned out on frames for the purpose, or on sheets spread on the floor. Allow them to remain until almost dry, take up and iron round the edges, pressing out all the points well, then hang up to air. If there is no convenience for having the curtains pinned out, partly dry them by hanging them at a safe distance from the fire, or in a warm room; then spread them out on a table, and iron all over. If curtains are lined, iron the linings first before stretching and pinning out to dry; and when ironing, iron from the middle towards the sides, so that if there is any fulness it may come to the edge where it will show least.

Plain and Spotted Net.—Wash in the same way

as lace, and put through thin hot-water starch. Iron plain net on the wrong side; stretch and pull it out, and then iron again. It must not be too stiff, and should look clear. When held up to the light, the little holes in the net should not be filled with starch. Iron spotted net in the same way, only a piece of flannel may be put under it to make the spots stand out better.

A Gentleman's Evening Tie.—Care must be taken in washing these to keep them a good colour. They may be washed along with laces or fine muslins, but must not come in contact with anything dirty. After blueing, and while still wet, put them through clear starch of a moderate thickness, rather thicker than for ordinary muslins; let the starch soak well through them, and then squeeze out with the hands. Shake them out well, put them between the folds of a towel, and pass them through the wringing machine. To prepare them for ironing pull them out well, and roll up from left to right, keeping the muslin the same width all the way along. If there are hems at the ends of the ties, notice which is the right side, and keep the right side inside when rolling. Cover each tie up as it is prepared, to prevent it becoming dry,

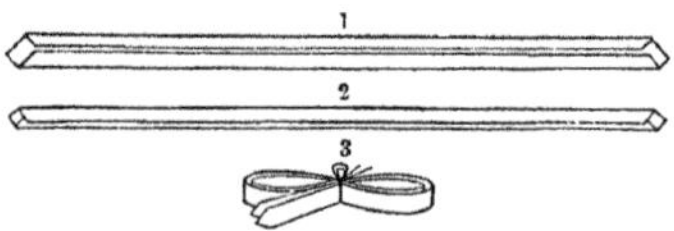

until all are finished, and it is time to iron them. To iron one of these ties, take a moderately hot iron, commence at the loose end of the roll, and iron carefully along from one end to the other, unrolling as required. Iron along several times until smooth and glossy, ironing on one side only. Turn over, and it is ready for folding. First turn down a small piece at the top of the tie, just sufficient to take in the rough edge of the material, and press it down with the iron. Next turn up a piece at the foot of the tie, rather larger than that at the top, and according to the width the points are to be (Fig. 1). Be careful to have both ends alike, and press down with the iron again. Fold down the top piece again, making the tie the same width all the way along. Measure the two points, and if they are exactly alike, iron along once more (Fig. 2). Fold loosely in four, and tie a thread round the centre to prevent it slipping (Fig. 3).

Chiffon.—Chiffon is washed in the same way as muslin, and after rinsing, put through very thin clear starch. Be careful not to twist it in any way, but enclose it in the folds of a towel, and either beat it between the hands until dry or put it through the wringing machine. Do not let chiffon he too long before ironing, it dries so very quickly; stretch it out to its proper shape, and iron it on the right side with a moderately hot iron. If it is a large piece, do not expose too much of it to the air at one time, but keep the part you are not ironing covered over to prevent it becoming dry. Pull out occasionally whilst ironing to keep it soft, and iron over again. It must on no account be made stiff, but ought to fall softly, and just have sufficient stiffness to prevent it looking limp.

SILKS, PRINTS, AND FANCY ARTICLES

Washing of Silk.—There are many silks which can be washed quite easily and made to look equal to new, more especially the soft silks, such as Japanese, Tussore, Foulard, &c., but corded and glacé silks will not be successful, and it is wiser to have these dry-cleaned.

If a number of different silks have to undergo treatment, commence by dividing them into lots—white silks by themselves, light-coloured ones in another heap, and the darker and brighter-coloured ones in a third lot apart.

To wash *white silk* prepare a lather of tepid water and soap jelly. Squeeze the silk well in this, and work it up and down in the water. Take two or three different soapy waters if necessary until the silk is quite clean. Never use the water too hot, as it would make the silk yellow, and never rub soap on white silk for the same reason. If the pieces of silk are small, or if they are silk handkerchiefs, a basin will be quite large enough for washing in, and then less soap will be required. At the same time the basin must be large enough to enable one to work comfortably.

After washing, rinse the silk thoroughly, first in tepid, and then in plenty of cold water, letting the water from the tap rush on the silk, or letting it lie in clear cold water for a short time. It is most important to get the soap well out of the silk, or it will look thick and feel hard when ironed. Pure white silk should have a little blue added to the last rinsing water, to bring back its clear bluish colour.

Coloured Silks should be soaked for a short time before being washed in cold water with a little salt in it.

If the colour is inclined to run, this will prevent it doing so to a certain extent. Silks of different colours should be soaked separately. Wash the silks in the same way as white silks, still using the water tepid, as hot would be more apt to draw out the colours. If the colour comes out very much, hurry through the process as much as possible, and do not let the silk lie about between the different waters, especially where there is a mixture of colours in the silk, as one colour would run into the other. It is better to put the articles as quickly as possible from one water to the other.

A little salt should be added to the last rinsing water to help to fix the colour, or with blues, greens, pinks, and reds a little vinegar sometimes restores and brightens the colour.

To Put a Gloss on Silk.—After rinsing put the silk through cold water with methylated spirits in it, allowing one dessert-spoonful of the spirit to half-pint of cold water. There is no occasion to prepare a large quantity of this, but there must be sufficient to soak the silk thoroughly. Then squeeze well out.

Wringing and Ironing.—In wringing silk be most careful not to twist it in any way, as it will then have a drawn look and a washed appearance when finished. Squeeze the silk between the hands, then shake it out, fold it evenly, and place it between the folds of a towel or piece of muslin, and afterwards either beat it between the hands or pass it once or twice through the wringing machine. Be careful that there is no starch on the rollers when putting it through the wringer. The silk may lie for some time rolled up in a towel, but must not be allowed to get too dry before ironing, as to sprinkle it with water afterwards would give it a spotted appearance. If it should happen to get dry, it will have to be put into water again, or damped all over with a wet rubber. Before ironing, smooth the silk out well on the table, lay over it a piece of muslin or old handkerchief, and iron over with a moderately hot iron. When slightly dry, remove the covering, and iron with the bare iron, first on one side and then on the other, to give the silk a gloss. If the silk feels in the least hard after ironing, shake it and rub it between the hands, and then iron again. The silk when finished should be as smooth and soft as when new. Some silks look better without being glazed. These should never be touched with the iron, but have something between them and it. If a very hot iron is put on wet silk, it will stick to it and crinkle it up. That is the reason why the silk should be covered when the ironing is commenced.

In ironing coloured silks do not use the iron too hot or it will destroy the colours ; and if the colour is coming out to any extent, spread a piece of clean cloth over the ironing sheet to prevent the silk staining it.

A Silk Slip.—Wash according to directions already given, and after rinsing put it through gum water in the proportion of two table-spoonfuls of the melted gum (see p. 290) to one quart of water. Add also a little methylated spirits to gum water, and let the silk soak in this for half-an-hour. This will give a gloss to the silk and also impart the slight stiffness which is found in new silk. Squeeze out with the hands, lay smoothly between the folds of a towel, and pass it through the wringing machine. Shake out and wrap again in a dry towel, and allow it to remain a few hours, if possible, before ironing. To iron the slip commence with the sleeves, ironing these on a sleeve-board if possible, but if this is not available iron first the upper and then the under half of the sleeve, then well up into the drawings at the top and at the wrist if there are any. If the sleeve is gathered or pleated, a little management with the point of the iron will be required to prevent its being creased. It is somewhat difficult to give definite instructions, as shapes and styles vary so much. The easiest way must always be taken, and that which crushes the material least.

Next iron the bodice part. Place the neck at the left-hand side and commence with the piece lying nearest the edge of the table, and work gradually along until the other side is reached. Iron up into any gathers with the point of the iron, and smooth well round the armhole. If the silk becomes dry damp it over with a wet rubber, but do not sprinkle it. When the silk part is finished, press out any lace or embroidery on the wrong side and iron any tapes. If there are any lace frills these may be goffered (see p. 284). Then dry the silk slip thoroughly before laying it away.

Washing of Prints.—When prints are being washed for the first time, and there is danger of the colour running, it is well to soak them in cold water with salt in it beforehand. Allow a handful of salt to one gallon of water. Wash them in tepid water, making a lather with boiled soap the same as for flannels. In fact, the water in which flannels have been washed, if it continues clean enough, will be suitable for the washing of prints and coloured things. Give them at least two soapy waters, squeezing and rubbing them gently with the hands until they are quite clean. Pay particular attention to the most soiled parts. If there is the least fear of the colour running, do not rub soap on them. After they have been washed several times, and when the colour is ascertained to be fast, the prints may be washed by the ordinary method for white cotton articles. Some prints will even stand boiling, but do not attempt this unless it is quite certain there is no danger of their colour being destroyed. When clean, rinse the prints, first in tepid water and then in plenty of clear cold water. Add salt or ammonia, one table-spoonful to a gallon, to the last rinsing water when the colours are not fast. Vinegar is good for restoring blues, and ox-gall for dark colours. The strength of the colour depends very much upon the quality of the material. If the colours have been properly mixed before being used for printing, they will stand soap and water perfectly ; if not, careful washing will not prevent them fading. When water becomes tinged with the colour of the material that has been washed in it, it must be poured away at once and not used for anything else. Goods of different colours which are not fast must be washed separately. After rinsing, wring them out, fold evenly, and pass them once or twice through the wringing machine. In all cases, when washing coloured articles, avoid the use of soda and washing powders.

Starching and Ironing.—When coloured things are only wished slightly stiff, they should be put through thin clear starch while they are still wet. Wring them again after starching, and then either roll up in a towel and let them lie some time before ironing, or hang them up to dry slightly. If wished very stiff, let them dry first, and then starch. Do not use the starch too hot or it will destroy the colours, and when ironing them do not use the iron too hot for the same reason.

Iron on the right side, except in cases where the pattern is raised or dull and a gloss would be unsuitable. When ironing any fancy article with sewed work, press out the sewed part on the wrong side over flannel.

How to Starch and Iron a Cotton Petticoat.—It is not necessary to starch the whole of the garment. It will generally be found sufficient if it is just starched about a quarter of a yard up from the foot, or to the top of any tucks or embroidery. The starching may be done before the petticoat is hung up to dry. Have a basin of clear starch, not very thick; dip the foot of the petticoat into this, squeeze the starch well through it, and then pass it once or twice through the wringing machine. In wringing put the band end through first.

Or the petticoat may be starched dry. Sprinkle it well with water down as far as the tucks or frills, and then dip the foot part into the starch in the same way as before. The petticoat being dry, the starch will not require to be quite so stiff. After starching and wringing, roll the petticoat up tightly with the starched part inside, and let it lie rolled up in a towel for some time before ironing. If the petticoat is made of rather thick material, it will be as well to hang it up to dry slightly before commencing to iron it.

To iron a petticoat or skirt of any kind well it is necessary to have a skirt-board. It will not only be better, but much more quickly done. Have the narrow end of the skirt-board at your left-hand side, and place it in a good light. Cover it with a small sheet kept for the purpose, and pin the sheet tightly underneath, so that there is no fear of it wrinkling up. If there is embroidery on the petticoat, put it on the board with the wrong side out to begin with, and the band of the petticoat towards the narrow end of the board. Iron the embroidery first, pressing it well out so as to raise the pattern. If there are two or more embroidered frills, commence with the lowest one; iron it first, then turn it back, and iron the second one, and so on. When the embroidery is finished, turn the petticoat on the right side. If there are frills on it, iron the plain piece under the frills first, then the frills themselves, except when they are made of embroidery, when they already have been ironed. Iron the plain top part of the petticoat last; let it be pretty damp, and iron it firmly, so as to get it smooth and glossy. If it has become in the least dry, damp it down with a wet rubber, or it will have a rough appearance when finished. If there are full frills, goffer them before taking the petticoat off the board. If there is more than one, goffer the top one first, and then the lower. When finished, remove the petticoat from the board, iron the waist-band on both sides and the strings, fold the petticoat neatly and hang it up to air.

A Princess Petticoat.—Iron the bodice part of the petticoat as a slip-bodice before putting it on the board; then proceed as above.

A Dress Bodice.—This should not be starched too stiffly or it will be uncomfortable to wear. It is therefore better to starch it when wet, and then wring it well. If very thick, hang it up to dry slightly before ironing. If it is made of thin material, merely roll it up in a towel, and let it lie for a short time.

To iron, commence with the linings—first the neckband, then the sleeves, and lastly the bodice. When ironing the lining of the bodice keep the neck at the left-hand side; commence with the part nearest the edge of the table. When that is ironed, go on to the next piece, and so on until the other side is reached. Do not iron the linings too dry or it will be difficult to get the right side smooth afterwards. Iron all seams out flat. Do the right side of the bodice in the same order, trying to make each piece perfectly smooth. A sleeve-board may be found useful when ironing the sleeves. If there is any lace, iron it before beginning the right side of the bodice. Leave any goffering that is required till the end. Iron round the seam at the armhole to make it soft and comfortable for the arm. Air well, and fold as little as possible.

Holland.—Wash in the same way as white cotton articles. A little tea may be added to the last rinsing water to preserve the colour. Or rinse in water in which a little hay has been boiled. After wringing finish off in the same way as prints.

Chintz.—First shake the chintzes, or brush them with a soft brush, to remove all surface dust. Then soak them in a plentiful supply of cold water overnight. If they are very dusty it is a good plan to change the water once or twice during this time. Then wring out and proceed with the washing. Although the colours in chintzes, and especially the better ones, are almost invariably fast, it is wise to take every precaution against their running the first time they are washed. Wash chintzes in the same way as prints, punching and pounding them well in the soapy water. A little liquid ammonia may be added to the water if it requires softening. A second soapy water will generally be found necessary, and the process of squeezing and pounding should be repeated. When the chintzes appear to be quite clean, rinse them well in plenty of warm water, and then in cold water until it is free from soap. Then wring tightly, and next put them through rather thick starch, and hang outside to dry. When quite dry, starch a second time in hot-water starch, pounding and squeezing the starch well into the material. Pass through the wringer once or twice, then shake out and hang up indoors until dry enough for ironing. Take them down, and roll up in a cloth until they can be ironed. Or if there are straight pieces of material, these may be mangled first. Iron with hot and heavy irons, finishing off with the polishing iron. Each iron should be well rubbed on a little bees'-wax before it is used, as this will make it iron smoothly and help to give a gloss to the chintz. Finish off with the polishing iron (see p. 300) if a very high gloss is desired.

Note.—Instead of starch, size is sometimes used for the stiffening of chintz. Take a penny packet of size and dissolve it in half a gallon of boiling water. When lukewarm put in the chintz and let it soak one hour. Then wring out and hang up until sufficiently dry to iron.

TO WASH GLOVES

Cotton Gloves.—If very much soiled rub them with soap and let them soak in tepid water for several hours. Paraffin soap is good, especially if the gloves are soiled. Then rub well and squeeze out the dirty water. Wash again with hot water and soap until perfectly clean. Pay particular attention to the most soiled parts. It is sometimes a good plan to put them on the hands and brush them with a nail brush. Rinse in tepid water and then in cold, adding a little blue to the cold water for white gloves. Wring out and hang up to dry. They may be pressed with a moderately hot iron when nearly dry.

Silk Gloves.—Wash these in the same way as other silk articles—rinse and hang up to dry. When nearly dry press with an iron.

Chamois Leather and Doe-skin Gloves.—Wash and dry according to directions given for chamois leather (p. 289). Rub occasionally whilst drying and pull them into shape. The best way to dry them is to put them on wooden hands sold for the purpose.

Woollen Gloves.—Wash and dry in the same way as other woollen articles. Pull them out well whilst drying or put them on wooden hands.

COLLARS, CUFFS, AND SHIRTS

Importance of having them well Washed.—The above should be washed according to general directions already given (p. 278), and dried thoroughly. It cannot be too strongly impressed that unless the process of washing is well carried out, no amount of care in the starching and ironing will make the articles look well. It is a good plan when washing to give the articles a good brushing on the washing-board. Collars especially are so liable to be stained with the heat of the neck that, unless they are thoroughly washed and rinsed, when they reach the stage of being ironed the iron will only show up the faulty work. A little extra trouble taken in the washing will save much future disappointment. Then again care must be taken in the drying. Dry in a clean place and dry thoroughly, or they will not take in the starch properly, and will be limp when finished.

All articles which are wanted very stiff should be starched in cold-water starch.

How to Starch Collars and Cuffs.—Before commencing the process have everything at hand that is likely to be required—a basin of cold water, a basin of cold-water starch (see p. 281), a plate, one or two clean towels, and a piece of clean soft rag to use as a rubber.

Mix the starch well up from the foot of the basin; put into it several of the collars and cuffs, or as many as the starch will cover easily at one time, and let the starch soak well through them. Squeeze them with the hands in the starch, and then wring as dry as possible and lay them on the plate, and do the others in the same way. They must not be put through the wringing machine, or too much of the starch would be taken out.

Take a collar or cuff at a time; rub it between the hands to get the starch well through the different folds of linen, draw out straight, and lay smoothly on the towel. Commence a few inches from the top of the towel, so that there is a dry piece to double over. Then proceed with the others in the same way; lay them close together on the towel, but do not put one on the top of the other.

Do not use the starch when it gets very low in the basin, but always have a plentiful supply to work with, so that it may not cake on the articles. When all are starched, put the basins of starch and water out of your way, and spread out the towel on the table to be ready for the collars and cuffs.

Roll up tightly and beat the bundle between the hands so as to bring the different folds of material together, and lay aside for an hour at least before ironing.

Method of Ironing Cuffs.—To carry out this process successfully it is absolutely necessary to have first a really hot iron and one which has been well dusted, the sides and top as well as the bottom, and then rubbed on a little bees'-wax or candle-end to make it run smoothly; and, secondly, a smoothly covered ironing table or ironing board without any objectionable wrinkles.

Do not take out more than one cuff or collar from the towel at one time, and keep the others well covered. If they get dry, they will not iron properly, and it is impossible to damp them over, as it would take out too much of the starch. Spread the cuff out on the table with the wrong side uppermost, and smooth away all wrinkles with a paper-knife. If there is any extra fulness on the wrong side, push it over to the edges, where it will not be seen. Iron once or twice across on the wrong side until slightly dry, then turn to the right. See that it is quite smooth before putting the iron down on it; iron it well, and then go back again to the wrong side. Iron slowly at first, until the cuff gets pretty dry and smooth; then iron more and more quickly backwards and forwards, until the cuff is quite dry and the surface glossy. Iron principally on the right side, as it is there that the most gloss is wished, but iron the wrong side smooth enough to prevent it feeling rough to the skin. Lift the cuff occasionally when ironing to let the steam escape, and dry the sheet underneath it with the iron before laying it down again.

When several cuffs have thus been ironed, they may be polished with the polishing iron (see p. 292), or if not, rounded into shape with the iron and placed near the fire to become thoroughly crisp and dry.

Collars.—These are ironed in very much the same way as cuffs, first on the wrong and then on the right side. When there are points to be turned down, be careful to iron them most on the wrong side of the collar, as that will be the side which will show most. When turning them down, make a mark first with the side of the iron, on the right side of the collar, then press down with the fingers. Do not iron down with the iron, as it is apt to cut the linen. Then turn the collar. When the whole collar is turned over, be careful to notice which is the right side before beginning to iron. Lift up any tabs there may be on the collars; dry underneath them with the iron, and then iron down again.

Eton Collars.—Iron the band first, stretch it well, and iron on both sides until dry, being careful not to iron the collar itself so as to dry it. Then stand the band up, and make the collar lie flat on the table. Iron round it slowly—first on the wrong side, keeping the band well stretched to prevent any creases where they are joined. Do not iron too long on the wrong side, or the right will become so dry that it will be impossible to iron it smoothly. Turn and iron the right side until dry; smooth and then turn with the fingers.

A Front.—Iron the neckband first on both sides until dry, or if there is a collar attached, finish it off before commencing the front. Iron the front on the right side only, and it is not necessary to iron the wrong; and if there is any fulness, smooth it away towards the sides before commencing to iron. Stretch the neckband well when ironing towards the neck to prevent creases. Then work the iron quickly up and down the front to get a good gloss. (For Polishing of Collars, &c., see p. 292.)

A Gentleman's White Shirt.—Have the shirt perfectly dry, and keep it on the wrong side until it is about to be ironed. Commence with the cuffs; place them evenly together, and gather them up in the left hand. With the right hand wet the cotton part just above the cuffs with cold water, as this will prevent the starch from spreading up the sleeve where it is not required. Then dip the cuffs into the starch, and squeeze the starch well through them. Starch right up to the top of the cuffs, but do not let the starch go any further. Wring out tightly, and rub with the hands in the same way as other cuffs.

Next starch the front. Place the two halves of it evenly together, and gather them up in the hands, commencing at the back of the neckband, and gathering down to the foot of the front. Wet carefully down the side of the front to prevent the starch spreading on to the body of the shirt, at the same time being careful that no drops of water fall on the front itself, which might cause blisters when ironing. Then dip the fronts and neckband into the starch and squeeze the starch well into them. A mere dip in and out again is not sufficient; the starch must be forced through the different layers of linen. Wring out and rub between the hands. After starching spread the shirt on the table with the front uppermost and the neck nearest the edge of the table. Smooth out the front and give it a light rub over with a clean dry cloth or rubber. Fold it double, the neck towards the bottom of the shirt. Place the sleeves across the back, smoothing out the cuffs, and double the shirt again so that the sleeves are inside. As it is now folded, sprinkle it well with water on both sides, roll tightly up from one end to the other, and keep covered over until it has to be ironed. A shirt should lie for an hour at least before being ironed, but must not be allowed to become too dry.

To Iron a Shirt.—First turn the shirt on to the right side, and place it on the table with the front uppermost and the neck towards the edge of the table. Turn the yoke forwards, so that it lies flat on the top of the back of the shirt, and iron the yoke first on the right side, then turn it back, slip the iron inside, and iron it on the wrong. Next iron the neckband, first on the wrong and then on the right, ironing it until quite dry. Finish it off well, particularly at the button-holes, and be careful not to iron down on to the front of the shirt. When these are done, fold the shirt down the centre of the back, keeping the front apart from it. Iron the back on both sides, always keeping the neck at the left-hand side. Open out, so that the whole of the back lies uppermost on the table, and iron round the back of the armholes, and this finishes the back.

Next fold the shirt double lengthways with the front inside to prevent its becoming dry, and place it on the table with the sleeves lying out to right. Throw back the upper sleeve, and commence with the under one. Iron the cuff first on the wrong and then on the right, in the same way as other cuffs, then run the iron up inside the cuff and iron the thick part over the drawings. Iron also the wrong side of the hems at the opening of the sleeve, and turn the cuffs into shape. Smooth out the sleeve, and iron first on one side, ironing well into pleats or gathers at the top and bottom, and put a pleat into the sleeve itself if necessary. Turn down the shirt at the neck so that the other side of the sleeve can be ironed, but do not change the position of the shirt itself.

Then iron the second sleeve in exactly the same manner, the ironed sleeve being turned back and underneath the shirt out of the way. When both are finished, place the shirt on the table with the front uppermost and the neck at your left-hand side. Arrange the back in pleats, and press them down with the iron. Then iron the breast of the shirt; slip a shirt-board up in between the back and the front, without disarranging the pleats down the back. Stretch the upper half of the breast on to the board first, drawing the other half as much out of the way as possible. Tuck the cotton part of the front underneath the board, so as to keep the breast firm. Smooth away all wrinkles on the breast with a paper-knife, pushing any fulness over towards the sides. Hold the neck firmly with the left hand iron slowly up the centre, then gradually towards the sides. As it becomes smooth, iron up and down more quickly, lifting the breast occasionally to let the steam escape. Keep stretching it well with the left hand to prevent any wrinkles forming round the collar. Do the other side in the same way, and then hold both firmly together, and iron quickly and firmly up and down the breast to get a good gloss.

When the breast is finished, slip out the shirt-board and arrange the cotton part of the front smoothly on the top of the back, putting a pleat down the centre where required. Damp it over if it has become dry, and then iron it smoothly. If the shirt has to be polished with the polishing iron, do so now; but if not, fold it.

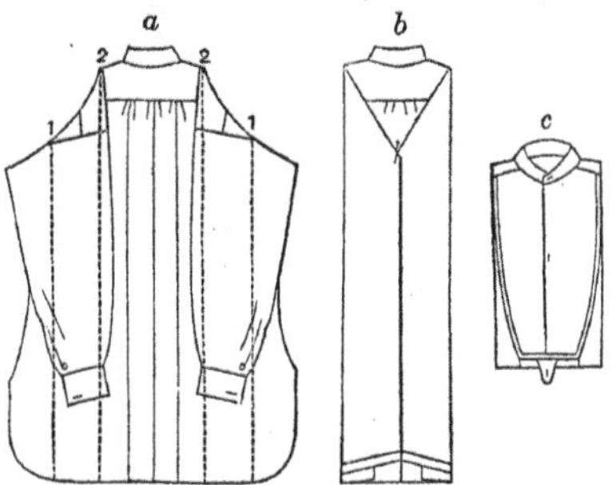

To Fold a Shirt.—First put a pin in the neck to keep the two sides together, then turn it over so that the back is uppermost and the neck at the left-hand side. Turn the sleeves down the sides of the back (Fig. *a*), noticing that both are turned in from exactly the same place on both sides. Turn over them a small piece from the sides by dotted line 1 (Fig. *a*); then turn over again from dotted line 2 (Fig. *a*), so that both sides meet down the centre of the back. Stretch them rather tightly, so that the front will have a curved look, and pin them firmly together (Fig. *b*). Hang up to air, and then fold so that the front only shows (Fig. *c*).

A Lady's Shirt.—After it is rinsed put it through rather thin clear starch and hang it up to dry. This gives a slight stiffness to the body part of the shirt. When quite dry starch the cuffs and collar in cold-water starch, being careful to wet previously just above the cuffs and below the collar with cold water to prevent these parts becoming stiff with the starch. If there is a plain band down the front, and this is liked stiff, dip it also in the cold-water starch. Rub the starch well in and then smooth the parts over with a clean rubber. Sprinkle the dry parts of the shirt with cold water and roll up tightly. Let it lie for an hour or two at least before ironing.

To iron the shirt, open it out and turn it on the right side. Commence with the collar, stretch it out, and iron first on the wrong and then on the right side. Next iron the yoke on both sides and then proceed to the sleeves. Iron these in the same way as the sleeves of a gentleman's shirt, or slip them on to a sleeve-board. Use a small iron for running up into the gathers at the top, and try to avoid creases. To iron the bodice place the shirt on the table with the neck at the left-hand side. Commence with the front lying nearest the edge of the table, smooth it out and iron it well. Next iron the back and then the other front. Finish off by ironing the parts round the armholes, also the hems on the wrong sides and any strings. The cuffs may now be polished if wished, then turn them into shape and hang the shirt up to air.

To Fold the Shirt.—First pin the two sides together at the neck, and pleat the front if desired. Then lay the sleeves down the sides of the back the same as in a gentleman's shirt (Fig. *a*); fold them upwards again so that the cuffs show above the neck, and pin them into position. Fold over the sides so that they meet down the centre, and pin them together. Fold quite loosely; any pressing would crush the sleeves.

INFANTS' AND CHILDREN'S CLOTHING

Preliminary.—In washing infants' clothing it is always better to keep the articles separate, and not to mix them with other clothes. Special attention must be given to them, and in dressing they require very dainty handling.

The water used in washing must be changed as soon as it becomes in the least degree dirty.

Neither soda nor washing powders must on any account be used, as they are irritating to the skin.

Baby's Robes and Robe Skirts.—If time permits, allow these to soak for an hour or two in tepid water before washing. When about to wash, wring them out of the soaking water, and wash in water as hot as the hand can bear. It is best to wash these carefully with the hands. Being fine, they will not bear being rubbed on a board or with a brush. Rub soap on them, and pay particular attention to the most soiled parts. If the material is fine, use melted soap (see p. 287). Go methodically over every part; wash first on one side and then on the other, and give them a second soapy water if they are not clean after the first. Then boil if necessary, and afterwards rinse, blue, and wring (see p. 278). Give them throughout very careful treatment, as the least unnecessary strain is apt to tear them or cause holes.

After wringing, put through the thinnest possible starch and wring again. Then dry partially, roll up in a towel, and let them lie a short time before ironing, but not long enough to become dry.

To iron a robe skirt cover a skirt-board with a fine sheet, and put the skirt on it with the wrong side out. Iron any lace round the foot and embroidery on this side, pressing it well with the iron to make the pattern stand out. Then turn, and iron the rest of it on the right side. If any of the muslin part has been dried with the ironing on the wrong side, damp it down before ironing it on the right. If there are any tucks, iron them first, stretching them out well before ironing, and getting them quite free from creases. Iron the plain part of the skirt from the bottom upwards, and keep drawing it towards you as you go along. Do not let it stick to the ironing-sheet, but keep lifting it up from time to time. Should it get dry before the ironing is finished, wet the end of a towel and damp the muslin over lightly with it. The muslin must on no account be ironed dry, or it will have a rough appearance, instead of looking smooth and glossy.

The skirt of a *robe* is ironed in the same way. Iron the embroidery on the front of the bodice before turning the robe on to the right side. After turning, finish the skirt of the robe before doing the bodice. If the bodice has become dry, damp it down before ironing. Iron as much of it as possible on the board, using a small iron so as to get into the corners well. Any frills that cannot be done on the board may be left until the robe is taken off. The embroidered flaps or side-pieces on the front of some robes are better left until the end and ironed off the board, the muslin part of them on the right side, and the embroidery on the wrong. Do the sleeves whichever way is found easiest. Sometimes they are wide enough to allow of the iron being slipped inside them, or they may be managed more easily by putting a roll of flannel inside and ironing over that. Goffer or crimp any frills that require it; iron out any strings, and then air well.

A Piquée Pelisse.—Wash according to general directions (see p. 278), and starch while wet in thin hot-water starch. Allow it to dry slightly before ironing.

Iron all embroidery first on the wrong side, over flannel, until it is quite dry. The piquée itself must be ironed on the right side to give it a gloss. Commence with the cape, iron it from one end to the other, and have the coat part of the pelisse turned back from under it so that the cape itself lies single on the table. Then iron the sleeves—lay out one at a time smoothly on the table, and iron first the upper and then the under part. Then lay the pelisse on the table with the neck at your left-hand side, turn the cape back, and iron the coat itself. Iron the piece nearest to you first, smooth out each piece as you go along, always keeping it lying the one way, and draw the coat towards you as you get it ironed. Press well with the iron to get a gloss. Double by the shoulders and sides, and finish off round the armholes; also iron the hems on the wrong side. Then finish by goffering any trimming that requires it; air well, and fold loosely.

Stays.—When washing these, place them on the washing-board and use a brush to brush them with. Being made of firm material, they will bear a good rubbing. Boil them if necessary, and after rinsing put them through thin hot-water starch. On no account make them stiff. Allow them to dry slightly, and iron first on one side and then on the other until quite dry. Stretch well while ironing, as the quilting is inclined to pucker. Hang up in a warm place to air before laying away.

Pinafores.—These should always be slightly starched; if left quite limp they will not keep their appearance any time, and will very soon soil. Muslin pinafores should be put through stiffer starch than those made of diaper and other fancy white material, and must always be starched wet. Diaper and other kinds of pinafores may be starched either wet or dry, and the starch should be quite thin. Pinafores made of muslin and other thin material should be wrung well and rolled in a towel for some time before ironing. Those made of thicker material may be slightly dried and then rolled up.

When ironing pinafores always commence with the embroidery, pulling it out well and ironing very carefully. The rest of the pinafore is as a rule very simple to iron. Always keep the top of the pinafore at the left-hand side, and iron the material single when possible. If the pinafore is joined up the back, iron it double—first the front and then the back, or iron it on a skirt-board. If there are tucks along the foot of the pinafore, stretch them out well when ironing to prevent them dragging. Iron as much as possible with the thread of the material. A small iron must be used for getting into all gathers. Always finish off well round armholes and iron out all strings, and run round hems on the wrong side. If there is a full drawn front on the pinafore it sometimes looks well crimped. Goffer or crimp all frills that require it, and fold neatly.

Knickerbockers.—After washing these, wring and let them dry slightly before ironing. On no account must the frills be starched, as the stiffness would irritate the tender skin of young children. Iron the frills first, then the waistband on both sides. Keep the waist at the left-hand side when ironing the legs, and iron first the front and then the back of them. Iron whichever way crushes them least. There is such a variety of shapes that it is difficult to give definite rules. Iron well into gathers, and hems on the wrong side. Crimp the frills, and then fold neatly.

Flannel Binders, Pilches, and Barracoats.—Wash and dry these according to general directions given for washing and drying flannels (p. 287). They should, when possible, be dried in the open air; it gives them a sweeter and fresher smell. When nearly dry, iron them all over with a cool iron to make them smooth and soft. Iron all strings and bindings, and be most particular to air well.

Knitted Socks and Bootees.—Wash these carefully in a lather of warm water and boiled soap, and rinse in warm water (see p. 287). If white, a little blue should be added to the last rinsing water. Pay great attention to the drying of these, as they are liable to shrink. Wooden blocks of different sizes are to be had for stretching them; they are put on to these while still wet, and allowed to remain until dry. A simpler block may be cut out of a piece of cardboard the exact size and shape required, and in some ways this is even better than wood, as in this case pins can be put through the cardboard and the sock stretched in length as well as breadth. Failing to get either of these, pin the socks out to their proper shape on a covered table or board.

Knitted Jackets and Drawers.—For the washing of these, see p. 287. When drying them, see that they are pulled out to a proper shape before hanging up. If they are not very thick, it is almost better to pin them out on a covered table or floor, and allow them to remain there until dry.

Wincey and Serge Dresses.—These are both washed in the same way. Shake well before washing to free them from all superfluous dust. Soak them in warm water with a little ammonia, and let them remain from twenty to thirty minutes. This softens them and makes them easier to wash. Wring them out and wash in the same way as flannels (see p. 287). Pay particular attention to the most soiled parts. Rinse thoroughly, adding a little blue to the last rinsing water for white or blue serge. Hang up to dry with the wrong side out, and if drying indoors turn and shake occasionally during the process. When nearly dry, iron with a cool iron. Wincey especially requires a good deal of pressure bestowed on it. Navy blue serge should be ironed on the wrong side only; it would not look well to glaze it.

Smocks.—Smocking must never be pressed with the iron, but only steamed. Iron the rest of the garment first, leaving the smocking to do last. It takes two people to steam it. Let a moderately hot iron be held with the bottom upwards by one, while a second holds the smocking firmly on the top of it, and draws it slowly over the surface of the iron until it becomes quite dry. The heading round the top of the smocking should be ironed with a small iron, and if it is a starched material, afterwards goffered.

Boys' Sailor Suits.—These require very careful washing. They are as a rule made of drill or jean, materials which are both very hard to wash. Being of a firm texture, they will stand a good deal of rubbing and a brush on the washing-board. They may be boiled after washing if there is no fear of any colour in them running. After rinsing, starch while still wet. The starch must not be stiff, as the material itself is of a stiff nature. Wring well, and dry slightly before ironing. Be careful to choose a very clean place for drying, and dry with the wrong side out.

To iron the trousers turn them on the right side, smooth them out on the table, with the waist at your left-hand side and the front uppermost. Iron the fronts of the two legs first, but not too dry; turn over and iron the back, then iron over the fronts again. Iron bands and hems on the wrong side, and press hard with the iron to get a good gloss.

In ironing the jacket, commence with the collar, and if this is of navy blue or scarlet, iron it on the wrong side only, or on the right with something laid over it; it should not be glossed. Next iron the sleeves on the right side, first the upper and then the under half. In doing the jacket itself, keep the neck at the left-hand side, commence with the piece nearest to you, and iron from one end to the other, smoothing out each piece as it is reached. Then finish off at the shoulders, round armholes, and the inside of the jacket. Blue linen suits must not be polished with the iron, but either ironed entirely on the wrong side or ironed with something over the material.

Silk Dresses, Pinafores, and Veils.—For the washing of these, see p. 292. After a silk dress is wrung, starch any lace there may be on it in very thin starch, and hang it up to dry for a short time. Iron the lace first on the wrong side, then any linings or double parts on the wrong side. Next iron the sleeves with a small iron, first the upper and then the under part, ironing well into the gathers. If the dress is smocked, leave the smocking to the last (see p. 299). If there is a bodice, iron it before doing the skirt. Do the skirt either on the skirt-board or by laying it double on the table, and ironing first the front and then the back. If the silk is very wet in parts, iron with something over it to begin with, to prevent the iron sticking to and scorching it. When the silk is embroidered, press out the embroidery on the wrong side after the silk is ironed. It is not necessary to goffer the lace on a silk dress, as it looks better falling softly. Goffering would be out of place unless merely for a narrow frilling on the neck.

Silk Pinafores are ironed in the same way as others (see p. 298). The lace on them may be slightly starched, but do not goffer it.

Silk Veils should be pinned out on a covered table or board while still wet, and allowed to remain until dry. If they feel in the least degree stiff after they are removed, rub gently with the fingers to soften the silk again.

Blankets.—These being small may be washed in the same way as white flannels (see p. 287). Dry in the open air if possible, and then air before the fire.

POLISHING

When about to polish, have ready at hand a polishing board, a basin of cold water, a piece of soft rag, and a well-heated polishing iron. Let everything be particularly clean and free from dust.

To polish *cuffs*, take one at a time; place it flat on the polishing board, dip the clean rag into the cold water, and then lightly wet the surface of the cuff. On no account must it be made too wet, or it will be apt to blister; and be careful that no drops of water fall on it. Hold the cuff in position with the left hand, and run the polishing iron up and down it with the right.

There are different kinds of polishing irons; the one like diagram on p. 274 is to be recommended. It is of a good weight, and has a rounded surface at the one end only. The opposite end is held up while in use, and the iron is swung backwards and forwards from the wrist, the rounded surface doing the polishing. Other kinds are to be had which are held flat while in use, and are worked quickly backwards and forwards on the surface to be polished.

Polishing at first gives the linen a streaky appearance, but it must be continued until the surface is evenly glossed all over. The iron must be changed when it cools. When all the cuffs are polished, turn them into shape. Polish *collars* in the same way, only be particular that you polish the proper side of those that are turned down, or have turned-down points. In polishing a *shirt*, slip up the polishing board without crushing either the front or the back. Polish the breast first, working the iron up and down the length of it, and not across. In all cases remember to wet the surface slightly before polishing. When the breast is finished, draw the board gently out, lay it across the shirt, place the cuffs on it, and polish them. Turn the cuffs into shape, and fold the shirt (see p. 297).

Different kinds of glazes are to be had for polishing linen, which are used instead of the polishing iron. They do not of course give such a high gloss, but by many people are preferred.

Directions for using them are generally given with the different kinds. Some are added to the starch, while others are in a liquid form and are rubbed on the surface of the linen when ironing.

Polishing irons should be treated with great care. Their surface is made of polished steel, and if it once gets roughened it will not do such good work.

DRESS—ITS CHOICE AND CARE

Without indulging in an inordinate passion for dress, which is likely to result in unjustifiable extravagance beyond her means, it is the duty of every woman to dress suitably and well, according to her position in life. Appearances count for a great deal in all phases of society, and in the matter of dress, as much as in anything else, appearances must be studied. The question of lack of means is often put forward as an excuse for general untidiness, dowdiness, and want of taste, but no woman, however limited her purse, need degenerate into what is contemptuously termed a "dowd." True, it is necessary to "cut one's coat according to one's cloth," and it needs not a little pinching and contriving in some cases to be able to do this successfully, but the result will always be found to be well worth the trouble taken in achieving it. In addition to the first and all-important question of good taste, such things as durability, general utility, and style have to be considered, and last but not least, the best way to take care of clothes in order to preserve as long as possible their pristine freshness. All these important phases of the dress question are fully dealt with in this chapter in a manner which it is hoped will be especially useful to those women for whom ways and means are all-important considerations.

The Art of Dressing Well.—Dress is an invaluable aid to good looks, yet, strange as it may seem, comparatively few women have acquired the art of dressing well. The reason for this is not hard to seek. If fashion sets the seal of her approval upon some particular style, every woman rushes blindly in its wake. No matter if the style be one that is only suitable for the tall and the slender, it is embraced indiscriminately by the short and the stout, whilst, with a hopeless lack of the sense of what is fitting, the portly dowager of fifty will be seen to deck herself in a mode only becoming to a young girl of eighteen.

There are some women who dress well instinctively. These realise that careful dressing can do a great deal towards enhancing their good points; whilst bad dressing can materially nullify any pretence to good looks they may possess. To dress well is to dress becomingly and suitably. For instance, however pretty a smart light silk gown may be, it would look unsuitable in the street on a wet and muddy day. However trim and well fitting a navy blue tailor-made suit, it would look woefully out of place at a smart garden party. Elaborate silks and laces are not the wear for the seaside be it said; whilst the rough-knitted jersey and very short-pleated skirt and high boots of the Scotch Highlands would present a most incongruous appearance if worn out of doors in town. A woman will exclaim, "What bad taste," if she sees a man wearing brown calf boots with a tall hat and frock suit, yet the same woman may think nothing of wearing a light flower-betrimmed hat of the picture variety with a tweed coat and skirt.

The Well-dressed Woman.—Suitability and good taste should be the aim of all those who wish to acquire the art of dressing well. The woman who dresses well plans her dress from the point of view of her own individuality. She no more thinks of slavishly following the dictates of fashion than she thinks of absolutely ignoring them. But she wisely adapts the fashion to suit herself, and does not try to adapt herself to suit the fashions. There is rarely a style but can be adapted in some way or other to suit individual needs. It is in rushing to the extremes of fashion that the woman of the present day more particularly errs.

How to avoid Dowdiness.—On the other hand, the well-dressed woman does not allow her appearance to become dowdy. If her purse is limited, she will adopt that style of dress that does not date quickly in preference to the most marked styles of the current season.

Simplicity should be the chief characteristic of the toilette of the woman of small means. Chiffons, laces, and other such ephemeral fabrics should be discarded for the more useful tailor suit for everyday wear. She should always be careful to avoid choosing very bright colours, no matter how well they suit her. Where a woman who can only afford one new gown, for instance, chooses a strawberry-coloured cloth—it will look very well when it is new; but her friends in time will tire of seeing her in it. Constant wear will emphasise the fact that she only has one dress, and when this has to do duty, say, for two or three seasons, she runs the danger of becoming known as "the woman in the strawberry-coloured dress." On the other hand, navy blue, black and other dark materials, seldom "date" a dress to the same extent as the brighter colours. Black perhaps is par excellence the most economical wear. The black costume may be varied with dressy blouses for dressy occasions, simpler blouses for everyday wear, whilst varying little touches in the way of new ornamental buttons and different trimmings do wonders towards renovating a black indoor dress which has seen better days. For evening wear black or white are the most sensible colours for the woman who has but one evening gown in her wardrobe. Such colours as pink or blue are very pretty when new, but constant wear of a coloured evening dress serves decidedly to emphasise the limitations of the wardrobe of its wearer.

Style and Colour.—Just as there are some women who dress well by instinct, there are others who seem to possess an instinct for dressing badly. Tall thin women will appear in gowns clinging so tightly to their forms as to accentuate their thinness. In addition, the ultra-tall woman will as often as not dress her hair very high on the top of her head, and wear hats remarkable for the abnormal height of their crowns. To make matters worse, the trimming on her gown will run in straight lines from almost the neck to the feet, and very often also one or more of her tailor-made dresses will be built of striped materials which will serve to emphasise both her undue thinness and her extreme height.

Short stout people, on the other hand, will garb themselves in the brightest of colours. Their gowns will as often as not be heavily trimmed, the trimmings running horizontally across the dress, serving effectively to "cut the height" of the wearer. Very often large patterned materials and huge checks are worn, whilst tailor-mades are liberally adorned with buttons the size of half-crown pieces. It should be remembered that all striped materials and the trimmings laid lengthways on a dress add to the height. They should therefore be avoided by the ultra-tall women. On the other hand, narrow stripes are becoming to the stout woman, whilst checks and large-patterned materials add to the breadth of her figure, and should therefore be avoided. A stout woman should never wear white or other light colours; these only serve to accentuate her stoutness, whilst dark materials tend to give her a much slimmer appearance. A style of dress at present in vogue with a front panel running from neck to hem is becoming to most stout figures, but the panel requires careful cutting. It should not be too broad, and should be made to taper as narrowly as possible at the waist-line. All unnecessary fulness in the way of pleats at the hips should be avoided; at the same time the dress should not be made to fit too closely to the figure. The skirt should stand out well at the hem, the fulness at the foot serving to make less prominent the width of the hips.

A stout woman should never wear a very short skirt. Her walking-skirts should only just clear the ground—if she attempts the very short "trotteur" skirt, which is becoming to the graceful figure and neat ankles of the young girl, she will make herself appear even stouter than she is. The skirt of the moment which clings tightly round the feet at the hem is particularly unbecoming to the stout woman. Her dress should be plain and well cut. Gathers and elaborate pleating should be avoided. On the other hand, the extra fulness afforded by pleats and gathers should always be made use of wherever possible by the thin woman in the planning of her gowns. She should avoid all severe harsh lines in dress, as these would only serve to emphasise the angularity of her figure. It may be said with truth that the very severe tight-fitting gown should only be adopted by women of perfect proportions.

Fashions within the last year seem to have been designed only to suit the very slim; the fashionable figure, in fact, at the time of writing is slender, and many have been the devices resorted to by possessors of plump figures to acquire the fashionable contour. All sorts of new corsets have been designed with the object of aiding the fair wearers in this direction. Some of these models have, in fact, been carried to almost ridiculous extremes. In length they reach almost to the knees, and one cannot help wondering how the wearer can bend or even sit down when encased in these latest outcomes of fashion's vagaries.

The wise woman who is endowed with unfashionable plumpness does not seek to reduce it in this manner. She chooses her corsets, indeed, with the view of improving her figure, knowing that there are many good makes of corset which will achieve this result without imposing upon her the penalty of general discomfort entailed by the species above-mentioned, but she does not strive to appear in gowns which in design and construction are only suitable for the schoolgirl. She knows that gowns of the "Pensionnaire" type are not for her, and adopts a style of dress more suited to her figure in accordance with the principles already laid down for her observance. La Mode of late seems to have devoted herself entirely to the needs of the *jeune fille*. A vogue for simplicity has come upon us; gowns are not only simple in design and construction, but they are characterised by that degree of extreme simplicity which, though most becoming to sweet seventeen, is trying, to say the least of it, to more mature forty. The woman who has attained the latter age must therefore refrain from adopting the exaggeratedly simple styles. Her dress may be simple without being childishly so, and it is in this respect that the greatest discrimination must be exercised. In all periods of history the best-dressed women have been those who made fashion walk hand in hand with common sense, and to no period does this apply with greater truth than to the present day.

Choice of Colour.—Many women are apt to nullify the effect of a really smart dress by selecting a colour which does not suit them. A few general hints in regard to colour may here be given. It may be taken as a general rule that where the tints of the hair and eyes are repeated in the costume, the effect is on the whole successful. Thus blue-eyed people rarely look so well as in the different shades of blue, more especially the shade that matches their eyes. A fair girl with a delicate pink and white complexion looks well in the various soft subdued tones of pink. The choice of colours for the girl whose hair is of the colour of ripe corn, and whose complexion is of a pink and white prettiness, is very varied; white, pale blue, pale pink, black, dark greens, red, dark brown (where she has brown eyes), all suit her well. The red or auburn-haired woman must be particularly careful in her choice of colour, and her dress should not be so much regulated by the colours themselves as by the varying shades of the different colours. Green, for instance, is considered an ideal colour for the red-haired woman, but it must be either a very dark green or a very faint delicate shade bordering on the tint known as *eau de nil*. Bright greens are altogether unsuitable. Brown may be worn by the red-haired woman, more especially if she has brown eyes. In other cases it is not so successful, although it always serves to bring out the pretty shades in her hair. The fact remains, however, that a red-haired woman to look her best in brown should have brown eyes. Black velvet is pretty generally becoming to the red and the auburn-haired, but the ordinary dull black cloths prove trying, and should be relieved by touches of white where possible. A red-haired woman always looks well, however, in a low-cut black evening gown, the black serving to accentuate the whiteness of her skin. Dark-haired women with creamy or sallow complexions look their best in bright colours such as bright reds, yellows for evening, &c. When they wear dark dresses, these should always be relieved by touches of bright colour. Cream suits this style of complexion better than white. Dark-haired women with delicate fair skins and pink and white complexions, however, require softer and less decided shades; white, dove greys, delicate pinks, heliotrope are eminently suited to this style, and if the eyes are violet, the shades of violet and mauve are particularly becoming. Grey is a colour which should be chosen with great discrimination. It has a very hardening effect upon the faces of people with very pallid complexions. As a rule, light greys should be relieved with black or white. Certain soft shades of grey are particularly becoming to elderly people. Youth and age, it should be remembered, are not the least important factors in deciding the colour of a dress, and the sensible woman who is advancing towards middle age will not err in affecting the style and colours which became her in her youth.

Very often a colour which proves unsuitable if worn as a whole dress will be perfectly becoming if a touch of it only appears upon the dress. For instance, though a girl with red hair should not wear a whole pale blue dress, a tie, a waist-belt, or a sash of pale blue upon a white dress would suit her quite well. White frilling or lace on the collar and cuffs of a dress is becoming to almost every woman, though many could not wear a whole white dress. On the other hand, touches of bright colour on a dead white dress serve to make it fitting wear for a sallow dark-haired person who would look simply ghastly in unrelieved white. It is in the satisfactory blending of colours, on the whole, that success in dress may be achieved. The very texture of the material itself should be studied. For instance, for evening wear red-haired and pale fair-haired women should wear the soft dull materials such as chiffons, ninons, net, soft silks, voiles, &c., in preference to satin, which is too hard for this type of prettiness, although it is most becoming to youthful-looking fair girls with very pink and white complexions and to the dark-haired types. Where the complexion is washed out, anæmic, or pallid, white satin especially should be avoided.

OUT-DOOR COSTUMES

One thing to keep in mind in regard to the selection of an out-door costume is this:—If the costume has to do duty for an extended period, by all means let it be good in quality. It is better to pay a fair price for a "tailor-made" at the start than to have a dress "run up" anyhow by some indifferent dressmaker on the strictly economical plan. This procedure nearly always turns out false economy in the long-run—what with the outlay upon making, material, lining and extras, the cost of the dress amounts to nearly the same as that of a tailor-made. The cut is more often than not indifferent, the fit unsatisfactory; and, last but not least, the costume in nine cases out of ten will often be altogether lacking in style. In many instances the dress will prove such a failure that the unfortunate wearer in sheer desperation will lay it aside, and, notwithstanding the fact that she can ill afford it, will be induced to buy a new gown by effecting some economy in another direction. It is false economy, therefore, to buy indifferent clothes at the outset. A woman should always have one good costume to fall back upon. It is not always necessary that this should be made to measure. The cult of the ready-made tailor gown has to-day reached the level of a fine art. For the trifling sums of from 5s. to 10s. 6d. these gowns are altered by expert fitters to suit individual figures. Of course those with what is known as "stock figures" will get the most satisfactory results, as very often a ready-made gown will fit them exactly without the slightest need for alteration. These fortunate people have the best facilities for practising economy in dress in that particular way. It is always advisable to go to a good class firm for costumes of the kind. The very cheap "ready mades" are bad investments. Very good "tailor mades" may now be had for three and a half to four guineas, but if the costume is bought at sale time it may often be had for much less.

SUMMER DRESSES AND THE HOME DRESSMAKER

A woman who is an adept with her needle will be able to eke out her dress allowance in a much more satisfactory manner than her sister who is less gifted in this way. Such a woman on a dress allowance of £12 a year will be able to dress much better than a woman whose allowance runs to more than double that amount. The summer season in particular is a time of triumph for the home dressmaker. Nothing can look more suitable in the hot weather than dainty linen, cotton, and muslin frocks. When it is remembered that linens and cottons may be had for an outlay of a few pence a yard, it will be seen that the cost of a gown made of these materials will be very small. A dainty cotton frock can be made for as small an outlay as 5s. upon the material.

One material which has been much in vogue of late years is particularly economical for summer wear. It is known as "mercerised lawn," and has the appearance of fine Indian muslin, only with a softer and more clinging effect, and is to be had in white and all the most delicate shades. To crown its other advantages it is of double width, and may be purchased for from 6d. to 1s. per yard. The material has the additional advantage of washing particularly well, having no tendency whatever to shrink in the wash. With the aid of a good paper pattern, a very pretty dress, good enough for any dressy occasion, can be fashioned out of this material by the clever home dressmaker at a cost of from between six or seven shillings, including trimmings, buttons, and other accessories. If the home dressmaker, in addition to being able to make herself dainty frocks of the kind, is able to save washing bills by laundering them herself at home, then she is fortunate indeed, and she will always be able to hold her own in the smartest company as a woman who dresses prettily and well.

(For the making of dresses from paper patterns, see Home Dressmaking.)

(For washing cotton dresses at home, see p. 293.)

EVENING DRESS

In selecting an evening dress due regard must be paid to the occasion for which it is required. A ball dress, for instance, would be quite out of place if worn at a dinner-party or at the theatre, whilst a dinner dress would hardly be suitable at a ball. Yet many women show a remarkable lack of taste and discrimination in this direction. Dresses worn at big balls and dances and receptions must necessarily be more elaborate than those worn at dinner-parties or at the theatre, excepting of course where the dinner-party precedes some large ball or some important reception.

Ball Gowns should always be of light and delicate colours, the soft, flimsy materials such as chiffon, ninon, and net being the prettiest and the most graceful for these occasions. The lighter and more ethereal-looking the fabric the more successful will a ball dress be. The corsage of a ball gown is of course cut low at the neck, and the sleeves are usually quite short, sometimes mere straps or bands of the material or its trimmings doing duty as such. The gloves worn with these gowns are extremely long, covering the whole of the arm; and shoes and stockings are worn to match. White is the ideal colour for the ball dress of a young girl, more especially where she is a débutante. Delicate shades of pink, pale blue, primrose, *eau de nil*, pale green, are also effective. Ornaments of some kind are usually worn in the hair. Dainty wreaths of flowers, choux or bands of ribbon, in accordance with the fashion of the moment, being particularly suitable for the wear of young women and girls; jewelled combs, sequin ornaments and jewellery being worn by the elder women.

Sensible people have realised that long trailing dresses are not conducive to the enjoyment of dancing, hence for the moment fashion has decreed that dance dresses should be short and without trains.

Dinner and Theatre Dresses.—Dinner dresses are not so elaborate as dance frocks. Sleeves are worn to the elbow as a rule, and the corsage is not so décolleté. In some cases demi-toilette, consisting of a gown with transparent yoke and sleeves, may be worn. This style is particularly suitable for theatre wear, more especially for elderly people. As a rule, ladies occupying the stalls, boxes, or dress circle of a fashionable West End theatre in London, and our other large towns, wear low-necked dresses; these are not, however, of the nature of ball dresses, and "demi-toilette" is every bit as appropriate. At the opera full evening dress is *de rigueur*, and the display made by the handsome gowns and costly jewellery worn by the lady members of the audience at the opera during the season is of itself a sight well worth going to see.

The General Utility Evening Gown.—An evening gown for a woman of small means has to be a more or less adaptable garment which can be made to do duty upon widely different occasions. A gown of this kind should never be pronounced in style or in colour. The material should be of some endurance. The various satin-faced materials, such as "satin charmeuse," which have been so much in vogue of late, are ideal fabrics for a general utility gown of the kind described, as they wear exceedingly well. The dress should be smartly cut and finished. A little extra expenditure on the initial outlay will be well worth while. The neck should of course be cut low, and the sleeves short for wear on very dressy occasions; but the gown should be furnished with two separate detachable sets of lace or net guimpes and sleeves. One lace guimpe could be cut low in the neck, only not so décolleté as the gown itself, to form a little lace chemisette coming above the décolletage; the sleeves of this guimpe should be of elbow-length. The second guimpe should be cut high in the neck, the sleeves being either to the wrist or to the elbow. A woman will thus be provided with a good evening dress which can be adapted for very dressy, moderately dressy, or demi-toilette occasions; and upon each and all of these occasions she will have the satisfaction of knowing that she is well and suitably dressed.

Evening Wraps.—Evening cloaks, coats, or wraps are necessarily indispensable adjuncts to evening dresses, but they must of course be chosen with due regard to the circumstances of the wearer.

A woman who lives in the suburbs, for instance, and cannot afford the outlay on a hired carriage, taxicab, or cab to take her to the theatre or to a dance in town, must necessarily go there by train or bus. In these circumstances a white or other light-coloured cloak would be useless. It would very soon get dirty, and as light colours show up the dirt very quickly, it would probably have to be cleaned after having been worn only two or three times. For the woman so situated a coat of some darker colour should be chosen. It need not necessarily be too dark. There are several shades of art blue and art green, for instance, which are most becoming as well as most useful. The cloak should be lined with white or some other light colour for the protection of the light gown underneath.

How to keep Gloves Clean when Going Out.—Light evening gloves are also apt to become very quickly soiled when travelling by train or omnibus. The wise woman will provide herself with a pair of cotton or woollen gloves (according to the season), of a size larger than those she usually wears and slip them over her other gloves whilst in the train. She will, of course, take them off when she reaches her destination, and the gloves underneath will be found to be quite clean and fresh, whereas if she had not taken this precaution, they would have unavoidably become soiled.

Hats are seldom worn with evening dress, but when a woman has to either walk or go by train or tram to the theatre, it is advisable that she should have some light head-covering, not only to obviate the risk of catching cold, but also to keep her hair tidy. A light crocheted woollen "fascinator," which is the name given to a kind of hood especially designed for evening wear, is admirably suited for the purpose, and may be purchased for two or three shillings. Silk, chiffon, and lace fascinators are more expensive, some of these dainty trifles being extremely elaborate and ornamental in design. A pretty lace scarf, or a white *crêpe de chine* motor scarf, would also be useful, only the scarves must be fresh-looking and clean, as many women spoil the effect of extremely dainty toilettes by wearing either a soiled scarf or a very bedraggled piece of chiffon over the hair. Fascinators are dress accessories well within the scope and skill of the home worker, and many a dainty little head-covering may be fashioned at home from one or two lengths of lace, chiffon, or silk with very little trouble.

DRESS FOR THE WOMAN WORKER

The women workers in our large cities are apt to err most lamentably in regard to their dress in office hours. Girl typists will be seen dressed in light fluffy dresses with short sleeves and no collars, their dress liberally adorned with imitation jewellery, to say nothing of the ubiquitous row of pearls worn round the neck. Such a dress is thoroughly out of place in a business office, and the girl who adopts it will handicap herself a great deal when it comes to the question of seeking for a new post.

Appearances go for a great deal in business, as much in fact as under any other conditions of life. An employer will as often as not put down the girl who is tawdry in her appearance as apt to be tawdry in her work, and the post will therefore go to a girl who, though perhaps she may be less efficient as a worker, will create a more favourable impression by being suitably dressed. A neat coat and skirt costume is the ideal dress for the city worker, with an alternative in the serviceable costume recently suggested by the manager of one of London's largest drapery establishments as the most suitable wear for the woman in business. This consists of a neat Norfolk costume, made of good face cloth or serge for winter wear, and of butcher-blue linen or other similar material for summer wear, worn with a neat turn-down linen collar. The costume is a particularly dainty and effective one. In addition it looks trim and thoroughly in keeping with business or office surroundings.

COATS AND WRAPS

The rain coat is rapidly taking the place of the ubiquitous mackintosh for wear in wet weather. It has this advantage, it can take the place of an ordinary coat to perfection, and for this reason it is especially useful on showery days. Mackintoshes do not look well except when worn during an actual downpour; a brilliant burst of sunshine will make them look woefully out of keeping. Very often the wearer will not wish to discard her coat when the weather clears up, as she will most probably have donned her oldest garments in preparation for a very wet day. It is in these circumstances, then, that a rain coat is especially useful. Very good rain coats may be had in serviceable tweeds, covert coating and other materials, also in the material known as "Cravenette."

Motoring Coats.—It is useless to make an ordinary coat and skirt costume do duty for a long motor drive, such as from London to Brighton, for instance. A special motor coat is absolutely necessary. Very useful tweed and cloth motoring coats may be had at moderate prices. The coats are usually semi-fitting, and rainproof in most instances.

UNDERCLOTHING

Women are at length beginning to understand that good well-cut underclothing is essential to the neat fit of a dress, and in this respect what may be termed a regular revolution in regard to underwear has set in. One ofter hears elderly people sighing for the good old days when clothing was regulated as much by common sense as by the style of the moment. We doubt if such days ever existed—they certainly did not in regard to underclothing. It is interesting to read the remarks of fashion writers in books dealing with subjects of dress published about twenty years ago. One writer loudly decries the underwear of the time from the point of view of health. She points out that clothing to be hygienic must be light, and speaks in no measured terms of disapproval of the practice of cumbering the body with heavy garments as a protection against cold. She also deals with the increased bulkiness of the figure caused by the fastenings of those under-garments which were worn drawn into a very substantial fulness by means of tapes round the waist. "The weight of the garments should not fall from the waist," she complained; "all hygienic garments should be designed so that the weight falls from the shoulders." This writer proved a veritable prophet in her generation, for all sensible women nowadays plan out their underwear with due regard to the principles she advocated. We doubt if the change is due to the improved present-day knowledge of the principles of hygiene, rather may we ascribe it to the vagaries of "Dame Fashion," who at present decrees that the fashionable figure must be slim. Bulkiness of underwear is naturally incompatible with slimness of contour, and hence for the nonce fashion and hygiene are walking hand in hand.

Sensible people no longer cumber their bodies with heavy underwear; light woollen combinations and a warm flannel petticoat are all the extra clothing they adopt in very cold weather. Sometimes they discard the petticoat altogether, and wear neatly cut and warmly lined serge or satin knickers under their walking costumes. Corsets are also now built on hygienic lines; the wasp waist is happily a thing of the past, and we hope that it will remain buried in oblivion.

There are several makers of woollen underwear who vie with each other in the lightness of texture combined with the maximum of warmth to be found in the material of which their goods are manufactured. Silk, and mixtures of cotton and silk and wool and cotton, for winter underwear are also to be had in several makes, and make satisfactory winter wear for those who cannot stand the all-woollen garments next their skin. Ready-made under-garments may be had in almost every size. All the leading firms are making a special feature of "out sizes," by which is meant sizes to fit women with ultra-stout figures. The good needlewoman can now fashion her own underclothing with a great measure of success. Patterns of all styles and sizes of underwear may be had from almost all the ladies' fashion papers in liberal profusion; the veriest amateur can cut well-fitting garments from them, as they are extremely simple in design as a rule, and can easily be adapted to suit individual requirements.

Lingerie.—Fastidiousness in regard to "lingerie" is characteristic of the present day, and every woman is anxious that her underwear should be as neat and as dainty as possible. Formerly longcloth and calico were considered the materials "par excellence" for "lingerie" under-garments, and strength of make was held to be of much more importance than good cut and daintiness of design. Nowadays, the tendeny of the modern woman is to go to extremes of luxuriousness in the fineness and daintiness of her underwear, and to ignore as far as possible the question of serviceability.

This is as much a mistake as to make durability an apology for lack of daintiness, more especially where both good qualities can be so admirably combined. It is advisable to avoid all cheap makes of underwear characterised by the elaboration of their trimmings. It stands to reason that the material of these must be of the very cheapest to allow of such elaborate ornamentation, and in most cases the garments will not survive a few visits to the laundry. When you have only a very little money to spend in this direction, the plainer the article the better and the more serviceable will it turn out to be. Fine longcloth, batiste, lawn, nainsook are the favourite materials for underwear. Perhaps a good nainsook is the most satisfactory in regard to the combined qualities of daintiness and good wear. Dainty laces are used as trimmings on all the finer garments, which are also embellished by means of fine hand-embroidery and the finest needlework. Fabulous are the sums of money spent in this direction. Some very pretty and at the same time inexpensive underlinen may be had in the plain hand-embroidered work of the Irish and French peasants; night-dresses, chemises, drawers, combinations worked in this manner are sold at very moderate prices. Ribbons are now largely worn with under-garments. They usually are slotted through rows of embroidery or lace beading. Although ribbons may be purchased very cheaply nowadays, the fashion tends to be a somewhat extravagant one, as they seldom wash satisfactorily. Messrs. Cash of Coventry, however, have supplied a need in this direction by their washable ribbons for underwear which come out like new from the hands of the laundress. These ribbons can be obtained from any drapers at prices varying from 1s. 1d. to 3s. per dozen yards, according to width. The colours are warranted to be perfectly fast. For trimming home-made under-garments, the plain hem-stitched and lace frillings sold by this firm are also remarkable for their good quality and durability; beading, open-work insertions, and edgings of all kind particularly suitable for trimming dainty lingerie may be had at the most moderate prices. All Cash's trimmings are sold in twelve-yard lengths at prices varying from 1s. the piece and upwards.

Underskirts and Petticoats.—At one time a silk petticoat was deemed a luxury only within the reach of the most affluent. Nowadays well-cut silk underskirts for wear with dressy toilettes may be had at prices well within the reach of the average woman's purse. In this connection fashion is apt to change to a certain extent. Sometimes rustling silk underskirts are worn; at other times, as at the present moment, underskirts of soft silk or satin are more fashionable. White lace-trimmed and embroidered petticoats are the correct wear with summer muslins and linen dresses. These may be had cut in the princess style at very moderate prices.

The Princess Petticoat.—One of the most noteworthy outcomes of the change of fashion in regard to underwear is the "princess" petticoat. This garment, which consists of a camisole and underskirt in one, has come to stay, for it is so comfortable that few once having worn it will discard it.

It is made to fit closely to the figure, and all unnecessary fulness is done away with.

In regard to lingerie petticoats of this kind they are very useful for wear with muslin and other summer dresses, forming a complete underdress of themselves, and thus doing away altogether with the necessity for any kind of dress lining.

Another style of petticoat which has perfection of fit as its leading characteristic is that known as the "Leewig" petticoat. These petticoats consist of close-fitting cotton, stockingette or spun-silk tops with detachable flounces. The flounces fasten easily to the petticoat by means of patent fastening devices, and the effect on the whole is neat in the extreme. Flounces of every description may be had to go with these petticoats, ranging in price from 2s. 11d. to £5, 5s. The petticoat tops have the additional advantage of washing perfectly, and thus from the point of view of hygiene, as well as from the point of view of economy, a petticoat of the kind is a good investment. The Leewig petticoats are the patent of Messrs. Charles Lee and Co., Wigmore Street, London, and are made to measure free of any extra charge.

FURS

The wear of furs has become so ubiquitous that there is scarcely a woman nowadays who does not possess some piece of genuine peltry, however small, cherishing it as one of her most valuable possessions.

In choosing furs the woman of limited means will require to exercise no little care and discrimination; skins which will not last more than a season will be of no use to her, however inexpensive they may be. Her object should be to obtain inexpensive yet good furs with good wearing properties.

Bearskin is a fur which should at once find favour with the woman who has to practise economy in regard to her purchase. It is not only one of the least expensive of furs, but it is also one of the most durable, and, as far as the dark bearskin is concerned, one of the most universally becoming. The light bearskins are not much worn, for the reason that on account of their shade they do not suit many people.

Marmot runs bearskin very close in regard to both wear and economy in the original outlay. **Squirrel** is also an economical fur, its soft grey tints being especially becoming to dark-haired women, and fair women with very bright and clear complexions. This season, however, there is every indication of a rise in price of squirrel, owing to the vogue for grey furs which was one of the features of the winter season of 1910. **Opossum** is a good durable and very inexpensive fur, chiefly used for trimming coats, although it was also a great deal worn last season in the form of ties and muffs. **Beaver** is a useful fur which shows signs of coming into fashion again, although it has not been much worn during the last few seasons. **Moleskin** is an inexpensive and becoming fur, but it has the disadvantage of wearing badly. This is also the case with one of our most beautiful and at the same time one of our most fashionable furs—**Fox. Black Fox,** which is the most generally becoming of the fox varieties, being perhaps the worst in this respect; the smoked fox wearing better than either the black, silvered, or the white. The vogue for silver fox was specially marked last season. **Skunk** is a beautiful soft fur, somewhat after the appearance of dark bearskin, but much more expensive.

The black woolly furs **Astrachan** and **Persian Lamb** are very durable. Neat little ties and muffs of astrachan are quite moderate in price, but as the fashion at present inclines to very large stoles and enormous pillow muffs, a set of the kind in either of these furs would be fairly expensive.

Sable is one of the most expensive of furs, but at the same time it is one of the most durable; a good sable tie will last for years. The **Russian** sable is the best and the most costly. Next comes the **Canadian** sable, and last the **Kolinsky,** which is much cheaper than either the **Russian** or the **Canadian** varieties.

A new fur called **Fisher** was introduced last season. This is very like sable in appearance, with the exception that the skin contains a few white hairs. It may be purchased for the same price as Canadian sable. **Mink** is a good wearing fur, somewhat darker than sable. **Stone Marten** also wears well. **Chinchilla** is a soft delicate fur of a pretty grey shade. **Ermine,** the Royal fur, is one of the most beautiful and becoming of furs, though delicate and costly. **Sealskin** is a fur which will always be fashionable for those who can afford it. Undoubtedly the most beautiful of furs, its soft sheeny appearance is unrivalled, and there are few whom it does not suit. Its price is, however, prohibitive to many—a good long sealskin coat being rarely obtainable for less than £100. There has been a great vogue during the last season, however, for seal musquash and seal coney, both of which, more especially the seal musquash, resemble the real seal in appearance. Seal coney is the less expensive of the two, and has been largely worn both in the form of coats and stole and muff sets.

The woman with little money to spend on furs cannot do better than purchase a good bearskin, marmot, or squirrel set. A fairly good dark fox stole and muff may be had for £7, 7s., but the bad wearing properties of the fox are usually against it. It is better to purchase all furs from a good furrier, as necessarily the quality of the skins will depend to a great extent upon the establishment at which they are bought. It is impossible to give any exact figures as to the prices of furs, as these are continually fluctuating. In regard to imitation furs, white foxaline or imitation fox sets may be purchased for a sum of about £2, 2s. Their appearance is very good indeed, the white foxaline resembling the real fur very closely, and in this respect it is superior to most other imitation furs.

It is always better to send good furs to a furrier to be cleaned in preference to sending them to an ordinary cleaner. Furriers remodel, reline, and renovate furs at very moderate prices, and often store them for the winter free of charge, if they are entrusted with work of the kind. (For Care of Furs, see p. 315.)

HATS, BONNETS AND VEILS

In her headgear, even more perhaps than in her dress, is a woman inclined to go astray when slavishly following the dictates of fashion. Thus the grotesque spectacle presented by a diminutive specimen of womanhood wearing a hat of immense proportions, the brim being so large as to completely hide her neck at the back, is only too common at the present day. Cartoonists may hold her up to ridicule, humorists may launch their wit at her expense—but all without avail. Her hat is of the latest fashion, so she feels quite happy, and goes her own sweet way.

A woman of taste shuns all extreme styles in millinery as in dress. Whatever the fashion of the moment, it is always open to modification, and headgear of at least a moderate style is always to be had. A woman has no excuse therefore for making herself grotesque.

One important thing to be remembered is that headgear should always be as light as possible. Heavy, stiff, ill-ventilated millinery is most injurious to the health of the hair. Although on the cold snowy days of winter there is nothing more becoming than the toque of fur, fur as a head-covering is not hygienic, more especially as fur toques are apt to fit very closely to the head. Young men become prematurely bald because their headgear is stiff and unhygienic, and unfortunately for them the styles of their hats vary but little in their essential points. There is such an abundance of choice in a woman's millinery that she need never choose a hat which by reason of its heaviness and its very close fit is unhygienic. A woman's millinery should therefore always be chosen with due regard to the all-essential quality of lightness. Heavy headgear if persistently worn will in time cause injury to the best head of hair.

A woman's hat should always be in keeping with her dress. Thus a neat toque or turban or a medium-sized hat plainly trimmed is the ideal hat to wear with a "tailor-made." Simple picture hats are suited to light cotton and muslin dresses, whilst more elaborate hats of all shapes are worn with smart afternoon toilettes, and all very dressy gowns for dressy occasions. A picture hat would be quite out of place on a motor drive or on a steamboat, be it said. For motoring distinctive motoring millinery should always be worn. Motor hats and bonnets are not now the hideous things they were when motoring first came into fashion. Indeed, a pretty face seldom looks prettier than when seen under a becoming motor hat (or bonnet) and veil. For wet weather special waterproof silk hoods are made to cover the hat or bonnet. These may be had at a price of from 10s. 6d. and upwards. Motor veils are also largely worn round the headgear on board ship and on stormy days at the seaside; indeed, there is no fashion introduced within recent years that has proved more useful than the motor veil. Both when motoring and on board ship, or on gusty days at the seaside, it serves the double purpose of keeping the hat on and keeping the hair tidy. With a motor veil well tied round one's hat, a gusty day is robbed of most of its discomfort to the feminine sex in the way of hat-pins falling out, hats blowing off, and tresses becoming loosened and falling about one's face in not always "picturesque" disorder. (For Home Millinery, see p. 432.)

Bonnets.—The bonnet, in the true sense of the word, has had its day. Formerly it was practically *de rigueur* for a woman as soon as she married to discard the youthful-looking hat for the more sober-looking bonnet, as a sign that she had attained the dignity of matronhood. Nowadays the old-time bonnet is only worn by elderly people, with the addition perhaps of the more old-fashioned matrons who still adhere to the traditions of their youth. Now and again there come signs of the reappearance of the bonnet in the millinery world, but these only herald the tentative advent of some picturesque styles taken from similarly picturesque periods, styles as a rule only becoming to very young faces, and for this reason usually short-lived.

For elderly people the present-day styles in bonnet wear are a great improvement upon those formerly in vogue. Dainty silk and lace creations are to be had trimmed with jet, ribbon, ostrich tips and other appropriate trimmings. The art of millinery is employed towards making them as youthful-looking as is compatible with the age of their wearers.

Veils.—Veils are not now the all-important adjunct of dress they were in former years. At the present day their wear is practically optional, limited to those whom they suit. The style of wearing veils is materially altered. A few years ago they were worn quite closely round the face, whilst now they are allowed to fall loosely from the hat, and when worn with large picture hats are becoming to most faces. The style is a great improvement from the point of view of the eyesight; the tightly skinned veil was most trying to the eyes, and even now large patterns and spots should be avoided. Dainty veilings may be had in many makes, the plainer the pattern and the finer the net the better for the eyesight. Large patterns on a veil are always injurious. When taken off, a veil should be pulled out smoothly, and wound round a piece of cardboard before being put away, or else rolled up carefully, the ends being kept even. When veils are to be worn with very large hats, their adjustment is much simplified by making a narrow hem at the top, and running very narrow ribbon through this. In this way the veil can be made to gather upon the ribbon, which is drawn tightly over the brim of the hat and tied at the back. Veils may now be worn to fall loosely over the chin, a fashion which much simplifies their arrangement.

GLOVES, BOOTS, AND SHOES

"One can always tell a lady by her gloves and by her shoes" is a familiar saying, and, like most familiar sayings, it has a very substantial amount of truth. To be "down at heel" is perhaps the worst form of shabbiness, and the woman who goes about with holes in her gloves advertises the fact that she is lacking in that refinement and neatness of dress by which a gentlewoman is always characterised. There are many false economies habitually practised by various households; but of all false economies, economy in footwear is apt to become the dearest in the long-run. Cheap boots are usually made of hard unyielding material; they are not only answerable for corns, bunions, blisters, and other similar ills, but their soles are little more effective than brown paper in resisting damp and wet—consequently many a severe chill and illness can be traced to their wear. In addition they lose their shape very quickly and require to be soon renewed. It is better to pay a good price for all boots and shoes, and the result will be much more satisfactory in the long-run. There should not be much difficulty in getting ready-made boots to fit nowadays, when half and even quarter sizes are to be had. The Americans have been largely responsible for this welcome innovation in regard to size, and American boots and shoes are, as a rule, neat and well fitting. One particularly good American make of boot, known under the trademark of the "Sorosis," has become very popular. The Sorosis boots and shoes are well cut and keep their shape very well. They may be had for the modest price of 16s. 6d., and are good for any amount of hard wear. Several good makes of walking shoes can be had for from 10s. 6d. and upwards. The cult of the "small" foot is not as universal as it was a few years ago. The greater participation by women in outdoor exercise, games and athletics is in a large way responsible for this, and women seldom nowadays are seen to attempt to squeeze their feet into shoes one or two sizes too small for them. A woman with a naturally large foot would, however, do well to always wear her boots with toe-caps, as these diminish the apparent size of the foot; she should never wear brown and other light-coloured boots or shoes, as they have exactly the opposite effect. Boots with very high heels and pointed toes should be avoided.

Evening Shoes are worn to match the dress. They are usually of leather, suede or satin. Satin shoes are the most fashionable at the present moment. Gold and Silver leather evening shoes are also very smart, and can be worn with almost any evening gown. (For painting white shoes gold or silver, see p. 318.)

Goloshes.—Rubber goloshes are very useful to slip over the boots and shoes in wet weather, in order to keep the feet perfectly dry. They may be had as complete overshoes or half goloshes; the latter cover the sole and toe-cap of the boot, only fitting over the heel by means of a piece of broad elastic.

The prices of goloshes vary slightly with the price of rubber; usually 2s. 11d. will buy a pair of goloshes, whilst half goloshes may be had for even less.

Snowboots.—Snowboots are not much worn in England; they should, however, form part of the equipment of every woman who contemplates going to Canada or other colonies where the snowfall is great. For wintering in Switzerland and other similar places their wear is also essential. They are made of cloth, usually trimmed with fur, and have india-rubber soles. They are slipped over the boot in snowy weather. They are not costly, and it is always useful to have a pair by for winter in case of an unusually heavy snowfall.

Creaking Boots.—Well-made boots rarely creak; the creaking boot or shoe is usually one of an inferior quality. Standing the boots overnight in salt and water, using just sufficient cold water to cover the soles after rubbing a little oil well into the leather, has often remedied this annoying defect. If this treatment does not do good at first, repeat for two or three nights.

Gloves.—Kid and suede gloves are those used for smart wear. In the summer silk and cotton ones may be worn with light dresses. The fashion in gloves varies to a large extent. Sometimes very long elbow-length gloves are worn in the daytime. At other times they are only worn to cover the hands and wrists. Their length of course depends altogether on the length of sleeves to gowns which is the fashion of the moment. The fashion of short sleeves to gowns is always liable to recur at regular intervals, more especially for the summer season, and glove-makers have therefore to carefully watch the trend of fashion before planning their stock. For evening wear, long gloves are nearly always in fashion—the long white suede and kid gloves being always appropriate wear for light toilettes and black gloves for black toilettes, although evening gloves are always worn as far as possible to match the gown, and may be had in most of the delicate evening shades.

In regard to the colour of gloves for outdoor wear, fashions are also constantly changing. At one time the various shades of tan were considered appropriate wear for all occasions in the daytime. Subsequently white kid gloves were *de rigueur* for afternoon and dressy toilettes. At the present time the tendency is as far as possible for the gloves to match the gown, and gloves are now manufactured in almost every conceivable shade. This is a fashion which may be carried to extremes of luxury beyond the reach of the modest purse, and for this reason it is not likely to become general. Light-coloured gloves, however, such as light beaver, biscuit colour, white, should be worn on dressy occasions.

From the point of view of economy, kid gloves are more useful than suede—the latter are apt to wear into holes more quickly, and do not look so fresh as kid gloves once they have been in the hands of the cleaners. Gloves should always be well fitting, and care should be taken to select those of the right size. Tight gloves are responsible for red hands and arms, whilst gloves which are too large give an air of untidiness to their wearer. Great care must be taken in putting on gloves for the first time, for on this will to a large extent depend their appearance on subsequent occasions. Never put on a new pair of gloves hurriedly—work all the fingers into the glove fingers before putting in the thumb, and above all see that the seams are not twisted, but that they are all in place. It is as well to rest the elbow on the table while gently putting on the glove. A little powder dusted into the fingers of the gloves before putting them on will often make them go on more easily. The buttons of new gloves should always be firmly stitched on before they are worn. One or two buttons will usually be found to be loose, and this is a very necessary precaution if neatness is desired. A very small piece of cotton wool placed inside the finger-tips of silk gloves will often prevent holes from coming as quickly as they are wont to do with gloves of this kind. All kid and suede gloves should be sent to the cleaners when dirty, home cleaning of gloves is unsatisfactory as a rule, and as gloves are cleaned for the small sum of 2d. a pair nowadays, the bother of cleaning them at home is hardly worth while. (For washing silk and cotton gloves, see p. 295.)

If after taking off delicate kid gloves they are stretched out straight and put away flat between sheets of tissue or other clean paper, they will keep their shape much better, and their wear will be materially prolonged.

STOCKINGS

Cashmere stockings make the most satisfactory all-the-year-round wear ; warm, closely woven cashmere stockings for the winter, and a much lighter texture for the summer. Large worked silk patterns on stockings are no longer fashionable. The finer the texture of the stockings the smarter are they supposed to be for present-day wear. Very finely woven lisle thread hose are much in fashion at the moment. These are quite plain without any pattern, excepting perhaps a small black silk clock which runs up the side of the leg. The effect is that of fine silk, and as lisle thread is much cheaper than the former material, it has to a great extent superseded it for dressy wear amongst people of moderate means, though silk hosiery undoubtedly is the acme of " dressiness " for very smart occasions.

Those who wear lisle thread hose would always do well to see that the soles and heels are of cashmere. Stockings of this description can be had in a great many makes, and from the point of view of both wear and comfort are far superior to those which are of lisle thread throughout.

Open-work lisle thread stockings are no longer so fashionable as they were. Although they are still largely worn, plain lisle thread stockings are considered smarter in every way. Those who suffer from tender feet, corns, &c., should never wear any other than cashmere or light woollen stockings.

Suspenders.—As a means of keeping up the stockings, suspenders are much more satisfactory than garters. They are more hygienic, inasmuch as they do not tend to restrict the circulation as in the case of a band of elastic drawn tightly round the leg. Suspenders now form an integral part of nearly all the new makes of corsets, and besides keeping up the hose, serve in a certain measure to keep the corset in place and so help to support the figure.

It is always well to ensure that the studs of the suspenders are surrounded by some soft silk or kid covering, otherwise they are apt to tear the stockings, forming what is known as a " ladder." Some stockings are manufactured with a small portion of the upper part of the leg of different and stronger material from the rest of the stocking. Stockings built in this way effectively resist the strain of the heaviest suspenders. Failing this, it is a good plan, if the stockings are fairly long in the legs, to double them over slightly at the top before fixing the suspenders. When thus doubled over they resist the strain of the suspenders much better than when they are put on in the ordinary way.

THE ACCESSORIES OF DRESS

It is in the accessories of her dress as much as in any other detail that the well-dressed woman justifies her reputation as such. With her, pins are not made to do duty for hooks and eyes, and there is never that ugly gap between waistband and skirt which is so often characteristic of the blouse and skirt toilette of the untidy woman. She is well up to date in such trifles as waistbands and dainty neck-wear, realising that even a gown which has seen better days may be effectively smartened by the freshness of such little details as lace jabots, pretty ties, or any other similar dainty trifles which may be the fashion of the moment. In one important detail the well-dressed woman holds her own. The fit of the collar of her gown is always above reproach. There is nothing that tends to impart an air of untidiness in dress more than an ill-fitting collar. The collars of ready-made blouses, for instance, run in certain sizes, and are apt to be too large on some women. Yet these women will seldom think of altering the collar before wearing the blouse, and the result is that they never achieve the effect of looking really smart. The fit and cut of the collar of a gown is not the least important adjunct to its style, and the well-dressed woman realises this. In the matter of collars, fashion is apt to show strange vagaries. One season they will be worn high, almost to the ears—at another gowns will be innocent of even the pretence of a collar band. One word of warning to the middle-aged woman in this direction. Very stiff and tight-fitting collars are injurious to the neck, causing it to become lined, and often making the skin of an unbecoming yellow colour ; these, like all other extremes of fashion, should be avoided. On the other hand, a woman who is getting on in years should always have a collar of some kind to her gowns. This need not be too high, but it should always be of medium height—the lower her collar the more it will detract from her appearance. Collarless bodices in the daytime are only becoming to the very young. This is a rule to be observed whatever the tendency of fashion. At the time of writing, what are known as the " Peter Pan " and " Claudine " collars are much in vogue. The Peter Pan is a plain turn-down collar of embroidery, net or lace; the Claudine collar is a pleated collar of the same shape and materials. Both are worn with blouses which are innocent of neckbands. This style of collar is very becoming to young girls of the " pensionnaire " style with round faces and full throats, but when adopted by the dowager of fifty it only succeeds in making her look absurd. Elderly women should avail themselves of the fashion for dainty net and chiffon frilling, which sewn on to the collar has a most softening effect upon even the most faded and wrinkled faces.

There has been indeed during the whole of the year 1910 such a variety of becoming neckwear to choose from, that the elderly woman has really had no excuse for succumbing to the vogue for the Peter Pan.

Dainty lace, net and muslin jabots have been introduced in endless variety, their coming into fashion being due to a large extent to the very deep and low openings with which the fronts of tailor-made coats were cut. The lace jabot has proved such a dainty dress accessory that the opinion may be hazarded that it will still hold its own, at any rate for wear with indoor toilettes. These jabots are simple of design and easy of construction, and the clever home worker may easily fashion them from any odd bit of lace, muslin, or net which she may discover in her odds-and-ends bag. Many women still keep to the neat linen collars and cuffs for wear with morning shirt blouses. It must be remembered, however, that these are only suitable for morning indoor and outdoor wear. For the afternoon something more dressy is required. Linen collars should fit as loosely as is compatible with neatness, and they should never be worn too high. The constant wearing of stiffly starched high collars is very bad for the neck, causing lines and discoloration of the skin.

JEWELLERY

Love of jewellery is innate with almost all womankind. Perhaps it is inherited from that passion for all kinds of ornaments displayed by our more remote and barbaric ancestors. It is certainly typical of the savage of to-day as shown in his love of gaudy bead ornaments and everything bright and glittering. The love of jewellery, therefore, is most certainly a barbaric instinct, but none the less it is an instinct which we most of us possess.

Her passion for jewellery will often make a woman err seriously in regard to good taste. In no respect can vulgarity or ostentation be more glaringly shown than in regard to an inordinate display of brooches, rings, bangles and other ornaments of the kind. Often at fashionable restaurants a woman will be seen with diamond rings half covering every finger of both hands, sometimes not even excluding the thumbs. Such a display may certainly be indicative of her wealth, but it serves even more to emphasise her lack of refinement and good breeding. Very little jewellery should be worn in the morning. Diamonds are totally out of place with a morning gown; with the exception of her engagement ring, which a woman never discards, she should keep diamond ornaments for afternoon and evening wear. A great display of jewellery in the daytime is never in good taste. For evening wear, however, one's taste for jewellery may be indulged, only excess of ornamentation should be avoided.

Brooches, pendants and bangles should be in keeping as far as possible. For instance, one should avoid wearing a turquoise necklet at the same time as an amethyst brooch and a ruby bangle. Pearls and turquoises go very well together, as do diamonds and opals—diamonds, in fact, go well with most stones. They are most becoming as a rule to brunettes and dark-haired women generally, whilst pearls are the ideal stone for fair women, and more especially for young girls. Jet jewellery is worn with very deep mourning.

There seems to be an inclination nowadays for women who cannot afford good jewellery to go in to a great extent for various imitations and shams. This is a very great mistake. Sham jewellery is yet another unfailing sign of vulgarity. If a woman cannot afford diamonds and precious stones she should be content with plain gold. It is better to possess a very little good jewellery than an abundance of paste and other imitation ornaments.

Care of Jewellery.—All plain gold bangles, bracelets, brooches and other articles of jewellery may be cleaned by washing in a lather of soap and water. They should be well dried with a towel, and gentle rubbing with chamois leather will serve to give an additional polish. Diamonds may be cleaned by rubbing with eau-de-Cologne. If very dirty, they may first be brushed gently with warm water and a little soap. The preparation known as "jewellers' rouge," to be obtained from the jewellers, is very good for polishing gold and diamond ornaments. Pearls and turquoises should never be allowed to go into water; turquoises in particular are liable to lose their colour if exposed to the wet. These stones can be cleaned with methylated spirits. Opals are stones which require particular care; they should never be exposed to too much heat, as this often makes them crack. They should be cleaned with powder, to be obtained from the jewellers for the purpose.

For cleaning jewellery set with small pearls, rub well with a chamois leather, and if very dirty, apply a little whiting with a small brush. Little boxes containing chamois leather and cleaning material for jewellery can be bought at any of the large stores. Jet may be cleaned by rubbing with olive oil and polishing with a chamois leather.

If before putting on any article of jewellery, the wearer would take the trouble to polish it gently with a clean chamois leather, she would find that it would keep clean for a much longer period.

SYMBOLISM OF STONES

The *Diamond* signifies light, innocence, life and joy.

The *Ruby*—divine power and love, dignity and royalty.

The *Carbuncle*—blood and suffering.

The *Sardius*—martyrdom.

The *Sapphire*—all heavenly virtues.

The *Topaz*—divine goodness and human faithfulness.

The *Emerald*—hopes of immortality.

The *Amethyst*—earthly sufferings and truth unto death.

The *Pearl*—purity, innocence and humility.

CARE OF CLOTHES

Care of Outdoor Clothes.—A woman who takes care of her clothes always manages to look tidy and neat, whatever the limitations of her purse, and she can eke out her dress allowance much more successfully than her careless sister who, either through ignorance or natural untidiness, fails to get the proper amount of wear out of her garments, which very soon lose their pristine freshness.

In respect to outdoor costumes, one sensible rule should invariably be observed. Never wear an outdoor skirt in the house if you wish it to keep in proper shape. Make a rule of changing it as soon as you come in from a walk; there is nothing more calculated to make a tailor-made skirt lose its shape and become shabby than constantly sitting about in it and wearing it indoors.

All cloth and serge dresses should be brushed directly they are taken off. The garment should first be brushed with a good whisk brush to get the dust off, then it should be laid on a table and brushed with a moderately hard clothes-brush, a hard brush being used to remove any mud from round the hem, and a soft brush to remove the dust from silk or velvet trimmings. Soft brushes should always be used for very fine cloth and velvet. Combined soft and hard clothes-brushes may be had, the bristles being hard on one side of the brush and soft on the other.

On a wet day particular care should be taken to change the outdoor dress. Letting alone all questions of catching cold through keeping on damp clothing, a skirt will become hopelessly creased-looking if worn when it is wet. It should be taken off at once, and hung up to dry in a warm atmosphere. If very much creased, however, it will require ironing with a moderately warm iron on the wrong side of the material to take the creases out. Dry skirts which are slightly creased should be hung out in the open air, or near—but not too near—the fire. The wear of tailor-made garments will be materially prolonged if they are sent occasionally to the tailor's to be pressed. A tailor's charges for pressing are not heavy, and more especially in the case of a pleated skirt which has become very damp and creased, a visit to the tailor will give it a new lease of life. There are many working tailors in a small way of trade who charge very little for pressing and renovating garments from time to time, repairing buttons and attending to other little details which require attention to keep the garment trim and neat. A tailor will also have all the necessary pressing appliances, and the result will be more satisfactory in every way than if the dress were ironed at home.

Care of Indoor Dresses.—Indoor dresses also require their share of attention. The busy woman need not wear an untidy or slovenly appearance in the house because she has domestic duties to attend to. She should keep a special workaday gown, it is true, but this should always be trim and neat. A plain butcher-blue linen with turn-down collar and tie makes an admirable house dress for morning wear in the summer; a neat plainly cut blouse and skirt serves an equal purpose in the winter. The linen dress could be one of these plain-cut princess gowns known as "tub frocks," which are likely to remain long with us on account of their extreme usefulness.

Overalls and Aprons.—The housewife should take the additional precaution of wearing an overall which will completely cover her gown whilst engaged in any housework. An overall is especially handy also to slip over an afternoon gown in the event of any light household task cropping up in the afternoon, and also in the event of cooking or superintending the cooking in the evening. It is better to have long sleeves to the overall if possible, though many women prefer overalls and aprons of the daintier sleeveless types. For light work one of these latter is quite sufficient. They may be bought in several styles from 2s. 11d. upwards, or can be easily made at home by even the amateur needlewoman.

Putting Clothes Away.—Dresses and skirts which when taken off are thrown carelessly over the backs of chairs, or are hung up one on top of another behind doors, very soon become soiled and shabby-looking. Cloth and serge dresses should be well shaken and brushed when taken off in the manner already described, and then hung up in a cupboard or wardrobe, the coats suspended on coat-hangers, and the skirts hung up by their loops. There should always be two loops for hanging sewn inside the waistband of the skirt. This helps a great deal to preserve the "hang" of the garment—one loop is not sufficient for the purpose. Some very simple combined coat and skirt hangers may now be had from the most of the leading drapers for the trifling cost of a few pence, and it is as well to use these where possible.

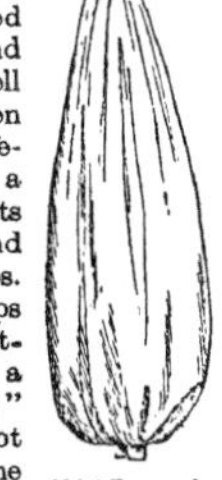

Skirt-Bag and Hanger.

Light-coloured skirts and all best skirts should be hung up in thin muslin or cotton bags made to open down the front. Several drapery firms sell combined hangers and skirt-bags at moderate prices. An old white petticoat can be admirably made to answer the purpose of a skirt-bag by drawing it in at the top.

Impromptu Cupboards.—In some small houses and flats where every inch of space is valuable, there is little room for heavy furniture such as wardrobes, and very often there are no cupboards provided, so that the putting away of clothes becomes a real problem, which is not always readily solved.

The clever woman is seldom at a loss, however, even in this emergency. Where there is an alcove or recess in the wall, for instance, she can, with the aid of two boards of wood for shelves, some dress-hooks and a few yards of chintz, make an excellent little impromptu cupboard. One shelf is placed at the requisite height from the floor, say six or seven feet, to form the top of the cupboard; the other shelf is placed a few inches from the floor. The chintz curtain is hung from the top of the cupboard to the floor, and is made to draw backwards and forwards. The dress-hooks are fitted to the top shelf, whilst boots and shoes and hat boxes may be put on the lower shelf, the cupboard being sufficiently high for the purpose. Odd corners in the room can also be utilised for hanging dresses by nailing a board with some dress-hooks across and covering the corner with a curtain. This method is not, however, so satisfactory as the alcove cupboard, and clothes should only be placed there temporarily to get them out of the way.

Curtains of impromptu cupboards of the kind should be thoroughly well dusted every day. Ottomans are also very handy articles to have in flats, and any small carpenter will put one together for a trifling sum. Covered with pretty light-coloured chintzes, they make very dainty-looking additions to the furniture of the room, and their usefulness in regard to the putting away of linen, clothes or hats is undoubted.

Silk Dresses and Underskirts.—Silk dresses should be carefully wiped over with a clean cloth before being put away. Stiff silk underskirts should never be folded away in a drawer, as the silk is liable to split at the folds. They should always be hung up. Starched cotton and muslin dresses should be folded away neatly and put in drawers. If hung up they will soon become limp and lose their freshness.

Hats should be brushed with a soft hat brush every time they are taken off, and put away on hat shelves in the cupboard or wardrobe, or else in a hat box, and well covered over with tissue paper. For travelling, special leather hat boxes fitted with cushions for a number of hats should be used. These can be had for from 12s. 6d. and upwards. If the hats have to be placed on the top tray of an ordinary trunk, it is a good plan to pin them to the canvas of the tray by means of hat-pins; this will prevent them from getting knocked about and tumbled.

Umbrellas should never be opened out to dry when wet. They should be turned upside down, resting on the handle. They should not be left tightly rolled up when not in use, or the covering will wear into holes at the folds. It is never a good plan to leave an umbrella in the hall stand. Very often another umbrella will be pushed through it by mistake, especially if the stand is overcrowded. A good way of keeping umbrellas is to make a case of holland or canvas to hold the number required, and hang it up inside the door of a cupboard or wardrobe where it will take up little or no room, placing the umbrellas inside.

For travelling, special umbrella-cases of leather or waterproof canvas should be used, if there are a number of umbrellas to be taken. These cases may be had at prices varying from 3s. 4d. and upwards.

Boots and Shoes should always be kept on trees when not in use, and they will retain their shape much longer. Wet boots should not be placed too near the fire to dry, or the leather will crack. Place them at once on trees and stand them in a warm dry place. Where there are no boot-trees available, it is a good plan to stuff the boots with pieces of old newspaper. It is always better to have two or three pairs of boots in constant wear, and not to keep on wearing one pair day after day until they become worn out.

Never allow boots or shoes to become "down at heel." Send them to be repaired as soon as the heels show signs of wear. Boots and shoes should not be left lying about under the bed or upon the bedroom floor. If there is not a place for them at the bottom of the dress cupboard, a little boot cupboard may easily be fashioned out of an old wine-case or orange-box. This should be varnished or enamelled, stood on its side against the wall, and a piece of chintz made to draw across it to form a miniature curtain cupboard. There will be room for a plank of wood to be fixed in the centre of the box, and the boots can be placed on the shelf thus formed, and at the bottom of the box. Boots which have to be stored for any length of time should be well vaselined before they are put away.

STORING WINTER AND SUMMER CLOTHES

Before putting away winter or summer clothes at the end of the season they should be well sorted out, and any garments that will not again be required should be given away or otherwise disposed of. It is an unwise policy to hoard up old soiled and disused garments which can never be worn again, more especially to keep them with other good garments. To do this in the case of cloth or woollen clothing is practically to invite the depredations of the moth. All serge, cloth, tweed and woollen dresses should be well beaten and thoroughly brushed with a good clothes-brush and then hung out in the open air for a few hours before being packed away. Nothing should ever be put away dirty, and care should be taken that all the garments are thoroughly dry, as mildew is apt to form upon clothes which are put away damp for any extended period. All the necessary cleaning and repairing should be done before laying clothing aside for the season.

Plenty of tissue paper should be placed between the folds of light silk and satin dresses, and stuffed into the sleeves to make them keep their shape. All cotton and muslin dresses should be washed and rough dried before being put away. White cotton and muslin dresses should be rinsed in blue water to keep them a good colour. No starch should be allowed to remain in any cotton dress that is put aside for the winter. When quite dry, fold the garments away carefully. If white garments are folded between sheets of blue tissue paper this will help to preserve their colour.

Furs.—Before putting furs away they should be well beaten with a very light cane or riding-whip to free them from dust; then they should be hung out in the open air for several hours.

They should not be put away damp, as damp, like dust, renders them liable to the attacks of the moth. They should be well powdered with cayenne pepper and then placed in thick brown holland bags, which, in their turn, should be sewn up in brown paper. Camphor or naphthaline sewn up in tiny muslin sachets and placed inside the holland bag with the furs may be used instead of the cayenne pepper. Camphor is very popular as a moth preventive, but naphthaline is much more effective, only its clinging odour is somewhat against it for this purpose. Some strips of Russian leather placed in the bag with the furs will also be found useful in resisting the inroads of the moth. It is an advantage if the furs can occasionally be taken out of their coverings in the summer and hung out in the sunshine. In fact, where there is sufficient wardrobe and cupboard accommodation to allow of their being hung up with plenty of space, and where the cupboard is warm and dry and free from damp, it will be quite sufficient to put them away in the cupboard without packing them, taking them out and shaking them as often as possible. A few balls of naphthaline might be placed upon the cupboard shelvec.

Fur-lined coats and cloaks should be well sprinkled with cayenne pepper and stored in special boxes lined with tar paper. Chinchilla is too delicate a fur to be either beaten or shaken.

In the case of really valuable furs, it is much better to send them away to a furrier to be cleaned and stored for the winter. The charges for fur warehousing are moderate, and the freedom from anxiety afforded by the knowledge that they are in expert care is well worth the small outlay entailed.

CARE OF MEN'S CLOTHES

Men's garments soon become shabby-looking if they are not properly cared for. Coats, waistcoats and trousers should be well brushed when taken off, and then carefully folded or hung in a wardrobe. Trousers should be placed in trouser-presses, or if these are not available they should be pulled out lengthwise, folded down the front of the leg and folded over before being put

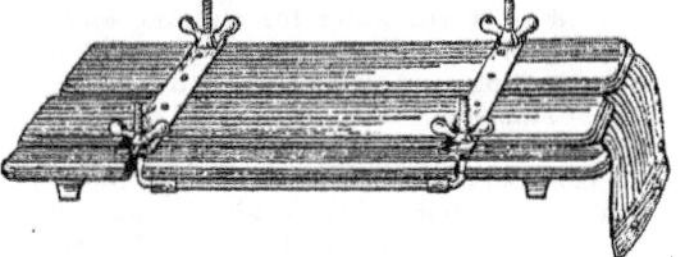

Trouser-Press.

away. A very good plan is to place the trousers so folded under the mattress of a bed, as the pressure thus afforded answers the same purpose as that of trouser-stretchers, and helps to prevent them from becoming baggy at the knees. Laying a damp cloth over the trousers after they have been folded down the front of the leg, and then carefully pressing them with a moderately warm iron is also effective. They should only be folded down the front before being ironed, and not folded over until afterwards. Coats and overcoats should be hung on hangers. Small single hangers can be had from any draper for from 2d. upwards.

Mending.—All men's garments should be kept in thorough repair; that is to say, all the small mending, such as sewing on buttons, repairing button-holes, darning underlinen and socks, should be regularly attended to. As men's socks are sold in so many different colours nowadays, it is always a good plan when buying new socks to buy at the same time wool to match them. It is a wise plan to stretch the heels and toes of socks and lightly darn them before use; they will be found to wear much longer in this way. (For general hints on Mending, see p. 407.)

All flannel and linen under-garments should be carefully gone over when they return from the laundry, and buttons sewn on and any other necessary small repairs executed before they are put away, as nothing is more annoying to a man when taking clean clothes from his chest of drawers to find that there are buttons lacking or holes undarned. Frayed collars and cuffs of shirts should be neatly clipped with a sharp pair of scissors. If the linen fronts and collars and cuffs of shirts have become very shabby and worn, they can be sent to have new fronts made. Most laundresses will undertake this renovating work for quite moderate charges. If, however, the shirts should be of the cheapest kinds sold, it might pay better to buy new ones. Cheap underwear is even a greater mistake with men than with women. Shirts in particular require so much treatment in the way of dressing and glazing at the hands of the laundress, that the very cheap kinds never wear satisfactorily, neither do they ever look as well when laundered as the better garments. (For Washing Shirts, see p. 295.)

Renovating Shabby Coats, Waistcoats, and Trousers.—There is nothing like rock ammonia dissolved in warm water for cleaning and renovating men's garments which have become shabby-looking and shiny. Use a good-sized lump of ammonia to about a pint of water, and when it has dissolved dip a clean whisk brush, or a clothes-brush with firm bristles, into the solution and thoroughly brush the garment; then hang in the open air to dry. If pressing is required, do this with a moderately warm iron, ironing the garments under clean brown paper. Velvet coat collars can also be cleaned by carefully sponging with ammonia solution.

Rents and tears in men's coats, overcoats, waistcoats or trousers cannot be satisfactorily darned at home. The garments should be sent to a *stoppeur* who is able to match the thread of the tweed or cloth, and repair the garment in such a manner that the darn is imperceptible.

Hats should be carefully brushed every day with a soft hat-brush. After being out in the rain the surface of a silk hat will often become rough and untidy-looking. To remedy this, pass a hat-brush which has been damped with cold water gently round the hat in the direction of the nap. This will distribute the moisture evenly. When the whole hat is thoroughly damped, brush evenly round with a hard brush. Leave the hat for a few hours, and when it is thoroughly dry, brush with the soft hat-brush as usual.

When a silk hat has become dull-looking through constant wear, it should be sent to the hatter's to be ironed. This is usually done for a very moderate charge, and is more satisfactory than ironing at home. Sometimes, however, brushing with a hot brush will have the required effect. Silk hats which have become soiled and greasy can be cleaned with a piece of clean flannel dipped in a solution of ammonia and water; gently wipe this round the hat in the direction of the nap. The whole cleaning and ironing process will be undertaken by a hatter for a trifling consideration. They also do the work very promptly, usually getting the hat ready while the customer waits. On the whole, a great deal of trouble is saved in this way. Felt hats are also cleaned with ammonia.

Boots and Shoes should not be allowed to litter a man's dressing-room. A small trunk or suit-case stand usually forms part of every dressing-room equipment. The suit-case is

Suit-Case Stand.

placed on the top of this, and the boots neatly ranged on the shelf underneath. Failing this, they should be put away in a cupboard or on shelves made for the purpose. All the boots should be placed on trees when not in wear, and if put away for any length of time, they should be well vaselined to prevent the leather from cracking.

Ties and Collars.—Collars should be kept in special round collar-boxes; ties should be folded neatly when taken off, and put away in a tie-case.

CLEANING AND DYEING

Cleaning and dyeing play an important part in the renovation of clothes, and old garments should not be thoughtlessly cast aside before the possibilities in this direction have been well weighed and considered. A dyed dress may be renovated and altered in more ways than one, so much so as to present the appearance of a totally new garment. Where a woman is an adapt at fashioning her own gowns, she will be able to effect much saving in this way. If, however, she has to have all her dressmaking done for her, then before planning extensive renovations of the kind, she would do well to take pencil and paper and calculate exactly what it will cost her. In addition to the dyer's account, dressmakers' charges will be found to considerably swell the sum total, which would in these circumstances sometimes amount to almost the cost of a new garment. For this reason a woman should either carry out the renovating of dyed garments herself, or if she is unable to do this, she should engage a good visiting dressmaker and needlewoman by the day and help her with it. It does not always pay to send out renovations unless the dress was originally a very expensive one. Dressmakers as a rule have not much liking for this work, they prefer new and more straightforward dressmaking; and for this reason, apart from the question of expense, their work in this direction is seldom satisfactory. There are exceptions to this rule, of course, but one is more liable to come across the rule than the exceptions.

Formerly to send clothes to the dyers or cleaners was somewhat of an undertaking, as each garment had to be religiously unpicked and taken to pieces, and when it came back from the cleaners, there was all the work and worry of putting it together again. Nowadays cleaners undertake to clean garments of the most elaborate character without so much as unpicking a stitch of them. Cleaning has, in fact, been raised to almost the level of a fine art; what is known as the "dry cleaning" process has been almost universally adopted, and all danger of the shrinking of cloth and woollen garments has been practically obviated. The most delicate fabrics pass successfully through the expert cleaner's hands.

In dyeing, however, the possibility of slight shrinking must always be reckoned with, and a woman should make allowances for this when planning out the renovation of a garment in this way. The time taken by professional cleaners to clean garments usually amounts to from eight to ten days, whilst for dyeing a fortnight is usually required. The latter rule does not apply, however, to garments which are being dyed black for purposes of mourning. All dyers give special concessions in regard to exceptional circumstances of the kind, and most of them can undertake to get the garments ready within two or three days.

Hints for Home Cleaning.—A great deal in regard to cleaning may be successfully undertaken at home. For this purpose there should always be a good amount of Fuller's earth, ammonia and benzine in the store cupboard. Special care must, however, be taken in regard to the storing of the two latter articles, as ammonia in its pure state is explosive when too much shaken, and benzine is inflammable. Petrol is also exceedingly useful for the home cleaner, but on account of its dangerous properties it should only be procured in small quantities as required; and it should never on any account be stored at home.

Cleaning Lace and Silk Yokes, Vests, Trimmings, &c.—It often happens that a cloth dress will have a white lace or net yoke, or vest, or other similar trimming which would naturally become dirty long before the dress is soiled. One does not care to send a whole dress to the cleaners for the sake of the trimming, more especially as the latter may be cleaned at home as follows:—

Lay the dress on a table over which a clean cloth has been spread; cover all the dress over with a cloth excepting the portion which is to be cleaned, then with a piece of flannel soaked in petrol rub all over the soiled part. Go over it again with a piece of clean flannel dipped in petrol, and leave in the open air to dry. Petrol, it must be remembered, is extremely dangerous in careless hands, as it is most inflammable; for this reason the cleaning should only be undertaken in the daytime, and in a room where there is no fire.

White Non-Washing Silks may be cleaned by rubbing with stale bread-crumbs mixed with a little powdered blue. White silk and other light dresses which have only been slightly soiled can be made quite fresh again by rubbing with stale bread-crumbs. Silk, serge, and cashmere dresses may be freshened by rubbing with a solution of fig leaves, made by boiling a handful of fig leaves in about a quart of water, and straining off when cool.

Taking Stains from Garments.—One general rule to be observed in taking stains from garments is this:—When rubbing with the cleansing preparation rub always in a circular direction, beginning in a circle just outside the stain round the outer part, gradually working in towards the centre. This prevents the stain from spreading any further.

Most stains, such as grease stains, fruit stains, and wine stains, may be removed from very fine garments by rubbing with a flannel dipped in ether. This may be obtained in small quantities from most chemists at prices varying from sixpence and upwards.

To Remove Paint Stains.—Rub when fresh with turpentine applied on a piece of flannel. If the stain is an old one, mix ammonia with the turpentine. Paint spots on velvet or velveteen can usually be removed with paraffin or pure alcohol.

To Remove Grease or Wax Stains.—Lay the garment out on a table over a clean ironing-sheet, place a piece of blotting-paper both over the stain and underneath it. Iron with a moderately hot iron. The blotting-paper will be found to absorb the grease and the stain will disappear. Good brown paper may be used instead of the blotting-paper with successful results.

Cleaning Light Blouses.—A simple and easy method of cleaning light blouses at home which has been proved successful is as follows:—

Take an ordinary hat box and line it with clean white paper, cover the bottom of the box with a layer of Fuller's earth. Place the blouse in this, covering it with another layer of Fuller's earth. Cover this with a sheet of white paper; close the box, rendering it as air-tight as possible, and put it aside for four or five days. When taken out of the box and shaken, the blouse will be found to be perfectly clean.

Renovating Shabby Garments.—Faded and shabby-looking stuff garments may be much improved by careful sponging with liquid ammonia. For all black fabrics ammonia is the best cleanser.

Cleaning Light Cloth Garments.—For children's light cloth coats, &c., a little fig dust well rubbed into the material, and allowed to remain on for a few hours before being brushed off, is an effective cleanser. For light cloth trimmings, cloth ball is also very useful. This may be obtained from any drapers for an outlay of from 10½d.

Ink Spots on Cloth.—When a cloth or stuff dress becomes stained with ink, the stain should never be allowed to dry into the material. Pressing blotting-paper on the wet stain will often be sufficient to absorb it. This, however, must be done at once if it is to be efficacious. Another way of removing ink stains from cloth is to sponge at once with milk, then with warm water; dry with a soft cloth, and iron on the wrong side of the material. (For taking out ink spots on cotton or linen, see p. 279.)

To Raise the Pile of Velvet.—When velvet has become shabby it may be renovated by holding the wrong side of the velvet over a jug of boiling water; this will cause the pile to rise. Another and perhaps a more effective method is as follows:—

Cover the flat part of a very warm iron with a damp cloth. Get some one to hold the iron for you, and then grasping the velvet firmly at

each end pass it backwards and forwards on the wrong side across the cloth. The steam from the cloth will cause the pile to rise, and the velvet will become almost like new. (For Washing Velveteen, see p. 289.)

To Wash White Coque Feather Boas.—Dissolve some Lux into a basinful of warm water, stir it into a lather, and place the boa in this, gently pressing the feathers between the fingers; rinse in clean water, shake well, and hang in the open air to dry in the sunshine. The feathers will have a straight appearance when wet, but will resume their fluffy appearance as soon as dry. They should be well shaken before hanging them up. In winter they should be shaken before a fire and then hung near it; only not too close, as they are liable to get scorched.

To Clean Ostrich Feathers.—Shake them well in a lather of Lux and water, or soap and

water. Dry slowly before the fire, and curl the feathers with a blunt penknife.

To Clean White and Light Felt Hats.—Rub the hat all over with calcined magnesia applied with a small soft brush; put the hat aside for a day or a night, then shake the powder off. If the hat is found not to be perfectly clean after the first application, repeat the treatment. For white felt hats, bran moistened with petrol and rubbed all over the hat makes a particularly effective cleanser.

Renewing Black Chip Hats.—After removing all dust from the hat with a soft brush or a piece of velvet (a velvet cushion such as is used for polishing patent and glacé shoes would do), rub in a little olive oil with another piece of old velvet.

Straw Hats.—White straw hats may be cleaned by rubbing with cut lemon, and afterwards rinsing in cold water. The straw should then be stiffened by brushing with a brush dipped in a solution of gum and water. To whiten white straw hats which have become scorched by the sun, dissolve a tea-spoonful of oxalic acid in half a pint of warm water and brush evenly round the hat, rinse and put in the open air to dry.

Black straw hats, after being thoroughly brushed to take the dust off, may be cleaned by applying black ink and liquid gum mixed in equal proportions with a small brush.

To Dye Straw Hats which have become irretrievably scorched by the sun or discoloured, brush all dust off with a good stiff brush, and paint the hat all over with hat dye or Aspinal's enamel of the shade required, using a colour brush for the purpose.

To Paint White Shoes Gold or Silver.—White kid and leather shoes which have become very soiled may be dyed gold or silver. To do this, purchase sixpenny-worth of gold or silver paint, and paint evenly all over the shoes with a paint brush. Leave them in the air to dry.

Tarnished Gold Braid may be freshened by rubbing with a little Fuller's earth.

To Clean Furs.—Furs may be cleaned by rubbing with warm bran. The bran should be placed on a piece of white paper in the oven to dry. It should not be overheated, or the furs will be spoiled. The white paper will form an excellent guide in this direction, for if it becomes the least bit brown it will be a sign that the bran has become too much heated. It should be well rubbed in and then shaken or brushed out. Fig dust may be used in the same way.

Cleaning White Furs.—Powdered magnesia warmed in the oven is a good cleanser for white and light furs. It should be well rubbed into the fur and then shaken out. After the first shaking it will be found advantageous to leave the furs in a box for a day or two, and then thoroughly shake out once more. For the coarser white furs ordinary flour warmed in the oven makes a very good cleanser. Spread some clean paper on the table, place the fur to be cleaned upon it, and well rub in the warm flour into the hairs. When the fur appears to be clean, shake well and lay aside in a box for twenty-four hours, when most of the surplus flour will be found deposited in the bottom of the box. Shake again thoroughly, and the fur will be ready for wear.

DRESS ALLOWANCES

It is wise of parents to give their daughters a dress allowance as soon as they attain a certain age, making them responsible for the purchase and upkeep of their wardrobe. This plan tends to give young people a practical insight into the value of money which will stand them in good stead when they in turn have to take the cares of a home upon their shoulders. Every woman should allot a certain sum of money each year for expenditure upon dress, and be careful that this sum is not exceeded. System in this as well as other questions of apportionment of income is essential where economy has to be practised. "I cannot say what I spend upon dress," a woman will often be heard to remark. "I buy new clothes when I need them, but my wants do not amount to much, and my expenditure must be very small." If this woman would make up her mind to note down carefully, say for a period of three months, her dress expenditure she would be astounded at the substantial total to which small sums expended here and there upon what seemed at the time to be mere trifles have amounted, and she will then begin to realise the necessity of the fixed dress allowance as a factor in restraining all unnecessary expenditure.

The cost of a woman's wardrobe will depend upon the social circle in which she moves, and the appearance which she has to keep up; also upon the extent of her aptitude with her needle, her ability to cut out, fashion, and renovate garments for herself, and the care she takes of her clothes. Much saving may also be effected by the woman who knows how to spend her money judiciously.

Buying at Sales.—The woman who has only a small dress allowance often makes the mistake of expending it upon cheap articles which may be good for show at first, but which are certainly bad for wear, and in her hankering after cheap finery she neglects essentials, with the result that she is never well dressed. "Little and good" should be the motto for the woman to whom shillings and pence are a matter of moment. She should know what to buy, and when and where to buy to the most advantage. The clever woman makes a point of buying the more expensive items of her wardrobe at the sales of the large drapery establishments. In the case of firms of high standing and repute, these sales are always genuine, and some really amazing bargains may be had during sale time. The large winter sales occur in January or February, and the summer sales at the end of July and in August. At the winter sales especially some wonderful bargains in coat and skirt costumes may sometimes be found. Very often a costume which was originally priced at seven or eight guineas will be marked down to as low a figure as £3, 3s. It will, in several cases, be of the latest style and cut, and one is sometimes puzzled as to the reason for the reduction. This may be due to the fact that the dress is of a colour only becoming to the few. Well, if it is secured by one of the few, that one will have every reason to be satisfied with her purchase. Care, of course, must be taken to choose a costume which will not "date" too quickly. Summer dress materials may also be purchased to wonderful advantage at sale times. The bargain-hunter at the sales must show method in her shopping if she wishes to make it a success. She should know what she wants to buy, and make up her mind to buy it, and not be led into spending her money upon those innumerable little unnecessary trifles which appeal to her natural feminine love of finery, and so prove such formidable weapons in the armoury of the expert salesmen at this season. After the sales are over, many a woman finds herself the possessor of a number of useless little odds and ends she does not want, but which she felt she must buy "because they were so very cheap."

Sales are the rocks upon which many good resolutions for economy are wrecked; on the other hand, they are inexpressible boons to the sensible woman shopper who knows how to shop upon a scientific basis. She has two things always before her—her requirements, and the limitations of her purse. This being so, she is careful to purchase only what she really needs, and thus she is able to eke out her allowance by careful and judicious buying at this period. If all women kept these two essentials well in mind at sale time, they would find that they could expend their money to great advantage.

The inability to "cut her coat according to her cloth" is the reason why a woman so often finds herself unable to make both ends meet on a small dress allowance. She is ever striving to vie in her dress with other women who enjoy double her income, and her efforts are doomed to failure at the outset. It is not much use, for instance, to spend all one's allowance on an expensive gown, only to have it ruined by wearing it in wet weather through not having sufficient money to provide either a good coat to cover it, or a tailor-made for ordinary occasions, and the appearance of the smartest gown is spoiled by shabby shoes or inferior gloves. A woman with little money to spend on dress must set a standard for herself, and not be led into trying to follow the standard of others, for this invariably leads to disappointment. It is surprising on how little money a woman can dress well if neatness and serviceability are the two objects she keeps in view, leaving the taste for indulging in the extremes of fashion to the woman who can afford to indulge herself in this direction.

But whatever her income, a woman with the exercise of a little forethought can avoid being old-fashioned and out of date in her dress. Even if she can only afford one new costume every two years, she can at least take care that what she buys is not only in fashion at the moment, but that it is not of a fashion so striking that it is doomed to be short-lived. Ordinary styles last generally well into two seasons. The first season they are adopted by a few—the second season they become general. It is an unwise plan to only adopt a style after it has become general, for this is a sure indication that it will die out very soon, and for a woman whose dress has to last her for two years, this is not a promising outlook. A woman therefore should strive to show some originality and some decisiveness in her choice of dress, and not be content to follow blindly where others lead. She must not disregard fashion altogether be it said; to do so would be to make oneself conspicuous, and the well-dressed woman is never conspicuous; but she should shun all styles which do not suit her, avoid all dress unsuitable for the position in life which she occupies, remembering that to be suitably dressed is to have solved the art of dressing well.

How to make her dress allowance suffice for her requirements is therefore a problem with which many a woman is confronted. A good manager, however, will by dint of careful contriving successfully cope with all her difficulties, very often making £15 a year go as far as £30 would go in less experienced hands.

The successful management of a dress allowance will depend to a great extent upon how far a woman can dovetail her requirements, making the purchases of one year fit in with those of the next. For instance, where she is only able to buy one new dress in a year, one year she will buy a good outdoor costume—the next year she will expend the money on an afternoon dress, each doing duty therefore for two seasons.

In this way she will be able to balance each year's expenses to a nicety, instead of spending only half her allowance one year and three times the amount of it the next.

It is difficult to set down hard-and-fast rules for expenditure upon dress in the year; as has been said before, the successful expenditure of a dress allowance resolves itself into a question of good management. As a guide, however, for those to whom the advice may be useful, we append some specimen lists of expenditure covering annual sums of £15, £25 and £40 a year. These amounts may be taken to be fairly representative, and the lists will give at least some general idea of judicious apportionment of the money spent upon the various articles detailed.

SOME SPECIMEN DESS ALLOWANCES

£15 a Year

	£	s.	d.
Costume	3	0	0
Dress	2	0	0
Coat or cloak	1	1	0
Boots and shoes	2	0	0
Underclothing	3	0	0
Hats	1	0	0
Blouses	1	10	0
Gloves, veils, &c.	1	0	0
Boot-mending, cleaning, &c.		9	0
	£15	0	0

In regard to the item £3 for a costume, this can be spent on a winter costume one year and the next year a best summer dress, costing £2, and two cotton dresses or linen skirts at 10s. each can be purchased. In regard to the £2 allotted for a dress, this can be expended upon an afternoon toilette one year, and on an evening toilette the next. It is always necessary to allow a good sum for boots and shoes, therefore £2 will not be a bit too much to put by for these, and the expenditure upon them will be pretty nearly the same each year. The amount spent upon underlinen will of course be varied according to the amount of wear to be had out of the articles purchased, and where a woman is able to make part of her lingerie herself, the expenditure will of course be decreased, for home-made underlinen not only costs less, but wears much better than that which is bought ready made. Any surplus from the £3, therefore, in any particular year, can be allowed for an umbrella or a sunshade, as the case may be. Nine shillings is not a very large amount to cover repairing and cleaning, but it can be augmented occasionally from any small sum that may be left over from other items. In regard to the £1, 1s. allowed for coat, this can be expended upon a good warm serge coat, which would also do duty as a rain coat one year, and the next year it might purchase a plain simple little light cloak or coat which would do duty for both day and evening wear, only the purchase would have to be made at sale time for anything like a presentable garment at the price to be had.

Many other little contrivances too numerous to mention can be resorted to in order to eke out a dress allowance of the amount named, but ideas in regard to these will come of themselves to the woman who takes the trouble to plan her expenditure in a sensible manner.

With the above few notes as a guide, the reader will be able to adapt the two following specimen lists for dress allowances of £25 and £40 a year respectively to suit herself.

£25 a Year

	£	s.	d.
One good costume	4	0	0
Summer dress	2	0	0
One afternoon dress	2	10	0
One evening dress	2	10	0
One wrap or coat	1	10	0
Boots and shoes	2	5	0
Hats	2	0	0
Blouses	2	0	0
Underclothing	3	10	0
Gloves, veils, neckwear	1	10	0
Umbrella or sunshade	0	10	0
Cleaning, boot-mending, &c.	0	15	0
	£25	0	0

£40 a Year

	£	s.	d.
One good costume	5	5	0
One best summer dress	3	0	0
Two lingerie dresses at £1 each	2	0	0
Afternoon dress	3	0	0
Evening dress	4	0	0
Wrap	2	10	0
Blouses	3	0	0
Underclothing (including dressing-gown)	5	0	0
Boots and shoes	3	0	0
Hats	3	0	0
Gloves, veils, and neckwear	2	10	0
Umbrella or sunshade	0	15	0
Repairing, cleaning, &c.	1	0	0
	£38	0	0

This leaves a balance of £2, which should be set aside to be added towards the same balance on the following year, and the two together with any surplus from the lingerie or other items will serve to purchase a useful set of furs.

The above list allows for new winter costumes and new summer dresses every year; but of course the winter costume of the preceding year always comes in for morning outdoor wear, the new toilette being kept for visiting and more dressy occasions. The same may be said in regard to the summer dresses. Where a woman engages in motoring to a certain extent, she will of course require a good motoring coat, bonnet, and veil. By spending a little less on her winter and summer dresses one year she will be able to supply this, or else she might forego the new wrap one year, and employ it on a motoring outfit instead. This will last her a good time, and will not require to be often renewed. A stylish evening or day wrap may often be purchased for the small sum of £1, 15s. In this case the surplus from the £2, 10s. allowed will go towards the purchase of a rain or dust cloak.

Where a woman can make her own blouses and summer and indoor dresses, her allowance, of course, can be made to go twice as far again. She should always be well in advance with her new things at the very beginning of each season, as in this lies the secret of being up-to-date as far as dress is concerned.

THE BRIDAL TROUSSEAU

Upon no occasion perhaps does the question of dress assume such importance to the girl and women members of a family as when one of their number is engaged in the preparation of her trousseau. However poor and humble the circumstances of the parents of the bride, they will strain every effort, depriving themselves even of necessaries if needs be, in order to see that their daughter goes to her husband well equipped in every way.

We have said good-bye to the days when every girl, as soon as she reached the mature age of fifteen or thereabouts, would pass most of her time laboriously putting the finest of stitches into the finest of garments to be set aside in the "bottom drawer" with sprigs of lavender placed between their dainty folds, pending the appearance of "Mr. Right" upon the scene to put the momentous question. How many a trousseau prepared in this manner has been fated to remain for ever undisturbed in the place into which it was laid with so much care and tenderness and so many happy thoughts of that bright future which looms golden in the mind of nearly every girl. Marriage is not to-day the sole idea of the young girl's life as it was in those days, and in any case, however anxious a girl may be to get married and settle down in a home of her own, she would never anticipate events by preparing a trousseau before any man had asked her to be his bride. Such an act indeed the modern girl would look upon with superstition as being unlucky—yet, when the momentous question has been asked, and once she is engaged, her thoughts are naturally full of the preparations she must make in this direction. Her girl friends will flock round her and beg to see the pretty things that she has prepared. Small wonder then that the engaged girl is anxious that everything she has will be the daintiest and the best procurable for the money her parents can afford.

People are not making the mistake nowadays of including a large number of dresses of every kind and variety in the trousseau. In most cases half of these dresses would be quite out of date before their owner had any opportunity of wearing them, and she would be doomed therefore, if not very well off, to spend the first few years of her marriage wearing *démodé* gowns.

A sensible idea adopted by many parents is that of including several dress lengths in the trousseau. These can be made up as required, and will be found not the least useful part of the trousseau. The number of dresses that will be absolutely necessary depend upon the social position the bride will be called upon to fill. For the ordinary middle-class girl of average means, in addition to her wedding dress and going-away dress, the following will usually be found sufficient:—

One good outdoor costume.
One good coat and skirt for morning wear.
Two afternoon dresses.
One light evening dress.
One dark evening dress.
One fur coat, or dressy coat or wrap.
One evening cloak.
One morning dress or skirt to wear with blouses.
Two or three light muslin and lingerie dresses, blouses, &c.

With several dress lengths added, this list of dresses should be sufficient for all ordinary requirements.

Where the wedding dress is afterwards used as an evening dress, the light evening dress may be dispensed with.

The specimen lists given below for trousseaux which may be purchased for an outlay of £65 and £130 respectively are capable of much variation. They are intended mainly as a guide to parents with marriageable daughters as to what form their expenditure should take. The £65 trousseau includes only the essentials of a wedding outfit, the various items mentioned being of simple and plain yet at the same time of fairly good quality. In the £130 outfit a little more scope for finery is allowed. A substantial proportion of the respective sums of money is allowed for underlinen, as lingerie of the very cheap variety is excluded from both lists.

TROUSSEAU FOR £65

	£	s.	d.
Wedding dress (to be used afterwards as best evening dress) and veil	8	8	0
Going-away dress (afterwards best visiting costume)	5	5	0
Wrap suitable for both afternoon and evening wear	2	10	0
Outdoor costume	4	4	0
1 dark evening dress	4	4	0
Good afternoon dress	3	3	0
Skirt for wear with blouses	1	1	0
Rain coat	1	1	0
Going-away hat	1	10	0
2 Hats at 12s. 9d.	1	5	6
Blouses	2	0	0
6 pairs short gloves at 3s. 3d.		19	6
2 pairs long gloves at 5s. 6d.		11	0
1 pair very long gloves at 7s. 11d.		7	11
1 pair boots		16	0
2 pairs walking shoes at 10s. 6d.	1	1	0
1 pair white evening shoes (for wear with wedding dress)		10	6
2 pairs indoor shoes at 5s. 6d.		11	0
Umbrella		15	0
Sunshade		10	6
Lingerie			
3 Night-dresses, longcloth and embroidery at 7s. 11d.	1	3	9
2 Night-dresses, fine nainsook and lace at 12s. 9d.	1	5	6
1 Night-dress, cambric and lace		15	9
6 longcloth chemises trimmed with embroidery at 3s. 11d.	1	3	6
4 French hand-made chemises with Valenciennes lace at 5s. 11d.	1	3	8
2 fine cambric chemises with lace at 10s. 9d.	1	1	6
6 Longcloth knickers at 3s. 11½d.	1	3	9
4 French hand-made knickers at 5s. 11d.	1	3	8
2 Cambric and lace knickers at 8s. 11d.		17	10
2 pairs corsets at 12s. 9d.	1	5	6
3 Camisoles at 3s. 3d.		9	9
2 Camisoles at 5s. 6d.		11	0
1 Camisole at 7s. 11d.		7	11
4 Flannel or nun's-veiling petticoats at 5s. 6d.	1	2	0
1 dozen pair stockings at 2s. (six cashmere, six fine lisle thread)	1	4	0
2 pairs spun-silk stockings at 3s. 6d.		7	0
4 White petticoats at 7s. 6d.	1	10	0
1 Lace or silk petticoat for wear with bridal dress	1	1	0
1 Dark petticoat		7	6
6 Merino, woollen, or silk-spun combinations at 6s. 6d.	1	19	0
1 Winter dressing-gown	1	0	0
1 Summer dressing-gown		15	0
2 dozen handkerchiefs at 10s. 6d.	1	1	0
	£63	13	6

This leaves a balance of £1, 6s. 6d., which may be expended upon veils and neckwear. In regard to the lingerie, if combinations are preferred to the chemises and drawers, the combined garments will of course be cheaper than the separate items. The above list represents all articles actually bought in their complete state. A substantial saving would be effected if the bride, aided by the women members of her family, could make some of the lingerie and simpler gowns herself. Many people cannot afford even £65 for a trousseau for their daughters. In these circumstances the help of the home needlewoman is a necessity; the wedding frock should be of the very simplest, and the frocks not home-made would have to be the plainest of their kind. With the sum of £65 to expend, however, with the addition of the help of really clever home-workers and plenty of time in which to prepare their work, a very good trousseau indeed may be had. For a comparatively small outlay upon materials, dainty light muslin frocks, an extra afternoon frock, and even a pretty tea-gown may be made without added extra outlay. It is always advisable to have the going-away dress and the outdoor costume, made at a good shop. In regard to both these a good tailor's cut is eminently desirable. With the money saved on garments made at home even a little extra expenditure may be made in this direction.

There are, of course, many articles nowadays of the ready-made species which can be had for ridiculously low sums, and might perhaps cost no more than those of home manufacture. In regard to a bride's trousseau, however, everything in it should be good. For this reason it is better to avoid purchases of the cheap "ready-made" variety if making one or two things at home will allow for an extra outlay upon the garments which have to be bought.

£8, 8s. is not a very large sum to allot for the wedding dress and veil, if the dress is to be made at a good costumier's. If, on the other hand, a known and tried dressmaker who makes up ladies' own materials is entrusted with the work, it can be made for even less, and the surplus would go towards some other purchase. If the wedding is to be a quiet one, the bride being married in her travelling dress, £4, 4s. of the sum allowed for the wedding dress might be expended upon a good white evening dress, the remainder being expended upon two pretty muslin dresses or else two useful dress lengths.

As a rule, the bridal dress is worn as a best evening gown afterwards, so the evening gown allowed on the list should be a black one if possible, as it is destined to play the part of a serviceable dress.

Many bargains, and good ones, may sometimes be had at sales both in regard to lingerie and to dresses; the discriminating shopper will be wise to make judicious use of her opportunities in this direction, and she will perhaps secure several of the items at a good deal less than the figures at which they are marked upon the following lists.

Trousseau for £130

	£	*s.*	*d.*
Wedding dress (to be used afterwards as best evening dress) and veil	10	10	0
Going-away dress (afterwards best visiting costume)	7	7	0
Good fur-lined coat or fur stole and muff	7	7	0
1 Cloth outdoor costume	5	5	0
1 Serge or tweed costume	3	3	0
1 Long coat suitable for motoring or rain coat	2	10	0
Demi-toilette dress	3	3	0
Evening dress	5	5	0
1 Afternoon dress	4	4	0
1 Evening wrap	3	0	0
1 Dress length, 6 yards cloth at 4s. per yard	1	4	0
1 Dress length, 12 yards silk or satin at 5s. per yard	3	0	0
1 Tea gown	3	0	0
Light muslin or voile summer dress	3	0	0
2 Linen costumes or cotton dresses at £1, 10s. each	3	0	0
1 House dress	2	2	0
Going-away hat	2	2	0
Motoring and travelling hat and veil	1	10	0
2 Hats at 12s. 9d.	1	5	6
Blouses	4	0	0
1 pair boots	1	1	0
1 pair walking shoes	1	1	0
2 pairs walking shoes at 12s. 6d.	1	5	0
2 pairs evening shoes at 10s. 6d.	1	1	0
2 pairs house shoes at 7s. 6d.		15	0
Umbrella	1	1	0
Sunshade		15	0
6 pairs short kid and suede gloves at 3s. 3d.		19	6
2 pairs short kid and suede gloves at 5s. 6d.		11	0
4 pairs long kid and suede gloves at 6s. 11d.	1	7	8

Lingerie

	£	*s.*	*d.*
6 Night-dresses at 7s. 11d.	2	7	6
4 Night-dresses at 12s. 6d.	2	10	0
2 Night-dresses at £1, 1s.	2	2	0
6 Chemises at 5s. 6d.	1	13	0
3 Chemises at 7s. 6d.	1	2	6
3 Chemises at 10s. 6d.	1	11	6
6 Drawers at 5s. 6d.	1	13	0
3 Drawers at 7s. 6d.	1	2	6
3 Drawers at 10s. 6d.	1	11	6
6 Spun silk, merino, or woollen combinations at 6s. 6d.	1	19	0
6 Camisoles at 4s.	1	4	0
5 Camisoles at 6s. 6d.	1	12	6
1 Camisole at 10s. 6d.		10	6
1 pair corsets	1	1	0

	£	s.	d.
2 pairs corsets at 12s. 9d.	1	5	6
1 Silk, satin or lace petticoat for wear with wedding dress	2	2	0
1 Silk petticoat	1	1	0
1 Moirette petticoat		10	6
6 White petticoats at 7s. 6d.	2	5	0
6 Nun's-veiling or flannel petticoats at 6s. 6d.	1	19	0
6 pairs cashmere stockings at 2s. 6d.		15	0
6 pairs fine lisle thread at 3s. 3d.		19	6
3 pairs silk stockings at 10s. 6d.	1	11	6
2 dozen handkerchiefs at 15s. 6d. per dozen	1	11	0
4 lace handkerchiefs at 10s. 6d. each	2	2	0
Good dressing-gown	2	0	0
Summer dressing-gown	1	1	0
2 Dressing jackets at 12s. 6d. each	1	5	0
1 pair quilted satin bedroom slippers		3	6
Veils, neckwear, scarves, &c.	1	10	0
	£129	6	8

The balance of 13s. 4d. may be expended upon a pretty night-dress case, and a brush-and-comb bag.

The trousseaux lists given comprise only the clothing. Travelling bags, trunk and dress baskets will of course make extra items in each case. All luggage should be as neat as possible.

SCHOOL OUTFITS

For a Girl

4 Night-dresses.
1 Dressing-gown.
1 pair bedroom slippers.
1 Night-dress bag and 1 brush-and-comb bag.
3 pairs woollen combinations.
4 pairs cotton combinations or 4 chemises and 4 pairs of drawers.
2 pairs knickers with 2 linings.
2 pairs stays with suspenders.
3 Princess petticoats.
6 pairs stockings.
1½ dozen handkerchiefs.
3 Bath towels.
3 Face towels.
Toilet requisites.
1 Writing-case with paper, &c.
1 Cash-box with lock and key.
1 pair school slippers, 1 pair for better wear.
2 pairs walking shoes, 1 pair boots.
1 pair gymnastic or tennis shoes.
1 pair goloshes or overshoes.
2 Linen bags.
2 School dresses or 2 skirts with blouses.
1 Sunday dress.
2 Evening dresses.
1 Gymnastic costume.
1 Coat for everyday wear.
1 Coat for Sundays.
1 Waterproof.
1 School hat, 1 Sunday hat.
1 Evening cloak.
1 Umbrella.
2 pairs woollen or cotton gloves.
1 pair kid gloves, 1 pair evening gloves.
Ties according to regulation.
1 Rug.
1 Music case (flat).

The above list represents ordinary requirements; special garments may be necessary according to the sports and games played at the school. At fashionable schools a larger outfit will be necessary.

For a Boy

1 Sunday dress suit.
2 Tweed suits (longs or knickers according to school regulations).
1 Overcoat. 1 Dressing-gown.
1 pair bedroom slippers.
Toilet requisites, brush, comb, &c.
3 White dress shirts, 4 flannel shirts.
8 Linen or flannel collars (according to school regulations).
3 Sunday collars (according to school regulations).
3 pairs underclothing (vests and drawers).
2 pairs boots, 2 pairs shoes, 1 pair slippers.
1 pair gymnastic shoes.
1 Rug. 3 Pyjama suits.
6 pairs socks or stockings (according to kind of suit worn).
1½ dozen handkerchiefs.
1 Black necktie, 2 school neckties.
1 Tall hat and hat-box for Sundays.
1 Umbrella. 1 pair garters.
1 pair kid gloves, 1 pair woollen gloves.
1 School cap. 1 pair cuff links.
Cash-box and writing-case.
1 School muffler.
3 Bath towels, 3 face towels.

Extras for Winter Term

2 pairs football shorts (blue).
2 pairs football shorts (white).
2 Football jerseys.
1 Football blazer and belt.
2 pairs football stockings. 1 Sweater.
1 pair football boots.

Extras for Summer Term

4 pairs white shorts or longs (according to school regulations).
2 pairs blue shorts.
4 Cricket shirts.
1 Blazer and belt.
2 pairs cricket shoes.

ETIQUETTE AND SOCIAL GUIDE

THE word "etiquette" simply means "ticket," and is the "label" attached by an unwritten convention to the best observances in the social life of well-bred people. In this chapter the fundamental principles of etiquette are described, and the chief rules which govern its observance are enumerated in a manner which it is hoped will be useful to many a woman who is in doubt how to act upon various social occasions.

Tact.—It has been said that the essence of all good breeding is *tact*. A tactful woman is essentially a woman who knows how to adapt herself to varying circumstances, who has that keen perception which enables her to see and do what is best upon occasions when discrimination between the wrong and the right methods of action is necessary. A tactful woman is one who will never hurt another's feelings. She will always respect the little foibles of her friends and refrain from holding them up to ridicule. When she entertains, she is past master in the art of asking the right people to meet each other and of making them all feel at their ease in her society.

"I like going to Mrs. Brown's; she does know how to make you feel at home," is a phrase often heard in speaking of a tactful hostess. On the other hand, "You will not enjoy yourself at Mrs. Jones'. There is always an atmosphere of stiffness in her house. You never feel at home there somehow," is a warning often given when reference is made to a hostess whose disregard for the comfort of her guests and want of tact generally is proverbial upon these occasions.

There are some people who have a genius for "rubbing their friends up the wrong way." The society of these women as a rule is shunned. Others are well known for their agreeable and charming manners. These women become popular with every one, no matter how plain and homely their appearance may be. Comment is often made upon the fact that plain girls as a rule get married sooner than their fairer sisters. The reason is not hard to seek. The latter have grown into the habit of looking upon homage and adulation as their right. "Self" is the keynote of interest in their lives, and in the worship of self they neglect to cultivate that all-potent charm of manner founded upon true innate unselfishness and tact, in which their plainer sisters as a rule excel. When beauty and tact are allied in one person, then her charm is indeed irresistible, while sad indeed is the case of the woman who possesses neither the one nor the other.

Manners.—In the cultivation of tact, good manners are essential. "Manners makyth Man" and woman too, for if good manners are so essential to man, are they not then indispensable to woman, whose great object in life is to please?

A lady's manners should be perfect upon all occasions. Manners cannot be donned and discarded at will. To be ill-mannered and churlish in the home circle and keep one's best manners, like a visiting toilette, to be donned for the benefit of strangers, is as ill-advised as it is inefficacious. Politeness assumed in this way invariably comes with an effort, and is only too often apt to degenerate into mere affectation.

Practise good manners with your own people if you wish to shine before strangers. The manners of a gentlewoman are always characterised by their perfect ease and naturalness, and how can this ease be possibly acquired if politeness is only assumed for special occasions? Much of that stiff, artificial demeanour displayed by so many of our young people is due to the fact that, instead of being taught good manners in their childhood, they are expected to assimilate the whole of the rules of etiquette, politeness and good breeding in the few months which immediately precede their coming out.

The effect of this mistaken training is lamentable in most circumstances, for the polish acquired in this way at the last moment is of so thin a veneer that it very often only serves to accentuate that native *gaucherie* which it was intended to conceal.

We all pay a silent tribute to the mother who initiates her little three-year-old toddler into the mysteries of how and when to raise his diminutive cap as soon as he is promoted to knickerbockers. All mothers should pay particular attention to the manners of their children. "As the twig is bent so will it grow," and by dint of careful training politeness becomes innate with the little ones, so that when they grow up their claim to the title of "gentleman" or "gentlewoman" will be recognised by all with whom they come into contact.

Etiquette.—Every gentlewoman should be thoroughly acquainted with that code of manners which falls under the general designation of the word "etiquette." To many people the word etiquette conveys the meaning of mere empty forms and ceremonies which can be honoured just as well in the breach as in the observance. This is a mistake. We have defined tact as a keen perception for seeing and doing what is best in varying circumstances. Etiquette tells us what to do to keep within the rules of politeness and good breeding. It is obvious, therefore, that in the practice of tact a knowledge of etiquette is all-important. Many an otherwise tactful woman has given offence by her ignorance of social rules, more especially in regard to the rule of precedence. A knowledge of etiquette in these circumstances would have saved her from making a mistake of a kind so often bitterly resented by the person at whose expense it is made.

Etiquette in Olden Times.—Every period of history has had its recognised code of manners, and though the etiquette of our forefathers differed considerably from our own social rules, yet the governing principles of true politeness have always had their foundation upon the practice of true kindliness, courtesy and consideration for others; for "Manners are not idle, but the fruit of loyal nature and of noble mind."

It must be said, however, that the ideas held by our forefathers upon the outward observances of refinement and culture as decreed by their laws of etiquette, differed very considerably from the standard of manners at the present day. Customs invariably change, and with the change of custom our ideas also undergo a considerable metamorphosis, so that what was allowable in former times would in many cases be looked upon with horror at the present day. In the same way our descendants will probably look back upon the twentieth century as a period of positive uncouthness as compared with the standard of increased culture they will have attained.

In a little book, intended as a guide to gentlewomen as to their behaviour and deportment upon all occasions, which was published in 1686, some interesting rules are laid down as to the etiquette and suitable behaviour of the lady of the period. This ingenious little volume, which bears the somewhat quaint title, "The Accomplished Ladies' Rich Closet of Rarities, or The Ingenious Gentlewoman and Servant Maids' Delightful Companion," casts a most interesting sidelight upon the manners prevailing in England just after the reign of the "Merrie Monarch." Indeed, it may be taken for granted that they were also *de rigueur* during that same interesting period which has generally been looked upon as one of the most picturesque epochs of our history, when courtliness and gallantry were raised to the level of a fine art. Yet from the manners of the times, as detailed in this book, it will be seen that much was permissible in the code of etiquette which prevailed in the seventeenth century which would be looked upon nowadays with amazement and disgust.

For instance, the following precept laid down for the observance of the lady in society, "If you are abroad at dinner let not your hand be first in any dish," is decidedly reminiscent of a time when knives and forks were not regarded as indispensable to the dinner-table equipment. And again, "Whenever you carve, keep your fingers from your mouth; throw not anything over your shoulder," would suggest that it was quite usual for a fair carver in the days of the Stuarts to convey surreptitiously the dainty morsels to her mouth through the medium of her fingers, instead of placing them upon the plates of her guests, and to summarily dispose of any excess of fat and skin upon a joint by promptly throwing it over her shoulder!

It requires an effort of the imagination to think of the stately dames of the period behaving in this fashion, and if such were the manners of the gentler sex, what must have been the polite behaviour of those cavaliers of the long perfumed ringlets and picturesque dress which outrivalled in its richness and elegance the attire of their ladies. Picture those effeminate white hands, adorned at the wrist with dainty lace ruffles, dipping for some coveted tit-bit in the gravy!

Evidently curiosity has always been the besetting failure of the fair sex; yet nowadays no lady would require the following caution: "Be not inquisitive (for that is uncomely) to know what such a Fowl or such a Joynt cost, nor discourse of Bills of Fare";—and even though inordinate love of the good things of this world might be her besetting sin, she would not require to be told, "Take not in your wine or other liquor too greedily, nor drink until you are out of breath. Eat not your spoon meat so hot that it makes your eyes water, nor be seen to blow it."

Some rules laid down for the deportment of a gentlewoman when out walking are worthy of comment:—

"Observe that you walk not carelessly or lightly, shouldering as it were your companions, nor strutting or jutting in a proud manner. Keep your head steady, your countenance not too much elevated nor too much dejected; keep your arms likewise steady, and throw them not about as if you were flying. Let your feet rather incline a little more inward than outward, lest you be censured splay-footed. . . . Do not run or go extreme fast in places of concourse, unless great occasion require it, for in such violent motions it is not always in your power to keep your body steady; nay, by too much haste you may chance to fall!" The following caution, "Wink not too often, nor cast your eyes ascance as if you squinted, neither keep them too reserved, nor scornfully turn them away when any object offers," would seem to indicate that in her behaviour out of doors the young maiden of the period was often apt to go to somewhat divergent extremes!

It is when we come upon a book of this kind, handed down through so many years, that we begin to realise the manners and habits of a bygone age. It indicates to us that then, as now, a code of etiquette was absolutely essential to the smooth working of society. The principles of etiquette will always remain the same, but its rules must needs vary with the passing of time and fashion. *Autres temps, autres mœurs*—"and other manners too"; but the personal qualities which make the effective foundation of all good manners are necessary if the "polish" imparted by etiquette is not to be only a superficial one.

Etiquette of To-day.—Though we do not now need to have such quaintly elementary rules of etiquette drawn up for our observance, yet the fact remains that it is against the simple rules of good breeding that the woman of to-day is too often apt to transgress. It is in little things more than anything else that good breeding tells, and the gentlewoman who wishes to justify her claim to that title should aim at making her manners upon all occasions, whether in the family circle or at social gatherings, in the drawing-room, at the dinner-table, out of doors, in private as in public, beyond reproach.

How a Lady should Behave out of doors.—In her behaviour out of doors the gentlewoman is quiet and unassuming. She shuns any exaggeration of dress and fashion which would make her conspicuous; it is not her aim to attract the eye of the crowd, but to escape its notice. She does not sweep the pavement with trailing skirts or address her friends in loud tones. Neither does she attract attention by her boisterous laughter. The aim of the gentlewoman is to escape notice out of doors; that of the ill-bred woman to attract it. Therein lies the difference.

It is the lady's privilege to bow first, if she should meet a gentleman of her acquaintance.

The bow should be a gentle inclination of the head, not a jerky nod, nor a movement so slight as to be almost imperceptible.

A lady should also be the first to offer to shake hands. It is no longer fashionable to raise the arm in an exaggerated manner when shaking hands.

It is not necessary to make introductions between friends out of doors, excepting in the case of a lady being out with another lady with whom she is staying on a visit. In this case she would introduce any friends she might meet to her hostess.

Driving.—A lady should always enter a carriage before a gentleman. If two ladies are driving together, the lady of highest rank should enter it first, unless she particularly expresses a wish that her companion should do so.

A visitor should enter the motor car or carriage before her hostess.

When two ladies and a gentleman are driving together, the ladies should take the front seat, the gentleman sitting with his back to the horses. In a motor car the ladies should also occupy the front seat.

A gentleman should be always the first to get out of a motor car or carriage, in order to assist the ladies to alight.

Young ladies should always leave the place of honour in carriage or motor to the elder ladies.

Etiquette of the Table.—In no circumstances are bad manners more noticeable than when displayed at the table, whilst, on the other hand, it is at the table more than anywhere else that good breeding tells. To eat badly is to commit one of the greatest offences against the laws of politeness, and of all vulgarities vulgarity at table is without exception the very worst. A woman's innate refinement will often protect her in this direction, and she is as a rule less apt to err against the rules of table etiquette than a man.

Apart from the elementary rules of table politeness, however, there are certain laws of etiquette governing the manner of eating articles of food which, though found as a matter of course on the dinner-tables of the rich, are usually absent from the tables of those only moderately blessed with this world's goods, for the simple reason that they are luxuries that cannot be afforded in the poorer household.

It is in these circumstances that a woman endowed with good breeding but little means finds herself at a loss at times when asked to join the dinner-table of her wealthier sister. A woman of refinement will generally pull through the ordeal without committing any very glaring *faux pas*—for if any uncommon dish (to her) is put upon the table, she will wait and watch how the others eat it. But the very fact of having to do this involves a certain awkwardness of demeanour caused by over-anxiety to do the right thing and to avoid a mistake.

A woman should not be placed in this equivocal position, however perfect her imitative powers may be. She should always know what to eat and how to eat it. With the elementary rules of table etiquette every gentlewoman is acquainted, but for the benefit of those who are not quite *au fait* we give here the principal rules, elementary and otherwise, governing the important question of manners at the table.

How to Eat.—When you have taken your seat at the table, remove your gloves, unfold your serviette, taking from it the piece of bread or roll, which you place at your left-hand side, then spread the serviette over your lap.

As soon as you are served at table, begin to eat; to wait for others is now considered ill-bred.

Soup should be eaten with a table-spoon, and taken from the side of the spoon. When the quantity of soup on the plate is so small that it cannot be easily taken up by the spoon with the plate in its normal position, gently tilt the plate—not towards you, but away from you—so that it can be taken up more easily.

Rissoles, mince, and other similar-made dishes should be eaten with a fork only.

All sweets, where possible, should be eaten with a fork alone.

A spoon and fork may be used for fruit tarts. Either the spoon or the fork should be raised to the mouth for the purpose of receiving the fruit stones. In the case of plums and other large stone fruit, it is better to separate the stone from the fruit with the spoon and fork before putting the fruit into the mouth.

In eating asparagus, where no small asparagus tongs are provided, a knife and fork should be used, and the points should be cut off and eaten with a fork.

Salad is always served on salad plates. It should be eaten with a knife and fork.

It is, of course, needless to emphasise that the bones of game or poultry should not be taken up with the fingers.

The knife should not under any circumstances be raised to the mouth. When eating cheese, small pieces of cheese are placed upon small pieces of bread and so conveyed to the mouth with the fingers.

In eating artichokes the outer leaves are removed with a knife and fork; the inner leaves can then be taken up to the mouth with the fingers.

Savouries, when possible, should be eaten with a fork.

Oysters should be eaten with a dinner-fork. Hold the oyster shell on the plate with the left hand, remove tho entire oyster with the fork, which is held in the right hand, and convey it to the mouth.

Fish is always eaten with a fish knife and fork. Failing these, it may be eaten with a fork and a crust of bread.

The skin and stones of grapes and cherries should not be ejected direct from the mouth to the plate. The hand should be raised to the mouth to receive them.

Strawberries when served without cream can be taken up by the stalks in the fingers. When served with cream, the stalks should be separated from the fruit with a spoon. Strawberries and cream are eaten with a spoon and fork.

Pears, apples, peaches and nectarines are eaten with a fruit knife and fork. The fruit is held on the fork with the left hand and peeled with the knife, which is held in the right hand; it is then divided into halves and quarters.

Oranges are divided into halves and quarters, and each quarter is peeled separately as required.

Pineapple is eaten with a dessert knife and fork, and melon with a spoon and fork.

Finger glasses containing water are placed on doyleys on the dessert plates. Both finger glass and doyley should be removed at the beginning of dessert, and placed at the side of the dessert plate. When dessert is over, the fingers may be dipped into the finger glass and wiped with the serviette.

General Hints.—Never crumble your bread or fidget with the table service; to do so indicates that you are unaccustomed to good society. When not eating, keep your hands away from the table.

Do not fold your serviette after dinner at a friend's house; leave it on the table before you. When staying on a visit, however, a serviette ring will be allotted to you for ordinary occasions; then the serviette would be folded and placed in the ring.

Never take a second helping of soup or fish.

A hostess should never unduly press a guest to partake of a certain dish, however hospitable her motive may be.

INTRODUCTIONS

A knowledge of the rules of etiquette governing introductions between friends is of the utmost importance for every woman, no matter what her social position may be. The chief things to be remembered in regard to making introductions are :—

1. Introductions should not be made indiscriminately without regard for the wishes of the persons who are introduced to each other. An introduction which is unwelcome to either one or the other of the parties should be avoided at all costs, as the person who does not desire the acquaintance may in some cases feel compelled to show by her manner what her feelings are upon the subject.

Before introducing one person to another, therefore, always find out if the introduction will be acceptable to both parties. If the persons are of different rank, it will be sufficient to consult the person of higher rank before making the introduction.

2. Always introduce a gentleman to a lady irrespective of any question of rank. Precedence in this manner is one of the privileges of the sex. Always mention the name of the person you are introducing first, thus: "Mr. X—Miss Z," would be the correct formula, Mr. X being introduced to Miss Z. This mere mentioning of the names of the party is sufficient, but when it is wished to adopt a less formal method the person making the introduction might say, "May I introduce Mr. X to you, Miss Z?"

3. If seated, a lady need not rise when a gentleman is introduced to her, unless that gentleman is her host, or else some clerical dignitary to whom she should show respect by reason of his office.

4. Upon being introduced both bow but do not shake hands. If a lady offers her hand to a gentleman, it is an act of grace on her part. When introductions are made between ladies, the lady of lower rank should be introduced to the lady of higher rank. An unmarried lady should be introduced to a married lady, unless the unmarried lady is of a higher rank than the married lady. Ladies only bow to one another as a rule upon being introduced, but should the lady of higher rank offer her hand, it may be taken as a mark of favour on her part. When ladies are of equal rank, the younger lady should be introduced to the elder one.

5. A hostess should shake hands with every one introduced to her in her own house. When a person introduces two of her very great friends to each other it would be quite correct for them to shake hands. In the same way when a young girl is introduced to an elderly lady, the latter usually shakes hands as a mark of kindness.

6. At a dinner-party it is customary for the hostess to present the gentleman to the lady whom he is to take in to dinner. It is not necessary for her to ask the lady's permission before doing so.

7. After dinner the hostess uses her own discretion as to what ladies she will introduce to each other in the drawing-room.

8. Gentlemen continuing at the table over the "walnuts and wine" talk with each other without introduction.

9. At afternoon At Homes, garden parties, and similar functions the hostess should use her own judgment as to what introductions should be made. She should introduce gentlemen to the ladies in order that the former may look after the needs of the latter in the way of taking them to the tea-room. Gentlemen should always realise what is expected of them on these occasions and act accordingly. Acquaintances made in this manner do not involve more than a bowing acquaintance afterwards.

10. The lady should always be the first to bow to a gentleman upon meeting him on subsequent occasions.

11. Ladies do not rise from their seats upon being introduced to each other on ordinary occasions, or At Homes, or in the drawing-room after dinner.

12. In ball-rooms the real responsibility for introductions rests much more with chaperons than with stewards. The latter can only interpret according to their judgment the advisability of introductions. If an introduction is sought by a gentleman he is bound either to dance, or at all events to show the usual civilities of the supper-room, to the lady to whom he sought to be introduced.

13. When two or three ladies call on the same afternoon at the same house, the hostess generally feels it necessary to introduce them to each other. Introductions so made will warrant a bowing acquaintance.

Letters of Introduction.—It is not wise to be too ready to give letters of introduction. Friends feel bound to show special courtesies and hospitality to a person introduced to them in this manner, however they may feel disposed towards her.

Upon hearing that an acquaintance has the intention of visiting some particular town, a good-natured woman will often be heard to exclaim, "Oh, I must give you an introduction to Mrs. X. She is sure to give you a good time," without pausing to think what Mrs. X would think of her suggestion. By giving introductions in this way, a woman must remember that she taxes both the courtesy and hospitality of the friend to whom the introduction is addressed. If her friend is in a superior rank of life, it is only right to ask her permission before sending the letter.

The letter of introduction should never be closed, and the bearer should leave it with her card without asking to see the hostess.

If the latter is well disposed, she should as soon as possible send an invitation to dinner or an At Home, or any similar function.

THE ETIQUETTE OF VISITING CARDS

There is much in the etiquette of card-leaving that is misunderstood, and many *gaucheries* are habitually committed, through ignorance, in contravention of the recognised rules governing this important social custom. The leaving of cards may be said to be the most efficient method of regulating a lady's visiting list, forming an unfailing index to her choice of acquaintance. It is also the means decreed by society for the exchange of the various civilities around which the social wheel revolves.

The principal rules governing the etiquette of cards are as follows :—

Style and Size of Lady's Card.—A lady's card should always be plain in type, unglazed, and free from any kind of ornamentation. In size it should be from 3¼ to 3⅝ inches wide and 2½ inches in depth. The name of the lady should be printed in the centre of the card, and her address in the lower left-hand corner. If she has a country as well as a town address, the second address may be printed in the opposite corner. If she has an At Home day, this should be printed or written across the top left-hand corner.

A married woman should never have her Christian name printed on her cards. If her husband is the senior member of his family, her name would be printed simply—' Mrs. Brown." If he has a father or an elder brother, then her husband's Christian name should be used before the surname—" Mrs. James Brown."

How to leave Cards when making Calls.—Ladies leave their visiting cards personally when walking, not by servants or through the post office.

When the Lady called upon is not at Home.—When a married lady calls upon another married lady and finds the latter " not at home," she should leave her own card for the mistress of the house, and two of her husband's cards, one for the master of the house and one for the mistress.

Excepting in the case of a first call, however, a lady very often nowadays leaves only one of her husband's cards in addition to her own, if he is very well acquainted with her friend's husband and they are constantly meeting.

When the lady called upon has a grown-up daughter or daughters, the lady leaving cards should turn down the right-hand corner of her card to indicate that she wishes to include the daughter (or daughters) in her call.

If the lady called upon is a widow, only one of the caller's husband's cards should be left.

If the lady who is making the call is driving, she should send her footman to inquire if the lady called upon is at home. If he is told that she is not at home, his mistress should hand him the cards to be left on her behalf.

When the Lady called upon is at Home.—When the mistress of the house *is* at home, the lady making the call should leave two of her husband's cards on the hall table upon leaving. She must not in this case leave her own card. If her husband is very intimate with her friend's husband and it is not a first call, it will only be necessary to leave one of her husband's cards.

Cards are never sent up with the servant when calling unless the call is of a *strictly business* nature.

Leaving Cards upon Newcomers.—When new people settle in a county district, the residents should be the first to either call or leave cards upon them. This they can do without having any previous acquaintance with the new people. The latter should never, even if they be of higher rank, call upon the residents first. They should return call for call and card for card, but if they do not wish to continue the acquaintance, they can intimate this desire by merely leaving cards in return for the call. The custom of calling upon new people is characteristic of county and country society, but does not prevail in London and other large cities.

In leaving cards upon a friend who is the guest of a person with whom the caller is unacquainted, there is no need to leave a card upon the hostess.

Except where the persons called upon are living in hotels, it is " bad form " for visitors to write upon the cards left the names of the persons for whom they are intended.

Card Etiquette for Brides.—A bride should not send out cards to her friends or give an At Home after the honeymoon is over. She must wait for them to call upon her. A newly married bride generally makes a point of being at home in the afternoons during the first fortnight after her return home in order to receive the calls of her friends.

Difference between making Calls and leaving Cards.—All the rules given above concern the etiquette of cards in " making calls." But there are instances in which cards are left apart from the ordinary social function of paying visits. In this case they are left as a mark of civility or acknowledgment of civility or hospitality received. When a card is simply left it is not necessary to ask if the lady is at home.

Calls should always be returned by *calls* and *cards* by *cards* within a week or ten days at latest, and care must be taken that a call is not returned by a " card " only, or a " card " by a " call." If a superior in rank should waive ceremony and return a call for a card, this mark of extra civility may be taken as a compliment by the recipient. If, however, she only repays a call with a card, it is obvious that she does not wish to improve the acquaintance.

Great punctiliousness should be observed in regard to the returning " call for call " and " card for card " etiquette, otherwise, apart from the *gaucherie* involved by ignorance of these social rules, a slight may be conveyed where there is no intention of showing one, and positive offence given to the person slighted in this manner.

Leaving Cards after Entertainments.—After the following entertainments cards should be left by all invited (whether present or not) within a week of the entertainment: balls, weddings, receptions, private theatricals, amateur concerts, dinners.

Dinner Calls.—Only after dinner-parties need you ask if the hostess is at home. In this case, what is called a " dinner call " is made. In the other cases card-leaving is sufficient. It is not necessary to leave cards after a luncheon party or an ordinary At Home.

Cards " To Inquire."—Cards to inquire after friends who are ill are left in person, and must bear simply the words written above the printed name—" To inquire after Mrs. ——." In the stage of convalescence there comes in return through the post an ordinary visiting card with the words written above the name, " With thanks for kind inquiries." In the case of an accouchement " to inquire " cards are either left personally or by servants.

P.P.C. Cards.—P.P.C. or *Pour Prendre Congé*—" to take leave "—cards are usually left upon their friends by people who are going away for a period of from three to six months, or who are leaving a neighbourhood for good. These cards should be left within a week or ten days of departure, either in person or by servants.

In large cities arrivers intimate their arrival by leaving cards upon friends who otherwise might not know of it. Ladies having a large circle of acquaintances very often in these circumstances send their cards to their acquaintances by a man-servant, or in some cases give a list of addresses to their stationers who undertake to send the cards out.

Wedding and memorial cards are now out of fashion.

Card Etiquette for Young Girls.—A young unmarried girl does not have cards of her own, but has her name printed underneath her mother's name on her mother's cards. This is also the case where there are several young daughters who are "out." It is always better form to have each name printed separately under the mother's name, though if there were four or five grown-up daughters the term "The Misses" would be permissible.

When young girls are chaperoned in society by friends, their names should be written in pencil under the names of the ladies chaperoning them on the visiting cards of the chaperons.

When a girl is on a visit without her parents, and wishes to call upon a friend, she should use a card on which her name and that of her mother's is printed, crossing out the mother's name in pencil. Unmarried ladies past their first youth should have their own visiting cards.

The Motherless Girl.—Very often through the death of her mother a young girl suddenly finds herself head of her father's house, and responsible for all its social observances. Though used to the routine of calls and card-leaving as discharged by her mother, she will find that in her case circumstances are slightly different. There are rules of etiquette governing a young girl's social observances when left in this position, and she should make herself *au fait* with these before embarking upon the additional social duties enforced upon her in these sad circumstances.

When a girl has no mother, her name is usually printed under her father's name upon his card, which in this case are of the style and size of a lady's card.

When returning a call upon a married lady who is not at home, one of these cards (with the name of father and daughter) should be left. If her father is well acquainted with the husband of the lady called upon, there is no need to leave one of his personal cards as well; but if, on the other hand, the two men are only slightly acquainted with each other, it will be necessary to do so.

If the lady called upon is at home, only one of the father's personal cards should be left.

In calling upon a widow, one of the cards with the father's and daughter's names should be left. If the widow has a daughter, a corner of the card should be turned down to include her in the call. If the daughter is middle-aged, a separate joint card of father and daughter should be left for her.

Leaving Cards after Entertainments.—After being invited to a ball, reception, or other similar function given by married people, a joint card of the father and daughter should be left within a week of the function; and as this comes under the category of card-leaving as acknowledgment of civility and hospitality, there is no need to ask if the mistress of the house is at home.

After a dinner, however, a call should be made, the father accompanying his daughter if possible. If he does not do so she should leave two of his personal cards on departure.

If an aunt or other relative of the motherless girl should come to live with her, the social duties would of course fall upon her as chaperon. In this case the girl's name would be printed on her chaperon's cards, and the etiquette observed would be the same as during her mother's life, until the chaperonage is dispensed with.

Gentlemen's Cards.—In size a gentleman's card is usually 3 inches wide and 1½ inches deep. His name should be printed in the centre of the card and always with the prefix "Mr." (if he has no higher title). Printing the Christian and surname without any prefix, as in "James Brown," is not considered good form. An officer in the Navy adds R.N. or R.I.M. (Royal Indian Marine) after his name, but no King's Counsel, Member of Parliament or Doctor of whatever faculty adds K.C., M.P., LL.D., D.D., to their card names. Baronets and Knights, until recently, were simply "Sir James Brown," without Bart. or Kt., but since the Lord Chamberlain's instructions that baronets attending Courts should have their rank of baronet on their cards, it is usual for them to indicate their rank on their printed visiting cards. Officers in the Army have the name of their club down in the left-hand corner, and the name of their regiment down in the right-hand corner.

In calling upon married people, a gentleman leaves two cards—one for the mistress and the other for the master.

A gentleman should not turn down the corner of his card; his call is upon the host and hostess, and not upon the young ladies of the house.

Calls are not made nor cards left by a gentleman upon new acquaintances, however pleasant they may have been to him at a dinner or ball in another person's house, without a clear intimation from the lady that a call at her house would be agreeable to her.

The same rules apply to gentlemen as to ladies with regard to leaving cards after entertainments.

Bachelors call upon bachelors after receiving hospitality, unless they are upon such intimate footing as to dispense with ceremony.

INVITATIONS

There are certain points of etiquette to be observed in regard to sending invitations. Invitations, it must be remembered, are of two kinds, formal and informal. All formal invitations are printed on special cards and worded in the third person—whilst for informal occasions, such as a luncheon party, or a small tea party, the invitation usually takes the form of a short note, or else it may be written on a visiting card. A hostess should guard herself from falling into the error of issuing an informal invitation for a formal occasion, or a formal invitation for an informal function—for to do either would indicate that she had a lack of that *savoir faire* which sets a hall mark upon social entertaining.

Dinner Invitations.—Dinner invitations are issued in the name of both the host and hostess. If the host is a widower with a young daughter, the invitations are issued in the name of both himself and his daughter. In the case of a brother and sister who live together the invitations would be issued in the name of both brother and sister. The following is the usual form for printed dinner invitations :—

> "*Mr. and Mrs. Black request the pleasure of Mr. and Mrs. Brown's company at dinner, on Tuesday, the 6th of January, at* 8 *o'clock.*"

The reply, if acceptance, should take the following form :—

> "*Mr. and Mrs. Brown accept with pleasure Mr. and Mrs. Black's kind invitation to dinner on the 6th of January.*"

Invitations to At Homes.—An invitation to an At Home should be sent in the name of the hostess only. At Home invitations are printed upon At Home cards—the name of the hostess, with the words "At Home" underneath it, being printed in the middle of the card, with the day and date underneath the words "At Home." The address should be printed on the right-hand corner at the bottom of the card, and any amusement provided for the guests should be added on the left-hand corner. The letters *R.S.V.P.* may be written or printed on the card, but in the case of an afternoon At Home it is not usual to add them, as answers as a rule are not expected to these functions. If an answer is required, however, the letters *R.S.V.P.* should be added. The name of the person invited should be written in ink on the top left-hand corner.

Balls and Dances.—Invitations to balls and dances are sent out on ordinary At Home cards, the word "Dancing" being printed in the corner of the card. The word ball should never be used on the card, the same form of invitation being used for both small dances and large balls entailing a most lavish expenditure.

An acceptance to a ball invitation is written on ordinary notepaper. The following is the usual form of acceptance :—

> "*Mr. and Mrs. Black have much pleasure in accepting Mrs. Brown's kind invitation for Friday, the 6th of November.*"

Garden Parties.—Invitations to a Garden Party should be issued in the name of the hostess upon "At Home" cards. Any outdoor amusement provided, such as tennis, should be written in the lower left-hand corner of the card. It is also usual to add the words "and party" after the name of the person invited. When Garden Parties are given on a very large scale, the invitation may take this form :—

> "*Mrs. A. requests the pleasure of Mr. and Mrs. B.'s company at a Garden Party on——*"

Weddings.—Wedding invitations are now very plain. Black lettering is much more used than the silver lettering which was formerly considered indispensable, although the latter still has a certain vogue. The invitations may be printed on sheets of notepaper which form a kind of combination of a notepaper sheet and envelope, having a flap at the upper end which is folded over and so posted; or they may be issued on a simple card with envelope to match, or printed on ordinary notepaper. The wording should be as follows :—

> "*Mr. and Mrs. Crane request the pleasure of Mr. and Mrs. Mason's company at the marriage of their daughter Laura, with Mr. Reginald Dark, on Monday,* 17*th June, at St. Paul's, Knightsbridge, and afterwards at* 2 *Eaton Square.*
> *R.S.V.P.*"

Acceptances and Refusals.—Formal invitations sent in the third person should be answered in the same manner if the answer is an acceptance. In sending a refusal it is always more courteous, however, to give some explanation, and this should in the case of intimate friends be written in the third person. Thus :—

> "*Mr. and Mrs. X. regret that absence from town prevents them from accepting Mrs. Z.'s kind invitation for the 4th of November.*"

is more courteous than :—

> "*Mr. and Mrs. X. regret that they are unable to accept Mrs. Z.'s kind invitation for the 4th of July.*"

Although printed cards of refusal are in use, it is always more courteous to send refusals in writing. In some cases it happens that though one member of the family invited to a dance or other party is prevented from some reason from accepting, yet the other members are able to accept. The circumstances in a case of the kind should always be explained by letter. Thus :—

> *"Dear Mrs. X.—I regret that I shall be out of town on the day of your dance, or I should have much pleasure in accepting your kind invitation. My sister, however, will be at home, and will be very pleased to accept.—Yours sincerely."*

General Hints regarding Invitations.—Formal invitations need not be given to luncheon parties, small informal At Homes, nor christenings.

One invitation card is sufficient for the husband, wife, and daughters of a family, but separate cards must be sent to the sons.

Invitations should always be answered promptly.

In inviting a friend to stay with her on a visit, a hostess should always be careful to specify the exact time the visit is to last.

The title, "the Honourable," is never written on cards of invitation.

PAYING AND RECEIVING CALLS

Paying Calls.—A strict observance of the etiquette governing the paying and returning of calls is all-important, as any neglect or ignorance of the rules of visiting exposes the offender to the danger of receiving the "cold shoulder" from her friends, sometimes to the extent of being excluded from all their dances, At Homes, and other entertainments.

A mother with grown-up daughters should be especially punctilious in this direction. Many mothers, once their daughters have attained years of discretion, show the inclination to shift most of their social duties upon the shoulders of their girls. This is a great mistake. Once her daughters are "out," a mother should be more than ever on the alert in regard to her social obligations if she has their welfare at heart. It should be her endeavour to see that they get asked out to the right places to meet the right people, and that every opportunity is given them of meeting desirable friends and making suitable marriages. If she withholds these opportunities from them by any laxity in the performance of her social obligations, then she fails most lamentably in one of her most important duties towards them.

Etiquette for the Visitor.—All calls should be returned within a week or ten days. If the person on whom the call is due has an At Home day, the call should be made on her At Home day. Afternoon calls, or "morning calls," as they are often designated, are made between the hours of 3 and 6 o'clock, a first or strictly formal call being usually made before 4.30.

If driving when making a call, a lady should send her footman to inquire if Mrs. X is at home.

If Mrs. X is not at home, she should give him the necessary cards to leave (see p. 330).

If walking when making the call, she should ask the servant who answers the door, "Is Mrs. X at home?" If the answer is in the negative, the necessary cards must be left (see p. 330).

If, however, the answer is in the affirmative, the visitor should follow the servant to the drawing-room, giving her name to the servant to be announced.

Never give a visiting card to the servant when the mistress of the house is at home.

The hostess will advance to meet the visitor and shake hands with her; the visitor should then take a seat and engage in conversation with her hostess.

A visitor should cultivate ease and self-possession in conversation and manners. A flurried manner will show that she is not accustomed to go out much into society.

When a second guest is announced, the first guest should take her leave as soon as possible afterwards.

It is not necessary for a lady to rise when introduced to another visitor.

When one visitor leaves, it is not necessary for the other to rise. Visitors who have been introduced to each other at an afternoon call merely bow upon leaving. They should also bow if they have spoken to each other without being introduced.

When the visitor is a gentleman, he should leave his hat and stick in the hall upon arrival. Formerly it was the custom for men to take their hats and sticks with them into the drawing-room when making calls, but this has now been superseded by the newer custom.

A gentleman visitor should hand round the tea and cakes to the ladies. When a lady rises to leave, he should open the drawing-room door for her. He should of course rise each time another visitor enters, as no gentleman should remain seated whilst his hostess is standing.

Receiving Calls.—A lady should always be careful to intimate to her parlour-maid early each afternoon if she will be at home or "not at home" to callers. When a servant is not sure that her mistress is free to receive visitors, and has to make the inquiry whilst the caller waits, if she comes back with the answer "not at home," it might often be interpreted by the caller as meaning that the lady called upon is at home to other people but not to her. For this reason it is always better to give definite instructions as to callers early in the afternoon.

The mistress of a house cannot be too careful in training her servants as to their correct attitude towards callers. Even the solitary "general" can be made to understand that it is great discourtesy to leave a caller upon the doorstep whilst she goes to find out if her mistress is in; and yet this has been done time after time in houses where the mistress is either careless in regard to the training of her servants, or else is not *au fait* herself in the social rules.

If a servant is in doubt as to whether her mistress is "at home," she should ask the caller to come in, saying, "Will you come in, please, while I inquire," returning as soon as possible with the answer.

When the mistress of the house is at home, the servant should reply to the inquiry in the affirmative, stepping aside to allow the caller to enter. On wet days she should relieve the caller of her umbrella, any extra wraps, such as mackintoshes, cloaks, &c., and then preceding her she should lead the way to the drawing-room. Outside the drawing-room door the servant should pause, making the inquiry, "What name, please?" She should listen attentively to the name given by the caller, then opening the drawing-room door wide, and standing well inside the doorway—never behind the door—she should announce the name of the visitor clearly and distinctly. Should the mistress, however, not be in the drawing-room, she should merely say "My mistress will be down directly," or words to that effect, and should at once go to apprise her mistress of the caller's arrival.

A servant should not knock at the drawing-room door before ushering in visitors.

The hostess should never keep a caller waiting while she hastily dons another dress. If she has intimated to her servant her intention of "being at home" she should naturally be prepared to receive visitors, and should if possible be in the drawing-room during the calling hours.

If she is in the drawing-room when the caller is announced, she should rise to meet her, shake hands, and offer her a chair near her own. If it is a first call and the two have therefore no intimate subject in common, she should lead the conversation to topics of general interest which are likely to appeal to almost every woman. It should be the aim of the hostess to put her guest at her ease, and encourage her to shine in conversation. The tactful hostess can converse and stimulate conversation without an effort, and without the assistance of the inevitable post-card or photograph album, which form the invariable resource of the hostess in suburbia who is unaccustomed to the etiquette of calls. (See the Art of Conversation, p. 352.)

The servant should know that tea should be brought up to the drawing-room as a matter of course, and should bring it in at the usual time. If, however, the call happens to be an unusually early one, and the hostess is anxious that her guest should be shown the usual afternoon hospitality, she should ring the bell and indicate that she wishes tea served at once and before the usual hour.

When the visitor rises to take her leave, the hostess should ring the bell to intimate to the servant that she should be ready in the hall to show her out. If there is only one caller, the hostess should accompany her to the drawing-room door, or even to the top of the stairs, waiting until she has gone down, as an additional mark of courtesy.

When one or two people call on the same afternoon, the hostess should rise to receive each caller.

It is always better to introduce the callers to each other where there are only two or three. Upon regular At Home days, when a number of guests are present, it is unnecessary to do this, the hostess using her own discretion as to what introductions she will make; but on ordinary occasions when two or three callers are in the room at the same time, it is always more courteous to introduce them, if only for the purpose of including them in the general conversation.

If, however, there is some potent reason why an introduction would not be feasible between two callers, a tactful hostess can manage to draw them both into the conversation without introducing them.

Tea is brought in by the servant, and placed upon a small table near the hostess. Care should be taken that the tea equipage is of the daintiest—the silver brightly polished, the tea-cups and saucers, tea-cloth and doyleys spotlessly clean, and that the cakes and bread and butter are daintily and tastefully arranged.

The hostess should pour out the tea herself; she should also hand round the cups to her guests, unless there is a gentleman present, when he would be naturally expected to perform the ordinary courtesies in this direction.

When there are two or more callers present, the hostess should rise and shake hands as each one takes leave, but she should not see each caller to the drawing-room door. If any one of the callers is of much higher rank than the others in the room, however, it is permissible for her to do so.

When the host is at home he might accompany each departing guest down into the hall. This would be a special mark of courtesy. In any case he should see each guest to the drawing-room door, waiting at the top of the stairs until she has descended.

The At Home Day.—Many people with a large circle of acquaintances set apart a day once a week or once every fortnight to receive their friends who wish to call upon them. This day thus set apart is known as an At Home day, and a lady always has her At Home day printed upon her cards. The At Home day must not be confounded with the "afternoon At Home." The latter is a social function or afternoon party on a large scale, whilst the At Home day is merely the regular day set apart by a hostess to receive calls, and even although the circle of acquaintances may be so large that the number of callers on an At Home day is sometimes very great, yet the two are quite distinct.

On her At Home days the hostess should of course be in the drawing-room all the afternoon ready to receive her guests; tea should be brought in at the usual time, and placed upon a small table near the hostess.

A plate-stand containing thin bread and butter, sandwiches, hot cakes, *petits fours*, or other small fancy cakes, and cut cake, should be placed near the tea-table. One of these stands is almost indispensable for afternoon tea, and the wicker ones can be obtained at very moderate prices. The sandwiches should be very deftly cut. They should be very tiny, and are usually in shape of a small triangle. Watercress, cucumber, egg, potted meat and jam sandwiches are the most suitable for afternoon teas.

Tea is usually brought in at about four o'clock upon an At Home day. The mistress can always ring for fresh tea when she requires it. Tea should never be served in the dining-room excepting on the occasion of large afternoon At Homes.

Some ladies make it a point of never being "at home" to callers except upon their At Home days. When a lady has an At Home day, her friends should contrive to make their calls upon that day.

At Home days are specially useful for people who, living in the town, have a large acquaintance in the suburbs, or *vice versâ*.

VISITING

The Guest.—When invited to stay at a friend's house, the visitor should keep two things well in mind:—

1. To conform to the rules of the household.
2. Never to outstay her welcome.

The time for the visit is usually specified by the hostess, and the visitor should strictly adhere to it. More often than not such a phrase as "Can you not stay a little longer?" is a mere *façon de parler* on the part of the hostess, and must not be taken literally.

In cases where the wish of the hostess is manifestly sincere, and she asks you as a favour to stay a little longer, do so if you can manage it, but always remember that it is better to leave too soon than to stay too long.

If you are just upon an ordinary visit to a friend's house, and perhaps the only visitor, your day will be well mapped out for you. Always be punctual in your attendance at meals. Be down in time for breakfast. In ordinary middle-class homes, where a certain routine prevails, breakfast is not served at all hours for the convenience of guests.

When visiting friends, a certain amount of tact is indispensable. Do not always be at your hostess's elbow when she is busy with household duties; know when to be at hand and when to make yourself scarce. If upon any occasion you see that you are in the way, and that your hostess is too much overburdened with a sense of duty towards you to leave you to your own devices, make some excuse in the way of letters to write or some other similar plea, and so leave her undisturbed to whatever work she has in hand.

Occasional little delicate attentions on the part of the guest, such as a gift of a few flowers, are much appreciated by a hostess, conveying as they do that the guest appreciates the trouble that is being taken upon her behalf.

Dress.—What dresses to take with you on a visit will depend altogether upon the position in life of your hostess. If she is in very humble circumstances it would be unkind to flaunt before her eyes fine clothes with which she cannot hope to compete. On the other hand, she would resent it if, knowing you habitually dressed well, you brought all your oldest and shabbiest clothes to wear when staying with her. Whatever the circumstances, your clothes should be always fresh and neat. A trim tailor-made for morning and outdoor wear is indispensable, with a good supply of plain and dressy blouses. An afternoon dress and hat, a smart demi-toilette for informal evenings at home, and an evening dress and cloak for going out to dinner-parties, &c., would meet the sum of your requirements for a week's stay.

Be careful that your boots and gloves are of the neatest. A lady is known as such by attention to these details.

Luggage.—A common error into which women, and especially young girls, fall when going away for a short visit is in regard to the enormous amount of luggage they take with them. This on occasions proves a source of actual annoyance to the hostess, especially if the luggage is of a large and bulky nature. It not only gives extra trouble to the servants in carrying it upstairs, but on many occasions a particularly unwieldy trunk has caused damage to the banisters and wall-paper when being conveyed to the visitor's room. In these days of neat compact luggage, such a state of things is inexcusable. A neat, light compressed cane dress-box for a week's or even a fortnight's visit is sufficient, with perhaps a small hat-box in addition, whilst often a good-sized handbag will meet all the requirements of a week-end visit. Whatever luggage you may take, be careful above all that it is light and of normal size. Let it be as smart and fresh-looking as possible. Shabby luggage invariably conveys an unfavourable impression, yet many women are apt to be very negligent in this important detail.

General Hints.—It should always be the aim of the visitor to give as little trouble as possible. She should in the first instance keep her bedroom neat and tidy. Many young girls have a habit of leaving their dresses here, there, and everywhere about the room—tearing up papers and throwing them anywhere; in fact, leaving their things in such a general state of disorder that it takes the housemaid quite a long time to put the room straight. This is very thoughtless behaviour on the part of the guest. She should be careful always to leave her bedroom scrupulously tidy. Upon getting up in the morning she might strip the bed of its bed-clothes, and open the windows wide, seeing that all her dresses are neatly put away before going down to breakfast. She should also be very careful not to leave books and needlework lying about in the various reception rooms.

Whatever untidy ways she may have fallen into at home, she should be careful to be most punctilious as far as orderliness is concerned when away. Many hostesses are caused excessive annoyance by the untidiness of their visitors—annoyance which is all the greater, as etiquette forbids them to express their disapproval.

It is always a mark of courtesy for a visitor to write a letter to her hostess as soon as possible after her return home, expressing the great pleasure she has derived from her visit. Many people dub this custom old-fashioned. This it may be, but at the same time it is one of the good old-fashioned customs which, happily for the laws of politeness, is still *de rigueur*.

Tips.—The question of tips is a vexed one and the cause of much perplexity to the average woman. Their amount will altogether depend upon the extent of the establishment of your hostess. Where only one servant is kept, for a week-end visit 2s. would be sufficient; for a week 3s. would about meet the case, and 5s. would be ample for a fortnight's stay. Where there are two servants, cook and housemaid, the housemaid only need be given a tip, for it is she who brings you your hot water in the morning, attends to your room and sees to your comfort generally. The same scale of tips as that mentioned for the one servant would be suitable for her.

Where there are both housemaid and parlourmaid, tips should be given to each upon the scale already mentioned.

A young girl is never expected to give so much as a married woman, but her tip should in no case be under 2s. Two shillings would be ample for a week's visit, where one or two servants are kept. In houses where there are three servants, she might give 2s. to the parlourmaid, and 2s. to the housemaid after a week's visit.

Where a butler is kept a married lady staying without her husband, or an elderly unmarried lady, would naturally give him 5s. after a week's stay. Young girls are never expected to tip men-servants.

The Hostess.—The hostess should do all in her power to make her guest's stay a pleasant one without unduly fussing over her. The latter attitude only serves to make the guest uncomfortable and mar her enjoyment. Let your guest enjoy a sense of freedom, and do not always give her the feeling of being tied to your apron-strings. Study her tastes and try to conform to them. See that everything in her room is in order for her comfort—that the writing-table is well furnished with notepaper and ink, and the pin-cushion supplied with pins. The window-curtains should be clean and bright, and a few flowers daintily arranged in vases would add materially to the cheerfulness of the room. One or two of the latest novels might also be placed on the table, and a cosy easy-chair on which she could recline and indulge in a quiet read would be much appreciated.

Attention to these little details go much towards contributing to the enjoyment of the visitor, betokening as they do the truly hospitable hostess. Above all, let your visitor "feel at home" in every way. This is the essence of true hospitality.

Country House Visiting.—House parties at country houses are very popular in society, and invitations for these are most eagerly sought after. The hostess usually specifies the time for which the invitation is extended. In the case of a visit of this kind, the obligation of leaving at the proper time and not outstaying your welcome is more than ever imperative. Necessarily the number of bedrooms is limited, and if a succession of visitors is expected, your room will be required for the next visitor.

During your stay you will generally find the morning hours free. Punctual attendance at breakfast is not necessary. Breakfast is served during certain hours, and each guest can serve herself when she comes down. Many take the morning meal in their bedrooms. Luncheon also is in most cases an informal meal, when unpunctuality is excusable, but never on any account be late for dinner. Be in the drawing-room at the required time beforehand, and never absent yourself after dinner.

Try to make your hostess feel that you are enjoying yourself, and be pleasant and agreeable to the other members of the party. Spare the servants unnecessary trouble on your behalf, and reward them suitably upon departing.

Tips.—Tips on the occasion of a country-house visit amount to a not inconsiderable item of expenditure, as the wealthier and higher the position of your hostess the higher the rate of tips expected by the servants. It is a general rule that men give more than women, and that very little is expected from young girls. The rule is to tip all those servants who perform special services for you. Thus where a husband

and wife are staying together on a visit, the husband tips the butler, valet, coachman, and any other servant who has waited upon him, whilst the wife tips the housemaid and the maid who may have assisted her in dressing (if she has not her own maid with her). The tips for the maids are usually calculated at the rate of a shilling per day for short visits, but the tip should never amount to less than 5s. Where a guest makes use of the services of her hostess's lady's-maid, she should give the latter 10s.

The men-servants in large houses as a rule expect gold from the gentlemen. An elderly unmarried woman, or a married woman on a visit without her husband, should also tip the butler and coachman—10s. to the butler, and 5s. to the coachman for a week's visit would be sufficient. A man, as a rule, would give double these tips.

In the shooting season tips to the gamekeeper form a very heavy item in the gentlemen's tipping list. Gold is absolutely *de rigueur*; for one day's partridge shooting the tip to the gamekeeper would be £1, whilst the loader would get from 2s 6d. to 5s. Any defalcation in this direction on the part of a guest would be repaid the next season by his relegation to an impossible place in the *battue*.

Dress.—Dress should be an all-important consideration to the members of a country-house party. Motoring and riding, as a rule, play a prominent part in the amusements afforded. In the summer, garden parties, lawn tennis and croquet are almost a foregone conclusion. It will be necessary therefore to take toilettes suitable for each and every function. A neat well-cut tailor-made is indispensable. It should be of the latest fashion, and made to clear the ground, as long skirts are particularly *outré* out of doors in the country. In the hot weather a good supply of dainty lingerie frocks will be found useful. For dinner full evening dress is always indispensable; the ladies as a rule also change their frocks for tea, smart afternoon dresses being worn upon this occasion. Care should be taken that the dresses taken upon a country-house visit are all fresh and neat. The woman of small means will find this question of dress a great tax upon her resources; but as she cannot hope to vie in her toilettes with her wealthier sisters, let her see that she is at least dressed suitably for all occasions. Though her dresses may be few in number, and in quality and style may not come up to the art of a Worth or a Paquin, yet if they fit well, and she is always suitably attired, she may rest happy in the knowledge that to be always suitably dressed is to have acquired the art of dressing well.

ENTERTAINING

Dinners.—Dinner-giving is one of the favourite methods of showing hospitality adopted by society; but rash indeed would be the host and hostess who attempted to entertain in this manner without a knowledge of dinner-party etiquette.

Invitations for large dinner-parties are issued three weeks beforehand; in some cases even this lengthy notice is extended, more especially if the party is of great social importance. For ordinary small dinner-parties, however, from a week to ten days' notice is considered sufficient. The invitation to a dinner is always issued in the name of the host and hostess (see Invitations, p. 332), and an acknowledgment (whether acceptance or refusal) should come promptly from the invited guest. People should always be more prompt in answering invitations to a dinner than in any other case. So much depends upon just the right number of guests being present and their suitable pairing; and how can a hostess make her arrangements in this direction if she does not know until the last moment which guests may be expected. Any discourtesy in this respect is not soon forgiven by a hostess, and the offender is very often excluded from her dinners in the future.

Punctuality at a dinner-party is another important rule. It is the height of discourtesy to keep a hostess and her guests waiting; always make a point of arriving fully a quarter of an hour before the time mentioned. 8.30 is the usual hour for large dinner-parties in town, though they may be given at any time between 8 and 9 o'clock. In the country, however, they often begin as early as 7.30.

Ladies take off their cloaks upon arrival in a room set apart for the purpose, whilst the gentlemen leave their hats and coats in the hall if there is no room set apart as a gentleman's cloak-room. The servant precedes each guest to the drawing-room and announces him or her in the usual way (see p. 334). Formerly a husband and wife upon being announced would enter the drawing-room arm-in-arm. This fashion is quite out of date now; the lady enters first, and is followed by the gentleman. The host and hostess come forward to shake hands with each guest.

Precedence.—The laws of precedence must be strictly observed at all dinner-parties (see p. 356). When dinner is announced by the butler (or parlour-maid where there is no man-servant), the host offers his right arm to the lady of highest rank and leads the way with her to the dining-room. The other couples follow in strict order of precedence, the gentleman of highest rank following last with the hostess. Husbands and wives should not be sent down together. In the dining-room the hostess takes the top of the table, the gentleman who has taken her in to dinner taking the place at her left hand. The host waits standing in his place at the bottom of the table until all his guests are seated—he indicates the places they are to take as they enter; the lady of highest rank seats herself at his right hand. At large dinner-parties a card on which the name of the guest is written is usually put before each place. A lady should always sit at the right hand of the gentleman who has taken her in to dinner.

At the conclusion of the dinner the hostess bows to the lady of highest rank, and the latter at once rises and leads the way from the dining-room, followed by all the ladies in the order in which they entered, the hostess following last of all. The gentlemen rise at the same time as the ladies, and remain standing until they have all gone out. The host or gentleman nearest the door opens it for them, and closes it after them. In the drawing-room coffee is almost immediately served to the ladies. Here the hostess may make what introductions she thinks fit between her lady guests. Coffee is taken to the dining-room a few minutes afterwards, and the gentlemen usually remain over their wine for about twenty minutes, after which they join the ladies in the drawing-room. The suggestion to rejoin the ladies is usually made by the gentleman of highest rank, who leads the way to the drawing-room, the host following last.

All the guests should shake hands with the host and hostess upon departure, and the host should conduct the lady guests who are unaccompanied to their carriages.

Selecting the Guests.—Much of the success of a dinner-party depends upon the discrimination exercised on the part of the host and hostess in selecting their guests. It is always as well to include one or two brilliant conversationalists in their list. Good talkers are invaluable at a function of the kind, and prove a great help to the host and hostess. Needless to say, people who are in any way uncongenial to each other should never be asked at the same time.

To give a successful dinner-party is not such an easy matter as it would seem. Everything depends upon the way it is arranged, and the arrangement should be well and carefully thought out beforehand. But "the best-laid schemes o' mice and men gang aft agley," and the guest who disappoints his or her hostess at the last minute is often the means of upsetting the most carefully-planned arrangements. Here again the tactful hostess should not be at a loss. If she has very many intimate friends and relations she can often prevail upon one of these to fill the gap as a very great favour without incurring the risk of giving offence. It would not do, of course, to give a tardy invitation of the kind to an ordinary friend or acquaintance. To do so would be to commit a discourtesy which would often be greatly resented by the person so asked.

Some Hints for the Hostess.—A hostess must avoid betraying any fussiness and nervousness of manner over little details that at times go wrong at a dinner-party, however well it may be organised. Some women sometimes fuss themselves into a veritable fever over trifling mistakes that more often than not no one else will have noticed. A hostess should always be calm and at her ease whatever happens—bright and alert to the exigencies of conversation, having the tact to divert it into different channels when it seems to bear upon subjects which might not be acceptable by all present. Given a tactful host and hostess, the right people as guests, a well-selected and well-cooked dinner, choice wines and good service, the success of the dinner cannot fail to be assured.

Luncheons.—There is a pleasing absence of ceremony about luncheons that commends itself to many, and for this reason luncheon parties within recent years have attained a considerable vogue. It is at luncheon that a hostess is in the habit of entertaining her more intimate friends, and the informal little gatherings at the luncheon hour are, as a rule, wholly enjoyable both for the hostess and for her guests.

Formerly at ordinary luncheons the servant, after having handed round the first dishes, would retire from the room leaving the hostess and her guests to serve themselves to sweets. It is more general now for the servants to hand round the dishes and remove the plates after each course, the guests helping themselves between whiles; whilst at strictly formal luncheon parties waiting is *de rigueur*. Where there are children in a family these are generally present at the luncheon table.

When expected guests arrive at the luncheon hour they are shown at once to the dining-room, but should they arrive beforehand, the hostess receives them in the drawing-room. The guests do not enter the dining-room arm-in-arm as for dinner, but singly, the ladies going first and the gentlemen following them.

All the ladies should not sit together, however; each gentleman should place himself beside a lady, if the places are not previously allotted by the hostess. The hostess usually leads the way with the lady of highest rank to the dining-room, or the host should do so if he is present, the hostess following last. The laws of precedence are not usually strictly in force, although it will be found that a woman of good breeding will invariably make way for one of higher rank than herself, so precedence is seldom altogether disregarded even at an informal luncheon party. Ladies should not remove their hats for lunch, but they may take off their wraps. When the host is present, the gentlemen guests usually remain in the dining-room with him for a short time after luncheon when the ladies have adjourned to the drawing-room. The hostess gives the signal for this adjournment to the lady of highest rank present, and the latter leads the way out, the hostess following last. Where the host is not present, however, gentlemen and ladies leave the room at the same time. Coffee is usually brought into the dining-room at the end of luncheon.

Formal invitations are very rarely given to luncheon parties, a verbal invitation in many cases being deemed sufficient. Very little notice is necessary, but in the case of a formal party a week's notice is sometimes given. The usual hour for luncheon is from 1.30 to 2. It is etiquette for the guests to leave as soon as possible after the adjournment to the drawing-room, unless they are specially requested to stay longer by the hostess. Strict punctiliousness must be observed in this respect.

Afternoon At Homes.—There is no more favourite social function for ladies, from both the point of view of the hostess and the point of view of the guest, than the afternoon At Home. It is a form of entertainment that recommends itself above all to the hostess of limited means, because it is one that can be effected upon quite a small scale, and at the same time enables her to make some sort of return for the hospitality she may have received from her wealthier friends.

The kinds and styles of afternoon At Homes are many and various. There is the large party given on the scale of an evening reception, when sometimes over two hundred guests are invited. An At Home given on this scale necessitates almost as much preparation as for an evening reception. Usually on these occasions some high professional talent is engaged for the entertainment of the guests. At large At Homes an awning should be put up, and a carpet set down at the front entrance, and cloak-rooms should be provided. Refreshments should be served in the dining-room from a long table or buffet, and the tea and coffee should be poured out and handed round by the maid-servants, the gentlemen usually helping themselves to champagne cup or other refreshment. (For refreshments given at large afternoon At Homes, see p. 252.)

The lady guests are escorted to the tea-room by the gentlemen.

At large At Homes the hostess should receive her guests at the drawing-room door, which should remain open, the hostess standing within the doorway. Servants should always be in attendance to call the guests' carriages as they leave, and the hostess does not ring the bell to signalise each departure as on the occasion of afternoon calls.

Small At Homes.—Small At Homes are those to which a small number of friends are invited, and as a rule no special entertainment is provided. The hostess receives her guests in the drawing-room as at afternoon calls (see p. 334). Tea may be served in the dining-room or in the drawing-room—generally in the former; although if the number of guests is very limited it is better to serve it in the drawing-room. It is handed round to the ladies by the gentlemen present.

At large At Homes entertainments of some kind are usually provided, but at small At Homes the hostess should be on the alert to entertain her guests. She should move amongst them freely and join in their conversation. The guests are free to move about as they like and speak to their various acquaintances on these occasions.

Invitations to large afternoon At Homes should be sent out a fortnight in advance, and for small afternoon At Homes a week in advance. (See Invitations, p. 332.)

Bridge Teas.—Afternoon At Homes are sometimes given for the purpose of playing bridge. Parties of this kind are known as Bridge Teas, and they usually begin about 3.30. It is necessary for the guest to arrive fairly punctually on these occasions.

For a Bridge Tea an informal note of invitation is usually sufficient.

Evening Parties.—Evening parties vary considerably as to their quality and extent, from the brilliant official or political reception graced by all the shining lights of diplomacy and politics, to the simple little social gathering at which the guests must rely solely upon the host and hostess, and the congenial company provided, for their entertainment. The strictly official and diplomatic parties are termed "Receptions," and are occasions of the utmost formality. All other evening parties are termed "At Homes."

At Homes may be given on a very large or upon a very modest scale. At the large evening At Homes some form of entertainment is usually provided for the guests, and an elaborate supper is one of the features of the evening; whilst for the smaller At Homes the entertainment is of quite informal nature, and only light refreshments are served.

At large At Homes the hostess should receive her guests at the head of the stairs or just inside the drawing-room door, whilst the host is in the drawing-room to welcome them as they enter. The approach to the front entrance should be carpeted, an awning should be put up, and a servant should be in attendance to open the carriage doors for the guests as they arrive, and to summon carriages and cabs for them as they leave.

Cloak-rooms should be placed at the disposal of both ladies and gentlemen, and tea and coffee should be served to the guests as soon as they arrive. The nature of the entertainment to be provided is usually specified on the invitation cards—professional humorists at the piano, raconteurs, &c. Pierrot troupes are now very much the vogue for evening At Homes. The hours for these evening functions vary from about 10 or 10.30 till about 1, although At Homes given on a Saturday should end at midnight. Supper is served usually about

11 o'clock. The host should take the lady of highest rank present in to supper. On ordinary occasions the hostess usually likes to see the principal guests in to supper before following herself; but if she does not require to do this she should follow the host with the gentleman of the highest rank. When a royal prince is present at a social function of the kind she should lead the way to the supper-room with the royal guest.

At small informal parties where light refreshments only are served, the gentlemen as a rule escort the ladies to the room in which is the buffet, and help them to whatever they require.

It is not necessary to take leave of the host and hostess after receptions.

Hiring Suites of Rooms.—In many cases a hostess is unwilling to turn her house topsy-turvy for the sake of a large reception or an evening party. In these circumstances she engages a suite of rooms at an hotel or elsewhere in which to entertain her guests. Most of the large hotels make the letting out of rooms for these occasions a special feature of their business, and will also undertake the entire catering if required. Rooms other than hotel suites may also be had suitable for the purpose; town halls, galleries, rooms belonging to various institutions, &c., are let for these occasions, and may be had for quite a moderate sum.

Caterers.—The large catering firms nowadays cater for all sorts of parties at a certain figure per head, sending their own trained servants, and providing cutlery, glass, decorations, napery, and everything necessary to the attendance and table equipment. When a hostess is giving a reception at her own home, she can do so with the minimum of trouble if she has secured the services of a good firm of caterers. The trained servants sent out by these firms are all experts in regard to the formalities required, and all the usual incidental details which prove such a source of anxiety to the hostess will be taken off her hands. In small establishments manned by a proportionately small staff of servants where an entertainment has been planned on a scale much beyond the average resources of the household, the caterer's aid is invaluable. And what is not the least recommendation of the catering system is, that everything is cleared away and the house restored to its normal order within the least possible time, and with the minimum of delay by the assistants who are sent down for the purpose, the household being usually enabled to resume its normal routine on the very next day. Only those who have experienced the usual domestic upheaval which follows any large entertainment will be able to appreciate to the full extent the benefit conveyed in this manner.

Bridge Parties.—"Bridge" forms the *raison d'être* of another very popular kind of evening party. A bridge party usually begins about nine o'clock, and all the guests should be punctual in their arrival. In most cases prizes are awarded to the winners in the game. There is a prize for ladies and a prize for gentlemen. In some cases second prizes are also awarded. The hostess should show a little discrimination in the selection of the prizes, choosing articles that would be likely to appeal to the recipients of both sexes. Sometimes very handsome prizes are given, but there is no need to go to great expense as long as the gifts are suitable. The card tables are usually numbered, and small cards are given to the guests as they enter, on which the number of each table is specified, together with the names of the four guests who have to sit at each table. Coffee is usually brought in to the drawing-room for the guests at the beginning of the evening. Either supper or light refreshments are served during the evening. In most cases supper is given at the end of the play about midnight or soon after, but in some cases it is served earlier in the evening, and the play resumed afterwards. The host leads the way to the supper-room with his partner in the game. The other partners follow, the hostess following last of all with her partner.

Balls and Dances.—Dancing has ever been, and ever will be, the favourite form of amusement amongst the young people of both sexes; it follows, therefore, that the most popular entertainment that can be given by a hostess is a ball or a dance. A ball is a dance given upon a very large scale. A great number of invitations are sent out; the arrangements for supper are most elaborate, the floral decorations are of the best, and a full band is engaged for the benefit of the dancers. To give a ball in the true sense of the word is to entail a very lavish expenditure; for this reason an entertainment of the kind can only be contemplated by a hostess who is abundantly furnished with this world's goods.

At a dance the arrangements are not so ambitious. The number of invitations issued seldom amount to more than 100 to 150; the decorations, though tasteful, are simple and not costly. The supper is not upon such an elaborate scale as that of a ball, and in many cases no set supper is given, light refreshments served from a buffet being considered sufficient, whilst the music is often supplied by a pianist unaided by other instrumentalists.

In issuing invitations for a dance, the hostess should be careful not to ask more guests than will be able to dance comfortably upon the floor provided. There is no pleasure in the crowded dance, when it is impossible for the dancers to take two clear steps at a time without getting into the way of some other couple. Excessive crushes detract materially from every one's enjoyment, and to avoid them should be the first consideration. A good floor in the dancing room is of the utmost importance. The floor should be level and well polished; for a small dance a smooth drugget of brown holland well stretched over the carpet will be found to meet all requirements, but in many houses nowadays the floors are of parquetry, the carpeting consisting solely of rugs which can easily be removed. In these circumstances, as a polished floor is the floor par excellence for dancing, the floor should be polished. (For a good method of Floor Polishing, see p. 66.) The hostess must have a certain number of rooms to place at the disposal of her guests. There should be a cloak-room for the ladies, with a maid or maids in attendance. Where a large number of guests are present, it is as well to have books of duplicate cloak-room tickets, a ticket to be attached to each cloak, and the duplicate handed to the owner. A good supply of needles and cotton, tape, pins, &c., should also be available, as scarcely a dance passes without some little accident in the way of torn skirts and flounces. The largest room should of course be devoted to the dancing. The halls and landings might serve as lounges. They should be tastefully arranged with cosy chairs, palms and flowers. At large dances there should be, in addition to the supper-room, a room set aside for light refreshments, which should be served throughout the evening. This extra room would not be required at smaller dances. A room should also be set aside in which the gentlemen can leave their coats and hats, as if the hall is utilised for the purpose it does away with all possibility of its being used for a lounge. Where the hall is so small, however, that it could not be used for a lounge in any case, the gentlemen might leave their coats and hats there, failing any other room. The doors of the dancing-room are usually removed for the occasion.

Where one of the reception-rooms has to be utilised as a dancing-room, there is not so much scope for decoration as in the larger establishments with a regular ball-room. The room should be well lighted, however, and it should if possible be decorated in one colour scheme. For instance, the lights could be shaded with pink shades, the mantelpiece and fireplace could be covered with banks of pink roses or pink carnations. At very large balls the floral decorations form a very considerable item of expenditure—the banisters are decked with veritable banks of flowers, floral arches are erected over some of the doorways; in fact, every available space is literally covered with tastefully arranged blossoms. A decorative scheme of the kind, however, is not as a rule within the ken of the average hostess, but she should make a point of introducing pretty floral decoration wherever possible to add to the charm of the surroundings.

It is always as well that some male friend or relation of the hostess should be deputed to fulfil the duties of master of the ceremonies. The daughters of the house also should afford their mother all the assistance in their power before giving themselves up to the enjoyment of the evening. Where a number of elderly people are present as chaperons, cards or any other similar entertainment might be organised in another room, when space permits, on their behalf.

Music.—The music should always be of the very best. A piano and one or two stringed instruments form an ideal combination, but where a piano alone is provided, at all events let the pianist be a professional well used to dance music. There is nothing more trying for the dancers than to be compelled to dance to an indifferent musical accompaniment. Some one should be at hand to take the pianist's place when the latter has to go to supper. This is an important detail which must on no account be overlooked. One of the daughters of the house, if a good musician, could well take the place for this short interval.

Receiving the Guests.—The hostess should stand at the head of the staircase or at the door of the dancing-room to receive her guests. She should shake hands with the guests as they arrive. Gentlemen and ladies do not enter the dancing-room arm-in-arm. The ladies go first, the gentlemen follow. Programmes with the order of the dances are handed to the guests, although at some of the largest private balls dance programmes have been to a great extent done away with. The dance is usually opened by the hostess herself, or if she has grown-up daughters, by one of her daughters. It is etiquette for the men present to ask the daughters of the hostess for at least one dance. The host should take the lady of the highest rank in to supper. The laws of precedence in regard to the other guests are usually waived at dances. As a rule, they pair among themselves and follow according to their inclination; but the host must always lead the way to the supper-room.

Fashionable Dances.—Among the favourite dances now in vogue are the valse, quadrilles, lancers, polka, two-step, cotillion and Sir Roger de Coverley. A dance usually begins from 9.30 to 10 o'clock; in the case of a small dance, carriages as a rule can be called between 2 and 2.30, but the larger dances are carried on till any time up to 4 in the morning. Cinderella dances are so called because they end at midnight. Where a dance is given upon a Saturday it usually takes the form of a Cinderella.

Public Balls.—Public balls are those for which tickets are sold. It is always as well to form a party to attend these functions, otherwise there is not much chance of an enjoyable evening, it being impossible to dance with people with whom one is unacquainted.

County Balls form the chief events of the season in the country. All the best people invite large house parties for the purpose of attending them, and the event as a rule is one of some social importance. Charity balls and ordinary subscription dances also come under this heading of public balls. The dances of the kind given in London are many and various, and the tickets vary in price according to the scale upon which the dances are given.

Private Subscription Dances.—Sometimes private subscription dances are got up amongst friends. The arrangements are usually in the hands of two or three ladies, who circulate the news of the dance and the price of the tickets amongst the people of their acquaintance. A room and a band are hired, and the arrangements placed in the hands of a firm of caterers. For a dance of this kind to be a success a great deal of organising capacity on the part of the promoters is necessary.

Etiquette at Naval, Military, and Hunt Balls.—These functions as a rule are brilliant in the extreme. In the first two cases the officers, and in the last case the members of the Hunt appear in uniform, and the scene is usually very picturesque. Large parties are usually formed for attendance at these balls. It is always necessary on these occasions for the guests to bring their cards of invitation with them and hand them to the official in charge.

Juvenile Parties.—Christmas time may well be called the children's season, for it is the pivot as it were round which all the juvenile parties revolve. Most of them take place during the Christmas holidays, and seldom is such whole-hearted enjoyment manifested by grown ups and little ones alike as on the occasion of a really well-managed juvenile party.

These parties vary a great deal as to the nature of the entertainment provided. Sometimes they take the form of regular miniature balls with dancing as the chief amusement, the tiny partners copying in every way the manners and etiquette of the grown ups. Parties of this kind are more suitable for boys and girls of from twelve years of age and upwards—the very tiny tots are apt to become too precocious by frequent attendance at miniature dances. On the other hand, attending an occasional juvenile dance is good for the little ones, inasmuch as it has a good influence upon their manners and goes a long way towards curing any tendency to excessive shyness they may possess.

The best form of juvenile party, however, is that in which dancing is combined with other forms of amusements in which the very little tots as well as the elder boys and girls may throw themselves whole-heartedly into the enjoyment provided. Old-fashioned games such as forfeits, blind man's buff, &c., can be indulged in, and these should always be organised by one or two of the younger grown ups who understand children, and are not above taking a part in the game themselves.

A magic lantern is also an entertainment appreciated by the little ones, and at Christmas time a Christmas tree from which presents are distributed, a lucky bag, or a bran pie will be found to appeal greatly to the juvenile idea of enjoyment.

The time for children's parties depends to a great extent upon the scope and character of the entertainment provided. Four till seven would be the correct time for an ordinary tea-party with games. Five to ten is a favourite time for parties on a more elaborate scale at which dancing combined with games and other entertainments are provided. For a juvenile ball, six to eleven is a favourite hour, very often the proceedings terminating with a grown-up dance as soon as the juvenile party is concluded.

Organising a Children's Party.—A children's party requires careful organising. The necessity for the company to include one or two grown ups, who can arrange games and take part in them themselves, has already been pointed out. Tea should be served about half-an-hour after the time notified for the arrival of the little ones. Plenty of bread and butter, cut cake and cakes of all kind should be provided. If the party is to be over very early and no other meal is given, it is better to have tea later in the afternoon, and to make jellies and creams a feature of the tea menu, not omitting bon-bons, which should always be provided at parties for the little ones, as they invariably prove an irresistible source of enjoyment.

Where several forms of entertainment are given, at least three rooms should be at the disposal of the little ones, one for tea and supper, one for dancing, and one for games. Tea and supper could be served in the dining-room, dancing could proceed in the drawing-room, and the games could be held in the morning-room or library. Failing this extra room, however, the drawing-room could be made to do duty for both dancing and games.

The games should take place after tea and last about an hour. After this the little ones should have a short time for dancing, then the conjuring or other entertainments could be giver. This order of course can be varied in accordance with individual requirements. Presents from the Christmas tree are usually given towards the end of the evening. (See Indoor Games.)

Light refreshments are usually provided for the children before they leave, whilst at juvenile balls a regular supper is provided. The light refreshments should include lemonade, sandwiches, jellies, creams, fruit, and ices where possible.

Garden Parties.—The summer season has its own special programme of entertainments which occur year after year with unvarying regularity. Chief amongst these is the garden party, a favourite form of entertainment with both young and old. June and July are the favourite months for town garden parties, August and September for those given in the country.

Invitations are usually sent out three weeks beforehand in the name of the hostess, and it is usual to specify upon the card any particular entertainment to be provided (see Invitations, p. 332). The success of the function of course will materially depend upon the weather; but guests are expected to turn up if it is fine or wet, unless there is a regular and persistent downpour of rain. Every hostess, however, should be prepared for eventualities, and the wise hostess takes care to have one or two rooms in readiness in which she can receive her guests, and in which tea and other refreshments can be served and entertainment provided. She will be able to regulate matters to such an extent that she can with no trouble transpose her garden party into a regular afternoon At Home, and send her guests away wholly satisfied with their entertainment however unpropitious the weather may have been.

Garden parties may be given upon a large or a small scale. For the simple little family affair where the guests number from twenty to thirty young people who have been invited to play a friendly game of tennis, the arrangements can be of the simplest. In this case tennis will be the *raison d'être* of the entertainment. The young people should arrive in suitable tennis attire, and simple refreshments in the way of lemonade and other cooling drinks, and ices where possible, might be handed round at intervals to the guests. Tea could be served either in the garden or indoors. One point to be remembered is that in the strawberry season there should always be an ample supply of strawberries and cream—there is nothing in the way of light refreshments which will be more appreciated by the young people. It adds materially to the enjoyment of the party to have a director of games who will arrange the different sets with due regard to the capabilities of the players.

Large Garden Parties.—At large garden parties the arrangements are upon a much more elaborate scale. A marquee is usually erected upon the lawn, and there tea, ices, and all kinds of light refreshments, including champagne cup, claret cup and strawberries and cream, grapes, peaches and melons are served. More often than not a band is engaged to play, and in this case a bandstand must be erected for the occasion. Smaller tents are often found here and there in the garden for fortune-tellers, palmistry, &c. The entertainments provided for the guests are many and various, and the number of people invited very large. The ladies should wear the lightest and daintiest of summer dresses. Laces and flimsy muslins are the most suitable materials for young people. Serges and stuff dresses would be out of place. The hostess receives her guests upon the lawn. They should all go up and shake hands with her upon arrival, and introduce the friends they have brought as "party" before they mingle with the crowd and seek out their acquaintances. The hostess does not at a garden party introduce people, but leaves them to find their own friends.

Refreshments may be served in the house, if preferred. In any case, it is always as well to serve a great part of the refreshments indoors in case of weather eventualities in the shape of unexpected thunder-storms, showers, &c., it being wiser not to place too much reliance upon the clerk of the weather even under the most favourable auspices. At very large garden parties given in the country during the season it is usual to provide special trains for the conveyance of the guests from town. In these cases the times of the different trains are specified on the back of the invitation cards. It is always courteous for the guests to take leave of the hostess before going, whenever possible. Garden parties as a rule last from 3.30 till about 7. The hours are generally specified upon the cards of invitation.

Picnics.—Of the many entertainments peculiar to the summer season, a well-organised picnic is perhaps the most enjoyable. Picnics should only be arranged when the fine weather seems to have well settled in, and in this respect one important thing the women of the party should keep in mind is to dress in accordance with the weather, if they do not wish their enjoyment to be altogether marred. This advice is sometimes a little hard to follow. In many instances a picnic is by way of being a notable event to one or two of the young girls amongst the guests. They will have provided themselves with dainty toilettes for the occasion. Judge of their chagrin therefore if the day dawns threatening and cloudy, if not actually wet. But if they are to have their full sum of enjoyment they must resist all temptation to wear their cherished finery and don some dress more suitable to the weather—otherwise throughout the day they will be worried about the chances of spoiling their fine clothes, and even if they do not actually do that, they run the risk of catching a heavy cold which will probably have the effect of preventing them from joining any other picnic parties of the season. It will be well, therefore, to be wise in time, and let no other consideration but common-sense prevail in the choice of their attire.

Good Organisation Necessary.—For a picnic to be a complete success, it is necessary that it should be well organised at the outset, and that no detail should be overlooked. A great deal in the first instance depends upon the selection of a suitable spot. England is replete with beautiful little country places abounding in romantic scenery. Very often some historical ruin is the centre of these rural spots; in the case of an excursion to one of these the picnic would therefore be instructive as well as amusing.

Then the riverside places abound in beautiful scenery, and present the additional attractive prospect of a pleasant row to vary the programme of the day. When one lives in the country, the opportunities for picnics are of course unlimited, but near every town there are rural spots easily reached by train or tram at small expense, and the prospect of a picnic may be said to be even more attractive to the dwellers in the town than it is to the dwellers in the country.

Small Picnics.—For a small party a picnic is a comparatively simple matter, one or two tea-baskets equipped with the necessary table requisites, such as cups and saucers, spoons, forks, knives, plates, methylated spirits lamp upon which to boil the water, a kettle which usually consists of a teapot and kettle combined, tins for the biscuits, cakes and bread and butter, salt, &c., will hold these and all the other necessary provisions. Nothing as a rule is forgotten in a properly equipped tea-basket, and the tins are usually labelled in accordance with the goods they are to contain, so there is no chance of anything being overlooked. Special sets of grease-proof paper plates and dishes are sold for picnics. They may be had in all sizes and include meat plates, dishes, pudding plates, tea plates, &c. A picnic-box containing a complete set of cardboard dishes and plates sufficient for a small picnic may be purchased for 9½d. Small baskets containing ample provisions for a picnic may also be had at very moderate prices from most caterers.

Large Picnics.—For large parties, however, tea or luncheon baskets will not hold sufficient. It is always as well to take one tea-basket on account of its handy equipment in the way of methylated spirits lamps, tins for condiments, &c., but a large hamper should be requisitioned for the packing of the provisions.

If the picnic is to be for luncheon, a properly equipped luncheon basket with glasses, knives, forks, &c., should be taken together with two other hampers, one to contain the wine, lemonade, &c., the other the table-cloth and various articles of food. In packing these baskets care should be taken to put the heaviest articles at the bottom of the basket and to place the things in the basket as nearly as possible in the order in which they will be required, leaving the table-cloth uppermost. It is as well also beforehand to make a list of everything that is to be packed, and to check this list before the provisions are placed in their respective baskets.

Packing the Provisions.—An important thing to remember in regard to a picnic is the fact that "too many cooks spoil the broth." One or two persons at most should be held responsible for seeing that the proper things are placed in their respective baskets. If too many interfere, the chances are that each one will show a tendency to leave the details to the others, with the result that many things will be overlooked. Very often a picnic is for tea alone; but if it is proposed to make a day of it, the host will often arrange for luncheon to be supplied at some rural inn first, and for the tea picnic to take place afterwards; or else the luncheon may be taken in the open air and tea subsequently provided at the inn. It is always as well for the host to have some knowledge of the locality of the place in which the picnic is given. He should always know the nearest country inn in the neighbourhood in the case of the provisions falling short, or some important table necessity having been overlooked, in which case the deficiency could be easily supplied.

The informal picnics where people wait upon each other are by far the most enjoyable. Wealthy people as a rule motor down to the spot selected, sending their servants beforehand to make all arrangements. The latter remain to wait upon the party, and are responsible for things going right in the way of food supplies. It cannot be denied that picnics are enjoyable under these circumstances, more especially to those who like to take things easily, but after all a picnic is an informal gathering at best, and to rob it of its informality is to rob it of half of its charm. At large parties it is of course necessary to have one or two servants to take charge of the provisions in transit, to unpack them, to open the wine, and to repack the things when finished with; but during the meal let them be as little in evidence as possible. The guests will far prefer to help each other and to help themselves.

Contribution Picnics.—Sometimes a picnic is organised by three or four people. In this way the individual expenses are very materially lessened. For a picnic of this kind, however, good organisation is more than ever essential if things are not to go wrong. The ladies should agree between themselves as to what part of the entertainment each is to be responsible for, and what provisions each is to supply. Only in this way can the dangers of both omission and overlapping be averted.

Boating Parties.—Very often a boating party is made the *raison d'être* of a picnic. The boats must be hired in suitable time, and care must be taken to include good oarsmen in the party. Either provisions are taken in tea-baskets or else one of the many riverside hotels is fixed upon beforehand for tea, and the rowing party makes this spot its destination. The party very often returns home by train on these occasions.

Steam Launch Parties.—Steam launches can also be hired by the day for picnics. Many people club together to share in the expense, and the company is as a rule a very large one. Generally a riverside place where tea may be had is fixed upon as the destination of the party, and they return home by launch also. On the whole, it may be said that outdoor parties of any kind given during the summer are of all forms of entertainment the most enjoyable, providing that the fickle clerk of the weather is in a sunny mood and that the company gives itself up whole-heartedly to the enjoyment of the hour, leaving the worries of the moment to take care of themselves.

WEDDING ETIQUETTE

The Engaged Girl.—When one of the daughters of a household becomes engaged to be married, there are many points of etiquette to be kept in mind, both by herself and her parents and the parents of her *fiancé*.

In the first place, after the announcement of an engagement, the father, mother and relatives of the bridegroom to be must at once make the acquaintance of the bride and her relations if they have not been previously acquainted. They should call upon the father and mother of the intended bride as soon as possible, and their calls must be returned with the utmost promptitude. It must be borne in mind by both families, that if they are to avoid that unpleasing state of friction which is often manifested between the relations-in-law of a young couple, they must begin by avoiding any little breach of etiquette which is likely to cause offence on either side, and which often is the beginning of actual lack of harmony between relations by marriage.

The bridegroom's relations will of course wish to make the acquaintance of their son's future bride. For this purpose it is usual for them to ask the latter upon a short visit, as soon as the engagement is announced.

The visit to her future relations is one of the most trying ordeals a young engaged girl has to undergo. She knows that at the best, the attitude of her *fiancé's* parents towards her will be one of criticism, and that they are inwardly debating within themselves whether she is really good enough for their son.

A tactful girl, however, will come triumphantly through this ordeal. She will always bear in mind that she is taking the son away from his people, as it were, and this will make her all the more considerate towards the family in which she is about to enter. She will refrain from monopolising all his time, for instance, and from flaunting that air of proprietorship which in some girls is particularly aggressive. She will encourage him to continue in all the little attentions he was wont to bestow upon his father and mother, and not exact the whole of his attention to herself. She will, in fact, so ingratiate herself with every one by her unselfishness and consideration that by the time her visit is over, she will be looked upon by all as a decided acquisition to the family, and her *fiancé* will have the satisfaction of knowing his choice is unanimously approved.

Conduct of the Engaged Couple.—An engaged couple should be careful not to advertise the fact too freely to the world at large. Any effusive demonstration in public is the height of bad form. A girl who insists, for instance, at a dance on dancing all the evening with her *fiancé* is guilty of a grave transgression against the laws of etiquette.

Engaged couples are nowadays allowed much more of each other's society than in olden times. Independence is the motto of the age, and the young girl acts up to it by going about with her *fiancé* to places of public amusement unchaperoned. To act strictly in accordance with etiquette, however, a young girl should always be chaperoned by one of her relatives on these occasions. It is a rule which is as often as not honoured in the breach as in the observance, but it is a rule which prevails all the same.

Where the engagement is to be a short one, it is better for the engaged couple not to go out much into society except amongst their relatives and friends. If the engagement is destined to be a long one, however, this rule cannot be observed.

Breaking off an Engagement.—In the case of an engagement being broken off, all letters and presents on both sides should be returned with the least possible delay.

Fixing the Wedding Day.—The choice of the wedding day remains with the future bride, as this has been her time-honoured privilege. There are certain superstitions in regard to weddings which she should do well to bear in mind if she does not wish to go against the prejudices of elderly and superstitious relatives. May, for instance, for some reason or other is considered an unlucky month for a wedding, and the Lenten season is as a rule avoided in regard to the celebration of marriage. In older times the solemnisation of marriage in this season was forbidden, so it may be said that the reluctance of the average bride to have her wedding in Lent has its rise in a tradition handed down from the past.

Forms of Marriage.—The wedding day fixed, the next thing to be thought of is in what form the marriage is to take place. There are four different modes of celebration of marriage in England. They are—

Marriage by Banns.
Marriage by Ordinary Licence.
Marriage by Special Licence.
Marriage by Registrar.

Marriage by Banns.—This is the form of marriage most usually adopted. Banns must be published on three consecutive Sundays in the parish in which the prospective bridegroom resides, and also in the parish in which the prospective bride resides, and both must have resided in their respective parishes fifteen days previously to the first publication of the banns. The marriage must take place within three months of the banns being published, or republication will be rendered necessary. The marriage must be solemnised in one of the churches where the banns were published, and the clergyman of the other church must give a certificate of such publication to the clergyman about to perform the ceremony.

By Ordinary Licence.—Marriage by licence is a convenient alternative to the publication of banns. In London application should be made by one of the parties to be married at the Vicar General's office at the Court of Faculties, or at the Bishop of London's Registry. In the country it is usual to apply to a clergyman who is also a surrogate, and he will obtain the licence by return of post from the Bishop's Registrar.

Fees.—The fee in London is £2, 12s. 6d. inclusive of stamp duty, and varies in the country from £1, 15s. to £2, 12s. 6d., according to the diocese. The licence is granted without previous notice, and is available as soon as issued, but one of the parties must declare on oath that there is no legal impediment to the marriage, and also that one of the parties has resided at least fifteen days in the parish in which the wedding is to take place.

Marriage by Special Licence.—A special licence can be obtained at an average cost of £29, 8s. by approval of the Archbishop of Canterbury after application at the Faculty Office. It enables a marriage to be celebrated at any time or place, and does away with the necessity of the residential qualifications.

Marriage by Registrar.—(1) *By Certificate.*—A marriage can now be celebrated in a Registrar's Office without any religious ceremony. Notice must first be given in the prescribed form by one of the parties to the intended marriage, if both have continuously resided in the registrar's district during the seven days immediately preceding the notice. If each has resided for so long in different districts, a notice must be given to each registrar. Twenty-one days after this notice the marriage can take place, and during this period the notice is publicly exhibited in the registrar's office. The fee for entry of notice is 1s., for issue of the certificate 1s., and for performing the marriage ceremony 5s.

(2) *By Licence.*—The Registrar, however, can grant a licence by which the ceremony can take place one whole day next after the notice. For instance, if notice were given on a Monday, the marriage could take place on a Wednesday. Fifteen days previous residence in the district is necessary on the part of either the prospective bride or the prospective bridegroom, and the notice need not be suspended in the office of the registrar as is the case when a certificate is applied for.

The cost of a licence is £1, 10s., and besides small fees for entries and certificate of notice, 10s. stamp duty. The fee for performing the marriage ceremony is 10s.

The arrangement of all these matters in regard to the ecclesiastical and legal part of the ceremony devolve on the bridegroom, and all fees are paid by him.

Marriages in Scotland.—In Scotland there are two forms of marriage, regular and irregular. The ceremony of what is known as a "regular marriage" is performed by a minister after the banns have been published on three consecutive Sundays in the parish in which the prospective bridegroom resides, and also in the parish in which the prospective bride resides. Custom, however, has made deviation from this law permissible, and in practice proclamation on one or two Sundays is deemed sufficient. Most frequently the Scottish wedding takes place in the house of the bride's parents, although a large number of weddings are now celebrated in church. As an alternative to having the banns proclaimed the bride and bridegroom elect may give notice to the registrar of the district in which they have resided for fifteen days immediately preceding the notice. The fee for entry of notice is 7s. 6d. The notice is publicly exhibited for seven days, after which period a certificate of publication of notice of marriage is granted (fee 1s.). This certificate must be given to the minister performing the ceremony. Where banns have been proclaimed the certificate of proclamation of banns must be given to him in like manner.

In "Irregular Marriages" no official celebration is necessary, the declaration of the consent of the parties to take each other for husband and wife being deemed sufficient. It is necessary, however, that either the husband or the wife should have resided in Scotland for at least twenty-one days before the mutual consent to marriage is made. The declaration should be made before witnesses, who will be able to testify to the fact that it was made when the parties apply for registration of the marriage. All irregular marriages should be registered within three months after the marriage, application for the purpose being made to the sheriff. Regular marriages require to be registered within three days. A registration schedule for the purpose must be obtained from the registrar of the parish in which the ceremony is celebrated.

Fees at a Wedding.—There is no set figure for the amount of the fee to be given to the officiating clergyman; these must be regulated by the position and means of the bridegroom. It should never, however, be under £1, 1s. This fee should be placed in an envelope and laid on the vestry table after the ceremony, with the inscription, "For the Rev. ——, with compliments and thanks."[1] The fee to the clerk should not be less than 10s. Then there are many and sundry fees to be given to vergers, and pew attend-

[1] If the clergyman is a relative, or a very great friend of the family, no fee is given, but it is usual to make him some present, generally a piece of silver, as a souvenir of the occasion.

ants, all of whom expect to be remembered on the auspicious occasion.

The Bridegroom Pays all Fees.—All fees in connection with the actual celebration of a wedding ceremony are defrayed by the bridegroom, and are paid previous to the ceremony or immediately after it. It is usual for the best man on these occasions to see to the paying of fees for the bridegroom. The latter either gives him the requisite amount beforehand, or else the best man lays out the money required, which is refunded to him afterwards.

Other Expenses of the Bridegroom.—In addition to the paying of all the necessary fees, there are several other expenses entailed upon a bridegroom. At the commencement of his engagement he has to present his future bride with a handsome engagement ring, in accordance with the never-varying custom. Then various gifts on the part of an engaged man to his *fiancée* during their engagement are always a foregone conclusion. He is also expected to give his bride a handsome present upon her wedding day, in addition to the all-important wedding ring. He has also to provide his bride and her bridesmaids with their bouquets, and he must give each of the bridesmaids a present, which usually takes the form of some piece of jewellery, such as a bangle, a brooch, or a pendant. In addition, the bridegroom has to provide the carriage to convey the bride and himself from church and afterwards from her parents' house to the station, although in the country as a rule the carriage is provided by the father of the bride.

In regard to their future home the bridegroom has to supply all the furniture, plate and linen. Large contributions towards the plate, however, are usually given in the form of wedding presents, so his expenses in this direction are often materially lessened.

Expenses of the Bride's Parents.—First and foremost amongst the expenses of the bride's parents comes the trousseau, which should be prepared with due regard to the position in ilfe which their daughter will occupy. All the linen should be marked with her married name. Then there are various At Homes and parties given before the marriage in celebration of the engagement. On the wedding day the bride's parents give the wedding reception and pay for all floral decorations in the church. If the service is a choral one, they must bear all the expenses of the choir. The bride's parents also pay for the carriages used by themselves and their household. They do not pay for the carriages of the guests invited to the wedding. Tips are as a rule expected by all the coachmen and footmen on the wedding day, and these usually amount to about 5s. in each case. In accordance with time-honoured custom they are all given champagne or other wine in which to drink the bride's health. Where wedding favours are given these are also supplied by the parents of the bride. The bride usually gives a handsome wedding present to the bridegroom on the wedding day.

The Eve of the Wedding.—The evening before the wedding it is customary for the bride's parents to invite one or two of the near relatives of both bride and bridegroom to dinner. The bridegroom and his best man are also present.

Bridesmaids.—The number of bridesmaids will depend upon the scale upon which the wedding is to be. Six bridesmaids make a favourite number for ceremonious weddings, with occasionally two little boys, or a little boy and a little girl, to act as train-bearers. At very quiet weddings one or two bridesmaids will be sufficient. The bridesmaids should be chosen from the relatives of both families, the sisters of the bride and bridegroom (where there are sisters) being usually asked to perform the office. The bridesmaids provide their own dresses, and in making the selection of the colour and style of dress to be worn by her bridesmaids, the bride should always be careful to select something that will be equally becoming to all. She should also bear in mind that the style of the dresses should be such as will enable them to be worn on future occasions.

The Bride's Dress.—The bride is as a rule dressed entirely in white, unless the wedding is a quiet one and she is married in her travelling dress, or else that it is her second marriage. Silk, satin, *crêpe de chine*, or ninon, chiffon or lace over silk or satin are the favourite materials for bride's wear. The dress is trimmed with orange blossom—and a long white veil is worn over a wreath of orange blossom. White gloves, shoes, and stockings are also worn; everything must be *en suite*, the bouquet she carries being also of white blossoms.

When the Bride is a Widow.—A bride who is a widow should not wear a bridal veil or orange blossoms. Brides who have been married before often wear their travelling toilettes for the ceremony. Delicate greys of all shades, fawns, and other light colours are usually selected. For a ceremonious wedding, however, a widow may wear white, but it should be relieved by some touch of colour. A widow is not attended by bridesmaids at her wedding. There is no obligation for her to be given away by her father or other male relations at the ceremony, although it is usual for either her father or one of her male relatives to perform this office on her behalf.

The Best Man.—The responsibilities of the best man, who should always be a bachelor, are many and varied. He is the right-hand man of the bridegroom, as it were. He should accompany the bridegroom to the church, and see that he does not leave the wedding ring behind him. He must see that all the arrangements in regard to the bridegroom's carriage, both for conveying him and his bride from the church, and from the bride's house to the station, are in order. He must be ready to relieve the bridegroom of all the little incidental worries in his power. For instance, the best man often actually sees to the taking of the railway tickets, and the safe conveyance of luggage for the honeymoon trip. The best man has also, as a rule, to attend to the payment of all fees incidental to the wedding, either before or after the ceremony on the bridegroom's behalf. He must also sign the register in the vestry afterwards.

Going to the Church.—The bridesmaids should arrive at the church a short time before the bride. If the bride's sisters are acting as bridesmaids they should drive to the church in the carriage with their mother, the carriage afterwards returning for the bride and her father; but when she has no sisters she generally drives to the church with her mother, her father, having preceded her, meeting her at the church door.

The bridegroom and the best man should arrive at the church before the bride, and stand together below the chancel steps, or kneel at a *prie-Dieu* until shortly before the bride's arrival. The best man should make it his care to see that the bridegroom is in good time at the church.

In the Church.—The bridesmaids assemble in the church, or inside the church near the west door, in two rows facing each other, waiting for the bride's arrival, and ready to fall in behind her.

The General Company.—The bridegroom's relatives should seat themselves at the right of the nave of the church, the bride's relatives seating themselves upon the left.

The Bridal Procession.—If the wedding is a choral one the choir and clergy march in silence to the west end, and are ready at a signal agreed upon with the organist to strike up the processional hymn. The bride enters the church leaning on the right arm of her father or guardian, and follows the choir to the chancel step, the bridesmaids, two and two, following her. The bridegroom takes his place at her right side with the "best man" standing behind him. He neither embraces nor shakes hands with the bride, but simply bows to her. The father stands at the bride's left hand. Her mother sits in the front seat with the nearest relatives.

And now the service begins. At the question "Who giveth this woman, &c.," the father bows to the clergyman, and stepping in front of the couple, joins their right hands together, and then goes back to his place. Now is the time for the gloves of the bride to be handed with her bouquet to the care of the chief bridesmaid, who holds them to the end of the service. The bridegroom should unglove as soon as the service begins. It always creates an awkward pause if the bridegroom has to hunt in his pockets for the ring. He should have it ready when required by the priest to place it upon the book. After the first blessing, the bride and bridegroom alone follow the priest to the altar, the others remaining at their stations, not chatting together, but reverently joining in the service.

When all is finished, the bride, leaning on her husband's left arm, and followed by her bridesmaids, father and mother, and the principal relations and friends, go to the vestry to sign the book and give congratulations. On going slowly down the church, the bride takes her husband's left arm, both recognising their friends with smiles or bows, the bridesmaids follow two and two, and then the bride's mother. The "best man" waits until the last to see everybody into their carriages. The Bishop of London has lately condemned the custom of throwing rice or confetti in the church porch or within the railings at the west end. Sensible people will approve the bishop's action and govern themselves accordingly.

The ceremonial described is that of the Church of England. The actual form of the wedding ceremony will, of course, differ in regard to different creeds, but in every case the social etiquette remains the same, whatever the religion of the bride and bridegroom may be.

Where wedding favours or button-holes are given to the guests, they should be distributed by the bridesmaids in the vestry and in the church. Wedding favours should be worn on the left side.

The Wedding Reception.—Formerly it was compulsory for a marriage ceremony to take place before noon, hence the origin of the "wedding breakfast" as the most suitable form of hospitality to show to the guests. But since the time in which the ceremony can be performed has been extended, fashionable marriages now as a rule take place about from 2 to 2.30, hence the old-fashioned wedding breakfast has been superseded by the afternoon reception or At Home. The invitations should be issued three weeks before the wedding day (for Wedding Invitations, see p. 332), and it is usual for the guests invited to give a wedding present to the bride or bridegroom. The presents have, as a rule, all arrived before the day, and a room is usually set apart in which they can be displayed for the benefit of the guests.

The arrangements for the wedding reception are of a similar nature to those for an afternoon At Home (see p. 339). The guests are received in the drawing-room, and they should at first shake hands with the host and hostess, and afterwards with the bride and bridegroom. The hostess should stand at the drawing-room door, and the bride and bridegroom should stand together in some prominent position in the room.

After the presents have been inspected the company adjourn to the luncheon or tea room in the following order: The bride and bridegroom lead the way, followed by the bride's father with the bridegroom's mother. Next come the bridegroom's father and the bride's mother. After them the best man with the chief bridesmaid, and the remainder of the bridal party. Then follow the general company without any prescribed order of precedency.

The Refreshments.—The refreshments provided at a wedding tea are similar to those for an afternoon At Home, but champagne is of course *de rigueur* at a wedding, and in the centre of the buffet stands the bride's cake. The room is cleared of furniture, and the buffet extends along the length of it, servants being stationed behind it to pour out tea, coffee, &c. The number of toasts which were formerly proposed at the old-time wedding breakfasts are now as a rule dispensed with, but the officiating clergyman or some old friend of the family briefly proposes the health of the happy couple; the bridegroom replies and the bride cuts the cake, a small portion of which is handed to each guest.

Wedding Luncheons.—The wedding hospitality sometimes is extended in the form of a luncheon, which is taken either sitting down or standing up. The latter is the more usual form, especially when the company is a very large one, the sitting-down luncheon being adopted when those invited consist mainly of the near relatives and most intimate friends of the bride and bridegroom. In the case of a luncheon the menu is naturally more extended and varied than that of a wedding tea. At a standing-up luncheon the gentlemen help the ladies and themselves to the various dishes, whilst at a sitting-down luncheon the servants wait as usual. At a sitting-down luncheon the bride cuts the cake after the sweets have been served.

Departure of the Newly-Married Couple.—As soon as the bride has cut the cake and the healths have been drunk, she retires to change her dress for the wedding journey, accompanied by the head bridesmaid, if the latter is a near relative, and the company adjourns to the drawing-room. When the bride comes down again the farewells are made, and the bridegroom leads her to the carriage. The old-fashioned custom of throwing a slipper after the bride "for luck" is still adhered to—rice is also thrown, but confetti should be avoided. It is most troublesome to get rid of, and besides the colour sometimes comes off, and if the bride's travelling dress is a light one it is liable to get spoiled by a too profuse confetti shower. If something must be thrown diminutive horse shoes of silver paper are now sold, and they are being largely used at weddings for the purpose. They do not cling to the clothing, and are much safer to use than either rice or confetti.

After the Wedding.—*The Wedding Trip.*—There is a tendency on the whole nowadays to curtail the wedding trip. Sometimes it lasts little more than a week, at other times it is abandoned altogether, the honeymoon being spent in the new home of the young couple. Formerly a wedding trip of from three to four weeks was considered *de rigueur.* At the present time the length of the trip is purely a matter of individual inclination and convenience.

Wedding Cards and Cake.—Formerly it was the custom to send out to friends and relations slices of wedding cake packed in small white boxes bordered in silver. Wedding cards printed in silver were also sent out in the name of the newly-married pair, and on these cards the maiden name of the bride crossed through with a silver arrow would also appear as a symbol that she had given up her maiden name for ever. Sometimes several hundred of these cards and packets of cake would be sent out, and to superintend their dispatch was quite a labour of love on the part of the bride's family after the wedding day. This custom, however, has now largely fallen into disuse, and is only kept up by old-fashioned people. Neither cards nor cake are now sent out by people who wish to be considered up to date. (For etiquette in regard to cards and calls for a bride, see p. 330.)

Wedding Anniversaries.—It is a pleasing custom among most married people to celebrate each year the anniversary of their wedding as it comes round by each giving the other some little gift. The husband often takes his wife out to dinner and to the theatre afterwards. In these annual celebrations neither relations, friends, nor acquaintances have any part—though in the case of a very near relative a congratulatory letter might sometimes be sent.

Silver and Golden Weddings.—Silver Weddings and Golden Weddings, however, are both observed, and usually an At Home or dinner-party is given in honour of the occasion. The Silver Wedding is the twenty-fifth anniversary of the marriage, and the Golden Wedding is the fiftieth. In the first case the invitations may be printed in silver, in the second case in gold; but they often take the form of an ordinary At Home card with "Silver Wedding" or "Golden Wedding," as the case may be, in the right-hand corner. Presents are usually made to the married couple by their friends and relatives on the occasion of both Silver and Golden Weddings.

CHRISTENINGS

A christening party is, as a rule, limited to the near relatives of the parents of the infant, and therefore partakes of much of the informality of a strictly family gathering. The invitations to a christening take the form of ordinary letters, and they should, if possible, be sent out a full week before the event.

The ceremony usually takes place in the morning, and the relatives invited upon arrival at the church seat themselves in the pews nearest the font. If the child is a boy it must have two godfathers and one godmother, and if a girl two godmothers and one godfather. The godmother (the chief godmother if there are two) holds the child during the first part of the service, and places it on the left arm of the officiating clergyman when he is ready to take it. When the clergyman asks for the child's name, the chief godfather should pronounce it, taking care to do so clearly and distinctly. When the child has been christened, the nurse, who is standing at the right of the clergyman, takes it from him. After the service the father accompanies the clergyman to the vestry to give the necessary particulars for the registration.

Fees.—The verger, pew-opener, and other church attendants will expect gratuities on the occasion of a christening. It is usual to give the officiating clergyman some souvenir of the occasion, which generally takes the form of a piece of silver, but money is not given as a rule. However, in many instances the parents present the clergyman with a cheque to be devoted to the requirements of the parish or to any good work he pleases.

Christening Presents.—The godfathers and godmothers must make presents to their godchild. Silver mugs, silver bowls, silver spoons and forks are typical presents for both godfathers and godmothers to make. In many instances the godmothers' presents consist of some simple yet good piece of jewellery when the infant is a girl, such as a pearl necklace, a jewelled cross, or pendant. Often also the godmother's present takes the practical form of a handsome robe and cloak. The presents are usually sent the day before the christening.

Tips to the Nurse.—Each of the sponsors makes a present of money to the nurse varying in amount from 5s. to £1 according to their individual means.

After the Ceremony.—The entertainment given to the relatives and friends of the parents after the ceremony may take the form of a lunch, a tea, or a dinner-party in the evening.

Christening Lunch.—If a lunch is given, it takes place as soon as the party have returned from church. The christening cake should occupy the central position on the luncheon table, and the health of the infant should always be drunk in champagne. The cake is cut at dessert.

No precedence is observed upon going in to luncheon, the hostess and other ladies go first and the gentlemen follow. The clergyman who performed the ceremony, if present, should sit at the hostess's left hand, and each lady should be placed at the right hand of a gentleman if there are an equal number of ladies and gentlemen. If the party is a large one the places should be indicated by little cards on which the names of the guests are inscribed.

Christening Tea.—The entertainment very often takes the form of a tea. This is served in the dining-room, the hostess receiving her guests in the drawing-room first. All go down to the tea-room together, the host and hostess included. The refreshments are the same as at an At Home, with the addition of the christening cake. Coffee and tea are poured out and handed round by the servants, but the host and hostess should attend to the needs of their guests in the way of handing cakes, &c.

Christening Dinner-Party.—In some cases the friends and relations are invited to a dinner in the evening. The precedence is the same as for an ordinary dinner-party. The christening cake is cut at dessert by the hostess, and the infant's health drunk at the same time.

FUNERALS AND MOURNING

The gloom cast over a family by the death of a dear one leaves the bereaved relatives without much heart for forms and ceremonies. Yet there are certain formalities which must be observed even in these last acts to be performed in tribute to the memory of the departed. The arrangements for the funeral fall naturally upon the head of the family. Women are spared as much as possible any share in the mournful details. Where it is the head of the family who has died, either the eldest son or the nearest male relation takes the matter in hand. But in some instances a woman is so alone in the world that she has to rely strictly upon herself to see that the last rites are faithfully and fittingly performed.

The funeral is at once placed in the hands of the undertaker, and is arranged on a scale suited to the means of the family. Any wishes expressed by the deceased as to his last resting-place are of course respected. A doctor's certificate should be obtained as soon as possible after the death (see p. 376). As soon as the day for the funeral is settled upon, letters should be written on black-edged notepaper to near relatives and friends who would wish to attend, apprising them of the date, hour and place. An announcement of the death, together with the date and time of the funeral, is also as a rule inserted in one or two of the chief newspapers. The undertaker will often see to this. In fact many details can be left in his hands, as he thoroughly understands the etiquette of funeral procedure. Friends and relatives at once begin to send wreaths and other floral offering unless the not very frequent request of "No flowers" has been made. Formerly it was not considered etiquette for the ladies of a family to attend a funeral: now they can do so if they wish. Needless to say black should be worn by all attending the funeral.

All the blinds of the house should be pulled down after the death, and they should be kept lowered until after the funeral has taken place.

If the funeral takes place in the morning it is usual to invite the friends to some light luncheon. If it occurs in the afternoon they should be offered tea upon their return to the house. Friends, as a rule, however, refrain from availing themselves of invitations, unless they have had to come from a very great distance.

Letters of Condolence.—Upon hearing of the death, letters of condolence should be sent by friends and relations. These should always be written on black-edged notepaper.

To Inquire Cards.—After the funeral, cards "With kind inquiries" should be left by friends. When the family feel once more able to receive calls they send out cards "With thanks for kind inquiries." Friends may call after the receipt of these cards of acknowledgment, but not before.

Periods of Mourning.—The etiquette in regard to mourning is not now so strict as of yore, and the periods of mourning have in most cases been materially shortened. More especially in regard to the regulation mourning wear has the change of fashion been most marked, for whereas crape was formerly worn for almost any and every kind of mourning, it has now been almost universally discarded excepting for widows' wear, whilst even in the latter case it is worn as a trimming only, and altogether put aside at a comparatively early date in the mourning period.

Mourning for Widows.—There are two accepted periods of mourning for a widow. In the case of the longer period mourning should be worn for two years, whilst eighteen months represents the time mourning should be worn during the shorter period.

Crape when worn is used as a trimming only, and it is only worn for the first six or eight months—sometimes it is not worn at all by widows, and in many cases chiffon or some other dull material takes its place.

The Widow's Cap.—The widow's cap and veil have been discarded in many cases. The usual period for wearing the cap is a year and a day. The veil may now be of chiffon instead of crape. Lawn cuffs and collars are worn during the first year.

Jewellery.—Diamonds may be worn quite early in the period of mourning, and gold jewellery after a year. Diamonds and pearls are often worn with very deep mourning.

Half Mourning.—In the longer period of mourning, half mourning begins after one year and nine months. In the shorter period half mourning may be worn after fifteen months.

For Father or Mother.—The regulation period in which mourning is worn for a parent is twelve months. During this time black with crape is worn for six months, black without crape for four, and half mourning for two months. The wearing of crape is optional, but black must be worn for the first ten months. After three months the black may be relieved by touches of white.

For a Son or Daughter.—The regulation period of mourning for a son or daughter is the same as for a father or mother.

Young Children.—For young children mourning is worn for six months, and for infants three months' mourning is sufficient.

Brother or Sister.—The period of mourning for a brother or sister is from four to six months. During the longer period black is worn for five months, and half mourning for one month. During the shorter period black should be worn for two months, and half mourning for the remaining two months. If in accordance with older customs crape is worn, the crape should be worn for the first three months, black without crape for two months, and half mourning for one month during the longer period. During the shorter period crape should be worn for two months, and black without crape for the remaining two.

The prevailing method, however, is to follow the first rule and discard crape altogether.

Jewellery.—Diamonds and pearls can be worn after one month—gold after two months.

For a Stepmother.—If the stepmother has filled the place of their own mother for her stepchildren from their childhood, they should wear mourning for her for the same period as if for their own mother. In other cases the period of mourning would be for six months—black for four months, and half mourning for two months.

For an Uncle, Aunt, Nephew, or Niece.—Mourning should be worn for either three months or six weeks. During the longer period black should be worn for two months, half mourning for one month. During the shorter period black should be worn for three weeks, half mourning for three weeks. Crape should not be worn for these relations.

For a Grandparent.—Mourning should be worn for either six or four months. During the longer period black should be worn for three months, and half mourning for three months—after six weeks it may be relieved with white. During the shorter period the time for the wearing of mourning and half mourning should also be equally divided. Formerly crape was worn for the first three months of the mourning period.

Jewellery.—Diamonds may be worn after one month—gold after six weeks.

For a First Cousin.—For a first cousin, black should be worn for one month, or black for three weeks, and half mourning for three weeks.

Relations by Marriage.—For relations by marriage the shorter of the two periods which prevail for blood relations is usually adopted.

Periods of Seclusion.—When persons in mourning should begin once more to enter upon social duties is a much debated question, and one which must to a large extent be governed by special circumstances. The general rules upon the subject are as follows :—

A widow should not accept invitations for a period of three months. During this time she should only visit her relations and very intimate friends. After this she may gradually resume her social duties, but she should not be present at balls or dances till a year has elapsed.

Parents, Sons, and Daughters.—A parent mourning for a son or a daughter should remain in seclusion for six weeks. Balls and dances should be avoided for six months. The same rules apply to a daughter who is mourning for a parent.

Brother or Sister.—For a brother or sister the period of seclusion is three weeks. Balls and dances should be avoided during the whole period of mourning if the latter is the shorter four months period; or during five months if the mourning is of the longer period.

Grandparents, Uncles, and Aunts.—For grandparents, uncles, and aunts, the period of seclusion is about a fortnight.

Notepaper and Cards.—During the period of mourning all notepaper and visiting cards should have black edges. The black edge is decreased in thickness as the period of mourning draws to a close.

THE ART OF CONVERSATION

The art of conversation is indispensable to a woman's social equipment. There is nothing more pleasing than the cultured conversation of a well-bred woman; nothing more wearisome than to listen to the trivial talk of a woman as lacking in breeding as she is in brains. It does not follow that the most learned people are the best conversationalists, although the exigencies of conversation require as a rule that a woman should be well read. Any woman with a fair education can cultivate the art of talking well, provided she has tact, a good memory, and a pleasant well-modulated voice. Harsh strident tones detract very materially from the charm of a conversationalist. Very often this defect is noticeable in girls who have been educated at large public schools, where the habit of shouting at recreation time is insensibly contracted. Every care should be taken to cure this habit of shouting, for although the voice may lack that actual sweetness of timbre which is such a potent charm, yet well-modulated tones go far to make up for this deficiency.

A good conversationalist is before everything a good listener. She does not monopolise all the talking, but will adroitly lead to a subject of particular interest to her friend, and then listen carefully to what he or she has to say, putting in an appropriate remark here and there as occasion warrants. The secret of conversation lies as much in the art of making others talk as of talking oneself. For a hostess good conversational powers are imperative. She must know the secret of drawing out her shyest guest and making her talk at her ease. She must also know how to make a conversation general, and discreetly change the subject if the topics touched upon seem likely to lead to discord.

Topics to be Avoided.—Religion and politics are topics of conversation which should always be avoided. They are subjects upon which difference of opinion is very rife, and may often lead to heated arguments which are as tiresome and unpleasant as they are ill-bred.

Slang and Word Clipping.—There is a growing tendency towards the use of slang in almost every class of society at the present day. Words are also clipped and abbreviated in such a manner as to almost render them unrecognisable. The gentlewoman would do well to avoid this tendency, as nothing jars upon the refined ear more than the mutilation of a good language, and no matter how inured we may become to colloquial slang, it never sounds well from a woman's lips. In whatever society slang or word clipping is used, the fact remains that it is contrary to all the laws of refinement and good breeding.

Pronunciation.—Words should be pronounced distinctly and never slurred. The omission to sound the letter *g* in the suffix "ing," as in the word "dancing," is almost as great a sign of lack of education as the omission or addition of the letter "h." Cockneyism should also be avoided. There is no more marked vulgarity than a Cockney accent. When engaging nurses for their children, parents should pay particular attention to their pronunciation. Children always adopt the accent of those who are constantly with them, and Cockneyism contracted in this way is most difficult to cure. Any defects in children's speech should be carefully observed and corrected by their parents if they do not wish the defects to become permanent. Whispering in company is considered the height of ill-breeding. People who have private matters to talk about should select a suitable occasion upon which to discuss them, and not offend others by excluding them from the conversation in this very marked manner.

Current Topics.—A woman should keep herself well informed upon current topics of interest. She should read the criticisms of new plays and the reviews of new books. She will do well to keep herself *au fait* with current literature, as this is to many an absorbing topic of conversation. She should in addition cultivate the faculty of remembering whatever she sees, hears, or reads.

Tact is the quintessence of good conversation. The tactful woman will never be at a loss to find a subject of interest to her listeners. She will discountenance scandal and other ill-natured small talk—and when in spite of all her efforts a dispute of any kind should occur in conversation between her friends or guests, she will pour oil upon the troubled waters of discord by quietly leading the conversation into a calmer and safer channel. (For how to address titled persons in conversation, see p. 354.)

THE ART OF READING ALOUD

If a correct accent and a good pronunciation are necessary in ordinary conversation, how much more are they indispensable for the woman who is called upon to read aloud for the pleasure and entertainment of others. Good reading is an accomplishment quite as worthy of cultivation and as capable of imparting pleasure to others as vocal or instrumental music.

Tone.—The cultivation of a correct tone of voice for reading is essential. There are some people whose voices for conversation are all that can be desired, but who if asked to read before a hall containing a large number of people fail to make themselves heard except by those who are sitting quite near them. In these cases the voice lacks what is called "carrying power" or resonance. There is nothing better for the cure of this defect in the voice than constant practice of reading aloud in the open air. Practice of this kind will gain timbre for a voice naturally dull or faint.

Delivery.—Articulation must of necessity be clear and distinct—each word should be uttered deliberately with due regard for its correct pronunciation. The sing-song method of reading should be altogether tabooed. This defect is often incurred by the reader letting his (or her) voice drop after every comma, semi-colon, and colon, to the same extent as after a full stop. Pauses after stops must of course be carefully regarded, but care must be taken not to give them more than their proportionate value: for instance, the reader must pause longest after the full stop, not so long after the colon, still less after the semi-colon, whilst after the comma the pause should be almost imperceptible. The interrogation mark, indicating a question, and the note of exclamation, expressing sudden feeling, require almost the value of the full stops. The reader should try to cultivate a natural manner. Whilst proper emphasis must be given to the passages which require it, any attempt at declamation should be avoided. Reading should be fluent and not faltering or hurried. There is nothing more annoying to the hearers than a reading rendered in staccato or jerky tones. Last, but not least, feeling and expression are essential attributes to good reading. The reader should be able to convey as much as is in her power to her listeners the intention of the author. Without feeling, reading is little more than a mechanical exercise—without expression it becomes both wearisome and monotonous, often to such an extent as to have the effect of sending the unfortunate hearers to sleep.

One final word of warning—defects of speech are much more noticeable in reading aloud than in conversation. A stutterer should never attempt to read before company until he (or she) is cured of this defect. Nothing can be more trying to people than to listen to a person whose delivery is marred by such an infliction. Reading aloud is excellent practice for the stammerer, but let her read aloud to herself until this defect is altogether cured.

THE ART OF LETTER-WRITING

The woman who can write exactly as she speaks, who can talk on paper to the recipient of her letter just as easily as if she were actually conversing with her, is mistress of the art of letter-writing, for in being able to write as we speak lies the secret of good composition, and therefore of good correspondence.

In writing letters a woman must of course be guided by the degree of intimacy which exists between herself and the person to whom her letter is addressed. In writing to her friends her powers of composition may have full play, whilst communications to slight acquaintances must of necessity be brief.

How to Begin a Letter.—Many women find it difficult to begin their letters—others find equal difficulty in concluding them. One sensible rule to observe in beginning a letter is to avoid starting off with the pronoun 'I." The stock phrase "I hope you are quite well," with which a number of women still begin their letters is as old-fashioned as it is ungraceful. If the letter must be commenced with a pronoun, commence it with the pronoun, "You," referring to the person to whom you are writing before referring to yourself.

Business Letters.—Business letters should of course be written in a business-like manner; they should be as brief and succinct as possible. Business letters when very short may be written in the third person. In other cases the first person should be employed, the beginning "Dear Sir," and the subscription, "Yours truly," being usually adopted. The name and address of the person to whom a business letter is sent should be placed either at the beginning of the letter on the left-hand side above the "Dear Sir," or at the end of the letter after the signature on the left-hand side. For business letters "Yours truly," and "Yours faithfully," are the usual forms of subscripton. In ordinary letters the subscription depends upon the degree of intimacy between the correspondents. Yours sincerely, and Yours very sincerely, are the forms most generally used.

Necessity for Spelling Names Correctly.—Care

should always be taken that the name of the person to whom the letter is addressed is spelt correctly. Some people are very sensitive as to the proper spelling of their names. A Mrs. Smyth, for instance, might resent it very much if a correspondent were to address her as "Mrs. Smith." It is always as well to ascertain the correct orthography of the names of acquaintances before writing to them.

Letters in the Third Person.—Letters to strangers may be written in the third person; but only if the communication is very brief. In other cases it is better to write in the first person as usual, as the constant repetition of names in a long letter written in the third person would not read well. In this case the letter should begin "Sir," or "Madam," and be subscribed "Yours truly." Invitations are generally written on cards, and in the third person (see p. 332).

Notepaper.—A woman should be very particular in regard to her notepaper, as this is one of the many little details by which her claim to refinement will be judged. The notepaper should always be of the best in quality and of medium thickness, and the envelopes should match it in every way, being of a size to exactly fit the sheet of notepaper when it is folded.

Crests and Armorial Bearings not used.—Crests and armorial bearings should not be blazoned upon notepaper. The address should be stamped clearly in plain lettering at the top of the first page. White, black, or violet are the favourite colourings for the lettering. Dies should always be used for stamping the addresses on notepaper. These can be specially made at moderate charges of from 4s. 6d. upwards, and can be used time after time, the stationer undertaking the stamping for a small charge.

Lever Embossing Presses.—A very convenient method, however, for stamping notepaper at home is by means of a lever embossing press. This is a small hand instrument into which a

Lever Embossing Press.

die is fitted, and by placing the notepaper over the die and depressing the lever, each sheet of notepaper can be stamped as required. This instrument is all the more useful to have at hand when it is remembered that in the best regulated household the supply of stamped paper is apt to run short, and pending the stamping of a fresh supply by the stationer very often plain paper has to be used. The possession of a lever embossing press renders such a state of affairs impossible—it is always at hand, and for this reason many women find it an indispensable adjunct to their writing-tables.

How to Address Persons of Rank.—It is essential that every woman should know how to address persons of rank in writing, both as regards the addressing of the envelope and the beginning of a letter. There is, of course, a great difference between the methods of addressing titled people employed by their friends and those employed officially and by strangers. For instance the friends of a duke would call him "Duke" when in conversation with him, whilst strangers would adopt the formal term "Your Grace." In writing the formal term would be "My Lord Duke," whilst a friend would write at the beginning of his letter "Dear Duke."

MODE OF ADDRESSING PERSONS OF RANK

In conversing with persons of rank, avoid the constant repetition of their title. The following table refers to the forms to be observed in *formal* communications:

(*a*) = How to address the envelope.
(*b*) = How to begin the letter.
(*c*) = How to refer to a person's rank when conversing with him.

ROYALTY—

The King: (*a*) To His Majesty the King; (*b*) Sir, under His Majesty the King; (*c*) Your Majesty.

The Queen: (*a*) To Her Majesty the Queen; (*b*) Madam, under Her Majesty the Queen; (*c*) Your Majesty.

The Prince of Wales: (*a*) To His Royal Highness the Prince of Wales; (*b*) Sir; (*c*) Your Royal Highness. Similarly in regard to other members of the Royal Family.

NOBILITY AND GENTRY—

Duke and *Duchess:* (*a*) To His (Her) Grace the Duke (Duchess) of ———; (*b*) My Lord Duke (Madam); (*c*) Your Grace.

Duke's *eldest son* has a courtesy title, and is addressed as if it were his by creation. Duke's *younger sons:* (*a*) To the Right Honble. Lord James ———; (*b*) and (*c*) Sir. Duke's *daughters:* (*a*) To the Right Honble. Lady Jane G. ——— (*b*) Madam; (*c*) Your Ladyship.

Marquis and *Marchioness:* (*a*) To the Most Honble. the Marquis (Marchioness) of ———; (*b*) My Lord Marquis (Madam); (*c*) Your Lordship (Ladyship). Marquis's children same as for those of a Duke.

Earl and *Countess*: (*a*) To the Right Honble. the Earl (Countess) of ———; (*b*) My Lord (Lady); (*c*) Your Lordship (Ladyship).

Earl's *eldest son* takes courtesy title and is addressed accordingly. Earl's *younger sons*: (*a*) To the Honble. Charles R———; (*b*) and (*c*) Sir. Earl's *daughters* same as for those of a Duke.

Viscount and *Viscountess* similar to Earl and Countess. *All* their sons and daughters are styled Honourable. (*a*) To the Honble. John (Mary) S———; (*b*) and (*c*) Sir (Madam).

Baron and *Baroness* and their children similar to Viscount and Viscountess and their children.

Baronet: (*a*) To Sir Edward D——— Baronet or Bt. (not Bart.); (*b*) Sir; (*c*) Sir Edward. His wife: (*a*) To Lady D———; (*b*) Madam; (*c*) Your Ladyship.

Knight: (*a*) To Sir John F———; (*b*) Sir; (*c*) Sir John. His wife, same as Baronet's wife.

Omit Kt. after the name on the envelope, and avoid in speaking the use of the surname.

THE CLERGY—

Archbishop: (*a*) To His Grace the Lord Archbishop of ———; (*b*) My Lord Archbishop, or Your Grace; (*c*) Your Grace.

Bishop: (*a*) To the Right Reverend; (*b*) My Lord Bishop; (*c*) Your Lordship.

N.B.—As a matter of courtesy the same form is usually adopted in addressing bishops, whether they are English Suffragan, or Colonial or Scotch, or Irish bishops.

Dean: (*a*) To the Very Reverend The Dean of ———; (*b*) Very Rev. Sir; (*c*) Mr. Dean.

Archdeacon: (*a*) To the Venerable the Archdeacon of ———; (*b*) Venerable Sir; (*c*) Mr. Archdeacon.

Clergymen: (*a*) To the Rev. C. D———; (*b*) Rev. Sir; (*c*) Sir.

If the Christian name is not known, leave blank: Rev. ——— D. ——— not Rev. Mr. D. ———. If a clergyman possesses the right to be styled Honourable or Right Honourable, this should precede his address as a cleric; *e.g.* The Right Hcuble. and Right Reverend ———

A *Canon* or *Prebendary* is addressed like ordinary clergymen except that Canon or Prebendary takes the place of the Christian name or initial.
The wives of bishops and other clergymen derive no title from the official rank of their husbands.

THE JUDGES, MAYORS, &c.—

The Lord Chancellor: (*a*) To the Right Honble. the Lord High Chancellor; or to the Right Honble. Earl Russell, Lord High Chancellor; (*b*) My Lord; (*c*) Your Lordship.

This style is also adopted in addressing the Lord Chief Justice, the Master of the Rolls, and the Lords of Appeal.

Vice-Chancellor: (*a*) To the Honble. ——— Vice-Chancellor; (*b*) and (*c*) Sir.

Puisne Judges: (*a*) To the Honble. Mr. Justice ———; (*b*) and (*c*) Sir, but "My Lord" when on the Bench.

Judges are usually Knights; but the above mode of address is more complimentary than that used in the case of Knights. Their wives are addressed as the wives of Knights.

Judges of the County Court: (*a*) To His Honour Judge ———; (*b*) and (*c*) Sir, but "Your Honour" when on the Bench.

Justices of the Peace: (*a*) W. Smith, Esq., J.P.; (*b*) and (*c*) Sir, but "Your Worship" when on the Bench.

Lord Mayor: (*a*) The Right Honble. the Lord Mayor of ———; (*b*) My Lord; (*c*) Your Lordship. His wife: (*a*) The Right Honble. the Lady Mayoress of ———; (*b*) Madam; (*c*) Your Ladyship.

In Scotland, Lord Provost takes the place of Lord Mayor. His wife does not share in his title.

[The chief magistrates of London, Dublin, York, Liverpool, Manchester, Birmingham, Bristol, Leeds, Sheffield, Newcastle, Cardiff, Belfast, and Cork are Lord Mayors; and those of Edinburgh, Glasgow, Aberdeen, Perth, and Dundee are Lord Provosts.]

Mayors: (*a*) The Mayor of ———, or in a memorial or other formal address, To his Worship the Mayor of ———; (*b*) and (*c*) Sir, but "Your Worship" when in Court.

Aldermen: (*a*) To Alderman Sir James ———, or To Mr. Alderman Jones; (*b*) and (*c*) Sir.

OFFICERS OF THE ARMY AND NAVY—

(*a*) The professional rank must always precede any other title; *e.g.* Admiral Sir William Eyton; Captain James Martin, R.N.; Lieut. Nairn, R.N. A lieutenant in the army is addressed simply as Esquire, but above that grade the rank is expressed; *e.g.* General Sir Edward King, Colonel The Honble. Arthur Bayne; Major Thompson; (*b*) If the officer is untitled begin the letter by writing "Sir" under the name and office. [Friends, of course, would write Dear Admiral, Dear General, &c., as the case may be.] The wives of officers, like the wives of clergymen, do not derive any title from the official rank of their husbands.

SPECIAL CASES—

Ambassadors take the title, as do also their wives, of "Excellency"; (*a*) To His Excellency the Earl of ———, Ambassador to ———; (*b*) according to rank; (*c*) Your Excellency.

Privy Councillors are addressed as "Right Honourable," but their wives not so.

Governors of Colonies: (*a*) To His Excellency ———, Governor of ———; (*b*) According to rank; (*c*) Your Excellency.

Cardinals : (*a*) To His Eminence ——— ; (*b*) and (*c*) Your Eminence.

Dowagers. Care should be taken to distinguish Dowagers by putting their Christian name before the title, thus : The Right Honble. Jane, Countess of Wigan.

Maid of Honour : (*a*) The Honble. Miss —— ; (*b*) and (*c*) Madam.

Obs. It is courteous to add to the ordinary address :—

(1) The letters indicating the order of knighthood that the addressee possesses, such as K.G., K.C.B., &c.
(2) The letters M.P. in the case of a Member of Parliament.
(3) The letters K.C. in the case of a King's Counsel.
(4) The letters indicating a Doctor's degree—D.D., D.C.L., LL.D., M.D., &c.

RULES OF PRECEDENCE

(1) The precedence of the members of the Royal Family depends on their relationship to the reigning sovereign, and not on their relationship to any of his predecessors.

(2) Ambassadors take precedence immediately after the Blood Royal ; envoys and ministers accredited to the sovereign after dukes and before marquises.

(3) The five degrees of honour among peers correspond with the titles—duke, marquis, earl, viscount, baron. Of those belonging to the same rank, seniority of creation settles the place in the scale of honour.

(4) Peers have precedence according as they are of England, Scotland, Great Britain, Ireland, or the United Kingdom.

(5) Precedence depends partly on rank and partly on place or office ; thus, the Lord Steward and the Lord Chamberlain of H.M. Household are above all peers of their own degree.

(6) Younger sons of rank A precede even the eldest son of rank B ; thus the younger sons of a Duke precede the elder sons of a Marquis or Earl, and so on.

(7) All sons of Viscounts and Barons precede Baronets, but the eldest sons and daughters of Baronets walk before the eldest sons and daughters of Knights of any degree whatsoever, Knighthood not being an hereditary honour. On the other hand, the eldest sons of Knights precede the younger sons of Baronets.

(8) The official precedence of a husband or father confers no personal precedence on his wife or children ; *e.g.* the Lord Chancellor or the Speaker of the House of Commons does not transmit any rank or place to his wife or children from his official position but only from his personal rank.

(9) Any one who is entitled to both personal and official precedence is to be placed according to that which implies the higher rank.

(10) Unmarried women take precedency from their father, "share and share alike," which is not the case with sons.

(11) Married women share their husbands' dignities, but can confer none of their own upon their husbands. Nor can the daughter of a peer, unless a peeress in her own right, transmit any rank or place to her children.

(12) Distinctions of birth, creation, or descent are a woman's own, and remain if she marry a commoner ; but if she marry a nobleman she must take her husband's place in the order of precedency.

(13) The wife of the eldest son of any degree precedes the daughters of the same degree, and both of them precede the younger sons of the next higher degree. Thus the wife of the eldest son of an Earl walks before an Earl's daughter, and both of them before the wife of the younger son of a Marquis ; and the wife of a Marquis precedes the wife of the eldest son of a Duke.

TABLE OF PRECEDENCE AMONG MEN

The King.
The Prince of Wales.
King's other Sons.
King's Uncles.
King's Nephews.

(Ambassadors. See rule (2).)
Archbishop of Canterbury.
[In Scotland, Moderator of the General Assembly if in attendance at a royal function.]
Lord High Chancellor, or Lord Keeper if a Peer.
Archbishop of York.
The Prime Minister.
Lord Chancellor of Ireland.
Lord President of the Privy Council.
Lord Privy Seal.
Lord Great Chamberlain.
Lord High Constable.
Earl Marshal.
Lord Steward of H.M. Household.
Lord Chamberlain of H.M. Household.
The last five rank above all Peers of their own degree.

Dukes.

Eldest Sons of Dukes of the Blood Royal.

Marquises.

Eldest Sons of Dukes.

Earls.

Younger Sons of Dukes of the Blood Royal.
Eldest Sons of Marquises.
Younger Sons of Dukes.

Viscounts.

Eldest Sons of Earls.
Younger Sons of Marquises.

BISHOPS.

(1) London, (2) Durham, (3) Winchester.
English Bishops, according to Seniority of Consecration.
[In Scotland, the Primus of the Episcopal Church immediately follows the Moderator of the General Assembly.]
[In Ireland the Bishops of the Disestablished Church are now placed on equality with those of the Roman Communion, all alike taking rank according to seniority of Consecration.]
Secretary of State and Chief Secretary to the Lord Lieutenant of Ireland, if at least a Baron.

BARONS.

Speaker of the House of Commons.
Commissioners of the Great Seal.
Treasurer of the Household.
Comptroller of the Household.
Master of the Horse.
Vice-Chamberlain of the Household.
Secretary of State and Chief Secretary to the Lord Lieutenant of Ireland, if below the rank of Baron.
Eldest Sons of Viscounts.
Younger Sons of Earls.
Eldest Sons of Barons.
Knights of the Garter.
Privy Councillors.
Chancellor of the Exchequer.
Chancellor of the Duchy of Lancaster.
Lord Chief Justice of the King's Bench.
Master of the Rolls.
Lords Justices of Appeal, and the President of the Probate Divorce and Admiralty Division.
Judges of the High Court of Justice.
Knights Bannerets made by the Sovereign in person.
Younger Sons of (1) Viscounts. (2) Barons.

BARONETS.

Knights Bannerets not made by the Sovereign in person.
Knights Grand Cross of the Bath.
Knights Grand Commanders of the Star of India.
Knights Grand Cross of SS. Michael and George.
Knights Grand Commanders of the Order of the Indian Empire.
Knights Grand Cross of the Royal Victorian Order.
Knights Commanders of the Bath.
Knights Commanders of the Star of India.
Knights Commanders of SS. Michael and George.
Knights Commanders of the Order of the Indian Empire.
Knights Commanders of the Royal Victorian Order.
Commanders of the Royal Victorian Order.
Knights Bachelors.
Companions of the Bath.
Companions of the Star of India.
Companions of SS. Michael and George.
Companions of the Order of the Indian Empire.
Members of the Fourth Class of the Royal Victorian Order.
Companions of the Distinguished Service Order.
Members of the Fifth Class of the Royal Victorian Order.

Eldest Sons of the Younger Sons of Peers.
Eldest Sons of Baronets.
Eldest Sons of Knights of the Garter.
Eldest Sons of Bannerets.
Eldest Sons of Knights according to their father's precedence.
Younger Sons of Baronets.
Younger Sons of Knights.
Esquires and Gentlemen.

TABLE OF PRECEDENCE AMONG LADIES

THE QUEEN.
The Princess of Wales.[1]
The Queen Mother.
Daughters of the Sovereign.
Sisters of the Sovereign.
Aunts of the Sovereign.
Wives of the Uncles of the Sovereign.
Nieces of the Sovereign.

DUCHESSES.

Wives of the Eldest Sons of Dukes of the Blood Royal.

MARCHIONESSES.

Wives of the Eldest Sons of Dukes.
Daughters of Dukes.

COUNTESSES.

Wives of the Younger Sons of Dukes of the Blood Royal.
Wives of the Eldest Sons of Marquises.
Daughters of Marquises.
Wives of the Younger Sons of Dukes.

VISCOUNTESSES

Wives of the Eldest Sons of Earls.
Daughters of Earls.
Wives of the Younger Sons of Marquises.

BARONESSES.

Wives of the Eldest Sons of Viscounts.
Daughters of Viscounts.
Wives of the Younger Sons of Earls.
Wives of the Eldest Sons of Barons.
Daughters of Barons.
Maids of Honour to the Queen.
Wives of Knights of the Garter.
Wives of Bannerets made by the King in person.

[1] There being no Princess of Wales at present the Queen Mother comes next in precedence to the Queen.

Wives of the Younger Sons of Viscounts.
Wives of the Younger Sons of Barons.

Wives of Baronets according to the dates of their husbands' creation.
Wives of Bannerets not made by the King in person.
Wives of Knights Grand Cross of the Bath.
Wives of Knights Grand Commanders of the Star of India.
Wives of Knights Grand Cross of SS. Michael and George.
Wives of Knights Grand Commanders of the Order of the Indian Empire.
Wives of Knights Grand Cross of the Royal Victorian Order.
Wives of Knights Commanders of the Bath.
Wives of Knights Commanders of the Star of India.
Wives of Knights Commanders of SS. Michael and George.
Wives of Knights Commanders of the Order of the Indian Empire.
Wives of Knights Commanders of the Royal Victorian Order.
Wives of Knights Bachelors.
Wives of Companions of the Bath.
Wives of Companions of the Star of India.
Wives of Companions of SS. Michael and George.
Wives of Companions of the Order of the Indian Empire.
Wives of Members of the Fourth Class of the Royal Victorian Order.
Wives of Companions of the Distinguished Service Order.
Wives of Members of the Fifth Class of the Royal Victorian Order.

Wives of the Eldest Sons of the Younger Sons of Peers.
Daughters of the Younger Sons of Peers.
Wives of the Eldest Sons of Baronets.
Daughters of Baronets.
Wives of the Eldest Sons of Knights of the Garter.
Wives of the Eldest Sons of Knights Bannerets.
Wives of the Eldest Sons of Knights.
Daughters of Knights.
Wives of the Younger Sons of Baronets.
Wives of the Younger Sons of Knights.
Wives of Esquires and Gentlemen.

PRESENTATION AT COURT

The reign of King Edward VII. saw many changes in regard to the ceremonies connected with presentations and attendance at Court, and it is presumed that the rules prescribed by our late king will be continued by King George. In Queen Victoria's reign presentations were made at "Drawing Rooms," which were held in the day-time. Now the evening "Court" has superseded the old-time drawing-room. The time at which these Courts are held is 10 P.M., and the Lord Chamberlain gives previous notice as to what time the company is expected to arrive. Attendance and presentation at the Courts are by invitation only, these invitations being conveyed through the Lord Chamberlain. Ladies who wish to be presented at Court can only be presented through one of their relatives or acquaintances who has already been presented. The one who makes the presentation must attend the same Court as the lady she is presenting.

Former Presentations.—Ladies who have been presented at any Drawing Room held during the reign of King Edward VII. do not require to be again presented to King George and Queen Mary. Whenever these ladies wish to attend a Court or make a presentation they should send in their names and the names of those whom they wish to present to the Lord Chamberlain, before the date by which the Lord Chamberlain gives notice that all names must be sent in.

Who may be Presented at Court.—All those of good social position and of good reputation are eligible for presentation at Court. No lady, however high her rank, would be admitted to Court if there were the least stain upon her reputation. The wives and daughters of members of the aristocracy, members of parliament, the various professions, bankers, merchants, in fact, all people of recognised substantial position are eligible for presentation, providing a lady who has already been presented is willing to fulfil this office for them.

Making Presentations.—The lady making the presentation must be personally responsible for the character of the lady she presents. She may present her own daughters or daughters-in-law and only one other lady in addition. Presentations at each of their Majesties Courts are limited by Royal Command.

Official Presentations.—Presentations may be made officially by the foreign ambassadresses, the wives of members of the Cabinet, and of other official personages in the several departments of the State. The restriction in regard to the presentation of one person only does not apply to official presentations.

Ladies have to be presented again upon their marriage and upon accession to titles. A lady having been presented on her marriage may attend any subsequent Court by invitation, but if she has no official position, she is only expected to attend a Court once every fourth year.

Preliminary Formalities.—Only married ladies may make presentations. An unmarried lady, however high her rank, does not possess this privilege. When a married lady desires to be presented she should write to the Lord Chamberlain requesting this honour, and stating in full the name and rank of her husband, and of her parents, and of the lady who is presenting her.

In the case of a girl débutante her mother or the relative who is to present her should make the application. It is necessary for a lady making a presentation to attend herself at the Court at which the presentation is to be made, though it is not necessary for her to accompany the person whom she presents. A married lady presented at a Court can herself make a presentation at the same Court, but the person presented by her must enter the Presence Chamber after her and not before her.

Etiquette of Presentation.—At the beginning of the year the Lord Chamberlain inserts a notice in the newspapers requesting those who wish to attend one of the Courts during the year to send in their names; usually the number of Courts to be held amounts to four, sometimes five. Ladies who wish to attend them send in their names, and also the names of the ladies they wish to present. The Lord Chamberlain then forwards to each lady a card to be filled up with full particulars, and when this has been duly done and all is found satisfactory an intimation is received from the Lord Chamberlain that her name has been put on the list for attendance at the Court, and the invitation arrives.

Privilege of the Entrée.—The Diplomatic Circle, Cabinet Ministers and their wives, and the members of the Household have what is known as the Privilege of the Entrée. They enter at the gate of the Palace situated outside Buckingham Gate. The rooms next to the Presence Chamber are allotted to them. Those who have the privilege of entrée are received by their Majesties according to precedency and before the general assembly. In regard to the general assembly there is no precedency as to which ladies enter the Presence Chamber, the earliest arrivals being the first admitted to their Majesties' presence. Those who have the privilege of entrée have also the privilege of making the first presentations.

Arrival at the Palace.—Upon arrival at the palace a lady leaves her cloak in the cloak-room. She must not forget to take her invitation card with her. After being divested of her cloak she goes through the hall and up the Grand Staircase of the Palace to the corridor, carrying her train upon her left arm. Her train must be carried in this way until it is taken down and spread out for her before entering the Presence Chamber. She will not have to touch it in any way as all this is done for her. In her right hand she holds her bouquet—in her left hand the invitation card. This she must be careful to hold right side uppermost so that the name can be read at once. When she has reached the corridor she must show the invitation card to the page in waiting, and then pass through into one of the saloons. If the saloons are full she takes a seat in the corridor until there is room for her to enter. From the saloons she passes in her turn to the Picture Gallery. Here her train is let down and spread out by two pages in attendance, and she crosses through the Gallery to the Presence Chamber, giving her card to the usher at the door. There is usually a long line of ushers, but the card is given to the nearest one and is passed on by him until it reaches the Lord Chamberlain. There will be a long line of ladies passing in turn to make their curtseys in the royal presence. The débutante will make one of that line, and she must pay particular attention to her deportment, because the least *gaucherie* will make her conspicuous. The skirt of her dress will be long enough in front to hide her shoes—these should never be shown in any circumstances; the walk should be a graceful, gliding movement, the feet gently pushing the long silken skirts forward to prevent any danger of tripping or other similar contretemps.

An Important Point.—One important point for the débutante to remember is that she must never stand still once she has taken her place in the line of ladies who have entered the Presence Chamber. She must keep walking, taking very tiny steps if necessary, and if the space between herself and the lady in front of her is so limited that the train of the latter is in her way, it is permissible for her to gently push it aside with her foot.

The Curtsey.—When it is her turn to curtsey before the King the Lord Chamberlain reads the name of the débutante, pronouncing the magic words "to be presented." The débutante must be right in front of the King as she makes her curtsey. Needless to say, the curtsey should be the perfection of grace, and requires a great deal of rehearsal beforehand. Keeping the body gracefully erect she should glide the left foot backwards, and bending the knees, but not the back, make the obeisance; the right hand containing the bouquet should be lowered slightly so that the bouquet may not be in the way. All appearance of nervousness and fluster should be avoided. Whilst paying her homage the débutante should endeavour to wear a cheerful expression, and as she rises from the curtsey she should gracefully incline her head to the King in acknowledgment, then beginning on the right foot as she rises she should take three gliding steps towards the Queen, curtseying to her in the same way. After rising and gently inclining her head as to the King, she must follow the line of ladies who have already been presented, making her way out of the Presence Chamber. When she reaches the door she must turn quickly, holding out her left arm with the elbow bent to receive her train, which the page will throw over it. She must be sure to do this quickly in order to catch it at the proper moment, or much awkwardness might result.

Ladies do not now step backwards when leaving the Royal Presence, nor do they curtsey to any other members of the Royal Family but the King and Queen. Formerly upon being presented to Queen Victoria each lady had to remove the glove from the right hand, and when the words "to be presented" were uttered by the Lord Chamberlain the Queen would extend her hand, and the débutante placing her own ungloved hand beneath Her Majesty's, would kiss it as she made her curtsey. Now a lady upon being presented does not kiss the King's hand, but only curtseys to the King and then to the Queen, who bow in return.

There are so many points of etiquette in regard to a presentation at Court that it is absolutely necessary for a lady about to be presented to take at least one lesson in deportment beforehand. Mrs. Wordsworth of 47 Harrington Road, South Kensington, London, who is one of the best-known authorities on Court etiquette and deportment, coaches débutantes for the occasion of their presentation. She teaches them how to hold their trains, how to walk, how to curtsey, and how to conduct themselves generally in the Royal Presence. A lady's first appearance at Court is apt to be somewhat of an ordeal when she is not quite *au fait* with the procedure, and even if she is fortunate enough not to make any actual *faux pas*, her fear of doing so will keep her mind in a state of constant perturbation. On the other hand, she will have acquired the ease born of self-confidence if she goes to Court fittingly prepared. By arrangement with Mrs. Wordsworth, classes for the purpose of instruction in Court deportment may be held by herself or her assistants at all provincial and country districts. Private lessons can also be arranged in the same manner.

Court Dress.—Ladies must wear full Court dress when attending or being presented at Court; the train to the dress must not be less than three and a half yards in length. The bodice must be low, and the sleeves short. The train may be of any shape, and it may either hang from the shoulders or from the waist. A presentation dress should be white, but it may be trimmed with coloured flowers if desired.

Plumes.—The head-dress consists of a veil of white tulle and plumes. All ladies, married and unmarried, must wear plumes. The married ladies wear three white plumes, the unmarried ladies two.

High Court Dress.—For the benefit of old ladies and those who suffer from delicacy or ill-health, the Queen has approved of a High Court dress which may be worn by those to whom for any of these reasons the ordinary low Court dress is unsuitable. The bodice is cut square or heart-shaped in front and filled in with white. At the back the bodice may be high or cut down the same way as the front. The sleeves to the bodice are of elbow-length. Ladies who wish to appear in High Court dress must first obtain the Queen's permission.

White gloves only should be worn, excepting in cases of mourning.

Bouquets are carried by both married and unmarried ladies.

CHURCH DECORATION

Women are often called upon to assist in the decoration of their parish church at various festivals, and if they do not actually help in the work they may like to send in some floral contributions. In doing this it is well to remember that all the colours employed in the decoration of the church have some special significance. Thus:—

White signifies innocence, glory, and joy.

Red stands for (*a*) the fire of love which the Holy Ghost kindles within us; (*b*) the blood of the Martyrs.

Gold signifies glory.

Blue signifies Heaven, knowledge, contemplation.

Purple signifies penitence and fasting.

Black, death and darkness.

Green, the hope and desire of Heaven.

In regard to floral decoration, therefore, white is the most appropriate colour for the white days, such as Christmas, the Circumcision, the Epiphany, and Easter. White and gold are generally used for the latter festival, the Easter Lily being a particularly appropriate flower for altar decoration on Easter Sunday. On Palm Sunday the altar may be decorated with palms; the general decoration may also include box, yew, and willow.

Red is the colour for Pentecost and feasts of martyrs.

Purple is the colour for Lent, with the exception of Good Friday, when black is used. As a rule there should be no floral decorations sent for either Advent or Lent; this rule is, however, generally departed from on the third Sunday in Advent, the fourth Sunday in Lent, and Holy Innocents' Day.

Christmas time is undoubtedly the festival of the year when church decoration assumes its most interesting aspect. Many church workers eagerly volunteer their service not only in regard to the decoration of the altar, but also in regard to that of the whole church. Holly is the leading feature of the church decoration, whilst ivy, rosemary, and bay enter into the general decorative scheme. Wreaths of holly, ivy, and other green leaves are twisted in and out around all the pillars, and wherever there is a window-ledge or recess it is banked with holly and green leaves. Very few people know how to make wreaths and festoons properly. It is always best to have a solid foundation of fine cording, and to make up bunches of holly and leaves, tying them to this cording foundation at regular intervals of a few inches the one from the other. The bunches of holly and leaves can be tied with fine twine, and the worker should have all the necessary implements, such as scissors, string, &c., ready to hand. If the wreaths or festoons have no foundation of the kind, and the various bunches are only tied together and joined to one another without the support of cord, they are apt to break away from each other and thus present an untidy appearance.

If several workers are engaged in decorating the church at Christmas time it is always as well to have some scheme of organisation by which each member is allotted a particular task; under these circumstances the work is brought to a quicker and a much more satisfactory conclusion.

LIST OF LADIES' CLUBS

The following is a list of the principal Clubs in London with the Entrance and Subscription Fees.

Abbreviations—A.F.—Annual Subscription or Fee.
E.F.—Entrance Fee.
C.M.—Country Member.

LONDON

Albemarle (Ladies and Gentlemen).—37 Dover Street, W. E. F. £6, 6s. A. F. £6, 6s.

Alexandra.—12 Grosvenor Street, W. E. F. £2, 2s. A. F. £5, 5s. C. M. £4, 4s.

Alliance.—61 Curzon Street, Mayfair, W. A. F. £3, 3s.

Austral (Ladies and Gentlemen).—38 Dover Street, W. E. F. £2, 2s. A. F. £3, 3s. C. M. £2, 2s.

Athenæum.—31 Dover Street, W. E. F. £5, 5s. A. F. £5, 5s.

Army and Navy.—2 Burlington Garden, W. E. F. £3, 3s. A. F. £5, 5s.

Empress.—35 Dover Street, W. E. F. £5, 5s. A. F. £5, 5s.

Empire.—69 Grosvenor Street, W. E. F. £5, 5s. A. F. £8, 8s.

Ladies' Imperial.—17 Dover Street, W. E. F. £5, 5s. A. F. £5, 5s.

Ladies' Park.—32 Knightsbridge, S.W. E. F. £5, 5s. A. F. £4, 4s. and £3, 3s.

Lyceum.—128 Piccadily, W. E. F. £2, 2s. A. F. £4, 4s. C. M. £3, 3s.

New Century.—Hay Hill, Berkeley Square, W. E. F. £2, 2s. A. F. £1, 1s.

New County.—21 *Hanover Square*, W. E. F. £2, 2s. A. F. £3, 3s.

New Era.—67 Curzon Street, Mayfair, W. E. F. £2, 2s. A. F. £3, 3s. C. M. £2, 2s.

New Victorian.—30A Sackville Street, W. E. F. £2, 2s. A. F. £3, 3s.

Pioneer.—5 Grafton Street, Piccadilly, W. E. F. £3, 3s. A. F. £3, 3s. and £2, 2s.

Sesame (Ladies and Gentlemen).—28 and 29 Dover Street, W. E. F. £6, 6s. A. F. £6, 6s.

University.—4 George Street, Hanover Square, W. E. F. £1, 1s. A. F. £1, 10s.

Victoria.—145 Victoria Street, S.W. E. F. £2, 2s. A. F. £5, 5s. C. M. £3, 3s.

Writers'.—Hastings House, 10 Norfolk Street, Strand, W.C. E. F. £1, 1s. A. F. £2, 2s. C. M. £1, 1s.

MANAGEMENT OF MONEY AND LEGAL GUIDE

How to keep within her income or allowance besides leaving a margin for savings and unforeseen expenses is a problem which many a harassed housewife has failed to solve. The simple rules in regard to the suitable apportionment of the allowance and the best methods of keeping check upon expenditure, which are given in the first part of this chapter, have been compiled as the result of actual experience—they have been tried and found successful. In addition, all that every woman ought to know in connection with the management of her affairs, including such important questions as banking, insurance, and those points of law which are liable to crop up in ordinary every-day life, are described and explained in as simple a manner as possible.

Allotment of the Income.—The value of money is one of the first things every woman should learn, and this is especially necessary in the case of those who have anything to do with household management, as the basis of all good housekeeping lies in the proper control of the household purse.

It would be a very good thing if every young girl could be taught to keep an accurate account of her own pocket-money as a preliminary to undertaking expenses on a large scale.

Successful management does not depend so much on the size of the income, but rather upon the spending of it to the best advantage. Those who get into trouble with a small amount would no doubt have similar difficulties if their income were doubled or even trebled.

First of all then it is important to ascertain the exact amount of your income, or at least how much of it may be safely expended on the various items which come under the heading of *Household Expenses.*

When starting housekeeping it is a good plan to portion out the income so as to make it cover all the expenses that are likely to occur for a period of, say, three months, six months, or a year. For this purpose each detail of expenditure must be jotted down under a distinctive heading, such as rent, food, clothing, education, &c., and a certain sum allotted to each division. Everything must be borne in mind, not only the *Current Expenses, i.e.* those which run on from day to day, such as rent and taxes, household expenses, insurance, charities, clothing, and perhaps school fees, &c., but also *Occasional Expenses,* such as holidays, travelling, recreation, hospitalities, possible medical attendance, and any special outlay. An effort should also be made to have a *Reserve Fund,* so that something at least, even although it may be a small amount, is saved each year. The list must then be added up and the amount of the expenses compared with the amount of the income. If the sum of the income exceeds that of the expenditure, things are quite safe, we are living within our means; but if it is less, one or other of our expenses must be cut off or curtailed.

Many schemes for the proportionate allotment of the income have been drawn up, such as the following:—

Rent and taxes	$\frac{1}{8}$
Household expenses	$\frac{3}{8}$
Clothing and charities	$\frac{1}{8}$
Education and travelling	$\frac{1}{8}$
Insurance, incidental and saving . .	$\frac{1}{8}$

But a table of this sort can only serve as a guide and not by any means as a hard-and-fast rule to go by. In fact, it is quite impossible to draw up any scheme which will apply to every household, as conditions vary so considerably.

This drawing up of a plan demands a certain amount of careful calculation, and perhaps just at first it will be impossible to arrive at the best division of the means at disposal, but if after a few months' trial this or that part of the scheme is found not to work well, it is easy to make alterations until the best possible allotment of the income is secured.

When the income is a fixed one this is comparatively easy; it is where it is fluctuating or uncertain that the greater difficulty comes in, and in this case one can only plan for a shorter time and count on the lowest sum.

To begin with, the amount necessary to pay for rent will vary in different places, and while one-sixth might be found necessary for a suitable house in town, in country districts one-eighth or even one-tenth of the income would be ample. It must be remembered that the amount of rent paid will very much influence the style of living, and that it is not wise to go beyond a sum that is in proportion to one's means.

Then, again, education fees will be very heavy

in some families, or special training fees in order to equip one or other of its members for a chosen career in life, while in other households this kind of outlay is practically nil.

Doctors' fees may never be required some years, while at other times they may be abuormally heavy.

Then expenses due to appearances amount to a considerable sum in some cases, and they cannot well be curtailed without damaging the reputation of the head of the house. This is especially noticeable in the households of professional men or women where a shabby, mean appearance either in dress or household appointments would materially injure their career.

With regard to clothing, where much can be made at home the expense is decidedly less, but where this is impossible a larger sum must of necessity be allowed.

Thus it will be seen that there are certain expenses which can be reduced in some houses and not in others, and that the plan must be made out accordingly.

It is best therefore for the head of the family to make out his or her own plan, always being careful to keep the expenses within a safe limit. The income should always overlap the outlay, and, in addition, there should if possible be a Reserve Fund, as mentioned above.

A certain sum having been apportioned to each set of expenses a system of book-keeping should then be started.

Where a husband and wife are at the head of the house it very often happens that the man pays all the expenses except those connected with clothing and the house-keeping proper, handing over to his wife a fixed sum weekly or monthly for these requirements. This will, of course, simplify the book-keeping for the house-mistress, although under all circumstances the method to be adopted is very much the same.

It is one of the duties of the mistress of the house to keep an accurate account of all money that comes under her charge. Many women have a strong objection to keeping accounts and content themselves with a rule of thumb method of managing their affairs; but this haphazard way of dealing with money is almost sure to lead to trouble sooner or later. A housekeeper who keeps accounts will be amply repaid for her trouble, and although at first it may seem irksome and almost too great a strain upon one's time and thought, yet when once a simple method of book-keeping has been mastered the entries become almost mechanical and cause no trouble. Correct accounts are a most valuable help against habits of extravagance, and a neat record of one's income and expenditure is a possession by no means to be despised.

An elaborate system of book-keeping is not necessary; in fact, the simpler the plan adopted the better. There should first of all be a *Cash-Box*. Every woman who has charge of money should furnish herself with a cash-box fitted with lock and key in which to keep all the money she has in hand. If this box has separate divisions in which to put gold, silver, and coppers, it will be all the more useful. This is very important when considerable sums of money have to be dealt with, and even when the amount is small it is always wiser not to leave money in open places. To lock it up is not a sign that we mistrust people's honesty; at the same time it is not fair to put temptation in any one's way.

The next thing is a *Cash-Book*. This should be of a very good size and be ruled with money columns. There are several different housekeeping books on the market, ruled off with different headings under which to put the different items, but these are, as a rule, too complicated, and a simple account-book can be made to serve the purpose admirably.

The cash-book should show three things at a glance: (1) the amount of money received to date; (2) the amount of money paid out to date; and (3) the balance.

On the right-hand page enter all payments made, putting the date to each day before beginning the entries. This is called the credit side, and is a record of all that goes out.

On the left-hand page enter all money you have in hand to begin with, then any money received or drawn from the bank with the corresponding dates. This is called the debit side and is a record of all that comes in.

This is all that is required for the daily entries, and ten minutes a day should suffice for the transaction if the work is carried out with regularity and accuracy.

Then at the end of the week or on a fixed day each week the account should be balanced.

To Balance the Account.—To do this first add up very carefully the columns on both pages, and then compare the amount spent on the right-hand page with the amount on the left-hand page. If the amount on the credit side is less than the sum entered on the debit side the money remaining in the cash-box should equal the difference. This is called the *Balance in Hand*, and should be added on to the right-hand page in order to make both columns alike.

After ruling off the account the cash in hand should be brought down to start the debit side of the next week's account. When a page is finished, whether it be the left-hand or the right-hand one, the entries on both sides should be stopped, and if one page has a blank space left a line should be drawn diagonally across it to show that no further entries should be made there.

The plan given on the next page will serve to show what is meant by the above explanation. It is intended as a guide to method only.

SPECIMEN PAGE OF CASH BOOK

	Week ending May 14—	£	s.	d.		*Week ending May 14—*	£	s.	d.
May 9	Amount in hand . .	0	15	0	May 9	Grocer	0	7	4
,, 9	Cash received . .	5	0	0	,, 9	Dairy	0	5	0
					,, 10	Newspapers . . .	0	0	9
					,, 10	Baker	0	3	6
					,, 10	Stationery . . .	0	4	8
					,, 11	Household repairs . .	0	6	1
					,, 11	Flowers . . .	0	1	0
					,, 12	Window-cleaning . .	0	2	6
					,, 12	Washing	0	4	3
					,, 12	Cab fares	0	4	0
					,, 12	Chemist	0	2	11
					,, 13	Servants' wages . .	2	12	0
							4	14	0
					,, 14	Cash in hand . . .	1	1	0
	£	5	15	0		£	5	15	0

This keeping of a cash-book is the simplest form of book-keeping, and if all that is required is a simple record of the food bills and working expenses of the household it may be deemed sufficient; but if the expenditure of the whole income has to be accounted for something more will be necessary. The drawback to this simple form is that there is no attempt at classification, and it does not show how the expenditure is being divided under the various headings of food, clothing, rent, &c., and whether the limits agreed upon at the commencement are being adhered to. To obtain this information the different items would require to be separately posted to another book, and this book would be called *The Ledger*.

To Post the Ledger.—At regular intervals all the items in the cash-book should be classified in another book. It is just a question how many headings should be made for household expenditure; an over-detailed classification should be avoided, as it makes too much demand upon our time. Here, again, simplicity coupled with accuracy should be aimed at.

The number of headings must vary according to circumstances, but the minimum might be the following:—

1. Rent and taxes.
2. Food account.
3. Other household expenses.
4. Clothing.
5. Education, books, and stationery.
6. Insurance and charities.
7. Travelling and holiday expenses.
8. Incidental expenses.

The ledger need only be made up once in three months, or at most once a month. We shall then have an exact statement as to where the money has gone, and if retrenchment is necessary it will serve as a distinct guide as to where we shall require to curtail expenditure.

The following table will serve as a guide to the arrangement of the *Ledger*.

Quarterly Expenditure

	£	s.	d.
Rent and taxes	15	0	0
Food Account	30	10	0
Other household expenses . . .	12	14	0
Clothing	11	18	0
Education, books and stationery .	14	0	0
Insurance and charities	8	17	0
Travelling and holidays	6	6	0
Incidental expenses	5	9	0
	£104	14	0

Or, if the mistress of the house has only the money spent on household bills to account for, a simple and more detailed analysis might be made out monthly in the following manner :—

Monthly Household Bills

	£	s.	d.
Grocer	2	2	0
Fishmonger	1	0	0
Baker	1	2	0
Butcher	2	10	0
Milk, eggs and butter	1	10	0
Greengrocer	1	0	0
Washing	1	8	0
Repairs	0	12	0
	£11	4	0

HOUSEHOLD EXPENSES

This term applies to all expenses connected with housekeeping proper, such as food, washing, fuel and light, servants, wages, cleaning materials, repairs, &c., so that the fixed sum which has been allotted under the above heading will require to be judiciously apportioned amongst the various items mentioned in order that it may be used to the best advantage.

With regard to the actual food allowance, there is great diversity of opinion as to what should be spent per week. Certain fixed standards have indeed been set up which have come to be regarded as reasonable, but these will naturally vary with individual circumstances, as, for instance, the number to be fed, individual taste and requirements, and the means at disposal.

The allowance for food is generally calculated at a certain sum per head. This sum will vary in accordance with the number of people to be provided for, a smaller amount per head being necessary in the case of a large family than in the case of a small one, the expense per head in the case of one or two people being much greater than in any other circumstances. For a grown-up family of moderate means, where all the members dine at home and meat is eaten every day, and all have good healthy appetites, 10s. per head per week would be thought a very fair sum to provide a nice table with good variety, a little extra being allowed for any visitors. If this sum is beyond what can be afforded a sufficiency of good nourishing food can be provided for much less, or from 5s. to 8s. per head, but this will require more thought and management, and such things as game and poultry would not figure largely on the bill of fare. It is generally necessary to allow the same amount for servants as for the other members of the family. Of course, there are many whose means are not limited who will consider the above figures ridiculously small, and who would require 15s. or even £1 per week to supply all their wants. The reason why a moderate amount in many cases proves insufficient is very often owing to waste of material, extravagance in buying, or lack of knowledge as to how to make the most of things.

A small food allowance presupposes favourable opportunities for marketing, as, for instance, in the case of people living in the country where garden produce is cheap and also farm produce, although, on the other hand, they may have to pay more for their groceries and butcher meat.

In order to use a food allowance to the best advantage, a certain knowledge of cookery and the dietetic properties of food is also necessary. The house-mistress must just make up her mind as to what is a legitimate amount to spend on food, and if it comes to having to curtail expenses there are always other ways of doing it, but there must be a sufficiency of good wholesome food before everything else.

It is not always an easy matter to cut down expenditure, and few people enjoy economising, yet in hundreds of cases it has to be done. Saving can be effected in many ways. For instance, one can discontinue the use of wine and other luxuries, reduce the number of servants, have washing done at home, make one's own clothes, and last, but not least, avoid spending money on trifles. This is a perfect habit with some people. Shop windows have such a fascination for them that they can rarely pass by without going in to buy some knick-knack or other, spending as much money in this way as they do on dress, and there is nothing to show for it. Sales are also a temptation to many: they are persuaded to buy an article or piece of material for which they have not the slightest need, simply because the price looks cheap, and they do not like to miss what seems to them a bargain, when in reality it is waste of money. The greatest point of all in cutting down expenditure is to prevent waste and to adopt economical methods without in any way being mean and stingy.

Payment of Household Accounts.—It is just a question whether it is better to pay ready money or to have weekly, fortnightly, or monthly accounts. If the ready-money system is adopted it means more entering up each day, and there is more detail work. A small note-book would require to be kept in addition to the cash-book in order to jot down each payment when it is made, as it is useless to burden one's memory unnecessarily. But it is not easy to pay ready money for everything, and upon the whole weekly payments, which practically amount to the same thing, are preferable, as they save the trouble of so many small payments. A set of house-books too save an amount of trouble, and seem to keep the matter in a more concise form. In small households this system should certainly be adopted, and especially so if the income is a limited one. Running up long bills is not economical, and if you wish to be well served you should make up your mind to pay the house-books regularly.

Of course there are special circumstances where it is not convenient to pay weekly, and where even the trades-people prefer a monthly payment, but the books should in any case be made up and checked weekly. If accounts are only rendered once a month it is much more difficult to keep a check on the items, and mistakes are apt to pass unnoticed.

The Checking and Filing of Bills.—Each bill as it is received should be carefully examined and the various items checked and verified. Bills should never be paid until this has been done. The small vouchers which ought to accompany all goods sent in by the trades-people must be kept for this purpose, and also all weight tickets such as would be sent with meat or coal. With regard to milk and bread, which are usually taken daily from a man at the door, it is a good plan to keep a small book or slate at hand in which the daily amount is marked down.

All bills, when they have been paid, should be receipted and kept for future reference. Occasionally a bill may be presented a second time, and this mistake may happen even with the best houses, and unless the receipt can be produced the payment will in all probability have to be made again. Loose bills can either be kept on files bought for the purpose, or they can be folded lengthwise with the name and date of payment outside, and then encircled with an india-rubber band. They must always be arranged in an order which will allow of ready discovery.

BANKING

The Business of a Bank.—The bank is a most important factor in both our commercial and social life. Nearly all payments in business are made through the medium of a bank, and almost every individual of any standing in private life has a banking account.

Besides taking charge of the money of his customers, it is a banker's business to pay cheques issued by them, to collect the value of cheques paid to them, to attend to and discount their bills, and, if necessary, to take charge of their securities, their jewels, or other valuable property. The money that is paid into a bank is not allowed to lie idle in its safes. If that were so there would be no profit in a banker's business. A large proportion is lent by the bank at a much higher rate of interest than is paid to depositors. The difference in this interest represents the banker's profits.

Interest.—Interest is a certain sum paid in return for the use of money. It is always calculated at so much per cent. (*i.e.* per hundred) per annum. Thus—

2½ per cent. = £2, 10s. in every £100, 6d. in every £1.
5 per cent. = £5 in every £100, 1s. in every £1.
7½ per cent. = £7, 10s. in every £100, 1s 6d. in every £1.
10 per cent. = £10 in every £100, 2s. in every £1.

Simple and Compound Interest.—The sum upon which interest is allowed is called the "principal." The interest allowed upon the original "principal" only is called "simple interest." When, however, the simple interest is allowed to accumulate and be added to the principal, it ranks as an increased principal, and interest calculated upon the larger sum obtained in this way is known as "compound interest."

Bank Notes.—Some banks have a right to issue bank notes to the public. These are printed on special paper and are equivalent to their amount in cash. English bank notes are issued for sums of £5 and upwards, while Scottish and Irish banks issue £1 notes as well. Bank of England notes are legal tender, and are accepted both in Britain and abroad almost as readily as gold. £1 Scotch or Irish notes are only of the value of 19s. 11d. in England.

How to Open a Banking Account.—Some women have a very vague idea of the formalities to be observed in opening a banking account, and of the difference between what is known as a Deposit Account and a Current or Credit Account.

In opening a banking account it is usually necessary to have an introduction to the bank from some person known to it. £50 is usually the minimum sum for which London banks will open an account; but there are, of course, exceptions, and accounts are opened for much smaller sums by most of the suburban and provincial houses.

The Deposit Account.—If it is wished to leave the money on deposit at interest the bank will have to be notified that a "Deposit" account is to be opened. The customer will then have to write her signature clearly and distinctly in the bank's signature book for purposes of identification, and she will receive a receipt from the bank known as a "Deposit Receipt." In London interest should be paid on the sum deposited at the rate of 1½ per cent. below bank rate (see p. 369); that is, if the bank rate is 4 per cent. she will obtain interest at the rate of 2½ per cent.

A week or a fortnight's notice is usually required by a bank before the withdrawal of money left on deposit. It is as well to ascertain what notice is required before banking money in this way. Many banks, however, are willing to pay the money without notice when necessary. The deposit receipt should be sent to the bank every six months in order that the interest may be calculated. The latter may be withdrawn or added to the principal as preferred.

Joint Deposits.—A deposit may be made jointly by more than one person. In this case all the names will appear on the receipts, and the money will not be paid *over* except on receipt of *all* the signatures; so it would, where desired, be convenient to have the receipt made out payable upon the signature of a certain one only.

If the depositor dies, the money can be withdrawn by the executor or administrator upon production of the probate or letters of administration.

It is never wise to be secretive in regard to money deposited with a bank, for if the depositor should die and the receipt were overlooked or lost, and consequently no demand ever made for payment, the bank would not think of communicating with the deceased person's relatives, and at the end of six years the unclaimed deposit would become the bank's own property.

Credit or Current Account.—A current account is one from which the customer may draw money by cheque at will, and into which she can make payments when convenient.

A woman should be careful never to vary her signature in signing cheques, but to keep it in every way the same as that by which she signed her name in the signature book. Until the officials at the bank become familiar with her writing all signatures on cheques are compared with that in the signature book for identification, and should there be any marked discrepancy between the two, difficulty in obtaining payment of the cheques might result.

The bank generally makes a charge equivalent to an eighth per cent. upon the withdrawals for the working of a small account.

After the customer has complied with the preliminaries of signing her name in the bank's signature book, and paying in the money, the bank will hand her a "paying-in" slip book, a "pass-book," and a cheque-book.

The Paying-in Book.—Each page of the paying-in "slip book" is perforated down the centre. Particulars of the amount paid in, whether by gold, silver, or notes, country or London cheques, are filled in on each side of the perforation, then the book is handed to the receiving cashier, who tears off the right-hand slip for the use of the bank, initialling the one that remains in the book, leaving it both as record and receipt in the hands of the customer.

The Pass-Book.—In the customer's pass-book the bank enters all records of the account in regard to sums paid in and withdrawals. In a little pocket in the pass-book are placed all cheques which have been paid away by the customer and returned to the bank in the course of business. It is as well to keep these cheques, as they form incontestable proof and receipts of money paid out. The pass-book should be left in the hands of the bank as much as possible in order that the accounts can be regularly kept.

The Cheque-Book.—The cheque-book is a book containing a certain number of stamped forms called "cheques," which every bank supplies to its customers, who are charged with the cost of the stamps. Each cheque is perforated so that it can be easily detached from the book. To the left of the perforation is a small counterfoil which remains in the book, and upon which a record of each payment by cheque is entered.

The cheque presents many mysteries to the average feminine mind. Briefly, a bank cheque is an order in writing to a bank from its customer to pay on demand a certain sum of money to a person whose name is given on the cheque. Each cheque is liable to a stamp duty of one penny, and the stamp is usually impressed upon the printed form. The person who draws the cheque is called the "drawer," and the person or firm to whom it is payable is called the "payee."

A cheque may be drawn "to order" or "to bearer." In the former case the "payee" can obtain payment at the bank named by writing her name across the back of the cheque. This is known as "endorsing" a cheque.

An order cheque always needs endorsing, whereas it is not necessary to endorse a cheque made payable to "bearer"; any person can obtain payment on presenting a "bearer" cheque.

Alteration on Cheques.—A cheque can be altered from "bearer" to "order" by running the pen through the former word and substituting the word "order." This may be done by the drawer or the payee, but only the drawer may alter a cheque from "order" to "bearer," it being necessary in this case to put his or her initials under the correction made. Any alteration in the amount must be initialled by the drawer.

Great care should always be taken in filling in a cheque. The first figure of the sum payable should always be placed close to the £ mark, so that there is no possibility of another figure being placed before it. In the same way the dots or hyphen separating the pounds from shillings should be close to the last figure of the pounds, so that there is no chance of adding a figure to the pounds total.

Crossing Cheques.—Cheques are crossed for greater safety and to ensure their being paid into a banking account. When crossed cheques are used the risk of fraud is greatly minimised. A crossed cheque cannot be exchanged for cash at the counter of the bank of the drawer; the payee must pay it into her own bank if she has one. If not she must get change for it from some one who has.

Different Methods of Crossing Cheques.—A cheque is crossed *generally* by drawing across its face two parallel transverse lines either with or without the words "and Co." between them. Cheques so crossed cannot be exchanged for cash at the counter of the bank. The payee must employ her banker to collect the money for her by paying it into her bank account. If she has not a bank account she must get some one who has one to cash it for her.

It is crossed *specially* (1) by inserting the name of the bank through which the payment is

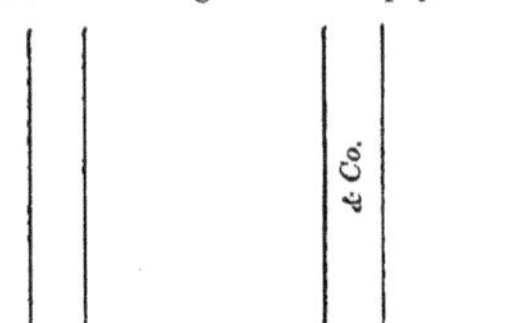

Examples of General Crossings.

to be made, in the crossing, or (2) by inserting the name of the person to whose account the payment is to be made, or (3) by inserting both the name of the bank and the name of the person to whose account it has to be credited.

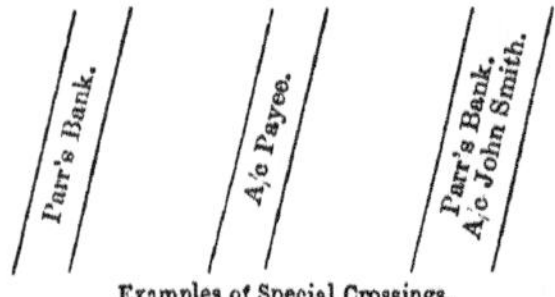

Examples of Special Crossings.

(1) Means that the cheque can only be cashed through Parr's Bank.
(2) Means that only the payee can get cash for the cheque, and only from the bank where he has an account.
(3) Specifies not only the account to which the cheque is to be paid, but the bank where such account is kept.

The crossing of a cheque does not affect its negotiability, and if a crossed cheque has been stolen after being endorsed, the person who takes it from the thief in good faith and gives value for it can enforce payment of it, even though the cheque has been stopped. The loss will fall upon the payee. In order to destroy the negotiability of a cheque, the words, "not negotiable" must form part of the crossing. Whoever then takes the cheque can have no better title to it than the person who gave it to him had.

As a still further safeguard to prevent the addition of figures, it is well to write across the cheque that the sum is under a certain amount. For instance, the words "under ten pounds" written across a cheque for nine pounds would clearly indicate that the amount was £9 and not £90, and all possibility of fraud would be prevented.

Dishonoured Cheques.—A cheque is said to be dishonoured when it is returned from the bank because the drawer has not sufficient money to his (or her) credit to meet it. Cheques returned in this way are generally marked "R.D." (refer to drawer) or "N.S." (not sufficient funds).

Stopping Payment.—A drawer can stop payment of a cheque after having parted with it by immediately notifying her banker in writing not to pay it on presentation. Full details as to date, amount, and name of payee should be given. A payee who has lost a cheque after having endorsed it should at once notify the drawer of this fact, so that payment is stopped before any one else has had time to cash it.

How to Write a Cheque on Ordinary Paper.—All cheques should be drawn upon the form provided by the banker; this tends to prevent forgery, and at the same time is more convenient to the customer, as the counterfoils in the cheque-book may be made a useful means of record. But there is nothing to prevent a cheque being drawn upon an ordinary sheet of paper if the customer so desires, though in that case the signature should be written across a penny postage stamp.

Cheques Payable to Self.—An order cheque may be made payable to the drawer. In this case it must be filled in "Pay to Self," and must be endorsed by the drawer.

Delay in Cashing Cheques.—Cheques should always be presented for payment as soon as possible. When the payee holds back a cheque for as long as six months, the banker will not cash it until he has obtained the consent of the drawer. Cheques are subject to the Statute of Limitations, and therefore payment cannot be enforced if they are presented after six years.

Overdrafts.—A customer who is able to furnish her bank with good securities may obtain an advance or "overdraft" from her bankers should she so wish it. On any of the following securities overdrafts may be arranged:—Consols, Colonial Government Stock, Municipal Bonds, railway debentures, good industrial stocks and shares, personal securities and life policies.

The money lent in this manner by the bank is debited with interest to an account called the "loan account." The whole sum is then placed to the customer's current account, and the customer has to pay interest on the whole sum borrowed, even though the necessities of her case may require part of the sum to lie to her credit in the current account.

Unless an overdraft has been arranged with her bank it is dangerous for a woman to draw cheques for a larger amount than the balance at her credit. By doing so she incurs the discredit of having her cheques returned dishonoured from the bank to the payee.

Circular Notes.—When a woman going abroad wishes to avoid the risk and trouble of carrying large sums of money she can obtain from her banker "circular notes," in each of which the banker requests his foreign correspondents to pay to the person named in an accompanying letter a certain sum. This letter is called "a letter of indication," and is signed by the banker and by the payee, in order to lessen the risks of personation and of forgery. It contains a list of the foreign banks at which the circular notes can be cashed. These notes are of no value without the letter of indication and *vice versâ*.

Bank of England.—The most important of all our banks is the Bank of England. It may be said, indeed, to be a national institution.

It fixes the rate of interest, is the bank in which the revenue collected by the Government from all parts of the country is deposited, and is the agent for the Government in transacting all such financial business as relates to the raising of Government loans whether for permanent or for temporary purposes. It also holds the cash reserves of other banks and manages the business in connection with the National Debt. Apart from these special circumstances, the Bank of England is in the same position as all other banks, transacting business as a private bank in the same manner as they do.

Bank Rate is the name given to the price at which the Bank of England states it is willing to grant loans.

The raising of the bank rate means that more will be charged upon loans and paid upon deposits. The lowering of the bank rate means that less will be charged upon loans and paid upon deposits.

The bank rate varies with the supply of and demand for gold. A high rate indicates that there is a scarcity of money in the market, and the bank rate is raised whenever there is likely to be an outflow of gold from England. When the bank reserve is high, and there is a great influx of money, the rate is lowered.

The London banks generally allow interest on deposits at 1½ per cent. below bank rate unless the latter is very low.

The Bank Return.—Every week the Bank of England issues a report as to its financial position. This is known as the "Bank Return," and every week each of the leading newspapers publishes an analysis of the bank return in what is known as the "Money Article."

The return is made up by the bank on Wednesday, and a copy posted up outside the bank on the following Thursday afternoon.

The Post Office Savings Bank.—The Post Office Savings Banks are established by Act of Parliament, and every depositor has the direct security of the State for the repayment of deposits.

Unlike ordinary banks, where it is very seldom that an account can be opened for less than £50, in the Post Office Savings Bank an account may be opened for one shilling.

For the savings of a woman of limited income the Post Office Savings Bank is the ideal medium, for interest at the rate of 2½ per cent. per annum is allowed on every complete pound deposited, and any sum from one shilling upwards, but excluding pence, is accepted as an ordinary deposit. The depositor can open her account at any post office in the United Kingdom. She is handed a book, at the beginning of which she must sign her name, address, and occupation, intimating whether she is married or single. In this book the Post Office officials enter each payment as it is made, stamping it with the stamp of the office into which the money is paid. This constitutes a sufficient receipt for any sum under £5; but for sums of £5 and upwards a receipt is received by post from the head of the Savings Bank Department in London. In this book all withdrawals are also entered. Money withdrawals can be made from any post office branch in the Kingdom. For sums of over £1 a withdrawal form must be asked for, and this, when filled in, is posted to the chief office of the Savings Bank Department in London, the depositor receiving in the course of a day or two a warrant for payment of the amount she wishes to withdraw. She can obtain payment of this warrant at any post office on the production of her bank book, into which the necessary entries have to be made. She can also pay money in to her account at any post office.

Any sum up to a pound may be withdrawn "on demand" at any post office by filling in a "withdrawal on demand form," but in these circumstances the depositor is required to hand over her book, which is sent to the head office of the Savings Bank Department for examination.

No charge for postage is made to the depositor, if in the United Kingdom, for any letter passing between her and the chief office on Post Office Savings Bank business.

No more than £50 can be deposited in one year except for investment in Government Stock or for the purchase of an Annuity or Insurance (see p. 372). Except for the same purposes no deposit can be made which causes the balance due to a depositor, including interest, to exceed £200.

Forms to which stamps may be affixed are supplied at the post office for the assistance of children and others who are unable to save more than a penny or two at a time. For each penny saved a stamp is purchased and affixed to the form. When twelve stamps have been affixed in this manner, the form can be handed in at any of the post offices as a shilling deposit.

It will be seen that the Post Office puts every facility in the way of people with limited incomes for saving their "mite," however small it is, with the added benefit of a fair rate of interest and also the advantage of economy in the working of its accounts, and absolute security.

Post Office Savings Bank Accounts may be opened on behalf of children under seven years of age, but in this case the money may not be withdrawn until the child has attained that age. All children of seven years and upwards might well be encouraged to save their money in this simple way. The sense of responsibility imparted by the management of their own little accounts will tend to inculcate a knowledge of the value of money, combined with a habit of thrift which cannot fail to stand them in good stead in later years.

DEBT

A debt is a certain sum of money owed by one person to another. The person who owes money is termed the debtor, and the person to whom the money is owed is known as the creditor.

Recovery of Debt.—If, after several applications for payment of a debt by the creditor, the debtor still fails to pay it, the usual means of procedure for the creditor to take for its recovery is to sue the debtor for it.

Where to Sue for a Debt.—If the debt is less than £20 the creditor *must* bring his action in the County Court. Where the debt is between £20 and £100 the creditor *ought* to bring his action in the County Court, unless he is certain that the debtor has no defence to the claim, in which case he may bring it in the High Court and obtain summary judgment against the debtor, a more expeditious way than the process of the County Court. Where debt exceeds £100 proceedings *must* be first instituted in the High Court, though in some cases the High Court will remit the action for hearing in the County Court.

Limitations of Actions for Debt.—Actions to recover ordinary debts must be brought within six years from the time when they became due, or within six years of the last payment or any part of the principal or interest, or within six years of the last acknowledgment in writing of the debt, which acknowledgment *must unconditionally* import a promise to pay: a conditional promise will cause it to be invalid as an acknowledgment.

In the case of debts due upon a bond or other instrument under seal, including mortgage debts and debts under a Bill of Sale, the period of limitation is twenty years, and in action for the recovery of money charged on lands for the recovery of the land itself the time limit is twelve years.

Bankruptcy.—The law of bankruptcy affords relief to insolvent debtors who, by surrendering their property for the benefit of their creditors, are in return relieved from liability in regard to their debts. A petition of bankruptcy can be filed by the debtor himself, or by his creditors. The Court then issues a " Receiving Order," by which the Official Receiver becomes the receiver or protector of the property until a trustee has been appointed by the creditors. Within seven days of the receiving order being made the debtor must furnish to the Official Receiver a statement of his affairs, and after he has furnished this statement he must attend for public examination before the Registrar, on which occasion he must answer questions on oath. Within fourteen days after the receiving order a general meeting of the creditors is held, and this meeting decides whether the debtor shall be adjudged bankrupt, or whether a composition or an agreement shall be accepted from him. If he is adjudged bankrupt, the creditors then appoint a trustee to wind up the bankrupt's estate. On the appointment of the trustee the property of the bankrupt passes to him, and it is his duty to realise the property and to divide the proceeds among the creditors.

Discharge.—At any time after he has been declared a bankrupt, but not until his public examination has been concluded, the bankrupt may apply for his discharge. The Court will, as a rule, grant the discharge provided that a good dividend has been paid to the creditors, that the bankrupt shows that his accounts have been properly kept, that he has not been recklessly extravagant or indulged in rash or hazardous speculation, or been guilty of misdemeanour in his business.

Until he does get his discharge the bankrupt labours under many disabilities; one of the chief of these is that should he obtain credit without disclosing the fact that he is an undischarged bankrupt, he is guilty of a criminal offence, and is liable to imprisonment.

Married Women and Bankruptcy.—A married woman carrying on a trade separately from her husband can be made a bankrupt.

INSURANCE

Insurance is a matter little understood and little entered into by women, who, however, are beginning to look into it more closely now that the passing of the " Workmen's Compensation Act " has made the insurance of servants by their employers a matter of almost vital necessity in every house.

Insurance may be defined as " a contract by which a person (called the insurer or assurer), in consideration of a lump sum of money, or of a periodical payment called the *premium*, undertakes to pay to another (called the insured or assured) a larger sum on the happening of a particular event. The deed in which the contract of insurance is contained is called the *policy of insurance*, the term policy being derived from a Latin word signifying promise.

Nearly every risk to which we are liable may be insured against, including epidemic illness, accident, and sickness. Football and cricket clubs frequently insure against loss in the receipts from the season's play. Organisers of bazaars and other entertainments do the like.

The more common forms of insurance are Life Assurance, Fire and Marine, to which may be added Accident and Burglary Insurance.

Life Assurance.—The word " assurance " is

really the correct term when a life policy is taken out, insurance being applied to all other policies; but colloquial use has made now the word insurance apply to both life and other policies, hence the term "insurance" is pretty generally used for both. In life assurance, in return for the payment of a stipulated premium payable at regular intervals, the insurance company undertakes to pay a lump sum to the person or persons for whose benefit the contract is made, upon the death of the person insured. Life insurances may also be taken out for a certain number of years at a much less premium than that charged for the whole life. If the person insured dies within this period the whole amount of the insurance is payable upon his (or her) death to the next of kin.

Careful attention to all the conditions laid down in an insurance policy is necessary. A very slight misunderstanding on the part of the person who is taking out the insurance may, in the event of loss, result in the company denying their liability on the grounds that the conditions have not been fully complied with.

Assurance or Insurance with Profits.—In an insurance which carries profits the company allows the policy-holder a share in the surplus or profits of the company. For this privilege a higher rate of premium is charged. At the end of every five or seven years a valuation is made of the properties or assets of the company and its liabilities. The surplus or profits of an insurance company represent the figure at which its assets exceed its expenses and liabilities. This surplus is ascertained and distributed at certain fixed intervals, usually every five or seven years. The profits so gained are called bonuses, and are distributed amongst the policy-holders in the form of bonus additions to their accounts. The policy-holder may either draw the bonus in cash, have it added to the amount for which he (or she) is insured, or use it as a fund for reducing the payment of future premiums. One or two insurance companies have adopted the practice of a yearly valuation and bonus distribution.

Insurance Facilities for People of Limited Means.—Formerly it was a somewhat heavy undertaking for men and women of limited means to insure their lives. Either quarterly or annual payments of the premium were the rule, and with some people, more especially those of fluctuating incomes, payments of a lump sum at these intervals was well-nigh impossible. Also, if the premiums were not promptly paid, the policies would expire, and the sum of money already paid as premium would consequently be forfeited. Much greater facilities are now being placed in the way of people of limited means and men and women workers.

Premiums can be paid in small sums and at short intervals. Many of the companies now accept small monthly payments with a time allowance of a fortnight in which to make each payment, and a system has been adopted for using what is termed the "surrender value" of the policy held—generally about one-third to one-half of the premiums already paid—as a fund for the continuance of payments which for a time the holder finds it impossible to meet, so that the policy may not lapse.

Should the investor desire to discontinue the insurance, many of the companies allow either the *surrender value* in cash or a fully *paid up* policy for a reduced amount, free from payment of any further premiums.

A number of the companies have also abandoned the practice of charging a higher rate for the insurance of women than that charged for insuring men, and the medical examination which was formerly always necessary before the making of an insurance contract has now to a large extent been done away with.

Endowment Insurance.—Endowment insurance secures the payment of a lump sum to the person insured when he (or she) attains a certain age stipulated in the policy. By regular payment of the premium, therefore, a young woman of from twenty to thirty could at the age of say forty-five be entitled to the payment of any sum from £100 upwards, according to the amount for which she is insured. Should she die before that age the whole of the insurance money would be payable to her heirs. In connection with this scheme of insurance many offices make a feature of annuities both "Immediate" and "Deferred."

Immediate Annuities are secured by the payment of a lump sum down to the Insurance Company. *Deferred Annuities*, payable after the person insured has reached a certain age, can be secured either by payment of a single premium, or by quarterly, half-yearly, or yearly premiums in accordance with the varying conditions enforced by different insurance companies. The "annuities" and "endowment" forms of insurance make ideal investments for the woman worker dependent upon her own resources, for by payment of a small sum annually, under either of the schemes, she can secure herself against penury in her old age, when she will no longer be able to work as in her youth.

Endowments for Children.—The object of the endowment of children is to afford parents the means of having their children educated and started in life. They by this means secure to every child which may be born to them a given sum, to be paid in each case on the child attaining any specified age, say from 14 to 21 years. The advantages offered to young married persons by thus securing a fixed sum for every one of their children, however great the number, must be obvious to every person who reflects on the care and anxiety attendant on providing for a numerous family. The necessary funds are thus furnished wherewith to meet the school expenses of sons and daughters, the support of sons at college, the dowry of daughters, and the entry of sons or daughters into the professions or commercial life.

Government Annuities and Insurance.—Immediate or deferred annuities, if not less than £1, and not exceeding £100, receivable half-yearly with Government security for the payment of the money at the proper time, may be purchased through the medium of the Post Office Savings Bank on the lives of persons of either sex, and of the age of five years and upwards. On the death of an annuitant a single payment equal to one-fourth part of the annuity is made to the representative, if claimed within two years.

Persons between 14 and 65 years of age may insure their lives through the medium of the Post Office Savings Bank for sums of not less than £5 and not more than £100, with Government security for the payment of the money. The lives of children below 14 years, but not under the age of 8 years, may be insured for £5 but no more.

Insurable Interest.—In order that a contract of insurance may be valid the insured must have what is called an insurable interest in the thing insured; that is to say, he must have a pecuniary interest in, or must be liable or accountable for, any loss arising in regard to it.

Thus a man may not only insure his own life, but he may also insure the life of another, providing he has an insurable interest in that other's life. A wife has an insurable interest in her husband's life, being dependent on him for support; so, too, are children dependent upon their father. But a husband has no such interest in the life of his wife, unless he has an income or other monetary advantage depending upon her life. A creditor has an insurable interest in the life of his debtor for the amount of the debt, and on the creditor's death he can recover the amount of the debt, even although it has been paid off. Employers have also an insurable interest in their workmen or servants, being liable to them in cases where they have sustained injury, or been killed in the course of their employment.

Control Exercised over Life Offices.—Every Life Assurance Company established since 1870 in the United Kingdom must deposit £20,000 in the High Court, and no certificate of incorporation can be issued until the deposit has been made. As soon as the insurance fund accumulated out of premiums amounts to £40,000 the deposit is returned. If the company carries on other business besides that of life insurance the receipts in respect of the life insurance must be kept in a separate account and be placed in a separate fund called the Life Insurance Fund of the company. This fund must exist solely for the security of holders of life policies, as though the company carried on no other business than that of life insurance.

Every Life Office doing business in this country must render annual accounts and reports to the Board of Trade. Copies of these must be furnished to policy-holders when required. It must be remembered, however, that the Board of Trade has no control over the conduct of a Life Office when once it has been started. There is, therefore, no guarantee that the business of any company is being properly carried on.

Stamps.—Policies of life insurance must be stamped as follows:—

	s.	*d.*
Where the sum insured does not exceed £10 .		1
Where the sum insured exceeds £10 but does not exceed £25		3
Where the sum insured exceeds £25 but does not exceed £500, for every £50 or part of £50		6
Exceeds £500 but does not exceed £1000, for every £100 or part of £100	1	0
Exceeds £1000, for every £1000 or part of £1000	10	6

On policies of insurance against accident or sickness the stamp is one penny. Policies of insurance against employers' liability are chargeable as agreements—this is, if under hand, 6d., if under seal, 10s.

How to Assure or Insure.—A person who wishes to assure his (or her) life must first apply to a Life Office, and the Assurance Company will send a proposal form to be filled up by the person who has to be assured.

In this proposal form it is required to give accurate answers to the questions therein set out, concerning his (or her) health, habits of life, and family history; sometimes a medical examination will have to be undergone, but under certain conditions many of the principal insurance companies have done away with the necessity for this.

The greatest care should be taken in faithfully answering these questions in the "proposal" or "declaration," for this proposal is the basis of the contract, and it is on the faith of the answers contained in it that the policy is granted; and excepting in the case of a "non-forfeitable" policy, if the answers are untrue, however innocently they may be made, the policy falls to the ground and the insurance money cannot be recovered, though the premiums paid may be returned unless the untruthful answers have been wilfully or fraudulently made. In addition to the declaration the Life Office usually requires a reference to one or two intimate friends of the person about to be insured. Their replies are treated as confidential. When all these requirements have been satisfactorily met, the Life Office grants the policy on payment of the first premium.

Accident Insurance.—Accident insurance is a contract by which the Insurance Company undertakes to provide against loss if the insured sustains accidental injury or disablement, either partial or temporary, and to pay the sum insured for to the personal representative of the person insured should his death result from an accident.

The rate of premium for accident insurance is determined chiefly by the occupation. According to the nature of the occupation the risks are divided into three classes—ordinary, medium, and hazardous.

To insure for £100 in case of death, with full benefits for disablement, the rates per annum in some of the principal offices are :—

	s.	d.
Ordinary risks	8	6
Medium risks	12	0
Hazardous risks	14	0

These rates only apply to accidents happening in Europe; but some offices issue "world-wide" policies which also indemnify for accidents taking place abroad at considerably higher rates.

Many newspapers and other periodicals contain free accident insurance coupons for sums varying from £100 and upwards. The conditions printed upon the coupon must be fulfilled in order for the insurance to be effective. Such newspaper insurances most often indemnify against accidents when travelling by rail or boat.

Fire Insurance.—Fire insurance indemnifies the policy-holder for any loss or damage to his property sustained by fire.

The maximum amount of compensation which can be claimed is stated in the policy, but indemnity is only given for the *actual damage sustained*. There is, therefore, no advantage in over-insuring property or in insuring it for its full value in each of several different offices. The latter procedure would only serve to benefit the insurance companies, for instead of one company being obliged to pay the full value of the property, the liability would be shared between the several offices with which it has been insured.

The rate of premium varies according to the property insured. On ordinary dwelling-houses the rate is usually two shillings per cent. and seldom less than 1s. 6d. per cent. In the case of factories, shops, &c., that entail more than ordinary risks, and in the case of theatres, distilleries, chemical works, and other such places which are exposed to peculiar danger, rates are fixed by special arrangement, the premium in extreme cases being £2 or even £3 per cent.

Fire insurances are usually effected for a year, the policy being renewable on the payment of another premium. Fifteen days, called "days of grace," are allowed at the end of the year in which to renew the policy. Should a fire occur during these fifteen days the company is still liable, provided that it is intended by both parties to renew the policy.

Insurance of Domestic Servants.—Under the Workmen's Compensation Act, 1906, every employer is liable to compensate his employees for injuries arising out of and in the course of their employment, although such injuries may be the direct results of carelessness on the part of the injured person, or even disobedience to orders.

As this act applies to all domestic servants, male or female, the master and mistress of every household should realise the responsibility which the keeping of servants entails upon them in this connection, for compensation up to £1 a week is payable during the servant's total or partial incapacity for work, and this may well involve the payment of an annuity for life, whilst if the injury results in death, a lump sum of money of as much as from £150 to £300 is payable (see law of Master and Servant, p. 377–78). It is essential for the master of a house to protect himself against liability, which might arise in regard to accident to his servants, by insurance. Most of the insurance companies make a special feature of domestic servant insurance. The usual premium payable for the insurance of an indoor servant amounts to from 2s. 6d. to 5s. per annum. Great care should be taken on examining the insurance policy that it indemnifies against all risks. It should in all cases declare that the insurance company indemnifies the employer against all liabilities under—

The Workmen's Compensation Act, 1906.
The Employer's Liability Act, 1880.
Fatal Accidents Act, 1846.
And at Common Law.

The following are the rates of premium chargeable for the insurance of domestic servants by the Royal Exchange Assurance Company :—

BENEFITS OF POLICIES

SCHEME 1 grants complete indemnity against legal liability.

Premiums

	s.	d.
Indoor domestic servants (male or female)	2	6
Gardeners	5	0
Grooms, coachmen, and stable hands (not hunting)	7	6
Chauffeurs and motor-car attendants	20	0

SCHEME 2B (the ideal policy) grants full wages during first four weeks' incapacity, and half wages thereafter in accordance with the Workmen's Compensation Act, and medical expenses not exceeding £5 for each accident.

Premiums

	s.	d.
Indoor domestic servants (male or female)	5	0
Gardeners	7	0
Grooms, coachmen, and stable hands (not hunting)	10	0
Chauffeurs and motor-car attendants	30	0

The liability to pay compensation to

CASUAL OR OCCASIONAL SERVANTS

may be covered by the addition of 25 per cent. of the premium chargeable for permanent indoor and outdoor servants under Scheme 1. Minimum extra premium 2s. 6d.

Burglary Insurance.—Burglary insurance is a recent development in the business of insurance. Generally speaking, the law in regard to fire insurance applies to burglary insurance. The rate charged in regard to loss by burglary or housebreaking is usually 1s. 6d. in every £100's worth of goods insured. If the insured wishes to insure against theft, either by strangers or by workmen or servants employed in his house, the rate is 2s. per cent. Against burglary, housebreaking, theft, and fire the rate is in some offices 3s. 6d. per cent. Thus if a householder effected such a combined policy on goods worth £2000, the annual premium would be 3s. 6d. for every £100's worth of goods insured; that is, £3, 10s. altogether. Every such policy must bear a penny stamp.

LEGAL NOTES

Husband and Wife.—Before entering upon the matrimonial state every woman should have a clear appreciation of what her legal status as a married woman will be, and to what extent her identity becomes merged in that of her husband.

Married Woman's Property.—Formerly the position of a married woman left much to be desired. Whatever personal property she possessed as a single woman would become her husband's upon marriage. If she had property in land it passed under his control, and he was entitled to draw all the rents and income derived from it. Also any money his wife earned in business, in the professions, or in any kind of employment became his. A wife had no power to make contracts. On the other hand, the husband was liable for any debts contracted by his wife before marriage.

The Married Woman's Property Act of 1882 served to place matters upon a much more equitable basis. Now a married woman can retain and control her own property, drawing all the income from it. She can keep any money she may earn in business or in any other employment. She can now take out an insurance policy on her own life or that of her husband; in fact, she is to all intents and purposes in the same position as a single woman in regard to the power of managing her own property.

Domicile.—The legality of a marriage usually depends on whether it was celebrated in accordance with the law of the husband's domicile, so that girls marrying foreigners, even in England, should be careful to ascertain beforehand from the consul of the country to which the particular foreigner belongs whether all the requirements of the foreign law have been fulfilled; as otherwise they may find that the husband may repudiate the marriage when he returns home. Many unfortunate English girls are trapped and ruined in this way.

Maintenance.—As long as the marriage relationship is undetermined, a husband is bound to maintain his wife. A wife is also bound to maintain her husband if necessary, but only if she has separate property which will enable her to do so.

Husband's Liability for Wife's Debts.—(1) *Before Marriage.*—The Married Woman's Property Acts, 1882, provides that the husband is only liable for his wife's debts contracted before marriage to the extent of the assets he received with her.

(2) *After Marriage.*—It is a principle of law that a wife can only pledge her husband's credit in so far as she is acting as his agent for the purpose. The liability of the husband for the debts of his wife in this respect vary according to whether they are cohabiting or not. If husband and wife are living together and the wife is in the habit of ordering goods for which her husband pays he will be considered as holding her out as his agent to pledge his credit, and will be bound to pay debts incurred by her. If, however, he warns the tradesmen not to supply her with goods, or if he gives her a sufficient allowance with which to pay her bills, he will not be liable. If husband and wife are living apart owing to the misconduct of the former, the wife can pledge the husband's credit for the supply of necessaries to herself.

Gifts and Loans between Husband and Wife.—A wife may give to and receive from her husband gifts of every description. Evidence should always be forthcoming, however, that a gift has been made more, especially if it does not leave the possession of the donor. With regard to loans made by a wife to her husband the Married Woman's Property Act, 1882, provides that "any money or other estate of the wife lent or entrusted by her to her husband for the purpose of any trade or business carried on by him or otherwise, shall be treated as assets of her husband's estate in case of bankruptcy, under reservation of the wife's claim to a dividend as a creditor for the amount of value of such money or other estate *after* but *not before* all claims of the other creditors of the husband have been satisfied." Thus, if a woman has lent money to her husband and he has subsequently been declared bankrupt, she cannot receive any payment until all the other creditors have been paid.

Marriage Settlement.—In spite of the comparative freedom now enjoyed by a wife in the management of her affairs, she is apt to be at times unduly influenced by her husband, and many a woman has been known to have lost the whole of her property in an effort to pay her husband's creditors; consequently, in order that she may continue to enjoy the benefit of income settled upon her at marriage unrestrained by any interference on the part of her husband, it is usual to insert a clause in the settlement called "restraint upon anticipation." Not only does this provision protect the wife from the influence of her husband, but it is also a safeguard against extravagance on her own part, for she is deprived of the power of selling, mortgaging, or charging her property in any way.

Legal Position of Married Women in Scotland.—Formerly the married woman in Scotland laboured under great legal disabilities. The whole of her personal property was subject to the *Jus Mariti* of the husband; that is to say, as head of the wife he was deemed to have sole right over her property. He could sell or even make gifts of it at his pleasure, and his creditors could seize it for payment of his debts. Only by a special pre-nuptial contract could his rights in this direction be modified. The husband could also draw all the rents and income derived from his wife's landed property. He was also, prior to the Married Woman's Property Act of 1877, entitled to any earnings his wife might derive in business, or by her proficiency in literature, the arts or any other employment. The Married Woman's Property Act (Scotland) of 1877 decreed that the wife could retain her earnings, and by a later Act in 1881 her condition was still further ameliorated. This second Married Woman's Property Act decreed that all property coming to a woman after the passing of the Act was her own, that all incomes, &c., from her estate might be paid to her, that property she held in her own right could not be seized by her husband's creditors in payment of his debts. But there is this important difference in regard to the legal status of a married woman in Scotland as compared with that of a married woman in England—whereas the Englishwoman has full power to manage her estates and make contracts on her own behalf, her sister in Scotland has no such powers. Her husband retains the right of managing her property, the wife having no power to act in this direction without his consent. She cannot enter into any contract or dispose of her property in any way, except by will, without his approval; she cannot sue at law or be sued; but, on the other hand, she cannot be imprisoned for debt. Only where a special settlement in regard to the administration of her property has been made before marriage can the husband's rights in this direction be restricted.

Women married before 1881 cannot participate in the benefits of the Act unless the husband signs a deed to the effect that he is willing the property should be held by his wife in accordance with the new law.

The Importance of Making a Will.—All persons, men or women, who possess property of any kind should realise the importance of making their wills in order to insure that their property is distributed according to their wishes after death.

For a will to be valid, according to English law, it must be in writing and signed at the foot or end by the testator, or, if the latter is too ill to write, the signature can be made by some other person under his direction, the testator affixing his mark. The will must be signed in the presence of two or more witnesses, who, in their turn, must attest and subscribe the document in the presence of the testator.

A will need not assume any particular form. Any writing duly signed and attested by two witnesses is sufficient.

A will cannot be made by any person under the age of twenty-one. A married woman may now make a will in the same form as that of a man, but she would have to make a new will in order to bequeath property acquired by her after the termination of her married life either by the death of her husband or her divorce from him. A will is always revoked by the marriage of the testator, so that both men and women with property should make new wills after marriage.

Executors.—It is always advisable for the testator to appoint an executor or executors to wind up her estate and distribute her property according to her will.

Administrators.—Where the deceased person has left no will, there can be no executors and no probate. The property, if "realty," will go to his heir-at-law, and, if "personalty," to his next-of-kin. But as it is desirable that some one should wind up the estate and distribute it among those entitled to it, the Court will appoint a person called an Administrator, and grant him "Letters of Administration."

Codicils.—With the exception of the cases above mentioned, a will can only be revoked by another will or codicil inconsistent with the former one. Where a codicil is made which, though not consistent with the first will, does not actually revoke it, the first will is valid in so far as it is consistent with the later will or codicil, but the later will is alone valid as to the parts where they are not consistent.

Wills in Scotland.—No set form of wording is necessary for the drawing up of a will in Scotland. It should be signed by the testator and attested by two witnesses.

Should the will, however, be what is termed a "holograph" will; that is to say, should it be written in the testator's own handwriting and signed with his signature, it will be valid *without* the attestation of witnesses. A holograph will unsigned would not, of course, be valid.

Intestacy of Husband.—Should a man die intestate, leaving a wife and children, one-third of his personal estate will go to his wife and the other two-thirds will be divided between his children. Should he leave no children the wife takes it all if the value is under £500; if over that value she takes £500 with interest at 4 per cent., and half the residue, the other half going to the next of kin.

A wife is also entitled on her husband's death to a dower for life in one-third of his lands.

Intestacy of Wife.—When a wife dies intestate the whole of her personal property reverts to her husband. He is also entitled to a life estate called "curtesy" in her freehold lands.

Parent and Child.—The parents of a child are said to be its natural guardians; that is to say, they have the right to the control of it until such time as the child attains the age of twenty-one, or marries, if the ceremony takes place before that age is reached. The primary right as guardian rests with the father, but he may be deprived of the care of them if, in the opinion of the Court, it is deemed to be in the interests of the children that they are taken out of his custody. After the death of the father the mother is the natural guardian of their children. Should the father, however, in his will appoint a testamentary guardian for his children, this delegated guardianship will over-ride the rights of the mother.

Maintenance.—The duty of a father to maintain his children until they can support themselves is a natural one, and unless the neglect to do so would bring the case within the criminal law, there is no legal obligation upon him. A number of statutes, however, deal with the subject. First of these was the Poor Law Act of '43 Elizabeth, c. 2, which cast upon parents "of sufficient ability" the duty of maintaining their children under a penalty, and this was extended to a later Act to the case of a man's step-children. The Act of '57 & '58 Vict., c. 41, imposes on parents the duty of providing adequate food, clothing, medical aid, and lodging for children in their custody until the boys attain fourteen years and the girls sixteen. The liability of the parents under the first statute ceases when the children attain the age of sixteen, unless they are from infirmity incapable of supporting themselves; but if the parents retain the children in their custody they are liable for their maintenance until they come of age.

Births and Deaths, Registration of—Births.—In the case of every child born alive it is the duty of the father and mother of the child, and, in default of the father and mother, of the occupier of the house in which, to his knowledge, the child is born, and of each person present at the birth, and of the person having charge of the child, to give the local registrar of births information of the birth within forty-two days and to sign the register. If the birth is not registered within three months many formalities must be gone through, and fees are imposed, and after twelve months a birth can only be registered by the Registrar General's express authority.

Registration of Deaths.—When a person dies in a house it is the duty of the nearest relatives of the deceased present at the death, or in attendance during the last illness, to notify the registrar within five days of the death; and, in default of such relatives, the obligation lies upon every other relative dwelling in the same district as the deceased. If there are no such relatives the information must be given by the occupier and inmates of the house in which the death took place, and by the person causing the body of the deceased to be buried.

Where the deceased has been attended during his (or her) last illness by a registered medical practitioner, the latter must sign and deliver to one of the persons required to give information concerning death a certificate stating to the best of his knowledge and belief the cause of death. This certificate must be delivered to the registrar when information concerning the death is given.

Vaccination.—Parents are required under a penalty of twenty shillings to have their children vaccinated before they are six months old, either by the public vaccinator or by some medical practitioner. If, however, the parent makes a statutory declaration within four months of the child's birth that he conscientiously believes the vaccination would be prejudicial to the health of the child, he will be exempt from the penalty, but he must deliver the declaration to the vaccination officer within seven days of obtaining it.

Master and Servant.—There are many points in the law of master and servant as applied to the domestic servants of a household which the average woman finds somewhat difficult to understand. The most important things to remember in this connection will be dealt with here briefly and explicitly in a way which it is hoped will tend to enlighten the housewife as to the exact scope of her responsibilities towards her servants.

Wife as Husband's Agent.—As all dealings with servants are mainly conducted by the wife as superintendent of the domestic side of the home, the mistress is more often than not regarded as having supreme control over them. She it is who engages them, allots their various duties, provides for their outings and holidays, and dismisses them when their work is unsatisfactory. This is a typical instance of the wife acting as her husband's agent, for where husband and wife live together it is the husband who is the legal head of the servants of a household. It is the husband who is liable for the payment of their wages, and the Courts would compel him and not the wife to pay them. He it is who is responsible for the contract of engagement, and upon him rests the onus of responsibility for injuries caused to other people by his servants' wrongful or negligent acts, and it is he who is liable to compensate his servant for any injuries they may have received in the course of their employment. The word "master" is therefore in no way the meaningless term it is supposed to be in the average home when applied to the control of servants, and although the mistress, as housewife, retains the active management of these members of the household, yet she can only be said to be acting upon her husband's behalf, for he is in every way responsible to and for them.

Notice.—Upon the engagement of a servant, what is known as a "contract of service" is entered upon between master and servant; that is to say, the master engages the servant to fulfil certain duties which the latter undertakes to perform for remuneration to be agreed upon between them.

Custom ordains that the contract of service may be terminated by either servant or master giving a calendar month's notice. In Scotland forty days' notice must be given. If the master chooses to discharge the servant without notice, he must, unless the dismissal is justifiable, pay to the servant a calendar month's wages in addition to the wages up to the day of dismissal. The wages payable in such a case would be the actual money wages, and no allowance need be made for board and lodging. Should a servant depart without giving the master notice, any wages earned by him (or her) since they were last paid are forfeited. The master may take an action against him (or her) for breach of contract.

Dismissal without Notice.—In several cases a servant may be dismissed without either notice or wages in lieu of notice. They are :—

(1) Wilful disobedience of a specific order. The disobedience must be wilful and the order specific. A mere casual neglect to obey a general order would not as a rule justify instant dismissal.

(2) *Incompetence.*—A servant must be able to perform the duties for which he or she was engaged, and which he or she undertook to perform upon engagement.

(3) *Habitual Neglect of Duty.*—Consistent neglect of duty may at times result in such serious consequences as to justify instant dismissal.

(4) Gross misconduct, insolence, or dishonesty.

(5) *Illness.*—If the illness is one that is likely to be of a very long period. A mere temporary illness constitutes no reason for the dismissal of a servant.

Temporary Illness of Servant.—A master is bound to pay the wages of his servants during temporary illness. He is not liable for medical aid unless he sends for the doctor or authorises him to be sent for. In this case he must pay the bill and is not entitled to deduct it from the servant's wages.

Ejecting a Servant.—If a servant refuses to go upon being dismissed, it is always better to call in a policeman to see that he (or she) leaves the premises. A master is allowed to forcibly eject a servant, but he must be careful in doing this, as there is no knowing how far the law may be exceeded, and a charge of assault consequently preferred by the servant. It is always as well therefore to have a policeman upon the scene to be witness that everything is in proper order.

When a servant is suspected of theft, it is as well also to call in a policeman to search his (or her) boxes. A master should never undertake this himself, as, if the theft could not be proved, he would be liable for damages.

Breakages.—A servant is not liable for breakages; hence, unless an agreement has been arrived at upon engagement that he or she is to be held liable under the terms of the contract, it is illegal for a master to deduct the value of the breakages from the servant's wages.

Master's Liability for Servant's Negligence.—Masters are responsible for the injuries caused to other persons and their property by the wrongful or negligent acts of servants, if such servants are acting within the scope of their ordinary duties and within the general scope of their master's authority. Thus if a chauffeur, while driving his master's motor car in the ordinary course of his employment, were by his negligence to collide with another vehicle, the master would be responsible for the damage sustained by that other vehicle. If, on the other hand, the accident occurred when the chauffeur had taken out the motor car not in the course of his employment, but for his own pleasure, the master would not be liable.

Servants' Characters.—A mistress (acting as agent for the master) is not legally bound to give a character to a servant; but if she gives one it must be true. Care must be taken that all the statements made are justified; the mistress should state all that she knows of good about the servant as well as of bad. The statements made in giving a character are said to be "privileged," and if an action for libel is taken by the servant the mistress is protected on this same score of privilege, even where the words complained of are untrue, provided that they were written without malice and in the belief that they were true. If, however, malice can be proved, the plea of privilege will be of no avail, and the servant will be entitled to damages.

It is very wrong of a mistress to give a good character to a servant whom she knows to be dishonest. Any employer engaging a dishonest servant by reason of such untrue character is entitled to damages from the person by whom the servant was recommended.

Master's Liability for Servant's Injuries.—A master is liable for any injuries sustained by his servants arising out of and in the course of their employment, even although such injuries may be the direct results of carelessness on the part of the injured person, or even disobedience to orders, though in the latter case the servant is not entitled to compensation unless death or permanent disablement should result from the accident.

The term domestic servants includes generally all those who are engaged in the menial work of a household either indoors or out-of-doors, though no compensation could be claimed by a relation of the master of the house engaged in doing menial work. The amount of compensation payable as fixed by the Workmen's Compensation Act, 1906, is as follows :—

In the Case of Death.—Where death results from the injury, if the servant leaves any persons wholly dependent upon his earnings, the persons so dependent are entitled to receive a sum equal to the servant's earnings in his (or her) employment during the last three years. If the servant has not been so long in the employment, they are entitled to a sum equal to one hundred and fifty-six times his (or her) average weekly earnings. In no case must this sum be less than £150, nor must it exceed £300; so it will be seen that should a servant meet death by accident, leaving relatives dependent upon him, £150 represents the minimum amount of the master's liability. If the servant leaves no dependents his master will be liable for the expenses of medical attendance and burial to the extent of £10.

Disablement by Accident.—Where total or partial incapacity for work results from an accidental injury sustained by the servant out of and in the course of his (or her) employment, he (or she) is entitled to receive a weekly payment during the incapacity not exceeding half of his (or her) average weekly earnings during the last twelve months if he (or she) has been so long employed, but if not, then for any less period during which he (or she) has been in the employment of the same employer, but in no case must the weekly payment exceed £1. Earnings in the case of an indoor resident servant would include not only wages but also an allowance for board and lodging.

In the case of accident to a servant who is under twenty-one years of age, and whose average weekly earnings are less than 20s., a weekly payment equal to the whole of the amount of his weekly earnings will be payable, but this weekly payment must not exceed 10s.

So it will be seen that in the event of disablement the master will be liable for weekly payments up to £1, and in the event of the injury being a permanent one the compensation would require to be paid during the *whole of the servant's life.*

The position of the master of the house, therefore, is one of somewhat heavy responsibility in this connection, but he can relieve himself of this to some measure by insurance. For a nominal sum per annum the chief insurance companies will take all risks. It is well worth an annual outlay of from 5s. to 7s. 6d. each year to be protected in this way, and it should be the first act of a master, after engaging a servant, to effect an insurance policy in his or her name. Care should be taken, however, that the policy covers all risks (see Insurance of Domestic Servants, p. 373).

Casual Labour.—Casual labour in the strict sense of the term does not come within the meaning of the act. Thus if, as often happens, a man is employed on one or even two odd occasions to perform some such menial duty as chopping wood, he could not claim compensation were he injured while so employed. On the other hand, the boy who is engaged to come daily to clean knives and boots, the charwoman who comes regularly once or twice a week, may be said to come within the scope of the Act, although their work may be said to be of a casual nature. The insurance companies also insure against risks entailed by labour of this kind.

The Law of Landlord and Tenant.—Before taking a house or any other property it is always advisable to have some idea of the chief points in the law of Landlord and Tenant, otherwise the intending tenant might often find himself faced with serious responsibilities which he had not the remotest idea of incurring. Few women have even a superficial knowledge of the legal points involved in the letting and taking of houses, the various kinds of leases and tenancies, the tenant's obligations to his landlord, and *vice versâ.* Yet a little knowledge in this direction has often been the means of a considerable saving of both worry and expense. Some of the most important rules covering the relation of landlord and tenant will here be dealt with.

Landlord and Tenant.—A landlord is the person from whom lands or tenements are taken, and a tenant is one who holds property from the landlord for a certain limited period subject to the payment of rent.

Varieties of Tenancies.—There are various kinds of tenancy: (1) A tenancy at will is a tenancy which either the landlord or the tenant may terminate at any moment without notice. (2) A tenancy at sufferance arises where a tenant continues in possession after the expiration of his tenancy. He cannot be regarded as a trespasser, but he is liable to be turned out by the landlord at any moment. If he retains possession after receiving from the landlord a proper notice in writing to quit, he is liable to be sued for double the yearly value of the property for the time he remains in possession; if he holds over after himself giving notice of his intention to quit, he may be sued for double rent.

(3) **A Tenancy from Year to Year.**—The law does not look with favour on tenancies at will, therefore when a tenant at will has paid rent or done anything else which may be fairly taken to show an intention to create a yearly tenancy, the tenancy becomes automatically a tenancy from year to year. Tenants ought, therefore, before entering into their tenancies, if they

wish the tenancy to be for less than a year, to make the agreement quite clear with the landlord; for though no term is specified tenancy will in the first instance be a tenancy at will; the mere payment of rent will convert it into a yearly tenancy, but this does not apply to weekly tenants.

Leases.—The contract by which property is let for a term of years is called a lease.

The leases in connection with the letting of dwelling-houses are usually either for three, seven, fourteen, or twenty-one years. People often prefer to have an agreement instead of a more formal lease in the case of tenancies of less than three years; but except for very short terms, it is generally better to have a lease stating clearly all the conditions under which the tenancy is held. A lease for a term of three years or less where the rent received amounts to two-thirds of the full improved value, can be made verbally if accompanied by the giving and taking of the premises, but such a plan is seldom adopted and by no means to be recommended.

In Scotland, where a lease is for more than one year, it must be in writing, specifying a definite term, and a definite sum as rental. A verbal lease can be made, however, for a year or less. Letters between landlord and tenant agreeing to a lease are also valid in certain circumstances. All leases must be duly stamped.

Covenants.—All leases contain a number of covenants or conditions which the landlord and tenant respectively bind themselves to observe. The very employment in a lease of certain technical expressions implies the creation of certain covenants. Thus the use of the word "demise" implies a covenant on the part of the landlord that the tenant shall be entitled to the quiet and undisturbed enjoyment of the premises, unless there is any express covenant in the lease with a contrary effect.

There are in most leases what are called "usual covenants," being covenants on which the landlord can insist when there is nothing to the contrary in the agreement for the lease. They are four in number:—

(1) Tenant to pay rent.

(2) Tenant to pay rates and taxes, except the landlord's property tax and tithe rent charge.

(3) Tenant to allow the landlord to enter the premises from time to time to see that they are in a proper state of repair.

(4) Tenant to keep the premises in a proper state of repair throughout the tenancy, and to deliver them up in such a state at the end of the term.

In addition to the usual covenants there are a large number of special covenants to be found in all leases, for the respective landlords and tenants can always agree to whatever additional covenants they please. These additional covenants fall into two general classes:—(1) Personal covenants; (2) Covenants running with the land. The latter kind are binding on all those to whom the tenant assigns the property, whereas the former are in general only operative between the respective parties to the lease.

Rent.—The principal duty of every tenant is to pay rent, whether there is a covenant to pay it or not, for if there is no agreement between the parties stipulating as to the exact sum payable, the tenant is bound to pay a reasonable sum for the use and occupation of the premises, unless, of course, there is an agreement that the tenant shall have the premises rent free, as might well happen if he is in the employment of the landlord, and has the right to occupy the premises as part of his remuneration.

The amount of rent payable in any particular case is usually arranged for in the lease or agreement which may also appoint times for the payment of the rent. But in the cases where there is no stipulation as to when payment is to be made, the law says that it is due on the last day of the year of the tenancy if the tenancy be for a year or more, and on the last day of the tenancy if it be for less than a year. As a matter of general practice the rents of houses are paid quarterly on the proper quarter days, and sometimes monthly.

Though the rent becomes due on the morning of the day on which it ought to be paid, it cannot be legally considered in arrear until midnight on that day.

Rates and Taxes.—Taxes paid by Landlord.—All rates and taxes are as a rule paid by the landlord in the case of *furnished* houses or flats. In the case of *unfurnished* houses the Landlord's Property Tax is in the first instance usually paid by the tenant; but he is entitled to deduct the amount so paid from the rent, so that it eventually falls on the landlord; similarly the tithe rent charge must in all cases eventually be paid by the landlord. There are also certain other rates and taxes which the landlord will have to pay, unless there is a special agreement by which the tenant binds himself to pay them. They include the sewers rate for permanent improvement to the sewers, the land tax, and the poor rates on property let for less than three months. Whenever the tenant is called upon to pay any of these rates he must do so, but unless he has agreed to pay them he may deduct the amount so paid from the rent. The landlord must pay rates and taxes when the rateable value of the premises does not exceed £10, or where they are let to weekly or monthly tenants.

Taxes to be Paid by Tenant.—There are, however, certain taxes which, in the absence of any agreement to the contrary between the landlord and tenant, must be borne by the tenant. They include the water rate, the county, borough, highway and general district rates, poor rates on property let for more than three months.

(unless the tenant is merely a lodger), and the ordinary assessed taxes.

The owners of unoccupied houses are not liable for payment of the poor rate, but if the tenant comes into possession after the levying of the rate he may be called upon to pay a proportionate part of it, according to the length of the period of his occupation.

Repairs.—As a general rule, the landlord cannot be called upon to execute repairs unless he has agreed to execute them. As for the tenant, where there is no express agreement as to repairs, he is bound to use the premises in a tenant-hke manner. Thus he must not do damage to the premises, and he can generally be compelled to do such repairs as are necessary to keep the premises wind and water-tight; but unless he has agreed to do so, a yearly tenant cannot be called upon to execute any substantial repairs, though a tenant under a lease would in such a case be compelled to execute substantial repairs.

In many cases it happens that the respective landlords and tenants agree together that each will be responsible for a certain portion of the repairs. Thus it is by no means uncommon for the landlord to agree to execute all repairs to the outside of the premises, whilst the tenant agrees to repair the inside. But the amount of repairs to be done and the person to pay for them is generally a matter of arrangement between the parties at the time of the execution of the lease or agreement.

The landlord is bound in letting furnished premises to see that they are in a fit state for habitation (see p. 381), but in the case of unfurnished premises he can only be made liable under the Housing of Working Classes Act, 1885, in respect of premises let at a low rental to persons of the working class and under the Housing Town Planning Act, 1909, in regard to dwellings let for three years at rent not exceeding £40 in London, £26 in certain districts with a population of 250,000 or upwards, and £16 elsewhere. As regards all other kinds of unfurnished premises, the landlord, apart from any agreement to the contrary with his tenant, is under no obligation to put the premises in a state of repair, or even into an inhabitable condition before the tenancy commences; and further, he cannot, apart from the agreement, be called upon to rebuild the premises if they are destroyed by fire during the tenancy, though the tenant can be compelled to pay the rent during the period in which the premises remain uninhabitable. It is advisable, therefore, for tenants about to take unfurnished premises to see that the landlord agrees to put them into a thorough state of repair before the commencement of the tenancy, and to insist upon a covenant being inserted in the lease or agreement to the effect that the payment of rent shall cease if the premises are rendered uninhabitable by fire.

In Scotland the landlord is bound in letting a house to put it in a habitable condition. If he does not do this the tenant may throw up his lease. In addition the landlord is bound to keep the premises wind and water-tight and the drainage system in order during the tenancy. The tenant in his turn must take good care of the premises, returning them to the landlord in the condition in which he found them.

Fixtures.—There are two kinds of fixtures—landlord's fixtures and tenant's fixtures. The tenant's fixtures are those in which a tenant is entitled to remove and take away with him on giving up the tenancy, unless, of course, they did not originally belong to him; whereas the fixtures he must leave behind, whether he has put them up himself or not, are called landlord's fixtures.

Garden Fixtures.—An ordinary tenant of a house, no matter how he may have improved the garden by the planting of plants, rose-trees, shrubs, and other horticultural embellishments, *cannot remove* these without the consent of the landlord upon the expiry of his tenancy, for by law they have become the landlord's property in consequence of the legal maxim "whatever has been firmly affixed to the ground has become part of the ground." This law, however, does not apply to market gardeners or nurserymen, if they have complied with the terms of the Agricultural Holdings Act and the Market Gardeners' Compensation Act. They may remove what they have planted.

Domestic Fixtures.—In regard to fixtures which tenants have affixed to property for their own convenience, the practical effect of the present rule is that the landlord may claim all buildings and other permanent improvements to his property; the tenant may remove ornamental and purely domestic fixtures belonging to him, such as tapestries and gas-brackets, &c., but he is only entitled to them if they can be easily removed, without material injury to the property. Practically the same rule in regard to the removal of fixtures prevails in Scotland.

Distress.—If a tenant falls in arrear with his rent the landlord may enter upon the premises and seize and sell a sufficient quantity of the tenant's goods to satisfy the debt. There are, however, certain things which he is not entitled to distrain, such as things in actual use at the time, the wearing apparel, bedding and trade implements of the tenant if under £5 in value, and the goods of a lodger where the latter has complied with the terms of the Lodger Goods Protection Act.

No distress may legally be levied between sunset and sunrise, or on any Sunday, Christmas Day, Good Friday, or any day appointed for a public thanksgiving.

Removal of Goods by Tenant.—If, after the rent has become due, a tenant fraudulently or clandestinely removes any of his goods from the premises the latter may follow and seize them within a period of thirty days after, unless they have been *bonâ fide* sold for value to a person without knowledge of the fraud.

Lodger's Property.—The goods of a lodger are protected from distress levied on his immediate landlord if he observes the conditions of the Distress Amendment Act, 1908. By this Act, if the superior landlord of the lodger's immediate landlord endeavours to distrain on the lodger's property for the rent due from the immediate landlord, the lodger must:—

(1) Serve on the superior landlord or his bailiff a written declaration that the property is his, and also stating what rent, if any, is due from him to the superior landlord, and undertaking to pay to the superior landlord any rent so due or to become due until the arrears of rent due to the superior landlord have been paid off.

(2) Annex to this declaration a correct inventory of the property.

In Scotland the landlord has what is termed "hypothec" or real right in security for rent over the furniture of his tenant. He may make the hypothec effectual by sequestration of the goods within three months of the date upon which the rent fell due. Sequestration may be followed by the sale of the goods carried out by an officer appointed by the sheriff. Goods are only subject to hypothec for each successive year's rent, and not for arrears. Where goods so subject are removed by the tenant, the landlord may obtain a warrant from the sheriff to bring them back. He is also entitled to prevent the tenant from removing his goods not only when the rent falls due, but also during any period of the tenancy, unless a tenant can give good security that the rent will be paid. Coin of the realm, bonds, bills and wearing apparel are not subject to the hypothec of the landlord.

Furnished Houses and Lodgings.—Where a tenant takes a furnished house or lodging there is an implied warranty in law on the part of the landlord that the premises are reasonably fit for human occupation. So if by reason of bad drains or any other cause the house is rendered unfit for habitation, the tenant is entitled to terminate the tenancy. If, however, the landlord has agreed to keep the premises in a state of repair, he is entitled to notice of want of repair and an opportunity to put it right, before the tenant is justified in leaving. This implied warranty as to fitness for human occupation only exists where the property is let furnished. If the property is let unfurnished, the tenant is not entitled to terminate the tenancy on finding the drains in a bad state, or the house unfit for occupation.

Flats.—The landlord is bound to keep the stairs in good condition.

Liability of the Landlord or the Tenant to Third Parties.—The tenant is liable for injuries to third parties caused by the dangerous condition of the premises. There is a statutory duty imposed on the owner or occupier to fence in or cover over all dangerous places or holes abutting on the highway, *e.g.*, to keep in good repair the area railings and coal-cellar covers on the pavement. When, therefore, a passer-by is injured by reason of these things being in dangerous condition, he has usually a right of action against the tenant and not against the landlord. The same is the case when the condition of the premises themselves is the cause of injury to other people or to their property. The landlord and not the tenant will, however, be liable (1) where he (the landlord) has agreed to keep the premises in repair, or (2) where he has let the premises in a dilapidated condition. Of course, if the injured party is a trespasser he has no remedy whatever.

Sub-letting a House.—The lessee of a house may sublet it unless he has bound himself by the terms of the lease not to do so. It is extremely common to find in leases a covenant to the effect that the tenant will not underlet or assign the house without the written consent of the landlord. The main difference between an underlease and an assignment is that the latter is for the whole of the remainder of the term of the original tenant's lease, whereas the former would only be for part of the term.

Where tenants agree not to underlet or assign without the consent of the landlord, it is advisable that they should insist on the following additional words being added to the covenant:—"But such consent is not to be unreasonably withheld in the case of a respectable and responsible person." If then the consent is unreasonably refused the tenant may assign without incurring the forfeiture of the lease.

Termination of a Tenancy.—Where a house has been taken for a stated period the tenant does not require to give notice to the landlord of his intention to quit. But where the tenancy is a yearly tenancy, or a monthly or quarterly one, notice is required, for a yearly tenancy does not mean a tenancy for a year, but a continuing tenancy from year to year.

Notice of Removal.—Where the parties have not come to any special agreement, the amount of notice proper for a yearly tenancy is half a year, and for a quarterly, monthly, or weekly tenancy it is a quarter, or a month, or a week respectively.

When to give Notice of Removal.—The law provides that a yearly, quarterly, monthly, or weekly tenancy can only be properly determined at the end of the year, quarter, month, or week of the tenancy; so that the tenant must give his notice the requisite amount of months or weeks before the *end* of the period of the tenancy. Thus he cannot terminate a yearly tenancy at any time by giving six months' notice. A yearly tenancy commencing on the 1st of January can only be terminated on the 31st of

December, so that the half year's notice should be given by the 1st of July. The tenant may not, by giving the notice at the end of August, terminate it at the end of the following February. The half year's notice required to terminate a yearly tenancy does not necessarily mean six calendar months. The notice should be for at least half a year—that is 183 days.

Other Ways of Terminating a Tenancy.—By Surrender.—When *both* parties agree to put an end to the tenancy before the completion of the term, the tenant must make a surrender to the landlord, which in all cases must be in writing and generally by deed.

By Forfeiture.—Most leases give the landlord the right to re-enter the premises and terminate the lease on the breach by the tenant of any one of the important covenants of the lease. Where such a right of entry is reserved to the landlord, he will be presumed by law to have waived it if he accepts the payment of the rent after he has gained knowledge of the breach of the covenant.

Responsibility for Fire.—If the tenant of a house has covenanted to repair, he must in every case remedy or rebuild in the case of damage to or loss of the premises by fire, unless he has been careful to make a special condition that liability for damage by fire shall not form part of the covenant. It is always as well for the householder to protect himself from loss or damage by fire by a clause of the kind, or by insuring his property with a good insurance company, or by seeing that a covenant for insurance by the landlord is included in the lease. (For conditions of Fire Insurance, see p. 373.)

Chimney on Fire.—Should a chimney catch fire in London the occupier of the house is liable to a penalty of 20s., even though the fire be caused by some one else's carelessness, though he can in the latter case recover from this person the penalty he has paid if he can prove the neglect. In towns outside London the penalty is only 10s., but it is not recoverable if the occupier can show the fire did not in any way arise from carelessness, neglect, or omission on his part or that of his servant.

Sanitary Regulations.—It is an offence to build a house without proper drainage in any urban district. Where any house is without a drain sufficient for its effectual drainage the local authorities must, by written notice, require the owner or occupier of the house, within a reasonable time, to make a covered drain emptying into the local authority's sewers or cess-pools under the direction of the authority.

Every house must be provided with one or more water-closets as required, furnished with a suitable water-supply, and all the necessary arrangements to ensure its efficient working. Where, however, there is not a sufficient sewerage or water-supply a 'privy'" or earth closet may be substituted.

Every house must also have a sufficient ash-pit, dust-bin, or other receptacle for ashes and refuse. Failure to comply with these regulations renders the occupier liable to a fine of £5, and a further fine of 40s. for each day the offence continues, or the sanitary authority may do the work themselves and recover from the owner or occupier. Closets, privies, and ash-pits must not be allowed to get into a condition which is offensive or injurious to health. The occupier of the house is in these circumstances liable to a fine of £5, or a further fine of 40s. for every day they remain in this condition.

Infectious Diseases.—Disinfection of Premises.—Every Local Government Board may make regulations enforcing the cleansing and disinfection of premises, bedding, &c., in the case of a house which has been visited by an infectious disease. It is an offence under the Infectious Disease (Prevention) Act, 1890, to knowingly cast infected refuse into any ash-bin or receptacle for refuse. Outgoing tenants are fined for leaving premises infected, unless they give notice of infection to the landlord.

The letting of a house where infectious disease has prevailed within a period of six months prior to the letting also involves a heavy penalty.

Removal of Refuse.—Local authorities have power to undertake or contract for the removal of house refuse from private premises; and where they have exercised this power it is an offence for any one else to remove or obstruct authorised persons from removing such refuse. But there is a provision exempting occupiers of houses from liability in respect of such refuse as is produced on their own premises and intended to be removed for sale or for the occupier's own use if it is meantime kept so as not to be a nuisance. If the local authority, after having undertaken or contracted for the removal of the refuse, unreasonably neglects to have it removed within seven days of being requested in writing to do so by the occupier of the premises, it renders itself liable to penalties.

House Duty.—This is known by the names of House Tax, House Duty, and Inhabited House Duty. All inhabited dwellings of £20 and upwards are chargeable. Liability to pay this tax falls upon the occupier and not the owner of a house. The rate of duty varies with the annual value of the house, and for ordinary dwelling-houses is as follows:—

On houses where the annual value of the premises does not exceed £40	3d. in the £.
Where it exceeds £40 but not £60	6d. in the £.
Exceeding £60	9d. in the £.

A lower scale is charged under certain conditions to lodging-house keepers and those engaged in trade.

Time for Payment.—In England the year calculated in the assessment of this tax is from April 5 to the following April 5, and in Scotland from May 24 to the following May 23; in all cases the tax is required to be paid on January 1 of that year.

Land Tax.—The tenant pays this in the first instance, but she is entitled to deduct it from the amount paid for rent, unless she has by the terms of the lease or agreement agreed to bear the charge herself. Persons whose incomes do not exceed £160 a year are exempt from the payment of land tax, whilst those whose incomes do not exceed £400 are exempt to the extent of one-half.

House and Estate Agents' Commission.—House agents are as a rule employed to negotiate the sale or lease of a house or property. Thus where a lease or a purchase has been effected through their agency they are entitled to a commission upon the proceeds of the same payable by the seller or lessor of the property.

This commission only becomes payable when the sale or lease has been effected in consequence of the agents' introduction.

The following are the usual fees and charges in London of House and Estate Agents and Auctioneers for letting house property, factories, shop property, &c.:—

When let on agreement for not more than three years, 5 per cent. on the first year's rent; when for a longer term, 7½ per cent., and, in addition, 5 per cent. up to £1000 and 2½ per cent. on the residue upon any premium or consideration. Also 5 per cent. on the purchase price of any plant, fixtures, fittings, &c., which may be purchased by the tenant. Where the rent is weekly, one week's rent is charged.

Income Tax.—The Income Tax is payable by all persons whose annual income exceeds £160. At present the amount levied is 1s. 2d. in the £ upon unearned incomes and on earned incomes of over £3000, and 1s. in the £ on earned incomes of between £2000 and £3000. On all earned incomes up to £2000 the tax is 9d. in the £. All whose incomes do not exceed £160 are entirely exempted from payment, whilst a rebate is allowed of the amount of the tax on £160 when the income is less than £400; £150 when less than £500; £120 when less than £600, and £70 when less than £700. A special allowance equal to the amount of the Income Tax upon £10 is allowed to Income Tax payers whose income does not exceed £500 in respect of every child under the age of sixteen. In addition to the ordinary Income Tax a Super Tax of 6d. in the £ is payable by persons whose total income exceeds £5000, for every £1 of income above £3000.

Rates.—Rates differ from taxes inasmuch as they are contributions levied by some local authority either for local government purposes or for the purpose of providing for the poor. Whilst taxes are levied by the Government and are of general application, the term "rate" also applies to a charge made by a public company (*i.e.* a water company) for services rendered. Under this designation can be classed the water rate and the gas rates.

Who Pays the Rates.—The occupier of a house and not the owner is generally the person who is primarily liable for the payment of the rates, though there are some rates which the owner must pay. In the case of a landlord and tenant the parties frequently agree between themselves that the liability shall ultimately fall upon the landlord.

Each locality has its own rates governed by its own needs. Rates are assessed on the net annual value of the property. The rateable value of a property is arrived at by deducting from the gross value the tithes, cost of insurance, repairs and other expenses incidental to property which detract from its gross value.

Gas and Water Rates.—The gas and water rates are usually a charge made by a public company for services rendered. Gas is usually paid for according to the quantity consumed as measured by the meter. The private Acts of most gas companies have provisions dealing with the testing of gas meters and the recovery of overcharges if the meters do not register correctly, but many of the Acts provide that allowances for the incorrectness of meters can only be made on the current quarter account. Water rates, however, are generally assessed, and are payable on the rateable value of the premises, though it is not unusual for an extra charge to be made when garden hoses are employed, or where there is otherwise reason to believe that an abnormal supply of water will be used.

The Hire Purchase System.—To people of limited means who cannot afford the disbursement of a substantial lump sum, the facilities for furnishing their homes on the hire purchase system present many decided advantages. Briefly a hire purchase agreement for the purchase of furniture or other goods amounts to this—the goods become the property of the person who hires them when he has completed the purchase by a specific number of payments made periodically. Until all the payments have been made the goods belong to the person who lets them out. Should default be made in payment, the owner may retake possession of his goods and all previous instalments paid by the hirer will be forfeited.

It is always as well, before entering into a hire purchase agreement, to see that it is being effected with a reputable firm. Many of the chief hire purchase traders belong to a society whose object is to see that the system is honourably kept up, and that the mere fortuitous failure to pay an instalment is not made the means of depriving the hirer of the benefit of his contract altogether. Firms belonging to this society will usually subject this rule to considerable modification in favour of a hirer who has a comparatively respectable character and position, and if there is reason to believe that his default is in the nature of a temporary suspension of payment only. As a rule it pays the hire furnisher better to conclude the sale with the hirer even for an extended credit than to take back goods in a second-hand condition and find a purchaser for them, more especially as a reputation for harshness would be fatal to his success in business in any restricted locality.

Stamps.—A hire purchase agreement requires a sixpenny stamp if its subject matter is of the value of £5. If below that, value no stamp is necessary.

Excise Licences.—The chief excise licences which concern the householder according to the position he occupies and the extent of his establishment are :—

The licence on male servants.
The licence on armorial bearings.
The licence on carriages and motors.
The licence on dogs.

Male Servant.—Every person who employs a male servant must obtain a licence, paying for such licence 15s. for each servant employed. The licence is annual and expires on the 31st day of December each year. The term "servant" in this connection applies only to what may be described as a personal servant, not to a workman or labourer employed in any handicraft or trade. But if a farm labourer is employed daily to drive a pony carriage, then a licence is necessary. It is also necessary in the case of a tradesman who employs a man to attend to a vehicle solely used for the purpose of pleasure. A gardener employed at a *weekly* wage and who works for his employer a number of hours *per day* cannot be employed without a licence even if he is at liberty to work for other people. Trade servants, including those engaged in hotels and refreshment houses, game watchers and persons not residing in employer's house engaged for a portion only of each day, are *not* servants in that sense and do not require to be licensed.

Penalties for Employing Male Servants without a Licence.—It is the duty of any person employing male servants to render a declaration to this effect to the Inland Revenue authorities in the month of January each year. The penalty for neglecting to deliver or refusing to deliver such declaration is £20, or for employing a male servant without a proper licence, or employing more male servants than authorised by the licence, is also £20.

Armorial Bearings.—The general regulations and penalties affecting the use of armorial bearings are the same as those which apply in the case of "male servants." The licence must be taken out annually, and the duty payable is £1, 1s., but if used on the carriage the amount is increased to £2, 2s. Any person wearing or using armorial bearings, even as an ornament, is bound to take out a licence. The wearing of a signet ring with a lion rampant engraved thereon renders the wearer liable to duty, so is the user of notepaper with a similar device printed on his notepaper.

Certain persons are exempted from making declarations, or taking out licences, either for the employment of male servants or the use of armorial bearings. These are : (1) Members of the Royal Family; (2) sheriffs and mayors of corporations serving an annual office therein in respect of any servants or carriages kept for the purposes of office during the year of service; (3) persons wearing by right of office any arms or insignia of members of the Royal Family, or of any corporation or royal burgh in respect of the use of any such arms or insignia; (4) any person ordinarily resident in Ireland, who is a representative peer on the part of Ireland or a member of the House of Commons, and not residing in Great Britain longer than forty days before and forty days after such session.

Carriages.—For every carriage which has four or more wheels and is fitted to be drawn by two or more horses or mules, or drawn or propelled by mechanical power, a licence costing £2, 2s. must be taken out by the owner. If a four-wheeled carriage is fitted to be drawn by one horse only, then the cost of the licence is £1, 1s. This amount is reduced to 15s. if the one-horse carriage has less than four wheels; the licence for all kinds of hackney carriages is 15s.

Vehicles Exempt from Licence.—Carriages which are kept but not used at any time during the year do not require to be licensed, neither do vehicles constructed and used solely for the conveyance of goods of trade or husbandry. These latter must have the Christian name and surname and address of the owner printed on them in letters of not less than one inch in length. If, however, a tradesman uses his trade vehicle for the purpose of giving his friends or his family pleasurable jaunts, and not solely for the purposes of his trade, he will be required to take out a licence; moreover, the vehicle must be *constructed or adapted* for trade purposes. Therefore a wardrobe dealer cannot avoid the duty if he conveys goods in a governess cart, even if he has his name and address painted upon it and does not use it for pleasure or any other purpose than in the exercise of his calling.

Motor Cars and Cycles.—A person employed to drive a motor car is a male "servant," and the employer is liable to an annual duty of 10s.

in respect of such a driver. The duties payable on motor cars are as follows :—

	£	s.	d.
Motor bicycles and tricycles	1	0	0
Motor cars not exceeding 6½ h.-p.	2	2	0
,, exceeding 6 h.-p. but under 12 h.-p. .	3	3	0
,, ,, 12 ,, ,, 16 ,, .	4	4	0
,, ,, 16 ,, ,, 26 ,, .	6	6	0
,, ,, 26 ,, ,, 33 ,, .	8	8	0
,, ,, 33 ,, ,, 40 ,, .	10	10	0
,, ,, 40 ,, ,, 60 ,, .	21	1	0
,, ,, 60 ,, ...	42	0	0

Registration of Motor Cars and Motor Cycles.—Every car must be registered and must bear a mark indicating its number and the County Council for which it is registered. The fee for registration is £1, but in the case of motor cycles it is 5s. The penalty for using a car without being registered or using a car the mark on which is obscured or defaced, is for a first offence a penalty not exceeding £20, and for a subsequent offence a penalty not exceeding £50 or three months imprisonment.

Licence of Drivers.—Every person driving a motor car must have a licence, the fee for which is 5s. The licence is good for twelve months, and must be produced by the driver when demanded by a police constable, otherwise the driver is liable to a fine not exceeding £5. No person under the age of seventeen years can obtain a licence for driving a motor car, but in the case of motor cycles the age limit is 14 years.

Any person who drives a motor car without being licensed is liable to a fine not exceeding £20 for a first offence, and for a subsequent offence to a penalty not exceeding £50 or three months imprisonment.

Regulations as to Lights, Bells, and Horns.—During the period between one hour after sunset and one hour before sunrise, the person in charge of a motor car must carry attached thereto lamps so constructed and placed as to exhibit lights in accordance with the regulations of the Local Government Board. Moreover, all motor cars must carry bells or other instruments warning of their approach. Failure to comply with these regulations incurs the penalty of a fine not exceeding £10.

Dog Licences.—With a few exceptions which will be detailed below, persons wishing to keep a dog must take out an annual licence for the purpose. The cost of each dog licence is 7s. 6d. The licences are issued by the Inland Revenue department, and may be obtained at any post office. A register of the persons licensed and the number of dogs for which they hold licences is kept, and is open to the inspection of police constables and justices of the peace. All dog licences expire on December 31, irrespective of the date of issue. No rebate is allowed if the licence is operative for less than a year. The licence does not apply to a particular dog; it is the owner who is licensed to keep the dog, and he cannot transfer the licence to another person, even if that person should become the owner of the dog.

Dogs Exempted from Payment of Duty.—In the following cases no licence is required :—

(1) For dogs under six months old.

(2) Hound puppies under twelve months old not entered or used with a pack of hounds.

(3) In the case of a dog kept and used solely by a blind person for his guidance.

(4) Dogs kept and used solely for the purpose of tending sheep or cattle. The number in this case is restricted to two.

Penalties for Keeping a Dog without a Licence.—A person keeping a dog without a licence or keeping more dogs than he is licensed to keep, or refusing to produce a licence on the demand of an Excise Officer or constable, renders himself liable to a penalty not exceeding £5.

Dog Owner's Responsibilities.—The most important question in regard to dogs from the point of view of the owner is in connection with the degree of responsibility which attaches to her for acts committed by her canine pet. The old saying that every dog is entitled to its first bite is not entirely accurate, but it gives a rough idea of the principles upon which the Courts have acted. In order to make an owner liable for an assault committed by a dog upon a person, the Court demands that there must be some evidence of knowledge on the part of the owner that the dog had a disposition to bite people. It would be possible to prove this knowledge in many ways, even although the animal may not have actually bitten any one before. Should a dog injure cattle his owner is liable for damage whether he was aware of the mischievous propensity of the dog or not.

Damage to Dogs.—A person is entitled to kill a dog in self-defence, and in certain circumstances in defence of his property. Thus a landowner may kill a dog which is actually chasing sheep or rabbits in a warren if the act is necessary for the safety of his property, *but not otherwise*; and a dog in pursuit of game may also be shot by the owner of the game, but not if the bird or animal pursued is out of danger.

Collars.—The Board of Agriculture has power to make orders for prescribing and regulating the wearing of collars by dogs when out of doors, each collar to have the name and address of the owner inscribed upon it on a plate or badge attached to it. By an order dated 22nd of October, 1906, the Board has exempted packs of hounds, dogs used for sporting purposes, the capture of vermin, or the tending of sheep, from this regulation.

Stray Dogs.—Where a police officer has reason to believe that any dog found in a highway or place of public resort is a stray dog, he may seize the dog and retain it until the owner has claimed it and paid all expenses incurred by reason of its detention. But the owner, if known, is entitled to a notice that the dog has been so seized, and will be liable to be sold or destroyed if not claimed within seven clear days after the service of the notice.

Railway Companies and Dogs.—When a dog is sent from one place to another by rail the railway company will only be liable to the owner when a dog is killed or injured as a result of the negligence or default of the servants of the company.

The company is, in addition, permitted to make conditions limiting the liability it is prepared to assume; but in order to make them binding upon the public it is necessary first that the conditions should be reasonable, and, secondly, there must be a memorandum of the contract between the parties signed by the consignor of the dog or his agent. A very usual form of such condition is one which limits the liability of the company to a small fixed sum, unless the full value of the dog is declared, and a certain percentage paid upon the excess value over the sum fixed. If, however, the railway officials allow the dog to be despatched without this condition being signed, the owner can recover the whole amount of the loss, whether he has paid an additional percentage or not.

Railway Companies' and Passengers' Luggage.—A railway company is liable to passengers for loss of their luggage. Of course, if the passenger carries the luggage in the carriage in which he is seated, he assumes control over it himself, and the company is then only liable for loss due to the negligence or wilful misconduct of their servants; whereas if the luggage is placed in the van, the company is liable for any loss or damage, no matter how caused, except damage arising through some inherent defect in the luggage itself, such as bad packing.

A railway company, however, is not liable for loss or injury to gold or silver articles, clocks, jewellery, watches, bills, money securities, pictures, stamps, maps, writings, plated goods, glass, china, silks, furs, or hand-made lace if the value exceeds £15, unless their value is declared by the passenger, and an increased charge paid. Railway companies may limit their liability in regard to carrying cycles, making a condition that such machines are carried at their owners' risk. But these conditions must be agreed to by the owner of the cycle and signed by him, and even then the company will be responsible for any loss caused through the negligence or fault of their servants, but they will not be liable as common carriers.

The liability of the companies for passengers' luggage begins from the moment the luggage is handed to their servants for conveyance to the van or carriage or to be labelled, and ends when the luggage is delivered to the passenger and placed on his cab. If the luggage is merely handed to a porter to look after it without any further directions, the company is not liable for damage that may occur to it. The luggage must be handed to the porter for immediate or present and not for future conveyance. A passenger must claim his luggage within a reasonable time.

PLAIN SEWING AND MENDING

SEWING has been from olden times an art the practice of which has been the special privilege of women. In many ancient stories and histories the typical woman is introduced to us plying her needle. Thus we see in the "Odyssey" Penelope awaiting her royal husband, Ulysses, working at her famous piece of linen or tapestry, and of the model woman described in Proverbs we are told: "She seeketh wool and flax and worketh willingly with her hands . . . she maketh herself coverings of tapestry . . . she maketh fine linen," &c.

We can see in our museums and palaces beautiful needlework done by women of all times; yet, strange though it may seem, for the last generation or two until quite recently needlework has been looked down upon by a certain class of people, with the most lamentable results, for this ignorance is usually displayed by those to whom the saving effected by a knowledge of practical sewing would come as an inexpressible boon.

Fortunately much is done nowadays in schools and training colleges for the teaching of needlework, and the girl of the present day, the mother of to-morrow, will know how to add to the comfort and happiness of her home by the clever and timely use of her needle.

It should be the duty of the head of every household to see that the house linen and the children's clothes are kept in order, and to mend them when there is no one else to do it. "A stitch in time saves nine" is one of the truest sayings, and a mother should teach her children to sew as soon as they can be safely trusted with needle and thread.

Every girl or woman can become a neat sewer, and it is important that to begin with she should know the making of every stitch as well as the different materials and their use. Our object here is to explain these essential factors in a simple and comprehensive manner in order to make them as easy as possible for the beginner.

THE WORK-BASKET AND WHAT IT SHOULD CONTAIN

First of all each worker must have her own work-basket independently of the household mending bag or basket. A wicker one is best, as it is lighter and easier to carry about. A light wicker portable work-table with two fixed trays and a handle is also useful where there is much mending to be done, and it can be bought for a few shillings.

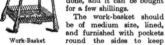

Work-Basket

The work-basket should be of medium size, lined, and furnished with pockets round the sides to keep sewing cotton, tapes, &c., apart and in order, the centre portion being allotted to the work itself.

The work-basket should contain:—

Two pairs of scissors—one large pair for cutting-out, with one blade pointed and the other round, the latter to be held underneath the material when cutting; and one small pair for cutting threads, for unpicking and any finer work. The rings of the scissors ought to be round and large enough for the fingers to enter comfortably.

A good thimble—a silver one to be preferred, and one that fits the finger comfortably.

A good supply of ordinary needles of the best quality. To test if they are good try to break one between the fingers. If the temper of the steel is first rate it will break off sharply, but with difficulty; if it breaks too easily, like a piece of glass, or bends, the needle is not good. The needles should be long-eyed to be easily threaded, and the holes ought to be well polished, so that they will not fray nor break the thread. For working the ordinary seams in plain needlework short needles are best, but for other work longer ones will be required. It will be useful to have an assortment of different sizes of needles from Nos. 5 to 12 to suit the various thicknesses of thread that will be used. There ought also to be a small supply of other kinds of needles, such as crewel needles, darners, chenille needles, Berlin wool needles, &c. It is a good plan to buy a needle-case fitted with the best quality of needles and containing all the different shapes and sizes that may be required.

A small emery cushion to polish rusty needles.

Five or six reels of white cotton, one of them

very fine to match No. 10 needles, and two or three reels of black cotton. (The numbers vary with different makers.)

A card or reel of white darning cotton for stockings.

A card or reel of black darning cotton for stockings.

A card or reel of tan darning cotton for stockings.

A few skeins of white embroidery cotton.

A reel of white silk, medium size.

A reel of black silk, medium size.

A reel of black silk, thick for button-holes.

Also a card or reel of cotton or silk of the colour of each dress, pair of gloves, stockings, &c., for mending.

Darning wool to match the stockings and underclothing.

A reel or skein of white and one of black linen thread may be very useful for sewing linen, holland, and other strong materials.

White crochet cotton for fancy stitches.

A box of mixed pins.

One or two bodkins for running in tapes and ribbons.

A stiletto for piercing holes to make eyelet holes, &c.

Pieces of tape, white and black of different sizes, linen and cotton.

Linen buttons in assorted sizes.

Pearl buttons in assorted sizes.

White and black hooks and eyes of different sizes.

A tape measure marked with inches on one side and centimetres on the other.

A small pin-cushion.

Machine needles, cotton, &c., should be kept with the machine outfit; they will be more handy in the machine drawer. The small articles, such as hooks and eyes and buttons, should be kept in a little box or a small bag; or a glass bottle with a screw lid is good, as the contents can so easily be seen.

SIMPLE STITCHES

General Hints.—Before describing the different stitches used in plain needlework it might be as well to give a few preliminary instructions.

The position of the body when sewing is very important. Whatever the work may be there is never any need to sit in an awkward position. The height of the chair ought to be in proportion to that of the table at which one is sitting, and if this is somewhat high a foot-stool may be used. There must be no undue stooping of the body, and the work must be held sufficiently high to prevent more than a slight inclination of the head.

Sewing should always be done in a good light; there must be no straining of the eyesight.

The work should never be pinned to the knee, as this causes the body to take an ungainly attitude, but should be fixed to a small weighted cushion on the table when it is necessary to keep it in a certain position.

The thread must never be bitten off with the teeth, but neatly cut with a pair of scissors.

Both thread and needle must be adapted to each other, and also to the material with which they are to be used. Fine cotton and fine needles should be used for fine material, and thicker needle and cotton for coarser material. The needle ought always to be chosen a little thicker than the cotton in order to make a hole large enough for the latter to enter easily. The end of the cotton which hangs loose from the reel should always be put through the needle first and the thread used the way it unwinds. It will be less likely to break and fray out if this is done. Never sew with a bent needle, as it will be impossible to make neat and even stitches, and if it becomes sticky pass it several times through the emery cushion. Be careful how you commence and finish each new seam. The thimble should be worn on the middle finger of the right hand.

The following explanations of stitches are made as simple and varied as possible. The best way to master a new stitch is to read each explanation twice through, study the illustrations of it thoroughly, and only then begin attempting it. Practice will show that this is not waste of time. It will be a little slower perhaps at the commencement, but the worker will soon find herself doing quicker and more accurate work.

Also be very exact in the measurements, one-eighth, one-sixth, one quarter, &c., of an inch; these will become so familiar with time and practice that they will hardly need to be measured.

Basting or Tacking.—Basting or tacking is used to keep the different parts of the garments together, or to fix the seams and patterns straight and securely before they are sewn. It is really a preparation seam, and should be

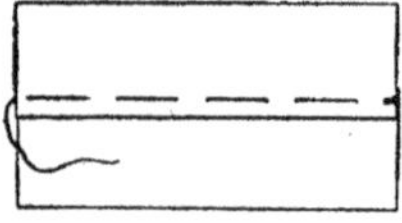

Basting or Tacking.

done most carefully, and never be overlooked under pretence that it is waste of time. It will be found in the long run that on the contrary it is a great saving of time, besides being the only sure means of producing neat and even work. Begin by making a knot at the end of a fairly long piece of cotton, as tacking threads are more easily taken out when there is a knot by which to take hold of them. Basting or tacking cottons should be used if possible, preferably pink, pale blue, or any colour that will not soil white material, and which will be easily seen. Hold the material lightly, yet firmly, so that it may not slip, and make the stitches just above where the line of running, hemming or seaming stitches will be. Begin at the right-hand side, put in the needle straight down, and bring it out on a horizontal line a quarter of an inch further on; pass over half an inch and put the needle in again and out another quarter of an inch farther, and so on, making the stitches twice as large as the intervals left between them. At the end of the seam put the needle twice in the same stitch, making what is called a back-stitch, so as to fasten off the thread.

Hemming.—Hemming is used to fasten down the raw edge of all materials, to fell, or fold down a seam. Nearly all articles of household linen and underclothing require hemming. The purpose of the hem is to strengthen and ornament the edge of the material. It can, if wished, be finished off prettily with fancy stitches or a lace edging. A great deal of hemming is done by machine; this certainly saves time and trouble and does for longer or coarser articles, but neat work done by hand is always more elegant, lasting, and valuable.

A hem is of different widths according to the piece of work for which it is used. It varies from the eighth of an inch hem at the end of a muslin frill to the one of three or four inches or more in width at the foot of a petticoat or a dress.

Laying the Hem.—The hem must be cut perfectly straight, to a thread if possible. Calico, muslin, and cotton materials generally tear to a thread, but as they are apt to pull crossways, especially those that are stiffened, one should first try on a piece of the material if it tears well. After tearing hold the material by the two opposite corners diagonally and pull it carefully until the raw edges are in a straight horizontal line again. This done, hold the wrong side of the material towards you. Turn down the raw edge towards you: this first fold should be one-quarter or one-third of an inch wide, according to the width of the hem. In muslin, nainsook, or any light materials the first fold should be exactly as wide as the hem itself so that the raw edges do not show through. Now fold over the hem for the second time to the desired width. Do the folding on the table if possible, making the hem of the required depth, and press down firmly with the nail of the thumb. Some people prefer to hold up the material in the right hand and fold it as they go along, pressing it down with the thumb of the left hand. This method, however, has the disadvantage of creasing the material, thus detracting from that "new" appearance which adds to the value of hand-made garments.

To ensure the even folding of wide hems it is a good plan to use a card notched to the width of the hem and to measure every three or four inches before pressing down for the second folding. In hemming serge or any material that will not crease, the first folding down should be tacked, and the card-measure applied to every stitch for the second folding.

Flannel hems are only turned down once.

When hemming the four sides of a square turn down the two opposite sides first, then the two other opposite sides, so that the corners may be alike. When the hem is turned down it should be tacked unless it is too small. Make the tacking stitches about one-eighth of an inch above the edge.

Sewing the Hem.—Hold the hem in your left hand. The cotton should be about the thickness of the threads of the material. Do not take it too long. Insert the point of the needle under the second fold of the hem at the right-

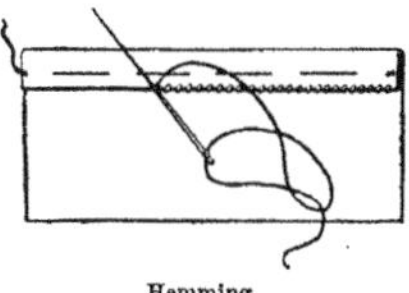

Hemming.

hand side, two threads from the edge of the hem. Draw it through, leaving an end of cotton half an inch long. Slip this end under the fold towards the left, and hold the hem securely over the first finger so that it does not slip.

Insert the point of the needle in the material just below the edge of the fold, two or three threads to the left of the place where the needle was first put in. Direct it slantingly upwards to the left, take two or three threads diagonally, and bring the needle out through the fold of the hem, on the same line and five or six threads apart from the first place the needle came through. Go on thus holding the needle slantingly, the point upwards until the cotton is finished. When taking a new length of cotton, tuck the ends under the fold of the hem.

To fasten off, work twice over the last stitch and cut the cotton close to the fold if it is a raw edge that will be covered. If it is a selvedge, or the top hem on a square hemmed on all sides, the hem should be continued to the end of the material, then the corners should be carefully seamed. At the end of the seam make a double stitch, insert the needle between the fold and the hem at the top, bring it out on the wrong side the length of the needle, and cut the thread close to the hem. If the cotton is lightly pulled when cutting it will disappear in the fold.

Avoid pulling the cotton in hemming or the material will be puckered; only pull it if the hem is a circular one, and convex, or if you fell a seam on the cross as on the sides of a chemise or a night-gown, when the stitches should then be very close together. If the hem is concave, as round a neck or an armhole, the material will need to be stretched to lie flat, or else it must be snipped with the scissors; this should be thought of when tacking, and in hemming the material should be carefully stretched on the left forefinger.

Felling.—This is the same as hemming. The term is always applied in connection with seams, where two pieces of material are joined together and one edge is folded in and hemmed down, as in the "run and fell" seam.

Running and Gathering.—Running is a stitch used for joining together two pieces of material, as in a run and fell seam; it is also used for making tucks. It does not make a strong seam, and should not be employed where there is much strain. It is a stitch something like tacking, only the stitches are much shorter and are all of the same size. If the material is thin, like muslin or soft like silk, several stitches may be taken up at once on the needle. Hold the work in the same way as for basting. Do not

Running.

knot the cotton, but begin at the right-hand side with a back-stitch. When ready to take a fresh needleful of cotton, first work over the last stitch twice with the old cotton, pulling the needle for these extra stitches through one piece of the material only, then cut off the thread, put the needle with the new cotton in the second last stitch; make a double stitch in the last two stitches also through the single material, then proceed with the running to the end. Fasten off with a back-stitch. For gathering, the stitches should be double the size of the spaces (see p. 395).

Seaming or Top Sewing is very like over-casting, only the stitches are finer and closer together. It is used to join two pieces of material together as in the sew and fell seam, and is worked over the edge of the material. When two selvedges have to be joined it is generally this stitch which is used. Place the two selvedges together with the wrong sides outwards and tack them about one-eighth inch down. For seaming, hold the work upright between the left thumb and forefinger. Begin at the right-hand end, leaving about half an inch of cotton to be worked over with the first few stitches. Sew over and over the two selvedges, making neat slanting stitches and just deep enough to hold the pieces together. There must be no knots made in seaming. When a new piece of cotton is required, work over the two ends with the first few stitches. The ends must remain near the surface of the seam, and the stitches must be taken underneath so as to

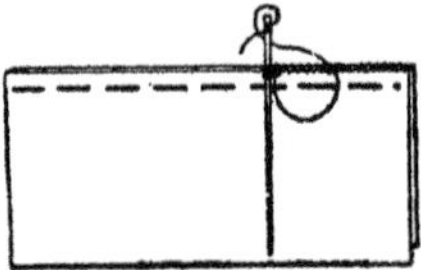

Seaming or Top Sewing.

hide them and make them secure at the same time. Then continue to the end of the seam. To fasten off, work backwards over the last three stitches exactly in the same holes so as to make three neat little crosses; after the third insert your needle to the right in the middle of the stitches and bring it out to the left at the end of the seam. Then cut off the cotton and take out the tacking threads. Open out the work on the table and flatten it carefully from right to left with the thumb-nail.

Stitching.—In stitching a short stitch is taken on the upper and a long one on the under side, then the needle is taken backwards through the hole made by the last stitch. Stitching is used to finish off neck and wrist bands, and for seams where a very strong even stitch is required. Stitching is always worked on two or more thicknesses of material. It is apt to tire the eyes, and should not be worked for too long at a time; in fact, long-stitched seams should be done by a good machine. When stitching by hand, if a straight line of stitches is required, it is better to draw a thread of the material. This requires a little skill and careful attention. Choose a thread thicker than the others if

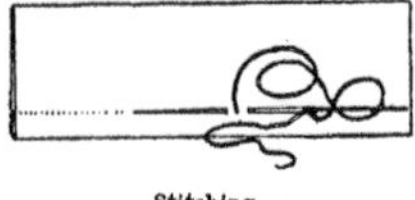

Stitching.

possible, keeping of course in the correct place where the stitching ought to be. Insert the needle under it about half an inch from the right-side end and bring it out. Secure it firmly between the thumb and forefinger of your right hand, and hold the whole width of the material where the stitching is to be worked in your left hand also between the thumb and finger. Then ease the material from the thread by rubbing it gently along, beginning at the right-hand side, with the thumb and forefinger of your left hand, and make it gently slip on the thread. When the thread breaks, which often happens in light materials, it is easily found again, as the material is slightly creased near the broken part. Take it up again half an inch from the broken end and go on drawing very gently.

Back-stitching is much the same as stitching, only the stitch is taken half-way back instead

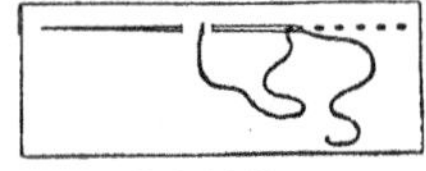

Back-Stitching.

of all the way, leaving a small space between each stitch.

Overcasting.—Overcasting is not used as a rule for any of the seams or any sewing worked on calico or linen materials. It is used for edges or seams in dress bodices, sleeves, and skirts when the raw edges cannot be hidden in any other way. It is difficult to overcast

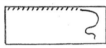

Overcasting.

very evenly. The stitches are usually worked from left to right as in illustration. Be very careful in overcasting not to draw the thread too tightly or the edge would curl. When the seam has to be snipped to allow it to curve outwards, the overcasting should follow the cuts, be done neatly over the angles, and two or three close stitches made inside the snips so that the material should not unravel near the seam.

DIFFERENT CALICO SEAMS

Seams are used to join together widths or pieces of material. They vary according to the materials or garments they are used for. There are six different kinds of calico seams:—

(1) **The Top-sewing Seam,** which is used for the joining together of two selvedges.

(2) **The Sew and Fell Seam.**—Used for calico garments, such as chemises, drawers, night-dresses, men's shirts, and any garments which need to be joined very strongly.

(3) **The Run and Fell Seam.**—Used for calico, muslin, and garments of lighter material.

(4) **The French Seam.**—Used especially for thin materials and silk, for making slip-bodices and outer garments, as overalls, pinafores, and any garments of which as little as possible of the seam must be seen on the right side.

(5) **The Mantua-maker's Seam.**—Used for fine materials, more especially used in dress-making for pockets, sleeves, seams of skirts, and any garments that have no lining. It is much used also for fancy articles, as silk bags, reticules, &c.

(6) **The Counter Hem.**—Used sometimes for under bodices, nightgowns, shoulder seams, infants' first shirts, and baby clothes in general.

Notes.—When making the seam in a garment the fell should always fall towards the back. The width of seams must always be the same throughout. If one breadth of the material is straight and the other gored, *i.e.* on the cross, the gored breadth should always be next to the worker. The corresponding seams in garments should always be worked to pair with each other; that is to say, if one seam is begun at the top the corresponding one must be begun at the bottom, as in sleeves, for instance.

The Sew and Fell Seam.—To make a sew and fell seam turn down an eighth of an inch on the wrong side of one of the pieces of material

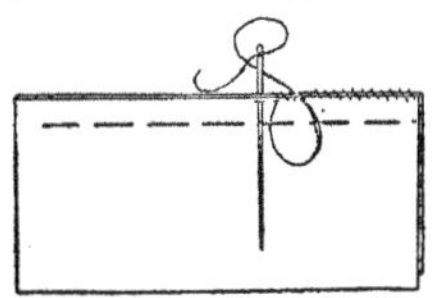

Fig. 1.

to be joined. Turn down an eighth of an inch on the right side of the other piece of material; turn back this folded edge nearly a quarter of an inch, still holding the material exactly in the same way. This double fold must always be on the front width of the material when joining the pieces of a garment together. If one side of the seam is on the cross, as in nightgowns, the double fold should be made on the straight side.

Put the two pieces of material together edge to edge with the right side outside and the folds inside, and tack an eighth of an inch from the top, beginning at the bottom of the garment. Then seam neatly together, beginning at the bottom of the garment (fig. 1).

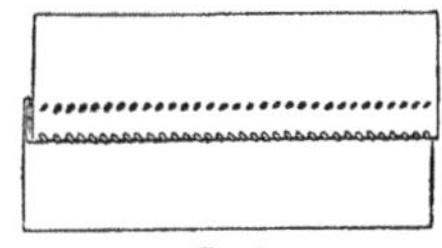

Fig. 2.

When the seaming is done, take out the tacking threads, open the seam, and press it down flat on the table with the thumb-nail in the same direction as the seaming has been worked. Turn over the work on the wrong side, tack down the fold and neatly fell it. Then take out the tacking threads (fig. 2).

The Run and Fell Seam.—The run and fell seam is simpler and easier than the sew and fell seam, and can often be used instead of it. To make a run and fell seam turn down an eighth of an inch on the right side of one of the pieces of material to be joined and crease it well down. Place the raw edge of the second piece of material under this crease so that the two right sides of the material are turned inwards face to face.

Tack the two pieces of material together beginning at the right-hand side a little distance from

Fig. 3.

the edge. Be careful to put the needle through the three thicknesses. Then run the two pieces neatly together just below the tacking thread, taking a back-stitch every six stitches or so. Take out the tacking threads and press the seam perfectly flat, so that the raw edge is

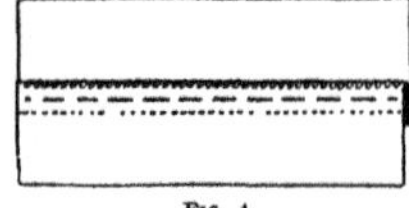

Fig. 4

hidden as in a hem. Tack the fold down neatly and then fell it (fig. 4).

The French Seam.—To make a French seam put the two pieces of material together edge

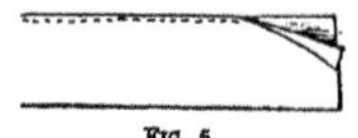

Fig. 5.

to edge with the right sides outwards. Tack, then run, with an occasional back-stitch an eighth of an inch down from the top edge (fig. 5). Remove the tacking thread, turn the

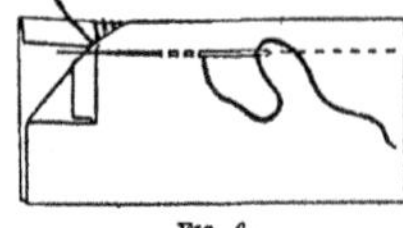

Fig. 6.

work over to the wrong side, and press the seam carefully so that it forms the top edge. Tack an eighth of an inch down from the top and run below this, being very careful to take in the raw edges on the other side (fig. 6). If the material is heavy, or if the seam has to be very strong, stitching may be worked instead of running.

The Mantua-maker's Seam.—Lay the two raw edges of the materials together, the right sides inwards, and so that the top width lies an eighth of an inch below the under width. Turn down that eighth of an inch of the under-width

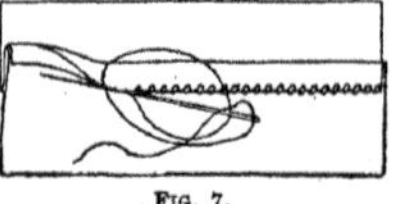

Fig. 7.

over the top width. Again turn down the two materials together an eighth of an inch deep. Tack through the whole thickness very carefully. Then hem, being very careful to take every stitch through the under-side (fig. 7).

Remove the tacking stitches. The seam will stand in a ridge instead of lying flat.

The Counter Hem.—For counter hemming, turn down a fold an eighth of an inch deep on the right side of one of the widths of material.

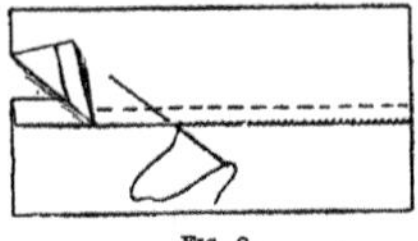

Fig. 8.

Turn down a fold an eighth of an inch deep on the wrong side of the other width of material. Place the two folded edges over one another and pin the seam down the middle, then tack down the fold on the right side. Turn over and tack down the fold on the wrong side, or, if the material lies easily, it may be tacked once only down the centre (fig. 8). Take out the pins and hem down the fold on the right side, then

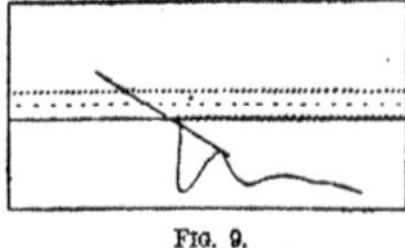

Fig. 9.

hem on the wrong side (fig. 9). Some people stitch this seam instead of hemming it down. In that case both rows of stitches should be made on the right side, and the tacking made so that the stitches should be very near the edge of both folds.

A False Hem.—A false hem is used to join a piece or strip of material on to another garment. It is meant either to lengthen a garment or to strengthen it. The material used for the false hem need not necessarily be the same as that of the garment. Cut and join together a strip of material long enough for the false hem required.

The joining should as much as possible be done on selvedges and *top sewn*. If that is not possible, fold down the raw edges of the materials to be joined half an inch wide. Put the folds down back to back, so that the raw edges be outwards, and overseam. Open the seam out so that the folds lie flat on each side.

When the strip is prepared, place it against the garment the right sides inwards, and the

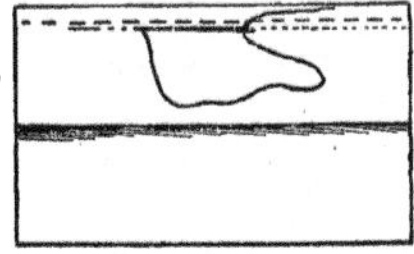

FIG. 10.

two edges even one with the other. Tack and run them together quarter of an inch at least from the top (fig. 10). Then turn over the false hem and fold it down half an inch above the seam, so that the latter does not show on the outside. Tack this fold carefully half an inch from the foot, then place the garment very flat on the table, with the wrong side uppermost, and fold in the raw edge of the false hem half an inch

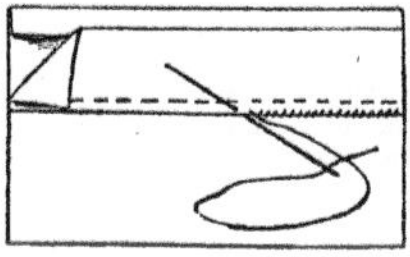

FIG. 11.

inwards. Tack it very carefully an eighth of an inch above the edge. Then hem it down (fig. 11).

DIFFERENT FLANNEL SEAMS

Flannel seams differ from calico seams in that they are not made with double folds, as the material is too thick. There are three different kinds of flannel seams :—

I. and II.—**The Open Flannel Seams,** used when a very flat seam is required, as in baby clothes, barracoats, flannel vests, bodices, &c.

III.—**The Closed Flannel Seam,** used for stronger garments, as flannel petticoats, flannel shirts, night-dresses, &c.

The Open Flannel Seam.—I. To make an open flannel seam, place the two pieces of flannel together, the right sides inwards, and the edges exactly parallel. Tack, then run them together a little more than an eighth of an inch down from the top. Take out the tacking threads. Open the seam out and turn down each edge of the flannel on to its own piece of material. Flatten at the join and tack down

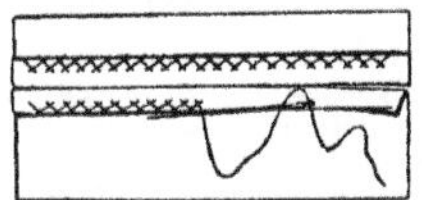

FIG. 12.

if necessary. Herring-bone each fold down, taking one thickness of material only, first the fold at the top and then the material below in turns (fig. 12). (For Herring-boning, see p. 397.)

II. There is another way of felling an open flannel seam. When the seam is run and flattened down, work only one row of herring-boning in the exact centre of the seam on the wrong side, one stitch above the join and one below alternately, being very careful to work through both thicknesses and show neat running stitches on the right side of the work. This seam is not so neat as the first, only it is quicker and quite strong. The raw edges are not wide enough to unravel.

The Closed Flannel Seam.—To make a closed flannel seam put the two pieces of flannel together with the right sides inwards, the top piece of flannel an eighth inch below the under. If one of the widths is gored, put the gored one on the top of the other. Tack one-sixth of an inch below the gored edge, then run and back-stitch just below the tacking. Take out the tacking threads. Fold the longer edge over the shorter one, making

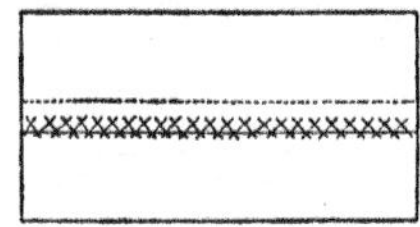

FIG. 13

the seam as flat as possible, and tack in position. Then herring-bone down and remove the tacking threads (fig. 13).

TUCKING

To Measure and Make Tucks.—Tucks are folds of material taken double and resting on the single material. They vary in width according to the material and the garment. In muslin, nainsook, cambric, &c., for baby gowns, fine blouses, rabats, handkerchiefs, &c., they are very small. In underlinen they are a little wider. In flannel petticoats they are often one or two inches deep; also at the foot of dresses, &c.

Sometimes they are arranged in sets with a space between or with a deeper tuck between. These sets should always be uneven in number, *i.e.* 3, 5, 7, &c.

They may also be graduated in size. For instance, the tuck above the hem would be the largest, the next one would be smaller, and so on until the top one, which would be smallest of all.

In making tucks it must be remembered that each tuck occupies three times its width, *i.e.*:—

1. The surface side of the tuck.
2. The under side of the tuck.
3. The width of material the tuck lies upon.

So for a tuck a quarter of an inch deep, you require to leave three-quarter inches width, not counting the space left between the tucks. Those spaces vary according to the width of the tucks and also according to taste; there is no definite rule. Generally, if the tucks are moderately narrow, the space should be the size of the tuck, so that a quarter of an inch tuck would require one inch of material, *i.e.* the three-quarter of an inch required for the making of it, plus a quarter of an inch for space. If the tucks are wide, the spaces should be a half or a third of the size of the tucks.

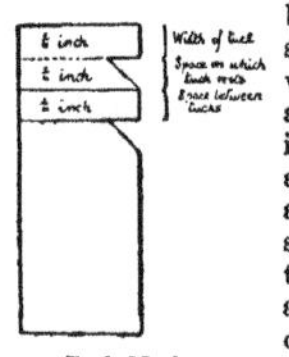

Tuck-Marker.

When tucks are very narrow or in sets, each tuck may touch the running stitches of the preceding one without hiding the stitches. But, again, this is according to taste. Tucks must never overlap each other.

When you have decided upon the size of the tucks, the best way is to make a tuck-marker by notching a piece of cardboad or stiff paper to the right depth so that each tuck may be very

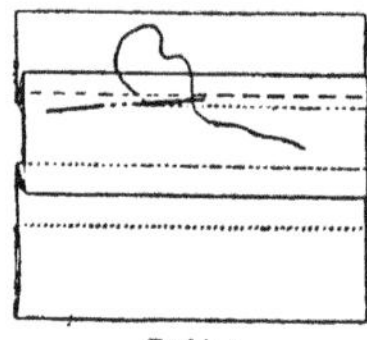
Tucking.

accurate. Carry the marker along the tuck as you tack it every three or four inches. Some people prefer to use a tape measure or a small inch ruler, but this is not such an easy form of measurement. The method of making the tuck-marker is shown in the diagram.

In fine materials it is sometimes a good plan to draw a thread where the running stitches are to be worked and work along that. Never draw a thread at the edge of the tuck, as it would soon wear out with washing and ironing.

For running the tucks fold them upwards, as the running stitches must be worked on the under side. Make the running stitches one thread below the tacking stitches. Make no back-stitches except in beginning and fastening off, and be careful to show on the top of the tuck a row of neat and even stitches.

PIPING

Piping is used for strengthening the neck and armholes of outer garments as overalls and frocks; also for trimming purposes.

For piping use a piece of cotton cord or fine string if proper piping cord cannot be procured. String does not look so well, as it is too stiff. The cord must be inserted in strips of material generally cut on the cross or bias (see p. 434). Measure from the cross-way edges one and one-eighth inches and cut strips along them until you have the length required for the piping. When one strip is cut it is quicker and surer to put it down again on the material cross edges to cross edges, and to cut the other strips from it. Stitch the pieces together a little more than an eighth of an inch from the top, then open out the seams and flatten them well. Be careful to stitch all the joins on the wrong side of the material. Any scraps of the material may be used for the strips, only be very careful to cut them of equal width.

When the strip is the proper length, turn down three-eighth of an inch on the wrong side of the material without stretching the work. Crease well down, then lift up the fold and place the cord along the crease. Turn the fold down

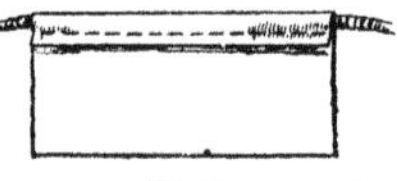
FIG. 14.

again and tack along through both thicknesses of material (fig. 14). The tacking stitches require to be smaller than ordinary tacking stitches. Place the narrow edge of the piping exactly on to the raw edge of the right side of garment and tack carefully through the three thicknesses of material. Run and back-stitch quite close to the cord, but be careful not to put the needle through it (fig. 15). Take out the tacking threads and cut the cords the required length. Turn over and press carefully so that the cord stands out along the top. Then fell the edge of the piping on to the material.

When the piping has to come in the middle of two thicknesses of material, as at the foot of a lined yoke, the cross-way strips of material should be cut three-quarters to one inch wide. Then fold in two and put in the cord as before. The piping must be placed first to the right side

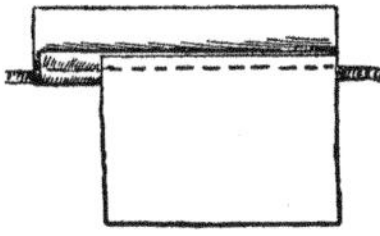

FIG. 15.

of the garment with the uppermost edges exactly even; then the bottom of the yoke on the top with the edge uppermost and even with the other two edges, so that the piping is between the garment and the yoke. Tack in position, then stitch through all thicknesses close to the cord. Then turn up the yoke, and hem down the yoke lining over all the raw edges on the wrong side of the garment.

Piping can be used to draw the tops of frills and flounces. A crease should be made where the material has to be drawn, the cord placed inside on the wrong side of the garment, then secured with running on the right side. When the running is done, hold the left-side end of the cord in your left hand and slip the material gently along with the thumb and forefinger of your right hand. Several rows of this piping and drawing make a very effective trimming.

GATHERING, STROKING, AND SETTING IN

Gathering stitches resemble running stitches, only in gathering you leave more threads than you take up, so as to make the gathers deeper and easier to keep in order and to give a fluted and grooved effect. You may take up two threads and miss four, or take four and miss six, according to the amount of material that has to be gathered into a given space. Gathering is worked on the right side of the material across the selvedge. It must be done very evenly. The cotton used in gathering should be coarser than the one used for ordinary sewing. Do not double the cotton, as it is apt to twist and knot, and if one thread breaks it looks untidy. The material gathered should as a rule be at least half as wide again as the band or yoke into which it is required to fit. Find the middle of the material and mark it with a pin or stitched cross. Divide again into quarters and mark them. Turn down the top edge a quarter of an inch, crease it well down, and then open it. The gathering stitches must be made along the crease. Begin the gathering at the right-hand side. If there are hems on the sides, leave them perfectly flat and never gather over them. When the end is finished, unthread the needle and make a knot in the thread. If the material to be gathered is wide and requires several gathering threads, begin those where the halves and quarters are marked. Begin and end each time as directed.

Place a pin at the end of the gathers and also before each new thread, with the point to the top edge. Hold the thread in your left hand and draw the gathers to the right with the right hand, leaving them slightly loose. Twist the cotton round the top and bottom of the pin about three or four times. The work is now ready for stroking.

Stroking.—Stroking is the placing of all the gathers evenly side by side. Hold the work in the left hand, the right side of the material towards you, and begin at the left side and work towards the right. It will be found easier to pin the right-hand side of the work on to a lead cushion (see fig. 16). Use a wool needle, as this will not scratch the material. Hold the

FIG. 16.

needle in your right hand slantingly, the point upwards. Raise each gather gently with the point of the needle and stroke down into the little ruck which lies between, moving it gently to the left. Hold the gathers firmly under your left thumb until they are all stroked. The top part above the gathering threads should be stroked in the same way.

Setting In.—Take the band or piece of material into which the gatherings have to be set, divide it into halves and quarters and mark as on the gathered part. Undo the gathering threads from the pins. Place the folded edge of the band exactly over the gathering thread and pin together the halves and quarters respectively. Loosen the gathers exactly to the size of the band and fasten the gathering threads again to the pins. Arrange the gathers evenly below the band with the point of the needle, putting in more pins if necessary and tack in position. Hem neatly, taking up each of the gathers on the needle. When all the gathers are set in take out the pins, thread each gathering thread and finish it off, passing it through to the wrong side and making two or three double stitches. Then turn over the work. Tack down the wrong side of the band exactly

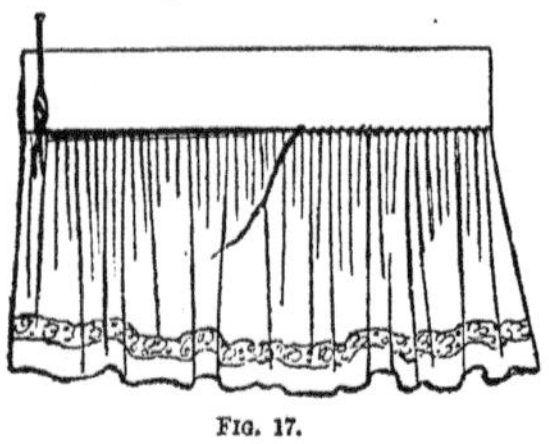

FIG. 17.

on the hemming stitches. Fell it, being very careful that the stitches do not show through on the right side.

When the band is stitched by hand it should be stitched after the first side of gathers are set in two or three threads above the gathers, and the felling done afterwards. A thread might be drawn previously where the stitching is to be worked.

If the stitching is done by machine it should be done through the whole band after it has been felled.

WHIPPING

Whipping is used principally for the gathering up of lace frills or for frills made of very fine material such as muslin or cambric. It is also used instead of hemming on the raw edges of very fine frills. These should be cut by the thread or torn across the selvedge. The width of the frill will depend upon the purpose for which it is to be used: for ordinary underclothing it should be from an inch to two inches deep. The length should be twice that of the hem or band to be trimmed, or even longer if the material of the frill is very fine, if the frill is deep, or there are corners to be turned. Make a hem as narrow as possible at the foot of the frill; or it may be hem-stitched. If several widths of material are required for the frill, seam them neatly together before beginning. If the frill is to be round as for a wrist-band, join the ends before beginning to whip. Divide the frill and the band on which it has to be gathered into halves or quarters according to length. Take a rather coarse cotton and a fresh needleful for each section of the frill. To whip the frill hold it as for hemming the top. To start it turn a very tiny hem down and work two or three hemming stitches. Hold the material between the thumb and forefinger of your left hand, keep the forefinger quite still, let the frill rest on it, and rub the thumb up and down so as to roll down the top raw edge, making a very tight and very neat roll.

When you have rolled down an inch insert the needle at the back of the roll very close to it, the point towards you slanting towards the left. The stitches should be slanting on the wrong side and straight on the right side (fig. 18). Put the needle

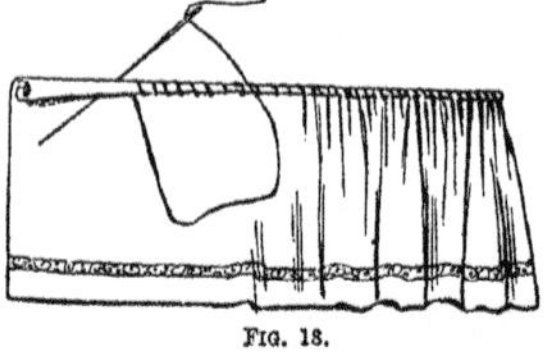

FIG. 18.

through one thickness only and never through the roll, or the cotton would not draw easily. The stitches must be very neat and regular, about one-eighth inch apart. Whip the inch prepared, and then roll another inch, and so on, drawing it up slightly as you go along. When the frill is whipped pin the halves, quarters, &c., on to the band exactly as for setting in gathers, the top right-hand side of the band against the top right side of the frill, holding the wrong side of the frill towards you. Secure the end of the whipping thread of the frill by twisting it round a pin as for gathering, and arrange the fulness evenly.

To sew the frill on the band begin at the right-hand side with two or three seaming stitches, then put the needle at the back, taking the smallest possible amount of the band and bring it out in front passing under the middle of each little roll. Each seaming stitch must be exactly on the whipping stitch of the roll (fig. 19). At

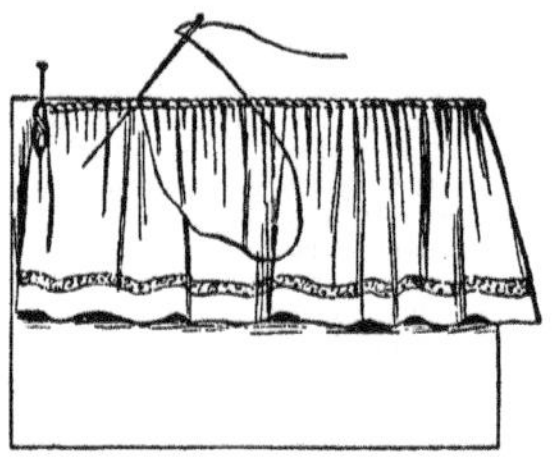

FIG. 19.

the end fasten off as in seaming. Finish off and cut off the whipping cotton. Raise up the frill on the right side and flatten the seam well with the thumb-nail.

FANCY STITCHES

Herring-boning.—So called because it is supposed to resemble the back-bone of a herring. This stitch is used principally for flannel seams (see p. 393) and for the seams of patches (see p. 415). It is a good plan to practise it first on a piece of canvas with coloured cotton or wool. To herring-bone a flannel hem begin at the left-hand side, hold the work as for hemming, and work from left to right. Put the needle under the fold close to the edge, bring it out on the top, and make one double-stitch. Then from the hole where the cotton comes out count four threads down (or their equivalent) and four to the right; insert the needle in the fourth and bring it out horizontally two threads to the left. Then from the hole where the cotton comes out count four threads up and four to the right, and again insert the needle and bring it out horizontally two threads to the left. The needle must always be held horizontally, and each stitch consist of two threads taken towards the left, which shows a double row of small running stitches on the other side. Finish off neatly. Keep the cotton well behind the needle and do not allow it to pass under the point. The stitches must lie smoothly without puckering the material. It is not easy to count the threads in flannel, but if the size of the stitches has been learnt on canvas it will be easy to keep them regular with a little care and practice.

Feather and Coral Stitching.—Feather and coral stitches are used to ornament both flannel and cotton garments. They are often worked in the centre of a narrow band, on both edges of a wider one, along a hem, or between tucks. For cotton goods use crochet cotton, coarse or fine,

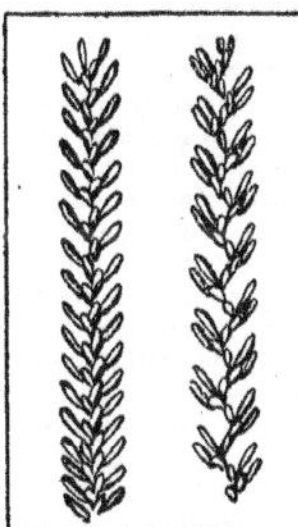
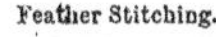

Feather Stitching.

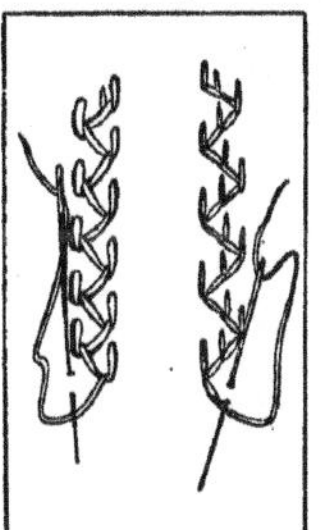

Coral Stitching.

according to the nature of the work. For flannel use flax thread or flannel silk. Work with a crewel needle.

The great point in both kinds of stitches is to make them very regular and to keep the middle rib on a straight line. As it is impossible to count the threads, a little practice is necessary to make the stitches regular. When making the stitches on the front of a garment always work downwards, and if there are several lines of feathering begin them all at the top, so that all the stitches lie in the same direction.

Single Feather Stitch.—Take the threaded needle and secure the end of the cotton by making two or three stitches in a seam at the back of the work where they won't be seen, then slip the needle through the front ready to begin the stitches. Hold the cotton under the left thumb; insert the needle a little distance to the right-hand side a very little higher than the place where the cotton comes out, slanting it to the left; bring it out a little below the place it was brought out before; be very careful to pass the point of the needle over the cotton held by the left thumb. This makes a little "**V**" towards the right caught at the foot.

Again hold the cotton under the left thumb, turn the needle to the right-hand side this time, and insert it as far again from the middle rib as it was inserted before to the right; slant it towards the right, and bring it out in the middle rib a little below the preceding stitch, being always careful to pass the point over the cotton held by the left thumb. This makes a little "V" towards the left also caught at the foot.

Repeat this, making a slanting stitch towards the right, then towards the left alternately, until you have the length required.

To finish off pass the needle and cotton to the wrong side close to the place it came out, being careful to catch the loop, and cut off close to the work. Be careful not to draw the cotton too tightly or it will pucker the material; it should rather be left somewhat loose to allow for shrinkage in the washing.

The Double Feather Stitch is so called because it consists of two stitches worked one below the other to the right, then two to the left of the middle rib. It is very effective and less stiff in appearance than single feather stitching.

The Treble Feather Stitch consists of three stitches worked one below the other, first to the right and then to the left alternately; it is rather more elaborate than the other kinds of feather stitching, but very pretty, especially worked in fine stitches on the top of a chemise or on the knee-band of drawers, &c. As the middle rib in both double and treble feather stitches curves somewhat right and left with each group of little stitches, care must be taken to make these curves very regular.

The Coral Stitch resembles feather stitch; in fact, one is often mistaken for the other, although they are worked in a different way.

Single Coral Stitch.—Use the same cotton, silk, needle, &c., as for feather stitching. Hold the needle straight down instead of slanting it either to the right or to the left. Bring out the needle to the front of the work and hold the cotton with the left thumb as before. Insert the needle a little to the right exactly on a line with the hole where it came out, and take a few threads straight down on a vertical line. Pass the point of the needle over the cotton held by the left thumb.

Again hold the cotton under the left thumb and insert the needle a little to the left exactly on a horizontal line from where it came out; take the same number of threads straight down on a vertical line and bring up the point of the needle over the cotton held by the left thumb, and repeat this working from right to the left until the length required is finished.

The Double Coral Stitch is worked in very much the same way as single coral stitch; only two stitches are made towards the right, then two towards the left, and so on. The needle is inserted a little more slantingly towards the left and the right than in the single coral stitch.

Blanket Stitch.—The blanket stitch, also called loop stitch, is a kind of button-hole stitch worked on the ends of blankets to prevent their unravelling and to give them a more finished appearance.

Turn down the raw edge of the blanket a little way and tack it very flat with a needle and cotton. A selvedge will not require to be turned down. The stitch may be worked in bright red, pale blue, or any pretty coloured wool.

There are several different patterns of blanket stitch which can be varied according to taste. To work the ordinary blanket stitch (fig. 20) begin at

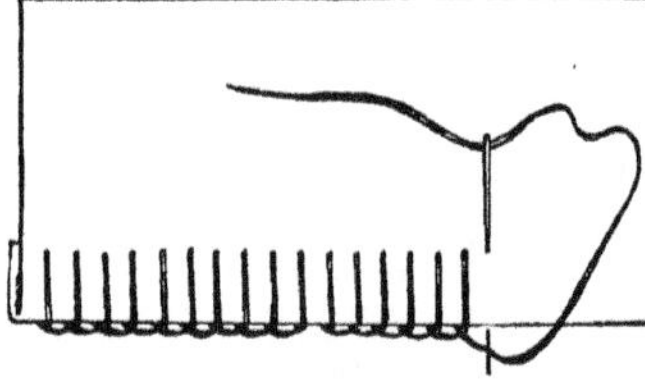

Fig. 20.

the left-hand corner and hold the work with the right side uppermost. Bring the needle through from the back to the front about half an inch from the edge or above the fold. Insert it again a quarter of an inch to the right, holding it vertically downwards, and slip the point over the wool. The needle and wool should be drawn straight downwards, but not too tightly, and so as to make a nice ridge of stitches along the bottom. Again insert the needle one quarter of an inch to the right of the previous stitch and bring it vertically down through the loop, and so on.

To turn corners, make three stitches (or five if necessary) quite close to each other at the top, and a quarter of an inch apart from each other at the foot.

Other blanket stitches can be made by varying the length of the stitches and giving them

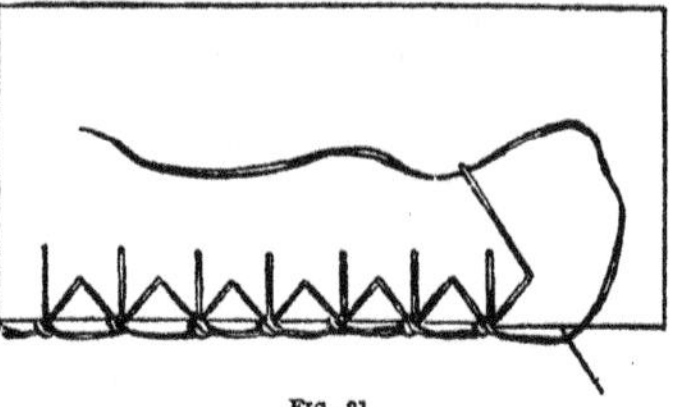

Fig. 21.

different slopes, as in fig. 21. This is a little more fanciful in appearance.

A Scallop Edge.—Scalloping may be used on a hem or as an edging for flannel garments. The stitch is generally worked on double material, as at the edge of a hem or false hem, but when used as a trimming only, as in a flannel frill, single material is sufficient. The scallops may be cut in cardboard (three or four together), placed at the edge of the material and traced lightly in pencil. A better and simpler plan is to use a transfer pattern and iron it on to the garment. Test a little piece of the transfer on an odd piece of the material to see if the iron is properly heated, and then be careful to pin it in a straight line on the garment about a quarter of an inch from the edge. The scalloping stitch is made in the same way as the blanket stitch, and should be worked with flax thread, washing silk, or fine well-twisted wool.

To begin with, run along the two edges of the scallops with ordinary embroidery cotton to outline the pattern. Thread a crewel needle with the thread or silk you have chosen; make five or six running stitches from right to left in the first scallop on the left to fasten in the end and bring out the needle at the left-hand point. Hold your thread or silk down under the left thumb; put the needle in just above the top row of tacking stitches, bring it out just below the bottom row of tacking stitches with the point above the thread. Draw the needle and thread through downwards, and see that the knot rests exactly at the foot of the scallop. Make the next stitch close to the first in the same way. The needle must be held perpendicularly with the point towards you, and as the bottom part of the scallop is wider than the top, the stitches must slant very slightly to the left to begin with, be straight in the middle, then slant very slightly to the right. A nice improvement is to work a spot in the centre of each scallop (fig. 22). This pattern can be found in transfers, or it is easy to mark a dot above each scallop and make it the centre of a tiny ring. These spots are worked in what is called satin stitch, sewing across in straight stitches. Commence with a small stitch at the side, increase towards the

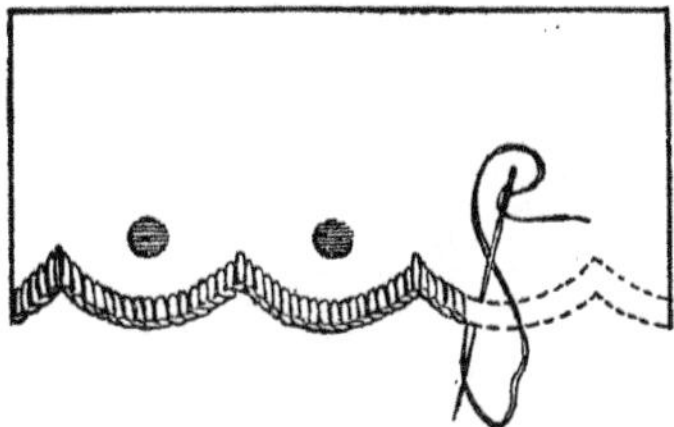

FIG. 22.

middle, and then decrease to the end. Slip the needle at the back through the stitches, make a very small back-stitch and cut off.

Another way of working a narrow scallop is to keep the top of the stitches in a straight line, as in fig. 23, the length of the stitches being graduated from very short at the corners to wide

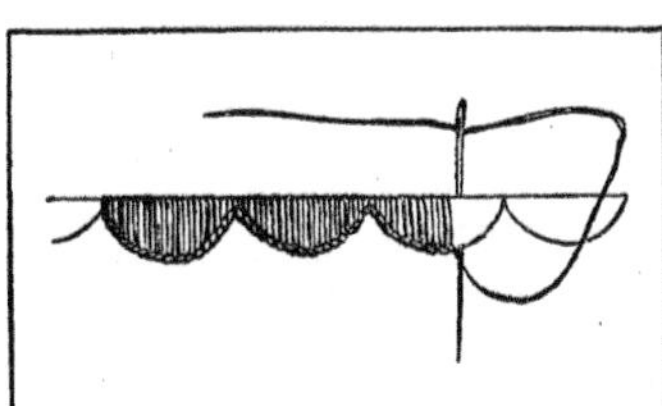

FIG. 23.

in the middle. All the stitches should lie vertically. If the scallop is wished thicker it may be padded before the embroidery is commenced. Make several chain stitches along the centre of them, a single one at the ends and two or three longer ones in the centre.

Hem-Stitching.—Hem-stitching is used in many cases instead of the ordinary hemming; it makes a very pretty trimming and is easily learnt. It can be done on any material from which the threads are easily drawn. Pocket-handkerchiefs, sheets, tea-cloths, &c., are all much prettier when finished with a hem-stitched edge. The width of the hem varies according to taste and the nature of the article being worked upon.

Before beginning to hem-stitch see that the edges of the material are perfectly straight. When you have decided upon the width of the hem, measure double that width from the edge of the material, plus a little more for turning in, and draw out four threads as explained for stitching (pp. 390–91). When the threads are drawn, lay the hem very carefully and tack it exactly where the first thread has been drawn out. In a square article tack down the two opposite sides first, then the other two sides.

A hem-stitch can be worked either from the right or from the left-hand end of the hem. If you begin at the right-hand end, insert the needle under the fold and take two threads of

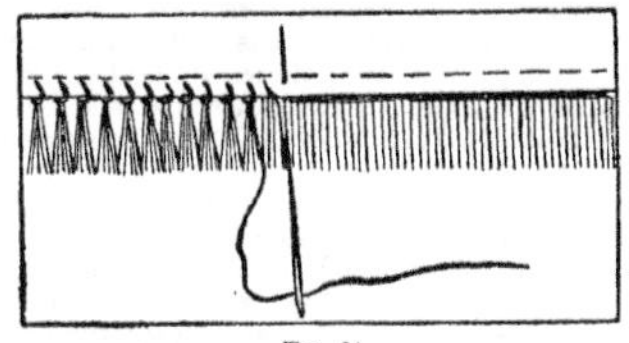

FIG. 24.

the material and slip the end of the cotton well under the fold. Hold the needle in a horizontal position, take up four of the loose threads on it, and draw the cotton through. Then put the needle again into the fold two threads up, holding it slantingly, the point towards the left (fig. 25). Again hold the needle horizontally, take four threads, and so on.

Be careful to draw the cotton rather tightly when holding the four threads so as to draw them well together; also do not pass over any loose threads.

Be careful at the corners where the loose threads are double to take eight threads on the needle, *i.e.* four on the wrong and four on the right side, and draw them well in so that the stitches do not appear larger. Seam the edge, and slip the needle through in position to begin the next hem.

When hem-stitching is worked from left to right bring out the needle and cotton in the fold

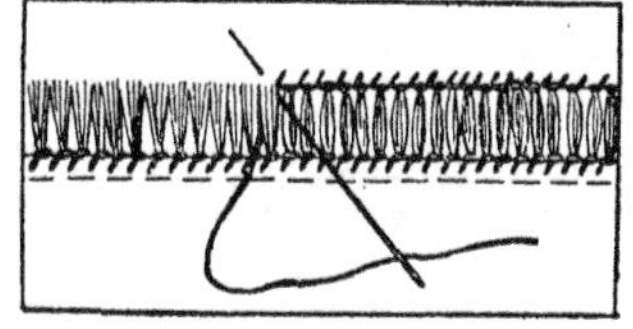

FIG. 25.

two threads up, then hold the needle horizontally and take up four of the loose threads towards the right. Hold the cotton under the left thumb, bring the needle back, and insert it in the space of open threads and bring it through two threads of the fold, holding it vertically, the point up, and so on (fig. 24). If there are more than four threads drawn, a second row of hem-stitching may be worked at the other side of the open space by turning the work upside down (fig. 25).

FASTENINGS

To Sew on Buttons.—Pearl buttons are much prettier for underlinen, but unfortunately they cannot bear the pressure of the mangle or wringer and are generally crushed under the weight of the machine. It is better, therefore, to sew linen buttons on all articles that undergo frequent washing. Linen buttons should be of the best quality or they will soon be crushed out of shape.

Before sewing on any kind of button make a back-stitch on the right side of the garment to secure the cotton, as a knot is not permissible.

Buttons should always be sewn on double material, so, if necessary, strengthen the place where the button has to come with a piece of tape on the wrong side, or a little square of the same material neatly felled on the wrong side.

It is a mistake to take very thick cotton for sewing on buttons, as it makes the beginnings

Pearl Buttons.

and fastenings off untidy, and the middle of the button too bulky.

If the button has two holes in it slip the needle in one of these, take the stitches through from hole to hole and through the thickness of the garment four to six times, then slip the needle between the garment and the button close to the middle, and "stem" the button, *i.e.* wind the cotton round and round four or five times, slip the needle to the back, make one or two back-stitches, slip the needle through half an inch of the thickness, and cut the cotton close.

Buttons with four holes can be sewn in different ways, as shown in the above diagram.

Linen buttons without holes can also be sewn on in a variety of styles as shown below. (1) By working stitches in a small circle. In order to get a perfect circle, the centre of the

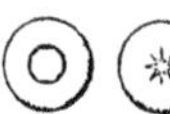

Linen Buttons.

button may be marked with the hollow end of a small key or anything that will serve the purpose. Prick round the circle with a needle to mark the place of the stitches, then sew round with small even stitches. The circle must be small so that the button-hole can lie very flat over the button. (2) The circle may have a cross in the middle. (3) A star can be made in the middle by working six or eight stitches all meeting in the centre. (4) Or, again, a horizontal bar of four or five stitches worked over in button-hole stitch like a loop. The last method is a very strong and secure way of putting on a linen button.

It is very important that a button should be sewn on exactly in its proper position. If the exact spot is not otherwise marked, place the button-hole side of the garment very evenly on the top of the corresponding button side and stick a pin through the hole. Then slip the button-hole carefully over the pin, put the pin in more securely, and sew on the button in the place indicated.

Button-holes.—It requires great skill and attention to make button-holes well. They should be worked on double material. If the material is single, strengthen it on the back with a neatly felled oblong of the same material, which should not be seen on the right side. All button-holes are cut in the same way. A pair of button-hole scissors may be used, although they are not a necessity. The slit of the button-hole should be a little longer than the diameter of the button to allow it to pass through easily. The best way to cut a button-hole is to make a crease in the material at the place it is to be made; insert the point of the scissors on the mark and cut very slowly and carefully the length required. Try to keep by the thread of the material, and be careful the scissors do not slip.

Use coarser cotton for button-holes than for ordinary sewing. For flannel or woollen materials use silk twist if possible; it makes a strong and pretty stitch.

Button-holes are made with two barred ends when they are in front of a chemise, night-dress,

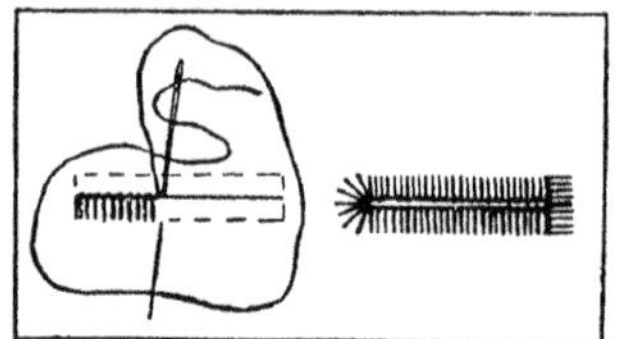

Button-holes.

shirt, &c., and with one round end and one barred at the end of a band for a dress, &c. In the latter case the round end comes against the button. Sometimes the holes are made with two round ends, but this is not so usual.

To work a button-hole some people begin by making either a line of small running stitches round it to prevent the edges from unravelling, or making one or two long stitches the length of the button-hole and working over these, but a little experience in button-hole making will render this preparation unnecessary. Sufficient cotton must be taken to work from end to end, as there must be no join in the sides of a button-hole. The cotton may be joined at a barred end but not at a round one.

To begin with, slip the needle between the two thicknesses of material, bring it out at the left-hand end of the button-hole four threads down from the cut edge. Draw the cotton through, leaving an end of an inch which can be caught in with the stitches. Work from left to right. Hold the opening of the button-hole over the left forefinger, insert the needle at the back and bring it half-way through to the front and through the same hole as before. With the thumb and forefinger of your right hand bring the double cotton from the eye of the needle, and pass it under the point from left to right; draw the needle out, pull the cotton upwards away from you, and tighten the little knot or loop which must lie exactly on the cut edge. This forms what is called a purl edge. Work the next stitch one or two threads to the right and again four threads down, bring the thread over the needle and repeat until you have reached the end of the hole. To make a barred end put the needle in at the bottom of the last side stitch and "strand" the ends, *i.e.* put two or three threads of cotton across to make the foundation of the bar. As the button-hole stitches are made four threads deep, you have eight threads on the two sides, plus one in the middle (the fifth) corresponding to the slit of the button-hole. The bar consists then of nine button-hole stitches, worked with the knots meeting those of the sides. These nine button-hole stitches must be worked through the two thicknesses of material like the side stitches. Then turn the work the opposite way, work the second side like the first, and, if necessary, make a bar at the other end.

To finish off insert the needle at the top in the hole of the last stitch; draw the cotton through to the wrong side, weave along the button-hole stitches, and cut the end close to the work.

To make a round end the stitches must be made in a semicircle close together, and radiating like the spokes of a wheel.

To Mend a Button-hole.—Cut off very carefully all that is left of the knots in the centre; draw out any little threads that come out easily without unravelling the material more than is necessary. If many threads come out, overcast the button-hole with fine cotton, then work it all over again with the same cotton or silk as was first used. As a rule, it is better to remake the barred ends; the general appearance of the button-hole will be neater.

Hooks and Eyes can be attached to garments in different ways; the most essential point is to put them on very neatly and securely. The positions will vary according to the make and fashion of the dress; the best way of sewing them on is as follows:—Use button-hole twist or cotton to match the colour of the material. Find the position of the hook and make a small stitch where it has to be put. Hold the hook in position with your left thumb and work round the two rings and through the material with close blanket stitches and then make several seaming stitches over the stem. Finish off with a back-stitch close to the hook, slip the needle through the material without showing it on the right side, and cut the cotton off close.

To sew on the eye mark its position exactly opposite the hook. Begin in the same way, and work round the two rings with blanket stitches, taking the stitches through the material. When both rings are covered and fastened on the material, blanket stitch the eye itself without going through the material.

The object of so covering the hook and eye with blanket stitches is to make them look neat and also to prevent them from coming unfastened so easily.

When the rings of the hooks and eyes are to be covered with lining or other material, it is

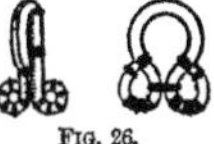
Fig. 26.

Fig. 27.

unnecessary to work them round with stitches. In this case it suffices to fasten them on very securely by making four or five stitches round each ring and two or three along the stem as in fig. 26. For the eye, make about four or five stitches at the foot of each ring, one where the two rings join and two or three at the sides. Finish off as before.

The hook is sometimes put with the tongue against the material and the back uppermost, as this is supposed to make a more secure fastening. Work two or three close seam stitches at the foot of each ring, two or three where the rings are joined together, and fasten off as before (fig. 28).

Little round rings are sometimes used instead of eyes. These should be fastened to the garment with four or five blanket stitches taken through the material, and then the rest of the ring is covered with blanket stitches.

Patent hooks are provided with little holes. Sew them on by making three or four stitches in each hole through at least two thicknesses of the material. Then three or four stitches quite at the point round the back of the thinnest part of the hook. Patent eyes are sewn on with three or four stitches taken from ring to ring

FIG. 28.

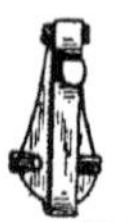

FIG. 29.

and through at least two thicknesses of material (fig. 29).

Eyelet Holes are used as outlets for a draw-string in an under-garment, in the neck of a pinafore, or in the neck and sleeves of infants' garments, &c. They are also used in dress-making instead of eyes, in which case they should be worked in silk, or, preferably, twist the colour of the material. Eyelets made as an outlet for a string in the neck of a garment should be made an inch apart in front of the garment if the neck is round. If divided in front or at the back, one eyelet should be made on the upper side of the garment half an inch from the left-side edge through the single material only; the other eyelet should be made on the wrong side of the garment half an inch from the right-side edge and through the single material only. Or, the string may be allowed to come out at the right-hand side, through the edge of the hem or the casing, when only the one eyelet hole will be required. When the place of the eyelet hole has been determined, pierce a hole with a stiletto or with the end of a small pair of scissors.

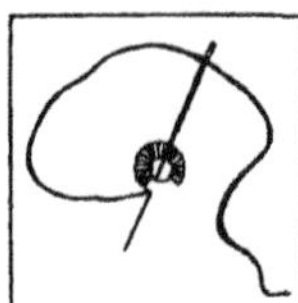

Eyelet Hole.

Do this through one or two thicknesses according to the purpose of the eyelet holes. Slip the needle with cotton or silk under the first thickness of material, and hide the end of the latter by pushing it in with the point of the needle. Then work from left to right over the raw edges of the hole with very neat and close overcasting stitches about four threads deep. When you have worked all round, run the needle and cotton through the stitches at the back and cut off close to the work. Button-hole stitches can be made instead of overcasting stitches, the knots or loops being brought to the inside edge of the eyelet.

A Loop can be made in conjunction with a hook instead of an eye, or with a button instead of a button-hole. When you have found the

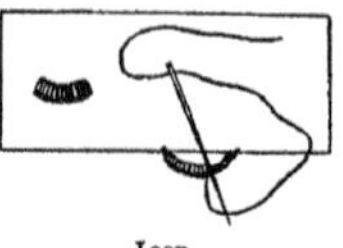

Loop.

place of the loop, pass the needle and cotton or silk through the double material, work about four stitches or strands about one-quarter of an inch long, then bind the strands together, working from left to right with close blanket stitches over the cotton or silk only. When the loop is intended for a button, it is generally put at the edge of the garment. Make the strands loose enough to receive the button; on no account must they be too long.

TAPES, BINDING, ETC.

Tapes.—Tapes are made in both cotton or linen, the linen being stronger than the cotton. They are to be had in various widths, and the size chosen depends upon the purpose for which the tape is to be used. Tapes are used as strings on aprons, children's pinafores, and various under-garments, &c., as loops for hanging towels, kitchen cloths, &c., and also for strengthening purposes.

Strings.—These must be sewn on perfectly flat. Turn down about one-eighth of an inch at one end of the string and make a second fold as far from the first as the tape is wide, but turned the other way. This second fold is to mark a little square where the stitches should be worked on the tape. Place the string on the edge of the wrong side of the material with the narrow fold downwards, and the second crease just meeting the edge of the material. Pin the string in position, fold it back from the edge of the material and on a level with it. Hold the string and material together very securely between your left thumb and forefinger, and seam the tape on to the material with very small stitches. Then turn back the string and fell neatly the three other sides on to the material. If the material is double, the stitches should not show through.

The free ends of strings should have a neat one-eighth inch hem on the wrong side, or the end can be made neat with blanket stitches taken rather deeply to prevent the tape from unravelling.

Another way of sewing on a string to a hemmed end is to place the narrow fold of the string two threads above the hem and work two neat rows of stitching on the right side of the material, one just above the hemming through the edge of the tape, and another at the edge of the hem through the hem and the tape. Fell the selvedge sides of the string without showing the stitches through on the right side.

When tapes are sewn at the edge of a hem, the first fold can be inserted under the hem in its proper place and tacked along the hem. The two selvedge sides of the string should be felled, and the stitching on the fourth side may be worked either on the edge of the hem on the right side, or further down if the hem is deep and if the edge is required to overlap the other side.

Loops.—To make a loop, measure the length of tape required and fold it in two. Turn in the raw edges and put one end in its place, either at the edge of the hem or to make a square. Fell round three sides (the two selvedges of the tape and the folded end), but do not finish off. Place the other end of the loop on the right side of the material and slip the needle through and fell three sides of the tape on the right side exactly on top of the stitches on the wrong side. Make a row of stitching through both tapes just above the edge of the material and finish off (fig. 30).

Another way is to sew the loop on the wrong side of the material. Fold the tape in two,

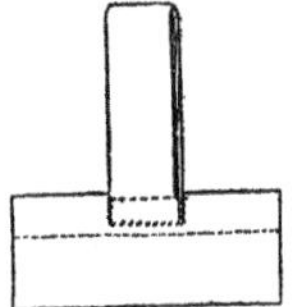
FIG. 30.

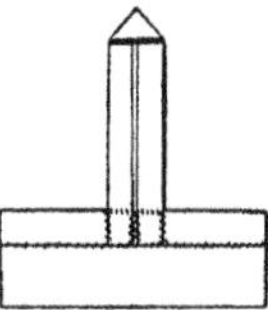
FIG. 31.

crease well, and open it again. Place the two ends side by side as in fig. 31, so as to form a three-cornered point. Prepare and sew the loops as before, either inserting them under the hem or felling them above. Notice that as the ends of the tape lie side by side you must sew them together when you have reached the middle, cross neatly under these stitches when you have come to the top and go on with the felling. Stitch or seam both tapes at the edge of the material.

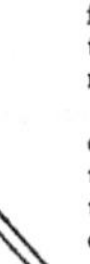
FIG. 32.

If the loop is sewn at the corner of a cloth the ends are turned down once only, and the loop placed so that the edge of the turning down should meet the hem (fig. 32). The point of the corner must be exactly at the joining of the two loops. Fell and seam the loop as before. Another method for a corner loop is to double the tape obliquely and place the ends so that they overlap each other. Place the raw edges uppermost, meeting the edge of the cloth and forming the basis of a triangle. Stitch firmly

FIG. 33.

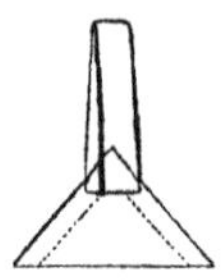
FIG. 34.

across both, then turn over and stitch round the corner (figs. 33 and 34).

Strengthening Tapes are used at the bottom of front openings of chemises and night-dresses, at the wrist openings of sleeves, and the hip openings of children's knickers, &c., to prevent them from getting torn. The strength and width will depend upon the garment and material on which it has to be sewn. To put on a strengthening tape at the foot of the opening of a chemise or night-dress cut a piece of tape one to one and a half inches long, and make a fold at the two raw ends. Place this at the bottom of the opening on the wrong side of the garment with the folds facing the material. Fell it neatly along the four sides without showing the stitches on the right side. For the wrist opening of a shirt or for children's knickers turn down a fold at the end of the tape, but on different sides. Fold the tape obliquely in the middle; this will bring the narrow folds on the same side. Place the tape on the wrong side of the garment, the folds facing the material, with the oblique fold exactly over the end of the opening. Pin in position, then tack, being very careful to keep the end folds on the thread of the material. Hem all round the edges of the tape,

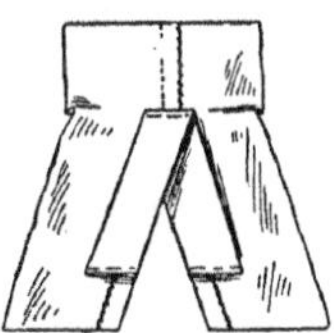
FIG. 35.

and at the edge of the opening work a few button-hole stitches for the sake of strength. If the material is double be very careful not to show the stitches on the right side (fig. 35).

Binding. — Binding is a process used to strengthen the edges of material by sewing a covering over them. This covering may consist of a strip of the material, or of tape, braid, ribbon, or a special binding. Flannel garments are frequently bound at the edges instead of being hemmed, tape, ribbon or Prussian binding being used. In tailoring the seams of coats and jackets are very often covered with a binding. In dressmaking, too, the raw edges of the material are often finished with Prussian binding or ribbon instead of being overcast. Binding can also be used instead of overcasting to strengthen the armholes of shirts, blouses, night-dresses, and such-like, when a piece of thin material cut on the cross should be used.

To sew on braid or ribbon binding fold it lengthways, crease it well along the middle, lay it over the edge of the material to be bound, one half to the right side and one half to the wrong, and tack it carefully in position with a needle and cotton. Hem first the right side, and then the wrong side. Some people can manage to hem only once on the right side and through the three thicknesses, but it is not to be recommended, as it is very difficult to make the stitches neat and to bring them through regularly. This can, however, be done with a sewing machine. To bind with the same material as the garment, cut and prepare the strips as for piping (see p. 394). The strips of material may be cut on the straight to bind a part that is on the straight also, but never to bind a part that is on the cross or slanting in the least, as it would be sure to pucker. They should be from a half to one inch in width, according to the thickness of the material to be covered. Fold them lengthways like the braid and make a crease; then for the first part, proceed as for putting on a false hem (see p. 393). Place the edge of the binding against the edge of the material on the right side and run it along about a quarter of an inch from the edge. Then turn it upwards, and flatten the seam well; fold it down at the crease, and fell it neatly on the wrong side. When there is a corner to bind round, make a small pleat in the binding on each side of the material at right angles with it; hem the fold of the binding in a neat diagonal line going from the inside angle of the hem to the outside angle of the material; slip the needle under the binding back to the hem, and continue hemming. Do the same at all the corners and on both sides of the work.

To Braid a Skirt.—Before using skirt braid it is a good precaution to soak it in cold water and allow it to shrink. This often prevents the foot of the skirt from puckering. It you do not care to do this, be careful to leave the braid looser than the material, as it is sure to draw in when moistened by rain or the dampness of the roads. If the ordinary flat braid is being used, fold it double and run or hem it on the wrong side of the skirt, placing it so that it shows below the edge of the skirt and so serves as a protection to the material. The stitches should be taken through both selvedges of the braid and one thickness of the material, but should not show on the right side. Or, instead of doubling the braid, it may be sewn singly and flat on the skirt, a small edge of one selvedge being allowed to show below the foot of the skirt. In this case two rows of sewing will be necessary—a row of hemming along the lower selvedge and a row of running worked through the braid and one thickness of the material close to the edge of the skirt. None of the stitches must be allowed to show on the right side. Brush braids must always be sewn on by the latter method.

PLEATING

To pleat material is to make it lie in flat, smooth folds, more or less deep according to the fulness required.

Pleating is extensively used in dressmaking at the top of skirts and in the arranging of frills and flounces. It is also used at the top of petticoats, aprons, overalls, children's frocks, &c. It is more suitable than gathering for thick material as it is less bulky.

Pleats like tucks should be arranged on the right side of the material and they must be very accurately measured. They are generally held in position by a band or yoke, or by a row of stitching as in a frill or flounce.

There are two kinds of pleating:—Kilt-pleating and box-pleating.

Kilt-Pleating.—For this kind of pleating allow material twice or three times the length of the band or piece of material to which it is to be attached.

When pleating for a flounce, the folds should all lie in one direction and be of equal size.

Kilt-Pleating.

A space may be left between the pleats if there is not sufficient fulness to allow of their being close together, but if, on the other hand, there is ample material, it may be necessary to make them overlap slightly. The size of the pleat will also depend upon the amount of material at disposal and the fulness required.

When once the size, &c., has been carefully gauged it is a good plan to make a measure by notching a card as in tuck-making, and to use that as a guide for the other pleats and spaces between them.

Tack the pleats as they are made about one-quarter of an inch from the upper edge, or if there are only a few they may be held in position with pins. Be careful to keep the material lying straight, and see that the three edges at the top are perfectly level.

In the making up of a garment pleats are often made to lie in opposite directions. They should always lie in the direction in which most fulness is needed, generally away from the front. Here, again, careful measurement is necessary in order to make both sides alike. Sometimes a pleat is stitched down part of its length so as to make it lie very flat, as in a kilted skirt.

When the pleats have to be put between the folds of a band, as on the top of an apron, make and place the band in the following way:—Fold in the edges of the band and join the ends neatly or leave them open as required. Mark the centre and pin it exactly to the centre of the garment. Tack it along in position through the one side, only making the folded edge of the band lie on the top of the tacking threads of the pleats. Then hem the band to the material, being particular to take all the stitches through all the thicknesses of the pleats.

When the right side is finished, turn over and tack the band down on the wrong side exactly on the top of the hemming stitches already made. Hem down without letting the stitches show through to the right side.

Some people prefer to stitch the band. If this is done by hand, stitch the right side only instead of hemming it two or three threads above the folded edge of the band (a thread might be drawn previously for this stitching), then hem down on the wrong side as above.

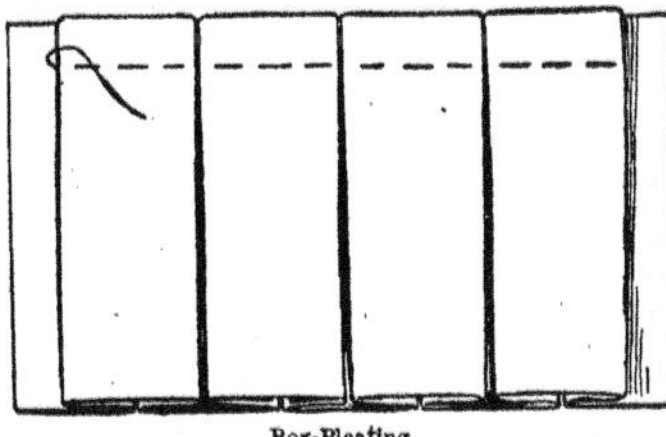

Box-Pleating.

Or the band may be stitched on by machine through the two thicknesses at once. Careful tacking will be required for this to prevent the work being twisted.

Box-Pleating.—This differs from kilt-pleating in that each alternate fold is made in a different direction. The width of the pleats may vary according to the purpose for which they are

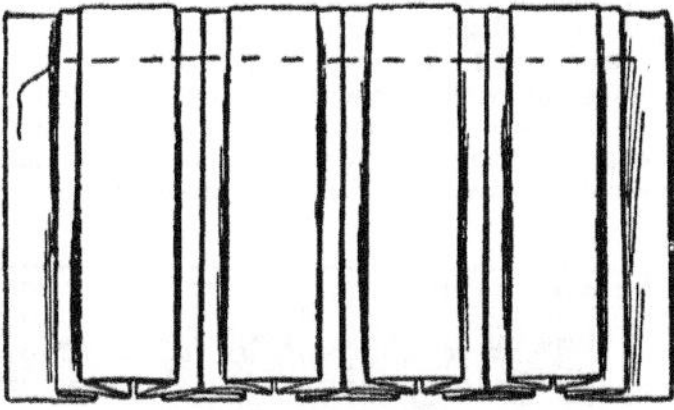

Double Box-Pleating.

used and the amount of material at disposal, but each couple must be exactly alike and careful measurement is again necessary.

Sometimes a double and even a treble box-pleat is made by laying one or more folds on the top of each other, first to one side and then to the other. Each upper fold should be slightly narrower than the one below it. A double box-pleat may be used in a very full flounce, when the pleats may be stitched half an inch from the top and the edge allowed to rise, the top being previously ended with a very narrow hem or some narrow trimming.

MARKING

In household linen the marking should be placed where it is easily seen when the article is folded, generally in the left-hand corner, unless it is embroidery, when the letter may be placed in a more conspicuous position.

Body linen is marked very much according to fashion and the style of the garment. If it is done by embroidery it should be placed where it can be seen on the front below the opening or trimming, or near the left shoulder, but if the marking is done in ink or with Cash's lettering, it should be in a less conspicuous spot, such as the inside of a band or the wrong side of a hem.

Stockings should be marked on the inside of the hem at the top or below the hem on the right side if done by hand.

There are several different ways of marking, as for instance:—

(1) Marking with ink.

(2) Marking with Cash's or other embroidered initials, monograms and names, or

(3) Marking by hand with a needle and thread.

(1) Marking with Ink is very suitable for collars and cuffs, also where there are large supplies of household linen, but it should not be employed for dainty articles (see p. 265).

(2) **Marking with Cash's Lettering.**—These can now be bought in many different designs and colouring, and special names can be ordered at so much per dozen (see p. 265). To sew them on, turn in the raw edges very evenly, tack in position, and then hem round very neatly.

Letters and monograms embroidered on fine cambric or muslin can also be bought separately. The price will vary according to the quality and design. Some of them are most elaborate and very decorative, and, if neatly placed, will have the appearance of being embroidered on the material itself.

They should either be hemmed on with very fine, almost invisible stitches, or button-holed round with fine sewing cotton.

(3) **Marking by Hand.**—For this many different stitches can be used from simple to very elaborate ones.

Cross Stitch is one of the simplest. Many years ago it was the general custom to mark personal linen, clothes, and napery with cross stitch; and we have all seen most elaborate canvas samplers with letters of the alphabet, figures, and the quaintest ornaments and mottoes, worked by our mothers and grandmothers when they were girls. In the present day there does not seem to be so much time for work of this kind, and once the stitch is learnt the letters themselves can very easily be copied from a printed design (see illustration).

Cross stitch consists of two oblique stitches placed one on the top of the other and crossed in the middle (fig. 36). It is most easily worked on a material in which the threads can be counted. If from the nature of the texture this is impossible, a piece of canvas should be tacked evenly on the top of the material where the marking is required and the stitches worked over that. The canvas must be more or less fine, according to the kind of material, and sufficiently large to take in all the letters. Blankets, for instance, would require rather a coarse canvas in order to make the letters look large and handsome, while table-linen would look better with a finer lettering. The threads of the canvas must be drawn out when the work is finished. Care must be taken when sewing that none of the stitches are taken through the threads of the canvas, but only through the holes. An expert sewer might be able to mark on any material without the aid of the canvas for a guide, but it is not so easy for an amateur.

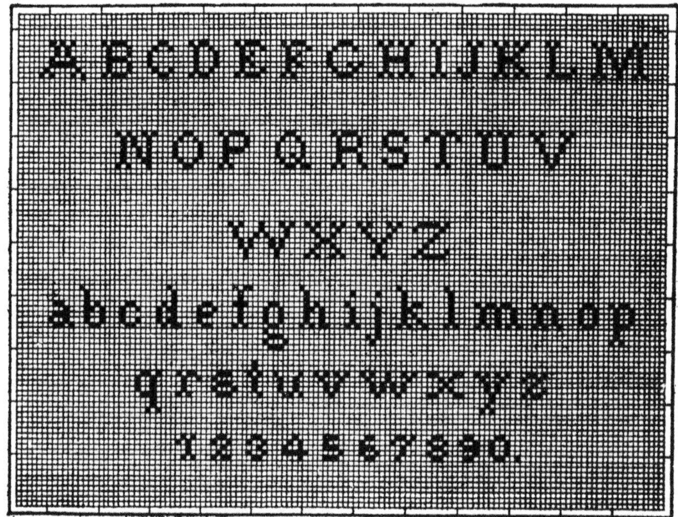

Cross-Stitch Letters and Figures.

The stitches are generally made over two

threads of the material, and care must be taken that all the stitches lie in the same direction. If larger letters are required the

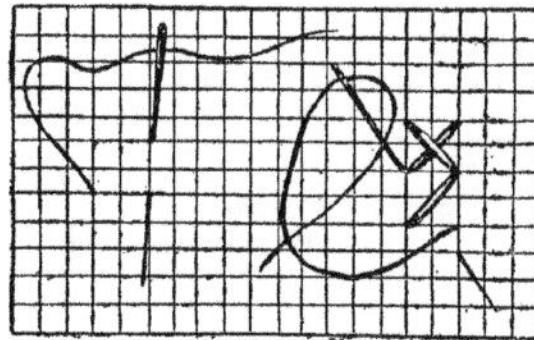

FIG. 36.

stitches must be worked over three or four threads accordingly.

To fasten off pass the needle straight through to the back and weave it through about half-a-dozen stitches. The back of the work must be kept as tidy-looking as possible.

Ingrain cotton (blue or red) or white embroidery cotton is the best to use for marking cotton or linen articles and a pretty coloured wool for marking blankets.

The Leviathan Stitch.—This is a little more elaborate than the simple cross stitch, as it has the addition of a vertical cross in the middle (fig. 37). It is most suitable for large letters or for initials.

The Eyelet Stitch.—This is another fancy stitch also used for a large style of marking. It

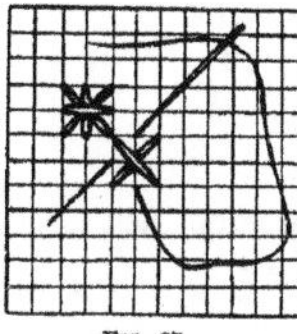

FIG. 37.

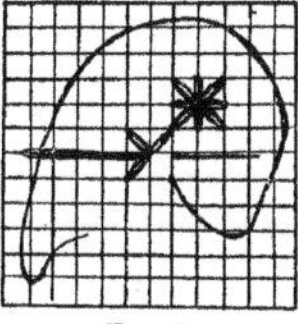

FIG. 38.

consists of eight stitches worked over two or three threads all radiating from one central hole (fig. 38).

Back Stitch and Chain Stitch are also very useful for marking, especially such articles as kitchen towels, ordinary sheets, &c., and anything that requires a whole word and several figures. The lettering can first be traced in pencil and then worked over in one or the other stitch.

Chain stitch is worked like feather or coral stitch (see p. 397), only it is done on a single line following a pattern (fig. 39). Bring out the needle at the beginning of the letter, and hold the cotton down with your left thumb. Put in the needle where it came out and bring it along the pattern the length of two or three threads; be very careful to bring it out above the cotton. Put the needle in again where it

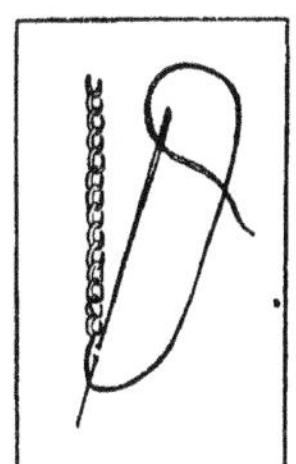

Fig. 39

came out last, bring it out the same length as before above the cotton, and so on, following the traced line so as to form the letter required. Back-stitch may be used in the same way.

These stitches are very useful for marking twill or any material where the threads cannot be counted.

MENDING

Mending, like sewing, is an art and one to which no woman should be a stranger. Though it is often considered a thankless task to have to repair an old garment damaged by accident or by use, it is none the less a necessary one, and a good piece of mending should be as worthy of exhibition as a prettily made new garment. The ability to mend skilfully and neatly is a gift every woman should covet.

A good mender means a good sewer and one who possesses plenty of common sense. Although numerous directions and rules can be given for the various methods of patching and darning, it requires some knowledge and skill to apply these—to know when it is better to put in a patch, or when a darn would be preferable; also how to make a darn that will be durable and at the same time not conspicuous, and, finally, to get the longest life possible out of each article that comes under our care.

As soon as a girl is old enough she ought to be taught to do her own mending and sometimes a little of the household mending as well. This more than anything else will teach her to be neat and orderly and to be careful with her clothes.

All holes and rents should be mended before the clothes are sent to the washing, and if it is not convenient to do this thoroughly they should at least be drawn together with needle and cotton to prevent the friction of washing making them worse. Table-linen must always be mended before washing, as mending it afterwards would crush and spoil its appearance. The same applies to anything that is starched.

When such things as buttons and tapes are wanting it is best to sew these on after washing.

A special supply of mending materials should be kept in a box in the linen cupboard, in a drawer, or in any other convenient place. It might contain pieces of linen, pieces of cotton, damask, flannel, woven material, &c., and any special material similar to the garments or household linen in use. It is a good precaution when buying clothes, especially clothes for growing children, to get a little extra material for altering and mending purposes.

There should also be a large portable mending-basket which would have to be prepared each week by the one who has the responsibility of the household mending. It should contain only the articles to be mended and the necessary materials for mending taken from the general supply.

A darning bag for the household would also be found a convenience. It might contain all the stockings requiring mending and be provided with a pocket to contain the special darning wool required.

DARNING

Stockings

To Mend Stockings.—Stockings should be mended very carefully in order to make them last as long as possible. There are different ways of mending them, and the style adopted must depend upon the degree of wear and the texture and thickness of the material.

The mending must be done in wool, cotton, or silk, according to the kind of stockings, and it must match them exactly in colour. The thickness of thread to be used will depend upon the kind of mending to be done. For strengthening purposes it is better to take it rather thinner than the thread of the stocking itself, but when there is a hole it may be of the same thickness.

Mending is usually done on the wrong side of stockings, except in cases where the feet are very tender, when it is better to darn them on the right side.

Strengthening a Thin Place.—If there is a worn or thin place in a stocking without any actual hole, it should be strengthened to prevent it wearing further. Turn the stocking on the wrong side and stretch the piece to be darned over the left hand, over a piece of smooth card-board, or over a darner or wooden egg sold for the purpose. The stocking must not be stretched too tightly or the darn will have a bulged-out appearance when finished.

Commence about an inch to the right of the worn piece, and insert the needle with the point pointing upwards and the thumb on the top. Take up one loop or thread and miss one alternately until you have as many stitches as you can hold on the needle. Then draw the needle through, leaving an inch of thread at the end. Continue in this way until you have reached the top of the weak place. Now turn your hand and hold the needle vertically with the point turned downwards this time and the thumb underneath. Work downwards, taking up the stitches which were missed in the first row and missing those which were taken up. A loop of the thread must be left at the end of each row to prevent the work dragging. For the first four or five rows make each row a stitch longer than the preceding one, then make the rows the same length until the thin place is covered, when the rows may be decreased in length to correspond with the other side. This prevents all the strain coming upon one thread of the woven material. If a new thread is required take it at the beginning of a row. Leave one inch ends while you are working,

Darner.

FIG. 40.

and when the darn is finished these may be cut off to quarter of an inch (fig. 40).

Note.—If the material is fine, as in a woven stocking, three or four threads or their equivalent can be missed and taken up alternately instead of one.

Strengthening New Stockings.—Some people darn over the heels of stockings when they are new in order to make them last longer. This is especially necessary in the case of children's stockings and boys' stockings in particular—when the knees might also be strengthened with advantage.

This strengthening darn should be done with wool a little thinner than that of the stockings. Use a long thin needle. Run lengthways over the stocking web, taking up one thread and leaving three. In the next row turn and take up the centre thread of those you missed and miss the three next and so on, always taking one and missing three alternately throughout the whole process. Leave a loop at the end of each row. Work pretty loosely so that the stocking does not pucker.

Note.—In fine stockings take up and leave more threads in proportion.

To Darn a Hole—Ordinary Method.—First prepare the hole. If it is a fine webbed stocking, pick or cut away carefully any rough frayed-out pieces, but not more than is necessary, as the smooth threads that are left help to strengthen the darn. With a coarser make or hand-knitted stocking pick out carefully the loose ends of wool and weave the longer ones in with a darning needle.

Turn the stocking on the wrong side and stretch the hole over the left hand or over a stocking-darner. A wooden or china egg is useful if the hole is in the toe or the heel of the stocking, but elsewhere it is inclined to make the darn bulge out.

A considerable portion of the material round the edge of the hole should be darned in order to strengthen it, so commence at the right-hand side a little distance from the edge of the hole.

Some prefer to commence at the left-hand side and to darn from left to right, but this is a matter of taste. Commence in the same way and make the same stitch as for the strengthening darn, increasing the length of the rows until the hole is reached, when they may be all alike. The hole itself must be covered with straight strands of the thread and the darning stitches extended a little way above and below. Then continue the strengthening; darn beyond the hole as on the first side. Be sure to leave loops of the thread at the end of each row, otherwise when the stocking is washed the darn will

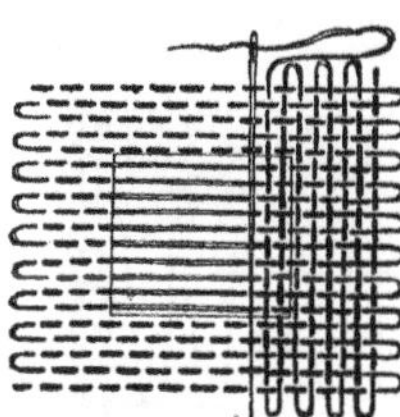

Fig. 41.

shrink and pucker. These first rows are called the warp rows, as they run the lengthways of the stocking.

Turn the work sideways so that the top and bottom of the hole become the sides and begin what is called the weft rows, those which run across the thread of the material. Commence at the lower right-hand corner of the darn and at the same distance from the edge of the hole as the warp rows were commenced.

Point the needle upwards and take up and miss alternately the stitches of the warp rows and continue thus until the other side of the darn is reached. When crossing the hole, the darn should form a lattice-work of threads and the darning must be carried as far to the right of the hole as it was to the left, and the rows decreased in length in a similar manner.

If the stockings are very fine two or three threads may be missed and taken up instead of one, only be very careful to slip the needle through any loose stitch at the top or at the bottom of the hole.

These darns may be made square if preferred, but it is not such a good plan, as the whole strain rests on one thread of the material (fig. 41).

If the hole is large it is a good plan to lace it across with a few threads of fine cotton or wool before commencing the darn. This will hold it together and keep it in shape.

A "Jacob's Ladder."—So called when a stitch breaks and drops down row after row until a ladder of threads is formed. This is easily mended if taken in time, but it rapidly extends and becomes very unsightly if neglected. If it occurs in a fine stocking, turn it on the wrong side and darn up and down the length of the material over the weak place and a little distance to each side. Be careful to catch up the dropped stitch or stitches and thus prevent them from running down further. Care, too, must be taken not to drag the threads, and loops must be left at the ends of the rows.

In hand or machine-knitted stockings of a coarser make the dropped stitch may often be taken up with a crochet hook and worked up each strand of wool, or steps of the ladder, as it were, in turn. The crochet hook is inserted in the bottom loop and the first bar is drawn through it, and so on with all the bars in turn. When at the top, fasten off securely with a darning needle. If several loops have run down, pick up each one in turn from right to left.

New Pieces in Stockings.—A good knitter will cut the worn-out heels and toes and even the whole feet from hand-knit stockings and knit new ones in. She can even knit pieces on the legs and seam them neatly in place.

In worn stockings, too, a good mender will be able to put patches cut from another stocking that is otherwise worn out. To do this, cut the sides of the hole even to a thread and pick out the ends of thread that are left. Then ravel out the top and bottom of the space until you have a row of loops strong enough to support a join. Next take a needle and fine soft cotton the colour of the stocking, and button-hole the sides of the hole very closely. Now cut a piece of webbing for the patch, making it quite even with the thread and a little longer than the hole into which it is to be fitted. This extra length allows for any drawing up in the fixing, and, if superfluous, can easily be unravelled to fit the space at the last. Neatly button-hole the sides of the patch with the same cotton as was used for the stocking, and then graft it in at the top (Grafting, see below). Now turn the stocking on the wrong side and overseam the edges together by the upper edges of the button-hole stitch. Turn the stocking again to the right side, ravel out the end of the patch until it fits the hole exactly and graft it in. Care must be taken to make the seams very soft and flat.

SPECIAL DARNING

Swiss Darning.—This special darning can only be done on articles of stocking-web tissue, either hand-knitted or woven—such as boys' stockings, golfing stockings, jerseys, &c. It is another method of thickening and strengthening any part that is thin. The stitch is worked on the right side of the material and, when well done, the direction of the stitches of the material is so carefully followed that the darn itself is scarcely seen. The wool used must be of exactly the same texture and colour as the article to be mended.

The piece to be mended should be lightly tacked on to a piece of cardboard to keep it in shape and secure. There must be no straining of the material.

If the webbing of the material is examined it will be seen that the stitches slant alternately upwards and downwards, and that they form ribs on the right side and loops on the wrong. The darning stitches must be worked in horizontal rows from right to left. Commence at the top right-hand side of the thin piece to be darned, and bring the needle out from behind between two of the stitches which slant upwards. Then insert the needle in a slanting direction upwards, pass it horizontally under the rib to the left and draw it out. Put it in again at the place where the first stitch was started, pass it under the next rib as before, and repeat in turn to the other end of the thin place. Now invert the work and make another row in the same way, covering the stitches that slant downwards this time, and repeat this working backwards and forwards until you have darned as much as is necessary. This is not a difficult kind of darning, and at the same time it is very satisfactory and effective.

Grafting.—Grafting is very useful in repairing socks, stockings, vests, jerseys, and similar garments of a material that is very regularly and not too finely woven. It is a very simple and neat method of fixing new feet or tops on children's stockings.

Ravel out the wool until the loops of both edges to be joined are quite whole and distinct. Then take a needle and wool exactly the same as that of the garment, match the loops on the right-hand side of the pieces to be joined and make a fastening. Lay the work over the fingers as for hemming, taking care that the loops of the two edges are exactly opposite each other. Insert the needle horizontally through two loops of the upper edge and draw out the thread. Next insert it one loop back on the under edge and bring it out one loop forward. Continue thus, taking alternately two loops at the top and two at the bottom until the end of the join is reached. If this is well done the seam should be almost invisible.

Stocking-Web Tissue.—Like Swiss darning, this is used for mending articles of thick stocking-web tissue either hand-knit or woven. It is really the weaving in of a new piece to the material to fill up a hole, and is preferable to the ordinary darn, as it is less noticeable.

The same stitch is used as in Swiss darning, only in the stocking-web darn a foundation composed of strands of cotton must be made on which to work.

This kind of darn is always worked on the right side of the material, and wool exactly the same as that of the garment must be used.

First prepare the hole by unravelling the loose ends of wool until there is an even row of loops top and bottom. Weave in the longer ends with a darning needle on the wrong side. Turn back the worn edges on the sides, leaving half a rib on each side of the holo at the top. Then tack a piece of cardboard at the back of the hole and under the place to be darned. Be careful neither to over-stretch nor contract the hole, but to keep it lying perfectly flat. The webbing, too, must be perfectly vertical so that the corresponding loops at the top and bottom of the hole are exactly opposite each other.

When the hole is arranged take a needle and coloured sewing cotton and connect the loops top and bottom, as in fig. 42, and in the following

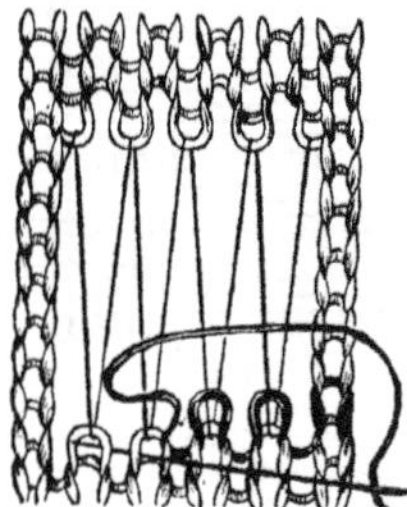

Fig. 42.

manner:—Make a knot and pass the needle through the card and first loop at the bottom right-hand corner of the hole. Pass it through the half and the next loop at the top, then back through first loop at the bottom, taking the next one also on the needle. Now pass it through the two next loops at the top, and continue in this way, taking alternate loops top and bottom until the loops are all picked up. Then pass the needle through the half loop at the edge of the hole and the card and fasten off.

Care must be taken to make the strands just the size of the hole. The strands will appear as a double row of threads, and the Swiss darn is worked on these.

Take a needle with the darning wool, slip it under the work and fasten it on at the right-hand bottom corner about two or three stitches from the edge of the hole. Swiss darn over these two or three stitches. Then put the needle through the first loop of the hole and draw it out. Pass it under the two cotton threads coming out of that loop and then back into the middle of the same loop. Now take up the next loop to the left and draw the needle out and repeat until the other side of the hole is reached (fig. 42). Swiss darn over two or three stitches in the webbing as on right-hand side. Next invert the work and work another row in the same way, and work backwards and forwards

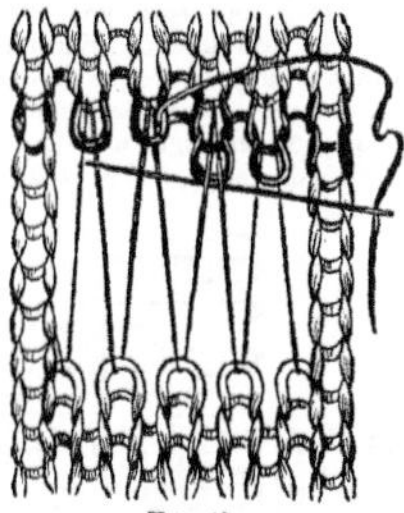

FIG. 43.

until the hole is filled up (fig. 43). Sometimes it may be necessary to push the stitches into place with the point of the needle, as they must lie in even horizontal rows. Join the new piece of webbing just made to the loops at the other side of the hole by grafting stitches (see p. 410). When finished, cut and draw out the foundation threads very carefully and remove the card.

DARNING OF LINEN OR COTTON MATERIAL

Thin Places.—To darn thin places, ravellings of the same material should be used when practicable. The darn can then be made almost imperceptible. If not, use cotton or thread as similar to the material as possible. Use long and thin needles for this kind of work.

Turn the work on the wrong side. Take up and leave one, two, three, or four threads according to the thickness of the material. Work the first set of lines along the selvedge way of the material rather close to each other and half an inch beyond the thin place on all sides. Alternate the stitches and leave loops as in the other darns. If the place is very thin, or if there is a hole in the middle, reverse the work when the first side is finished and cross it. When crossing take up the mending cotton only. Take up one thread and leave one, and so on

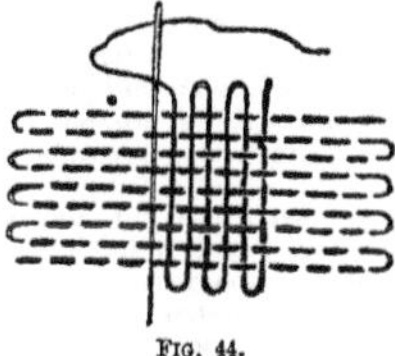

FIG. 44.

(fig. 44). Alternate in the next row: continue as far as necessary. Finish off as before.

This darn may also be made diamond-shaped or with a waved edge, which prevents all the strain coming on one thread of the material.

Cross-cut Darns.—*A cross-cut tear* is so called because it is made across the thread of the material. It may occur in table-cloths and doyleys that have been cut with a knife or in other linen cut by laundry machinery.

To mend this kind of hole begin by trimming off the ragged edges of the cut, then prevent the cut from opening by drawing it together on the wrong side with a few stitches. These must be made rather loosely with very fine sewing cotton. For darning take ravellings of the material or proper darning cotton. Measure half an inch at both ends of the length of the cut, and make two parallel creases on the

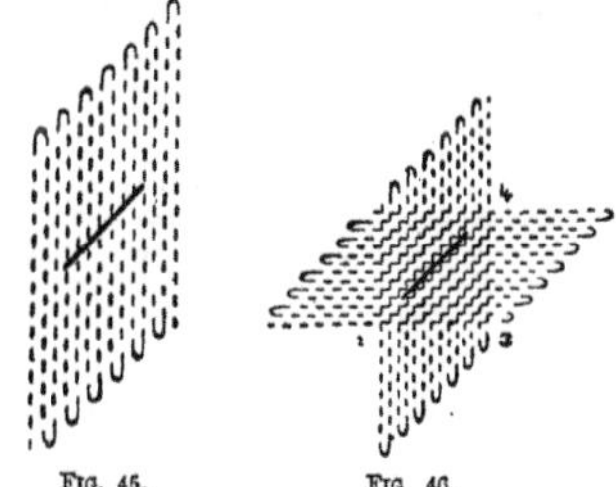

FIG. 45. FIG. 46.

thread of the material. Then make two creases perpendicular to these and this will give a square holding the cut diagonally in the middle (fig. 46).

Put in the needle at the corner No. 1 of this

square and work downwards, taking up two threads and missing two until you reach the corner No. 2. Count the number of stitches already made and continue in the same line, making the same number of stitches again. For instance, if you have seven stitches from 1 to 2, make seven stitches beyond, and this finishes the first line.

Then count two threads to the right and two upwards and begin the second line there. All the lines must have the same number of stitches, and as this row is one stitch shorter at the bottom it must be one stitch longer at the top. The stitches must be alternated as in other darning, and a small loop must be left at the ends.

When you reach the slit the stitches of each row must be taken under it so as to keep the raw edges on the wrong side. This may make some of the stitches uneven, but it must be done as neatly as possible.

When you have reached the corner No. 3, cut off the darning thread. The darn will be in the shape of a rhomboid (fig. 45). Turn the work sideways. Begin again at No. 1, work to 4, and continue on; double the number of stitches. This line and the following must have the same number of stitches as those of the first rhomboid. Commence one stitch further up and increase one each row so as to make a rhomboid as before.

In working the second rhomboid, when you reach the square the stitches should meet those of the first rows of darning and form neat little V's or steps. When the darn is finished, carefully remove the tacking stitches.

Unless the tear is quite small it is a good plan to tack a piece of cardboard at the back before beginning to darn.

Hedge-Tear Darn.—The hedge-tear darn is used to mend triangular tears often caused by the material catching on a nail or hedge.

As in other darns, take ravellings of the material if possible; if not, what resembles the material most in make and shade. Cut off any loose threads round the tear and draw the edges together with very fine sewing cotton.

Begin on the left-hand side about three-eighths of an inch from the end of the tear, take up two threads and leave two, making stitches above and below the tears. Begin the second row two threads to the right and two threads above the first row, taking up the threads that have been left and leaving each two threads corresponding to the spaces. All the rows must be exactly the same length. Leave one-eighth inch loops as in other darns. When passing the hole, keep the edges of the tear on the wrong side as much as possible.

When you have reached the corner of the tear, continue working to the right as much as half the width of one side of the tear. Cut off the thread and turn the work sideways so that the undarned end of the tear lies at the left. Commence darning at the left and three-eighths of an inch away from the end of the tear on the other side. Work towards the right, making

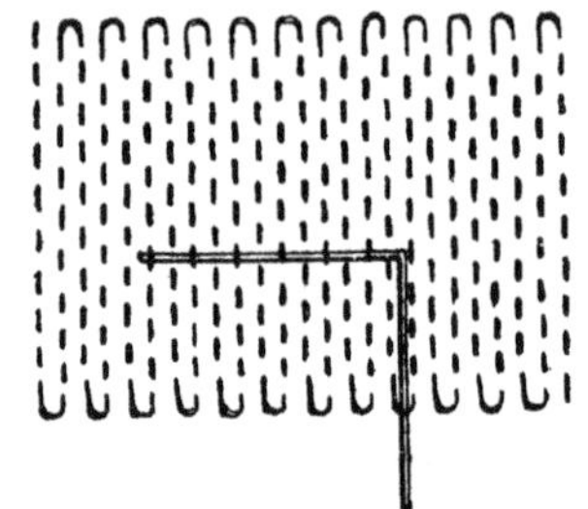

Fig. 47.

rows exactly the same length, and with the same number of stitches as in the first piece of darning.

Half-way along the tear you will meet the stitches of the side already darned, and this should form a square of V's or little steps as in the cross-cut darn. All the stitches must show through neatly on the right side (fig. 48).

When finished, remove the tacking stitches.

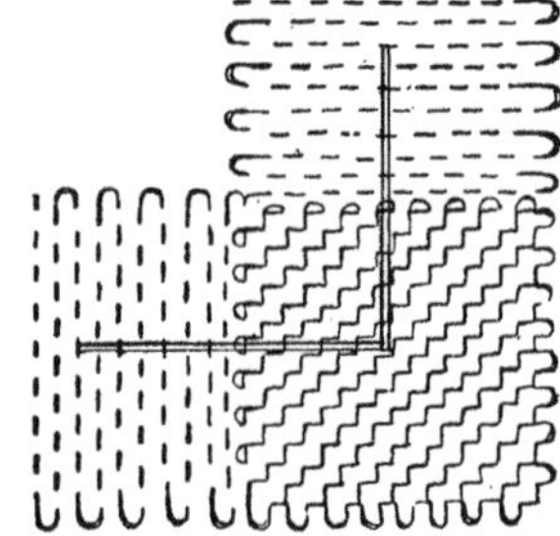

Fig. 48.

The weakest part of the tear will now be strengthened with the crossed row of stitches.

This darn also may be worked over a piece of cardboard if it is found easier.

PATCHING

Patches are used to cover holes or a worn or torn piece of material, and they are a means of making household goods last much longer than they otherwise would do. They are as a rule preferable to darns as they are less conspicuous.

A good housekeeper will have at hand plenty of material at different stages of wear for all patching purposes. The patch should be of the same strength as the material to be mended: it is therefore unwise to employ a new piece of the *same* material. If a new piece of material must be used, it should be thinner in texture than that of the article to be patched. If it is calico, print, or anything of a stiffish nature, it should be washed before being used, to make it softer.

Patches may be of any size and any shape required, but square and oblong ones are the most generally used. Circular and triangular patches are sometimes worked on flannel or woven material, but, if possible, they should be avoided unless they can be quite hidden. The patch must at all times be cut large enough to well cover the hole or worn part, and a little extra allowed for turnings.

The chief points to attend to in putting in a patch are—first, to fix it well, and, secondly, to make the corners lie very flat and without wrinkles. This once mastered, with care and perseverance the work is fairly easy as the stitches are all of the simplest.

The thread of the patch must in all cases lie with the thread of the material, and the sewing also must be worked by a thread.

There are several different kinds of calico and linen patches, *i.e.*—

(1) Seam and fell patch.
(2) A patch hemmed on both sides.
(3) A run and fell patch.
(4) A shaped patch.

(1) Seam and Fell Patch.—Cut the patch large enough to cover the hole and the thin part of the material surrounding it, plus an extra inch on each side. Be careful to cut it very evenly and with the threads running in the same direction as the material on which it is to be laid. Commence by turning down a narrow fold all round the patch on the right side, the selvedge side first and then the other two. Mark the fold by the threads of the material and see that the corners are perfectly straight. Place the patch on the wrong side of the garment with the folds facing it; see that the warp and woof of both materials lie in the same direction and that the hole comes in the middle of the patch. Pin the four corners carefully in position, then tack and hem round very neatly, beginning in the middle of one of the sides, and making a stitch exactly at each corner. When finished take out the tacking stitches and turn the work over to the right side. Slip the scissors in the hole and cut diagonally to within one-third of an inch of each corner. Cut away the worn-out part very evenly to a thread, leaving one-third of an inch of edging all round. Then turn in the raw edges very evenly with the aid of a needle, snipping them in the corners to the depth of one-eighth of an inch to prevent any puckering. Then tack round and see that all lies flat and smooth.

Fold back the garment so that the fold and the patch form a double edge. Overseam very neatly, beginning with the middle of one of the sides, and be particular to make a stitch exactly at each corner. When finished remove the

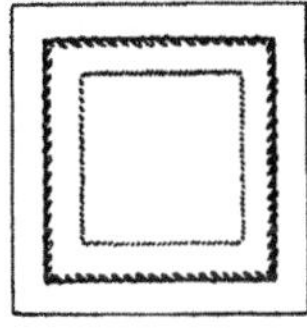

Fig. 49.

tacking threads and flatten the work well (fig. 49).

The first side may also be seamed instead of hemmed.

A patch may be laid on the right side of the material instead of on the wrong; this is a matter of individual choice.

(2) A Patch Hemmed on both Sides is more quickly made and is often used for old things where a large patch is necessary. Cut and prepare the patch as before, and lay it either on the right or wrong side of the material as is most convenient. Tack in position and fell down the first side. Turn over, cut away the worn part, and turn in the edges as in fig. 49.

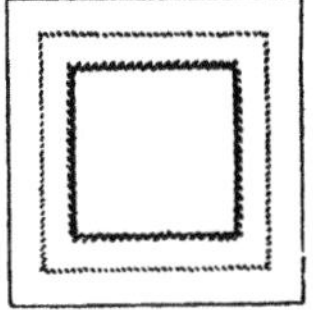

Fig. 50.

Fell or hem the second side, take out all tacking threads, and flatten well (fig. 50).

(3) Run and Fell Patch.—This patch is best suited to large holes. It is somewhat more difficult to arrange than Nos. 1 and 2, but if neatly done the results are very satisfactory.

Take the article to be patched and outline the hole with four well-marked creases on the right side of the material. The creases ought to be made at least an inch beyond the worn part on each side and even with the thread of the material. Cut the patch to a size to correspond exactly to this marked space and allow a little extra for turnings. Turn in the raw edges on the wrong side, crease them well down, and open out again. This is merely to make a mark as a guide for the sewing.

Place one of the sides of the patch against the crease on the fabric—the two right sides together and the two creases precisely one on the top of the other. The patch is not placed *over* the hole, but lying quite to one side of it. Run the two pieces together from corner to corner and exactly along the creases. Then turn the patch over, allowing it to take its proper position.

Now sew along the second side in the same way, being most particular about the turning of the corner so as to avoid puckering. The hole may be made a little larger if necessary so as to allow the fingers to be slipped inside. Sew the other two sides in the same way and then

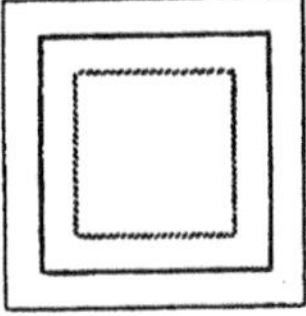

FIG. 51.

turn the work over. Cut away the worn part and fell down the edges inside (fig. 51).

(4) **A Shaped Patch.**—This is sometimes required if a hole occurs near the seam of a garment, as for instance under the arm of a night-dress or chemise or in the side of a slip-blouse.

Unpick the seam for about one inch beyond the length required for the patch. Cut a patch the size required and tack it carefully in position and straight to a thread of the material. Hem or fell the edges which lie on the garment, and then cut the remainder to the curves of the seam. Turn the work over, cut away the worn part and fell neatly. The rest of the patch will thus become part of the seam in place of the worn part which has been cut away.

If both sides of the seam of the garment are worn a similar patch must be put on the other side. They should, if possible, be exactly alike; they will then join more neatly at the seam (fig. 52).

Print Patch.—When mending print or any other material with a marked design the patch must be cut so as to match exactly the pattern of the material. For this reason it is sometimes necessary to cut the patch larger than it need otherwise be, and the hole need not always be in the middle. Sometimes, too, it will be found better to cut the patch of an uneven shape, as the stitches will show less if they are not in straight lines.

Having cut the patch to the best shape possible, turn down the edges on the wrong side, to the depth of about one-eighth of an inch, and place it on the *right* side of the garment following the thread of the material and the lines of the pattern; put a pin in each corner and then tack carefully in position.

Then fold back the material from the patch so that the edge of the material and the edge of the patch form a double edge, and overseam round very neatly, holding the patch nearest you. Commence at the centre of one of the sides and be particular to make a stitch exactly in the corners. Fasten off, slipping the needle through to the wrong side, making one or

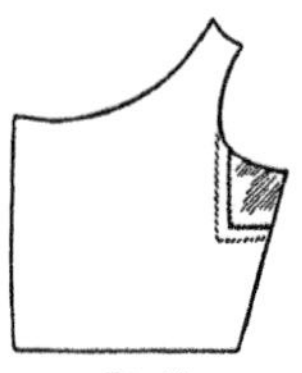

FIG. 52.

two back-stitches, and smooth out the seam so that the patch lies perfectly flat. This is the only seam which shows on the right side of a print patch.

Turn the work over to the wrong side and cut away the worn pieces to within a quarter of an inch of the edges as in other patches. Then begin at one corner and overcast the two raw edges together with neat blanket stitches. The stitches must not show through on the right side.

Flannel or Woven Material Patches.—Flannel patches differ from those made on cotton or linen in that the raw edges are never turned down, as the material is too thick. They are worked with herring-bone stitches instead of being felled. The patch itself may be square, oblong, triangular, or round, according to the shape of hole to be covered.

Square and Oblong Patches are worked the same way and are preferable to the other shapes when it is possible to use them. Cut the patch according to directions given for calico patch, and notice that the way of the nap, *i.e.* the fluff on the flannel, corresponds with that of the garment. Place the right side of the patch downwards on the wrong side of the garment, the threads of the material running in the same direction, and the middle of the patch over the middle of the hole. Put a pin in each corner and then tack down carefully with fine sewing cotton. Herring-bone round the edges, beginning in the middle of one of the sides. Commence by inserting the needle between the two thicknesses of material and four threads up from the edge of the patch. Be careful with the corners to make them all alike. Finish off by making one or two back-stitches over the last herring-bone stitch and slipping the thread through between the two folds of material.

Turn over to the right side. Cut away the worn part of the garment to within one quarter of an inch, or about eight threads off the herring-bone stitches, which show through like running stitches. This will allow four threads for the herring-bone on the right side, and four threads for the space between those and the other stitches. Now herring-bone the garment on to

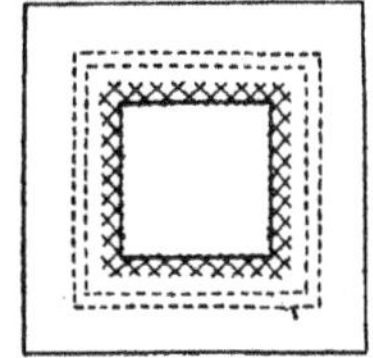

Fig. 53.

the patch, beginning in the middle of one of the sides. Work the corners as before and finish off (fig. 53).

A Triangular Patch is sometimes found more practical than a square or oblong for mending under armholes or at the neck of a garment. It is prepared and placed in the same way as a square patch, and the corners must be neatly finished. Care must be taken when tacking

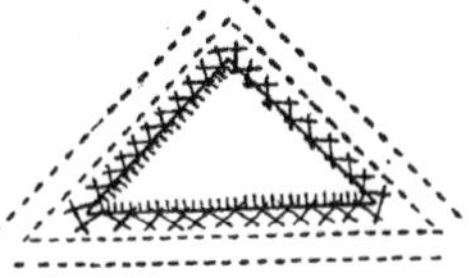

Fig. 54.

and herring-boning along the crossway sides, as the material will be inclined to stretch (fig. 54).

A Circular Patch is most suitable for a hole occurring in the elbow of a garment. It is a little more difficult to manipulate, as the edges are apt to stretch. Prepare and place it as above and tack it very carefully in position. The herring-boning will differ a little from the regulation stitches, as they cannot be worked to a thread; and as the inner circle is narrower than the outer one the top stitches must be made closer than the bottom ones on the wrong side, and on the right side the bottom stitches closer than the top ones (fig. 55).

Patching of Woven Material.—Woven material can also be patched in the same way as flannel if the garment is old and the hole to be mended very large. Darning in this case would not be

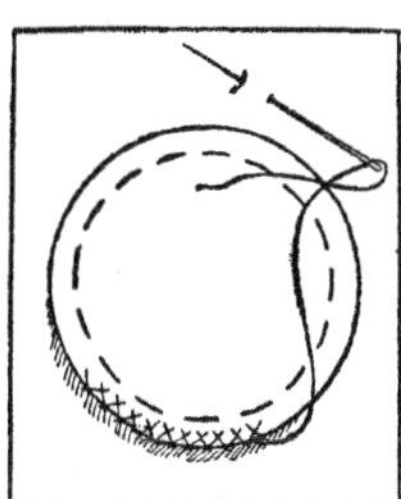

Fig. 55.

suitable. Fix the patch according to directions given for a flannel patch and herring-bone with fine wool instead of cotton.

SPECIAL MENDING

Fine Muslin should be mended in the same way as other cotton material. Any darning should be done with very fine soft cotton, and if a patch has to be inserted the hems should be made very narrow, and, where possible, hidden with a tuck.

Blankets.—These are such precious articles that they should be darned and patched as long as possible, and when they become too shabby to put on the top of the bed they can be used as under-blankets or binders. All thin places should be darned with wool of the same colour. If the place is very thin a piece of thin open flannel might be put at the back and the darning done over that. When there are actual holes, patching is better than darning, and the herring-boning should be done with fine wool instead of cotton. If the sides of the blanket become ragged and shabby they should be trimmed with a pair of scissors, then a narrow fold made and herring-boned down; or, the edges may be worked over with blanket stitch in the same colour of wool as the ends of the blanket.

Woven Under-garments.—These are also very precious articles, and ought to be mended and made to last as long as possible. Each week when they come from the washing they should be examined, and at the first signs of wearing must be carefully darned. It is also important to mend all under-garments at the end of a season if they are to be laid away for some time.

If a thin place occurs in a heavy woven material a piece of thinner woven material of an elastic nature may be put at the back and the darning done over that, or the worn piece may be cut away and a neat patch inserted. Hand-knitted underclothing is best mended with the stocking-web darn, or a new piece might be knitted in.

The wear of woven garments may be much increased if the parts which undergo most friction are carefully strengthened before the garment is worn.

Table-Linen.—Mend according to general directions given for mending linen materials. The question as to whether a patch or darn is best must depend upon the position and size of the piece requiring repair. The aim must be to mend so skilfully that the damaged part is as little observed as possible.

A hole must always be patched unless it is quite small, when it may be filled up with darning. In patching the pattern of the damask must be matched as closely as possible as in print patching. If a hole occurs in the middle of a table-cloth it is sometimes a good plan to fix in a centre taken from an old serviette.

Flourishing thread is the best to use for darning purposes, or a linen thread that is not glazed. Instead of darning by the ordinary method, a clever worker will copy the design of the damask by missing and taking up more or less of the warp strands of the darn, but this is very trying for the eyesight and could only be undertaken by an expert worker.

When the corners of a table-cloth become worn or torn in the washing, they should be rounded off very neatly and hemmed. The four corners should be made alike.

Mending of Tweed or other Cloth.—This mending being applied to outer garments, it is very important that it should be very neat and show as little as possible on the right side. As a rule, for thin places and holes it is better to tack a patch at the back and darn over it on the right side. Ravellings of the same material should be used. When finished put a damp cloth over the wrong side and press it well with a hot iron. If there is a lining the back seam must be unpicked and the patch slipped between the cloth and the lining. The darn must be pressed before the lining is sewn together again.

If the garment is not lined, the raw edges of the patch can be darned into it neatly at the back; but this should only be attempted by really good workers, as, even if the stitches do not show through very much, the work is apt to pucker.

An easier way is to overseam or blanket stitch the raw edges of the patch and press them well with a hot iron.

Fine Drawing.—This stitch can be used for mending a rent or cut in cloth of a close texture which does not unravel easily. The stitch itself is very simple, and, if carefully made, should be almost imperceptible. Use a thread of the same material if possible, or, failing that, silk or wool to match it. Silk must never be used on a dull fabric as the stitch would be perceptible; in fact, if the material is very fine there is nothing better than a human hair for mending a cut of this kind.

If the edges of the tear are very much unravelled, work the longer threads in, then cut the rest quite straight. Hold the work flat over your left hand between your thumb and first finger with the right side uppermost, make a knot at the end of the thread and bring out the needle on the right side of the tear close to top and keeping the two edges very well together. Point the needle the other way and bring it out, and similarly through the other side. Draw the thread closely to make the edges of the cloth meet, but not to overlap (fig. 56). Continue taking a stitch on each side

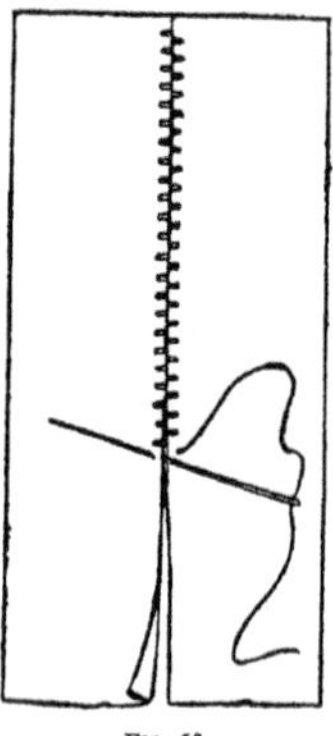

FIG. 56.

alternately till the join is finished. Finish off with one or two back-stitches. Press the join under a damp cloth with a hot iron.

Old German Seam.—This is very similar to fine drawing and can serve the same purpose. The stitches are made much closer together; they should not be more than two or three threads apart.

Stoting is often used by tailors for mending a tear in material that does not easily fray out. Take a thread of the material and make a knot at the end. Fold back the material so that the edges of the tear are outside and perfectly even. Hold the work as for seaming, and begin quarter of an inch at the left of the tear. Work from left to right, making very close stitches and taking up a very small amount from each edge. Continue to one quarter of an inch beyond the tear on the right-hand side. Finish off with about six stitches to the left, crossing the last six seaming stitches. Iron on the wrong side with a damp cloth over the material. If the work is well done the tear should be almost invisible.

The "Stoppeur."—There is a special kind of darning for tweeds and cloths done by the "stoppeur." "Stoppeur" is to mend a hole so that it is absolutely invisible on the right side, and only loose threads are seen on the wrong side. It is done with threads exactly like those of the material, and the design itself is copied. This is rarely done by an amateur; but if an awkward hole or cut occurs in a good garment, such as a tailor-made gown or overcoat, it is worth while to send it to the professional "stoppeur," who will mend it for a very reasonable charge.

To Mend Silk.—It is not easy to mend silk nicely, as, like fine muslin, it is only used for dressy garments and fancy articles, all of which are more or less conspicuous.

As a rule, it is best to darn it finely with silk of the same colour, or to put a patch on the wrong side and to darn over that. If there is a decided hole, then it may be better to insert a patch in the same way as on a print article. As far as possible in the mending of light silk seams and tucks should be made use of to hide part of the patch. Lace insertions, too, especially in children's frocks, come in very useful for the mending or hiding the insertion of a patch.

To Mend Gloves.—The style of mending must depend upon the material and texture of the gloves. The thin places in cotton, silk, or woollen gloves must be very neatly darned with fine cotton, silk, or wool of exactly the same shade and texture. Little wooden eggs of different sizes can be bought singly or by the half-dozen for slipping inside the fingers when mending gloves. There are also small sticks with rounded ends for the same purpose.

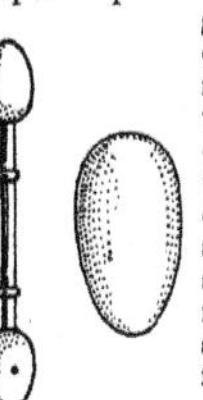

Glove-Menders.

Split seams in cotton and silk gloves must be stitched on the wrong side of the glove with fine silk or cotton of the same colour. Care must be taken not to pucker the seam and to commence and finish off the thread securely without knots.

If a woven or knitted glove splits between the fingers or at the wrist owing to its being too tight, darn the opening neatly so as to allow a little more width. If the same thing happens to a kid glove, take some silk of the same colour and button-hole stitch the edges of the slit, working round and round several times if necessary to fill up the space. Then turn the glove on the wrong side and close the hole by catching the end loops together, either with overcasting or with button-hole stitches.

If there is a decided hole a better way is to procure a piece of the same kid from an old glove and to cut a patch of a suitable size. Put this under the hole or slit and over-seam all round the edges on the right side with very close stitches. Use fine sewing silk of the same shade as the glove. Turn to the wrong side and herring-bone down the edges of the patch with pretty large stitches. The stitches on the patch should be taken through the single kid only, so that only one set of stitches show through to the right side; and these must be of the very smallest. Suede, chamois, and all sorts of skin gloves can be mended in this way.

SEWING BY MACHINE

No household should be without its sewing-machine. Although good handwork is always more valuable, and in many cases it cannot be replaced, where there is a large amount of sewing to be done, some more rapid method of getting through the work must be resorted to.

There is no limit to the work that can be done on a good sewing-machine, and when we consider the hours of hand-sewing it can save, not to speak of the work which would otherwise have to be given out or bought "ready made," the initial expense in buying the machine should never be grudged.

Not only will a machine do the long plain seams, but it has now so many accessories that it can be made to hem, braid, tuck, gather, quilt, bind, &c., as well.

It is very important to buy a good machine and one by a reliable maker. It is a mistake to be led away by a cheap price or to buy one second-hand; in most cases it will be found that a second-hand machine is worn out in some part and will be an endless source of worry. Invest in a really good article; it will give endless satisfaction and will last a lifetime if reasonable care be taken.

There are two different kinds of machines: (1) those that sew with a single thread—the Chain-Stitch Machines, and (2) those that have two threads—the Lock-Stitch Machines. There is something to be said in favour of both kinds. In the former there is less mechanism, and the working of the machine is very simple. The work can easily be undone when required, and provided the ends of thread are well fastened, the stitching is perfectly secure. It is particularly good for light work, such as the sewing of silks and muslin. A little hand chain-stitch machine can be had so small and light in weight that it can easily be carried about or can be packed up for travelling without any trouble.

The lock-stitch machine gives a double stitch, as there are the two threads, one above and the other below in the shuttle. The work is very strong and secure and can only be undone with difficulty.

Both kinds of machines can be worked either

by hand or by foot. The special advantage of the treadle machine is that both hands are left free to guide and arrange the work.

The treadle machine is objected to by many on the grounds that it is bad for a woman's health, but the evils have been much exaggerated, and unless the machine is a particularly heavy one and it is worked for hours in the day, there is nothing to be feared. If there is only a small amount of sewing to be done a small hand-machine will no doubt serve the purpose, but if it is wanted for use in a large household it is almost wiser to buy one with the treadle, as this can always be detached and the machine worked by hand if desired.

Full instructions for the use of the machine are given with each special make; in fact, most makers offer lessons free of charge to each purchaser, and this will be found of great assistance, as it is difficult to learn from any printed directions. There are, however, several important points to be borne in mind when using any machine, and a few general hints may be found useful.

One is apt to attribute to the machine all the faults of bad work, when in reality it is often nothing but inexperience on the part of the worker.

(1) The machine must be kept clean and in good order. It ought to work easily and with little or no noise; in fact, some of the newest makes are almost silent. If it works heavily it is almost a sure sign that it requires oiling. It wears a machine to work it when insufficiently oiled, to say nothing of the difficulty in working, being very tiring for the worker. Oiling must be done regularly and the best machine oil used. This is very important, as oil of an inferior quality is almost sure to clog. By means of a little oil-can oil all the parts where there is friction—these are generally indicated by little holes in the machine—and then wipe off any superfluous oil with a soft duster.

The machine must always be kept free from dust. There is always a certain amount of fluff coming off the different fabrics that are sewn, and this lodges in the various parts of the machine, so that it is well to wipe it over when the work is finished.

Then from time to time a more thorough cleaning is necessary. Use a little petrol instead of the ordinary oil and work the machine several minutes. Then clean the other parts with petrol, wipe off with a soft cloth, and grease in the usual way.

A machine should be kept covered when not in use.

(2) The furnishings used with the machine should be of the best. The needles must be good and well proportioned to thickness of thread and material. It is always well to keep a supply of different sizes in reserve, and if these are stuck into a piece of greased flannel this will preserve them from rusting.

The sewing thread, too, must be good and of a smooth and even make. It is impossible to produce a good stitch with a poor quality of cotton; besides, if there are knots or badly-twisted parts, there will be the continual annoyance of breaking the thread. The thickness of the thread must also be proportioned to the size of the needle, and in the lock-stitch machine the shuttle thread should always be a little finer than the upper one.

(3) The tension must be right. Very careful attention should be given to the instructions regarding this, because unless properly regulated it will be impossible to work the machine satisfactorily.

When beginning to work the machine it is always better to test the stitch on an odd piece of material before starting on the work itself.

DARNING BY MACHINE

The Singer Sewing Machine Company have introduced a new method of darning by machine which ought to be an immense boon to the busy housewife. The process is very simple, and the special attachment which can be bought for 3s. can be used on any lock-stitch sewing-machine.

Full particulars can be had by writing or calling at any of Singer's shops, where a special lesson will always be given to purchasers free of charge. Both woollen and cotton goods can be darned by means of this little appliance, and the expert worker will be able to darn curtains and lace so as to match the texture of the material. The work is quickly done and has a very neat and smooth appearance when finished.

HOME DRESSMAKING

In this article no attempt has been made to go into the more scientific side of dressmaking, including such subjects as drafting patterns, making fitted bodices or tailor-made garments; such knowledge can only be acquired by taking a thorough course of technical lessons—it cannot be imparted by books.

The woman who wishes to make a study of dressmaking in all its branches should undoubtedly arrange to take lessons either privately or at one or other of the many technical schools. It is for the assistance of the woman who wishes to eke out her dress allowance by making her own skirts and blouses and simple frocks, with the aid of one or other of the many paper patterns which are now so easily procurable, that this article has been written, and we trust that the many hints embodied in this chapter in regard to the adaptation of stock patterns to individual figures, and the cutting out and making of simple yet smart garments will be of real practical use to the home worker.

Economy of Home Dressmaking.—The extravagance of the present age in regard to dress has been made at various times the subject of much comment in the newspapers. Men correspondents have aired their so-called grievances in the form of letters to the press, complaining that where their grandmothers in their time could do with one or two new dresses every year, their wives and daughters are not content with less than half-a-dozen. On the surface there would appear to be a certain amount of justification for this complaint, which will, however, bear the brunt of more searching investigation. The fact is that we enjoy so many advantages to-day in the way of reduced cost of dress material and accessories that, on comparing the cost of dress fifty or sixty years ago to what it is now, the balance of expenditure will be found to be pretty evenly adjusted. Nowadays a woman would hold up her hands in horror if called upon to pay six or seven shillings a yard for the material of her most ordinary gowns; yet this was looked upon by our grandmothers as a very moderate expenditure indeed. Neither would the woman of to-day dream of spending a small fortune on the heavy silk brocade of which the best gown of every self-respecting woman of our grandmothers' time was invariably built. Good dress materials are now well within the reach of the most modest purse; and where a woman can make a large number of her gowns herself, she will manage to dress very well indeed on a comparatively small outlay.

Not the least remarkable aspect of the present era in dress is the rapid growth of home dressmaking. In former times the home-made dress was usually an object weird and wonderful in its clumsiness and lack of style. Nowadays the rapid advance made in the science of dressmaking has come to the aid of the home dressmaker, with the result that she is able to turn out very creditable and well-fitting gowns.

Paper Patterns.—The now well-known paper patterns are the outcome of this progress in the dressmaking art. Patterns well drafted and well designed and, above all, well cut may be purchased for a few pence. These patterns have been designed by expert dressmakers and fitters, and with their aid many women and girls manage to keep up a very good wardrobe upon a very small dress allowance indeed. Nowadays there is scarcely a woman who has not attempted to make a blouse for herself at some time or other and with success. In olden times a woman had to use her own brains in the designing and cutting of her gowns. Nowadays the brains of the experts who design the various patterns are at the command of every woman who chooses to avail herself of the opportunities offered. All she has to do is to carefully note and follow the instructions given with the pattern. If she is careful in regard to these, her work cannot very easily go wrong.

The necessity for getting a good and reliable pattern before attempting to make a dress or a blouse is obvious. Among the many patterns which have found favour with the home worker, those sold by Messrs. Butterick & Co. of 83 and 84 Long Acre, London, W.C., deservedly take a prominent place. These patterns are to be had in nearly every size, and the instructions for their use are so concise and so clear, that women with only the most elementary idea of dressmaking can turn out really smart garments for themselves with the aid of Butterick patterns.

If it is a woman's first attempt at dressmaking, she should select a shirt blouse or a plain skirt of the simplest description on which to try her

" 'prentice hand." Once she has turned out a really successful shirt blouse or a plain unlined skirt, she may attempt more ambitious things, for in dressmaking, as in every other science, once the rudiments are mastered the rest will become easy.

In ordering a blouse pattern it is necessary to give the correct bust measurement. In sending for a skirt pattern the waist measurement, and, what is even more important, the measurement round the hips about five inches below the waist-line should be given.

Dressmaking Accessories.—Having secured a good pattern, the home dressmaker should turn her attention to the other necessary accessories. She will require a pair of sharp cutting-out scissors, a pair of small button-hole scissors, good needles and thread, a measuring tape, and a tracing wheel for tracing the pattern lines and

Tracing Wheel.

marks in the material. Tailors' chalk or coloured thread could be used for marking heavy materials on which the tracing would not show. A good treadle sewing-machine is of course a very valuable accessory to dressmaking; there should also always be a plentiful supply of pins.

The table on which the material for cutting out is laid should be large enough to allow for the various pieces of the pattern to be spread out full length upon it. The pattern should be pinned to the material or adjusted in such a way as to prevent it from slipping out of place.

A Useful Dressmaking Board.—It is an important rule of dressmaking that all the different pieces of a garment should be tacked together on a table, or, failing this, some other smooth flat

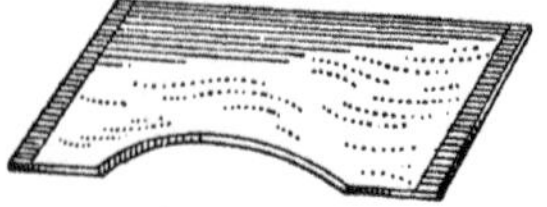

Dressmaking Board.

surface. A plain piece of board will answer the purpose quite well. It should be after the style and size of an ordinary drawing-board, with one side scooped out to form a curve, as shown in the illustration. If there is no member of the family sufficiently versed in the art of home carpentering, any joiner will supply and cut out the board for a trifling sum.

When seated at work the worker should take the board upon her knees; the curved part will fit into her waist. She should place her feet upon a footstool in order to support the board more firmly. In this way she will have a very effective little impromptu table at her command upon which all her tacking can be done with the greatest ease.

Dress-Stands.—A woman who makes her own gowns will find her work much simplified if she has a good dress-stand for fitting purposes. This she can have made to her own measure, or, if it has to do duty for several members of a family, one of the expanding dress-stands, which can be adjusted to any figure, will be found most useful. In arranging the pleats of a skirt at the back and securing an even hang all round, a dress-stand is almost indispensable. Separate bodice-stands may also be had padded for pinning for an outlay of only five or six shillings. The padded stands are undoubtedly the most useful ones to have.

Dressmaking Stitches.—The home dressmaker must of course have a knowledge of the simple needlework stitches, such as tacking, basting, running, gathering, hemming, seaming, sewing, stitching, back-stitching, slip-stitching, &c., for description of which refer to needlework section (p. 388).

Tailor's tacking is the stitch used in conveying the different notches and perforations of a pattern through the different breadths of the

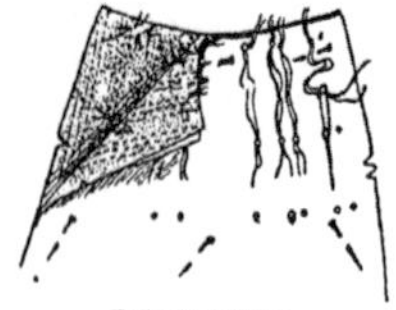

Tailor's Tacking.

material to be cut when chalk cannot be used. With a double thread of basting cotton baste through pattern and material with one long stitch and two short ones, leaving the long stitch loose enough to form a loop, then take hold of the two pieces of material, separating them about a quarter of an inch and cut them as shown in illustration. Coloured cotton is usually used for tailor's tacking.

Blouse Patterns.—Blouse patterns are cut in different stock sizes according to the bust measurement, and when the proper bust measure is given the pattern will fit if a woman is of correct proportions. There are many figures, however, which differ from the average. One woman may have an unusually high waist, another may have an unusually long one. Again, the arms of another may be very short in proportion to the rest of her figure, whilst in another case the arms may be unduly long. The following simple instructions and diagrams for alteration of patterns will be found useful in all these cases.

One important thing to remember is that in all cases in which an alteration is necessary, the alteration must be effected *on the pattern* before it is placed upon the material for cutting.

Before cutting out pattern be sure to read carefully all instructions on pattern envelope. In most patterns diagrams of all the separate pieces of the patterns together with instructions for cutting out are given.

If a blouse pattern is too long-waisted and requires shortening, a tuck should be made in both front and back pieces in the position

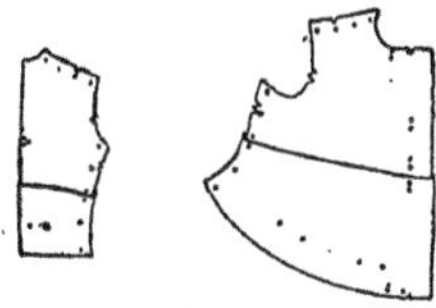

FIG. 1.

shown in fig. 1. If the pattern is too short-waisted and requires lengthening, cut pattern across as shown in fig. 2, lay the divided portions upon another piece of paper separating them far enough to make the pattern of the

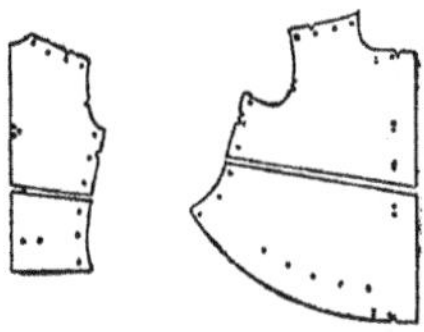

FIG. 2.

required length, and paste them on the paper, cutting out a new pattern according to the altered outline.

For widening the shoulder should be raised, and increased turnings allowed at under-arm seams.

In the Butterick patterns an allowance is always made for fitting at shoulder and under-arm seams. With other patterns, however, this is not always the case, and it is most necessary to carefully read the directions sent with the pattern in order that you may allow extra width for fitting and finishing if no allowance is made.

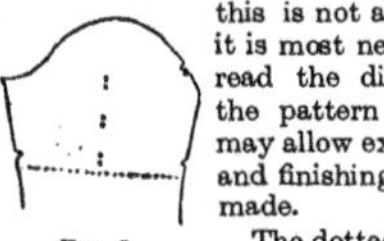

FIG. 3.

The dotted line in fig. 3 shows where to make a tuck in the blouse sleeve for shortening it, or to cut it across for lengthening it.

To shorten a two-piece sleeve pattern make tucks in each piece above and below the elbow of the size required as shown in illustration. If the sleeve need lengthening cut across the pattern in the same places, separating the pieces to the required distance.

GENERAL DIRECTIONS FOR MAKING BLOUSES

When all the necessary alterations have been made in the pattern it should be carefully pinned to the material, and before taking the pieces off mark all seams, notches, or perforations in the pattern with chalk, or use the tailor's tacking stitch in coloured thread through both breadths of the material (see p. 420). If the blouse is to fasten at the back, the front portion of the pattern is laid to a lengthwise fold. If, as in the case of shirt blouses, the fastening is to be in front, the edge of the front portion of the pattern should be laid to the selvedge or to a straight thread running parallel with the selvedge.

In cutting out sleeves be careful not to cut both sleeves for one arm; this is a mistake very often made by the beginner.

When the blouse has been cut out, baste pieces together with notches evenly matched; slightly stretch the shoulder seam of the front piece or pieces whilst basting to make the blouse fit evenly at the neck. Also stretch the neck portion of the blouse whilst basting on the collar. All parts of unlined blouses should be sewn together with French seams (see p. 392) for the sake of neatness. When French seams are used, however, the blouse will set better if the seams are opened up from the bottom to the waist-line—the sides of the opened-out seams should be neatly turned over and hemmed. If the blouse is sewn into a small "basque band," sometimes called a "belt stay," at the waist, this will dispense with any unnecessary fulness below the waist-line, and the blouse will set better and not pouch out loosely over the waist-band, as blouses are often inclined to do.

Failing the belt-stay, a draw-string inserted at the back of the blouse should be used. This should be just at the waist-line; if placed too high it will show above the waist-belt; if too low the blouse will pouch out untidily at the back. Another effective way of keeping a blouse in place is to stitch a webbing band to the back and to fasten it round the waist before putting on the skirt. If, in addition, two strong hooks are sewn upside down on the webbing band and two eyes sewn on the skirt-band to fasten with the hooks, bodice and skirt can be securely kept together in this way without any danger of the blouse riddling up or the skirt slipping beneath the waist-band.

Making the Sleeve.—The seams of blouse sleeves should be first basted, and then very carefully sewn together. The top part of a blouse sleeve is gathered over the shoulder. The gathering must be made between the notches shown in the sleeve pattern, and each sleeve must be carefully sewn into the armhole with the notches in the top of the sleeve even with the notches in the armhole. The sleeve is also gathered at the wrist into the cuff. To finish off the armhole neatly a narrow piece of cambric cut on the cross should be stitched in the same seam that stitches the sleeve into the armhole, and afterwards turned over and stitched around to form a binding to the armhole, as shown in

Binding a Sleeve.

illustration. If the top of the sleeve is not too full, however, it can be sewn in with a French seam.

The sleeves of shirt blouses are nearly always made to open a few inches up the arm; the position of this opening varies with fashion. Sometimes the opening may be at the inside arm seam and sometimes at the back of the

Fig. 4.

sleeve. For a shirt cuff the sleeves are slashed at the wrist and an overlap and an underlap sewn on, as shown in fig. 4. The overlap should be adjusted so as to entirely conceal the underlap.

The Collar.—Collar patterns are always given with the blouse patterns. Collars are cut on the straight of the material and slightly curved to fit well into the neck. For short necks the collar must necessarily be rather low, and therefore very little curve is required, a straight band being often found sufficient. High collars, however, require to be well curved. With shirt blouses detachable linen or muslin collars are often worn over a plain neck-band. For dressy blouses, however, when high collars are worn these should be boned when finished to make them set well. It is always better to have collar supports which can be removed with little trouble when the blouse has to be washed or cleaned. The celluloid collar supports are admirable for this purpose. They should be sewn in on either side of the collar with the top coinciding with the line of the neck from the ear and the bottom of the support slanting slightly forwards. Collars of dressy blouses usually fasten at the back, and a collar support should be sewn at each side of the fastening. When the collar fastens in front a collar support should be sewn at each side of the front fastenings. When ordinary collar boning is used, be careful that this is finished off very neatly and covered with some soft covering, as in many instances painful and unsightly sores upon the neck have been caused where this important detail has been neglected.

From a plain shirt blouse pattern may be evolved many a blouse of a much daintier kind. The fastening may be made at the back instead of at the front, the latter being cut to the fold of the material. Such blouses may be made of silk, lace, muslin, net, *crêpe de chine*, or other dainty materials, and prettily trimmed with lace and insertion or hand embroidery. The plain shirt blouse is capable of many stages of evolution, and a well-fitting pattern should be carefully kept, as in time the home worker may evolve many ingenious ideas for making use of it in some new way. With plain loose blouses a separate blouse slip should be worn instead of lining. Blouse slips need not be boned; they can be of cambric, lawn, or washing silk, and are very easy to make.

Buttons and Button-holes.—Shirt blouses are usually fastened in front with buttons and button-holes. Care should be taken that buttons and button-holes are even. To ensure this, take a piece of light cardboard, make a notch in this corresponding to the distance required between each button-hole, and, beginning at the waist-line, mark the position of the button-holes by means of this notched card, marking each with a pin. The waist should be taken preferably as the beginning of the measurement, as there should always be a fastening at the waist-line, and this can be assured in this way. Make corresponding measurements for the buttons on the left side of the blouse front. (For making button-holes, see p. 400.)

Skirts.—Skirt patterns may have three, five, seven, nine or more gores; skirts with only three gores require darts in order to be fitted to the figure. A beginner often finds difficulty in arranging these darts, therefore it is better that she should select a skirt with five or seven gores for her first attempt.

As has been said before, when ordering a skirt

pattern particular attention must be paid to the measurement round the hips. If the hips are large in proportion to the waist, then order by the hip measurement, as although this entails receiving a pattern with a slightly larger waist, the latter can easily be taken in. For the length of skirt take your measurement from the waist to the floor in front, at the back, and over the hips. For walking length about two inches will have to be deducted from the measurement thus obtained. Now compare length obtained by measurement with the length of the pattern. If the pattern is too long, make it shorter by

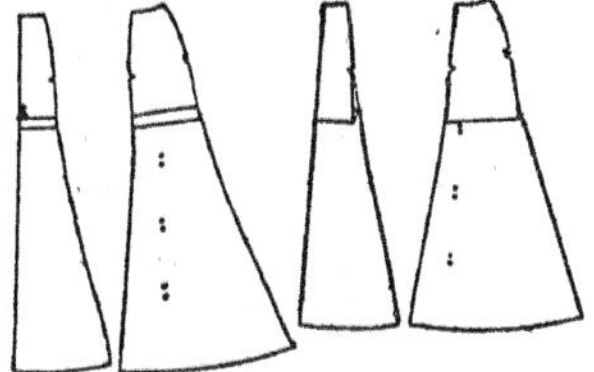

Fig. 5.—Lengthening and Shortening Skirt Patterns.

putting a tuck of the necessary size in each piece of the pattern about six inches below the hip-line. If it is too short, lengthen it by cutting across and separating the pieces to the distance required. Pin all pattern pieces carefully to the material, and mark all notches and perforations before taking the pieces off. In the case of women who are not of average proportions, alteration in length is not the only alteration which will have to be made. The skirt of the woman with a prominent abdomen, for instance, is apt to stand out in front unless properly cut. Although only a very simple alteration is necessary to secure a perfect fit, few women go to the trouble of finding out how this alteration can be made, and are surprised if their skirts hang badly through lack of it. An extra allowance should be made at the top of the front and side gores when the abdomen is

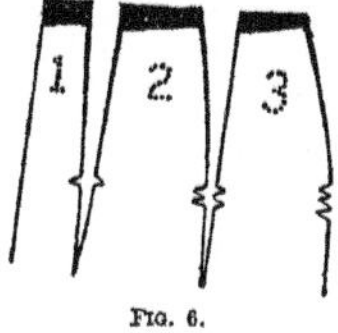

Fig. 6.

prominent, the extra depth being gradually diminished until it is reduced to next to nothing at the hips. Fig. 6 will convey a good idea of the alterations to be made; the extra length at the top of the skirt will prevent it from standing out in front. Care must be taken not to make the waist smaller when extending the gores; in order to avoid this the side edges of the gores must be increased as shown in illustration. When a skirt has to be altered in this way it is better to cut it out first upon some cheap coarse lining and fit it on before cutting the material.

To cut out Skirt Patterns.—If the material has a pile or "up and down," all tops of gores must be laid in the same direction when placed upon the material; if there is no up and down, the gores may be arranged for cutting with the top of one gore fitting in with the bottom of another. The front piece of pattern is marked with a notch on one side, the side without the notch being placed to a lengthwise fold; the other patterns are marked with notches on each side, thus the first side gore has one notch on one side and two notches on the other, the second side gore has two notches on one side and three on the other, and so on. The edge of a pattern piece with the less number of notches must always be placed to a selvedge or straight thread from the hip downwards, the hip of course being shaped to the figure; thus in a gore which has two notches on one side and three notches on the other the side with the two notches would be placed to the straight selvedge or straight thread, whilst the side with the three notches would naturally fall on the slant or the "cross" of the material.

The Pile of Cloth.—All woollen and cloth skirts should be cut with the pile running towards the bottom of the garment, but velvet or plush garments should be cut so that the pile runs upward. In cutting out the various pieces of the garment care must be taken that in each one the pile runs in the same direction.

Stripes, Checks, and Plaids.—In cutting the various pieces of a garment in striped, checked, or plaided materials care must be taken that the stripes, checks, and plaids are properly matched. For this reason a greater quantity of material will be required than in the case of plain stuffs. It is important in these cases to select a position for the top of the material. All the pattern pieces should then be placed with their upper parts in the direction selected. It is as well to place the pieces of the garment already cut on the material next to the adjoining piece which is to be cut. This will form a very good guide as to the best method of cutting the next piece. In matching plaids and patterns in this way a little waste of material is often unavoidable.

Stitching the Seams of Skirts.—The different pieces of the skirt should be carefully basted together before stitching. Lay the skirt on a table while putting it together. The straight side of each gore should always be held towards the worker. The straight edge of the gore always goes to the bias edge of another gore, excepting at the back, where the two bias edges come together. Care should be taken not to stretch the bias edges whilst basting. All the seams should be basted from the top downwards; the skirt should then be tried on and any unevenness at the hem corrected. If possible, it is as well to place the skirt on a dress-stand, or for the person who is to be fitted to stand upon a stool and get some one to mark on the bottom of the skirt with pins or chalk in an even line the exact length required. All skirts, excepting those of very light flimsy materials, such as ninon, &c., should be stitched by machine. In all cases they should be stitched from the top downwards. In machining side-back seams always have the back next the "feed" of the machine and the side-back next the pressure foot. When the seams have been stitched, press them open and overcast them. (For Overcasting, see p. 391.) When stitching seams of very light materials, such as washing silk, fine muslin, stitch a piece of tissue paper in the seam. This can be afterwards pulled off, and will prevent the material from puckering.

Finishing the Top of Skirts.—The waist-band may be made of cotton belting. If single belting is used it is stitched on the right side, and the raw edges on the wrong side are faced with silk or Prussian binding. Where the belting is double, this should be opened out, one end being stitched at the front of the skirt, the other taken over the back. Another way of finishing the top of the skirt is by means of a "cording"; this method is especially suitable for stout figures. To do this cut on the cross a piece of strong silk or other stuff one inch and a quarter wide; it must be a perfect bias. Place a medium-sized cord along this strip of silk or stuff, double the silk over, and run the silk and cording together, taking care not to stretch either the top of the skirt or the cording. Baste skirt and cording together by placing the side having the narrow seam of silk against the right side of the skirt with the cording towards the bottom. After basting, back-stitch to the skirt by hand, the right side of the skirt towards you, then turn in the edge to the inside and finish off neatly.

Plackets.—The placket of a skirt may be placed either at the side or at the back. The opening of the placket should be only as long as is necessary for the skirt to be slipped on and off easily. The seam should be opened out about ten or twelve inches from the waist according to the size round the hips, but in all cases the shorter the placket the better. Two strips of material, each half an inch longer than the placket opening, should be cut. One strip must be about four inches and the other strip about two inches wide. The wider strip is doubled over and sewn to the left side of the skirt to form an underlap, whilst the other strip is faced to the right side (see fig. 7).

Pockets are seldom worn nowadays, as there is not much room allowed for them in the tight-fitting skirt of the moment. Where a pocket is found indispensable, however, it should be made of lining to match the skirt and placed in the placket either at the side or at the back of the skirt. It usually takes the form of a kind

Fig. 7.

of pear-shaped bag, and is cut with the centre of the pocket to the fold of the material. Open it out and cut slip for pocket in the centre, where pattern has been placed against the fold. Face the opening with a piece of the dress material. Fold again after facing, stitching all round except at the opening; finish with French seam, and back-stitch pocket in the placket by hand.

Finishing the Bottom of the Skirt.—Never turn up the hem of a skirt before the waist-band has been adjusted. The bottom of the skirt may either be turned over and hemmed, or finished with a false hem. In turning over the skirt for the hem care must be taken that the latter is of the same depth all the way round. To ensure this take a piece of cardboard, make a notch in this of the depth required, and, using this as a measure, turn up hem all the way round to the depth of the notch. If the skirt is hemmed, the fulness at the top should be gathered slightly before basting it to the material. Baste carefully before stitching. The skirt may be hemmed by hand or machine-stitched. The hems of cloth and serge skirts are usually machine-stitched, sometimes being finished off with two or three or more rows of machine-stitching. Needless to say, the rows of stitching must be perfectly even or the appearance of the skirt will be spoiled.

In accordance with present fashions stiffening is not much used in the hems of skirts. Where an interlining is preferred, bias strips of lining or canvas are inserted in the hem. It is better to avoid very stiff interlining, as the latter very soon cuts the material. The edge of the skirt may be finished off with braid or binding to prevent it from cutting. Brush or velvet braiding are very good for the purpose. (For Method of Braiding Skirts, see p. 404.)

Making a False Hem.—A false hem may be made with pieces of material cut on the cross, or in the shape of the bottom of the skirt. In the latter case it is necessary to take the skirt pattern as a guide in cutting out. If the hem is faced with bias strips the odds and ends of material left over from the cutting can be utilised. A bias facing should always be stretched slightly at its lower edge and shaped to the skirt by pressing. Before putting on a false hem turn up the lower edge of the skirt on the wrong side and baste it; turn up also the lower edge of the false hem. This should be turned under and basted to the wrong side of the skirt (fig. 8). The

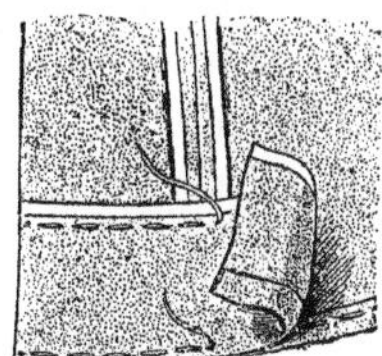

Fig. 8.

raw edge of false hem at the top may be turned in or bound with binding ribbon or braid. When it is basted into position, stitch skirt and false hem together. The hem should be well pressed with a warm iron on the inner side when finished, and all fulness at the top shrunk out by damping and then ironing.

Pressing Seams.—There are many details of dressmaking which the amateur more often than not altogether neglects; chief amongst these is the pressing of seams. Careful pressing is of the utmost importance to the appearance of the finished garment. Special skirt, bodice, and sleeve boards may be bought for the purpose, but, failing these, the home worker can press her garments quite well without them. Skirts and coats require a large flat surface, and should be ironed on a large ironing-board on a table. Sleeves, however, should always be pressed on a rounded surface. Failing a sleeve board, either an old broom-handle or a rolling-pin covered first with an old piece of blanket and then with a smooth white cloth, would make a very good substitute; a large round ruler might also be made to answer the purpose. The seams of cloth garments should be damped before pressing. It is not necessary, however, to damp the seams of lighter and softer materials. All darts should be pressed over a tailor's cushion where possible. Seams of silk and velvet garments should not be pressed upon a table or board. When it is necessary to press seams in silk or velvet, hold one end of the seam in the left hand, and let some one else hold the other end. Then with the right hand run the iron along the seam, pressing it open or closed as desired; in this way the iron touches only the seam. If no assistant is at hand, lay the iron on its side and use both hands to draw the seam across the edge of the iron. The hem of a silk skirt may be

Tailor's Cushion.

pressed in the usual way on the table or board, but do not have the iron hot, and press only the hem.

GENERAL HINTS

Shrinking Materials.—It is important to remember that all woollen materials should be shrunk before they are cut and made up. If this is not done, the dress will probably not only shrink if exposed to rain, but it will also spot. When buying woollen materials always inquire if they have been shrunk. If not the shrinking will be usually undertaken at the shop at which the material has been bought for a small charge per yard, or it may be accomplished at home in this manner:—Lay an ironing blanket evenly upon a good-sized table. Place the material face downwards upon the blanket, having first cut off the selvedges. Then take a strip of heavy unbleached muslin or drilling one yard wide and two yards long, wet and wring this out, and then place it over the material. Now press several times with the hot iron, shrinking only a small portion at a time. After doing this remove the muslin and press directly on the material until dry. Double-width material should be folded the right side inwards whilst being pressed. Some of the thinner woollen goods will not stand pressing in this way. It is as well always to experiment with a small piece of the material. If it is found that it becomes shrivelled up, it is a sign that water should not be used; press instead with a moderately warm iron.

An important point for the home dressmaker to remember is that some light summer washing materials, such as drill, duck, piqué, linen, spotted muslins, require shrinking as much as woollens, for if this is not done dresses of these materials will in most cases shrink a great deal after their first visit to the laundress.

There is another important detail in regard to dressmaking in which the home dressmaker often fails, *i.e.* neatness in finishing. A carelessly finished garment reflects but little credit upon its wearer. Neglected turnings and frayed edges, badly adjusted hooks and eyes, crooked button-holes, puckered hems, all betoken the careless worker. Every part of the garment should be neatly and carefully finished.

When making a skirt never forget to sew two little loops made of ribbon binding, skirt lining, or black tape to the inner side of the waist-band, one at each side of the waist, by which to hang up the skirt. This is only a little thing, but it helps to keep the shape of the skirt much longer than if it were hung up by the material itself.

Trimmings.—These play an important part in the fashioning of tasteful garments, and must be chosen with discrimination and taste. The skilful worker can transform quite a simple little blouse or skirt into very dressy garments indeed by the judicious addition of trimmings. Ornamental buttons may be utilised with great effect. These may be had in all kinds of shapes and designs, and are also often made of the same material as the dress. In this latter case the home worker must make the buttons herself, purchasing button moulds of the size required. These may be bought at any draper's and are covered by cutting out pieces of the material and gathering them on to the moulds.

Hand Embroidery is a very favourite trimming for blouses. A good transfer pattern should be procured and ironed on to the part to be embroidered. These patterns are often given away gratis by fashion papers, and should be carefully treasured in case occasion for using them arises. The transfer should always be tacked or pinned in the position required, the right side next to the material, and then pressed with a moderately hot iron. The iron must not be too hot, however, or the blue ink of the pattern will become obliterated, whilst if too cold no impression will be made. Very often in the case of blouses made of the heavier materials, instead of embroidering a transfer design, a most ornamental effect is achieved by applying a very narrow braid to the outline. The braid should be slip-stitched on with silk to match it, pressing well on the wrong side when finished. All passementerie and other similar trimmings should be carefully tacked in position before actually sewing them to the garment.

SOME SIMPLE PATTERNS

The following are smart yet simple styles which may be easily carried out by the home dressmaker. Patterns similar to those illustrated may be obtained upon application to The Butterick Publishing Company, Long Acre, London, W.C.

A Shirt Blouse.—Fig. 9 shows a very simple yet up-to-date little shirt blouse well within the scope of the amateur worker. It is finished with a simulated box-pleat in front and four tucks running from the shoulder on either side. The back is finished with two long forward-turning tucks to give the effect of a large box-pleat. The pattern may be had in bust sizes 32, 34, 36, 38, 40, 42, 44, and 46 inches. Two yards of material 44 inches wide will be sufficient to make the blouse for a woman of 34 or 36-inch bust measurement. The pattern is cut out with allowance for tucks, the position of the tucks

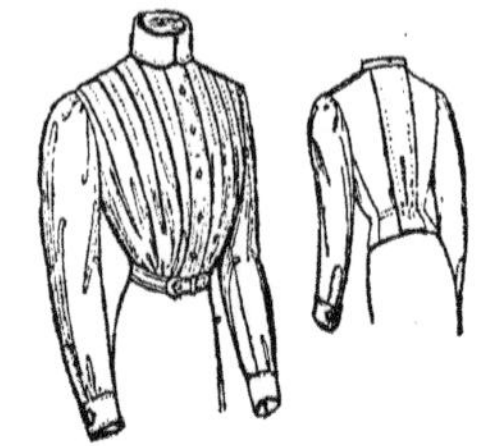

Fig. 9.—A Butterick Pattern.

being marked on the pattern with lines of perforations.

To cut out the Blouse.—All pieces with large triple perforations should be cut to a lengthwise fold; these include the back and the belt-stay. All the other pieces must be cut with the large double perforations lengthwise.

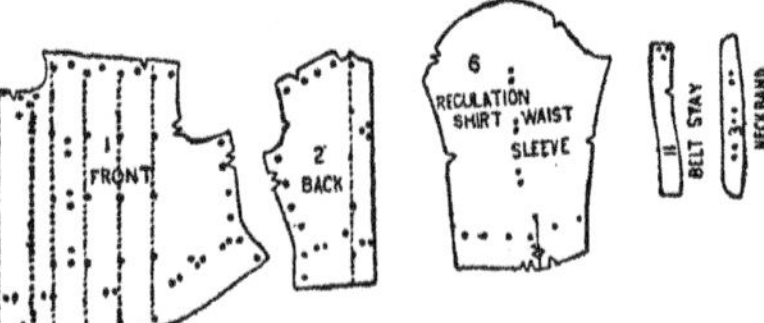

Pattern Pieces of Fig. 9.

To Make the Blouse.—To make the box-pleat fold under the edge of the right front at notches, stitching quarter of an inch from the fold, and make a backward-turning tuck, creasing the material for the purpose at the line of small triple perforations. Make a three-quarter inch hem on left front piece, turning hem under at large single perforation. On each side of the front make four backward-turning tucks, creasing the material for the purpose at the lines of small single perforations marked on pattern, stitching three-quarters of an inch from each crease, extending the tucks yoke depth. In the back make a forward-turning tuck on either side, creasing on lines of small single perforations and sewing three-quarters of an inch from each crease. Then gather the fronts and back at small double perforation in waist-line and three-quarters of an inch above, terminating gathering-in line with single perforations just above.

Baste seams with notches matched, gather sleeves at top between notches and at bottom into cuff. Join sleeve seam and baste sleeves into armholes with corresponding notches in top of sleeve and armhole. If the blouse is cut with a sailor collar, the neck must be cut slightly lower in front.

If the blouse is finished with a belt-stay, cut the latter out with the triple perforations on pattern to a lengthwise fold, and sew it under gatherings at waist-line with the notches at the bottom of the belt-stay meeting the under-arm seams.

The blouse should always be tried on before the seams are actually stitched, and any little arrangement of the fulness or other adjustment can be made.

A Useful Overblouse.—The overblouse given in the illustration (fig. 10) makes a very useful little garment, as it may be slipped on over a blouse which has already seen good wear, giving it quite a rejuvenated appearance. It can also be worn over a specially made guimpe or underslip and be fashioned out of ninon, net, lace, silk, cashmere, or velveteen, in accordance with the taste of the wearer. One and seven-eighth yards of material forty-four inches wide, or three and three-eighth yards of material twenty-seven inches wide would be required for women of from thirty-two to thirty-six in bust measure. It is very easy to make, as the garment is cut in one piece. Before cutting out make necessary alterations on pattern, lengthening or shortening the waist about two and a half inches above the waist-line. The latter will be indicated upon the pattern by a line of small double perforations. For wide material place the pattern with the edge having large triple perforation to a lengthwise fold. To avoid piecing when narrow material is used, cut with edge having large triple perforation lengthwise, allowing three-eighths of an inch for seaming. Cut trimming band for neck with triple perforation to lengthwise fold. Baste seams with perforations and notches matching. Turn hems under at each side of back. Gather along double perforations at waist-line and three-quarter inch above, terminating gathering-in line with large single perforations.

Fig. 10.—A Butterick Pattern.

Sew notched edge of sleeve-band to bottom of sleeve with seams even and notch on upper side.

Sew trimming band on flat with neck edges and front centres even.

There are many ways in which the overblouse idea may be extended and developed from the renovation point of view. By the addition of a skirt tunic it becomes transformed into a useful overdress. This may be carried out in ninon, lace, or net, and, worn over an old evening dress, will serve to give the latter quite a new lease of life. Light overdresses of the kind look especially well over satin, and as this material has had a certain vogue during the past two seasons for evening wear, it may be presumed that many a woman will have hidden away in some corner of her wardrobe a satin dress which in ordinary circumstances would have been put aside as having fulfilled its mission, but which, if she is wise, she can easily utilise in this very simple way.

A very useful and at the same time dainty evening gown can also be made by attaching the overblouse in semi-princess style to a simple five-gored skirt. This would look very well carried out in ninon and worn over a silk or satin underslip, whilst made in soft silk it would be a very simple style suitable for a young girl's evening gown.

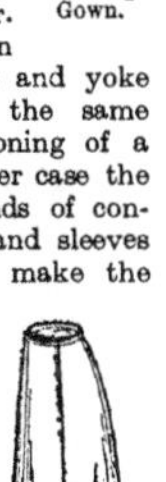

Evening Gown.

In cutting out the overblouse of soft material for evening wear, extra width should be allowed for gathering. If of very thin transparent material it is advisable to cut out an underbody of the same shape in silk or satin, only the latter should be quite plain and the overblouse gathered on to it. Three rows of gathers edged with a tiny frill, as shown in illustration, make a very effective finish for evening wear. Carried out in cashmere and worn over a simple guimpe, the sleeves and yoke of which are faced with lace, the same idea may be applied in the fashioning of a pretty afternoon gown. In this latter case the trimming should consist of the bands of contrasting material as finish to neck and sleeves instead of frills and gathers. To make the whole dress five yards of material forty-four inches wide would be required for women of thirty-six-inch bust measure, and for underbody of evening gown one yard of forty-five-inch material would be necessary.

A Simple Skirt.—The gored skirt pictured in illustration is a very simple pattern that may easily be attempted by the home dressmaker.

Fig. 11.—A Butterick Pattern.

Before cutting out on woollen stuffs the material should be shrunk (see p. 425) and the selvedge cut off.

The diagram (p. 428) shows the pieces of the skirt pattern. Some inexperienced amateurs have made the mistake of thinking that the single pieces joined together would make a whole skirt. Naturally they only represent the half; the second half of the front gore is obtained by placing the front of it indicated by three large perforations in the pattern to a lengthwise fold; the other pieces are cut in duplicate. As already pointed out, notches are made in each piece of the pattern to mark the

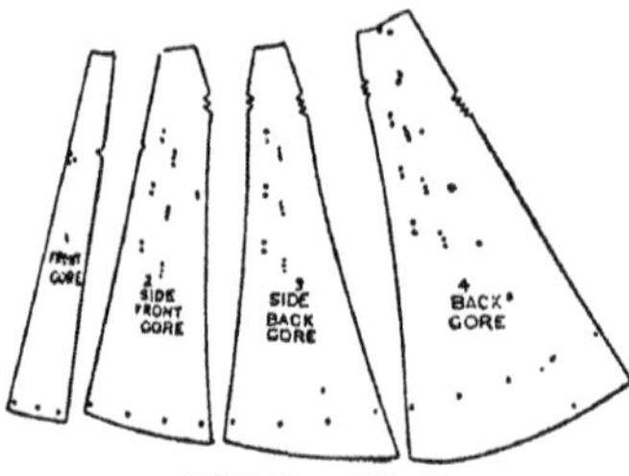

Pattern Pieces of Fig. 11.

position of the gores. In cutting the material these notches must be carefully marked, and in basting the skirt the pieces with a corresponding number of notches must be tacked together. Full instructions for cutting and making correctly are always given upon the pattern envelope.

For an average-sized figure four yards of material forty-four inches wide will be required.

A Princess Underslip.—The vogue for such ethereal fabrics as ninon, voile, lace, and net for afternoon and evening wear, together with fashion's mandate that the figure must be slim, and that therefore under-garments must be well fitting, has tended to decidedly extend the sphere of usefulness of that very comfortable and neat garment the "princess" underslip. There can, indeed, be no more useful accessory to the wardrobe, for instance, than one of these slips in black or white satin, for it can be worn under almost any kind of gown, and is at the same time dressy enough for the smartest occasions. Soft satin, it must be remembered, is an excellent material for wear, and is also washable, two very excellent recommendations for the woman with a small dress allowance, whilst made out of nainsook or batiste the slip is very useful for wearing with summer lingerie dresses.

For a slip with flounce six and a quarter yards of material thirty-six inches wide with four and one-eighth yards flouncing, eighteen inches deep will be required. Ribbon beading and lace can be used for trimming if desired.

..Jcks running igiven in fig. 12 may be made The back is finise flounce, with long or short

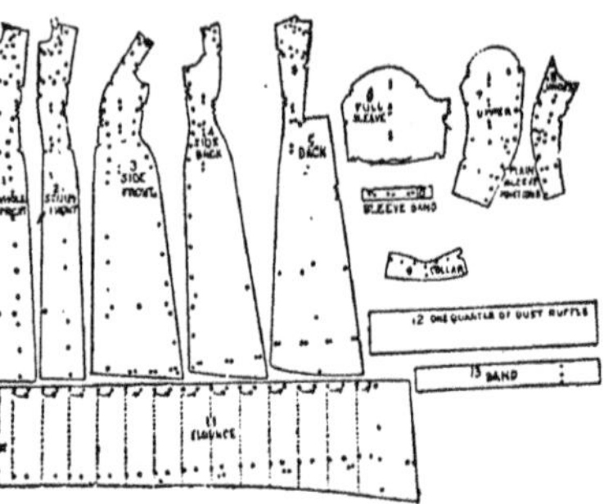

Pattern Pieces of Fig. 12.

sleeves, low or high neck, or the flounce may be made to button on to the skirt, so that two or three different flounces suitable for varying occasions may be made to go with the one garment, thus affording a pleasing variety in wear.

Two alternate fronts are given in the pattern pieces. The piece marked (1) is placed with the triple perforations to a lengthwise fold where no seam in front is desired. For narrow material and where there is to be a centre seam use the piece marked (2). The other pattern pieces consist of side-front, side-back, back, two styles of sleeves, sleeve-band, collar, one quarter of dust ruffle, flounce and band to be used when the flounce is made to button on to the garment. If the under-garment is to be made of satin or silk, and the dust ruffle is to be accordion pleated, cut the latter from pattern piece numbered 12 according to instructions given below, and send it to an accordion pleater, who will do the work for a small charge. The pattern is adaptable to either the medium sweep or the round length.

Fig. 12.—A Butterick Pattern.

If flouncing is desired, cut the pattern of flounce (No. 11), with front edge having a cluster of four small perforations on a fold and lower edge at border; if of other goods in either length, cut with front edge on lengthwise fold. Cut "12" the depth and four times the length of its pattern, "13" twice the length of pattern lengthwise; piece with large triple perforation on lengthwise fold; other pieces with large double perforation lengthwise.

To Make.—Gather sleeve along top between notches. If full sleeve is used, gather this at bottom also. Join parts with notches matched, and, furnishing an opening at centre-back, seam above cluster of four notches for back closing, or at centre-front seam just below lowest single notch for front closing. If flounce is to be pleated, make thirteen backward-turning pleats at each side by creasing from each small single perforations in top to corresponding perforation below, and bring creases over to large single perforation, as indicated by small arrows on diagram.

If a gathered flounce be preferred, gather top of flounce and dust ruffle, and join dust ruffle to bottom of gores. Sew flounce to slip at line of large single perforations, or, if flounce is to be buttoned on, join ends of band; sew one long edge of band to top of flounce and sew other long edge over seam. Work equally spaced button-holes on band, and sew corresponding buttons to slip as far above large single perforations as required for top of flounce to come at perforations when adjusted.

Then sew the upper edge of a row of insertion to the slip so that it will cover the band when slip is buttoned on. Trim with edging, insertion, and ribbon beading.

For an inverted pleat at back, crease from large single perforations near waist-line to corresponding perforations below, and bring both creases over to back edges of extensions.

Try on, bringing closing edges of slip together, and making alterations if necessary at outlet seams.

A Useful Evening Cape.—The Toga cape has supplied a long-felt want on the part of the home worker, for it is a simple pattern of an evening cape easy to cut and easy to

FIG. 13.—A Butterick Pattern.

make, yet at the same time bearing the all-important hall-mark of style. It is a fashion also which promises to die hard on account of its general all-round usefulness. Satin, cashmere, or other soft and easily draped material is the best to use in making this cape. The material should be as wide as possible to avoid the necessity of a centre seam. Three and seven-eighth yards of material fifty-four inches wide, or four and three-quarter yards forty-four inches wide, or seven and three-eighth yards of twenty-seven-inch material would be required. There is only one piece to the pattern.

To Cut.—If material without nap or distinct

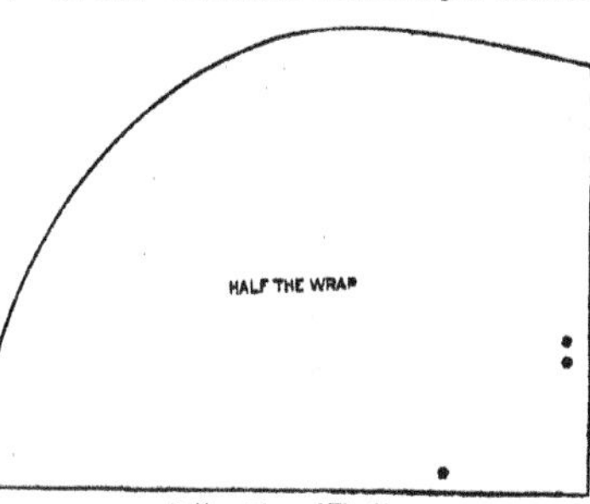

Pattern Piece of Fig. 13.

up or down is used, cut with back edge (part of pattern showing double perforation) to a crosswise fold: if the material has a distinct up or down cut with edge having a double perforation crosswise, allow three-eighths of an inch on this edge for seaming.

To Make.—Tack the two edges of the top together to form a loop at the point indicated by single perforation on pattern. Try on to see that it hangs well and that the tacking comes just at the back of the neck with the fulness hanging in folds as illustrated. The simplest method of adjusting the front of the cape is to allow it to hang straight, a pretty ornamental buckle being used as a fastening. Trim with hand embroidery or fancy braiding and fasten a tassel to the lower end of loop. The wrap may be lined if desired.

A Simple Morning Dress.—In the chapter upon the "Choice and Care of Dress" it is said that every woman should have a simple but neat dress for morning wear, especially when she has a number of little household duties to attend to. This dress should be made preferably of washing material and should be cut just long enough to clear the ground, or even shorter if required. It should fit the figure neatly, yet loosely enough to be comfortable and to allow free movement of the limbs. All these important qualities, which are so indispensable for a really useful house dress, will be found in fig. 14.

This pictures a morning dress composed of a neat blouse bodice attached to a plain seven-gored skirt in semi-princess style. The skirt may be finished off with a flounce at the foot or else may be left quite plain, according to individual taste. For the dress without the flounce four and seven-eighth yards of material forty-four inches wide would be required for a woman of thirty-six-inch bust measure, one and a quarter yards extra material of the same width being necessary for the flounce. The dress may be made up with or without a lining. We shall explain the latter method as being the easier of accomplishment by the home worker.

FIG. 14.—A Butterick Pattern.

Before cutting out blouse bodice, try on to see position of waist-line; if the latter is too high or too low make the necessary alterations by slashing or pleating pattern (see p. 421). Also make the necessary alterations on skirt pattern. This latter can have either inverted pleats at the back, or be finished with gathers, or else be left perfectly plain. If the last-named method be preferred

Pattern Pieces of Fig. 14.

it will be necessary to cut off back edge of back gore of pattern at the line of small single perforations.

To Cut.—If two bias edges are to meet at each side seam, for striped or plaid material cut the side and back gores with line of small triple perforations lengthwise, or if a bias edge is to meet a straight edge, for plain material cut these gores with large double perforations lengthwise. Cut all pieces with edges having large triple perforations on a lengthwise fold, and other pieces with large double perforations lengthwise. Either a bishop sleeve or a leg of mutton sleeve may be used—patterns of both styles are usually given.

To Make.—Baste seams and join gores with notches and perforations matching. Finish off right front of blouse with box-pleat, gather sleeve at top between notches. If the bishop sleeve pattern is used, slash up at the wrist, and finish with a lap seven-eighth inch wide. Gather sleeve at bottom between notches. Turn under end of cuff in line with large single perforations for a hem. Gather the front and back of blouse at the bottom and also one and a quarter inches above, terminating gathering at large single perforations. Either a turn-down collar or a high standing collar may be used. Roll the former at line of perforations, or sew on the latter with ends meeting at centre-back.

If flounce is used, it should be cut four times the length of pattern. Fold under top of this seven-eighths of an inch and gather half an inch from fold, or if a heading is not desired, cut off top of flounce half an inch and gather at top. Sew flounce along gathering to skirt with lower edges even.

For inverted pleats crease the back gore on line of large single perforations, and bring creases to centre seam. If preferred gathered at back, gather gores between small double perforations (see diagram).

Join the skirt to the blouse with front and back centres even.

Sew a belt one and a half inch wide when finished flatly over joining of skirt as illustrated, and join loose edge of front gore to belt.

A Kimono Dressing-gown or Jacket.—For a simple yet pretty style of dressing-gown, the now familiar kimono is difficult to beat. The trend of fashion also leaves it practically untouched, for it bids fair to remain a long time with us, if only for its usefulness, which is undisputed.

If it is wished to keep strictly to the kimono idea, a material with a floral pattern is the best to use. Pretty Japanese silks, prints, or cottons with floral designs make up very effectively, a band of some plain contrasting material being used as a finish. For warmer garments plain flannels and nun's veiling may be used.

FIG. 15.—A Butterick Pattern.

For the dressing-gown given in our illustrations four and one-eighth yards of material forty-four inches wide will be needed for women of thirty-six-inch bust measure, with two yards of contrasting material twenty or more inches wide for trimming bands. A dressing-jacket may be made from the same pattern by cutting off the front and back pieces and the front trimming band at the line of large single perforations running across the pattern pieces. A long or a short sleeve may be made. For the latter cut off the sleeve pattern at the line of small single perforations.

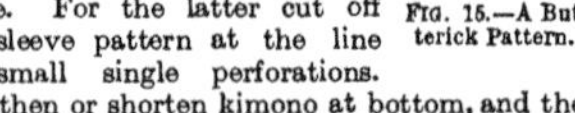

Lengthen or shorten kimono at bottom, and the sleeve near notches in side edges. A two-and-a-half-inch hem is allowed both for dressing-gown and dressing-jacket. Cut all pieces having large double perforations lengthwise of the material

To Make.—Gather sleeve along top between notches. Join parts with notches marked. Try on, bringing front edges of fronts together,

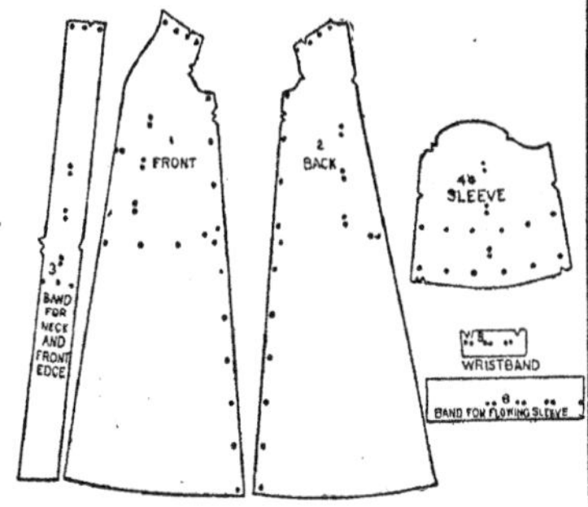

Pattern Pieces of Fig. 15.

making alterations, if necessary, at seams. Sew bands of contrasting material to neck and front edges of garment, and sleeve-bands to sleeves. For the dressing-jacket two and three-eighth yards of material forty-four inches wide, or two and three-quarter yards thirty-six inches wide, with one and three-eighth yards contrasting material twenty inches or more wide for bands, will be required.

This pattern is also capable of development into a useful theatre coat when satin, one of the heavier silks, or cloth in some pretty art shade is used. The kimono shape has long been in favour for evening wear, and its popularity is by no means on the wane. When used in this way the garment should be neatly lined with satin, silk, or polonaise. The sleeves may either be gathered into a cuff or allowed to fall loose according to individual taste. Needless to say, it should be finished off very neatly, and the facings of neck and sleeves should be interlined with stiff muslin or other kindred material.

Note.—When ordering any of the patterns illustrated from the Butterick Publishing Company, mention *The Woman's Book,* and quote number appearing under illustration.

Useful Measurements

12 inches	1 foot
3 feet	1 yard
36 inches	1 yard
100 centimetres	1 metre
109 ,, ...	1 yard
1 metre . . .	about 40 inches
8 finger-lengths . . .	1 yard

HOME MILLINERY

This chapter has been written for the benefit of the amateur and home worker, and not for that of the woman who wishes to earn her living as a milliner. For this reason, therefore, only the principles of simple millinery, well within the scope of the average woman who is obliged to eke out a small dress allowance by making or trimming most of her own or her children's hats, are detailed. How to make a pretty bow or rosette, how to sew on feathers, how to make and sew in a head-lining, and to line the brim of a hat, are all first steps in millinery which must be mastered by the home worker, and by means of numerous illustrations and diagrams we have endeavoured to explain these essential preliminaries in as clear a manner as possible.

A description of the more intricate work, such as the making of wire frames, &c., has been omitted, as a course of special lessons under a teacher would be necessary to acquire proficiency in this.

It is not within the scope of a book of this kind to deal with the latest styles in regard to hats, for fashion varies to such an extent that even the latest style in millinery at the time of writing would probably be *demodé* by the time this article had passed through the printer's hands. There are certain principles of millinery, however, which cannot alter. These are fully dealt with; and if they are carefully studied and successfully put to practical use by the home worker she will find it quite easy to adapt them to the prevailing modes. The knack of arranging flowers and other trimmings can scarcely be taught. It comes as the result of natural taste and artistic instinct. We cannot all be originators of artistic ideas in millinery, but at least we can endeavour to copy the ideas of others.

This can be done by carefully studying the shop windows and fashion papers, noting the prettiest styles and endeavouring to apply them to our own needs. In this way and by constant and persevering practice, artistic efforts may be achieved by every woman who puts her heart into her work.

MILLINERY EQUIPMENT

Apart from the special requirements for each hat the necessary implements and material for home millinery are few and inexpensive.

If millinery is undertaken regularly at home it will be well to lay in a supply of the following, and then it will not be necessary to buy small quantities each time a hat has to be made or re-trimmed.

Millinery Pliers.

(1) Millinery pliers, 1s. per pair, used for cutting wire instead of scissors.

(2) Millinery or straw needles of various sizes.

(3) Steel pins, long and slender, with sharp points.

(4) Silk wire, 1¾d. a ring; satin wire, 2d. per yard, black and white.

(5) Ribbon wire for wiring ribbon bows, 1d. per card, black and white, and cotton wire, ½d. to 6d. per ring.

(6) Black and white sarcenet for head-linings, 1s. 3d. per yard, or thin cotton.

(7) Black and white china ribbon for running through head-linings, ½d. per yard.

(8) Soft and stiff muslin in both black and white, 2¾d. to 6¾d. per yard.

(9) Buckram, 6¾d., or spartra, 1s. ¾d. per yard, for making shapes, bandeaux, &c.

(10) Strong sewing cotton, Nos. 16 or 20, or sewing silk in black and white, and any special colour to suit the hat that is being trimmed.

The home milliner will also be well advised to keep a piece-box into which odds and ends of lace, silk, ribbon, &c., can be put. Little pieces of this description will often be found of service and be the means of saving many a penny.

HEAD-LININGS

Every hat or bonnet should have a head-lining to make it tidy, and also to prevent the rough straw or edges catching the hair. This should be put in before any trimming is commenced, although in the case of the brim requiring lining this would naturally come first.

A head-lining is generally made of black or white sarcenet, but any light weight and soft finished quality of silk, such as thin glacé, China or pongée, will do equally well. In very light lace or net hats a net or chiffon lining can be put in, while in cheap hats a soft cotton or muslin will serve the purpose. For dark hats, black or a colour to tone with the material must be used, while white is the best for light-coloured hats, although sometimes a colour to match the straw is used for the crown. This is sometimes necessary if the straw is of a very transparent make. Odds and ends of silk and ribbon may often be utilised for this purpose.

The lining for a hat should be cut in two pieces, a round or square-shaped piece for the crown and a long-shaped piece to go round the sides. The side lining may be cut either on the cross or on the straight. For the breadth measure the height of the crown and two inches over, and for the length measure the inside circle of the crown, allowing one and a half inches over for the join. Commence to sew the lining in at the centre of the back either by stabbing through the crown or sewing it in as in fig. 1, sewing with an overcasting stitch

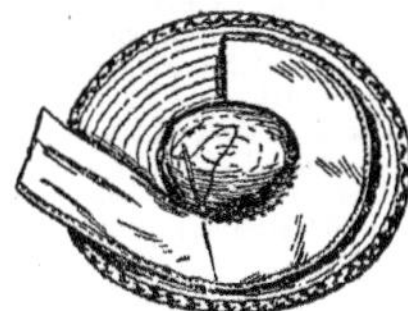

FIG. 1.

from right to left. The stitches must not show on the right side. Where the head-lining meets at the back slip the needle through the lining and slip-stitch or hem the two sides together. Make a narrow hem on the edge of the lining, and draw this up with narrow China ribbon after the hat has been trimmed.

The crown top lining may be either square or round and of a size to fit the hat. Line it with tissue paper, and either paste it in with a very little paste or sew in with a tacking stitch, *i.e.* a long stitch inside and a very small stitch on the outside of the crown.

The lining of a bonnet is put in in the same way, only the ends of the lining are not joined together, but hemmed down at the base of the bonnet.

If the home milliner does not wish to take the trouble of making her own head-linings, most of the large drapery establishments sell them ready for sewing in. They will cost from 6d. to 9d.

BANDEAUX

A bandeau is used to make a hat fit more comfortably, to make it smaller or larger, or to raise it off the head in one part or another. It is also used for sewing on trimmings.

A bandeau is generally made of buckram or spartra wired at the edges and then covered with velvet or silk. Velvet is largely used for the purpose, as it clings to the hair. For a very light hat three thicknesses of stiff net may be used instead of buckram, wired at the edges and then bound with silk or velvet cut on the cross. It can then be covered with tulle or chiffon. This will not of course be so strong as the buckram bandeau.

To Make a Round Bandeau.—This is used to make a hat either smaller or larger and also to raise it off the head. Cut buckram or spartra on the cross one and a half inches deep and of a size to fit the head, allowing one inch for joining. Join into a circle and wire top and bottom with silk wire, using a button-hole or wire stitch. (see fig. 2). Be careful to lap the wire one inch

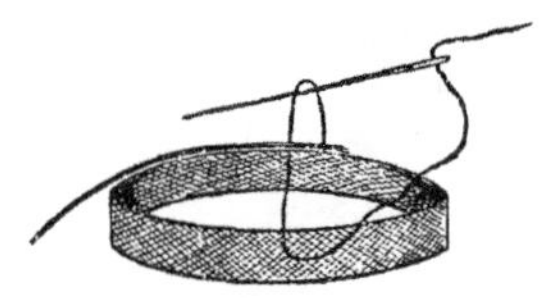

FIG. 2.

at all joins. Then cut some velvet on the cross four inches deep and of a length to go round the bandeau, allowing for turnings. Place the strip of velvet inside the bandeau with a half-inch turning above the edge. Tack in position through velvet and buckram (fig. 3). Then bring

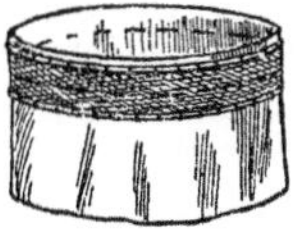

FIG. 3.

the velvet up on the right side, turn in the raw edges, and slip-stitch the two together. This bandeau should be stab-stitched into the hat after the head-lining is sewn in.

Black velvet is most generally used for all bandeaux, although they can be made of a colour to match the hat.

A Small Bandeau.—This is made in the same way as the circular bandeau. It is used to tilt the hat off the head in the front, back or

sides as the shape requires. Any trimming that is desired may be attached to it.

A Flat Bandeau.—This is one of the most fashionable bandeaux of the present day. Cut a circle in buckram ten inches across and cut away the centre two inches from the outer edge. Wire round both edges the same as in the other bandeaux. Cover with velvet on one side only. Turn the outer edge over to the wrong side and sew it down, then notch the inner edge, and catch down the notches on the wrong side of the buckram (fig. 4). Place the bandeau with the raw edges next the hat and tack it into position. An easy way to find correct position is first to

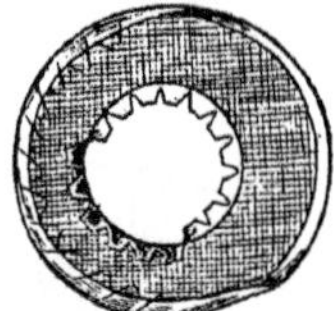

FIG. 4.

place the bandeau on the head (velvet side next the hair), and then to put the hat on the top. Take off hat, holding the bandeau in its proper position.

VELVET

Most people know that there is a pile on velvet; that is to say, one way will feel rough and the other smooth when it is stroked with the hand.

In cloth the pile or smooth way always runs down, but in velvet it is just the reverse, as it runs up. There are two ways of finding out the up and down of velvet—by feeling it or by looking at it. Either pass your hand very gently over the surface and feel how the pile runs, or hold it up to the light and see how the light affects it. It should appear dark; if it looks light it is the wrong way of the material.

Velveteen should not be used in millinery as it is too heavy.

The greatest care must be taken in cutting and placing velvet to have the pile running the same way in each piece, or one piece will look lighter than another.

When covering a hat the velvet should shade from the front to the back. It is always best to cut out all the pieces together, and then a mistake is not so likely to be made.

When lining or binding a hat with velvet the brim should be held with another piece of velvet to prevent the fingers marking it.

When fixing two pieces of velvet together needles or fine steel pins should be used, as the ordinary pins would make marks on the smooth surface. It should always be tacked or sewn with silk, as cotton will also mark it, and the tacking threads should not be pulled out roughly, but cut here and there with a pair of scissors and then gently drawn out.

To Cut Velvet or Silk on the Cross.—Lay the material on the table with the right side uppermost and the selvedges running the length of the table. Take the bottom left-hand corner and fold it across to the right until the selvedge threads run straight with the weft threads (fig. 5), and cut through the fold. The fold

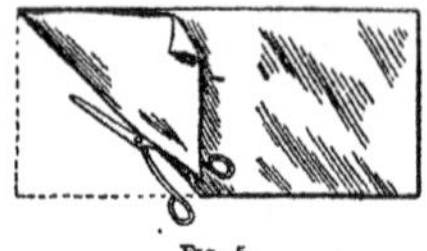

FIG. 5.

is the exact cross of the material; if the exact cross is not cut the bind or whatever the crossway pieces are used for will not set smoothly when put on the hat.

To Join Silk and Velvet on the Cross.—Cut the strips of the material off the cross-cut end and of the width required. The joins in a crossway piece of material always run on a slant, which

FIG. 6.

means that they are joined on the straight of the material. Place the two selvedges or two slanting pieces together so that a pointed and a blunt end are together as in figs. 6 and 7. Velvet is better joined by hand with small back-stitches

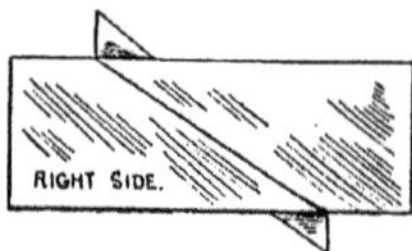

FIG. 7.

made about half an inch down from the selvedge. Care must be taken that the dark shade in both pieces runs the same way. Silk may be joined by machine.

To Hem Velvet.—There is a special stitch for hemming velvet called the "Catch Stitch." Turn down the velvet once and commence sewing at the left-hand corner. First take a stitch on the turning without going through to the other side, then a very small stitch just below the turning taking up a mere thread of the back of the velvet. No stitches must show on the right side (fig. 8).

Roll Hemming Velvet.—In this method the velvet is turned down twice and the stitches do

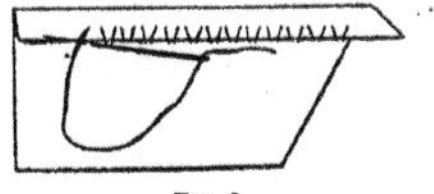

FIG. 8.

not show. Turn down less than quarter of an inch to the wrong side, then turn over again quarter of an inch, thus hiding the raw edges. With a needle and silk take up one or two threads on the back of the velvet and a long stitch on the under part of the double fold. Draw the thread as tight as possible without puckering, when the stitches should be invisible and the hem have a round appearance.

A Rouleau.—This is generally put on the under-brim of a hat about one inch from the edge, to cover the hat and to give the brim a more finished and softer appearance. A velvet rouleau a shade darker than the hat itself always looks well.

Take a crossway strip of velvet about an inch wide and turn the raw edges over to the wrong side, making them meet in the centre. Lace

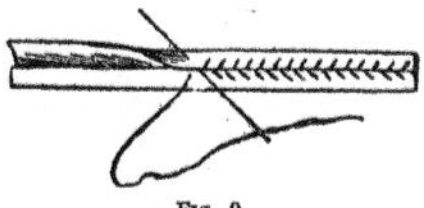

FIG. 9.

them together, taking a stitch first under one side and then under the other (fig. 9).

To Make a French Fold.—Cut a piece of velvet on the cross three times the width the fold is to be when finished. Fold over one edge, then fold over the other edge, turning one edge over more than the other (fig. 10).

Next turn over the narrow turning halfway on to the wider turning, so that no raw edges show,

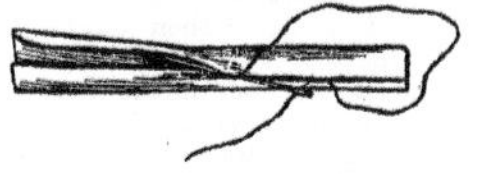

FIG. 10.

slip-stitch this fold down, taking great care that the stitches do not show through on the right side.

Velvet Ears.—Cross-cut ends of velvet are frequently used in the making of bows, as the material is too thick to allow of many loops. They are also economical, as they use up the small pieces of velvet.

There are several different ways of making these :—

Fig. 11.—Take a strip of velvet, turn the long point over to meet the shorter one, pile to pile, and stitch across the open side. Then turn

FIG. 11. FIG. 12.

inside out, push the blunt end of a pair of scissors into the point, and fix in position with a few slip-stitches. Hem the remainder of the strip on both sides.

Fig. 12.—Take a straight end of velvet and turn over one of the points crossways pile to pile. Sew the side edges together and turn inside out, pushing the point well out.

Or take a cross-cut end and line it with a piece of velvet or silk the same shape. Put the two right sides together and sew round with the exception of the straight end. Turn inside out and finish as before.

OTHER PRELIMINARIES

Wiring the Edge of a Hat.—The edge of a hat is usually wired to keep the brim in shape. When a hat in unlined and without a binding or facing of any kind, wire of the same colour as the straw should be used. A medium-sized satin wire is best, as there is more thickness for the stitches to sink into and be hidden. The wire should be placed at from a quarter to half an inch from the edge of the brim on the under or wrong side of the straw.

The wire, when possible, should be stab-stitched on; that is to say, the stitches taken through from one side to the other so as not to bend the hat or wire. The size of the stitch will depend upon the kind of straw ; a smaller stitch will be required for the finer makes than for those of a coarser quality. In machine-made hats there is often a double row of straw round the edge between which the wire can be slipped, and then the straw can be caught down to keep the wire in position. Some of the finer makes of straw, such as Panama and Leghorn, are strong enough to enable the wire to be simply sewn to one of the braids without taking the needle through to the wrong side.

Care must be taken to make the stitches as invisible as possible, and strong silk of the same colour as the wire should be used for sewing.

To join the wire allow an extra inch for overlapping and cut off with the pincers. Unwind the silk of both ends and push back the cotton under covering, trimming it off where it is not required. Then re-wind the silk over the two ends together tightly and neatly.

In all good hats, and especially those of a fine make of straw, it is usual to cover the wire with a rouleau of velvet, silk or tulle, unless the brim of the hat is lined entirely. In this case the cotton-covered wire will serve the purpose, and it may be sewn on with a loose button-hole stitch.

To Bind the Edge of a Hat.—Whatever material is used it should be cut on the cross. First wire the edge of the brim, unless the hat is very firm and does not require the extra stiffening; then cover the wire with a piece of muslin cut on the cross to prevent it showing through and marking the velvet or whatever material the binding is made of. Cut the material twice the width required plus one inch for turnings. Join neatly on the cross and get the necessary length.

Tack down half an inch turning on each side of the strip and fold the bind in half. Slip a pair of scissors inside, and with the blunt point stretch the fold to enable the bind to lie flat on the round of the hat. Then pin in position, arranging that a join does not come in the front, and tack round the outer edge through the hat and the two thicknesses of material, rather stretching it on. Slip-stitch the bind on to the hat first on the upper and then on the under side of the rim.

Linings for Hat-Brims.—At the present time tulle, net, soft silk, satin, and velvet are the most fashionable for lining the under-brims of hats, but of course any soft material can be used. Figs. 13, 14, 15 illustrate three very pretty methods of preparing a lining, and the material for these can be cut either on the straight or on the cross.

For fig. 13 measure round the edge of the hat and allow half as much again for the fulness.

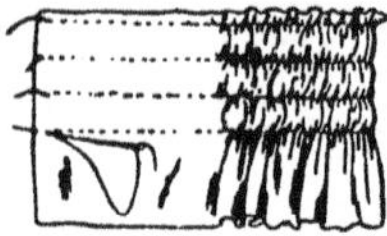

Fig. 13.

Cut the width the widest measurement of the brim, plus one and a half inches for turnings.

Put in gatherings at equal distances apart, and fix on to hat; by the outer and inner gathering sometimes the centre gathering also has to be fixed. Slip-stitch the join neatly together.

In fig. 14 allow same width round as in fig. 13, but in the width the tucks must be allowed for. For each tuck allow twice its width.

In fig. 15 cord is required. The cord can be bought in many sizes at a penny a bundle in black and white. Cut material the same size

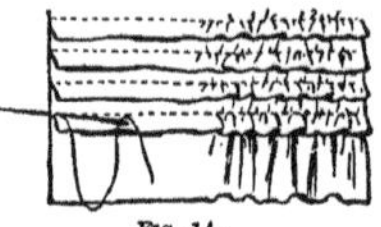

Fig. 14.

as for fig. 14. The cord can either be put in after the tucks are made or the tucks may be made over the cord.

Plain Under-Brims made of satin, velvet, or silk are very much used nowadays. These should be cut out and put on in the same way

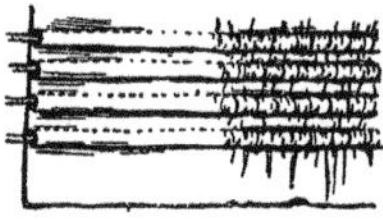

Fig. 15.

as in covering the under-brim of a buckram shape (see p. 440).

Ruching.—A ruching may be made of silk, net, tulle, ribbon, lace, &c., and consists of a succession of box-pleats made along the length of the material and fastened down in the centre.

When made of single box-pleats three times the length of the finished ruching will be required, for double box-pleats five times, and for treble seven times as much. Thus, to make one yard of ruching of double box-pleats, five yards of ribbon or other material would be required.

The single box-pleat is formed by making a pleat in the ribbon to the right and another to the left, leaving one to one and a half inches between, and making the inner folds of each meet at the back, but this simple pleating is seldom used for millinery purposes.

For a *double box-pleated ruche* start by making a pleat towards you and then another exactly on the top; make another pleat away from you at about one and a half inches distance and another exactly underneath. Tack the pleats in position along the centre, and continue thus until the required length is made.

Care must be taken to make the pleats of equal width.

The *treble box-pleat* is made with three pleats to either side.

To give the ruche a lighter appearance raise the top pleat on each side and tack them together a little way in from the edge (fig. 16).

When a ruching is made of silk the edge is usually mushed or frayed out. The silk must be cut on the cross in strips four and a half or five inches in depth, and then joined to get the required length. A yard of silk will make a ruching for a fair-sized hat. Fray out the edges

FIG. 16.

with a pin to the extent of a quarter or half an inch, drawing out the threads the way of the silk. Make up the ruching as above, and when the edges of the pleats are tacked together this will form a very light and feathery-looking trimming and one which is very serviceable.

Quilling consists of a number of pleats placed nearly on the top of each other and fixed along one edge. It is used principally for the fronts of babies' bonnets, and can be made of ribbon, chiffon, or lace.

A Chiffon Quilling.—Cut a piece of chiffon twice the depth required, fold it in half, and pin to keep it in position. Place the strip lengthways on the table and commence pleating at the end farthest from you. Make one pleat about half an inch deep away from you, make another the same size but underneath the last pleat, so that one pleat is on the top and one underneath. Make the next pleat on the top, placing it so that it covers up half of the first pleat made. Continue thus first pleating on the top and then underneath, making the pleats all the same size and placing each one to centre of the last. Sew along the raw edge to keep pleats in position.

THE MAKING OF BOWS AND ROSETTES

General Hints.—The ribbon must be handled very lightly if the bow is to have a fresh appearance. The novice usually errs in experimenting too much, with the result that the daintiness which marks first-class millinery is altogether wanting.

When making bows for the first time it is as well to commence by practising on strips of stiffish muslin, or old ribbon, or even with tissue paper, and then when the knack of making loops has been acquired the new ribbon may be handled without fear.

If the bow is in ribbon it is better, if possible, to keep it in one piece; it can then be unpicked, ironed out, and renovated and made up in a different way when wanted. This can of course only he done with good ribbon. In any case, it is better not to cut the ribbon in separate loops.

Do not be too sparing in the quantity of the ribbon used or you will spoil the effect. A bow should have a nice firm and rounded appearance when finished, and in order to obtain this the two ends of each loop must be pleated in *opposite* directions. The pleated ends must be secured by winding them round and round with strong cotton or linen thread.

When pulling the loops into position do so by placing the forefinger into each loop, being careful not to flatten it down or it will be wanting in that smart and stylish appearance which is so necessary.

The number and size of the loops will depend upon the style of bow that is required, but all the loops and ends must appear to come from one centre; there must only be one root to the bow, and that must be as tight as possible. A single stitch or two may be taken where necessary to keep the loops in place, but these must always be under a fold and invisible. It may sometimes be found better to mount the loops on a small tab of stiff net.

Although there are many different styles of bows, and fashions are apt to vary in this respect, if you succeed in making one shape well you will be able to make them all with very little difficulty.

Wiring.—When the loops are long and it is wished to have them standing out well in a certain direction, the ribbon should be wired. The wire may be pinned down the centre of the ribbon on the wrong side, made up with the loops, and then fixed in position with one or two stitches taken on the back of the loops. Ribbon wire is the best to use; or a fine lace wire the same colour as the ribbon may be neatly tacked along the centre of the ribbon on the wrong side.

A Bow for the Back or Front of a Hat.—From two to two and a quarter yards of ribbon about six inches wide will be required. Commence at one end of the ribbon, leaving four or five inches

FIG. 17. FIG. 18.

to form an end, then pleat into small pleats and twist round with cotton (fig. 17). A needle can be used if desired to keep the fastening tight. Then measure the length of loop required and pleat the other end in opposite direction from the first pleats (fig. 18). Make three more loops in the same way, and arrange them so that two of the loops lie in an opposite direction to the

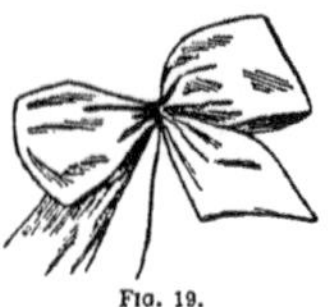

FIG. 19.

other two, then leave an end to match the one left at the beginning (figs. 19 and 20). The tie over should be made of a separate piece of ribbon, and can be large or small according to

FIG. 20.

fashion and on the straight or cross of the material.

Bow for the Side of a Hat.—About three yards of ribbon seven inches wide will be required. Make in the same way as the above, only it is usual to have all loops and no ends. The loops which lie towards the front of the hat may be a little shorter than those which lie towards the back. The tie over should be rather broad, and is better put on after the bow has been fixed to the hat. Unless the ribbon used is very stiff, a bow like this would require to be wired.

Bows of Piece Silk, Velvet, &c.—A bow made of silk cut from the piece is generally cheaper than one made of ribbon. A fairly large-sized bow can be made with one and a half or two yards of silk at 1s. 11d. per yard. The silk should be cut on the cross in strips about nine inches wide and then joined together in one length. Hem the edges with sewing silk the same colour and then make up the bow the same way as in ribbon. If the bow requires wiring, make a fold at the edge of the silk and stitch along twice to form a casing, then slip in a silk wire before making up the bow.

When bows are made of piece velvet the material must be cut on the cross and joined in the same way as for a silk bow. When making the loops, fold and pleat through two thicknesses, as if done separately as in ribbon the wrong side of the velvet would show too much. Velvet bows are often lined with silk or ribbon of the same or a contrasting colour ; when this is done the bow should be made up as a ribbon bow.

Lace Bows.—Lace insertion made into a large bow makes a very effective trimming for a hat. The lace should always be wired before making it up. Use fine lace wire to match in colour if the lace is fine, and the ordinary silk wire for a strong make and when a very firm bow is required. Fix the wire into position with a loose button-hole stitch along both sides of the lace on the wrong side and across the ends, which are generally mitred. Make up the bow in the same way as a ribbon bow.

The Butterfly Bow.—This kind of bow should be made fairly small, as it is supposed to represent a butterfly. It consists of two loops and two upstanding ends in the centre. Make it in the same way as other bows, only commence with a loop instead of an end. Make a second loop the same size and lying in the opposite direction, and then a third exactly in the middle of these two. Sew the end under and stab stitch through the root to make it very secure. Place a tie-over through the third loop, pulling the loop sharply up, and cut slanting across to form the two ends.

Butterfly Bow.

The Alsatian Bow.—This is made in a slightly different manner from other bows, and when finished it has a very flat appearance. It is made with two loops each side and a broad

Alsatian Bow.

tie-over, and is used for sailor hats of all sizes, for turned-down mushroom shapes, and also for nurses' bonnets.

Cut off two lengths of ribbon, one length four inches longer than the other. Take each piece separately, and fold the cut edges to the centre so that they just touch. Then lay the one on the top of the other, and pleat them together once in the centre, stitch into position, and cover the stitches with a broad tie-over.

To Finish the Ends of Ribbon.—This may be done in the following different ways :—

(1) By cutting them across diagonally.

(2) By leaving them straight and fraying out some of the silk to form a fringe. If a small piece of the selvedge is cut off at each side this can be done quite easily.

(3) By making a wide hem at the ends and three or four pin tucks (very small) just below it.

(4) By cutting the end like a fish tail.

(5) By embroidering or braiding a small design on the ribbon.

Lace Quills.—These are usually made of piece

lace. Pieces left over from making the yoke of a blouse or dress will often be enough to make very pretty quills. A piece of lace nine inches long and about two inches wide will make one of a nice size.

First of all cut out a paper pattern the shape of a quill, place it on the lace, taking care that the pattern of the lace comes well in the centre of the quill. Cut round pattern, leaving quarter-inch turnings, wire all round with silk wire, turning the quarter-inch turnings over the wire. Leave about three inches of wire at both ends and twist them together to make a stem. Cover the edge of quill on the right side with fancy braid, ruching, straw, jet, or any other fancy trimming.

Lace Quill.

Rosettes.—There are two kinds of rosettes, those formed of a succession of loops of ribbon or ribbon velvet, and those made of silk, tulle, or net, &c.

To Make a Ribbon Rosette.—Rosettes can be made of any width ribbon from one inch to six inches wide; whatever the width the making is exactly the same.

Commence as in fig. 21 and make a loop, then make a second loop quarter of an inch from

FIG. 21. FIG. 22.

the first one, and continue making loops in this way until there are a sufficient number for a rosette of the size required (fig. 22).

Cut a small circle of net or buckram and wire round, then fix the loops to this, as in fig. 23, beginning at the outer edge and working towards

FIG. 23. FIG. 24.

the centre. It should have a nice round compact appearance when finished (fig. 24).

Crossway Silk Rosette.—Cut the silk on the cross the width required and join pieces together until you get sufficient length. Fold the edges together and gather along with a strong cotton. Draw up and fix on a round foundation of net

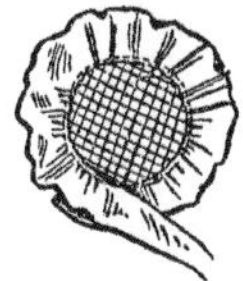

FIG. 25.

FIG. 26.

or buckram, commencing at the outside edge and working towards the centre (figs. 25 and 26).

Tulle Rosette.—The tulle should be used on the straight. For a fairly large rosette take one yard of tulle and fold it lengthways. Make the first fold the depth required, then make another fold on top, then another and another, and so on until all the material is used, pleating it up like a fan (fig. 27). Pin the folds into posi-

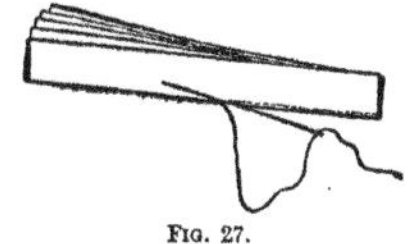

FIG. 27.

tion and put in a gathering thread at the lower edge. Draw up and sew together or fix on foundation. The rosette will now have rather a flat appearance, as the folds will cling together, so pull it out to make it look round and fluffy.

Rosette of Narrow Ribbon.—These should be mounted on a small round of stiff net or muslin. Tack the ribbon on this in small loops, commencing at the outside edge and working towards the centre. Make the loops stand up as much as possible, and let those in the middle be a little longer and higher than those at the edges. This makes a neat tight-looking rosette suitable for the trimming of children's bonnets and hats.

SEWING ON TRIMMINGS

All trimmings must be sewn on with as few stitches as possible and these few stitches must be firm and strong. The sewing must never be overdone; if too many stitches are used, the trimmings will have a set and ugly appearance, instead of being light and graceful. This is especially noticeable in the sewing on of flowers and feathers.

Feathers and Quills.—First sew the quill of the feather on to a small piece of stiff net or buckram (fig. 28). Then pin it in position on the hat with a hat-pin. Do not put the pin through the feather itself, but put it first into the hat, then over the feather and into the hat again. When making a hat for yourself this should be done before the glass. Then having fixed the feather in the right position, stab-stitch it through the net, taking the needle backwards and forwards until the feather is quite secure. Fix the tip of the feather in position with a *tie-stitch.* First tie the cotton on to the tip of the feather (fastening it on to one of the cotton loops at the back if it is an ostrich plume), leaving an end, then take a stitch through the hat and bring the needle back again. Tie the two ends of the cotton together in a firm knot and cut off. The feather must not on any account be tied tightly down.

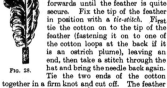

Fig. 28.

Flowers must be arranged as naturally and as artistically as possible. Small flowers, such as violets, cowslips, forget-me-nots, button roses, &c., look best when arranged in clusters and the large flowers in sprays. Cut off any unnecessary length of stem; bend up the remainder and sew over and over on to the hat. Fix the flowers themselves into position with a tie-stitch. The heavier flowers should be mounted on a wire.

In wiring, carry the wire up the length of the stem to the flower itself, then wind it round the stem and bring it down to the bottom again. When flowers are wired they do not require so much sewing to the hat, as they keep so much firmer.

When many flowers are used it is better to make them up first into a spray or wreath, using fine wire to fasten them together, and then tie-stitch them here and there on to the hat.

Ruching.—Sew this on to the hat from behind or take the stitches through the pleats where they will not be seen.

A Rouleau of Velvet, &c.—This should be slip-stitched on to the hat with a fine needle and silk the same colour as the hat.

Bows.—Put the needle through the back part of the tie-over and stab-stitch it through the hat. Repeat this several times until the root of the bow is secure. Then arrange the loops becomingly, handling them lightly, and fix them in position with invisible tie-stitches.

A RIVER OR COUNTRY HAT

Material Required.—A hat shape, 1½ yards muslin embroidery 20 inches wide or 1 yard 36 inches wide, 1 yard plain muslin, trimming of ribbon or flowers.

Making.—Buy a simple hat shape in buckram or spartra similar to fig. 29. Spartra is the better material of the two, as it does not spoil so readily with damp. Although it is possible to make these shapes at home, they can now be bought so cheaply that it is scarcely worth the trouble. A hat for the river or country should be trimmed in such a way that it will not get out of order quickly, therefore it is better to have something quite simple, and if colour is introduced it should be capable of change to suit various costumes. Nothing is prettier for the purpose than white embroidered muslin, which can easily be washed or cleaned when it becomes soiled.

Fig. 29.

Lay the embroidered muslin on the table with the right side uppermost and place the hat shape on the top with the front to one of the corners, so as to have the material for the front on the cross. Cut round, allowing an extra half-inch for turnings. Remove the hat, mark the size of the crown in the centre, and cut out, again allowing half an inch for turnings. (In order to get the exact size of the brim and crown a piece of paper may be pinned on to the shape, cut out, and then used as a pattern.) This piece is for covering the upper brim, so cut a piece the same size for underneath. Line the two brim pieces with plain muslin and tack together. Slip the material for the upper brim over the hat and notch the inner edge to fit the base of the crown. Tack the notches down to the crown of the hat. If the brim of the hat bends down very much it will be necessary to cut the material at the back and make a seam to make it lie smoothly. Stretch the embroidery well over the brim of the hat, fold the turning over the edge, and pin to keep it in position. Catch-stitch down to the wire or buckram shape with even stitches. Lay the under-brim piece of embroidery on to the shape and fix into position with pins. Notch the inner rim and sew the notches up to the inside of crown. Make a turning on the wrong side of the outer rim and slip-stitch round to edges of top covering, commencing at the back of the hat. The edge may be further finished with a rouleau of velvet or a narrow braid.

To Cover the Crown.—Cut a round of the embroidery eighteen to twenty inches in diameter, line it with plain muslin and gather round the edges with strong cotton (fig. 30). Draw up and slip over the crown of the hat. Tack round edges close to the brim, and put a few stitches in the crown to keep fulness in position. Or, if preferred, the crown of the hat may be covered quite plainly by stretching it down to the base with the fulness arranged in small pleats. Put in head-lining before trimming.

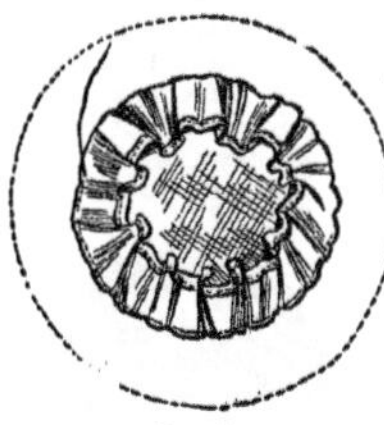

FIG. 30.

Trimming.—This may be made of ribbon or flowers, or a coloured scarf may be tied round and finished with a bow and ends at the side. Fig. 31 shows a trimming of ribbon, and this

FIG. 31

could easily be made up separately from the hat, and if two or three were made up in different colours of ribbon they could simply be fastened to the hat with a strong pin and changed when required to suit different costumes. A wreath of pretty flowers or of flowers and ribbon could be used in the same way.

FLOWER TOQUES

The "flower toque" is an almost universal favourite for dainty wear, and when properly made looks very smart and pretty.

A variety of flowers can be used for making a toque of the kind, and they may be chosen in accordance with the season—primroses, violets or hyacinths for the spring, roses for the summer, geraniums for the autumn. For the last-named season very pretty little toques have been made of grapes; in fact, the home worker will find that there is abundant material to hand with which to carry out pretty ideas, and the more her dexterity increases, the more ideas she will get. The flowers can be used either with or without foliage.

The foundation of the toque may be either of wire (green wire if it can be procured) or stiff millinery net.

Although the directions given below apply specially to the making of a toque of roses, the method is very much the same whatever kind of flower is used.

A Rose Toque.—*Required.*—A wire or net shape, roses, foliage, green tulle or net, ribbon or velvet.

Method.—Choose a shape that suits you well; it should be rather small in size. Prepare it first by swathing it or covering it over with green tulle or net of the same tone as the foliage used. Then commence sewing on the flowers. Cut the stems of the roses and leaves quite short so that they can be sewn flat to the shape. Commence at the top of the crown and sew the roses tight through the centre to the shape. Place them close together until the whole of the top is

FIG. 32.

covered with flowers, introducing a few leaves if wished (fig. 32).

If there is a distinct turned-up brim to the toque, this might be covered with foliage only or with foliage and tulle, and a twist of tulle should be put round between the crown and brim. Or if the brim is very narrow and bending downwards, it might be covered with dark green or black velvet, which is always becoming next the face.

The toque may be left plain, or finished off

FIG. 33.

with a smart bow of ribbon or velvet at the side (fig. 33), or with loops of narrow velvet and a standing-up spray of roses, or with an artificial osprey, according to what is most becoming.

FUR IN MILLINERY

Fur was never more fashionable than it is to-day, and it is employed largely both in millinery and dressmaking.

The fact of its being so much in demand has raised its price considerably, and it is not every one who can afford a new hat or toque of the most fashionable shape every year. But it is wonderful what can be done with odds and ends of fur, and how, in millinery especially, they can be utilised and made into something quite stylish. All small pieces of fur should be kept as well as old fur ties and muffs, as they can often be made into a toque when good for nothing else. Or, if not sufficient to make the whole hat, they might at least cover the brim, while the crown could be made of cloth or velvet to match the costume that is being worn.

The Cutting of Fur.—Fur should always be cut on the wrong side and with a sharp-pointed knife. Place the fur on the table with the skin side uppermost and mark with a coloured pencil

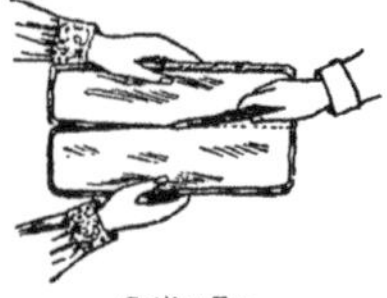

Cutting Fur.

or chalk where you wish the cutting to come. Then get some one to hold the fur stretched out while you cut through by the marked line.

To Join Fur.—Place the two pieces with right sides together, being careful that the fur all lies one way, or the join will show. Place a piece of cardboard two or three inches long between the pieces, with the edge close to where the join is to be. Push down the hairs of the fur so as to leave edges of skin clear to sew through. Then overcast the two pieces together with a fur-sewing needle and strong sewing cotton, No. 24 or 30. Make the stitches rather deep and close together and draw them tight, moving along the cardboard as required.

To Make a Fur Toque.—*Required.*—Pieces of fur, a wire shape, brown tulle, brown satin.

Method.—A wire frame of the turban shape is the one most suitable for a fur toque. First cover the frame all over with a thin brown lining or net, then prepare a strip of fur wide enough to cover the brim and long enough to go round. Join it into a circle and place it on the frame, arranging that the join comes where it will not show. Pin it in position and then tack with a turning over the top and underneath the brim. The under part of the brim which comes next the hair is generally made of brown satin, as it is cooler for the head, and also because fur would so quickly wear if it were on that part. Then take a piece of fur large enough to cover the crown, and do not cut it up more than is necessary, as next year, when remodelling, the hat will be much easier to arrange if there is

Fur Toque.

some allowance for alteration. Stretch the fur smoothly over the crown, arranging any fulness in small pleats at the sides. Tack it in position from the wrong side as far as possible to avoid catching in the hair with the cotton. A fold of tulle or chiffon should be placed between the brim and crown to cover edges. Finish off with a pretty feather mount, a handsome quill, a rosette, or other ornament, according to fashion and individual taste, or, if preferred, the toque may be left perfectly plain.

THE MAKING OF STRAW HATS

These are made either by hand or machine. As the home-made straw hat will not be subjected to the stiffening and blocking process that the bought one receives, it will be more successful if made over a wire frame, wearing better and keeping its shape longer than if made without this support.

As said before, shapes can be bought so cheaply—the average price for a wire one being 1s., or, if made to order, 1s. 6d. to 2s.—that it does not repay the trouble to make one, and the amateur always finds this a difficult job.

It will be wise to commence with a simple shape similar to fig. 34, which has no peculiarities in form, and if this is a success something more difficult may be attempted, and a close examination of any straw hat will show you how to proceed.

Choose a frame which suits you well, light in weight and of the size you wish. The straw for covering is sold in bundles of twelve yards, in any colour and many different styles, and the price will vary from 1s. to 5s. per bundle, according to quality and make. Two bundles will cover a medium-sized hat, or three might cover two smaller ones. Choose a nice pliable straw, as it will be easier to work with than the stiffer makes.

If the straw is very stiff and dry it is a good plan to moisten it first by wrapping it in a damp cloth and leaving it over-night. This will enable it to be stretched and pulled more readily without breaking. If the straw is a kind that unravels quickly, the end should be wound round with strong thread of the same colour before commencing.

To Cover the Brim.—First pin the straw neatly round the edge on the upper side of the brim, starting at the back and fixing it to the outside wire. The straw must be perfectly flat and lie easily. Sew on to the outside wire, taking small stitches on the right or upper side and larger underneath. In fixing the second row do not cut off the straw, but let it continue on. The second row is sewn to the inside edge of the first row of straw. Continue sewing round and round until the crown is reached, lapping each row one quarter of an inch over the

Fig. 34.

edge of previous row, hiding the stitches as far as possible beneath the pattern of straw (fig. 34).

If the brim is wider at the front than at the back, it should be widened by a few extra rows of straw put on and sloped away under the outer row at the back or sides of the hat.

Cover the under-brim in the same way, starting at the back and working up to the head-line. When fixing the straw on under-brim the needle should always be put in slanting, so that small stitches are made on both sides.

To Cover the Crown.—The top of the crown should be covered with a circle or plaque of straw made in the hand and not straight on to the shape. To make this plaque, wind the cotton tightly round the straw to make a firm point to start with, then draw the braid of straw around this to form the centre, easing it in to make it flat. In the loosely made straws a drawing thread is sometimes put at the edge of the straw to facilitate the process, or the outer edge may be stretched (fig. 35).

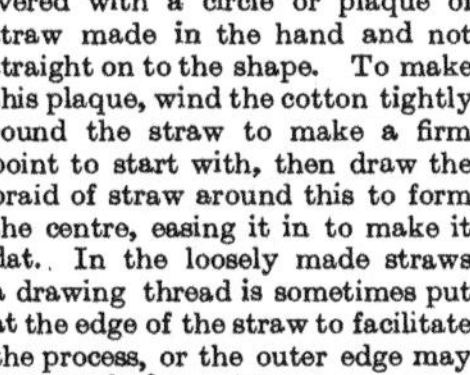

Fig. 35.

When the centre circle is well formed, continue sewing the straw in rows round and round, taking small stitches on the right side and larger ones on the wrong. Each row must be stitched and eased to the previous one so that they lie perfectly flat. If this top piece is made too tight it will bulge out when placed on the frame. At the beginning the rows should overlap each other considerably, and as the circle increases the edge may be extended nearer to the edge of the preceding row. When large enough, fasten off the end of the straw so that it will not unravel, and slope it gradually under the last row. Make the plaque about half an inch more in diameter than the top of the frame, and then sew it on to the wires in two or three places.

Side-Band.—This is formed by sewing a row of straw to the edge of the crown piece, commencing at the side or back, or where the join is likely to be hidden by trimming. Leave an end of straw of about one inch at the beginning, and this can be caught and covered by the second row. Continue sewing one row under the other until the side is covered, easing the straw smoothly on to the shape and finishing the end by turning it up under the preceding row. Tack the side-band to the last row of the brim, and the hat will be ready for its head-lining (p. 432) and trimming.

Trimming.—This style of hat may be trimmed in a variety of ways, but for hard wear there is

Fig. 36.

nothing more useful than a scarf drapery or a good ribbon trimming with a stylish bow at the side or front (fig. 36).

MUFFS

The tendency at present is for muffs to be very large and either oblong or square; but fashion changes very rapidly, and the directions given below are for an ordinary medium-sized muff which can easily be manufactured at home. Although black satin is used in the construction of it, the material may be varied to suit individual taste and requirements. Black or other coloured velvet, for instance, trimmed with fur is always effective, or a piece of the same material as the costume worn would also look well. Then, again, for evening wear a lighter-looking muff might be made of *crêpe de chine* edged with marabout or ermine.

The lining may be made of any coloured silk which will tone with the outside. A white or light-coloured lining is always best for smart wear, as it does not soil the gloves.

Strips of fur from one to four inches wide can be bought at most of the big drapers, the price of course varying according to the value of the special kind of fur.

Muff of Black Satin and Fur

Required.—1½ yards black satin, fur edging, 1½ yards coarse calico, down or wadding.

Method.—Divide the length of satin into two equal parts, measuring 27 inches by 20 inches, and sew each of these pieces together by the raw edges, so that they form a round. Cut two pieces of calico, about half an inch smaller in length and width than the satin, and sew them together in the same way. Slip the two calico circles one inside the other, and stitch the two together at one end. Fill equally all round with down, and sew up the other end. Slip this down bed into one of the satin circles, turn the raw edges of the satin over on to the

FIG. 37.

calico, and fix firmly into position. Sew on the fur round each end, making the joins come at the bottom of the muff. Slip in the lining and hem it in half an inch from the edge (fig. 37).

CHILDREN'S MILLINERY

Baby Girl's Bonnet

Required.—½ yard satin, ½ yard muslin, ½ yard sarcenet, 3 yards ribbon (3 inches wide for rosettes and strings), 2 skeins embroidery silk.

Method.—The shape shown in illustration is very comfortable, easy to make, and requires little fitting. Three measurements are required—round the child's face, across the back of the neck from ear to ear, and from the forehead to the back of neck. When possible it is easier to take the measurements from an old bonnet, and to make each new bonnet a trifle larger than the last.

Average measurements would be :—

Round face	14	inches.
Forehead to back of neck .	11	„
Round neck from ear to ear .	11	„

Cut out a paper pattern similar to fig. 38, join at the notches, pin or tack up the seams and try on the child. If it fits well, unpin the pattern and cut out in the satin, muslin, and sarcenet. All the pieces must be the same size, and turnings must be allowed everywhere

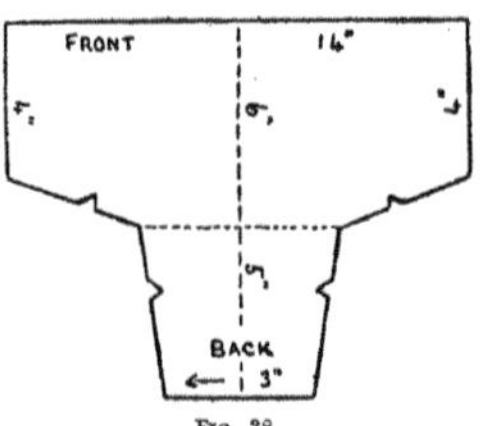

FIG. 38.

except at the seams where the notches are. First tack the satin and muslin together, fix the side seams and sew them firmly together. Turn the satin over the muslin all round the raw edges and catch-stitch the raw edges of the satin to the muslin.

To make the revers, take a piece of muslin the length of the front of the bonnet from end to end and four inches wide, and shape as in fig. 39. Then cut out in satin, allowing an extra half-inch for turnings, and place the two together, tacking the satin down over the muslin.

The revers can now be embroidered with any simple pattern, or it may be trimmed with a ruching of ribbon, passementerie, or swansdown edging. After it has been trimmed, line in the back with sarcenet and fix it to the bonnet.

Make two rosettes (see p. 439) out of the ribbon, sew them to each side of the bonnet, and use the remainder of the ribbon for the strings. Cut one string longer than the other, and sew in at each side of the bonnet on the wrong side. Join up the seams in the sarcenet head-lining, slip it inside, turn in the raw edges one-quarter inch from the edges of the satin, and hem neatly all the way round (fig. 39).

FIG. 39.

A quilling of chiffon or ribbon can be put round the front of the bonnet; it gives it a softer appearance, but does not suit all children.

This shape of bonnet may be made up very prettily in other materials; they are often made of material to match the coat the child is wearing. Embroidered muslin is especially pretty, and should either be left without lining or lined with a very thin cambric which will wash easily.

In winter, if the bonnet is required warmer, it may be interlined with flannel or delaine, or with a layer of wadding or domet. Although the inside lining is generally made of sarcenet, any soft material can be used, such as satin or silk from the lining of a dress or coat.

Baby Boy's Hat (age six months)

Materials required.—¾ yard satin, 20 inches wide, 5 yards satin ribbon about 2½ to 3 inches wide (3½ yards to be used for the ruching, 1½ yards for strings), ¼ yard stiff muslin, ½ yard sarcenet, ½ yard book muslin.

The only measurement required for this is the size round the child's head. An average size would be 21 inches.

Any kind of material can be used for this style of hat as long as it is not stiff and hard. Satin wears well, as the dust does not cling to it. Boys' hats are usually made with less trimming than baby girls' bonnets.

Making.—After having measured the child's head, cut a piece of muslin that length plus turnings and 2½ inches wide. Fold in half widthways and then join into a circle.

Twenty inches of satin is needed for the crown of hat. Cover the band with the satin that is left over, both inside and outside, tack the outside on firmly, but leave the satin inside loose, as this is hemmed down after the band has been fixed on the crown.

Take the 20 inches of satin and make it into a circle; in the middle of this circle cut a round hole 3½ inches in diameter. Gather round the edges of this hole, and fix it on to a button about the size of a shilling. A piece

Fig. 40.

of cardboard will do to make the button, and it should be covered with two thicknesses of satin.

Now line the top piece with the book muslin. Lay the satin as flat as possible on the muslin and cut the muslin the same size. Gather the two together one half-inch from the raw edges. Draw up to the size of the head-band (fig. 40).

For the Head-lining.—Cut a round 14 inches in diameter from the half-yard sarcenet, gather round the edge also to the size of the head-band. Tack it into the satin crown. The crown is now ready to be fixed on to the band. Pin on the band, letting the raw edges of the crown come between the band and the satin lining; stitch on firmly.

Make a ruching of the satin ribbon (see p. 436), and sew on to the band. Fix on the strings

Fig. 41.

at each side so that they come just underneath the ruch, and make the right-hand string rather longer than the left. Hem up the satin on the inside of band, and the hat is finished (fig. 41).

Silk Hat for Little Girl

Required.—2 to 2½ yards washing silk, 2 rings of washing wire, 1 large reel of sewing silk, ⅛ yard of stiff net, ½ yard book muslin.

Making.—Silk hats, or Liberty hats as they are usually called, are generally made of washing silk, such as China or Japanese silk. The only measurements required are the size round the head and the width of the brim.

Cut a lengthwise strip of the silk 11 inches deep, and this will make a brim 5 inches wide when finished. Fold in half lengthways and fix with a few pins. Measure one inch from the fold and half an inch from the raw edges, and put in a row of machine stitching or a row of running in both places. Measure half-way between these two rows and put in another row. Then put in more rows as in diagram, so as to form casings to take in washing wire. At one end of the

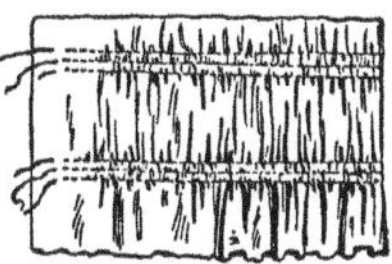

Fig. 42.

strip do not take the stitching quite to the end, as it will be easier to join it to the other end if this is left plain (fig. 42). Then insert the wire in the casings, putting in two pieces at the same time where the casings come together.

Join the head wire to the size required to fit head, and then join the others so that they lie in a flat circle when placed on a table. Join the silk neatly over the wires by slip-stitching.

Next cut a band in stiff net, the size of the head in length (average twenty inches) plus one inch for joining and two and a half inches deep. Wire this top and bottom, and cover with a circle of stiff net or buckram, and bind the lower wire with a piece of silk. Fix the brim to this crown by stab-stitching it through.

The crown piece of the hat is formed by cutting a round of silk eighteen to twenty inches in diameter and gathering it round the edges. Slip this over the hat and fix it round the base of crown. This round of silk may be embroidered, tucked, or have insertion let in as desired.

Put in a head-lining and then trim the hat with ribbon or some of the silk with which it is made. If piece silk is used a simple twist round the hat with a nice full rosette at one side and a smaller one catching up the brim will be all that is necessary (fig. 42). Or in ribbon, a twist round

Fig. 43.

and a nice soft bow in the front or at the side. A rosette of soft lace with a wreath of daisies or tiny pink rosebuds makes another dainty trimming for those who prefer flowers. Silk elastic should be fastened to the inside of the hat or white ribbon ties if they are preferred. The trimming should be of the simplest and daintiest description.

VEILS

A Wedding Veil.—Unless this is made of real lace, Brussels net is usually bought for the purpose. Two yards of net two yards wide will make a fairly large veil. A hem two inches wide should be made on the right side of the veil. Be careful in laying the hem to turn over two inches twice and not to make a narrow fold to begin with or the raw edges would show through the thin net. Pay particular attention to the corners. The hem should be kept in position with a row of running stitches made in filoselle silk. A small design may be embroidered in the corners, or a narrow fancy border all the way round looks very effective. The veil may also be decorated with sprays of flowers.

When real lace is used for a wedding veil it will be very much more becoming if it is lined with the finest white chiffon.

A wedding veil can be worn over the face or not as desired; the style of wearing it alters somewhat each year. It is generally kept in position with a wreath of orange flowers.

When the veil is worn over the face, two small wreaths are sometimes worn, one under the veil and the other on the top, then when the veil is thrown back, the flowers underneath make a softer line round the face.

When the veil is worn off the face it is either twisted round the head in the form of a turban or pleated up in a manner to suit the wearer.

A Confirmation Veil.—This can either be made of Brussels net like a wedding veil or of fine lawn. One and a quarter yards of fine lawn at 1s. per yard would be sufficient. A narrow hem should be made all the way round.

Make a mark in the centre of one of the sides and sew on a tape or ribbon twelve inches at each side of this centre mark. These tapes are tied at the back of the neck under the veil, and a kind of cap is formed in this way.

HEALTH AND THE TOILET

A WOMAN should cherish her health as her most valued possession, for good health is assuredly as potent a factor in promoting her happiness as ill-health is in destroying it. It is one of a woman's first duties therefore towards herself and towards her household to keep in that perfect physical state of well-being which does so much to help her with the trials and worries of everyday life, for a healthy body and a healthy mind are as a rule synonymous. The healthy woman, by very reason of her vitality, permeates cheerfulness and happiness around her. Whilst good health is the most potent minimiser of all our troubles, ill-health may be said to be the originator of most of the evils of ill-temper, irritability, and morbid despondency. Hence, if we would be happy, first and foremost it should be our aim to keep well.

How to keep well.—By strict attention to the laws of hygiene much may be done in the way of keeping our health and guarding against the inroads of disease. Yet how many women are there who possess even a superficial knowledge of the principles of hygiene? and how many more, having this knowledge, go so far as to put it into practice? This may be due in the main to an ignorance of the importance of hygiene, and a failure to realise the fact that it is only possible to maintain good health by a strict observance of the fundamental health laws.

Cleanliness may be regarded as the basic principle of hygiene. This applies not only to cleanliness of person, which is of course essential, but not sufficient in itself for the preservation of health. In order to keep well it is necessary also that we should have pure food, pure air, pure water—cleanliness and wholesomeness, in fact, in all our surroundings. Neglect any of these essential factors and the health, and through the health the appearance, will suffer in the long run.

It should be a woman's aim in life not only to be healthy in body and mind, but also to always look her best. The two as a rule go together. A healthy body and a healthy mind have more effect upon the personal appearance than can at first be appreciated. All successful culture of beauty must have for its foundation that purity and wholesomeness of living which in its turn forms the groundwork of good health. Of what avail, for instance, is the possession of classic features if the beauty of the face is marred by a muddy complexion and unsightly skin blemishes; or of what use a well-built figure if it is hidden by stooping shoulders and an ungainly gait? On the other hand, a woman with the bloom of health upon her cheeks, and the signs of physical well-being in her upright carriage and the elasticity of her step is indeed "a thing of beauty and a joy for ever," however plain and commonplace her features may be.

Personal Cleanliness.—Personal cleanliness is essential for the woman who would not only keep hygienically sound in body, but who wishes also to enjoy the aid to beauty furnished by a clear and good complexion. It is useless to expect the complexion to be good when the care of the physique and person is totally neglected. Strict attention in the first instance is required to the eliminating organs of the body. It should be seen that these are regularly made to do their duty. Where gastric disturbances are habitual no amount of external care will free the complexion from blemishes. As soon as the skin becomes muddy and unhealthy-looking, therefore, the first step is to ascertain whether there is any functional disorder to which this state of things may be attributed. Most often it can be traced to faulty digestion, which is in its turn attributable either to unsuitable diet or insufficient mastication of food. Insufficient mastication of food is often caused by bad and diseased teeth, which are so rendered powerless to perform their natural functions. The care of the teeth plays an important part in our personal hygiene, and it is a subject which is fully dealt with on p. 464.

BATHS

The first consideration in regard to her personal cleanliness should be the daily bath. The temperature of the bath should of course be adapted to individual requirements, but it must be remembered that the warm bath with a liberal use of soap is essential for cleansing purposes. A cold bath, where it can be taken, acts more as a stimulant than a cleansing operation, but it disagrees with many people, and regular cold bathing with some would do more harm than good. An unfailing test as to whether the cold bath is beneficial to the individual can be found in the reaction which sets in afterwards. If a glow of heat is felt after bathing it may be taken as a sure sign that it has done good. If, however, shivering fits occur, the cold tub should be altogether avoided. Much of the stimulating effect of a cold bath may be obtained by thoroughly sponging the body with cold water after a warm bath has been taken. This procedure is effective in minimising the tendency to catch cold, which often arises from leaving a warm bathroom for a room of a much cooler atmosphere. Cold baths are baths of a temperature below 60 degrees Fahrenheit; warm baths are from 92 to 98 degrees Fahrenheit, whilst hot baths exceed the latter temperature. In Turkish and Russian baths variations of temperature play an important part in the cleansing process, producing a copious action of the skin which effectually cleanses it of all its impurities and secretions. These baths, however, prove entirely unsuitable to some constitutions, and should not be taken excepting under medical advice. Where they can be taken the general effect upon the tone of the skin and complexion is most beneficial.

"Do not be sparing with the soap and water" is a good maxim to be observed in taking the daily bath. Where the water is hard it should

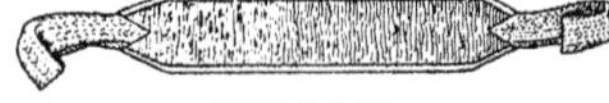

Loofah Bath-Strap.

be softened with a little borax, some Scrubb's Cloudy Ammonia, or a prepared water softener, such as Lavender Bath Salts. A few drops of toilet vinegar or eau de Cologne also added will have a wonderfully refreshing effect. Good vigorous rubbing and scrubbing are the next essentials. A loofah bath-strap or a flesh-brush should be brought into requisition for this purpose. The friction of either will cause the skin to feel a healthy glow. Then again, a brisk rub

Flesh-Brush.

down with a large bath towel when the bathing process is over will give a pleasant feeling of invigoration, doing more than anything else to stimulate the pores of the skin to healthy action.

Hip and Sponge Baths.—Most houses and flats possess bathrooms in these days of up-to-date conveniences. Failing a regular bathroom, the daily ablution should be performed in a hip or a sponge bath. One advantage possessed by these is that they admit of the bath being taken into the bedroom, and thus all risk of catching cold from being exposed to varying atmospheres in going backwards and forwards to and from a bathroom is obviated. These small baths can be had at all prices ranging from 10s. and upwards.

Rubber Camp-Baths.—For travelling, rubber camp-baths are very useful. These are usually made to fold into a small compass and can be packed in waterproof cases. They range in price for 11s. 6d. and upwards, according to size.

Sea-Baths.—Sea-bathing is very invigorating, and when making a stay at the seaside it is as well to bathe as much as possible. If bathing in the sea does not agree with you, the same symptoms of shivering that manifest themselves after a cold bath are apparent. Under these circumstances, needless to add, sea-bathing should be avoided.

It is unwise to let the salt water get into the hair when bathing, for it has the effect of rendering it harsh and dry, and giving it a faded appearance. Before going into the water the hair should be tightly coiled and pinned on to the top of the head, and a well-fitting waterproof or oilskin cap worn over it. This is a precaution which should be taken by every woman who wishes to keep her hair bright and glossy at the seaside. Constant saturation of the hair by salt water during the summer months has such ill effects upon its appearance that it sometimes takes months to bring it once more to its normal condition.

Salt Baths at Home.—A salt bath may be enjoyed at home by adding salt to the bath water in the proportion of four pounds of salt to every sixteen gallons of water. Brills & Tidman Sea Salts are very good for the purpose. They can be obtained at 1s. 4½d. and 9½d. the dozen packets respectively. Ordinary table salt can also be used in this way.

Care of Sponges.—Sponges may be kept in very good condition if they are not allowed to lie in soapy water and the soap is well rinsed out of them after use. It is better, too, if they can be hung up to air and not left lying in a damp condition. A piece of tape can easily be threaded through the sponge and tied so as to form a loop to hang it up by.

If a sponge should become slimy and sticky it can be cleaned by soaking in salt and water or strong ammonia and water. Allow it to remain in either of these for several hours, squeezing it occasionally, then wring out and rinse in plenty of cold or tepid water.

THE SKIN AND COMPLEXION

Wrinkles and their Causes.—The skin is a mirror, as it were, in which all the defects in our personal hygiene are plainly featured. Want of cleanliness, chronic stomach disorders, such as indigestion and constipation—sedentary living, unrelieved by any sort of exercise—all show themselves in the dull and muddy complexions and unsightly skin blemishes with which so many women are afflicted, and which they so often try in vain to cure. Hygienic care of the body is the first essential for the woman who wishes her skin to be pure and her complexion healthy. Perfect cleanliness internally and externally must be the rule for those who wish their complexion to be pure and healthy.

Habitual constipation is one of the most relentless foes the complexion can have. It arises from a variety of causes of which sedentary habits, want of exercise, unsuitable diet are the most prolific.

A glass of pure cold water taken upon rising in the morning, and half-an-hour before each meal, a glass of hot water or lemon and water before going to bed at night, a little fruit taken at breakfast-time, gentle friction of the bowels after the morning tub, a good walk in the open air, and some simple physical exercises (p. 455), together with strict attention to diet, will do much towards ameliorating this state of affairs. In many cases a glass of hot water taken upon rising and half-an-hour before each meal is efficacious.

Overwork and worry are powerful deterrents to all culture of beauty. No amount of care can undo the havoc wrought by unstrung nerves or a worrying disposition. Do not worry over petty things. Remember that "every cloud has its silver lining." There are times in this life, it is true, when trouble comes upon us with a heavy hand, yet the minor, every-day worries are more often than not of a woman's own making, and it is the habitual worrying of a discontented disposition which, more than anything else, leaves its mark upon the face with so remorseless a hand. Try and cultivate a more cheerful outlook upon life if you would permanently rid yourself of these vexing little lines between the brows.

There are lines, however, that are imprinted upon the face by laughter. These lines have a character all their own—they give the face a cheerful, happy expression, and add to rather than detract from its beauty. But it is the wrinkles that arise from impoverishment of the subcutaneous tissues caused by ill-health, faulty hygiene, and worry, which we must set ourselves to cure, in the first place, by removing the cause; in the second place by strengthening and nourishing the skin and keeping it in good condition with the aid of gentle massage treatment.

Very few women know how to wash their faces properly. A mere superficial dab with a soapy sponge is often deemed sufficient for the purposes of cleanliness. The soap is not properly washed off and a hurried and perfunctory drying serves to complete this portion of the toilet. These women are surprised that their skin becomes coarse and ill-nourished-looking, besides showing a tendency to wrinkle. The skin of the face is constantly giving off waste matter through its pores, besides receiving dust, dirt, and other impurities upon its surface. By the mistaken treatment thus described the pores of the skin become clogged up with the soap which is left to dry on the face, and are so prevented from doing their eliminating work properly—blackheads and pimples are the inevitable result.

It is above all important that the face be washed in soft water. Hard water is most deleterious in its effect upon the skin and complexion. It can always be detected by the difficulty in getting the soap to lather in it—thick crusty flakes forming on the surface of the water and clinging to the sides of the bath. After washing in very hard water the skin experiences a feeling of roughness which is decidedly unpleasant. This alone should indicate in one measure the injury that can be done by its constant use.

Rain water is the best to use, but this is not always available. Borax and oatmeal are both good water-softeners—boiling will also tend to soften hard water to a certain extent. One of the simplest of water-softeners, however, and one of which the properties in this direction are but little known, is to be found in lemon juice. Two tea-spoonfuls of the juice of a lemon added to a basinful of warm water will be found sufficient. Lemon juice has the added recommendation of being congenial to most skins, whereas oatmeal and even borax would be too drying for many. Oatmeal is especially suitable for very greasy skins. The most pleasant way to use it is to place a quantity in a small muslin bag, sew this up, and place it in the water a little time before it is required. The same bag will do duty for three or four days, after which the oatmeal will have to be renewed.

The face should be well washed in warm soft water twice a day—in the morning and at night. The night toilet is of the utmost importance, as, if it is neglected, the dust and dirt accumulated during the day will fill up the pores of the skin and prevent its healthy action. A good pure soap and hot water should be used. Sponges or face flannels should be thoroughly clean. It is better, however, to wash the face with the hands, rubbing with a brisk circular movement. In the morning toilet soap will not be necessary. A few drops of tincture of benzoin added to the water makes an excellent skin tonic.

When coming in from a walk, a game of tennis, or any other similar exercise on a hot summer's day, do not make the mistake of at once washing the face in cold water to get cool, as this is very bad for the skin and complexion. Instead, rub a very little cold cream into the skin; allow this to remain on for a few minutes, then wash off in soft warm water.

To Whiten Neck and Arms.—It is as well to bathe the neck and arms in milk every night for a few nights before going to a dance. When going out in the evening the appearance of the neck and arms will be much improved if, after washing, glycerine and rose-water mixed in equal proportions is well rubbed into the skin; then dust over with some good powder. Allow this to remain on for some time, then wipe gently off, when the skin will be found to look beautifully fresh and white.

Rough Elbows.—The skin often assumes a coarse and scaly appearance at the elbows, being extremely rough to the touch. To remedy this, in the first place the habit of leaning the elbows upon desk or table must be abandoned. Plenty of friction is necessary to rejuvenate the skin. Rub some common salt well into the elbows at night, then wash in warm water, and after drying apply a little cold cream. In the morning rub briskly with a good rough loofah.

For Red Arms.—Rub the arms every night with diluted lemon juice in the proportion of two-thirds lemon and one-third water. Bathing the arms in milk at night-time is also an efficacious remedy.

MASSAGE

Every woman should know how to massage her face and neck, as persistent massage serves not only to keep the dreaded wrinkles at bay, but also to give tone to the complexion, preserve the contour of the face, and correct any tendency to undue plumpness or leanness. There is nothing like massage for filling out ugly hollows in the cheek and neck, or toning down over-flabby cheeks, which are every bit as unsightly as the unduly thin ones. Massage, to be effective, it should be remembered, must be persistent. It is not sufficient to practise it only when the inclination seizes us. Make a point of massaging the face thoroughly once or twice a week, whilst gentle massage movements should be used every night when applying skin food or other emollient.

After having given the face its usual wash with soap and warm water, dry it well, and with the tips of the fingers apply a coating of good skin food. Only use as much skin food as the skin can comfortably absorb.

Now, seated in front of a mirror, it is time to begin operations.

Place the tips of the first and second fingers of each hand so that they meet in the centre of the chin, begin massaging each side of the chin from this point, continuing the movement upwards and outwards, following the contour of the face. All movements in face massage should be *circular and upwards*. Rub the food in gently, but firmly, with the tips of the fingers.

Next turn your attention to the lines which are apt to form at the corners of the mouth. To prevent or cure these, rub the skin food in very firmly with the *palms of the hands* with an upward and circular movement, beginning at each side of the mouth and extending over the cheek. This movement will also serve to fill out the hollows in the cheeks if they are unduly thin, and reduce their plumpness if they are inclined to be fat and flabby. After this movement, gently tap the cheeks with the tips of the fingers. This will serve to give them tone, stimulate the circulation, and have a beneficial effect upon the complexion generally.

Then turn your attention to the little lines which form under and at the corners of the eyes. All movements round the eyes should be very gentle, as the skin here is very elastic and inclined to stretch.

Rest the tips of the first and second fingers of each hand on the temple, and with the tips of the second fingers massage under the eyes from the nose and upwards to the temples across the little network of wrinkles that form at the corners of the eyes. If the skin wrinkles very much under the touch of the fingers as the movement is in process, it is a sign that the touch is too heavy. The movement must be very slow and very gentle—a rough movement will do more harm than good.

Now it is time to attack the horizontal wrinkles which do so much to mar the beauty of the forehead. Rub firmly across these wrinkles with a light, upward, and circular movement; rub persistently until the food has worked its way well into the skin. Then with the tips of the first and second fingers rub firmly across these ugly little vertical lines between the brows, stretching the skin out smoothly. The nose then requires its share of attention. The pores of this organ are apt to become coarse and large. To correct this cover the finger-tips with skin food and massage from the base of the nostrils along each side of the nose upwards, afterwards gently applying the skin food along the nose and upwards towards the brows.

Now with a piece of clean white rag wipe away all superfluous skin food from the pores. For most skins it will be found advantageous after this treatment to sponge the face in soft warm water to which has been added from eight to ten drops of tincture of benzoin or any other good astringent skin tonic, drying it gently with a soft towel.

Massaging the Neck.—Attention should be given to the lines which form upon the neck and to any tendency there may be to the unsightly "double chin." Massage will correct and prevent both.

Cover the neck with skin food, and with the tips of the fingers rub gently across the horizontal lines, which are often the result of wearing very high or very stiff collars, then massage firmly round the throat, afterwards gently tapping the flesh under the chin several times. This will do much to tone the flesh and prevent undue flabbiness. Wipe off all superfluous skin food when the massage is finished. After the massage the following simple exercise will do much towards strengthening the muscles of the neck and checking any undue tendency to the formation of a double chin. Crane the neck, stretching the chin forward as far as it will go, then keeping it still stretched; bend the head slowly backwards as far as it will go till it almost touches the shoulders at the back, then bring the head slowly forward again until the chin is allowed to rest on the chest. Repeat the movement several times, then vary it by turning the face with the chin raised in the same position first to the right until the face is looking over the right shoulder, and then to the left in the same manner. Where the double chin is pronounced skin foods should not be used; the neck should be well massaged with the fingers, and a chin-strap should be worn at night.

When the neck has become dark and discoloured-looking through the constant wearing of high collars and furs, rub a little lemon juice diluted with water (one-third water to two-thirds lemon juice) into the skin every night, when it will soon regain its normal colour.

The benefits of face and neck massage have now become so universally recognised that the weekly visit to a "beauty specialist" forms an established routine engagement for many women of the wealthier classes who, instead of practising complexion treatment at home, can afford to pay for treatment by experts. Half-an-hour a week spent at an establishment like Pomeroy's in Bond Street, London, for face treatment and massage will be found to have the most beneficial results in preserving the healthy tone of the skin. The fees average 7s. 6d. for each face treatment, or 30s. for a course of six. One treatment would do much to initiate the home masseuse into the mysteries of massage, making an excellent foundation for the home treatment which is to follow. The skin foods and other complexion specialities of this firm may be had from the principal chemists throughout the country.

OTHER TREATMENT

The Steam Face-Bath.—For some skins, more especially those with coarse open pores, it will be found beneficial to give the face a steam bath about once a week. To do this, fill a basin with very hot water, to which the juice of half a lemon has been added. Cover the head with a large towel, bend over the basin, letting the towel completely screen the face, and remain in this position until the face has become thoroughly steamed. Then wash in soap and water and rinse it well.

The pores will now be cleansed. As they will have been thoroughly opened by this treatment, to contract them once more fill another basin with warm water to which about twelve drops of tincture of benzoin should be added, and bathe the face again for a few minutes. Then splash it all over with cold water, and dry with a soft towel. A little good face cream gently rubbed into the pores with the finger-tips will complete the treatment.

Electrolysis is the best-known method of removing disfiguring superfluous hair. It should always be applied by an expert. Most of the skin and complexion specialists have expert operators in electrolysis for the purpose of removing superfluous hair.

CLOTHING

The proper choice of suitable clothing for varying seasons forms an important factor in regard to our health.

In winter the clothing should be light and warm—never heavy; in the summer it should be light and cool. All clothes should fit sufficiently loosely to give the limbs and respiratory organs their full freedom. In so far as protection against cold is concerned, woollen fabrics are superior to all other materials. Light woollen combinations or vests should be worn next to the skin in winter, and even in the summer when athletics, outdoor games, or any kind of violent exercise is indulged in, it is as well to wear a light woollen undervest, for wool is the only fabric which can be depended upon to absorb perspiration; and there is less risk of catching cold than when wearing linen or cotton next to the skin, as those fabrics become extremely damp after exercise, and very often a severe chill is the result.

The Jaeger underwear possesses both the qualities of warmth and lightness of texture in addition to that of durability; and so from a hygienic point of view is excellent. There are agents for Jaeger clothing in almost every town in the United Kingdom, so that it is easily obtainable.

Colour should also play an important part in the selection of our clothing for the different seasons. For summer white is the ideal colour, as it is the one that absorbs the least heat. This is the reason why in tropical climates white is as much worn by men as by women. On the other hand, black or dark-coloured garments attract the sun and absorb the greater amount of heat. These dark colours are ideal for winter wear, but they should not be much worn in summer.

The Corset.—*Tight-lacing.*—Few women realise how very injurious to their health this practice is. Tight-lacing has the effect of compressing the body to the point of deformity, and severe injury to the internal organs is often the result.

Happily the "wasp" waist is no longer the fashion of the moment, but there is a tendency to unduly compress the hips and lower portion of the body, which may often have most injurious results. Great care should be taken in the selection of corsets. It is wrong to economise in this direction. A little more money spent on the corset and a little less on dress and finery would have the effect of resulting in a much cleaner bill of health for many a woman who is accustomed to stint herself in this direction. Cheap corsets should never be worn; they are usually stiff, hard, and unyielding, not giving freedom to the movements of the body. The best corset-makers are now, however, building their corsets with more regard to the hygienic laws than was manifested years ago. Good corsets now are fairly elastic and pliable. They are well planned and built, and are stocked in almost every size. It is always as well, if possible, to have the corset fitted, as this will ensure perfect ease in wear. Various makes are specially adapted for very full and very thin figures, and it is as well to bear this in mind when making a selection. Where the corset is fitted, the corsetière will, of course, adapt it to the special requirements of her customer.

It is as well to avoid the varying extremes of fashion in this direction. Though at one moment the "wasp" waist may be the decree, at another "no hips," and slenderness almost to emaciation will be *de rigueur*, no woman who respects her health will become fashion's slave. By doing so she will often only succeed in making herself grotesque.

The sensible woman always knows how to strike the happy "medium" whatever the fashion may be; there is no more pleasing sight than a good, well-proportioned figure well and sensibly corseted with due regard to the natural laws.

Boots and Shoes.—Suitable footgear is a most important consideration. The question of fit is paramount. The boot must be made to fit the foot, and not the foot distorted out of all shape to fit the boot. Ill-fitting boots serve to deform the feet if their wear is persisted in, causing corns, bunions, enlarged joints, and ingrowing toe-nails and often other ills (see p. 464).

Tight boots also impede the proper circulation of the blood, and chilblains in this way are often caused. The practice of wearing very high heels is particularly reprehensible. A woman wearing boots or shoes of this description cannot possibly walk in a natural fashion; the weight of the body is thrown forward upon the toes, being robbed of the support which the heels would have given it in the more natural circumstances; the heel of the shoe is placed in the middle of the foot under the arch of the instep—the result is to spoil and weaken the arch of the foot, and rob it of its natural spring: the gait becomes awkward, jerky, and ungainly in the extreme, and that freedom and swing of movement typical of a healthy and graceful carriage is conspicuous by its absence.

Well-cut boots and shoes with medium-sized heels and round toes are the ideal footwear. Very pointed toes are responsible for a great many of the toe deformities. It is not at all necessary that the footwear should be clumsy in order to be hygienic. Boots and shoes can be made just as neatly and as daintily with moderately sized heels as with high ones. They should have good strong soles, and not the thin brown-paper mixture which is so often characteristic of the cheap boot. It is a bad plan to economise in shoe leather—many a fatal chill has been traced to wet feet as a result of wearing poor shoes in inclement weather. In all cases where the soles of the boots or shoes are not waterproof, goloshes should be worn. Mothers should make their young daughters realise the importance of keeping their feet well protected from damp. Girls are apt to be very neglectful in this direction, and much ill health and even chronic invalidism in after life is very often the result. (For Waterproofs, Raincoats, see p. 306.)

FOOD AND DIET

The question of food and diet is an all-important one, but it is a question in which we must be guided to some extent by common-sense. Constitutions vary, and one woman's meat is only too apt to prove another woman's poison. In these days of dietarian extremists, of which the vegetarians form a typical faction, it proves sometimes very hard to strike an even balance for oneself in regard to the food question. It may be at once said that extremes in diet as in all other things are harmful, and should be avoided. For most people an all meat diet would be as injurious as a strictly vegetarian one. Special diets are of course prescribed in special circumstances, but apart from these exceptions, as a general rule a mixed meat and vegetable diet is the most suitable in a temperate climate like ours. One important maxim to bear in mind is "Avoid everything that disagrees with you, no matter how pleasing it may be to the palate." Various forms of diet must of course be adopted to suit individuals in special cases. For instance, the woman who is inclined to obesity should avoid sugar and all starchy foods, confectionery and pastries; whilst, on the other hand, the ultra-thin woman's diet should consist to a large extent of the very foods that the stout woman should avoid.

The normally healthy woman, so long as she is guided by the maxim never to take anything that disagrees with her, need not be hampered by any of these restrictions, but, and this is all-important, her meals should be taken at regular intervals and she should never eat between meals. It is the average woman's tendency to err particularly in regard to the quantity of food she takes. She either eats too much and too often, or else she eats too little. Nowadays people are more inclined to err in the former respect than in the latter. Three good meals a day are ample for the sustenance of health and strength, and the harmful practice of eating between meals should be abandoned. Dainties and sweets of various kinds should not be partaken of indiscriminately at any hour to the prejudice of the appetite at meal-time. Eating between meals more often than not is the basis of loss of appetite, indigestion, and other similar troubles. A great many people err in this respect, more especially in regard to our five o'clock tea. There is no harm in indulging in "the cup that cheers," with perhaps a thin slice of bread and butter or a biscuit, but there is a growing tendency to make quite a full meal at this time-honoured afternoon function, and where dinner or even supper follows at a two or a three hours' interval at most, the practice is one calculated to do harm to the strongest digestion.

It may be said at once that tea and sometimes coffee are taken to excess in the average middle-class home. They are both prolific causes of indigestion, and many a faulty digestion can be traced to excessive indulgence in either. Girl and women workers are the most inclined to indulge in the tea habit to excess. The evil in their case is increased inasmuch as our women workers as a rule are those who err not only in taking insufficient food at meal-time, but also in not selecting it with due regard to its nutritive properties. Hundreds of girl clerks may be seen in our great cities at the luncheon hour taking a meal of buns or pastries, supplemented with a liberal allowance of tea.

Economy practised in regard to food is false economy, and it is doubtful whether, even from a monetary point of view, it proves economy in the long run. A few years ago, perhaps, it was difficult to get a good meal for an expenditure well within the limits of the city worker's purse, but to-day things have undergone a remarkable change in this direction. At most of our light refreshment shops, for instance, a well-cooked chop or a steak may be obtained for the sum of sixpence. Taking into consideration the fact that the average price of tea is twopence a cup at least, and that pastries are as a rule twopence each, the fallacy of the tea and cake diet from the point of view of saving is obvious. It is a bad principle in any case to attempt saving on our meals. There are many other little details in which economy may be practised, but economy practised in regard to the food question is apt to cost very dear in the end. There is no need to partake of a heavy meal at luncheon time. Where the work is of a sedentary nature heavy eating in the middle of the day is injudicious. The diet might consist of eggs one day, meat and vegetables on another day, and fish the next, and so on; but let the cup of tea be absent from the mid-day meal.

We should always regulate the quantities of our meat and vegetable foods in accordance with the varying seasons. Thus in summer time fresh green vegetables, fruit, new-laid eggs should play an important part in our diet, and meat should not be taken in such large quantities as in the winter.

Too much stress cannot be laid upon the importance of good cooking. Bad cooking robs food of many of its most nutritive properties, whilst good cooking appeals to the palate, giving a healthy tone to the appetite, and in this way stimulates the digestive forces. Over-indulgence in sweets or pastries is ruinous to a good complexion, and all highly seasoned dishes and pickles, chutney, and other similar condiments should be avoided. On the other hand, fruit and green vegetables may be indulged in to the heart's content with the most beneficial results. Oranges especially are notable as complexion beautifiers. The woman who takes four or five oranges a day will find them most useful as digestive stimulants. Apples too are invaluable aids to a good digestion. Needless to say, the fruit should be in perfect condition. Both unripe and over-ripe fruit should be rigidly avoided.

SLEEP

Sleep is one of the essentials of life, for neither health nor strength can be maintained without it. When for some reason or other sleep cannot be obtained, the nervous and muscular system very rapidly become exhausted, for neither the brain nor the body can procure the needful rest from the wear and toil they are subject to during the day. During sleep the physique is not only resting but building up a fresh reserve of strength—it is, as it were, undergoing repair; for the muscular system as well as the brain recuperates itself under the influence of absolute rest, storing up nutriment brought to it by the blood in preparation for the next day's toil and activity.

Periods of Sleep.—Infants, children, and old people require longer periods of sleep than others. From fifteen to twenty-eight years of age nine hours' sleep should be taken. After twenty-eight until old age, eight hours will be sufficient.

The bedroom should be quiet, dark, cool, and well ventilated, and the window should be kept open at the top, summer and winter, to let the fresh air in. If you feel cold, put extra covers on the bed and a warmer dressing-gown whilst doing your hair, but never seek added warmth at the expense of ventilation.

Time for Sleep.—There is much truth in the old adage—

> "Early to bed, and early to rise
> Makes a man healthy, wealthy and wise."

The truth of it is borne out again in the fact that the sleep obtained before midnight is often designated as "Beauty Sleep." Regularity in the bed-time hour is not possible to all, but where it is possible its results are most beneficial. We have all experienced that jaded feeling which is the result of keeping late hours for some nights running, and even though we try to make up for it by sleeping several hours later in the day we never feel quite the same as if we had had our rest at the normal hour.

There are a number of people, such as journalists and those of the theatrical profession, who, from the nature of their calling, are bound to reverse the natural order of things, turning day into night and night into day. These should be careful always to make up their full eight hours of sleep. Care should be taken that when they have to rest far into the day-time, their bedrooms are well darkened, and that they are not disturbed by any sounds of the rush and bustle of the daily household work. (For Insomnia, its Causes and Cure, see Home Nursing.)

EXERCISE

Regular and systematic exercise is absolutely necessary for the maintaining of good health. Exercise taken in the open air is the most beneficial, the healthiest women being those who engage in outdoor sports such as golf, tennis, hockey, &c., for these not only keep the muscles of the body in good condition, but they entail a certain amount of time spent in the open air, and the more fresh air a woman is able to breathe the better it will be for her health, and incidentally for her complexion and her good looks in general. Walking exercise is especially good; it has been said that every woman and girl should walk at least five miles daily, but very few attain that standard. Nowadays when buses, trams, &c., are to be found at every turn, and transit of every kind is so accessible and so easy, a woman is inclined to walk as little as possible, to the general detriment of her health and good looks. Many women workers are compelled to lead sedentary lives. If these women would only make up their minds to walk to and fro from their offices and places of business instead of taking tram or bus, they would find their health materially improved. Even if doing so entailed their getting up half-an-hour earlier every morning, the little self-denial practised in this way would be amply repaid by the abundant benefits to be derived.

For the woman in easy circumstances walking is equally necessary, however much she may be tempted to take her outings in carriage or motor. The aimless, shambling walk without set purpose will not do her any good. In walking one should always have an object in view, the stride should be firm and light, the carriage erect. Needless to ay, high-heeled shoes should be altogether tabooed, as they throw the whole weight of the body upon the toes, instead of the pressure being first upon the heel and the ball of the foot, and last upon the toes, as is necessary for the natural movement in walking. Walking up and down a room for about ten minutes daily with a book well balanced upon the head will do a great deal towards improving the carriage of the head and shoulders. Some good physical exercises morning and evening will be found most beneficial; in fact, where the life is a sedentary one, it may be said that they are necessary for the maintenance of health (see below).

BREATHING

Few women have realised the value of deep breathing as an incentive to vitality and health; fewer still know how to breathe correctly. In breathing the lips should be kept closed and the breath inhaled and exhaled through the nostrils. Six to ten deep breaths taken regularly every morning upon rising will act as a wonderful tonic to the system. Standing erect with the hands upon the hips, inhale a deep full breath whilst slowly rising upon the tips of the toes—then slowly exhale whilst bringing the heels to the ground again. This breathing exercise should be repeated at least six times every morning or evening, and the number of breaths could be gradually increased to ten or twelve with the utmost benefit. Through the day-time, when working, walking, or indulging in any kind of exercise, a woman should practise the art of breathing correctly, inhaling and exhaling the breath through her nostrils and not through her mouth, as is the habit with many.

SOME SIMPLE PHYSICAL EXERCISES

The following simple physical exercises may be practised at home with much benefit. Any particular exercise or exercises may be selected and practised by a woman in accordance with her particular requirements.

First Exercise.—*Position.*—Stand with head erect and shoulders well squared, arms hanging at the sides, the finger-tips touching the thighs, heels close together and toes turned out (fig. 1).

Bend the forearms upwards, with the palms turned inwards and the fingers pointing to the shoulders (fig. 2).

Throw out the arms sideways parallel with the shoulders, keeping the palms downwards (fig. 3).

Second Exercise.—Stretch out arms sideways

PHYSICAL EXERCISES

FIG. 1. FIG. 2. FIG. 3. FIG. 4. FIG. 5.

FIG. 6. FIG. 7. FIG. 8. FIG. 9. FIG. 10.

FIG. 11. FIG. 12.

FIG. 13. FIG. 14. FIG. 15.

(fig. 3), then bend forearms until the hands are in front of the shoulders (fig. 4). Then quickly stretch arms sideways.

Third Exercise.—Bend arms as in fig. 2, then stretch arms upwards (fig. 5).

Fourth Exercise.—Bend arms as in fig. 2, then from this position stretch them forward, with the palms inward and the fingers well extended (fig. 6).

The above exercises are especially good for chest development.

Fifth Exercise.—Stretch arms upwards (fig. 5), then, with the feet firmly on the floor and without bending the knees, bend the body slowly backwards (fig. 7). This exercise has most beneficial effects in strengthening the back. The beginner should take up her position at first near a wall against which she can support herself by her hands as she bends.

Sixth Exercise.—Stretch the arms upwards (fig. 5), then, without bending the knees, bend forwards until the tips of the fingers touch the floor in front (fig. 8). The knees must not be bent under any consideration. If you cannot touch the floor at first, bend as far as you can without bending the knees; the rest will come with practice. This exercise is of enormous value in giving suppleness to the figure, reducing obesity and strengthening the abdomen. It should be performed regularly by those who are inclined to stoutness. After practising Exercise V. and Exercise VI. separately, practise both movements one after the other, bending backwards and forwards in turn several times.

Seventh Exercise.—Trunk-twisting movement. Place the hands behind the neck, the finger-tips just meeting (fig. 9), twist the body slowly to the right (fig. 10). Then after turning slowly to the front again, twist the body to the left in the same manner. This exercise gives suppleness to the figure and has a most beneficial effect upon the internal organs.

Eighth Exercise.—Lie down on floor with arms extended behind the head and the feet well together. Gently raise the left leg as high as it will go (fig. 11), then slowly lower it to the floor again. Raise and lower the right leg in the same manner. Repeat several times, then raise and lower both legs together (fig. 12). This is also an effective exercise for reducing superfluous flesh and curing constipation and digestive troubles.

Ninth Exercise.—Bend the knees as in fig. 13, placing both hands on the ground in front of you. Then, without bending the arms, throw out the legs to the rear (fig. 14). Bend the arms until the chest nearly touches the floor (fig. 15). Then straighten the arms until the position is again the same as fig. 14. Return to position shown in fig. 13.

This exercise is also very good for digestive troubles.

The Value of Housework.—Housework is a source of exercise which has a decidedly health-giving value. Turning mattresses and making beds are very ordinary and seemingly uninteresting household duties, but from the point of view of health they are good; the more energy and interest a woman displays in following the ordinary routine of her domestic duties, the less danger does she run of becoming a victim to nerves and other kindred feminine complaints. She must not overdo things, however, as it is as harmful to work too hard as to work too little, but if she goes through with her light household duties cheerfully and willingly, taking pleasure in her work, they cannot but be productive of physical benefit to her. It is not every one who can indulge in tennis, golf, and other similar outdoor and health-giving exercises, but there are very few women who have an excuse for not availing themselves of the exercise to be had in the daily routine of household work. Let them therefore, if they value their health, make the most of their opportunities in this direction.

CARE OF THE HAIR

No woman who values her appearance can afford to neglect her hair, for a fine, well-kept head of hair forms indeed a "woman's crowning glory," whereas dull-looking, ill-kept tresses tend to show more than anything else that she lacks that dainty and scrupulous care of her person which should prove one of the chief characteristics of her sex.

Brushing the Hair.—The hair should be thoroughly brushed for at least from five to eight minutes each morning and evening, and even longer if it is particularly thick and luxuriant. Care should be taken in the selection of the brushes. These should be of medium hardness—extremely hard brushes do more harm than good. A moderately stiff brush might be used for the hair, and a softer one for the scalp. Part the hair in two divisions from the centre of the forehead to the nape of the neck, then brush it at each side with firm, even, and rapid but not unduly heavy strokes. Few women understand the knack of hair-brushing, and more harm than good is done by an unduly harsh treatment with the brush. The brushing should be sufficiently brisk and vigorous to set the oil glands of the scalp in action. A healthy glow is felt over the head and scalp when the brushing is properly done.

Combing the Hair.—It is as well to take out the tangles with the comb *before* brushing, taking care not to break the hair by pulling it too hard. The teeth of the comb should not be too sharp; they should be firm and strong, however, and not easily breakable. Tortoise-shell combs are the best, but these are not within the reach of every purse. Very good combs can be obtained for the expenditure of from 1s. 6d. to 2s.; but great care should be taken in their selection. The scalp should never be scraped with the comb, as this induces irritatien and dandruff; neither should "back-combing," which is the name given to the process of fluffing out the hair by combing it back from the ends to the roots, in order to give it the appearance of an added thickness, be much practised.

After thoroughly brushing and combing the hair at night it is best to do it up in one or two very loose plaits, in order to give it a much-needed rest from the strain to which it has been subjected by the exigencies of the coiffure during the day-time. When the hair is tightly braided it cannot enjoy the benefit of this rest.

Scalp Massage.—Much benefit can be derived from gently massaging the scalp with the tips of the fingers, using a quick, circular movement. Part the hair in the middle, massage gently from and round the parting, then separate the hair in strands, and massage the scalp from and round the smaller partings thus made. The friction so caused stimulates the oil glands, and does much to promote their healthy action. This massage may take place night or morning, but preferably in the morning, when the scalp is not tired. For very dry hair a little cocoa-butter might be applied with the tips of the fingers during the massaging process; it should be rubbed gently into the scalp and not allowed to go over the hair.

Washing the Hair.—Too frequent washing of the hair is injurious, as it has the effect of removing the natural oil. No hard-and-fast rule can be laid down as to how often the hair should be washed; it is a matter which depends upon the nature and quantity of the hair and the condition of the scalp. People with abnormally greasy hair, for instance, require to wash it once in a fortnight or three weeks to keep it in a good condition; whilst dwellers in the town are compelled to wash their hair more often than people who live in the country.

On the other hand, people with dry hair should wash it as seldom as is compatible with perfect cleanliness. A good plan for those whose hair tends to dryness is to rub oil well into the scalp twenty-four hours before washing. This will obviate any tendency of the hair to become harsh and brittle after the shampoo. One important point to remember is that soap should never be rubbed on to the hair during the washing process. The best way to wash the hair is to dissolve a little good soap in hot water (Castile Soap is very good for the purpose), beat it into a lather, and then rub it well into the scalp until a lather is formed all over the head. Continue this operation in fresh hot water, still rubbing the lather well in. Then thoroughly rinse in hot water until all the soap is removed. A final rinsing can be given in cold water if required. Be careful to thoroughly dry the hair after washing, as a failure to do this often causes the dandruff which is so prejudicial to the health of the hair. Many good shampoo powders are sold which can also be used in this way. The yolks of one or two eggs beaten up to a froth and mixed with hot water also make a very good shampoo.

If people would only realise the cleansing properties of thorough brushing they would not need to wash their hair so often. It is most important, however, that the brushes should be kept scrupulously clean. Attention to these details go a long way towards keeping the hair and scalp in a healthy condition.

Where the hair is inclined to be unduly dry and brittle, a little Rowland's Macassar Oil or cocoa-butter should be well rubbed into the scalp twice a week. The former preparation should be used sparingly, two or three drops being sufficient to impart a delightful gloss. For unduly greasy hair a little bay rum rubbed into the roots twice a week will be found to have beneficial results in most cases.

Soda should never be used in washing the hair, for although it gives it a pretty, fluffy appearance, and tends to make fair hair look fairer, yet it is very injurious, having a most drying and irritating effect upon the scalp, causing the hair to split and break, and after a time to fall, if constantly used. Occasional tipping (i.e. cutting the ends of the hair) and singeing is beneficial when the hair is broken and the ends uneven, but the old idea that constant tipping and singeing was absolutely necessary to keep the hair in good condition is now altogether exploded.

Toilet Brushes.—It is very important to keep hair brushes very clean. They should always be kept under cover and not allowed to lie about exposed to the dust. Then wash them once a week or as often as occasion requires. Put sufficient hot water into a bowl or basin to cover the bristles of the brush and add a good teaspoonful of borax, a lump of soda, or enough ammonia to make the water smell rather strongly. Allow this to become luke-warm. Remove all hairs from the brush and dab it up and down in the water until it looks quite clean. The water must not be allowed to come over the back of the brush, or it is liable to loosen it and destroy the polish on the wood. Rinse thoroughly in cold water, which will prevent the bristles from becoming soft. Shake out the water, wipe the back of the brush with a towel, and dry as quickly as possible in the open air or in a warm atmosphere.

Soda should not be used for fine and expensive brushes as it might spoil the appearance of the backs; borax or ammonia are safer materials.

Polished wood or ebony backs can be rubbed up with a little furniture polish when the brushes are dry; tortoise-shell or ivory backs with a little sweet oil.

To Wash Combs.—Make a lather of soap and water. Take a small nail brush with crisp but not unduly hard bristles, and apply the soapsuds to the comb, brushing from the back of the comb to the edges of the teeth (left to right) with a brisk even movement. This brings out the dirt more effectively than by brushing the comb lengthways. Rinse well in cold water. Never let the comb lie in hot water—doing this is apt to bend it and make it brittle.

Falling Hair.—Falling hair may as a rule be regarded as a sign of ill health, hence it is necessary that any bodily condition which may be discovered as tending to produce the affliction in question should be duly corrected. Among lotions which may be used for strengthening the growth of the hair and preventing its falling out is that used by the late Sir Erasmus Wilson. It consists of :—

Strong liquor of ammonia . . .	½ an ounce.
Chloroform	½ an ounce.
Oil of sesame.	½ an ounce.
Oil of lemon	½ an ounce.

Spirits of rosemary being added up to 4 ounces.

A little of this should be rubbed into the scalp with a small sponge every other day. The hair should be parted from the nape of the neck to the forehead, and the tonic well rubbed into the parting thus made. Then the hair at the sides should be separated into strands, and the tonic applied to the scalp at the smaller partings. This tonic is especially good for dry hair.

For greasy hair the following preparation should be used :—

Cantharides	2 drachms.
Oil of lemon	½ an ounce.
Red lavender	2 drachms.

Spirits of Rosemary up to 4 ounces.

A little paraffin well rubbed into the scalp at night-time with the tips of the fingers in some cases acts as a very efficient tonic.

One important point to remember is that the hair and scalp should be well shampooed before first beginning to use a hair tonic if the utmost benefit is to be derived from its use.

Grey Hairs.—As a rule fair-haired women do not become grey with advancing years as soon as their dark-haired sisters, and the woman with dark hair is also the one most liable to be afflicted with *premature* greyness.

Premature greyness can in many cases be arrested, whilst the greyness that comes of advancing years must necessarily take its course. The woman whose locks show a tendency to become grey before she has attained the age of thirty should at once consult a good hair specialist, and so try to nip the mischief in the bud.

Grey hairs, like wrinkles, are often caused by constant worry or disorder of the nervous system, and the general health requires attention if the progress of the wintry locks is to be arrested. It has been said that constantly washing the hair with soda is very conducive to premature greyness. An excessively dry condition of the scalp should be avoided, and some good nourishing hair tonic regularly applied.

Dyeing the Hair.—The woman who wishes to dye her hair to hide the grey of advancing years would do well to think before she takes this step. Locks that are dyed serve in some inexplicable manner to emphasise the lines on the face, and thus, if she manages to conceal age by art in one direction, she only succeeds in emphasising it in the other. The young woman, however, whose locks present early the pepper and salt appearance which is often a prelude to complete greyness, cannot be so much blamed if she attempts to conceal by art what natural means have failed to cure. One word of warning, however, in this direction—never attempt the dyeing process yourself; go to a good and experienced hairdresser who knows from experience of the safest preparations, and who is an expert in applying them in the proper manner.

The amateur hair dyer has often awakened in the morning to find her locks turned green or some other weird colour. All her efforts to alter their appearance has been unavailing, and she has been compelled to go to a hair specialist in the long run. Needless to say, all her trouble and anxiety would have been saved if she had followed this course in the beginning.

False Hair.—False hair enters so largely into the scheme of fashionable hair-dressing that a few words on the subject will not be amiss. False curls, plaits, twists of all kinds are requisitioned in the present-day coiffures, even by those whose locks are naturally abundant. The wearing of masses of false curls over the natural hair cannot but be harmful to the scalp, which becomes unduly heated as the fresh air, so essential to the health of the hair, is excluded. The weight of a light, false plait or twist wound round the head is almost imperceptible, and so additions of this kind to the natural locks cannot do much harm, but it is heavy masses of curls and coils which should be avoided. If some addition is required to the tresses, the best way is to save up one's hair combings until there are sufficient for a plait, a switch or coil, and send them to a good hairdresser to be made up. The combings must be kept in a well-closed box, and they should not be kept too long before being made up, or they will become dull and lose their colour.

The Coiffure.—Whatever care may be given to other details of the toilette will be nullified to a certain extent by an ill-dressed head of hair. The clever woman realises that her looks depend a great deal upon the suitable arrangement of her tresses, and she takes pains to dress her hair to suit her face. When she possesses a pretty forehead and well-arched eyebrows she dresses her hair well away from the brows, knowing that it is the style which will suit her best.

If her face is unduly long, with prominent features, she shuns the middle parting, which could only add to its length. If, on the other hand, it inclines to undue squareness or plumpness, she avoids the pompadour, which would only tend to accentuate these defects.

There is nothing more unsightly than ill-kempt, straggly tresses, unless it is the hair brushed up so stiffly and strained so tightly as to give an appearance of being pulled out by the roots.

Those who are wise realise that the hair is a frame, as it were, to the face, which can be made to beautify the picture it surrounds, or else to detract very materially from its beauty.

The best coiffures invariably convey an idea of naturalness of arrangement, although artificial waving and other expedients may have been resorted to in order to bring about the desired results.

Waving and Curling the Hair.—It is not given to us all to have naturally wavy or curly hair. For those who are so fortunate as to possess it, the difficulties of hair-dressing are materially lessened, for wavy hair has a way of arranging itself naturally and becomingly with very little care. It has the advantage also of never looking really untidy, although "artistic untidiness" is generally the effect of curly tresses, for the little curls rebel at being unduly restricted by hairpins and ribbons, and have a knack of breaking away from the restraint of these accessories of the coiffure upon the least provocation, but with the happiest results.

Where the hair is inclined to be fluffy much may be done to simulate the natural wave. Of all forms of artificial waving that of doing up the hair in good waving pins is perhaps the most satisfactory for the woman who dresses her own hair.

Nowadays, it is true, very excellent waving and curling tongs and irons are sold, but to use them satisfactorily requires the knack of a trained coiffeur. The home use of curling and waving irons of all kinds should be discouraged, for the hair is often invariably impoverished by constant burning with hot tongs. It requires an expert to use them properly. If you must use them, take a course of lessons in waving from a good hairdresser, or, better still, go to the hairdresser once a week or once a fortnight to have the hair waved. What is called the "Marcelle" wave will last a week or even a fortnight with fluffy hair, and the hairdresser's charge as a rule does not come to more than 1s. 6d.

The Use of Waving and Curling Pins.—Of curling and waving pins those sold by Messrs. Hinde are perhaps amongst the best. They can be obtained from almost any hairdresser or draper in the United Kingdom, and are very easy to use. Upon getting up in the morning separate the part of the hair which is to be waved into strands, and twist each strand round a waver. By the time the toilet is complete and it is time to begin the coiffure, upon taking out the pins it will be found that the hair is well and naturally waved. If the hair is inclined to be abnormally greasy, it will not wave quite so quickly, then it will be necessary sometimes to leave the pins in over-night. This should not be done often, however, as the hair needs rest during the night-time, and should not be subjected to any unnecessary strain if this can be avoided. A little rum or spirit of any kind rubbed on to the hair before waving will very often act as a most effective curling fluid; often also by slightly warming the pins in the flame of a candle or a gas jet before using, the hair will be found to wave much more quickly. Fringes are very little worn at the present day; a few stray curls here and there on the forehead are the utmost concession made by fashion to those who find a fringe of some kind necessary. One of Hinde's curlers will be all that is necessary for the curling of the present-day fringe. Where the hair is unusually dank and greasy two might be used, but care must be taken to avoid the very stiffly curled fringe which is now so terribly *démodé*.

Dressing the Hair.—In almost every successful coiffure the front and back portions of the hair are dressed separately. After having waved the hair, part it first of all from ear to ear. This will separate the front and back portions.

Comb up the back portion towards the centre of the back of the head, and if the hair is long tie it in the required position, or fasten it with a hair-binder. It is better not to tie short hair, as more can be made of it if left loose. Then take the front portion, shaking it down over the face, and comb it well. If the pompadour effect is required, separate the hair into three divisions, gently fluff the centre part of the division with the comb, turn it up and fasten into position with an ornamental comb. Do the same with each of the side pieces, taking care not to leave a parting on either side. With fluffy hair the pompadour effect can be achieved without the aid of a pad; with very straight hair a light pad is necessary—it must be a very light one and the hair must not be strained too tightly over it.

If a parting is required, part in two in the middle, take up each side separately, gently push the hair forward, and keep it in place with side-combs. The harsh, even parting is a thing of the past nowadays; the hair is always parted loosely, and a little wave made to fall over the forehead on each side. If preferred the parting can be made to come to one side.

These preliminary steps carefully attended to, the foundation of a good coiffure is made; the hair can now be done in the style preferred.

Fashionable Coiffures.—In the winter season 1909–10, a style of hairdressing known as the "Turban Coiffure" was introduced into England from Paris, and became pretty generally adopted by all those who wished to be "in the fashion."

A typical English Coiffure.

This style of head-dress, however, though admirably suited to our fair neighbours across the Channel, was by no means universally becoming to English faces. The foundation of the coiffure was a large turban frame which fitted the head like a cap; the hair was drawn through a hole at the base of the frame and arranged over it in a flat chignon or turban, whilst a straight band of hair drawn round the chignon so formed completed the coiffure. By reason of its general unbecomingness to English faces the reign of the "Turban" was short-lived. English hairdressers met together in conference to deliberate whether it was not possible to design coiffures in England instead of adopting the Paris styles. As a result of their deliberations, a typical English coiffure has been introduced which bids fair to lead the fashion for some time to come.

The curls which were so great a feature of the fashion in coiffures during the early part of 1909 have been revived, only with a difference. They are much larger, and are generally built on frames still retaining something of the turban shape. These are encircled by a coil of hair drawn in many cases through tortoise-shell rings, which form part of the back-comb. As an alternative a straight flat slide is worn at the base of the hair. For evening dress three short ringlets are allowed to fall over the nape of the neck at the back. These ringlets are as a rule absent from the coiffure in the day-time, although for very dressy occasions they may sometimes be worn; on these occasions, however, the dress collar would have to be low.

The arrangement of the very dressy form of the new coiffure can seldom be effected by a woman herself without the help of a lady's-maid, and some extraneous aid to her own locks in the form of curls, switches, &c. The simpler forms, however, do not require so much elaboration, although the same idea is maintained, and a woman can effect the fashionable arrangement of her tresses without even the aid of a hair-frame in the following way.

If the hair is long and plentiful, after arranging and waving the front portion, take up all the hair at the centre of the head at the back and tie it or fasten it with one of Hinde's hair-binders in the centre of the head, leaving the under portion of the hair hanging loose over the shoulders. Then separate the bound portion into strands, making several large curls, take up the under portion and coil it loosely round the curls, fix one of the fashionable hair-slides in the hair just above the nape of the neck, and the coiffure is complete.

With short hair, the hair should not be bound. It should be separated into two portions in the way already described; the under portion should be well pinned back while the upper portion is being curled, then it should be divided into two strands, which should be made to cross one over the other at the back and twisted round on either side of the head to give the appearance of one complete strand.

A woman sometimes finds it very difficult to make the fashionable curls by twisting strands of hair over her fingers; the curls are apt to break and become loose when made in this manner. Messrs. Burnet & Temple, Ltd., of 3 and 4 Fitchetts Court, London, E.C., have brought out a very simple and ingenious device by which curls and puffs can be made with the

least amount of trouble. This consists of a small wooden stick round which the hair is rolled; the stick is fitted with grooves through which a safety hairpin is inserted, fastening the curl in place when the stick is removed.

It must be remembered that fashions in millinery have a most decided influence upon fashions in hairdressing; a woman must nowadays dress her hair to suit her hat, and the latest evolution of the coiffure may be ascribed to the vogue for very large and picturesque head-gear which has prevailed for so long. As a relief from large hats, the turban toques are equally fashionable, and the simpler form of hairdressing described is suitable for either the one form of millinery or the other, the only difference being that the *bouffant* and waved effects at the sides should be more elaborate when wearing a large hat than with the toque. In this latter case the side dressing may be comparatively simple.

Combs and Slides.—Ornamental combs and slides play an important part in the present styles of hairdressing. The slide is particularly useful as well as an ornamental accessory. Placed as it is at the back of the coiffure, it prevents the hair becoming caught in the hooks or buttons of a high collar, and helps to keep the curls trim and tidy. Combs have very deep, wide borders, which serve to convey the appearance of hair-slides when placed in the hair. Very large tortoise-shell hairpins are also worn; in fact, it may be said that as waving and curling is a feature of present-day hairdressing, the popularity of combs, fancy pins, and other similar accessories will largely increase, as they are most effective in accentuating the deep waves and curls, and at the same time serve to keep them in place, imparting a "finished" appearance to the coiffure.

CARE OF THE HANDS

Many a woman who is on the whole particular in regard to her general appearance is apt to neglect the care of her hands. This is a great mistake, as ill-kept hands and nails are unsightly in the extreme, whilst a well-groomed hand is not only pleasant to the eye, but is also one of the best indications of refinement a woman can possess.

Housework is often made the excuse for lack of care in this direction. The average woman is apt to entertain the idea that well-kept hands are incompatible with the proper fulfilment of domestic duties. This is quite a fallacy, for with a little care the busy housewife can keep her hands in as good condition as the lady of leisure, who can afford to spend half-an-hour or an hour at her manicurist whenever she feels so inclined.

Thin rubber surgeon's gloves should be worn when doing work which necessitates the hands being constantly in and out of the water, such as washing dishes, scrubbing, &c. A pair of old gloves should always be kept in readiness for wear when dusting, sweeping, or performing other similar duties. They should, if possible, be a size too large, so as not to restrain the circulation in any way. Gloves should also be worn when engaged in gardening and other out-of-door work.

How to Keep the Hands Clean.—Cleanliness is, of course, the first essential in this portion of the toilet. The hands should be well washed in good soap and warm water softened with a little borax or some good toilet vinegar night and morning, and, whenever necessary, during the day. A good nail-brush with firm bristles should be used for scrubbing the nails, and pumice stone or lemon or both for removing stains from the hands and fingers. When the hands become soiled and greasy after the performance of household duties, a little cold cream or white vaseline should be rubbed well into them before and after washing, in order to keep the skin smooth and soft. On home washing days, when there is a great deal of laundry work to be done, after being immersed for a long time in the wash-tub the hands are apt to assume a rather harsh, wrinkled appearance. This can be cured by dipping them into a little vinegar; they should then be rubbed with cold cream, as after the performance of other household duties.

After washing and drying the hands before going to bed at night, glycerine and rose-water, or red lavender, mixed in the proportions of two parts glycerine to one of red lavender, should be rubbed into the skin. To do this thoroughly it is well to rub the mixture well into the palms and then rub the hands together as in washing.

When the work of the house has been abnormally heavy, and, in spite of all precautions, the hands have become a little rough, it is advisable to wear a pair of large chamois leather gloves at night, or a pair of old kid gloves one or two sizes too large. Gloves of the normal size would not do. They would only restrict the healthy circulation of the blood, and *red*, not white hands would be the result.

Drying the Hands.—The importance of thoroughly drying the hands after washing cannot be too highly estimated. A neglect of this causes the skin to become red and coarsened, and in winter time chapped hands and often chilblains are the result. Many a busy housewife is content, after hurriedly washing her hands, to dry them perhaps on a kitchen roller towel, the latter being most probably wet already through constant use. Every bit as much care should be taken in drying the hands as in washing them. They should be dried first with an ordinary linen towel, and then well rubbed with a soft Turkish towel. An added precaution to take would be to dust them over with fine oatmeal, a little Fuller's earth, or any good toilet powder.

For the treatment of chilblains, see Home Nursing.

Care of the Nails, Manicure.—Every woman should be able to manicure her hands and nails for herself. The process is a very simple one and only requires a little care and the proper implements.

The following articles are necessary for the use of the home manicurist :—

A packet of orange sticks for pushing back the skin.
A small nail file.
A small brush.
A pair of curved nail scissors.
Some good cold cream.
A box of nail powder.
A nail polisher.
Some fine emery or sand-paper.

Cases containing the orange sticks, nail file and brush and polisher can be obtained from any perfumers for the small sum of 10½d. or one

Curved Nail-Scissors.

Nail Polisher.

shilling, whilst most leather merchants sell compact little cases containing the curved scissors as well for from 2s. 6d. to 3s. 6d. The manicure powder can be obtained from all perfumers and chemists in boxes of from sixpence upwards. It is as well of course to get as good a set of implements as possible, as a little additional money spent on the original outlay will pay in the long run.

To Manicure the Nails.—Take some warm water and make a good lather of soap-suds. Add a few drops of Eau de Cologne or toilet vinegar and the juice of half a lemon. Soak the fingers for from five to ten minutes in the soap-suds. This process has the effect of softening the nails so that they are ready for attention. Then after having rubbed a little cold cream well into the skin round the base of the nails, press the skin well back with the orange stick, not only at the base but all round the nails. By doing this those half-moons which are so dainty and attractive a feature of well-kept nails are brought into view. The cuticle of the nail should never be touched with the scissors unless it is absolutely necessary to use them to cut a hang-nail.

The nails should now be cut round the edges if necessary, and filed into shape with the little file. The curve of the nail should be trimmed to follow that of the finger-tips. The ideal nail is of an oval form, and although we do not all have the good fortune to possess oval finger-tips, a little careful manipulation in the trimming of the nails will do a great deal in giving them an oval appearance as far as possible. Constant practice works wonders in the proper manipulation of the nail file.

After the nails have been carefully filed, a little of the sand-paper should be used to smooth away the rough edges.

Finally the nail powder should be applied with the brush, and the nails should be gently polished with the polisher. The latter consist of a little instrument somewhat in the shape of a miniature iron with the flat part covered with chamois leather. If no polisher is available, it is often sufficient to rub the nails against the palm of the hand.

After this treatment has been gone through, the nails will assume that pink and polished appearance which adds so much to their beauty, and which is quite easily attainable by the expenditure of a little care.

The manicuring process should be gone through at least once a week. Every day, however, the cuticle of the nail should be pushed back with the orange stick after washing, or even with the towel. The polisher should then be used with light rapid friction, and this daily attention will keep the nails in proper condition.

A very good substitute for ordinary nail-polishing powder can be obtained from Messrs. Pritchard & Constance, of 64 Haymarket, London. It is sold under the trademark of "Amami" Polishing Stone, for the moderate price of sixpence. Amami Nail-Polishing Stone is no trouble : merely rub on the moistened palm of the hand, first the stone, and then the finger nails ; the thumb nails should be done separately. A lasting pearly polish appears at once. The substance of the stone, in addition to being quite harmless, tends to preserve in good condition both the nails and the cuticle.

Where the nails are unduly dry and brittle, a little olive oil rubbed into them at night will do wonders in restoring them to good condition.

CARE OF THE EYES, EYEBROWS, AND EYELASHES

Not only are the eyes the all-essential organs of sight, but they have also been described as the "Mirror of the Soul." They reflect our thoughts, our intellect, our emotions, and our sympathies, giving to the face that spiritualness which forms its chief beauty. They can be made indeed the most formidable weapon in the armoury of woman's charm, and yet they are the very organs of her body which she is the most inclined to abuse and neglect.

The average woman thinks nothing of straining her eyes over books or needlework in an indifferent light. It is bad for the eyes even in a good light to strain them over small print or minute stitches for hours at a stretch. The eyes require rest as much as the other organs of the body, and if they are required to do more than their fair share of work they are bound to suffer in the long run.

In the evening, when artificial light is required, be careful to sit with your back to the light, so that it is thrown on the pages of the book, and not straight into the eyeballs. The light should be shaded. Dark green shades are the most restful to the sight, and lamps and lights should be covered with them wherever possible.

Electric light, which is apt to be dazzling in its brilliancy, should always be shaded in green or some other soft colour.

From the point of view of our personal hygiene the care of the eyes and eyebrows, eyelids and eyelashes, should receive daily consideration.

The eyes are naturally at their best, of course, when the health is at its best. Nothing can impart to the pupils the brilliancy of good health. Very often drugs such as belladonna are resorted to to give them the sparkle and shine which for some cause they lack. This is a most injurious practice, and can be productive of nothing but harm.

When washing in the morning care should be taken that the secretions which have accumulated in the corner of the eyes during sleep are removed. These, be it noted, should be washed out with warm water. It is inadvisable to rub into the corner of the eyes with a towel in order to dislodge the secretions, as inflammation is very often caused in this way. At night-time also care should be taken that the eyes are given their proper share of consideration in the evening toilet.

Use of the Eye-cup.—When the secretions which accumulate round the eyes during the night are found to be so unduly heavy as to be difficult to dislodge in the morning, to thoroughly purify the eye it will be found necessary to use an eye-cup. This is a little glass cup made in the shape of the eyeball. It should be filled with warm water in which a pinch of boracic powder has been dissolved. Hold the cup towards the eye, lower the head slightly to meet it, and it will be found that the eye-cup fits round the eye exactly. Tilt the head backwards and forwards, holding the cup into position, and open and close the eyelid in the water until the eye is thoroughly cleansed. Dab gently with a small piece of soft rag to dry, and repeat the treatment with the other eye. The eye-cup can also be used at night to remove the dust and dirt which have accumulated during the day. In all cases where the nature of the daily occupation forces the eyes to go through a heavy strain, such as literary work, constant typeing, proof-reading, dressmaking, &c., the daily use of the eye-cup will prove a most beneficial tonic.

Eye-cup.

When the eyes have been so severely strained that they are red and inflamed round the rims, and the secretions are so extensive that it is sometimes difficult to open the lids in the morning, a lotion should be used after bathing. This should be prescribed by a good oculist. In all cases of persistent trouble with the eyes an oculist should be at once consulted. There are people who, upon the first signs of eye-strain, rush to the nearest optician, buy a pair of glasses, and think that they have done all that is required. This mode of procedure may answer with luck, but most often it results in permanent injury to the eyesight. There is nothing more injurious for the eyes than unsuitable glasses. Glasses should only be made to the prescription of a good oculist who, after thorough examination and testing of the patient's sight, knows exactly what is required. Very often glasses are not required, and a simple lotion will set the trouble right. So those who, upon the first little trouble with their eyes, are inclined to at once buy spectacles, should be wise and find out first if they are really needed before they ruin their sight for life.

Eyebrows and Eyelashes.—Well-marked eyebrows and good lashes are invaluable aids to beauty, and although it is not possible for us all to attain the high arched brows and long curling lashes which form the ideal of the artist, yet with care we can train our brows and lashes to something very near it.

Where the brows and lashes are thin, vaseline or cocoa-butter well rubbed into them at night serve to promote their growth; but the treatment must be persisted in regularly to produce results.

When the eyebrows are unduly straight, by careful manipulation with the fingers when applying the vaseline, and pinching the hair with a semicircular movement upwards, they can be trained into something like the arched brows we all covet. The vaseline should be applied to the eyelashes gently and carefully, either with the tip of the first finger or the end of a match covered with a piece of soft rag. It should be applied under the lashes, which should be gently coaxed outwards and upwards to induce them to curl at the tips. When this has been done, dab the eyelids gently with a piece of clean soft rag to remove all superfluous vaseline, which, if allowed to remain, might cause the lashes to stick together. Under no consideration attempt to touch the lashes with the scissors under the impression that by clipping their growth will be improved.

The hair should never be dressed to fall very low over the forehead so as to cover the brows. A coiffure of this kind tends to wear away the eyebrows and impede their growth.

Brushing the brows with a small brow-brush night and morning goes a long way towards improving their appearance.

There is not much use in having pretty brows, however, if we mar them by continual frowning. The frowning habit grows upon one imperceptibly, and it is a habit very hard to correct. Persistent frowning brings those unsightly little lines between the brows which does so much to spoil their beauty. They can be removed in time with persistent care and treatment (see p. 450); but a habit once contracted is hard to get rid of, and no matter how often the little lines are effaced, if the frowning habit continnes they will reappear.

CARE OF THE TEETH

Too much stress cannot be laid upon the extreme importance of the proper care of the teeth. Indigestion and other gastric troubles are often traced to decayed and defective teeth. To masticate food properly good teeth are of paramount importance. To keep the teeth and mouth clean is one of the surest methods of keeping them sound. Care should be taken, therefore, that all particles of food which collect between the teeth are dislodged by aid of the tooth-brush.

The teeth should be brushed at least twice a day, night and morning, and also after meals if possible. A good tooth powder should be used, and the teeth brushed not only across, but also up and down, the teeth of the upper jaw being brushed downwards, and those of the lower jaw being brushed upwards. Attention should also be paid to the gums. They should be brushed as carefully as the teeth. The mouth might be also rinsed with a good antiseptic mouth wash every evening. Calvert's Carbolic Tooth Powder or precipitated chalk are very good for cleansing purposes, and used in conjunction with a mouth wash, in accordance with the directions given, will serve to keep the mouth and teeth in a clean and wholesome condition. Where tartar accumulates upon the teeth to any great extent, it should be scraped off by a dentist. It is superfluous to add that when tooth decay does make its appearance the dentist should at once be consulted and the ill thoroughly remedied. It is not generally known that a milk diet is very injurious to the teeth; the milk, becoming acid on the gums, destroys the enamel. This may be obviated by using a good pinch of carbonate of soda in the water with which the teeth are brushed.

The care of her teeth is apt to be too much neglected by the average woman; and yet it is quite a simple matter to keep them clean and healthy, and a little care in this direction brings its reward an hundred-fold. Leaving all questions of health apart, bad and badly-kept teeth spoil the prettiest face, whilst good, well-kept teeth have often the effect of redeeming a countenance from actual plainness.

CARE OF THE FEET

Regular care of the feet is as important as regular care of the hands.

The toe-nails should be kept well trimmed, but they should not be cut too short. Unlike the finger nails, they should be cut straight and not in a curve, as it is injurious to cut too far down into the side of the toe-nail. Doing this serves to increase the tendency of the nail to grow inwards at the corners where such a tendency exists. Boots with pointed toes should never be worn, as they compress the toes inwards in accordance with the shape of the boot, in some cases to such an extent that the great and little toes very nearly meet. The pointed shoe or boot is the cause of bunions, corns, and nearly every foot deformity. When corns and bunions make their appearance they should be at once treated, as, if neglected, they not only cause a large amount of pain, but in some cases actually cripple the sufferer. (For treatment, see Home Nursing.)

To Cure Ingrowing Toe-Nails.—An ingrowing toe-nail can very often be cured in its first stages by the following simple means:—With a sharp pair of scissors make a V-shaped incision in the centre of the top of the nail, and insert a piece of cotton wool between the nail and the toe at the corner in which the nail shows a tendency to grow into the flesh. The nail will gradually grow at each side towards the incision until the latter is closed, and the tendency to grow inwards at the corner of the toe will thus be effectively checked.

Perspiring Feet.—Some people are afflicted with feet that perspire to an abnormal degree. This is an extremely unpleasant affliction, arising very often from some defect in the general health. It frequently occurs in children, often disappearing altogether as they grow older; but with adults, as a rule, the trouble is more persistent.

In all cases strict cleanliness must be observed. The feet should be bathed at night in warm water to which a little Condy's Fluid has been added in the proportion of a tea-spoonful of Condy's Fluid to a pint of water. They should be bathed in this way after any considerable exercise has been indulged in. Light woollen stockings should be worn—never cotton ones—and these should be frequently changed. Sometimes it will be found necessary to put on a fresh pair of stockings every day. Strict attention must also be given to the general health. In many cases it will be found that a good tonic will be beneficial.

Tired and Sore Feet.—There are some kinds of work which entail a woman being a great deal on her feet, and often her feet become very tired and sore in consequence. There is nothing more refreshing in these circumstances than to sponge the feet with a little methylated spirits. This treatment will cause the soreness and fatigue to disappear, and will, in addition, be wonderfully refreshing.

CARE OF THE EARS

Wax should never be allowed to accumulate in the ears. When the wax has become so hardened that it is difficult to dislodge, take enough soda to cover a threepenny piece, dissolve this in a dessert-spoonful of water, and gently drop it into the ear at night. This will serve effectively to loosen the wax. In no case attempt to dislodge wax by means of hair-pins or any other sharp instrument. Much injury can be done to the ears in this way. In many cases it will be necessary to syringe the ear with a special ear syringe.

MAKING UP

How far it is justifiable to have recourse to art as an aid to good looks is, and has ever been, a much debated question. Before, however, trying to improve her appearance by the aid of "make up," a woman should pause and think, for once she has started making up there will be no going back; she will have to continue to do so. The pity of it is that it is most often the women whose skins and complexions leave nothing to be desired who are the first to have recourse to the aid of the rouge-box, and who thus inevitably ruin their natural complexions in the cult of the artificial.

There are some women, however, who, from chronic ill-health or other causes, have such sallow, unpleasing-looking skins that one cannot blame them for seeking some sort of an aid to beauty—that is to say, if they make up so cleverly that the most practised eye cannot detect it. The art of make up lies in concealing the fact that art has been called in as an aid to nature. It is the clumsy and vulgar display of rouge, the emphasising of the fact that the complexion is false, that jars so much upon persons of refinement. On the other hand, one cannot help but admire the woman who makes up so cleverly that no one can tell her complexion is not natural.

The first care of the woman who makes up must be to do it well; secondly, and by no means less important, she must never allow herself to be seen without her make up. She should make up the first thing in the morning, and not follow the example of some women who make a point of donning their complexions with their visiting toilettes. A woman who acts in this way cannot conceal the fact that she has recourse to art, as the difference between her natural complexion and her artificial one will be too marked to escape general notice.

How to Make Up.—If a woman must make up it is necessary that she should know how to do so without injuring the texture of her skin in the process. Before attempting to apply the rouge, the face should be thoroughly washed with soap and warm water. After drying rub some good skin food well into the skin pores and wipe it off with a piece of soft rag. Then apply a small quantity of the rouge to the cheeks, finishing the process by dusting some good powder over the face. Take off all superfluous powder with a clean face chamois leather.

Rouge may be had in the form of liquid, powder, or paste.

Powder.—Powder for the face is now in such general use that it has almost ceased to be regarded as a cosmetic. Yet in spite of this, great care must be taken in its application. The face thickly coated with powder is not pretty to look upon, and the pores of the skin become very much coarsened as a result of its indiscriminate use. Then some of the cheaper powders contain very injurious ingredients. Some face powders are, however, great boons to very greasy skins, but they must only be lightly dusted over the face with a clean powder puff or face leather, and then all superfluous powder should be dusted off. Care should be taken to use only the pure powders, avoiding all preparations containing mercury and arsenic. The Poudre Simon is one of the best face powders to be had. It should be used sparingly in conjunction with Crème Simon if possible. The Crème Simon, which is not the least bit greasy, should be gently massaged into the skin, and then rubbed off and the powder applied afterwards.

Care must be taken to remove all traces of powder and make up before retiring to rest at night. To do this some good cold cream or white vaseline should be rubbed lightly over the face with a gentle massage movement, then wiped off with a piece of clean soft rag, and the face washed with soap and warm water.

Papiers Poudrés.—The little leaflets known as Papiers Poudrés are invaluable to the woman who is a great deal out of doors in the warm weather. They consist of diminutive sheets of paper finely powdered at one side and enclosed in a booklet from which they are easily detachable. One of these little leaflets gently passed over the face when it is greasy and perspiring will remove not only superfluous moisture, but all dust and dirt. The Papiers Poudrés may be purchased from most chemists.

THE CHILD

WITH mothers who wish conscientiously to fulfil their duty towards their children in every way a certain sense of responsibility is ever present. They do not always know how to act in varying circumstances which may crop up, whether in connection with the rearing of their children in infancy, the care of their health in childhood, or the important question of education in later years. It is said that knowledge comes with experience, but too often this knowledge will have been only too dearly bought! The advice in regard to the management of children contained in this chapter is the result of experience, and it is trusted that many a mother who is in doubt in regard to any particular question of child management, may find a way out of her difficulty by referring to these pages, and so take advantage of the experience gained by others.

PREPARING FOR MOTHERHOOD

Very soon in the married lives of most young wives comes a time when the knowledge is brought home to them that they are to be called upon to fulfil woman's noblest mission—the mission of motherhood. To the really womanly wife, the thought that she is to become a mother will be sweet indeed, joy tempered with a sense of reverence maybe at the great responsibility of the little life to be entrusted to her care. That there should be a little nervousness at the prospect, too, is perhaps not unnatural, but it should be but passing when it is remembered that, by careful living during the months prior to baby's birth, nature will be materially assisted, and will, in her own way, reward the expectant mother who has helped her.

A woman can never sufficiently realise the importance of those months before her little one is born. She should remember that if she builds up her strength during this period, she will not only be much better fitted for the ordeal before her, but she will also fulfil her responsibility to the little life in her keeping, for it is well known that upon the care taken of herself by the mother during pregnancy will largely depend the future health of her child.

The expectant mother should lead a simple and regular yet gently active life, a strict observance of the laws of hygiene being more than ever important at this period, when not only her own welfare, but also that of her child must be secured. Too much stress cannot be laid upon the necessity for plenty of pure fresh air, wholesome food taken at regular meals, sufficient exercise, judicious rest, and hygienic and cheerful surroundings. If any of these are wanting, then the health of both mother and child will be needlessly jeopardised.

Pure Air.—Plenty of pure fresh air is the first important essential. Enjoying the benefit of the air out of doors is not sufficient—indoors all the rooms should be fresh and well ventilated. The bedroom window especially should always be kept open at the top. Plenty of fresh air at night will do a great deal to obviate that tendency to sleeplessness which often manifests itself towards the end of the period of waiting.

Exercise.—Sufficient exercise, including the daily walk in the open air, is also a necessity. The woman who thinks her whole day should be spent reclining upon a couch, and imagines herself incapable of exertion of any kind, is storing up much future ill for both herself and her child. She must have regular exercise, going cheerfully through the performance of light household duties, though any straining in the way of reaching up to high shelves, lifting heavy weights, &c., must, of course, be avoided.

Though exercise in moderation is beneficial, it should not be indulged in to excess. A woman should not take such long walks as to cause exhaustion, nor should she indulge in violent exercise such as is afforded by tennis and other similar games. Riding and cycling should also be given up. The enthusiastic follower of all kinds of athletic pursuits should take special warning, for if she continues to indulge in these pastimes to any great extent, she will use up all her strength and energy and will therefore have no reserve to draw upon when the time comes when both will be so greatly needed. Another important thing to bear in mind is that during the first three months and the last few weeks of pregnancy travelling by bus, train, or tram should be avoided as far as possible, for the disturbing influence of the severe jolting often experienced in this way is most injurious, and a miscarriage at times may be the result.

Diet.—Strict attention to diet is all-important. Meals should be taken at regular intervals.

Eating should not be indulged in between meals. Heavy and highly seasoned foods should be avoided, also pastry and other sweet things likely to cause that much-dreaded ill—indigestion. Plenty of fruit and green vegetables should be taken, as these will tend to prevent constipation. Very fattening and starchy foods should be only taken sparingly. Excessive tea or coffee-drinking is most injurious—though, if taken in moderation, tea is really an excellent beverage. Plenty of milk should always be taken if possible. Good cooking is essential. The diet should also be pleasantly varied, as the distaste for food so often resulting from monotony must be avoided at all costs. It is a mistake to think that stimulants are necessary during this period. Indeed, they are apt to be actually harmful at times, and should never be taken excepting under medical advice.

The Daily Bath.—This is most important in pregnancy. There is less likely to be kidney trouble when the bath is taken regularly. Any puffiness of the face or limbs should, however, be reported to the doctor, as early treatment will often prevent tiresome complications later on.

Rest.—The maxim "Early to bed and early to rise" should be religiously observed by the expectant mother. At least eight hours of sleep should be aimed at. Ten o'clock is a good hour for retiring, 7 or 7.30 o'clock a good time for rising in the morning, and unless there is trouble with "morning sickness," breakfast should be taken downstairs. A freshly-made cup of tea taken before rising is often helpful. Every day an hour's rest should be taken in a darkened room on bed or sofa after the mid-day meal. Rest of the body is not the only essential, for rest of the mind is almost as important in every way. On account of the severe strain to which her nervous system is being subjected, a woman is more inclined to give way to irritability and nerves at this than at any other time. She should guard herself against this tendency by being firmly determined never to worry over trifles, and doing her utmost to maintain an attitude of calm equanimity. Self-control should be aimed at upon all occasions, and a cheerful, happy, and contented frame of mind should be cultivated. Any tendency to morbid despondency must be sternly combated. It must be remembered that cheerful and beautiful surroundings do more than anything else to foster cheerfulness of mind, a fact that should be remembered by friends and relations. Any sudden news entailing either excessive grief or excessive joy is harmful, and shocks of any kind should be avoided. Late hours and all kinds of excitement should be altogether abjured. Going to At Homes or theatres means spending a number of hours in stuffy, ill-ventilated rooms and in an atmosphere of excitement which is far from beneficial. The expectant mother should be prepared to forego these amusements, realising that a power of self-sacrifice is not one of the least attributes which will qualify her for the noble mission of motherhood. All social intercourse, however, need not be abandoned during these months of waiting. Simple little social gatherings and the society of bright and cheerful friends will do good. It is the constant striving after pleasure and excitement, the strain of keeping up with an endless round of social engagements, which is harmful. All morbid and sensational literature should be avoided. Let the woman who is to be a mother cultivate beautiful thoughts by reading wise and beautiful books. Let her frame of mind be such as will fit her to guide the mind of the little life entrusted to her care. Such, no doubt, has been the mental attitude of the mothers of many of our wise men and brave heroes, and such should be the mental attitude of the mother who wishes to qualify herself in every way for the high calling of motherhood.

Dress during this period is an important consideration. In the first place hygiene and comfort must be studied, and as far as possible an effort must be made to avoid appearing conspicuous. In regard to the wearing of corsets, opinions differ, though it is generally acknowledged that it is wiser not to discard them. To wear tight stays would be foolish and harmful, and corsets of the straight-fronted type must be altogether tabooed. There are special corsets, however, particularly suitable for maternity wear. These are very lightly boned, opening at the sides, and expandable. They are very comfortable and afford great support to the figure. If the breasts become very enlarged and tender, what are known as "bust corsets" should be worn over the regular stays. They may be obtained from most drapers for a very small outlay. All clothing should be warm and light, whilst compression of any part of the body should be avoided. Suspenders should be worn instead of garters, as the latter tend to impede the circulation. High-heeled shoes are always injurious, but they are more than ever so at this time. While care is taken to dress hygienically and sensibly, a woman should not give way to the inclination of being careless and indifferent in regard to her personal appearance. She should endeavour to dress both indoors and out of doors as neatly as possible under the circumstances.

It is inadvisable to spoil good clothes by altering them and attempting to adapt them to the increasing figure. Good gowns tinkered about with in this way can seldom be worn afterwards. It is also most injurious for a woman to endeavour to squeeze herself into tight gowns at those times. She will naturally wish to avoid looking conspicuous, but she will only make matters worse by resorting to the measures above described. Special maternity dresses with adjustable bands are made at all the leading ladies' costumiers and outfitting establishments, and every woman who prizes her health as well as her appearance should invest in one or two of these garments at such times. It is quite easy to ask for the lady at the head of the costume department at one of these establishments and explain to her what is wanted. The dresses are fitted by expert fitters who thoroughly understand their work, and such a garment cannot fail to prove satisfactory in every way. Ladies also make a mistake in wearing heavy loose voluminous cloaks at these times. A well-fitting skirt specially made and a long coat are the ideal outdoor wear for the expectant mother. None but dark colours should be worn, as light colours only serve to attract attention to the figure.

Indoor gowns should be made of voile and other light-weight materials, as these do not tend to look bulky at the waist. Skirts to indoor dresses should also be specially made mounted upon elastic bands, the front gore extending above the waist-band so that it can easily be let down, with pleats at the side that can be let out. These skirts can often be undertaken at home by the good needlewoman with the aid of a suitable pattern. A prettily made tea-gown is also a very useful garment for indoor wear.

INCIDENTAL AILMENTS

A woman is very prone to various nervous and digestive disorders at this time, and though these can be greatly minimised by careful living, yet they are apt to occur in some form or other in spite of every precaution, and always call for judicious treatment. Chief amongst these ailments are :—

Morning Sickness.—During the early months especially vomiting is apt to occur almost at the same time every morning. Strict attention to the diet must be paid. The action of the bowels must also be properly regulated. Rest in bed daily until the time when the vomiting is apt to occur has passed will often prove a good preventative. Very often nausea and sickness occur after meals. If this trouble is persistent a doctor should be consulted, and the patient should be put upon a special diet.

Sleeplessness is another common feature of the condition, especially during the later months. As a rule, it will be found much easier to resume one's rest after a thorough rousing and a cup of hot milk, with maybe ten minutes' light reading, than to toss from side to side endeavouring in vain to court the sleep one needs so badly. Material comfort will also help, and, besides *two* pillows beneath the head, try a third, placed (parallel with the others) beneath the ribs, so that, while lying on the side, the arm can be placed between the two sets of pillows without suffering undue pressure. Heavy meals at night should be avoided, and the bedroom should be properly ventilated.

Toothache may, during pregnancy, generally be relieved by taking fifteen to twenty grains of phosphate of lime, incorporated in the food, twice daily.

Heartburn is due to indigestion, and rich food should be strictly avoided by those subject to this distressing complaint. Take occasionally some calcined magnesia (the dose to be advised by chemist or doctor), or half a tea-spoonful of bicarbonate of soda in a wine-glassful of warm water.

Constipation will probably cease if fresh fruit be eaten each morning on rising. See to it that sufficient drink is taken also, particularly of cold water, early in the day. If possible, overcome the constipation by attention to diet rather than by drugging, but on no account allow it to continue, or your recovery may be considerably retarded after baby's arrival.

Nervous Worry may evidence itself by a tendency to magnify trifles, which at other times would pass unnoticed, into positive calamities, while noises, sights, and smells which, under ordinary circumstances, would be accounted nothing, will sometimes thoroughly upset a woman in this condition.

She will also often give way to tears upon the least provocation. A regular simple mode of life with the avoidance of all excitement and determined effort to exercise self-control will do much to remedy this state of things.

Varicose Veins and swelling of the feet are apt to occur. In these circumstances it is necessary to rest with the feet up as much as possible. The legs should be bandaged; crêpe bandages are much the best for the purpose, as they are light, elastic, easily washed, and give great support. They should be three inches in width and cost about 1s. 8d. each.

THE MOTHER'S REQUIREMENTS

Early selection should be made of the room in which the lying-in is to take place in order that everything is in readiness. The room chosen should be as large and airy as possible, and situated preferably in a quiet part of the house, where there will not be undue disturbance from street and other noises. Cleanliness and freedom from germs is indispensable, and a few days before the room is likely to be required it should be thoroughly cleaned. The bed should not be placed with one side to the wall, but in a position which will allow plenty of space at either side. A screen will be useful to keep off draughts. A fire should be laid in the grate, so that it can be lighted when needed and a kettle placed in readiness in which water can be boiled, as plenty of hot water will be required.

Do not leave everything until the last moment,

or in an emergency unsuitable and unnecessary purchases will likely be made. As a rule, the nurse or doctor will give instructions as to what to provide, but if not it will be wise to have the following in the house :—

Three yards gamgee tissue.
One pound absorbent cotton wool.
Two or three packets sanitary towels (2s. 6d. size).
One bottle Lysol (disinfectant).
One pot good vaseline.
One or two dozen nickel safety-pins.
Two and three-quarter yards fine linen towelling for binders.
A mackintosh sheet one yard square (this must be mackintosh on both sides).
A bed-pan (slipper shape preferred).
Some yellow soap (Castile or Primrose).
A reel of white linen thread.
A bottle of caster-oil.
A small supply of brandy.
One dozen night-lights (eight hours size).
A rubber hot-water bottle.
Night-dresses and bed-linen (well aired).
A supply of bedroom towels.

BABY'S OUTFIT

This should be all in readiness about two months before baby is expected. The number and style of the little things will to a large extent depend upon the social position of the mother and the means at disposal, and the following suggestions are only offered as a guide.

Baby's Bassinette or Cot.—This is an absolute necessity, as a baby should never be allowed to sleep in the same bed as its mother. There are several different kinds of cots at prices ranging from a few shillings to several pounds. There is no need to buy anything elaborate unless one is willing to spend a large sum.

For a simple bassinette perhaps there is nothing better than one of the Japanese travelling baskets. The two pieces should be comfortably lined with

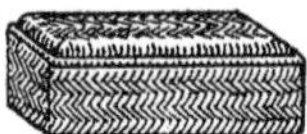

Japanese Basket.

quilted sateen or some good washing material, and while one piece serves as the bed, the other can be placed over the end to act as a shade and screen. This improvised bassinette has also the advantage of being very light and easily moved about, and, again, if travelling has to be done it will form a receptacle for baby's little wardrobe.

Then there are also the basket and metal cots. These are generally trimmed with pink or blue sateen covered with white muslin and lace or with a simple covering of some pretty light-coloured washing material. There must always be a curtain or hood to protect the little sleeper from the light or a draught, and the cot must also

Basket as Cradle.

be raised above the ground on a steady stand. It is best to have it the height of the mother's bed.

A well-made wicker bassinette costs from 3s. 6d. and upwards, and a stand 5s. or 6s. extra, while the metal cots swung on a stand can be had for 10s. and upwards. If bought ready trimmed they will cost from about 30s. extra, according to the material chosen and the amount of work put on it. Many, however, prefer to trim their bassinette at home, and for a few shillings it is quite possible to make a very dainty little bed. The accompanying illustration shows one of the simplest styles. Pink and blue are the favourite

Trimmed Bassinette.

colours for trimming a bassinette, although some prefer to keep them all white. Cotton sateen with a covering of plain or spotted muslin are the usual materials employed. The inside must first be lined with quilted sateen or with plain sateen and a domette interlining. Cut the muslin frill half as full again as the size of the cot and deep enough to allow of a wide hem. Or it may be edged with some pretty lace. There should also be a frill of the coloured sateen under the muslin, but this will not require to be so wide. Draw up both frills, sew them to the edge of the cot.

The curtain is made with muslin lined with the coloured sateen and is generally trimmed with lace. It should be two and a half or three yards in width and long enough to clear the ground by four or five inches. Draw it up with a strong tape at the top and fix it to the arm of the cot. Then finish off with rosettes of coloured ribbon.

The other requirement for the cot will be a tiny hair mattress, a little rounded pillow to fit the head part, some warm soft blankets, a piece of mackintosh, and a dainty cover made of the same sateen and muslin as the covering of the cot, and prettily trimmed with lace, or if the weather is cold a light eiderdown quilt may take its place. There should also be a tiny hot-water bottle—an ordinary ginger-beer bottle with a tight screw and a woollen bag will serve the purpose.

The little mattress may either be stuffed with hair, or, if this is too expensive, dried fern leaves, cocoanut fibre, fine shavings, or chaff all make good substitutes, and it is much wiser to use one of the cheaper materials and renew frequently than to stuff the mattress with hair and go on using it in an unhealthy state.

The Basket.—This is used to hold all the requirements for the baby's toilet, and is generally lined and trimmed to match the bassinette. A flat unlined basket can be bought for from 2s. 6d. upwards, and one on a stand for about 7s. 6d.—the trimming usually costs 7s. or 8s. extra. Here, again, the work of lining can easily be done at home when expense is a consideration. The inside should be fitted with two or three pockets to hold the smaller articles, and there must be a pretty cover to lay over the top. Sometimes the high baskets are made on casters, when they can be easily moved about.

Untrimmed Basket.

Trimmed Basket.

The basket should contain the following:—a tiny hair brush, a fine soft sponge, good pure soap in a soap-box, refined Fuller's earth or fine talcum dusting powder, a closed puff-box, a pot of white vaseline, boracic lint and some old soft handkerchiefs, a pin-cushion with good supply of safety-pins, needles, white cotton, a thimble, a pair of scissors, narrow tape, a bodkin. Then on the top might be laid a set of clothes ready for the little stranger's arrival—a flannel binder, a knitted woollen vest, a flannel nightgown, soft napkins, a fine white shawl, and a square of flannel.

Other Requirements.—A little bath, one or two soft bath-towels, and two bathing aprons for nurse.

THE LAYETTE

Essentials in Clothing.—All clothing must be warm, porous, and light. Warm, because heat is as important as food to the young life, and we must do our utmost to guard our little ones against chills; porous, to allow the pores of the skin to act freely and thus keep it in a healthy condition; and light so as not to encumber movement nor cause any waste of power. The garments must at the same time be elastic, fitting the part closely but not too tightly, in order to leave room for growth and the regular expansion of the little frame. Wool in some form or other is the substance best adapted to meet all these requirements; it is far better than the muslins and lace so invariably associated with a baby's outfit. The material should be as fine and soft as possible. Wincey, delaine, nun's veiling, and viyella are all suitable for the upper garments, as they will wash and keep their colour well, while the finest flannel may be used for underneath. Another advantage of the woollen outfit is that the garments can easily be washed at home. It is also more economical as far as washing is concerned, because the clothes do not crease nor soil so quickly, and if the rule is followed that all clothing be aired in the fresh air and afterwards by a fire before being put on again, a petticoat, a dress, and a night-dress will often last a week.

It is also important to have the clothes simply made so that they may be readily put on and taken off and washed without difficulty. The weight, too, must be evenly distributed. White is always to be preferred to any colour, especially for the young infant.

There have been many attempts at reform in infants' clothing, but old customs die hard, and although woollen garments are more generally introduced into the layette than formerly, there are still some mothers who insist upon having the little beings decked out in a mass of starched lace, frills, and embroidery. However, as a rule, baby is now dressed in a more common-sense way; ornamentation has to a large extent given way to comfort and utility, and the welfare of the little body comes first. The old style of low neck and short sleeves is rarely seen; the pretty little lawn shirt, the first garment to be put on, is also a thing of the past, and is replaced by a wool or silk vest, while the dainty embroidered caps are also condemned as fitting too closely to the head to be healthy.

Although woollen garments are recommended, there is no need to have them clumsy and ugly. The material may still be fine and the stitches small, while the little frocks give ample scope for embroidery and dainty needlework. In fact, there is no objection to cambric and silk frocks still being worn as long as there is a sufficiency of woollen clothing underneath.

First Clothing Required.—The mistake is often made in providing too much clothing, and it is forgotten that the baby will outgrow the first little garments in a few weeks and that it is really a waste of money to buy an unnecessary amount. There must, of course, be a large enough supply to keep the baby in a clean and healthy condition and to allow for frequent washing.

The following list includes all that is necessary for the first three months, but of course it may be indefinitely enlarged, according to fancy and the means of the mother :—

Four vests of fine woven or knitted wool or of silk and wool.
Three binders.
Four long flannels or barracoats.
Four woollen night-dresses.
Four monthly gowns—delaine, nun's veiling, or other woollen material.
Six flannel squares (Pilches).
Twenty-four Turkish towelling napkins.
One or two small Shetland shawls.
Four pairs knitted shoes.
One large Shetland or knitted shawl
One woollen hood.

In addition to the above there might be two or three pretty embroidered muslin or silk gowns for special occasions.

White petticoats are now little used, and are only required under a light robe. A carrying cloak and bonnet is often preferred to the large shawl and woollen hood for out of doors. When this is the case, one or two little woollen jackets for wearing under the cloak should be supplied. Prettily embroidered head flannels may take the place of the small shawls for indoor use, but they are not so light.

Although it is not usual to prepare the short clothes before the birth of the baby, the following will be required after the first three months :—

Four larger vests.
Two pair flannel stays.
Four pairs woollen drawers.
Four woollen petticoats with bodices.
Four woollen dresses.
Four night-dresses.
Four pairs woollen socks.
Twenty-four larger napkins.
Six bibs.

Here, again, the list may be supplemented by the addition of some silk or embroidered muslin dresses. A coat and bonnet might also take the place of the shawl and hood for out of doors. Although called short, they ought to come below the feet to begin with, and can be shortened after another three months by making a few tucks.

On Making the Layette.—What a world of pleasure does a mother take in making with her own hands the tiny garments which must be in readiness for the arrival of "Baby," and how many loving thoughts are interwoven with the minute stitches in which it is her pride to excel. More especially is this the case when preparing the layette for her first child, for then there are no elder children to claim their share of attention. A mother should not, however, permit the preparation of baby's trousseau to encroach too much upon her time. She must remember that it is a mistake to spend hours and hours stitching and sewing to the injury of her health, and that she would be much better spending the time or part of the time at least in taking healthy exercise in the open air. On the other hand, sewing for baby in moderation will prove an interesting and pleasant pastime, and the little flannel garments especially can very easily be undertaken by the expectant mother. A treadle machine must on no account

* No. 32940. Infant's Long-Clothing Set.

be used, although there is not the same objection to an easily worked hand-machine being employed for the longer seams.

Of course, if there are other willing hands to

* Patterns of this set of garments may be obtained from Weldons, Ltd., Fashion Publishers, 30 & 31 Southampton Street, Strand, London, W.C., price 6d., post free 7d. Pattern numbers should be quoted when ordering.

help, there is no reason why the whole of the layette should not be made at home, and certainly by so doing many a shilling will be saved and better material procured.

Good patterns should always be used when cutting out baby garments. Those who undertake this work cannot do better than write to Weldon's for their Infant's Long-Clothing set of patterns, consisting of seven different pieces as illustrated, price 6d., post free 7d., and also for the Short-Clothing Set consisting of six different

* No. 37950. Infant's Short-Clothing Set.

pieces at the same price. Full directions for making each garment are given with the patterns, also particulars as to the amount of material required. They have been proved most satisfactory by those competent to judge.

The tiny garments should be made of the finest material that can be afforded, and the utmost nicety is required in their manufacture. They must be sewn together with the most delicate needlework, the seams must be narrow, and no part of the garments must be hard or made in such a way as to cause discomfort. There must be no lumpy buttons or hooks to press on the tender flesh, but fine soft tape should be used for the principal fastenings. Care must be taken in the making of arm-holes and sleeves so as to avoid any pulling or straining, and there must be no tightness anywhere. Everything must be made to look as pretty as possible for the little stranger.

The Binder.—This is the first article of clothing put on the baby. It should be made of a strip of flannel torn across the material. It should be six inches wide, so that half a yard of flannel will make three binders. They must not be hemmed or sewn in any way. The binder is used to give warmth to the abdomen, and it also forms a foundation on which to pin the diaper. It should be rolled round the little body quite easily and fastened with a safety-pin with a shielded point, or by means of a few stitches.

The Vest.—This may either be hand-knitted or woven and should be made of the very finest wool, or of silk and wool. It should have high neck and long sleeves if for winter wear, and be long enough to cover the abdomen. It is always better to have the fastening at the side, and French tape or baby ribbon is always better than buttons.

Napkins and Pilches.—Napkins are best made of Turkish towelling. They should be half a yard wide and three-quarters of a yard in length, and made single, as they are more easily washed. The two opposite corners should be folded together so as to form a triangle. The folded side of this triangle is put round the infant's waist and fastened with a safety-pin to the binder. Then the point is brought up between the legs and fastened in front. The first pilch is made of

* No. 37947. Head Flannel and Pilch.

flannel and is worn over the napkin for safety's sake. It might either be in the form of a square and put on in the same way as the napkin, or it might be shaped as in illustration. A mackintosh pilch is sometimes used to save frequent changing, but this is most reprehensible, and generally shows laziness and lack of attention on the part of the nurse. The mackintosh acts as a sort of compress and is most unhealthy. It might be used for an hour or two on any special

* Patterns of this set of garments may be obtained from Weldons, Ltd., Fashion Publishers, 30 & 31 Southampton Street, Strand, London, W.C., price 6d., post free 7d. Pattern numbers should be quoted when ordering.

occasion when an accident is to be dreaded, but under no other circumstance.

The Barracoat or Flannel Petticoat.—This is the next article of clothing. It should be made with the body and skirt in one and should fasten on the shoulders. It is a mistake to make it too long, as it only adds weight—a few inches below the feet will be quite sufficient. Sometimes a second petticoat is worn made of fine lawn or nainsook, but this is not necessary with a woollen frock.

The Frock.—The material of which this is made must vary according to circumstances, and, as said before, some woollen material is best. Nun's veiling is suitable for summer wear, while for winter wincey or viyella will be better. For daintier wear or special occasions white silk trimmed with lace or a dainty embroidered muslin might be used.

Woollen Bootees and Drawers.—Little woollen bootees should be worn night and day. They can either be knitted or crocheted, and should be warm and roomy. When the clothes are shortened, the bootees should be long enough to come well up the legs for protection. Woollen drawers are also useful for slipping on when the baby is taken out of doors, and sometimes they are made all in one with the bootees.

Bibs.—These should be made of a material which does not readily absorb moisture. Soft Turkish towelling with a scalloped edge are best for ordinary wear, while one made of embroidered silk can be worn for best.

For Outdoor Wear.—For the first three months there is nothing more comfortable than a shawl and a little knitted bonnet, although many mothers prefer the cloak made of fine cashmere or silk trimmed with swansdown or silk embroidery. Care must be taken when the cloak is used that the weight of it does not hang from the baby's shoulder. A little knitted jacket should always be worn underneath the cloak.

Gloves.—When the child is older the tiny hands should be protected with gloves without fingers. These should be tied in at the wrist and fastened in place with a safety-pin.

(For Children's Clothes, see p. 495.)

For those who wish to buy the little garments ready made, most of the large drapery establishments will supply lists giving the prices of the various articles, and special ladies' outfitters are always ready to give all the necessary information as to quality and prices.

THE MONTHLY NURSE

It will first be necessary to decide whether to engage a trained nurse or an untrained one, a choice which will doubtless be influenced by such considerations as income and mode of living; for, naturally, the trained midwife expects a higher fee than her self-trained colleague. Moreover, she will not undertake any ordinary household duties, knowing full well that mother and babe will make such demands on her time as to leave no leisure for her to attend to any matters outside the sick-room.

It is not unusual for a doctor to give particulars of several nurses to patients whose accouchements he undertakes. Before closing with any one of them, it is always well to obtain references from previous patients similarly circumstanced to yourself, that you may ascertain whether, besides being skilled at her work, the nurse of your choice is also a pleasant woman to live with. You do not want any one whose presence is likely to prove irritating, nor who will be lacking in both tact and sympathy.

The nurse is usually paid by the week or month, and will expect, in addition to her fee, laundry expenses, as well as her fare, should she come a long distance. If she is engaged to attend the patient some weeks before the expected event, it is usual to pay half-fee for the period of waiting.

A good deal of possible friction will be saved if at the time of engagement there is a clear understanding as to exactly what duties the nurse may be expected to perform. The bedroom is in her sole charge and she will see to the dusting of it, but she will expect the relaying and lighting of the fire to be done by the maid. Attendance in the way of bringing up hot water, meals, &c., will also have to be given by the latter, as the trained nurse cannot be asked to do housework of any kind. Details such as the washing of napkins, &c., are also points which will have to be settled with the nurse upon engagement.

If possible, the nurse should take her meals in a room by herself; she should not be expected to join the servants in the kitchen. The meals should be served preferably in a dressing-room adjoining that of the patient, as in these circumstances, especially during the first days after the confinement, she will be at hand in case of need.

Baby's Arrival.—Once these arrangements are complete, everything will be in readiness for baby's arrival. The nurse will have probably taken up residence in the house a few days beforehand, and will thus be able to notify those in attendance as to when the doctor should be summoned. The management of the confinement will now be in the hands of the doctor and nurse who have undertaken the case, and their instructions should be carried out in every way.

If baby arrives unexpectedly when neither doctor nor nurse are present, the person in attendance should see that he is placed in a position to breathe properly and that he is not being suffocated with clothing. Afterwards well wash his eyes with plain warm water and clean pieces of old linen, and then cover him with a soft warm blanket, and he will take no hurt for some time, until experienced assistance can be procured.

THE NURSERY

Whenever possible, there should be a room set apart for the children of the house, a room in which they can play and spend happily the hours they are not sleeping or out of doors. Let the nursery be one of the largest and healthiest rooms in the house, not a room in the attics which is liable to be too hot in summer and too cold in winter, nor yet one in the basement which will be dark and possibly damp as well.

The ideal nursery has a south or south-west aspect; it is lofty and spacious, with a fireplace, a good window that opens top and bottom, and a cheerful outlook. Unfortunately, it is not always possible to find a room fulfilling all these requirements, but we can always do our best, remembering that fine healthy children cannot be reared in dark and cheerless rooms, so let us give them all the sunshine and good air we can if we wish them to develop physically and mentally, for they are like the flowers which droop and grow pale if they are left in the dark.

The walls should be washable throughout—distemper, enamel paint, or varnished paper are all suitable coverings. A light harmonious colour is best, giving a feeling of restfulness. If paper is used, it must be of a very simple pattern; in fact, there is nothing so charming as the plain coloured wall. Monotony can be avoided by the use of a simple coloured frieze with a few figures of animals, birds, or flowers, &c., and designed by some good firm. All intricate patterns and multiplicity of design must be avoided; papers covered with pictures that tell stories only tire and confuse the child's mind. There might also be a few good pictures on the walls of objects that will interest children, but never permit anything in the way of rubbish—rather leave the walls bare. Pictures must not be hung too high.

The best floor covering is cork carpet, as it is warm and washable and very durable. Indian matting and linoleum are also good, but the latter is cold, and rugs would be required. Uncovered floors are not good, unless of the real parquet flooring, as splinters are apt to come off the wood and get into the little one's hands and feet—and carpets are not hygienic.

As for furniture, the less there is the better, and what there is should be of the simplest description. It must be of a kind that is easily washed and cleaned, with as few sharp angles as possible, and arranged so as to leave open floor space for the children to have a full clear run in which to exercise their limbs. A good steady table for meals, a few chairs, a low chair for nurse, a roomy cupboard, a toy-cupboard, a low kindergarten table with a little chair for each child are the principal articles required.

A nursery guard should be firmly fixed to the fireplace, and one that covers the grate right over is the best. It is a convenience, too, to have a

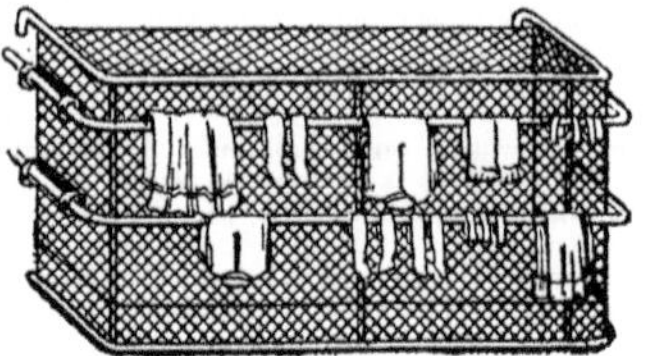

Nursery Fire-Guard.

rail on the outside on which little garments can be put to warm.

A good cupboard for the nurse's use is very necessary, or it might be a cupboard and chest of drawers combined. If meals are taken in the nursery this will hold the children's special china, table linen and so forth, sewing materials and many other odds and ends.

The toy-cupboard, too, is very essential if the children are to be taught to be tidy, and it is well to allow a special shelf or division for each child. It must also be low enough to be within their reach. A low kindergarten table with the little miniature chairs will also be found useful when the children are at an age to draw, paint, work with clay, or amuse themselves with other quiet occupations.

Another useful addition to the nursery is a play-pen in which a child can be put to crawl about

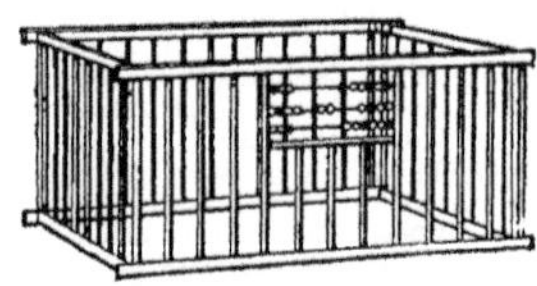

Play-Pen.

without any danger of its hurting itself. A washable crawling rug will also be useful, and a cosy hearth-rug will give an appearance of comfort to the room.

When curtains are used they must be made of some washable material. Casement curtains are really the best, as they do away with the necessity of having blinds.

A high window should have one or two bars fixed across it for safety.

A reliable clock and a thermometer must not be forgotten, and if bathing is done in the nursery there should be a good draught-screen.

Cleanliness and Ventilation.—It is very important that the nursery be kept thoroughly clean; there must be cleanliness in every detail.

The room must be swept and dusted every day, and the floor washed once a week. Care must be taken on the day that the washing is done that the children do not return to it until the floor is dry. Choose a time when the children are out of doors, or when they can spend several hours in another room. After the washing is done, both door and window must be left wide open so that a current of air may dry the room, and a good fire must be kept burning unless the weather is warm and bright.

The best time for cleaning the fireplace in the nursery is in the evening, when the children are in bed and nurse has finished with the room. The fire can then be raked out, the grate cleaned, and all made ready for putting a match to the fire in the morning. The floor of the room might also be swept in the evening, leaving only the dusting to be done next day.

Good ventilation is also very important in the nursery, and fresh air must be admitted freely. During the day all windows should be kept open in warm weather, and in cold weather either one window must be left open a little way, or a simple Hinck's-Bird ventilator (see p. 8) inserted. When the children are out the windows might be thrown wide open. Opportunity might also be taken while the children are out of drying any wet towels, &c., but this ought on no account to be allowed when the nursery is occupied, as it would make the air of the room too moist and might be hurtful to young children.

The Night Nursery.—The apartment in which the children sleep, whether it be the room occupied by the nurse as well or a special room set apart for the children by themselves, must be chosen and furnished as carefully as the day nursery. The same rules as regards ventilation and general arrangement will apply here.

The furniture should be as scanty as possible and of a kind that will wash. There must be a cot or little bed for each child and also a bed for

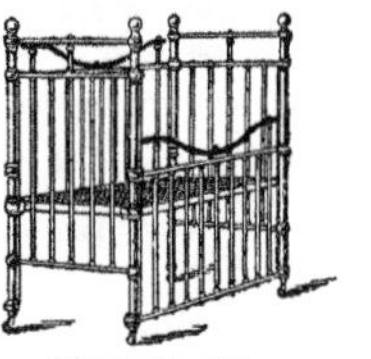

Cot with Drop-Side.

the nurse. There is nothing nicer than the little white enamelled beds with a spring or wire foundation, as they can be so easily washed and kept clean. A cot is always best when it is made with a drop-side; the bed is more easily made, and it is also a simpler matter to get at the child. Very young children should have their cots covered with a net to prevent them getting over the sides and hurting themselves.

The most suitable bedding is a good hair mattress and a low soft pillow. It is most important that the mattress should be fresh and clean; it should be taken to pieces periodically and thoroughly aired and renewed if necessary.

The covering must be warm, but as light as possible—an under-blanket, one or two upper blankets, and an eiderdown or light cover will be necessary. Good cotton sheets will also be required for the older children, but none for the baby's bed. A mackintosh sheet should also be supplied for the bed of a very young child.

The floor of the night nursery should be covered with linoleum or cork carpet or left bare, and two or three rugs should be supplied for putting at the side of the beds.

The nurse will also require a dressing-table for her own use and a chest of drawers or other receptacle for keeping her clothes.

There should also be one or two chairs, one low chair and a screen. If the bath-room is close at hand a wash-stand will not be required.

Casement curtains of a pretty green or other soft shade will be the best for keeping out the light, and will do away with the necessity for blinds.

Apart from the actual furniture required, the children's sleeping-room should be left as empty as possible. There should be no boxes stored under beds nor on the top of wardrobes, no garments left hanging on pegs, nor a quantity of books, pictures, and ornaments, which only help to collect dust.

The window should be left open night and day, and when heating is necessary it should be by means of an open fire and not a stove. Gas should not be left burning in the bedroom at night, but a night-light may be used if a light is needed.

THE NURSE

Choice and Qualifications.—Too great care cannot be taken in the choice of a nurse for the little ones. There is hardly any position so full of trust and responsibility, and when a mother realises that the health and character of her children in after life will to a large extent be determined by the treatment they receive in the first years of their life, she will make every effort and even sacrifice rather than let them be under the control of an ignorant or unprincipled woman.

A good nurse ought to be fond of children, good tempered, and thoroughly trustworthy. She must be healthy and active, bright and happy-looking, and capable of gentle firmness. It is important also that she speaks well and has no defect or peculiarity of any kind, as children are very quick to imitate both the bad and the good.

Personal cleanliness is another important

some time, until experienced assistance can be procured.

THE NURSERY

Whenever possible, there should be a room set apart for the children of the house, a room in which they can play and spend happily the hours they are not sleeping or out of doors. Let the nursery be one of the largest and healthiest rooms in the house, not a room in the attics which is liable to be too hot in summer and too cold in winter, nor yet one in the basement which will be dark and possibly damp as well.

The ideal nursery has a south or south-west aspect; it is lofty and spacious, with a fireplace, a good window that opens top and bottom, and a cheerful outlook. Unfortunately, it is not always possible to find a room fulfilling all these requirements, but we can always do our best, remembering that fine healthy children cannot be reared in dark and cheerless rooms, so let us give them all the sunshine and good air we can if we wish them to develop physically and mentally, for they are like the flowers which droop and grow pale if they are left in the dark.

The walls should be washable throughout—distemper, enamel paint, or varnished paper are all suitable coverings. A light harmonious colour is best, giving a feeling of restfulness. If paper is used, it must be of a very simple pattern; in fact, there is nothing so charming as the plain coloured wall. Monotony can be avoided by the use of a simple coloured frieze with a few figures of animals, birds, or flowers, &c., and designed by some good firm. All intricate patterns and multiplicity of design must be avoided; papers covered with pictures that tell stories only tire and confuse the child's mind. There might also be a few good pictures on the walls of objects that will interest children, but never permit anything in the way of rubbish—rather leave the walls bare. Pictures must not be hung too high.

The best floor covering is cork carpet, as it is warm and washable and very durable. Indian matting and linoleum are also good, but the latter is cold, and rugs would be required. Uncovered floors are not good, unless of the real parquet flooring, as splinters are apt to come off the wood and get into the little one's hands and feet—and carpets are not hygienic.

As for furniture, the less there is the better, and what there is should be of the simplest description. It must be of a kind that is easily washed and cleaned, with as few sharp angles as possible, and arranged so as to leave open floor space for the children to have a full clear run in which to exercise their limbs. A good steady table for meals, a few chairs, a low chair for nurse, a roomy cupboard, a toy-cupboard, a low kindergarten table with a little chair for each child are the principal articles required.

A nursery guard should be firmly fixed to fireplace, and one that covers the grate right over is the best. It is a convenience, too, to have a

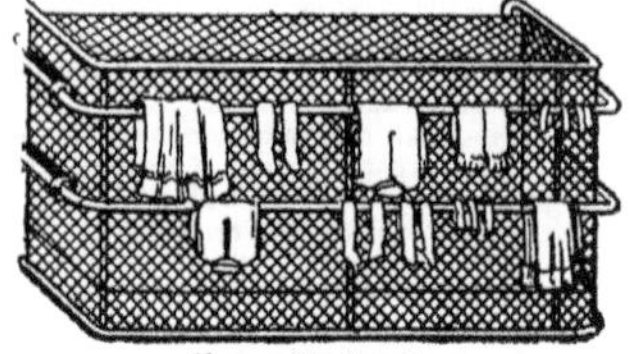

Nursery Fire-Guard.

rl on the outside on which little garments can be put to warm.

A good cupboard for the nurse's use is very necessary, or it might be a cupboard and chest of drawers combined. If meals are taken in the nursery this will hold the children's special china, table linen and so forth, sewing materials and many other odds and ends.

The toy-cupboard, too, is very essential if the children are to be taught to be tidy, and it is well to allow a special shelf or division for each child. It must also be low enough to be within their reach. A low kindergarten table with the little miniature chairs will also be found useful when the children are at an age to draw, paint, work with clay, or amuse themselves with other quiet occupations.

Another useful addition to the nursery is a play-pen in which a child can be put to crawl about

Play-Pen.

without any danger of its hurting itself. A washable crawling rug will also be useful, and a cosy hearth-rug will give an appearance of comfort to the room.

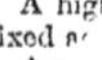

When curtains are used they ... made of some washab... are really th... necessity of ...

A high ... fixed ...

A ...

be...

The room must be swept and dusted every day, and the floor washed once a week. Care must be taken on the day that the washing is done that the children do not return to it until the floor is dry. Choose a time when the children are out of doors, or when they can spend several hours in another room. After the washing is done, both door and window must be left wide open so that a current of air may dry the room, and a good fire must be kept burning unless the weather is warm and bright.

The best time for cleaning the fireplace in the nursery is in the evening, when the children are in bed and nurse has finished with the room. The fire can then be raked out, the grate cleaned, and all made ready for putting a match to the fire in the morning. The floor of the room might also be swept in the evening, leaving only the dusting to be done next day.

Good ventilation is also very important in the nursery, and fresh air must be admitted freely. During the day all windows should be kept open in warm weather, and in cold weather either one window must be left open a little way, or a simple Hinck's-Bird ventilator (see p. 8) inserted. When the children are out the windows might be thrown wide open. Opportunity might also be taken while the children are out of drying any wet towels, &c., but this ought on no account to be allowed when the nursery is occupied, as it would make the air of the room too moist and might be hurtful to young children.

The Night Nursery.—The apartment in which the children sleep, whether it be the room occupied by the nurse as well or a special room set apart for the children by themselves, must be chosen and furnished as carefully as the day nursery. The same rules as regards ventilation and general arrangement will apply here.

The furniture should be as scanty as possible and of a kind that will wash. There must be a cot or little bed for each child and also a bed for

Cot with [illegible]

the nurse. There [illegible] white enamell[illegible]

covered with a net to prevent them getting over the sides and hurting themselves.

The most suitable bedding is a good hair mattress and a low soft pillow. It is most important that the mattress should be fresh and clean; it should be taken to pieces periodically and thoroughly aired and renewed if necessary.

The covering must be warm, but as light as possible—an under-blanket, one or two upper blankets, and an eiderdown or light cover will be necessary. Good cotton sheets will also be required for the older children, but none for the baby's bed. A mackintosh sheet should also be supplied for the bed of a very young child.

The floor of the night nursery should be covered with linoleum or cork carpet or left bare, and two or three rugs should be supplied for putting at the side of the beds.

The nurse will also require a dressing-table for her own use and a chest of drawers or other receptacle for keeping her clothes.

There should also be one or two chairs, one low chair and a screen. If the bath-room is close at hand a wash-stand will not be required.

Casement curtains of a pretty green or other soft shade will be the best for keeping out the light, and will do away with the necessity for blinds.

Apart from the actual furniture required, the children's sleeping-room should be left as empty as possible. There should be no boxes stored under beds nor on the top of wardrobes, no garments left hanging on pegs, nor a quantity of books, pictures, and ornaments, which only help to collect dust.

The window should be left open night and day, and when heating is necessary it should be by means of an open fire and not a stove. Gas should not be left burning in the bedroom at night, but a night-light may be used if a light is needed.

THE NURSE

Choice and Qualifications.—Too great care cannot be taken in the choice of a nurse for the little ones. There is hardly any position so full of trust and responsibility, and when a mother realises that the health and character of her children in after life will to a large extent be determined by the treatment they receive in the first years of their life, she will make every effort and even sacrifice rather than let them be under the control of an ignorant or unprincipled woman.

A good nurse ought to be fond of children, [illegible] tempered, and thoroughly trustworthy. [illegible] be healthy and active, bright and [illegible] and capable of gentle [illegible] qualification, and as regards dress this must always be neat and tidy and very simple in style. Some people insist upon their nurses wearing white, but this is not always advisable. For one thing, the continual glare of everything white, especially out of doors, is not considered good for baby's eyes, and then the washing is a consideration, as white, if worn at all, must be clean. A nice soft grey or navy blue is preferable, or grey might be worn in summer and blue in winter. The morning-dress should be of linen or other washing material, and for the afternoon alpaca, beige, or serge would be suitable. An apron must always be worn indoors. The out-of-door costume must be quiet and neat—there is no occasion for her to wear the uniform of a hospital nurse—in fact, this should rather be avoided—a jacket or coat to match the dress in colour and a hat or bonnet with a ribbon trimming are perhaps the most suitable. White gloves should always be worn when taking out a baby.

A nurse should be a good needlewoman. She may not be called upon to make new garments for the children, but she is generally expected to keep their clothing in order and do little renovations.

A knowledge of laundry work and simple nursery cookery are also useful acquirements, and if she has experience in treating the simple ailments of children, or knows what to do in a case of emergency, she will be all the more valuable to her employer.

Unfortunately, it is not always easy to find all the above requirements in one woman. It very often happens that the one who is competent is not good-tempered and resents any interference, or that the good-tempered one lacks knowledge. This makes it all the more important that the mother should always take the chief supervision; in fact, it is one of her first duties, and she ought under all circumstances to reign supreme in her own nursery, and no matter how clever and experienced the nurse may be it is never right to give her the full control of the children.

Duties.—As regards the duties of the nurse and the order in which they are to be performed, it is almost impossible to set down any rules which will suit all cases. There must be a plan and a time-table, but it is for every mother either to make her own, or to do so in consultation with her nurse, and then to see that it is adhered to. The duties will naturally vary with the size of the family and the number of servants kept, and the mode of living. When there are several children and two nurses are kept, the head nurse will have the entire charge of the infant. She will also be responsible for the care of the other children, but the under-nurse or nursemaid will assist with their dressing, &c. She will be responsible for the order and management of the nursery, the arrangement of meals, &c. The under-nurse will do all the rough work, including cleaning, washing of dishes, carrying coals, and work under the direction of the head nurse. When the nurse is single-handed and there are several children, she will either require help from the housemaid in the cleaning of her nurseries, or the mother must be prepared to take the children for a certain time each day in order to give the nurse some freedom to do a little washing or cleaning. By this means she ought to be able to get through much useful work.

FEEDING

There is unfortunately a growing disinclination among mothers to nourish their infants as nature intended. Selfishness is as a rule at the root of this very unmotherly feeling. The mother who nurses her infant will require to lead a more or less quiet life for nine months, forgoing many social engagements, and rather than deny herself in this respect a mother will sacrifice the welfare of her little one by depriving it of its natural food. Vanity is also often the reason for objection to nursing. The plea is made that it "spoils" the figure, whereas, as a matter of fact, to nurse a baby for the first few weeks of its life is to materially assist nature in her restoring process, and shapeliness in consequence is regained sooner than in other circumstances. Nursing is good for the mother as well as for the child.

There are many instances, of course, when it is impossible for the mother to nurse her child, but if it is possible she should look upon it as her first duty towards the little one to do so.

That the mother's milk is lacking in quantity or quality is not now accounted any argument in favour of neglecting altogether the duty of breast-feeding. In these circumstances a baby may be brought up partly on its mother's milk and partly on the bottle. The mother who finds it exhausting to nurse altogether can, for instance, feed it herself in the day and give it the bottle at night. In this way the little one is not altogether deprived of its natural food. Time was when "the mixing of milks" was regarded as most unwise, but that is now past, and it is universally recognised that baby may be given the bottle as well as partially breast-fed with very satisfactory results.

Should there be evidences of consumption or other disease likely to be hereditary, consult the doctor as to the advisability or otherwise of artificially feeding baby.

The breasts must be carefully tended during pregnancy, if the mother intends to feed her baby. See that the corsets do not flatten the nipples, which should be hardened by bathing them night and morning for the last couple of months, and afterwards applying a mixture either of lavender water or pure eau de Cologne.

The infant should be put to the breast directly after it has been washed, as the first milk will act as a mild purgative for the little one. During the first two days of its existence an infant does not require to be fed more than once every four hours. Afterwards it must be fed every two hours with the utmost regularity in the day and about three or four times in the night for the first two or three months—after that every two and a half hours, and then every three hours until it is weaned.

Great care must be taken to keep to regular hours for baby's meals. If the child is allowed to feed at all times and at all hours directly it utters so much as a cry, not only will it be bad for the infant, but the mother must needs lead the life of a veritable slave to her baby, never being able to count on so much as half-an-hour of freedom, and, what is more, she will be forced to neglect in a certain measure both her husband and her home.

A little patience exercised at first in adhering firmly to a rule will do away with the necessity for such a state of affairs. Even young babies will realise the quality of firmness in their mother when once they come into contact with it. At night-time in particular will a mother have trouble with the infant whom she has unduly pampered in this respect, and the longer this pampering goes on the more difficult will it become to cure the bad habits so formed. Very often consideration for her husband who needs his rest so much will induce a mother to nurse a baby whenever he cries at night in order to keep it quiet. It may be taken that the infant of a few months old is a reasoning being in so far that, as soon as he knows crying will ensure the gratification of his wishes, the more he will resort to this expedient. In these circumstances it is better to sleep with the child in another room for a few nights, and train it in the way it should go in this respect. With a little patience proper habits may be formed, although the mother who has been firm in the training of her little one since infancy is not likely to be troubled in this way.

Of course, there are exceptions—delicate children will require feeding more frequently than healthy ones, and the doctor's advice will have to be taken in this respect, but here again regularity should be aimed at.

Weaning should take place when the infant is nine months old, and in any circumstances the mother's nursing should not continue beyond ten months. Prolonged nursing is both bad for the mother and bad for the child.

It is better to accomplish the weaning gradually, beginning by giving the new food at one or two meals only at first, gradually substituting it for the natural nourishment at other meals until at the end of a month the mother can leave off nursing altogether. This gradual weaning is more than ever important when it takes place in the hot summer weather. Whilst nursing, a mother should take plain nourishing food, avoiding everything that is rich or highly seasoned.

Bringing up by Hand.—When it is quite impossible for a mother to nurse her baby, it will be necessary that the little one be brought up by hand. There is the alternative, of course, of engaging a "wet nurse," but this is not always advisable, for many reasons. The milk used should be the special "nursery milk," which is always sent from the dairies in sealed bottles. It must be diluted with barley water and sweetened with a little sugar, and freed from germs by boiling. This should be done by placing a jug containing the milk into a saucepan of water and putting this on to boil. The milk will be ready when the water has boiled for fifteen minutes.

The boat-shaped feeding-bottle is the best kind to use, and infinitely preferable to the bottle with the long rubber tube. The latter is unhygienic, because it is so difficult to keep the tube clean, and any milk left in will turn sour, diarrhœa being often caused in this way. It is of the first importance that feeding-bottles should be kept thoroughly clean. When baby has finished his meal, any milk that he has left should at once be thrown away, and the bottle should be rinsed out, first in cold water and then in hot water in which a tiny piece of soda has been placed. It should then be cleaned out with a special bottle-brush, well rinsed, and left in a basin of cold water until required. Two or three bottles should always be in use, so that there is always one ready when required.

Boat-shaped Feeding-Bottle.

Exceptional care is required in bringing the baby up by hand, the least thing wrong in the food causing diarrhœa, which often proves fatal to infants. It is one of the duties of the monthly nurse before leaving to carefully instruct the mother and also the nurse in regard to the feeding and general care of the infant.

The following "Feeding Charts" and Recipes have been prepared by Mrs. Bernard Mole, Principal of the Hampstead Nursery College, and will give an idea (1) of the proportions of milk and barley water to be given to babies up to the age of ten months; (2) the gradual adding of other foods at nine months to eighteen months with some useful recipes; and (3) a suitable diet for babies of eighteen months old and upwards.

INFANTS' FEEDING TABLE

Maximum

Age	Milk	Barley water or boiled water	Total quantity	Time, every
1 month . .	1 oz. 2 drs.	1 oz. 6 drs.	3 oz.	2 hours
2 months . .	2 oz. 4 drs.	2 oz. 4 drs.	5 oz.	2½ hours
3 months . .	3½ oz.	2 oz.	5½ oz.	2½ hours
4 months . .	4 oz.	2 oz.	6 oz.	2½ hours
5 months . .	5 oz.	2 oz.	7 oz.	3 hours
6 months . .	5½ oz.	1 oz. 4 drs.	7 oz.	3 hours
7 months . .	6½ oz.	1 oz.	7½ oz.	3 hours
8 months . .	7½ oz.	4 drs.	8 oz.	3 hours
9 months . .	8 oz.		8 or 9 oz.	3½ hours
10 months . .	8 oz.		8 or 9 oz.	3½ hours

After 9 months, broth, bread and milk, rusks, Robinson's patent barley may be given.

NOTE.—1 tea-spoonful equals 1 drachm ; 2 table-spoonfuls equal 1 ounce.

DIET CHART

(9 to 18 months)

At 9 *months* leave off mid-day bottle and give broth with bread-crumbs in it, or fine sago, custard, or lightly-boiled egg (yolk only) poured over sieved crumbs.

At 10 *months* leave off breakfast bottle, and give bread and milk (sieved crumbs).

At 11 *months* leave off tea bottle, and give "Nursery Rusks" soaked in boiling water, and warm milk poured over.

At 12 *months* leave off supper bottle and give Robinson's Patent Barley.

Keep on with 10 *p.m. bottle till* 12 *months*, then give warm drink of milk to take its place.

At 13 *and* 18 *months* give good dinners of broth and crumbs followed by some nourishing milk pudding and a drink of cold water.

DIET CHART

(After 18 months

	7.30 A.M.	12.30 P.M.	6 P.M.
Monday . .	Bread and dripping Bread and jam 6 oz. warm milk	Minced meat and gravy, potatoes Suet pudding	Robinson's patent barley
Tuesday . .	Fried bread Bread and marmalade 6 oz. warm milk	Vegetables and gravy Milk pudding and baked apple, &c.	Bread and milk
Wednesday .	Bread and milk Bread and jam	Soup and milk pudding Fruit	Robinson's barley
Thursday . .	Fried bread Bread and marmalade 6 oz. warm milk	Vegetables and gravy Fairy pudding	Bread and milk
Friday . . .	Bread and milk Bread and jam	Fish Milk pudding and fruit	Robinson's barley
Saturday . .	Porridge Bread and marmalade	Stew gravy Boiled batter	Bread and milk
Sunday . .	Eggs Bread and butter 6 oz. warm milk	Gravy and vegetables Fruit and milk pudding	Robinson's barley

NOTE.—Tea : bread and butter, cake, or jam, and warm milk.
Lunch : warm milk and biscuit.

SOME NURSERY RECIPES

Receipt for Fine Sago

2 tea-spoonfuls fine sago. | 1 teacup cold water.

Method.—Simmer all the morning (not less than twenty minutes), add a little brown sugar and milk.

Mutton, Veal, and Beef Broth

½ lb. of meat. | 1 pint of water.

Method.—Shred meat, add salt, simmer in double saucepan three to four hours. Another method for the nursery. Shred meat, add pinch of salt and water. Stand all the morning. Warm up to 130° and serve.

Custard

6 oz. milk.	1 tea-spoonful sugar.
1 egg.	

Method.—Beat egg, pour on hot milk in which sugar has been added. Stir till wooden spoon is coated.

Note.—Must not boil or will curdle.

Bread and Milk

1 slice of bread.	6 oz. milk.

Method.—Rub the bread through a sieve, place in cup and pour on boiling milk in which a little brown sugar has been added.

Note.—After twelve months old, cut bread with crust into cubes.

Boiled Egg

Method.—Carefully drop egg into boiling water, let it stand in hot water for eight minutes, and the yolk and white will be jelly-like consistency. Pour on to crumbs and serve.

Note.—Must not boil or white will harden.

Another method. Boil three minutes and use yolk only.

Albumen Water

1 white of egg.	½ pint of water.

Method.—Stir in slightly-beaten white of egg into half a pint warm water, add little sugar.

Whey

½ pint milk.	½ tea-spoon rennet.

Method.—Heat milk to 100° F. Stir in the rennet and allow it to cool (not less than seven minutes). Stir up with fork and strain through muslin. Heat up again to 70° F. to get rid of rennet. Strain before using.

Barley Water

2 table-sp. coarse pearl barley.	1 pint of water.

Method.—Wash barley in strainer by pouring hot water through. Put barley in jug and cover with a pint of boiling water. Stand all day and strain off quantity for use.

Nursery Rusk

Cover rusk with boiling water and let it soak. Add warm milk and a little brown sugar when ready for use.

Diet for Older Children.—After the child is over three years old, the diet may be gradually enlarged until it is able to take simple dishes of all kinds. The food must always be simple and well cooked, and never highly seasoned.

The most substantial meal should be in the middle of the day, when one of the following dishes might be served: fish either steamed or stewed or made up in some simple way with butter sauce, game (if not high), and poultry, roast, boiled or broiled meat. Salted meats and spiced salt fish, pork and liver should be avoided, also rich stews and highly-seasoned sauces of any kind. There should also be a liberal supply of vegetables in season.

In winter especially the dinner should commence with a little soup; in fact, with young children a good broth or milk soup might quite well take the place of the meat course once or twice a week if it is followed by a good nourishing pudding.

As the pudding is generally the favourite dish with the little ones, care must be taken to have it well cooked and light, and some cooks are very apt to be careless in this respect. A suet pudding in some form or other is one of the most nourishing dishes that can be given—the plain suet dumpling served with golden syrup or brown sugar, the dumpling with a few currants or raisins in it, the suet pudding with fruit inside, or the jam roly-poly are all excellent *if well cooked.* Even the simple milk pudding requires care in the preparation, because unless the starchy substance of which it is made is thoroughly cooked, it will not be wholesome.

Variety must be studied as much as possible; if the same dishes are served day after day the children become tired of them and do not take sufficient for their proper nourishment.

Fruit in some form should be given every day, and as some children can take more of this than others, it is the duty of the mother to watch what agrees with each child. As a rule fruits are more easily taken stewed than raw. Stewed prunes, apples, or figs, baked apples and baked bananas can vary the winter diet, while in summer there will be the various fresh fruits in season.

The older children's breakfast should consist of porridge or some other cereal food with good milk, followed by eggs or a simple fish dish, or toast and bacon fat, with cocoa, hot milk, or milk and coffee to drink. If breakfast is served very early a glass of milk with a biscuit, oatcake, or piece of gingerbread might be given in the middle of the forenoon.

Then for tea—bread and butter with syrup or jam, some plain cake or biscuits, and either cocoa or warm milk to drink.

The supper taken in the evening must be very light in character—warm milk with bread and butter, a well-cooked milk pudding, a dish of rice, or some milk soup are all suitable.

THE CHILD'S TOILET

Bath.—Perfect cleanliness is another essential in the healthy life of the child, as without this the skin will be unable to discharge its functions. One cannot use too much water, and the somewhat common fear that more than one bath a day is weakening is quite wrong; the error made is more likely to be on the side of too little washing rather than that of too much.

All children should be bathed at least once

daily, and the habit must be begun from infancy. Each child must be provided with its own sponge and flannel or other washing requisites.

For an infant the temperature of the water should be about 100° F. for both the morning and evening bath, and this may be continued for the first six months. As it gets a little older the temperature of the morning bath may be reduced to 80° or 85°, and after three years old to 65° or 70°. With older children the morning bath should be given very quickly with plenty of friction by rubbing, and they will also require a hotter bath in the evening at least twice a week if it cannot be managed oftener. Or they may have a warm bath in the evening, and a quick sponge over with cold or tepid water in the morning.

A little child must always be bathed in a warm room, and if, when older, he is taken to a bath-room, care must be taken to guard against chills.

A bath must never be given directly after a meal. An hour at least must elapse between the taking of food and the bath. This is why it is generally found more convenient to give little children their supper after their bath, either sitting at the nursery fire or in bed.

The same would apply to bathing in the sea. Mothers should see that their children never run off to bathe directly after a meal. Boys especially must be warned, as they are inclined to jump into the water at any odd time.

Neither must children be forced to go into cold water against their will, especially into the sea. A bath or bathe under these circumstances can do no good and often much harm, and there is generally a gentler way of getting them accustomed to the water.

Some children cannot bear cold water, especially if their circulation is poor or they are delicate in any way. A mother must use her own judgment and discretion in this matter, and both baths and bathing should always be under her supervision or instruction, and be given by some reliable person.

To Bath an Infant.—The best time for the morning bath is about 9 or 9.30, and about one and a half hours after it has had a meal. By this time the nursery will be thoroughly warm and there will not be much danger of chill. First put in readiness everything that is required. There should be a nice warm Turkish bath-towel without fringes and a fine face towel; the little garments should be hung up to warm in front of the fire, and baby's basket with all the toilet appliances should be at hand. Put a folding-screen round the chair and fireplace so as to shut out all draughts from door and window, and see that both door and window are closed for the time being. The little bath might be put on a stand so as to avoid unnecessary stooping.

Put in sufficient water to cover the baby's chest. Care should be taken to put in the cold before the boiling water, otherwise if the bath is of tin, the foot of it will retain the heat and baby's skin might be injured. A large apron should be worn when giving the bath; one made of Turkish towelling is the best. Castile or other pure soap must be used, and nothing of a cheap fancy nature. A soft sponge or a very soft piece of flannel should be used for washing. Needless to say, the sponges must be kept in a very clean and fresh condition.

When the infant is undressed, sponge and soap the head first very gently, and being careful that the soap does not trickle into the eyes. Careful attention must be paid to the eyelids, ears, and nostrils.

Then wash the rest of the body, after which baby may be lowered gently into the bath. The left hand and fore-arm must support the back and head of the baby while in the bath, while the right hand does the sponging; or one of the patent hammock baths might be used—they have a piece of stout webbing stretched across the bath from side to side on which the baby rests, while both hands of the nurse are left free. Two or three minutes will be quite long enough for the baby to be in the water; it should then be lifted into a warm soft towel for drying.

Rub gently all over with the towel, using the fine towel for the face and neck, and then rub with the hand, as this helps circulation. A little powder should also be used to such parts as the creases of the thighs, the armpits, under the knees and the throat.

The dressing must be performed as expeditiously as possible, and by the time this is finished the baby will be ready for its meal and a nap.

Clean Habits.—A word might be said about the training of the infant in the habit of personal cleanliness. From infancy the nurse or mother should make a practice of holding the child over a vessel every two hours and especially after sleep. If this is done with regularity the infant very soon gives warning of its wants, and at three months the napkin ought to be wetted very rarely during the day, and at a year old might be dispensed with except for night-wear. Of course there will be exceptions, and some children are more difficult to train than others. A napkin should be changed at once when it has been soiled; if left on for hours it hinders the formation of cleanly habits. The shaped pilch should be continued for some time after the napkins have been given up.

Care of the Hair.—During infancy the hair should be soaped and washed every day, dried with a soft towel and brushed with a very soft brush. When the hair has grown, once or twice a week will be sufficient for washing, and care must be taken that it is thoroughly dry before the child is put to bed.

Oils and hair-washes are quite unnecessary for

children's hair; in fact, it will grow better without them, and good and regular brushing with clean brushes should be relied upon for keeping it pretty and soft. It is a mistake to let a little child's hair grow too long, as it just heats the head unnecessarily. Neither should there be any tight plaiting or putting up in curls at night—there is no harm in plaiting it loosely, but the head must be left perfectly at rest during the hours of sleep. It is important that each child should be provided with his own brush and comb.

Care of the Mouth and Teeth.—This is very important, and even the mouth of the tiny infant must receive attention and be washed twice a day at least. This may either be done before or directly after the bath. Twist a piece of fine lint or gauze round the finger, dip it into a weak solution of boracic acid and water, and carefully and gently rub the mouth and gums with this. As soon as the first tooth appears the use of the tooth brush must be commenced—a very soft one at first—and this must be dipped into the boracic acid solution and used very gently. A good pinch of carbonate of soda in the water is also a good thing, and it preserves the teeth against the injurious effects of milk. Tooth powders and pastes are not necessary for the first teeth, but a little precipitated chalk or other simple tooth powder may be used by older children.

The chronic ill-health and low vitality of some children can often be traced to their teeth, and they are never too young to be impressed with the importance of keeping them clean, not only for the sake of appearance, but also for the sake of health. The most important times for cleaning are morning and evening, more especially the latter; to preserve the teeth and gums it is particularly essential that the mouth should be clean before going to bed at night.

It is wise to commence periodical visits to a good dentist at a very early stage, just to make sure that all is in order and that the children's teeth are growing in a proper manner. By paying attention to the first set of teeth, the second set have a better chance of being sound and good.

Nails.—The nails of children must not be neglected. If kept clean and neatly trimmed, they are likely to remain a pretty shape in after life. The toe-nails also must not be forgotten, as when left too long they often cause trouble in walking.

Sleep.—Sleep is one of the great essentials of child life. A very young infant will sleep twenty hours out of the twenty-four; in fact, attention to its wants will take up all the time it need be awake, and the more it sleeps the better. After a few weeks it begins to require less sleep, until at between three to six months it will likely be awake for six or seven hours, whilst in the second year twelve hours' sleep at night and two hours in the day will generally be sufficient. A sleep in the middle of the day should be encouraged as long as possible; if it is continued until the sixth or seventh year so much the better; it will result in a stronger body and better nerves. A child who does not get a sleep in the day often becomes so weary and excited that it cannot sleep at night.

It is very important, too, that all children should be in bed at an early hour, and that their hours should not be upset, except under some very special circumstances. For the first three years bed-time should not be later than 6.30 P.M. Children of from three to five should be in bed by 7 o'clock, and then the time for sitting up should be increased very slowly until between the ages of thirteen and fourteen the child is going to bed between 8.30 and 9 o'clock.

An infant may be allowed to sleep a great deal out of doors in its pram or bassinette. Be careful that this is placed out of a draught and sheltered from the sun. The baby must always be in a lying-down position when sleeping; when older and able to sit up, it must on no account be allowed to sleep in this position or injury may be caused to the spine and neck. The baby must be very comfortably wrapped up and placed on its side. It is a good plan also to change the side on which it sleeps and not to lay it repeatedly in the same position.

A child should not be hushed or rocked to sleep, and an empty india-rubber teat or comforter should never be employed to keep it quiet. Neither should it require some one to sit with it until it goes to sleep, or be taken up and brought into a lighted sitting-room because it happens to waken up and cry. These are all bad habits which are quite unnecessary, and if once commenced are very difficult to break off. It should not be necessary either to insist upon silence in the house after the baby has gone to bed; the child who has learnt to sleep while talking and even music is going on in an adjoining room will soon sleep through any sound, and not be easily startled.

As the child grows older the question of accustoming him to sleep in the dark will also have to be considered. There will be no difficulty on this score with healthy normal children who have been trained from infancy to go to sleep almost as soon as they are laid in their little cots, but as the child grows older his powers of imagination become an important factor to be reckoned with. Some children are highly nervous and subject to night terrors—although patience and firmness on the part of the mother will help a great deal towards curing this condition, yet it would be absolute cruelty to force a child subject to nervous fears to sleep in the dark. There are many grown-up people who dread darkness—is it to be wondered at, therefore, that some children manifest the same weakness? Such fears, it is true, are often caused by injudicious management on the part of parents and nurses. For instance, threats such as "I'll ask the bogies to come and take you," or else stories of naughty little boys and girls being stolen from home at night-time, are quite sufficient to fill even the least nervously-inclined children with fear. Let a mother see to it, therefore, that her children are not frightened in this way, and that their little imaginations are not distorted by injudicious stories of wicked people, witches and ghosts, which are so often related to them by well-intentioned but stupid people, who cannot appreciate the harm they are doing.

All over-excitement of any kind should be avoided; the healthier and more childish the life led by the little ones, the less prone will they be to over-excitability and nervousness; a nervous child requires the greatest care and management, and it is only the patient and careful mother who, whilst doing her utmost to convince her little one that his fears are groundless, will see that he leads a healthy life in every way; who will be able by care and good management to counteract a tendency to nervousness, which will get worse as the child grows older if no effort is made to check it.

Even an infant may be taught that the night is to be passed quietly if, when it is necessary to attend to its wants, everything is done without excitement and with as little light as possible.

Fresh air is the best sedative, and the child who has been out of doors during the day, who is well fed and made comfortable in bed, ought to go off into a quiet and refreshing sleep without any trouble, unless there is something physically wrong.

As said before, the covering of the beds must be warm and light (see p. 475) and regulated according to the temperature and climate. A little child must never be allowed to suffer from cold, nor lie awake for that reason. In very cold weather very little children, or children with poor circulation, should have their beds warmed with a hot bottle before they are put into them. The window in the sleeping-room should always be open. Rather have a fire when cold than shut the window, as a fire is always a good ventilator. No gas must be left burning during the night. If for any reason a light is required, it is better to have a night-light.

Children are very apt to kick off the bedclothes at night, and for this reason flannel sleeping-suits are better than nightgowns, even for girls, or tapes may be sewn to the corner of the top blanket and fastened to the bedstead. On no account must a child be allowed to sleep with its head under the clothes.

About 10 o'clock the nurse or mother should always see that the children are sleeping properly before she goes to bed, and the little ones ought to be lifted and their wants attended to until this is no longer necessary.

Whilst dealing with this subject a word of warning may well be given to mothers. In spite of the most careful training, some children form the habit of wetting their beds at night. Very often a child afflicted with worms will do this as a result of the irritation that sets in. Attention must be directed to ridding the child of the worms before he can be cured of this habit. Very often, however, a child will be liable to this distressing tendency in spite of every precaution and care and without any apparent reason or cause. In these circumstances it is more often than not that he is afflicted with some bodily defect. Medical advice should at once be sought, and punishment should never be administered for what the child cannot help. All such cases demand careful treatment and management.

Fresh Air and Exercise.—*The Walk out of Doors.*—If children are to thrive they must be out in the open air as much as possible. The importance of this cannot be too strongly emphasised. Of course, some judgment must be shown as regards weather and in choosing the hours for the daily walk. It would be wrong to send out very young children in snow or rain, if a very cold wind were blowing, or in very great heat.

In summer weather even the new-born infant may be taken out of doors after the first few days, although, of course, in winter more precautions must be taken, and a time must be chosen when the sun is shining. The little one might then be accustomed more gradually to a change of temperature by wrapping it up and taking it into a cooler room for a short time.

For the first few walks the tiny infant should be taken out in its nurse's arms and a ten to fifteen minutes' airing will be sufficiently long; after that the time might be increased gradually. When the monthly nurse leaves, the baby should be taken out in a bassinette-perambulator, or one in which it can lie as comfortably as in its little cot.

The choice of the first pram is very important. It must be one on four wheels and well swung, so that there is no vibration which might injure the child's spine. It ought also to be fitted with a mattress and pillow, protected and covered in the same way as the bed (see p. 470). There should also be a hood or canopy, to protect from the sun or inclemencies of weather. The baby must be comfortably placed in his pram, a warm bottle being put in if the weather is cold, and a light and warm covering. The perambulator must be wheeled very steadily, and on no account must it be jolted down steps, even one or two, while the baby is in it. This bassinette-perambulator must be used until the baby has gained sufficient strength to sit up without causing any strain on the spine. The same pram can then be adapted accordingly. A mail-cart should not be used until the child is between a year and eighteen months old, and care must always be taken that the little legs do not dangle, and also that they are well protected from the cold.

When a child is being wheeled out of doors it must always be protected from the hot rays of the sunshine, from cold wind, or from snow or rain.

As soon as the child is steady on its legs it should be encouraged to walk a little out of doors, as this helps to keep up the circulation—just a little to begin with and increasing the distance very gradually. The mail-cart must not be discarded too early, because although it is all-important that children should be out of doors, it is very wrong to drag them along when the little legs and bodies are tired. Of course, when there is a garden or field into which the little ones can be turned to play and run about in fine weather, the life out of doors is very much simplified—it is the town-bred child who is to be pitied in this respect.

Other Exercises.—The exercise that an infant can take is very limited, but still it has its little movements, and these should not be checked but rather encouraged, as they help to develop its muscles. When the child is a little older it should be put on the floor on a rug and allowed to kick and roll about, and, later on, to crawl. Care must always be taken that it is well protected and not hampered with its clothing. The habit of tossing a baby up and down is a very bad one; it should not be excited, and there is no occasion to hold it and nurse it all its waking hours. Neither should it be hurried into walking—in fact, there is no occasion to teach walking, as the baby will learn by itself as soon as the little legs are strong enough and able to bear the weight of the body. The use of the play-pen is excellent for this, as the baby will soon drag itself up the sides and begin cautiously to move round. Then later on a baby-walker might be used (see illustration); the baby stands inside

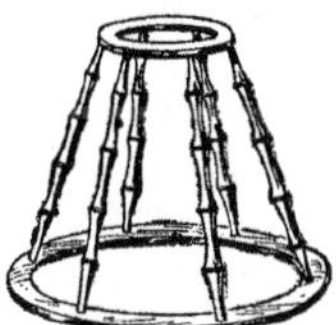

Baby-Walker.

this and pushes it along. It is always better to let them learn to walk gradually rather than to press them forward, as some children are naturally more backward than others in this respect.

At about four or five years old some simple movements in calisthenics or Swedish gymnastics may be started, but they must not be continued for too long. As soon as possible, too, the child should be taught to hold itself erect and to move gracefully. Dancing is very valuable in this respect, as it develops grace and gives lightness of movement.

Swimming is another excellent exercise for young children, if done in moderation and the child is strong enough. Then later on the child should be encouraged to take part in outdoor games, the amount to be always carefully regulated by the mother, as the tendency in many cases, especially with girls, is to go beyond their strength.

CHILDREN'S AILMENTS

Symptoms of Illness.—It should be taken as a general rule that the less medicine given in the nursery the better it will be for the little ones. A warm bath and a suitable aperient form the best panacea for most childish disorders. For the more serious ailments, or when in doubt in regard to treatment of ordinary disorders, a doctor should be consulted. Never on any account administer drugs without medical advice. The health of many a child has been ruined by the administration of sleeping draughts by unscrupulous nurses.

A great deal of the anxiety connected with the rearing of children lies in the difficulty sometimes experienced in discriminating between the various symptoms of illness which appear. When a child appears to be ailing it may happen that the indisposition is only a slight and temporary one; on the other hand, the symptoms might be the premonition of sickening for bronchitis, measles, or some other illness to which children are more or less liable. Every mother should keep a clinical thermometer in order that she may be able to take the child's temperature and so recognise feverishness when it is present. In taking the temperature of children the thermometer should be placed not in the mouth, but either in the armpit or groin; it should be allowed to remain there ten minutes, and upon taking it away the temperature will be found to be accurately noted. The normal temperature is 98·4°; in fever it will rise to 100° and over. When a child is feverish the safest plan is to at once put it to bed, seeing that it is kept warm to obviate the risk of chill, which might be caught if it is exposed to cold or draught or allowed out in the open air in its feverish condition, often with fatal results.

In infantine disorders a great deal is often indicated by the nature of an infant's cry—the low, wailing cry indicating cold is quite distinct from the sharp impatient cry of hunger and the moaning of pain, whilst a half-smothered, hoarse cry is often indicative of bronchitis or other chest troubles. An infant's breathing is often a guide to its condition; for instance, hurried breathing followed by wheezing denotes bronchitis, then there is the sharp fighting for breath and crowing sound associated with crowing croup.

There are many other signs which indicate a child's condition of health, too many to be entered upon fully in a book of this kind. Suffice it to say that, in addition to the symptoms mentioned, when a child's little face has the flush of fever, when it has the pinched and wan look of pain, when its eyes become either vacant or wild in their expression, it may be taken that it is suffering from disorder of some kind which might turn out to be serious if neglected, and the utmost precautions should therefore be observed, and medical advice sought in case of need or doubt.

Teething.—The first teeth should begin to appear at six months, the two front teeth or incisors of the lower jaw coming first, the upper incisors making their appearance in another month, and the other teeth by degrees until the end of the second year. Some children, however, are very backward in teething. Most healthy infants cut their teeth without much trouble, but often the gums become very swollen and sensitive, and the infant is feverish and fretful. Rubbing the gums with the fingers has a soothing effect, also the child may be given an india-rubber ring to bite, but care must be taken to keep this clean. At night-time a warm bath will often give relief. The feverishness which is usually present at the time of teething makes a baby very susceptible to chill, and this is what principally causes the many infantine ailments, such as diarrhœa, &c., generally associated with the teething period. At this time, therefore, additional precaution against the danger of catching cold must be taken. During teething a quantity of saliva dribbles from the child's mouth. This should not be allowed to go through the clothing or bronchitis may result. Change the bib frequently—a small piece of mackintosh placed underneath it will keep the clothing dry.

Diarrhœa.—This may usually be ascribed to some fault in the diet and occurs frequently at the teething period. If the infant is being brought up by hand, add a dessert-spoonful of lime-water to its bottle; if it is being nursed by the mother, give dill-water and lime-water mixed—a tea-spoonful of each.

Constipation should never be neglected, as it may lead to convulsions and other ills. This complaint is most prevalent with infants brought up by hand. Care must be taken that the proper proportion of barley water is in the bottle. Give baby a drink of water first thing in the morning. Massage of the abdomen will do good. An enema may be given, but only very occasionally. The administration of purgatives is inadvisable as a rule, although a tea-spoonful of salad oil may sometimes be given. The child should be trained early in the forming of regular habits.

Babies of a year old and upwards may be given with advantage the insides of well-cooked fruit, such as apples, bananas, &c.

Thrush is an affection of the mouth due to the formation of a parasitic yeast which forms white patches on the gums, cheeks, and throat. The condition is most common in hand-fed infants, being often caused by dirty bottles, dummy teats, and general bad management. The treatment should be an improvement in the general management of the baby, a little honey and borax or some glycerine of boric acid should be applied to the white patches by means of a camel's-hair brush or a little cotton wool.

Convulsions.—These are due to some irritation in the nervous system, often occurring during teething—and may be caused by indigestible food, constipation, worms, or even a pin in the clothing. The treatment is to detect and, if possible, remove the cause. The child should at once be stripped and placed in a hot bath of about 100° F., the hot water reaching the nape of the neck. An enema should be given next, more especially in the case of worms, and medical aid should be obtained. If the convulsions are caused by teething, the gums may be lanced with advantage. The approach of convulsions may generally be anticipated when the infant grinds its teeth in sleep and is subject to severe facial twitchings.

Crowing or Spasmodic Croup.—This is due to a spasm in the larynx of nervous origin, and is most common among rickety children at teething time. A loud crowing sound is indicative of the attack, which is most distressing while it lasts and usually occurs at night. The child fights for breath, its fingers are clenched, its face livid. A flannel or sponge wrung out in hot water and applied to the throat will often give relief. Make the child sit up and give half to a tea-spoonful of ipecacuanha wine to induce vomiting, giving another dose after ten minutes if this does not act. Medical advice should be obtained, and great care taken in regard to general management and diet.

Chills should never be neglected, as otherwise bronchitis, pneumonia, or pleurisy may result. When a child is seen to have a serious chill put him straight to bed, giving him a warm drink and an aperient, if needs be. Take his temperature, and if it is above normal for twelve hours it will be advisable to call in medical aid.

Little Ulcers.—When these appear on the tongue or lips give half a tea-spoonful flower of sulphur in a little treacle and apply glycerine and borax.

Weak Legs and Ankles.—These are too often the result of forcing a child to walk more than is good for it at too early an age; the little legs become "bandy" and scarcely seem to support the body. See that the child is not too much on his feet, and bathe the legs and ankles regularly in salt and water.

Ringworm.—Shave off the hair round the affected part and paint with iodine. Apply a coating of iodine daily until the ring-worm disappears. If the case is a bad one, it should be under medical treatment.

Worms.—Children are often affected with these; the best cure is to give an enema of two pints warm water with two table-spoonfuls common salt added to it—and a dose of caster-oil after. If very persistent, feed the child on rice pudding for a day or two.

Sleep - Walking, or Somnambulism.—Sleep-walking generally occurs in highly-strung school children who are over-worked. The treatment should be in medical hands, and meanwhile the windows and doors must be guarded and the child not left to sleep in a room by himself.

Prolapse or descent of the lower bowel so that it appears externally sometimes occurs with children. The cause is prolonged straining at stool from constipation, or other source of bowel irritation. The prolapsed bowel should be at once washed and then gently squeezed back by grasping it with a clean piece of old linen smeared with vaseline or olive oil. After the replacement of the bowel has been accomplished, a diaper should be folded and passed between the legs; this should then be secured in front and behind to a waist-belt. In future the child should pass its motions lying down, all strong aperients must be avoided, and any prolapse corrected directly after the motion.

TRAINING AND EDUCATION

Early Training.—With the mother first of all must rest the responsibility of the early training of her little ones. It is during the first seven years of a child's life that the most lasting impression is made on the little mind, and that the greatest influence is brought to bear for evil or for good. Great educational authorities assert that these first years of childhood are of the utmost importance in education, both mentally and morally, and if they are wisely ordained the good influence of early training and teaching will manifest itself throughout life; the adverse influence of bad training having equally lasting effects.

The most valuable training for a child, therefore, is that which begins at his mother's knees. Let every mother bear this in mind, let her remember that the shaping of her child's character rests in the main with her, and let her not spare herself in seeing that her responsibility in this respect is faithfully and conscientiously discharged.

A child should be made to learn early the lessons of obedience and self-control. This requires the utmost patience on the part of the mother. She must make it quite clear from the first that when she expresses a wish it must be obeyed, and never waver from her attitude of gentle firmness. A child very soon learns if its parent's word is law, or if he can make her alter her mind by means of a little coaxing.

It is very hard at times for a mother to resist the pretty childish graces which are often put forward as an inducement for her to waver from some precept or excuse some fault, but once she gives way to such blandishments, she may give up all idea of ever having her children under perfect control. The knowledge that when mother says a thing she means it does more than anything else to win the respect and confidence of the little ones. For this reason all promises must be religiously kept and in the same way all threats of punishment fulfilled. Broken promises and empty threats are equally harmful. The first beget in the children a lack of confidence as well as a sense of injustice, whilst the second cannot possibly have any effect upon the child who knows perfectly well that they will not be carried out.

Parents should be careful to set a good example to their children upon all occasions, both in their powers of self-control and their courtesy of demeanour towards each other. Never give way to temper before a child nor enter into quarrelling or argument of any kind. It must be remembered that in little ones the imitative faculties are developed to an almost abnormal extent, and that a child's character will receive lasting impressions from those with whom he comes into contact in early childhood. Let an effort be made, therefore, that he shall never learn anything but good from his surroundings.

A mother should not allow her children to be too much in the company of servants; and, what is very important, she should be particular to choose a nurse who speaks the King's English correctly, as a bad accent or Cockneyism is very soon acquired by the little ones, and exceedingly difficult to cure.

The children should be as much as possible with people of refinement. During the years which intervene between babyhood and the age when lessons may begin, it a good plan to engage a lady to be with the little ones for a few hours daily, taking them for their walks, and making their deportment and manners her special care. There are very many ladies having home ties which prevent them from taking any resident position who would be only too pleased to obtain a post of the kind. For the mother who has a number of social duties which preclude her from spending as much time with her children as she would wish, such a plan has much in its favour.

In most families the children join their parents at luncheon, this being the dinner-hour for the little ones. This is a very good custom, as it enables them to acquire the manners and deportment to be observed at table. A mother should begin early to train her child in this direction. Bad manners should always be punished by banishment from the dining-room, and a solitary meal in the nursery. Properly trained children can be allowed to sit at the luncheon table when friends are present without any qualms of anxiety being felt by the parents as to how they will behave, whilst ill-mannered children will be a source not only of shame to the parents, but annoyance to their guests.

It is not good for children to be banished altogether to the nursery, but, on the other hand, it is very bad for them to be too much with grown-up people. Nowadays it seems to be the fashion for mothers to take their children about with them everywhere. Dressed like little fashion plates, they are taken to pay calls, to At Homes, to luncheons and dinners at restaurants—they are, in fact, treated as regular little men and women of the world and encouraged to show off upon all occasions. The little girls might be miniature ladies of fashion by the airs and graces they are trained to assume. To every right-feeling mother there can be no more sorry spectacle than that presented by an over-dressed precocious child laying herself out for admiration and attention and conducting herself with all the *savoir faire* of a woman of thirty. The ill-advised mother who is responsible for this is guilty of little less than cruelty to her child, whom she has robbed of the best joys of childhood by turning her into a little woman before her time.

Grown-up people should also be very careful in regard to their conversation before children. Many things heard from the elders are stored up in the small memories, and are apt to come out upon the most awkward occasions. Never indulge in scandal or gossip of any kind before a child. Many parents err most flagrantly in this respect, heedless of the fact that by so doing they are sowing the seeds of unkindness and ill-nature in the hearts and minds of the little ones.

The simpler the life led by the children the happier they will be. Simple meals, regular hours, and plenty of healthful exercise should be the keynote of the régime of both nursery and school-room. How pleasant it is to see the enjoyment manifested by children so brought up at the most simple treats and pleasures. They are real children in every sense of the word, and in later life they will have none but happy recollections of a childhood passed in this way.

Pocket-Money.—A too liberal allowance of pocket-money should never be made. There is nothing more conducive to extravagance in later years than an unlimited supply of pocket-money during childhood. The exact sum given must of course depend upon circumstances. For children of from seven to ten years of age 2d. to 3d. per week represents a fairly good average. At a boarding-school the allowance of pocket-money should depend upon the prevailing régime. A parent should make a point of obtaining enlightenment in regard to this from the head master or mistress, regulating the allowance accordingly. Boys or girls at school should neither have more nor less pocket-money than that received by their companions.

Punishments.—The injudicious administration of punishments has served to spoil the character of many an otherwise well-disposed child, often turning a girl or boy of a really affectionate and pliable disposition into a hardened little rebel. How few parents are there who know how to punish judiciously and wisely, and, what is of more importance, to give a punishment in proportion to the offence committed.

The precept that a child is more easily led than driven should always be well borne in mind. The parents' rule should, therefore, be a gentle though a firm one, and the child must be brought to realise the benefits of not transgressing in any way against that rule, together with the penalty attendant upon transgression when it occurs. A child must always realise *why* he is being punished, and be able to appreciate the justice of the punishment. If he is easily made to understand the penalties attending certain acts, he will be more likely to avoid them.

Take, for instance, the tiny toddler of two years whose powers of inquisitiveness are such that he develops an uncontrollable desire to touch and handle everything with which he comes in contact. Many distressing accidents have occurred through the mother failing to teach him that when he touches a certain forbidden object there is always a penalty attached to his disobedience. For instance, there is a jug of hot water placed within the reach of master baby. He shows an inclination to handle it. The wise mother will not at once put it out of his reach, but will say warningly, "Don't touch that—very hot—baby will burn himself," carefully watching him to see that he comes to no harm. Baby probably makes up his mind to disobey, but he will touch it tentatively, with the result that he does not burn his little fingers as he would have done without his mother's warning, but at the same time experiences a very disagreeable sensation, and so realises the result of disobedience and will not offend again.

A child should not be indiscriminately slapped for every little fault. Many parents look upon the most ordinary childish behaviour as naughtiness, sternly repressing any tendency to high spirits. The constant habit of boxing a boy's ears, or slapping and shaking a little girl upon the least provocation is most reprehensible. It tends to foster a sense of injustice in the minds of the little ones, and will serve to lay the foundation of a stubborn and dogged disposition. There is nothing more harmful to the childish mind than that it should be labouring incessantly under a sense of wrong. Children will rebel against all those by whom they think they are being treated with injustice, whereas with judicious management they can be as often as not most easily led. This explains the fact that some governesses and tutors have succeeded where others have failed. The former have mastered the art of the proper management of children through not only being just but through being able to look at things from a child's point of view; also being able to discriminate between big and little faults, making their charges realise the justice of punishment when deserved. There has been much argument for and against corporal punishment in the bringing up of children, but it may be safely said the more it can be avoided the better. It is true that in case of a baby who is too young to understand reasoning, and who; for instance, shows a tendency to make his mouth the receptacle for buttons, pennies, or anything else he can find, one and only one sharp tap will often be effective in deterring the child from repeating the attempt, though even in these circumstances prevention is better than cure, and the mother would do well to keep all these kinds of things out of the child's reach.

With the older children, however, the maxim "Spare the rod and spoil the child" should be taken in its moral rather than in its literal sense. No fault should ever be allowed to go unchecked. It is worse than useless to punish a child for a fault on one day and allow it to go unreproved the next. In very special circumstances a whipping may be necessary, but never give it unless after due deliberation you have come to the conclusion that other methods of punishment will fail. Never punish a child in a moment of anger at one of his offences. There is no more unedifying sight than that of a parent who has completely lost her self-control administering punishment to a child, a punishment which under the circumstances is likely to be out of all proportion to the offence. Give the anger time to cool down so that you will be able to see the fault in its normal proportions, then summon the little offender, and after reasoning gently with him and showing him the error of his ways and explaining to him why punishment has to be given, pass sentence. It may be said that constant whipping has the effect of spoiling and hardening many a little nature. A child can be punished in many other ways. Being obliged to stay at home while the others go out with mother, being debarred from some favourite game, or being sent to bed an hour earlier than usual, all are punishments which tell with children. Never punish a child by its fears. To lock up a nervous child in a dark room, for instance, is as cruel as it is inadvisable; such an action may be the cause of much harm and actual illness to the child.

Mothers should always make a rule of giving punishment themselves to their children. Never allow a nurse or other servant to slap a child. The roughness of some nurses when out with their little charges has often caused comment on the part of onlookers, and ladies, total strangers, have been known to remonstrate with them on their rough usage of the children in their charge. Such a state of things would not exist if the mother made it clear upon engaging a nurse that impromptu punishments such as slapping and shaking were altogether forbidden. At the same time the mother must carefully investigate every cause for complaint and be careful to uphold nurse in maintaining discipline, never neglecting to mete out punishment when deserved.

For the older children who are in charge of a governess the same rule must apply in regard to the punishment of all the more serious transgressions.

Just as delinquencies on the part of small offenders must be met with prompt punishment, so must any special little acts of good conduct have their reward. A word of encouragement here and there is of the utmost value in helping a child to be good. Let not this encouragement be withheld, and be ready to reward the little ones for any special pains taken in overcoming some fault, or performing some—to them—difficult task. Discretion must also govern the form which the reward must take. Parents are too apt to give money or sweets indiscriminately on these occasions, encouraging involuntarily a love of extravagance and even greediness in their children. Gifts of the kind now and then will do no harm, but do not let the rewards always take this form. Such treats as a walk or a picnic in the country, permission to invite some little friends to tea will be appreciated by children who are brought up in a becomingly simple manner, and who will hail with delight any little departure from the ordinary routine.

CHILDREN'S LITERATURE

1. Why do we wish our Children to Read?—This will depend largely upon our own attitude to literature. If, next to a living soul, a book is to us the most powerful influence in life, if we have realised it to be "the precious life-blood of a master spirit," then at least one reason is not far to seek. It is that books may become to them what they have been to us in maturer years—one of the most potent influences in life. Life, we have to remember, is larger than literature, and if man's business here is "to know for the sake of living, not to live for the sake of knowing," then surely reading, which has been called "a knowledge of all knowledges," has a large claim upon his attention.

But this conscious preparation for the future is second in importance to the present happiness of the child. That a child should be happy, and that it should find a large part of its happiness in its interests, cannot be disputed.

When one thinks of the intense present

interest a child can find in literature, and of the powerful influence good books can have in after life, one is impelled to ask might not more be done at home to cultivate a taste for a type of literature much neglected by the present generation ?

Is it not a mistake that as soon as a child begins to read himself he is little read to either at school or at home ? The ordinary reading lesson of a child of eight is in no way calculated to arouse his intellect, or to excite his imagination, or in any way to whet the literary appetite. How then is this to be done ? Either we must continue to read aloud to our children, or we must put within their reach literature in so simple a form that they can read it themselves.

2. What do we wish them to Read ?—It will be interesting to form a child's ideal library chronologically, the chronology of course having reference not to the publication of the volumes, but to the age of the little readers.

The library will consist chiefly of nonsense, narrative and morals. Yes, morals, for children exult in them. The sense of moral distinction is keen. No more pregnant words exist for him than good and bad, cruel and kind, fair and mean, true and false. Therefore, morals must be regarded as a requirement in children's literature.

We might begin our library by placing ten books on the lowest shelf of our imaginary bookcase, suitable for children between the ages of three and seven. The first volume should be a good collection of Nursery Rhymes liberally illustrated with story-telling pictures. The order in which we arrange the next six books does not matter. Not one of them is a continuous story, and portions from each may be read at pleasure. But it were wisdom to read these volumes from beginning to end before adding further to the library. Three are in prose—a selection from "Æsop's Fables"; a collection of Fairy Tales; "Tommy Smith's Animals." Three are in verse—"The Nonsense Songs and Stories of Edward Lear"; "The Poems of Jane and Ann Taylor"; "Struelpeter."

The interest and value of "Æsop's Fables," *wisely selected*, cannot be commended too highly, and one would wish the dissemination of the truths they contain to be broadcast. The volume of "Fairy Tales" should contain the prime favourites of the nursery, and be written as you would tell the tales to a child on your knee. "In Fairyland," by Louey Chisholm, is a favourite collection. "Tommy Smith's Animals" is not universally known, but it ought to be. It seldom fails to arouse interest and evoke enthusiasm. The writer is Edmund Selous.

The immortal "Struelpeter," consisting of stories first told by a child-loving doctor to his little patients, is well known.

Less well known are "The Nonsense Songs and Stories of Edward Lear." It is a true work of imagination. All children may not but many will revel in these tales.

"The Original Poems of Jane and Ann Taylor," edited by E. V. Lucas, is a treasure-house.

Seven books now occupy our lowest shelf. There is still room for three. The two books which might be placed next on the shelf are "Alice in Wonderland" and "The Water Babies," abridged by Amy Steedman. These are the first continuous tales that our imaginary child will hear. Of "Alice in Wonderland" nothing need be said. That it is a prime favourite with little children admits of no question.

Now to read aloud "Water Babies" in the original to a six-year-old is an exhausting process. There are words for which simple synonyms must be found and paragraph upon paragraph which must be omitted. The ingenuity of the reader and the patience of the little listener are alike taxed. An abridgment such as the above may be read more easily than any other book on the same shelf, and there are few books that will give such joy.

Only one vacant space is now left. Surely there is no doubt that before the child is seven years old we want him to know much of the life of Jesus and many of the stories that He told. A suitable book for this purpose has been a long-felt want, but at last there appeared "A Little Child's Life of Jesus," by Amy Steedman, and for it countless mothers must be thankful.

The above mention of an abridged "Water Babies" opens the question of the redaction of the classics generally. One hears it asked, "If a child reads tales re-told, will he read them later in the original ?" One can only hazard a guess as to the consequence of early familiarity, but it may be pretty generally expected (1) that those who in any case would have read the originals will still do so; (2) that a number of those who would not have done so now will, as a result of having had their appetites whetted by a foretaste of what the originals have to offer; (3) that those who will not would not have done so in any case, and that for them it is surely better to have read the stories in simple form than never to have heard them at all.

One may, therefore, believe in the abridged classic, carefully selected and reverently retold (1) because there is more opportunity of reading to children before they reach eleven years of age than later, and there does not seem without these redactions a library of literature sufficient to satisfy the cravings of little boys and girls; (2) because when children themselves begin to read, it is almost impossible to find books they can read with ease, and we do not want literature to be in any sense a reading lesson.

Although the above book-shelf is designed for children between the ages of three and seven, it is not meant that at seven the little library is to be left behind, but its volumes will represent old friendships. There are many children who would rest content with a shorter catalogue, and others who would cry that it might be lengthened, but few boys or girls of six would be mentally overfed or starved with a book-shelf equipped according to the above suggestions.

The higher shelves of the imaginary book-case we shall suppose to be for boys and girls from seven to eleven years of age. There might be placed the "Told to the Children Series," of which the first four volumes in the following complete list are included among the books recommended for younger children. This Series, although enjoyed by many older readers, is primarily designed for children under eleven. To guide choice the volumes have been tabulated according to their simplicity of subject-matter and manner of telling, and variety has been studied for the sake of any who should read the Series consecutively.

Nursery Rhymes.	The Faerie Queen.
Æsop's Fables.	Stories of Roland.
Nursery Tales.	Stories from Chaucer.
The Water Babies.	Stories from the Ballads.
Stories from Grimm.	Stories of William Tell.
Tanglewood Tales.	Stories from Shakespeare.
Simple Susan.	Stories of Siegfried.
Robin Hood.	Stories from Wagner.
Robinson Crusoe.	Little Plays.
Pilgrim's Progress.	The Iliad.
Arabian Nights.	The Odyssey.
King Arthur's Knights.	Stories of Three Saints.
Uncle Tom's Cabin.	Stories of Beowulf.
Stories from Hans Andersen.	Celtic Tales.
Old Testament Stories.	Don Quixote.
The Heroes.	Undine.
Gulliver's Travels.	More Tales from Shakespeare.
Guy of Warwick.	
The Rose and the Ring.	Stories from Dante.

The omitted volume "Stories from the Life of Christ" might be read after "Jesus, the Carpenter of Nazareth," by Robert Bird.

The "Children's Heroes Series," edited by John Lang, is also to be warmly recommended, and the "Shown to the Children Series" is notable alike for letterpress and illustration. A little volume, "Ruskin for Boys and Girls," by Mary Macgregor, is so captivating as to arouse interest in the series to which it belongs. "Grandmother's Favourites," edited by Amy Steedman, and "Old-Fashioned Tales" and "Forgotten Tales of Long Ago," edited by E. V. Lucas, are what their titles indicate and are all charming.

Other volumes I have every confidence in recommending are, "The King of the Golden River," by Ruskin; "The Gold Thread," by Norman Macleod; "The Princess and the Goblin," "The Princess and Curdie," and "At the Back of the North Wind," by George Macdonald, and "Black Beauty" by Anna Sewell; "In God's Garden," "Knights of Art," and "Legends of Italy," by Amy Steedman, and Jacob's "English Fairy Tales." A modern writer of Fairy Tales who might be introduced to those to whom she is unknown is Mary de Morgan. Her volumes, "The Necklace of Princess Fiorimonde" and "On a Pin-Cushion" deserve to be far more widely known than they are.

All histories by H. E. Marshall should find a place on these shelves. Boys and girls alike read them as they read story-books. Room must also be found for the delightful Jungle Books of Rudyard Kipling. The "Laughter of Peterkin," by Fiona Macleod, will fascinate the imaginative child. A place must also be reserved for those delightful Animal Stories by Ernest Thompson Seton and by William Long.

A good anthology should find a place on every bookshelf. The children's favourite is "The Golden Staircase" by Louey Chisholm, which is also published in four parts as "Poetry for the Four, Five and Six-Year-Old," &c. Other excellent collections are "A Treasury of Verse," by M. Edgar, and "A Book of Verses," by E. V. Lucas.

3. How do we wish our Children to Read?—(1) We must insist that the child thinks as he reads. This is more important than to teach him thoughts. (2) Every book that is worth reading once is worth reading twice, and this habit can be formed in the child while he is still being read to. (3) As the child cannot omit judiciously he must read his books word for word. (4) He must read with his whole attention. In no way should he regard a book as a toy. (5) And, lastly, expressions of appreciation should be encouraged. He should be urged to give a book a fair trial. If it does not appeal to him let him put it aside, but never let his attitude be that the book is not a good one. A great deal can be done while the child is little to influence his attitude towards books by paying attention to how he reads.

Education.—A child develops early his powers of observation; he begins to take an interest in his surroundings and to inquire into the why and wherefore of things, and it is at this time his real education begins.

Parents very often show a remarkable lack of foresight by endeavouring to check the natural bent for inquiry taken by the little people, treating their questions as troublesome and a nuisance, and not even attempting to answer the most simple inquiry. This is a great mistake. It must be remembered that facts of which we seldom think, because they are so familiar to us that their existence is accepted as a matter of course, are entirely new to the child whose observant faculties are beginning to develop, and the questions asked are usually the result of a real desire for knowledge. The incessant "why" of children is apt to become tiresome, but a mother should never lose patience. It would be a clever woman indeed who could answer all the questions put to her by a child.

She would have to be a veritable walking encyclopædia to do so; but she should do her best to answer them as far as is in her power. If she is not quite sure of the right answer to give, she should not take the course adopted by some mothers of making up a reply to keep the child quiet. Instead she should say, "I couldn't answer that, dear, just now, but I shall find out for you by and by," never failing to keep her promise in this respect. A good encyclopædia and a reference book are almost indispensable on the family book-shelf; without them many of the little one's questions will have to go unanswered. There are some questions asked by children, it is true, to which it is not at all feasible that an answer should be given. Again, in these circumstances do not tell the child untruths, or get cross and impatient with him, but tell him gently that you cannot give him the answer now as he is too little to understand. To judiciously gratify the natural bent of a child for inquiry and cultivate his powers of ehservation is to give him the best teaching he can have during his early years. A child should never be put to book learning too soon. Reading and writing can be taught well enough when he is in his sixth or seventh year, and even then the lessons must be gradual and such as will not keep him long at his desk. Never force children to learn lessons too early. Very sharp children especially will stand in danger of having their brains overtaxed if they are too much pushed forward in this respect. Let the child be out as much as possible in the open air, enjoying healthy exercise, building up strength for his little body. All this time he will be learning—learning to take note of all that goes on around him, and this is all the education that matters in very early childhood.

Let the mother who is her child's teacher set to work in a manner that will make teaching seem to him as play. It may indeed be play, but instructive play for all that, and to be able to teach in this way a mother will need to acquire not a little knowledge herself. Educational authorities have now recognised the value of nature study in the instruction of the young. What useful lessons can be given in long country walks by a mother who can tell her child the history of the things he sees, showing him the difference between the various kinds of leaves and flowers, telling him all about the different trees, the birds, the various little dwellers in the ponds and in the fields. What moral tales can be pointed out also—what better object lesson can there be than in the industry and providence of a little colony of ants or of a hive of bees?—what better foundation to education can a child have than a habit of being able to take note of all these things and understand them? Such a training will be to him of more value than all the spelling lessons and multiplication tables laboriously learned and repeated with mechanical precision. Try to cultivate a child's reasoning powers before you tax his little memory. In this way the best results will be achieved.

When the time comes for the child to set to work in earnest to learn to read and write, the same principle of making work as much like play as possible should be observed. Such methods are embodied in the best kindergarten system, notably the Froebel System. A mother may often find it advisable to send the little ones to a kindergarten school for an hour or two every day, or else to engage a governess well versed in the Froebel method if she is not free to do the teaching herself. If she does elect to teach herself and she is acquainted with this method, so much the better. If not, she may easily obtain instruction at one of the Froebel institutes, but generally her own method will be as effective as any other if she only keeps before her the one guiding principle not to make the lessons a series of monotonous repetitions of words learned by rote, but to make them as interesting as possible, graduating them in accordance with the child's powers of comprehension, so that he can assimilate them naturally without any strain upon his memory.

As boys and girls get older the same care must be maintained in seeing that their brains are not overtaxed in any way. Remember that a child's mental development should never be forced to the detriment of his (or her) physical well-being. It is a great deal to be deplored that some parents and teachers are slow to recognise the fact that a great amount of study is very bad for some girls and boys. These as a rule are only too eager to learn, taking to their books as ducks take to water; nevertheless, this avidity for learning must be checked if the evil results of undue mental strain are to be avoided. It is more natural for normal healthy boys and girls to shirk some of their lessons than to be eager to have a double dose. Overstudy is responsible for much ill-health amongst young people. It unfortunately happens that at the age of fourteen to fifteen, just when our children require most care if they are to grow up well and strong, they have to enter for some public examination, in preparation for which a certain amount of cramming is required. The passing of such an examination is often looked upon as a matter of almost life and death by both children and their parents, with the result that the former are encouraged to study during all their leisure hours and often until late at night, forgoing all healthful exercise and recreation in order that they may make sure of passing well. This is a very wrong policy indeed, and to it may be ascribed many a nervous breakdown amongst our girls and boys. Never tax a child with learning beyond his (or her) powers. When any special course of study is necessary, see that it is strictly kept within the limits of working hours.

Sufficient exercise and recreation are essential for both the mental and physical well-being of our children, and they must not be forgone under any circumstances. When children must enter for examination, let them begin their preparations a long time beforehand in order that there may be no undue rush at the end. For the University Locals, for instance, one year's preparation is not one bit too much, yet many parents expect their children to get ready for them in three or four months.

If, although given ample time for preparation, a child is still unable to limit his studies to regular hours, then it must be taken that the task is altogether beyond his (or her) powers, and it should either be put off for another year or else altogether abandoned if needs be.

Parents should strive early to discover any special aptitude displayed by their children, in order that they may do their utmost to bring out their talents in any particular direction. Their education should be planned first and foremost from the point of view of utility, special attention being given to knowledge that will prove useful to them in later life.

For instance, study of the classics should not be pursued to such an extent as to leave little time for foreign languages in the case of those destined for a commercial career. When a child has reached the age of thirteen or fourteen, a parent should see that his studies are directed towards specialisation for the career of his choice. The same applies to those girls who will have to earn their own living as they reach a suitable age. Too often parents spend all their time and money upon the education of their boys, whereas little trouble is expended upon the training of the girls; a few years at a boarding-school and perhaps a year at a "finishing" school too often represents the sum total of the education of the average girl, who, thus poorly equipped, is often expected to go out into the world and earn her own living in an age when specialisation is exacted if one has to earn a living wage. Such treatment is decidedly unfair; when a girl has to work for herself she has less odds in her favour than a boy. Is it not all the more essential, therefore, that she should go out into the world fittingly equipped to hold her own in the career she has chosen? There are many careers now open to women, full details of which are given in another part of this book, but in connection with each trade or profession a certain amount of specialisation is necessary if it is to be followed with success.

A girl's education, therefore, requires to be mapped out as carefully as that of her brothers, more especially if she is required to turn it to advantage in later life, but, and this is of the utmost importance, the study of domestic science should not be excluded. Needlework, cookery, and household management should form part of every girl's curriculum. A mother should make this training her special care. Too often nowadays girls are taught to look down upon housework of every kind, with the result that when called upon to undertake the management of a home of their own they are totally unfitted for the task. Such mistaken policy is much to be deplored; a woman should not only be able to hold her own in all branches of the womanly art, but she should also take a pride in being able to do so.

Value of Accomplishments for Girls.—In the education of girls accomplishments should take a prominent place, and all talent for music, singing, painting, &c., should be carefully brought out. An accomplished lady is not only an ornament in society, but she serves to contribute in a large measure to the happiness of her own home. Accomplishments are always useful to a girl, and should she by any circumstances be compelled to earn her own livelihood, they can always be turned to good account.

In selecting a school care should be taken to ascertain whether there is good instruction in music, drawing, painting and dancing; and in regard to the first three whether the pupils are prepared for the examinations of the chief colleges of music and art. If lessons are taken at home from private teachers, care should be taken to ascertain that these are well qualified in every way. It is a great advantage for little girls to learn dancing at a very tender age. This helps to make their little limbs and bodies supple and pliable, and their carriage and deportment graceful. Much of the native *gaucherie* of childhood is eliminated by early instruction in this art. As girls get older, fencing is also an art which is worth cultivation, as its practice secures an alertness and lightness of movement which is not so easily acquired in any other way. Gymnastics are also essential, not only from the point of view of health and physique, but also from that of carriage and deportment. In most of our towns, girls' classes are held at the large gymnasiums, the fees for the course of instruction being very moderate indeed. A girl should also be encouraged to take part in healthy outdoor games, such as hockey and tennis. She should never be allowed to stoop when sitting over table or desk, as this habit is responsible for those unsightly round shoulders which do so much to mar an otherwise good figure.

The doctrine of "self help" should be early inculcated in the minds of girls and boys alike, and in this way they will be prepared for the responsibilities of later life. Parents should remember that by giving their children a good mental and moral education they are endowing them with what will prove to be a most valuable asset in life, the importance of which cannot be too highly estimated. Let them see, therefore, that they do their duty in this direction as far as is in their power, and they will be happy in the knowledge that they have left no stone unturned to send their children out into the world fittingly equipped for the career of their choice.

The Governess.—For their early education children are often placed by parents under the care of a governess, and many girls receive their entire education from childhood to young womanhood in this way. Parents cannot use too much discrimination in choosing the lady to whom they are to trust the tuition of their little ones, but, incomprehensible though such a course would seem, as a rule they place economy before all other considerations, and where they would pay their cook £25 a year without a qualm, they grudge even £20 a year for the salary of their governess. This point of view is altogether wrong. Can parents ever be sufficiently grateful to the lady who conscientiously fulfils her duty towards her charges by giving them a good foundation upon which to build their future education? Is the welfare of their children a matter of such indifference to parents that they grudge even a living wage to her to whom the children will owe so much, if her task is well done? The erroneous economy practised in this respect is responsible for the large number of uneducated young women who fill the position of "nursery governess." They are content to do indifferent work for indifferent wages; in fact, in many cases they are not much above the level of the ordinary domestic servant, being called upon to combine the duties of governess, nurse, and general help, with the result that the children are not only badly taught, but badly cared for as well.

Such a state of things should not be; it is much better to let the children remain in the care of a good nurse, taking their first lessons from their mother until they are of an age to be put in the charge of a fully qualified lady. When children are six or seven years old, if properly trained, they have been taught to do little things for themselves, and the care of them does not entail so much work and worry as that of the very little ones. There are well-educated ladies fully equipped for teaching in every way who are quite willing to take "entire charge" of children of six years old and upwards, and who would certainly not wish to be classed as "nursery" governesses. There would be more room for the many well-educated girls and women who find it so hard to get positions, if mothers would realise the fact that those in charge of the tuition of even very little children must be ladies of good education if they are to adequately fulfil the important task entrusted to them. There are also many other considerations by which parents should be guided in engaging a governess. The day of the harsh, unsympathetic disciplinarian is passed, or should be, with parents who have the welfare of their little ones at heart. A young bright girl who is fond of children is infinitely preferable to an elderly spinster whom age and care will probably have hardened, and who often has but little sympathy with or understanding of youth.

Employers cannot be too tactful in their treatment of their governess. It must be remembered that a lady so situated fills a rather anomalous position in a household, being of the family and yet not of it. They should remember that she is a lady, and treat her accordingly. Children and servants should be taught to look upon her with respect. Some people make a practice of constantly finding fault with the governess before the children. Such conduct is as harmful as it is ill-bred. The authority of the governess must be upheld in every way by the parents, who must punish the children for any serious breach of discipline that is reported to them.

Having assured themselves of the efficiency and reliability of the lady they have chosen, they must be content to place their confidence in her. But they must first take particular care of assuring themselves of her reliability. A mother can exercise gentle supervision during the first week or two of the lessons without in any way appearing to do so. In this way she will be able to form a fair judgment in regard to the character of the governess—whether she is just and has the power of self-control. If she has not these qualities, she is unfit to fill the position she occupies, however great her learning may be.

In most houses the governess will join in all the family meals with the exception of dinner, which she will take by herself in the school-room or another sitting-room. She should have her evenings free as much as possible.

Choice of a School.—When a child is of an age to begin study in real earnest, the question of the choice of a school should be entered into. The first point to be considered is whether a boarding-school or a day-school should be selected. It may as a rule be said that, in the case of girls especially, it is better to keep the child at home, if possible, until the age of fifteen has passed. The years between the age of thirteen and fifteen are usually most critical ones in respect to both the moral and physical development of boys and girls. It is during these years that they require the utmost care, both physically and morally, and by whom are they likely to be so well guided in both respects than by their mother. With boys, however, such a course is not always possible, more especially if they are to be sent to some well-known public school situated at a great distance from home, or some special college which has an age limit for admission, such as the Osborne Naval College, where no student must be over thirteen years of age at the me of entry.

BOYS' SCHOOLS

Preparatory Schools.—These undertake the preparation of boys for public schools, eight being the usual age of admission. The school selected should preferably be one where day boarders are received. It is always as well to be informed as to the conditions obtaining at these schools in regard to the eligibility to scholarships for public schools, as in some cases only those pupils who have been at least part of the time resident at the preparatory school are eligible. Special entrance scholarships to the various public schools may be won at many of these preparatory establishments. A list of well-known preparatory schools may be found in the Public Schools Year Book (Swan Sonneschein & Co., 2s. 6d.).

The Public Schools.—In its narrowest sense the term " Public School " is limited to the great foundations of Winchester College (founded 1387), Eton College (1440), Rugby School (1587), and Harrow School (1571). But the name is now popularly extended in England to such institutions as are modelled upon one or other of these historic foundations, and in some cases possess venerable traditions. They always give a first-class education, leading on to the great universities or to " the Services," and are officered by a staff composed of high university graduates; and afford a common life for the pupils and all the means for the pursuit of athletics, which has become more and more a passion with the youth of England. No country in the world has institutions comparable to the great Public Schools of Great Britain.

With the exceptions natural to even the best of human institutions, the " public school man " bears a stamp, moral, mental and physical, which is easily recognised.

These schools are usually organised in three departments: (1) *Classical*, preparing for the universities, certain professions, and higher branches of the Civil Service; (2) *Modern*, preparing for the army, engineering, and the leading positions in commercial and industrial pursuits; and (3) *Junior*, for the younger boys who have not yet decided whether to enter the Classical or the Modern side. The usual age for admission, except to the Junior School, is twelve, with fifteen as the extreme limit; pupils remain as a rule till nineteen. Application for admission has often to be made three or four years or even longer beforehand. Entrance Scholarships and Exhibitions are in some cases fairly numerous, but they are rarely won except by boys who have attended a preparatory school practically connected with some public school, or who have worked with a private tutor, whose tuition has been especially directed towards this particular object.

Grammar Schools.—Those with whom means are an important consideration cannot do better than send their boys to one of these schools, where the average fees are much lower than in the case of the public schools. In connection with most of these schools there are numerous entrance scholarships, which cover the cost of tuition and books, and perhaps part of the cost of maintenance as well, and not infrequently there are leaving scholarships to help the holders to a university or university college, or to professional education at a medical school, &c.

Before selecting such a school it is well worth inquiring what provision there is of leaving scholarships and exhibitions, and if any particular career in life is already in view for the pupil, it should be seen whether the school makes special provision for such requirements—whether, for instance, if it is intended to keep the pupil at school till eighteen or nineteen, the upper forms of the school are so arranged as to afford suitable instruction for pupils of that age. If the top form of a school has an average age of about sixteen, the school will usually lead more suitably to ordinary business in the city, clerkships in banks, or to the lower branches of the Civil Service—whereas if the average age of the scholars in the top form is eighteen, the school will probably give suitable preparation for the universities and professions, the army, or the higher branches of the Civil Service.

Private Schools.—Great care and judgment must be expended upon a selection of a school of the kind. The qualifications of the head teacher and staff in the way of university diplomas, teaching degrees, &c., should be considered; it should be seen that the number of qualified members of the staff is adequate to the variety of ages and attainments of the pupils, and that the provision of apparatus, class-rooms, laboratories, &c., is adequate. Above all, special inquiry should be made as to the results of the teaching when submitted to the test of public examination.

Of course the scope and aims of private schools vary widely; some give an excellent preparation for the universities; others for more professional studies (law, medicine, agriculture, applied science, &c.); others for the Civil Service (first or second class clerkships, the excise, customs, post office, &c.); the army or the navy, &c., and these points must be taken into consideration in selecting such a school.

University Education.—Admission to the universities cannot be obtained by students under sixteen years of age. A university training is of particular use to those who wish to follow any of the learned professions. It is somewhat costly, however, although scholarships and exhibitions are numerous, and form a solution of the expense difficulty for those who are fortunate enough to obtain them. But even though he be the proud winner of a scholarship, a young man will have to be of frugal and economical habits if he hopes to make any headway. The great difficulty lies in the fact that in the leading universities the wealthier classes predominate, and young men of limited means are apt to feel acutely their inability to be "in the swim." It requires sound common sense, total absence of pride, an ability to economise, and, above all, strict attention to work, to make a university career a success under such conditions.

A fairly well-educated candidate has an excellent chance of obtaining a scholarship. Besides university scholarships and exhibitions, most of the public schools have awards at their disposal to help their pupils to the universities, whilst public bodies such as the London County Council are increasingly devoting their funds to a system of senior scholarships, with a similar end in view. The city companies also offer exhibitions to help students at Oxford or Cambridge.

GIRLS' SCHOOLS

A mother cannot expend too much care upon the selection of a school for her daughters, both in regard to the tuition provided and to the pupils with whom she will have to associate. This most especially applies to boarding-schools, for in the case of day-schools a girl remains under home influence, which is more successful than anything else in checking the danger to be derived from unsuitable companions.

Private Schools.—As regards these, what has been said in the case of boys' schools applies with even more force to those for girls. Some of them are excellent, whilst others are unsatisfactory and even inefficient, and the tests which have been recommended in connection with the choosing of private schools for boys should always be applied. Inquiry should be made to ascertain that the school is conducted upon up-to-date methods, and that ample provision is made for the girls in the way of healthful exercise, outdoor games, and athletic training. Also that suitable food is provided. Fees at private schools vary to a great extent, but it is by no means the case that the more expensive schools are superior to the less expensive ones. It is always better, where possible, to select a school that has been recommended by friends who have sent their daughters there, and whose reliability and good judgment are beyond dispute.

High Schools.—In most of our towns of any size there are good high schools for girls which have been established by public companies, and are able to offer a good education at a moderate cost, so that, except in rural districts or the smaller towns, a parent ought to be able to procure a good education for girls at a fee of between ten and twenty guineas per annum, although of course this figure can be very easily swelled by the many "extras" which are so often necessary in the education of girls. The schools are "day" schools, but in connectoni with many of them there are licensed boarding-houses for boarders. They in most cases provide for girls an education as thorough as that received by boys in public schools of the highest class.

Convent Education.—Various Anglican and Roman Catholic Sisterhoods supply an excellent education for girls. Mostly there is no question of creed for admission, nor is religious instruction given where not desired; still the religious atmosphere must have its influence, although no bias may be intentionally imparted; on the other hand, the sisters are mostly ladies, who devote their lives to the work of education, and the example of their culture and refinement is of incalculable value. Education at most of these establishments is based upon modern methods, pupils being prepared for the university locals and other examinations.

Colleges.—There are now colleges for girls which approach the rank of university institutions. Amongst these may be mentioned Queen's College, Harley Street, London, W., which gives a course of instruction to pupils up to the age of twenty or even higher, with the intention, not of preparing for particular examinations, but of fitting pupils for their duties in society; the fees are thirty guineas a year for tuition, with extras; boarders seventy-five guineas extra.

The Cheltenham Ladies' College (established in 1854) gives special preparation for the B.A. and B.Sc. courses of London University, as well as for the Cambridge Higher Local and other advanced examinations, and has highly successful departments in Art, Music, and Gymnastics. The fees are from twelve to twenty-four guineas per annum, while there are fourteen boarding-houses whose fees vary from fifty-four to ninety-three guineas. Each year there is awarded at least one scholarship of from £25 to £45 at St. Hilda's Hall, Oxford, which was originally founded to receive the elder students of Cheltenham College.

University Education.—At Oxford and Cambridge women are examined and classed, but degrees are not yet granted them. At the other universities women are admitted to degrees on the same terms as men almost without exception: London University led the way in 1878; the Scotch Universities followed suit in 1892; and Durham in 1895. Trinity College, Dublin, also has admitted women on the same terms as men. The younger universities have throughout their existence received women; and the University of Wales admits them to a share in the management of the university, exactly as it does men. In most cases special provision has been made for the residence of women students, while usually they have shared the tuition offered to the men (though sometimes they have their own lectures, as at Cambridge and Glasgow).

There are four halls of residence for women students at Oxford, *i.e.* Lady Margaret Hall, Somerville College, St. Hugh's Hall and St.

Hilda's Hall. At Cambridge there are two residential colleges, *i.e.* Girton and Newnham. Scholarships and exhibitions are offered each year in connection with these colleges.

In connection with the London University the "Schools of the University" for women are Bedford College, the Royal Holloway College, and Westfield College.

Coming out of a Daughter.—It is a great event in the life of a girl when she puts up her hair for the first time and goes into long frocks; for when she does this she has left her childhood for ever behind her. In most families eighteen is the accepted age for a girl's introduction into society—in some cases seventeen years represents the momentous epoch. The coming out of a daughter is usually signalised by a dance given by her parents. In higher social circles it is also marked by her presentation at Court (see p. 358).

Very often, however, her *début* is made at a house other than that of her parents, in which case she should always be under the chaperonage of her mother or some other relation. The conventional dress for the *débutante* is nearly always white, though within the last two years colours of the lighter and more delicate shades have been worn upon this occasion. Tradition, however, dies hard, and white is still and ever will be first favourite in this respect. The dance toilette with low neck and short sleeves is of course *de rigueur*.

Before her daughter's coming out a mother should be careful to accustom her to the ways and manners of society. She should allow her always to be present at small afternoon parties and At Homes, and all other functions at which it is permissible for a girl who is not yet out to attend. Particular care should be taken to see that she is quite *au fait* in the dances of the season. It must be remembered that a graceful dancer is an acquisition to any ball-room, whereas the girl who is *gauche* in any way will prove a severe trial to her partner.

The first dance of a *débutante* will be the forerunner of invitations to many others. It is needless to caution a mother that she should exercise discretion in allowing acceptance of all of these. In the first place only invitations from people of whom the parents approve in every way should be accepted, and in the second place no girl should be allowed to launch at once into too great a whirligig of parties, balls and dances. This kind of thing is apt to be overdone during a girl's first season, and although youth is proverbially energetic, yet there are some girls who would be unequal to a strain of this kind. The wise mother will not let her pride in her daughter's success surmount the important consideration of care for her health, and will exercise a judicious cutting of the party list where necessary. (See also Etiquette of Balls and Dances.)

CHILDRÉN'S CLOTHING

As compared with the fashioning of her own garments, the cutting out and making of children's clothes presents a comparatively easy task for the home worker.

A clever needlewoman can with good patterns save many a penny spent on her children's clothing. Material is cheap to buy; it is the making that costs so much. Very often, too, larger garments, provided the material is good and suitable, can be utilised to make frocks and coats for the little ones.

Daintiness and simplicity are the chief qualities which should characterise their clothing wherever possible. The needlework may be of the finest, the materials of the best, but any extreme elaboration in trimming and ornamentation should be avoided. Simplicity pertains to childhood, and in no respect does this simplicity shine to greater advantage than in the matter of dress. The unfortunate befrilled and beflounced little mites who are continually dressed up in silks and finery quite unsuitable for their years and are always "on show," as it were, miss much of the happiness of childhood. They are not allowed to romp and play like other children for fear of spoiling their fine clothes. Soon they become self-conscious, sometimes even affected, and as a result develop into miniature little men and women of the world before they enter into their teens.

Naturalness and simplicity are the great charms of childhood, and a mother is a very poor friend to her child if, however fond and loving her motives, she gives rein to her maternal pride by continually decking the little one out in extravagant clothes, thus installing into the child's mind an abnormal sense of the importance of dress and finery.

Let the little one's clothes be always spotlessly clean, neat and well-fitting, but remember that the more simply a child is dressed the better she will look, whilst an over-dressed child will invariably lay her parents open to the charge of vulgarity.

Children's clothing must also be of a kind that will protect them from cold or heat. A wise mother will see that flannel or wool in some form or other is worn next the skin. If woollen combinations were worn all the year round there would be much less chance of the little ones catching cold. The texture of the garment may of course be altered to suit the season of the year, a thinner make of wool being worn in summer than in winter.

It is also important that the clothing should be large enough to permit of growth; there must be no tightness nor restriction, and at the same time the garments must not be too large and bulky. This is sometimes difficult with growing children; they have no sooner been provided with a set of clothes than they seem to have outgrown them. For this reason it is a mistake to provide large numbers of anything; rather give just enough to allow for the necessary changing and washing, and let the child give them constant wear. This would no doubt mean frequent renewals, but it will be renewals in small quantities, and this is much to be preferred to having to alter garments which have scarcely been worn, or perhaps discard them altogether.

Another mistake made in the dressing of children is to give them too many different garments and thus burden their little bodies and hamper their movements. Rather give a few and see that the material is of the right warmth, than pile on a number of unnecessary articles of clothing.

Three or four complete coverings ought to be quite enough for both girls and boys. With little boys, for instance, it is a mistake to continue the petticoat stage, and at eighteen months,

Boy's Tunic.

if they have reached the running-about stage, the long tunic or smock with the little drawers or knickers below might well be started. They can be made in serge, wincey, delaine, or any good washing material.

Boy's Blouse.—When the little boy is older a blouse may take the place of the smock. This is a garment which can very easily be made by the home worker. Almost any material can be used for this—serge, cloth, linen, print, drill, velvet, or silk. Short trousers would complete the costume, and as a rule these are best made in the same material as the blouse, except in the case of white silk blouses, which can be very well worn with navy blue knickers.

Sleeping Suit.—These should be started with little boys as soon as good habits have been formed. In fact, they are very often used for little girls as well—especially when they are inclined to kick off the bed-clothes at night. If a good pattern is obtained, it is very simple to make. Viyella, wincey, or fine shirting are the most suitable materials.

Child's Seaside Overall.—This is one of the most useful garments designed for the use of the tiny tots during recent years. It is worn by the little ones over their dresses when at play, and forming, as it does, a combination of overdress and loose knickers, it effectually protects the

Seaside Overall.

frock underneath from all dust and dirt. For babies who have reached the "crawling about the floor" stage it is an ideal garment. Galatea, gingham, and holland are suitable materials for the making of these overalls.

The Yoke Frock.—Perhaps there is nothing more serviceable for the little girl of from two to ten years than the simple yoke frock. This usually consists of two breadths of material gathered into a yoke, and as with the exception of the yoke no fitting is required, a frock of this kind is an extremely simple one to make.

It is always as well to cut the skirt of the frock fairly long, in the first instance, making a number of hand-sewn tucks above the hem. This can be let down by degrees as the child grows, and a frock of this kind has been known to last for years. (For Making Tucks, see p. 394.)

Frocks of a more dressy nature for party and best wear may be made from a simple yoke dress pattern. If instead of gathering, the skirt is arranged back and front in a series of vertical tucks from the yoke to the waist, a pretty little empire frock can be made. For party wear the sleeves can be made short and lace insertion applied in different designs on the yoke and at the hem, whilst a pretty sash can be tied round the waist. In fine white cambric or washing silk a frock of this kind can be made to look very dainty indeed and fit for any dressy occasion. For a little girl of six, two yards of material forty-four inches wide will be required.

Embroidery flouncing is much used in the making of lingerie dresses for the tiny tots.

Yoke frocks made of flouncing should be cut more in the empire style, that is to say, the entire armhole should be cut in the yoke, the flouncing hanging straight from it without the usual slightly curved piece under the arm.

The Djibbah.—This is an admirable style of garment for a little girl, and it is easily cut out and put together, as the sleeves are made in one with the rest of the garment and there is only one seam under the arm. It is also very comfortable to wear, as it slips over the head and there is no trouble with buttons or other fastenings.

It can be made useful for different purposes; either it may be worn over a frock as a simple overall, or, in summer, with a little muslin or silk top, it will serve as a frock by itself. The little tops can very often be made from a silk

Djibbah.

or muslin dress which has become too short. The dress should be cut off at the waist and fastened on with a draw-string.

Illustration shows a djibbah designed by Mrs. Drew, 32 Comely Bank, Edinburgh, who makes a speciality of children's clothing of an artistic character.

Letting in Insertion.—Open-work insertion is a favourite ornamentation for the best lingerie frocks for the little ones; the insertion should be added after the frock has been made up, and evenly laid on as required. To make it open-work after it has been basted on, take a pair of scissors and cut the back of the material upon which the insertion has been laid, being careful not to cut the latter; turn back the edges and hem neatly.

Hem-stitching Frocks by Machine.—Hem-stitching makes a very dainty finish to little lingerie frocks, but it is not every mother who has the time to do this fine work by hand. Very effective imitation hem-stitching can be done, however, by machine in this manner:—After the hem has been turned over, cut it away from the rest of the skirt about a quarter of an inch above the place where the stitching of the hem would come. Then fold up enough blotting-paper or any other kind of soft paper to the thickness of one-eighth of an inch, and insert it between the edges of the piece cut off and the lower edge of the skirt from which it has been cut, which are placed one on the top of the other as in sewing a seam, and having loosened the tension of the machine, make a quarter-inch seam, sewing both through the material and the paper. When the seam is finished, cut the paper carefully close to the stitches and pull it out. The upper edge is folded back, the hem edge folded over, and the hem is stitched with a row of fine machine stitching close to the edge. Another row of fine stitching should be made over the edge of the upper part.

Shoes and Stockings.—The clothing of children's feet and legs is a very important matter. Woollen stockings are the best for all ordinary occasions, and the texture may vary in thickness according to the season of the year. They must fit well, because if too tight they will cramp the foot, and if too loose they will be liable to cause blisters. The practice of putting short stockings or socks on children is a very risky one, and the cause of many a chill and serious illness. It is very necessary to keep the legs warm, and only in warm weather is it permissible to leave them bare.

Properly-fitting boots are also most essential. It must be remembered that in the child the bones consist chiefly of gristle, and are easily put out of shape if under pressure of any kind. It is always better when it can be managed to have the boots made to order, but if bought ready made the greatest care must be taken with the fitting. They must be neither too large nor too small, the sole ought to be broad enough for the expansion of the toes, the heels low and the toes nicely rounded. Lacing boots are as a rule better than those that button. If the boot is badly shaped it is not only the foot that suffers, but the leg and spine as well. Sandals have been much worn of late years, but those are only suitable for summer wear.

(For Children's Millinery, see p. 394.)

HOLIDAYS AND TRAVEL

THERE was a time when English people were content to spend their holidays at home, never stirring beyond the limits of their own native town or village. To-day things have changed, and the annual migration to the country, seaside, or continent is now a typical feature of English family life. The progress made in the emancipation of womanhood is also typified by the number of women and girls who travel alone. It is for the use of these women, and for mothers who have a great deal of the worry and care attendant upon the organisation of their children's holidays, that the hints given in this chapter are primarily intended.

THE ANNUAL HOLIDAY

The annual trip to the country or seaside is the object of much saving and contriving and endless preparation on the part of both pater and materfamilias, as well as much eager anticipation upon the part of the little ones, yet how seldom does it turn out to be a complete success.

To begin with, going away with the children will not afford materfamilias any appreciable respite from her daily round of domestic duties; very often indeed it will mean added work and anxiety. Paterfamilias also is apt to be worried with innumerable little trivialities consequent upon the care and management of a young family, which takes away a great deal from the enjoyment to be derived from a respite, however brief, from the daily business routine.

The conclusion to be arrived at is obvious. Since it can never be a complete holiday for parents to be always with their children, sometime or other during the year they would do well to have a short holiday to themselves, away from their family. If no more than a week can be managed for this, at any rate let this week be altogether free from all domestic cares of any kind. They should never attempt to make a holiday for themselves out of the children's holidays, for they will be doomed to disappointment. Parents may derive pleasure and happiness from the enjoyment of their little ones, but the very planning of that enjoyment will prevent them from having any real rest. They should make up their minds, therefore, to keep their own holidays entirely distinct from those of the children if they are to derive any real benefit therefrom. The advisability of the annual holiday *à deux* for parents has been a great deal discussed in the columns of our leading newspapers, many of which have conducted a lengthy correspondence upon the subject. The result has always been a concensus of opinion in its favour. Furthermore, it has also been advocated that pater and materfamilias should spend a portion of their holidays apart from each other as well as apart from the children—the wife going to her friends or relations, the husband spending it in the pursuit of a favourite pastime, such as shooting, fishing, golf, &c. There is much to be said in favour of this arrangement.

When, for instance, a man's ideal holiday consists of either a long cross-country walking tour, clad in a serviceable suit of tweeds and with no other luggage than a knapsack on his back—or else when he thinks nothing is more enjoyable than to adopt a fisherman's life for the time being, going out in a sailing boat with a fishing fleet—in short, when his sole idea of enjoyment is to "rough" it in every way possible, it stands to reason that a woman would be out of place in a holiday of the kind. The sensible materfamilias will realise this, and will allow her husband to spend at least a week in his own sweet way. Having done this he will enter with much more zest into the scheme for the rest of the holidays.

It has been suggested that a four weeks' holiday should be divided up as follows —

One week to be spent by husband and wife separately and apart from their children.

One week to be spent by husband and wife together.

Two weeks to be spent with the children.

During the fortnight that the parents are away, the children might be sent to a farm-house in the country in the charge of a governess or nurse.

This plan is not, however, always feasible, and in families where the children go to a boarding-school the parents will generally find it advisable to take their holiday during term time.

In other cases people have not the means to enable them to take separate holidays, the family vacation of two or three weeks being the utmost they can afford. In these circumstances more care than ever must be taken in planning out the holidays that there may be a time of enjoyment for parents as well as for the children. If the former make up their minds to spare themselves as much worry as possible by careful organisation and arrangement, and to enter wholeheartedly into the amusement of their little ones, much will be done to achieve this desirable end.

THE CHILDREN'S HOLIDAYS

In planning the holidays for the family careful calculation must be made of the money that can be spent, allowing ample margin for the hundred and one little odd expenses that are apt to crop up when one is away from home. Nothing mars enjoyment more than the knowledge that one has miscalculated expenses, and that many pleasant little excursions have to be denied and other economies practised as a result.

Great care should be taken in the selection of both locality and rooms. Where there are children, if the seaside is chosen, preference should be given not to a "show" place, where it seems to be the sole aim of the visitors to change their toilettes several times a day and be always on parade, but to a place where there is a vast expanse of sandy beach, where the little ones can dig and build sand castles to their heart's content. Places on the east coast of England are generally bracing, whilst south-coast resorts are warmer and more relaxing, and this fact should be borne in mind, as very bracing air agrees with most people, but is too strong for some, who are better in a more relaxing atmosphere.

It is better as a rule to take a good suite of rooms in preference to a furnished house. In the latter case the housewife will have more than the usual worries of house-management, for she will have the care and worry of looking after other people's furniture with the responsibility for breakages, a number of which invariably occur whatever precautions are taken; and when the inventory is checked at the expiration of her tenancy, she may find that she has quite a lot to pay in this respect.

In some cases, however, the family of little ones is so large that it is not always possible to obtain suitable apartments for their accommodation. In these circumstances it will become necessary to take a furnished house. Care should be taken that the latter is as compact as possible in every way, so that housework is reduced to a minimum. It will be necessary in the case of taking a house to take one's servants also. It might be possible to allow each of these, however, a short holiday in turn, if care is taken in selecting a house that is easily worked. Sometimes an exchange of houses may be arranged.

In taking a house it is as well to avoid one with very old furniture and fitted carpets, as a house of this kind will be very difficult to keep clean. In the case of fitted carpets, it should be insisted that these are lifted and well beaten and cleaned, and the floors thoroughly well scrubbed before taking up the tenancy. (Law in regard to Furnished Houses, p. 381.)

In selecting rooms it should be ascertained that they are clean, airy, light, and well ventilated. Many people who go to the seaside are apt to sacrifice one or the other of these important essentials to health and comfort for the sake of having their windows looking on to the sea front. This is a mistake: where large and comfortable rooms may be had facing the sea, well and good, but everything should not be made subservient to a sea view. Health and comfort must be considered. Lodging-house keepers as a general rule trade upon the idiosyncrasy of holiday-makers to have rooms on the front at all costs, by asking exorbitant prices for the smallest apartments which boast so much as a narrow side-window looking on to the sea.

If better rooms can be found in a road leading to but not actually on the front, preference should be given to them. Proximity to the beach is of course an important consideration where there are little ones, and if not actually on the front, the rooms should be chosen as near to it as possible.

In the better-known and more fashionable seaside resorts in England £1, 1s. a room per week represents the average charge for August; in some places this is the figure for both July and August, and in others for August and September in accordance with the months constituting the "season" at each individual resort.

Boarding-houses are quite unsuitable for children. In the first place, their presence is often in a measure resented by the other guests; in the second place, the fare is not always suited to juvenile needs, and where any exception to the general rule is made in their favour, the charges for extras mount up to a remarkable degree.

When the holidays must of necessity take place during the busy season, it is essential to engage the rooms some time beforehand. A visit of inspection should always be made and a clear understanding as to terms arrived at. Be careful to find out what items will fall under the very elastic term of "extras," which is often made to apply to a great many other items in addition to the usual light, &c. It is better, indeed, to make an arrangement for all charges to be "inclusive," paying a little more if necessary.

The Country.—A few weeks spent at a farm-house in some pretty country place forms an ideal holiday for the children. Here they can roam about in the fields and woods at will—the life on a farm is full of interest to them. They love to help to feed chickens and pigs and other denizens of the farmyard, and great is the interest they take in the daily round of the farmer's work. Then what pleasant drives may be had through country lanes in the pony cart or trap, which is usually to be hired at almost every large farm at a very moderate figure; and what splendid picnics may be organised with very little trouble in the woods and meadows.

Farm-house apartments must be taken beforehand, as they are very quickly snapped up during the summer months. When you have settled upon one or two likely districts, it is a good plan to write to the postmaster of the village, asking him to recommend one or two good farmhouses where apartments are let. Then upon the first available day a visit of inspection should be made. Be careful first of all to see that the sanitary arrangements are good and up to date. In many country places, for instance, it will be found that the lavatory is in the garden. This is an obvious drawback, more especially in case of illness, and careful inquiry should be made in regard to this before taking the rooms. However pretty and picturesque these may be with their old-time ingle-nooks and chimney-pieces, if the sanitary arrangements are not perfect they are best avoided.

There are many advantages which a holiday at a farm-house possesses over one at the seaside. In the first place, rooms are much cheaper, and the food is usually good. Very often no more than one or two families at most will be taken, and the farmer's wife will be willing to do the catering as well as provide lodging at a moderate inclusive sum per head, consulting always the tastes of the family and the special needs of the children. Not having a large number of guests to cater for as in boarding-houses, the guests are not restricted to the set menus that form the order of the day at the latter-named establishments.

Dinner will usually be in the middle of the day unless a late meal is especially desired, and the food will be plain, but pure and wholesome and usually well cooked. Careful inquiries in regard to the quality of the cooking should be made before hiring the rooms. The reputation of a bad cook travels fast, and if the postmaster is not *au fait* in regard to the qualifications of the farmer's wife in this respect, it will be found that the village shopkeepers will be only too ready to enlighten the visitors and to recommend some other place, as it is to their interest visitors should make as long a stay as possible and return again the next year, and this they certainly will not do if their surroundings are either uncomfortable or uncongenial. From the point of view of economy a holiday at a farmhouse for the children is much to be recommended, as, apart from the lower charges for board and lodging, incidental expenses are also very much less.

General Hints.—The sole secret of making the children's holiday a success is to see that they have plenty of occupation. The nature of this must of course vary with the place where the holiday is spent. The amusements to be had in the country naturally differ considerably from those at the seaside. From the point of view of occupation and amusement, more varied interests as a rule will be found by the sea. Bathing, paddling, boating are all sources of great delight to the children, and, as a rule, the entire mornings may be spent on the beach, part of the time being occupied in bathing or paddling. In regard to the last-named amusement so dear to the little ones, a mother should be careful to see that they wear shady hats when paddling and that their heads are not exposed to the pitiless rays of the sun during the warmest part of the day. The little legs and feet should also be well dried with a rough towel when the children come out of the water. It is a most reprehensible habit to allow them to run about with wet feet and legs to be dried up by the sun for the mere sake of getting sun-burnt.

The children should be encouraged in following pet hobbies such as shell and seaweed collecting, photography, &c., and the parents should show a sympathetic interest in these and be as helpful as possible in their suggestions. They may be allowed to have a run on the sands before breakfast, but bathing should not be indulged in before the early morning meal. They should never be allowed to remain more than from five to ten minutes in the water. Dinner should always be in the middle of the day, and half-an-hour's rest should be taken after this midday meal. Then the little ones will be ready for a walk, a drive, or any little excursion that may have been planned. For wet afternoons and evenings, good games should be organised in which both grown-ups and little ones take part.

If the children are kept thoroughly occupied in this manner during the whole of the vacation, the time will pass pleasantly and happily—if not, the holidays are apt to drag painfully for both children and parents. It must be remembered also that in this variable climate of ours wet weather during the holidays is a factor which has constantly to be reckoned with, hence it behoves parents to go to the seaside prepared for eventualities of the kind, planning out a complete scheme of amusement for the wet as well as for the fine days.

THE WOMAN WORKER'S HOLIDAY

Those who are working all the year round, whether it be at teaching, in an office, or in any other of the callings now open to women, will require to get the utmost out of the short respite afforded by the holidays from the routine of their workaday life. The holidays should be looked upon by them as a real rest and period of recuperation, during which they can lay in a fresh store of health and strength for their next year of work.

One word of warning in this respect. People who habitually lead sedentary lives must not rush all at once to the opposite extreme during vacation time. Walking fifteen to twenty miles a day, for instance, when one is unaccustomed to such exercise, can only mean a heavy strain upon the strength and do more harm than good. Rushing about from one place to another in the effort to cram all the sightseeing possible into a week or two weeks is also harmful. It is wiser to take things easily at first, taking the first two days to acclimatise oneself to one's surroundings, and increasing gradually the measure of exercise taken as the time goes on. The woman who has only a week or a fortnight's holiday will find it harder to keep to this rule than the woman who has from a month to six weeks, but she should keep to it as far as possible.

When a tour through any part of the country is arranged it should be done by easy stages, overtiring of any kind being avoided. Women nowadays show a tendency to rush away to crowded resorts where prices are high, and neglect the many beautiful little spots with which our country abounds, notably in Devon, Cornwall, and Wales, where it is possible to spend the vacation in the pleasantest manner with the minimum amount of outlay. The one thing that deters people from exploring regions to them unknown lies in the fact that their ignorance of the place involves also ignorance of the nature of accommodation to be found there in the way of board and lodging, and as both good housing and wholesome food are indispensable in ensuring the success of a holiday, they prefer returning year after year to the same spot than to embark as it were upon a voyage of discovery. For those so situated, the booklet "Holiday Resorts," published by the Teachers' Guild of Great Britain and Ireland, will be found very useful. It contains a long list of recommended addresses throughout the United Kingdom and abroad, which has been specially compiled for the use of teachers on their holidays.

Boarding-Houses.—In England the "pension" or boarding-house system has greatly developed during recent years. Boarding-house life is both suitable and enjoyable if proper care is employed in the judicious selection of an establishment. As a general rule, it is inadvisable to take rooms in a house that has not been recommended by some friend, although some people are remarkably quick at forming judgment upon inspection as to whether a particular place will suit them or not. It must be remembered that at most frequented resorts during the busy season it will be practically impossible to engage a room at a boarding-house for a day to see if it will suit; it will be necessary to take it for a week at least, and a week of discomfort will prove so much time of the holiday practically wasted for all the good it will do. Another thing to bear in mind is—do not go to a fashionable seaside resort in August under the impression that you will get good board and a comfortable room at 30s. a week. August is essentially a month of inflated prices, when boarding-house keepers reap their harvest. All accommodation offered under two guineas a week will as a rule turn out to be poor, the latter sum representing the minimum charge during the season of all reliable establishments. Of course, this does not apply to the less fashionable resorts or places which do not boast of piers, bands, concerts, and the other manifold attractions of the up-to-date seaside towns, but in even the smaller seaside resorts prices in August are higher than at any other time.

THE COUNTRY COTTAGE

In several of our country villages pretty little cottages may be found in many cases at as low rentals as £12 a year. With many the country cottage has formed the solution of the holiday problem, not only for the summer vacation, but for week-ends throughout the year. A little place of the kind is kept up at very little expense. A woman or a man and wife can often be found to look after it and keep it in order in return for having the use of it rent free when the owners are not in occupation. The furniture required is of the simplest and need represent very little outlay. Many people who have tried the experiment claim that, in spite of money spent in rent, upkeep, &c., the possession of a cottage of this kind enables them to have much longer and more frequent holidays and at a lower cost than in any other circumstances.

THE HOLIDAY ABROAD

In these days of facilities for cheap and easy travel and of tourist agents who conduct carefully-planned-out tours abroad at a minimum of expense, the proportion of English people who spend their annual holiday upon the continent is decidedly on the increase. The advantages of such a holiday are manifold. To begin with, the average English woman who never stirs beyond the limits of her own native shores is apt to become too insular and narrow-minded in her ideas. There is nothing that has a more educating effect than travelling in foreign countries and mixing with people of other nationalities, nor is there anything more calculated to broaden our outlook upon things.

The continental holiday nowadays is even within reach of the business woman who earns no more than 30s. to £2 a week salary. What more pleasant change can she derive than by spending a week or a fortnight in Belgium, the most accessible country for people of limited means. It will cost her little more than a holiday spent at a seaside resort at home, where £2, 2s. is the minimum season charge for board and lodging, to say nothing of railway fares and other incidental expenses.

Unfortunately there are many English women who never show to advantage when travelling in other countries. They fail to adapt themselves to their surroundings, not being able to realise the fact that, though many of the customs of the foreigners are different from ours, yet they have a perfect right to practise them in their own country, and that it is the stranger who must conform with the customs of the country in which she is a visitor. The truth of the saying "In Rome one must do as Romans do" has yet to be realised by many an English woman who, when travelling, has the knack of leaving her good manners behind her. In this respect she does not err in so marked a manner as Englishmen abroad, whose aggressive personality, loud voice and manner, and still louder dress were at one time so much held up to ridicule by the French caricaturist. It must be admitted, however, that this type of John Bull has become greatly modified during recent years, though a want of adaptability to their surroundings is still to be noted amongst a large proportion of English tourists.

The traveller should begin by reconciling herself to the fact that it is impossible for her to have everything as she has it at home, and she must make up her mind to conform for the time being with other tastes and other methods of living. The cooking at foreign hotels and pensions, for instance, will seem strange at first; but though it is different from what she has been used to, it is nearly always very good, and she should not spoil her pleasure and that of others by grumbling at it and wishing for some English dish not on the menu. A gentlewoman, it is true, would not be likely to err in this respect, and a gentlewoman at home will almost invariably be a gentlewoman abroad, but there is no denying the fact that many women show a peculiar aggressiveness and intolerance when travelling which they rarely display when at home. Many women also when out of their own country seem to develop an eccentricity in dress as marked as it is unusual, for at home their toilettes will be irreproachable on all occasions. Here, again, is an anomaly which, however inexplicable, is nevertheless existent, there being a number of sinners in this respect.

A woman should always bear in mind that a large number of foreigners never have an opportunity of visiting our mother country, hence the sole idea they have in regard to the character and appearance of English people must necessarily be gathered from their observation of the manners and habits of the English tourists and travellers they occasionally come across; and it stands to reason if English travellers are constantly offending against good manners and good taste, the impression formed of the English in general will be a very erroneous one. Travellers should always bear this fact in mind, and by being as circumspect in their behaviour and—as far as the exigencies of travelling allow—as careful in their dress as when at home, they can do much to remove the bad impression made by the agressive type of Britisher who so often frequents the continent, and does his best to earn for English people generally an unmerited measure of disapprobation.

Dress.—The traveller should endeavour to be neat and well groomed on all occasions. For an itinerary tour her dress will have to be strictly limited to what is most useful. A neat serge or tweed coat-and-skirt costume for travelling is the first essential. With this a becoming small hat and a trim blouse should be worn. Boots should be clean and well polished and gloves neat and tidy. Plenty of lingerie blouses, an extra pair of boots, a pair of indoor shoes, the necessary underlinen and a dressing-gown should be packed away in the suit-case, and for evenings at the hotel or pension one of those dainty little crêpe de chine or voile princess dresses which would seem to have been designed mainly with the needs of the traveller in view, so little room do they take up. A dress of this kind may be rolled up tightly without becoming creased in any way if care is taken first to adjust the folds. The boots should have good thick soles, as there is nothing more tiring than constant walking about in thin shoes. Strong comfortable boots are especially essential for walking tours, and, needless to say, short skirts should be worn.

When making a stay at a fashionable resort, such as Ostend or Trouville, one will require to be smartly dressed, and an ample supply of frocks for all occasions will be necessary.

It is always advisable when travelling abroad to be prepared for great differences of temperature within a comparatively small area. A change of winter underclothing and a warm coat are often very welcome even during the summer months.

Combined Coupon Tickets.—By means of the "Rundreise" or combined ticket system, the tourist may effect a reduction of from 20 to 30 per cent. on her fares. This system prevails in Belgium, Holland, Germany, Austria, the Balkan States, Turkey, Switzerland, Denmark, Norway, Sweden, France, Italy, and Sicily, and full particulars in regard to it may be obtained from any of Messrs. Cook's offices, or from the offices of the Belgian State Railways, 53 Gracechurch Street, London, E.C. These tickets give the passenger the right to stop not only at the principal stations on many lines of the countries through which she is travelling, but at any out-of-the-way place. In the latter case it is usually necessary to get the coupon for that section stamped by the stationmaster immediately after leaving the train. In Switzerland and Germany, however, the passenger is allowed to break the journey at any place without this formality. She has perfect freedom in planning out her own itinerary, subject to certain regulations in regard to time and distances. Only hand luggage is allowed free to travellers using Rundreise tickets.

Season Tickets available for five and fifteen days, which enable the holder to travel as often as she likes all over Belgium in every direction on all the Belgian railway lines (2890 miles in extent) are issued in England at the Belgian Mail Packet Booking Office, 53 Gracechurch Street, 72 Regent Street, London, and at all Belgian stations at 11·75 francs (9s. 5d.=$2·35) 3rd class, 20·50 francs (16s. 5d.=$4·10) 2nd class; 30·75 francs (24s. 7d.=$6·15) 1st class, compartment reserved or saloon cars.

An unmounted photograph of the holder, measuring one and a half inches square, must be supplied to be affixed to the ticket. About a quarter of an hour's notice should be given to obtain the season tickets.

Similar season tickets available fifteen days are issued at double the above prices.

In Switzerland season tickets are issued which are available over most of the principal railways; they do not, however, include all the mountain railways, although in some cases reductions are allowed on the latter to holders of these tickets. They may be obtained in London from the General Agent of the Swiss Federal Railways, 11B Regent Street, from the L.B. & S.C. Railway Continental Traffic Manager's Office, London Bridge, and the Great Eastern Railway Continental Traffic Manager's Office, Liverpool Street. The fare for fifteen days is £3, 8s. 1st class, £2, 8s. 2nd class, and £1, 16s. 3rd class. The Swiss Federal Railways also give a list of local diligence rates over the passes, and of addresses of the best hotels.

Hotels and Pensions.—It is always better to go to an hotel or pension which has been recommended by friends upon whose judgment you may rely. Failing this the traveller cannot do better than expend a shilling upon the little book "Holiday Resorts," already mentioned. This contains extensive lists of recommended addresses of good hotels and pensions with moderate tariffs in most places abroad, and should therefore be a great help to the woman whose expenses must be carefully weighed and considered.

In the season at fashionable resorts both hotels and pensions are subject to inflated prices, the latter being always cheaper than the former. It is always better to engage rooms beforehand, and in much frequented places it is as well to order by wire the day before, prepaying for a reply as to whether the rooms have been reserved.

When making a stay of a week or more at an hotel an arrangement for inclusive "pension" terms should be made if possible. In most Swiss hotels "pension" terms can be arranged for three or four days. When not on "pension terms," ask for the bill every few days and carefully check it. It is always better, if leaving in the morning, to ask for the bill the eve of your departure, so that you have time to see if the charges are correct. Tips, as a general rule, should not amount to more than 10 per cent. of the bill for a week's stay at an hotel, being distributed amongst the chambermaid, concierge, head waiter, boots, and any one who renders special service. For a long visit the percentage would of course be considerably lower. Not less than one franc to each servant is given for a short stay.

Tips after long Sea Voyages.—For tips after long sea voyages, gold for the table steward and the stewardess is *de rigueur*. After a voyage to America or Canada, 10s. at least should be given to each. For very long voyages, as to Australia, double the amount should be given. Smaller tips are given to any other of the servants on board who render special service.

General Hints.—Travellers on the continent should have at least a slight practical knowledge of the language of the country which they visit, for although English is spoken and understood at the chief hotels and pensions and the larger shops of the principal towns and resorts on the continent, porters and cabdrivers show a decided inclination at times to double their fares for the benefit of those who show that they are unable either to understand what is said to them or make themselves understood. Baedeker's manual of conversation will be found useful in assisting the traveller to at least make her wants known in an intelligible manner. Failing this, she should have some other handy little guide to conversation to which she can refer. The Baedeker Guide Books to travelling on the continent are also of inestimable use to the traveller who is planning out her own tour. It is always better, however, when going abroad for the first time, if totally ignorant of foreign languages and if unaccompanied by an experienced traveller, to join one of the tours conducted by Cook's or any other tourist agency Not only are the whole tours carefully organised and planned out by experts, the tourist being saved worry of any kind, but they are conducted at the minimum of expense, the charges including board and lodging as well as fare. Particulars of tours can be obtained from any of Messrs. Cook's offices, and from Dr. Henry S. Lunn, 5 Endsleigh Gardens, London, N.W., Messrs. Dean & Dawson, 17 St. Paul's Churchyard, London, E.C., and other tourist agents. (For Luggage Abroad, see p. 505.)

Money.—The traveller abroad should make herself acquainted with the coinage of the country which she is visiting. English money

can be usually changed by the purser on the steamer by which she is crossing. It is not advisable, however, to change too much money, because in most places English gold is readily accepted, the change (if any) being given in the foreign currency. It is only with the small coin that difficulty will be experienced. The woman, for instance, who is taking a short trip in France or Belgium with £10 for expenses will only require to change £1 of this into small French money for the needs of the journey, tips to porters, cab fares, &c. For the rest she can obtain change as she requires it at either her hotel or pension or at any shop where she wishes to effect a purchase. She should be careful to ascertain, however, that the change is correct. The change in French money for £1, for instance, would be 25 and not 20 francs, and sometimes advantage is taken of the ignorant in this respect (see Foreign Money Rates). For wealthy people who allow themselves unlimited money during their holidays, the Circular Note System is of the utmost convenience (see p. 368).

Foreign Travel as an Educator.—Besides the general broadening of the mental horizon, foreign travel offers a pleasant and rapid method of acquiring a knowledge of other tongues, especially if a lengthened stay can be made. This is now so generally recognised by parents that many send their children abroad for the latter years of school life. Within the last few years large numbers of boys and girls have been sent to families abroad, their parents in England receiving in exchange a child to be taught English. This custom has become so popular that an agency has been opened in Paris to negotiate suitable exchanges. All the necessary information in regard to this may be obtained from Monsieur Toni Matthieu, Echange Internationale, 36 Boulevard Majenta, Paris.

In addition to this, travelling scholarships are offered by various educational bodies which entitle the holder to a sum of money to be spent on a visit abroad. The advantages of their studying a foreign language are obvious. Not only does this system offer opportunities for acquiring a good accent and ease of expression, but the more intimate and personal knowledge gained by admission into a cultured house open to the student the doors of acquaintance with the true spirit of the language and its literature.

Should the parents not be able to take their children, or should no suitable escort be found, they may safely be sent alone if notice is given to one of the societies formed for helping and protecting young travellers. These societies have a very complete organisation throughout Europe, and can arrange for the traveller to be met at the different points and placed in the right train to continue her journey, met at the final destination, and seen into safe hands. The service is generally rendered gratuitously, and is absolutely without distinction of class, creed or nationality. Among such societies may be mentioned the pioneer of the movement, *Les Amies de la Jeune Fille*. Similar work is also done by the Catholic International Association for the Protection of Girls, the "Station Work" department of the National Vigilance Association and Guild of Service for Women, and the Jewish Association of Protection. All these work in harmony, and particulars can be obtained on application to The Secretary, National Vigilance Association, St. Mary's Chambers, 161A Strand, London.

LUGGAGE

What luggage to take and what not to take always forms a vexed question with the holiday-maker. The great maxim to be observed is to take only as much as is absolutely necessary, but individual needs vary so largely that this maxim is capable of a somewhat elastic interpretation. We often read in the papers of some enterprising American lady who has travelled round the world with no more extensive wardrobe than the tweed dress she was wearing and a small handbag containing linen and toilet accessories. Though we may wonder at and even admire her enterprise, few of us would be tempted to go and do likewise. An English woman when travelling always likes to feel fresh and natty, and this cannot be accomplished unless she has garments with her suitable for all occasions.

It is in the quality of her luggage more often than in its quantity that a woman is apt to err. Many will travel with a trunk so heavy and unwieldy as to be a positive nuisance, and not all the grumbling of porters and cabmen, nor the damage done to walls in carrying the box up and down stairs, will make them see the error of their ways. Then, again, some women are never happy unless, in addition to their ordinary luggage, they are encumbered with a number of cardboard hat-boxes, paper parcels, string bags, and other paraphernalia, some portion or other of which they invariably manage to lose.

With proper luggage there is no need to put up with the nuisance of worrying about the safety of innumerable small packages. Modern luggage is specially constructed with regard to convenience, and the old-fashioned trunk which, in spite of its unwieldiness, was remarkable for its lack of efficient accommodation for clothes and hats, is happily a thing of the past.

The up-to-date trunk is light and compact. In the better kinds a number of adjustable little compartments are to be found in the upper tray, with grooves which enable the packer to make the divisions larger or smaller as required. Flat trunks may be obtained which hold dresses full length, but which are so light that their size does not form any drawback. These are specially suitable for long voyages. On the latter it should always be remembered to have a flat cabin trunk containing the clothing and everything needed on board ship. This can easily be kept in the cabin, whilst all the other luggage must be stored in the hold. Care must be taken that the cabin trunk holds everything that is likely to be needed, and the traveller, before packing, should make a careful list of her requirements, seeing that each article on the list is placed in her trunk. On the whole the flat trunks are always more convenient than the dome-shaped boxes for any kind of travelling, as they can easily be put out of the way under a bed if need be when in rooms or hotels.

Neat leather or canvas hat-boxes may now be obtained fitted with cushions at the top, bottom, and sides upon which to pin the hats. There is little fear of millinery becoming spoiled or crushed when packed in one of these, and the woman who likes to have plenty of variety in her headgear should never travel without one.

For a fortnight's trip a roomy dress-basket and a hat-box will be all the luggage needed. Dressing-cases are also very useful in travelling, but it is not every woman who is fortunate enough to possess one.

When travelling with a large family of children the maxim "as little luggage as possible" will not apply. There are so many things necessary for the comfort of the youngsters—special cooking appliances, occasionally a special bed or cot, perambulators, mailcarts, and other important essentials. As, however, the children's holiday is rarely a migratory tour, but merely a certain number of weeks' sojourn at one place, the amount of luggage necessary should not form a great drawback. In these days of cheap "luggage in advance" rates much of the expenditure upon cabs may be curtailed, or a family omnibus may be hired from home to the station at a comparatively small cost, whilst at most seaside places outside porters deliver the luggage from the station to one's rooms at a small charge per package. In regard to the children's luggage it is more than ever essential to draw up a list of all the articles that will be required, and to take care when packing that nothing is forgotten.

Luggage on the Continent.—In the case of travelling on the continent, it is a mistake to carry an amount of hand luggage. This is always a nuisance. In the first place, it is subject to rigorous inspection by the Customs upon arrival, and the contents are apt to be well tumbled about during the process of inspection, more especially when, as is usually the case, there are hundreds of people awaiting their turn for their baggage to be examined. The same applies to landing in England from the continent—too much luggage should certainly be avoided; it is best to limit the baggage to one fair-sized yet very light trunk which can be registered through to its destination. There is, indeed, a great advantage in the continental system of registration, for once the traveller has taken her registration receipt she will not need to worry about her baggage beyond claiming it at the "Customs," being present when it is examined. It may be further remarked that the Customs examination in many countries on the continent is very lenient where registered luggage is concerned. In most cases the mere formality of opening the box is proceeded with, the traveller being asked if she has anything to declare—the box being closed again when she replies in the negative.

The dutiable articles in most places on the continent are tobacco, tea, spirits, soap, new clothes, confectionery, lace. A passenger's allowance of very small quantities of dutiable articles, however, is made in most cases. The registration of luggage may be effected on most of the railway systems throughout the different countries.

The maxim "no hand baggage" cannot be applied, however, to all circumstances. In regard to itinerary tours which comprise constant railway travelling from one place to another with "Rundreise" tickets (see p. 502), or in countries where no free allowance of luggage is made upon the railways, it is wiser to have only luggage which may be taken in the railway carriage, as this, of course, is free. This might consist of a flat suit-case which can easily be put away under the seat and a light hat-box. A heterogeneous collection of small parcels should always be avoided.

Luggage may be sent in advance from England to places where it is intended to make a long stay by means of the Continental Daily Parcels' Express, who have their offices at 53 Gracechurch Street, London, E.C., 72 Regent Street, London, W., and at Dover. This company undertakes the forwarding of passengers' luggage to any part of the continent by "Grande Vitesse," or mail service, at very moderate charges. A large number of tourists will find it a convenience to send their heavier luggage in advance in this way.

When the summer holiday is to be spent in such pastimes as mountaineering, walking tours, in countries like Switzerland, the tourist will have to rely upon the ever-useful knapsack for immediate requirements, sending on her luggage in advance to each place at which she is to find a *pied-à-terre*. The needs of travellers in this respect are met in Switzerland by the system of posting unaccompanied luggage. Not more than 44 lbs. can be sent, and the charge is 7d. per 22 lbs. On the mountain routes the travelling is made by means of "diligences" (coaches). In connection with these, 33 lbs. of free luggage is allowed and 22 lbs. on the passes.

In regard to bicycles a deposit of from five per cent. and upwards is in many cases levied upon cycles taken into a country, the deposit being returnable when the passenger leaves. It is important, therefore, that she keep her receipt carefully, for she must produce this before the deposit is returned. In France a permit for three months must be obtained. This will cost three francs, but if a longer stay is made the cycle tax of six francs will have to be paid. On most railways throughout the continent cycles are charged as ordinary luggage.

Packing a Trunk.—There is an art in packing a trunk which comparatively few women have mastered. This art may be defined as the ability to pack the largest number of articles without creasing or spoiling them in any way within the least possible compass. A good packer will manage to pack away in one trunk the same quantity of clothing that an indifferent packer would find it difficult to get into two.

The first important thing to remember is that all heavy articles, such as boots, shoes, books, &c., should be placed at the bottom of the box. They should be packed quite tightly together, and any empty corners filled up with stockings and other small woollen articles. Sponge-bags and toilet accessories should be also placed in the bottom layer if there is no separate dressing-bag for these.

When the bottom of the trunk has been packed quite neatly and tidily, forming as flat a layer as possible, the underlinen, neatly folded, should be placed over it to form the next layer. Over this should be placed coat-and-skirt costumes and dresses. They should be folded very carefully, with sheets of tissue paper between the folds, and rolls of tissue paper should also be inserted in the sleeves. At the top of the trunk should be placed the light silk dresses and blouses and evening gowns. These should be carefully folded and the sleeves stuffed with tissue paper. Hats should always be packed in a separate box if possible. It is impossible to pack millinery properly in an ordinary trunk, and indeed the headgear of the present-day fashionable dimensions can rarely be made to repose in safety on the upper tray of even a fair-sized dress-basket. One or two small or moderate-sized hats may, however, be placed on the top of the latter if needs must, but they should be carefully pinned with hat-pins to the canvas of the tray, and any bows or similar trimmings should be stuffed out with tissue paper to prevent them becoming crushed.

Hand-mirrors will seldom get smashed if placed within the folds of woollen garments. The same applies to any breakable articles. Bottles containing liquid of any kind should be avoided if possible when travelling, but if it is necessary that these be taken, they should be well rolled up in cotton wool and afterwards packed in neat little paper parcels. One or two extra waterproof sponge-bags into which they can be placed will also be found useful. These bottles should not be placed near any of the better articles of clothing in case of accident, although, if carefully packed, breakages seldom occur. Before packing care should be taken to see that all stoppers are firmly screwed down and that the bottles are tightly corked, for should the cork or stopper come out, a certain amount of damage to clothing must inevitably result in spite of all precautions in the way of cotton-wool wrappings. It is always as well to place the bottles within the folds of an old dark dressing-gown, and as near the bottom of the box as possible.

Veils, gloves, lace scarves, all should come upon the top tray of the trunk. Neat little satin or silk sachets with the name of the contents embroidered thereon are the handiest receptacles for these.

When packed, the trunk should be well locked and strapped. Either hanging or adhesive labels should be used, and on them the address should be clearly written. Care should be taken to pull off all old labels, as when these are allowed to remain in any numbers they are liable to cause confusion, especially when travelling on the continent. It is a good plan to have two labels. The porters have enormous quantities of luggage to deal with in a given time, and the labels often suffer from rough handling.

When packing for a trip on the continent it will be found necessary to include many small articles which would not be necessary when travelling at home. A spirit-lamp and kettle will be found most useful. In some pensions a sufficient supply of hot water may not always be available for washing purposes, though of course this does not apply to the large hotels. Then, again, one often likes to indulge in the "cup that cheers" either en route on the train journeys between various places, or in the early morning. Care must be taken, however, not to take more than the small quantity allowed by the Customs Regulations of the different countries. Soap, candles, matches, tapes, buttons, scissors, shoe-laces, safety-pins, needles, and cotton all should be available—to say nothing of the ever-useful corkscrew. If one is accustomed to use special toilet preparations in the way of face powders, &c., a supply of these should also be included. It is a mistake, however, to take a number of articles if you are going to a place where they can easily be procured, and at which you intend to make a more or less prolonged stay. It is for the itinerary tour in particular that strict attention in regard to all the little accessories that make for comfort is needed.

HOME PETS

There is scarcely a British home, from the mansion of the rich to the cottage of the poor, which does not boast of some pet, if it be only the humble domestic cat. The care of pets is a problem, therefore, which must present itself sooner or later to the average housewife. Dumb animals are often sadly neglected, not always willingly it is true, but most often from sheer ignorance of the best way to treat them both in illness and in health. The following notes upon the characteristics of our household pets with directions in regard to their diet and general hygiene, together with hints as to the best methods of treating the common ailments to which they are subject, are intended to give practical guidance to the housewife in all the most important problems in regard to the care and management of her pets with which from time to time she may be called upon to deal.

DOGS

The dog is the most companionable as well as the most faithful of our pets, and, properly trained, he may also become a most useful member of the household.

In purchasing a dog it should be remembered that some breeds are eminently suited for a hardy outdoor life, and for this reason would not thrive as household dogs in a town; on the other hand, others make admirable indoor pets, provided of course that they have a certain amount of good daily exercise out of doors. "Lap dogs"—a designation which include all the tiny breeds of dogs which form ladies' pets —do not require so much exercise, although they are all the better for it.

Guard Dogs.—Some dogs are especially noted for their qualities as guardians of their master's house and property. Chief amongst these are the Mastiff, Bulldog, Great Dane, Retriever, Newfoundland, and Airedale Terrier. The Mastiff, Great Dane, and Newfoundland are best kept out of doors on account of their size, and for this reason are more suitable for country than for town life. The Bulldog makes a very good indoor dog. Of the smaller dogs, Fox Terriers, Irish Terriers, Skye Terriers, and Bull Terriers make splendid guard dogs.

Companionable Dogs.—The St. Bernard is a most faithful companion and very gentle with children. By reason of his size this dog should also be kept out of doors. The Collie is most companionable and sagacious. To keep in health it requires a very large amount of exercise, and is therefore best kept in the country. The Newfoundland is also companionable and fond of children. Deerhounds, Bloodhounds, Setters, Sheep Dogs are also faithful companions. They are best suited to an outdoor life.

Dogs to keep Indoors in Town.—In choosing a house dog for town it should be remembered that the small short-haired varieties are best on account of the less trouble entailed in keeping them clean. Long-haired dogs bring in mud from the street on their coats, and will often roll on the carpets and furniture in their attempt to get rid of it. Few people will take the trouble to brush the dog as he comes in from his walk, yet this should always be done if he has been in muddy or dusty roads.

The most useful dog for indoor town-life is undoubtedly the Fox Terrier. Sagacious, easily taught, faithful and companionable, he makes as a rule a good watch-dog, and his short coat is easily kept clean. The Irish Terrier is also a most useful dog for town, although he requires careful training on account of his fighting propensities. As has been said before, the Bulldog makes a very good indoor dog and guardian of the house. Skye Terriers and Aberdeen Terriers make capital little house dogs, only the coat of a Skye Terrier is rather a drawback as it requires very careful attention in regard to brushing, combing, and grooming generally. The Basset Hounds and Dachshunds are also excellent little indoor dogs. Spaniels are generally all-round useful dogs, and the Poodle is one of the most sagacious and teachable of our pets.

Pet Dogs.—Pugs, Pekingese, Pomeranians, Griffins, Yorkshire Terriers, King Charles Spaniels, Italian Greyhounds, Maltese Terriers are the principal dogs which rank as ladies' pets. These as a rule are pampered little individuals, accompanying their mistress in her drives and reclining on silken cushions in her boudoir and drawing-room, yet when properly trained and not allowed to become fractious and snappy (a result as a rule of over-feeding) they make charming little companions, with the most ingratiating ways.

Management of Dogs.—It must be remembered that the good qualities of a dog are enhanced by careful training and his faults cured in the same way. It is always better for this reason to rear our pets from puppyhood if we would obtain the most satisfactory results.

Strict cleanliness and judicious feeding are the two great essentials in the management of dogs. Dogs kept in the house should be washed once a fortnight if possible in summer, and once a month in winter. Outdoor dogs do not require such frequent washing. Plenty of warm water and good carbolic soap should be used when bathing a dog; the animal should be well immersed and the soap well rubbed over his coat, thoroughly rinsed off, and, last but not least, he should be well dried. All dogs should be carefully groomed daily. This is most essential with the long-haired varieties, such as Collies, Skye Terriers, &c. For these a strong broad-toothed dog-comb should be used as well as a brush.

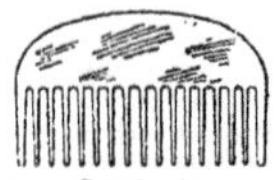

Dog-Comb.

Dog-Brush.

Regular and careful grooming often does away with the necessity of such frequent bathing as would otherwise be needed.

Vermin.—If cleanliness in the way of washing and grooming is not strictly attended to, the animal will often be pestered with vermin as a result. Carbolic soap should be used in washing dogs which are afflicted in this manner. In very bad cases the dog should be rubbed all over with oil a few hours before the tub is given. This should be allowed to remain on until washed off in the tub.

The Kennel.—When a dog is kept in a kennel, he should be given fresh straw every week, and this straw should be shaken and turned over every day and all soiled straw removed. In summer a piece of matting can be used instead of straw. Do not keep him chained up for a long time at a stretch if it can possibly be avoided. A dog should always have plenty of exercise; besides, the kennel will soon get foul if he is chained up all day.

Dog-Kennel.

Needless to say, the kennel must be kept clean, being washed out at frequent intervals. A dog-kennel should always be as roomy as possible, and it should never be allowed to rest right on the ground, on account of the danger of the dog catching cold from damp. The door of the kennel should, if possible, be at the side. When it is in the front the animal cannot get away from the rain and snow which in stormy weather blows through the opening. With the door at the side he can curl up in the corner away from the entrance, and so avoid it. For indoor dogs an old wine-case filled with straw makes an excellent bed. The tiny pets should be provided with little dog-baskets.

Feeding.—Many mistakes in regard to feeding are made by the average dog-owner; it is either a case of "killing with kindness" or semi-starvation through unsuitable food. The mistake first mentioned is the one most often committed, more especially in regard to the strictly house pets. Tit-bits of various kinds are given to them at all hours of the day, to say nothing of sugar, the excessive eating of which is most injurious. Pet dogs should never be allowed in the room at meal-time, particularly when they are versed in the art of "begging" or other similar blandishments, which make it hard to refuse them the tit-bits they covet. A dog should not be fed between meals. Two good meals a day are ample for most of our canine pets. To lap dogs, however, three smaller meals should be given daily. These may consist of meat, vegetables, and Spratt's dog biscuits, with a regular supply of bones. The latter are very good for the dog's teeth. Only large bones should be given—never bones of poultry or game. These are apt to injure a dog's stomach, as they are often swallowed whole. Meat should only be given at the chief meal. Animals which have little exercise should not be given large quantities of meat; it is a mistake, however, to exclude it altogether from a dog's diet. The biscuits can be given dry or soaked. They should always be broken up. The diet should be varied as much as possible—meat scraps from the table with vegetables make a good and suitable meal where one or two indoor dogs are kept, but the amount of meat should be regulated by the amount of exercise they get. Never allow food to be left lying about in the vessels; at meal times give only what is sufficient. Plenty of drinking water must always be at hand, and the drinking vessel must be kept scrupulously clean. Drinking-troughs should not be stood out in the sun in hot weather; the water should be kept in as cool a place as possible.

Above all things be guarded against the mistake of killing your pet with kindness, as is so often the case with strictly pet dogs, such as Pugs, Pomeranians, &c. The poor little animals have to pay in the long run for the indiscriminate pampering they receive at the hands of their mistresses. Their little lives are not only rendered miserable by ever-recurring disease, but in most cases they are materially shortened.

Exercise.—Never forget to let your pets have sufficient exercise. To keep them indoors all day long falls little short of actual cruelty. If you would have them keep strong and healthy, let them be your companions in your daily walks; remember that exercise is almost as necessary to them as food. The dog should be trained early to follow well out of doors—this is all the more necessary in regard to dogs kept in towns—for the very real dangers of traffic are always present, and it is not safe to take a dog out in the crowded streets if he does not follow well or answer to his mistress's call.

When quite young a dog should always be taken out on a lead. All dogs when out of doors

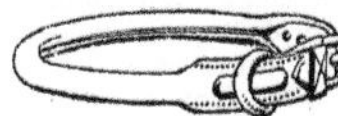

Collar for Long-haired Dog.

must wear collars with the name and address of their owner inscribed thereon. The collars of long-haired dogs should be rounded in order to preserve their fur. When sending puppies or small dogs away long distances by train they

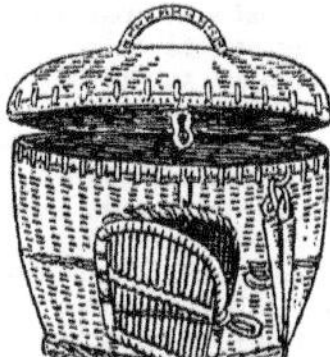

Dog's Travelling-Basket.

should be placed in a basket with plenty of room for ventilation allowed. Special baskets are sold for the purpose at moderate prices.

Puppies.—Puppies require very careful tending if that great ill of puppyhood, "distemper," is to be avoided. A puppy of a few weeks old when taken from the care of its mother should be fed at least six times a day. The last meal should be given to it late at night; after a late meal he is more likely to rest and refrain from disturbing the slumbers of the household by his yelping. Between six and eight weeks of age is the usual time for weaning puppies.

Milk thickened with meal is the best food after weaning. Later Spratt's puppy cakes soaked in milk may be added. The meals should be decreased as the puppy gets older, and at five months three meals daily will be sufficient. When he is teething, bones and a very little meat should be added to his diet. Puppies at this time are apt to get destructive, tearing up whatever they come across. For this reason it is well to supply them with plenty of bones to gnaw at, and old boots, shoes, balls, anything which they can tear up and destroy at their will.

Care of the Mother.—The period of gestation is between eight and nine weeks, and during this time the animal should be well fed, and a small dose of olive oil occasionally administered. When the time approaches for the puppies to be born, a bed should be provided for her in some quiet, secluded place, which is warm, airy, and free from draught. The bed should consist of a roomy box or basket into which plenty of clean straw has been placed. Beyond the preparation of the bed, the animal can in most cases be left quite alone until the puppies are born. It is as well, however, especially in the case of a valuable dog, to arrange for the attendance of a skilled veterinary surgeon in the event of complications arising. After the puppies are born, fresh straw should be placed in the box, and the mother should be coaxed to take a little warm beef-tea. Then she should be left undisturbed as much as possible for a few hours. She should have three good meals a day while nursing, consisting of easily digestible food and a little raw meat at first.

Training Dogs.—A puppy should be trained early in the ways of obedience and cleanliness. If he contracts bad habits in his early life and these are left unchecked, it will become increasingly difficult to cure him as he grows older. He should be kept clean and given frequent baths, care being always taken to thoroughly dry him afterwards. He should be supplied with a nice warm bed and kept as free as possible from draughts. Violence and impatience are quite out of place in the training of puppies. By patience, firmness, and perseverance on the part of the owner a puppy will soon get to know who is master; only firmness and perseverance on the part of the master or mistress are essential in order to achieve the desired result. The little creature must be first made to understand what is wanted and then made to do it. A too liberal use of the whip is inadvisable. A well-known authority on dogs has said that one good beating, if thoroughly deserved, will do good, inasmuch as it will not be forgotten by the little culprit, but to beat the dog on the smallest provocation will spoil his temper and often make him snappy and then ferocious in time. Such a method of training can only be productive of harm. Whilst some dogs are very fond of going into the water after stones, &c., others are afraid to do so. In these circumstances they should never be thrown in, as this will only increase their fear in this direction. Very often a dog may be persuaded to take to the water by seeing other dogs go in, more especially if these dogs are his daily companions; but he should never be forced to do so.

Ailments.—A dog which is well housed, suitably fed, and well cared for hygienically should always keep healthy. There are, however, certain ailments to which our canine pets are subject which will sometimes make their appearance in the best-regulated kennels. Unless the ailment is of a strictly minor order it is always better to at once call in a qualified vet. We owe it to our faithful companions and pets that they should have the best attention in sickness. It is as well, however, to be able to recognise the symptoms of the various canine ailments, so that the sufferers may be properly treated in the way of housing, feeding, warmth, &c. We shall therefore describe the symptoms of the chief ailments to which dogs are liable, together with the particular management and attention required to effect a speedy cure.

Administering Medicine.—Small dogs can be taken on the knee of the person who is administering the dose; very large dogs, such as Mastiffs, usually require a man to handle them.

Sometimes the pills or medicine may be mixed with food. When giving a pill, see that it is placed well on the back of the animal's tongue, closing its mouth quickly until the pill is swallowed.

Canker.—This appears in the form of acute inflammation of the ear. The dog will be seen to hold its head on one side as if in pain and to keep on scratching his ear. He must be prevented from doing this as much as possible, as the scratching will only increase the inflammation. The ear should be regularly treated with a good antiseptic solution. If taken in time, this treatment will often be sufficient to ward off a bad attack. Severe cases require special treatment, and a veterinary surgeon should at once be consulted. Very often ear inflammation occurs through accumulation of dust and dirt inside the ears of the dog, which he endeavours to dislodge by scratching. Those who have the welfare of their pets at heart can prevent this state of affairs by gently wiping the inside of the ear of the animal with a piece of soft rag, thus freeing it from all dust and dirt, whenever it is seen to scratch its ear or to be suffering from undue irritation.

Distemper.—Some people think that it is necessary for *all* dogs to have distemper. This is quite a fallacy. If a dog is well housed and kept free from all source of infection, it will seldom have it. Distemper is a most infectious disease and can be contracted from other animals or infected sources, such as bedding, &c.

Symptoms.—It is some time before the symptoms make their appearance, all that is noticeable at first being the fact that the animal is not well. The symptoms are similar to those of a cold—the appetite is poor, a watery discharge comes from nose and eyes, there is a rapid rise of temperature, the discharge from the eyes increases to such an extent that the eyelids often become almost glued together. In all bad cases of distemper it is best to seek the advice of an experienced veterinary surgeon, as many severe complications often ensue.

The patient should at once be isolated and kept in warm and comfortable surroundings. Very careful feeding upon light nourishing food is necessary: the diet should include plenty of milk and beef-tea. All the dog's surroundings should be thoroughly disinfected. Too much emphasis cannot be laid upon the necessity for cleanliness and warmth.

Eczema.—Eczema is often found in over-fed pets, more especially in older dogs. The skin eruption appears most often under the thighs and about the ears and back of the animal. Intense irritation is set up which is accelerated by the continual scratching, and painful sores often result. Careful dieting and regular exercise are necessary. The sores should be treated with boracic ointment. The animal should be kept very clean, and a tonic should be prescribed by a veterinary surgeon to improve the general condition of its health.

Fits.—These occur most frequently in puppies, and may be very slight, consisting merely of convulsive movements of the muscles, or else they may take the form of severe convulsions, with foaming at the mouth, rolling eyeballs, and all the other usual accompanying severe symptoms. Nothing can be done while the attack lasts. Dogs subject to fits should be kept on a very light diet, and aperient medicine should be regularly administered. Sometimes after an attack a dog will rush away at a tremendous speed foaming at the mouth, having altogether the appearance of a mad dog. He will hide himself and not return till the attack has quite passed over. This after-effect of an epileptic seizure may easily be mistaken for rabies, so in order to avoid the disastrous consequences of such a mistaken impression on the part of a stranger it is as well to tie him up until he has altogether recovered.

Hydrophobia.—As has been already pointed out, foaming at the mouth must not be taken to indicate hydrophobia. This dread disease has been stamped out in England, and it is very seldom that a case of hydrophobia is heard of. The surest indication of the disease is a complete change in the disposition of the animal. If, for instance, a good-tempered dog becomes suddenly snappy, ferocious or irritable, and it seems to frequently rub the sides of his mouth with his paw as if to dislodge something from it, it should be looked upon with suspicion, and kept tied up until it can be ascertained if there is any danger of its being attacked by this disease.

Mange is a highly contagious skin disease caused by an animal parasite. Sometimes the parasite takes up its abode on the surface of the skin. In this case a number of small red spots appear which form into sores, the hair falls off in quantities, and an unpleasant odour emanates from the skin. When the disease assumes this form it is known as sarcoptic mange. In follicular mange the parasite is to be found in the hair follicle. Though this form of mange is not so contagious as the sarcoptic form, it is more difficult to cure. Expert veterinary advice should at once be sought when either form of mange makes its appearance. The dog should be at once isolated. Give it a thorough bath and then apply the dressing prescribed to the entire surface of the animal's skin. This is usually composed of sulphur and slaked lime, or sulphur and train oil, the proportion of sulphur used being usually double that of the other ingredient. Allow the dressing to remain on for a few days, then wash it off. If necessary, the process should be repeated. In most cases of sarcoptic mange the destruction of the parasite will be effected after two or three applications of the dressing. The treatment for follicular mange is much more protracted, and the animal should always be sent away to the care of a veterinary surgeon until the cure is effected.

Rheumatism most frequently occurs in old dogs. It is sometimes brought on by confinement in damp and draughty kennels or sleeping on damp bedding, but most often by exposure to wet and cold. Most often it takes a chronic form, and is manifested in extreme stiffness of the joints, the animal having difficulty in walking. There are intervals of great pain and considerable stiffness and lameness, whilst at other times the dog will appear to be quite well. Sometimes the attacks are exceptionally severe. The affected parts should be carefully massaged with some good liniment every day, the dog should be given a warm and comfortable bed, and doses of iodide of potassium with salicylate of soda should be regularly administered.

St. Vitus' Dance.—This disease takes a somewhat similar form to that which it displays in human beings, its presence being indicated by the same twitching of the muscles. Warmth and careful dieting are essential. The patient should be prescribed for by a veterinary surgeon, and medicine regularly administered.

Worms.—A large number of dogs suffer from these internal parasites, as they often pick up the eggs of the various worms with their food and water. Tape-worms are the most frequently prevalent, although they are also infested with round-worms in several cases.

Treatment for Tape-Worms.—The infested dog should be starved for twenty-four hours, then a good vermicide should be administered. This treatment should be followed by a dose of castor oil or some other aperient within two or three hours.

Round-Worms most usually infect puppies, and fits may often be traced to their presence. Puppies should be kept without food for three hours before the vermicide is administered. No aperient is necessary unless the animal is an adult.

CATS

The Care of Cats.—Puss is one of the most common of our domestic pets, and perhaps it is for this reason that, with the exception of valuable animals which are bred for show purposes, she is often sadly neglected. Very few people think of feeding her regularly; one or perhaps two saucers of milk will be allowed her daily, and the rest of her food she is supposed to make up with mice or anything else she can forage for herself.

This is quite a wrong way of bringing up our feline pets: it is simply encouraging them to thieve whatever dainties they can get hold of. A cat who is left to hunt for her own food will not be too particular as to where she finds a meal, and the larder will suffer in consequence.

Properly trained, a cat will become a most docile animal, and a respecter of its master's property, but first of all she must be fed. Milk is not the sum total of all her requirements; she should have at least two good meals daily in addition to the milk allowance. The scraps from her master's table, including bits of meat, gravy, and plenty of green vegetables, will usually be sufficient; but the meals must be given regularly. Bread and milk in the morning, scraps left from the mid-day meal of the household, and another meal of scraps at night will be sufficient, whilst kittens require more frequent feeding. Cats should always have access to grass, which they eat with relish, as this is good for them medicinally. Drinking water should also always be within pussy's reach, as milk is not sufficient to quench her thirst. Cats are very fond of all kinds of fish, and their fancy in this direction should be indulged whenever possible.

The cat, more especially the common short-haired cat, is really one of the hardiest of our domestic pets. Persian and other long-haired cats require more care, and are apt to be more delicate than the ordinary short-haired varieties. A cat can easily be trained in habits of cleanliness, only the training must begin from kittenhood. When a cat is kept in a house where there is no garden, it should always be provided with a good-sized tin tray covered with earth; needless to say, the earth should be frequently changed. Cats are said to become very attached to the houses in which they are brought up, and they have often been known to run away and get lost after a household removal. An old-fashioned plan to prevent this is still often followed. As soon as pussy arrives in the new house, butter is rubbed well over her feet and legs. She will at once begin to lick off the butter, and by the time she has finished this engrossing occupation it is said that all idea of flight will have been abandoned. When a cat is expected to have kittens, a warmly-lined basket should be provided for her in a quiet place. In most cases it will be found necessary to get rid of some of the kittens, but one should always be left, as, apart from any questions of cruelty, it is bad for the mother to have all the young ones taken from her.

Different Kinds of Cats.—The most beautiful of our feline pets are undoubtedly the Persian and Angora varieties. Of these the blue Persians are perhaps the handsomest. Then there are black, white, and tabby Persians all with the beautiful long soft silky fur which is the chief characteristic of their breed. Persians require much more attention than our ordinary common cat, as they are more delicate of constitution; but they are such gentle and beautiful animals that any extra care expended upon them is abundantly repaid.

Other varieties of cats are the Manx, the Siamese, and the Abyssinian. The Manx cat has no tail, and in the colouring of its coat it resembles the British cat. The Siamese cat has a light-coloured body and a dark face, tail, and legs.

The ordinary cat keeps her own coat in good condition by cleaning it with her tongue. Long-haired cats, however, should be brushed and combed daily. During the moulting season this is more than ever necessary, for when long-haired cats moult, if they are not strictly attended to, they will often swallow quantities of hair which may accumulate in the stomach and kill them. The danger of this is obviated by regular and careful grooming.

Common Ailments.—Our ordinary cat is as a rule very hardy; nevertheless there are many ailments with which puss may be overtaken, and as it is said that some of the diseases which attack cats, notably consumption, may be communicated to human beings, the reason for the greatest care is all the more evident.

Colds.—These should not be neglected, as they may often develop into more serious ailments, They are usually indicated by fits of sneezing and catarrh. Keep the cat thoroughly warm and out of draughts, and give her warm milk to drink until the cold has run its course.

Diarrhœa.—Give a tea-spoonful of castor oil, and keep the patient on a very light diet for a day or two.

Distemper.—A veterinary surgeon should be consulted. In addition to administering the medicine he prescribes, pay great attention to diet, give plenty of fish and strengthening food. Isolate the animal, as the disease is infectious.

Puss is generally ailing and out of sorts before the actual symptoms appear. These usually manifest themselves in the form of sneezing and a watery discharge from the eyes and nose.

Fits.—These occur most frequently with kittens, especially when teething. Nothing can be done while the fit lasts, but a dose of castor oil should be administered when the convulsions are over. Be very careful how you lift up a cat in convulsions, always using a good thick cloth for the purpose. Place it at once in its basket out of harm's way. Get veterinary advice as to the general health of the little animal.

Other Diseases.—Cats are also liable to consumption, mange, canker of the ear, eczema, and other diseases. In all cases skilled advice should at once be sought.

CAGE BIRDS

No more cheery pet can be kept in a household than a little feathered songster if it is well tended and its cage kept bright and clean. To keep a bird and yet be wholly ignorant of the right method of caring for it is not only folly, but in many cases this ignorance amounts to actual cruelty. The sum of the requirements of our pet birds is very small, but they should be rigidly attended to. Cage birds suffer more almost than any other pet from the consequences of neglect. Their being kept in confinement produces a certain delicacy which is certainly not one of their characteristics when enjoying the freedom of their natural state.

Before keeping a canary or any other similar pet it must be borne in mind that no cage bird will thrive unless it has a roomy cage, plenty of good suitable food, and clean fresh water both for drinking and bathing purposes, and its cage and surroundings are kept thoroughly clean. Last but not least, the cage must be hung in a bright position, where the little songster may obtain plenty of bright light—not artificial light be it said; there is nothing more unhealthy, for instance, than for a bird to be placed near a gas-jet. Care must also be taken that the cage is well away from all draughts. Given strict attention to these first essentials and also a knowledge of the more common ailments to which our feathered pets are subject, the little captives will thrive and gladden the household with their bright song. They will come to know the hand that tends them, and with a little patience on the part of their keeper they may in time be tamed to almost as great a degree as any other household pet.

Canaries.—There are many varieties of canaries, chief amongst which are the Yorkshire, the Norwich, the Border, the Lizard, the Crest, the Belgian, and the German. Of the English birds the Yorkshire Canary is the most graceful, whilst the best songsters undoubtedly come from the Harz Mountains in Germany. As a rule, the latter are inclined to be delicate when brought over to England: where they are successfully reared, they undoubtedly make the best songsters. In regard to singing, amongst the English birds a mule is often a much better songster than a pure-bred canary, and mule birds are also usually fairly hardy.

Choosing a Canary.—In choosing a canary, care should be taken to go to none but a reputable bird-dealer. Many bird-dealers will send a bird to the customer's house on approval for a day or two in order that she may be able to judge its singing capacity. A reputable bird-dealer as a rule will be pleased to help the purchaser in every way in his power, and will give much valuable advice. In other cases it is always better for the purchaser to take some friend with her who thoroughly understands cage birds and their different points and qualities.

The prices of canaries vary to a great extent. As a rule, however, a very good bird may be had for from 10s. 6d. and upwards, and often 7s. 6d. will purchase a hardy little songster.

The Cage.—The cage should be as large and roomy as possible and furnished with at least three perches, one at each side near the food and water-troughs, and one higher up in the cage. The bottom of the cage should be fitted with a sliding tray which can be taken out, cleaned, and covered with fresh sand daily. A little vessel for water and another one for food are placed at each side of the cage; in most cages a little recess is built out on either side to hold these vessels with an opening in the cage bars through which the bird can reach its food. In others the food and water vessels are placed on stands inside the cage.

Canary Cage.

A cage made of ordinary wood and wire is very suitable, and can be purchased for from 5s. and upwards. Brass cages are more expensive and more ornamental, but they become dangerous if the bars are not kept thoroughly dry, on account of the verdigris which forms upon them. Enamelled cages may also be had at all prices. In addition to the food and water vessels, a larger vessel should also be placed inside the cage in which the bird can take his daily bath. All vessels must be kept scrupulously clean and should be washed out daily. It is always as well to keep two complete sets of perches, so that while one set is being scrubbed with soap and water, the other set can be placed in the cage. Perches should never be returned to the cage before they are thoroughly dry.

Food and Water.—Canary seed is the chief food for canaries. The seed should be clean and free from grit. The food vessel should always be cleaned before placing the seed into it in the morning. A little fresh green food should also be given daily. Water-cress, groundsel, lettuce, or chickweed are all appreciated by our pets. In the winter, when green food is scarce, a small piece of apple should always be placed between the bars of the cage for the bird to peck at. By way of a delicacy a lump of sugar might also be placed between the bars of the cage: this dainty is much appreciated and serves to keep the bird's beak in good condition; a piece of cuttle bone for the bird to peck at should also be placed between the bars.

The bottom of the cage should always be covered with good rough sand or gravel put in fresh every morning, to aid the canary in grinding its food. Fresh water should be given every morning for drinking and for the bath. In summer fresh water should be given twice daily. The water vessels should be kept scrupulously clean. For the bath an ordinary saucer or a glass vessel such as is used sometimes for packing potted meat would fulfil all requirements.

Breeding.—Much interest may be derived from the home-breeding and rearing of canaries. Care should be taken to select a hardy pair for mating, and they should be paired about the middle of March. It will be necessary also to buy a breeding-cage. This may be procured

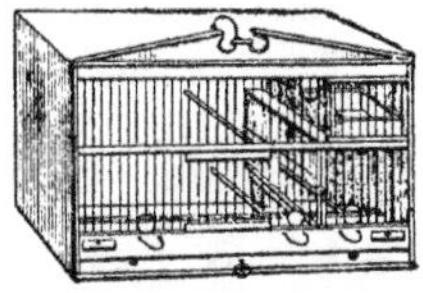

Breeding-Cage.

for a few shillings, and is divided into two compartments by a movable wire partition. The cock and the hen are put into separate compartments, and as soon as the cock is seen to feed the hen through the bars the partition is withdrawn and the cage thrown into one.

The breeding-cage is fitted with a nest-box, and nest-building material should be placed between the bars. As soon as the first egg is laid it should be taken away and a little china egg substituted, and so on with each egg until three have been laid, when they are returned to the nest and the hen sits upon them. Hard-boiled egg mashed up with bread-crumbs should be given daily during the hatching time, in addition to the seed, and plenty of good green food. When the little birds are old enough to leave the nest they may be placed in a separate compartment, where they will be fed by the cock. In addition to the egg, they may now have a little crushed seed, which they will learn to pick up for themselves. When they can feed themselves they may be placed in another cage.

Taming Canaries.—A canary will thrive much better if it can be so thoroughly tamed that it can be allowed to fly about the room for a certain time each day, and may be relied upon to return to its cage of its own accord. One person only should undertake the taming of the little captive in this respect, because it is necessary that the bird should get to know and care for the hand that tends him if any headway is to be made in the taming process. A great amount of patience is required to accomplish this—the bird should be taught to perch on its owner's finger, to feed from her hand. Then the cage-door can be opened and the bird allowed its liberty. At first it will require to be gently coaxed back to its cage by the display of some fresh green stuff or other dainty; but gradually it will return to it of its own accord. Care, of course, must be taken that no cats or other pets liable to harm the little wanderer are allowed in the room. A cat, if taught very young, may be trained to become quite friendly with a canary or any other bird, and to refrain from any attempt to harm it. Much more antagonistic pets than cats and canaries have been known to live together in harmony as a result of careful early training.

Birds in the Aviary.—Several birds of various kinds may be kept together in an aviary, and their rivalling notes will often make a most

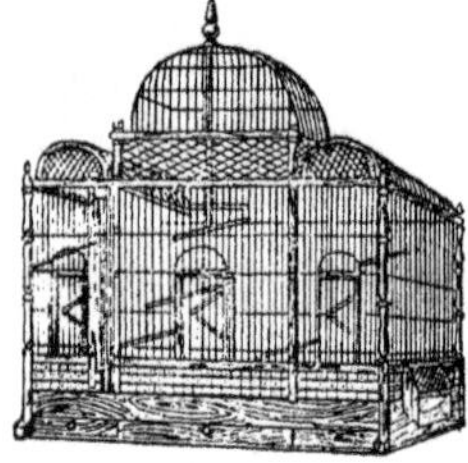

Aviary.

delightful harmony. An aviary must on no account be overcrowded. If any of the inmates disagree, it is better to separate the offender from his companions and place him in a cage by himself. Strict cleanliness must, of course, be the rule.

Other Cage Birds.—Amongst other British birds which may be kept successfully as pets are the Bullfinch, Chaffinch, Goldfinch, and Linnet. The Goldfinch is a very fine songster, and the Bullfinch may be trained to pipe tunes. The Chaffinch can also be trained as a songster, and the Linnet has a very pleasing note. All these birds are fed upon the same seeds as Canaries, and the general treatment is in most ways the same. The Goldfinch, however, needs plenty of hemp and maw-seed, and a Bullfinch needs a more varied diet than the other finches. In addition to a good seed mixture, he should be provided regularly with groundsel chickweed, a little egg occasionally, and meal-worms and other insects when they can be procured. The Chaffinch also requires insect food now and then.

The Soft Bills.—It is not as a rule advisable to keep birds which belong to the class known as "Soft Bills," although as songsters they are unrivalled. But to enable them to thrive in captivity they require the utmost experience and care on the part of those who tend them.

The Nightingale.—The Nightingale takes first place as a songster. It requires a large and roomy cage; the top and back should be of wood and the bars of osier. Shredded raw meat, chopped eggs, meal-worms, beetles, ants' eggs comprise its diet, the principal aim being to make its food partake as much as possible of the nature of that which it enjoys in its natural state.

The Skylark.—The Skylark, if properly tended, thrives well in captivity. Its cage should be a roomy one, and should always contain some green turf. Ants' eggs, meal-worms, meat, and one of the preparations sold as lark food should constitute its diet.

The Blackcap is another good songster, and has to be fed and treated in a very similar manner to the Nightingale.

The Thrush should have a very large roomy cage, which should be cleaned every morning. Its diet should consist of fig-dust moistened with milk and water to form a paste, shredded raw meat, worms, and snails. A stone should be placed in the cage to enable it to break the shells.

The Blackbird.—The Blackbird has a very soft clear note—the treatment of a blackbird in captivity is the same as that of a thrush. Starlings can also be managed in the same manner, as can Magpies, Jackdaws, and Jays. Large roomy cages are the first essentials for all these birds. It is useless to expect them to thrive in an unduly confined space. Strict cleanliness and attention to diet is also essential. On the whole, Canaries and Finches are the most suitable birds for home pets; and we would advocate that no one undertakes the care of birds of the soft-billed variety without having first served an apprenticeship, as it were, in the successful rearing of Canaries and Finches.

Parrots.—Of all the foreign birds which are imported to our shores parrots are perhaps the most popular as home pets. These birds possess the power of imitating human speech and afford

an abundance of interest and amusement in this way. When purchasing a parrot, care should be taken that the bird is thoroughly acclimatised, as there is a great amount of mortality amongst them. Upon being brought over here it takes a person of the utmost experience to tend them and train them in accordance with the necessary change of diet and conditions. For this reason never purchase a parrot from any other but a recognised bird-dealer who can guarantee that it has spent at least a season in this country.

The Cage.—A parrot's cage should be large and roomy. In no case should it be less than eighteen inches in diameter. The cage should be furnished with a swing which must be of sufficient height for the bird to be able to stand upon the perch without his head touching the swing. It is always advantageous to be able to allow a parrot to come out of his cage occasionally for exercise if he is sufficiently tame; this can be done with safety if the flights of one wing are clipped. The cage should be placed out of doors on fine sunny days, and during summer it is good for parrots to be put out occasionally during a shower, as many birds object to bathing themselves. In very dry hot weather a little water might also be sprayed upon them once or twice a week, only care must be taken that they do not catch cold afterwards. A strong tinned wire cage may be had for from 12s. 6d.

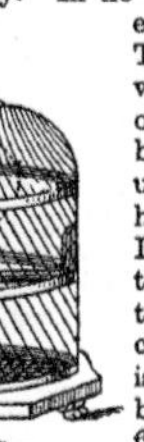

Parrot-Cage.

Feeding.—The chief food for parrots is grain such as hemp, wheat, eats, Indian corn, sunflower seed, and canary seeds, and they also appreciate dainties such as fruit, green stuff, carrot, &c. Banana they are especially fond of. It is a good plan to give them a small piece of banana or other similar dainty every day, only they should not be furnished indiscriminately with scraps from the table. Parrots are also very fond of sop food such as bread and milk, and where, as in some cases, they object to water the sop will form a good substitute. Messrs. Spratt sell a very good parrot-seed mixture.

Water.—Parrots require very little water, but it is a mistake to think that water is harmful to them. The water-tin should not be left in the cage all day, but it should be filled with fresh water and offered to the bird at least twice daily. If a water-tin is left all day in the cage of a parrot who for some mistaken reason has been deprived of water for any length of time, he will drink too much of it and so become ill. To this fact may be ascribed the origin of the idea that water is harmful to parrots. A bath should be put ready for the parrot once a week. It should be taken away, however, if the bird shows no inclination to bathe. In warm weather it is a good plan to stand the cage out in the rain for a little.

Grit.—Grit of some kind is always necessary. Spratt's Parrot Grit Mixture is very good. A piece of cuttlefish bone should also be always put in the cage.

Feather-Eating.—The objectionable habit of feather-eating indulged in by some parrots is caused, according to a well-known authority, by skin irritation set up by parasites, improper diet, or want of occupation, more commonly by the latter. A parrot should be given twigs to gnaw to keep it well occupied, and it should not be kept in a little-frequented room, or the habit will certainly be brought on by ennui, as the parrot is a sociable bird and likes plenty of company. An empty reel of cotton is a favourite toy with "Polly," and it will sometimes keep him amused for an hour at a stretch.

Different Kinds of Parrots.—Amongst the chief varieties of parrots which are brought to our shores are the Grey Parrot, the Rose-breasted Cockatoo, Blue-fronted Amazon, Ring-necked Parrakeet, and the Blue and Yellow Macaw: of these the Grey Parrot is the best talker, although the Blue-fronted Amazon can in many cases be made to rival it in this respect. The Macaws are usually kept chained, having a parrot-stand on which to perch, as they are too big to be kept in an ordinary cage.

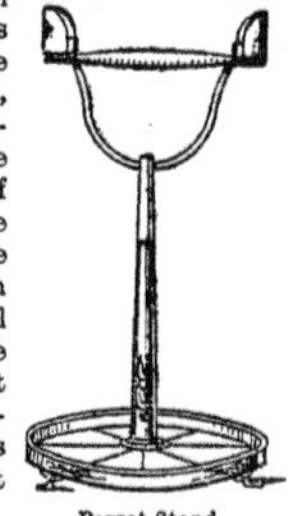

Parrot-Stand.

Ailments of Cage Birds.—If birds are thoroughly well cared for they will seldom cause much anxiety in regard to health. If strict attention is paid to their diet, cleanliness, and general hygiene, and, above all, if they are kept free from draughts, they will be found as a rule to keep well and to give very little trouble. It is as well, however, that every one should know how to treat the more common ailments with which our feathered pets are afflicted, and the following brief notes should be useful in this connection.

Moulting cannot be exactly classed as an ailment, as all birds moult—that is to say, cast their feathers once a year, generally late in summer or early in autumn, but it is important that great care should be taken of our pets during the moulting season. They should be well fed and kept warm and free from draughts. A little maw-seed should be added to the usual food—a rusty nail or a little saffron placed in the drinking-water. Either will form an efficient tonic.

Nails and Beak.—Birds' nails should not be allowed to grow too long or they may get caught in the wires of the cage, and often injuries to the toes may be caused in this way. Take the bird in your hand and, holding it on its back, lift it up to the light, when you will be able to see the veins in the claws and thus avoid cutting as far as these. Cut with a sharp pair of scissors. Take good care to hold the bird firmly, so that it cannot wriggle whilst the nail-cutting is proceeding.

Colds.—Colds are nearly always the result of draughts. They often bring about loss of voice for a time. Put the cage in a warmer room which is at the same time free from draughts, and add a little hemp to its diet—a few drops of glycerine and whisky may be added to the water with advantage.

Asthma.—Where a cold results in asthma, the condition of the bird is most serious. The complaint is indicated by heavy breathing and wheezing. The bird should be kept in a warm, moist atmosphere and a cloth placed round its cage. Egg and bread-crumbs with maw-seed should form its diet. Asthma is one of the most fatal diseases that attack our pets—unless taken in time a cure is hopeless. It should be avoided by keeping the bird well out of draughts.

Diarrhœa.—This is often caused by unsuitable diet or too liberal a supply of green food. Give a tiny drop of castor oil in the beak. An egg diet consisting of the yoke of a hard-boiled egg mashed up with some biscuit is often effective, or scalded rape seed may be given instead.

Constipation is often caused through an insufficient supply of green food. Often drops of glycerine added to the drinking-water will be found effective, and the cause should be removed by at once increasing the supply of green food. A little apple should be given where no green food is available.

Egg-bound.—When a hen bird after sitting for some days on a nest does not lay, but appears instead generally out of sorts, she will be found to be egg-bound. She should be held over a jug of hot water, and then the vent should be anointed with a little olive oil. Two drops of olive or castor oil should also be given internally.

POULTRY-KEEPING

A LARGE amount of interest and pleasure may be had out of poultry-keeping, where there is sufficient space for a good run and the tending of fowls is thoroughly well understood.

Poultry-keeping on a large scale for profit will not here be dealt with. Suffice it to say that it is a business which should not be too readily undertaken by any one but an expert on account of the anxiety and great risks entailed. Where, however, a householder, with a certain amount of spare ground at his command for the erection of a suitable hen-house and run, keeps a few fowls for the purpose of supplying the table with fresh, new-laid eggs daily, it is a different matter. Poultry kept in this way will, if properly tended, more than pay for its keep—in fact, it will show a good margin of profit if the stock is judiciously kept up and renewed.

The Hen-House.—A suitable house and run must, of course, be provided. Excellent houses are supplied by the manufacturers of poultry appliances at very moderate prices. Cheap poultry appliances are a mistake, and it is money thrown away to buy them—the cheap house is bound to be made of poor quality, unseasoned timber, which will swell in wet weather so that the doors and windows will not shut, and shrink in the summer until there is a creak letting in draught between every board. The difference between two apparently similar houses at a £1 and 40s. is in the wood, as a rule—and the purchase of the better one will pay in the long-run. If the timber is good to start with, atmospheric conditions will have no effect upon it, and the house can be stood in the sun with impunity. Furthermore, a coat of paint now and then will make the house look like new, and it will fetch a fair price if at any time it is necessary to sell it. The roof of a wooden poultry-house should be of weather-board well painted or creosoted. Felt covering to the sides and roof is not to be recommended, as it is generally put on cheap makes to cover deficiencies in the wood.

A closed-up poultry-house with the usual ridge ventilation requires to be not less than 5 feet by 4 feet by 5 feet to be healthy accommodation for six fowls. One side of the house should have as large a window as possible, covered only with wire netting, as it is essential that the house should be properly ventilated.

As the dampness of our climate is one of the worst enemies of our poultry, a house well raised above the ground is to be preferred to a low pattern with no floor. The nests should be placed on a level with the floor. If the house is of a pattern which comes directly into contact with the ground, old railway sleepers placed under the woodwork will help to keep it in good condition.

Cleanliness.—Cleanliness in the poultry-house and run is essential. All poultry-houses and their runs should be cleaned out daily. A sprinkling of sifted ashes, sawdust, or peat-moss dust should always be thrown under the perches. The perches should be regularly taken out and cleaned, and the inside of the house should be limewashed at least three times a year.

Grit and Lime.—It is absolutely necessary that grit in some form should be supplied to fowls. This is indispensable in assisting them to digest their food. In every run a heap of gravel or broken stone, crockery or oyster-shell, must be placed, also some old mortar rubbish or similar substance. Laying fowls require a considerable quantity of lime to provide material for the egg shells, and this may be given in the shape of oyster-shells broken up, ground bones, or, best of all, mortar rubbish. The laying of a shell-less or soft-shelled egg is a sure sign that the birds are neglected in this respect.

Nest-Boxes.—These are often made too small. Good nest-boxes for small varieties can be made out of orange-boxes, which cost only a few pence each. They are already divided into three nests, are very strong, and need only the addition of some strips of wood along the openings in the sides. The advantage of such nests over more elaborate and costly ones is that they can be thrown away and replaced with new ones, if necessary, without compunction. The nests should be filled with straw, and each should contain a china egg.

Perches.—All perches should be arranged at a uniform height, which should not be greater than 4 feet from the ground. If they are placed at different heights, all the birds will endeavour to crowd on the highest perch, and will fight for possession of it. Perches should be round and small enough to be comfortably grasped by the toes of the fowls. They should be easily removable for cleaning purposes.

Site.—With regard to a site, wherever possible, poultry-houses should be so situated that they get all the sun in the winter, and yet are not too hot in the summer. A south-east or south-west aspect will meet the case, the choice to be decided by the prevailing wind of the district, away from which the houses should be turned.

Poultry Runs.—In cases where the fowls have a run out over a paddock, very great care is needed not to overstock the ground. Twelve birds to the acre seems to be the greatest number which can live healthily for an indefinite period of years. Ordinary hen runs should be enclosed with wire netting. They can be made by driving posts not less than 6 feet high into the ground at certain distances and attaching wire netting to them. Good portable hen runs

Indian corn (or maize) are the best grains. For soft foods these grains are ground into flour. Wheat ground in this way is known as middlings, sharps, pollards, or thirds, different names for the same thing given in different parts of the country. Oats treated in the same manner produce ground oats, barley meal, ground barley. Pea meal and bran are also good soft foods.

Middlings, bran, and pea meal mixed with warm water make an excellent morning meal of soft food for the cold months of autumn and winter. A mixture of ground oats and middlings is also good. The scraps of meat food should be given with this meal. The evening meal should be of grain and oats. For laying birds nothing can be better than oats,

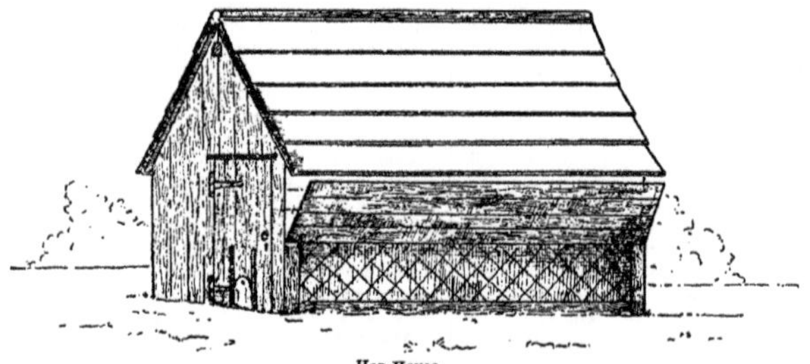

Hen-House.

may also be bought at moderate prices. A run 10 feet long by 6 feet wide will hold six fowls. The suburban poultry-keeper with very little space at his command will be well advised if he adds a roof to his run. His object will only be to produce a regular supply of new-laid eggs, and there is little doubt that he will attain his desire with greater certainty if he keeps his birds dry and well sheltered. Coal ashes should be spread over the floor of the run to keep it dry.

Food and Feeding.—To ensure the health of the denizens of the poultry-yard it is essential that they should have proper and suitable food. It must be remembered that a food which may be very suitable and even necessary in winter may be totally unsuitable in summer, and that birds penned will not thrive on a diet suitable for those enjoying a large range. Fowls to be fattened for the table must also be fed in a special manner. In short, the food must be of the right description to serve the particular purpose required. Laying hens will eat more than idle ones, and in winter the fowls will eat more than in summer.

Various kinds of grain, soft food (ground-up grain), vegetable and meat foods are necessary.

Grain and Soft Food.—Oats, wheat, barley,

whilst wheat is a good all-the-year-round food. Indian corn (or maize) is the best fattener, but is not to be recommended for any fowls except in very cold weather, because birds fed too exclusively on it are apt to acquire a soft, yellow, oily fat instead of the desirable firm, white flesh. For growing birds a judicious blending of oatmeal, Indian corn, wheat, and barley is desirable.

Meat Foods.—Grain and soft foods do not constitute the sum-total of the foods required by fowls. Quite as important and by no means so easily secured in the average poultry-yard are insect and animal life. Fowls which are at liberty forage themselves for a great deal of their meat food. They eat with avidity all manner of grubs and caterpillars, earth-worms, shell-snails, and slugs, as well as ants' eggs, beetles, and flies, and there is no doubt that birds thrive best when they have the opportunity of searching, stalking, and scratching for these desirable tit-bits. It is absolutely necessary that fowls should have a daily supply of animal food in some form or other. Cereals alone are not sufficient to fulfil all the necessary functions, and if the birds are confined they must receive something in addition, even if it takes the shape of meat from the butcher. For the small poultry-yard the house scraps, in which bits of meat and bones are always to be found, will be sufficient. "Save the scraps for the chickens" must therefore be the mandate to the powers that be in the kitchen. Cut green bone is very valuable as a meat food for fowls where meat and bone scraps from the table prove insufficient; also bullock's liver, tripe, or raw scraps may be had very cheaply from the butcher's. A small allowance of meat food minced finely and mixed with the soft food should be given daily. It is better to do this than give a larger quantity once or twice a week. Meat acts as a stimulant with fowls, and is especially valuable as an incentive to laying. It will be found to work wonders on backward pullets. If birds do not lay, it is very probably because they are low in health through their not having sufficient meat in their diet. A judicious meat diet will, in most cases, obviate all necessity of having the recourse to the spices and strong stimulants which are so much used for the purpose of bringing hens on to lay and increasing egg production.

Table Scraps.—Care must be taken in sorting the table scraps given to the fowls that they do not consist too largely of fat and bread-crusts. These contain very little egg material, and only serve to fatten without stimulating. Apart from the meat scraps, potatoes and potato-parings mix well with the soft food.

Green Food.—Fowls eat quite a lot of grass if they get the chance, and a daily supply of green food is as indispensable to birds in confinement as is animal food. The green stuff may take the form of a few handfuls of grass, a cabbage or lettuce hung up in the run at a height where it can be conveniently pecked at, or, in fact, almost any garden produce. Under this category we may include potatoes, carrots, and other roots, none of which come amiss if boiled till soft and mixed with the meal in small quantities. The cores of apples with the seeds (which will be eagerly devoured) and the peel can be given if everything else fails, but it is necessary to mention that too free use of apples leads to a bad kind of diarrhœa in fowls. Birds which have free access to the apple heaps in autumn in the orchards of the West get in sad plight from this cause.

Number of Meals.—Two meals a day—one early in the morning, the other in the evening—are ample for fowls which have a paddock or other space to roam about in, whilst birds in confinement should have a third and lighter meal, mainly of green stuff at noon. The soft food should be given at the morning meal, mixed with any scraps, green bone, &c., to constitute the meat allowance. The evening meal should consist of grain. For the morning feed just as much soft food should be given as the fowls will run after eagerly—this will be about 2 oz. to 3 oz. per bird. For the evening meal 2 oz. of grain per head for the small breeds, 2½ oz. to 3 oz. for the large ones, will be sufficient.

Birds in the fattening pen intended for the table should have not less than three square meals daily, and young chickens need feeding four to six times a day.

Cost of Feeding Fowls.—This depends, of course, partly upon whether the food is purchased in an advantageous market, also upon how much *has* to be bought. Presuming that *all* the food has to be purchased, and that this is done in the cheapest market, we may estimate as follows for six laying fowls, weekly :—

6 HENS—1 WEEK.

Meal (2½ oz. each daily), say 6 lbs. barley meal, at 3s. 4d. per bushel of 48 lbs.. .	about 5d.
Grain (2¾ oz. each daily), say 7 lbs., at 3s. 9d. per bushel	„ 5½d.
Meat, 14 oz. greaves at 11s. per cwt. . .	„ 1d.
	11½d.

Green food and grit will have to be added to this sum, if not available in the form of scraps, and odds and ends of rubbish.

Water.—All water-vessels should be rinsed out and refilled with pure water twice daily. The water should never be allowed to stand in the sun, neither should snow water be given.

Hints on Buying Fowls.—When starting a poultry run it is necessary of course to buy young birds. It is by no means easy for a novice to tell the age of a fowl—a fact of which an unscrupulous vendor will take advantage. It may be said that, broadly speaking, the legs of a young hen are smooth and delicate, her comb and wattles soft, and her feathers close. Old hens often have hard, horny-looking legs with hard spurs, a stiff bill, and rough comb and wattles, while the feathers may be loose and inclined to droop behind. Any of these indications may, however, be deceptive, so that the buyer must, unfortunately, be somewhat dependent on the word of the seller as to the exact age of his pullets. For this reason it may be better to buy in the spring chickens fully fledged, when their age can be almost exactly arrived at, feed them well, and wait for the eggs.

For Winter Laying.—As very few pullets commence to lay before they are six months old, and the majority not until from one or two months older, to secure a supply of new-laid eggs in the winter it will be necessary to buy chickens hatched late in February or early in March. It is important that the pullets should have begun to lay before the first real frost sets in. Once they have commenced to lay, cold will seldom check them if they are sensibly fed, but they will often be deterred by cold from commencing egg production. When winter eggs are the chief concern, the majority of the pullets should be killed off after Christmas, as they get broody or stop laying, and they will be found to make excellent roasting birds even though nearly or quite a year old. Their places should be taken by chickens hatched from their eggs, thus ensuring a new generation of birds every year to provide the household with winter eggs. Hens, *i.e.* birds in their second winter and onwards, never lay in September, October, or November, because they are then moulting. It is known, however, that picked pullets, well forced from birth and hatched early, will not moult, but will lay instead.

Varieties of Fowls.—In deciding upon what fowls to keep it will be necessary to bear in mind for what special purpose they will be required. Certain breeds of fowls make the best layers, others are better for table purposes, whilst others in varying degrees are suitable for both. The following are very good fowls for laying purposes: Anconas, Andalusians, Minorcas, Leghorns, and Hamburgs. All of these are non-sitters, and lay white eggs. Ascels, Dorkings, Game, Indian Game, La Flèche, Poland, and Sussex are good table fowls. These are non-sitters, and lay dark-coloured eggs. Orpingtons, Langhams, Redcaps, Wyandottes, and Plymouth Rocks are sitters and good for both laying and table purposes. Houdans are non-sitters and good for laying as well as table purposes. Brahmas and Cochins are good layers of dark-coloured eggs, but are such inveterate sitters that they always show a marked inclination to become broody after having produced only a small number of eggs. The hens of both breeds make capital mothers.

Fowls for Small Runs.—Orpingtons, Minorcas, Leghorns, Cochins, Faverolles, Plymouth Rocks, and Wyandottes stand confinement well, and are therefore particularly suited for a small run in a kitchen garden or back yard.

Where the space is very limited chicken-hatching should not be attempted, and it is better, in these circumstances, to keep a few hens of the non-sitting breeds, without a cock. However, even the small poultry-keeper who keeps hens merely for the eggs they provide for the table requires to renew his stock every year if the egg supply is to be good and continuous, and if the fowl run is not unduly small a brood can easily be raised once in the year for effecting this purpose.

Making a Pen.—If the fowls have their liberty, a dozen hens of the heavier sitting breeds may be put with one cock. Of the non-sitting breeds, eight to ten hens is sufficient, if fully fertile eggs are expected. Eight or six hens respectively will be enough if the birds are confined.

The best results come from running March-hatched pullets with a cock in his second season, or from running a cockerel with hens in their second season. It must be remembered that the better the stock the better the chickens will be. If none but the strongest and healthiest birds are selected for stock, the chickens will inherit the good qualities of the parent birds. It does not matter how nearly related the latter are, so long as they are strong and healthy. In-breeding, in fact, is absolutely necessary in some cases to fix definite characteristics, and as long as the strongest and healthiest are selected for stocks no harm will come from breeding them together.

Selection of Eggs for Hatching.—Apart from the selection of eggs from particular hens, it is important that only eggs of fair average size, say, not less than 2 oz. in weight, of good shape, and with clean, smooth shells should be put on one side for hatching. None of the eggs should have been laid longer than three weeks at the outside, and the fresher they are the better.

The Sitting Hen.—Care must be taken in arranging a suitable nest for the sitting hen. The nest should always be made, if possible, on damp ground. To make a good nest, throw down a heap of mould in a corner of the sitting-house, place some bricks around it to keep it together, scoop out the centre slightly and place therein some soft straw, and the nest is complete.

If a number of hens are sitting together in the same house, it may be necessary to separate them with wire netting in some way, or to cover each over with a basket. Three cheap sitting-boxes can be made out of an orange-box, the nests being prepared with mould and a little straw as above suggested.

A heap or box of dry ashes should be within reach of every sitting hen for her to dust herself in.

The number of eggs to be placed under a hen varies from ten to fifteen, according to the time of year and the breed. In cold weather it is undesirable to give more than can be comfortably covered. If the outer eggs are merely covered by the feathers, and the season is inclement, a good hatch will not be secured.

Suitable eggs for settings may be had for from 5s. and upwards per setting (usually about fifteen eggs) from most poultry-rearers. The price will of course vary in regard to the quality of the eggs.

The period of incubation is twenty-one days. A hen should be allowed to get accustomed to her nest before the eggs are placed under her. This can be done by placing a couple of nest eggs in the nest and placing her on it at dusk. She should then be left for twenty-four hours, and when it is found she has quite settled down, the eggs for the sitting can be placed under her.

Food for Sitting Hens.—The food given should be wheat, soft food being unsuitable. It is sometimes difficult to get a hen—particularly a broody turkey hen—to eat; indeed, we have known one of the latter to die on the nest from this cause. In such a case they must be crammed daily with soft food, mixed as dry and crumbly as possible. We always like to see a hen feed freely, walk about a little, and take a dust-bath before returning to the nest. No fear need be entertained that harm will come to the eggs from a thorough cooling. They may be allowed to get stone cold, and will still hatch satisfactorily, especially at the commencement of incubation, and the more air in reason they get the stronger will the chickens be.

Broken Eggs.—If by chance an egg gets broken in the nest, all those in contact with it must be washed in warm water, and the nest renovated with clean earth and straw. A cracked egg may be repaired with a small piece of sticking-plaster or stamp-paper.

Towards the end of the three weeks (twenty-one days) of incubation, the nest, if very dry, may with advantage be sprinkled with rain-water, with a watering-can with rose. Under natural conditions, the eggs would be more or less exposed to rain during the temporary absence of the hen, besides benefiting from wet which may fall on the ground around them, and there is no doubt that ample moisture is an important factor towards a successful hatch.

Testing Eggs.—A simple and efficient instrument for testing the fertility of eggs is made by cutting a hole, the shape of but slightly smaller than an egg, in the centre of a piece of cardboard. The cardboard must be covered with black paper, or painted black. At night, if the egg is placed against the hole in the cardboard and held up to the light of a good lamp, the contents can be plainly seen on the seventh day. Infertile or "clear" eggs are almost transparent and similar to those new laid, and the novice can compare with a known unincubated egg if doubtful of the appearance they have. Those which contain chickens will appear quite dark and opaque, except at the larger end; possibly, if the light is strong enough, small branching blood-vessels will be seen. Addled eggs look very dark and cloudy.

Feeding and Rearing Chickens.—Chickens do not require any food for the first twenty-four hours of their existence. During this time both

Poultry Coop.

hen and choikens should be left alone. The first meal for the chicks should consist of a little baked custard, or hard-boiled eggs chopped fine, mixed with double the quantity of bread-crumbs and moistened with milk. The hen should be given a feed of Indian corn, then both hen and chicks should be taken to their coop, which should be placed on a piece of clean short grass. The coop will have to be placed on a board every night and imperviously closed if the presence of

Poultry Coop and Run.

rats is suspected. Coops are also sold with little runs attached. These are very useful when it is desired to keep the chicken within bounds.

During the last few years a revolution has taken place in the methods of feeding chickens. In the past meal messes were considered to fulfil all requirements. In the present the rage is all for "dry feeding," as it is called, and the loud praises of all poultry-keepers who have tried it testify to the benefit of the reform.

Now, instead of feeding the chicks on ground meal, small seeds, such as canary, millet, dari, and small wheat, are given. These seeds should be of the best and should be given whole, not crushed. It will be found that the chicks can be reared entirely from the beginning on this natural dietary supplemented with animal food.

Some authorities strongly recommend that a little baked custard be given during the first day or two, in lieu of the old-fashioned hard-boiled egg, and it no doubt makes a valuable addition to the dry food. If the chickens have their liberty they will find for themselves all the necessary grit, animal life, and green food. If confined, these items must be added to their menu by their owner. Ants' eggs and maggots will be much appreciated. Chopped nettles suit them very well, and finely-chopped onions and leeks have a wonderfully stimulating and apparently tonic action, and should be given freely. Chickens require grit just as much as adult fowls.

The chickens should be fed every two hours for the first three weeks. The first meal should be as early in the morning, and the last as late in the evening as possible. The grain should be thrown on the ground, the soft food placed in saucers, which together with the drinking-vessels should be kept clean.

Many poultry-rearers believe in giving the chickens Spratt's Chicken Meal as soft food for the early morning meal, giving the mixture of the various small seeds at the other meals.

Fattening Fowls for the Table.—Of the pure breeds, Dorkings, Game, Langshans, Wyandottes, Orpingtons, Plymouth Rocks, and Sussex are the most useful table-fowls for family purposes. The birds should be penned up in a warm, dark, quiet place for fattening. Fowls will fatten very well if confined in any place where they get no exercise, and are out of sight and hearing of their comrades.

Feeding for Fattening Purposes.—Oatmeal is the best food, maize having a tendency to produce a yellow, oily fat. Three meals daily, as far apart as possible, should be given, consisting of oatmeal mixed to a crumbly state with (if possible) milk. "Scraps" from the house, particularly finely chopped fat trimmings, may be mixed in with advantage. A supply of water and some coarse sand or fine gravel should always stand before the birds. As much as the fowls can eat should be given at each meal, *but no more.* Food should never be left standing in front of them. Care must be taken that the troughs are kept clean and the food is not allowed to become sour.

A bird will be at its best after three weeks' penning. If left longer than this it will "go off," and the food given be wasted. In view of this fact, it is important that fowls should be penned up so as to be at their best exactly when wanted.

Killing.—Dislocation of the neck, if properly done, is undoubtedly the most humane method of killing a fowl. The system of "wringing the neck" is not to be recommended, an easier and more certain mode being to hold the bird by the legs and give it a very sharp blow at the back of the neck with a small but heavy stick. For the average poultry hand, who does not understand correct dislocation, perhaps the best way of all to bring about a merciful and instantaneous death is to pierce the brain with a knife. The bird must be hung up by the legs, the mouth opened, and the blade of a penknife thrust firmly through the back part of the roof of the mouth. An incision should be made in the neck, and the bird should be left hanging for a short time until the blood has drained out if great whiteness of flesh is desired; but bleeding is not absolutely necessary.

A fowl plucks much more easily when still warm.

The best time to kill is first thing in the morning before the early meal, as the intestines will then be free of food. A fast of not less than three hours is absolutely necessary, or the birds will not keep for long, and the flesh will lack firmness.

COMMON AILMENTS OF THE FOWL

The majority of the complaints from which poultry suffer are brought on by lack of cleanliness, cold or damp, or a faulty dietary. In the well-kept poultry-yard disease should be rare. When a bird appears to be unwell it should at once be isolated from the others, as most of the ailments of the fowl are infectious.

The following are some of the most common ailments amongst poultry :—

Cramp.—This is a frequent complaint with chickens, caused by exposure to cold and wet, or too close confinement on a boarded floor. The toes of the little birds become contracted, and they will often sit down to relieve the feet.

Treatment.—The birds will usually recover if placed for a few hours in a hamper near the fire. Their legs may be rubbed with turpentine to hasten the cure.

Diarrhœa.—This may be caused by exposure to wet and cold, sudden change of food, or unsuitable food.

Treatment.—A case of simple diarrhœa is best treated first by starvation, a dose of castor oil being given if the bird is very bad. A drop or two of tincture of opium will also cure it. The most suitable food until the ailment is completely past is boiled rice, and plenty of grit should be put within reach of the invalid. As diarrhœa in its initial stages is very difficult to distinguish from the fatal fowl enteritis and enteric, or inflammation of some portion of the intestines, a disease which would cause the death of the whole stock in a short space of time, it is advisable that all symptoms of diarrhœa should be looked upon with the greatest suspicion, the invalid isolated, and the other fowls removed to fresh ground if possible. If the bird is undoubtedly inflicted with inflammation of the intestines, it should be killed at once, and the body burnt, as a cure is almost hopeless and certainly not worth attempting.

Egg-binding.—When a hen is unable to pass her egg she is said to be egg-bound. A hen who is egg-bound will be seen to go frequently to the nest and come out again without having laid, her wings and tail will be drooping, and she will be evidently in pain. This will be caused by an unusually large egg which she is unable to pass.

Treatment.—Hold the hen over a vessel of hot water so that the steam can reach the vent, and apply a little olive oil to the vent; a dose of castor oil may also be given with advantage. The hen should be kept as quiet as possible.

Gapes.—This causes a great deal of mortality amongst chickens, and is caused by small worms which live in the windpipe. The chicken gasps for breath, and needs to be speedily relieved of the worms, which choke it. This disease never occurs amongst carefully housed chickens, and is in part due to neglect.

Treatment.—If taken early, a morsel of camphor the size of a grain of wheat given daily, and a little camphor put in the drinking-water, combined with improvement in diet and housing, may effect a cure. In bad cases it may be necessary to insert a feather, stripped to within an inch of the point, and dipped in a weak solution of tobacco water, quickly into the windpipe, turning it round and drawing it out again together with some of the parasites. Another remedy is to put the fowl in a box for a quarter of an hour at a time, placing a small piece of sponge soaked in eucalyptus oil in with it, the process to be repeated constantly throughout one or more days as found necessary. The breathing of air strongly impregnated with eucalyptus will cause the death of the worms.

Leg Weakness.—*Cause.*—The body of the bird is too heavy for the strength of its legs, consequently it constantly subsides into a sitting position.

Treatment.—The constitution of the bird must be built up on nourishing food and meat. The food should be little in quantity, but of the best, to overcome this form of weakness.

Difficulty in Moulting is due entirely to weakness and general debility.

Treatment.—Birds should be kept in a warm house and fed liberally on animal food. As much saccharated carbonate of iron as will cover a threepenny piece, given mixed with the soft food daily to each individual, will act as a tonic, and help to build up the constitution.

Roup.—*Cause.*—A very contagious disease of the respiratory organs, actually a species of catarrh, symptomised by offensive discharge from the nostrils, &c., and caused by exposure to wet and *very* cold winds.

Treatment.—The affected bird should be immediately isolated and placed in a warm house. Feed on oatmeal mixed with ale or stout, and give plenty of green food. Some iron tonic, as recommended in the previous paragraph, will be beneficial. The head and eyes must be washed morning and evening with warm water, to which a few drops of carbolic acid have been added. The disease runs its course very rapidly, and may spread throughout the entire yard. If in a week the bird is not almost well, it is better to kill it and burn the carcase. In all cases of contagious diseases the attendant should be careful that he does not throw food to healthy fowls with hands unwashed since he handled a sick bird.

Scaly Legs.—*Cause.*—A very small insect which burrows under the scales and forms little cells, temporarily disfiguring the legs, and causing considerable irritation.

Treatment.—The best cure is to brush the legs twice daily with a hard tooth or nail brush dipped in paraffin oil. A fortnight's daily attention will usually get the legs right. The appearance of this ailment should suggest the advisability of a thorough cleaning out, disinfection, and lime-washing of all poultry-houses.

Vermin.—*Cause.*—Neglect and uncleanliness, particularly absence of an efficient dust-bath. Fowls generally have a few fleas in summer, but with proper attention vermin should not be sufficiently prevalent to cause annoyance to the bird.

Treatment.—The addition of some flowers of sulphur to the dust-bath, and the dusting of the hen with insect powder, will alleviate these troubles. In very bad cases it may be necessary, to dress the hen on head and beneath wings and thighs with paraffin. These attentions will be of little avail, however, unless the poultry-house is thoroughly cleaned out and the walls and perches and all crevices lime-washed. Fleas breed in dust, consequently none should be allowed to accumulate untouched for more than a few days at a time.

RECREATIONS

INDOOR GAMES AND ENTERTAINMENT

Every woman should include a knowledge of good indoor games and entertainments amongst her accomplishments. To be able to play well is almost as essential as to be able to do one's work thoroughly. The most popular people with children and the younger "grown-ups" are almost invariably those who are good organisers of games. We have all of us experienced the dullness of those long evenings that drag for want of something to do or for want of co-operation in amusement. Let us take a typical case. One member of the family may have an interesting book—her evening will most probably be spent to her satisfaction; another may be engaged in writing letters. This is an agreeable task for some; in any case it is a task which prevents time hanging on one's hands. Well, let us suppose that the one or two remaining members of the family have nothing to do. They cannot keep up a conversation for fear of disturbing the others. They literally have to sit gazing in the fire yawning the time away until bed-time. Now dullness and want of occupation are especially bad for young people, and the wise head of a family will never allow such a state of affairs to prevail. She will make a point of seeing that all the evenings of her young people are spent pleasantly and well by encouraging them to co-operate in their amusements by having games in which all may join. Other young people may sometimes call in in the evenings, and the greater the number of players the more fun there will be. In fact, friends will soon make a habit of dropping in on various evenings, knowing that they will always be amused. The wise mother will encourage these impromptu visits, as she will realise that the social spirit is as the breath of life to the young folk, and that if opportunity is afforded to her sons in particular to spend their evenings pleasantly at home, they will not be anxious to seek their amusement abroad. It may indeed be said that dull evenings have been the means of breaking up many an otherwise happy home circle. The thoughtful house-mistress will therefore take this to heart and keep her young family together by entering with zest into their amusements and occupations, and making herself an adept organiser of all kinds of home fun.

Theatricals.—Amongst the favourite entertainments provided at children's parties theatricals may be said to take a foremost place. To begin with, the pleasure of preparation almost equals, if it does not excel, that of the actual performance. The word "rehearsal" has a mysterious yet potent charm for the young people. It is synonymous to them with many pleasant little gatherings which may be arranged in turn, at the houses of the various players and at which they go over their parts, arrange about the costumes and all the various other details which have to be attended to.

For home theatricals to be a success there must always be some good organiser to take charge of the whole proceedings in regard to choice of play, choice of performers, costumes, and scenery. Without this chaos would inevitably result. The organiser must also act as stage manager, allotting to each player his or her part. In this respect her task will be somewhat difficult, for very seldom yet has a little company of players been known to assemble without five or six of them at least wishing to play the principal rôle.

In this respect the stage manager's word must be law. Having once made her decision in regard to the allotting of the parts, she must be careful never to deviate from it, whatever pressure may be brought to bear upon her, unless there should be very good reason for her doing so, such as the utter incompetency or unsuitability of any particular player concerned. But the careful stage manager will think well before she gives out the parts, and thus avoid making mistakes which are often the means of hurting the feelings of the person chiefly concerned, and which might well have been avoided.

Home theatricals, if properly arranged, involve very little expense. Fancy costumes can be made of the cheapest materials, such as art muslin and sateens, whilst if the piece to be presented is a modern one the dressing is even yet more simplified. Friends and relations will willingly lend articles from their wardrobes in order to assist in the success of the presentation.

The size and shape of the room in which the theatricals are to be given are most important considerations. A large drawing-room with a curtained alcove or folding-doors in the centre is the most suitable for the purpose. The stage will be on one side of the folding-doors or curtains, while the members of the audience are seated on the other side. Rows of chairs should be neatly arranged in the auditorium, and in a manner which will allow for as good a view as possible of the stage to be obtained. Of course, where there is no raised platform the people seated in the back rows will not see so well as those in front, and for this reason the latter position should as far as posible be allotted to the tiniest of the juveniles with the grown-ups who are in charge of them.

On the night of the performance complete order must reign behind the scenes. The players should be dressed and in their places at least ten minutes before the curtain goes up. They should be letter perfect in their parts but at the same time "stage fright" is a factor which must be reckoned with, and for this reason there should always be a "prompter" concealed from the audience who, keeping the MSS. of the play in front of her, will follow the dialogue carefully, giving assistance when necessary in a clear low voice. The words should never be whispered nor too loudly spoken: a happy medium is acquired with experience.

The stage manager should always have a list of any "properties" required in the piece, such as walking sticks, flowers, or the inevitable letter upon which the plot of so many a play depends. It would be disastrous, for instance, if the heroine were supposed to discover an all-important letter upon her writing-table, and when the time came for her to find it the letter was not there. Few young amateurs would have the presence of mind to cope with such a difficulty. The stage manager should see therefore that everything is in its place before the curtain rises, or else appoint some one to do it for her.

All the players must be well acquainted with their exits and entrances. It would not do for any one, for instance, to appear to go through a blank wall or a window instead of through the door, but this is a mistake which is very commonly made, to the amusement of the onlookers. In the ordinary drawing-room screens have to play an important part in the arrangement of the exits. Four screens, two on each side, can be requisitioned for the wings, and a small steady table placed in each recess (see illustration) for moderator lamps—preferably of the self-extinguishing pattern, in case they should be upset by an untoward accident—to make up for the deficiency of footlights, though these can be provided by the aid of a little ingenuity, *e.g.* candle reading-lamps with shades and reflectors, begged or borrowed from accommodating neighbours. Cocoa-tins cut in half and night-lights will serve the purpose equally well. Here, again, the inventive genius of the promoters of the enterprise will have to be called into play.

By the judicious arrangement of the screens it will be possible for exits and entrances on both sides of the stage.

Very little expense need be gone into in the way of scenery. If it is an indoor scene, as the room of a house, as long as the furniture on the stage is suitably arranged no scenery will be required. Simple outdoor scenes can also be very easily planned. I remember seeing a most admirable representation of the fairy scenes from "The Midsummer Night's Dream" given at a Christmas party by some very talented children. In this the background to the scene was hung with green art muslin, to which were tacked trailing boughs of ivy and other foliage. Stiff brown paper covered the floor, loose foliage being scattered here and there in realistic fashion, whilst green art muslin spread over footstools and cushions, and artistically decorated here and there with more leaves, did admirable duty as the green bank upon which Titania sleeps. Palms and other plants were judiciously arranged along the sides of the stage near the wings.

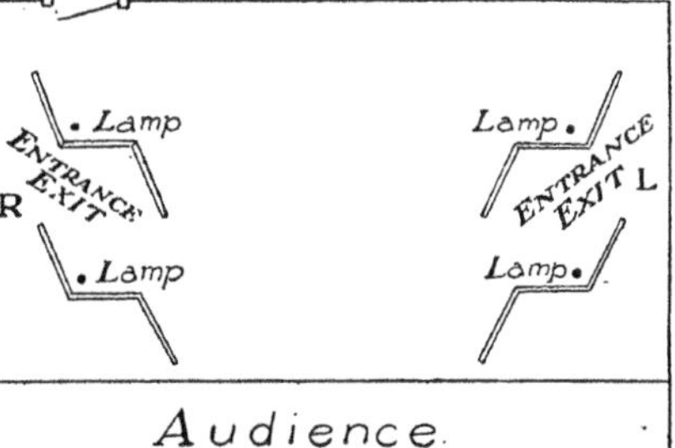

Plan showing arrangement of Screens for Exits and Entrances.

The dresses, which were correct in every detail, were all fashioned out of art muslin. As this material is procurable at 2d. a yard it can be imagined that they were not costly, although very graceful and pretty. All these garments were cut and made at home from copies of the "Midsummer Night's Dream" pictures. The most costly item was the expenditure entailed by the hiring of a mechanical donkey's head at 5s. 6d. for the night.

How to Make a Drop-Curtain.—An essential piece of stage furniture for amateur theatricals is the drop-curtain. It can be made from two equal widths of some serviceable material such as dark cretonne, supported by brass rings on a stout bamboo rod, to either end of which are attached large steel eyes (A A).

The bamboo rod should be cut to such a length that when the eyes have been added, the whole can be fixed to steel hooks screwed into the picture rail on either side of the room.

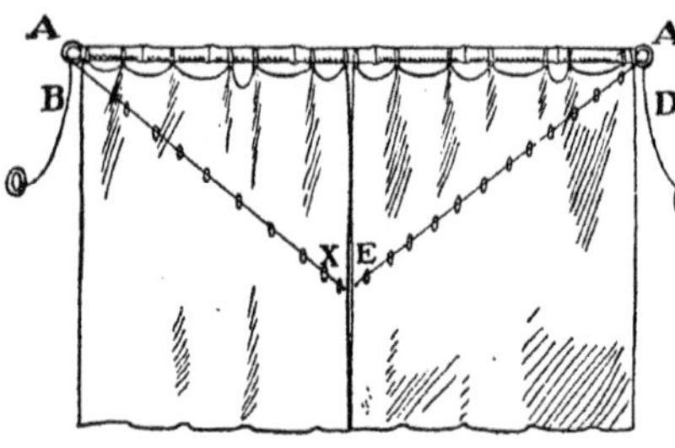

Back View of Drop-Curtain.

Should any difficulty be experienced in procuring a rod of sufficient length, the difficulty may be overcome by the use of two shorter pieces joined at the middle by iron sockets.

In the case where it is intended to give the performance in either a schoolroom or a small hall, a curtain of a much larger size and of stouter material would be required, and this latter can be supported on a length of strong gas barrelling held in position by brackets nailed to the wall at each end.

The arrangement for raising or lowering the curtain is shown in the diagram, in which A A is the rod. A number of small brass rings is then sewn to the back of the curtain, as at A X and A E. Top rings, much larger, are also attached to the curtain and passed along the rod. Cord is next run from X and E respectively through the rings at A, and allowed to hang loose as at D and B. The bottom of the curtain should be weighted with shot.

The Choice of Plays.—The choice of plays will necessarily depend upon the age and talents of the performers. Simple one act comedies with three or four persons at most are the best to attempt at first. Good dialogues are very amusing, and their production involves very little trouble and expense. For children the plays selected should be as simple and pretty as possible. For the very tiny tots nothing will be found more suitable than the simple fairy tales, such as "Little Red Riding Hood," or tales from history, as "King Alfred and the Cakes." Some very pretty children's plays are included in the book "Little Plays," by Lena Dalkeith, which are published at 1s. and 1s. 6d., and may be obtained by ordering through any bookseller.

Very often the "grown-up" organiser of juvenile theatricals will herself have a taste for dramatic writing. She will then be able to arrange any of the various fairy tales in accordance with her own ideas. The elder children will be found to be somewhat more ambitious in regard to their histrionic efforts. They will as a rule wish to emulate the "grown-ups" as far as possible in their selection of plays. Some of the simpler comedies and farces will be found very suitable, although a certain amount of discretion must be exercised in their choice.

Messrs. Samuel French & Co., of 24 Southampton Street, Strand, London, publish a large selection of plays for amateurs, and their list includes the following simple little pieces:—

"Aunt Jane," by G. H. Pugh, is a very suitable little play for schoolgirls. There are three characters; the *mise-en-scène* is of the simplest and such as can be arranged with the utmost ease in any ordinary room. The plot turns upon the expected arrival of an unknown aunt to take charge of her little nieces. There is much conjecture as to what she will be like. One of the nieces forms the idea of dressing up as Aunt Jane for the benefit of her sister, representing her as a very unpleasant person indeed. Finally the deception is discovered by means of a letter from Aunt Jane announcing that she is unable to arrive on that particular day. The tone of her letter indicates that she is a very nice aunt indeed, and the curtain goes down on two reassured and happy little nieces. The dialogue is brisk and amusing, whilst it is at the same time simple and easily memorised.

"Nursery Rhymeia" or "The Party," "The Prince and the Pie," by Alfred Paxton (eight characters), "The Waxworks' Revels," by William Heighway (eleven characters), are suitable for a more ambitious performance by a large number of children at a Christmas party, for instance.

Sometimes the performers will consist only of boys. In these circumstances preference should be given to plays in which only male characters are required, such as in Miss Keating's "Plot of Potzentausend."

One great thing to be borne in mind in regard to home theatricals is to obviate as far as possible all danger of fire. Candles should not be used as footlights. It is better to do without footlights at all than run any risks in this direction. Where there are electric light pendants conveniently placed, nothing will be found easier than to arrange these in such a manner that their full light is reflected on the stage. These, with the safety-lamps in the wings, should be all sufficient for lighting purposes in an ordinary room.

Apart from the necessary wigs and other paraphernalia, "make up" is not always necessary when the theatricals take place in a room of ordinary dimensions where there is no limelight. In large rooms and halls, however, make up will be necessary. In his book "Home Fun," Mr. Cecil H. Bullivant gives very minute and clear directions in the art of "making up." He also gives many valuable hints in regard to the making of home scenery, with the minimum of outlay. The amateur theatrical enthusiast cannot do better than purchase a copy of this book, which will tell her everything most useful to know in regard to these two very important essentials in dramatic representation.

The Pastoral Play.—In the summer no more charming entertainment can be devised than a pastoral play rendered by children. Hostesses with suitable garden space would do well to keep this fact in mind. A pastoral play may also prove a most enjoyable finish to a garden party. The grounds should be prettily decorated with Japanese lanterns, &c.; the performance should, if possible, be given on a raised portion of lawn or ground with a slope towards the audience.

Mention has already been made of the suitability of the fairy scenes from the "Midsummer Night's Dream" for juvenile performance. These are also admirably suited for open-air representation. "Under the Greenwood Tree," by Major Philip Trevor, is a very pretty little play, especially suitable for performance out of doors. The scene is a woodland glade, where a number of children are taking part in a "costume" picnic, headed by little Molly, Marchioness of Storr, the child owner of the forest. Molly is dressed as Berengaria, Queen of Richard I.; the others may wear any fancy dresses. In the course of their revels the children discover Robin Hood and Maid Marian in the trunk of a tree. They come to life for a spell, and Robin tells them about the days of King Richard. Many bright songs are introduced, and a feature of the play is a pretty Maypole dance.

Plays for "Grown-Ups."—The choice of plays for grown-up performers is practically unlimited. Light comedies in one act, such as "Time is Money" and "Compromising Martha," will be generally found to be most suitable for home performance.

It should be remembered that when a copyright play is to be performed in public for charity or other purposes, the authorised permission for the performance must be obtained and a fee (usually one guinea) paid. This does not apply, however, to performances given in private houses where no money is taken for the seats.

TABLEAUX VIVANTS

For tableaux vivants a good stage manager is above all essential. Upon her rests the responsibility of posing the actors and arranging the setting of the "living picture" in as effective a manner as possible. The subjects chosen for the tableaux should be those that can easily be recognised by the audience, such as characters and scenes from Shakespeare, historical scenes, favourite fairy tales, representations of famous pictures or tableaux from famous plays. "Three Little Maids from School," "Bubbles," "The Sign of the Cross," "Cinderella," "The Geisha"—all make pretty pictures easy of representation. For the first-named picture three girls in Japanese costume should be grouped in attitudes typical of Yum-Yum's "Three Little Maids from School" song in the "Mikado." For "Bubbles" only one juvenile actor is necessary. He should have as far as possible the same cherubic type of countenance as that of his prototype in Millais' famous picture. Costume and pose should also be very closely copied. A very simple tableau is the "Geisha." A girl dressed in a brightly coloured kimono seated on the ground in oriental fashion, holding a Japanese sunshade over her head. "The Sign of the Cross" has long been a favourite tableau with amateurs. The poses of Mercia and Marcus have become familiarised to most of us by means of the many pictures published of the late Wilson Barrett's play. One tableau might represent Mercia holding the cross aloft and Marcus bowing down in reverence before it, whilst another could be illustrative of the well-known picture, Mercia leading Marcus to the "Light Beyond." "Cinderella" is an ever-popular subject for tableaux. She might appear in her tattered dress, seated on the floor gazing into the cinders with her hands clasped round her knees. There are many other fairy-tale tableaux dear to the heart of the little ones, such as "The Prince Discovering the Sleeping Beauty," "Dick Whittingtou resting on his way to London," &c., &c., judicious selections from which should present no difficulty to the stage manager with artistic ideas and a taste for grouping. When the pictures are historical, illustrated books on costume should be studied, such as "British Costume during Nineteen Centuries," by Mrs. Charles Ashdown.

The stage manager must before all choose suitable exponents of the various characters to be depicted. No tableau should last longer than three or four minutes at most, and the various scenes should follow each other as quickly as possible. Careful attention should be given to the lighting effects, and a drop-curtain should be arranged as for private theatricals, a person being stationed at either side for its prompt raising or lowering at a given signal.

The thoughts of each character must be concentrated on the part undertaken and the onlookers absolutely forgotten. As far as possible the actors should forget that there is a certain amount of strain in the immovable poise, otherwise limbs will twitch and the balance and pose be in peril. With sufficient practice it will not be difficult to remain in the attitude fixed upon for the few minutes after the curtain is lifted. Impersonators should not be afraid to breathe regularly, for this prevents artificial rigidity.

CHARADES

One of the most popular indoor entertainments for winter evenings, or indoor parties, both with children and "grown-ups," is to be found in charades. Not only do they afford amusement to the audience, but the players themselves obtain a good deal of fun from their efforts to baffle those who are listening to them.

Suppose, for instance, that a "party" is composed of some twenty people. About five or six of them are selected to go outside, choose a word, which can easily be split into syllables, each making a word in itself. When they have chosen their word they must go in and act it, giving a different scene for each syllable, and finally a scene for the whole word, which latter the audience are required to guess when the play is over.

The players must not waste too much time in planning how best to act the words, or the audience will show signs of impatience. This can also be averted by the hostess arranging for a musical or other little "stop-gap" to fill up the time which must necessarily elapse between the moment when the players retire and their subsequent appearance.

Having thought of a little sketch which will take in all the several parts of the word chosen, the players arrange impromptu scenery and start the first act, taking care to bring in the first syllable, and yet not giving it undue prominence. This care must be observed all the way through the charade, as the fun is much greater when the listeners cannot guess the word too easily.

If the word chosen is "Indignation," it is split into three syllables—In-dig-nation.

These words having been acted, in the last scene the complete word is brought in, and as it is through this act the audience will listen most carefully for a clue, the players, if they wish to baffle them, should do their best to bring in a variety of words with the same number of syllables as those contained in the word they are acting, in order to mislead the listeners.

If preferred the various scenes need have no connection at all with each other, a complete little play being acted for each syllable and for the complete word. This often proves the most enjoyable method, and one that renders the word much more difficult to guess.

The more impromptu the organisation of charades the more enjoyable they will prove. The players should always "dress up" if possible, table-cloths, bed-covers, shawls, and scarves may be requisitioned; the homelier the materials to hand the more comical at times the effect will be. In all cases good fun should be aimed at, for charades are most successful when played in a broadly comical spirit. This applies in the main to impromptu charades, for when they are prepared for a long time beforehand as a feature of entertainment for a party, they should be prepared with as much care in regard to acting, staging, dress, and other important details as is entailed in the rehearsals and preparation of an ordinary play.

A stage manager should always be appointed, preferably one who is quick to decide upon a word, and who is adept in the planning out of suitable scenes. The following words, being easily subdivided, are suitable for charades, and may serve as a guide to the selection of others: Brace-let, care-ful, care-less, can-did, car-pet, case-ment, dor-mouse, eye-glass, fire-work, grate-ful, kid-nap, mis-take, night-mare, out-fit, sun-shine, ac-ci-dent (axe-sea-dent), baron-et-cy (baron-ate-sea), con-flag-ration, high-way-man, in-spec-tor, night-in-gale.

Thus from the word "grateful" a very pretty charade for children could be acted in this way:—

Scene I.—Cinderella is seen dressed in her rags, gazing into the cinders in the grate. Presently the shrill voice of one of her sisters is heard calling "Cinderella, Cinderella!" The sister then comes into the room angrily and scolds Cinderella, asking her why she is wasting her time gazing into the *grate*, when she ought to be helping her to dress for the ball. The sister should wear a loose dressing wrap, and her thin wisps of hair should be done up in curl papers in grotesque fashion. Presently the other sister comes in, also in grotesque déshabille, and joins in rating Cinderella. Then the two step-sisters begin to fight with each other (the dialogue here can be made very amusing) until, finally, Cinderella rises in disgust and follows them into their room to help them dress for the ball.

Scene II.—Ante-room of the ball-room in the prince's house. Comical scene between Cinderella's sisters, who have been obliged to sit out most of the dances, and who cannot even get into supper because the room is *full*. They discuss the mysterious princess who has arrived at the ball and her wonderful glass slipper.

Suddenly one of the sisters exclaims, "Why, what is the matter? there is the princess alone running away from the palace as fast as her feet can carry her." The clock strikes twelve.

Scene III.—Cinderella's household once more. The baron, his wife, Cinderella and her sisters are all upon the scene. They discuss the proclamation of the prince, declaring he shall marry the girl whose foot the mysterious glass slipper will fit. Quarrelling takes place between the two sisters as to who has the smaller foot. Baron and his wife join in the argument. Baron declares that neither of them has so small a foot as Cinderella. The proud sisters and their mother now turn round and abuse both Cinderella and the Baron. Herald's voice outside proclaiming, "Oyez, Oyez, make way for his royal highness the prince." Prince enters with herald—shoe is tried on first one sister and then the other. They make comical endeavours to get it to fit, but to no purpose. Then the prince says, "Have you not another daughter?" Sisters reply contemptuously, "Oh, she is only a little cinder slut; it would be waste of time to try it on her." Cinderella advances, however, and asks for the shoe; she sits down whilst the herald tries it on her. It slips on with the greatest ease. She stands up, throws off her rags, and appears in the light dress of the princess. Delight of the prince, who embraces her, exclaiming, "I shall always be *grateful* to the little glass slipper."

PARLOUR GAMES

The parlour games here described are suitable either for children's parties, for impromptu little gatherings of young people, or for any quiet evening in the family circle. It will be found, as a rule, that amongst a number of young "grown-ups" the simpler and more childish the game the more the enjoyment to be derived from it. I have known a game of "hunt the slipper" keep a gathering of young people of ages varying from sixteen to twenty-three amused for over an hour. No game has therefore seemed too simple for inclusion under the general heading of "Parlour Games."

Dumb Crambo.—This game can be made even more amusing at times than charades, because in this case the word must be acted in dumb show, and those who choose the word often make a point of choosing one which will call upon all the ingenuity of the actors to represent it correctly without speaking. Half of the players go out of the room whilst the remaining half think of a verb, such as weep, skip, fly, &c. When they have chosen their word, one of their number goes outside to the other players, giving them a word which rhymes with the word which they are to act; thus, if the word chosen was "drop," she could say it was a word that rhymed with crop, and so on. With this clue the actors must come in and act in dumb show the word they think to be the right one. If they are wrong, their audience hisses and they have to go out again. If they have guessed right they are clapped, and at once they take the place of the others who have to go out and act the word in their turn.

Forfeits.—There are several games which entail the giving of forfeits, and as these are always a source of unparalleled delight for the young people, the method of crying forfeits, together with some of the favourite tasks imposed, will be described. Anything may be given by way of forfeit—a handkerchief, ring, bracelet, tie-pin, &c. The winner of the game, or the person who has escaped the forfeit penalty, takes charge of all the forfeits which have been collected. She then sits down with the players around her and chooses one of their number to impose the penalties. The latter has to kneel down with her face on the knees of the guardian of the forfeits, who holds up each article in turn, saying, "Here's a pretty thing, and a very pretty thing, and what is the owner of this pretty thing to do?"

The person who has to impose the tasks must exercise her ingenuity in suggesting things which will promote the most fun. Above all, should she try to think out "catch" forfeits or tasks which, through some ingenious turning of words, will seem almost impossible at first sight to perform, but which, when correctly interpreted, will turn out to be quite simple. Some well-known forfeits are:—

"To stand on one leg in one corner of the room, sing in another, dance in another, and cry in another."

"To bite two inches from the poker." This is a well-known "catch," and is done by snapping your teeth as for a bite two inches away from the poker. Many a player when set this task has stood for a long time in bewildered perplexity to the hilarious enjoyment of the onlookers.

"Put two chairs together, take off your shoes and jump over them." Another "catch": to do this put two chairs together, take off your shoes and jump over the *shoes*, not the chairs.

"Call your sweetheart's name up the chimney."

"Place the poker against the floor so that you cannot jump over it." Also a well-known "catch" penalty: to do this place the poker next the wall.

"Recite three verses, each one from a different poem without stopping."

"Hop upon one foot three times round the room."

"Put yourself out of the room through the keyhole." Write your name on a slip of paper and put it through the keyhole.

"Kiss a book inside and outside without opening it." Kiss the book first inside the room, then take it outside the room and kiss it again.

"Translate into French a sentence given by each member of the company." This is usually productive of great fun, as not only most nonsensical sentences are given, but also sentences which are most difficult of translation, especially by the elementary French scholar.

"Stand upon the fire." Write "the fire" on a piece of paper and stand upon it.

"Kiss the person you love best in the room." This may be done by kissing your reflection in the looking-glass.

"Give imitations of a donkey, a cow, a pig, a dog, or a cat."

"Waltz round the room blindfolded."

"Put out the fire in one minute." Write "the fire" on a piece of paper and put it out of the room.

The above forfeits will give indications as to the kind of tasks that may be set. Many ingenious tasks may be thought out in the home circle. The one chosen to "cry the forfeits" should always be an adept in calling them, or else the fun will lag.

Musical Chairs is a very favourite game for children's parties; it is a game also which is entered upon with zest by most young people upon any occasion when they find themselves gathered together in any numbers. It has often been the means of turning a dull evening into an extremely merry one. First of all some one must be able to play the piano. She need not be too particular as to the quality of her playing, but the more at ease she is with the piano keys the greater will be the enjoyment of the game, for she will rattle along when she is expected to stop playing, and stop when she is expected to play, so that the delightful confusion of the game will be increased to a remarkable degree, whilst with a slower, hesitating pianist the fun would be apt to lag. A row of chairs is arranged down the middle of the room, alternate chairs facing different ways. The chairs must be one less in number than the people who are playing. As soon as the music starts the players must dance round and round the chairs, and directly the music ceases each player must seat herself. Of course as there is one chair short one of the players will be left out, and the fun begins with the scrimmage to obtain seats as soon as the music stops. For each player who is left out a chair is taken away until there is only one chair left. Of the two people who remain to contest this chair the one who is first seated when the music stops wins the game. Sometimes musical chairs is played with forfeits, each player having to give a forfeit as she falls out of the game, the winner "calling the forfeits" at the end.

Consequences.—Any number of players can join in this table game, which is usually productive of much fun. To each player is given a pencil and a piece of paper, and the game is played as follows :—

All players are told to write down an adjective that can be applied to a gentleman. Having done this they fold over the paper at the top to hide what they have written. Then each player hands her slip to the neighbour on her left so that each receives a different slip to write on. On this they must now write a gentleman's name, after which they must pass on the papers in the same manner as before, and this must go on until they have finished all that is to be written. Consequences usually run in the following order :—

Give an adjective applicable to a man.
Give a man's name.
Give an adjective descriptive of a woman.
Give a woman's name.
Say where they met.
Say what he said to her.
Say what she said to him.
Say what he gave her.
Say what she did with it.
Say what she gave him.
Say what he did with it.
Say what the consequences were.
Say what the world said.

When all these questions have been answered the papers are opened and read aloud, and it can be imagined that, owing to their changing hands so frequently and no single one of the players being aware what the others have said, their contents are very funny.

Literary Consequences.—This game is played in a similar manner to Consequences, each player being provided with pencil and paper, only, instead of the name of a person, that of a book is taken. It is played as follows :—

(1) Each player writes down the title of a book.
(2) The sub-title.
(3) The author.
(4) His collaborator.
(5) Where published.
(6) What the reviewers said about it.
(7) The consequences.
(8) What the world said.

It can be well imagined that the sequence is apt to be somewhat funny at times.

Composite Drawing.—This is a game not unlike consequences, only drawing must take the place of writing. Each player is handed a piece of paper and pencil. On this she draws the head of a man, woman, child, bird, beast, or fish. When finished, the paper is folded over carefully to hide the drawing and then handed on to the player on the left. Then a body is drawn, the paper is again folded over and passed on, and the legs and feet are drawn. When the papers are opened out some very amusing results may be seen, such as a cat's head upon the body of a lady with the legs of a horse.

General Post.—This is a most amusing game for a number of players. One of the party is blindfolded and called the postman. Another of the players directs the game, and is called the postmaster-general; the others are seated round the room. The postmaster gives to each player the name of a town—needless to say, these names must be carefully remembered by all.

Then the game begins. The postmaster calls out the names of various towns to which he wishes to post a letter. The players who bear the names of these towns must immediately exchange seats. For instance, if he says, "I wish to send a letter from London to Dublin," the players who have been named after these towns must at once get up and change places whilst the postman tries to take one of the vacant chairs. If he is successful in this the player whose seat he has taken must become postman. When played with zest this game soon becomes a most enjoyable romp, which can be entered into heartily by both young and old.

Variations of Blind Man's Buff.—There are many variations of this simple and amusing game. As is generally known, the game which earned this name originally is played by blindfolding one of the players with a handkerchief or scarf. All the players dance round the blind man, running away from him when he gets too near. The blind man must not only catch one of them, but also be able to identify his captive. If he can do this the latter must take his turn at being blind man.

Another way of playing the game is to give the blind man two spoons. With these he must feel his captive in order to identify him instead of feeling with his hands. This, of course, makes the task much more difficult.

In yet another version of the game the blind man is made to stand in the centre of the room; he must have a stick in his hand. The players form a ring, and dance around him until he taps the ground with his stick. Then he points his stick towards one of the players, who has to answer any question the blind man asks, and the latter to guess his identity by his voice. Needless to say, the players must disguise their voices as far as possible in order to baffle their interlocutor. As soon as the latter has guessed the name of the person whom he has questioned, he can change places with the latter, who must be "blind man" in his turn.

Musical Buff is yet another version of this game. A person is stationed in each corner of the apartment, then one of the party is blindfolded and led into the centre of the room. The director of the game points to each of the four in succession, and each says in a separate clear tone the word "Come." When the word has been said by each in turn, the blind man endeavours to find his way towards the person who spoke last.

Proverbs.—One of the party retires while the rest decide upon a well-known proverb. When he returns, he stands in the centre of a semicircle. Some one taps three times with a stick, and at the third tap each player shouts one word of the proverb loudly and simultaneously. This is repeated three times, and it is amazing how difficult it is to distinguish even the most well-known proverb in the uproar.

Should one word give the key to the player not in the secret, the individual who speaks it takes his place. For instance, in the proverb "All is not gold that glitters," it may happen that the word "glitters" provides the keynote. Therefore, he or she who speaks it takes the place of the one who guesses.

The proverb must contain as many words as there are players, and each shouts only the one word allotted to him.

Another way of playing the game is for the person who has to guess the proverb to ask each player in turn a question. Each must introduce in her answer a word from the proverb.

The Game of Shadows.—A white sheet is stretched against the wall, with a lamp immediately before it. All other lights are extinguished. One of the company sits on a chair or steel with eyes fixed on the sheet. Behind him the company files noiselessly, the while he endeavours to identify them by means of the shadows silhouetted on the screen.

Simple disguises are allowable and increase the fun. For example, a boy may don a girl's hat, a girl a boy's; or a skirt or shawl may be draped over an Eton suit, thus concealing the wearer's identity. The one whose shadow betrays her takes the place of the player who identifies her.

Gardeners.—Two rows, headed by a chosen captain, face each other. In turn they fire at each other the names of vegetables, flowers, or fruit beginning with the letter A, and using in turn the other letters of the alphabet—asparagus, artichokes, apples, &c.

The players on each side set their wits to work to aid their captain when he shows signs of faltering. They are not allowed to speak aloud, their promptings being given in whispers, and this is where the fun comes in, for, when one is excited and eager to give a word, it is very difficult to remember to whisper, especially when placed at the tail of the line.

When a gardener and his side pause to remember a word the opposite side counts twenty slowly; if at the end of that time their opponents still fail, they forfeit a man. The game goes on until one captain has secured his adversaries' followers. Should any one except the leaders speak aloud, he or she is obliged to cross to the other party.

When a captain surrenders he is obliged to go to the end of the line, and the next man takes his place and responsibilities.

Tidings.—Each player adopts some trade or profession. One member reads out the social gossip from a daily paper. When he pauses and points at one of the rest, that one must reply quickly some sentence regarding his calling or the stock he sells, for instance—

Reader.—"The ball that took place at the residence of the Hon. Mrs. Mortimer last evening was distinguished by the presence of His Majesty the King.

"A number of débutantes were present, the majority of whom were dressed in—" Here the reader glances at the carpenter, who answers, "Shavings."

Reader—"Their headgear consisted of" (glances at the fruiterer)—

Fruiterer—"Pine-apples."

Reader—"Their jewels were necklaces" (glances at the ironmonger)—

Ironmonger—"Of nails."

Reader—"The dancing took place in—"

Tobacconist—"A cigar box."

Reader—"The walls of which were richly decorated with—"

Lawyer—"Red tape."

Reader—"The band was composed of forty instruments all—"

Doctor—"Medicine bottles."

Reader—"His Majesty's first partner was—"

Fishmonger—"A whiting."

Reader—"Who was most becomingly clad in—"

Chemist—"Silver scales."

Reader—"Her bouquet was composed of—"

Draper—"Reels of cotton."

Reader—"And her tiny feet were cased in—"

Mason—"Bricks."

Reader—"Her dancing was as light as—"

Plumber—"A gas escape."

Reader—"And her charming smiles showed to view a perfect set of—"

Bootmaker—"Black heels."

It can be imagined from this example the merriment and laughter similar answers evoke.

The Lawyer.—The party is divided into two rows, through which walks the lawyer. He asks a number of questions, and the answers may contain any words except "yes," "no," "white," "black."

The person to whom he puts his query does not reply, but the one immediately opposite does.

The lawyer exchanges places with the one who makes the first mistake.

An Example

Lawyer (pointing to Mary)—"Your hair is very long; is it your own?"

Tom opposite bawls, "False."

To Jessie—"Do these pretty boots pinch your feet?"

Jack—"Of course, they are two sizes too small."

To John—"Did you use your razor this morning?"

Jane—"He hasn't any hair to cut."

To Timothy—"Is your nurse waiting to put you to bed?"

Elsie—"Naturally; he goes to bed at seven."

To Dick—"What would you like on your next birthday?"

Ethel—"A rattle."

To James—"What is your favourite pastime?"

Alice—"Putting dolly to bed."

To Freda—"What is the colour of your face?"

Andrew (afraid to say "white" for fear of forfeit)—"Green."

The Lover's Coming.—All the members of the party save one are massed together at the end of the room. The leader walks close to them, and throws a light rubber ball towards any person she likes.

The person must be prepared to catch the ball. As the leader throws it she accompanies the action with these words, "My lover comes thus"—the ball is tossed in a way to illustrate the manner of the supposed lover. The thrower terminates her sentence by a letter of the alphabet. The one to whom the ball is thrown has to provide an adjective beginning with the given letter as she catches the ball, thus:—

Leader—"My lover comes g" (throws ball).

Catcher—"Gaily" (tosses ball back).

Leader—"My lover comes h."

Catcher—"Hopping."

Leader—"My lover comes o."

Catcher—"One-eyed."

Leader—"My lover comes s."

Catcher—"Smirking."

Excitement is caused by the difficulty in producing a word at a moment's notice and being ready to catch the ball at the same time.

Telegrams.—Each player is provided with paper and pencil, upon which any twelve letters are written, with sufficient space left between for words.

The leader gives a topic such as a wedding, accident, invitation, &c. A watch is placed on the table, and from ten to fifteen minutes given, during which each player concocts a telegram from the letters supplied by his left-hand neighbour.

At a signal the telegrams are thrust under a hat and read out in turn by the leader.

Example I.—Topic: a sensational robbery.

S.	B.	O.	B.
H.	M.	J.	P.
K.	I.	P.	H.

From these letters may be devised the following telegram:—"Serious burglary; one box hairpins missing. Jane prostrate; kindly inform police —Henry."

Example 2.—Topic : a catastrophe.

C.	A.	S.	D.
P.	B.	C.	A.
B.	Q.	D.	W.

"Cat ate Sunday dinner. Please bring cheese and bread; quite distracted—Wifie."

The funnier the telegram, the greater the laughter when it is read out.

The Fan Fight.—The players divide into two lines. A piece of tape is stretched across the room, and before every two players a feather is placed. Each player possesses a Japanese fan, and the object is to lift the feather and waft it on to a stretch of newspaper, which marks the opponents' den.

The dens are guarded by goalkeepers, also armed with fans, and their business is a lively one.

Feathers must not be blown or pushed with the hand, as happens sometimes when the excitement of the game makes one forgetful of all else but the threatening direction the feather is taking. Only the fan is to be used.

The feathers should be of different colours. When one of a side succeeds in driving a feather into the opposite den, he and his adversary retire from the game, but naturally they share the prevailing excitement and watch every movement of their respective sides, cheering and encouraging them to win.

When the feathers belonging to one side are all captured in a den, the other side is conqueror.

Magic Hieroglyphics.—For this seemingly mysterious achievement a confederate is required. He must know that—

A is shown by one tap because it is the first vowel.
E is shown by two taps because it is the second vowel.
I is shown by three taps because it is the third vowel.
O is shown by four taps because it is the fourth vowel.
U is shown by five taps because it is the fifth vowel.

Consonants are revealed by means of sentences, which the wizard speaks in a natural and unostentatious manner.

The confederate is banished from the room while the party decide upon the word he shall be called upon to guess. Monosyllables are preferable.

When he returns the wizard is armed with a wand, by means of which he proceeds to make imaginary pictures on the carpet.

Supposing the word to be "orange." He begins with four taps, and the confederate, who is all attention, knows that the word begins with the fourth vowel, O.

The wizard, flourishing his wand, remarks with extreme innocence :—

"Rather fatiguing work, as you perceive."

The confederate says to himself R.

One tap is the next sound for A.

And some sentence such as—

"No one can imagine the mental strain," supplies the letter N to his alert companion.

The wizard's query, voiced in a mocking tone—

"Getting near it ?" supplies the letter G.

A few more imaginary pictures, and two taps, which represent the letter E, and the confederate with an air of profound relief wipes his brow and declares confidentially that the word is "orange."

Result.—The company applaud loudly, and are thoroughly mystified.

The Auction Game.—This is a most fascinating resource for a wet wintry afternoon, and its preparations are interesting enough to keep a whole houseful of young folk occupied and amused. A large piece of cardboard is cut into twenty-five squares, and on each is pasted a picture of some article taken from advertisements in old newspapers, magazines, or catalogues. The pictures are numbered, and on the back a price in keeping with the article is written.

The more variety there is among the stock for sale the better. It may contain anything from a thoroughbred Persian to a set of nine-pins, and the prices may be copied from the catalogues, &c.

When this is done, a mint of paper or card-board money is manufactured. The range of coin corresponds to the prices of the articles. Should the most expensive of these be marked £100, the paper money must include that amount. Upon each disc of cardboard is written its value.

The guests having arrived, the capital is divided among them in equal portions. If there has been no time to manufacture the coin, imitation money can be purchased quite cheaply, and this lends a greater reality to the game.

The first thing is to secure an auctioneer amongst the party, who possesses a ready flow of language, and is not troubled by shyness. An amiable uncle or other grown-up relative will do capitally.

The auctioneer stands on a chair or stool and cries out the article before him, treating it as if it were real.

He is provided with a hammer, and the company begin an eager bidding for the thing that takes their fancy.

The players, as may be expected, are as anxious as people in a real auction to obtain what they covet at the lowest price possible.

Should a member offer more than he is able to pay, and succeed in being the last to name the highest price, he pays a forfeit of threepence to each of the other buyers, and the article is again placed on the auctioneer's table.

The winner is the individual who has got the best value for his money, and has the most capital in hand by the time the twenty-five articles are sold.

It is a good plan to offer prizes—a good one for the discreet and careful buyer, and a "booby" for the poor foolish spendthrift, who has nothing to show at the end of the game.

Excitement and eagerness are increased by the cry of the auctioneer, "Going, going, gone," and the beat of his hammer.

If he is able to introduce funny narratives concerning the articles into his harangue, so much the better.

For instance, a pair of boots, fashioned from the corpse of the King of Prussia's pet calf, and the black kid gloves which King Charles II. wore at the funeral of his great-aunt; the mouse-trap that once held prisoner a rodent of aristocratic lineage and purple blood; the ash-tray into which the burnt cigar of Peter the Great is supposed to have fallen—all should go at a high price.

The Whistle, another excellent game, is played in the following manner:—

One of the company is blindfolded, and a long ribbon, through which is threaded a whistle, is pinned to his back, and he is told that he must catch the blower and discover the whistle.

Of course he has no idea that it is on his own person.

He is swung into the centre of the room, and his playmates make surreptitious dives at the whistle and raise it to their lips, taking care not to stretch the ribbon so that he will feel the tug.

Perfect silence should be maintained by those eddying round him; they move on tip-toe, with bated breath, but now and then sounds of stifled laughter are heard.

The "blind" man seeks high and low for the possessor of the whistle, his ears strained to catch the direction of the sound. He may succeed in embracing a youth or damsel, but his search round the neck, waist, or in her fingers for the missing whistle is futile.

It will be long ere he guesses the secret, if he ever does, and the delight of young and old at his expense is hilarious.

The Poet's Corner.—This is an excellent and ingenious pastime for young men and women who have out-grown the old-world games of "Hunt the Slipper" and "Hide and Seek."

The "poets" are each given a slip of paper and pencil, at the head of which they write any question they like. When this is written, the papers are folded, so that the sentence is concealed and passed on to the left-hand neighbour, who, without looking at the question, writes any word she likes beneath so long as it is a noun. This is again concealed and passed to a third party, who must compose a rhythm or stanza, which includes both question and noun. As these have no relation to each other, some ingenuity is needed to link the two in a verse.

For example, suppose the question given is as follows:—

Question—"What is the time?"
Noun—"Chair."

Verse.

"*What is the time?*" Grandfather asks.
This is one of the pleasant tasks
He sets the children from his *chair.*
And round eyes at the timepiece stare.
Little Alice reads the time—
The old clock helps her, and chimes out nine.

Or—

Question—"What is your age?"
Noun—"Cigar."

Name Divinations.—This is a clever puzzle game, which seems to the beholder to be steeped in magic and mystery. In order to discover the name or birthplace of a person, the following table of five columns is necessary:—

(1)	(2)	(3)	(4)	(5)
A	B	D	H	P
C	C	E	I	Q
E	F	F	J	R
G	G	G	K	S
I	J	L	L	T
K	K	M	M	U
M	N	N	N	V
O	O	O	O	W
Q	R	T	X	X
S	S	U	Z	Y
U	V	V	Y	Z
W	W	W		
Y	Z			

The manipulator shows the table to the individual whose name he wishes to discover, asking him to point out the column or columns that contain the initial letter. A glance at the table will show that if it is in only one column it must be the top letter. Should it be found to be in more than one, it is discovered by adding the first letters of the columns in which it is stated to be, the sum supplying the alphabetical position of the letter. For example, take the name "Elizabeth."

Elizabeth glances at the table and looks for the columns in which her initial letter occurs. It is obvious that she must be careful not to overlook this repetition. She informs you that it is to be found in columns 1 and 3. Now, the columns mentioned are topped by the letters A and D, which are the first and fourth letters of the alphabet. Add these together and you get 5. *E is the fifth letter.* In case you forget it, write it on a slip of paper. The next letter, Elizabeth informs you, occurs in columns 3 and 4. These are headed by D and H=4+8=12.

The twelfth letter is L. Columns 1 and 4 contain I, headed by A and H=1+8=9. *The ninth letter is I.* Z is found in columns 2 and 4 and 5, headed by B, H and P=2+8+16=26. *The twenty-sixth letter is Z.* The next letter exists only in column No. 1, therefore it is A. The next letter exists only in column No. 1, therefore it is B. The next letter exists only in columns 1 and 3. The top letters of these, A and D=1+4=5. *The fifth letter is E.*

T is found in columns 3 and 5. Top letters D and P=4+16=20. The twentieth letter is T.

H occurs in column 4, therefore it is the top letter, H.

Result—Elizabeth.

Wizard Photography.—The wizard, who possesses a confederate, is banished from the room. During his absence the latter produces a piece of paper, and declares his intention of taking a photograph of any individual among the company upon it, in such a manner that it shall be visible to the wizard alone, who, upon examining it closely, will call out the name of the original.

Naturally every one considers that this must be quite an impossible proceeding, and for that reason every one becomes very curious and watchful, making up his mind to discover the trick.

The confederate fixes upon one of the company, poses her to his satisfaction, tells her not to look grave, &c., just as professional photographers do, and when she is quite ready and gazing at the sheet of paper, which is held out in the manipulator's left hand, he passes his right over it, snaps his fingers, and tells her that the wonder is accomplished.

He hastens to wrap the "plate" in his handkerchief, and, calling in the wizard, hands it to him, retiring to a seat where the latter can observe him without appearing to do so. The wizard, looking very mysterious and wise, bids the company maintain an unbroken silence while he unwraps and examines the "plate."

His confederate meanwhile imitates as nearly as possible the position of the original of the photograph.

Should she cross her feet, toss back her hair, rest her chin on her hand, or perform any other trivial action, the confederate does the same, quite naturally so as not to arouse any suspicion or notice. All attention being concentrated on the wizard, his actions will not be observed by any one save the manipulator, who is led by the position he assumes to guess the individual whose likeness on the "plate" is supposed to be visible to him alone.

Few would realise until they try the game the wonder and admiration of the guests for the wizard who successfully achieves his purpose, and the means employed are seldom, if ever, discovered.

The Missing Ring.—A plain curtain ring is threaded through a piece of tape or ribbon, knotted at the ends. The guests form a circle round a central figure. The ring is passed swiftly along through hands gripping the tape, while the master of ceremonies counts one, two.

At three, all fists must be threaded by the tape and perfectly motionless, and the man in the centre, who is permitted to observe the circuit of the ring, is called upon to say which person has possession of it. Should he guess rightly, he changes places with the individual.

Apples and Nuts.—Mix a number of hazel nuts and apples together on a table removed from the wall; hand a tea-spoon and table knife to each of the guests. Bid them at a given signal move to the table, with the knife in the right hand, the spoon in the left, and scoop up one apple and one nut. This is no easy matter on a smooth surface, for the probability is that the fruit and nuts will roll to the floor.

When they are secured, they must be conveyed to a dish at the other end of the room. He who performs this feat successfully the most times wins, and the apples and nuts are awarded him as a prize.

Amiable Dog.—The party is divided into two lines. The first player begins by saying, "Our little dog is amiable." The first player on the opposite side must answer quickly with another adjective beginning with the same letter thus, "Our little dog is artful." Meanwhile, the first player counts ten. If in that time his opponent fails to respond, he is obliged to go over to the opposite rank. Other letters of the alphabet may be used. The side that gains all the "men" wins.

Bouts Rimés.—This is a very amusing writing game. The players are provided with pencils and paper and each one is required to write down a line of poetry. After this is done the paper is folded down, but the last word of the line is written under the fold, so that it can be seen by the next person who has the slip. The latter must make her line of poetry rhyme with this word. As can well be imagined, the verses when complete nearly always make most comical reading.

Waxworks.—This is a game dearly loved by the little ones. The leader of the game must arrange all the others in various positions, giving them different characters or actions to represent. Thus one may be told to represent a Chinese mandarin. She will squat on the floor, her hands raised above her head. A couple of players will be placed in position for a waltz, others may be told off to represent marionettes, well-known advertisement pictures, cat chasing a mouse, &c., &c. When the groups are all arranged, the director of the game goes to the piano and begins to play a lively air. As soon as the music starts the waxworks must move into action—the nodding mandarin begins to nod, the dancers to dance, the marionettes to act, the cat to chase the mouse, &c., &c. When the music stops they must at once relapse into immobility. No matter what their position at the time, the more difficult it is to at once become motionless, and the more ridiculous the attitudes of the various players when the music stops, the more fun the game will be. Those who do not stop at once with the music must pay a forfeit. Sometimes in playing this game the players are divided into two parties, one party of players helping to pose the others for their parts and keeping watch in regard to those who are subject to forfeits, and helping the leader in this way. When the players are very numerous this is decidedly the better method to adopt.

Coffee-Pot.—One of the players goes out of the room whilst the remainder choose a word which has two meanings, such as "can," which can be used in the sense of "can" the verb and "can" the noun. When they have chosen the word the player comes in and asks each of the company a number of questions in his endeavour to guess the word. The word coffee-pot has to be used in the answer instead of the word selected, thus if "can" were the word selected and the answer were "I cannot do so," the player should reply, "I coffee-pot not do so."

CHRISTMAS PARTIES

At Christmas parties, at which guests of all ages are found, it is sometimes a perplexing riddle to the hostess to know how to entertain them all. Musical items which may delight the older members of the company may only serve to render younger folk restless and dull, and dancing is not always possible in rooms of limited size. Moreover, there are still many young folk who are unable to set their feet nimbly to waltz or two-step, and would much prefer a romp to whirling round in time to a measure.

Self-consciousness and shyness are usually very evident when the party enters the drawing-room, and this coating of ice, if not thawed quickly, will rapidly freeze into impenetrable restraint and gloom. At such times a good game, quickly organised, is invaluable. The rules should be explained by the hostess in so simple a manner that the youngest person can follow them, and everything necessary should be arranged beforehand to avoid awkward delays and pauses.

The hostess can make her selection of games from those detailed in the list of indoor amusements. Let the revels be of the simplest. "Musical Chairs" and "Hunt the Slipper" are great favourites with the children—any game which entails the crying of forfeits are also highly appreciated. A feature should always be made of a Christmas tree and the distribution of toys. This may be done in many ways. Either one of the grown-ups could dress up as Father Christmas in the traditional red robe, a long white wig and beard, and hand the presents to the little guests, or else the gifts could be distributed by lottery. For this each article upon the tree should have a ticket pinned to it on which a number is written. Duplicates of these tickets should be placed into a bag, and each little guest should be asked to draw a number, receiving the gift to which the number he or she has drawn corresponds. Plenty of excitement attends this method of distributing Christmas presents. Then the presents may be obtained by means of "lucky dips" in the bran tub. For this a large tub is half filled with bran in which the various gifts are hidden, and each little guest is allowed a "dip," becoming the proud possessor of whatever gift he or she withdraws.

The Christmas Postman.—Another novel manner of distributing Christmas presents is the following:—

Each gift is tied up in a neat brown-paper parcel upon which is written the name of the child to whom it is to be given. One of the elder children of the hostess is dressed up as a postman carrying a big sack containing the gifts over his shoulder. After tea, at the time arranged for the gift distribution, all the little guests are assembled together. The child who is to enact the rôle of postman is taken outside and dressed up for the part. Presently there is a loud rat-tat at the door—a postman's knock. The hostess goes to answer the door and comes back saying, "The postman wishes to see Miss X." The little guest bearing the name mentioned is led outside and the door closed behind her. The postman then hands her the parcel containing her gift, and she comes back into the room again all excitement and curiosity until she reaches her place and other eager fingers help her to undo the string and find out what the parcel contains. Then comes another rat-tat and another little guest is asked for, and so on until all the presents are distributed.

Decorating the Christmas Tree is a labour of love with the grown-ups. The tree should be as large a one as possible and firmly planted in a small wooden tub painted green. The space immediately round the tree should be kept clear by an impromptu partition consisting of four posts connected by a rope or chain. This will prevent the little ones getting too close to it when the candles are lighted, and obviate any risk of accident by fire. All risks in this direction should be minimised as far as possible. Many a children's party has ended in disaster through neglect of this all-important precaution. No romping of any kind should be allowed whilst the present distribution is taking place. Indeed it is better to make a rule that the little guests should be seated where they may obtain a good view of the tree, and forms should be arranged opposite, but not too near the tree for this purpose. There should always be a fairy queen doll in a white and gold or white and silver spangled dress at the top of the tree. With the little girls this proves to be the most coveted present—many a little heart beats high in anticipation of winning so pleasing a gift. The heavier gifts should not hang from the tree, but should be arranged neatly along the top of the tub in which the Christmas tree stands. The decoration of the tree itself should be as light and bright as possible. Plenty of golden and silver balls and other ornaments sold specially for the purpose should adorn its branches, such as Father Christmases filled with sweets, bon-bons, Christmas stockings, flags, &c., &c. Boxes of Christmas-tree ornaments may be obtained from most large stores and sweet shops from 1s. each and upwards according to quality. Pieces of cotton wool resting lightly upon the branches give a very pretty "snow-flake" effect, but here again the utmost care must be taken that they are not placed anywhere near the candles, as cotton wool is most inflammable. A penny box of frosting should also be brought into requisition and sprinkled upon the branches of the tree. This will give a most pretty shining effect when the candles are lighted. A Christmas tree is by no means an expensive item if the ornaments and gifts are chosen with care and discretion. Little things, however simple, please little people. It is the excitement of having gifts distributed in the manner characteristic of the Christmas season which appeals to them, and not the value of the gifts themselves.

Some Novel Tea-Parties.—There are a number of novel and enjoyable little functions that may be planned by those whose means are limited, yet who are obliged to make some return for hospitality received. "The Advertisement Tea" is one of the most entertaining of these, and its preparation does not entail much trouble. A large number of pictorial advertisements should be neatly cut from magazines and other periodicals. All letterpress of any kind which might serve as a clue to the name of the advertiser should be cut away from the pictures, which should be neatly pinned to the wall in a way that will not damage the wall-paper. Each advertisement should be numbered. After tea the guests should be taken into the room where the pictures are displayed, and seats should be arranged for the players in such a way that each one will be able to have a good view of them. Strict silence should be enjoined, and to each player must be handed a slip of paper and a pencil on which she must mark down the number of each picture, writing after it the name of the advertisement which the picture represents. Two prizes should be given—one for the lady and one for the gentleman who puts down the highest number of correct names.

Book Teas.—These are always entertaining functions. They can be given in a variety of ways, one of the most amusing and the least expensive of which is the following method :—

In each letter of invitation it should be explained that a book tea is to be given under the following conditions :—

(1) Each guest must illustrate the name of a book by some accessory or ornament to his or her dress.

(2) No accessory must cost more than a shilling.

(3) Two prizes to be given—one lady's prize and one gentleman's prize for the most original idea for illustrating a title.

(4) Each guest must hand to the hostess a slip of paper upon which is written the name of the book she is supposed to represent.

When all the guests have arrived, the hostess gives each a number to pin on the front of her dress. She then bids them all be seated, and, after enjoining strict silence, asks them to each write down upon a list the names of the books represented, after the number of each impersonator. This must be done in quarter of an hour, and the papers handed in to the hostess. After tea the different lists are compared with the names upon the list of the hostess, and the guest who has made the greatest number of correct solutions wins the "guessing" prize, which is awarded at the same time as the prize for the most original idea.

Upon arrival each guest must be shown into a dressing-room in order to dress for the part.

The following are instances of some successful methods of title illustration adopted at one of these teas :—

One guest represented "The Lilac Sunbonnet," by Crockett, by wearing a lilac sunbonnet.

Another came as "Vanity Fair." She carried in one hand a looking-glass, her cheeks were rouged, and a powder puff dangled from a chain round her neck.

Another came as "The Scarlet Letter," by N. Hawthorne. An enormous "L" cut out in scarlet paper was pinned to the front of her bodice.

Some hostesses make it a stipulation that only "new books" must be represented. Needless to say, a good knowledge of books is one of the essentials to winning the "guessing" prize.

Book teas can also be given for children. The titles should, of course, in this case be illustrative of children's books.

General Knowledge.—Upon a table in one of the reception rooms arrange plates containing a sample of some household commodity, such as ground rice, starch, arrowroot, flour, &c.

A ticket bearing a number should be placed upon each plate.

After tea give each of the guests a pencil and a piece of paper, and ask them to write down the correct name of each article after the number of the plate which contains it. But they must on no account *taste* the article; they may only smell it. It is surprising how difficult it is to guess correctly by smell and touch only, and the game becomes a very interesting one indeed. A prize is awarded to the person who guesses the largest number of the articles correctly.

TELLING FORTUNES BY CARDS AND DICE

There is no more amusing diversion for a frivolous half-hour's entertainment than that of fortune-telling by cards. Young or old enjoy it, and with a ready tongue the combinations presented may be so varied that quite surprisingly good predictions can be made.

Surround the whole business with as much mystery as possible. Insist that all shuffling be done by the subject himself, and that cutting is always carried out with the *left* hand.

Learn the meanings of the cards by heart. This is not difficult, and by doing so one is enabled to tell a fortune *quickly*—always a more impressive proceeding than telling it card by card.

These are the generally accepted meanings of the cards :—

Clubs.—Ace of Clubs, *wealth and prosperity.* King of Clubs, *upright, affectionate.* Queen of Clubs, *deeply in love.* Knave of Clubs, *generous and sincere.* Ten of Clubs, *a fortune from an unexpected quarter.* Nine of Clubs, *obstinacy; disputes with friends.* Eight of Clubs, *a love of money.* Seven of Clubs, *fortune and great happiness.* Six of Clubs, *a lucrative partnership.* Five of Clubs, *marriage with a wealthy person.* Four of Clubs, *inconstancy.* Three of Clubs, *a second or third marriage.* Two of Clubs, *opposition.*

Spades.—Ace of Spades, *a love affair; if reversed, a death.* King of Spades, *an ambitious person.* Queen of Spades, *a treacherous friend.* Knave of Spades, *indolent,* but *well-meaning.* Ten of spades, *an unlucky card.* Nine of spades, *the worst card in the pack; sickness, or loss of fortune.* Eight of Spades, *opposition from friends.* Seven of Spades, *sorrow.* Six of Spades, *great fortune.* Five of Spades, *success; a happy marriage.* Four of Spades, *illness; small loss of money.* Three of Spades, *an unfortunate marriage.* Two of Spades, *a death.*

Hearts.—Ace of Hearts, *pleasure; if with Spades, quarrelling; if with Diamonds, news of an absent friend; if with Clubs, merry-making.* King of Hearts, *nice, but hasty and passionate.* Queen of hearts, *fair, affectionate.* Knave of Hearts, *the subject's dearest friend.* Ten of Hearts, *the antidote of bad cards that lie near it, but confirming the good.* Nine of Hearts, *wealth; this is also the wish card.* Eight of Hearts, *feasting and merry-making.* Seven of Hearts, *fickle.* Six of Hearts, *generous, easily imposed upon.* Five of Hearts, *waverer; changeable.* Four of Hearts, *marriage late in life.* Three of Hearts, *imprudent; hot-headed action, which has disastrous consequences.* Two of Hearts, *extraordinary success and good fortune.*

Diamonds.—Ace of Diamonds, *a letter; the card next to it will indicate its nature.* King of Diamonds, *hot-tempered.* Queen of Diamonds, *a coquette.* Knave of Diamonds, *a selfish person.* Ten of Diamonds, *money.* Nine of Diamonds, *a roving person.* Eight of Diamonds, *marriage late in life.* Seven of Diamonds, *a gambler.* Six of Diamonds, *early marriage.* Five of Diamonds, *friendship.* Four of Diamonds, *unhappy marriage.* Three of Diamonds, *quarrels, law-suits, and disagreements.* Two of Diamonds, *a serious love affair.*

There are two effective ways of fortune-telling.

For the first, ask your subject to shuffle the cards very thoroughly and to wish all the time. Then cut them into three piles with the left hand. Should the wish card (the Nine of Hearts) be one of those cut, it is a lucky omen.

Notice two other cards and their possible bearing on the wish. Now, after lifting the cards and putting them together with the left hand, proceed to divide them into piles in this fashion—

The first pile is to yourself. The second, to the house. The third, to your wish. The fourth, what you do expect. The fifth, what you don't expect. The sixth, sure to come true. The seventh foretells the happenings of to-night.

Arrange these piles, as you deal out the cards one by one, in a semicircle. Then proceed to read them off by their meanings.

Another and rather more complicated method is to ask the person whose fortune in being told which King he will be (if it is a woman, one would naturally ask which Queen).

After the wishing has been done as before, the fortune-teller lays out the cards in rows—seven in a row.

To read the fortune the teller must start from the King or Queen chosen, counting seven from him or her in every case.

The King or Queen of the same suit will always be the lover or sweetheart of the one whose fortune is being told, and the Knave being their thoughts, it is, of course, quite easy to discover their feelings.

It is rather a good plan to write the meaning of the cards on an old pack. By using this a few times a rapid flow of ideas will much more readily be induced. It might be mentioned that a too strict adherence to rule is by no means either necessary or desirable in fortune-telling. Tell what the combination of cards suggests to you—quite irrespective of the exact meaning of each—and you will be infinitely more amusing and obtain much greater fame as a wizard.

A Throw of the Dice.—Although forecasting of the future from dice is one of the most ancient methods of prediction, it is curiously enough almost unknown in modern days. For this reason it is of special value to the home entertainer, and will prove infinitely simpler than the cards, the meanings being easier to learn as well as fewer in number.

First chalk a magic circle on the table, then obtain a small cup or box to shake the dice in.

Three dice only should be used.

The person whose future is at stake must shake and cast the dice in the circle. This, as in card fortune-telling, should be done with the left hand.

Three tells you of an approaching accident; four, a rise in your position; five, that you will make the acquaintance of one who will be a friend; six, predicts loss; seven, a scandal; eight, a reproach that is not undeserved; nine, a wedding; ten, a christening; eleven, trouble for one you love; twelve, an important letter; thirteen, tears; fourteen, beware of an enemy; fifteen, good luck and happiness; sixteen, a journey; seventeen, a water journey; three sixes, or eighteen points, is a very good sign. It means great profit in business, or something the person wishes for very much.

FORTUNE-TELLING BY DOMINOES

A fairly unique accomplishment is to reveal the future by the aid of dominoes, and there is something sufficiently fascinating and mysterious about this mode of revelation to fill the uninitiated with awe at the powers of the exponent.

Each small oblong has its secret meaning by which some happening vital to the subject is illustrated. It is a matter of little difficulty to commit these to memory; and in this, as in other methods of divination, the fundamental principle is that of comparison and calculation.

The dominoes used range from double-six to double-blank, and by these are symbolised the various vicissitudes of fate likely to befall mankind. The exponent places his paraphernalia upon the table, and, having turned them with their black spots facing the surface, proceeds to shuffle them. When this is done, the subject is requested to draw three pieces, one at a time. Between the choice of each the dominoes are shuffled.

The first supplies an impression; should it be drawn a second time, the impression becomes a conviction. The third, however, may lessen or wholly contradict its degree of importance, and this is where calculation and comparison in blending the signs are essential to a successful justification and interpretation of these symbols.

Double-six is an emblem of matrimonial happiness and financial prosperity.

Six-five is almost equally fortunate. Perseverance and concentration are rewarded by ultimate success.

Six-four implies a comfortable income, and secures happiness in marriage.

Six-three demonstrates that fate smiles upon the love and marriage of the subject.

Six-two.—Prudence, hard work, and a certain amount of good luck, or exposure and shame for any wrong-doing.

Six-one promises two marriages to the young subject, the first of which will not be as happy as the second. Should the subject be of middle age, this domino foretells the speedy arrival of good things, and the fact that he or she will never be left lonely and uncared for.

Six-blank is, alas, a sign of great trouble—sickness, death, or heavy money losses.

Double-five presages that all achievements will be rewarded with a large amount of success, but inordinate wealth is not prophesied.

Five-four is almost as unfortunate a draw as six-blank. Should a young girl lift it, it means that her future husband will be poor and leave her a widow. Further, he may be of extravagant disposition, in spite of his poverty.

Five-three indicates a tranquil and contented existence. Sufficient money and matrimonial affection of moderate strength, the couple being incapable of passionate devotion.

Five-two conveys a warning that love and marriage are destined to an unhappy termination.

Five-one portends social popularity, but financial worries and losses.

Five-blank is supposed to demonstrate egotistical and avaricious characteristics, tendencies to swindling and intrigues, also a warning to remain unmarried.

Double-four.—The man who earns his livelihood by manual labour may regard this domino as a sign of future security and prosperity, but to him whose profession needs mental achievement it is rather disastrous. Troubles and disappointments await him.

Four-three.—Matrimony and moderate income.

Four-two proclaims an early marriage and moderate income.

Four-one.—Wealth or many friends.

Four-blank.—A sure warning that single life will be the best and happiest. It counsels that any secrets imparted to another will be indiscreetly revealed.

Double-three.—Enormous riches.

Three-two foretells prosperity in matrimony, travels, and speculations.

Three-one.—Some danger and unhappiness. The necessity for acting with extreme caution in all matters.

Three-blank.—Domestic unhappiness, such as a quarrel or incompatibility of temperament of husband and wife. The absence of harmony in the home.

Double-two promises average happiness and income.

Two-one.—Two marriages, if the individual be a woman; financial failures to a commercial man.

Two-blank.—The intrigues of unscrupulous persons will meet with temporary success. It also denotes poverty, and an indolent husband. The individual will return safely from all journeys undertaken.

Double-one.—An existence free from money worries; peace and constancy in love and marriage.

Double-blank seems to favour the deeds of unprincipled persons, and foretells want of integrity in lover and husband.

DIVINATIONS BY TAROCS

Tarocs differ from the numeral cards used for bridge, whist, &c., in several ways. A pack consists of seventy-eight cards, made up of twenty-two emblematic pictures and fifty-six ordinary.

These latter are grouped into four suits of fourteen cards each:—four *coat cards*—king, queen, chevalier, and valet; and ten *pip cards*, numbering from 1 to 10.

The twenty-two emblematic cards are known as the *Major Arcana*, and are divided into three groups of seven, which equal twenty-one cards. The twenty-second stands for the highest point successful achievement may reach. The *Major Arcana* contains:—

1st Division

1. The Juggler—emblematic of the male inquirer.
2. The High Priestess—emblematic of the woman inquirer.
3. The Empress—emblematic of the action, initiative.
4. The Emperor—emblematic of the will.
5. The Pope—emblematic of the inspiration.
6. Lovers—emblematic of the love.
7. The Chariot—emblematic of the triumph, providential protection.

2nd Division

1. Justice—emblematic of justice.
2. The Hermit—emblematic of prudence.
3. The Wheel of Fortune—emblematic of destiny.
4. Strength—emblematic of fortitude, courage.
5. The Hanged Man—emblematic of trial and sacrifice.
6. Death—emblematic of bereavement.
7. Temperance—emblematic of temperance.

3rd Division

1. The Devil—emblematic of immense force or illness.
2. The Struck Tower—emblematic of ruin and deception.
3. The Stars—emblematic of hope.
4. The Moon—emblematic of hidden dangers, enemies.
5. The Sun—emblematic of material happiness, marriage.
6. Judgment—emblematic of change of circumstances.
7. The Foolish Man—emblematic of inconsiderate actions.

The remaining card, No. 22, which belongs to this division, is

The universe, emblematic of success.

The *Minor Arcana*, divided into two groups of four, corresponding to the suits of ordinary playing cards:—

Sceptres relate to diamonds, interpreted as enterprise.
Cups relate to hearts, interpreted as love.
Swords relate to spades, interpreted as misfortune.
Pentacles relate to clubs, interpreted as interest,

The four *coat cards* stand for different conditions of existence:—

King, emblematic of man. Divine world (spirituality).
Queen, emblematic of woman. Human world (vitality).
Chevalier, emblematic of youth. Material world (materiality).
Valet, emblematic of childhood. Transition stage (life in growth).

The remaining cards of these suits (1 to 10) are important according to their relation to the *coat cards* and their numerical value. These are divided into four groups:—

(1) 1, 2, 3 of each suit appertain to man—abstract qualities, creation, and enterprise.
(2) 4, 5, 6 of each suit represent woman—opposition, reflection, and negation.
(3) 7, 8, 9 of each suit represent youth and materialism.
(4) The four tens of each suit represent the stage of transition.

In order to tell fortunes by means of tarocs, the manipulator must be perfectly conversant with the design, class, and interpretation of each card.

Process of Divination.—The complete pack is

used. Shuffle and cut into three parts, each composed of twenty-six cards, thus :—

26 26 26

Take the *central* pack and place on the *right*.

The inquirer shuffles the two remaining packs, which equal fifty-two. These are dealt out in a similar fashion—three groups of seventeen cards, thus :—

17 17 17

Again remove *central* pack to the *right*.

Deal out the remaining packs, which equal thirty-four, in three groups of eleven, thus :—

11 11 11

It will be seen that seventy-eight cards divide equally in the first deal.

In the second deal, however, only fifty-one cards are used, so that there is one over. This card is shuffled with the third deal.

Two cards are now over, and these are placed as discards, until the central pack of the last deal of eleven is put on the right, when they are shuffled with the remaining twenty-two discards. The cards will now be as follows :—

26 17 11

Discards = twenty-four, making in all seventy-eight. They are next placed beneath each other in sequence, thus :—

A. 26—emblematic of the supernatural, spiritual.
B. 17—emblematic of the thoughts and calling of the individual.
C. 11—emblematic of the physical and material.

The tarocs of pack A, B, and C are now lifted separately, and placed on the table from left to right in rows. Each taroc has its meaning, and from its relation to its fellows the manipulator is able to present a brief sketch of character, inclination, and futurity.

Another simple method is to shuffle all the cards and request the inquirer to cut. The manipulator then proceeds to draw the first seventeen tarocs, uncovering only the eighteenth and last card of the pack. These two cards create what degree of sympathy is shared between himself and his client, the keynote being given by the symbolic meaning attached to the card. The seventeen cards are now revealed from left to right, their interpretation being given separately. In order to reach a proper signification, they are then compared as follows :—

The first with the seventeenth.
The second with the sixteenth.
The third with the fifteenth,

and so on, each process increasing or taking from the first manifestation.

ORGANISING ENTERTAINMENTS FOR CHARITY

Though the organisation of charity entertainments involves real hard work and a great deal of anxiety for the organisers, yet it may well be classed as a pastime owing to the large amount of pleasure afforded to all who take part in it when their efforts are successful.

Charity entertainments are many and various, ranging from the simple penny reading, village concert or bazaar, to the more ambitious theatrical entertainment for which a theatre or hall has to be hired, or the concert or "fancy fair" given in one of the large town halls. The larger the scale upon which the entertainment is planned the greater the amount of work there will be. For large entertainments it is always as well to appoint a committee of organisation consisting of at least four members, each of which will be responsible for some particular part of preparation, to be allotted to them by the chief organiser who will superintend the whole.

Small entertainments for local charities which do not involve so much preliminary outlay and for which a certain amount of profit is usually assured, may be organised by one person, but even in these circumstances she should be able to count upon the co-operation of a number of willing helpers, and she should always avail herself of their services to the full, and thus by sparing herself the necessity of worrying over the hundred and one minor details, will be able to devote all her energies to the carrying out of the more important part of the work.

In the first place influential patronage must be secured. Persons of high social standing should be approached, more especially those who are interested in the special charity for which the entertainment is to be given. If the request is placed before them in a tactful manner they will in most cases give permission for their names to be included in the list of patrons.

Then steps must be taken to give publicity to the event. If the lady or gentleman who is in charge of this important department has some journalistic associations, and might therefore be able to influence press paragraphs, so much the better. It will be necessary also to commence advertising the event in the principal papers a few weeks beforehand, and it is better, if possible, to insert a small advertisement daily during the last week. Neatly-worded paragraphs describing the most striking features of the entertainment should be sent to the editors of all the papers in which the advertisement appears, together with a polite little note requesting the favour of a paragraph and pointing out that the entertainment is advertised in his paper. Then, at least twelve days beforehand, tickets of admission to the entertainment should be sent to the editors, with printed programmes and any further particulars to which attention should be drawn.

Strict accounts should be kept of each item of expenditure involved. While nothing should be grudged which will help to ensure success, all extravagance of outlay should be avoided. How many so-called "charity" entertainments have been given, for instance, in which, after paying all the incidental expenses, not a farthing has been left over for the charity. In the case of theatricals each performer should be asked to provide or hire her own costume, make up, &c., as her contribution to the charity. If this course is not pursued, then the expenses will soon mount up. They should all go to the same costumier, if possible, and in most cases the latter will make a substantial reduction if mention is made of his name in the programmes. A reduction will also be made in the charge for hiring scenery for the same consideration. The same may be said in regard to the printing, which in the case of small local charities may often be obtained free of any charge whatever. A theatre is often lent for the performance free, with the exception of the cost of lighting, orchestra, and attendants' fees, all of which will have to be met. Nearly always the use of a large hall may also be obtained free for the purposes of a concert or bazaar, if tactful application is made in the proper quarter.

Bazaars should always be planned upon as original lines as possible to make them a success. A pretty idea is for all the stall-holders to be in the costume of some historical period; for instance, it might be called an "Elizabethan Fair," and all the stall-holders would have to be dressed in Elizabethan costume. In the stalls themselves the illusion should also be kept up as far as possible. The refreshment room should be decorated in Elizabethan style with simple little tables and settles, and the waitresses dressed in the simple costume of the Elizabethan serving-wench. The fortune-telling booth should by no means be forgotten, as to have their fortunes told forms an irresistible attraction to the feminine members of the community at least. Fortunes might be told either by palmistry or cards, both are largely appreciated. Part of the tent might be partitioned off for the purpose of telling fortunes by the teacup. This would be a novelty, as each consultant of the "wizard" would first be obliged to partake of the "cup that cheers" before her future is foretold. The woman who has not enough articles to equip a stall should bethink herself of the possibilities of the bran tub. Presents of all kinds and varieties should be hidden away in a tub half full of bran, and 3d., 6d., or 1s. charged for a dip, in accordance with the value of the articles therein. Then, again, if the sales are not brisk at any particular stall, the possibilities of the "raffle" must not be lost sight of. Very often articles will fetch a much higher price when raffled than if sold in the ordinary way. Tickets bearing different numbers should be made out in duplicate, one set being sold and the others placed in a bag or hat and well shaken up together. From these a person must be asked to draw a number. The person possessing the duplicate of the number drawn has won the prize. Raffling is looked upon by some people as one of the most enjoyable features of a bazaar, and these will make a point of expending all the money they have to spare upon tickets for the various raffles. There are no end of pretty fancy articles for sale at bazaars that can be made by clever fingers.

A Roller-Skating Carnival always forms an irresistible attraction, and its successful results are even more assured than those of a bazaar by reason of its novelty. A local skating rink should be hired and tickets of admission sold under condition that all the skaters must be in fancy dress. Prizes should be given for the best and the most original costumes.

Whist and Bridge Drives, for which tickets are sold, are often sources of great help to local charities. There must be a fairly large number of players, and the tickets should be charged at 2s. 6d. to 5s., there being first and second prizes for the successful winners possessing 5s. tickets, and first and second prizes of lower value for those with 2s. 6d. tickets.

There are, in fact, no end to the enjoyable functions which may be organised in the cause of charity, and in each case it may be said that much of the success of the function will depend upon the capability for organisation displayed by its promoters.

OUTDOOR GAMES

LAWN TENNIS

Lawn tennis is one of the favourite outdoor games with young people of both sexes. It forms the *raison d'être* of many a pleasant garden party in the summer months; it is a game in which both men and women can join, and from its purely social aspect, if for no other reason, it is well worth cultivating by the modern woman.

We are not all sufficiently fortunate to have enough lawn space at our disposal for the formation of a tennis court. The wise mother, however, will see that her children are initiated into the mysteries of the game when at school; also as they get older she will arrange for them to join some good lawn tennis club, of which there are several in nearly every town or suburb. Moreover, she would do well to show her interest in the pursuits of her young people by joining the club with them, and by obtaining in this way a health-giving respite from the many and arduous duties which fall to the lot of the average house-mistress.

The fees of membership vary in different localities, although £1, 1s. per season would represent the average. Girls who have to spend their days teaching or in an office, or at some other equally sedentary occupation, cannot do better than become members of clubs of the kind and spend their summer evenings in playing tennis. The small sum expended will prove to be well invested, and the benefits to be derived from this healthful deviation from the ordinary routine are well worth some small sacrifice. It often happens, however, that the members of some clubs are all "crack" players, and the beginner would therefore shrink from exposing herself to adverse criticism of her play. In these circumstances she should remember that, in London and many other large towns, portions of large parks or public grounds are set apart for the purpose of lawn tennis—and both tennis court and net may be hired at from 3d. to 1s. an hour. The facilities so offered are not always taken advantage of, for the very good reason that a large number of people are not aware of their existence. Before joining a tennis club, therefore, make inquiries in order to ascertain if there are any places in your district where tennis courts and nets are to be hired. If there are, then try to get a friend or friends who are good tennis players to go regularly with you until you have attained that proficiency which can only be achieved by practice.

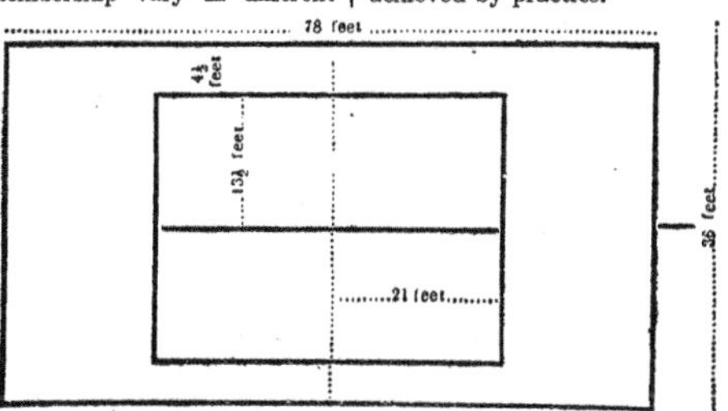

Plan of Full-sized Tennis Court according to the Regulations of the Lawn Tennis Association.

The Court.—The piece of lawn upon which the court is marked must be thoroughly smooth and level. It should never be on a slope. The lawn requires to be kept in good condition, and requires regular rolling and mowing. The lines indicating the court are marked in whitening by means of a "Lawn Tennis Marker." There are many different kinds of markers to be had, most of them consisting of a little tank upon wheels, the tank containing the whitening which by a patent device is conveyed to the "marking wheel."

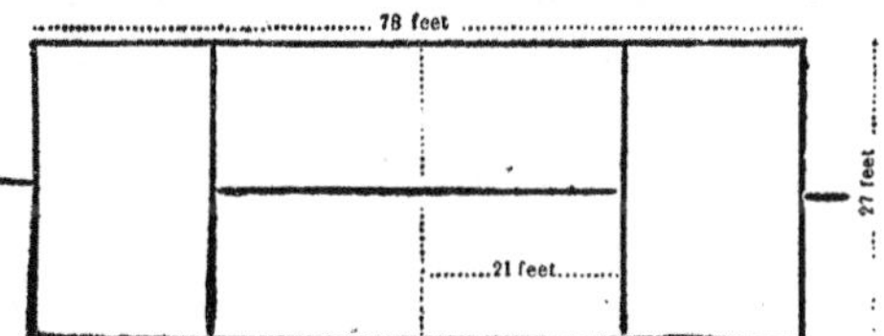

Plan of Single-handed Tennis Court according to the Regulations of the Lawn Tennis Association.

In simple language the game of lawn tennis consists of hitting balls across a net by means of rackets. As is well known, lawn tennis may be played by two, three, or four players. For the single-handed game (*i.e.* two players) the court is slightly differently marked than for the other games. The difference is shown in the accompanying diagrams.

programmes and any further particulars to which attention should be drawn.

Strict accounts should be kept of each item of expenditure involved. While nothing should be grudged which will help to ensure success, all extravagance of outlay should be avoided. How many so-called "charity" entertainments have been given, for instance, in which, after paying all the incidental expenses, not a farthing has been left over for the charity. In the case of theatricals each performer should be asked to provide or hire her own costume, make up, &c., as her contribution to the charity. If this course is not pursued, then the expenses will soon mount up. They should all go to the same costumier, if possible, and in most cases the latter will make a substantial reduction if mention is made of his name in the programmes. A reduction will also be made in the charge for hiring scenery for the same consideration. The same may be said in regard to the printing, which in the case of small local charities may often be obtained free of any charge whatever. A theatre is often lent for the performance free, with the exception of the cost of lighting, orchestra, and attendants' fees, all of which will have to be met. Nearly always the use of a large hall may also be obtained free for the purposes of a concert or bazaar, if tactful application is made in the proper quarter.

Bazaars should always be planned upon as original lines as possible to make them a success. A pretty idea is for all the stall-holders to be in the costume of some historical period; for instance, it might be called an "Elizabethan Fair," and all the stall-holders would have to be dresed in Elizabethan costume. In the stalls themselves the illusion should also be kept up as far as possible. The refreshment room should be decorated in Elizabethan style with simple little tables and settles, and the waitresses dressed in the simple costume of the Elizabethan serving-wench. The fortune-telling booth should by no means be forgotten, as to have their fortunes told forms an irresistible attraction to the feminine members of the community at least. Fortunes might be told either by palmistry or cards, both are largely appreciated. Part of the tent might be partitioned off for the purpose of telling fortunes by [illegible]e teacup. This wo[illegible] eac[illegible] consultant of the [illegible] be [illegible]liged to partake of t[illegible] bef[illegible] her future is foretol[illegible] has [illegible]ot enough articles to bet[illegible]nk herself of the possi[illegible] tul[illegible] Presents of all kinds [illegible] bo[illegible]dden away in a tub ha[illegible] 3d. [illegible]d., or 1s. charged for a wit[illegible] the value of the artic[illegible] ag[illegible], if the sales are not brisk sta[illegible] the possibilities of the " be[illegible]st sight of. Very often [illegible] a [illegible]uch higher price when raf[illegible] in [illegible]e ordinary way. Tickets [illegible] nu[illegible]bers should be made out i[illegible] set[illegible]eing sold and the others pl[illegible] ha[illegible] and well shaken up togethe[illegible] a[illegible] [illegible]rson must be asked to dr[illegible] Th[illegible] person possessing the du[illegible] [illegible]umber drawn has won the priz[illegible] loo[illegible]ed upon by some people as on[illegible] en[illegible]yable features of a bazaar, a[illegible] m[illegible] a point of expending all th[illegible] ha[illegible] to spare upon tickets for ra[illegible]es. There are no end of p[illegible] ar[illegible]cles for sale at bazaars that c[illegible] by[illegible] clever fingers.

Roller-Skating Carnival always ir[illegible]sistible attraction, and its succes[illegible] ar[illegible]e even more assured than those o[illegible] b[illegible] reason of its novelty. A local sk[illegible] sh[illegible]uld be hired and tickets of admi[illegible] u[illegible]der condition that all the skaters in [illegible]ancy dress. Prizes should be give[illegible] b[illegible] and the most original costumes.

[illegible]hist and Bridge Drives, for which a[illegible] sold, are often sources of great help c[illegible]harities. There must be a fairly large o[illegible] players, and the tickets should be a[illegible] 2s. 6d. to 5s., there being first and p[illegible]zes for the successful winners posses t[illegible]kets, and first and second prizes of low f[illegible] those with 2s. 6d. tickets.

[illegible]There are, in fact, no end to the e[illegible] f[illegible]nctions which may be organised in th[illegible] o[illegible] charity, and in each case it may t[illegible]at much of the success of the funct[illegible] d[illegible]epend upon the capability for org[illegible] d[illegible]isplayed by its promoters.

OUTDOOR [illegible]AMES

LAWN TENNIS

Lawn tennis is one of the favourite outdoor games with young people of both sexes. It forms the *raison d'être* of many a pleasant garden party in the summer months; it is a game in which both men and women can join, [illegible]ed from its pu[illegible] [illegible]eason, it is wo[illegible] [illegible]oman.

We are n[illegible] [illegible]ough law[illegible] [illegible]ation of [illegible] [illegible]owever, [illegible]

into the mysteries of the game whe
also as they get older she will arra
to join some good lawn tennis cl
there are several in nearly every tow
Moreover, she would do well to show
in the pursuits of her young peop
the club with them, and by obta
way a health-giving respite from t
arduous duties which fall to the
average house-mistress.

The fees of membership vary

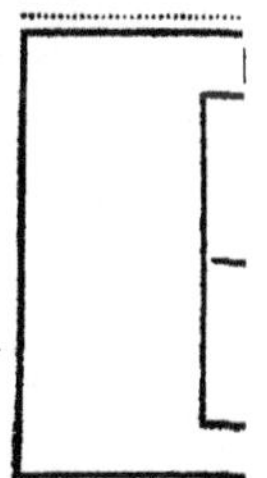

Plan of Full-siz

localities, although £1, 1s. per s
represent the average. Girls w
spend their days teaching or i
or at some other equally seden
tion, cannot do better than beco
of clubs of the kind and spend
evenings in playing tennis. The
expended will prove to be well
the benefits to be derived from
deviation from the ordinary rout

For the single-handed game the court must be 27 ft. in width and 78 ft. in length—for the three and four-handed games it must be 36 ft. in width and 78 ft. in length. In both cases it is divided across the middle by a net, the ends of which are stretched to the tops of two posts which stand 3 ft. outside the court on each side. The height of the net is 3 ft. 6 in. at the posts, and 3 ft. at the centre. At each end of the court, parallel with the net, and at a distance of 39 ft. from it, are drawn the base lines, the extremities of which are connected by the "side lines." Halfway with the side lines and parallel with them is drawn the "half-court" line, dividing the space on each side of the net into two equal parts, called the right and left courts. On each side of the net, at a distance of 21 ft. from it, are drawn the service lines. The half-court line need not be drawn beyond the service line. In the single-handed game (*i.e.* two players) the service lines extend to the side lines, whilst for the three- or four-handed games, within the side lines at a distance of 4½ ft. from them, and parallel with them, are drawn the service side lines.

Rules of the Game.—As with every other game, lawn tennis has its recognised code of rules, which must be followed. The opponent players stand on opposite sides of the net. The player who begins the game by serving the ball over the net is called the "server," the one who returns the ball the "striker out." Players take it in turns to serve in alternate games. In the three-handed game the single player serves in every alternate game. In the four-handed game the service of the first game is given by one of the partners on either side, the second game by one of the partners on the opponent side, the third game by the partner of the one who served in the first game, and so on until the set is finished. The server must stand with both feet behind the base line and within the limits of the imaginary continuation of the centre service and the side lines. She must deliver the service from right to left courts alternately, beginning from the right.

The ball served must drop within the service line, half-court line, and side line of the court, which is diagonally opposite to that from which it was served, or upon any such line.

A Fault.—If the service be delivered from the wrong court, or if the server is not standing as directed above, or if the ball does not go over the net, or goes beyond the service line, or if it drop out of court or in the wrong service court, there is what is known as a "fault" in the service. If the server makes two consecutive faults, a stroke is won by the other side.

A Let.—It is a "let" if the ball served touch the net provided the service be otherwise good, or if a service or fault be delivered when the striker out is not ready, or if a player is obstructed by any accident not within her control. In case of a "let" the service or stroke counts for nothing and the server may serve again.

The "striker out" must not return the ball before it touches the ground in her first return stroke. The server wins a stroke if the "striker out" volley the service, or fails to return the service or the ball in play (except in the case of a let), or return the service or ball in play so that it drop outside any of the lines which bound her opponent's court, or otherwise lose a stroke.

The striker out wins a stroke if the server serves two consecutive faults or fails to return the ball in play (except in the case of a let), or returns the ball in play so that it drops outside any of the lines which bound her opponent's court.

Scoring.—On either side winning the first stroke the winning side scores 15, for the second stroke 30 is scored, for the third stroke 40. If both sides win one stroke the score is 15 all, if both win two strokes the score is 30 all, if both win three strokes the score is "deuce"; the next stroke after "deuce" won by either players is called advantage for that player. If the same player wins the next stroke she wins the game. If she loses the next stroke the score is again called deuce, and so on till either player wins the two strokes immediately following the score of deuce.

Tennis Racket.—A great deal depends upon the quality of the racket. It should never be too heavy—13½ oz. represents a good average weight for ladies' use. It should be made of good strong gut not too tightly strung. Many new patents in rackets have lately been introduced. In one the racket has two centre strings of wire. Balls also should always be of good quality. To fulfil the requirements of the lawn tennis laws these should not be less than 2½ in. nor more than $2\frac{9}{16}$ in. in diameter, and not less than 1⅞ oz. nor more than 2 oz. in weight.

Net and Posts.—Nets should be of the best quality procurable. An inferior one will not last. They should be well taken care of, never being allowed to remain out in all weathers, but removed from the posts and rolled up carefully when the game is over. The posts which possess a winding apparatus by means of which the net can be evenly stretched between them and fixed in place are the best to use.

CRICKET

Cricket has long been regarded as England's chief national sport, and it is a game in which most young people like to excel. Though essentially a boy's and man's game, girls are by no means debarred from entering into it, and many a cricket match is arranged and played at our large girls' schools, there being much competition for membership in the school cricket eleven.

A cricket match is played by two sides of

eleven players each, each side being under the direction of its captain. The game consists of the defence of the wicket by the batsmen of the one side against the bowlers and fielders of the other, whose mission it is to endeavour to knock down the wicket with the ball. Cricket may be played with double or single wickets, the former method being the most universally adopted.

For the double wicket game there must be a batsman at each side of the wickets. The play of the defending side is termed their "innings." When a batsman hits the ball far enough, the batsmen run across each to the other one's wicket, and keep on running backwards and forwards as long as there is no danger of the batsman being bowled out while away from the wicket. Each time they run to each other's wickets is counted a "run." The side which scores the greater number of "runs" wins the game. As each batsman goes out his place is taken by another batsman, until ten have played. When the tenth is out the other side begin their innings.

The wickets are pitched opposite and parallel to each other at a distance of 22 yds. Each wicket must be 8 in. in width, and consist of three stumps with two bails on the top. The wickets must not be changed during a match unless the ground between them becomes unfit for play. The ground at each wicket must be marked out according to the rules of the game with bowling crease, return crease, and popping crease—the bowler must keep within the limits of the bowling and return crease, and the batsman within those of the popping crease. In addition to bowlers and batsmen the fielders play an important part in the game of the attacking party. They each have their certain definite positions allotted to them; it being their mission to stop the ball and throw it in. Chief amongst these may be mentioned the wicket-keeper, who must stand behind the stumps. He must be on the alert to stump the batsmen who miss the ball and are over the crease, and run them out when the ball is returned from the fielders, to take "catches," and prevent "byes."

Before the commencement of every match two umpires must be appointed, one for each end. The umpires are the sole judges of fair or unfair play. They must pitch fair wickets, arrange boundaries where necessary, and the allowances to be made for them, and change ends after each has had one innings. The batsman is declared "out"—

If the ball is caught by the bowler or a fielder before it touches the ground.

When he is "bowled," *i.e.* if the wicket be bowled down, even if the ball first touch the striker's bat or person.

If he is "stumped" out—that is to say, if in playing at the ball, provided it be not touched by the bat or hand, the striker is out of his ground and the wicket is put down by the wicket-keeper with the ball, or with hand or arm with ball in hand.

If with any part of his person he stop the ball.

If he "hit the wicket" with his bat or any part of his person or dress.

When under pretence of running or otherwise either of the batsmen wilfully prevent a ball from being caught.

If the ball be struck by any part of his person or he wilfully strike it again, except it be done for the purpose of guarding his wicket, which he may do with his bat or any part of his person except his hands.

If he is "run out"—if the wicket be knocked down by his opponents with the ball while he is making his runs: he is out if he has not grounded his bat inside the popping crease before the ball hits the wicket for which he is making.

The bowler bowls an "over" or six successive balls from one end. Then a bowler at the other end also bowls an "over."

It is "no ball" if the bowler does not have one foot behind the bowling crease when bowling, but the batsman is entitled to run just the same. If the ball is lost, six runs are allowed to the striker.

HOCKEY

Hockey is a great deal played by girls and women, usually forming one of the sports taught at girls' schools. There are also a number of ladies' hockey clubs throughout the country. The game is played with hockey sticks and an ordinary cricket ball painted white. There are twenty-two players, eleven on each side. Usually five of these eleven are "forwards," three "half backs," two "backs," and one the goal-keeper. To score a goal the ball must be driven between the goal posts. The ground must be marked in the shape of a rectangle, the long sides of which are called the "side lines" and the short sides the "goal lines." In the centre of each goal line are placed the goals, which consist of two upright posts placed four yards apart connected by a cross-bar. Behind the goals at either side a net is placed. Fifteen yards in front of each goal a semi-circle is drawn with its sides terminating at the goal line. This is called the "striking circle," and in order for a goal to be scored the ball must be struck from a point within this circle.

The game is started by two of the players (one from each side) striking the ground in front of the ball three times with their sticks. This is known as a "bully," and the play must be restarted by a "bully" each time a goal is scored. The side which scores the greater number of goals wins the game.

The player must not hold, carry, or send the ball in any direction except by means of her hockey stick, but she may stop the ball with her foot and catch it with her hand if she drops it immediately afterwards.

The rules for the game of hockey for women in England are drawn up by the All England Woman's Hockey Association, of which Miss M. A. Julius, 7 Onslow Avenue, Richmond, is the secretary.

Dress.—Loose blouses or jerseys and short serge skirts should be worn. Boots or shoes should have good, thick, strong soles, and boots as a rule are preferable to shoes, as they serve in a measure to protect the ankles from injury by knocks with the hockey sticks.

ROUNDERS

Rounders is a very popular game for the play-ground, and one in which any number of players may take part. The game is played in an imaginary round or circle, on which four bases are marked by posts placed at equal distances from each other. In some cases trees are situated in convenient parts of the ground to do duty as bases. The players are divided into two sides. The members of the side who are "in" stand in a line at the post marking the home base and one member of the other side acts as bowler, the others taking up various positions on the ground as fielders. Each member of the "in" side takes it in turn to strike the ball sent by the bowler, generally with the open hand, though in some forms of the game a bat is used. When she has struck it she must at once run to the post or tree marking the first base, it being the object of the fielders to get her "out" by hitting her with the ball while she is running between the bases. No two players may stand together at any base but the home oase, so that when a player is stationed at the first base from home, directly another player hits the ball and begins to run she must at once make for the next base. The great object of the game is to obtain as many rounders as possible, that is to say, that each player should endeavour to hit the ball far enough to enable her to run to all the posts and home again without stopping. The side which wins the greater number of rounders wins the game.

If a ball is caught before touching the ground by the bowler or any of the fielders, the side of the striker is out, and the others must take their turns as batsmen. Each player as she reaches home takes her stand at the end of the line of players waiting for their turn to act as batsman, and she bats the ball in her turn again until she is out. When all the players on the innings side are out, the next side comes in.

BASEBALL

This may be called the American Rounders, and is a very favourite game in America. It is played by eighteen players, nine to a side. The field is diamond-shaped, the bases being stationed at the four corners. The pitcher stands opposite to the home base six feet from it and bowls to the batsmen of the "in" side, whilst the other members of the "out" side are stationed as fielders in various positions over the ground, one taking up his position as "catcher" behind the home base. The batsman when he has hit the ball must run to the first base. Each round of the four bases makes a "run," and the side which scores the greater number of runs wins the game. Should a batsman fail to hit the ball after it has been bowled to him three consecutive times he is out. When three of the batsmen have been bowled out the innings is over. If the batsman is hit by the fielder with the ball whilst running between the bases he is out. Each side is allowed nine innings.

CROQUET

Croquet is played with croquet mallets and balls on an oblong-shaped lawn upon which a number of hoops and arches are set in a definite order. Six hoops are used in the new standard settings. Each player has a mallet and a ball; the balls are of different colours in order that they may be easily distinguished in play, and the mallets bear corresponding colours. Two or more players may take part in the game, four or eight being favourite numbers. The object of the player is to send her ball through each hoop until the winning peg is reached, and to keep her opponent from making progress. This can be done by means of "Roquet," by which the player when she has passed through a hoop strikes with her ball that of her opponent. When she has done this the player must place her own ball against the ball which she has struck, and then hit the former with her mallet, the force of the stroke serving to move both balls. There is a great art in this stroke the knack of which is only gained by experience. For instance, one kind of stroke will send both balls in the same direction, whilst another kind of stroke will send them far apart. The object of the player should be not only to send her opponent's ball as far away from its destination as possible, but also to place it in a position where it will be useful to her or to one of the other players on her side. The player is not now allowed to put her foot on her opponent's ball to keep it steady when making the stroke. Many people, however, still play croquet in the old-fashioned way.

When a player has passed through a hoop, or taken "Roquet," she is allowed another turn. If she misses a hoop, sends a ball out of bounds, or fails to move her opponent's ball when playing it against her own after "Roquet," her turn is over.

The rules of croquet are drawn up by the

Croquet Association. A copy of the rules, with diagrams of standard settings, price 4d., may be obtained from Horace Cox, Bream's Buildings, London, E.C.

BOWLS

Bowls is a very popular lawn game. It is played with bowls which have a bias on one side, and a small ball called the jack. The play is begun by one of the players bowling the jack across the lawn to give it its position. Then turns are taken alternately by members of each side. The object of each player is to bowl her ball as near as possible to the jack, and to knock away that of her opponent, if possible. In bowling the side with the bias should always be held towards the player. When all have had their turn the score is taken. The side which has the nearest bowl to the jack counts points in accordance with the number of bowls they have nearer the jack than the opposing side. The number of points that make the game can be settled beforehand by the players.

BADMINTON

Badminton is very like tennis, only it is played with special Badminton bats and shuttlecocks instead of balls. It has the advantage of being a game which can be played either in or out of doors, only in the latter case it cannot be played in a strong wind. It is mostly played in covered courts, and in these circumstances makes an admirable winter game. The shuttlecock is sent over the net in the same manner as in tennis, only the game must necessarily be a volleyed one. Should a player fail to return the shuttlecock which is served to her, a point is scored against her, also against the server who sends the shuttlecock into the wrong court. The shuttlecock must not touch the net or posts or fall out of bounds. The game usually is fifteen, but when both sides have scored thirteen, five extra points may be played for.

A Badminton net stands higher than a tennis net, being 5 ft. in the middle and 5 ft. 1 in. at the sides.

GOLF

Golf is becoming a very favourite game for women, though the golfer is apt to find her hobby a somewhat expensive one at times. Besides the initial outlay on golf clubs, balls, and other accessories, tips to caddies have to be considered, whilst if the golfer is to have any chance of pursuing her favourite pastime she must of necessity belong to a good golfing club.

The game is played with small balls and clubs of various shapes on uneven ground. The course has at intervals of 150 and 500 yards a number of smooth greens each with a hole in it, and the object of each player is to get her ball into each of these holes in turn and so round the course with the least number of strokes. The one who wins at the greater number of holes wins the round.

For the first stroke the ball is placed on a small mound called a "tee." Sometimes two players on each side strike the same ball alternately. The match is then called a "foursome."

Golf is essentially a game which must be acquired by practice. Little help can be obtained by an amateur from books. The rules of the game have been drawn up by the Golf Club of St. Andrews, and the beginner should obtain a copy of these. There are a number of ladies' golf clubs in country places, health resorts, and the suburbs, at which an entrance fee, which varies from one to three guineas, in addition to the year's subscription, must be paid.

HOME NURSING AND "FIRST AID"

No woman, be she princess or peasant, should consider her education complete without some knowledge of nursing, and although, to some extent, one believes in the "Born Nurse," it is certain that the necessary knowledge must be acquired, either by study, by practical experience, or by attending some of the excellent lectures which are given in various parts of the country by trained nurses and for which only a nominal fee is charged. Perhaps a knowledge of nursing is needed most by middle-class women, as the professional nurse is expensive, and it is only the very poor who are eligible for the ministrations of the district nurse.

Even if a woman is fortunate enough not to have to use her nursing knowledge for members of her own family, how valued a friend she may be, how useful a neighbour! Who so much in demand as the calm, quiet woman, who can act in a sudden emergency, knowing how to apply simple remedies and having the power to discern between slight ailments and serious symptoms: she will not only know when the doctor should be sent for, but can also be relied upon to faithfully carry out his orders. Calmness in a crisis is the result of knowledge.

THE SICK-ROOM

Choice of Room.—It often happens that a person is taken ill in a room which is quite unsuitable for an invalid, and he may have to remain there either because there is no other place available or because he is too ill to be moved. In this case the room must be made as like the ideal sick-room as possible. If you are able to choose a sick-room, select one at the back of the house, as it is quieter, and if it looks out on to a garden, so much the better. There is something very soothing in the sounds and scents from a garden, and most people like to listen to the songs of birds and to the rustling of leaves. The room should be large and lofty, and it is an advantage to have windows on opposite sides, so that when there is a strong wind blowing in one direction, a window on the other side can be opened. A room with a south-eastern aspect is best, as it will have plenty of sunshine, and sunshine, like fresh air, means life to the patient. The old plan of darkening a sick-room is a bad one. Unless the eyes are affected, or there is cerebral trouble, a patient should be encouraged to tolerate the light. Of course, a patient's bed can be moved, or the window curtain arranged so as to prevent "the sun getting in his eyes."

Ventilation and Warmth.—Good ventilation is an absolute necessity in the sick-room, and to ensure this there should be an inlet for fresh air and an outlet for what is impure. This can be arranged by opening the window at the top. The warm foul air escapes at the top, and the fresh air enters between the sashes. The windows should be opened wide and not just a few inches. The idea that night air is injurious is a false one, as often the air is purer at night than in the day-time; there are fewer fires and consequently less smoke. If the room is small, keep the window wide open. If the patient is in a draught, put up a screen, or if there is not one available it can be improvised by arranging a sheet over a clothes-horse. The sick-room should always be fresh, even to an outsider coming in from the open air. It should at the same time be warm, but not over-heated. A temperature from 56° to 60° Fahr. is usually high enough, but in some cases it may be necessary to have it as high as 65° Fahr. A thermometer should be hung in the room near the patient's bed and the temperature noted from time to time. There should also be a fireplace, as a fire in an open grate is an excellent ventilator. A complete set of fire-irons is not required. A small poker and tongs are all that are needed. Choose a time when the patient is awake to make up the fire, and if it must be made up while he is asleep, wear old gloves and take up the coal in the hands, or put a number of pieces of coal in a paper-bag beforehand and place this on the fire when necessary. When there is a fire in the room the grate will, of course, need to be "done up" once a day, but afterwards it can be kept tidy with a brush or a duster kept for the purpose.

Cleanliness and Arrangement.—Everything in a sick-room should be kept scrupulously clean. The floor should either be bare or covered with oil-cloth. In this way it can be kept clean by frequent dusting or wiping over daily with a damp cloth, and then occasionally washed with soap and water. Small rugs or mats can be laid down, and they should be placed so as to deaden the sound of footsteps. These can easily be taken out of the room and shaken.

The walls should be covered with a prêtty light paper.

It is better to avoid drapery as much as possible, and what there is should be of washing material. There should be no unnecessary furniture in the room, and it should be of the kind that is easily kept clean. One or two easy-chairs are useful, also a sofa, but in the case of infectious diseases upholstered furniture should be banished as far as possible.

On a table or chest of drawers place a tray, on which have a basin of water and a clean tea-cloth to wash the medicine glass or feeder. The medicine bottles and glass can be kept on this table, but all lotions, linaments, or poisons should be kept on the washstand. Somotimes a lotion, intended for outward application only, is given in mistake for medicine. The risk of doing this is lessened if lotion and medicine bottles are kept apart. Have a small table close to the patient's bed. This should be covered with a dainty white cloth, and on it might be placed a small bunch of very fresh flowers in a vase that will not easily fall over; also a table-napkin to place under the patient's chin while he is being fed. It is nice to have a tiny tray on this table on which a clean spoon can be kept, or the medicine glass or feeding-cup put down if the patient has to be raised, or can only take his nourishment slowly. Later on, during convalescence, a drink or a little fruit can be placed on the table for the patient to take as he wishes, and when he is able to read a book this might also be placed within reach.

There should be plenty of nice fresh flowers in the room, but avoid choosing those with a very strong scent, and never keep stale flowers in the vases. It is better to remove all plants and flowers at night.

Bed and Bedding.—The bedstead should be, if possible, behind the door with the head to the wall and a space on either side.

The window should be at the side of the bed. Never, if you can help it, have the head of the bed against the window, as the patient will be sure to complain of the draught. If it happens to be in this position, and the room is too small to allow of its being moved, then turn the patient with his head to the foot of the bed if possible.

In winter, when the weather is cold and dull, have the bedstead as near the fire as you conveniently can. It is nice when the fire is at the side of the bed, so that the patient can have a good view of it. There is something very cheering in a bright fire.

A single iron bedstead with a wire spring is the best, as it will be easy for the nurse to reach the patient. The only advantage in a full-sized bed is that the patient can be moved from one side to the other while the bed is being made. There should be a good, thick, soft mattress of hair or wool—hair for choice. Flock and feather beds are not good, as they get lumpy and full of hollows when they cannot be properly shaken.

The sheets should be large enough to be well tucked in under the mattress. A draw sheet is usually needed. This should be a yard wide and two yards long. An ordinary sheet doubled answers the purpose quite well.

The number of pillows required by a patient differs very much, but a bolster and two soft pillows or three pillows are usually needed. When the patient is lying quite flat, the second pillow may not be required, but it is often useful to put under his shoulders, or to support his back when lying on his side, or when one pillow gets very hot it is nice to be able to replace it by a fresh one.

Have warm soft woollen blankets. Cheap blankets made of cotton mixture are quite out of place in the sick-room, as they are heavy and not warm.

The same applies to heavy cotton quilts; they are undesirable on all occasions, and are impossible for an invalid, as their weight is most trying and tiring. Very light, thin bed-spreads should be used; small plain ones without frills are best, as they can be easily washed. A clean sheet makes a very good bed-spread.

All bed-linen should be of snowy whiteness.

THE NURSE

The woman who undertakes sick-nursing must learn to be observant; she must also be very accurate when making statements about her patients to the doctor and conscientious in carrying out his instructions. Often the nerves may be all "on edge" from the strain of nursing, especially if the patient is a very dear relative, and for this reason it is the duty of the nurse to take care of her own health. For the patient's sake as well as her own she should always try to take her meals regularly, and, if possible, out of the sick-room. She should also get some hours' sleep in another room.

Dress.—The nurse's dress should be of washing material, and she should always wear an apron. The dress should be short enough to clear the ground, and if the sleeves are short so much the better, as it is often necessary to wash the hands, and long sleeves are in the way, unless they can easily be turned up. Silk petticoats and rustling garments of all kinds are quite out of place, neither should jingling bracelets nor long chains be worn, as they are not only noisy but dangerous, being liable to catch on a table-cloth or quilt and cause an accident. The nurse should always wear quiet shoes with india-rubber heels if possible, or, if nursing at night, she might wear felt slippers. She should always walk softly but firmly, and never tip-toe about the room.

If the nurse has had some rest in the day, and comes on fresh for night duty, she can wear her day clothes, but if she has been with the patient all day and has to remain all night as well, she must undress, or at any rate take off all tight garments and put on a dressing-gown so that she can get some rest on a sofa, or in an easy-chair.

Night-Duty.—If the patient's condition allows it, it is better to have a little bed in the room and to go right into it, getting up about every two hours to give medicine or nourishment, or do what is necessary. Of course, this cannot be done in a serious case where a patient is delirious or requires constant watching. In an illness of this kind it is imperative for the one who is on charge at night to have some good sleep during the day in order to be very much awake and alert, as the patient is often at his worst at this time, and especially in the early hours of the morning when his vitality is very low. Some light and nourishing food must also be taken during the night, as this will tend to counteract the bad effect that overstrain, want of sleep, and anxiety may have on the body.

Relieving the Nurse.—It sometimes happens that a number of anxious relatives are desirous of staying with a person who is very ill in order to do what they can to help. Now this is a great mistake: for one reason they use up the fresh air so greatly needed by the patient, and for another they all become tired, and thus render themselves unfit to perform nursing duties properly. Where there are several friends to help, they should take it in turn to relieve each other in the sick-room. Except when help is needed in lifting the patient, or in rendering him some special service, it is better that only one person should be in attendance at a time. When the one in charge of a patient leaves another to take her place—perhaps a friend who has offered to take night duty—she should leave some written instructions, such as the time when food and medicine are to be taken, &c.

Example

Food.	Medicine.	Stimulant.
Milk, 2 A.M.	11 P.M.	12 A.M.
Bovril or Beef-tea, 4 A.M.	3 A.M.	4 A.M.
Milk, 6 A.M.	7 A.M.	8 A.M.
Benger's, 8 A.M.		

Poultice every four hours. Last poultice put on at 12 A.M.

The friend should be instructed to tick off the various items as she gives them, and she in turn should leave a short written report such as the following:—

Example

12.30 A.M.	Patient restless.
2 A.M.	Slept an hour.
2.30 A.M.	Patient sick.
3 A.M.	Complained of pain.
4 A.M.	Perspired profusely.
6 A.M.	Slept for two hours.

From the above it is easily seen that patient had a bad night.

The Professional Nurse.—As a rule the doctor will say when a trained nurse is needed, but it is always as well to obtain the services of one in a very serious case where special orders are given, or where a patient requires attention night and day. A nurse must be treated with every consideration. Her meals should be served in the dining-room, and some one should relieve her while she takes them. It is the duty of the people who engage her to see that her food is regularly and properly served, as otherwise her health will suffer, and she will be unfit for her duties. When on night duty she should be asked what refreshment she would like to have. As a rule it is tea or coffee and some sandwiches, or something that she can take easily.

When only one nurse is in attendance, it is usual for her to do the night duty. Before going off duty she attends to the patient's toilet and does what is necessary for him before she leaves. She is often busy during the greater part of the morning. If possible, she should go out for a walk each day. She generally goes to bed soon after lunch, and should not be disturbed for seven or eight hours.

Some nurses take their own fees, but more often these are paid to the association for which they work. The fees vary from two to three guineas a week. Laundry and travelling expenses have also to be paid.

Sometimes a visiting nurse can be engaged. She goes in once or twice a day to attend to the patient generally, or to carry out any special order. She will have a tariff of charges, and her fees vary according to what she does, or the time she spends at a call. It is sometimes more convenient to have a visiting nurse where the sleeping accommodation is limited.

THE DOCTOR

People do not often care to change their doctor. The family doctor is looked upon as a true and trusted friend. From him people expect not only professional attendance, but all round sympathy and advice, and as a rule they are not disappointed. Of him Louis Stevenson says: "He is the flower (such as it is) of our civilisation."

When it is necessary to choose a doctor, if possible choose one who lives fairly near, and before engaging him ask him what his fees are, so that there may be no misunderstanding on this point. Except among the poorer classes the doctor does not often receive payment at the time of his visit; as a rule the bill is sent in quarterly or half-yearly, and sometimes only once a year. When the bill is sent in it should be promptly paid. A doctor has many bad debts—not among the poor, but among the upper and middle-classes. There is no more strenuous life than that of the doctor, and he should receive every consideration.

Having chosen a doctor in whom you can place your confidence, be sure that you follow his instructions, as the treatment is useless unless carried out.

A trained nurse is never expected to express an opinion as to diagnosis unasked. Of course, a doctor would not expect such a strict observance of etiquette on the part of relations or friends, but at the same time it is only polite to defer to the doctor in all matters concerning the patient. Do not tell the doctor that you believe the patient to be suffering from one thing when he has diagnosed something quite different. Then do not worry the doctor by giving him the various opinions of yourself and friends, but instead report to him faithfully every symptom or change you have noticed since his previous visit.

Consultations.—In the case of serious illness or uncertain diagnosis, it is only natural that the patient or his friends should wish for further advice, and no doctor will object to a consultation if he is approached in a right manner. When it has been decided to have a second opinion, speak first to the doctor. The matter should then be arranged without the slightest friction. The doctor will probably have a fellow-practitioner with whom he would like to consult, or he may be willing to meet a doctor whom you suggest. If the case is very grave and urgent, and especially when it is a question of surgical interference, the doctor himself will be the first to suggest sending for a specialist, and he will probably wish to call in some one from his own hospital. In this case the doctor—with the consent of the patient's friends—arranges the matter, and the specialist and doctor visit the patient together and consult as to what is best to be done. The specialist's fee must be paid at the time of the visit. It should be placed in an envelope beforehand and handed to the doctor, who gives it to the specialist. The amount is arranged between the two doctors, and usually varies according to the position of the patient.

CARE OF THE PATIENT

How to Make the Bed.—When a patient is too ill to be taken out of bed the bed must be made while he is in it. This can be done quite easily if one knows the way. If the under-sheet has to be changed, roll up the fresh one lengthwise to half its width and place it near the bed ready for use. Then remove the bed-spread and top blanket, and draw out the top sheet from under the remaining blanket. Untuck all other bed-clothes. Turn the patient on his side by means of the draw-sheet. Wash and rub his back, and then pull the night-dress down smoothly while he is in this position. Next roll the draw-sheet and then the under-sheet as close as possible to the patient. Put in a fresh under-sheet and draw-sheet with the rolled parts quite close to the patient and on a line with the sheets that are to be removed. Then gently roll the patient on to his other side. He will then be lying on clean sheets. The soiled sheets are easily removed on the other side of the bed, and the fresh ones unrolled and tucked in under the mattress. When the sheets have to be put in in this fashion, care should be taken that the rollings are made as flat as possible so that the patient can be turned over them without discomfort. The rollings should always be uppermost, as it is easier to grasp and unroll the sheets from the other side of the bed. If a mackintosh is in use and there is only one, it should be drawn out carefully, washed and dried if necessary, and then rolled in with the draw-sheet when the bed is made. Of course, it is more convenient to have a second mackintosh. Always make sure that the under-blanket, under-sheet, mackintosh, and draw-sheet are quite smooth and free from wrinkles; also that the blanket and sheets are firmly tucked in under the mattress. The

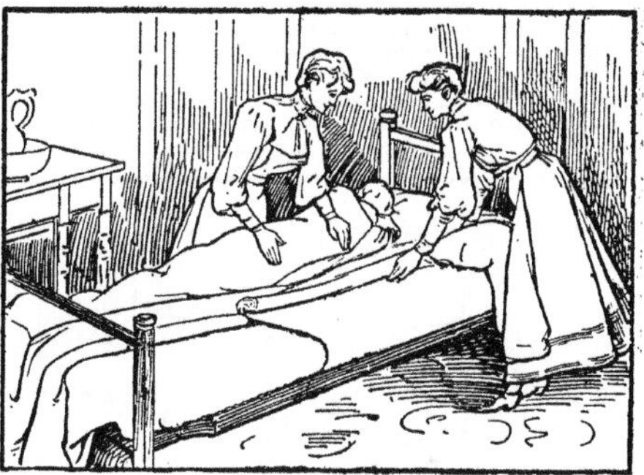

Changing Sheets from the Side.

patient should be covered with a blanket while his bed is being made.

After the under-sheets have been changed, put the top sheet over the blanket already covering patient. With one hand hold the sheet in position, and with the other draw out the blanket and put it over the sheet. Next put on the rest of the bed-clothes.

When it is not necessary to change the under-sheet, the bed is quickly and easily made when the patient is on a mattress. He is just rolled over from side to side and the draw-sheet either drawn through or changed. If it happens, as it sometimes does, that the patient is on a flock or feather bed and has to remain on it, he must be rolled as far as possible to one side, and the bed must be gently shaken, and the flocks or feathers pushed into the hollow in the middle. He is then rolled to the opposite side of the bed, and the second side is shaken in the same way. It is possible for one nurse to make the bed and roll in the sheets, but it can be done better and more quickly by two people, and an amateur nurse should always have assistance.

Sometimes a patient cannot be turned from side to side. In this case the clean under-sheet can be put in from the head of the bed. It should be rolled up widthwise. The patient's head and pillows are raised by one nurse, while her assistant pushes down the soiled sheets and rolls in the clean one. The head and pillows are then lowered into position, the shoulders and then the other parts of the body are gently raised, the soiled sheet is pushed downwards to the feet, and the clean sheet is gradually unrolled until it covers the bed. The draw-sheet would, of course, be rolled out with the under-sheet, and would have to be put in afterwards. One nurse would raise the lower part of the body while the other nurse rolled in the draw-sheet.

Changing Sheets from the Top of the Bed.

If a patient is not very ill, he can often lift himself enough for his draw-sheet to be put into place. To raise the lower part of his body he should be instructed to press his head firmly on to his pillow and his heels into the bed.

When a patient can only be raised a very little, the clean draw-sheet can be fastened to the edge of the soiled one with safety-pins. One nurse pins the two sheets together and gently raises patient's body, and a nurse on the other side of the bed draws the two sheets through quickly. Both nurses pull on to the sheet together to ensure its being straight. It is then tucked firmly under the mattress on both sides of the bed.

When a patient slips down towards the foot of the bed, he can be lifted back into position on the draw-sheet. It must be untucked and rolled up quite close to the body on each side: a nurse on either side of the bed must grasp the sheet where it is rolled up and near its upper and lower margin. In this way there is a better purchase than if the hands were close together. Both nurses must lift together, and the patient must be instructed to lift his head at the same moment. If he is unable to do this, a third person must pass her arm under the pillow and so support the head, while the others lift. Of course, an injured limb would need to be supported. A patient can also be lifted by two persons —one on each side—joining hands under his shoulders and buttocks.

Great care should be taken to arrange the pillows properly. It is quite easy to see when the pillows are comfortable. When a patient is propped in a sitting position care should be taken that the back, neck, and head are properly supported, otherwise there will be great discomfort. An injured limb has always to be supported on a pillow. When a patient has his legs drawn up, a pillow should be put under the knees.

In some illnesses patients have to be kept between blankets. When this is the case put a warm soft blanket loosely over the patient. Put a sheet on the top, and let it come up a little higher than the blanket, as it is not pleasant to have the latter against the face. Bed-clothes should not be folded over the patient's chest—their weight is exhausting. The extra lengths can be folded over or tucked in at the foot of the bed.

Change of Bed.—An invalid can often be lifted on to another bed, or on to a sofa while his bed is made. He should be lifted in the under-sheet, which must be strong, and if the patient is heavy the under-blanket must be used as well. Enough of the top bed-clothes should be left to keep the patient warm, and one small pillow can be placed under the head. The number of bearers needed in lifting will depend upon the weight of the patient. The under-sheet should be rolled up close to the body on both sides. The bearers grasp the rolled parts of the sheet and lift gently and together. It is better to have the bed or sofa on which the patient is to be lifted placed at the side of the bed.

When a patient is well enough to sit up while his bed is made, a comfortable chair should be placed near and a large thick blanket spread over it. Another blanket should be wrapped round his body and legs as he is helped out of bed, and when he sits down he should be enveloped in the blanket which was spread over the chair. If the weather is cold, he should have on a bed-jacket and warm socks before he steps out of bed.

Water-Cushions and Beds.—In a long illness or where the patient is very thin or helpless, a water-cushion is necessary. It should be placed under the lower part of the body to keep pressure off the back and hips. A cushion twenty-eight inches by eighteen inches will usually answer the purpose very well. It should be filled with water at about 90° Fahr. or less if the weather is very hot. The empty cushion should be rolled under the patient in the same way as sheets are changed and then filled. A funnel should be used, and great care must be taken not to spill the water. Continue pouring in water until there is sufficient in it to prevent any part of the patient's body pressing on the floor of the cushion; it must not be too full or it will be hard. A ring water-cushion is often very useful.

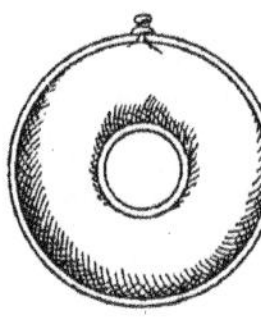

Air-Cushion.

Air-cushions are also used, but they are apt to get very hot and are not so good as water ones.

Sometimes a full-sized water-bed is necessary. In this case boards havé to be placed across the bedstead from side to side, to support its weight and to keep it perfectly straight.

The Patient's Toilet.—The daily bath is needed in health and is even more necessary in a long illness. Before commencing to bath a patient see that the room is warm, and put everything that is likely to be required in readiness, *i.e.* basin of hot water, a face sponge, a flannel for washing the body, some good soap, a can of hot water, a pail for emptying water, methylated spirits, powder, &c. Have a night-dress airing at the fire; there should always be two in use—one for day and one for night. A fresh draw-sheet should also be in readiness in case it is needed. Commence by removing the bed-spread and drawing out the top sheet; then slip a large bath-towel under the blanket. If the room is warm only one blanket is needed over the patient while he is being washed. If he is at all collapsed or likely to feel cold, put a hot bottle to his feet before you commence to wash him. A patient should never be hurried, but at the same time he should be washed as quickly and deftly as possible, as otherwise he will be tired before his toilet is finished.

First wash and dry the face, then the neck, hands, and arms. Next wash the lower limbs under the blanket, tucking a towel close up to the part that is being washed to avoid wetting the bed-clothes. Turn the patient towards you a little way to wash and rub the hip on the further side. Next draw the bath-towel from under the blanket, roll patient on his side, lay the bath-towel up close alongside him and wash the shoulders and back. The lower part of the back and the hips must receive special attention, and should be rubbed with methylated spirits and powdered after drying.

When washing the feet, turn back the bed-clothes from the foot of the bed, let the patient draw up his knees, place a mackintosh and towel under the feet, and put the foot-bath on the bed. The feet can then be put right into the bath.

When the washing is complete put on the patient's night-dress and replace the sheet and bed-spread. The night-dress should always be quite loose, so that it can be easily put on. In some cases it is necessary to have it opened up the back as far as the yoke or collar, which is just slipped over the head. Only one garment should be worn in bed, but a warm flannel bed-jacket should be at hand to put on if the patient sits up or has his arms out of bed. Long loose flannel jackets are the most useful, especially in rheumatic fever and pneumonia cases, where the slightest movement causes great pain. They should be quite plain, the sleeves should be large and loose, and tied at the wrists with tapes.

In a serious illness it is sometimes impossible to wash a patient properly, although the doctor may order frequent sponging to reduce the temperature. In this case a loose flannel jacket would be the most convenient garment to wear, as the removal of a tight night-shirt would be too exhausting for the patient.

Care of the Teeth.—In these days great attention is being paid to the hygiene of the mouth, and it is most important that a patient's teeth should be kept clean. With a little help he can often clean his own teeth, even when not able to sit up in bed. Place a towel under the chin, moisten the tooth-brush and dip it in the dentifrice, and hold the bottom of the soap-dish in position for rinsing the mouth.

When a patient is too ill to brush his teeth, this must be done for him. A soft tooth-brush is the best thing to use dipped in warm water with a few drops of liquid dentifrice, a little carbonate of soda, or weak Sanitas lotion. Clean not only the teeth and gums, but the tongue and roof of the mouth as well. This might be repeated two or three times a day.

Care of the Hair.—This must also have its due share of attention. In a short illness the daily brushing and combing are generally sufficient, and it is easy to keep a man's head clean. A woman's hair should be plaited—one plait on each side, but if the hair is thin and short it is sometimes better to brush it up on to the top of the head. In a long illness the scalp should be rubbed frequently with some good and reliable hair-wash to keep it in good condition. If there is much hair only half of it should be done at a time. A patient's hair-brush and comb must be kept scrupulously clean. When the hair itself has to be washed, spread a mackintosh and large bath-towel over the pillow.

Consideration for the Invalid.—In a very serious case it is better to keep the patient as quiet as possible, and to allow no visitors, unless it is some one whom the patient particularly wishes to see. Even then the visitor should be warned that he is to talk as little as possible and told not to speak of subjects likely to cause excitement. When the worst is past and during convalescence it often cheers a patient to see a few friends, but no visitor should be allowed to make a long stay, as even in convalescence a person is often so weak that over-excitement may mean loss of sleep—"Nature's sweet restorer"—which is so sorely needed after a serious illness.

Never allow a visitor to sit on the bed. It shakes and irritates the patient and causes great discomfort, if not actual pain, and it makes the bed look untidy.

Well-meaning people often cause trouble by calling to inquire after an invalid, and unless one can be of real use to the patient or his friends it is kinder not to call until the worst is over. There is always extra work where there is sickness and no one has time to talk to visitors. In the case of a serious illness a daily bulletin might be put on the front door, and this will save not only the extra work entailed in answering the door to callers, but, what is more important, it will prevent the patient being disturbed by the constant ringing of the bell. In fact, it is always better in the case of serious illness to put up a notice asking visitors not to ring, but to go round to the back or side-door, where soft knocks can easily be heard by the servant. Of course, many small houses and flats have no side-door. In a case of this kind some plan must be thought out by the friends to ensure quiet to the patient. Necessary noises can be borne more easily than unnecessary ones. Although a person may be very ill he has not lost all reasoning power, and he is naturally vexed and irritated if he thinks that people are not doing all that is possible to give him the necessary peace. Ringing of bells, banging of doors, and rattling of fire-irons, crockery, or newspapers are unnecessary noises which should not be allowed. The clicking of knitting-needles is another sound which might be annoying to a patient. It is a rhythmic sound like the ticking of a clock, and might even be soothing in some instances, but an observant person can easily see what vexes and what pleases and should act accordingly.

Then, again, do not read aloud to a patient unless you are quite sure he wishes it. Some people like being read to when they are ill; to them it is soothing, while to others it is quite the reverse. Of course, when a patient is very ill and the temperature is high there should be no reading aloud, as it would cause undue excitement, and even when there is a change for the better it is important that the patient should get all the sleep he can to make up for past wakefulness, and too much reading would serve to deprive him of a measure of this much-needed rest. Whispering is a bad habit which should never be permitted in the sick-room. The patient will wonder what is being said that he may not hear, and will probably come to the conclusion that he has some very serious symptoms.

An Insensible Patient is like a child and is dependent on his nurse for everything. She must see that he is warm, and that his bed is dry. If hot bottles are necessary, they should be covered, as serious burns have often been caused through neglect in this respect.

In a case of this kind the vitality is very low, and persons easily get bed-sores unless the greatest care is taken. These can easily be prevented, but they are difficult to cure when once they develop. A water-pillow is valuable to keep the pressure off the back and hips. It is also important to examine the patient about every two hours, and if the draw-sheet is found to be wet it should be changed, the back and hips washed, well dried, and rubbed with zinc ointment. The position of the patient should be changed frequently in order to relieve pressure on any particular spot. If he has been lying on his back for two hours he might be placed on his side for the next two hours, a pillow being placed along the back for support. This change of position also prevents the lungs from getting congested. A patient who is allowed to lie long on his back will often contract serious chest trouble. The friends at once conclude he has "caught a cold," and, in consequence, wish to close the windows, whereas the trouble is due to his having been left too long in one position. An unconscious patient can often breathe better on his side, so if he can breathe equally well on either side he can be turned from side to side alternately and need not lie on his back at all.

Nourishment must be given very slowly and carefully with a tea-spoon, very little being given at a time. The spoon should be kept in the mouth until the contents are gone, as it encourages the patient to swallow. Be quite sure that the drink is swallowed before giving more, and do not go on feeding if you find he cannot swallow, as what is given will only get into the air passages, and may cause suffocation. The head should always be turned a little to one side for feeding, as the food is less likely to go the wrong way. It can be kept in position by a small pillow nicely adjusted, or with the nurse's arm passed under the pillow.

Nursing an Infectious Case.—The patient must be isolated. A room at the top of the house should be prepared, and, if possible, the entire floor should be kept for the patient and his attendants. All carpets, drapery, and unnecessary furniture should be taken out of the room before the patient is taken into it. The furniture which remains should be of the plainest description, and the few covers or curtains that are allowed should be of washing materials that can be well boiled. A sheet kept well saturated with carbolic (1 in 20) should be hung over the doorway outside the sick-room. The room must be kept scrupulously clean, and there must be good ventilation without draughts. Unless the weather is very hot there should be a fire. All crockery used by the patient must he kept for him, and should be washed in the room or in a room adjoining. The food should be brought up and placed on a table outside the sick-room, and any that is left should be burned.

The patient must be washed every day, the greatest care being taken that he does not get a chill. It is important that the skin should act properly and so help to eliminate impurities, as otherwise too much work will be thrown on the kidneys. When the patient's linen—either bed or personal—is changed, the soiled articles must be put into a bath containing carbolic (1 in 20) or some Jeyes' fluid. They should afterwards be boiled for half-an-hour, and then dried in the open air.

All discharges from the patient must be received in vessels containing a disinfectant. Japanese handkerchiefs, or pieces of rag which can be burnt should be used in place of ordinary handkerchiefs.

The person attending the patient should not mix with the other members of the family. She should wear a dress of washing material and be careful to wash her hands frequently. She should keep her nails short and clean and should frequently wash her mouth with boracic lotion. If she goes out she should have a bath and change her clothes, and she ought not to enter a shop or any public conveyance.

Before the patient joins the family he should have a number of hot baths, and should be washed all over with carbolic (1 in 20). He must afterwards put on clean clothes. The nurse must be very thoroughly disinfected in the same manner. All her clothing worn in the sick-room must be boiled or stoved.

The patient's nail-brush, tooth-brush, papers, &c., should all be burned. All crockery, forks, spoons, &c., used in the room should be well washed in strong disinfectant, and, if possible, boiled afterwards. The bedding and blankets, and any of the patient's garments that cannot be boiled, must be sent away to be stoved by the Sanitary Authorities. If carpets and woollen drapery have been left in the room, they must be treated in the same manner.

The room must then be disinfected. All articles left in it should be spread out and well exposed—drawers and cupboards being left open. This disinfecting can be done by the Sanitary Authorities, who either fumigate with sulphur or spray with formalin. The room must remain shut up for twenty-four hours, and for a day or two afterwards the windows and door should be left wide open to allow the air to blow through. The room and its contents should afterwards be very thoroughly cleaned. All paint should be washed with soap and water, the ceiling white-washed, and the walls re-papered, the old paper being first stripped off and burned.

To fumigate a room with sulphur the chimneys and windows must be closed, and all crevices covered with strips of brown paper. These are generally pasted on, but this is not necessary where there is varnish: the paper need only be wetted and it will adhere quite well, and is more easily removed. Put about one pound of sulphur or more broken into small pieces, according to the size of the room, into an iron dish or pan. Stand this in a bath containing water, as a precaution against fire. Sprinkle with a few drops of methylated spirits and set it alight. Leave the room at once, close the door, and cover all cracks with strips of brown paper.

Routine of a Day's Work.—Sometimes after a bad night a patient may sleep for some hours in the early morning. When he wakes he will need refreshment. If on solid food and able to take ever so light a meal, he should have his hands and face sponged before being propped up to take his breakfast. If very ill he will of course only be able to take liquid diet. The fireplace should be done up next and a supply of coals brought in for the day. While the servant is doing this, the nurse could take the opportunity of performing any duties that would take her out of the room. The next thing should be the patient's toilet. After he has been washed, &c., the room should be put in order and made to look as cheerful and bright as possible. By this time the doctor will probably be due. When a patient is taking solid food let him, if possible, have his dinner after the doctor has been. This visit is generally an event which causes some excitement to the patient, and he is almost sure to hurry his dinner or not take it properly if he is expecting the doctor, and if the visit is paid in the middle of dinner the meal will probably be spoiled. The patient should be allowed to rest in the early afternoon, and at about four he can have a cup of tea unless this is forbidden. In the early evening the temperature, &c., should be again taken, and the patient should have his hands and face sponged, and, if necessary, his back should be attended to. If he is allowed, he might sit up in a chair and have his bed made in the evening; he might even be able to sit up for an hour or two.

It is, of course, quite impossible to lay down any hard-and-fast rule as to what is to be done during the day, as so much depends upon a patient's condition and the special treatment that is ordered. In some cases one is constantly having to perform special nursing duties for a patient, and many things may happen to make it impossible to do things at stated times, but as far as possible do everything regularly, whether it is giving nourishment—one of the most important duties in sickness—taking a temperature, washing the patient, or doing whatever the doctor orders.

Convalescence.—Convalescence is often the most trying time for both patient and nurse. Do not think that when the worst is over there is no further danger. For some time afterwards the greatest care is needed if a patient is to regain his lost strength and not fall a victim to some other disease, such as phthisis, which often follows pneumonia, measles, typhoid, &c. The invalid's low condition makes him an easy victim to disease germs, which, like mean cowardly people, are always waiting to attack the weak. The patient will need the same care in feeding, and it may be necessary to take great pains to tempt his appetite, as he will require plenty of nourishment. On first getting up he should not be dressed, as he will be very weak and inclined to faint, but put on a warm dressing-gown and a pair of socks and wrap him well round in a blanket. At first he should only sit up for a quarter or half-an-hour, the time being gradually increased as he gets stronger. He should always be in a well-ventilated room, and, if possible, should take rest on a balcony or in a garden.

Friends must be admitted with caution and not allowed to stay too long, especially towards evening. Try to keep your patient cheerful and free from worry; this is not always easy, as frequently he may be inclined to become irritable and very exacting. Do not, however, despise him for his capricious way, for his indecision of character, but nurse him back to health with the same patience as was shown to him during his hours of pain.

He should only be allowed to resume his ordinary duties gradually, and for a time should rest a little in the afternoon, take his breakfast in bed, and retire early.

A change of air, to the sea or country, is needed after a long acute illness.

FOOD

There is nothing more important in an illness than diet, and much depends on a patient taking his food properly. In this the doctor's orders must be strictly carried out. Many a person has died through improper food being given by foolish friends, as, for instance, solid food given to any one suffering from gastric trouble or typhoid fever.

Liquid Diet.—When a patient is very ill he is usually kept on a liquid diet and milk is generally ordered, as it contains all the elements necessary to life, and is easily assimilated. Sometimes as much as three pints of milk are ordered to be taken in twenty-four hours or a teacupful every two hours. It often happens, however, that a patient is unable to take as much as this, and when this is the case, it is better to let him take a smaller quantity and digest it rather than force him to take a larger quantity which will only cause sickness or indigestion. When only a little milk can be taken at a time, the feeds should be more frequent. Four or five table-spoonfuls might be given every hour, or even a smaller quantity every half-hour.

Some people have a great dislike to milk and often cannot digest it unless diluted. This may be done by mixing it with soda-water, plain water, or thin barley-water. It is also well to vary a milk diet as much as possible. Sometimes the milk may be given hot, at other times cold, or it can be flavoured with a little strong coffee, cocoa, or else tea can be made with milk. Sometimes for a change a patient may like Horlick's Malted Milk or The Allenbury Diet, or, again, the plain milk might be made into junket.

When the digestion is very bad the doctor may order the milk to be peptonised. This can be done with Fairchild's peptonising powders, and the directions are found on the box containing the powders, or Benger's Food, which is also pre-digested, might be given for a change. This also must be prepared according to the directions given on the tin.

When there is difficulty of digestion, the feeds should be taken very slowly—merely sipped.

In cases of extreme exhaustion more nourishment may be needed, and then eggs may be beaten up in the milk, or a little strong beef essence. Brand's essence or Panopeptin may be given between the feeds.

When brandy has been ordered give it in a little soda-water, plain water, or in a small quantity of milk. It should never be put into a tumblerful of milk, as it will flavour the whole and may be objectionable to the patient, and he would be unable to take such a large quantity. Brandy should not be poured out long before being taken, as it loses its stimulating properties and becomes useless.

It should be remembered that beef-tea is not so much a food as a stimulant, and should be given alternately with other food. Milk can be given alternately with beef-tea, invalid bovril, veal or chicken broth, or the white of an egg can be lightly beaten up and given with soda-water or plain water.

In cases where only a little is taken, give nourishment in a concentrated form, such as strong beef-essence, or Panopeptin, &c.

In most cases it is a good thing to give the patient plenty of water, but it must not be given instead of nourishment. When there is great thirst, barley-water flavoured with lemon may be given.

Feeding a Helpless Patient.—In feeding a helpless patient put a table napkin under his chin and then place one arm under his pillow and gently raise his head. Use a small teacup or glass for the feeds if possible, as a patient usually prefers this to a feeder. When the latter has to be used it must be most carefully washed and

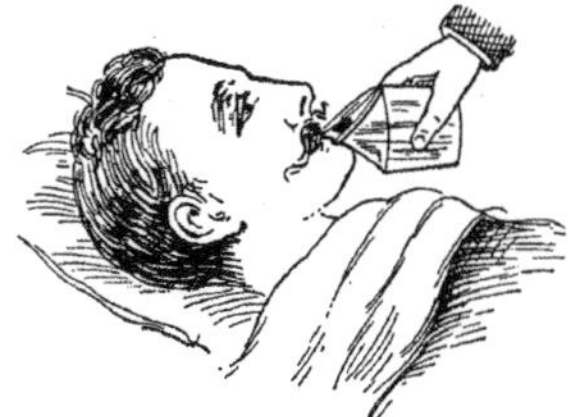

The "Ideal" Feeder.

frequently scalded, as, unless great care is taken, some particles of food will be left in the spout. The "Ideal" feeder is to be recommended, as it has no spout, which is an advantage.

Regularity in Feeding.—When a patient is on fluid diet only, his feeds should be given at regular intervals by night as well as by day. It must also be remembered that his strength is at its lowest ebb in the early hours of the morning, and care should be taken that he has some nourishment at that time. If he is at all cold, give a warm drink, and a stimulant if this has been prescribed. If a patient is having a good sleep he may sometimes be allowed to miss a feed, but if very exhausted he must never be left too long without nourishment.

Diet in Convalescence.—From fluids a patient goes on gradually to light solid foods. At first it may be that his milk or beef-tea is only thickened with a little arrowroot or cornflour, then he may have bread and milk, a lightly boiled or poached egg, or some milk jelly or pudding. After this would follow fish, either boiled or steamed, then chicken boiled, steamed, or roasted, and a little later a steamed or grilled chop. Always try to give the food which is most nutritious and most easily digested. When the diet is restricted prepare the foods allowed in the most varied ways possible.

The most easily digested vegetables are cauliflower, chicory, spinach, boiled lettuce, sea-kale, and celery. Most vegetables should not be given at first.

All fruit given should be fresh, and, as a rule, it is better stewed than raw. A little fresh cream may be given with the fruit, as this is a good way of supplying the invalid with fat. Stewed apples with cream or stewed prunes and cream are both very good dishes.

On pp. 558–59 are given a few recipes, specially suited to invalids, and many dishes suitable for the convalescent stage will be found in the "Guide to Cookery" (p. 116), while those who wish to study the subject more fully might consult a special book on invalid cookery, such as the "Art of Cooking for Invalids," by Florence B. Jack.

As soon as solid food is allowed, the meals should be given regularly at the ordinary hours. A patient is sure to take his food better when this is done. He will only be able to take small meals at first, and must have good nourishing drinks in between. He must also be fed during the night. The quantity he needs will vary according to how much he takes in the day, and whether he sleeps or not at night. If a breakfast-cup of milk, thin arrowroot or Benger's is given the last thing, and the patient sleeps well, he may not need feeding again until the early morning, but if he is wakeful and does not take food well, he will need nourishment every two or three hours. It is most important that a patient should take his food well in the early stages of convalescence.

Preparation of the Meal.—Whatever food is given should be the best of its kind, and never stale or tainted in any way. It is also important to have it well cooked, and all utensils used must be kept scrupulously clean. The cooking should not be done in the invalid's room, as the smell of the food would be sure to spoil his appetite.

Never ask a patient what he would like, but find out what his tastes are in some other way and indulge them as far as possible, always providing that they do not incline towards prohibited articles of diet.

A bad appetite can often be stimulated with a tasty little meal that comes as a surprise. The meal must also be daintily served. Always have a perfectly clean and pretty tray-cloth, and use nice bright glass, china, silver and cutlery. If there is a garden from which a fresh supply of flowers may be had, a small bunch of freshly gathered flowers or even a single sweet-smelling bloom might be placed on the tray. Take care that a hot meal is really hot, and also have the plates properly warmed.

Do not give a patient too much at a time; a piled-up plateful might set him against the food, whilst a second helping can easily be given.

When a meal is to be served, have the patient comfortably propped up beforehand, and see that he has on a warm bed-jacket or other wrap. A jacket is always better than a shawl.

Keeping the Food.—Never keep food in the sick-room if you can help it, but, if possible, put it in a cool larder, only taking enough in the room for immediate use. At night when it may not be possible to leave the room, the nourishments might be placed on a little table outside the door on the landing and near an open window if convenient. Only light nourishment is given at night, and jugs of beef-tea or milk may be kept outside on the window-ledge if the weather allows. The jugs must then be covered with clean muslin—a large bead on each corner will generally serve to keep a piece of muslin in position, but if the wind is high or there is danger of dust and smuts, small plates or saucers will be better.

Beef Juice

Ingredients.—From 4 to 6 oz. lean juicy beef—salt.

Method.—Choose a piece of beef from the rump or upper part of the round and see that it is freshly cut. Remove all fat, broil the meat quickly on both sides for one or two minutes to set the juice free. Then cut it in strips and squeeze out the juice with a lemon-squeezer or vegetable-presser into a warm cup. Add salt if necessary, and serve at once, as it does not keep well.

Beef-Tea

Ingredients—

½ lb. lean, juicy Beef.	A pinch of Salt.
½ pint Cold Water.	

Method.—Wipe the meat with a damp cloth to make sure of its being quite clean.

Then place on a board, and with a sharp knife scrape or shred down as finely as possible, keeping back any pieces of fat and skin.

Put it into a basin with the salt and water, stir it well up, cover the basin with a plate, and, if time permits, let it stand for half-an-hour.

Then pour all into a clean lined saucepan, place the pan over rather a slow fire, and, with two forks placed back to back, whisk it well until it almost reaches boiling point. Then draw the pan to the side of the fire, put on the lid, and allow the beef-tea to simmer as slowly as possible from ten to twelve minutes.

Strain and remove the fat from the top with a piece of paper.

Steamed Fish

Ingredients—

1 filleted Haddock, Whiting, or Sole.	A pinch of White Pepper.
A pinch of Salt.	A little Butter.
	A squeeze of Lemon Juice.

Method.—Cut the fish into neat pieces and place them on a greased plate.

Sprinkle with a little salt and white pepper, if it is allowed, and squeeze over some lemon juice, which helps to keep the fish firm and white, and also aids digestion. Cover the fish with a piece of greased white paper and then with a lid or basin. Place this over a pan half full of boiling water, and cook from twenty to thirty minutes, until the fish loses its clear, transparent appearance, and looks quite white. If the pieces are thick it will be better to turn them once during cooking. The liquid that is on the plate when the fish is cooked is the juice from the fish, and should be served with it.

This is the lightest and simplest mode of cooking fish for an invalid.

Sometimes a white sauce is made (see p. 146) and poured over it. The liquid in this case should be added to the sauce.

Stewed Fish

Ingredients—

1 filleted Fish—Whiting, Haddock, Sole, or Plaice.	½ oz. Butter.
1 table-sp. Bread-crumbs.	1 tea-spoonful chopped Parsley.
½ gill Cold Water.	White Pepper
1 gill Milk.	Salt.

Method.—Wipe the fish with a damp cloth, and cut it into small, neat pieces. Take a clean lined saucepan, rinse it out with water to prevent the fish sticking to it, and place the pieces of fish at the foot. Sprinkle over them a little salt and white pepper, pour on the milk and water; put the lid on the pan, and let the fish cook slowly by the side of the fire until it is ready, which will be from ten to fifteen minutes. Lift out the pieces of fish on to the plate on which they have to be served, and keep them hot. Add the bread-crumbs and the butter to the water and milk in the pan; stir over the fire for a few minutes until the bread-crumbs swell and thicken the sauce. Sprinkle in the parsley, finely chopped, and then pour this sauce over the fish.

Chicken or Veal Panada

Ingredients—

¼ lb. breast of Chicken, or ¼ lb. fillet of Veal.	1 or 2 table-sp. Cream.
1 tea-spoonful Cold Water.	A pinch of Salt.

Method.—Wipe the meat, and cut it into small pieces, free from fat and skin. Put it into a cup or small basin, with a pinch of salt and the cold water; tie over it a piece of greased white paper, and steam slowly from one to one and a half hours. Then lift out, and put the contents of the basin into a mortar; pound well, and rub through a fine wire sieve. Put the sieved mixture into a pan, add the cream, and heat through. This may be served on a piece of toast, or even cold. If considered too rich, use a little more water in the cooking, and omit the cream.

Stewed Pigeon

Ingredients—

1 Pigeon.
½ oz. Butter.
½ pint Stock.
½ tea-spoonful Flour.
Pepper and Salt.
½ slice Toast.

Method.—Prepare and truss the pigeon as for roasting, and coat it over with the flour. Melt the butter in a small stewpan and, when smoking hot, put in the pigeon, and brown it on all sides. Then lift it on to a plate, and pour away all the grease that is left in the pan. Pour in the stock, and, when warm, return the pigeon.

Put the lid on the pan, and allow the bird to stew very gently from one to two hours, according to age and size. When quite tender lift it out on to a neat square of toast, and remove the trussing string from it.

Reduce the gravy in the pan by allowing it to boil quickly without the lid, until there is just enough left for serving. Keep it well skimmed, that it may be quite free from grease, and then pour it round the pigeon.

Garnish with a sprig of parsley or a little water-cress.

Raw Beef Sandwiches

Take two ounce of lean, juicy beef. Wipe it with a cloth, and with a sharp knife shred it down as finely as you would for beef-tea. Pound this in a mortar, with any seasoning that may be allowed, and rub through a fine wire sieve. Spread between thin slices of bread, with a little butter on it, if it is allowed, and cut it into neat strips.

These sandwiches are generally ordered for special cases.

A Cup of Arrowroot

Ingredients—

½ oz. Arrowroot.
½ pint of Cold Water.
1 tea-spoonful of Sugar.

Method.—Put the arrowroot into a small basin, add to it a table-spoonful of the cold water, and break it with a wooden spoon until quite smooth. Then pour on the rest of the water, mix well, and pour into a small lined saucepan. Stir this over the fire until it boils and thickens, and then let it boil from seven to ten minutes longer, to thoroughly cook the arrowroot. Sweeten to taste, and serve in a cup or small basin.

A little nutmeg may be grated over the top of it, and wine or cream added as wished.

Note.—Milk may be used instead of water.

Tapioca Pudding

Ingredients—

¾ oz. Tapioca.
½ pint Cold Milk.
1 Egg.
1 tea-spoonful Sugar.
Flavouring (if wished).

Method.—Put the tapioca into a basin, and pour the milk on to it. Cover the basin, and let the tapioca soak about an hour. Rinse out a small lined saucepan, turn the tapioca and milk into it, and stir over the fire until it comes to the boil. Then simmer slowly until it turns quite clear, stirring it every now and then. The time will vary from twenty to thirty minutes, according to the size of the tapioca used. If it becomes too thick whilst cooking, add a little more milk. When ready, remove the pan from the fire, and sweeten and flavour to taste. After it has cooled a little, stir in the yolk of egg, and lastly the white, beaten to a stiff froth. Pour the mixture into a small greased pie-dish, wiping round the edges of the dish. Bake in a moderate oven until nicely browned. Sprinkle with sugar and serve at once.

Note.—Sago pudding may be made in the same way.

Apple Cream

Ingredients—

2 baked Apples.
½ gill of Double Cream.
A squeeze of Lemon Juice.
Sugar to taste.

Method.—Remove the pulp from two baked apples, and rub it through a fine wire or hair sieve, scraping the sieve well underneath. Put the pulp into a basin, add to it the cream, a squeeze of lemon juice, and sweeten to taste with castor sugar. Beat this well for a few minutes and serve in a small glass dish.

Egg Drink

Ingredients—

1 Egg.
1 tea-spoonful Sugar.
1 table-sp. Sherry.
1 teacupful of Milk.

Method.—Break the egg and remove the speck. Add to it the wine and sugar, and beat together with a fork, but do not make them too frothy. Heat the milk in a small saucepan, and, when almost boiling, pour it on to the egg, &c., stirring all the time. Serve hot.

Note.—The wine may be omitted. The yolk of egg only may be used, and soda-water instead of milk.

Oatmeal Gruel

Ingredients—

1 table-spoonful fine Oatmeal.
½ pint Cold Water.
Salt or Sugar.

Method.—Put the oatmeal into a clean basin and pour the water over it. Cover the basin and let it stand for at least half-an-hour, stirring occasionally. Then strain the liquid off into a small lined saucepan, and press the oatmeal as dry as possible. Stir over the fire until boiling, and boil from five to seven minutes. The thickness of the gruel is very much a matter of taste; if too thick, more water can be added; or if too thin, use more oatmeal. Season to taste with salt or sugar.

A small piece of butter may be added and wine or brandy if required. Serve very hot. Milk may be used instead of water.

SPECIAL APPLIANCES

A Bed-Cradle.—When the weight of the bedclothes has to be kept off the patient, a "cradle" is needed. This may be bought for 4s. or 5s., or, if only for temporary use, one may be easily improvised. When required to go over the body, it can be made from an ordinary wooden hoop of a convenient size. Cut the hoop in two and place the two arches thus formed side by side about half a yard apart. Join them together at the top with a piece of wood across the centre and at the bottom with a piece of wood on either side. Or another way is to make the two halves of the hoop cross each other, joining them in the middle with a nail. If the "cradle" is only needed to protect an injured limb, an ordinary kitchen-stool or a strong bandbox with the lid and bottom removed can be made to answer the purpose. Whenever a "cradle" is used, the part it protects must be covered (under the cradle) with a small light blanket or a piece of flannel.

Bed-Cradle.

A Bed-Rest is a contrivance for supporting a patient's head and back when he is sitting up in bed. There are several different kinds. Those with an iron frame painted white with white canvas laced in are good, as they can be easily washed and kept clean. Or a wooden one with a cane centre is comfortable and easily adjusted. A bed-rest can also be improvised if it is only required for a short time by placing a chair on its side with the back towards the patient. Pillows must, of course, be placed between the patient and the bed-rest.

Bed-Rest.

A Bed-Table.—This is convenient to put in front of a patient when he takes his meals in bed, and it is also useful for holding a book or writing materials during convalescence. The simplest kind is made like a tray on four legs hollowed out a little in front. Another but more expensive table stands on the floor and has a revolving top which can be turned round in front of the patient when required.

Bed-Table.

Table with Revolving Top.

A Pulley is useful in helping a patient to raise himself. One can be made with a stout piece of rope attached to a strong screw in the ceiling. To the lower end of the rope a bar of wood should be attached for the patient to grasp when he wishes to lift himself. A roller towel fastened to the foot of the bed can also be made to do duty as a pulley.

Hot-water Bottles are frequently needed in illness. There are several different kinds. The stone ones are cheapest, but india-rubber ones are much more comfortable, while those made of tin and copper will keep hot the longest. An india-rubber bottle is useful in applying heat to almost any part of the body, and it can even be used instead of a poultice. If it is put over the patient, it must not be filled too full, or it will be too heavy. When not in use, the india-rubber bottle should be filled with air—it is less likely to perish when this is done. Great care should be taken that screws or corks are quite secure, and all hot-water bottles should have flannel covers.

Bed-pans.—These are used for patients who are unable to get out of bed. The most ordinary shapes are the round and the slipper, and they may be had either in enamelled tin or stoneware. The round one is easily passed under the patient when the body is slightly raised. When the slipper is given, the patient's knees should be drawn up, when the thin end of the slipper can be gently passed under the back. Care should be taken to warm the bed-pan before administering it, either with hot water or before the fire. If the patient is thin, a little pad of flannel or cotton wool should be put on the edge to prevent pressure. In giving a bed-pan a nurse should pass her free hand under the patient's back to raise him. If the patient is very heavy and helpless, two people are needed—one to raise him and the other to pass the bed-pan. Never use a bed-pan on which the enamel is worn, nor one made of ware which is cracked, as both might cause serious injuries. The india-rubber bed-pan, which is also an air-cushion, is very useful where there is incontinence. It is very comfortable, and can be left under patient for any length of time. It must, of course, be emptied when necessary, care being taken not to spill the contents. The receiver part should be lined with a piece of soft, but strong, paper before it is put into position, as it is much more easily emptied when this is done.

Enemata.—An enema is often ordered when there is constipation, or when it is necessary to empty the lower bowel. It is usually given with a Higginson's syringe. This is a tube with a bulb in the middle which acts as a pump. At one end there is a bone nozzle which has to be passed into the rectum; at the other end there is a piece of metal which acts as a valve. The metal end is put into the basin of fluid which is to be injected; the ball in the centre is squeezed, the water is drawn up and is passed into the bowel.

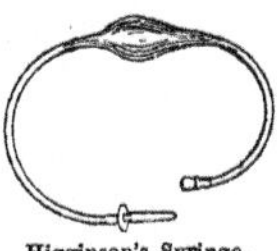

Higginson's Syringe.

Before inserting the nozzle be sure to expel all air from the syringe. To do this put both ends of the syringe into the fluid, and squeeze the bulb a number of times, until there are no bubbles in the water. If air is injected into the bowel, it will not only cause pain and discomfort, but will probably cause the fluid to be returned. When an enema has to be given, the patient should be placed on his left side with the knees drawn up. In case of accidents it is well to put a mackintosh covered with a towel under the pelvis. Where a patient is in a very feeble condition, and there is likely to be difficulty in retaining the injection, the pillow should be taken from under the head and placed under the thighs. Sometimes the patient cannot be turned, and the enema has to be given as he lies on his back. In a case of this kind, place the bed-pan in position before commencing to give the enema. A patient should always be told to do his best to retain the enema while it is being given, and for a few minutes afterwards. The nozzle must always be smeared with vaseline before use. It is not always easy to pass it into the rectum, but force should never be used. It should be passed slowly and gently. The fluid should be injected very slowly, as it is then much more likely to be retained. Sometimes there seems to be a resistance in the bowel, and the fluid cannot be passed in; in this case withdraw the nozzle, squeeze the bulb, and re-insert the nozzle. Always keep the metal end of the syringe under the water in the bowl. For this reason a little more fluid should be mixed than is required. If the metal end is uncovered, air will enter the syringe. If this should happen by accident, then the nozzle must be withdrawn, both ends of syringe must be put in the fluid, and the syringe refilled. The nozzle has again to be inserted and the remainder of the fluid injected. Of course, *an enema should only be given when ordered by the doctor*, and when an amateur nurse is in attendance he would naturally give very minute instructions and be willing to give all the information desired.

The most ordinary enema is soap and water. About a quart is usually given to a grown-up person; children are given about one pint, and a small infant would only be given an ounce. To make a soap and water enema take a piece of soft soap about the size of a hazel nut, pour on boiling water and stir well until the soap has dissolved. Cold water must be added until the water is the right heat—100° Fahr. The best plain yellow soap may be used instead of soft soap.

Turpentine Enema.—This is prepared by adding from half an ounce to an ounce (one or two table-spoonfuls) of turpentine to a pint of soap and water, barley-water, or thin gruel, according to the doctor's order. Turpentine mixes best with thin gruel, but whatever is used great care should be taken that the turpentine is well mixed.

A Salt Enema is made by adding a table-spoonful of salt to a pint of thin gruel or water; the latter is generally used.

Castor oil Enema.—Mix two table-spoonfuls of the oil with a pint of soap and water.

Olive oil Enema may be mixed in the same way, or the oil may be injected first and followed up with soap and water. It is sometimes a good plan to inject the olive oil (about eight table-spoonfuls) at night, and if the patient lies on his right side it can be retained without discomfort. The oil softens the fæces, and when a soap enema is given in the morning there should be a good result. The olive oil can be warmed by standing the vessel containing it in a larger one of hot water for a few minutes. It should be about blood heat. A small syringe might be used.

Starch and Opium Enema.—A half to a tea-spoonful of laudanum is mixed with eight table-spoonfuls of thin starch. This injection is intended to be retained, and should be given cool. Sometimes raw starch is ordered. This is frequently given with a ball syringe. To fill the ball syringe, squeeze the ball in the palm of the hand, put the point of the nozzle into the fluid, then gradually loosen the ball. In this way the syringe is filled. The nozzle is injected as far as it will go, and the ball gradually compressed until it is empty. The ball must remain compressed until the nozzle has been withdrawn; if it is loosened beforehand, some of the fluid will be drawn back into the syringe.

Glycerine Enema.—Pour from a tea-spoonful to a table-spoonful of glycerine into a small vessel and stand it in a larger one containing warm water for two or three minutes to take off the chill. There are special glycerine syringes, but a small ordinary glass one answers

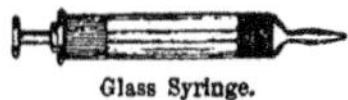

Glass Syringe.

the purpose quite well. Fill the syringe with glycerine, and then expel the air by holding the syringe with its point uppermost and gently pushing up the piston until the glycerine reaches the point of the syringe. Sometimes a glycerine suppository is ordered. It is cone-shaped and easily given.

Nutrient Enemata.—It is necessary in certain diseases of the stomach, or after an operation, or when there is vomiting and food cannot be taken by the mouth, to give nourishment by the rectum. The fluid given should be about the consistency of cream, and may be composed of strong beef-tea, milk, beaten-up eggs, Benger's Food, Horlick's Malted Milk, or whatever the doctor orders. As the food will not pass through the stomach, it should be artificially digested before being given, as it is then more easily absorbed. It can be peptonised or artificially digested with liq. pancreaticus (Benger's) or with Fairchild's peptonising powders. Failing these a pinch of salt should be used to each feed.

For injecting food it is best to use tubing and a glass funnel. Have two feet of soft india-rubber tubing and attach it at one end to a glass funnel. The other end is joined by means of a small glass tube to a soft india-rubber catheter

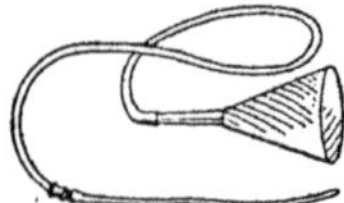

Tube with Glass Funnel.

(No. 12). The catheter and funnel would answer the purpose, but the longer length of tubing is more convenient. Have the nutriment ready in a cup or small jug and at a temperature of about 99° Fahr. Put the funnel, tubing, &c., into a basin of warm water and bring all to the bedside. Then remove the appliance from the water, smear the catheter with vaseline and insert slowly and gently into the rectum about five inches. Pinch the tubing just below the funnel and pour in the nutrient, then gradually drop by drop let it escape into the tube. Not less than ten minutes should be allowed for giving the above quantity, and longer if more is ordered. A trained nurse would be able to give the enemata without assistance, but an amateur would be glad to have some one to pour in the fluid for her. The patient must be kept in the same position and quite still for some time after having a nutrient enema. It should be given about every four hours—not oftener.

When a patient is being fed by the rectum he should be given a soap and water or plain water enema every morning. This is necessary to keep the lower bowel free from debris. The nutrient injection must not be given until a good half-hour after the enema. Tubings, nozzles, catheters, and funnels should always be boiled for a quarter of an hour after use. A Higginson's syringe can be cleansed by syringing hot water through it. A very good one can be boiled, but an inferior one would probably spoil in the process. When not in use the syringe should be oiled and hung up by a piece of string attached to the metal end.

Saline Injection.—This is sometimes ordered in cases of collapse. Allow a tea-spoonful of salt to a pint of water—temperature 100° Fahr. This is best given with the funnel and tubing, but could be given with a Higginson's syringe, when a glass funnel is not procurable. The outside of an ordinary glass syringe will answer the purpose, and the tubing of a babies' feeding-bottle can be made to take the place of catheter and tubing.

Inhaler.

Inhalations.—Sometimes a doctor will order certain drugs to be inhaled. The inhaler, which can be purchased at a chemist's, is filled with boiling water and the drug added. A jug can also be made to answer the purpose. A towel should be wrapped round and made to cover all the top except the spout from which the steam escapes.

Applied Steam.—When it is necessary for the air to be warm and moist a steam-kettle and tent may be ordered. A tent can be improvised with a clothes-horse and sheets. The top and three sides of the bed should be covered in. When a clothes-horse is not at hand, a long broom-stick can be fixed to each corner of the bedstead to make a framework for the tent. Care should be taken that the air of the room is very fresh, as steam tents are apt to get "stuffy." The kettle should be placed just outside the tent and the steam directed towards the patient by means of a long spout, care being taken that the steam does not go too near the face. If the fireplace is conveniently near the tent, the kettle can be kept boiling on the fire; if not, a spirit

Steam-Kettle.

or oil-stove must be used. Special steam-kettles can be bought, or a long spout to fix on to an ordinary kettle can be obtained for fourpence or sixpence. A long spout can also be improvised with brown paper in an emergency, but this soon softens with the steam, and has to be frequently renewed.

Spit-Cups.—When there is expectoration a spit-cup is needed. Those with adjustable tops are the best. Some disinfectant should always be put into them, as this prevents the sputum from getting dry. If there is no disinfectant at hand or if the smell is objected to, strong soda-water can be used. The cup must be kept scrupulously clean.

Spit-Cup.

THE TEMPERATURE, PULSE, AND RESPIRATION

In illness it is most important to ascertain the temperature of the body. This is taken by a small glass clinical thermometer which is self-

Clinical Thermometer.

registering. The mercury should always be shaken down before use. It registers quickest in the mouth and should be put under the tongue. If a patient is unconscious it can be taken in the axilla, which must first be wiped dry, and the arm should be held close to the body, as otherwise the thermometer might slip out of position and fail to register properly. In children the temperature is best taken in the axilla or groin. It is lowest at about four in the morning and highest between six and eight in the evening. In some cases it is only necessary to take it twice a day—morning and evening. In very serious cases it should be taken every four hours, and sometimes oftener. The normal temperature is 98·4° F., and anything much above or below that indicates illness. In rheumatic fever, typhoid fever, and pneumonia the temperature will sometimes rise to 105° F. and 106° F., and unless means are taken to reduce it, it may go up to 108° F. or even 110° F. In cases of this kind very prompt measures have to be taken. Always cleanse a thermometer well after use. It should be washed in (1 to 20) carbolic if it is being used for more than one patient. A patient suffering from phthisis should always have a thermometer kept specially for him.

The normal pulse rate in an adult is from 70 to 80 per minute. It is much quicker in children. In illness it is often very quick, and in some cases goes up to 180. Always use a watch with a seconds hand when taking a pulse and count for a full minute. Note if it is feeble, irregular, or bounding. With a high temperature there is usually a quick pulse; a very quick pulse with a sub-normal temperature is a bad symptom; it means that the patient is becoming collapsed.

The normal respiration is from 18 to 20 per minute. In a long and serious illness it is a good plan to register the temperature, pulse, and respiration on a chart.

MEDICINES

Care and Administration. — The medicines should be kept on a little tray and always away from liniment bottles. Keep them well corked. In giving medicine, shake the bottle and read the directions carefully, no matter how many times you have given the medicine. Pour it out from the side not labelled, as otherwise some drops may run down and make it impossible to read the directions. As far as possible give the doses regularly and at the times stated. Measure in a proper medicine glass, and when drops are ordered use a minim glass. If medicine is ordered to be taken after

Medicine Glass. Minim Glass.

food be sure you give it after, and if before food then give it before, otherwise it will not have the desired effect. If for any reason a dose has to be missed, do not give a double dose on the next occasion. Wash and dry the medicine glass after use.

Castor oil can be given in a little hot coffee. Pour a little coffee in the medicine glass, then the castor oil, and then a little more coffee. It can be given in the same way with orange or lemon juice or with brandy. If given in milk it should be well beaten up. Cod-liver oil can be taken in the same way. A little salt taken afterwards will help to get rid of the taste. Keep a separate glass or cup for giving oils, and wipe it afterwards with a bit of old linen. Then wash by itself in a little very hot water.

Salts, which must always be well mixed, are given in a small quantity of hot water before breakfast, one or two table-spoonfuls being the dose. Pills, if they cannot be swallowed, may be put inside bread or jam. Pills are generally given at night. Powders may be mixed with butter or jam, or put in a little milk. They are sometimes put inside little cachets of wafer paper.

When a sleeping draught is ordered, settle the patient for the night before giving it, and see that the house is quiet afterwards.

Liquid Measure

1 drop	1 Minim.
1 tea-spoonful	1 Drachm.
1 dessert-spoonful	2 Drachms.
1 table-spoonful	4 Drachms or ½ oz.
2 table-spoonfuls	1 oz.
1 wineglassful	About 2 oz.
1 teacupful	4 to 5 oz.
1 breakfast-cupful	About 8 oz.

BATHS

Special baths are sometimes ordered in cases of illness, and they must be given with great exactitude.

The following are the rules as regards temperature :—

Cold Bath should be	33° to 65° F.
Cool Bath ,,	65° to 80° F.
Tepid Bath ,,	80° to 90° F.
Warm Bath ,,	90° to 100° F.
Hot Bath ,,	100° to 112° F.

Before giving a bath see that the room is warm, and close the window for the time being. Have ready a bath thermometer, hot blankets, towels, and hot bottles or bricks. When a bath is ordered, it is easily given if the patient can step in with a little assistance; if he is too ill to do this, the bath is generally given under the doctor's special direction or by a skilled nurse, as the lifting is a very difficult matter for the amateur. He should be well dried with a hot towel, and a warm flannel nightgown should be slipped on as quickly as possible. He should then be wrapped in a warm blanket and put back to bed with hot bottles, placing them over the blanket which is covering him. Then give a hot drink. The uses of a hot bath are various; it is given to relieve pain and to induce perspiration. A patient should be carefully watched while in a hot bath, as he may become faint. Great care should be taken that he does not get a chill. He should remain in the bath about twenty minutes.

Mustard Foot-Bath.—Use from one to two ounces of mustard to a gallon of hot water. Mix the mustard first in a little cold water and add it to the bath. Keep the feet in until the skin has reddened. A hot bottle should be put to the feet afterwards. This foot-bath can easily be given in bed. (See "Patient's Toilet.")

Soda Bath.—Dissolve from a quarter to half a pound of soda in a full-sized bath.

The Sulphur Bath.—Dissolve four ounces of sulphurate of potash in thirty gallons of water. It should be made weaker for children.

Hot Air and Vapour Baths.—A special apparatus can be bought for giving a hot-air bath, or it can be given with an Allen's steam-kettle with the boiler removed. Have a blanket at the bottom of the bed. Take off the patient's nightgown, and wrap him loosely in a small blanket. Put a mackintosh under him, then place a cradle over him, and put a mackintosh over the cradle. Remove the ordinary bed-clothes and put hot blankets over the mackintosh. See that the patient is entirely covered except his face. The lamp is next lighted and placed on a stool at the foot of the bed. The tube from the lamp is passed under the cradle, care being taken that it does not touch the patient, or he may be badly burned. The blankets must be tucked in well all round the bed, and must fit up closely to the tube so that the hot air does not escape or the cold air enter. A thermometer should be hung up inside the cradle to measure the temperature, which should be from 110° to 150° F. Give hot drinks, or, if the patient is very thirsty, he may have a cold drink of lemon water—either hot or cold drinks may help him to perspire. The drinks must be given as he lies in bed—he must not sit up or take his arms out of bed. At the end of twenty minutes remove the lamp and slip out the mackintoshes and cradle. Leave him wrapped in his blanket for about an hour. Then rub him down quickly with hot towels, remove the blanket in which he has been wrapped and the others if damp. Wrap him in a warm flannel gown and put a hot bottle to his feet. The ordinary bed-clothes can be put back, but the patient must have blankets next him.

A Vapour Bath can be given in the same way as above, but in this case use a steam-kettle. Moist heat cannot be borne over 100° F. to 110° F. These baths are usually given in cases of nephritis, inflammation of the kidney, and in rheumatism. In both cases the patient should always wear flannel nightgowns and be kept between blankets. When a patient can sit up, a hot-air or vapour bath can be given as he sits in a cane-bottomed chair with blankets wrapped round him, a lamp being placed underneath the chair. Or a vapour bath can be given by putting a bucket of hot water under the chair.

Hot Pack.—This is ordered to induce perspiration. Place a small light blanket rolled up lengthwise in a bath, pour boiling water over it, and wring out as hot as possible. It is better for two people to do the wringing. Have the patient on his side, place the rolled part of the blanket close to his back. Roll him gently over and envelop him entirely in the blanket with the exception of the face and head. Cover with a hot dry blanket, on the outside of which place hot bottles. Put on more warm blankets and give warm drinks. At the end of twenty minutes remove the wet blanket, dry the patient with warm towels, change any blankets that are damp, putting in fresh warm ones, and then put the patient into a warm flannel night-dress. He should be left for a time rolled in a warm blanket under the bed-clothes, and fresh hot bottles should be put in.

Cold Pack.—Proceed as for the hot pack, but instead of the hot blanket use a sheet wrung out of iced water. Spread another sheet over the patient and rub this down with pieces of ice to keep it cool. Take temperature frequently. The patient may remain in this about twenty minutes unless he shows signs of collapse. He should then be dried, and the wet sheets and mackintosh removed. Then wrap him in a warm blanket and put a hot bottle to the feet if they are cold. The greatest care must be taken, and the treatment must always be stopped if the patient shivers or becomes blue. The ice may be omitted.

Cold or Tepid Sponging.—This is often ordered to reduce the temperature. Remove the night-gown and protect the bed with a bath-towel or blanket. Cover the patient with a blanket. Take a large sponge and sponge the whole body and limbs with long steady strokes from the top downwards. Turn the patient gently on his side for the back to be sponged. The sponging which is done under the blanket should be continued for about twenty minutes, when the temperature should be taken. If the patient perspires very freely afterwards, care must be taken to avoid a chill. It is a good plan to put hot bottles to the feet while sponging. *Hot sponging* will often reduce the temperature equally well, and is more comforting to the patient.

POULTICES AND FOMENTATIONS, &c.

A Linseed Poultice.—Have ready a piece of flannel the size required, and a basin and broad knife for mixing. Put the knife into the basin and pour over boiling water to heat them. Empty the water and pour in sufficient boiling water for the poultice. Add enough linseed to make the poultice of the right consistency, and beat until it no longer adheres to the basin. If too wet it will scald, and if too dry it will not be sufficiently hot. Turn the mixture on to the flannel and spread quickly with the knife to about three-quarters of an inch in thickness, cover with muslin, and turn the edges of the flannel over to make the poultice neat. Cover with cotton wool and bandage if necessary to keep it in position. Brown paper or muslin may be used instead of flannel.

A Jacket Poultice.—This is intended to go right round the patient's chest and back. For an adult it is better made in two parts, care being taken that it meets on both sides. It can be kept in position by a broad binder, which should be rolled under the patient as he lies on his side. The poultice for the back is put on first and held in place while the patient is gently rolled on his back; the other poultice is put on the chest. The binder is adjusted and fastened with safety-pins. Instead of the binder a "pneumonia jacket" of brown wool made up

Pneumonia Jacket.

on muslin could be used to keep the poultices in position. Being left open down one side and on the shoulder it is easily made to fit closely, and can be fastened up firmly with safety-pins. This jacket should be changed for a fresh one when the poultices are left off. A jacket poultice for a child can be made all in one, and should be quite light and thin. Poultices should be changed about every three or four hours. Although continuous poulticing is not so common as it used to be, a doctor often orders a poultice to be put on for an hour night and morning, and during the rest of the time the patient is wrapped in a "pneumonia jacket."

A Linseed and Mustard Poultice.—Add one part of mustard to seven or eight of linseed. Mix the mustard first in a little cold or tepid water, and add to the linseed while mixing with the boiling water.

A Mustard Poultice.—Make with one part of mustard to two of flour. Mix flour and mustard together to form into a smooth paste with cold water; spread on brown paper or old linen. Lay a piece of muslin over poultice and hold to the fire to warm a little before applying. Sometimes a doctor will order only mustard and water to be used. A plaster made in this way should only be kept on for a quarter of an hour or twenty minutes.

Mustard Leaves, which can be bought from the chemist, are sometimes ordered. Moisten a little in tepid water before applying. A mustard leaf must only be left on for about a quarter of an hour, and, when used for a child, muslin must be laid over it before it is applied. When a mustard leaf or plaster is applied, turn a corner of it up very soon afterwards to see that it is not blistering the skin—it is intended to redden but not to blister. Always rub off any mustard that may be left sticking to the skin after a mustard plaster is removed, and rub on vaseline or cold cream. Mustard is often applied over the heart in cases of collapse.

A Charcoal Poultice.—Make in the same way as a linseed poultice, adding one part of charcoal to five parts of linseed. Spread on old linen and cover with thin gauze.

Bread Poultice.—Put some stale bread into a small clean saucepan with hot water and let it boil for a minute. Strain off the water and spread on old linen.

Hot Fomentations.—These are used when it is necessary to apply moist heat to any part of the body. Place a strong towel over a large basin. Take a piece of flannel the required size (it should be large enough to be applied double), put it on the towel, and pour boiling water from the kettle over it. Grasp the ends of the towel and wring the flannel as dry as possible. If the flannel is left too wet it may scald. Give it a quick shake out and lower it gradually on to the part as hot as can be borne. Cover with jaconette or brown paper and a layer of cotton wool. If the fomentation has to be put on the chest or abdomen it can be kept in position with a broad binder. Fomentations are generally changed frequently, and must never remain on when cold. Cotton wool should always be put on when the fomentation is discontinued.

Turpentine Fomentations.—Make in the same way as above, pouring over one or two tablespoonfuls of turpentine before wringing it. Sometimes the turpentine is sprinkled over the flannel after it has been wrung out, but this may cause blistering, and the other method is safer.

Laudanum Fomentations.—Sprinkle some laudanum over the hot flannel after it has been wrung out and just before applying it.

Blisters.—Sometimes a blistering fluid is ordered and sometimes a plaster. Wash the skin well with soap and water, and if fluid is ordered paint it on with a camel's-hair brush and on the exact spot indicated by the doctor. Take care that the fluid does not trickle down, or other blisters may be formed. Cover with a piece of lint or old linen and cotton wool, and, if necessary, bandage. Sometimes the blister forms quickly (in two or three hours), but occasionally it takes twelve hours. If there is no blistering at the end of twelve hours apply a fomentation or poultice. When formed the blister must be clipped with a clean sharp pair of scissors. These should be boiled before and after use. Let the fluid escape into a vessel, or into cotton wool. Dress with ointment spread on the smooth side of lint. Change the dressing night and morning. If more blisters form they must be treated in the same way. A blistering plaster is sometimes ordered instead of the fluid. It must be cut the necessary size and covered with cotton wool. Should it not adhere to the skin, keep in place with adhesive plaster or a bandage.

Ice Applications.—These are ordered to allay inflammation or to arrest hæmorrhage. The easiest way to apply ice is in an ice-bag, which can be bought from a chemist, or a bullock's bladder may be washed and made to do duty. Break the ice into small pieces and half fill the bag, squeezing out the air before inserting the cork. Flannel or lint should always be placed between the skin and an ice application, and the bag should not be allowed to remain on after the ice has melted. The bag should be examined frequently to see that there is no leakage.

Notes on Ice.—Ice should be kept wrapped in a clean piece of flannel and placed in a cullender put over a basin, so that the water can drain off as the ice melts.

To break ice pierce it with an ordinary hat-pin or fine skewer.

When ice is being given to a patient to suck, tie a clean piece of muslin over a glass or teacup and put small pieces of ice on the top. Give them to the patient in a small silver tea-spoon. Ice is given to stop sickness and when there is great thirst.

AFTER DEATH

When all is over remove one pillow and straighten the limbs. Gently close the eyes, and, if necessary, put on little pads of wet wool or linen, which can be removed later. Place a small pad under the chin to keep the jaw from dropping. If this does not answer, a jaw bandage must be applied and allowed to remain for several hours until the jaw is fixed. Half-an-hour or an hour should elapse before the "last offices" are performed. This time can be occupied in getting ready what is needed, and in making the room tidy. The washing should be done quickly, the body being sponged under the blanket in the same way as if the patient were living. All must be done with gentle reverence. Put on a clean night-dress and white stockings. Tie the legs at the ankles and knees and fold the hands over the chest. The hair should be arranged neatly and to look as natural as possible. If there is a flock or feather-bed it should be removed—the mattress only remaining. If there is a mackintosh it should be washed and left under the sheet. Roll in a clean bottom sheet, and put a clean one over the top. Cover the face with a clean soft handkerchief. Remove all soiled linen from the room; the medicine bottles should also be emptied and removed, and the patient's sponge, nail-brush, tooth-brush, &c., removed and burned. The room should then be dusted, a clean cover put on the dressing-table, and a few fresh flowers brought in. The window should be left open from the top and the blind may be drawn. If there are children in the house it is better to lock the door, in case they should go into the room. Death is an alarming sight for little ones, and a sight from which they should be spared if possible.

It is wise afterwards to get the bedding baked, even when the case has not been infectious, or to have it remade. It should always be done after cancer, or where there has been a foul wound, and, of course, after all forms of tuberculosis. The sanitary authorities will often disinfect bedding, &c., free of cost.

"FIRST AID" IN SICKNESS AND ACCIDENTS

It is certainly highly desirable, if not absolutely a matter of duty, that every woman should be prepared to render efficient aid in the event of accident or sudden illness. A little timely knowledge will enable her, if not to actually alleviate the pain of the sufferer, at least to prevent further harm being done until the doctor comes. This knowledge is all the more essential owing to the fact that the immediate treatment of an injured person, or of some one taken suddenly ill, has a very important bearing on the after progress of the case.

The information contained in the following paragraphs is intended to act as a guide in emergencies when a doctor is not immediately available, or in cases of simple ailments when his aid is not needed.

"FIRST AID" IN SICKNESS AND TREATMENT OF COMMON AILMENTS

Acidity.—This is a form of indigestion, which is due to an excessive formation of acid in the stomach. The symptoms are heartburn and a rising of wind and of bitter stomach contents into the mouth. Relief is obtained by taking a tea-spoonful of bicarbonate of soda in a tumbler of hot water or 30 drops tincture of rhubarb three times a day after food, or ½ to 1 tea-spoonful of tincture of gentian taken in about 1 table-spoonful of water before meals.

Bed-Sores.—These can be prevented to a large extent by careful nursing (see p. 554), and in the nursing profession they are generally regarded as a disgrace. There are, however, a few cases where bed-sores will develop in spite of all one's efforts to avoid them, and they are by no means easy to cure. They ought to be washed with carbolic lotion about 1 in 40, with boracic lotion or a fairly strong solution of Condy's Fluid and water. The wound should then be covered with a piece of lint spread with boracic ointment, and this may either be fixed on with narrow strapping or simply laid on the place. Care must be taken to avoid pressure on the part by the use of a circular air-cushion, or by turning the patient on the other side if possible. Very superficial bed-sores will often heal when well dusted two or three times a day with equal parts of starch and zinc powder. No dressing need be applied, but clean linen should be next the wound.

Blackheads.—This is the name of a skin disease which is common in youth. The symptoms are pimples on the face and back which have black spots in the centre. Recent research shows "blackheads" to be due to a microbe; the black spots are not dirt as formerly supposed, but are caused by diffused pigment. The treatment consists in the free use of hot water and soap, followed by an application of the following lotion: Take 1 tea-spoonful each of precipitate of sulphur, tincture of camphor, and glycerine, and mix with 4 ounces (8 table-spoonfuls) rose-water.

A sand soap should be used once a week—the ordinary "Monkey Brand" is excellent for the purpose. The general health requires attention, and a doctor should be consulted.

Bilious Attack is a popular name for *migraine*. Migraine is not really dependent on disorder of the liver. The symptoms are headache, defective vision, and vomiting of a few hours' duration only. The causes are eye-strain combined with excessive mental work and lack of exercise. In reality it is a disturbed circulation in the brain which causes the headache, defective vision, and vomiting. The *treatment* should be to go to bed in the dark and sip some hot tea, and after the vomiting is over to sleep. If attacks are frequent, the eyes should be tested and suitable spectacles worn if any defect is detected, plenty of fresh air, exercise, and plain diet should be secured, and reading in a bad light or in a railway train avoided. Nausea, headache, pale motions, and high-coloured urine are the chief symptoms. The treatment is a free purge and spare diet, followed by more exercise and fresh air. If of frequent occurrence a doctor should be consulted.

Boils are abscesses in the skin. They contain a central core formed of a fragment of dead skin. The cause is debility combined with some local cause, such as the chafing of a collar.

Ichthyol and resorcin ointment applied at a very early stage will often check the mischief. When once developed, a cold-water dressing made of pink boracic lint will help to relieve the pain. They are best treated by lancing and touching the interior with pure carbolic, and not by the application of a linseed poultice, as this is apt to induce a crop of boils in the surrounding area. The general health should also receive attention, especially in regard to diet, fresh air, and regularity of the bowels.

Bronchitis may be acute or chronic, and either an independent affection or due to some other disease, especially certain fevers. The disease consists of inflammation of the lining membrane of the bronchi, which are the tubes into which the windpipe opens. The treatment should be confinement to bed in a room the air of which is moistened by a steam-kettle and kept at an even temperature of 60° in winter and 65° in summer. A few drops of terebene may be added to the water. Special care is required between two and four in the morning not to let the temperature of the room fall. The diet should be light, and plenty of barley water and lemon drinks allowed. Counter irritation over the upper part of the chest is at times useful. This is effected by the application of mustard leaves or of turpentine liniment. Medicine is required to make the skin act and to check the useless cough in the early stage, and the best for this purpose for an adult is probably ten grains of Dover's Powder at bedtime. Except in very mild cases the treatment should be in medical hands from the onset.

Bunion is caused by the prolonged use of pointed-teed boots. By such boots the big toe is thrust towards the centre line of the foot and the base of the toe exposed to pressure unduly. The frequent repetition of pressure always excites the growth of the part pressed on, and the swelling thus caused is known as a bunion. Hot fomentations may relieve the pain or the joint may be painted with iodine if it is not inflamed. Relief may also be obtained by placing a pad of cotton wool between the big and second toe. This takes the pressure off the joint. In severe cases a surgical operation may be resorted to.

Cold in the Head.—The symptoms are too familiar to need description. The prevention of colds may be effected with some success by an open-air life, sleeping with the window open, cold baths in the mornings, plain diet, and by suitable clothing and sound boots; the stuffy room is the place in which the cold is caught. The following will sometimes check a cold in the early stages: a hot lemon drink made with the juice of a large lemon, a pint of boiling water and sugar to taste—drink as hot as possible—menthol snuff, and camphor pillules to suck. An attack may also be treated by inhaling menthol or eucalyptus.

Chilblain is due to the paralysis, by cold, of the blood-vessels in the affected part. The fingers, toes, ears and more rarely the tip of the nose are most often attacked, and certain people with a sluggish circulation are more prone to chilblains than others; many children grow out of them. In the first stage of a chilblain the part is white and cold; in the second stage, congested, hot, red and itching. The treatment should be preventive; in cold weather loose woollen gloves should be worn and tight boots avoided, exercise encouraged, and the skin kept clean and dry. When the first symptoms appear rub the affected part with the following mixture: one small cupful brown vinegar, one small cupful turpentine, one small cupful methylated spirits, one egg—shake all these together in a bottle and it will be found an excellent remedy. It is also good for bruises and pains in the muscles. An application of tamus communis or ichthyol ointment is also very good. Relief from itching can be obtained by soaking the parts in hot water.

Constipation, or Costiveness, is present when the bowels are not relieved thoroughly once a day.

The treatment of constipation may be summed up in one word — prevention, whereas the popular method is to allow violent purging to alternate with several days of constipation, or to produce chronic dilatation of the large bowel by frequent copious enemata.

To have to resort to a pill is in itself a confession of failure. First, then, acquire a regular habit of obtaining relief for the bowels at the same time each day. This should always be after a meal, because the taking of a meal is a natural stimulus. The best time is after breakfast. Regular exercise must be taken, and fresh air must be obtained as much as possible, to improve the muscular tone. A cold bath in the morning and massage of the abdomen are often useful. The diet should contain sufficient laxative materials, such as honey, prunes, wholemeal bread, and fruits that contain seeds. In obstinate constipation, however, to continue the use of much fruit rich in seeds is a mistake, as it aggravates the condition. It is when the use of these avoids the necessity for medicine that they do good. When the above methods fail, medicine will be required. This medicine must be as little irritating as possible; castor oil, liquorice powder, senna and Apenta water are all good. Cascara in tabloid form is a little more irritating, but is good and widely used. As soon as the bowels are regular the medicine can be discontinued, provided that it is resumed if the bowels do not act regularly without it. All strong aperients must be avoided as much as possible, and left off when the need for them no longer exists.

Corn is an overgrowth of the horny layer of the skin caused by repeated pressure, such as that due to a tight boot worn daily. Between the toes, where perspiration is often copious, the soft variety develops. Soft corns can be quickly cured by the following treatment:—Powder well between the toes and put in a tiny piece of old soft linen. Starch and zinc or starch and talc powders can be used. Powder and linen should be renewed night and morning.

When the corn is over a joint a felt plaster will give great relief, or the corn may be destroyed by painting it night and morning with a saturated solution of salicylic acid in collodion, and by protecting it with the plaster. Many other remedies have been tried for corns, such as soaking the feet in hot water and cutting with razors, the use of a file, and the application of galbanum plaster, but the salicylic collodion is preferable.

Cough is a symptom of irritation which is generally situated in some part of the respiratory tract, such as the throat, bronchi or lung substance, but may be due to irritation of some distant organ, *e.g.* the heart and stomach, or to disturbance of the brain, as in a hysterical cough. The folly of attempting to apply a cough cure for all coughs alike is thus apparent. In the old and young, suppressing a cough with some soothing syrup containing opium is very easy and very dangerous; a cough should not be suppressed, but treated by removal of its cause, and if there be some tenacious secretion in the bronchi, the secretion requires thinning by ipecacuanha wine, sweet spirits of nitre, and salines: the cough will then loosen and relief be obtained. Half a tea-spoonful of oxymel of squills in a little water, or paregoric in small doses will also give relief. A hot lemon drink might also be tried. If, on the other hand, the source of irritation is in the throat, the use every three hours of astringent gargles, such as alum of a strength of half an ounce to the pint, followed by a dose of glycerine and lemon juice, may give relief. Unless the cough shows signs of ceasing within a few days, medical advice is requisite.

Cramp is a painful spasm of the voluntary muscles most commonly occurring in the calves. The condition may result from cold, as in bathing, or be due to irritation of the stomach or intestines, as in severe diarrhœa or arsenical poisoning. Cramp in the hand is generally due to strain of certain muscles overworked in the course of the daily work, as in writer's cramp and other forms of trade cramp. For simple cramp in the calves the best treatment is to push forward the heel and draw back the toes, or brisk friction with the hands or with compound camphor liniment also. Other forms of cramp require medical aid. So-called "Swimmer's Cramp" is a spasm of the arteries by which the circulation is seriously obstructed and heart failure induced. The treatment is warmth and stimulants. Colic corresponds to cramp, but attacks the involuntary muscles instead of the voluntary.

Diarrhœa has many causes. These belong to one or other of the following groups: (1) irritation of the bowel by its contents being abnormal; (2) irritation of the nervous system; (3) irritation of the skin by a chill. Group (1) includes the causes of most importance to us: they are errors in diet, intestinal worms, hard fæcal lumps due to previous constipation, and certain poisons. Group (2) includes fright or other painful emotion. Group (3) explains itself. In addition to these, diarrhœa may result from disease of the bowel, *e.g.* cancer or tuberculosis in it, or from some general disease, like typhoid fever or blood-poisoning.

The first thing to do in the *treatment* of diarrhœa is to take the temperature, and if this is either above or below normal, whatever the age of the sufferer, a doctor is required at once. Or if blood be present in the motions a doctor is required also. In cases of diarrhœa with a normal temperature, treatment for a few hours can be safely attempted. First consider the cause. Is there (1) an irritant to cause it, such as those given above; or (2) has there been a fright; or (3) a chill very recently? If the answer is (1), the removal of the irritant is to be attempted; nature is already doing so by diarrhœa; we must aid nature by a suitable purge. This must not be of an irritating character, as there is some irritation already. The safest is castor oil. If vomiting is present, the best is grey powder for a child, or half-grain doses of calomel given hourly for four to six hours for an adult. If there is much griping, in the case of adults it will be safe to add to the castor oil ten minims of laudanum. The application of fomentations to the abdomen will also be grateful. An enema of half a pint of warm olive oil may be tried. Collis Brown's Chlorodyne is also very good for simple diarrhœa.

In later life the diet should be spare, *e.g.* soda-water, toast, arrowroot and jelly. It is wise to put the patient to bed. If diarrhœa is thought due to cause (2), if the patient be put to bed he will soon be well. If, on the other hand, cause (3) is regarded as responsible, the sufferer should go to bed with hot bottles, hot fomentations or bran poultices or turpentine stupes to the abdomen. He should have a spare diet and some brandy. If in the course of a few hours improvement in these cases is not occurring, a doctor is required. If he is not obtainable, two to four bismuth lozenges should be given every three hours, and also a starch enema if necessary.

Ear-ache may be due to a wisdom tooth, or to inflammation of the middle or outer ear. If examination of the teeth shows nothing wrong, a little warm glycerine may be dropped in, or one part carbolic to thirty of glycerine. An eighth part of laudanum could be used with warm glycerine. If relief is not soon obtained, or if though the pain ceases ear discharge begins, medical aid is necessary. Chronic discharge from the ears always requires medical attention. If from one ear only, it may be due to a foreign body in the ear that has been neglected. Ringing in the ears may be due to some medicine which is acting on the auditory nerve, *e.g.* quinine and salicylates. If no medicine is being taken a doctor should be consulted.

Gum-boil.—An abscess between the gum and the jaw due to a decayed tooth. A hot weak solution of permanganate of potash can be used. The boil should be encouraged to burst internally by holding hot water in the mouth, and should be lanced as soon as matter has formed.

Hay Fever is an affection of the nose, due to the irritation of the pollen of grasses. It attacks certain people only and runs in families. The symptoms resemble a common cold, and asthma may be present as a complication. The treatment should be the avoidance of the hay-fields when the grass is ripe, and the use of tonics and soothing applications to the nose, such as Friar's balsam, a drachm to the pint of boiling water; inhale the steam: or creosote, ten drops to the pint of boiling water; inhale the steam. Menthol snuff often gives relief, and the nose might be rubbed with a menthol cone.

Headache may be due to one of various causes, some simple, others serious. Tablets containing phenacetin four grains and caffeine one grain give relief quickly. Eau de Cologne dabbed on the forehead, rubbing with a menthol cone, or a mustard leaf applied to the back of the neck and kept on until the skin is red, are all good. The patient should rest in a quiet, dimly-lighted room, and a cup of tea may be sipped slowly. If headaches are frequent a doctor should be consulted, as the trouble is often due to eye-strain, and spectacles may be needed.

Heart-burn is a symptom due to acidity in the stomach and not to anything wrong with the heart itself. The treatment is a tea-spoonful of bicarbonate of soda in half a tumbler of water. This usually gives immediate relief for the time. The diet, however, requires regulating, new bread, farinaceous and sweet food being the commonest causes of this disorder.

Hiccough is caused by spasm of the diaphragm, due generally to irritation of the stomach. Sipping cold water and also holding the breath as long as possible may relieve it. If these methods fail, a tea-spoonful of bicarbonate of soda in a half-tumbler of water should be taken. Obstinate hiccough in the course of a serious illness requires medical care.

Hoarseness.—This may arise either from over-use of the voice or from exposure to cold. A cold-water compress on the throat at night sometimes gives relief. Eucalyptus, menthol, and camphor pastilles are good, or the following simple remedy may be tried: beat up the white of an egg, add the juice of a lemon and about a teacupful of water, and sip slowly.

Indigestion or **Dyspepsia** is readily induced by unsuitable food, irregular or hurried meals, imperfect mastication or mental worry, over-eating or over-drinking. The *symptoms* vary in different cases, and include loss of appetite, nausea, vomiting, a feeling of weight after eating, and pain. Pain is felt in front in the lower part of the chest, or at the back in the left shoulder blade, and it is usually increased by food. There is often flatulence, and the food "repeats," causing a bitter taste in the mouth, sore throat, and cough. The mental effects of chronic dyspepsia are even worse: the mind is gloomy and apt to concentrate attention on the bodily symptoms, thus aggravating the condition. The *treatment* should be mainly preventive. Let the food be simply cooked and well served, varied and palatable; let the meals be eaten slowly and, if possible, amid pleasant companions. After the chief meal of the day rest amid pleasant surroundings is highly beneficial; breakfast should be a substantial meal, and eaten slowly, even though it may be necessary to rise somewhat earlier; luncheon for most busy people should be light. Between meals it is unwise to eat or drink, as the stomach requires rest like every other organ. The teeth must be seen to, regular exercise in the open air taken, worry avoided, the bowels kept regular. Tincture of gentian taken in doses from ½ to 1 tea-spoonful in about a table-spoonful of water before meals is a simple but excellent tonic. The sinking feeling that some people get at about eleven in the morning can be remedied by taking a cup of bovril and a biscuit or piece of toast.

No fixed rules can be laid down in regard to the kind of food to be eaten. "One man's meat is another man's poison"; experience is the best guide. The articles most commonly found indigestible are pastry, pork, new potatoes, new bread, sauces made of melted butter, very hot or very cold dishes or drinks, and malted liquors. An occasional attack of indigestion requires a purge, a spare diet for a few days, and comparative rest. If the attacks of indigestion are frequent, or if there is abdominal pain, a doctor should be consulted.

Influenza is an infectious fever due to a germ —the *bacillus influenzæ.* Infection is conveyed in the air, and also by direct contact between the sick and the healthy. The incubation period is two or three days. The *symptoms* begin suddenly with a rise of temperature to 103° or more, prostration, and pain in the back and head. After the onset the symptoms differ in different epidemics. In some the chief symptoms are bronchitis, with running at the eyes and nose, in others vomiting and diarrhœa, and in yet others severe headache, sleeplessness and delirium, and sometimes sore throat. The duration of the attack is short unless complications occur, of which pneumonia is the most serious. Owing to the severe prostration, convalescence takes longer than in most fevers, and other diseases are apt to begin at this time, especially consumption. As to the *treatment* required: the patient should be isolated and put to bed. The diet, which should be nourishing and easily digestible, is best given every two hours by day and every four hours by night. Hot milk and bovril are good. If vomiting is severe, peptonised food may be necessary. Until the temperature is normal the patient should be confined to bed. This point is of more importance than is popularly thought, many of the serious after-effects of influenza being due to neglect of this simple precaution.

In the early stages ½ to 1 teasp. of ammoniated tincture of quinine may be taken in a little water, or ten drops of Karswood creosote on a handkerchief and inhaled may prevent or help to cure influenza. A good seaside holiday before work is resumed is strongly recommended.

Lice lay eggs or nits, that are attached to the hairs by a ring of cement, which makes them very difficult to remove. The affection is by no means confined to the children of the poor. The best treatment, short of removal of the hair, is the application of some lotion, which dissolves the cement, followed by the thorough use of a fine-toothed comb. In many hospitals a lotion of vinegar and methylated spirits in equal parts is used. The hair is thoroughly soaked in this lotion, and then rags steeped in it are placed on the hair, and the whole is enclosed in a mackintosh bathing-cap for the night. Carbolic lotion (of a strength of 1 in 20) is also used in the same way, but though efficacious, it has the drawback that the absorption of some of the carbolic causes the urine to be green next morning. This, however, is not serious, for once or twice, in a child otherwise healthy. Care should be taken to keep the lotion out of the eyes. "Izal," which is non-poisonous, is a good substitute for carbolic. If the odour can be tolerated, thoroughly soaking the hair in petroleum will destroy the lice and loosen the nits. Sores in the scalp should be treated with white precipitate ointment. In bad cases with numerous crusts, after cutting off the hair, a linseed poultice smeared with olive oil should be applied. This will remove the crusts, and white precipitate ointment may then be applied. Lice on clothing can be destroyed with sulphur fumes.

Lumbago is an affection characterised by severe pain in the muscles of the loins. The pain is of sudden onset, and sufficiently severe as a rule to confine the sufferer to bed. It is recognised by an increase of pain on stooping. The cause is usually chill. It is uncertain whether it is of rheumatic origin or not. Labouring men suffer most from it. A hot soda bath is beneficial. An application of Chillie paste gives relief, also an ointment of wintergreen oil and menthol. This latter is applied to the affected part and covered with oil silk. A broad flannel bandage can be worn.

Neuralgia, literally pain in a nerve. The nerves most commonly attacked are those of the face, the ribs, the loins, and the back of the thigh. The pain is of a most intense character; it comes and goes, often without apparent cause, affecting only one side at a time, and is not accompanied by any rise of temperature.

In facial neuralgia, the ear, the eyesight, the teeth, and, especially the wisdom tooth, require careful examination, though many cases have occurred in which tooth after tooth has been removed by a dentist without relief having been obtained. It is therefore wise to consult a doctor before submitting to the removal of sound teeth. Exposure to cold and damp often determine an attack. Neuralgia is also common in the course of certain diseases.

The *treatment* should be the improvement of the general health. Regular habits and a course of tonics, *e.g.* iron, arsenic, quinine and hypophosphites, all do good in certain cases. A country holiday is still better; the seaside, however, is not recommended. Tablets—Phenacetin 4 grains and caffeine 1 grain, followed with a cup of hot bovril, will often give relief. A full, nourishing diet is needed. Oil of wintergreen and menthol ointment will also relieve the pain.

Palpitation of the heart is present when the beating of the heart makes itself felt. The chief *causes* are sudden emotion and indigestion, especially acidity with flatulence. The *symptoms* are either attacks of frequent and irregular action of the heart with a feeling of fluttering in the chest, or a more forcible action in which the whole chest may feel shaken. These symptoms are accompanied by giddiness, anxiety, pain in the chest, and other symptoms. They are apt to come on at night and awake the sufferer from his first sleep. The *treatment* during an attack should be a dose of bicarbonate of soda, one to two salt-spoonfuls taken in some hot peppermint water, or a tea-spoonful of sal volatile in half a tumbler of water. Between the attacks the causes of indigestion should be avoided, especially heavy and late suppers, tea, tobacco, rich and sweet food, constipation, &c. There is no ground for fearing the heart is diseased; it is the stomach that is out of order.

Piles or Hæmorrhoids are varicose veins at the lower end of the lower bowel. They form small tumours projecting into the bowel, and may gradually pass through the anus and appear on the exterior. The more important causes of these are constipation, congestion of the liver, and the abuse of aperient medicines, especially such as contain aloes. If piles are extruded, they must be washed and replaced by steady pressure applied with the aid of a clean rag smeared with vaseline on one side. When inflammation occurs, it is better to rest in bed and have a light diet. A dose of liquorice powder from ½ to 1 tea-spoonful, or 1 tea-spoonful of confection of sulphur, should be taken.

Hazeline applied on a soft piece of rag should give relief, or an ointment of hazeline, menthol, and cocaine. Resinal ointment is also very good.

The bowels should be encouraged to act last thing at night, as then the irritation caused by the action will pass off during the night.

Sciatica.—This is neuralgia of the sciatic nerve, and the same treatment as that indicated for neuralgia may be adopted. Ointment of wintergreen oil and menthol is an excellent remedy, also Chillie paste. Massage is also good, and hot fomentations may be applied to allay the pain.

Shivering is due to irritation of the nervous system by many different causes, some of which are trivial, others serious.

The duration of shivering varies from a few seconds to a couple of hours, and is often succeeded by sweating and flushing. The temperature of the body as a whole is usually rising during a shivering attack, although the patient feels cold, and it is falling during the flushed sweating stage, although the patient then feels hot. In children the more serious causes, which produce shivering in the adult, often cause convulsions. The *treatment* during the shivering should be hot blankets, hot bottles, hot drinks, and during the subsequent hot stage, if the sweating is excessive, the patient may be rubbed down with a soft towel. A rigor or shivering attack is generally the onset of an illness more or less serious, and the doctor should be sent for.

Sleeplessness may arise from many causes that may be summarised thus:—(1) Pain and other sources of irritation; (2) poisons in the blood which irritate the brain; (3) mental disturbance by worry, excitement, or strange surroundings. The treatment is largely a matter of the detection and removal of the cause, though certain aids to sleep may often be adopted with benefit. There are two chief varieties of sleeplessness, (*a*) difficulty in going to sleep at the beginning of the night's rest, (*b*) a habit of waking in the small hours, with difficulty in dropping off to sleep again.

Sufferers from variety (*a*) should pay attention to the following points: The hour of retiring should be the same each night. The mind and body should both be healthily tired, without being over-fatigued. Hence those engaged in sedentary occupations often sleep better for a short evening walk each night. Study pursued till bedtime or an exciting novel may cause a sleepless night. Heavy suppers or strong coffee late at night promote insomnia. Fruit late at night is also said to be a cause. Soothing applications to the skin are often of great service, *e.g.* friction with a flesh-brush or a warm bath. Warmth to the feet may be required in the form of extra covering or a hot bottle. The position of the head should be high in full-blooded people, in heart disease or asthma, and low in childhood and anæmia. Monotonous mental impressions promote sleep; thus thinking of a familiar rhyme over and over again, counting, reading a dull book, or, still better, having it read to one in a monotonous voice, picturing a flock of sheep coming through a gap in a wall one by one, are familiar examples that have their use.

The use of alcohol as a nightcap before retiring to bed is a habit that cannot be recommended, but a cup of hot milk or bovril can be taken in bed the last thing.

Sufferers from variety of insomnia (*b*) who wake in the small hours should take a little food, preferably warmed, *e.g.* milk or beef-tea. A spirit-lamp or special burner in connection with the gas of the bedroom should be at hand for the purpose. Any tendency to flatulence or constipation should receive appropriate treatment. Drugs used to procure sleep are only safe when medically prescribed.

Sore Throat, Quinsy, Tonsillitis are terms in popular use to denote many forms of throat affection. When the throat becomes sore it may be a symptom of the onset of some fever, which is most likely to be the case in childhood Hence a child with a sore throat should be isolated in a bedroom at the top of the house. The throat should be examined in a good light, and if any white patches can be seen, no time must be lost in summoning the doctor. If no white patches are present, it will be less necessary to consult a doctor at once, but the appearance of a rash next day should be looked for on the chest, as scarlet fever has to be thought of. Meantime a light diet and plenty of soothing drinks should be given, and a mild aperient at night.

In adults with bad teeth sore throats are very common. These take the form of either *tonsillitis*, known as ulcerated throat, or of *quinsy*, that is, an abscess in one tonsil. The tongue becomes coated, swallowing difficult, the temperature rises to 102° F., the limbs and head ache. The attack lasts about a week; if an abscess forms it may burst, but time and suffering is saved by having it lanced. The possibility of the attack being the onset of a fever has to be borne in mind. The same mode of isolation and dieting should be employed as that given above.

A gargle of permanganate of potash and boracic should be used hot—1 tea-spoonful of boracic powder to 1 cupful of a fairly strong solution of permanganate of potash. Formamint lozenges can be sucked, or the throat may be painted with glycerine and tannin. Eucalyptus, menthol, and camphor pastilles are also good.

Clergyman's Sore Throat is a chronic inflammation of the throat due to over-use of the voice. An astringent gargle, such as alum, five drachms to the pint, should be used, the voice rested, and the general health toned up. A cold compress will often relieve this form of sore throat.

Stiff Neck is commonly due to a chill. It should be treated by rubbing in oil of wintergreen or camphor ointment and by wrapping up the neck in flannel. Hot fomentations will also give relief.

A Stye.—This is a small abscess on the eyelid. Apply warm boracic fomentations—take a piece of soft linen and wring it out of a solution made of 1 cupful hot water and ½ tea-sp. boracic acid. A little boracic ointment may be put on the lid at night. When the stye is ready to be opened, pull out an eyelash from the centre. Take care the discharge does not get into the eye. Swab with boracic lotion, use a piece of clean rag and burn it afterwards.

Toothache should as far as possible be prevented by taking care of the teeth. When present it may be treated in the following way. A mild aperient should be taken. Menthol rubbed on outside will often relieve the pain. When the teeth are aching and there are no hollow ones, relief may be obtained by rubbing tincture of pyrethri on the gums. All decayed teeth should receive attention; if they are too bad to be stopped, they should be extracted. Bad teeth often cause various stomach troubles and rheumatism, and predispose to phthisis.

Varicose Veins are veins which, having been unequal to bear the pressure of the blood within them, have become dilated and tortuous in consequence. The condition is most common in the legs, especially of tall people who have much standing. The *symptoms* produced are pain, numbness or stiffness in the affected part. The nutrition of the skin often suffers, and swelling, eczema, or ulcer of the leg are then likely to develop. The *treatment* should take the form of some support; either an elastic stocking or a bandage may be worn. Crêpe bandages are excellent—they are light and easily washed. It is important that the pressure these exert should be greatest at the foot and least at the knee; hence the stocking presents an advantage over the bandage. Cold applications are also good—they act as a tonic.

Warts are outgrowths from the skin, due to a cause not yet known. They occur at all ages. They may occur in crops or singly. The *treatment* should be attendance to cleanliness and to the general health. The warts, unless present on the face or in large numbers, should be destroyed by some caustic. Glacial acetic acid painted on every night till the wart is completely destroyed is an efficient remedy. The skin around the wart should first be protected with vaseline, and the acid should then be applied on the end of a wooden match. A sore is often left, which soon heals if it is protected from the air with a little boracic ointment spread on linen. A saturated solution of salicylic acid in collodion painted on every night is also a good remedy. A strong solution of ordinary washing soda will often soften and remove warts. Whatever chemical is used, the treatment must be thorough, or the wart will only be stimulated to grow. *Warts on the face* should not be touched except by medical orders.

"FIRST AID" IN ACCIDENTS AND EMERGENCIES

Apoplexy or Stroke is caused by a blood-vessel in the brain breaking and allowing the blood to escape into, and to destroy, the surrounding brain substance. It is most common in middle-aged men who are gouty or intemperate, and in people who suffer from rheumatism and kidney disorders.

The symptoms are a sudden loss of consciousness from which the patient cannot be roused; the breathing is noisy; the limbs may be convulsed down one side and are usually limp on one side and stiff on the other.

The treatment during the attack consists in loosening the clothing round the neck and placing a pillow under the head. Hot bottles may be applied to the feet, but they must be well protected, as burns easily result. By turning the patient on his side the noisy breathing is often improved. A pillow placed along the back will keep him in position. Apply cold water to the head, and ensure a plentiful supply of fresh air. No stimulant must be given.

Bruises.—Moisten or bathe the part with Pond's Extract or arnica lotion.

Shutting Door or Drawer on a Finger.—This often causes very severe pain. The first treatment should be cold and pressure. Wrap a cold-water bandage round the finger and keep it raised, then later on place the finger in water as hot as can be borne. In severe cases the doctor should be sent for.

Bites.—(1) **Insect Bites** should be treated by the application of dilute ammonia; failing this, a strong solution of washing-soda or the blue-bag should be used.

(2) **Dog-bites** require cauterising, and a doctor should be seen at the earliest opportunity. They can afterwards be dressed with boracic ointment.

(3) **Snake-bites.**—A ligature should be firmly tied around the limb between the bite and the heart, and close to the former. The wound may be sucked, though with some risk, especially if

the lips are cracked; the saliva must be spat out at once, and the mouth should then be well rinsed.

The wound should then be bathed with dilute ammonia or a fairly strong solution of permanganate of potash, and a clean handkerchief wrung out of the solution placed over it. Give stimulant freely—brandy, whisky, or sal volatile. The sooner a doctor can be procured the better, as the wound requires cauterising. In England the viper is the only poisonous snake, and its bite rarely kills. The faintness it often causes is frequently due not to poison, but to fright.

Black Eye is due to rupture of the small blood-vessels of the eyelids and to the escape of blood into the surrounding tissues. The escaped blood undergoes chemical changes which alter its colour, and in time it is absorbed. The process may be hastened by applying hot fomentations. For the first few hours cold should be applied to check the escape of more blood.

Burns and Scalds.—Only when very slight should these be treated without a doctor. The depth to which a burn penetrates is of less importance than the area it involves. (1) Treatment when *severe*. Wrap the child in a blanket and put it to bed at once without removal of the burnt clothes. Apply hot bottles, wrapped in flannel, to the feet, and place one on each side of the child. Give it brandy and hot water, the right dose of which is a tea-spoonful of brandy if under two years of age and half a tea-spoonful more for each year that the child is over two, until a dose of three tea-spoonfuls has been reached. The brandy should be given in two table-spoonfuls of hot water or hot milk. Any part of the burnt surface which is exposed to the air should be at once protected by clean rag or unstarched muslin, soaked in olive or carron oil, and, failing this, put it on dry or wrung out of boracic lotion made by dissolving about one table-spoonful boracic crystals or powder in one pint boiling water. Nothing further should be attempted till the doctor comes. Plenty of hot water should be ready, as it may be decided to place the child in a hot bath in order to combat shock and soak off the burnt clothing. (2) Treatment when *slight*. Cover the part with a piece of clean rag or boracic lint soaked in carbolic, carron, or salad oil, and cover again with a bandage.

Next day boracic ointment spread on clean linen should be applied. Blisters should never be pricked without a doctor's permission, and when it is done the scissors or needle must be boiled before use.

Treatment of Scalds of the Mouth and Throat.—This accident results from children drinking from the kettle. The doctor should be sent for, and no attempt should be made to treat the burnt mouth until he comes, but the child should be wrapped in a shawl and nursed by the fire. Have ready plenty of boiling water, as a steam-kettle may be needed. A little olive oil may be given.

Choking.—In the milder forms of choking the best treatment, if any is required, is a smart slap between the shoulders. Fish-bones sometimes become fixed in the throat. They are best dislodged by copious draughts of water or by eating some bread and butter.

In the more serious cases of choking when a piece of food presses against the wall of the wind-pipe and causes suffocation, medical aid must at once be summoned, while some one near should pass the forefinger to the back of the throat and try to dislodge the obstacle. The finger must be passed to the side of the throat, as on no account must the piece of food be forced downwards. A small child can be held by his feet—head downwards and shaken and slapped on the back. This will sometimes dislodge the obstacle.

Concussion of the Brain.—This is generally the result of a blow or a fall on the head. When slight the effects will be very transitory—a feeling of dizziness or a loss of consciousness for a moment or two. In more severe cases the patient will lie in a completely unconscious state, similar to a faint. Any tight clothing should be removed or loosened; the feet should be slightly raised and cool applications should be made to the head. Perfect rest and quiet must be assured, and the doctor ought to be summoned. No stimulants must be given, but some warm tea as soon as the patient can swallow will do good. Sometimes a person will recover consciousness quickly, and will walk away apparently quite well, but soon afterwards will become increasingly drowsy. This is a most serious symptom and points to cerebral hæmorrhage. The doctor must be sent for at once.

Dislocation is the displacement of one of the bones that forms a joint. Pain, deformity and impaired movement result and continue as a rule until the dislocation is reduced. The joints most liable to dislocation are the jaw, finger and shoulder. The *jaw* is often dislocated in yawning too widely, when the sufferer finds he cannot close his mouth. Dislocation generally occurs on one side only. The treatment, after protecting the operator's thumbs by wrapping them up well in handkerchiefs, is to press on the back teeth of each side firmly with the thumbs whilst the fingers are placed outside the mouth, and below the jaw, and the chin pressed well upwards by them. The *finger*, when dislocated, may be treated by a steady pull so made as to tend to straighten the finger.

N.B.—Dislocation of the thumb, shoulder and other joints should not be treated beyond placing the affected limb in as comfortable a position as possible until the doctor comes. If the pain is severe, warm fomentations may be applied.

Drowning may cause death after two minutes' submersion, but life is often saved by persevering treatment of the right kind. The Royal

Humane Society have issued most valuable instructions which may be summed up by saying, first, clear the air passages; secondly, perform artificial respiration; thirdly, restore the warmth of the body whilst medical aid, blankets and dry clothes are sent for.

The air passages are best cleared by placing the patient on his face with a pad under the chest and applying pressure to the back over the lower ribs for three or four seconds. Then turn him on his side and apply pressure again to the ribs, and repeat these methods alternately until the water and froth no longer issue from the mouth.

The patient should then be turned on his back, a rolled-up coat placed under his shoulders, and the tongue drawn well forward. The braces or stays are then loosened and artificial respiration begun. The method usually adopted is that of Sylvester—

The operator stands at the head of his patient, grasps both arms just below the elbow and draws them up above the head, when he pulls on them, as this often stimulates inspiration. The arms are kept in this position while one, two are counted. The arms are next grasped just below the elbow, and then carried down against the sides of the chest and firmly pressed together. The chest is thus compressed and the air expelled. One, two is again counted and air then drawn into the lungs, by drawing the arms up over the head as before.

It may be necessary to continue this method without interruption for two hours. Meanwhile, if assistance can be obtained, the circulation should be stimulated by briskly rubbing the legs. As soon as natural breathing begins it may be discontinued, and treatment then directed to promoting warmth. Hot blankets, dry clothes, and hot bottles are required; hot coffee or brandy are given as soon as the patient can swallow. Later on injuries due to the patient having struck against piles or rocks may require attention.

Epilepsy is a disorder characterised by fits in which the sufferer is unconscious and may also be convulsed. In *minor epilepsy* there is a lapse of consciousness for a few minutes, in which unconscious acts may be performed, but in which the sufferer does not usually fall. In *major epilepsy* the unconsciousness is accompanied by convulsions and by falling, hence the name, falling-sickness.

A fit may be divided into the onset, the rigid stage, the convulsive stage, and the stage of recovery. At the onset there is in many cases a warning sensation, but in other cases the patient is struck down unconscious without the least warning.

The *treatment* during the fit is to prevent the convulsion injuring the patient. There is no fear at this stage of his injuring other people. The clothing should be loosened, the head, arms and legs pressed firmly against the ground, and a cork, tooth-brush handle, or other gag placed between the teeth to guard the tongue. When the convulsions have ceased, if the patient seems inclined to sleep let him do so. No attempt must be made to give anything by the mouth.

Fainting is due to a deficient blood supply to the brain, usually caused by a temporary weakness of the heart's action. The symptoms are too well known to need description. The duration of the attack is usually short, but it may last longer, and in rare cases ends in death. The treatment for a faint should be loosening the clothing, giving fresh air, putting the head down very low (no pillow) and the feet up, and applying smelling salts and wet handkerchiefs or eau de Cologne to the face. Brandy is rarely necessary, but thirty drops of sal volatile in a little water is a useful stimulant.

The practice of bending forward the head between the knees is one that is useful in *preventing* fainting, but it should not be resorted to after fainting has taken place.

If the faint is prolonged, medical advice should at once be sent for; meantime mustard to the heart and warmth to the feet should be applied.

Foreign Body in the Ear.—Should a bead or other such body be introduced, the head should be turned on one side with the affected ear downwards and a smart tap given to the head on the opposite side. This treatment may shake it out, but will probably fail. Syringing should be tried next, and if this fails nothing more must be done till the doctor comes, as any attempt to remove it by a hair-pin or other instrument will almost certainly drive it in against the drum and do much harm. When a seed like a pea has been introduced, syringing must not be attempted because it makes the pea swell and great pain is thus caused. When an insect has entered the ear it cannot of course go further in than the membrane of the drum, but by kicking against this great pain is caused. As insects breathe air they are readily drowned, and the ear therefore should be filled with warm glycerine and laudanum, and wool placed in the outlet. An hour later syringing should be practised to wash the dead insect out, and if this fails a doctor is required.

Foreign Body in the Eye.—This is best dealt with by closing both eyes and rubbing the normal one; a flow of tears is thus induced, which often dislodges the foreign body. If this fails, the lower lid should be drawn down, and if the body can be seen, it should be dislodged with the tip of a clean handkerchief or clean camel's-hair brush. Eversion of the upper lid, that is, turning it up to expose the inner surface, requires practice and is best not attempted. Splinters of iron, grit, &c., embedded in the cornea, should not be touched till a doctor is obtained, but a drop of castor oil should be applied to the inside of the lower eyelid, and the eye should be bandaged up to prevent the sufferer doing damage by rubbing it. *Lime* in the eye is best treated by dropping in castor oil or weak vinegar and water. Water alone is bad treatment.

Foreign Body in the Nose.—Blow the nose with the nostril on the unaffected side firmly closed. If this fails, sneezing may be induced by the application of snuff to the nostril of the unaffected side. Or, warm water containing a tea-spoonful of salt to the pint may be injected from a syringe into the nostril of the unaffected side, whilst the mouth is held open. If this simple treatment is not successful, the child should at once be taken to a doctor, as serious mischief might arise if not properly attended to. An instrument must on no account be used.

Fractures may be simple or compound. In the former the bone only is broken; in the latter case the skin is broken as well, so that germs can reach the broken bone. The first aim in a simple fracture must be to prevent further damage from being done by keeping the part that is broken in as natural a position as possible until the doctor comes. If the patient must be moved an effort should be made to get the broken bone into position and then to secure it either with bandages or with both splints and bandages. These should be put on over the clothing if possible, as then no other padding will be required. If it is found necessary to remove the clothing, this must not be pulled, but rather cut off, if it cannot be done otherwise without causing pain. When the fracture is compound the wound must have the first attention (see Wounds).

A splint may be very quickly improvised in a case of emergency—a piece of wood, a ruler, a broom-handle, a golf club, a piece of card-board, or even folded newspapers or brown paper will make excellent splints; in fact, any firm substance which will keep the broken ends of the bone together in a fixed position. When a splint is not applied over the clothing it must always be padded.

A bandage must never be applied over the fracture itself, unless the skin is broken at this spot.

Frost-Bite.—Even though the part appears lifeless, recovery can often occur provided the temperature be raised very gradually. The patient must not enter a warm room, and the affected part should be rubbed, preferably with snow. When the part comes to life, inflammation may be expected, which may be treated with fomentations or by wrapping up the inflamed organ in wool. The avoidance of alcohol or hot drinks in the early stage is also important.

A Frozen Person.—There must be no sudden application of heat. To bring the patient into a warm room in a benumbed condition or to place him in a warm bath is to cause death. Place him in a cold room, remove the clothing, wrap the body in a blanket, and with gentle friction of ice-cold water, snow or tincture of camphor, endeavour to re-establish circulation. This should be carried on some time, and some nourishment and stimulant, such as cold beef-tea, milk, ordinary tea, weak wine and water, given if the patient can swallow. When life returns put him in a cold bed in a cold room; as improvement shows itself heat may be established very gradually.

Hæmorrhage or Loss of Blood may be from an artery, a vein, or a capillary. In arteries the blood escapes from a wound in a bright scarlet intermittent stream; in veins it escapes in a dark continuous stream; in capillaries as a steady oozing. Owing to these facts it is widely taught that arterial hæmorrhage should be arrested by compression of the wounded artery at a spot nearer the heart, whilst venous hæmorrhage should be treated by pressure over the vein further from the heart than the wound; but so many amateur attempts at this method have ended in failure that it is safer to recommend direct pressure on the wound by the thumb and subsequently by a pad and bandage. A firm pad can always be improvised by placing a smooth pebble or cork in a clean handkerchief and folding it up. The limb should always be raised and all tight clothing loosened. If pressure on the wound itself fails to arrest hæmorrhage, additional pressure may be applied — nearer to the heart than the wound for arterial hæmorrhage, and further from the heart for venous hæmorrhage.

When the wound is too extensive to apply pressure to it, and arterial hæmorrhage is present, a *tourniquet* improvised as follows should be applied higher up the limb. A pad is placed over the main artery and secured in position by a handkerchief folded into a scarf and firmly tied. A stick is then inserted beneath the handkerchief on the opposite side to the pad, or it may be included in the knot of the bandage. By twisting the stick round and round the bandage is steadily tightened until hæmorrhage is arrested, when the stick must be prevented from unwinding by a bandage at each end.

A tourniquet or tight bandage must not be kept on longer than is necessary; the pressure should be gradually slackened as the bleeding ceases.

Slight pressure usually suffices to stop capillaring hæmorrhage. A pad of lint or clean linen soaked in hazeline or Friar's balsam can be applied, or, failing these, ice or a cold-water compress. Water as hot as can be borne will often check hæmorrhage.

If there are symptoms of collapse, keep the patient on his back with the head low—keep the limbs raised, and apply warmth. Give stimulants in very small quantities.

Bleeding may occur from a site to which pressure cannot be applied, *e.g.* the nose, lungs, stomach, &c. The treatment for these must be considered separately.

Nose Bleeding.—The patient should sit in a chair with the arms raised and the head well bent back. The collar should be loosened, and cold may be applied to the back of the neck and cold water to the nose. In severe cases a doctor will be required.

Blood-Spitting.—The treatment is complete rest in bed, talking in a whisper only, a little ice to suck, and a sponge-bag containing ice may be placed over the chest. Coughing should be checked as much as possible. No stimulants should be given.

Vomiting Blood may be due to blood that has come from the nose or the lungs and been swallowed, but if not, it is due to bleeding from the stomach and may be very severe. The patient should then be kept lying still, a little ice, but very little, should be given him to suck, and no medicine given by the mouth, as anything which may cause vomiting will increase the bleeding.

Stomach, Rectum, &c.—In cases of bleeding from the stomach, rectum, bladder, or womb, the patient should be kept lying down until the doctor arrives.

A Fit of Hysterics.—This is a nervous disease caused by excitement and weakness. It sometimes resembles an attack of epilepsy, but there is never complete loss of consciousness, and it generally ends in the patient beginning to laugh or cry. The case must be dealt with firmly and gently, but there should be no show of sympathy. A dash of cold water on the face will generally put an end to the attack. The general health should have attention.

Pins are often swallowed owing to the foolish habit of holding them in the mouth. A bowl of gruel should be taken, and an emetic avoided. In the vast majority of cases no harm results.

Poisoning.—Poisons are divisible into two main groups: (1) those in which an emetic is on no account to be given; (2) those in which an emetic should be given as soon as possible. Group (1) includes the *corrosive poisons* which, from their caustic action, eat into the stomach wall and may perforate it. In all other cases of poisoning in which the poison has been swallowed an emetic should be given, unless the patient is unconscious.

How to Act in a Case of Poisoning.—(1) Send at once for a doctor. (2) Preserve any poison bottle, medicine, food or vomit just as it is till the doctor arrives, otherwise the most essential evidence will be destroyed. (3) If the nature of the poison is known, it is possible to apply treatment specially adapted to it. (4) If there is no clue to the nature of the poison, follow these directions:—

(*a*) Note if the lips or clothing are burnt. If they are, the poison is a corrosive one, and an emetic must not be given. When the poison is known to be acetic acid, nitric acid, oxalic acid, or sulphuric acid, half an ounce of chalk, whitening, or wall plaster may be given mixed in half a pint of water. In a great emergency the plaster may be scraped from the ceiling.

(*b*) If the patient is unconscious, an emetic must not be given. The patient should be aroused either by speaking to him, shaking him, or flicking him with a wet towel, but not by holding smelling salts to his nose, as these may do harm to the air passages before the patient is aroused by them. If he is unconscious and the breathing is weak, artificial respiration (see p. 575) should be resorted to at once.

(*c*) Unless a corrosive poison has been taken, or the patient is unconscious, an emetic should be administered promptly, even though the exact nature of the poison is unknown. The best emetic is a table-spoonful of mustard in a tumbler of tepid water, though copious draughts of tepid water or salt and water (two table-spoonfuls to half a pint tepid water) may be used if necessary. The action of the emetic should be aided by the introduction of the fingers or a feather well down into the throat.

(*d*) In all cases of poisoning, if the patient can swallow, it is good treatment to give milk, or beaten-up eggs, or strong tea or coffee, salad or cod-liver oil. This may be done both before and after an emetic has acted. These remedies act as antidotes to many common poisons, and some of them also salve the irritated lining of the stomach.

(*e*) Lastly, treat the shock, which many poisons cause, with warmth and stimulants, and do not let the patient go to sleep until the doctor has arrived.

Ribs Broken.—This injury may result from a direct blow or a crush. The symptoms caused are shallow breathing, with pain on drawing a deep breath. Rarely the broken rib punctures the lung; bright red frothy blood is then coughed up. The treatment should be to tighten the clothing so as to give the ribs support. This may be effected in a man by pinning up the back of the waistcoat. The arm of the affected side should then be placed in a sling and the patient sent to the doctor. If he is coughing up blood, the treatment must be different; pressure will then aggravate the injury. The patient should then lie down till the doctor comes, or, if necessary, be carried to him on a stretcher or coster's barrow.

Ring, Fixed.—To remove a ring which is firmly fixed on the finger, the latter must be made smaller by expelling the blood it contains. This may be done first by shaking the hand above the head as high as can be reached, and then by bandaging the finger as tightly as possible from the nail downwards. By repeating this manœuvre the ring can often be slipped off with a screw-like motion. If not, some stout packing thread should be wound around the finger from the nail downwards until the ring is reached; one end of the thread is then to be passed under the ring and brought out through it. The thread around the finger is now unwound by using the end that is through the ring; by this action the ring should slip steadily towards the nail. Or the finger may be put into cold water and well soaped. If these methods fail, the file is the only resort.

Splinters.—If on the surface, they may be removed with a needle; if embedded in the skin, apply a hot fomentation for a few hours, then remove the splinter with a needle, if a pair of splinter forceps are not obtainable.

Sprains are the ill effects presented by tendons and ligaments which have undergone a strain. There is generally severe pain in the part accompanied by swelling. The sprained part should be kept raised, and hot fomentations should be applied to relieve the pain. A bad sprain is often worse than a broken bone, and a doctor should always be called in, or the after effects may be serious.

Strangulation.—In all cases of strangulation from whatever cause death is usually very rapid. Promptitude of action is the great point. Immediately a person is found hanging he should be cut down, one hand severing the cord while the other supports the body and prevents it being injured by the fall. Then any rope or handkerchief round the neck must be removed, and if the body is warm, steps should be taken to restore animation. Loosen any articles of dress and at once go on with Sylvester's method (see p. 575). Should there be assistance at hand, cold water may be dashed on the chest and the body briskly dried.

Suffocation by Gas.—Remove the sufferer at once from the deadly atmosphere into pure air and commence artificial respiration (see p. 575). Friction and warmth to the body should also be applied, and all tight clothing removed.

To rescue a person from a room filled with poisonous gas involves some difficulty, and should only be done after taking a deep respiration and covering the mouth and nose with a cloth soaked in vinegar and water. A rush should then be made for the window and a pane broken and the face put to the aperture, and then a second window broken if possible to create a draught.

Sunstroke exists in two forms: (1) Heat Exhaustion; (2) Thermic Fever. Heat exhaustion may result from exposure to heat of any kind. The symptoms are collapse, pallor, sweating, rapid feeble pulse, hurried breathing, and subnormal temperature. Death may occur from heart failure, though complete recovery is the rule. The *treatment* should be plenty of fresh air, and if there is much depression a stimulant may be given sparingly.

Thermic fever rarely occurs except from exposure to the direct rays of the sun. The symptoms are loss of consciousness, which may become very deep. This loss of consciousness may be the first symptom, the victim falling as though struck down, but usually dizziness and nausea occur for a short time previously. The case may soon terminate in death, or recovery may occur, the onset of which is indicated by a return of consciousness and a fall of the temperature. The *treatment* should be the loosening of all tight clothing and the application of cold to the whole body. This may be applied by sponging every few minutes with well water, or better by the application of ice. A sponge-bag full of ice should be placed against the head. A wet pack is sometimes beneficial, or a mustard leaf applied to the nape of the neck.

Wounds.—It must be remembered that the first application to a wound will materially affect its future progress. The amateur must therefore attend to the following rules:—(1) Arrest bleeding; (2) cleanse the wound; (3) bring the cut edges together when this can be done with safety; (4) provide for the escape of discharges; (5) keep the injured part at rest.

The first of these rules is discussed under Hæmorrhage (see p. 576). The cleansing mentioned in the second rule is necessary, because germs are the chief cause of wounds not healing.

Wash the hands with soap and hot water before dressing a wound, then use boiled water cooled, or water to which a little Condy's fluid or a few boric crystals have been added along with clean linen or boracic lint for the dressings.

With respect to the third rule, the question whether to bring the cut edges together or not is often difficult to answer. When in doubt it is better to leave the wound open, as in some wounds closing up is the worst treatment possible. In clean cuts, however, the edges should be brought together, preferably by the stitches of the surgeon, but failing a surgeon, resort must be made to strapping. A dry dressing just wide enough to cover the cut should be applied first, and over these strips of strapping should be applied in pairs, each pair making a cross, the centre of which is over the wound. The lowest corner of the wound should not be covered by strapping, so as to enable any discharge that may form to escape. Over the strapping a pad of wool is placed, which is secured by a bandage, and the dressing is then complete.

When it is decided not to bring the edges of the wound together, a dry dressing should be applied, unless there is a large raw surface, as in the case of many burns, when boracic or eucalyptus ointment spread on lint or clean linen is preferable. The dry dressing should be impregnated with antiseptics; boric lint or cyanide gauze are two of the best preparations, but when these are not obtainable, clean linen rag may be used and the antiseptic provided by dusting the wound with boric powder. A pad of sterilised absorbent wool should be placed over the dry dressing, and the whole enclosed with a bandage. Rest must then be secured for the injured part by the use of splints, slings, or by confinement to bed.

The After-Treatment.—Clean cuts should be left alone after the first dressing until the wound has healed. Wounds, the edges of which have not been brought together, should be dressed daily; the wound should be syringed or bathed with a mild antiseptic at blood heat, and then bandaged up as before. The bandage and wool, if not soiled, may be used again, but the dressing in contact with the wound should be renewed daily. The great point to be borne in mind in the dressing of wounds is the necessity for absolute cleanliness.

THE FAMILY MEDICINE CHEST

SUGGESTED CONTENTS

Boracic Powder or Crystals.
Menthol Cone.
Old linen that has been boiled.
Pink lint and Cotton Wool (absorbent).
Glycerine.
Tincture of Iodine.
Friar's Balsam.
Sal Volatile.
Senna Pods or Confection.
Smelling Salts.
Castor Oil.
Olive Oil.
Vaseline.
Boracic Ointment.
Linseed Meal.
Permanganate of Potash Crystals.
Court Plaster.
Carbonate of Soda.
Essence of Peppermint.
Clinical Thermometer.
Medicine and Minim Glass.
Clean pair of Scissors—kept wrapped up.
Rubber adhesive Plaster (1 spool ½ in. wide).
Jeyes' Fluid or Sanitas.
Carbolic Oil.

PERIODS OF QUARANTINE

The *quarantine period* is the time during which one exposed to infection must be isolated before he can be said to be free of all risk of having the disease. For convenience of reference we append a table of these times :—

Disease.	Age most likely to catch it.	Incubation Period.	Quarantine Period.
Chicken-pox	Childhood	12–19 days	20 days
Diphtheria	2–15 years	1–7 days, usually 2	8 ,,
Influenza	All ages	2–6 days	7 ,,
Measles	Childhood	10–14 days	16 ,,
German Measles . .	Youth	11–18 days	21 ,,
Mumps	Childhood	14–23 days	24 ,,
Small-pox	All ages.	12 days	16 ,,
Scarlet Fever . . .	5–10 years	1–7 days, usually 3	10 ,,
Typhoid or Enteric Fever	Young adults	5–21 days	—
Whooping Cough . . .	Childhood	5–18 days	21 ,,

HOME GARDENING

GARDENING is not only an interesting hobby, but it is also a health-giving occupation which many women could take up with advantage.

It is not necessary to undergo a training in gardening, or to have a great deal of spare time in order to make a small garden attractive, for nature responds to any fairly well-directed effort to grow plants, and the obviously beneficial effects of the work, not only in beautifying the home, but in improving the health, spirits, and character of those who make gardening a hobby, are in the highest degree encouraging. In the following pages the management of a suburban garden in all its aspects has been carefully considered, whilst the culture of flowers has been dealt with in a simple manner which should prove useful, especially to the amateur.

A SUBURBAN GARDEN

The most common cause of failure in suburban gardening is the cramming in of many kinds of plants, irrespective of their habit and their suitability for the conditions under which they have to grow.

Another mistake made by those who have only a small garden of, say, from three to six square rods is of trying to grow flowers, fruit, and vegetables together. In view of the fact that constant supplies of vegetables are brought to the door of suburbanists daily, it is seldom wise to give up the precious space of a very small suburban garden to them. There is certainly great value in vegetables, but they should only be grown where the conditions are favourable.

So far as fruit is concerned, it is equally open to doubt whether it is worth the while of suburbanists with a very small garden to attempt it. The most that should be done is to try a few cordon trees on the party fence. Larger trees will take up more room than can be spared. On the whole it is better to restrict a small suburban garden to ornamental plants, with which may be included grass.

Vegetables and fruits may, however, be planted in larger gardens, especially if they are big enough to be divided into two or more sections.

Planning the Garden.—There is room for the display of a considerable amount of taste and ingenuity in laying out a small garden. The beginner should not go along the line of least resistance, which generally leads to a border round the sides, a grass plot in the middle, and nothing more; in most cases a little more can be done.

Suppose the garden to be a rectangle, a little longer than it is broad, at the back of a row of terrace houses with a low wall or fence on both sides. A piece of painted or creosoted wooden trellis, about two feet high, might first be attached to the wall to secure greater height for creeping plants and also greater privacy. A foot-deep band of galvanised wire attached to the trellis, but not so securely as to be quite firm, will serve to discourage the invasion of cats. The trellis and the wire together will cost very little.

A walk at one side only of the garden will suffice, and it will of course follow the line of the border. If six inches of brick-bats and clinkers are first rammed in and then surfaced with two inches of gravel, the walk will do admirably. It should be a little higher in the centre then at the sides, so that rain will run off. The border ought to be four feet wide and the path three feet, then the width can be completed with a grass plot and another four feet border.

Borders, path, and grass plots need not be carried uninterruptedly to the other end of the garden, but might be stopped a few feet away in order to form a garden "cosy corner." This might be screened by a trellis five or six feet high, with a narrow border at its foot in which to put plants for covering the trellis. This trellis must not go completely across the garden; an opening the width of the path must be left in order to make an entrance, and here an arch should be set.

In one angle of this enclosure a summer-house might be set, or a pretty rustic bench with shrubs, or one or two selected trees, such as Laburnum or Lilac, and this will develop into a shady and secluded spot, delightful on the evening of hot days. It adds greatly to the attraction of a suburban home to have some such quiet place as this. A few seeds of Mignonette and Night-scented Stock should be sprinkled in patches near the summer-house, as the perfume will be highly agreeable on summer days and nights.

If there is to be a greenhouse it might stand

at the opposite side of the enclosure to the summer-house, or a small rockery might be formed.

If a Rose is particularly wanted for the arch, the glossy-leaved Dorothy Perkins is to be recommended. Whether it succeeds or not depends on the purity of the air. A charming arch plant that nearly always succeeds is the small, white-flowered Clematis Montana. Care should be taken to deepen the soil and to manure it well for whatever climber is planted. A thorough drenching of water or liquid manure twice a week in hot weather will be a great help to the plant.

As regards shrubs for the summer-house corner, the Aucuba is one of the most suitable, as it will grow under conditions that would be unfavourable to most shrubs.

Grass Plots.—If a grass plot is to be formed, the simplest way is to get an estimate for laying turfs from a local florist. The total cost, including labour, ought not to exceed £1 per square rod; less for a quantity. Or, the grass plot may be sown from seed. Two things are absolutely essential to success: first, a level fine bed of soil; the second, pure seed of a specially prepared mixture. The ground should be dug over in winter and the soil thrown up in lumps and allowed to remain thus for a few weeks; then in favourable weather, towards the end of March or beginning of April, it will crumble down beautifully into fine particles, and can be raked perfectly smooth and level. It should be made firm during the levelling process, or it may sink in parts later on and give an uneven sward.

The seed should be bought from one of the large seedsmen, and the soil and district should be described when the order is given. One pound of seed per square rod will be sufficient. Choose a still day in April for sowing, or September is another suitable month. Rake the soil lightly over after sowing, and finish with rolling if possible. The soil should neither be too dry nor saturated with moisture. Birds must be thought of and circumvented. Covering with fish netting, or stringing black threads a few inches apart on short sticks, will suffice for protection. Whatever is used can be removed when the grass is an inch high all over. Then roll the plot. This will crush down the young grass, but will do no harm, and by pressing the soil round the roots it will encourage the emission of new fibres. When the grass is from three to four inches high, the tops should be clipped off, preferably with shears or a scythe, as this will encourage a further break of grass from the base. The lawn is now secure, and regular rolling and mowing will steadily improve it. Rolling is best done after rain, and is most effective in the spring, when the ground is comparatively soft. Mowing is best done when the grass is dry or nearly so. In the case of young grass the cutter should be set rather high, so that the grass is not sheared off quite low down. This might bare the roots, and they would suffer in hot weather. It is not a bad plan to let the grass fall and lie on young lawns; it causes a brown appearance as the cut grass dies, but, on the other hand, the roots are mulched and shaded.

A neat, straight edge is a nice finish to a grass plot, and care should be taken to prevent the encroachment of the grass on the path and border.

Herbaceous Plants for Suburban Gardens.—The selection of plants for the borders will give food for much consideration. In these days hardy herbaceous plants hold the sway in large gardens, and there is no reason why suburban amateurs should not grow a few representatives of this large, popular, and beautiful class. A border four feet wide will not, of course, give the scope for fine colour effects which are procurable by a judicious use of fine perennials. There is not room for large groups. But handsome clumps of some good plants can be grown if the soil is well dug and manured. Let us summarise a few of the best. Double and single Pyrethrums thrive, and there are few plants more beautiful. They are suitable for small borders, because their habit is neat and compact. The foliage is graceful without being far-spreading. The flowers are thrown up well on long stems. They are useful for cutting on this account. On the whole, we certainly commend Pyrethrums to suburban amateurs. Columbines are delightful plants, the habit being neat and the flowers elegant, as well as charming in colour. Snapdragons are admirable in every way. They grow freely almost anywhere, bloom profusely, and are brilliant in colour. If the ordinary kinds are considered too large, recourse may be had to the smaller sections, which are equally as beautiful as the larger. Pentstemons are very graceful, and the flowers are as charming as those of any hardy plant in existence. These splendid plants are growing in favour every year, and suburbanists should make a point of becoming acquainted with them. Many of the Michaelmas Daisies are too large for small borders, but others are not. Chrysanthemums will do yeoman's service. They are compact in habit, and produce charming flowers.

Montbretias are graceful and free-blooming plants, with slender spikes of brilliant flowers rising from a mass of narrow leaves. The perennials already named, if supplemented by a few bulbs and clumps of Annuals, would suffice for the majority of small suburban borders, and they are but a few of the many splendid plants available.

Annuals for Suburban Gardens.—Such popular hardy Annuals as Clarkias, Godetias, Linums (Flax), Nasturtiums, Sweet Peas, Nemophilas, Saponarias, Silenes, Poppies, Candytufts, Convolvuluses, Eschscholtzias, Bartonia, Cornflower, Sweet Sultans, Portulacas, Leptosiphons, Linarias, Love-in-a-mist, Larkspurs, Mignonette, Phacelia, Virginian Stocks, and Night-scented Stock; also such beautiful half-hardy kinds as Asters, Ten-week Stocks, Marigolds, Phlox Drummondii, Nemesias, Scabiouses, Salpiglossis, and Zinnias are excellent for suburban gardens. (For Hints on Culture, &c., see p. 584.)

Bulbs for Suburban Gardens.—Bulbs play a prominent part among spring flowers; it is difficult to say what we should do without Daffodils, Tulips, and Hyacinths. These beautiful bulbs come into a bedding scheme which consists of two annual plantings—one in autumn, the other in late spring. The beds are cleared of the summer flowers in October, and planted with bulbs, which make way in their turn in May for a fresh lot of summer plants. Amateurs may put clumps of bulbs in their mixed borders for the sake of a spring display, which will be at its best when the herbaceous plants are only just starting to grow. And they may also plant bulbs in beds, interspersed, if desired, with Arabises, Aubrietias, and Forget-me-nots, all of which can be cleared away in May to make room for half-hardy Annuals or orthodox bedding plants, such as Begonias, Carnations, Geraniums, Pansies, &c. For the culture of bulbs, as well as hints on choice of varieties, see p. 587.

Roses for Suburban Gardens.—Roses cannot be recommended unreservedly as plants for suburban gardens. Their beauty of form, their glorious colours, their fragrance render these magnificent flowers supreme. Unfortunately the plants do not care for town life. Impure air has a marked effect upon them. The leaves get coated with smuts, and the buds refuse to open. The plants may flower fairly well once or twice, but they steadily decline. Whether success can be achieved in suburban gardens or not depends more on the atmosphere than on anything else.

Something turns upon culture, however. If the soil is well prepared, and strong plants of vigorous sorts are put in, the prospects of success are brighter than in a poor soil and with weak varieties.

It is wise to make the most of the limited energies of the plants by restricting them to a few shoots and flowers. Half-a-dozen branches will be better than twice that number. The clusters of flower-buds may be thinned down to one in each case, except in certain bunch-flowered varieties.

Suburbanists who are in doubt as to whether Roses might be expected to succeed in their gardens should try a few vigorous varieties first of all, and if the results are satisfactory they could increase the collection.

Carnations in Suburban Gardens.—The Carnation is a genuine town garden plant. Some of the most famous of Carnation growers have cultivated their favourites in or near a town. The fact is the Carnation has none of that susceptibility to the influences of impure air which makes the Rose so tantalising. Many amateur gardeners love to take up one particular flower and concentrate attention upon it. They find that they get more satisfaction from this than from spreading their energies over a large number of kinds. To those of this class who garden near towns the Carnation may be warmly recommended. The collection may be grown either in the garden or under glass, or partly under both conditions. (For Cultural Hints, see p. 591.)

Auriculas in Suburban Gardens.—As in the case of the Carnation, so in that of the Auricula, some of the most successful growers and exhibitors have been town or suburban gardeners.

It is a tiny plant, retiring and modest. But it has a charm, a winsomeness, which appeal powerfully to lovers of refined flowers. It is a dainty little floral gem, pretty in form, pleasing in colour, and delightful in perfume.

LARGER GARDENS

We have spoken hitherto of quite small suburban gardens at the back of terrace houses. More may, of course, be done in the larger gardens belonging to semi-detached and wholly detached villas further out. When these are situated in purely residential districts, even Roses can be grown successfully.

There may be a somewhat more elaborate plan, and in some cases fruit and vegetables may be introduced. Flowers, however, should be given the pride of the place. Vegetables are excellent in their way, but they do not add one iota of the pleasure and interest to a home that flowers are capable of yielding.

Herbaceous Borders in larger Gardens.—One advantage which the large garden will enjoy over its smaller neighbour is the capacity for providing a good border. This will permit of introducing large clumps of such plants as Paeonies, Delphiniums, Hollyhocks, Ox-eye Daisies, Phloxes, and other richly coloured plants. The border will not only be beautiful and interesting as a whole; it will yield large and constant supplies of flowers for carrying into the house.

Shrubs.—The suburbanist with a fair amount of room can also add to the interest of his garden by planting more shrubs, as many of the best will thrive in gardens where the air is fairly pure. A great deal depends on the preparation of the soil, which should be trenched and manured so as to get a depth of about two feet. The majority of the flowering shrubs bloom in Spring, but some excellent kinds can be got which will blossom at other seasons; indeed it is possible to have beauty almost throughout the year, as a few actually flower in winter. We must not expect much bloom in winter, but there are a few kinds which will flower in that quarter.

One of these is the Glastonbury Thorn, which flowers in late autumn or Christmas—there is also the Japanese Quince, which flowers generally in late winter. The winter Jasmine, too, is a pronounced winter bloomer. Daphine Mezereum is a delightful winter and early spring shrub. It has small pinkish, very sweet flowers, and does not take up much room. It does well in Suburban Gardens. Some of the Magnolias are early bloomers, and among them the beautiful species Stellata ranks very high.

Forsythia suspensa is a very early bloomer, and in mild winters is out before the spring quarter begins. It produces long, slender flowers and grows almost anywhere. It is one of the best of early-flowering shrubs.

The flowering Currant is another valuable plant to the amateur; it grows freely and blooms profusely. The Rhododendron is, of course, the queen of spring flowering shrubs, but it must have space, suitable surroundings, and is scarcely suitable for an enclosed garden.

One of the most beautiful of the Spiræas, namely, arguta, is an early bloomer, and should

Pruning Shrubs after flowering, removing bloomed wood. A shows the bloomed wood to be removed; B, B show young shoots that must not be cut off.

find a place in all collections of good flowering shrubs.

The majority of flowering shrubs are at their best in spring, but there are, too, several good shrubs that are distinctly summer blooming. The Spiræas are among the finest of summer flowering shrubs; some of the species are true shrubs. Of such are Douglasii, which has rose-coloured flowers; Bullata, which has pink flowers; Artchisoni with pale yellow flowers.

We do not get much autumn bloom among the shrubs, but we get abundance of berries, and they are bright and cheerful. We get them on the Aucubas, on the Dogwoods, on the Spinder Tree, on the Pernettya, on the Snowberry and the Japanese Rose.

Soil for Shrubs.—If any shrub-lover is importing soil in order to improve the natural medium of his garden, he cannot do better than arrange that the greater part of it be decayed turf. Practically everything will grow in it. Some leaf mould is helpful, but it need not consist of more than a quarter. In the absence of leaf mould, road sweepings could be added to the loam with advantage.

Pruning Shrubs.—Those that flower on the wood made the previous year should be pruned after flowering, the wood that has bloomed

Pruning Shrubs in spring for those that flower on current year's growths. A, A, A shoots to be cut out; B, B, B shoots to be retained; C, C, C show how to disbud to avoid undue crowding of young wood.

being cut away to make room for new. But those which flower on the young wood of the current year may be pruned in spring.

Trees.—The suburbanist who has a fairly large garden may perhaps like to have a selection of ornamental trees not too large in growth. The Almonds are useful because of their early bloom. The double scarlet Thorn, the Scotch Laburnum, various Hollies, the Lilac, the Mountain Ash with its sprays of bright berries, and Prunus Pissardii (for its purple leaves) are all worth considering.

These trees never attain to very large dimensions; at the same time they have beauty of flower, berry, or foliage to recommend them, and are suited to owners of small gardens.

Lovers of the class of trees called Conifers (because they bear cones) may like to include a few, and they are certainly very useful. Some are deciduous, others evergreen. A well-known example of the former class is the Spruce, and of the latter the Cypress.

One of the most useful of the Conifers for a small garden is Cupressus Lawsoniana, a graceful, hardy, and inexpensive, if somewhat sombre tree, of which there are many varieties differing in habit from the type. The Douglas Fir, Wellingtonia gigantea, the Maidenhair Tree and the Cedar are a few popular Conifers.

ANNUALS

That large class of plants which botanists distinguish as "Annuals" comprises some of the most popular of garden flowers. It embraces the Sweet Pea, China Aster, the fragrant Ten-week Stock, the brilliant Poppy, the perfumed Mignonette, the dear little blue Cornflower, the bright Candytuft, the Chrysanthemum, the Convolvulus, the Night-scented Stock, &c.

Annuals may be dealt with in three groups:—hardy, half-hardy, and tender. A hardy Annual is one that passes the whole of its career in the open air; a half-hardy Annual, one that is raised under glass and afterwards planted out; a tender Annual, one that lives out its life under glass.

Hardy and half-hardy Annuals may be used for bulb beds, mixed borders and banks. Perhaps they prove the most useful as clumps near the fronts of mixed borders, but a few selected kinds may be utilised to make up beds of themselves; and if the hints on culture which are given here are followed they will probably vie with any other beds in the garden.

There is another use to which many beautiful Annuals can be put, and that is to cover porches, arches, and fences, or to droop from window-boxes. The Canary Creeper, the half-climbing forms of Tropaeolum, and the Convolvuluses are all popular.

Having indicated some of the uses to which Annuals may be put, we may now pause to consider a few important cultural points, and then give selections of the best kinds and varieties.

Cultural Points.—Dealing first with the soil, we may say that it presents a very simple problem. Annuals do not require the deep, rich soil which Roses and herbaceous plants demand; indeed, it is a positive disadvantage in the case of many, notably Nasturtiums, because it causes growth so luxuriant that the plants flower poorly. There are few classes of garden plants for which we would prefer a light shallow soil to a heavy, deep one, but the Annuals certainly constitute one. We see, then, that as far as Annuals are concerned we may easily be too kind. We may waste labour and manure. We may make the plants grow too well—or, rather, too strongly. There is no need whatever for digging more than a spade deep, and the amount of manure used should not exceed the very modest quantity of one barrow-load per square rod.

An ounce of bone flour or sulphate of potash to the square yard, spread on whenever the ground is dug, but preferably in February or March, will, however, be beneficial, leading to the production of abundance of flowers and to the enrichment of their colours.

It is an excellent plan to rough-dig the ground in winter, leaving the surface quite lumpy, and then to spread on some wood ashes and soot. Towards the end of March, or in the early part of April, the surface may be raked down, and the soil will probably fall at once into a fine tilth, admirably suited for the small seeds.

If the Annuals are to be grown in beds by themselves, consideration should be devoted to finishing the soil off neatly. Have the sides raised above the surrounding grass and clear of the verge, so that a neat edge can be kept with the shears. A border of some dwarf plant, such as Thrift, or Pinks, or an Annual like the Sweet Alyssum will be an appropriate finish to the bed.

Arrangement in Beds.—Coming to the arrangement of the plants in beds, they could either be put in lines or clumps. The latter look more graceful and informal. If, however, the grower

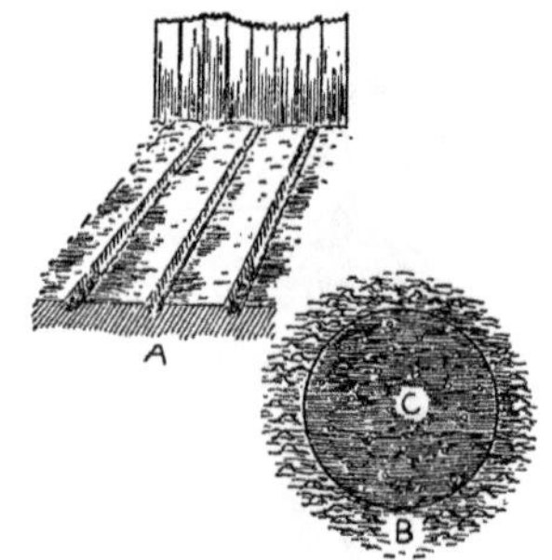

Annuals—Sowing Seeds. A shows how to sow seeds in drills; B shows how to sow them in patches or clumps; and C shows the seeds scattered thinly on the prepared soil.

prefers to sow in lines, it will be found convenient to get a board about ten inches wide, and use it for getting straight rows. A drill can be formed by turning the rake on end, teeth outward, along the edge of the plank, then the latter can be simply turned over and another drill drawn. This is quicker than constantly resetting a garden line.

With respect to clumps, the grower can do one of two things—form a shallow saucer by a quick rotary motion with the palm of his hand, or make a circle by pressing the rim of an inverted flower-pot into the soil. The clumps must not be made too close together. The rings or patches should be at the least a foot apart for small things, and two feet for large ones.

There is room for the exercise of considerable taste in associating the different plants in a bed of mixed Annuals. The colours may be contrasted, for one thing. Then, different height and habit may be considered. It is not wise to put tall things in the centre and arrange the others in regular tiers to the edge, as that may look stiff. Certainly we would not so far depart from this—the common—plan as to have short things in the centre and tall ones at the edges; but a tall, loose-growing plant may be used here and there to impart lightness to a group of short, compact plants.

The seed should be sown very thinly. If small, it may be covered half an inch deep; if large, an inch at least.

Annuals must be regarded as real objects of interest from the first, and regularly attended to, and not treated as though they differed from every other class of plant and required no attention after sowing. If a period is chosen for sowing when the weather is mild and genial, from the end of March to mid-April, and the soil is moist and crumbly, seedlings should be visible in about ten days. If they do not appear within a fortnight, the grower should want to know the reason why. Sometimes slugs attack the seeds, so that the plants never show through the ground at all, and often in such cases suspicion fastens on the seedsman.

Other Important Points.—If the seed has been sown thinly, the task of thinning the seedlings will not be a very irksome one. It may be done twice—the first time when they are about an inch high, and the second when they begin to crowd each other after being thinned to a couple of inches apart. Few people are bold enough in thinning seedlings. Very few Annuals should be nearer than nine inches to each other when they come into flower.

Hoeing among the plants is splendid practice. It cleans and aerates the soil, and promotes rapid growth. Staking will not be required in the majority of cases. If needed at all one bamboo or other stake attached to the main stem will generally suffice.

If there is one practice which conduces more than another to continuous flowering, it is the picking off of faded flowers before they have time to ripen seed. The logical conclusion from this, of course, is that if flowers must be regularly cut it is just as well to take them while they are fresh.

Watering will also be advantageous in dry weather. Watering entails considerable time and labour; besides being a source of expense, the necessity of it should be reduced as much as possible. Hoeing and mulching with a few inches of cocoa-nut fibre refuse, decayed manure, or lawn mowings, both tend to reduce the necessity for watering.

The following are a few of the most useful and valuable of the Annuals:—

Candytufts.—These are particularly useful, because they come early into bloom, and will grow almost anywhere. A good strain of carmine is one of the brightest and most useful Annuals we have. They grow to about twelve inches in height and can be had in crimson, purple, white, &c.

Chrysanthemums.—The varieties of annual Chrysanthemum called Morning Star and Evening Star, which are different shades of yellow, are very desirable. The amateur should also grow Chrysanthemum Burridgeanum, which will give some darker shades.

Clarkias.—The elegans rosea variety ought to be included whatever else is left out.

It is a very graceful plant, one of the earliest to come into bloom, and one of the last to go out. It grows from eighteen to twenty-four inches in height and can be had in rose, purple, &c.

The Eschscholtzias are very bright, and will grow anywhere. Californica and Mandarin are orange, Rose Cardinal rose. These plants have very finely-cut foliage. Height about twelve inches.

Godetias.—These should be regarded as indispensable. They are not very early bloomers, but they last a long time. They will stand drought better than most plants if they are raised sturdily. Height from twelve to eighteen inches in crimson, rose, white, &c.

Love-in-a-Mist.—There is a splendid variety of this, called Miss Gertrude Jekyll, which ought to be got. It is worth trouble to procure, being double the size of the old one, and a lovely shade of pale blue. The plant blooms incessantly for three or four months, and does not mind dry soil. Height from twelve to eighteen inches.

The Rose Mallows are splendid plants for dry soils, blooming profusely and long where most other plants would fade quickly. Height about thirty inches—crimson in colour.

Mignonette is a general favourite. There are various kinds, red, white, and yellow, and it grows to about nine inches in height.

Nasturtiums.—There is now a large number of these. The Tom Thumb varieties, such as Empress of India, are very vivid. The variegated leaf variety is interesting and attractive. It rambles freely, and is well worth growing. Sunlight is a yellow of medium height, but self-supporting. The Ivy-leaved Nasturtiums are also good things.

Night-scented Stock.—This should be sown in patches near the windows of the house, so that the delicious odour which it exhales may enter the windows. It is a somewhat straggly grower, and the colour is not bright, but it is very persistent, lasting quite into the autumn. The colour is lilac, and it grows to about twelve inches in height.

Shirley Poppies.—There are beautiful singles that one can buy in mixture. They are brilliant but ephemeral, and some of the giant doubles, which can be had in scarlet, white, striped, pink, and other colours, should be grown. They are splendid plants in beds, for their leaves are handsome, and when the huge flowers are thrown up well above the foliage on tall, strong stems, there are few garden plants to excel them. Height twelve to thirty inches.

The Sweet Pea.—The greatest of all Annuals is the Sweet Pea. It is not surprising that the plant should enjoy great favour; it is a vigorous grower, is hardy, thrives on most soils, remains long in beauty, has beautiful flowers with a wide range of colours, exhaling a delicious perfume. It will yield far more blossoms than any other plant which can be grown in the open gardens of this country.

The seeds should be sewn in shallow trenches or drills. The depth will vary slightly according to the texture of the soil—the stronger it is the shallower the cutting should be. In any case the trenches must not exceed four inches and never be less than two inches. Another important point is the distance at which the seed should be placed. It is exceedingly difficult to lay down a hard-and-fast rule, but if the distance varies from one to two inches it is almost impossible that the grower can go far astray. The plants can be grown either in single or double rows, but the former method is to be preferred.

It is imperative that the plants be given early support. Sticks should be placed to the seedlings before they attain the height of four inches, and to these preliminary sticks the young plants should be carefully attached with bass. Before the plants reach the top of the twiggy sticks the permanent ones must be put in position, or ordinary large meshed, galvanised wire, or a specially-made wire framework.

If the soil is good it is not likely that the plants will require any water until they are showing buds; in any event it is wise to defer watering until it becomes imperative. When watering is done it should be such a soaking that the ground will be moistened to a depth of about three feet. This done, the grower should not make the slightest attempt to water a second time until the soil is again quite dry. When the plants are in full bud and bloom, waterings with liquid manure will be essential.

HALF HARDY AND TENDER ANNUALS

These are raised in a frame or greenhouse in early spring, and planted in the garden when the weather is warm enough—say, in May or the early part of June. If the amateur has no glass the seedlings must either be bought or sown out of doors, but not before the beginning of May.

Those to be started under glass are best sown in boxes, and if a special compost can be prepared it should consist of equal parts of loam and leaf mould, with an eighth of coarse sand. It should be pressed firmly into boxes three or four inches deep, which can be bought from a grocer or oil and colour merchant, as a rule, at a very cheap rate. Sow in drills about half an inch deep, with the soil in a moist but not sodden state, and cover the boxes with squares of glass if possible, but, with or without glass, with sheets of newspaper, which may be removed when germination has taken place.

The remarks as to soil and planting made about hardy Annuals apply to the half-hardy. A deep, rich soil is not necessary for the majority.

Soot, wood ashes, bone flour, superphosphate, and sulphate of potash impart fertility as well as yard manure. Of course, the ground should be well worked and pulverised. The other general remarks made under hardy Annuals apply.

Among the best half-hardy Annuals are the following:—

Asters.—These rank very high, and are well worth cultivating. There are several types, and all can be bought in mixtures or in assortments of from six to twelve separate colours. The Dwarf Bouquet, Pæony flowered, Quilled, Victoria, Comet and Ostrich Plume will be found particularly valuable for garden decoration, owing to their graceful habit, and large, fleecy, richly-coloured flowers.

Marigolds are old favourites, and Nemesia Strumosa Suttoni a new one.

The Phloxes rival Verbenas, and the Salpiglossis has a grace of habit and a diversity of coloration of its own. Its large bell-shaped flowers are quaintly beautiful.

Stocks are quite indispensable. They can be bought either in mixed colours or in assortments of several distinct hues. The Dwarf German is shorter than the Giant Perfection, but the latter produces the finest spikes of bloom.

Zinnias are very brilliant. They like a little bottom heat to start in. Although slow beginners without warmth, they grow rapidly when once in swing, and are splendid garden plants.

Tobacco Flowers.—These are sometimes biennial or perennial in duration, but are generally grown as Annuals, and the same remarks apply to Petunias. Both plants should be grown, the former for perfume and evening bloom, the latter for their large, richly-coloured flowers.

The **Tender Annuals**, which are used for greenhouse decoration in pots, are not numerous. The Balsam, of which the Camellia flowered is one of the best types, is one of the most familiar examples. Petunias are much in demand for pot culture. Asters and Mignonette are both suitable for winter blooming, also the Rhodanthes and Ten-week Stock.

BULBS

In present-day gardening bulbs hold a position of their own among the flowers of spring, and if it were not for their charming colours and sweet fragrance our gardens would lose much of their charm. Much has been done by cultivation within recent years, and some of the lovely forms which are now the commonplaces of the garden were undreamed of fifty years ago.

Very little need be said about the functions of the bulb and the leaves. In practice the main things to know or remember are :—(1) That the green leaves are the food manufactories of the plant, and that if they are removed before their work is completed, there will be so much less food in the storehouse, which is the bulb. There are bulb-growers who think they may cut off the leaves directly, or very soon after, the flower has faded. It may be done once with comparative impunity, the only result being rather weaker growth the next season and a poorer flower, but the treatment must not be repeated.

(2) That the bulb is the cupboard of the plant where the food is kept. After a bulb has been a certain time out of the ground it will begin to show signs of growth, and the ends of leaves will appear from the top. This means that the plant has had to draw on its food supplies, and, if the supplies are not replenished, it will become weaker and weaker and ultimately die. This is the reason it is important to put the bulb in the ground in good time, so that it can make roots before it makes any top growth.

Another point to be remembered is that light seems to unduly stimulate the growth of the leaves ; therefore a bulb when it is potted should be first of all placed under a covering of ashes or fibre, or sand outside, or else in a dark, well-ventilated cellar.

Cultivation.—Like any other plant, the bulb responds to care and attention, so we can all do something to improve it. But there will be exceptions, for there are particular varieties which in practice fail to respond to our efforts, and we have the sad experience of seeing them gradually fade and die away. Those which fail are not the same in every garden. These likes and dislikes of certain kinds every one must find out for herself, just as in matters of food we can never tell what will agree or what will disagree with us until we try it.

Bulbs may be utilised in many different ways ; they may be planted in a border of mixed plants or in a bed by themselves ; they may be grown in grass or under trees in an orchard, and also in window-boxes and pots, or in bowls and glasses in the house.

Bulbs in Borders and Special Beds.—When bulbs are planted in clumps in mixed borders, all that can be done is to dig out as large a space as is possible, to the depth of a foot or eighteen inches, and mix a little bone meal in the soil below the bulbs. If the soil is stiff and clayey, some lighter soil or something that will help to keep it porous must be added, as no bulb likes stagnant moisture about its roots. If, however, it is very light and the drainage good, a layer of old cow manure placed at six inches below the base of the bulb is advantageous, and Rainit in addition to the bone meal should be added to the soil.

When the planting is done in special beds these should be from three to four feet wide and as long as convenient, and in such a position that they will be protected from cold winds. The ground should be " double dug," and lime and bone meal added. The bulbs in these beds must be planted in rows about nine or ten inches apart to allow a hoe to be worked between them from time to time during their growth. In January, if the weather is very severe, place a covering of some kind over the beds. Heather is good. Do not remove it until the hardest frosts are past and there is an inch or two of green leaves above the ground.

Keep the surface of the beds clean and hoe them frequently. The hoe should be run between the beds about once a month, and do not leave off until the hoe will spoil the blooms.

Bulbs in Grass.—There are two ways of planting :—

(1) By flaying large, irregular patches, and then loosening and enriching the soil with bone meal, or, when it is poor, with a very little superphosphate as well, then placing the bulbs in this prepared ground so that they will hold themselves up and not tumble over when the soil is replaced.

(2) By using such a tool as Barr's Special Bulb-Planter, which is most effective. First make a hole with the planter and put a little

Planting Bulbs in Grass. A, bulbs ; B, opening through turf. Bulbs six inches apart.

good, light, prepared soil at the bottom of the hole for the bulb to root in, then place the bulb itself on this, and put back the little circular bit of turf that is released from the cup (of the planter) when a second hole is made. After the first shower of rain it will be impossible to tell that the ground has been disturbed. It is always better to plant one sort by itself. A mass of almost any flower is effective. Try to avoid stiffness in planting. The more irregular the individual patches are the better, and so arrange that a few stray bulbs are placed singly here and there near the outside of the clumps. They must not be planted too far apart or the effect will look thin.

Time for Planting.—All bulbs should be planted before the end of October if the best results are to be got from them. Of course, they may be planted in November and even early in December, but they will not be so strong or so large as if they were put in the ground earlier. Those that are wanted for forcing and early blooming may be planted as soon as the month of August. Planting in grass should not be attempted until the ground is softened by autumn rains. Attention to this detail is very necessary.

Method of Planting.—A safe rule to go by is to plant large bulbs six inches deep and small ones four inches, but in light soil these depths may be exceeded slightly.

A question which has reference to planting is the length of time that the bulbs ought to be

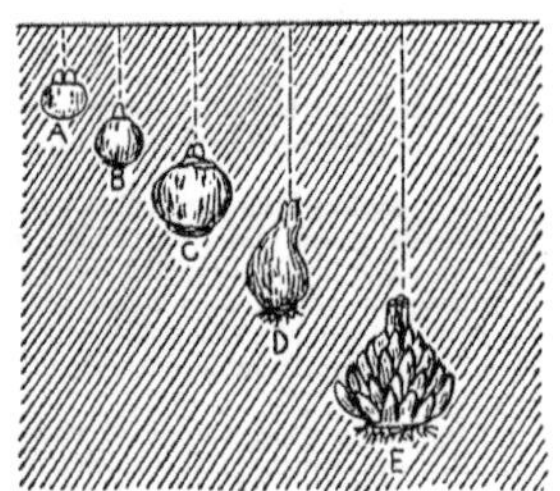

Depth at which to Plant different Bulbs. A, Snowdrops, Crocuses, or Scillas; B, Jonquils, Tulips, &c.; C, Hyacinths; D, Narcissi, Gladiola, &c.; E, Liliums.

allowed to remain without lifting. Except in the case of poor "doers," it is best to leave them alone for two years without disturbance; the blooms are finer and earlier the second season.

Lifting and Storing.—April is the flowering month, and in May when the blooms are over the leaves should be tied up, but do not cut them off until they turn yellow. As soon as the leaves assume a yellow hue and begin to lie flat upon the ground, the time has come to lift these bulbs which require removing from the ground. Too late lifting must be avoided—far better to be a little too soon. After the bulbs are lifted they must be thinly spread out in a cool, airy place, either in trays or on plates, until they are thoroughly dry. If the getting-up season has been wet they must be looked at every second or third day and turned. When quite dry they may be stored in trays or open bags until they are wanted to be planted. In the case of valuable varieties the bulb is sometimes split up when it is dried, and the offsets are planted separately. It is best only to take off those offsets which come off naturally by themselves, or which can be separated by a very slight outward pressure or pulling away.

Offsets should be planted as soon as possible; the smaller they are the greater is the necessity. Except in the case of expensive bulbs, the growing of small offsets is scarcely worth the while of any amateur. At any rate, offsets should be planted by themselves in beds in the kitchen garden or in some vacant space in August.

If by any chance the cultivator is late in taking up his bulb and they have begun to make new roots, they must be planted at once without being dried off. In the case of offsets this is of even more importance than for the parent bulb. The best advice, therefore, with regard to offsets is to plant early.

The following are a few of the most suitable bulbs for growing out of doors:—

Crocuses.—Very hardy, very cheerful, very easy to manage is the little Crocus. There are yellow, purple, white and striped Crocuses. The golden yellow is particularly bright, and it has comparatively large flowers. They are charming in lines to beds and borders, also in grass and under trees. They are so cheap that they can be planted in any quantities.

Daffodils and Narcissi.—These are easily-grown plants. They will thrive in most soils, but luxuriate in a deep, cool, substantial medium. They may be used in beds, borders, woodland and grass with equal effect. The variety of these bulbs is so enormous that the task of making a selection from mere names is a very difficult one; the amateur should consult a good bulb-dealer before making his choice. Some of the cheapest are among the best.

Two little practical details are worth noting. It must be remembered that all the beautiful red cups and red edges burn very soon if exposed to hot sunshine, and if such varieties are used they should be put in position where they will have a little shade. Secondly, attention must be given to the time the different kinds bloom, either to ensure a sequence of bloom or to have a big simultaneous display, as may be desired.

Glory of the Snow.—This ranks with the smaller bulbs, such as Scillas and Snowdrops. There are several species and varieties, all blue, blue and white, or white. The first of these is the true Glory of the Snow. It has delightful blue flowers with a white centre, grows to about the same height as the Snowdrop, and is in bloom at the same time. It is a hardy, attractive, inexpensive, and accommodating little bulb, and may be represented in gardens where such little gems are loved.

Hyacinths are loved by everybody. In pots, in glasses, in the soil of the open gardens, the Hyacinth is equally at home. Any cool, moist soil will grow Hyacinths well. Water is the life-blood of these plants; they must never be stinted for moisture, whether indoors or out. It is wasteful to dot odd bulbs about the garden, because they produce no particular effect. Clumps should be formed, and if they are thought to be a little stiff they may be associated with Chalice Daffodils, which are generally in bloom at the same time.

Scillas are very modest flowers, but they have their uses. Sibirica, the blue Squill, is a pretty and serviceable little plant. It blooms, together with its white variety, in February. Bifolia is a charming little plant which flowers in March. There are several varieties of it, including a white (alba) and a pink (Pink Beauty). The wild "Bluebell," or Wood Hyacinth, is a Scilla, and its specific scientific name is variously given as nutans and festalis. There are pink and white varieties of this also. It is an April bloomer. The Spanish Squill (*Scilla hispanica*), blue, and its varieties bloom in March. There are several different shades of blue, likewise red, rose, and white.

Snowflakes.—These are great favourites and they are easy to grow. The summer Snowflake grows about eighteen inches high, and has large white flowers. The spring Snowflake flowers a few weeks earlier, and also has white flowers tipped with green. Another variety has yellow tipped flowers.

Tulips.—Hardy, brilliant, easy to grow, the Tulip is one of our most valuable bulbs. It will give us a vivid blaze of colour if we grow some of the bright varieties in masses, but it will also give us many delicate and dainty little pictures if we choose the softer-hued sorts and grow them in selected positions.

By making a suitable selection we can have Tulip blooms for fully three months.

We might classify the sections as follows for outdoor flowering: *March bloom*, Van Thols; *April*, Early Dutch; *May*, Darwin and Cottage. The Van Thols are pretty enough, and make nice little patches of colour among Scillas, but they only grow a few inches high, and have small flowers. The Darwin and Cottage sections have flower stems two feet long, surmounted by immense blooms.

BULBS IN BOWLS AND GLASSES

This form of growing bulbs has become very popular within recent years. It is very simple and has proved to be entirely successful. Any earthenware receptacle that holds water may be used, and any of the fibrous mixtures sold by bulb merchants, such as cocoa-nut fibre or moss fibre, may be employed for the root medium. The medium does not matter much so long as the after-treatment is right. A few small pieces of charcoal should be mixed with the fibre to keep it sweet.

Pot firmly and just cover the bulb with whatever medium is used, taking care that it is neither too wet nor too dry. A good test is the old one of taking a handful and closing the hand upon it and then opening it; if the lump just holds together, but falls asunder directly it is touched, then all is well and potting can proceed.

The number of bulbs to be placed is best left to the taste of the individual; but they should neither be overcrowded nor look meagre. Care should be taken to avoid filling the vases quite full of fibre, as if that were done particles would be constantly falling over and making a mess. If this is guarded against, vases will be found perfectly clean.

The next stage is to put them in an airy cellar or room until the roots are formed and from one and a half to two inches of top growth is made. It is desirable that the store be frost-proof, but the bulbs will endure a little hardship.

Never bring bulbs directly from the cold to a warm greenhouse or room—always try to arrange for an intermediate step. Then bring them into heat or a warm sitting-room as required.

For this method to be successful the bulbs will require constant care to see that they are neither too dry nor too wet. Always stake or tie up the leaves of bowl plants in good time. Thin green sticks and green bast are the most suitable, or special wire supports may be used for heavy flowers, such as hyacinths. Care must be taken not to spoil the natural appearance of the flowers when fixing the support.

Bulbs may also be grown successfully in bowls filled with clean pebbles or shell gravel and water. They must be treated in the same way as Hyacinths in glasses—that is, put in a dark cupboard for six or eight weeks, and then placed in the window. Narcissi, Tulips, Hyacinths can all be grown in this way, also the smaller bulbs, such as Crocus, Snowdrop and Scilla, but these are not quite so effective. Some of the larger Lilies, such as the Joss Lily or Sacred Lily, can be grown very successfully in gravel.

Hyacinths can also be grown in glasses, although this mode of culture is not so popular as it used to be. Care should be taken to choose smooth, symmetrical bulbs, which will fit the necks of the receptacles. The water may come close to the base without touching it. One or two pieces of charcoal will help to keep it pure; should it become thick and smelly it will be wise to pour it away and substitute fresh, but this should be done very carefully, so as to avoid injuring or drying the roots. The glasses should be kept in a dark cupboard until the roots reach the bottom of the receptacle. A wire support, looped at the base to clasp the neck of the bottle, will be necessary to keep the plants from toppling over.

HARDY HERBACEOUS PLANTS

The old style of flower gardening, with its

ribbon borders and tender plants put out in beds late in May, is supposed to have passed away for ever. The tendency in flower gardening nowadays is to have an expanse of well-kept turf, and to surround the grass with borders filled with chosen hardy flowers.

Forming a Border.—In the first place it is wise to make borders as wide as possible. When the different kinds are bunched, none show to advantage. Their individual beauties are lost. Secondly, the ground for a herbaceous border should be thoroughly prepared; that is to say, it should be dug to double the depth of a large-sized spade, and have a liberal dressing of manure incorporated. It should be dug in autumn or winter if possible, so that it may have time to settle down before planting time comes in March and April. Thirdly, and not least important, careful consideration should be devoted to the selection and arrangement of the plants.

Three cardinal points may be urged on makers of herbaceous borders: (1) To avoid putting in any plants without considering the proportions and colours of its neighbours; (2) to allow sufficient room for every plant to display its individual characteristics; and (3) to arrange the plants in groups which are beautiful in themselves, and likewise make a harmonious whole.

Forethought is very necessary. It is hard for the amateur to realise that the little plants which she puts in in spring will, at the end of three months, have extended several feet.

The leading idea should not be to cover every square inch of surface at the earliest possible moment. That inevitably leads to ultimate overcrowding. Bare earth in spring and early summer is not in the least offensive so long as it is not weedy. With clear spaces between the different groups the hoe can be plied freely and conveniently when the ground dries after every shower, to the swift destruction of weeds, and the immense benefit of the proper occupants of the border.

Later in the year confusion is often caused by the falling about of the growths of tall plants in windy weather. This should be corrected at once by staking and tying. In this connection the amateur may be advised to remember that tight "bunching-up" is undesirable, and that a tie near the bottom of a plant, and another near the top, will generally held it more evenly and securely than one in the middle. Plants with flower stems which droop gracefully should not be held as straight and stiff as soldiers on parade.

It has been mentioned that spring is a good time for planting herbaceous borders, but it may be done in autumn or winter (except when the ground is hard with frost), if more convenient.

The amateur should not allow herself to be tied down by definitions. "Herbaceous plants" has come to signify perennial plants, but there is no reason whatever why beautiful annuals should not be included.

It is sometimes difficult to ensure a fine and continuous effect in a small border without making two plantings, but the little trouble involved in this is so amply compensated by the results obtained that it should never be grudged. As an instance it is not easy to get spring beauty in border groups without introducing bulbs, such as Tulips. Now these brilliant flowers become unsightly when the bloom is gone, because of the fading of the foliage. If they are left in the border, they mar its beauty; if they are taken up and the ground left bare, the gaps are noticeable. The proper course here is undoubtedly to form a reserve of good Asters and Stocks, which may be planted out when the Tulips fade. There is no need to wait until the latter have lost their foliage. They can be transplanted to a reserve bed directly the bloom is over, which, in the case of the late-flowering sections now so popular, may be the end of May or the early half of June.

The Ivy-leaved Geranium is another plant which comes in useful as a successional plan, and the first half of June is an excellent time to plant it out. A very pretty effect is produced if low stumps, over which the plants may ramble, are put in the border.

Even more valuable, because of the ease with which it can be raised in quantity from seed in winter or spring, and its long period of blooming, is the Snapdragon. It can be planted out at almost any period of the summer, flourishes in nearly all soils, and is very brilliant in colour.

One last suggestion for maintaining the beauty of borders may be made, and that pertains to the autumn. It is to grow a selection of Chrysanthemums in a spare plot throughout the summer, and when some of the larger of the herbaceous (that is, stem-losing) plants fade and become unsightly, to cut them down, and plant the Chrysanthemums near them. Herbaceous borders are often ugly and untidy after August, simply because the summer-flowering plants are past their best, and there is nothing to carry on the display. The provision of autumn-blooming plants, such as Michaelmas Daisies and Golden Rod, when the border is first formed, will do something to prevent this, but the introduction of the Chrysanthemums can still be effected with advantage.

Anemones.—Many of the Anemones are dwarf plants, more suitable for the rockery than the herbaceous border, but there are two notable exceptions, the Crown and the Japanese Anemones. The former bloom in spring and summer, and the latter in late summer and early autumn. One can buy roots of these, or seeds. They grow about a foot high, and make the most beautiful beds and border clumps imaginable. The Japanese Anemone grows about three feet high, and the best varieties have single white, pink, or rose flowers about two inches across. It is very graceful and beautiful, and, as it thrives in most kinds of soil, and spreads freely, it ought to be specially marked.

Campanulas.—The fact that the Canterbury Bell is a Campanula can hardly fail to prepossess amateurs in favour of this genus. When they have studied it a little they will find that it contains plants very little less valuable than the old favourite named. Some are quite dwarf; others are of medium height; while still others are nearly as tall as Hollyhocks. The Campanulas are mostly either blue or white. Some are annuals, others biennials, and yet others perennials. The first are best raised from seed sown in spring, the second and third from seed sown in early June.

Canterbury Bells.—The rise of some modern flowers has not caused old favourites like the Canterbury Bell to decline, nor is it likely to do so, considering how powerful its claims are. Its compact habit, great profusion of bloom, brilliant colours, duration and cheapness combine to render it indispensable. There are blue, rose, and white varieties, and there is a duplex-flowered form which is commonly called the cup-and-saucer Campanula.

No flower gardener of limited means can afford to ignore the Canterbury Bell. It will give striking beauty to the beds at the cost of a few pence. As fast as the flowers fade they can be picked off, and fresh buds will form in abundance.

The Carnation.—The Carnation is a prime favourite with almost every lover of flowers. We may include the Pink and Picotee with it in a general sense, and when we do so we widen its appeal.

It is of attractive form and colour with delicious perfume, and there are few gardens worthy of the name in which the Carnation is not represented.

The Selfs and Fancies are the two most suitable classes for garden culture. The former are one coloured, the latter are yellow or white flowers irregularly marked with another colour. The Picotees have a clearly defined line of colour round the edges of the petals. Carnations are beautiful both for beds and borders. Strong plants make very attractive objects with their tufts of greyish green foliage, large flowers and brilliant colours.

They can be grown from seed by sowing out of doors in early summer, but the flowers will not possess any marked quality. It is better to get young plants, and put them into the beds or borders from the end of March to June. If the soil is poor it ought to be dug two spades deep and manured.

The plants may be put eighteen inches apart and dressed firmly into the ground. The flower stems will need support, and special stakes, which are not expensive, should be bought.

Pinks are propagated by means of young shoots pulled out of their sockets.

The Carnation is hardy, but damp often kills plants out of doors, especially in wet heavy soils.

Pinks are not so particular as to soil as Carnations, and plants, if allowed to remain even three years in the ground, will flower well each season. They are very hardy and capable of resisting the severest weather. They are among the most desirable plants to grow in any garden.

The Chrysanthemum.—The Chrysanthemum is the Golden Flower, the national floral emblem, of Japan. This fact must have its interest second only to the Rose as a popular flower in Great Britain.

The fact that this magnificent plant is at its best at a period when every other great flower is practically over is one of the utmost importance. That the Chrysanthemum is really a hardy plant is conclusively proved by the evidence of thousands of plants which have lived for years out of doors, passing unscathed through severe winters. The truth is that the Chrysanthemum is hardy or not according to the conditions under which it is grown. It is always well worth while to grow a collection in the garden for late as well as for early blooming. Severe early frosts sometimes mar the flowers, but in most years no harm is done. The plant is easily grown and tractable, and with modifications in our system of culture we can get considerable variation in growth. The initial step will be the purchase of a few plants from a nurseryman, and this is likely to become an annual occurrence, for we shall want to add more varieties to our collection; besides, new ones are always coming out.

It is well to order Chrysanthemums in the autumn or winter, even if they are not wanted until the spring, especially if novelties are being bought. The reason is that certain varieties, and particularly new ones, are in great demand, consequently there is a risk of not getting the sorts that are wanted unless they are ordered early.

Cuttings cost less than rooted plants, and are procurable in autumn; but those who buy in November have the care of the plants all through the winter.

Amateurs who are in this position will be well advised to buy plants early for spring delivery. They will be quite safe in the hands of a respectable nurseryman. If the plants are received in March, they will be sturdy little specimens, established in small pots, and well supplied with roots.

Chrysanthemums are so beautiful for garden decoration that we find it difficult to understand why they are not used more. In part it is doubtless due to the fact that they are generally regarded as indoor plants, and not hardy.

No small advantage connected with the plant is that it may be transplanted from one place to another even when in bud, so long as the precaution is taken of well watering the soil first, and taking the plant up with a good deal of earth. The work is best done in showery weather. Plants so shifted soon re-establish themselves, and in a few days are growing freely. In due season they bloom well. The importance of this lies in the fact that a succession of flowers can be arranged in a border without over-crowding. Instead of cramming the Chrysanthemums into the border, there to half smother themselves while they are waiting to take the place of earlier flowers when the latter shall have faded, the Chrysanthemums can be planted in good soil in some spare plot, with plenty of room to grow into healthy and vigorous specimens. Earlier things can be cut down when they are over, and the Chrysanthemums planted near them. This greatly extends the beauty of a border. Similarly, beds may be planted with Chrysanthemums after summer flowers have faded.

Although Chrysanthemums are often allowed to look after themselves year after year, no trouble being taken to divide them, or to give fresh soil, outdoor plants benefit by attention. The clumps may be split up, and when they start growing in spring, planted in fresh, manured soil. But probably the best plants are got by raising a few fresh ones from cuttings every spring. This does not involve much trouble, and it ensures young, vigorous plants which will produce abundance of large, brilliant flowers. Soakings of water in dry weather, and occasional doses of liquid manure will of course benefit the plants.

The Pompon and Single varieties are the most generally useful for outdoor culture, owing to their branching yet neat habit and abundance of bright flowers. They can be cut from freely, and will prove quite capable of yielding a great deal of material for room decoration, as well as making a brilliant display in the garden.

The Dahlia.—This is a plant of very free growth. Provided it is raised sturdily and given free soil, it grows with refreshing vigour, and soon shows a great array of bright and cheerful flowers. They show a variety in colour—brilliant carmine, rich crimson, pure white, clear yellow, a delicate blush, a bright rose, maroon. Some are bicolours, and there is a section with flaked flowers.

There are many different kinds of Dahlias, but the amateur will get his best effects from the Cactus, Pompon, Single and Paeony flowered sections. There are, however, some large double Dahlias, which are good from the garden point of view.

It is useless to grow Dahlias in poor shallow soil—if the best results are expected. One must have deep, richly cultivated land. The Dahlia loves plenty of good food, and it loves moisture. A heavy soil will suit it better than a light one.

In mild districts Dahlias may be planted early in May. Plenty of room should be allowed. Six feet from plant to plant will not be too much. At the same time as they are put in a support in the form of a stout stake standing four feet out

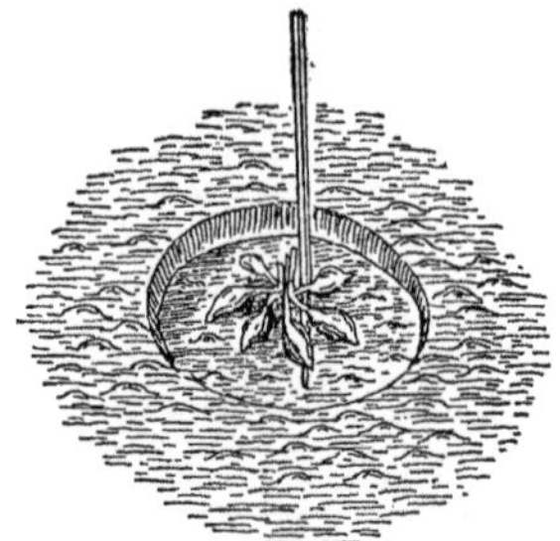

Planting Dahlias. How to plant old tubers and fix stakes before replacing the soil.

of the ground should be inserted. These look rather obtrusive at first, but cannot well be put in at a later stage without injuring the roots. The soil should be slightly basined around the stem, not mounded.

Dahlias in Autumn.—In a cool, mild, moist autumn the Dahlias may remain in beauty until November, but the first sharp frost that catches them will blacken the foliage and stop the growth. When this happens it is useless to retain them; the sooner they are cut down the better, as they will never recover, but will die quite away. The stem may be severed just above the ground, and the top growth cleared away. Some growers let the roots lie in the ground throughout the winter. No harm will follow if the soil is warm and friable, but in cold, damp soils the tubers may decay. It is decidedly safer to lift them, and after letting them stand upside down on their stumps for a day or two, in order to facilitate the escape of moisture, to store them. They pass the winter best in a dry, frost-proof place. If increase is not desired and nothing but garden decoration is thought of, the stools may be replanted intact in spring, and with a certain amount of growth-thinning they will give fairly satisfactory results; moreover, they will flower early, if that is considered an advantage.

Delphiniums.—Plants with stems four or five feet high, the lower part furnished with broad, much-cut leaves, and the upper position with bright blue flowers. They are not difficult to grow and are beautiful for borders. They require careful stalking. There are several varieties, and can be had in all shades from palest lavender to deepest indigo.

Evening Primroses.—These are characterised by great profusion of bloom, and are bright border plants. The principal drawback is a tendency to straggle, but this is not so marked in one or two of the modern varieties. The most compact Evening Primroses are the species Fruticosa and its variety Youngi, both yellow flowered. The latter is perhaps the most useful that we can have, as in addition to its closeness of growth it has the merit of producing a great mass of brilliant flowers.

Pansies.—Considering that it is a lowly plant, incapable of yielding those bold masses of colour, which the modern flower gardener loves so much, the pansy remains a decided favourite, especially in Scotland where the humid climate seems to suit its growth. But it will succeed with very little coaxing in moist, clay soils, even in the extreme south of England.

The work of the cultivator is easier if he plants fairly early, say by the end of March. At that period the nights, if not the days, are always cool; moreover, heavy showers may be expected. A liberal rainfall and cool nights between them are a great help in getting Pansies well established. If planting is not done until May or June far more attention is needed to get the plants into free growth. Pansies bloom for a long time and increase very rapidly. The hardy kinds will take no harm by being left out of doors all winter.

Phloxes.—A most beautiful and valuable class of garden flowers. They bear their flowers in bunches at the summit of slender stems clothed with narrow, lance-shaped leaves. The colours are very beautiful, soft and refined. Some flower early and others late in summer.

Primroses and Polyanthuses.—These are hardly herbaceous plants in the ordinary acceptation of the term, because they are not leafless throughout the winter. On the contrary, they grow in mild spells, and are at their best in spring, when the majority of true herbaceous plants are just awakening from their winter sleep. Primroses and Polyanthuses may be introduced into herbaceous borders with great advantage, as well as into ordinary flower-beds; they can be shifted into beds and borders in autumn, when the herbaceous and annual plants are fading, and moved out again in the spring, when other plants are coming on.

Pyrethrums.—These are valuable in more ways than one. They are among the earliest of the border plants to bloom, and they bloom very profusely. The foliage is distinctly handsome, and the colours are brilliant and varied. They are easily grown and are very hardy.

Gladioli.—One of the most beautiful of late summer flowers. A neat, somewhat close grower, with sword-shaped leaves and arching flower stems closely studded with funnel-shaped flowers.

Irises.—These stand forth as among the most valuable of border plants. The Flag section are particularly vigorous in growth, and have large brilliant flowers. They will grow almost anywhere. Others require a very moist situation.

Michaelmas Daisies.—Very useful in borders, as they bloom when other flowers are beginning to fade. They have vigour of growth, free blooming and bright, varied colours.

Ox-eye Daisies.—A species of Chrysanthemums. There is not much variety about these flowers, but they are useful in borders. They flower well and are easily grown.

Paeonies.—These are among the finest of our hardy plants. The number of varieties has grown rapidly within the last few years, and they can now be had in many shades of pink and red as well as white. They require abundance of room to look well.

Violas.—Sometimes called the tufted pansy, and the name is not inapt, inasmuch as the growth is tufty and the plants are at least as much Pansies as Violas.

The plants are distinguished by dense, compact growth, relatively large flowers, rich and diversified colours, and great profusion and persistency in flowering. Violas are admirably adapted for forming a groundwork for other plants. They can be utilised for this purpose in herbaceous borders and in rose-beds. If planted in autumn along with bulbs, many charming effects can be made. They can also be used for forming edgings to beds and borders.

It is desirable to avoid planting in straight lines. When Violas are employed for an edging to wide borders, an irregular line in the inside should be followed, so that the occupants of the border may extend forward amongst the Violas at different points. If one will have a ribbon border of Violas, let nothing else be associated with them, and let the varieties be most carefully selected for the purpose.

To get the best out of Violas, plants should be bought in spring, and planted in deeply-dug, well-manured soil. The earlier this is done the better, because when planted early they have a good chance of getting well established before the hot weather comes. The plants enjoy depth, coolness, moisture, and fertility. They may be planted about nine inches apart.

Constant cuttings should be practised throughout the summer. The flowers will be found useful in the house, and, apart from that, the regular picking will prevent seed-pods forming, and so keep the plants growing.

ROSES

There is a charm about a beautiful Rose garden which appeals irresistibly to every lover of flowers. It is not necessary to win a prize at a Rose show to enjoy Roses when they are used in free, informal, natural ways. People who love Roses must not allow themselves to be unduly influenced by what they see and hear at shows. They must learn about beautiful garden Roses—what they are, and how to manage them in order to get lovely garden scenes, together with abundance of flowers for bowls and vases.

There should be nothing stiff, stilted, and formal about Roses, whether in the growing of them or the utilisation of them. We should look upon them as cheerful, delightful, affectionate companions. To put the trees in stiff rows, grow them on a level, and prune them back to mere stumps, like a blackthorn hedge, is to rob them of all chance of showing whether they possess natural beauty. The Rose of our love is not the Rose of the show tent, but of the flower-bed, arch and pillar. It is the Rose that swings golden, and pink, and crimson clusters lightly in the summer breezes.

There are many different types of Roses :—

We read of Perpetual Roses, Tea Roses, Hybrid Tea Roses, Damask Roses, China Roses, Moss Roses, and Monthly Roses. But even these are not all, for we find a reference to the Austrian Brier, the Japanese Rose, the Province Rose, the Ayrshire Rose, and many more with more or less forbidding botanical names. The average flower gardener would be ill-advised to trace the great classes back to their source; this is the duty of the botanist, and those who love Roses for their garden beauty will rather content themselves with considering how they can best utilise the beautiful material which awaits their attention.

Roses can be used in a variety of ways. They may be planted in a border with other flowers, in a special bed by themselves, or in small plots in the grass. They can also be used for climbing up walls, or covering arches, pillars and fences. Ready-made arches, both of rustic timber and metal, can be purchased at moderate prices, and these will be admirable in suitable places, such as over divisions of garden walks. Rose pillars are very beautiful, and they are quite inexpensive. Let the reader imagine a stiff ribbon border, with the plants all on a level, and then imagine a border of various kinds of plants, informal and irregular, with Rose pillars rising here and there. How much more graceful and pleasing is the latter than the former.

If possible we must find room for a bed of Roses. This must not be filled with stiff, straight standards or with hard-pruned dwarfs, but with bush Roses of vigorous growth and free-flowering character. The stronger sorts must be selected, which will form real bushes without much cutting and still bear handsome flowers. There are many good varieties suitable for this.

Whether we grow Roses on or in arches, fences, walls (for we must not forget the dwelling-house), or beds, we must give them abundance of good food if they are to produce those generous masses of bloom which we want. Starvation will not do, half-measures will not do. We must have strong, healthy plants, growing in rich soil.

The beginner in gardening should buy the plants and not attempt budding or striking from cuttings, both of which require experience. The plants should be procured in the autumn, and directly the order has been sent off the ground must be prepared. The best time to plant is about the beginning of November.

Soil and Planting.—Roses like what is called "holding" soil, such as strong loam or clay. Light, sandy, gravelly or chalky land is not so good.

The ground ought to be treated in this way :- (1) Mark a strip two feet wide right across one end of the bed ; (2) take out the soil to a foot deep and wheel it to the other end of the bed ; (3) spread a coat of manure in the trench and dig it into the subsoil ; (4) fill up the trench with the topsoil from another two-feet strip ; (5) so proceed until the end of the bed is reached ; and finally (6) fill up the end trench with the loose soil that came from the first strip. This greatly enriches and deepens the ground. Road scrapings are good, and this material is generally procurable in the suburbs of a town. Allow the soil a week or two to settle down, and then plant the Roses, not deeply, but work the soil very firmly about the roots. Give generous doses of liquid manure throughout the summer and soap-suds at all times when available. Hoeing the soil among the roses is also good practice. Any trouble that is taken with the soil will be amply rewarded.

Pruning.—As regards newly planted dwarf or standard Roses, it is generally agreed that the branches are best pruned back to three or four buds about the end of March : fresh shoots soon break from the short stumps left. Experts differ as to whether climbing Roses should be cut back in the same way. Some advocate that the long canes should be cut back to the ground, while others declare that this is not necessary. If the Roses are planted in rich, deep soil, shortening is not so necessary. As regards general pruning —that is, when the plants are well established—growers may proceed on the following lines :—

(1) **Dwarfs.**—Prune varieties which form summer shoots of about the thickness of lead pencils, back to within six buds of the base every spring—but allow varieties which form shoots as thick as the finger to extend two or three feet—and merely trim the tips and the weak breast-wood which forms on the main stems.

(2) **Standards.**—The great majority of the Roses which are grown as standards form summer shoots of about the thickness of a lead-pencil, and may be cut back to four buds about the end of March each year.

(3) **Climbers with long Canes.**—Climbers which

form long, strong, upright canes, such as Crimson Rambler and Carmine Pillar, do not need much pruning. When, however, considerable numbers of canes have formed, and are getting thick and tangled, the old ones may be cut right out to give more room for the young ones which have pushed from the base.

(4) **Climbers with much Side-wood.**—There are several valuable climbing Roses, which throw many vigorous young side-canes from their main rods; and these are particularly valuable for walls, because they cover a considerable surface in a short time. They do not need cutting back when established, but will be the better for an annual trimming, thinning out tangled shoots.

A golden rule in pruning is to prune strong growers lightly and weak growers severely.

Different Kinds of Roses.—In the catalogues Roses are generally divided into the following different classes: (1) Hybrid Perpetuals, H.P., (2) Tea Roses, T., and (3) Hybrid Tea, H.T.

The H.P.'s form a considerable class and comprise the largest flowered and most brilliantly coloured of all roses. They have two well-marked flowering periods, the first being the end of June or the early part of July, and the second the first half of September. They are not continuous bloomers like the Teas. There are, however, one or two varieties, notably the lovely pink Mrs. John Laing, which bloom over a much longer period than the majority. The H.P.'s are of mixed parentage, the Monthly, Bourbon, and Damask Roses having all been used as parents for them. They are mostly green stemmed with five rough leaflets. As a class they are very strongly scented, although all are not equally fragrant.

Tea-scented Roses differ very considerably from the H.P.'s. The young shoots of the Teas are red or brown, and they are beautiful from the time they have made their first few inches of growth. They are more continuous in blooming than the H.P.'s.

Almost every bit of new wood on a vigorous, healthy Tea will bloom, and as such wood keeps coming for several successive months, it follows that flowering is practically incessant. They have neat flowers and long stems, and are delightful button-hole flowers. They possess a piquant, refreshing, agreeable, but not powerful perfume. While they differ in degrees of vigour, the majority are extremely vigorous, and the more they are cut the better they will bloom. The amateur will be well advised to give the Tea Roses the lion's share of his ground.

Hybrid Teas.—This is the variety which has shown the greatest development within recent years. They are the most valuable of dwarf trees. As a class the H.T.'s are distinguished by strong growth with a fair amount of young spring colour (although not quite so much as the Teas), profuse blooming, large flowers, and bright, clear colours. They are not, as a whole, quite so neat in the bud as the Teas, nor are the expanded flowers so full and brilliant as the H.P.'s, but they have a beauty and character of their own. Their long flower stems make them particularly valuable for cutting. Like the Teas, they are continuous growers and bloomers; indeed, one or two, notably the rich and fragrant Grüss an Teplitz, are rarely without flowers.

Noisettes.—This section is not important in point of numbers, but it includes two or three climbing varieties of considerable value. They bear flowers in clusters.

Climbing Roses other than Noisettes.—There are several beautiful climbing Roses which do not come into the Noisette class, such as the Sweet Briers, Polyanthas, Singles, and Banksian.

Special Selections.—The following are a few selections of varieties for various purposes. These are carefully chosen to unite vigour of growth with bright colours. Many, too, are perfumed, but the grower will not find such fragrance in all the pillar Roses as in the old Cabbage Rose.

SELECT ROSES FOR ARCHES AND PILLARS

Ards Rover, crimson.
Carmine Pillar, carmine.
Crimson Rambler, crimson.
Dorothy Perkins, pink.
Félicité Perpétue, white.
Euphrosyne, pink.
Leuchstern, carmine.
Mrs. F. W. Flight, pink.
Penzance Brier Lucy Bertram, red.

SELECT ROSES FOR WALLS

Alister Stella Gray, yellow.
Gloire de Dijon, yellow.
Longworth Rambler, crimson.
Madame Alfred Carrière, white.
Reine Marie Henriette, red.
Wm. Allen Richardson, copper.

SELECT ROSES FOR BEDS

Anna Olivier, white or buff.
Antoine Rivoire, cream.
Caroline Testout, pink.
Frau Karl Druschki, white.
Grüss an Teplitz, crimson.
Gustave Nabonnand, flesh.
La France, peach.
Liberty, crimson.
Madame Abel Chatenay, rose.
Marie van Houtte, lemon, tinted pink.
Mrs. John Laing, rose.
Mrs. R. G. Sharman Crawford, rose pink.

The above lists will meet the requirements of those who only want a small collection of Roses.

TENDER BUDDING PLANTS

These are plants which can only be grown out of doors in the summer, and unless the amateur is the possessor of a frame or greenhouse they are not such a useful section, as in most cases it would mean buying the special plants each season. A few of them may, however, be mentioned, as they are general favourites.

The Geranium.—In the days of the ribbon border, which consisted of a row of scarlet geraniums, a row of yellow calceolarias, and a row of lobelias, this was considered the queen of flowers, and florists vied with each other as to who would produce the finest specimens. Although this is now a thing of the past, the geranium still holds its own; it is a plant which can never drop out of our garden; it is too persistent in blooming, too bright and varied in colour ever to go out entirely. It is useful in greenhouses, in window-boxes, tubs and vases. A few clumps of, say, a dozen plants might very well be arranged in mixed borders.

Zonal Geraniums are generally planted in spring, and at that period they are undeniably tender, although it takes more than a slight frost to kill them in autumn, when the stems have grown thick and woody. The spring plants have been made tender by being grown under glass.

There are many varieties of Geranium, some attractive by reason of their foliage, and others that are admired for their flowers. In mild districts they may be planted outside in the middle of May, but in cold localities the planting should be deferred until the end of the month. Old plants may be preserved through the winter by lifting them from their beds in autumn before the frost has touched them. Then prune off both branches and roots, leaving no more than short stumps, and hang up the plants in a cellar or attic where they will be safe from frost. Provided that the plants can be kept sound, the plan is excellent, as fresh growth starts in spring and nice plants soon develop.

Geraniums will thrive in almost any kind of soil. They grow the most rapidly in rich soil, naturally, but there is such a thing as over-luxuriance. Very free growth means large, succulent plants, which do not flower very well, especially in a wet season. Geraniums with beautiful foliage rarely have really fine blooms, but they can be associated with other plants which are attractive by reason of their flowers.

Ivy-leaved Pelargoniums.—This section of the geranium still enjoys great favour. It is grown in the garden, in the conservatory, in vases, and in window-boxes. Its habit is loose and flowing. It droops flower-laden streamers from the summit of pillars and from window ledges. Its flowers are large and abundant, and they come in a long succession throughout the summer. The leaves have not the brilliant markings of the ordinary or Zonal Geranium, but the ivy shape is attractive. They may be given a somewhat better soil than the Zonals without fear of their making such exuberant growth as to flower badly. The Ivy-leaved Pelargoniums can be bought with single or double flowers, but the latter are much the more largely used. As they are tender, like the Zonals, they ought not to be planted before mid-May.

Calceolarias.—The Calceolaria is another component of the old-time ribbon border. The bedding type retains its stems after flowering, instead of dying down, and is therefore termed shrubby. It is indeed an evergreen, and although not quite hardy, it is by no means a tender plant. There is no great range of colours among the shrubby garden Calceolarias, although they are not all yellow. There are white, orange, red, and violet species in addition to the yellow. The Golden Glory is one of the finest. It is a splendid plant with large trusses, and the colour is bright yellow. Clumps of Calceolarias may be placed in selected positions in beds and borders, and they may be used in window-boxes also. They are so bright and cheerful that they merit attention for these purposes, and if used with discretion they do not overweight the garden.

Young Calceolarias are much more hardy than young Geraniums, and consequently they may be planted out a month earlier, without much risk of injury from frost. If planted early in good moist soil they have a chance of getting well rooted before the hot weather comes on. The plants may be set a foot apart. They will soon begin to flower, and will retain their beauty all the summer.

Lantanas.—These charming plants are very useful to bedders, and any amateur can grow them with ease. In foliage they resemble Heliotrope, and the flowers are borne in close heads. The colours are brilliant and varied. Inasmuch as the plants bloom freely and continuously and will grow in ordinary soil, they are undeniably useful. They have the defect of a straggly habit of growth, but this can be corrected by pinching in the early stages.

The Lantanas are useful for window-boxes, tubs, and large vases, as well as for beds.

Lobelias.—The blue Lobelia is a lowly plant, growing only a few inches high, of dense habit, and blooming so profusely as to cover itself with flowers. It is useful for putting round the edges of beds and for window-boxes. It can be sown from seed, but it is better to buy cuttings. May is a good time for planting. They are best planted in tufts about two inches thick, the clumps about three inches apart; they will then fill out and make a continuous line of colour. They will not spread, however, in a poor, dry soil. The ground should be moist and fertile. Given good land, the plants will remain in bloom until autumn.

Begonias.—Nothing in the way of dwarf plants can well be more beautiful than Tuberous Begonias. The foliage is handsome, the flowers are glorious, the form is beautiful, while the colours are as lovely as they are varied. Pure, snow-white, lemon and deep yellow, blush, soft pink and dainty rose, salmon, orange and brilliant scarlet—all these are present.

If the plants are healthy and growing, they will keep on flowering throughout the summer, and as long in autumn as the frost will keep away.

Amateurs who want to have a thoroughly successful bed of Tuberous Begonias ought to procure tubers in early March, bury them in a box of moist cocoa-nut fibre refuse or leaf-mould, and put them in a house. The heat and moisture will start them into growth quickly. If the material is moist, roots will push into it freely.

If the plants are six to eight inches high at the end of May, with a good mat of fibres, they will be in perfect condition for planting. The roots should not be shaken clear of the fibre when they are removed from the box; on the contrary, as much as clings to them must be allowed to remain.

The plants may be put eighteen inches apart in heavy, rich, moist soil, but somewhat closer in lighter, drier ground. They may be settled in with a good watering, and if the weather should keep dry after planting it will be well to give further waterings until they have got nicely into growth.

Regular hoeing will suffice to maintain steady progress. Flowers will come, and will keep on coming—in fact, there will be a steady stream of lovely blossoms. But the culminating display will be in the cool days of September, and (if frost permits) early October. The plants will be laden with brilliant blossoms, and the bed will be one of the sights of the garden. Fading flowers should be picked off regularly throughout the season.

The problem of wintering the plants is a simple one, as they will lose their leaves and stems by a process of natural decay. The tubers can be lifted, dried, and stored in any dry frost-proof place until spring.

Fuchsias.—The hardier of the Fuchsias, such as Corallina and Riccartoni, are sometimes introduced into beds and flower borders, but one can hardly speak of them as bedding plants in the ordinary sense. When they are used in the garden they are generally planted permanently, and cut to the ground every autumn. In cold districts it is well to cover the root-stocks with litter in November. This should not be removed, nor should the dead branches be cut off until the Fuchsias begin to grow in the spring. The garden Fuchsias are particularly graceful plants.

Heliotrope.—There is no reason why lovers of the fragrant "Cherry Pie" should not introduce it into their flower-beds. The richer hues, such as purplish blue and violet, will be found the most effective in beds.

Heliotropes are tender plants, and ought not to be put into the garden before the end of May. While they are not really particular as to soil, they do not grow to perfection in a close, retentive medium. On this account the soil ought to be thoroughly broken up, and if it is of a stiff, holding character it will be well to lighten and disintegrate it with burnt refuse, leaf-mould, road sweepings, or thoroughly decayed manure. The plants will require pegging down as they grow, and to allow room for this they should be planted eighteen inches apart.

WALLS AND FENCES

In small gardens the fence or wall area is very valuable, and it is most important to make use of every inch of space. This applies particularly to town gardens, and yet where plants are wanted the most they are often used the least. Beautiful flowers can never have a greater influence than when relieving the desolating and depressing bareness of terrace houses in towns and suburbs; moreover, the garden ground is almost invariably limited in such districts.

Probably the most common cause of house fronts being bare is that the people who occupy the dwellings have not acquired a love for gardening and an interest in plants. We must just hope that as time passes more and more will come to think of the exterior as well as the interior of their homes—will want pretty plants on the outside as well as attractive wall-papers within, and enjoy the pleasure of throwing open a bedroom window in the morning to look down on a pretty and fragrant display of flowers.

There is no good reason why the walls of town and suburban houses should not be covered. It is true that some beautiful plants that we should dearly like to recommend, such as the magnificent Crimson Rambler Rose, will not thrive, even with the most skilful and assiduous attention. But, as we shall see, there are other plants which will succeed.

Before considering the best plants for walls, however, let us take into account the principal things that make for failure and success.

The first practical point is improvement of the soil. The soil-area under a wall is often only a few inches wide and deep; the "soil" itself is half stones. Deepen the area to at least two feet, increase it if possible to a square yard for each plant, put in half-a-dozen good heaped spadefuls of turfy loam and manure, and the whole prospect is changed. With the increased body of soil there will at once be more moisture and more food available, but it will be advisable to give occasional soakings of water (and they should be real soakings, not driblets) in summer, together with weekly applications of liquid manure.

Our next important point is the period of planting. Failures often follow because the plants are put out in late spring, when the sun has become powerful.

Those who want to succeed with climbers and creepers should be encouraged to begin their operations earlier. The plants ought to be put in by the end of March (except in the case of tender annuals); then they will be nicely rooted by the time the hot weather comes, and will not merely be able to stand the heat, but will grow the better for it.

Planting Roses against a Wall. A, centre of plant kept open; B, the roots spread out in a wide shallow basin before covering in.

A third point is pruning.

Broadly speaking, an amateur can never do harm by cutting back a newly-planted climber, but may see the plants do badly if this is not practised. Cutting down is not generally done, because a person objects to buying a plant and then throwing away seven-eighths of it; he thinks it wasteful. It is the reverse. If a plant is cut back to within a few buds of the ground, the vigour of the roots will be concentrated on those buds, and strong shoots will result; moreover, shoots will come freely from the underground buds.

Given deep, fertile, moist (but not sodden) soil, early planting, and bold cutting back, wall plants will thrive in most places.

Among the many plants which can be used for this purpose, the following few might be mentioned:—

Roses.—For special varieties for growing on walls, see p. 595.

Clematises are very beautiful. There are different types of this flower, and some require more drastic treatment than others in respect of pruning. The Jackmanii, deep blue, the Madame Edouard André, red, and snow-white Jackmanii are three of the most useful, and they never do so well as when they are hard pruned every year. The flowering shoots of one year may be cut close back to their base in the spring of the following season, soon after they have started growing; and the plants will then push strong new shoots, which will produce far better flowers than would be borne on the weak shoots that would spring from the old flowering growths. With Fair Rosamond, Miss Bateman, and The Queen hard pruning must be avoided; all that is needed is thinning and trimming when the plants get crowded and tangled. The white Montana is also a useful, though small, Clematis.

Jasmine.—The yellow, winter-blooming Jasmine, nudiflorum, is a thorough suburban plant, and it is really attractive. It bears its small yellow flowers during mild spells throughout the whole winter, blooming in advance of the leaves. It is quite suitable for training against a low fence.

There is also a large form of the common, white, summer-flowering Jasmine, and there is a variety with golden leaves.

Honeysuckles.—Perhaps the best of these is the variegated Japanese, which has prettily veined leaves. Flexuosa is one of the best of the Honeysuckles that are grown principally for their flowers, and is very sweet. Then there is the winter-flowering Honeysuckle, which produces its sweet white flowers in February or March.

Dutchman's Pipe.—This quaint flower always interests people.

Ceanothus is a very attractive wall shrub. There are several species and varieties, mostly with pale blue or lavender-coloured flowers. They bloom profusely in summer, and may be grown successfully on south and west walls. The variety Gloire de Versailles is one of the best.

The Japanese Quince.—This will thrive in the suburbs and is one of the most valuable of wall shrubs. It blooms abundantly in winter and early spring. The typical species is bright red, but there are several varieties.

Veitch's Virginian Creeper.—This is too vigorous for the dividing wall, but may be planted to cover the walls of the house. It is of neat habit and will cling naturally to brick or stone walls by means of its own suckers, clothes the walls in a pleasing mantle of green in summer, and changes to warm red in autumn.

Variegated Ivy.—This is very suitable for the higher part of the party wall, and the kind called Hedera Helix rhombea is to be recommended. It is more vigorous in growth than most of the variegated sorts, and the leaves are prettily margined. To get the utmost vigour in Ivy, one must get the Irish, but that is green-leaved.

Kerrya Japonica.—The double variety of this plant must not be overlooked when the claims of comparatively dwarf plants are being considered, as they will be for certain positions. This is the plant which bears double yellow flowers nearly as large as Gardenias. It is very bright and cheerful, and it is easily grown.

Annual Ramblers.—Much can be done to beautify walls and fences in summer with annual flowers, notably Convolvuluses, Everlasting Peas, and Tropæolums (including Nasturtiums), and of those best raised under glass and planted out in May may be named Canary Creeper, Ornamental Gourds, and Maurandya.

Other handsome wall plants are procurable. Some amateurs may like to try the old *Wistaria sinensis*, the large-leaved Vines, or the Passion Flower, which, although not quite hardy, may be used.

WINDOW AND ROOM PLANTS

The cultivation of beautiful flowers in windows and rooms is one of those delightful pursuits which appeal to all classes.

Success in the cultivation of room plants turns partly on the choice of material and partly upon care in ventilating and watering. A great many plants will remain in health for months and even years in a light, airy room, but would become unhealthy in a week in a dark, stuffy one. There are one or two plants, notably the Aspidistra, which will stand almost anything, but the majority will not. Most plants do badly in rooms lit by open gas-burners if the window is not kept open at night. Ventilation is good for plants as well as for human beings.

It is not wise to choose very tender plants, because rooms, however warm during the day, are often cold at night. It is not prudent to rely on ferns, unless they be grown in a case, because the air is likely to be too dry for them.

If a tender plant is grown it should be removed from the neighbourhood of the window when the family retires to rest, and in cold weather covered with several thicknesses of newspaper. Should it happen to get touched by frost, it should not be stood near the fire, but placed in a cool shady place and sprinkled with cold water. This will save it if anything will.

The following are a few of the plants which will thrive in rooms with proper care and attention:—

Foliage Plants.—Palms.—These may be maintained in health for years in living rooms, even if gas is burned, with ordinary care and attention. They should be kept in or near the window in order that they may get plenty of light, being turned occasionally to bring a different side near the light. A compost of three parts fibrous loam, one part each of leaf mould and decayed manure, and a tenth of coarse washed sand will suit them. They should be watered when the pot rings hollow under the knuckles and at no other time. During mild showers they might be stood out of doors for an hour or two, as the rain will cleanse and freshen them. An occasional sponging with soft, tepid water will also do them good. This attention to the foliage is of great benefit to palms. Re-potting once a year will be ample, and this may be done in spring. When they have got to the largest convenient size of pot, top dressing may be substituted. The plant may be turned out of the pot, the outer casing of soil crumbled away, the drainage re-arranged, and the plant replaced in the pot, fresh earth being rammed down the sides and packed on the top. The pot should not be filled quite full; an inch of space must be left for water—two inches in the case of a large pot. It is also essential that the pots should be stood in saucers of water, in order to prevent the mess that would be made by water escaping through the drainage at every watering, but the water should not be allowed to rest in the saucers all day, except in summer; and even then periodical emptyings will have to be resorted to, so as to avoid an overflow.

An ounce of superphosphate to the gallon of water, applied once a week or so, or a pinch of one of the advertised fertilisers spread on the surface and watered in, will do good.

Ferns.—Every grower of room plants likes to have a few ferns.

The Crested Ribbon Fern and the Maidenhair are two that will thrive with care. The Maidenhair is not an easy plant to manage in a room, as it does not like changes of temperature; at the same time it has been known to remain in excellent condition for several years. Great care in watering is necessary, and the plants must not be allowed to get frozen. The Ribbon Fern does very well with care. It is charming in a small state for the table. The Sea Spleenwort, the Lady Fern, the Male Fern, the Shield Fern, and the Hart's Tongue may also be tried. The best time for repotting ferns is the spring, when the new fronds are seen to be moving. The compost recommended for palms may be altered to the extent of reducing the quantity of loam by one half and substituting peat.

If a Maidenhair should fall into ill-health it is advisable to cut it hard back, and let it break again.

The Aspidistra.—The Parlour Palm, as it is often called, is not a true palm. It is one of the most valuable of house plants, because it will thrive under most conditions and does not succumb quickly to unfavourable circumstances.

Most people prefer the variegated Aspidistra to the plain green, and are generally disconsolate when a variegated plant loses its silvery patches. They should learn that this is generally due to providing too rich a soil. The more luxuriant the growth the greater the likelihood of a preponderance of green. Plain loam and sand will suffice; manure and leaf-mould should both be avoided.

The transference to the open air during showers, the sponging of the leaves, and careful watering are all beneficial.

The India-rubber Plant.—This is not quite so successful in a room, as draughts and changes of temperature cause the lower leaves to fall. But with care success is possible. It should have the same treatment as palms.

The Parlour Fig.—This plant has broad, deeply-cut foliage, with very thick leaf-stalks. It will keep healthy in a room for a long time if carefully watered. It will not endure draughts like an Aspidistra.

Berried Plants.—There are two berry-bearing plants admirably adapted for room decoration, namely, *Ardisia crenata* and the Winter Cherry. The former, although little known, is the better of the two, so far as endurance is concerned at all events. Its berries are much smaller than those of the Winter Cherry, and are darker in colour. They hang on the plants for many months, and a plant will retain its beauty in a room for more than half a year if it is properly watered and the room ventilated. The Ardisia will thrive in the palm compost.

Flowering Plants.—The number of flowering plants available for rooms turns on whether there is a glass-house or not. The owner of a greenhouse will be constantly bringing nice plants that are just beginning to bloom into the rooms. They may be plants that would not thrive in a dwelling-house all the year round, but are quite suitable for embellishing it for a few weeks.

Bulbs will be valuable in the winter. They may be grown in water, in pots of earth, or in vases of peat-moss litter, as directed on p. 589. White Roman Hyacinths must be particularly borne in mind, because they are so beautiful both for the dinner-table and the window.

The beautiful white Arum Lily, too, must not be overlooked. If it is kept in a pot throughout the year care should be taken to give it abundance of water, as it is a semi-aquatic plant, and soon suffers from drought. There is no need to keep it in the house all the summer through. It may be stood out of doors when it ceases flowering. That it is a grand room plant is proved by the sight of splendid old plants which bloom freely every year. The Godfrey is a splendid variety.

Early Tulips, and Daffodils of the Trumpet and Chalice sections, are very useful for rooms. The Duc Van Thol Tulips will give very early flowers; and of the Narcissi, *obvallaris* (Tenby Daffodil), Golden Spur, and Henry Irving will be among the first in flower.

The Zonal Geranium is one of the most successful of window plants. It is so gay and so accommodating and a profuse bloomer. There are many beautiful varieties. There are also the ivy-leaved and scented-leaved Geraniums, which are both pretty and sweet. They are quite summer plants.

Marguerites are stock favourites for windows, both inside and out. Their strong points are their free and persistent blooming and their attractive foliage. They are easy to keep healthy so long as the leaf-mining maggot can be kept at bay.

WINDOW-BOXES

For those who have very small gardens or perhaps no garden at all, flowers in window-boxes form a special attraction, and if well attended to they certainly help to make the outside of a house bright and attractive.

An effort should be made to keep the boxes filled with suitable flowers all the year round, and even in the winter the flowering plants can be replaced by pretty evergreens, such as the Golden Privet, Winter Cherry, and Dwarf Holly Bushes, &c.

If boxes are used they must be made to fit the sill, but there is no objection to their over-hanging a little in front, provided that there is no fear of over-balancing. There must be a strip at each end, thickened in front, to keep the box clear of the sill, and level. A number of holes should be bored or burnt in the bottom of the box to permit of water escaping. These holes may be covered with pieces of broken flower-pot.

The boxes can then be filled up with good soil.

Some people prefer to have plants in pots on their window-sills, because of the facility for making changes. There is no real objection to this, but the grower must remember two things: the first, that blocks or a strip of wood must be placed along sloping sills to raise the front of the pots and bring them level, otherwise the plants cannot be properly watered; the second, that a support will be required to prevent their being blown off. A framework to fit the window can easily be made, and if it is faced with virgin cork the pots will be hidden.

For spring decoration of window-boxes there is nothing prettier than bulbs (see p. 587), and these can very well be buried between the plants already there. Hyacinths, Tulips, Snowdrops, Crocuses, or Daffodils will all give pleasure.

When bulbs are used in window-boxes it is a good plan to associate coloured Primroses with them, as the latter bloom later than most bulbs, and maintain the display. They are beautiful flowers, and will be at their best from the middle of April to the middle of May.

All the popular, free-flowering plants, such as Geraniums and Ivy-leaved Pelargoniums, Fuchsias, Marguerites, Begonias, China Asters, Chrysanthemums, *Campanula isophylla*, and Creeping Jenny will be available for summer and autumn bloom.

It is a mistake to crowd too many different kinds of plants into the boxes; they only spoil each other; the great point is to choose what will bloom best in the particular aspect, and to try to get a nice succession of flowers.

Another important point in window gardening

is to keep the plants well watered and never to allow the soil to become too dry. Even although rain may fall, it very often happens that the boxes do not get much natural watering. The watering ought to be thorough ; a mere surface watering of the soil does more harm than good, as it only attracts the roots upwards. A little liquid manure or a sprinkling of Clay's fertiliser from time to time will help to improve the soil and keep the plants flourishing.

INSECTS AND OTHER ENEMIES

The best of plant cultivators are troubled by insect enemies, although perhaps less severely than the worst. Careful cultivation combined with tidiness and cleanliness are great preventives. There should be no heaps of rubbish near the flower-bed, such as an accumulation of weeds, heaps of stones, prunings of plants, &c., as these will just be hot-beds for insects to breed. Insect-eating birds, such as starlings, blackbirds, and tits, should be encouraged, and, finally, when insects do appear prompt action should be taken in all cases.

The following are some of the preparations used for the destruction of insects, slugs, &c.

Lime.—This can be applied either dry or in a liquid state. It is perhaps best applied in the form of dry freshly-slaked quick-lime. Lime-water may be made by putting a lump of lime of the size of a cocoa-nut in a pail of water in the morning, and straining off the liquid when it is clear.

Paraffin Oil and Soap Emulsion.—Boil one pint of soft soap in two pints of water, and stir in, after removal from the fire and while still boiling hot, half a pint of paraffin oil; the working in of the oil when the soap is boiling will go far to ensure amalgamation. Dilute with five gallons of water. The mixture must be thoroughly worked up by filling a syringe from, and emptying it into, the vessel repeatedly. It is best sprayed lightly on the plants towards evening with a fine syringe.

Soap-suds.—Make in the same way as above, omitting the paraffin. Lifebuoy soap may be used in some cases instead of soft soap.

Quassia Water.—Take half a pound of quassia chips and soak them in half a gallon of cold water for two or three hours. Then boil slowly eight or ten hours. Strain and add water to make five gallons. Melted soap is sometimes added as well.

Tobacco Water.—Steep one ounce of strong shag tobacco in one quart of water and strain when the water is well coloured. Some soft soap may be added. Tobacco is also used in the form of snuff dusted on infested plants.

Sulphur.—This may be used in the form of the yellow powder known as flowers of sulphur, or as sulphide of potassium. The latter is very cheap and may be applied conveniently in solution. Dissolve one ounce of the chemical and two ounces of soft soap in five gallons of water, and spray the mixture on the plants in as fine a state as possible.

Special Preparations.—In recent years the most common means of keeping insects down is by vaporising preparations of nicotine, which is the poisonous principle of tobacco. The substance, and a small appliance for vaporising and distributing it, are sold together in handy packets, varying in size according to the number of plants to be treated. The packets can be bought from all seedsmen and florists, and they are not expensive. One that is extremely well known is the "XL ALL." Another is West's. These preparations must always be used strictly in accordance with the instruction given.

The following are some of the most common garden pests with simple remedies for their destruction.

Greenfly.—This attacks all kinds of plants and will work more havoc on a weak specimen than on a strong one. It increases at a tremendons rate. Syringe the plants well with soap-suds or paraffin oil and soap emulsion. Tobacco water and quassia water are also good. When the points of shoots are affected they should be dipped into quassia water. Flowers in pots may be dusted with Keating's powder.

Red Spider.—This is a tiny mite which forms colonies on the under leaves of many plants and spins webs. Sulphur solution syringed on the plants will sometimes check it. Failing this try tobacco water or soap and paraffin emulsion. The leaves must be sprayed on the under as well as the upper side. The red spider is almost invisible to the naked eye, but the effect of its operations is only too plain in the loss of substance and green in the leaves, and in the appearance of red or bronze patches or the foliage turning yellow. Another excellent remedy is to spray the plants with common salt diluted in water at the strength of one ounce of salt to two gallons of water. If this is done in the cool of the evening once a week, and the plants syringed next day with clean water, it will have the effect of keeping them clean.

Thrips.—These little black insects do considerable damage to the tips of flower stems, young foliage and flower buds, very often rendering the first opening flowers useless. Treat in the same way as greenfly.

Earwigs attack and eat young foliage, but are more destructive to flowers, concealing themselves at the base of the petals upon which they feed. An excellent trap consists of a hollow bamboo thrust into the soil beside the plant; the earwigs will secrete themselves in this at night, where they can be captured and killed by means of a wire pushed down the hollow of the bamboo. The old-fashioned flower-pot trap, filled with dry hay or moss, is also a simple and good way of catching them.

Fungoid Enemies.—There are several fungi which attack plants, but mildew is the most common. This coats the leaves of indoor plants with a grey powder, and they lose their substance and fall. These fungi, and particularly mildew, are commonly the result of faulty ventilation and if the plants are in a draught. They also come when the air is close and heavy. A spraying of sulphur is the best remedy. It is best to carry the plants outside for the purpose, as the solution will stain paint. The fungoid disease of chrysanthemums, known as "rust," may be attacked by the same means.

Caterpillars.—Syringe the plants or bushes with soap-suds or with paraffin and soap emulsion.

Slugs.—Lime is a valuable deterrent and slugs detest it in all forms. It is best applied at night when the slugs are likely to be feeding. Two applications should be made at intervals of about twenty minutes, because the slug can slough his skin and so get rid of one dose of the hot powder; but the second catches him at a hopeless disadvantage and finishes him off. Lime and water poured on the beds after dark will thin the slugs down. Soot spread thickly on the soil round the plants and then worked in is also good. It must not be used in a fresh state or it will destroy as many plants as slugs.

Worms in Pots.—Lime-water will generally bring them to the surface, when they can be removed.

Mice.—In gardens where mice are numerous all seeds should be thoroughly coated with red lead prior to sowing, as the mice do not like this. Several traps ought also to be set in and near their haunts.

Leaf-mining Grubs.—These are hatched from eggs deposited by flies between the upper and lower skins of the leaf. Cinerarias and Marguerites are specially prone to their attack. Spray the plants with tobacco water or a special insecticide.

Mealy-Bug.—This is a very offensive insect, as it clothes the stems and foliage of plants with a filthy white mass, making them disagreeable to handle as well as unhealthy. It does not spread as fast as greenfly, but it is more difficult to destroy. Treat in the same way as greenfly.

Wireworm is one of the most dreaded of pests. While some soils are quite free, others are badly infested with it, and until they are removed no plant is safe. The ordinary remedies do little good, but trapping may be tried. Slices of carrot, turnip, or potato should be buried about an inch below the surface and left over-night. If a small wooden skewer is put in each they will easily be found and examined the next morning. When the ground is very much infested it should be treated with gas-lime. When the soil is worked in the autumn the gas-lime may be sprinkled on it after digging in the proportion of at least half a pound to a square yard. The winter rains will wash it in and kill wireworm and other larvæ. As this is injurious to plant life, nothing must be planted for nine months after the application.

GARDEN TOOLS

The amateur gardener will require little beyond the following:—

Hoe.—One from six to seven inches wide will be the most suitable for general purposes. Price about 2s.

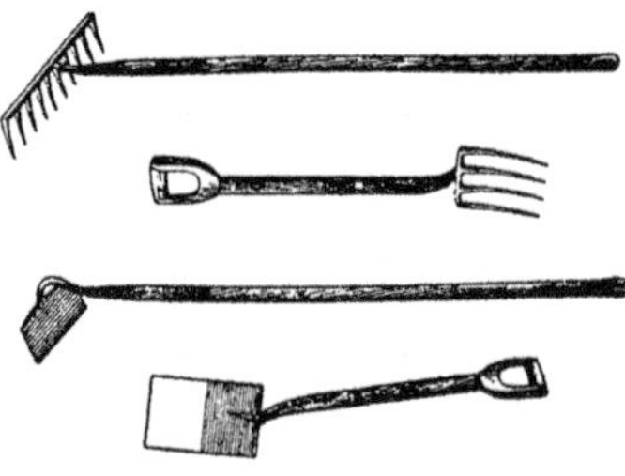

Rake, Fork, Hoe and Spade.

Rake.—Choose one about twelve inches wide. Price 2s. 6d.

Spade.—No. 3 is a very convenient size for general use. Price 3s. to 5s.

Fork.—A large fork will be required for turning the soil of borders. Price about 3s.—also a small one for weeding, 1s.

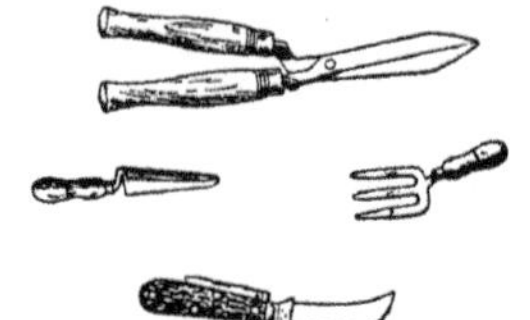

Shears, Trowel, Weeding Fork and Pruning Knife

Trowel.—For planting purposes—1s. to 1s. 6d.

Shears.—For cutting edges and trimming hedges—3s. to 4s.

Watering-Can.—One of galvanised sheet iron with a movable rose will be the most useful—2s. 6d.

Knife.—For pruning—2s.

Hammer and Nails.—For nailing plants to wall. Hammer 1s. 6d., and nails 3d. per lb.

A pair of strong gloves and pair of scissors.

If there is a lawn to keep in order a mowing-machine will also be required. They may be purchased from 25s. upwards, but an effort should be made to buy one of first-rate quality as it will give much more satisfaction.

A basket for holding the smaller tools, one or

Garden Basket.

two open baskets for carrying purposes, a reel of wire, a syringe, a foot-rule, and a broom will also be found useful.

Garden tools should always have a place for themselves where they can be kept in a dry and clean condition. Many of them can be hung up, and they will require little space.

Water-cans should be turned upside down when not in use; and if any tools are not likely to be used for a while, they should be rubbed with grease to prevent them rusting.

To Send Flowers by Post.—When cutting flowers for travelling one must be guided somewhat by weather conditions, but, generally speaking, they should be cut and placed in water five or six hours before being packed. If they are cut in the evening it must be before the dew begins to fall. Place the flowers in water and stand them in a dry place. If the weather is wet, place them in vases or jars in the house where there is just a trifle of heat. They will be found to dry quickly if treated in this manner. The packing must be done carefully. A flat hamper is the best for the purpose, as it is light, and moisture does not accumulate as it does in boxes. Failing this, a light wooden or strong cardboard box can be used. If the weather is very hot and dry, line the basket with waxed paper, as this prevents too much evaporation. If the weather is very damp, then use very soft tissue paper, and this will absorb a fair amount of moisture. Do not pack the blooms too tightly; on the other hand, if the basket is not full, it must be padded with tissue paper to prevent the flowers shaking. Never use damp cotton wool in packing. The packet must be marked, "Flowers with care." Immediately on arrival the flowers should be unpacked and placed in tepid water slightly salted.

HOUSEHOLD REPAIRS AND UPHOLSTERY

It is a source of great economy in a household when one of its members shows an aptitude for executing simple home repairs, and can also turn her hand to upholstery work and carpentry. Not only can the money, which would otherwise have to be expended in hiring workmen to do the various odd jobs, be saved, but the home upholsterer can add to the beauty of her surroundings by making pretty curtains and hangings, and fashioning dainty little articles of furniture at a comparatively small cost. Many useful hints in regard to home upholstery and repairs are given in this article, and the various methods of painting, papering, and distempering walls are fully described.

The Household Tool Chest.—It is always useful to have a certain number of simple tools ready at hand for doing the various odd jobs which are required from time to time in every home. Although small chests ready fitted with tools can be bought, this is not a plan to be recommended unless one is prepared to pay a high price, and even then it will be found that many of the tools supplied are never required.

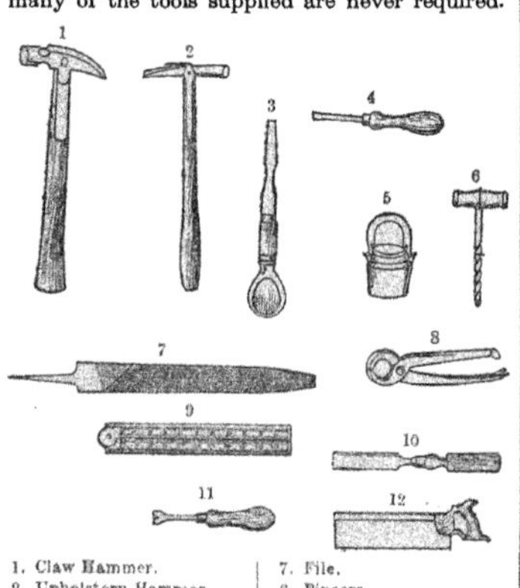

1. Claw Hammer.	7. File.
2. Upholstery Hammer.	8. Pincers.
3. Screw-driver.	9. Foot-rule.
4. Brog or Bradawl.	10. Chisel.
5. Glue-pot.	11. Tack-lifter.
6. Gimlet.	12. Saw.

It is much better to buy the few necessary tools of a first-class quality, and with care they will last for years.

The following will in most cases be found useful:—

2 Hammers—one strong and heavy and the other small and light for upholstery or light carpentry.

1 Screw-driver.	1 Gimlet.
1 Saw.	1 Bradawl or Brog.
1 Pair pincers.	1 Glue-pot.
1 Tack-lifter.	1 File.
1 Foot-rule.	A strong knife.
1 Chisel.	

Also an assortment of tacks, nails, screws, hooks, &c., suitable for the purpose in hand, which can be bought as occasion arises. A nail-box should have different divisions in which the various kinds of nails can be kept separately.

Tools must be kept carefully or they will be unfit for good work. They must be protected from rust, and if they are not likely to be used for some time they should be rubbed over with a little grease.

To Prepare Glue.—Break some glue into small pieces and put it into the inner part of the glue-pot with cold water to cover it. Allow this to soak some time and then pour off any superfluous water. Then half fill the outer vessel with water, place the double pot at the side of the fire, and allow the glue to melt gradually, stirring occasionally with a stick. The glue must be applied with a brush or with a small pad made by tying a piece of flannel on to the end of a stick.

TO PAPER A ROOM

This is not a very difficult matter unless the room is a very lofty one. Like all other work it requires practice before it can be done very skilfully, and the amateur would be wise to try her 'prentice hand on an attic or small room before she attempts to paper one of more importance.

New wall-paper must never be put on the top of old, as this is most unhygienic. So the first step to take is to strip the wall of its old covering. Take a pail of hot water and a large white-wash brush and go over the wall with this, soaking the paper well. Allow the damp to soak in, and then scrape the paper off with an old knife or a piece of slate. If there are any holes in the plaster, fill these up with plaster of Paris made into a paste with water or size, or paste a piece of white paper over them. Next wash the wall over with a coating of weak size, and when this is dry the wall will be ready for papering.

Size is a jelly-like substance (8d. per lb.), generally used in the proportion of one pound to one gallon of water. This must be melted slowly over the fire and kept warm while in use.

Wall-papers are usually twenty-one inches wide, and are sold in lengths of twelve yards, so it will not be difficult to calculate the quantity required. If a patterned paper is chosen, an extra allowance must be made for matching the pattern on the various strips, but the amateur should choose either a plain or a striped paper in order to avoid this extra trouble of matching the pieces. Cheap wall-papers can be bought from 6d. to 1s. per piece, and, of course, there are many at a much higher price.

In addition to the paper, the following will be required: a pair of large scissors, a pail for paste, a paste brush, one or two soft dusters, or another dry brush for smoothing on the paper, and some good paste.

To make the paste :—

Take one pound of flour and mix it to a smooth paste with cold water; then add more water until the mixture is of a creamy consistency. Boil this over the fire in a saucepan and add a little size or glue which will make the paste more tenacious. It is a good plan also to add a little alum (one and a half ounces), as this will prevent the paste from turning sour. The paste should be of the consistency of gruel when ready.

The paper must be cut in lengths according to the different parts of the room it has to cover, making it two inches longer than the actual measurements in every case. Then trim off the margins close to the pattern on one side and leave half an inch on the other. The pasting must either be done on a kitchen-table, or on newspapers spread on the floor. Paste one piece at a time, putting weights on one end of the paper if it is inclined to roll up. Be careful to paste all smoothly, and pay particular attention to the edges. Thin paper may be hung at once; a thicker make should lie for two or three minutes to soften it, as it will then be less likely to tear in the lifting. When carrying the paper to the wall loop up the lower end of the paper with the two pasted sides together to prevent it from catching on anything. Then place one end to the top of the moulding or ceiling, and the left-hand edge to the corner line, cutting off any unevenness if necessary. When these two edges are well in position press the surface to the wall in every part with a duster or clean dry brush, first down the middle and then outwards to the sides. Avoid any rubbing which might spoil the colour of the paper. Unfold the lower part of the paper, and continue it right down to the top of the skirting-board length, where any surplus must be cut off. A few wrinkles and blisters may appear at first, but these will disappear when the paper dries and contracts. Place the next strip of paper so that its trimmed edge covers the margin of the first strip. It is always best to make two cut edges meet at the corners. Short pieces above doors and windows must be neatly fitted, and if there are any irregular parts to be covered use plenty of paste, as this will soften the paper and enable it to be moulded into any shape.

DISTEMPERING

This is painting with whitening and size mixed to a paste with water, and some colouring matter added. It is generally applied to plaster. When used in a natural white colour it is called white-washing.

To Prepare White-wash.—Take six pounds of whitening (cost about 3d.), put it into a clean pail, cover it with water; let it stand twenty-four hours and pour the water off. This may be repeated several times if the wash is desired very white, but for ordinary purposes once is sufficient. Then add half a pound size dissolved in half a gallon of hot water and mix all to a creamy consistency. Add also one table-spoonful of powdered alum and enough washing blue to make it a natural white colour. Strain the wash and use when cold: it should be almost like a jelly and slightly sticky. It must be kept well mixed when in use. The above quantities will be sufficient to white-wash a small room or a good-sized ceiling.

Coloured Distemper is made by adding some colouring pigment to the above white-wash, such as yellow ochre for a cream tint, yellow ochre and black for stone colour, vermilion or Venetian red for pink, indigo for blue, and so on. These colours can be bought at any colour shop, and must be mixed smoothly with a little water before adding them to the wash. Add a very small quantity at a time, and then test the colour on a piece of paper. It must be remembered that the colour will look very much deeper in the pail than it will when dry on the wall.

Patent preparations can now be bought which will save the amateur the trouble of mixing the distemper, and these are quite inexpensive and easy to use. Full directions are given with each.

If the distemper is not to be used at once, a little water should be poured on the top to prevent a skin forming. It must always be well stirred up before use.

To Distemper a Wall.—The dust must first be brushed off and the wall then washed over with clean warm water and a brush. The water must be changed as soon as it becomes dirty. Then give the walls a coating of thin size and let them dry. If there are any cracks or holes, they must be filled up with plaster of Paris and whitening made into a paste with water and size, using one part plaster of Paris to three parts whitening.

For applying the wash use a good distemper brush, which will cost about 6s. Commence at the top of the wall and work downwards with even strokes backwards and forwards. Too much wash must not be taken up at one time or there will be splashing, and the work must be done as quickly and expeditiously as possible. The brush ought only to be put into the distemper half-way up its bristles, and then the surplus should be pressed out before applying

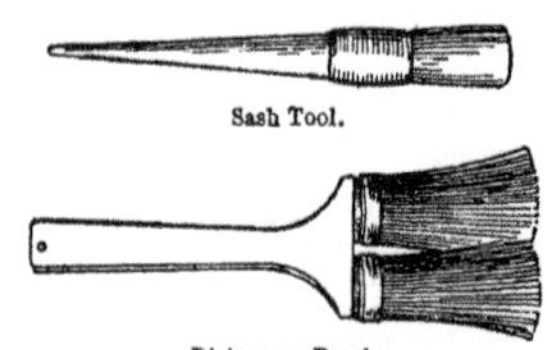

Sash Tool.

Distemper Brush.

the brush to the wall. Doors and windows should be kept shut while this work is being done to prevent the wash drying too quickly and looking patchy. When finished, a current of air may be allowed to pass through the room.

To White-wash a Ceiling.—This can only be done after considerable practice, and unless the ceiling is small and low the work should scarcely be attempted by a woman, as it means too much climbing about on steps and stretching of the arms and body. The ceiling must be prepared first, in the same way as a wall, by washing and then applying a coat of thin size. The white-wash should be put on in very even strokes along the length of the ceiling, the brush being worked evenly backwards and forwards. White-wash dries so quickly that unless it is applied quickly the work will have a patchy appearance.

PAINTING AND ENAMELLING WOOD

This work is very much simplified nowadays, as all colours can be bought ready prepared, and it is much better for the amateur not to attempt mixing the colours herself. Oil and colour men will supply any colour from about 6d. per pound, and sometimes they will lend a brush as well, only if painting is done to any great extent it is much better to possess one's own brushes. Brushes are expensive articles, but good work cannot be done without them, and there is no economy in buying cheap ones. Fibre brushes, for instance, are sold at a much lower price than those made of bristles, but after they have been used a few times the fibres begin to drop out.

In order to obtain satisfactory results in painting, the article to be painted must be thoroughly clean and the surface smooth. Remove all dust, and wash the surface thoroughly with soap and water; then allow the wood to dry, and fill up any holes with putty or cement. If there is any roughness this should be smoothed down with sand-paper. The professional painter will very often remove an old coating of paint before putting on another, especially if the former is blistered or broken in any way. This is done by the application of heat or some stripping fluid. It is work that can scarcely be undertaken by the home worker, and in many cases it is not necessary. When painting new wood a first coat of weak size will be necessary to prevent the paint soaking into the wood. The paint must be well stirred with a piece of stick before commencing and then applied with a brush with smooth, steady strokes. It must not be laid on too thickly, but well brushed in with the grain of the wood until no brush mark is visible. Two brushes are usually required, a small one for the intricate parts and a larger one for the wider surfaces. These brushes are called sash tools. The tips of the brushes only should be put into the paint. If two coats of paint are required the first must be allowed to become quite dry before the second is applied. New wood requires at least two coats, and sometimes a coat of varnish is put on the top.

Enamel Paints which are prepared with varnish are much used nowadays. They have a very smooth and glossy appearance when dry. They are used in the same way as other paints, and are especially useful in renovating plain wood furniture, water-cans, light wooden articles, &c.

When paint is not in use it should have a little water poured over the surface. This will keep it liquid and in good condition for future use.

CARE OF PAINT AND VARNISH BRUSHES

Before using a new brush it should be soaked in water for some hours. This swells the bristles and renders them less likely to fall out. Paint brushes that are in constant use should be kept in a tin with water or sufficient turpentine to cover the bristles. When they are finished with squeeze the paint well out on the edge of the paint pot, wipe the brushes with a rag, clean in turpentine, and then wash with plain soap and water and put aside to dry. Varnish brushes should be kept in the varnish while in use and then cleaned in the same way as paint brushes.

Old paint brushes can be cleaned by soaking

them over-night in strong soda-water and then washing them out thoroughly. The bridles of the brushes, whether of cord or metal, should not be allowed to soak in the water.

TO STAIN FLOORS

If it is a border round a room that requires staining, measure the distance from the wall all round and make a mark with chalk or a large-coloured pencil, always remembering to allow for an inch or two of staining to come under the carpet on all sides. Then knock down any nail heads with a hammer and fill up holes and crevices with a little putty, making the floor quite even. Sweep the floor over just before putting on the first coating of stain.

For a simple stain take two ounces of permanganate of potash in crystals and dissolve it in one pint of boiling water. Apply this with a soft pad on the end of a stick, putting it on the way of the grain. Be careful not to soil the hands. Allow the first coating to dry, and then apply a second in the same way until the floor is dark enough. A floor that is stained for the first time will require more stain than one that is just being renewed. Leave the floor to dry, and then rub over with a flannel dipped in linseed oil. Leave again for a day and polish with bees'-wax and turpentine (see p. 65).

The above is a very simple and inexpensive staining, but it will be found satisfactory.

Ready-prepared stains of various kinds can also be bought from any colour merchants. They can be had in different shades, but walnut stain is perhaps the most suitable for a sitting-room. Some of these stains contain varnish, others require a coat of varnish put on the top. The former are on the whole the best to use. When putting on the stain apply it to one or two boards only at a time, as it dries very quickly and is apt to have a marked appearance, unless each small piece is finished before another is started. Be careful not to splash the skirting-board, and if an accident should occur wipe off the stain at once and wash the board. It is always better to use two brushes when applying the stain, a small one for painting near the skirting-board and a larger one for the other parts. After the staining is finished the floor should not be walked on for a day or two, and it should be kept as free from dust as possible. A plank supported on two footstools may be placed across the doorway.

TO ENAMEL A BATH

First thoroughly wash the bath with hot water, soap, and soda to get rid of all grease, and let it become quite dry. If there are any rough surfaces, rub them down with fine sand or glass-paper and brush away any dust this may make. Then take some good bath enamel and give the bath its first coating. White, cream, eau-de-nil, or flesh-coloured enamel may be used. Allow the enamel to become quite dry, and smooth it over again with the sand-paper if necessary. A second coating of the enamel must then be applied and allowed to dry as before. Two coatings are generally sufficient, but in some cases three may be necessary. It is very important to let one coating dry before putting on another, or the work will not be successful. Some enamel may take one or two days to dry. When finished fill the bath with cold water and allow it to remain two days. This will harden the paint and take away the smell.

TO MEND CHINA

Broken china that is to be used for liquids or to be frequently washed requires to be mended with rivets, and this can only be done by an expert. The rivets will cost 2d. each.

In the case of ornaments the pieces may often be united with cement, and with care will hold together for years. The cement may either be bought ready prepared or can be made at home. The following are two different methods of making it :—

(1) Take a little plaster of Paris and mix it to a creamy paste with beaten white of egg just before use.

(2) Take half an ounce gum acacia, dissolve it in water and strain. Add enough plaster of Paris to make a creamy paste just before use.

Both these cements must only be mixed in *very* small quantities as required.

China should be mended as soon as possible after it is broken; if allowed to lie about the fine points or edges get rubbed or broken, and in consequence the joining will not be so close and will show more. Wash the broken pieces very carefully and then make them thoroughly dry and as warm as the hand can bear by putting them in the oven or near the fire. Use as little cement as possible—just enough to coat the two surfaces to be joined, and apply it with a match or fine piece of stick. Any surplus cement must be squeezed out and rubbed off at once. After pressing the two pieces together try to place the china in such a position that the weight of the pieces will tend to keep them together. If it is a plate, for instance, it might be propped up between two piles of books. Sometimes a binder is necessary, and an india-rubber band can be used with good effect. One piece must always be allowed to dry on before joining another, so if there are a number of fragments they might be joined in pairs one day and the next day two pairs put together, and so on until all is in shape.

BURST PIPES OR BOILER

Accidents of this kind usually occur after a frost if the water in the pipes has been allowed to freeze. The expanding of the water in freezing breaks the pipe, but it is only when the thaw comes that the water runs out.

When a leak occurs anywhere the stop-cock should at once be shut off so as to prevent more water from leaving the cistern. It is important, therefore, to know where the stop-cock is and also to see that it is kept in a turnable condition. Every second that is wasted may mean serious damage, and on no account must this special tap become so stiff that it cannot be moved.

Another plan is to flatten the pipe just at the break and thus check the flow of water. To do this slip a piece of wood or other resisting substance between the pipe and the wall and hammer the pipe sharply on to it. By this means the plaster of the wall need not be injured.

The accident of a burst pipe can generally be avoided by keeping the house warm enough. Where pipes are exposed to a very cold atmosphere it is a good plan to keep a gas jet or a small lamp burning on frosty nights.

An empty house, where there are no fires, is the one most likely to suffer. In this case it is safer to turn off the water-supply at the main and to empty the water out of the pipes if frosty weather is feared.

A more serious accident still is the bursting of a kitchen boiler. This is due to the boiler having run dry and the fire being kept on. If, on account of frost or any other reason, the hot water ceases to run, the kitchen fire should at once be put out.

GAS ESCAPES

An escape of gas may be caused by a break in the pipe—perhaps the result of a nail having been driven into it—by a badly-made joint having broken or given way, or because a screw-joint has become loose. The usual method of applying a lighted match or taper in order to find out the place of escape is a very risky one, and it is safer to avoid it altogether unless the escape is a very small one. If it is a big escape the safest plan is to turn off the gas at the meter and to allow a good current of air to pass through the room where the smell occurs. Then turn on the gas again for a few minutes, and you will no doubt be able to trace the hole quite readily by the smell or perhaps hear where it filters through the pipe.

A small hole can always be mended temporarily by patching it up with a good layer of soap or lard. Another way of stopping the escape is to flatten the pipe close to the faulty spot, but this may have the disadvantage of shutting off the gas from other parts of the house. If a pipe breaks in any part it may be temporarily mended by slipping in a piece of india-rubber tubing over the two ends and fastening it on with string.

The above are only temporary makeshifts, and the damaged pipe should be properly attended to at the earliest possible opportunity.

TO RE-MAKE A WOOL MATTRESS

When a wool mattress becomes slumpy it should be re-made; in fact, from a hygienic point of view this should be done every year.

Take the mattress into an unused room (one without a carpet is best) and spread it on a sheet on the floor. Take off the rounds of leather on the mattress, open one end and empty the wool on to the sheet. Then have the cover washed, starched and ironed. Pick the wool apart with the fingers or with a machine for the purpose. It is rather a tedious business to do it with the fingers, and sometimes it is possible to hire a machine from an upholsterer. The French housewife generally does this piece of work in her garden. When ready replace the wool in the case, keeping the mattress very even, and sew up as before. For sewing on the rounds of leather a long needle threaded with twine will be required.

TO RE-MAKE FEATHER PILLOWS

This should be done periodically when the covers become soiled. The simplest and tidiest method is to prepare the new or clean tick first by rubbing the inside over with bees'-wax or yellow soap, as this will prevent the points of the feathers from working through. Then make an opening in the old pillow the same size as that in the new tick and sew both openings together. Shake the feathers from one to the other, pin the seam before undoing the stitches, and the old case can be removed and the seam sewn up without any feathers flying about the room. Some people turn the feathers into a bath and wash and dry them before re-making the pillow, but this is rather a laborious and unpleasant operation. If the feathers require special cleaning it is better to send the pillows to a bedding manufacturer to have them properly re-made.

TO MAKE BLINDS

The simple blind on a roller is very easily made by the home worker. For material there is considerable choice in self-coloured or printed linens and hollands. If the blinds are being made for the front of the house, it is better to have them all alike, while for back or side-windows this is not so necessary.

When taking measurements take the length of the blind and six inches over to allow for a hem and a piece to go round the roller at the top. For the width measure the size of the roller less half an inch, so that the blind will be quarter of an inch narrower than the roller on both sides. Very often it is possible to buy the material the exact width required, as the rollers are generally made in regulation sizes, but, if not, allowance must be made for a one and three-quarter inch hem on each side.

It is very important to have a blind cut evenly; if badly cut it will pull up and down badly. Both top and bottom must be cut by the thread, and all hems must be measured exactly with a foot-rule or inch-tape, and a small pencil or chalk mark made where the hem has to come. The side hems must only be turned over once and then tacked down with herring-bone stitch (see p. 397). For the bottom hem mark a half-inch turning and a one and three-quarter inch hem. The latter will be wide enough to allow of a lath being slipped in, into which one end of the cord is fixed by making a hole through material and wood.

To fix the blind to the roller put a tack at each end on the raw edge of the material, turn the roller round until it is covered with the material, and then sew on with a needle and strong cotton. By this means the roller is quite covered and there is little danger of the blind tearing away.

It is not often that a blind is left perfectly plain as above; it is more usual to trim the edge with a piece of fringe or with some strong appliqué lace. When ornamentation of this kind is added, the blind itself must be cut shorter to allow for the width of the trimming. Sometimes a piece of lace insertion is let in as well just above the lath, or fancy-shaped medallions of the appliqué lace.

A MANTELPIECE DRAPERY

Perhaps the simplest way of hiding an ugly mantelpiece is the somewhat old-fashioned one of covering it with a cloth drapery of some sort. A plain board must first be made to fit on the top of the mantel-shelf, and this should extend

Drapery for Sitting-room Mantelpiece.

an inch or two beyond the edges all round. Underneath this shelf should run a thin iron rod fitted into eyes, and on this rod, curtains are run by means of rings. There is very considerable choice of materials for covering, such as serge, tapestry, silk, or velvet, but care must be taken to have it in keeping with the colour scheme of the room. A border of the material must first be made wide enough to cover the shelf and to hang down about a foot on the front and ends. If the material is light in texture it should be lined with sateen of the same colour to enable it to hang properly. A pretty fringe or gimp will be required to finish off the edge. It is always best to have this border separate from the board, as it can then be taken off and shaken when the room is cleaned. If made wide enough to tuck in between the shelf and the mantelpiece, there will be no danger of its slipping off. Underneath this border should hang curtains made of the same material and lined if necessary. These also should be edged with the same gimp or fringe along the foot and up the front edges. The curtains must be made wide enough to cover the entire fireplace, and if they are fixed to the rod by means of small rings they can be drawn backwards and forwards at pleasure. A more handsome effect can be produced by having the top border and edges of the curtains prettily embroidered.

Another Method of Draping a Mantelpiece.—A board must first be made as above with a one-inch strip of wood fastened underneath the front and sides. Cover this tightly with serge, sateen, or cloth of a colour to match the drapery and tack it underneath. The covering must be laid on very smoothly, the straight of the material running straight across the board. Commence tacking at the centre and work gradually towards the ends. If any wrinkles should appear they can generally be removed by damping the place and pressing with a hot iron. A valance is put on beneath this and fixed to the under-strip of wood. This can be of an ornamental character; a piece of pretty silk or wool tapestry, or some hand embroidery is the most suitable. A piece of buckram stiffening should first be put on; take the measurements carefully and make it two inches less in depth than the outer valance. Cover the buckram on both sides with thin sateen and tack it on to the strip of wood beneath the mantel-board. The top valance must also be lined with silk or sateen and finished along the edge with cord or fringe; fasten this on the top of the buckram background, and finish all neatly with an edging of gimp and studs or fancy nails. If curtains are required they can be fitted up in the same way as for the other mantelpiece border (see above).

When a bedroom mantelpiece requires covering, it is a good plan to make the drapery of some cotton material which can easily be washed, such as printed linen or cotton. The board might be tightly covered as above with a dark-coloured sateen and a buckram stiffening for the valance of the same colour below. The valance might then consist of a box-pleated flounce of the material about twelve inches in depth, and then curtains, if they are required, should be simply hemmed or finished with a narrow gimp which can be easily washed.

Mantelpiece Drapery for a Bedroom—board covered with dark satin; drapery made of chintz or printed linen with box-pleated valance; curtains edged with a narrow gimp.

HOW TO LAY LINOLEUM

Except in the case of a large room it is not a very difficult matter to lay a floor with linoleum. If the room is very large and the linoleum thick, it will be better to have the work done by expert workmen; in fact, in most cases when the linoleum is bought new the laying will be done free of charge. Still a few hints for the lighter pieces of work may be found useful.

First place the linoleum on the floor close to one of the skirting-boards. If it does not fit perfectly close any unevenness must be trimmed off with a knife. A very sharp hook-knife is the best for the purpose, as it will not slip out of position so easily as an ordinary knife. Fasten the linoleum in position with a few half-inch brads. If more than one width of material is required for covering, another strip must be joined to the first one, and if a patterned linoleum is being used care must be taken to match the pattern before cutting. When the edges are not exactly even, overlap one a little and trim off the surplus material with a knife. If the knife is held with the blade slanting towards the edge of the linoleum, this will give a slightly rounded edge which will fit all the more closely. Unless the edges of the joins are made to meet very exactly, water will soak through when washing is being done and cause the linoleum to shrink and rot. At the same time the two edges of a join must not be so tight that they require forcing down, as this would cause blisters. Fix the edges of the join with brads, driving them in as close to the edge as possible without tearing the linoleum, and put them in pairs, one facing the other. If there is any likelihood of the floor being damp, tarred paper should be laid beneath the linoleum.

A BOOT CUPBOARD

A very neat and easily-made boot cupboard can be manufactured out of an empty orange-box, which can generally be procured from a grocer without any trouble. By setting the case on end the division in it will form the shelves.

First tighten all the joins by driving in a few small nails or strong tacks, and cover over the heads of these with a little putty. Then take a very hard brush and brush the wood well in order to remove all sawdust and splinters. Line the inside with some stout wall-paper, leather paper, or ordinary brown paper fixed on with strong paste or glue. Allow this to dry, and then cover the outside with some pretty chintz or self-coloured sateen, fixing it in position with small tacks or brads. Or, the wood on the outside may be smoothed over with glass paper and painted with two coats of Aspinal's enamel.

A curtain must then be made to cover the front. This may either be of chintz to match the outside or a self-coloured serge to match the paint or sateen with which the outside is covered. About a yard of material 50 inches wide will be required, and 2½ yards of ball fringe or other edging. Make a deep hem at the foot and sew the trimming all round with the exception of the top. Turn in the top to the required length, and fix it to the top of the cupboard with small brass-headed nails, arranging the material in box-pleats. Or, make a casing, draw up the curtain to the correct width with strong string or cord, and then fix it in position.

THE MAKING OF CURTAINS

The question of material for curtains in the various rooms has already been discussed under House Furnishing, the first section of this book, but a few hints for making may be useful for the novice who would like to make her own draperies.

Serge or Tapestry Curtains.—When measuring for a pair of curtains take the length from the curtain pole to the floor of the room plus six inches to allow for turnings, top heading, and a small amount for resting on the floor or looping up. When measuring for the fringe or other trimming take the length round the curtain with the exception of the top, plus half a yard to allow for turnings and easing on when sewing. Select material of from one and a half to two yards wide so as to avoid having a seam down the length of the curtains.

Commence by cutting the top and bottom of

the material perfectly even, because unless this is done the curtains will not hang well. Then lay a half-inch turning on the right side and along the bottom and two sides of the curtains. Tack or baste the fringe on to this turning, easing it on very slightly to prevent any dragging of the material, and stitch on with the machine. Two rows of stitching will likely be required to make the heading of the fringe lie flat, one along the outer and another along the inner edge. Some fringes have a double heading, between which the edges of the curtain can be slipped. In this case a turning on the material would not be required. If a fancy border or braiding is used instead of fringe this would be put on in the same way, easing it on *very* slightly

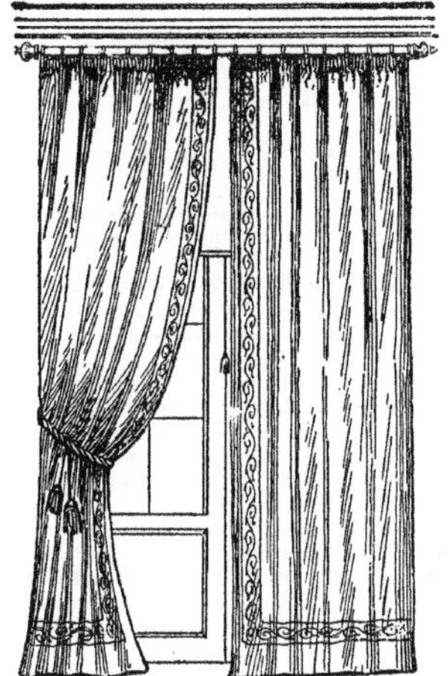

FIG. 1.—Serge or Tapestry Curtains—with fancy border stitched on, two rows of drawings at top with small heading, hooked on to curtain pole.

and then stitching it along the two edges. The trimming should be put an inch from the edge at the sides and from two to three inches from the edge at the foot, the turning on the material being made the necessary width. Care must be taken to turn the corners very neatly. Tacking before sewing is very important. When economy has to be studied one side only of the curtains need be trimmed, the side next the wall being left plain with its selvedge edge.

To finish the top of the curtains, turn over two inches of the material on the wrong side and make two rows of drawings a little way from the top and about half an inch apart. Run a cord or piece of strong string through this and draw up the curtain to the width required. Tack a piece of upholstery tape over the drawings, arranging the fulness evenly, and then stitch along both edges with the machine. Finish off neatly with a needle and cotton and be careful to secure the ends of the drawing string. The upholstery tape should be the same colour as the curtains if possible, also the sewing cotton with which it is stitched.

Iron those parts of the curtain which require pressing, such as the edges and heading, and then sew curtain hooks on to the upholstery tape at intervals of about three inches apart or according to the number of rings on the curtain poles (fig. 1).

Curtains are sometimes lined if the material of which they are made is very thin or a specially heavy curtain is required. Self-coloured sateen to match the curtains or a special lining cashmere is very good for the purpose. The lining should be tacked on all round, leaving it a little full to prevent dragging, and then stitched in position at the same time as the fringe.

Linen or Cotton Curtains.—These are suitable for a bedroom, as they can so easily be washed. They can be made in a variety of ways. The simplest is to finish them off with a hem all round, a three or four-inch hem at the foot, and a one or one and a half inch hem at the sides. Or they may be trimmed with a cotton fringe or fancy edging in the same way as serge curtains.

If a fancy cretonne or printed linen is being used, a nice finish is a border or plain sateen in a pretty contrasting colour, or if the curtains are lined with sateen this might be brought

FIG. 2.—Plain Curtain with top turned over.

over to the right side to form a border. This would require to be carefully arranged and well tacked before any stitching is done.

The top of cotton curtains may be finished in the same way as those made of serge, or when they are light in weight, rings which can be slipped over a narrow brass rod might be used instead of hooks. If the curtains are made of some light-coloured material which requires frequent washing, they should be finished at the top in the same way as muslin or lace curtains, as they will iron more easily if the drawings can be undone.

A valance is sometimes used to finish the curtains at the top. The simplest way of making this is to allow an extra twelve inches when cutting the length of the curtains and to turn this piece over at the top before putting in the runnings. A fancy border stitched along this a few inches from the edge will make an appropriate finish (fig. 2). Another method of putting on the valance is to cut a separate piece

FIG. 3.—Chintz Curtains—edged all round with ball fringe. Drawn valance stretching across window, also edged with ball fringe.

and to arrange it right across the window (fig. 3). This may either be drawn or box-pleated. If drawn, allow half as much again as the width of the window for the length of the valance; if box-pleated, twice the width of the window will be required. A valance is usually made from twelve to fourteen inches deep and is finished along the foot with a ball fringe or trimming to match the curtain.

Instead of a valance a stiffly-shaped piece, called a pelmet, is sometimes used to cover the top of the curtains. This is a little more difficult to make, but still, unless the window is a very large one, it is within the scope of the home worker. A piece of stiff buckram, from eight to ten inches deep and the length of the width of the window, must first be cut, then covered very smoothly with a piece of the curtain material and lined at the back with self-coloured sateen. The edge may be finished with ball fringe and a pretty gimp or other trimming to match the curtains.

Very careful measurements must be taken when cutting the buckram shape in order to get a straight edge, as any unevenness would be very noticeable. Instead of the straight pelmet, a shaped piece, as shown in fig. 4, might be made,

FIG. 4.—Top of Curtains covered with a shaped Pelmet.

but this is a little more troublesome to make and should only be attempted by an experienced worker.

Lace and Muslin Curtains should be finished on the top by turning them down about two and a half inches and stitching a broad tape along the line. A narrow tape should then be run through this casing and secured at one end. This can then be drawn up to the width required, and will be easily undone when the curtains require washing. Safety-pins with hooks attached should be used for fixing the curtains to the rings on the curtain pole.

Madras or plain muslin curtains should be made very full, as they will hang more gracefully. They must also be cut considerably longer than stuff curtains to allow for shrinkage in the washing. The edge can be finished with ball fringe, or sometimes a frill of the material is preferred. It is possible to buy the frilled material by the yard, or the frill can be made and sewn on to the curtain muslin. When cutting the frill allow double the length of the curtain to be trimmed for length and make the strips from four to five inches wide. Join the required number of strips together and make a narrow hem along one side. Turn down the other edge, draw it up with a strong cotton and sew it to the edge of the curtain, arranging the fulness evenly.

Casement Curtains.—In many of the modern houses casement curtains take the place of blinds. They should be made very simply of one of the special cloths sold for the purpose. Casement cloth is to be had in cotton, linen, silk, and woollen materials, and in a variety of colours and patterns. Cream colour is perhaps the most suitable. They may either be gathered into a heading and rings attached for running on a brass rod, or the rod may be passed through a casing at the top and the rings dispensed with. The former method is, however, better if the curtains are to be drawn backwards and forwards. These casement curtains are arranged in different ways and made different lengths according to the style of window under treatment. When the window is divided with a cross frame two pairs of curtains are used, one to cover the upper and the other the lower sash of the window. Or, again, they can be made the full length of the window, two or three pairs perhaps being required for a casement-shaped window. Some windows, again, have long casement curtains at the side and short ones as well to cover the windows. If the window-sill is broad the curtains should just touch it, but if narrow they might be brought a few inches below. The curtains can either be finished round the edges with a plain one and a half inch hem or with a hem-stitched border. They should always hang straight and never be looped up.

The woman who is clever with her needle can also make them look more artistic with some pretty embroidery, an open-work embroidery being particularly suitable for art-linen curtains. A little work of this kind will add very much to the charm of the curtains. Another pretty method of decorating casement curtains is by means of a stencil design. This is particularly suitable for little tussore or shantung silk curtains which are so much in fashion at present. It must be borne in mind, however, that stencil work will not wash well, and that it will mean dry cleaning each time the curtains require renewing, if the colours are to be preserved.

Stencil plates can be bought made of thin iron or zinc, and these can, of course, be used over

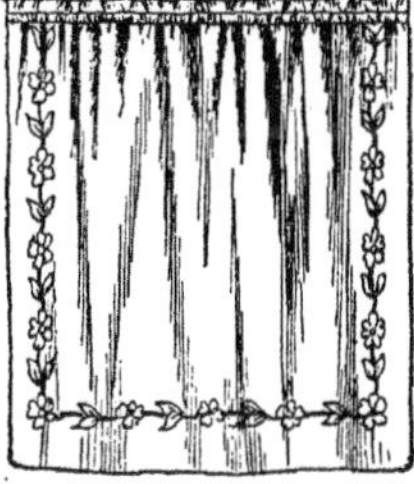

Small Casement Curtain with Stencil Design.

and over again, or a suitable design can first be drawn and then cut out of thin card-board or stiff manilla or wax paper. Various transfer designs can be used for the purpose: a conventional pattern generally looks best. Spread a sheet of clean blotting-paper on a drawing-board, place the silk over this and the paper design on the top, and fix all very evenly in position with drawing-pins. Care must be taken to fix the stencil quite firmly. Stencil paint is then applied with a small brush, the choice of colours being a matter of taste. Allow the paint to dry, and then carefully remove the design. The pattern is sometimes outlined with a fine embroidery stitch to give it a more finished appearance. Stencil paints or dyes are sold in small tubes and must be diluted with water; the ordinary paints are not suitable for the work.

TO RE-UPHOLSTER A CHAIR

Small chairs are not very difficult to re-upholster, and an amateur might quite well attempt one that is simple in form.

Very often the cover of a chair becomes dirty or worn, and it has to be hidden out of sight for this reason and because it means considerable expense to have it sent away to be re-made. Loose covers are not much used nowadays, and, at the best, they soon get out of order and become shabby looking. Many pretty materials can, however, be bought for covering the seats of chairs. An oddment of good tapestry can often be picked up very cheaply at a sale, and nothing wears better or, what is better still, some very good art linen or serge worked with a pretty design can be used. The clever embroiderer will very soon transform an ugly set of chairs—chairs in a bedroom, for instance—and make them match the colour scheme of the room and look quite artistic.

The old cover must first be taken off the chair that is to be covered, as it is never a good plan to put a cover over anything that is dirty, a pair of pincers or a small tack-lifter being used to take out the small nails that fasten the cover. At the same time attention should be paid to the manner in which the covering has been fixed, as this will be a guide for attaching the fresh one. The old cover can then be used as a pattern for cutting out the fresh material. When using a patterned material be careful to centre the pattern when cutting the cover, otherwise it will look one-sided. If the stuffing of the chair has become flattened through long use, remove the under cover, which is generally made of linen or cotton, tease out the hair, and put a layer of fresh hair on the top in order to raise any hollow places. A layer of sheet wadding might also be put over the hair; it will make the top of the seat fuller and softer. Then cover this with a piece of fresh linen or calico. Next place the new cover on the top, centre the back and front, and fix them temporarily with small tacks. Do the same at the sides, and then tighten gradually all the way round, fixing the material in position with very small headless tacks. Always work from the centre of each side towards the corners. Trim off any superfluous material, and then cover the edges with a narrow gimp fastened on with brass-headed nails or coloured studs.

When the webbing supports of a chair give way, it will be necessary to take out the entire seat and to fix new webbing. This must be bought from an upholsterer's, and the best and strongest quality obtained. First remove the old webbing, fix on one end of the new on the old marks with small clout nails or strong tacks, then stretch well and nail down the second end before cutting. Nail on the other pieces in the same way, and when putting in the cross-way pieces, interlace them, as this will give greater strength and elasticity. A piece of new Hessian sacking should come next to cover the webbing, and then the hair for the seat should be teased out and replaced and the covers fixed on as above.

CAREERS FOR WOMEN

In olden times the careers open to women were few; nowadays the professions which have *not* opened their gates to the woman worker are fewer still. The natural result of this extension of the field of work for women is that in all careers in which a woman may take part a high standard of proficiency is exacted. There is no room for the untrained worker. This is only just, for if women are to work side by side with men in fields of labour which at one time were open to men only, it stands to reason that they should be as fully equipped as the men workers.

This is essentially an age of specialisation, and sensible parents are beginning to realise the fact that girls nowadays as well as boys require to have their capabilities tested at the age when they begin to show in what direction their talents lie, and to have their careers marked out for them, for whether a girl marries or not it is highly desirable that she should be able to take her place in the ranks of women workers should there ever arise the need for her to do so.

In the following articles an attempt has been made to put before parents, in as clear and concise a manner as possible, the many vocations for which, by careful training, a girl may be fitted, together with details in regard to cost of training, necessary qualifications, and, last but not least, the prospects offered in each career.

THE TEACHING PROFESSION

With the rapid strides made in education within recent years a much higher degree of efficiency is exacted from those who adopt the teaching profession. Nowadays there is no room for the inefficient and the ill-equipped teacher; indeed, in many cases the supply of trained and experienced teachers exceeds the demand, and there are many branches of the profession that are perilously near to being overcrowded. The fact remains, however, that there is always room for really gifted teachers. There are many women who, in spite of all their knowledge, lack the power of being able to impart this knowledge to others. It should be remembered that there are a number of attributes beyond mere learning which are essential to a successful teacher. The gift of imparting knowledge, the ability to win the sympathy and respect of pupils, the power of maintaining discipline, and, last but not least, a strict sense of justice—all are necessary for the teacher who would follow her profession with success, whatever branch of teaching she may choose to adopt.

PUBLIC SCHOOL TEACHING

This, as applied to women teachers, may be divided into two branches:—

(1) Teaching in the Elementary and Secondary Schools under Local Authorities.

(2) Teaching in the High Schools.

Elementary School Teaching.—For women elementary school teaching offers good prospects, and has this particular advantage that the training is very cheap, and under the new regulations is such that will fit students for many pursuits other than teaching if they find this unsuitable or distasteful to them. In all cases special training, generally extending over two years, must be taken at a recognised training college, but before entering a college the Preliminary Examination of the Board of Education, or its equivalent, must be passed. It will thus be seen that a certain amount of preliminary training is necessary. This may be taken in several ways. A girl whose parents are in good circumstances may follow her education in the ordinary way at a school or college where she may be prepared for the examination. The daughter of parents of limited means, however, will be wise to avail herself of the many facilities for cheap training put within her reach by the Board of Education.

For the girl so situated, the first step to be taken after attaining the age of sixteen is to get an appointment as bursar, or an engagement as pupil teacher, or recognition as student teacher. The candidate in each of these cases must be suitable in respect of character, health, and freedom from personal defects, such as lameness or deafness.

Bursars.—A bursar is a girl attending full time at an efficient training school who intends to become a teacher in an elementary school, and who receives from the School Authority, aided by the Board of Education, such financial help as will enable her to continue her education for a year, after reaching the age of sixteen or seventeen, at the same school where she has been receiving continuous instruction for the three years immediately before her application for a bursarship. The bursar must receive continuous and suitable instruction throughout the year of her bursarship, and within two years of her appointment as bursar must enter for the "Preliminary Examination for the Certificate." The bursar must subsequently either enter a training college or serve for a year as student teacher in a public elementary school.

Pupil Teachers receive training in teaching as pupil teachers in elementary schools, together with instruction approved by the Board. Except in rural districts, no girl may be a pupil teacher before the age of sixteen, and as a rule must serve two years. In rural districts girls may, with the consent of the Board of Education, be engaged for three years from the age of fifteen. To enable girls who wish to qualify for elementary school teaching to become pupil teachers, provision has been made for their education and partial maintenance by most of the Education Committees of our large towns. The scholarships they offer give free education for two years either in special classes, or, more often, in secondary schools, and a maintenance grant of from £10 to £20.

Candidates must be suitable in respect of character, health, and freedom from personal defects. Those candidates who hold one of the certificates above mentioned, or feel they could pass the special and perhaps easier examination of the Board, should send in their names to the authorities of the elementary school in which they wish to serve early in June, as the usual date for admission is August, and the names of candidates must be submitted not later than July 1st. Those who hold training scholarships will have all the necessary arrangements made for them.

Student Teachers.—A student teacher is one who is employed in a public elementary school during not more than eight meetings in any one week for the purpose of gaining practical experience in the art of teaching, together with such further general education which may be available. To obtain recognition as a student teacher on the staff of a school the candidate must, immediately before her application for such recognition, have been a bursar, or have been in attendance for not less than three years at an efficient secondary school. If she has not been a bursar, she must be over seventeen years of age and have passed the Preliminary Examination for the certificate, or some other examination accepted by the Board of Education as a qualification for admission to a training college.

The above-mentioned methods of preparatory training for elementary teachers before they take the preliminary examination which renders them eligible to enter a training college will commend themselves especially to those of limited income, as grants are made by the Board of Education in respect of each recognised pupil teacher to the elementary school at which they are trained. Pupil teachers also receive small salaries varying in accordance with the arrangements made by the different authorities. The pupils, however, whose parents are in better circumstances and who have prepared for the Preliminary Examination as ordinary scholars at an ordinary school, will find it a great advantage to engage in elementary school teaching for a few months before taking up their training at a college, as valuable experience is always gained in this way.

Preliminary Examination.—This examination is open to pupil teachers and bursars who have completed their apprenticeship or entered on the last year, and to all others who have not taken preliminary training as pupil teachers or bursars who are over eighteen years of age. Candidates who pass this examination are now eligible to enter a training college where they will be prepared for the final teachers' examination; or if they do not intend to work for the teacher's certificate, they will be eligible for employment in elementary schools as uncertificated teachers. Training Colleges are of two kinds—Residential and Day. There are thirty-four Residential Colleges for women in England and Wales, and twelve Day Training Colleges. There are also fifteen Day Colleges where both men and women may receive their training. The course in a training college usually extends over two years, but those who wish to work for a degree must take a three years' course. A student who holds a degree or who has passed some other examination recognised by the Board of Education may enter a students' training college for one year. At those day colleges, which are closely attached to a university, the course lasts three years, and is so arranged that at the end of it students may become graduates of the university. This, however, entails very heavy work, as the student has not only to prepare for her degree, but must at the same time receive her professional training.

Fees.—The fees paid at training colleges are small, the fee at a residential college for a two years' course being as a rule £20 to £30. This covers both tuition, board, lodging, washing, and medical attendance. Books cost £5 or £6, and there are usually small charges made for sports, papers, magazines, &c. In Roman Catholic colleges the fees are lower. At a day college the usual tuition fee is £10 a year. Day students receive a maintenance grant from the Government of £20 a year. A course of training for day students is also provided at many of the University Colleges, £10 a year being the average fee.

A graduate in arts or science of any university in the British Empire may be recognised as a certificated teacher, provided she holds a certificate of proficiency in the theory and practice of teaching.

Prospects.—Students who have obtained their certificates at the end of their training are qualified teachers, and are eligible for posts in elementary schools, training colleges, and pupil teacher centres. Salaries vary considerably with the locality. One of the highest scales of salary in the country is as follows :—

Trained Assistant Mistress . .	£85 to £125
Untrained but Certificated . .	75 to 125
Head Mistress	120 to 265

Head Assistants get fron £10 to £15 more than ordinary assistants. The salary of the Head Mistress depends upon her length of service and the size of the school.

Secondary Schools.—In order to qualify as teacher in a secondary school, a candidate must have a degree or its equivalent, and after graduation must go through a course of special professional training in accordance with the regulations of the Board. The special training must extend over a year at least.

The following qualifications are accepted as equivalent to a degree: A Tripos Certificate of the University of Cambridge, provided that the examination is the one that would, if taken by a man, entitle him to a degree under the usual conditions without further conditions, or an Oxford diploma, which is one, if taken by a man, that would entitle him to a degree; also a certificate showing that she has passed the second Public Examination of the University of Oxford, or that she has obtained in the Examination in Modern Languages an honours certificate of the Oxford or Cambridge Higher Locals, provided they include the subjects required by the Board. Diplomas or certificates in the theory and practice of teaching in secondary schools are now granted by the following Universities: Oxford, Cambridge, London, Durham, Liverpool, Leeds, Wales, Edinburgh, St. Andrews, Aberdeen, Glasgow, Dublin, and by the College of Preceptors and the National Froebel Union.

Training.—Grants of £100 are now made by the Board of Education under certain conditions to training colleges in respect of every group of five recognised students who have completed a course of training during each year ending 31st of July. Courses of training for the teachers of secondary schools are provided at many universities or institutions, including the following: University of Oxford, Cambridge Training College for Women, at the Universities of Birmingham, Durham, Manchester, Liverpool, Leeds; at the University Colleges of Bangor, Cardiff, Aberystwyth; at the following institutions in London: Bedford College, Baker Street; Maria Gray College, Brondesbury; Mary Datchelor College, Camberwell; Catholic Training College, Cavendish Square; London Day Training College; Clapham High School; Froebel Institution; Cheltenham College, Cheltenham, and also at St. George's Training College, Edinburgh.

Prospects.—The commencing salary of a teacher in a secondary school in London is usually £120, rising in some cases to £250; head mistresses receive from £300 to £600. Salaries vary according to locality and size of school. Lower salaries are as a rule given in the provinces.

High School Teaching.—The branch of public school teaching which doubtless appeals the most to gentlewomen is that of teaching in the high schools. The candidate for a post of the kind should remember that a high standard of proficiency is exacted. A certain specified course of training must be followed which is necessarily expensive, and even then, unless she has great ability as a teacher, competition for a high school post is so keen that, however high her attainments, she will be superseded by others who excel in the actual art of teaching.

The intending high school teacher will find that skill in sports and outdoor games will be counted not the least among her acquirements. Games are nowadays a typical feature of the curriculum of all our girls' schools, and in the choice of the younger form mistresses especially, preference is often given to the candidate who is a good organiser, or an expert player of the most popular games in which girls may participate.

Not the least pleasant side of the life of the high school teacher is to be found in the friendships which she will form among her pupils and their parents. Although the scholars will be drawn from many social grades, they will be mostly of a class with which a gentlewoman may mix socially, and for this reason the life of a high school teacher will have a greater appeal for the woman of refinement than the life of a teacher in a public elementary or secondary school.

Prospects.—The initial salary for assistant mistresses varies in many localities. The average commencing salary is £100, in London £120, rising at the rate of £10 to £220 and sometimes to £250. The salaries of head mistresses of the larger schools range from £180 to £300 and upwards in accordance with the locality and the size of the school.

Training.—This will extend over at least four years, as a high school mistress must have a degree or its equivalent; three of the four years will be taken up in preparation for the degree. When this has been obtained she must take a year's training in the art of teaching and work for her teacher's diploma. The cost of training will average about £100 a year for a resident student. If the student lives near one of the training colleges, however, the cost will be materially reduced, and only the tuition and examination fees will have to be paid. Then will follow the cost of the year's training for the teacher's diploma. This may be taken at the colleges already mentioned in connection with secondary schools. The cost of training for an out student will average from £20 to £25 a year.

Teachers in Scotland.—In Scotland the training of elementary and secondary school teachers is directed by the Provincial Committees of Edinburgh, Glasgow, Aberdeen, and St. Andrews, and there are good training colleges in all these towns. The regulations are very similar to those in force in England and Wales, and will be found in the "Regulations for the Preliminary Education, Training and Certification of Teachers," issued by the Scotch Education Department. Candidates for elementary school teacherships must not be under sixteen or over eighteen years of age when they are junior students. At eighteen the Preliminary Examination for the Teacher's Certificate must be passed. For those who intend to become secondary school teachers the training necessary for preparation for a degree is less costly than in England. Those with degrees must take one year's special training in teaching in order to become secondary teachers. Bursaries in preparation for elementary school teacherships are granted at the discretion of the training authorities. Salaries are on a lower scale than in England—£83 for an assistant mistress, and £100 for a head mistress being considered a fair rate of pay. In a few of the high schools salaries are paid at a higher rate, some of them averaging the scale prevailing in English schools.

Kindergarten and Lower Form Teaching.—At one time it was a general idea that any girl or woman with a smattering of education, however superficial, was competent to teach young children. Happily nowadays the fallacy of this idea is recognised. The kindergarten system of teaching has become perfected, and is generally adopted as the best method of teaching little ones.

A very thorough training must be undergone by the would-be kindergarten teacher before she becomes eligible for a post. This training must have a good general education as a primary foundation. A candidate should also have passed some public examination such as the Oxford or Cambridge Senior or Higher Local, or the London Matriculation. The course of training in kindergarten work as a preparation for the certificates of the National Froebel Union must next be taken. There are two certificates, the elementary and the higher. Both are recognised by the Board of Education, and one of them must be taken before a post as kindergarten or lower form mistress can be obtained. All those who wish to obtain the better posts in kindergarten work, such as the management of a kindergarten, should study for the higher certificate. The elementary certificate is sufficient for assistant kindergarten mistresses. There are several training colleges in the United Kingdom where students are prepared for the Froebel examinations. The full course of training extends over two years and a term, the first year being taken up in preparation for the elementary certificate. All information in regard to the Froebel examinations, names of training colleges, &c., may be had on application to the Secretary, the National Froebel Union, Norwich House, Southampton Street, Bloomsbury, London, W.C.

Prospects.—There are numerous posts obtainable in kindergartens connected with high schools, kindergartens, private schools, and the lower forms of secondary schools, elementary schools, &c. The commencing salary for an assistant mistress averages from £60 to £70.

Teachers of Foreign Languages.—There are good prospects for the teacher who has thoroughly mastered some foreign language. This should have been acquired in the first instance by a term of residence in the country, as fluency of conversation, with purity of accent, are as indispensable as the mere learning.

Holiday courses in France for English teachers are arranged every August, and particulars of them can be obtained by applying for the "Table of Holiday Courses on the Continent," prepared by the special inquiries office of the Board of Education, Whitehall, S.W.

If desirous of teaching in schools, the language which the teacher is to make her speciality should be included in the syllabus of her examinations for her degree. A diploma gained at an examination taken in the country itself is more than valuable. The prospects for the teacher of languages are very good, but a high degree of proficiency is exacted. Posts may be obtained on the staffs of high schools, colleges, and private schools, and it is also possible to establish a connection as visiting teacher in schools and private families.

Teaching the Deaf.—This opens up a promising field for women and should especially appeal to those with large sympathies as being a real philanthropic work, the results of which are such a boon to those who are so sadly afflicted. The deaf are taught either by the "oral" or the "silent" system. Children who have been deaf from infancy are also dumb for the reason that they have never heard others speak, and therefore cannot imitate their speech as in the case of children who can hear. By the oral system they are actually taught speech by watching the lips of others as they speak. This training naturally takes a little time, but when the pupils have thoroughly mastered the language of the lips they can be educated in the same way as children who can hear.

By the silent method the deaf and dumb are taught to communicate with others by means of signs and the finger alphabet.

Needless to say, a girl must have very special

qualities if she has to undertake this difficult branch of teaching with success. She must also be endowed with an abundant fund of patience and sympathy, both of which qualities are necessary in teaching normal pupils, but how much more so in the case of those who are so sadly afflicted. She should have had a thoroughly good education and a training that would have enabled her to teach in ordinary schools before specialising in this particular work. The special training, which should extend over a year at least, should be taken at one of the training colleges where the students are prepared for the certificate of the Joint Board Examination for Teachers of the Deaf. Training may be had at the Training College for Teachers of the Deaf, 11 Fitzroy Square, London, W., and at Eaton Rise, Ealing. The London County Council awards scholarships tenable at the special training colleges for those who intend to become teachers in the County Council special schools. Many posts are to be had in Institutions for the Deaf and Dumb in England and abroad, and also in the schools under County Councils. To obtain a post in the latter, the student must have obtained her elementary teacher's certificate. For this purpose she can train at a training college for the elementary certificate in the ordinary way and afterwards may take a third year of training specially designed to prepare for the work of teaching the deaf at a training college or other institution approved by the Board of Education, or she may be admitted in the first instance to a two years' course which is specially designed on its professional side to prepare for teaching in a school for the deaf. She must take the Board's Final Examination with certain modifications, taking, instead of certain other subjects, the syllabus adapted to her special course of training.

The same rules apply to those who wish to qualify as teachers of the blind or the mentally defective. Teachers of the blind may be trained at the Smith Training College, Upper Norwood, for a fee of £65.

Women as Lecturers.—This is another branch of the teaching profession which is open to women who have taken their degrees. The posts in connection with lecturing are many and varied. Perhaps the most coveted are those obtainable in universities and the principal ladies' colleges, whilst in high schools and other public schools good posts are also to be had.

The lecturer must be first and foremost a specialist in her particular subject, be it in Science, Classics, History, or Modern Languages. In regard to the first named, she will have to be a demonstrator as well. To obtain a post in a university or a college connected with a university the would-be lecturer should have graduated with honours. This would involve four years' training at a university. For an arts lectureship the B.A., and for a science lectureship the B.Sc., degree should be taken. In connection with university extension lecturing there are also many posts available to women. This work is most varied and interesting and has a somewhat wider aspect than college lecturing, although from the very nature of the work it is more likely to be irregular and intermittent.

The salaries paid to lecturers in colleges are good, varying, of course, with the standing of the college. £200 a year is a fair average figure. The earnings of the university extension lecturer will depend upon the work with which she is entrusted. Some lecturers may hold two or three courses in different districts in a term, whilst others may only be called upon to give one course, consisting of a lecture once every week. The fees are good, amounting in many instances to £25 for a course of ten lectures.

PRIVATE TEACHING

Private Schools.—Nowadays a high standard of proficiency on the part of teachers is exacted in the best private schools, and although there are some schools which still pursue old-fashioned methods, employing unqualified teachers at sometimes nominal salaries; yet, thanks to the progress made in education within recent years, these are now decidedly in the minority. A good many of the larger private schools are modelled upon the principles of the great public schools for girls, and in these establishments the teachers must necessarily be highly efficient, degrees and diplomas being always a *sine quâ non* now of their engagement.

Training.—The same training as that taken for teacherships in public schools will be necessary for those seeking employment in the best private schools. For lower form teachers an Oxford or Cambridge Senior or Higher Local Certificate will be sufficient. In some of the lower grade schools these certificates will be deemed sufficient for the higher form mistresses. By degrees, however, most of the best private schools are recognising the fact that it is highly desirable that teachers should have a certain definite training in teaching in addition to the usual university certificates. As a rule, however, those who have gone through their full course of training as teachers will prefer a post in a public school to one in a private establishment, as, with the exception of a few cases, the salaries and prospects are so much better in the former than in the latter.

The salaries in large private schools vary to a great extent. In some of the best establishments they reach the standard of salaries paid in large public schools, but in the majority of cases they are considerably lower.

The Governess.—At one time every girl who wished to earn her living would seek a post as a governess, for although salaries were very often small, yet the standard of proficiency exacted by parents was correspondingly low. As long as the governess had a fair amount of general knowledge, was acquainted superficially with one foreign language, could teach elementary music, and dabble in painting or drawing as a mere beginner, she was deemed competent to undertake the education of children. Small wonder, therefore, that the ranks of governesses were swelled by the uneducated and the inefficient, whilst salaries depreciated to an almost negligible quantity.

It must be confessed, however, that in many cases parents went to the other extreme, expecting their governesses to be able to teach their children almost everything in the way of languages and accomplishments in addition to the ordinary routine of lessons. Sensible parents realise the fact that a good teacher must be thoroughly proficient in the subjects which she teaches, and that it is impossible to specialise in every branch of education and in all accomplishments as well. Yet in spite of this, one often sees even now in the papers advertisements for such a prodigy at a salary of £20 a year!

With the present-day progress of education, the majority of parents recognise that a governess to be a good teacher should have had a definite training upon lines which will fit her for the work in view. They also appreciate the fact that well-qualified women are entitled to at least a living wage, and that it is impossible for any woman to have a thorough knowledge of the whole gamut of arts, languages, and sciences.

In the best families a governess is employed for ordinary subjects, with the addition of perhaps one or two accomplishments, whilst visiting masters or mistresses are engaged to teach other accomplishments.

There are many qualities beyond the mere ability to teach which it is essential that a governess should possess if she is to be happy in the position she occupies. Chief amongst these must be classed tact and common-sense. Very often a girl who has been brought up in refined and cultured surroundings will imagine that she is being subjected to all sorts of slights and snubs; she will resent the fact, for instance, that she is not asked downstairs to dinner at night, but is expected to take her meal in the schoolroom. Surely this is unreasonable. She should remember that she is not one of the family, and that her employers are entitled to spend at least a certain portion of the day in privacy and free from the presence of a stranger. The sensible girl or woman, instead of being ashamed of her position, should take pride in the work with which she is entrusted, and should endeavour to win the affection as well as the respect of her employers. Tact should be exercised upon all occasions. She should know when to be at hand and when to make herself scarce. Her position is one of dependence, it is true, but by her own common-sense she will be able to lessen many of its disadvantages. In refined families every consideration is shown to the feelings of a dependent. In the houses of unrefined people, however, the life of even the most tactful girl can be made unhappy by the want of consideration and tact displayed by her employers. The timid gentle-natured girl should never take a position of this kind. It may be said that girls of excessively timid dispositions seldom make good teachers. They are not disciplinarians as a rule, and are seldom able to hold their own. Gentleness is indeed a very necessary quality on the part of the governess in dealing with her charges, but the gentleness must be coupled with firmness and never allowed to sink to vacillation or timidity if any sort of discipline is to be maintained.

Training.—One or two accomplishments and conversational knowledge of at least one language will prove a most valuable part of the equipment of a governess. In the case of the younger children a knowledge of Swedish drill will also be useful. The girl who wishes to be trained as a teacher of the younger children cannot do better than take a course of training in the Froebel method (see p. 618). She should also have the Oxford or Cambridge Senior Local Certificate. For these examinations she can be prepared at almost any good school, as preparation for the University Locals generally forms part of the curriculum of most of our best schools nowadays.

The governess who will have entire charge of little children should be well acquainted with the care and hygiene of little ones, symptoms of ailments, &c. She should also be able to give her little pupils a thorough grounding in drawing and music.

For teaching girls of twelve and upwards a Higher Local Certificate is very desirable, although an Oxford or Cambridge Senior Local will often be sufficient. If possible, a training in the actual work of teaching should also be taken. There are some colleges where a speciality is made of training girls as governesses in private families. At the Cheltenham Ladies' College a full course of training is given to those who wish to be governesses to either young or older children. For the latter the training extends over two years and a term; for the former there is a one year course. Full particulars may be had upon application to the college.

Prospects.—It might be said that these in many cases will depend upon the governess herself. So long as there are highly educated girls who are so ill-advised as to take merely nominal salaries, so long will salaries in many cases be maintained at a low level. A girl should remember that the expensive education which she has had to take to qualify herself for teaching demands something more than a mere nominal fee. Governesses who have taken a special course of training and possess certificates of efficiency may always command good salaries, and, as a rule, it will be found that these will not be grudged. Salaries vary to a great extent. Sometimes £200 a year is paid to resident finishing governesses, but such salaries are usually paid by members of the higher classes to ladies who are required to train their daughters to take their proper place in society. A governess of this class must be *au fait* in all the usages of society—should be able to instruct her charges in the art of conversation, whilst the teaching of accomplishments would form an important feature of her régime.

The certificated governess for elder children in an ordinary family should at least earn £40 a year, whilst the well-trained governess for younger children who has taken her Froebel Certificate should receive a salary of £30.

Owing to the various standards taken by different families, salaries are bound to fluctuate to a certain extent, but all who take up this profession should see to it that a certain definite minimum salary is secured.

TEACHERS OF GYMNASTICS, DRILL AND GAMES

For girls with good constitutions and the necessary training and capabilities, the teaching of gymnastics, drill and games proves an eminently suitable and remunerative profession. It is healthy in as much as teachers of gymnastics, from the nature of their occupation, have abundant health-giving exercise, and so escape from that sedentary life which teaching as a rule involves. The work has the additional charm of variety, and a thoroughly efficient gymnastic and drill mistress may command very good fees.

A most careful and comprehensive training is required before a girl can fit herself for the position of gymnastic teacher; in addition, the girl who wishes to take up physical training in order to put it to practical use should be one who is likely to be a good teacher when the training is completed. That cheerful yet respect-compelling personality, which is so powerful in influencing pupils for good when possessed by the ordinary teacher, is more than ever valuable in the case of the gymnastic and games mistress.

Training.—The course of study to be followed by a girl who wishes to become a teacher of gymnastics covers a wide field of knowledge both theoretical and practical; it includes :—

Physical exercises and drill with and without dumb-bells, Indian clubs, &c., including Swedish and German drill, breathing exercises, military drill and sword drill; gymnastics proper—that is to say, exercises on gymnastic apparatus, such as parallel bars, horizontal bars, trapeze, vaulting horse, ladders, giant's stride, &c.

Medical gymnastics, *i.e.* gymnastics with remedial apparatus for correcting and curing physical weakness and deformities—massage, fencing, swimming, out-door games, dancing, voice production.

The theory of gymnastics has also to be studied, the course comprising anatomy, physiology, hygiene, and in some cases nursing and ambulance work.

The best age for a girl to begin her training is seventeen. She should not begin younger than this, but the sooner she begins after the age of seventeen has been reached the more successful as a rule will her training be. A woman should not go in for training as a gymnastic teacher after the age of twenty-eight, when she has lost some of the suppleness of her first youth. A good constitution is of course essential, and a medical man should be consulted before a girl decides to take up gymnastics and physical culture as a career.

The best all-round training can be had at those colleges at which both the German and Swedish systems of gymnastics are taught. To thoroughly qualify herself for the position of teacher the student should go in for the examinations of one of the following bodies who grant certificates of membership to successful candidates :—

The British College of Physical Education (Mem. Brit. Coll. Phys. Ed.); Gymnastic Teachers' Institute (M.G.T.I.); National Society of Physical Education (N.S.P.E.).

Most of the Physical Training Colleges prepare their students for these examinations. When successful students are enabled to write the magic letters of membership of one or other of these institutions after their names, they may be said to be fairly equipped for their teaching careers.

There are many good Physical Training Colleges in England and Scotland at which a student can go through the necessary course to qualify as a teacher of gymnastics. The Liverpool Gymnasium Training College, 171 Bedford Street, South, Liverpool, is particularly notable for the success achieved by pupils, a number of whom have secured posts as gymnastic teachers in County Council and Board Schools, also public appointments as inspectors or trainers of physical education. The college is residential, but a few day students are received. The course of training is two years. The subjects included are :—

Anatomy, Physiology, Pathology, Orthopedics, Massage, Ambulance, Sick Nursing, Hygiene, Theory of Gymnastics, Theory of Games, Educational Gymnastics (Swedish and Anglo-German systems), Remedial Gymnastics (Swedish system), Fencing (French), Dancing, Swimming, Rowing, Hockey, Cricket, Tennis, Lacrosse, Rounders, Vigoro. Badminton, Net-ball, Basket-ball, Children's Games, Elocution, Needlework and Cutting-out.

The fees for resident students per term is

twenty-five guineas, for non-resident twelve guineas.

Good training may also be had at Madame Bergman Österberg's Physical Training College, Dartford Heath, Kent; the Southport Physical Training College, Southport; St. Bride's Physical Training College, Bride Lane, London, E.C.; Physical Training College for Women, South Western Polytechnic, Chelsea, London, S.W.; Manchester Physical Training College, Rusholme, Manchester.

Prospects.—The openings are good for the fully-trained teacher who can be personally recommended. The growing importance attached to physical culture as a factor in preserving health has created a demand for well-qualified teachers. Every year more schools engage a resident gymnastic and games mistress. Only ladies who will make good teachers and disciplinarians should enter for the gymnastic teaching profession, which requires much tact, good common-sense, and good authority. So many people take up this profession who are quite unsuitable for it, that it would appear on the surface to be becoming overcrowded; it is these incompetents who will in time swell the ranks of the unemployed. There are not too many really capable teachers, and these will always find their value.

The salaries vary, the minimum being £40 for a resident instructress, or £90 for a non-resident instructress, but some salaries run into hundreds a year. A visiting teacher in schools can also make a very good income if she succeeds in establishing a good connection, and a thoroughly well-trained teacher with good business ability and organising powers may found a school of her own in a town where one is needed.

Note.—For Teachers of Domestic Subjects, Art, Music, &c., see under separate sections.

LITERARY AND SECRETARIAL WORK

JOURNALISM

The profession of journalism has an irresistible fascination for most women who are at all proficient with the pen; it is a profession, however, which is not so easily accessible as other callings. There is an element of uncertainty about it also which should be well considered before deciding to adopt journalism as a career. In the newspaper world this uncertainty is particularly evident. Papers change hands, new proprietors bring in new editors, new editors engage new staffs, and the members of the old staff, however efficient and conscientious they may be in their work, are thrown out of employment.

The really clever journalist and writer, however, can always find a demand for her work; but in all professions the mediocre worker of only average ability preponderates. It is to the mediocre worker that this warning is given. If she manages by good fortune or influence to acquire a position in a newspaper office she may jog along comfortably enough until one day a staff upheaval comes, in the way of a change of editorship or some other similar contingency. Once she is thrown out of employment in this manner she will find it difficult to get another position of a similar nature, and a journalist somehow always finds it very difficult to settle down to less interesting work, so strong is the fascination of "Fleet Street" for those who have once been within its precincts.

Many women journalists, however, have followed this profession with brilliant success. They have set the stamp of individuality upon their work. They have specialised upon certain subjects and become known as authorities upon those subjects. For the work of these women there is always a demand, and the large income made by those favoured few is enough to hold out dazzling prospects to the beginner who is anxious to follow in their footsteps.

There are many things to consider before finally deciding to adopt journalism as a career. First and foremost it is important to realise the fact that a good writer does not necessarily make a good journalist. Other things are required in journalism besides fluency with the pen. The journalist must possess what is rightly known as the "journalistic instinct" if she is to pursue her career with any measure of success. She must have a keen sense of "news" and "news" subjects. For instance, she must have the power of realising the news value of the different subjects dealt with in her morning paper, with the faculty of being able in her mind to quickly summarise and analyse their comparative possibilities from the point of view of public interest. The efficient journalist can tell to a nicety what news is worth "following up," what subjects the public would like to hear more about. She appreciates the fact that good news stories and subjects for interesting articles lurk in most unexpected corners—a chance sentence in the speech of a well-known public man, a remark uttered by a well-known judge, a declaration by a well-known scientist, all may be rich in news possibilities, and to miss them might be to miss the opportunity of a good article or a good news story.

A journalist must keep in touch with current events. She should also keep watch on future happenings. The "Future Arrangements" column, describing important public engagements for the near future, which appears every week in most of our daily papers, should be carefully studied, and the contents cut out and pasted in a diary for reference. A woman journalist should be well informed upon all the principal subjects of the day. She should know also how to store up information for future reference. It has been said with truth that the scissors and the paste-pot are almost as formidable weapons in the armoury of a journalist as the pen; well, this is how the woman who wishes to become a journalist should make use of them in order to derive the utmost value from her reading. Every day as she goes over her morning paper she should carefully mark in pencil all the subjects of special interest therein. During the day she should cut out all the paragraphs she has marked, writing upon them the name of the paper from which they are taken and the date of their appearance. The very small cuttings should be pasted upon pieces of white paper, with the date carefully inscribed on the paper. All these cuttings should be carefully filed alphabetically so that they can be referred to at any moment, and a list of the cuttings should be kept in an alphabetical index-book. A very simple way to file cuttings is as follows:—Procure from a law stationer's a number of foolscap envelopes with the flap opening across their entire length instead of at the top. Those sold by general stationers usually have half of the pocket portion ungummed, so that they require pasting down before using. On the left-hand corner of each envelope write distinctly the subject of the cuttings to be inserted. Thus an envelope marked "Aeronautics" would include cuttings on balloon, airship, and aeroplane flights and records. These envelopes with their contents should be filed by placing them upright in the drawer or drawers of a desk, arranging them alphabetically. The writing on the left hand of the envelopes can be easily seen at a glance when opening the drawer.

Failing a desk, they could be stored upright in an ordinary box of a size into which they would just fit, neither too large nor too small, or an ordinary ABC concertina file might be made to answer the purpose. Proper filing cabinets may be had at very moderate prices, but, failing everything else, the cuttings may be filed in an ordinary cardboard box as already described.

No woman who has not tried to keep a cutting file in this way can realise what an enormous aid it proves to her work. If she cuts her papers judiciously and well—it requires the journalistic instinct to do this, be it said—it is surprising what a large amount of valuable information on important subjects she will have ready to hand for purposes of reference. Most successful journalists have proved the value of a systematically kept up "cutting file." In it they have found material and suggestions for articles which have helped to bring "grist to the mill." The woman who wishes to be a journalist, therefore, cannot do better than begin to practise the systematic filing of all sorts of literary matters which are likely to prove of future use. It will benefit her in more ways than one, for it will serve to give her an insight into the kind of news and literary fare the public wants. She will recognise the varying style of articles printed in the different papers and periodicals, and if it is her aim to be an outside contributor she will not waste her time in sending editors articles wholly unsuitable for their publications.

A woman journalist should therefore be well informed in regard to current events and topics of interest. She should not only know how to read, but also how to turn her reading to the best advantage. In addition to her "cutting file" she should have as many reference books at hand as possible. "Whitaker's Almanack," "Who's Who," "Hazell's Annual," Jack's "Reference Book," and a good Encyclopædia should, if possible, find a place on her book-shelf. She should be well acquainted with the names of famous authorities on various scientific subjects and the leading questions of the day. In a word, she should not only be well informed, but she should also be an adept at putting her knowledge to good account.

Journalistic Positions for Women.—There are many positions upon the staffs of newspapers or periodicals which may be filled by women. A woman may be either on the indoor or the outdoor staff of a paper or on both. On the indoor staff such positions as editor of the ladies' column or page, exchange editor, assistant to the editor, news editor, or literary editor may be filled.

On the outdoor staff a lady may be engaged solely in attending fashionable social functions, or she may be a lady reporter. Without being on the staff of a paper a woman may make a name for herself as a writer on "Special Subjects." There is always a market for the articles of the woman specialist, whether her subject be Dress, Household Pets, Sport, or Woman's Suffrage.

Editing a Woman's Page.—A good all round knowledge of special subjects of interest to women, such as "Dress," "The Home," "Society," is essential, a facile pen, and the ability to sub-edit, arrange, and "make up a page." The woman's page of a paper is usually of the utmost value on account of the advertising revenue it brings. For this reason there is scarcely a daily paper nowadays that does not possess its woman's page or column. It will be seen, therefore, that the editress of a woman's page should not only be able to write fluently on subjects of interest to women, but she must also possess a keen eye towards the advertising interest. Whilst avoiding the crudeness of what is known journalistically as the "puff paragraph," she should be able to give graceful and interesting descriptions of even the most uninteresting of advertisers' specialities, which call for editorial notice. In addition to being a good journalist, she should also be a good business woman. The combined qualities will make her invaluable both to the advertisement as well as to the editorial department, and to secure the co-operation of the latter in addition to that of the former is to make her position doubly sure.

Salaries for this particular work vary in accordance with the position of the paper. On the small provincial journals £2 a week would be considered a fair rate of pay, whilst on the large London dailies the editor of the "Woman's" page may earn an income of from £5 to £10 a week and upwards.

There are very seldom vacancies to be found on the principal ladies' weekly papers, all of which have well-known women writers on their staffs, but on the smaller weeklies and on the staffs of magazines openings may often be found. In these instances, however, the scale of pay is considerably less than in the case of the dailies and larger periodicals.

Training.—The best training for this kind of work is that received by practical experience as secretary and assistant to a fashion editress. Girls have risen to the position of editress in this way, but they have always been girls with brains who knew how to make the most of their opportunities.

Society Editor and Social Reporting.—A certain acquaintance with the manners and usages of good society is necessary for this particular work, with a good memory for faces, quickness of observation, and a facile graphic pen. The journalist who deals with society functions is sometimes known as the "Society Editor." She should dress well, and cultivate a pleasing, tactful manner. Self-possession and *savoir faire* are very important attributes in work of this kind, where a woman will have to mix at times in the highest social circles. A good social connection will be a great recommendation in obtaining a post as "Society Editor." The position is a very well-paid one, particularly in London with its unending round of social functions, but the expenses in the way of dress, &c., are very great. During the season the work of reporting also is apt to become most arduous. The very special qualities required for the suitable filling of the post of society editor are possessed by comparatively few women, and for this reason this branch of journalism is not so overcrowded as others. A woman who possesses all these qualities is a most valuable member of a newspaper staff.

Exchange Editor.—The position of "Exchange Editor" on a daily paper may be successfully filled by a woman. It is a position, however, which is as a rule only obtainable by a girl who has gained a certain amount of experience of the inside of a newspaper office. The intelligent girl who has filled the post of secretarial assistant to the editor or the news editor is the one most likely to be promoted to a position of this kind, as it is essentially one which can only be filled by a woman with a certain amount of journalistic training. First and foremost it is essential that the exchange editor should have the "news instinct." She must be able to tell to a nicety what news is worth following up, and also be able to make suggestions for good articles and new stories.

Every day she has to carefully read all the chief morning and evening papers published in Great Britain and Ireland, together with certain of the foreign papers, if these are not dealt with in the foreign editor's department—also the chief technical papers and other weeklies on the days on which they are issued. On these papers she must mark for cutting all news that has to be followed up, all paragraphs which might suggest a news story of any kind, and in some cases write down her suggestions for the benefit of the news editor or any other editor whom they may concern.

She will also have to cut out all references to and dates of future engagements for the use of the news editor. The responsibility of the position lies in the fact that the "Exchange Editor" must not miss either a subject which requires following up, or a subject which holds out any possible suggestion.

The exact routine of the work varies in different offices, but its principles remain the same. In some newspaper offices there will be two exchange editors. One will be on duty in the early morning until about 3 P.M., and the other from 3 P.M. and during the evening; the work in this way will be well divided. In many offices the foreign papers are dealt with in the foreign editor's room, and the exchange work for the news editor is done by one of the news editor's assistants. Everything will depend of course upon the size of the staff. Salary for work of this kind varies to a great extent; and as the post is one which depends a great deal upon promotion in the office, no set figure can be given. As it is a position of some responsibility £4 a week should be the minimum figure, rising to £6 or more. A woman will have to show remarkable sharpness and aptitude before she is entrusted with this work, and, as has been said before, it is a post that can only be obtained by a woman with experience of the inner side of the newspaper office.

Secretary to Editor.—This is a position of some importance and trust. A girl may be secretary to the editor-in-chief or to any of his subordinate editors—the news editor, literary editor, &c., &c. The scope of an editorial secretary's duties are very large. When she is secretary to the editor-in-chief her work will not only consist in dealing with his correspondence; often she will have to do "Exchange Work" on his behalf, read and give her opinion upon articles submitted, arrange the editor's appointments, interview people for him; in fact, there is no limit to the extent and variety of her duties. If she is secretary to the news editor she may also, besides dealing with his correspondence, have to watch the newspapers and the news tape machines on his behalf, drawing his attention to any news of importance coming over the machines. In her charge will be all invitations and tickets of admission to social functions. These she will have to acknowledge or refuse as the case may be, keeping the invitations ready to hand filed under their respective dates.

The extent of responsible work with which an editorial secretary is entrusted will depend to a great extent upon the capability she displays. She may never rise beyond the level of a shorthand typist, but if she is tactful, clever, and makes the most of her opportunities, she will become invaluable to her chief and be in all probability promoted to the position of editor's or news editor's assistant, where the scope of her duties will be considerably enlarged.

Two pounds a week is a good commencing

salary for an editor's secretary. This may be increased to as much as £4 and upwards, where promotion to the duties of an assistant is obtained. Habits of system and order and a knowledge of the various filing systems are invaluable in a post of this kind, where so many manuscripts have to be dealt with.

Women Reporters.—Reporting holds out many prospects for women in the world of journalism, but at the same time a woman reporter to succeed must have special talents and capabilities. Some women never rise above the level of junior reporters, earning from £1, 10s. to £2, 2s. a week. These show no special talent in their work beyond taking a good shorthand note if needs be, and being able to take an accurate report of lectures and meetings; but the really clever woman reporter is invaluable upon a newspaper staff.

The successful woman reporter is intelligent, energetic, and tactful, with abundant powers of description and a facile pen. She is prepared to live a strenuous existence, and her day is one of endless activity. Her work is of a nature which cannot be limited to regular set hours. The successful woman reporter has ideas; she can suggest a good news story and follow it out to its conclusion, whilst her enthusiasm in her work is unflagging, and in this way she often compares to advantage with a man. Her powers of intuition and her tact are so much greater than that found in the average man reporter that she is at times entrusted with very special duties, success in the achievement of which have often brought her into prominence and served to secure her a much higher position. As an interviewer in particular does a woman's tact stand her in good stead. A good woman reporter must be able to report upon anything and everything from a Royal wedding to a riotous suffrage demonstration. She must be ready to work at all hours should she be called upon to do so. She must be prepared to endure discomforts and even rebuffs at times. A woman reporter should have no false pride. She must know her way about and be well informed generally. The very special qualities necessary to make women good reporters are not often found, but women possessing them have achieved brilliant success in this calling.

In London the rate of pay for a woman reporter varies from £4 to £6, 6s. a week. This rate is sometimes exceeded, the salary varying to a large extent according to the capabilities of the worker. As an instance, one very clever lady reporter, who is only twenty-five years of age, is to my knowledge earning £8, 8s. a week on the staff of one of our large London dailies.

Good salaries may also be earned on the leading newspapers in Edinburgh, Glasgow, and Birmingham. On the smaller provincial dailies the rate of pay is very much less. Broadly speaking, there are comparatively few openings in the provinces at present. London is essentially the Mecca of the Woman Journalist.

Outside Contributions.—The incursions of many women into journalism are limited to what are termed in journalistic circles "outside contributions"; that is to say, they submit articles, short stories, &c., to editors for their approval. The great thing in work of this kind is to watch carefully the style of articles published by the different papers and only submit articles of a similar style. A woman who makes a point of studying her papers and magazines thoroughly will soon get an idea of the kind of matter used by the various publications. She should remember that brightly written articles with a certain topical interest stand a much better chance of acceptance than articles upon general subjects with no particular bearing upon questions of the moment. One guinea per thousand words is an average rate of payment for the work of an unknown writer, the scale of payment rising to £3, 3s. a thousand, whilst £5 a thousand represents a fair payment for very special work. A woman writer should always endeavour to take up a special subject and write upon it until she becomes gradually known to editors as an authority on this particular subject. If she achieves this result she will have no difficulty in finding a market for her literary wares.

Short Stories represent a promising field for the would-be journalist who has a gift in this direction. At the present day the popularity of the "short story" for magazines is on the increase, and editors are always willing to publish really good work. The art of short story-writing is, however, only possessed by few. Those fortunate ones who are able to write a really readable short story should make a study of the literary fare which appeals to the public taste if they wish to see their MSS. accepted, for in journalism it must be remembered that it is not what the writer likes but what the public likes that finds a ready market.

Sending MSS. for Consideration.—All MSS. sent up for editorial consideration should be written on one side of the paper. It should be typed if possible; some editors announce that they will only read typed manuscripts. Whether this rule prevails or not the chances are that all neatly typed MSS. will be examined first. If it is impossible to have it typewritten, then let the writing be as clear and as legible as possible. All pages should be numbered in their proper sequence, and the name and address of the author should be inscribed on the top left-hand corner of the first page, or at the end of the MSS. A stamped and addressed envelope should always be enclosed if the return of the MSS. is desired. Do not make the mistake of writing long verbose letters to the editor discussing the merits of your contribution or your ambitions towards a literary career. Hundreds of young girls make the mistake of imagining that effusions of the kind may induce the editor to look more favourably upon their contribution. Never was there a greater mistake. An editor is a man of business, not a man of sentiment. It is his business to supply the public with the literature they require, and not to go out of his way to give enterprising young lady journalists their first chance.

Sub-editing.—Posts as sub-editors on magazines or other periodicals may be successfully filled by women. A good knowledge of grammar and composition is essential together with an aptitude for extracting the essence of copy which has to be cut down to facts only, owing to the exigency of space. Aptitude for this work comes with practice only. No amount of teaching can impart the skill which is the result of experience. A sub-editor should be able to work quickly in times of stress. There is always a certain "rush" of work incidental to getting a publication ready for press; through this she must keep a cool head, or many vexing mistakes may result from her not being able to do so. The sub-editor must know how to prepare copy for the printers and to read and correct proofs. She should also be acquainted with printers' technical terms, the styles and sizes of type, paper, &c. She must know how to measure drawings for illustration blocks, and also know how to make up not only pages, but the entire publication if required.

A sub-editor should also understand the laws of libel, and so be able to recognise any statement which might be construed into libel and cost her paper a great deal in damages if allowed to appear. Sub-editorships on the larger periodicals or on daily papers are seldom filled by women. On the smaller weeklies, woman's magazines, on general magazines, and the smaller periodicals such positions may be obtained, but chiefly by the intelligent girl or woman who is first engaged to fill the position of secretary to the editor and afterwards drifts in to the more responsible position. Let it be said, however, that it is only the girls and women with brains and initiative who can get on in this way. The girl upon whom the editor can rely to act for him in his absence, settling important and unforeseen details on his behalf, renders herself invaluable to him, and her progress is assured; whilst the woman who is merely content to do what she is told, displaying no power of initiative when occasion for its use arises, will just as surely remain where she is, never rising out of the rut of her own particular routine work.

The rate of salary varies according to the paper. As compared with the responsibility of their work, women sub-editors are not as a rule well paid. On some periodicals with limited circulation, ladies have filled the post of sub-editor for as small a salary as £1 weekly. As a rule, however, work at this rate of payment has been undertaken only with a view to the valuable experience afforded, the worker seizing the first opportunity to obtain a more remunerative post. £2 to £4 a week may be taken as average salaries to be earned by a woman sub-editor, except in exceptional cases. £3 to £4 a week would be considered a fair rate of payment in London.

The "Special Writer" and "The Free Lance."—By far the most lucrative journalistic employment for the woman who is not actually a member of the staff of any newspaper or periodical is that of writing upon "special subjects." To do this, it is of course necessary to have an expert knowledge of the subject in question, so much so as to be looked upon as an authority upon it. A woman special writer may be a "free lance" or she may receive a retaining fee from as many as half-a-dozen papers for a weekly, fortnightly, or even a monthly contribution, and she can command £2, 2s. to £3, 3s. per column for her work.

The term "free lance" is used to indicate a journalist who is not attached to any particular paper, but is a fairly regular contributor to many. A great deal of hard work and perseverance is necessary before a woman can achieve any success as a "free lance." First she must make her work known to the different editors. She should try and think out some really good ideas for an article or series of articles in the first instance. When she has her plan well thought out she should write the first article of the series and call upon the editor to make her suggestion. Good ideas are always considered, and the writer stands a far better chance of having her work accepted if she can put forward some good well-thought-out scheme suitable for the paper to which she takes it. She should be careful, of course, to take her idea or scheme to the right person. Amongst amateur journalists, as a rule, there is a very vague idea of the *personnel* of a daily newspaper staff. Many women think that the editorial department of our large dailies is run by an editor, a sub-editor, and one or two reporters. It would be difficult indeed to get a newspaper published at all with such a small staff. The average editorial staff of a London daily is made up as follows:—

Editor-in-Chief.
News Editor.
Literary Editor.
Foreign Editor.
Sports Editor.
Night Editor.
Chief Sub-Editor.
Editor of Ladies' Page.
"Leader" Writers and "Special" Writers.
Dramatic Critic.
Musical Critic.
Reporters and Sub-Editors.

It will be seen, therefore, that whilst most ideas should be taken to the editor-in-chief, news items should be submitted to the news editor, literary items to the literary editor, fashion items to the fashion editress, and so on.

News contributions are paid by lineage, three-halfpence a line being the average price for ordinary news, and threepence a line for special and exclusive news.

Training for Journalism.—Although many qualifications are necessary to make a journalist, a facile pen and good powers of description are indispensable, and it is useless for a woman who has not the gift of writing to embark upon this career. Journalism is the profession of all others for which proper training can only be obtained by practical experience.

There are several schools of journalism at which valuable knowledge may be gained, but no amount of training will ever be equal to one year's experience of the inside of a newspaper office.

The very best training for the girl who wishes to take up newspaper work would be for her to obtain a position as typist or secretary in the editorial department of a newspaper office. A clever girl will make the most of her opportunities by careful observation of what goes on around her. She will seize eagerly upon any chance of filling reporting engagements in times of great stress when help is needed. If she does her work well and is tactful and obliging her chance will come one day. Many a girl from humble beginnings has risen to quite an important position in this way. But it is only the girls who do their work conscientiously and well, who are always tactful and obliging, to whom the chances come. Many a clever and even brilliant worker has been passed by in promotion owing to her disobliging disposition and want of tact. Journalism is a profession of ups and downs, quick promotions and rapid changes. It is a profession which presents brilliant prospects and heart-breaking disappointments, and it is only the woman with real capability, who is not afraid of hard work, who can count upon any measure of success.

ADVERTISEMENT WRITING

The art of advertising has made great strides within recent years, and with this progress has come an increased demand for really good advertisement writers. It is not often that a woman turns her attention to advertisement writing as a means of income—a woman who can use her pen with any small measure of success has literary aspirations, as a rule. Well, she need not altogether give up these literary aspirations, but while she is hankering after the unattainable, the money to "keep the pot boiling" is slow to come, and one must live. If she would turn some of her literary talent to account by qualifying as an advertisement writer, she would find plenty wherewith to keep the "pot boiling" if she only set about her work in the right way.

Writing advertisements is not such an easy matter as one would imagine. It requires a peculiar knack of constructing forcible and sales-compelling phrases. It requires the faculty for concentrating upon the essence of an argument and giving only the details that tell. An advertisement writer should be an adept at writing good headlines, and at the display and arrangement of type. She should have a thorough technical knowledge in addition to her literary aptitude, and also understand the relative values of display and illustration, being able to adapt her copy to suit the class of readers to whom it is intended to appeal.

Little has yet been written or said in regard to the prospects for women in the field of advertisement writing. Too many are apt to confuse advertisement writing with advertisement canvassing, with the result that few give a second thought to the possibilities held out for the good advertisement writer. The business of the advertisement canvasser is to get advertisement orders for the paper she represents, and although the ability to suggest a good advertising idea to a client will stand her in good stead, inasmuch as it increases the scope of her usefulness to her employers, it is not indispensable, the essential qualification being of course the ability to obtain orders.

Advertisement canvassing does not enter at all into the curriculum of the woman who takes up the career of an advertisement writer and specialist pure and simple. It is true that if she obtains a position as special advertisement writer on a newspaper the style of her copy will most certainly tend to affect advertisement orders, as an unwilling advertiser is often brought to book by a really good advertising suggestion, but here her responsibility ends.

The truth is being rapidly brought home to large advertisers that certain phases of advertising are better dealt with by women. Many costumiers, milliners, and drapers have their advertisements designed by women, because they have realised the fact that it requires a woman writer to bring out the best selling points in advertising all those things so dear to the heart of womankind in general. Who indeed is more capable of expounding to advantage upon the special qualities of furs, silks, hats, gowns, and woman's wear in general than one of the feminine sex who has an intimate knowledge of the subject and understands just the kind of arguments which will most likely appeal to women like herself? To the gradual recognition of the qualification of a clever woman writer for work of this kind is due the fact that a good deal of the booklet and special catalogue designing, as well as the advertisement writing, for large drapery and millinery firms is gradually being entrusted to women.

A woman may be either a "free lance" in advertising or she may obtain a good staff appointment; several large firms employ lady advertisement writers on their staffs. The advertisement writing for many of our chief publishing companies is also in the charge of ladies, whilst many newspapers, magazines, and periodicals employ lady advertisement writers.

The salaries for those filling staff appointments vary from 30s. to £4 or £5 a week, the first-named salary being essentially that of a beginner, £3 to £4 being the most usual figure for the tried and trusted worker. Of course, these figures admit of a great deal of expansion in certain exceptional cases. The advertising genius who, besides supplying the matter for advertisements, is capable of planning out an entire advertising campaign, from the ordinary form letters to full-page advertisements in the leading dailies, being able to handle facts, figures, and the business as well as the literary side of the campaign, bringing the whole to a successful conclusion, can practically demand her own terms, but such advertising geniuses are rare amongst women, who as a rule are apt to under-value rather than over-value their capabilities, and through over-conscientiousness in this matter are loth to undertake large responsibilities. It may be said that it is this lack of initiative which debars most women, in whatever profession of business they are engaged, from rising to the heights which they might otherwise have attained.

A woman who wishes to take up advertisement writing as a career must possess some power of initiative from the very beginning. Take the "free lance," for instance. Commissions from advertisers will not come to those who sit down quietly waiting for the "plums" to fall into their lap. An advertisement inserted in the "Want" columns of a suitable paper might sometimes be productive and result in perhaps one or two single commissions, but a living is not to be made by chance work of this kind. When a lady is thoroughly well qualified as an advertisement writer, possessing a certificate or other similar proof of efficiency from the institution at which she pursued her studies, she should set about getting work by watching carefully the advertising of the large firms in her neighbourhood—not only their paper and magazine advertising, but also their booklets, catalogues, or other printed matter. She should study well the various kinds and degrees of their merchandise, and think out good ideas for a striking advertisement, a good booklet or other literary matter. The ideas must, of course, be novel ones. Then she should write to the firm in question enclosing her suggestions, and asking them for an appointment. She should do this in the case of several of the chief firms of her neighbourhood, and if she receives only two replies from firms who wish to adopt her suggestions her trouble will be amply repaid.

Booklet designing and writing is very remunerative work. One guinea, as a rule, is the price paid to a beginner, whilst a more experienced writer could command a fee of £5, 5s. for designing and supplying copy for one little booklet. A woman who wishes to establish a connection must be unfailing in her energy and a hard worker. She must never be discouraged, but keep on plodding until her end is obtained. Then she will be able to lead a life of comparative ease, for the expert advertisement writer can turn out copy with very little trouble, added to which the work of advertisement writing is full of interest and variety. New ideas are constantly suggesting themselves, and there is a certain fascination in working them out to their conclusion.

As has been said before, the number of staff appointments as "advertisement writers" for women is increasing daily, and for those who prefer steady and regular work at a fixed salary, however small, a position on the staff of some firm or newspaper is preferable. Such positions are mostly obtained by recommendation, although a staff appointment may often result from introductions received while "free lancing." The *Daily News* is the best advertising medium for a position of the kind.

Training.—It has been seen that to succeed as an advertisement writer a woman requires the qualities of energy, initiative, patience, and perseverance, besides the necessary technical training in her work. The girl or woman who requires to be guided in every step she takes had better give up the idea of embarking upon a career of the kind, for her time will be wasted. A certain technical training is necessary also. The Americans have long ago realised the truth of this, and they have innumerable institutes and schools devoted solely to training in advertisement writing and business methods. In London a thorough training in advertising may be had at the "Dixon Institute," 193 New Oxford Street. This is a Correspondence School, so that the training is accessible to any one residing in the United Kingdom or abroad. The course is a most comprehensive one, covering the entire ground from the A.B.C. of advertisement writing to the planning and carrying out of an advertising campaign. The beginner is instructed in the technicalities regarding the various styles and sizes of types and display types, proof correcting, different kinds of borders, blocks for illustrations, and the various illustrating processes. Step by step the students are taken through every phase of advertising. The lessons are very carefully graduated, and the tuition may be said to be in every sense personal to each pupil, every effort being made to study their individual idiosyncrasies, and direct their training in the most profitable manner. The fee for the whole Advertising Course is £6, 6s.; whilst £9, 9s. is the fee for a combined course on advertising and business methods.

It is advisable to take a course of this kind before embarking upon the career of an advertisement writer and specialist. Of course, some girls and women are so fortunately placed as to be brought up in the atmosphere of advertisement writing, as it were; the secretary to an advertisement manager, for instance, if she is intelligent and observant, can pick up many hints and go through a training of actual experience. Now and then she may suggest an idea for an advertisement which will prove so good and effective that her capabilities in that direction will become recognised; gradually more and more copy will be entrusted to her, until she imperceptibly slips into the place of "special advertisement writer," her duties being restricted to writing advertisements. But these are only special cases; the average woman is not so fortunate, and for her a thorough course of study is essential if she is to make any headway. Natural talent is valuable, but where it is combined with the knowledge which a thorough training alone can impart, its value is increased by almost cent. per cent.

SECRETARIAL WORK

The post of "private secretary" is one particularly suited to a clever, tactful girl or woman, and there is always a certain demand for competent secretaries, which the stress and bustle of present-day life tends steadily to increase. All the leading professional men, such as consulting physicians, specialists, dentists, barristers, authors, and dramatists—also our great philanthropists and merchant princes employ secretaries, sometimes one, sometimes more, and they rely a great deal upon the intelligence and capability of the persons they employ in this capacity. These posts are in many cases filled by women.

The growth of women's institutions, clubs, political societies, &c., has also created an increasing demand for the lady secretary.

Secretarial posts in charitable and philanthropic institutions are also filled by women. There are great opportunities in secretarial work for really competent workers, but for competent workers only. The army of incompetents who do more than anything else to lower the standard of women's earnings will find that in the domain of the private secretary at least they cannot encroach. There are some instances, perhaps, when a good secretarial position has been obtained by influence—and the long-suffering chief has put up with the delinquencies of his factotum through goodness of heart or dislike of change—but such instances are rare. A secretarial position entails too much responsibility for it to be placed in inexperienced or inefficient hands.

Qualifications and Training.—First of all the girl who aspires to a secretarial post must have had a thoroughly good general education, supplemented by the special training which is required to adequately equip her for her career. This latter should include a thorough and practical knowledge of shorthand and typewriting. No mere smattering of shorthand will answer the purpose. It is not sufficient to be able to take down a quick shorthand note if one cannot read one's notes afterwards. The competent secretary should also have a good knowledge of précis-writing and research work; she should be conversant with at least two languages, and know how to keep accounts. Book and document indexing should also be included in her secretarial training; she should also know how to read and correct proofs if she is to make an efficient secretary for a literary man. System and order are invaluable qualities for a private secretary. She should know where to lay hands at once upon any document required, and for this purpose should be acquainted with one or two of the best filing systems and be able to put them to practical use.

The time taken in special training will depend a great deal upon individual circumstances. A brilliantly clever girl, for instance, would learn her work much more quickly than a girl of only average capability. A year at least should be given to the study of shorthand. In this constant and daily practice is required. Once the elements of shorthand are mastered, the student should make a point of attending speed classes every day. At Pitman's Metropolitan School, Southampton Row, London, a feature is made of these speed classes. In these classes the student has to take down from dictation at certain fixed speeds, the speed of dictation varying from the ordinary speed of writing from dictation in longhand to the highest speeds attainable in shorthand, and, what is of the utmost importance, students are required to carefully transcribe their notes. At Pitman's school a regular secretarial course may be taken, the fees varying in accordance with the amount of subjects included in the course. A very good training may also be had at the Woman's Institute, 92 Victoria Street, London, S.W. This includes all the subjects with which either a private or an organising secretary should be acquainted, the fee being £35 for a course of three terms. This course will in most cases prove sufficient training for an intelligent girl, who should, however, supplement it with regular shorthand speed practice. At the end of her course the student will receive a certificate of efficiency in all the subjects of general secretarial work.

The Society of Arts and London Chambers

of Commerce also hold examinations for which the chief commercial and secretarial schools prepare their pupils. Certificates from either of these examining bodies will prove most useful in obtaining a post. The cost of training in secretarial work averages from £25 to £50, and more if very special and thorough training is undergone. Principals of Colleges as a rule do all in their power to secure posts for well-qualified pupils. In addition to Pitman's School and the Woman's Institute, good secretarial training may be had at Clark's College, Chancery Lane, London, and Kensington College, Kensington, London, W.

Salaries.—An efficient private secretary may command a salary of from £100 to £200 per annum; the salary of a residential secretary would range from £50 to £150, or even more in special circumstances; good organising secretaries of societies are also well paid. Needless to say, these salaries can only be obtained by thoroughly efficient workers.

LIBRARY WORK AND INDEXING

The field for women librarians is at present somewhat restricted, though there is every indication of future development in this direction. Library work is work for which well-read and well-educated women should be particularly well fitted. It is work, however, which requires very special training. The librarian should possess a good memory for facts and figures; she should have had a thoroughly good education, and must, in addition, be well versed in bibliography, cataloguing, classification, and indexing. A thorough training is indispensable; there are no openings for untrained workers. In regard to public libraries, women chiefly at present occupy positions as assistant librarians, though in some instances the post of head librarian is filled by a woman. The librarians of all the women's colleges are women, former students being usually selected to fill the post. In the Board of Education library there are assistant lady librarians. A lady is at the head of the *Times* Book Club Library, with a number of women assistants under her control. Most of the large newspaper offices employ lady librarians and assistant librarians, and posts of this kind are usually very well paid.

The library work of a newspaper office involves special work in the filing and indexing of newspaper cuttings. Experience of this work is best gained by obtaining a position as assistant in a newspaper library when the ordinary training as librarian has been concluded. To fill a position as head librarian in a newspaper office, or indeed in any kind of library, a woman requires great powers of initiative and organisation in addition to a thorough knowledge of her work.

Training.—There are not many institutions at present where good training in library work may be had. Classes in general library work are held at the London School of Economics, Clare Market, W.C. Students are prepared for the examinations of the "Library Association." The full certificate of the Library Association, however, can only be gained by those who have had practical experience in a library, although the classes of the school are open to all. The fees amount to £10, 10s. a session for admission to all the classes. Any of the subjects may, however, be taken separately at separate fees. The University of London grants a yearly studentship of £25 for girls who have matriculated or hold the certificate of the Joint Board tenable for three years at the Library of the School of Economics.

A good way of training is to give one's services as assistant in some library for little or no remuneration, thus serving an apprenticeship, and at the same time qualifying for the examination of the Library Association and fulfilling the condition in regard to actual experience of library work.

The salaries for librarians range from £50 a year for an assistant to £150 a year for a head librarian. In one or two large London newspaper offices the figure of £200 to £250 is reached by head librarians, whilst assistants begin at from £65; £78 to £156 in some cases being paid to an experienced assistant. These posts, however, are not as a rule easily accessible, preference in filling vacancies being usually accorded to members of the staff.

Indexing.—Indexing, which should be thoroughly understood by the competent private secretary and librarian, may also be taken up as a separate profession. Only women endowed with an abundance of patience and perseverance should take up work of this kind, which from its nature is apt to become monotonous and brain-fagging to those of a highly strung nervous or impatient temperament. Accuracy and power of concentration are essential attributes for the indexer. A good technical training in the actual work is necessary. A woman requires to be an expert at the work if she is to make a living as an indexer.

Indexing is fairly remunerative work. It is not, however, always easy to obtain, but if a woman has once obtained a staff position or established a connection as a "piecework" indexer, she will in all probability keep it, for the essential qualities of accuracy and precision so necessary in indexing work are comparatively rare; so much so that an employer will be loth to part with a really good reliable worker in any circumstances. Perhaps this forms one of the reasons for the comparatively small number of vacancies to be found. A year's training in indexing is usually necessary, although in some few cases six months will prove sufficient. For technical and complicated indexing eighteen months to two years training would be required.

For indexing alone the openings are not very numerous at present, and the opportunities for good training are comparatively limited. In London a thorough training may be had from Miss Petherbridge, 52B Conduit Street, W., for an inclusive fee of £25 for a year's course.

The indexing of all our Parliamentary papers is in charge of a lady, and some of the Government offices and County Councils employ lady indexers. Lady indexers are also employed in connection with the libraries of newspaper offices. At present indexing is most useful when allied with secretarial or library work; but though the openings for indexing employment alone are not numerous at the moment, they are likely to increase, and with the increased demand the facilities for training will doubtless become more numerous. £52 to £104 a year is an average rate to pay for the indexer who holds a staff appointment. Indexing, however, is most commonly paid for as "piecework." Two shillings a printed page is paid for the indexing of Government Blue Books. In books and other general publications the rates of payment vary. To make "piecework" indexing remunerative, a woman would require to establish a large connection. A reputation for accuracy and neat work will help her best to do this.

MEDICINE AND NURSING

At one time it seemed that the difficulties which barred the progress of women who wished to qualify as medical practitioners were insurmountable, but gradually one by one these obstacles have been overcome, and nowadays the path of the woman who wishes to qualify for the medical profession is a comparatively clear one.

Women are now admitted to the medical examinations of all the Universities of Great Britain with the exception of Oxford and Cambridge; also to the examinations of the Royal College of Physicians, London, and the Royal College of Surgeons, England, the Society of Apothecaries of London, and the Conjoint Colleges of Scotland and Ireland. This article gives full information in regard to time and cost of training for the professions of medicine and nursing, as well as a careful survey of the prospects afforded to women in both careers.

Some Important Considerations.—Before a girl decides to train for the medical profession, there are several things which she must carefully consider. In the first place five years is the minimum time which can be spent upon training, six years as a rule being required. During this time she must be sure of £130 a year at the least to cover her medical training, board, and clothing expenses, including examination fees, books, instruments, &c. £130 a year would indeed leave very little margin, and the girl who is not an adept at making small economies would find it somewhat difficult to make ends meet even on that sum. £150 to £200 would really be a more satisfactory allowance; but £130 represents the minimum. Of course, if a girl is living at home she will only need the necessary sum for college fees, examination fees, books and instruments. Also if she succeeds in gaining one of the scholarships attached to nearly every medical school, the cost of her training will be materially reduced. The training for the medical profession is longer and more expensive than that required in preparing for any other career, and the time at which a start may be made in putting it to a practical use upon an income-earning basis is therefore considerably deferred. Again, the girl who wishes to make a success of the career of medicine must possess certain indispensable qualities. In the first place she must have a thoroughly healthy constitution to enable her to stand the stress of both training and "practice," when the training has been completed. In addition, she must have a thoroughly healthy and well-balanced mind, and be free from that tendency to nerves and hysteria which characterise so many members of her sex. A good education is, of course, indispensable, as a preliminary examination in general subjects must be passed before a girl can even enter upon her career as a medical student. And last, but not least, she must be endowed with an abundant fund of good common-sense.

Savoir faire and a knowledge of social life will also stand the medical woman in good stead; for this reason it is as well for a girl not to take up her medical studies directly she leaves school, but to spend a year going out into society, travelling, and altogether enlarging her social aspect. She should do her best to gain an insight into character and to study the idiosyncrasies of the men and women with whom she comes into contact. When she has started practice much of her success will depend upon her tact in dealing with the fads and foibles of her patients; in these circumstances keenness of perception in diagnosing the character of the patient will be as useful as keenness in diagnosing the disease from which he or she is suffering.

It must be remembered that during her five years of studentship her time will be occupied by hard work and study; she will not be able to go to too many social gatherings if her work has not to be interfered with in any way, so that she must make the most of her opportunities, in the year allowed between the interval of leaving school and taking up her studies, to glean what knowledge she can gain of social life in its different phases.

Choice of a Qualification.—Before a woman can practise as a doctor her name must be placed on the Medical Register of the General Medical Council, and no one can be placed thereon who has not one or more degrees or diploma of one of the examining bodies already mentioned after having completed the five years' course of study required by the General Medical Council. University degrees, more especially those of the London University, are held in the highest repute, and a student should work for these wherever possible. If, however, she has any doubts as to her powers in this direction, she should content herself with working for a diploma of one of the other bodies, as it is considered that the attainment of a diploma is of greater certainty than that of a degree, so it is as well to make certain of the former, especially as the latter can always be tried for afterwards.

As the regulations of the various examining bodies differ to a great extent, it will be necessary for a student to decide before beginning her course of study which degree or diploma she wishes to obtain.

Regulations.—Every medical student should be registered at the office of the General Medical Council, 299 Oxford Street, London, W., within fifteen days after the commencement of her professional studies. In accordance with the requirements of the General Medical Council a preliminary examination in general subjects must be passed previous to registration.

The following examinations are accepted by the General Medical Council when the certificates include the required subjects :—Oxford and Cambridge Junior and Senior Locals. Higher Local Examinations, Responsions, Moderations, Previous and General Examinations, Matriculation Examinations of the British and most of the foreign and colonial Universities; the College of Preceptors. First-Class Certificate (the required subjects to be passed at not more than two examinations) the College of Preceptors' Preliminary Examinations for Medical Students—the required subjects to be passed at one time.

Any of these preliminary examinations will fulfil the requirements of all the examining bodies with the exception of the Universities. In order to prepare for the degree of the London University it will be necessary to pass the Matriculation Examination of the University of London, or any examination accepted by the University in lieu of Matriculation. In entering for the degree of the Irish University the student must pass the Matriculation Examination of the University of Ireland. The University of Durham allows any registered medical student to take the first and second professional examinations, but before entering for the final examination a further examination in arts is required, unless the student has already passed the Entrance Examination of some University.

Chief Medical Degrees Open to Women

University of London—M.B., B.S., M.D., M.S.
University of Durham—M.B., B.S.
University of Ireland—M.B., C.H., M.D., M.S.
Scottish University Degrees—M.B., Ch.B., M.D.
Royal College of Physicians and Surgeons—L.R.C.P., M.R.C.S.
Society of Apothecaries—L.S.A.
Conjoint Colleges of Scotland—L.R.C.P.

The following qualifications are also open to women :—

M.A.O. and B.A.O.—Master and Bachelor of Obstetrics (R.U.I.)
University of Cambridge—Diploma of Public Health—D.P.H.
Royal College of Physicians, Diploma of Membership, London—M.R.C.P.
Royal College of Surgeons, England—Diploma of Fellowship—F.R.C.S.
Royal College of Physicians and Surgeons Ireland—F.R.C.P.S.

Training.—The course of study for the London University degrees of M.B., B.S. extends over five and a half years. Three different examinations have to be passed. The first examination after one year's study, the second eighteen months later, and the third three years later.

Courses for the Scotch University degrees, M.B. and Ch.B., the Irish and Durham degree, the Diplomas of the Royal Colleges of England, the Triple Qualification of the Conjoint Colleges of Scotland, and the Qualification of the Society of Apothecaries, London, extend over five years.

Chief amongst the medical colleges for women are those at London, Edinburgh, and Glasgow, which are exclusively for women students. There are several other medical schools in the provinces connected with provincial universities, but none for women only, the women being admitted as fellow students with the men.

Women are admitted to the medical classes on the same terms as men at the following Universities :—

Universities of Dublin, Manchester, University College of South Wales and Monmouthshire, Cardiff (University of Wales), Leeds School of Medicine (with the exception of the Infirmary, which is not open to Women), University of Birmingham, College of Medicine, Newcastle-on-Tyne, and the Universities of Bristol, Sheffield, Liverpool, Aberdeen, St. Andrews, Dundee, Dublin, Belfast, Cork, and Galway.

M.D. Degrees.—The London M.D. Examination is only open to students who have passed the M.B., B.S. of the University of London, two years previous to entering for the M.D. Examination.

There are no special courses arranged for the M.D. Examination in London, as candidates have generally spent most of the interval in obtaining experience in Medicine, and in reading up the special subject for which they intend to enter for the examination.

The London M.S. (Master of Surgery) may

also be taken in no less than two years after the London M.B., B.S. Examination. Experience in the practice of surgery is the chief training required for the examination. The M.B., B.S. degrees of the University of London are the qualifications in both Medicine and Surgery.

Candidates for the Scotch M.D. degree must have passed the M.B., Ch.B. Examinations of one of the Scotch Universities, and be of the age of twenty-four or upwards. They must pass an examination subsequent to one year after receiving the degrees of Bachelor of Surgery, and must have been engaged at least one year in attendance in the medical wards of a hospital, or in scientific work bearing directly on her profession, and at least two years' practice. Each candidate must submit for approval of the Faculty of Medicine a thesis on any branch of knowledge comprised in the second, third, or fourth examination for the degrees of Bachelor of Medicine and of Surgery which he may have made a subject of study after having received these degrees.

London.—" The London (Royal Free Hospital) School of Medicine for Women " is the great medical training centre for London, and was the first women's medical school in the kingdom. It is under the presidency of Mrs. Garret Anderson, M.D., and the opportunities for practical experience afforded to students, both at the Royal Free Hospital, the practice of which is reserved for the students of the school, and at the New Hospital for Women, are unrivalled. The whole course of medical study for the University of London, the Royal College of Physicians and Surgeons, the Society of Apothecaries, London, and the Conjoint Colleges of Scotland and of Ireland can be completed at this school. The greater part of the course for the Durham University and the University of Glasgow can also be taken. The Universities of Calcutta, Madras, and the Punjab also accept the certificates of the School as qualifying for their examinations.

Cost of Training.—The fees for the entire course for the M.B., B.S. degrees of the University of London, including Laboratory and Library fees, come to about £170 if paid down, and about £10 more if paid in annual instalments. To this must be added the cost of books and instruments, which comes to about £30. Then a two months' course of Practical Midwifery must be taken in the External Department of the Royal Free Hospital. Students must reside during the two months required for the course at the special house in connection with the hospital maintained for the purpose. The charge for Board and Residence is 25s. a week. Students are also required to attend the practice of one of the Fever Hospitals of the Metropolitan Asylums Board, for which a separate fee must be paid, and they must also receive special instruction in Lunacy at the Bethlehem Royal Hospital.

The entire cost of training would therefore amount to about £250 for the whole course, inclusive of extras.

There are many scholarships offered for competition which serve to give material help to the winners in defraying the cost of training. Chief amongst these are *The School Scholarship*, value £50, which is offered annually, and is open to candidates who have passed the London Matriculation Examination or a Preliminary Examination in arts recognised by the General Medical Council and are not holding any other scholarship.

St. Dunstan's Medical Exhibition.—The Governors of the St. Dunstan's Educational Foundation offer annually an Exhibition of £60 a year for three years, extendable for a further period of two years. Candidates must not be more than twenty years of age and must have passed the London Matriculation Examination.

The Bostock Scholarship for Women, value £60 a year, awarded by the Reid Trustees every fourth year, tenable in the first instance for two years, subject to extension for a further period of two years.

The John Bryon Bursary, value £20 a year.

The Fanny Butler Scholarship, value £40—£10 a year for four years, open only to candidates willing to practise in connection with the Church of England Zenana Missionary Society, 27 Chancery Lane, W.C.

The Helen Prideaux Prize of £40.

The Mabel Webb Research Scholarship in Pathology, Physiology, or Chemistry, value £30 for one year, and extendable for two or three years.

Several other minor prizes are awarded.

Several of the chief Missionary Societies are also willing to make grants towards the medical education of ladies who wish to take up medical missionary work when qualified. (See under Medical Missionaries.)

A reduction in fees is made for students entering the school with grants in aid of training from Missionary Societies.

Edinburgh.—The Edinburgh School of Medicine for Women, Surgeons' Hall, Edinburgh, prepares students for the Edinburgh University degrees, M.B., Ch.B., and also for the examinations which are held conjointly by the Royal College of Physicians and Surgeons, Edinburgh, and by the Faculty of Physicians and Surgeons, Glasgow. These examinations admit to the Scottish " Triple Qualification." The classes are also recognised by other universities and colleges.

The minimum cost of education and examinations for the Edinburgh University degrees (M.B., Ch.B.) is about £150; for the Triple Qualification, £115. There are several bursaries available to students, and the Carnegie Trust Fund is also open to them as well as to students of the other universities of Scotland.

The students receive their Clinical Instruction in the wards set apart for the purpose in the Royal Infirmary, also in the Royal Hospital for Sick Children, the City Hospital for Infectious Diseases, and at Bangour Asylum for the Insane.

Training in Glasgow.—The Queen Margaret College is the Women's Department of the University of Glasgow. Here women may prepare for the degrees in art, science, and medicine. For the medical degrees of M.B. and Ch.B. not less than five years' study is required. Students entering on a course of medical study must have previously passed the necessary preliminary examinations, and be registered in the books of the General Medical Council as medical students.

Students are prepared for the M.B., Ch.B. degrees of Glasgow University, the Scottish "Triple Qualification," and the London and Irish University degrees. The fees for the five years amount to about £125, exclusive of examination fees, books and instruments, and in addition a matriculation fee of £1, 1s. must be paid every year. The benefits of the Carnegie Trust Fund and a number of bursaries and scholarships are available to students.

Prospects.—The prospects for the qualified woman practitioner are becoming gradually extended now that a great deal of the old-fashioned prejudice against the "woman doctor" has been removed. In the first place, there is none of that "under-cutting of fees" which has to be adopted by women in most other professions. The Medical Council has decreed that emoluments for women doctors must be on the same basis as those for men, and this rule is always kept. The great object of the newly qualified woman doctor should be to get experience. This can be obtained nowhere better than in hospital work, and before setting up in practice for herself a woman would do well to take a staff appointment in a hospital for at least a year. A number of hospitals have opened their doors to resident women physicians. The salaries vary from £30 to £150 a year, and board and lodging is given.

The New Hospital for Women, 144 Euston Road, W., has a complete staff of women physicians and surgeons. There are also posts for medical women in London at the Clapham Maternity Hospital and School of Midwifery, the Chelsea Hospital for Women, St. John's Hospital for Diseases of the Skin, the Belgravia Children's Hospital.

In Edinburgh women physicians and surgeons are on the staff of the Hospital for Women and Children, Whitehouse Loan, Bruntsfield, and Dispensary for Women and Children; in Glasgow women medical officers are employed at the Victoria Infirmary Dispensary and the Samaritan Hospital for Women. Posts are also held by medical women at hospitals in Birmingham, Brighton, Bristol, Hull, Leeds, Liverpool, Manchester, Nottingham, Reading, and in many other places throughout the country. Various sanatoria and asylums have also recognised the claims of the woman doctor, and appointments in these are as a rule well paid. Private institutions are also appointing women doctors, and there are posts in connection with the Post Office, Factories, Girls' Schools, &c.; these appointments are as a rule remunerative, and many women prefer to take permanent posts of the kind to setting up in practice for themselves, more especially those who do not possess the necessary capital to tide them over the period of waiting which starting in practice always involves.

Private Practice.—No woman who has not sufficient capital to tide her over two or three years should think of starting in practice for herself. To start a practice means a period of waiting for the man practitioner; this period is more likely to be prolonged than decreased in the case of a woman. But a woman can do a great deal towards forming a clientele besides putting up a brass plate on her door and waiting quietly for the arrival of her first patient.

To begin with, she should not start in a neighbourhood without having first received some very good introductions to some of the most influential people in the place. Then she must take the trouble to make herself known socially: she should dress well, go about everywhere; in fact, make as many friends as she can. It is doubtful whether in these circumstances the woman with an abundant fund of tact and *savoir faire*, who creates for herself a social status, has not the advantage over the average young man starting in practice for himself, who is usually remarkably lacking in the necessary "push," and takes little trouble to cultivate the acquaintance of men and women unless they come as patients to his door.

There are several women doctors who have settled in practice for themselves with great success and are now making incomes of from £800 to £1000 a year, but these are only now reaping the reward of years of waiting and hard work. As a rule, when a woman has managed to establish herself as a practitioner, she may count upon making £150 a year as a beginning, once the inevitable waiting period has passed.

The extent to which the initial income will increase will depend chiefly upon herself and upon the wisdom she has employed in the selection of a suitable neighbourhood for her purpose. In London and the larger provincial towns lady doctors have done well, and there are still good openings for well-qualified women physicians. In the smaller provincial towns the prospects are not so good, as there is still an overwhelming amount of prejudice to overcome. In the larger towns in Scotland the prospects for women doctors are also good. Perhaps the best openings to be found at present are in the Colonies, South Africa, Canada, New Zealand and Australia presenting an especially promising field.

Assistant Doctors.—Medical practitioners with very large practices often employ assistant doctors, and in this particular field there are abundant prospects for the qualified medical woman. Women assistants are employed by medical men as well as by medical women; the fees are good, varying with the quality and extent of the practice, and an abundance of experience is to be had in this way. To begin as an assistant doctor is a good preparation in all ways to starting in practice for oneself.

Medical Missionaries.—There are also good openings for women in India, China, the East, as medical missionaries in connection with the various missionary societies. The commencing salary as a rule averages about £120 a year.

The Society for Promoting Christian Knowledge is prepared to give assistance, at a rate not exceeding £75 a year, for a period not exceeding four years, for a complete course of Medical and Surgical Training to ladies who are communicant members of the Church of England, offering themselves for work as Medical Missionaries in connection with some Missionary Society of the Church, or under the direction of a Bishop of the Church, among Heathen or Mohammedan Races. For further information address the Secretaries, S.P.C.K., Northumberland Avenue, London, W.C.

The London Missionary Society occasionally has vacancies for ladies possessing medical qualifications for work in India and China. Apply to the Rev. A. N. Johnson, 16 New Bridge Street, E.C.

The Zenana Bible and Medical Mission, King's Chambers, Portugal Street, Kingsway, W.C., assists ladies who wish to go to India as Missionaries.

The Church of England Zenana Missionary Society desires to obtain the services of ladies possessing medical qualifications for work in India and China. Apply to the Secretary of the Candidates' Committee, C.E.Z.M.S., 27 Chancery Lane, W.C.

The Church Missionary Society is prepared to help towards the cost of training ladies for Missionary work on special conditions. Apply to the Rev. R. Elliot, M.A., L.R.C.S.I., Secretary, Medical Committee, C.M.S., Salisbury Square, E.C.

The Society for the Propagation of the Gospel sends out qualified medical women for medical work among the women of India, China, and Borneo. Women are accepted as medical probationers previous to their training. Application should be made to the Candidates' Secretary, S.P.G. House, Tufton Street, Westminster, S.W.

Women doctors are also appointed in connection with the Lady Dufferin Fund. A small, but at the same time a comfortable, income may be derived from posts of the kind, and the work, though hard, is varied and full of interest.

Medical School Inspectors.—Under the Education Act of 1907 the local education authorities are obliged to provide for the medical inspection of children before or as soon as possible after their admission to a public elementary school, and on such other occasions as the Board of Education may direct. These appointments present good openings for the medical woman. The salary begins at from £200–£250, rising to £300 or more a year. The Diploma in Public Health will qualify a woman for a position of this kind, and will render her eligible also for the post of Assistant Medical Officer of Health or an Inspector of Midwives under the Midwives Act (see p. 654).

Quarantine Officers.—Women are now being appointed as quarantine officers at Suez.

HEALTH VISITORS AND SANITARY INSPECTORS

Many Local Authorities have in recent years appointed women as Health Visitors. The special duty of a Health Visitor is to visit the houses in the poorer districts, and there to give advice upon the feeding and care of children, and to assist in improving sanitary conditions generally. The checking of the unnecessarily large amount of infant mortality among the poorer classes may be said to be the chief *raison d'être* for the appointments of the health visitor. Her mission is essentially that of an adviser, and therefore to be successful in her work she requires an abundance of tact, good judgment, discrimination, and perseverance, for, unlike the Sanitary Inspector, she has no power to enforce the observance of the health laws.

Training.—The Council of the Royal Sanitary Institute have established an examination for Health Visitors. The syllabus includes general structure of the body, personal hygiene, air, water, food, clothing, the dwelling, elements of home-nursing, care of infants and young children, prevention of communicable disease, first aid, treatment of injuries, ailments and accidents. The fee for the examination is £2, 2s. A course of lectures to prepare students for the examination is given at the Institute. Training may also be had at the National Health Society, 52 Berners Street, Oxford Street, London, W., and in Edinburgh and Glasgow at the Nurses' Training Colleges.

The training is not a costly one, seldom involving an expenditure of more than ten guineas. The commencing salary is usually about £50, rising to £100 or £150 in certain cases. Those who wish to qualify as Health Visitors would do well to write for information to the Secretary of the National Health Society, 53 Berners Street, London, W., and to the Secretary of the Royal Sanitary Institute, Parkes Museum, Margaret Street, London.

Women Sanitary Inspectors are also appointed by local authorities, and although their number is at present comparatively small, yet there is no doubt that the openings in this direction will be gradually extended. There is no doubt that workshops and factories where girls and women are employed are much better inspected by women, and the recognition of this fact is due to the admission of women into the ranks of sanitary inspectors. The sanitary inspector is under the authority of the Medical Officer of Health. The details of her work will vary in accordance with the methods of the Medical Officer under whose direction she may be, but it is her chief duty to see that the provisions of the Public Health and the Factory and Workshops Acts are carried out. She will be required to inspect all the factories and workshops, laundries, &c., where female and child labour is employed, seeing that the provisions of the Acts in regard to cleanliness, ventilation, drainage, overtime, &c., are complied with. She must see that there is proper sanitary accommodation and that there is no overcrowding. The inspection of tenement houses will also in many cases fall within the scope of her duties.

The work is of a most responsible nature, involving as it does the enforcing of compliance with the law, and the woman who undertakes it must count tact as one of her qualifications. Her general education must have been good and supplemented by the special training necessary. She will require to have the certificate of the Sanitary Inspectors' Examination Board of London in England and of the Sanitary Association of Scotland.

The candidate must also be able to produce evidence of training by either having previously held office as sanitary inspector or Certificate of Instruction from an institution recognised by the Board.

The examination for the certificate of the Sanitary Association in London consists of two parts, Preliminary and Technical. The Preliminary Examination, which is both writing and oral, is upon the following subjects :—

English (including writing, spelling, composition and dictation) and arithmetic.

The technical examination is upon the following subjects :—

1. Elementary Physics and Chemistry in relation to Water, Soil, Air and Ventilation.
2. Elementary Statistical Methods.
3. Municipal Hygiene or Hygiene of Communities, including Prevention and Abatement of Nuisances, Sanitary Defects in and about Buildings and their Remedies, Water Supplies, Sanitary Appliances, Drainage, Refuse Removal and Disposal, Offensive Trades, Disinfection, Food Inspection.
4. Statutes, and the Orders, Memoranda, and Model By-Laws of the Local Government Board, and the By-Laws in force in the Administrative County of London.

Every candidate must forward to the Secretary of the Board, not later than fourteen days before the commencement of the Examination, notice of her intention to present herself for examination, and half the appointed fee. The remaining half of the fee must be paid not later than seven days before the date of the examination.

Candidates for the technical examination must pass the preliminary examination, unless they shall have passed an examination recognised by the Board in substitution for it; and must forward to the Secretary of the Board not later than fourteen days before the commencement of the examination :—

Evidence of having attained the age of twenty-one years, a recent testimonial as to personal character; if possible, from a Clergyman, Medical Officer of Health, or other person holding an official position. Evidence of having passed a recognised alternative examination, in the case of candidates who claim exemption from the preliminary examination.

The examinations are held twice a year, the fee for the preliminary examination is £1, 1s., and for the technical examination £2, 2s.

The necessary training may be had at the Royal Sanitary Institute, Parkes Museum, 90 Buckingham Palace Road, London, S.W.; the National Health Society, 53 Berners Street, Oxford Street, London, W.; the Bedford College for Women, Baker Street, London, W.; the Heriot Watt College, Edinburgh; the University College of South Wales and Monmouthshire, Cardiff; the Alexandra College, Dublin, and many other provincial centres, a list of which may be had from the Secretary of the Royal Sanitary Institute upon application.

The work, though arduous at times, is not excessive, the hours averaging about eight daily, with the exception of Saturdays, which are half holidays, Sundays, the usual bank holidays, and the summer vacation (about a fortnight to three weeks). The commencing salary is £80 per annum, rising in some cases to £185. Those who wish to train as sanitary inspectors cannot do better than write to the Secretary of the Public Health Society, London, the Sanitary Institute, London, or any other of the bodies mentioned for detailed particulars.

SURGEONS

It requires very special qualities to make a successful surgeon, and the number of women surgeons is very limited. The prospects for women in this branch of the medical profession are necessarily restricted, and the woman surgeon will have to work hard for a number of years before she can look for any return. The practice of surgery entails a large measure of responsibility, and public opinion is slow to acknowledge a woman's capability to undertake work in the execution of which so much nerve, coolness, and skill are necessary. If a woman elects to practise as a surgeon at home, therefore, prejudice will prove one of the most formidable opponents she will have to encounter.

The outlook abroad, however, is much more favourable, especially in regard to those countries in which the women may only receive medical or surgical aid from members of their own sex. In India women are in charge of the surgical work in some of the chief hospitals, but the competition for these posts is necessarily keen.

Training.—After completing her general medical education, which will take not less than five years (see article on medical training), the student must prepare for one of the examinations for a degree or Fellowship in surgery. It will require at least two years to prepare for this. It will be advantageous to obtain a post as assistant surgeon in a hospital, as valuable experience may be obtained in this way. Qualified women doctors may enter for the higher examinations in surgery of the English and Scotch Universities at which they have graduated. Women may also enter for the Fellowship of the College of Surgeons, Glasgow, and for the Fellowship of the Royal College of Surgeons, Ireland.

The training is on the whole a costly one, seldom averaging less than £250. Unless a woman has good private means, it will be almost useless for her to set up in practice for herself, as it will be a number of years before she can even hope to earn sufficient professionally to pay her way.

PHARMACY AND DISPENSING

Pharmacy is rapidly developing as a field for the woman worker; but it is a profession which demands very special qualifications if it is to be taken up with any measure of success.

Needless to say, a good all round general education is an important preliminary to the special training necessary. This should be supplemented by the indispensable qualities of thoroughness and perseverance, to say nothing of a high standard of intelligence, a special taste for the subjects bearing upon pharmacy, and a love of and enthusiasm for the work. In the study of pharmacy thoroughness above all is essential; no mere superficial knowledge will carry a girl through her qualifying examinations, and those who show an incapacity for going to the root of things had better pause and think before they take up the work for which a thoroughly practical training is above all essential.

Training.—The period of special training must extend over at least three years. During three years the law exacts that the student must be apprenticed to a qualified chemist. In England and Scotland both training and qualifications are identical, as students must prepare for the examinations of the Pharmaceutical Society. In Ireland the training extends over four years, and the certificate of the Pharmaceutical Society of Ireland must be obtained. There is, however, very little scope for the lady chemist in Ireland. Prejudice is still somewhat deeply rooted there, and many Irish girls make a point of coming to London to take the English qualification, and embark upon their careers either in England or in Scotland.

A preliminary examination in general subjects must be passed before or during the apprenticeship. Many qualified women chemists take pupils and apprentices, and a list of these ladies, together with a copy of the regulations for training and examinations, may be obtained upon application to the Secretary of the Pharmaceutical Society, Bloomsbury Square, London, W.C.

After her three years' apprenticeship has been completed, the student may enter for the "Minor" or qualifying examination of the Pharmaceutical Society. She should prepare herself for this by taking a course in laboratory practice and various other special subjects at a good College of Pharmacy at the end of the third year of her apprenticeship. If she passes this examination, she will be entitled to describe herself as "Chemist and Druggist," and will be licensed to dispense and sell poisons. The title of "Pharmaceutical Chemist" is obtained by passing the "Major" examination of the Pharmaceutical Society, which can be taken after a further six months' preparation.

The cost of the training will amount to about £100, and this, of course, is exclusive of board and lodging if the student has to leave home in order to pursue her studies. In addition, in most cases there must necessarily ensue a period of waiting before the lady chemist is able to make use of her talents upon a money-making basis. It will be seen, therefore, that a girl must possess a certain amount of capital to enable her to embark upon this profession. Every lady pharmacist should belong to the Women Pharmacists' Association, particulars of the membership of which may be obtained from Miss Margaret Buchanan, Pharmaceutical Chemist, Gordon Hall, Gordon Square, W.C. In connection with this association, a very efficient employment and information bureau has been established, where useful advice upon all subjects bearing upon this profession may be obtained, and through the medium of which employers are put into touch with employees. Regular meetings are held at which lectures by well-known pharmacists are given. Everything is done by the society to encourage co-operation amongst its members, and, by arrangement with one of our best-known insurance companies, insurance in respect of annuities upon superannuation is obtainable by members upon the most favourable terms.

Prospects.—By far the greater number of lady pharmacists are employed as dispensers in hospitals, infirmaries, or other institutions. Some have started a business for themselves, taking pupils and apprentices, or are employed as assistants by chemists. A certain number are employed as dispensers to medical men or women, whilst some large wholesale houses now employ qualified lady chemists.

In certain cases a good business with medical women may be secured. £118 per annum (outdoor), £70 per annum (indoor) would represent the average salary obtainable in hospitals and other institutions, where only one lady pharmacist is employed, for eight or nine hours' work per day. In many cases the dispenser only works five days a week. Where two or more dispensers are employed the head one would probably receive from £10 to £20 more, and the others from £10 to £20 less. An annual holiday of two or three weeks is allowed. Hospital hours are usually from 9.30 A.M. to 5 or 6 P.M.

The salary of assistants to chemists averages from £50 to £80 a year. The position of dispenser to a medical man does not, as a rule, offer very many opportunities for the qualified lady chemist, for the reason that the qualification of the "Society of Apothecaries" is often deemed sufficient for a post of the kind. This is obtained by passing what is known as the "assistant's examination" of the above-named society. The examination fee is £5, 5s., and at least six months' training in chemistry and dispensing is necessary. Needless to say, women with this lesser qualification can only command very small salaries, the sphere of work being necessarily limited. Parents very often decide upon their daughters taking this examination upon account of the small expenditure involved; but it is a wholly mistaken policy, for if pharmacy is to be taken up at all, it should be taken up thoroughly. There are so many women now qualified and legally registered as pharmacists that it is becoming daily more difficult for women only partially equipped to earn a living wage.

DENTISTRY

Comparatively few women have as yet taken up this profession. There is no doubt that the woman dentist is as yet something of a novelty, and, as in the case of surgery, there is a certain amount of prejudice to be overcome before dentistry takes a firm place as a recognised profession for women.

At present no woman should start practice as a dentist unless she has a fair amount of capital to tide her over those years of uncertainty which must elapse before she establishes a good connection. The training also is costly and somewhat lengthy.

Women are admitted to the Examination in Dentistry of the Board of the Royal College of Physicians and Surgeons, the London Society of Apothecaries, and of the Royal College of Surgeons of Edinburgh, Glasgow, and Ireland. Dental students must register their names at one of the offices of the General Medical Council in the same way as medical students. A preliminary examination must be passed. After registration a dental student must pass at least four years in the acquirement of professional knowledge, but it is usual for students to spend five or six years in preparation for their last examination instead of the regular four. Not only dental surgery, but mechanical dentistry must be studied.

Training is taken at a Dental Hospital and may be had at the National Dental Hospital, London, and at the Dental Schools of Edinburgh and Glasgow. The average cost of training in both the mechanical and surgical branches amounts to about £210, exclusive of books and instruments.

The woman who wishes to take up dentistry as a profession should apply to one of the Royal Colleges of Surgeons for a copy of their Regulations for the Licence in Dentistry.

NURSING

Amongst what are known as the essentially womanly professions, that of nursing must needs take the foremost place. Many girls, however, decide to embark upon a career of the kind from purely sentimental reasons, losing sight altogether of practical facts. They have read of the deeds of Florence Nightingale and others, and are fired with the desire of following the example of their heroines in their own humble way.

This desire is very laudable and much to be commended, and where a girl has a special aptitude for nursing such high and generous motives cannot fail to make her career in every way a success—but she must have *that special aptitude.* No girl should dream of embarking upon the nursing profession without it, and she must, in addition, have a thoroughly sound constitution and a healthy, cheerful mind. She must be tactful, energetic and persevering, not afraid of work, and always ready to accord that sympathy to her patients which is looked upon by them as one of a nurse's greatest attributes. It must be remembered that the training involves much hard work, whilst the income which may be commanded by a fully qualified nurse is comparatively small in proportion to the amount of responsibility entailed.

On the other hand, it is a profession full of

interest and variety, and the possibilities of doing good by ministering to the sick and alleviating and helping them to bear their suffering are practically unlimited.

To a girl who has had no experience of what discipline and hard work means, her first year as a probationer will prove a most trying ordeal. She should endeavour, therefore, to prepare herself for life as a probationer by accustoming herself while at home to a useful daily routine, spent in the performance of such domestic duties as she may be afterwards called upon to undertake. A thorough practical knowledge of domestic science is invaluable to the probationer. If upon entering the hospital she is well versed in the art of bed-making, cleaning out rooms, cooking, &c., &c., she will not be at a loss when called upon to perform duties of the kind, more especially if she has been sensible enough to put herself into thorough training in this respect by going through the practice of the regular and systematic performance of these duties in her own home as a preparation for her career in the hospital.

Probationers are seldom admitted into a hospital under the age of twenty-three, so that between the time of leaving school and entering into hospital training, a girl has ample opportunities for preparing herself in this way. The value of a good general education cannot be too highly emphasised, in addition to which hygiene, anatomy, and other branches of knowledge bearing upon her future profession should be most carefully studied. Habits of method and good organisation should be cultivated, as these will be found invaluable. Above all, the girl who wishes to become a nurse should take care of her general health, rising early, taking regular and sufficient exercise, and accustoming herself, in fact, to a certain daily system of routine, which will do as much as anything else to prepare her for those habits of punctuality, method, and discipline which form the chief characteristics of hospital life.

There are several branches of the nursing profession which a woman may take up—hospital nursing, including nursing in the military and naval services, private nursing, district nursing, midwifery, mental nursing, and massage. Many gentlewomen are now also training as children's nurses, and there are also very good appointments as nurses to be had in the Elementary Schools.

HOSPITAL NURSING

Training.—To obtain this, application must be made for admission as probationer to a hospital. The rules for the admission of probationers into these institutions vary to a considerable degree, and it is as well therefore to make inquiries as to the conditions of admission prevailing at several hospitals before selecting the one at which to make the application.

In several hospitals a preliminary course of training has to be undergone in a training school in connection with the hospital before the probationers are admitted into the hospital itself. This course extends over a short period of a few weeks, after which an examination is held, and those who pass this examination are admitted as probationers into the hospital itself. The usual age limit for admission of probationers is from twenty-three to thirty-five years.

The training, with the addition of service exacted by most hospitals, extends over a period of from three to four years. During the first year the probationer will be engaged in the heavier routine work of seeing to the cleanliness of the wards, sweeping, dusting, polishing, bedmaking, &c. In most hospitals from the first a small yearly salary of about £8 is given, and this is often raised to £20 during the third year. Most hospitals bind their probationers down to a term of three or four years' service. Some girls, however, who do not wish to bind themselves in any way until they have found out if the profession is likely to suit them, enter hospitals as paying probationers; that is to say, they pay a weekly fee for the privilege of being admitted into the hospital for a certain short period, at the end of which they can leave if they wish or enter as probationers in the ordinary way.

Application for Admission as Probationer.—When a girl has selected a hospital which she is desirous of entering as probationer, it will be necessary for her to send in an application for the purpose to the matron of the institution. She will receive in return an application form on which are printed several questions which she will be required to answer. This form will have to be filled in, and a doctor's certificate as to the soundness of the applicant's health; also her birth certificate will require to be sent with the application form. In many cases a medical examination will have to be undergone before admission into the hospital.

If it is decided to receive the applicant as a probationer she will be required as a rule to enter at first for a short period "on trial." After this period has elapsed and she has proved herself fitted for the work, she has to sign an agreement with the hospital for two or three—sometimes four years—according to the method of training prevailing at the different institutions.

Much of the scientific side of the training is to be had during the first year. The probationer must attend and take note of the lectures given by physicians and surgeons of the hospital—and by the sisters and teachers. At several hospitals an examination is held at the end of each course of lectures. With each succeeding year of her probation she will be given more responsible work, and when the probationary period is over and she has been granted her certificate, she will be qualified to remain in the hospital as a staff nurse. Her commencing salary would be about £25, over and above her board and lodging, rising to £40 when she is promoted to the position of staff nurse or ward mistress.

The salaries of matrons of hospitals average from £180 to £250 in accordance with the position which the hospital holds. In some of the larger hospitals the salary reaches the figure of £300. Needless to say, before the position of matron is attained a large amount of experience and capacity for organisation is exacted. (For Hospital Almoner, see under Social Work.)

General Hints.—A large hospital should always be selected for training, at any rate a hospital with over one hundred beds, as the best and most varied experience is to be had at the larger institutions. In many cases it will be found that there are no vacancies at the first hospital applied to. This should not deter a girl from trying at other institutions until she finds one to which she may be admitted as probationer. The chief hospitals in the large provincial centres offer training as good in every way as that which is to be had in London. A girl should always be careful to study the regulations of the hospitals to which she applies. Holidays, time off duty, and attention to the comfort of the nurses in the way of housing, separate bedrooms, are all important matters, and it will be found that it is at the largest and most important institutions generally that a nurse will receive the most consideration in this respect. There is no room in a work of this kind to give a lengthy list of hospital training schools with particulars as to regulations, &c.; we have merely dealt with a few of the larger and better-known institutions. If more detailed information is needed, the would-be hospital nurse will find it in a little book edited by Sir Henry Burdett, K.C.B., K.C.V.O., entitled "How to Become a Nurse," and published at 2s. by the Scientific Press, Ltd., London, which is one of the most handy guides to the nursing profession which may be obtained.

The following is a list of some of the chief London hospitals, with particulars in regard to age of admission, time of training, and number of beds:—

The London Hospital, Whitechapel Road, E., contains over 900 beds, and the nursing staff, including private nurses, numbers over 700. Candidates desirous of becoming probationers must receive a preliminary course of training for seven weeks at Tredegar House, 29 Bow Road, E.

The full term of training is two years, and two years of service are required after two years of training, the engagement with the hospital thus extending over four years, dating from the day a probationer enters the hospital.

Ordinary probationers must not be under twenty-three or over thirty-three years of age. A number of paying probationers are admitted for training if they are not under twenty-two nor over forty years of age. Probationers receive a salary of £12 the first year, and £20 the second year. Staff nurses receive salaries of from £24 to £27 per annum, sisters £30 to £40 per annum, private nurses £30 to £45.

Guy's Hospital, London.—Over 600 beds. Time of training three years, after six weeks' instruction at the Hospital's Preliminary Nursing School (fee £6, 6s.). Salary £8 for the first year, £12 for the second year, £18 for the third year. A staff nurse receives a salary of £25 for the fourth year, £28 for the fifth year, and £30 for for the sixth and subsequent years.

St. Bartholomew's Hospital.—Number of beds 680. Time of training four years (three years' training and one year's service), after a preliminary trial of a month. Applicants must be between twenty-three and thirty-five years of age. A preliminary examination must be passed. At the end of the first year they have to pass another examination, and if they do this satisfactorily they are admitted as "staff probationers" for the rest of the term. Salary £8 the first year, £12 the second year, £20 the third year, and £30 the fourth year. Staff nurses, £35–£50. Paying probationers between twenty-one and forty years of age are taken.

Great Northern Central Hospital, Holloway Road, N.—Over 160 beds. Time of training, three years after two months' trial. Age of admission, twenty-three to thirty-five years. Salary first year £8, second year £12, third year £18, fourth year £28.

King's College Hospital, Portugal Street, London.—Over 200 beds. Time of training three years; age of admission, twenty-three to thirty. Salary first year none, second year £15, third year £20, increasing to £36 in the sixth year. Sisters' salaries rise to £50.

The above are only a few of the many institutions offering excellent training to probationers. There are also Children's Hospitals in connection with which probationers may enter into training much younger than in the case of the ordinary hospitals. This is also the case with many of the general and other hospitals in the provinces.

In Scotland, also, there are a number of good hospitals at which training may be had. At the Edinburgh Royal Infirmary there are nearly 900 beds. The training extends over three years, and probationers must be from twenty-three to thirty-five years of age. Sisters retiring at the age of fifty-five receive a pension. At the Glasgow Royal Infirmary there are over 500 beds; the training extends over three years after the preliminary course. Candidates must be between twenty-one and thirty years of age. At the Stobhill Hospital, Glasgow, there are nearly 2000 beds. Course of training, three years. Age limit, twenty-two to thirty-two.

There are many considerations by which the

would-be probationer should be guided in her choice of a hospital. For instance, if she wishes to specialise in the nursing of any particular disease she must train at a place devoted to the treatment of the disease before or after taking a course of general training. Nursing of infectious diseases must be learned at one of the Fever Hospitals. At the Greenwich Hospital probationers may specialise in foreign diseases. Other hospitals devote special attention to midwifery, whilst Children's Hospitals are best for the training of those who wish to specialise in children's illnesses.

Poor Law Infirmaries.—There are now very good posts to be obtained as nurses in the Poor Law Infirmaries. Thorough training may be had at the large infirmaries in London and the larger provincial towns, which will fit a nurse not only for this special work but for any other branch of nursing. The age limit for admission of probationers is usually twenty-one to thirty-two years. As in general hospitals, an agreement of service for from three to four years must be signed if the probationer has satisfactorily executed her duties during her two or three months' trial. Pensions under the Poor Law Superannuation Act are granted in several cases.

Army and Navy.—A nurse who has completed her full course of training at a recognised hospital is eligible for an appointment in either the military or the naval nursing services. Candidates for a nursing appointment in Queen Alexandra's Imperial Military Nursing Service must be nurses possessing certificates of not less than three years' training and service in medical and surgical nursing in a civil hospital having not less than 100 beds. They must be between twenty-five and thirty-five years of age, of British parentage, or naturalised British subjects. The matron-in-chief will be required to satisfy the Nursing Board that, as regards education, character, and social status, the candidate is a fit person to be admitted to Queen Alexandra's Imperial Military Nursing Service. The candidate will be required to fill in the form of application which will be forwarded to her, and to produce her certificate of registration of birth; or, if this is not obtainable, a declaration made before a magistrate by one of her parents or former guardians, giving the date of her birth, certificates of training (in the original), medical certificate, and dental certificate.

Good powers of organisation and administration are called for on the part of the army nurse. The system of organisation and the regulations are quite different from those in force at an ordinary hospital.

All army nurses must give a period of service abroad, this period varying from three to five years, according to the climatic conditions. Women who wish to be army nurses should apply to the matron-in-chief, Q.A.I.M.N.S., War Office, Whitehall, S.W.

The rates of pay of Queen Alexandra's Imperial Nursing Service are as follows:—

Staff Nurse.—£40 per annum, rising by annual increments of £2, 10s. to £45.

Sister.—£50, rising by annual increments of £5 to £65.

Matron.—£75, rising by annual increments of £10 to £150.

Principal Matron.—£175, rising by annual increments of £10 to £205.

Matron-in-Chief.—£305, rising by annual increments of £15 to £350.

Allowances are also made in respect of board, washing, uniform, lodging.

The allowances made in respect of board, washing, uniform, lodging (when quarters are not provided), and fuel and light are as follows:—

Board and Washing Allowance.—£39 per annum at home and £54, 12s. abroad for all members.

Lodging Allowance.—£41, 1s. 3d. for staff nurses, sisters and matrons; £54, 15s. for principal matrons; and £73 for matron-in-chief.

Fuel and Light.—£11, 3s. for staff nurses, sisters and matrons; £16, 4s. 3d. for principal matron; and £22, 5s. 10d., for matron-in-chief.

An allowance for uniform of £8 per annum at home and £9 per annum abroad is made to all members excepting the matron-in-chief. An outfit allowance of £8, 8s. is made when proceeding on active service. Where the necessary establishment of servants is not provided, a servant allowance is also made.

Charge pay is granted to a matron or sister at the rate of £30 per annum when in charge of 300 beds or over, £25 per annum when in charge of 200 to 299 beds, £15 per annum when in charge of 100 to 199 beds.

Queen Alexandra's Imperial Military Nursing Service Reserve.—Posts may also be obtained in Queen Alexandra's Imperial Military Nursing Service Reserve, which has been organised for the purpose of keeping a reserve of nurses for the Imperial Military Nursing Service in case of war. Candidates must be certificated nurses between twenty-six and forty-five years of age, having trained for not less than three years in a hospital. They receive the small retaining fee of £2 per annum, and must be prepared when called upon to enter service either at home or abroad, and when on active service work under the same conditions that govern the Military Nursing Service.

Territorial Force Nursing Service.—Certified nurses may also become enrolled as members of the Territorial Force Nursing Service, provided that if engaged in a hospital they obtain the consent of the matron. Candidates must not be under twenty-three years of age. Unlike the Army Reserve Nurses, they will not be called upon to serve abroad, but will be required to serve in the territorial hospitals in the event of the calling out of the Territorial Force. The commencing rate of pay upon mobilisation would be £40 per annum for a nurse, £50 for a sister, and £75 for a matron. Allowances are made for board, lodging, washing, light, and uniform.

Queen Alexandra's Royal Naval Nursing Service.—Candidates for appointment as nursing sisters must produce certificates of training for at least three years at a large civil hospital in the United Kingdom, in which adult male patients are received for medical and surgical treatment, such hospital being also provided with a matron and staff of nursing sisters. Candidates must be of British parentage or naturalised British subjects. The limits of age for appointment are not under twenty-five and not over thirty-five.

Head sisters will, as a rule, be appointed by selection from the list of nursing sisters. All nursing sisters will be required to undergo twelve months' probation before they are confirmed in their appointments. Head sisters and nursing sisters are eligible for pension.

The salaries and allowances will be as follows:—

Head Sisters.—At Haslar, Plymouth and Chatham, £125 to £160 by annual increments of £5. At Malta, Gibraltar and Hong Kong, none borne, but an allowance of £10 a year will be made to the sister acting as head sister for the time being.

Nursing Sisters.—£37, 10s to £50, by annual increments of £2, 10s. Each head sister and nursing sister will be allowed in addition, in lieu of board, &c., at home from 15s. to 19s. a week, and abroad from 21s. to 35s. a week.

Furnished apartments, fuel and lights will be provided for the staff.

Each head sister and nursing sister will be provided with uniform.

A head sister may be granted leave for forty-two days in the year, and a nursing sister for thirty-five days.

Those who wish to become nurses in the Naval Service should write for full information to the Director-General, Medical Department of the Navy, Admiralty, 18 Victoria Street, S.W.

Mental Nursing.—For mental nursing very special qualifications of character are necessary. She whose vocation it is to "minister to the mind diseased" must be able to control her temper upon all occasions, however sorely it may be tried; she must be a good disciplinarian, firm yet gentle, cheerful and sympathetic. By the brightness of her own disposition she should endeavour to dispel as far as possible the gloom that settles over many of the clouded minds with which in the course of her work she must daily come into contact. No small measure of responsibility falls to the share of the mental nurse, and she must have sufficient presence of mind to be able to successfully cope with any emergency that may arise. In addition she must have a good sound constitution and a fair amount of physical strength.

The training of a mental nurse extends generally over three years. As a rule three months' preliminary trial is exacted. Examinations are held at the end of the training period. Where a mental nurse has already undergone training in a general hospital, she will not be required to undergo the full three years' training, and qualified nurses are often admitted at once as sisters in the mental hospitals. The age limit varies with the different institutions. Training is not to be had at all the asylums, although the system described is almost universally adopted. Before applying for admission, therefore, the would-be mental nurse should be careful to select an institution at which the full term of training, concluding with the necessary examinations, may be had.

The rate of payment of probationers is from £17 to £18 for the first year, increasing to £28 to £30. Pensions are granted in most cases.

MIDWIFERY

This branch of nursing presents openings for many women, and has this advantage that the training can be taken up later in life than in the case with the training of the ordinary nurse probationer. Midwifery therefore constitutes a good opening for women of middle age who are debarred from entering a hospital in the ordinary way on account of the age limit. Amongst the poorer classes midwives attend cases of child-birth independently of the doctor. Midwives employed among the higher classes take maternity cases as "monthly nurses" under the superintendence of a medical man.

It is not advisable for a girl to take up midwifery too young. Twenty-five is a good age at which to enter for the examination, and no student under the age of twenty-one is accepted for registration. All the qualities so necessary for a nurse are even more necessary for the midwife. Her work is highly responsible. It will be her lot to act in many emergencies, therefore she must have plenty of nerve and presence of mind. Good health is also essential, as the work is apt to be most arduous, often entailing long night vigils, when but little sleep can be taken.

Training.—The proper training of midwives has become compulsory since the passing of the Midwives Act, which came into force in April 1910. Much preventable mortality had occurred in former times owing to the ignorance of the women who were deemed competent to take charge of maternity cases. Happily this state of things has now been altered, and the compulsory training and registration of those who take up the work of midwifery has conferred an inappreciable boon upon the community at large. The training extends for from three to six months, and the cost seldom averages more than from £10 to £28 or £30. The regulations for training are drawn up by the Central Midwives Board, Caxton House, Westminster, London, S.W., from whom all particulars may be obtained. It is better, as a rule, to give six months to the training. Actual attendance at a number of lying-in cases is necessary. The training may be taken at a lying-in hospital or training institution recognised by the Board, or from a certificated midwife. Examinations are held by the Central Midwives Board every few months at London and some of the provincial centres. There are a number of training schools for midwives at which training may be had.

The following are some of the lying-in hospitals at which pupils are taken for midwifery and monthly nursing:—

City of London Lying-in Hospital, City Road, E.C. The course for midwives is four months, and for monthly nurses two months. The fee for midwifery training (including board) for those who wish to become registered midwives is £29, 8s.

Clapham Maternity Hospital (36 beds). Fees eleven guineas for three months' training, and less for trained nurses.

General Lying-in Hospital, Lambeth, S.E. Fees, twenty-five guineas for a three months' course.

Queen Charlotte's Lying-in Hospital, Marylebone Road, N.W. Fees, £35 for five months' training. For monthly nurses the fees are £24 for sixteen weeks.

Edinburgh Royal Maternity Hospital, Edinburgh. A three months' course for the monthly nursing certificate may be had for £13, 13s. (including board, &c.). For the midwifery certificate there is a six months' course at a fee of about £22, and a shorter course for trained nurses for fifteen guineas.

Glasgow Maternity and Women's Hospital.—Courses of three, four, or six months may be taken. Fees, £13, 13s., £15, 15s., and £21.

National Lying-in Hospital, Dublin.—Training six months. Fees, £18, 18s. There is a shorter course for certificated nurses.

At the Midwives' Institute, 12 Buckingham Street, Strand, London, W.C., classes are held to prepare pupils for the examinations. There are certain societies which offer free training or training at reduced terms for those who wish to work amongst the poor. Such societies are the Rural Midwives' Association, the Midwives' Institute, 12 Buckingham Street, Strand, and the Association for Promoting the Training and Supply of Midwives.

Prospects.—Midwives practising in rural districts independently of a doctor receive from 5s. to 20s. for each case. Good salaried appointments may also be had under the Poor Law and in connection with many of the district nursing associations. The midwife working under the Queen Victoria Jubilee Nurses' Association will receive a salary of from £70 to £100 a year. There are also good openings as teachers of midwifery in several training schools for midwives, hospitals and institutions. The woman who wishes to practise as a monthly nurse amongst the middle and higher classes must have a good connection amongst medical men. Salaries are very good, ranging in most cases from £8, 8s. for the month, and the nurse is often asked to remain in attendance on a case longer than this unless, of course, she has another case to attend. If she is asked to take up her residence in the house of her patient before she is actually required, it is usual to give her half fees.

The Midwives Act is also responsible for another appointment for which trained midwives are eligible, *i.e.* Inspectors of Midwives under local authorities. The salaries of midwife inspectors are good, ranging from £100 to £300.

PRIVATE NURSING

Private nursing may be undertaken either in connection with a private nursing institution or hospital, in co-operation with other nurses, or by a nurse alone.

In institution work the nurse joins the institution for a certain period, and she is sent out to attend private cases by the superintendent or matron, who receives the fees for her services, granting her a yearly salary of about £30. In private nursing in connection with a hospital, the nurse is retained on the staff of the hospital, being sent out to attend private cases. Her board, lodging, and uniform are provided, in addition to salary. They are not always provided in the case of a private nursing home. She may also join a Nurses' Co-operation, in which case she will be able to draw her own earnings, less a percentage of 7½ per cent. to be paid to the superintendent. It requires a great amount of energy and hard work to succeed as a private nurse—apart from any nursing institution. A nurse must have a very good connection amongst medical men with large practices.

Although this work is remunerative there are several disadvantages to be faced when nursing is undertaken by a woman single-handed. There may, for instance, be seasons when little or no nursing is to be had, followed by a period of exceptional activity. The nurse will have to fall back upon her savings (if she have any) during the first period, and, however willing and energetic she may be, she will be unable to attend every case for which her services may be sought in the second period. The nursing problem is, therefore, apart from cases of regular patients amongst chronic invalids, a very difficult one to tackle alone, and for this reason it is always better in the long run to join a good nursing home or Nurses' Co-operation.

District Nursing.—Perhaps this constitutes one of the most laudable branches of the nursing profession, as the district nurse undertakes the nursing of the poor in their own homes. The best work is obtainable in connection with the societies founded for the organisation of district nursing, chief amongst which is the Queen Victoria Jubilee Institute for Nurses, 58 Victoria Street, London, S.W. There is also a branch in Edinburgh at 29 Castle Terrace. Three years' training in a general hospital is necessary, with six months' extra training in district work. After this an examination must be passed, and the successful candidate is appointed at a commencing salary of £70 a year, or £30 a year with board and lodging and uniform, in towns where there are several nurses working and a house is provided for them. In these circumstances the nurses are under the direction of a superintendent, who has a higher salary than the ordinary nurses.

There are many other district nursing societies, including the Ranyard Nurses (see also under London Biblewomen and Nurses' Mission) and those of the Church Army. Salaries vary according to the different associations.

Village Nurses.—This may be called a branch of district nursing, as it also comprises the nursing of the poor in their own homes. Village nurses are employed in the more remote village districts. Only a short course of training in general nursing and midwifery is necessary.

Educated women would do well to go in for "district" in preference to "village" nursing, as the ranks of the village nurses are largely filled by women of the cottage class who have taken a course of training and work in connection with an institution, such as the Ockley Nursing Association, which has been organised for the nursing of the poor in their own homes by members of their own class.

Massage and Electricity.—Women may specialise with advantage in this branch of nursing. To married women or widows, or those who through some reason are debarred from completing a full course of hospital training, it should especially appeal as a means of livelihood, as the cost of training is small, averaging from £10, 10s. and upwards, the course usually extending over three months.

Those who wish to take up massage must have that special aptitude for the work which characterises the successful masseuse. They must also possess good health, as the constant practice of massage means a certain tax upon the strength.

The most successful masseuses are mostly those who have trained as nurses and specialised in massage at the completion of their training. In any case a good knowledge of nursing is a great help. Massage may be learned at one of the many physical training colleges, from medical men, or from trained masseuses. Much valuable experience may be gained in a hospital for paralysis and nervous diseases where massage and electric treatment are largely practised.

Examinations in massage are held and certificates awarded to successful candidates by the Incorporated Society of Trained Masseuses, 12 Buckingham Street, Strand, London, from whom all particulars may be received.

The masseuse who sets up in practice for herself will need to have a good connection amongst medical men, for nowadays few people will employ a masseuse who has not been recommended by their doctor. (For Face Massage, see p. 450.)

Nurses in the Colonies.—Those who wish to obtain work as nurses in the colonies should apply to the Secretary, Colonial Nursing Association, Imperial Institute, London, S.W., for a form of application. There are good prospects in the colonies for trained nurses who have also taken the midwifery certificate. Salaries range in most cases from £60 per annum, including board and lodging.

WOMEN IN HORTICULTURE AND IN AGRICULTURE

NOT the least striking feature of the general progress made by women in employments which were at one time deemed man's sole prerogative is to be seen in the realms of horticulture and agriculture. Women now take up with success all branches of farming and gardening. Special colleges are devoted to the training of women in these outdoor pursuits, and it is a significant fact that the horticultural college at Swanley, which was first accessible to both men and women students, now opens its doors to women only.

The woman who is fond of an outdoor life need not now be debarred from following the bent of her inclination by pursuing a remunerative and congenial outdoor occupation. Everything is at hand to facilitate her progress. Training is within easy reach. Old-time tradition has been set at naught by the success of many women pioneers, and the reaction which has set in during the last few years in favour of healthy outdoor sports and the benefits of an athletic training for women and girls in general, has resulted in an universal recognition of the fact that women may engage in most horticultural and agricultural pursuits without incurring that stigma of " unwomanliness " so often hurled in former times at the unfortunate woman who had an idea beyond her needlework, her cooking, and the management of her household.

LADY GARDENERS

Amongst the many outdoor occupations available to the woman worker, that of gardening must take a prominent place. There is at present a great demand for really capable gardeners and garden designers, a demand which is no doubt due to the general revival of the art of gardening, or rather should it be said of " art in gardening," which has taken place all over the country within recent years. Public gardens are planned and laid out with care and taste, large private gardens are designed with the utmost attention to beauty and artistic arrangement; even the little suburban garden is conspicuous by its perfectly kept piece of green lawn and the tasteful arrangement of the borders and shrubberies. Schools of gardening are being opened in all parts of the country for training gardeners, and, what is most important from the point of view of the woman worker, the demand for good women gardeners in particular is steadily growing, difficulty being found to fill a number of the posts available.

Needless to say, a woman must be well trained if she wishes to succeed as a gardener. Gardening is not to be learned in a year. For ordinary purposes at least two years' training in a good gardening college should be taken, and this should be followed up by a year's practical experience as assistant to a head gardener or market gardener. If possible, three years should be given to the training. By the third year a woman should have formed some definite idea as to the particular branch of gardening she wishes to take up, so that during the last year of training her study can be centralised upon the particular branch selected.

A well-trained woman may succeed either as a garden designer, an expert adviser upon gardening, a head gardener, a jobbing gardener, a market gardener, or a practical teacher of gardening. She must, of course, be guided in her selection according to her individual circumstances.

Schools of Horticulture.—There are many good horticultural colleges and schools all over the country at which women may be trained as gardeners. At **Swanley Horticultural College, Kent,** training may be had in every branch of horticulture. The college, which was formerly open to both men and women, is now restricted to women students only. The full course extends over three years, and instruction in the practical as well as in the scientific side of gardening is given. The fees, including board and lodging, are from £80 a year. Students are prepared for the examinations of the Royal Horticultural Society and of the Board of Education.

At **Studley Castle, Warwickshire,** a complete training may be had in every branch of horticulture and agriculture. The college is situated about 2½ miles from Studley station, Midland Railway, on a branch line between Birmingham and Evesham. It is the aim of this institution (1) To provide a training for girls in practical market gardening, including buying, growing, packing, and selling, so that they may be able to conduct a business of their own on sound financial lines.

(2) To train women who will be landowners to take a practical and intelligent interest in their estate and gardens.

(3) To train women to take posts both as forewomen and head gardeners.

Instruction is given in every branch of practical gardening, including French gardening, dairy work, poultry and bee-keeping, fruit bottling and preserving, carpentering, and a special course is also given in domestic economy.

Pupils are prepared for the Royal Horticultural Society's examinations, the National Dairy Diploma, and the examinations of the British Dairy Farmers' Association.

Fees.—Full training with board and residence at the college:—

Horticulture. Dairy Work and Poultry. Domestic Economy.	Cubicle, £60 to £80 a year. Study Bedroom, £100, £120, and £150 a year.

Bee-keeping is optional and may be combined with either of the above courses, at an additional charge of £5, 5s. a year.

Short Courses of Ten Weeks	Cubicle from	£20
	Study Bedroom,	£30 to £40
Short Courses of Six Weeks	Cubicle from	£12
	Study Bedroom,	£18 to £24

Fruit Bottling and Preserving:—

	£	s.	d.
Two weeks' Course, including Board and Lodgings	£5	5	0
To Resident Students	0	10	6

Carpentering:—
£3, 3s. a year or £1, 10s. a term.

Use of Microscopes	5s. a year.
" Gardening Tools	5s. a year.
" Carpentering Tools	5s. a year.

Laundry (exclusive of Silk and Muslin Blouses and Skirts), £2, 2s. a term.

Glynde School of Gardening.—A thorough training in practical gardening may be had at the Hon. Frances Wolsey's School for Lady Gardeners at Glynde, near Lewes, Sussex. For the woman who means to take up gardening as a livelihood no better or more complete training could be desired than that to be had at this school, which possesses the additional advantage of a minimum of expense in fees. These amount to £10 per annum for practical instruction, with £2 extra for attendance at lectures. Elementary science courses and preparation for the Royal Horticultural Examination may be arranged for slightly higher expenses. Lodgings conveniently near the Gardens, where several students board together, can be secured at 17s. a week for board and residence.

The chief characteristic of the school is the feature made of practical teaching. It is worked on the basis of a private garden, and not a school. Attention is given to the routine of garden work, including the care of grass, paths, and beds; mowing, sweeping, and general tidiness; digging, trenching, and other ground operations; raising plants from seeds and cuttings, their subsequent treatment; the culture of herbaceous alpine plants and roses, forcing violets, Dutch bulbs, &c.; watering, ventilation, and other points of glass-house management. Students are also taught fruit-growing and how to pack flowers and vegetables for market. Only a small number of students are taken, and these are required to furnish the highest references before obtaining admission to the school.

Royal Botanic Society's School.—At the Royal Botanic Society's School of Gardening, Botanic Gardens, Regent's Park, instruction is given in every branch of garden work. The course, which lasts three years, includes both the practical and the scientific side of horticulture. The Royal Botanical Society's diploma is awarded to students who successfully pass their examination. The course extends over three years. The fees for the first year are £20; for the second year £15; and for the third year £10.

Edinburgh School of Gardening, Corstorphine, Edinburgh.—At this school, which is situated about two miles from Edinburgh, instruction is given in all the branches of practical and theoretical gardening. Students are prepared for the Royal Horticultural Society's Examination. Students are non-resident. They can, however, obtain rooms in the village at very moderate charges, or go backwards and forwards from Edinburgh every day. The fees are £15 a year. Courses in horticulture, botany, chemistry are 5s. extra per term. Students take part in every detail of practical work—hoeing, digging, and preparing the ground, planting out, pruning, potting, care of glass houses, &c., &c. The course extends over two years.

The Head Gardener.—At a meeting on the subject of "Women in Horticulture" held in connection with the "Women's Congress" at the Japanese Exhibition, Shepherd's Bush, in July 1910, Miss Jessie Smith, a well-known authority upon horticulture, laid stress upon the fact that to succeed in gardening a woman must rise above the level of the labouring gardener. There is not a living to be made in mere manual gardening only. A woman will never be able to earn enough by manual gardening to keep herself in any comfort. Her only chance is to be a head gardener with working men under her, or to specialise in one of the other branches already enumerated. To achieve this end a power of organisation and initiative must form part of her qualifications, and her training must be a thoroughly practical one. When she has completed her college training she should have at least a year's practical experience, even if she has to pay fees to a head gardener or a market gardener for the privilege of obtaining this experience by practical work under his or her direction, or if she has to make an arrangement to give her work " on mutual terms."

The head gardener must possess the power of controlling the men (or women) under her, making them work well and willingly for her. Above all, she must be familiar with every branch of the work, and know how it is to be done, before she can take it upon herself to direct others. The importance of a period of practical work after completing her college training cannot be too greatly emphasised. Six months or more spent in travelling in order to study the gardening methods of other countries will also be found of the utmost value. The commencing salary of a head gardener (resident) averages £30 a year, increasing to £100. The head gardener on a large estate is usually given a cottage, rent free, and a right to a portion of the garden produce.

Garden Designing or Landscape Gardening.—Garden designing, or, as it is sometimes called, " landscape gardening," may be said to be one of the highest branches of the art of gardening. It is a branch, however, which requires very thorough training and an amount of patience, perseverance, and hard work on the part of the woman who wishes to qualify as a garden designer. She must be prepared also for her training to be extended over a longer period than that necessary for other branches of gardening. To thoroughly qualify herself she should first take a course of at least two years at a good horticultural college, during which time she should acquire a good knowledge of land surveying. After this course she should devote at least two years to the study of architectural design and building construction. It must be remembered that the garden designer has to deal with vast stretches of ground, not with miniature little plots. Large public gardens, and the gardens belonging to the large private landowner, have all to be designed and planned in keeping with a certain architectural system; the grounds of a house have to be in keeping with the architecture of the house they surround. Summer houses and other structures have to be built. More than a passing knowledge of architecture is therefore of considerable importance. Six months of a year spent in travelling upon the Continent, studying the various styles of gardens in the different countries, will form a beneficial finish to the training of the garden designer.

Prospects.—No woman should attempt to go in for garden designing, or, as it is often called, " landscape gardening," unless she has a certain amount of capital to tide her over the inevitable period of waiting involved before her work becomes known. Women landscape gardeners are employed by many of the municipal authorities, and once a woman has obtained a post of the kind she will probably keep it, and for this reason there are not many openings in this direction. When starting on her own account a woman should advertise for work in the gardening and other papers. Sometimes it will be a long time before her first order comes, but when it does come it will be in most cases the forerunner of others.

It is, of course, much easier for a woman with a large social connection and influential friends to get on in this direction; apart from the chances of work from municipal authorities, which are few, the unknown woman with few friends will find it a very hard struggle. No woman similarly situated should begin with landscape gardening alone. She should start nurseries, or if she have sufficient capital, a market garden, and gradually develop the garden designing in connection with her other business. When once a garden designer has established a connection the work is remunerative. Fees from £1 to 4 or 5 guineas are given at consultation, and a lump sum when the work has been carried out, varying with the size and extent of the garden scheme. Garden designing brings bigger fees than any other branch of gardening, and where the work is regular a good income may be made. Work of the kind is apt to be uncertain, however, excepting in the case of municipal and other large appointments, and some initial capital is absolutely necessary. A woman's prospects will depend entirely upon her capabilities. The field of labour is limited, but up to the present there has been very little competition, and therefore a clever woman should be able to make a good income if she is prepared to spend at least four or five years upon training.

The training, if it extends over four to five years, will be fairly costly. £80 to £100 a year represents the average charge for board, lodging, and training at the big horticultural colleges; to this will have to be added fees for special architectural courses. Needless to say, a woman should not train as a garden designer unless she has that sense of the artistic and taste for art generally which must characterise this as well as any other form of designing.

Miss Lorrie G Dunnington, of Belgravia Chambers, 72 Victoria Street, S.W., an expert garden designer, takes a limited number of pupils for training. It is essential that the pupils should have had a previous training in practical horticulture. The course, which extends over three years, includes garden design, plan drawing, surveying, architectural design, building construction, and general office routine. The fees are £80 per annum, for no less than three years, or £100 for one year's training. Two years at a good horticultural college, and three years' training under an expert designer like Miss Dunnington, who can give the necessary instruction on surveying, architectural design, building construction, should constitute an admirable training for the woman garden designer.

The Expert Adviser.—There are many people who cannot afford to employ a garden architect, but who are at the same time glad to have expert advice on various problems which may crop up in regard to their garden—where to plant new shubberies, plan out artistic borders, lay down a new lawn, make provision for a tennis court, and how to make certain necessary alterations without interfering with the general garden scheme. In these circumstances they are glad to be able to consult an expert, and a woman who establishes a good connection as such will find the employment a lucrative one. She must be able both to advise on matters upon which she is consulted, and, if her advice is adopted, to see that the work is properly carried out in accordance with her ideas. A good connection socially is an advantage for women who wish to make a livelihood in this way.

Jobbing Gardening.—This is the branch of the gardening profession which provides most scope for the good all round woman worker whatever her social status. It is, in fact, the branch which is most accessible to all. It is particularly suitable for the girl or woman whose circumstances require that she should live at home, going out by the day to do the work. The best scope for the jobbing gardener is to be found in the suburbs in the neighbourhood of large towns. She should begin by sending carefully worded personal letters to the owners of houses with gardens, offering her services; also she should insert an advertisement in the local paper. She can begin by herself charging 5s. a day for her work. As her clientele increases she will be able to employ a boy for the rougher work, and she can gradually raise her charges to 7s. 6d. and then 10s. 6d. a day. As her work increases she will require to employ men or women gardeners; the latter could in many cases be pupils, sending them to different houses under her supervision when her employers become too numerous for her to give each one her personal attendance every day. Quite a reasonable income may be made in this way. A good business woman and a good organiser will soon find that she has as much work as she can do with. She will be entrusted with the buying of plants on her employer's behalf, and in many cases will be able to start a small nursery garden in connection with the business. On the whole jobbing gardening presents the most satisfactory branch of gardening work open to the average woman, and it has this advantage that the initial outlay upon the business is small, and work may soon be had by those who set about getting it in the right way. A girl will require at least two years' training at a good gardening school and a further year's practical experience with a head gardener before she should undertake work of this kind. It is work in the course of which she will be constantly learning something new, and as her connection grows it will be work which will require organising power before everything else, and will give her experience which will stand her in good stead in any other higher branch of gardening which she may afterwards undertake. The outlay on training will not be great. Her training is best taken at gardening schools like Glynde College, Sussex, where a feature is made of practical work, and the fees do not amount to more than £10 in the year.

Market Gardening.—Unless a woman has capital it will be practically useless for her to start as a market gardener, as this is a business which requires a large amount of initial outlay before any returns can be expected. The capital to be expended should be supplemented also by a small income upon which a woman can live until her business gets beyond the "making expenses stage." She should have enough to keep herself for at least four years, or else it will be quite useless for her to hope to earn her livelihood in this way. Only a woman who is prepared to work early and late, at all hours and in all weathers, with little intermission in the way of holidays, and who has had a thorough training at a good horticultural college and at least two years' experience of practical work under a market gardener, can hope to make market gardening a success. In addition to this she must have good business ability, a knowledge of the best markets for her goods, and an abundance of patience and perseverance, without which her enterprise must needs spell failure.

An analysis of the initial outlay she will have to make will cause many a woman to think before she makes up her mind to embark upon this career. To begin with, land is dear. She will require at least two acres. Then she will require sheds for packing and potting; also houses will have to be built and equipped with heating apparatus; money will have to be expended upon stock. Anything from £800 to £1000 will represent the sum to be expended.

The woman who has a small sum to invest and who possesses a thorough knowledge of her work, combined with business ability, will be able to make not a fortune, but quite a satisfactory income out of market gardening. She must, of course, be guided by several important considerations in the selection of locality. Her market garden must be properly situated in a thriving locality close to a railway station to decrease costs and facilitate transit, and near a good market for her goods. None but a good business woman can hope to make market gardening pay. and the woman who has not received a thorough training in gardening, and who does not possess good business ability, cannot hope to succeed, and she should give up any idea of entering upon a business which requires the utmost skill and care in management before it can be brought to a profit-earning basis.

French Gardening.—This is a branch of gardening which has come into prominence of late, though in England as yet the art is practically in its infancy. Once the system in this country is well developed, it promises to become the most paying form of market gardening, and a few women have already taken it up with success.

It must be remembered, however, that if capital is necessary for the ordinary market gardening, it is doubly so for French gardening, which involves a much greater initial outlay upon glass, straw, matting, manure, &c., &c.

Hard unceasing work will also be involved, and the cost of labour will have to be reckoned with. A woman wishing to start a business of the kind should begin in a very small way, and extend her business as opportunity offers. No more than a quarter of an acre of glass should be attempted in the first instance, and she will require the help of at least two men.

The position of the garden is of the utmost importance. If the venture is to be a successful one, the commercial aspect of the case, such as proximity to favourable markets and to the railway station, must not be lost sight of. A good water-supply is all-essential, to say nothing of an abundance of manure.

In conclusion let it be said that, apart from all question of capital, the woman who has not had a thorough training in this branch of horticulture, and who has not sound business capabilities, should not embark upon an enterprise of the kind.

Training may be had at most of the horticultural colleges, a special feature being made of it at Studley Castle, Warwickshire, and at the Royal Botanic Society's School of Gardening, Regent's Park.

Teachers of Gardening and Nature Study.—A rapidly growing field for the woman horticulturist may be found in the realms of teaching. A great reaction has taken place in favour of the teaching of nature study in our schools. It has been realised that to make a child take an interest in the animal, bird, and plant life around her, inculcating at the same time in the little mind a love of nature, nature study is of all forms of teaching the most suitable for the little ones, and the most likely to be productive of good results. With the realisation of this fact has come a corresponding demand for teachers of gardening and of nature study, and it is a demand which at present exceeds the supply. So great is the demand for nature study teaching that ordinary teachers now often find it necessary to take a course of instruction in nature study in order that they may impart at least the elements of it to their pupils. There is also a steady increasing demand in secondary schools for "Gardening Mistresses," who, in addition to practical outdoor work, are competent to impart a knowledge of the scientific side of gardening. The woman who has taken her full horticultural course at one of the best horticultural colleges is most likely to obtain a post as teacher of gardening and nature study, as when vacancies occur applications for teachers to fill them are usually sent to the chief colleges. For school teachers who wish to extend their knowledge of nature study for the purpose of tuition, the Swanley Horticultural College, Kent, have instituted a special nature study course. The lessons are given out of doors in the months of July and August, and students are taken on occasions into the country so that they may study birds, pond life, insects, wild flowers, trees and grasses in their different environment. The fee for a fortnight's course is £5, 5s., inclusive of tuition, board and lodging, and expenses of excursions.

In addition to employing gardening and nature study teachers, several large schools are giving over their gardens to the care of women gardeners. For a resident woman head gardener in a school £30 or £35 a year is considered a good initial salary.

FLORISTS

A florist's business is one admirably suitable for women of taste and refinement, but at the same time it is by no means the simple undertaking usually imagined. It is essentially what is known as a "season" business; that is to say, there is every year a period of very great activity, and during this time the florist has to toil from early in the morning until late at night; there is no restricting the work to a set period of hours per day. No woman should embark upon this business, therefore, who is not prepared for hard and strenuous work. To make a successful florist a woman must not only possess the art of arranging flowers to the best advantage; she must also be proficient in all the mechanical parts of the work. A thorough training is absolutely necessary, and this can be obtained in no better way than by practical work at a florist's, where all the details, such as wiring, making up, packing, can be learned. A thorough knowledge of buying, keeping accounts, drawing out estimates is essential, and business ability is not the least attribute of a woman who wants to start for herself in this trade. She should be able to keep a keen eye upon costs, reducing them to a minimum, thereby increasing her profits. She must also show great discrimination in the choice of a locality for her business, seeing that there is no undue competition in her immediate neighbourhood.

As a general rule, a woman should only train to become a florist if she wishes to set up in business for herself. The earnings of florists' employées are uncertain, as often they are only employed during the busy season, and then their pay seldom averages more than 35s. to £2 a week.

A florist's business can be made to include many profitable side issues. For instance, a florist may undertake the care of the conservatories, window-boxes, and even the small gardens of the locality. For this, of course, a practical horticultural training is necessary in addition to the training in ordinary florist's work.

Training.—Training may be had at the Women's London Gardening Association, 62 Lower Sloane Street, S.W., where the instruction is practical in every way. The fees are £25 for the full course. Many florists will take lady pupils upon payment of a satisfactory premium—£20 to £30 is a very usual sum.

WOMEN AS FARMERS

By K. M. Courtauld, Principal of Colne Engaine Farm, Earls Colne, Essex

In writing about farming as an occupation for women, I am faced with a difficulty at the outset. I have myself been farming for over twenty-one years, and I have found the free, open-air life so enjoyable and the work so intensely interesting, each day and each season bringing an endless variety of occupations, that I should like to recommend the life to every woman who is fond of the country.

But, on the other hand, I have known of so many failures! Not only of women, but also of men who have taken small farms with high hopes which have been doomed to disappointment. I have seen debts and difficulties accumulating, the land deteriorating, the place getting more and more out at elbows, the tenant more and more depressed and embarrassed, and at last the struggle is given up and he leaves the farm thoroughly out of heart and having lost his money.

In the face of such examples I feel the responsibility of advising any woman to take up farming without serious consideration.

It seems to me there are three essentials without which it is hopeless to think of farming successfully:—

First.—A thorough practical knowledge and experience of the business.

Second.—Sufficient capital.

Third.—The capacity for hard and persevering work and country tastes.

I believe that, given these qualifications, a woman is more fitted to take a large farm than a small one. I am not, of course, speaking of small holdings worked as market gardens, poultry or fruit farms, but of ordinary farming; these are businesses in themselves. The only persons likely to make a small farm pay are men who have begun life as agricultural labourers, who have worked on the land since they left school. I know several such men who have got together a little money and taken a small farm. They work harder and longer hours than they did when they were working for wages, and they are probably no better off, if as well. Their standard of living is that of the labourers in the district, but they like to feel that they are their own masters, and they struggle on, working ten or twelve hours a day in summer and as long as it is light in winter, living on twelve or fourteen shillings a week. And if a stroke of bad luck comes to them, they have no reserve fund to draw upon; so unless they take the hat round amongst their neighbours for help, they are reduced to great straits.

Now this is not a life I could recommend to any woman, or, indeed, to any man, who had not been used to field work from childhood. I can see no reason why a woman should not manage a large farm—where brains are more important than muscles, where the actual manual labour is done by farm hands, and where her province is to direct and overlook others, to plan out the cropping and working of the land, to see that the stock are properly cared for, to buy and sell to the best advantage, in short, to do the work of a yeoman or gentleman farmer. In this she would find plenty of scope for all her energies. Much depends on attention to detail, on strict economy both of money and labour.

There is an old saying that "the foot of the master is the best fertiliser for the land"—certainly the more personal supervision the master can give the greater will be the chances of success.

I have said that one of the first essentials to success in farming is a thorough practical knowledge of the business, and I shall be probably asked how this is to be obtained. Now I am quite a believer in scientific farming, but science will not take the place of practical experience, although it will be most useful in supplementing it. I have heard of students who have learnt all about the manuring of roots and who could tell you the exact proportions of the various artificial manures which gave the best results, and yet who did not know a swede from a marigold. That sort of knowledge is useless. At least two years spent on a farm would be required to get an idea of the general routine of farm work. You want to learn by experience when a field has been properly ploughed, when it is in a fit condition to sow, and, if it is too rough or too foul, what to do to bring it round. You want to know what is amiss when a crop is not growing as it should do; is it suffering because the soil is poor or wants draining, or because the field has not been properly ploughed and harrowed beforehand, or has the corn been attacked by wireworm or some such pest?

You want to make yourself a judge of stock—go to market week after week, and as each animal comes into the ring, make a guess what it will fetch, and see how near you are to the price at which the auctioneer knocks it down.

Go to the Corn Exchange and see the various samples offered for sale and hear what the buyer has to say. Notice how one sample is not clean, *i.e.* has weed seeds and inferior grains and rubbish mixed with the good corn; another is slightly "clung" or damp; another is too soft or a little fusty in smell; or, in the case of barley, how it has been spoilt by the grains being cracked by bad thrashing.

By all means attend classes on farming subjects, read books and agricultural papers. I think a course of veterinary instruction would be most valuable, and pick up as much information as you can, but do not leave out the practical work, which is the most important.

If you can learn how to do the work yourself so much the better. If you can plough or milk yourself, you are in a better position to find fault with your man if he does his work badly, in the same way that a lady who can cook is better able to tell her cook where she has made a mistake.

It always appears to me that the girls who would be most likely to succeed as farmers, and for whom it would be easiest to obtain the necessary experience, are the daughters of farmers or squires, or landowners living on their own property. These girls are already used to a country life; they must have picked up a good deal of knowledge of farming subjects, and they might even be able to start in a comparatively small way while still living at home under the guidance of their fathers or brothers.

Perhaps I may say a few words as to how I started farming. I remember when I was still at school telling my father I would like to be a farmer, and he took the suggestion about as seriously as if I had said I should like to go into the army. However, some years later he had the farm where I am now living thrown upon his hands through the tenant leaving, and he engaged a neighbouring farmer whom we had all known well for many years to act as his bailiff. As my father had no time to give to farming, he agreed that I should go over to the farm frequently and see how things were prospering, and this I used to do two or three times a week for some years. This is how I first got an insight into the business of farming. Some time later when I was able to leave home he handed the property over to me, rent free, and made me a present of the stock to make what I could of it, and I have been living there and farming the land ever since.

For the first three or four years I still had some help from our old bailiff, who was managing other land for my father; later on I engaged a working bailiff on my own account. I cannot say that I have made money out of farming, but I have found that it has provided me not only with congenial work and interest, but with many advantages. For instance, I have my house and garden rent free; I get corn and hay for my horses, milk, butter, eggs, poultry, fruit, and vegetables at cost price. Then there are excellent opportunities for sport: I have the shooting over the land and plenty of room for summering hunters. I have also done much to improve the property. Amongst other things I have planted a great deal of fruit which bids fair to be the most paying crop I grow.

The question of capital is an important one. A very fair allowance is £10 per acre, and this should be allowed for the farm alone. No woman should start farming unless she has enough to live on economically for a year or two, and that in addition to the amount invested in the farm, as there is nothing more disadvantageous to successful farming than being cramped for money. To be unable to engage extra labour when it is particularly needed, to be obliged to sell produce at a poor price because one cannot afford to hold it, is courting failure.

I have said that one essential to success is a capacity for work and country tastes. I think many women who have lived a great part of their lives in town, and who think with delight of beautiful summer days spent in the country, imagine that they would enjoy life on a farm without really grasping what it means. All of us enjoy going out into the fields on a beautiful spring or summer morning, but it is a different thing to spend day after day working in sodden yards trying to make your stock as warm and comfortable as possible, or walking over the heavy fields with several pounds of clay on each boot, coming in wet through perhaps twice in one day. It is no use for a woman who does not like getting up early, who cannot stand the sun without a sunshade, and who will not wear thick boots, taking to farming; and at the best one must be prepared for many reverses and discouragements. Depending as he does upon the weather, the farmer too often sees his most carefully laid plans brought to nought. If you cannot get on with the work you most want to do, you must look out for some other job. If the weather prevents your sowing one sort of crop, you must have patience and hope to get in something else later on. There is no business that requires greater foresight, adaptability, and patient care than farming, and yet it often seems as if every outsider thinks he can teach the farmer his business, if you judge from the extraordinary suggestions and criticisms you sometimes read in the papers. One very amusing reference to women as farmers in England was made in the newspapers not long ago. The writer had been speaking of Miss Binnie-Clark's farm in Canada, and goes on to say, "Women of education at any rate cannot compete with men agriculturalists in England, because they cannot (according to convention) go and pinch fat beasts at markets and bargain for them over pints of beer in smoky inn tap-rooms. But in Canada there is no necessity for them to do business in that way."

Well, I can assure the writer that there is certainly no more necessity in England than in Canada. Whether this was the way English farmers did their business fifty or sixty years ago I cannot say, but it would now be quite as true to say that the country gentleman of the present day dines at four o'clock and then sits and drinks port wine until he falls under the table!

The idea that a woman cannot attend market or go to sales and buy on her own account is quite erroneous. I may say that I have done so for many years and have never met with anything but the greatest courtesy and consideration from my brother farmers, and if I have asked for help or advice it has never been refused me.

Another objection that has been raised to women farming is that they will not be able to manage farm labourers. This also is quite untrue. You would probably find that the same woman who would make a good mistress to her indoor servants would be equally able to manage farm men. Be careful to be absolutely fair and just to all alike; never show favouritism. If you have to find fault speak out strongly, the more forcibly the better, but do not nag or worry about trifles. Agricultural labourers have some odd prejudices and superstitions, and are generally reserved with strangers. Every one outside their own county is a "furriner," and at first is looked at with a certain amount of suspicion, but after living amongst them for a time you get to understand them.

With regard to wages, hours of work, &c., it is best to follow the custom of the neighbourhood, as the men are apt to resent innovations, even when they appear to you to be to their advantage.

In conclusion I should like to advise any woman who intends to start farming to make up her mind beforehand exactly what branch she would prefer. Perhaps the most paying at the present time is a dairy farm having a good milk round; it is more profitable and far less troublesome to sell milk direct than to make cheese or butter, although sometimes the surplus milk in summer may be profitably turned into cheese or butter.

Some farms are particularly suitable for fattening bullocks or rearing young stock; others are noted as good sheep farms. I myself think an arable farm, where all kinds of corn can be grown and a few stock of all sorts kept, is the most interesting. Where one is not dependent on one special branch there is the chance that if one thing does badly another may do well. If wheat is down, hay may be dear, and if mutton is cheap, beef or pork may be selling well, or it is "Up horn, down corn," as the old adage says.

DAIRY WORK

Dairy work is not much taken up by educated women apart from its connection with general farming. There is one sphere, however, in which this work offers fair opportunities, and that is in regard to teaching. County Councils pay women teachers and travelling lecturers a fair rate of salary ranging from £80 to £150 a year. Posts as dairymaids may also be taken by gentlewomen in model dairies on large country estates. These posts are, as a rule, fairly well paid, salaries ranging from £30 a year with lodging, fuel, and dairy produce.

There are also good prospects in the colonies for women well versed in dairy work, more particularly when they have also had a good training in domestic science generally.

Training.—Six months to one year's training should be taken at a good college, where the pupils are prepared for the examinations of the Royal Agricultural Society, the British Dairy Farmers' Association, the British Dairy Institute, and other recognised bodies. The cost of training will not amount to more than £36 for a year, and half that sum for six months. Excellent training is given at the Midland Agricultural and Dairy College, Nottinghamshire, and at the British Dairy Institute, Reading.

BEE-KEEPING

By Bertha La Mothe

Bee-keeping is an occupation which may be taken up by women of all classes and all ages. It is also an occupation particularly suitable for those women who, from force of circumstances, are debarred from going out into the world to earn their living, and yet must bring their share of grist, however small, to the family mill. It has all the advantages of healthy outdoor work without any of its disadvantages. No heavy work such as forms a feature of most agricultural occupation is entailed; neither is work out of doors in bad weather involved, for in winter bees may be left quite to themselves.

Besides being a profitable occupation, bee-keeping forms a most interesting hobby, but many people are debarred from embarking upon it owing to the fact that bees have stings. This is a disadvantage which is a great deal magnified. It is true that inexperienced people should not handle hives unless under the guidance of an expert, but when once a woman has learned to manipulate a hive of bees the danger of stings is very small. The beginner should always wear a veil and gloves at first. She will very soon discard the latter, but it is better always to wear a veil, as bees sometimes get caught in the hair and are liable to sting if they cannot disentangle themselves.

At certain seasons bees are easier to manipulate than at others; in spring, when they have few stores to guard, this is especially the case, but towards autumn, when their honey has been taken away from them, they are not so good-tempered. For about five months in the year during the winter the bee-keeper has no need to worry at all with her hives. During this time, therefore, some other occupation may be taken up.

To make a success of bee-keeping a woman must necessarily have some business capacity. April is the best month to start an apiary. Care should be taken in selecting a good district where there are plenty of orchards and such crops as clover and sainfoin. Lime-trees are also very good. In districts with few orchards and unsuitable crops the returns are not so good. In suitable localities profits should be made at the rate of from £1 to £1, 10s. per hive. No very large outlay is necessary. A new hive and stock of bees can be bought for from £2 to £3, and a second-hand hive for much less. Profits are not only made by selling the honey itself, but also by selling queens and swarms, stock on frames, &c. A ready market is found for honey in most localities at prices ranging from 8d. to 1s. per lb.

Training and Prospects.—Training may be had at Studley Horticultural College, Warwickshire, and many lady bee experts receive pupils. A short course on "Bee-keeping" may also be had at Swanley Horticultural College, Kent, for £3, 3s., non-resident. Certificates are awarded by the British Bee-keepers' Association. A first-class certificate-holder is qualified to take pupils, and this forms another remunerative branch of the bee-keeper's occupation. County Councils' Schools often employ lecturers on bee-keeping as part of their winter courses in Nature Study. For these fees of from 10s. to £2, 2s. per head may be had. The bee expert who can secure some lecturing in winter and can obtain pupils to share her practical work in summer stands to show a very fair rate of profit for the year. She must, of course, be prepared for hard work during the season, as there are periods of intense activity, but it is work amply rewarded by the interest it brings apart from all questions of monetary return.

POULTRY-KEEPING

By N. Edwards,
President of the Ladies' Poultry Club

After having seen something of poultry-keeping in the United States, Canada, France, Belgium, Holland, Switzerland, and Germany, I have found that in the United Kingdom we have the greatest advantages in regard to our climate and soil. In parts of North America fowls have to be kept under cover from three to six months of the year, when snow is deep upon the ground, and in summer the great heat is very trying to growing chicks. It is impossible for certain insects to live in the sandy soil found in parts of France, Germany, and Belgium, which in England form a large part of the nutritive food of the fowls. However, if accommodation be provided suitable to the climate fowls may be kept in a healthy condition in almost every part of the world; where snow lies deep for many months good houses and large scratching sheds must be provided; where the heat is intense, as in India, large well-ventilated houses painted white are necessary. On sandy soils meat must be given to supply the want of insect life, and so on; whatever is lacking naturally must be supplied artificially.

For egg production all the year round we should be able to compete well with any country, as we suffer from no great extremes of climatic change; but in spite of our huge advantages we imported in 1909 eggs worth nearly seven and a quarter millions of money, the value of which came in the following order: the greatest from Russia, then Denmark, Austria-Hungary, France, Italy, Germany, and Canada. The value of table poultry imported in the same year was about £920,000. The National Poultry Organisation Society has done a great work in starting egg-collecting depôts, which no doubt will in time be established in every county. With greater co-operation in and between our villages and diminished railway rates, we should have a most flourishing industry which would gain for us the position we hold in regard to high-class birds for stock and exhibition for which we stand pre-eminent.

Improvements are going on all over the world in the quality of pure-bred birds, and the sums paid annually to British fanciers and stock breeders reach very high figures. The demand comes from every quarter of the globe to this country, where we have the finest types and best-grown birds and a climate well suited to rearing.

By slow degrees the daughters of farmers in the United Kingdom are becoming more alive to the fact of their great advantages. With plenty of land on which to work, and no rent to pay for the keeping of poultry upon that land, with food at lower rates than others can obtain, they stand out as having the widest and best opportunities of all the different classes of women poultry-keepers. Many ladies who have a small piece of ground are able to supply the home table profitably with eggs, and where sufficient land is available enough chickens for the year's supply can be raised if a little time daily is given to the birds. It is a curious fact that almost every country house of any size has a garden kept so well that there is always a good supply of fruit and vegetables for the home table, while the poultry and eggs have all to be bought. By a little good management on the part of the lady of the house this need not be, and the table would be as well supplied by the products of the poultry yard as it is by the garden produce.

Poultry-keeping as a business for men and women is sometimes regarded from a very curious point of view; magical results without labour, time, or capital are expected. A girl once ordered a brooding hen and sitting of ducks' eggs which she was sending to a cottager for the work of hatching and rearing to be done, and on the proceeds she expected to take a trip to Switzerland. The magic hen was to convert an outlay of about ten shillings into at least ten guineas.

Fifteen years ago I started in a very small way, with only twenty fowls and half an acre of land, intending to make a business of one of the many branches of poultry-keeping, and as the best returns appeared to be obtained from pure-bred fowls, the sale was taken up of sittings and eggs, newly-hatched chicks, and birds for stock, exhibition, and export. My capital was very limited; however, before this was exhausted the poultry had begun to pay, and each season the plant was enlarged from profits, and now twenty-eight acres of land are in use and thousands of chicks and eggs, and about one thousand stock birds are sold annually. The work at first, single-handed, was very hard, but a determination to succeed overcame all difficulties, and I have never regretted the day I embarked in poultry-keeping.

Whatever is required in starting any other commercial concern is indispensable in this, and for the girl who expects to make a large business of poultry-keeping a thorough training is necessary. She should have a certain amount of business capability and plenty of enterprise. I have found amongst workers that women excel in that part where extra care in detail is necessary; and in the running of incubators containing over three thousand eggs at work throughout the hatching season, also in rearing one thousand chicks annually, women have done better work on my farm than men, *i.e.* in rearing and management of incubators. It is becoming much more general to have women for the management of poultry than it was formerly, as they are found particularly well adapted to the lighter part of the work, and on exhibition farms do extremely well. Many are successful as lecturers at home and in our colonies, several are noted fanciers who have won challenge cups at our largest shows, and each year the catalogues show a great increase in the number of women exhibitors.

It will now be readily seen that poultry-keeping offers opportunities to women of all classes, and when properly managed gives greater profits than from any other stock kept upon a farm.

Prospects.—The opportunities for women in poultry breeding are :—

(1) It is the work for the woman at home.

(2) It offers openings in both public and private appointments.

(3) It affords advantages as a business in table poultry and egg production to the daughters of farmers and of clergymen, or others who have land at their disposal.

(4) It can be made a successful financial business for those who take it up solely for the work of fancy and utility breeding.

In regard to poultry-keeping for profit the daughters of farmers have the greatest advantages; with plenty of land on which to work and no rent to pay for the keeping of poultry upon that land, with food at lower rates than others can obtain, they stand out as having the widest and best opportunities of all the different classes of women poultry-keepers. Apart from starting a poultry farm, there are openings for women poultry-keepers as instructors in Agricultural Schools, County Council Lecturers, private tuition, &c., &c.

It is best in poultry-keeping to start in a small way. Those who are taking up poultry breeding on a scale which requires a substantial capital to cover expenses of rent of house, land, stock, &c., will require to aim higher than at merely providing the market with fresh eggs, chickens, and ducks for the table. They should go in for breeding of utility and fancy poultry, selling them for stock and exhibition purposes, and when the scope of the business is sufficiently large they will be able to inaugurate a good export trade. Good profits may be made from the sale of newly-hatched chicks and sittings of eggs. After the close of the hatching season fresh eggs can be sold when prices are high, and when low perserved in water glass and sold in winter at a good profit, but, of course, at lower rates than fresh eggs.

The initial capital required is from £50 to £500 in accordance with the scale upon which the business is started; the quantity of land from two to twelve acres. A capable business woman will often succeed in paying expenses in the second year of her enterprise, and from thence onwards carry on the business at a profit.

Training.—The woman who wishes to make money out of poultry-keeping must necessarily have a good training, otherwise her chances of success are very remote indeed. Most of the Agricultural Colleges include poultry-keeping in their curriculum, but this should always be supplemented by practical work on a poultry farm. Most lady poultry farmers take pupils for varying fees. At Coaley Poultry Farm, Gloucestershire, courses of instruction in practical poultry-keeping varying in lengths from three to twelve weeks may be had. Fees, including board, are :—

For the three weeks' course . . .	£10 10 0
For the twelve weeks' course . . .	£31 10 0

This course may be divided into three different seasons of the year.

An examination is held at the end of a twelve weeks' course, and certificates are now awarded. The examiner for the utility, practical, and theoretical work is the agricultural expert for the counties of Monmouthshire and Gloucestershire.

Practical Daily Work (according to the seasons).—Preparing food, feeding adult stock, hatching with incubators, hatching with hens, testing eggs, preserving eggs for eating, rearing chickens in brooders, rearing chickens with hens, fattening fowls, killing fowls, plucking fowls, shaping fowls, dressing fowls, trussing fowls, cramming fowls, preparing birds for exhibition, packing sittings of eggs, packing newly-hatched chickens, varieties studied with club standards.

Pupils learn how to start poultry-keeping on the most modern and practical lines, with the best and latest appliances. Each person has an incubator to work, chickens to rear in a brooder, fowls to kill, truss, and dress.

Excellent advice upon poultry-keeping may also be obtained from the Secretary of the National Poultry Organisation Society, 12 Hanover Square, London, W.

DOMESTIC SCIENCE

WITHIN the last few years educational experts have awakened to the value of domestic science in the training of girls, whether it is to qualify them for one of the many posts which a thorough knowledge of the domestic arts will place within their reach, or whether it is to fit them to undertake the duties of housewives when they are called upon to rule over homes of their own. Special training schools in domestic subjects are now to be found in almost every large town in the United Kingdom, where girls may receive a thorough training to prepare them to earn a livelihood in any of the branches of domestic science, or where they may take short courses in order to put their learning to practical use in their own homes. It is also significant of the trend of opinion in regard to this important branch of a girl's education that a special course in domestic science has been included in the Women's Department of King's College, London University. Domestic science subjects include cookery, sewing, home dressmaking and millinery, laundry work and housewifery. There are good posts to be had for women who have had a thorough training, and also for those who have specialised in any one of the chief domestic arts. Needless to say, before taking up the study of domestic science a girl should have had a good secondary education, more especially if she wishes to qualify as a teacher.

HIGHER EDUCATION OF WOMEN IN HOME SCIENCE

The special domestic science course now included in the Women's Department of King's College, London University, is well worthy of special notice, more especially in regard to those who wish to earn their livelihoods in the higher posts, such as head teachers, Government inspectors, &c. The training is one that assures a high standard of merit in all who have taken the King's College Course, and in the annual report of the college for 1909 it is said :—

"Outside the strict undergraduate course the most noticeable addition is that of the students in the new Home Science Department. These, as so often with pioneer students, are an interesting and varied group of thoughtful women. After a year's trial it is possible to say that the movement is proving its value and importance as a new development in the higher education of women. A distinct advance can be observed in the attention given to it by leading educational authorities, and in the interest shown by those concerned in the education of girls, as, for instance, head mistresses. There is already a demand for women trained in this way to teach in schools greater than the College has been able to meet. From the College point of view the introduction of this course has strengthened the staff and furnished an appeal to the interest of a new set of students."

The syllabus for the Higher Education of Women in Home Science and Economics comprises two courses :—

(1) A one year's course for students of graduate standing.

(2) A three years' course for students whose general education has reached the standard requisite for entry on university courses of the usual undergraduate type.

The fees for the first is thirty guineas, and for the second course thirty guineas per annum. There are one or two scholarships in connection with the course, full particulars of which may be had upon application to the Vice-Principal of King's College (Women's Department). A reduction is made in favour of teachers. A diploma is awarded by the College to students who take a complete course and pass an examination to the satisfaction of the council. The tuition includes instruction in applied chemistry, the practical domestic arts, sanitary science and applied hygiene, economics, &c. The main object of these courses is to provide a thoroughly scientific education in the principles underlying the whole organisation of home life, the conduct of institutions, and other spheres of civic and social work in which these principles are applicable.

Either course will be useful for women who wish to qualify as teachers or lecturers in domestic subjects, or who wish to fit themselves for the post of matron in a large institution, or who are anxious to find work in the colonies. There is a special course for inspectorships or other Government appointments.

TEACHERS OF DOMESTIC SUBJECTS

Training and Prospects.—There are many posts available for teachers of domestic subjects, more especially in cookery, laundry work and housewifery in elementary and secondary schools, technical institutes and evening schools. Teachers of domestic subjects in elementary schools must have first-class teaching diplomas in housewifery, cookery, and laundry work or dressmaking, gained at a training school recognised by the Board of Education, and this is essential even if they are only required to teach one subject. The training extends over two years, and the fees are usually about £50 for the entire course. The charges of the National Society's Training School for Teachers of Domestic Subjects, Hampstead, represent the average, and are as follows :—

Cookery, £30—course of forty-two weeks; Laundry work, £10, 10s.—course of twenty-six weeks; Housewifery, £8, 8s.—course of thirteen weeks.

Those who wish to enter a special training college to be trained as teachers of domestic subjects must not be less than eighteen years of age. They must have had a good English education and have an aptitude for teaching. They are usually required to take an examination in general knowledge unless they possess a certificate from a public examining body. In colleges especially devoted to the training of teachers for public elementary schools, the Board of Education require each student to make a declaration that she enters the training college with the intention of eventually becoming a teacher of domestic subjects, either in a public elementary school or in some other school approved by the Board for the purpose.

The training in needlework, dressmaking, and millinery is less expensive.

These subjects are largely taught in secondary schools, and good posts in this connection may be had. Needlework forms a part of the curriculum in almost every girls' school, whether public or private; dressmaking is now also largely taught in private as well as in public schools, so that in this respect there are many openings for teachers of needlework and dressmaking. Classes for needlework, cutting-out, and dressmaking can also be formed, and, if properly managed, will prove remunerative. There are many ways in which a thorough practical knowledge of needlework may be turned to advantage on a money-making basis. The training in plain needlework, dressmaking, and millinery is very moderate. At the National Training School for Teachers the fees are as follows :—

Plain Needlework, £7, 7s.—course of twenty weeks; Dressmaking, £7, 7s.—course of twenty weeks; Advanced Dressmaking, £8, 8s.—course of twenty weeks.

Posts as teachers are also available in day schools for domestic economy. In these the pupils have mostly won scholarships granted by the local education authorities and have entered the school to train for domestic service. Cookery, laundry work, needlework, and dressmaking are the principal subjects taught. Domestic science teachers and lecturers are also employed at evening technical classes under local authorities, especially in country districts.

In order to obtain the higher posts in domestic work, such as teachers and head teachers in training colleges, a three years' training in as many subjects as possible should be taken. There are Government inspectorships of domestic science schools that can also be filled, but these positions are necessarily few, as the number of appointments is limited. As is the case with most other Government inspectorships, two years' probation must be undergone before a definite appointment is secured.

Salaries vary to a great extent in accordance with the locality and the school. £70 a year would represent a fair average figure for ordinary teachers' posts in elementary or secondary schools.

Salaries of teachers in day schools for domestic economy average from £90 to £140. Those of lecturers and teachers in technical classes vary according to the particular districts.

Head mistresses of schools of domestic economy receive salaries of from £100 a year and upwards, whilst the salary of a Government inspector in domestic science averages £200 a year.

Cookery.—Though to obtain a post as teacher of cookery in an elementary school under a local authority it is necessary to take training in housewifery and laundry work as well as in cookery, there are posts available for the student who has taken her first-class cookery diploma alone. In many large institutions there are posts to be had as head cook and head of the kitchen staff which can only be filled by one well versed in organisation as well as in the culinary art, and posts of this kind are largely filled by women. In connection with many schools of domestic science, as well as with private schools, posts as cookery teachers, lecturers, and demonstrators may be obtained. The principal gas and electric light companies also employ lady demonstrators of cooking in connection with their various exhibitions and show-rooms.

Private cookery classes have also been organised with success in a few cases, but as a rule it is inadvisable to start upon a private venture, as cookery lectures and demonstrations organised under the auspices of the County Councils are now held in almost every populous district, and the charges are so low that it would be impossible for any private enterprise to compete with them in this respect. In some country districts, however, cookery classes have been successfully organised by a committee of ladies, but in these cases a certain minimum attendance has been guaranteed.

Private cookery schools can also be started with advantage if a suitable locality is selected. Preference should be given to a high-class residential district where there is no competition in the shape of other schools to be encountered. In these circumstances a good connection may be formed amongst married ladies who wish to add to their knowledge of cookery, or to learn new dishes to teach their cooks. Special classes could be given for cooks to teach them some new or special dish. For this reason the principals of the school should make a point of being *au fait* in every innovation, being careful to keep their cookery up-to-date. Their advertising literature and catalogue should be well designed. They might, for instance, advertise various courses of lessons, *i.e.* lessons for housewives, lessons for cooks, lessons for prospective brides, &c.

In the afternoons demonstrations of cookery might be held, when 1s. to 1s. 6d. admission could be charged. Novelty should be the keynote of these demonstrations. The teacher should always endeavour to display some novel dish—some novel method of cooking or novel and useful cooking appliances. A very remunerative side-line may be effected in the sale of cooking appliances, and in this connection a good addition to the income may be made by using the appliances of firms who are anxious to place their wares before the public, and who are willing to pay well for an advertisement of the kind. Only really useful and really efficient utensils, however, should be used—appliances that can be safely recommended.

Dress of Cookery Teachers.—This must always be plain, neat, and clean. No more fitting costume could be had than a short skirt and bodice (or blouse) of washing material. Over this a plain white linen apron long enough to cover the dress, with a "bib" fastened by means of straps crossing over the shoulders should be worn. A very dainty effect is also achieved by means of clean white linen over sleeves. A regulation cap is usually worn. The cookery teacher should be very particular in regard to the care she bestows upon her hands. Her hair should also be kept particularly neat and tidy.

Domestic science training may be had at the following colleges in addition to the National Society's Training College, already mentioned :—

In London.—The National Training School of Cookery, 72 to 78 Buckingham Palace Road, S.W. The Polytechnic, Battersea, S.W.

Edinburgh.—Edinburgh School of Cookery and Domestic Economy, 3 to 6 Atholl Crescent.

Glasgow.—Glasgow and West of Scotland College of Domestic Science, 86 Bath Street, Glasgow.

Dublin.—Irish Training School of Domestic Economy, St. Kevin's Park, Kilmacud, Stillorgan.

Leeds.—Training School of Cookery and Domestic Economy.

Liverpool.—Training School of Cookery, 23 Colquitt Street.

Manchester.—Municipal School of Domestic Economy.

Newcastle-on-Tyne.—Northern Counties Training School of Cookery and Household Economy.

A full list of training colleges and schools of domestic science is published in the Englishwoman's Year Book.

HOUSEWIFERY

Training in housewifery may be had at all the above-mentioned institutions and also at other establishments which differ from those above-mentioned, inasmuch as their main object is to train students for the ordinary domestic duties of home life. The work of the cook, housemaid, parlourmaid, and housekeeper are all taught by actual practice, so that a woman so trained, when worried with the servant question, need never be very much put about, as she can set to and do the work herself. The training, moreover, will enable a mistress to manage her servants well and superintend their work in a proper manner. Women who wish to earn their living as lady servants may obtain all the training necessary at establishments of this kind.

Such training may be obtained at the Fegerne School of Household Management, Temple Ewell, near Dover. Here all the work of the establishment is done by pupils. Fees are 25s. a week, including board and lodging.

St. Martha's College of Housecraft, 4 Chichester Street, St. George's Square, London, S.W., is a home school run upon the same lines, and has been established to help Catholic gentlewoman and others who require a short practical and inexpensive training in domestic work as a profession, or for use in their own homes. The course of training is six months, and the inclusive fee for board, residence, and tuition is thirty guineas.

The Guild of Dames of the Household, Cheltenham, is an association which affords good training for lady servants. Fees, fifteen shillings weekly, including board.

Lady Servants.—There is no doubt that domestic service as a livelihood is declining in popularity amongst all classes of workers; it is not to be wondered at, therefore, that educated ladies do not take to it too readily as a career, yet under favourable circumstances it should appeal to many gentlewomen who are versed in practical domestic science, for it presents many opportunities for the capable and willing worker. The servant question nowadays is one of great difficulty. Girls and women of the original servant class are now filling our factories and our shops. Service to them is synonymous with bondage. They prefer to have their evenings free, and are content to work under much less favourable conditions than they would if in service, so long as their work is limited to certain set hours.

It may be said that the long working hours form in every case the disadvantage of domestic service. Life has often to be spent in a basement. Some mistresses are none too thoughtful for their servants' comfort, and even the one evening out a week is given grudgingly as a great concession. The best class of mistress, however, is always distinguished by her consideration for those working under her, and it is with this class of mistress that work can be done under the most favourable conditions. As a rule, where lady servants are concerned, employers are only too willing to afford them consideration, realising that they are qualified ladies who have undergone a thorough course of training and are therefore highly efficient. They are therefore only too anxious to keep them and study their comfort in every way. The success or non-success of the lady servant will depend to a great extent upon her powers of adaptability to her work. The woman who considers domestic service beneath her and does her work with an injured air, having always an "I am as good as you" expression upon her face when addressed by her mistress, will never attain success. Her life will seem to her one long hardship, and she will always be labouring under an undefined sense of grievance. On the other hand, a menial position in a household is unsuited to a woman, unless, as in the case of a head cook or housekeeper in a large establishment, she is at the head of all the other servants, having her own sitting-room in which to take her meals, or unless if she is an ordinary servant, her fellow-workers are ladies also. Finally, a great deal will depend upon the disposition of the worker. If she is one who is always willing to make the best of things and is able to adapt herself with a good will to varying circumstances, she will find happiness and independence in whatever domestic position she may take up.

The present unsatisfactory state of the servant question has created a demand for lady cooks in many instances. More especially is this the case in very large private houses, ladies' clubs and colleges. In these circumstances the position of the lady cook is at its best; she usually has her own suite of rooms in which she can take her meals and spend her spare time by herself. To satisfactorily fill a position of this kind, besides being an expert cook, a woman must also be a good organiser. She will have control of all the kitchen staff; often she will require to do some of the housekeeping as well. Such posts at present are few and far between; but there is no reason why the openings in this direction should not be increased, and why the lady chef should not take the place of a man chef in many cases. She should be able to earn an income of from £40 to £80 and sometimes £100 a year.

In small households lady cooks are sometimes employed, but as in this case the kitchen life will be that of ordinary servants in most middle-class homes, a position of this kind is only suitable where other lady servants are employed. Wages are paid on the scale of ordinary servants' wages.

Amongst givers of dinner-parties there is also a demand for the visiting cook, who will take upon herself the responsibility of preparing a whole dinner, with the help of a kitchen-maid to do the rough work. In the first instance she will be asked to draw up a menu with list of cooking requirements for approval. Then when the menu has been approved or various alterations have been suggested, she must superintend the whole cooking of the dinner, seeing that each dish is served promptly in its turn, and remaining until the entire meal has been served. Good fees may be commanded by the experienced cook. These average from 15s. to £1, 1s. per dinner, the latter fee being given to those with the highest qualifications and credentials.

To cook a dinner and see that it is served without a hitch is no mean achievement. It requires great experience and powers of organisation to do this properly, and it should never be attempted by the girl fresh from her training school until she has had good practice in cooking dinners of many courses. She must cultivate calmness of temperament, presence of mind in emergencies, power of maintaining discipline amongst those who work under her, and, above all, order, method, and punctuality, without which qualities any scheme of organisation must necessarily fail.

Children's Nurse.—This career opens out many opportunities for ladies. Parents are beginning to realise the urgent need of having persons of refinement to care for their children, and, in addition, persons who have had a certain definite training and are therefore competent for the work. There is necessity for specialisation in this as well as in other careers. The would-be nurse must go to a recognised school or training home, and gain her certificate of merit; it is useless for the untrained worker to expect to gain her livelihood in this profession.

The girl who would become a nurse must in

the first instance be fond of children. She must possess an abundant fund of patience and perseverance, and, in fact, have a vocation for the work. Before undertaking it a girl should well realise what it means. She will have to take entire charge of the little ones, make most of their clothes, do all the mending, and care for them in sickness; she should be able to recognise and treat the various childish ailments, and should have a thorough knowledge of child hygiene. In some cases she will have to give the little ones their first lessons, and in these circumstances a knowledge of kindergarten methods will be most useful. There are colleges over the kingdom where training may be had. This generally takes one year, although in some colleges there is a six months' course. The cost of training averages from £60 to £80 a year. The training is not only useful for those who wish to become children's nurses, but it is also valuable for girls who are to marry, and who in all probability will have children of their own to care for. The course of instruction usually includes the care and feeding of babies from a few days old and upwards; the management and routine of a nursery, nursery cookery, the cutting-out and making of children's garments, mending, nursery laundry work, nursery hygiene, and kindergarten methods of teaching.

The following are some of the best-known institutions where training may be had:—

The Norland Institute, 10 Pembridge Square, London, W. (The course includes three months' training in a children's hospital.) Sesame House, Acacia Road, St. John's Wood, London; The Hampstead Nursery College, Hampstead, London, W. (Roman Catholic)—Principal, Mrs. Bernard Mole; Princess Christian College for Training Ladies as Nurses, 19 Wilmslow Road, Willington, Manchester. Full particulars as to terms, course of training, &c., may be had upon application to any of these institutions.

Prospects.—The commencing salary of a lady nurse should not be less than £25 a year. An experienced head nurse can earn from £40 to £70 in many cases.

Housekeepers and Matrons.—A good training in housewifery and domestic science is necessary for the housekeeper of the present day. A short course of cookery should also be taken. There are very few positions available nowadays in the ordinary middle-class household; but in houses where a large staff of servants is kept the housekeeper still holds sway. Experience and a thorough knowledge of the domestic arts, as well as good organising capacities, are always necessary to successfully fill a position of this kind. The same may be said of housekeepers and matrons in large schools and public institutions. The housekeeper is usually required to superintend the cooking and catering and keep the accounts in regard to both. She will also have charge of the plate and linen, seeing to the necessary mending of the latter, or, if there is a sewing-maid, seeing that the mending is promptly and efficiently executed. In short, it will be realised that no inefficient untrained person can fill a post of this kind. Those who have had experience in the management of their own households must not think that the knowledge so gained is sufficient to enable them to take an important post. Though the practical experience they have gained is very useful, they should supplement this by short courses in housewifery and cookery at one of the domestic science schools.

LAUNDRY MANAGERESS

The best way to obtain a post of this kind is to take a course of practical training for three months in a laundry. Most large laundries take pupils for three months' training at an average fee of £10, 10s.; to this must be added the cost of board and lodging during the training period. The success of the student will depend a great deal upon how she uses her powers of observation, and whether she makes the most of all the facilities afforded her and studies the work to the most minute detail. When a student shows decided aptitude for the work, she will often be allowed to stay on after she has completed her course of instruction, and if the proprietor desires to retain her services, he will pay her a small salary and give her in all probability the charge of a department. It is always advisable to stay a year at the laundry after the training has been completed in order to get experience. After this a woman will be able to take a post as assistant manageress in a laundry or institution, and then aim at the post of manageress in due course. Training should always be taken at a large laundry, for in these the most varied experience may be had.

The following laundries take pupils, and are typical of the kind of institution at which training should be taken:—

The Wimbledon Laundry Co., Cranbrook Road, Wimbledon, London; The Anglo-American Laundry, Tooting, London; The Craigmillar Laundry, Edinburgh.

There are many qualities necessary to assure the success of a laundry manageress; of these business capacity and good powers of organisation are essential. Each department must be run with regularity of clockwork, books must be kept in order, and expenses checked. Tact in dealing with the complaints of difficult customers is also very necessary, and, above all, the power of maintaining discipline and gaining the respect of the large number of workers employed.

The salary of a laundry manageress usually commences at £2, 10s. a week, rising to £5. It is work, therefore, which is well paid, and in this respect compares very favourably with all other branches of business open to women. The hours of work in a laundry are long, usually from ten to twelve hours daily, but the work is full of interest and there are many compensations. Good posts may also be obtained in various institutions where they pay fair salaries—usually £50 a year with board and lodging. In ladies' colleges also there are posts available, where the rate of pay is on much the same scale.

Another recommendation which a post of this kind should have to the woman worker is the fact that the working years are more than in the case with most other employments for women. In fact, in selecting a manageress preference is in many cases given to the middle-aged woman who is experienced at the work. A girl should not take up laundry work too young—twenty-one years of age should be the limit—and she should have had a good general education and a knowledge of book-keeping and commercial arithmetic.

WOMEN'S WORK IN THE COLONIES

There are many openings in the colonies for educated women, more especially in Canada and South Africa. Emigration, however, is a serious step to take, and no woman should decide upon it before taking the advice of one of the best emigration associations. From these full information as to the kind of work which is best for the colonies, together with particulars as to the best way of getting employment, &c., may be had. Many societies advance passage money to girls, or make a grant towards it.

Intending emigrants to Canada should apply for information to the British Women's Emigration Society, Imperial Institute, London, S.W., and those who wish to go to South Africa should write for particulars to the South African Colonisation Society, 115 Victoria Street, London, S.W.

The best openings for women workers in our colonies undoubtedly present themselves to those who are well skilled in domestic science. In many of the country districts of Canada servants are scarce, so that the services of women helps are generally at a premium. The woman help in Canada will be required to know every branch of domestic work, including cooking, laundry work, mending, dressmaking, &c. Her position is infinitely better than that of the "lady help" at home, for she is always treated as one of the family, sharing in the pleasure as well as the work of her employers. Canadian life is homely and free in every sense, and little store is set upon social distinction of class; educated women workers are always treated as equals.

Some horticultural and agricultural knowledge on the part of the emigrant to Canada will stand her in good stead. Work in the gardens as in the fields may well become her province. In fact, there is scarcely a thing to which she should not be able to put her hand. Apart from the favourable prospects for home workers, capable girls very soon get married in our colonies and thus have houses of their own to direct. There are many establishments that give training to girls who intend to emigrate.

At the **Horticultural College, Swanley,** intending colonists may have a very good training in both indoor and outdoor work. Fees, £70 a year; shorter courses may be taken.

The Stoke Prior Colonial Training College, Bromsgrove, also offers training in all domestic subjects, including dairy work and poultry rearing. The training lasts from three to six months according to the course chosen, and the fees for board and tuition are from 17s. 6d. for a single room, and from 12s. 6d. if the room is shared, per week.

Then there is the **Arlesley Training College,** near Hitchin, Herts, which offers a very thorough training to ladies in all branches of Colonial housework. It is under the patronage of Lady Francis Balfour and Lady Buxton and other ladies who are much interested in the scheme. Besides the ordinary domestic subjects, the management of a garden, farm, or poultry-yard, bee-keeping, pig rearing, riding, driving, carpentry, a knowledge of ambulance and home nursing, &c., are all taught. The age limit for entrance in the college is from eighteen to thirty. The fees are £50 for a six months' course, or £80 for a year's course, including residence. A full course lasts two years. For fuller particulars apply to the Principal of the College.

Ordinary domestic training may be had at any school of domestic science, but training in poultry-keeping, dairy work, gardening, &c., are all essential in many cases for the "home help." If a girl takes good training in all these branches she is almost certain of obtaining profitable appointments. Girls who go out to the colonies to be married should also have some sort of training of the kind, as this will be necessary for the proper management of homes of their own.

Domestic helps earn good salaries, according to their capabilities; the thoroughly trained girl would earn as much as between £52 to £60 a year; the less experienced worker beginning at from £24 to £30. First-class head cooks in large town establishments, hotels, &c., earn very high wages, ranging from £60 per annum, and often rising to £120 in the case of hotels and restaurants.

School teachers and governesses are well paid in both Canada and South Africa, there being more openings in the former than in the latter country. A thorough teacher's training must be taken and the necessary certificates gained to obtain a post of the kind. (See Teaching

Profession.) Many posts are to be had in the state schools of Canada and in the high schools of Cape Colony and Natal. Assistant mistresses in elementary schools receive salaries of from £144 to £170 a year, and head mistresses from £200 to £300. It must be remembered, however, that the cost of living is higher than it is in the mother country. In South Africa salaries are lower, and the cost of living very much greater than in Canada; teachers therefore should take none but resident posts, for in these circumstances they will not have to pay for board and lodging, which are always exceedingly high items of expenditure. In many cases the passages of teachers from England to South Africa are paid by the schools. Posts as governesses and nursery governesses are well paid in both colonies.

When a girl goes out to Canada or one of the other colonies and has no fixed place to go to, she ought to arrange, if possible, to board at one of the branches of the G.F.S. or Y.W.C.A., as many of the cheaper hotels and boarding-houses are not desirable. Particulars of the different hostels in the colonies can be obtained by applying to Mrs. H. R. Mill, Honorary Secretary, Y.W.C.A. Emigration Department, The Hollies, Mill Hill, London, or to the Honorary Secretary, Mrs. Joyce, G.F.S. Emigration Department, St. John's Croft, Winchester.

Women have started and are running farms in Canada with success, but to do this requires very exceptional qualifications and a thorough agricultural training. In regard to clerical and other office posts these offer few prospects for the English girl, as the colonies themselves provide a sufficient number of this class of worker. The restaurant and hotel businesses pay well, and the woman with capital might turn her attention to an enterprise of the kind. Smart milliners and dressmakers are also in request, and girls who are versed in either dressmaking or millinery may obtain very good positions with large firms in the principal towns, or, if they have capital combined with skill and business ability, they can start a business of their own with good prospects of success. This, however, should not be done until one has a good knowledge of the country and especially of the local requirements.

Hints on a Colonial Outfit.—When choosing an outfit for abroad the kind of climate one is going to must be taken into consideration and also the life one expects to lead. In most cases it is a mistake to buy a great many clothes, unless one is quite sure of what is required and also the special rates of transit, as the expense of carriage is as a rule very heavy, and especially so if the journey happens to lie across country. In most places, too, it is possible to buy what is wanted and of a kind best suited to the needs of that special locality.

The woman who goes out to the colonies should provide herself with a reasonable amount of plain sensible clothing.

A good supply of underclothing is always advisable, and six of everything should be the smallest number provided. Woollen garments are indispensable, and these ought to be very warm if a winter in Canada is anticipated, while a specially thin make will be required for summer wear and for warm climates. All underclothing ought to be plain and neat rather than of a flimsy character, as the trouble of washing must be taken into consideration, and the woman colonist must, as a rule, be prepared either to do her own or else be able to afford a big washing bill.

Two neat costumes should form part of the outfit—one of which might be made of navy blue serge of rather a light make for spring and autumn wear, and the other might be made of some warm grey material or a tweed mixture for colder weather. Both of these would be found useful when travelling.

A good supply of neat well-fitting shirts or blouses should be provided for wearing with these costumes.

Two good travelling coats will also be necessary —one light in weight, which will serve as a protection from dust or a light shower of rain, and the other a warm storm coat, which will be a wrap in the coldest weather; a blanket coat would be very suitable for the purpose, as it is both light and warm.

A girl who is going to do domestic work will also require some strong working dresses made either of cotton or linen, which can easily be washed. A supply of large working aprons or overalls should also be taken.

The amount of finer clothes taken will depend entirely upon the life that is about to be led. If this is uncertain it is wiser just to take one simple evening dress, and perhaps a thin cloth dress along with two or three dressy blouses, and perhaps one or two lengths of pretty material which can be made up when necessary. A tussore silk dress is always useful; it is easily washed and looks fresh and new every time.

Suitable hats can generally be bought on the spot, and as they are difficult to carry, a large number should not be thought of. One or two hats and a close-fitting travelling-cap will be all that are required. Sun-hats can generally be bought locally for a few shillings.

There should also be a fair supply of boots, shoes and house slippers of a comfortable make and not too thin.

Such etceteras as gloves, stockings, ribbons, ties, handkerchiefs, belts, collars should be provided pretty liberally, but flimsy finery of all kinds should be avoided; it is quite spoilt after being packed up for some time, and in a simple Colonial life is out of place.

WOMEN IN BUSINESS

YEARS ago the woman in business was an unknown quantity; to-day she is an accepted fact. There is scarcely a business career nowadays which cannot be entered by a clever woman, and from the typist at £1 a week to the manageress or the proprietress of large commercial enterprises we find women working side by side with men, in many cases with equal advantages. There is still, however, a deplorable tendency to make women work longer and at lesser salaries than men in the mere clerical positions. For this many girls have themselves been responsible, a number of them working for pocket-money only. Happily women are beginning to realise the evils of undercutting in salaries, and it only needs a co-operation among all women workers to assure their being paid at least a living wage. In this article some of the principal branches of business open to women are considered.

LADY CLERKS

Shorthand Typist.—The girl who wishes to become a shorthand typist should first of all have had a good general education. Then she must have spent a year or two years in special training for her work. Too much stress cannot be laid upon the fact that a thorough education is essential in all cases as a basis upon which to build up the special work which is to follow. There seems to be a kind of idea that a girl can take a post as shorthand typist after very little training, and a post in an office is often thought to be the one refuge for the half-educated girl. Never was there a greater fallacy. It has been said that the ranks of typists have become overcrowded, and salaries have been correspondingly lowered. This is only in regard to the inefficient workers. There are a number of girls who can perhaps take down a letter correctly if not dictated at a high speed, and transcribe it without serious mistake, but beyond this they have not an idea. If they were asked to compose a letter on their own account or had to show initiative in any way, they would be hopelessly at a loss. Workers of this kind can never hope to earn good salaries, for the very reason that there are hundreds of others who would be able to step into their shoes at a minute's notice.

This is not the case with the intelligent worker who has thoroughly mastered her work in all its branches, who is not only an expert shorthand note-taker and transcriber, but who can save her employer a great deal of his time by being able to compose good business letters from a few words of instruction. A girl of this kind will always have some power of initiative—she will not have to be told again and again what to do, and she may be trusted to deal tactfully with any emergency that may arise. She will always be business-like, neat in her work, and conscientious in carrying out her instructions.

Typists who show capabilities of this kind, and whose work is valuable in every way, can always command a good salary, whilst those who are content to be mere machines will always be badly paid.

Training should be taken at one of the many business colleges with which all our large cities abound. Shorthand is now taught at many schools as an extra subject, but it is seldom that one can get speed practice to the same extent as in a business school. Proficiency in stenography can seldom be acquired in less than a year at least, but even to learn it in this time constant speed practice is necessary. Intelligent students have been known to teach themselves shorthand, but the process is necessarily a slow and a difficult one. Every opportunity should be taken to read shorthand, and it is a good plan also when reading newspapers and magazines to trace the outlines of the words in shorthand under the printed lines as you go on. All opportunities for practice, such as taking down sermons, lectures, and speeches, should be taken when they present themselves. In the business training course at a college the student will learn how to write business letters, &c., &c. She will, in short, be given just that training which will be most useful to her in an office.

Besides shorthand and typewriting, training should also be taken in book-keeping, and the principal methods of filing should be learned. Thorough knowledge of commercial French or German will prove an invaluable asset, for a much higher salary will be received by the girl who can correspond in a foreign language.

A typist's duties will consist of taking down letters in shorthand and transcribing them on the typewriter. Often she will be required to write short letters herself from a brief word of instruction. She will have to file letters systematically, being able to produce them at once when required. She will also be expected to answer telephone calls for her employer in most cases, and this is a fact worth remembering by those who are not accustomed to the use of the telephone. Often she will be required to keep note of her employer's appointments, and sometimes some of the book-keeping will fall to her share. The duties will vary in different offices. In large offices the stamping of letters, posting up of letter-book, &c., are performed by boys or junior clerks, whereas in the smaller offices some of these duties would fall upon the typist.

Prospects.—An expert shorthand typist who can correspond in a foreign language can nearly always earn £2 a week and upwards; 30s. to 35s. a week is the usual salary of the thoroughly efficient shorthand typist who is not proficient in languages. For a girl with ordinary qualifications, £1 to £1, 5s. per week would represent the average salary, a junior typist receiving about 15s. weekly. A girl's salary will increase according to how useful she makes herself to her employers. In many cases a typist's salary has been known to reach £4 a week, but the recipient has always had exceptional qualifications and been entrusted with responsible work.

Book-keepers.—The same principles laid down for the observance of shorthand typists must be taken to heart by the girl who wishes to become a book-keeper. Book-keeping by itself, however, does not present such a wide scope as when it is allied with shorthand and typewriting. Needless to say, the girl who wishes to be a book-keeper must be strictly accurate and have a special talent for figures. She should also be a very neat writer, as all entries in the books must be neat and legible. Training in book-keeping can be had at any commercial school, or at evening classes at technical institutes.

Thirty shillings a week is considered a good salary for a woman book-keeper, but the beginner would necessarily get less.

Some Hints in regard to answering Advertisements and Business Interviews.—The applicant for a post should remember that employers can often form a judgment as to the qualifications of a clerk by her letter of application. Great care should be taken, therefore, to pen a neat, legible, and well-worded letter, confining it strictly to the business point at issue. An employer does not want to know how difficult you find it to get work, or if you are an orphan, or if your mother is an invalid. He *does* want to know, however, what business experience you have had, what is your speed in shorthand and typewriting—if you can keep books and are used to any particular filing system, and if you can correspond in French or any other language. Make your letter brief, business-like, and to the point. Detail carefully all your qualifications, mention how long you were with your last employer, give references if desired, and ask for the favour of a personal interview. If a business interview is arranged, be at the office punctually at the appointed time; take great care to present a neat, well-groomed appearance, for this will count a great deal in your favour. If you are asked to take down notes in shorthand and transcribe them as a test, do so quietly and without flurry. Make up your mind to do your very best undeterred by the nervousness which is invariably felt upon these occasions. Let the answers to any questions you may be asked be always courteous and to the point. Employers are quick to appreciate a business-like demeanour, and this fact should always be borne in mind by applicants for a business post.

ACCOUNTANTS

Accountancy is another profession to which educated women might well turn their attention, only its practice necessitates the possession of several qualities which are not inherent in the average woman. The accountant requires a clear, deductive mind and great taste for mathematics, sound business capabilities, and a thorough training. She should have had a thoroughly good general education, followed by at least three years' special study of accountancy work.

Women are admitted to the membership of the London Association of Accountants and can obtain the qualifying distinctions of F.L.A.A. or A.L.A.A. given by this Association. The member's certificates of this Association are recognised by the Board of Trade.

To prepare for the examination the student should become articled for a period of from three to five years to a certified accountant who is a member of the Association. The premium will probably amount to 25 guineas.

Women can also prepare for a provincial Bachelor of Commerce degree at the Victoria University, Manchester, and the Universities of Birmingham, Leeds, and Liverpool. The study, if day classes are taken, will last three years, or five years if evening classes only are taken. The fees will probably amount to about £20 for each year.

For the girl of slender means preparation for the Accountancy Certificate of the London Chamber of Commerce may be had by attending the classes of the London County Council's Evening Commercial Centres. The cost for these classes is practically nil, seldom amounting to more than 2s. 6d. for the session.

BANK MANAGERESS, CASHIER

Within the last year a new profession has opened its gates to women, the profession of bank manageress. On March 14, 1910, Mr. Thomas Farrow founded the first bank for women in the United Kingdom at 29 New Bridge Street, Ludgate Circus, London, and in this bank the staff and advisory committee are composed wholly of women, and only women customers are accepted. It may be taken that this may lead to other similar ventures, so that the woman who has had a good commercial training may put it to account in this way. A bank manageress must necessarily be a woman of great capabilities and tact, and with sound business knowledge and training.

In a bank managed only by women it will be seen that not only the post of manageress, but also those of clerks and cashiers, are available. The woman's banking movement is well worth watching by capable women workers; if it develops to any great extent we may see women's banks throughout the kingdom, and further openings for women workers will thus present themselves.

The payment to the staff employed in the first bank for women has been fixed on a liberal scale.

HOUSE AGENT

The house agency business is eminently suitable for women, yet few have so far taken it up, owing no doubt to the long and thorough training involved.

It is absolutely useless for any girl to enter the ranks of house agents if she is not in the first place a good business woman and has not a thorough knowledge of every branch of her work. In addition a knowledge of the law is very essential for the house agent, for without it she might often land her clients into serious difficulties. A knowledge of surveying and valuation is also necessary.

There is a good future in the house agency business for clever women with the requisite training. A girl who wishes to start as a house agent must be in earnest and not do things by halves. She must have plenty of tact. The woman house agent, in fact, should be a lady in every sense of the word, with a good education and good manners; she should also be able to mix in good social circles. It is much easier for a lady of good social connections to start upon work of this kind, for friends will entrust their business to her, and her work will increase as her success in dealing with the business becomes known. Mrs. Arthur Holland, the well-known lady house agent, once remarked, "Very often I have talked over and secured an important contract in a drawing-room over the tea-cups with much more ease than I could have done in the office." Another argument in favour of the lady house agent is the fact that it is the lady of the family who takes or lets a house—the husband seldom bothers with these matters. Is it not fitting, therefore, that business should be discussed with another lady? Indeed, more often than not a lady has the advantage over a man in this respect, for she has considerable grasp of detail, and she may often obtain in this way concessions for her client which a man might well overlook.

The girl who is to be a house agent should also take instruction in house decoration, structural alterations and costs, for with this knowledge any one can gauge the possibilities of a house, and can advise the owner that at such and such an outlay a house can be made more attractive and command in many instances higher rent. Besides advising owners how to deal with their property, the girl who knows something of decoration and alterations can suggest improvements to the intending tenant.

A house agent should have a thorough training in every branch of her business, from the taking of an inventory to the drawing out of a lease. In England there are as yet difficulties in the way of training. The best way to train, however, is to become an articled pupil for three years to a house agent. This will cost, as a rule, 100 guineas. In addition, careful coaching should be taken in all points of law bearing upon the business.

It is essential to have some capital before starting a house agency business, but no capital will be of any use unless you have the requisite training and sound business capacity. Apart from women starting in business as house agents right away, it will soon be recognised that there is a great deal of work connected with house and estate agency for which they are eminently adapted. Take the checking of inventories, for instance; this can be quite well done by ladies, and already a number of house agents employ ladies to do this particular work.

Prospects.—House agency is a business which should open up very good prospects for clever women, for the reason that it is not overcrowded by women workers. It presents no sort of opening, however, for those with mediocre talents, but only for those with a thorough training and first-class capabilities.

HOUSE DECORATION

Women with the artistic sense cannot do better than turn their attention to house decoration as a means of livelihood, either with the view of obtaining a post with a firm of house decorators, or starting a business of the kind for themselves. There are certain qualifications which are, however, indispensable. In the first place a keen sense of form and colour and an eye for detail and arrangement are absolutely necessary. The house decorator must be able to originate effective schemes of decoration for clients, and to carry out schemes devised by them. In addition she must have a thorough knowledge of the business side of her work, the-comparative cost of various decorative schemes, different styles of furniture, fittings, &c. She must be able to draw up estimates and keep accounts, also to direct and supervise the work of workmen. The house decorator must have a knowledge of the typical furniture of various periods, and what style of decoration will go best with each. She must recognise the various kinds of cloths and brocades, the difference between the many varieties of carpets, and the properties of each in regard to durability, &c. She must also have a knowledge of antiques, both in regard to furniture and ornaments.

Training.—It will be seen that this knowledge cannot possibly be acquired without the necessary training. The only way of obtaining this is by serving an apprenticeship with a good firm of decorators, preferably with a lady decorator. Mrs. Keighley, the well-known lady decorator of Church Street, Kensington, London, takes pupils at a fee of 300 guineas for a three years' course of training. A shorter course of twelve months may also be taken, and the charge for this is 50 guineas. Students may do much in the way of acquiring knowledge by visiting the various museums, such as the South Kensington, and the Victoria and Albert, to study specimens of old furniture. A knowledge of architecture and design will be especially useful.

Prospects.—To start a business, capital will be necessary and also a certain social connection. As in the case of the house agency business, the lady who belongs to a good social circle and has a number of friends will stand the best chance. If a girl has no capital or good social connection she should strive to obtain first a position in a firm of decorators and gradually work her way up until she is able to set out for herself as an "adviser," or, if she can raise the capital, in a business of her own. She would probably begin at a salary of £1, 10s. a week, rising to £2 a week as her experience increases.

The woman who starts in business for herself must, of course, have that business aptitude which is so indispensable for the successful conducting of any kind of trade.

DRESSMAKING

This is a profession in which women always stand a good chance of success. A clever dressmaker is practically certain of a good clientele. Smart clothes are a necessity for the feminine world, and the demand for them always exists, so that no business can be started under more favourable auspices than that of dressmaking.

Whether a woman wishes merely to be an assistant in a dressmaking firm, or wishes to start a business of her own, her training should be a thoroughly practical one—she must learn the work from the beginning. She may take a course of lessons at a dressmaking school, but she should always supplement this by going into the workroom of a good dressmaking firm in order to get the necessary experience.

The conditions of apprenticeship vary. To enter many firms of high standing premiums of £50 to £100 must be paid. With ordinary apprenticeships, however, no fees are taken, and after six months a small weekly sum is paid to the apprentice. Every branch of the business is taught—from sewing on buttons to fitting a dress.

For the girl who wishes to be an assistant the post of fitter should be aimed at if her talent lies in this direction. Fitting is the most important branch of the business, an experienced fitter being able to earn £5 a week and upwards, whilst the salaries of first bodice and skirt hands seldom rise above £150 a year, though in some cases £200 a year is earned.

The woman who wishes to start in business for herself should be naturally gifted for the work. She should have a keen sense of beautiful lines in fitting and of the art of drapery; she should also recognise the principles which govern a good cut. This knowledge is absolutely necessary if she has to direct fitters and workers.

Prospects.—Many women commence by making frocks for their friends. If they are really good workers their clientele increases, and after some time they are able to secure trained assistance. Cash payments should be made a rule, and certain modifications in regard to price may be held out as an inducement to customers, for expenses are lessened when money comes in regularly.

By degrees the dressmaker beginning on these lines will find her business grow until she has quite a large connection. To start a West End business a fairly large capital is necessary—members of the wealthier classes are notoriously neglectful in regard to the prompt settlement of accounts, and, as a rule, a certain period of credit must be allowed. Business ability is a necessity for the dressmaker, who must also be alive to the possibilities of good advertising and other matters bearing upon her trade. No woman should enter the dressmaking business unless she is prepared for very hard work. The beginner with few assistants will often be obliged to sit up far into the night in order to finish the work entrusted to her, as it is fatal for the beginner to break promises made to her customer. A clever woman, by beginning in a small way and extending her business as opportunity presents itself, will by degrees build up quite a prosperous business yielding her a good annual income.

MILLINERY

As with dressmaking so with millinery—apprenticeship is the surest way of learning the business. To be apprenticed to a good milliner a girl would have to pay a premium of about twenty guineas or less, but rarely more than this sum. The period of training is not so lengthy as that required for dressmaking, a millinery apprenticeship lasting, as a rule, for from six to nine months. It is always wise after the apprenticeship is over to stay on a little longer in the shop in order to gain experience; during this time the worker would earn a small salary, beginning at 10s. a week and rising to 30s. a week. If she does not wish to open a business of her own she could try and obtain a post as head milliner in either a millinery shop or a large drapery establishment with a millinery department. In this position she will be required to direct the work of the millinery workers and apprentices, supervising the whole working department. Head milliners often receive a salary of £3 a week.

The woman who wishes to start a business of her own must have business capacity in addition to her knowledge of the actual work. It is business capacity that counts the most in all businesses—the power of organisation, of directing others, and checking expenditure and preventing waste. The good business woman knows that it requires more than mere knowledge of millinery to obtain success as a milliner, that there are many details, such as choice of locality, &c., which determine the fate of such a business enterprise, and it is generally to the neglect of one of these important questions that the unsuccessful milliner may ascribe her failure.

BEAUTY SPECIALISTS

This is a business which promises the most interesting developments, and is full of interest and variety. There are now many women who are drawing large incomes from businesses of the kind, and who, by their enterprise, have encouraged many others to follow in their wake.

A business of this kind is only successful in large towns where the wealthier classes are well represented. In smaller towns the clientele would not be extensive enough to make it pay. It is necessary also to start in a fashionable district where house rent and other expenses would be high, therefore a capital of at least £500 would in most cases be necessary.

Those who go in for this business must necessarily be women of refinement. A dainty, lady-like appearance, well-kept hands, a soft, gentle voice are invaluable assets for she who would obtain a post as assistant in a business of the kind. Beauty culture appeals especially to women of the leisured classes. An air of exclusiveness and refinement must necessarily pervade the establishment of the beauty specialist if she wishes to appeal to these classes especially.

The chief treatments applied at these establishments are face and neck massage and complexion treatment generally, including removal of blackheads, electrolysis, manicure, and sometimes hair and scalp treatment. A thorough knowledge of all these branches is necessary for the girl who wishes to qualify as an assistant. There are some girls who will never make good masseuses, as they lack that light and delicate touch which is so necessary, and no beauty specialist will accept a girl as a pupil who does not promise to be an adept at the work.

Training.—Training can only be obtained at the establishment of a beauty specialist. Terms of training vary; sometimes they are very moderate indeed, as girls of refinement with the necessary qualifications are difficult to find. It is the rule also with most establishments that no pupils are accepted unless they bind themselves to become assistants of the firm for a certain period, generally three years. In these circumstances the terms are usually very favourable, one firm having been known to take an especially promising pupil for a small fee of £5, and give her a salary after three months' training. From three to six months is generally the period of pupilage, after which a salary is given. Students must also sign an agreement to the effect that when they leave the establishment they will not start a business of their own within a given distance of the place where they have trained.

Salaries are very good, commencing as a rule at £1, 1s. to £1, 10s. per week and rising as the usefulness of the assistant increases. Head assistants and manageresses receive higher salaries; the amount varies in the different establishments. The girl who wishes to become a pupil cannot do better than write to a firm of beauty specialists, such as Mme. Pomeroy in Bond Street, London, asking if there is a vacancy for a pupil and upon what terms training may be had.

HAIRDRESSING

More women might turn their attention to the business of hairdressing with advantage. It is essentially feminine work, yet work which has for a long time been to a certain extent monopolised by men. Within recent years, however, ladies have set up as hair specialists with success. They have studied not only the art of hairdressing, but also the hygiene of the head, and the value of various preparations in curing scalp troubles. With hairdressing nowadays are also often associated the various methods of complexion treatment and massage, manicure and chiropody.

To make a good hairdresser a girl must in the first place have an innate gift for hair arrangement and the facility to distinguish the styles best suited to the various types of faces. The best way of learning the business is to take a course of instruction at a hairdresser's. The terms vary with the different establishments. In some the apprenticeships last a year, in others longer, whilst short courses, varying from three to six months in duration, may be taken. The last named are useful for ladies who wish to set up a private connection by beginning to do hairdressing for their friends, and also for those who wish to be ladies' maids. The fees for a two years' course would probably amount to from £25 to £30, shorter courses being naturally much cheaper. The pupil is instructed in every branch of the work, from brushing and combing, cutting, clipping, and shampooing the hair to the carrying out of the fashionable coiffure; making and dressing of wigs, and all kinds of false hair work. The study of the hygiene of the head and the properties of the various hair washes and hair dyes must by no means be neglected by the woman who wishes to start a hairdressing business of her own.

Prospects.—The posts of assistants are not highly paid, the pay rarely exceeding £2 a week, whilst 10s. to 15s. a week represents a commencing salary. Besides posts in ordinary establishments, there are hairdressing departments in most of our large drapery and general stores, which are often managed by ladies. A woman may also form a good private visiting connection for hairdressing at fees of 5s. a visit. There are no end of ways in which the art can be put to practical account by the good business woman.

OPENING A TEA-ROOM

Many ladies who have opened tea-rooms are carrying on quite a profitable business, whilst others have lost all their little capital in the endeavour to start an enterprise of the kind. The reason is that ladies of limited means who could cook a little and make sweets and cakes have rushed headlong into the business, fondly imagining that the little knowledge they possessed was sufficient for success. Never was there a greater fallacy. The first thing necessary to make a tea-room pay is sound business capacity. Servants can be engaged to do the cooking and see to the other details, and the success or failure of a tea-room will depend not only upon the cooking, though this is of course important, but chiefly upon the way it is managed. Choice of locality is an important consideration—choice should be made of a spot where there is little competition from neighbouring establishments, and where a certain proportion of customers may be assured. City tea and luncheon rooms, for instance, should not be opened in a main street, but in a side thoroughfare which is well frequented, near important business houses from which it is easily accessible.

The outlay on furniture need not be great, and every inch of space should be utilised to the best advantage. A long seat can be made to run the length of the wall, consisting of a large plank of wood fitted up by a carpenter and daintily covered with dark green art serge or cretonne of a pretty pattern. Tables can be of the cheapest, as dainty cloths can always be kept over them to hide their surface. They should be of various sizes to hold two, four, &c.

The chief thing in starting a business of the kind is to establish a distinctive note about the place which will answer well for the purpose of advertisement. It is a good plan, for instance, to call the rooms after the name of a flower and to carry out the scheme of decoration in accordance with the floral idea. Thus in "Daffodil" Tea-rooms the decorative scheme would be one of green and yellow. Should there be a shop frontage to the rooms a few dainty boxes of sweets, or ornaments if sweets are not sold, should be tastefully displayed upon billows of yellow art muslin. Vases containing daffodils might be arranged here and there—in the spring the natural flowers and at other seasons artificial ones could be used. At the back the window could be partitioned off from the interior by dainty little yellow curtains hanging from brass rods. Inside the room wall-paper and tables should be green, and a bunch of daffodils in a green vase might be placed upon each table.

In regard to the cooking a feature should be made of home-made rolls and cakes, and the service should be characterised by daintiness and refinement.

This is only a rough idea of what could be done by a woman with taste for arrangement. Menu cards might also have a daffodil painted upon the cover. Neat little cards enclosing a typical tariff might be sent round to the various residents, or offices (if in the city). Tea-rooms at pleasure resorts should be advertised in the local paper, and the advertisement should be well and carefully drawn up.

All these details require organisation, management, and careful counting of costs. Book-keeping will have to be most carefully done, and the duplicate check-system should be adopted for the making out of bills. In a tea-room managed by ladies, ladies are usually engaged as assistants. No assistants will be necessary where three or four sisters or friends are engaged in the business. If the cooking is not done by one of their number, a cook will have to be engaged, and in any case a servant for the rough work. Lady assistants in tea-rooms receive salaries of from about 15s. to £1 a week.

The amount of capital required will depend to a great extent upon the business capabilities of the organiser. £200 should be sufficient for most purposes, and clever women have been known to found a successful business with half that sum. In most tea-rooms some sort of lunches, if even only of cold meats, should be provided. In the city lunch is a necessity, and hot dishes must always figure on the menu.

The principal business of city tea-rooms is done in luncheons—but these need not be expensive. One joint and two made dishes should figure daily on the menu. This will be usually found sufficient with the choice of two sweets, cakes, &c. In the strawberry season strawberries and cream might be provided.

A woman with sound business instinct will rarely make a failure of a venture of this kind, because before starting out she will have counted the various ways and means, and will not rush rashly into any enterprise unless it can be started under the most favourable auspices.

SWEET-MAKING

This makes a very pleasant and profitable home occupation for the woman who is well acquainted with the method of turning out dainty and toothsome confectionery, and who has had a good business training enabling her to cut down expenses to a minimum, and be able to calculate to a nicety the sweets that can be sold at a profit and those which would not pay for the making.

It is a well-known fact that the ingredients used in sweet-making come very expensive when only small quantities are made, and in many cases the ready-made sweets can be bought for a lower price than that represented by the cost of making them. The object of the sweet-maker must therefore be to obtain a large clientele. This of course she will not be able to do at first, as the quality of her wares must become known before there can be any large demand for them; so she must feel her way gently, commencing with the less expensive sweets, such as toffees, candies, &c., which do not cost much to make, and can always be sold at a profit.

And now comes a question of utmost importance, and upon which a great measure of the success of the business will depend—the packing of the sweets. Few women realise how tasteful packing of confectionery appeals to almost all classes of shoppers. For a long time English sweet-sellers lagged behind in this direction, until the firm of Fullers gave them an object lesson in the best way of appealing to the public taste. Every one is now familiar with the style of packing which has proved in itself one of the most successful advertising appeals of the firm to the public—plain fancy white boxes, stamped with the legend "Fuller" in neat lettering, carefully wrapped in white paper stamped with the same legend, and finally tied round with ribbon of a tasteful shade, the whole giving an air of taste and refinement which proves irresistible. It may be hazarded that many a box of sweets intended as a present has been sold by virtue of the tasteful ribbon bow by which it was decked. Let the woman sweet-maker therefore take these principles to heart. Her boxes need not cost much. She can get them wholesale from a box manufacturer (a list of names can be found in a directory). The plainer and simpler they are the better, but let them at any rate be distinctive in style. Perfectly plain white boxes with narrow gold or silver rims are always effective. In these the better kinds of sweets should be packed in neat little frilled paper sweet-cases, whilst candies and tablets should be neatly done up in wax-paper. The result of this arrangement will be twofold, for it will not only add to the dainty appearance of the sweets, but it will make for economy, inasmuch that less sweets will be required to fill each box.

The sweet-maker must have some small capital with which to lay in a supply of sweet moulds, cases, boxes, and other necessary implements. For a large business she will have to lay out at least £10 on these, but one must look before one leaps, and when beginning in a small way the following will usually be found sufficient, as they can be added to as the business increases.

A good sugar thermometer is one of the first things to be bought, and this will cost from 4s. 6d. to 5s. 6d. Success in sweet-making depends very largely upon boiling the sugar to the right degree, and it is only with the thermometer that this can be determined with exactness and little trouble. The amateur method of testing the boiling sugar by dropping small portions into cold water may succeed; but very often it does not, and waste of good material is very often the result. A small marble or slate slab is another very useful accessory; but sometimes the top of a marble washstand can be utilised until funds will allow of the correct article being invested in. One or two strong enamelled saucepans, a wooden spatula, weights and scales or a small balance, a wire fork and ring for lifting the sweets, some grease-proof and wax-paper, along with the necessary boxes and paper cases, will complete the preliminary outfit. Then by degrees special moulds, cutters and other apparatus may be added to suit the requirements of the special recipes that may be learnt.

It is, of course, necessary for the sweet-maker to be thoroughly well versed in this particular branch of the culinary art. The woman who has a decided gift in this direction will learn all that is necessary by taking a sweet-making course at a good training school. The fees for tuition vary in different schools, but as a rule they average about 10s. 6d. per lesson, two or three recipes being learned at each. Careful and constant practice of the recipes is very important. Cake-making usually forms part of the course, and the business might also be extended to comprise this branch of confectionery if feasible.

Once she is thoroughly proficient in the art, the sweet-maker must set about making her wares known. She can begin by selling to friends and acquaintances, as already advised;

but it will be necessary for her to secure a wider public if the business is to be made to pay. A neatly-worded advertisement distinguished by some characteristic illustration or design should appear once or twice a week in the principal local paper. All the advertising literature should be characterised by refinement as well as good selling arguments. Neat little price lists should be prepared giving full particulars of the wares sold, and on the cover of this should also appear the same pretty design that is used in the advertisement.

Prospects.—There are good prospects of success principally for the good business woman who is gifted with taste and has good social connections. Quite recently in a large theatre under the management of a lady, the whole of the sweets sold in the theatre were made by a lady sweet-maker living in a country Vicarage. Such an order, it will be seen, forms almost a livelihood in itself, and the lady sweet-maker should always aim at obtaining orders of the kind which will enable her to cater for large communities. Above all she must make *good* sweets of many different varieties.

Some Sweet Recipes.—The following recipes will be found useful by those who wish to take up this business, and might serve as a basis upon which to build up a more extensive list which will become necessary as the clientele increases.

American Candy

Ingredients—

1 lb. Loaf Sugar.	3 oz. Butter.
1 gill Water.	Flavouring.
½ lb. Glucose.	

Method.—Put the sugar, water, and glucose into a saucepan, and melt them slowly over the fire. Then boil with the thermometer to 290° Fahr. Add the butter broken in pieces, and boil again to 305°. Pour the mixture out on a greased slab; add flavouring to taste. Fold over and over with a wooden spoon or spatula, and when sufficiently cooled work well with the hands, and pull out into a long roll until it begins to stiffen. Then cut in pieces with a pair of scissors and wrap in waxed paper.

Note.—A little colouring may be added to the candy if desired.

Apricotines

Ingredients.—Equal quantities of apricot pulp and castor sugar; and some crystallised sugar.

Method.—Take some good tinned apricots, lift them from the syrup and drain them on a sieve for half-an-hour. Then rub them through a hair sieve and weigh the pulp. Put this pulp into a lined saucepan with an equal quantity of castor sugar. Bring to the boil, and boil until fairly thick, when the mixture will begin to draw away from the sides of the saucepan. It must be stirred all the time, and must not cook too quickly. Drop small pieces about the size of a half-penny on a wetted tin, and sprinkle with crystallised sugar before they harden. When firm put two together, the flat sides against each other; roll in sugar, and put them in little crimped paper sweetmeat cases. Small sweet moulds may be used for shaping the sweets; these should be wet with cold water and sprinkled inside with granulated sugar before the fruit pulp is poured into them.

Note.—Other fruit pulp can be used in the same way, but it must be one with a substance, such as apples, plums, peaches, &c. Currants, strawberries, and the like are too juicy.

Quince pulp lends itself very well to this purpose, and makes a delicious sweet. The fruit must be stewed to a pulp with as little water as possible.

Caramel Walnuts

Ingredients—

½ lb. shelled Walnuts.	1 lb. Loaf Sugar.
½ lb. ground Almonds.	1 gill of Water.
½ lb. Castor Sugar.	Lemon Juice.
1 Egg or two yolks.	Small Paper Cases.
Flavouring.	Colouring.

Method.—Put the walnuts on a tin, and toast them in the oven for about ten minutes. Then make some almond paste. Sieve the sugar, and put it into a basin with the ground almonds, a squeeze of lemon juice, and one egg or two yolks. Work all into a smooth paste with the hands, and turn out on a sugared board. Add a few drops of vanilla or any other flavouring that is preferred and work again until well mixed. Then divide this paste into small pieces the size of a hazel nut, and roll them into balls. Put a half walnut on each side of these balls, and press them well in. Proceed thus until all are finished.

Various Colours.—A nice variety is made by dividing the almond paste into three portions before the flavouring is added and making them up in different colours; keep one portion its natural colour and flavour with vanilla, colour a second portion pink by adding a few drops of carmine or cochineal, and flavour with essence of strawberry, and make the third green by using a little spinach green, and flavour with essence of almonds or ratafia.

The colouring and flavouring must be worked well into each separate portion. The flavouring may, of course, be varied according to taste. A few drops of liqueur may be used instead of a flavouring essence.

To Make the Caramel.—Put the loaf sugar, lemon juice, and water into an iron saucepan or sugar boiler, and boil quickly without stirring until a golden brown colour. Then remove the saucepan quickly from the fire, and dip the bottom of it into cold water, to prevent the caramel burning. Dip the walnuts into this one at a time; lift them out with two forks or with a wire fork or ring, and place them on an oiled slab or dish. This must be done very quickly, as the caramel soon hardens. It is better if two people can be engaged with it—one to drop the walnuts into the caramel, and one to lift them out. Everything must be ready too before beginning. When all are done, remove the walnuts from the dish, break off any superfluous caramel, and place the sweets in small paper cases.

Caramel Dates and French Plums

These may be prepared in the same way as caramel walnuts, and make a nice variety. Very good soft fruit must be chosen, because, if dry, the caramels will be hard and tasteless. Remove the stones from the dates or plums without cutting the fruit in two or breaking it in any way. Then fill the centres with an almond-shaped piece of almond paste, and roll slightly with the hands to form a neat shape. Allow these to dry for a few hours, and then coat with caramel and finish as above. A green or pink filling looks particularly pretty with this kind of sweet.

Chocolate Caramels

Ingredients—

1 lb. Loaf Sugar.	½ lb. Chocolate.
1 gill Water or Milk.	6 oz. Glucose.
1 gill Cream.	Vanilla.
¼ lb. Butter.	

Method.—Put the sugar, milk and glucose into a saucepan, melt slowly and then boil to 245° F. Cut the chocolate into small pieces, and melt it in another saucepan without any water. This is best done in an earthenware saucepan in the oven, or by placing the saucepan inside another containing hot water. Add the butter to the chocolate, and when quite melted add these to the sugar, &c., and boil all together to 245° or 250°. The mixture must not be stirred after the chocolate is added, but must be boiled very carefully to prevent it burning. Flavour with vanilla and pour out in a shallow oiled tin. Mark in squares with the back of a knife or with a caramel cutter, and when nearly cold cut the mixture right through. Wrap the caramels in wax-paper.

Coffee Caramels

Make in the same way as chocolate caramels, using sufficient essence of coffee to flavour instead of the chocolate, and three ounces of butter instead of a quarter of a pound. The coffee and butter must not be added until the syrup has boiled to 245°, and after that the mixture must not be stirred.

Cocoa-nut Drops

Ingredients—

1 lb. Loaf Sugar.	1 gill of Water.
½ lb. Glucose.	6 oz. Dessicated Cocoa-nut.

Method.—Put the sugar, water and glucose into a lined saucepan, bring to the boil and skim. Put the lid on the pan and boil rapidly for five minutes. Then remove the lid and boil to 240° F. Take the saucepan off the fire, and add the cocoa-nut and a little flavouring if wished. Arrange in small rocky heaps on a papered tray and leave them to dry.

Note.—If liked, the mixture may be divided in two portions and one part coloured pink.

French Jellies

Ingredients—

2 lbs. Loaf Sugar.	Colouring.
5 gills Water.	Flavouring.
2 oz. Gelatine.	Granulated Sugar.

Method.—Soak the gelatine in the water for half-an-hour, then put it into a saucepan with the sugar, bring to the boil, and boil for twenty minutes, stirring all the time. Divide into two portions, and colour and flavour according to taste. For instance, colour one half pink with a little carmine or cochineal and flavour with raspberry or strawberry essence, and colour the other half a pale yellow and flavour with lemon, or colour green and flavour with peppermint. Turn each portion into a wetted soup plate or pie-dish, sprinkle with granulated sugar, and leave until the next day. Then turn out, cut in neat square or oblong-shaped pieces, and roll them in granulated sugar. Leave spread out until dry and crisp on the outside.

Ginger Tablet

Ingredients—

2 lbs. Demerara Sugar.	1 oz. Ground Ginger.
2 gills Cold Water.	

Method.—Put the sugar and water into a lined or copper saucepan and stir till they come to the boil. Remove any scum, and then boil till a little dropped in water will form a "soft ball," about 245° F. Take the saucepan off the fire, add the ginger, and keep stirring until the mixture begins to turn thick. Have a flat oven tin lined with greased paper, pour the mixture into this and let it remain until cold. Cut or saw into neat pieces of equal size. A better way of shaping the tablet is to lay four iron rods, which are sold for the purpose, on a marble or stone slab so as to form a square and to pour the tablet in the centre of this. By this means the edges will be kept even and the pieces will be more regular in shape.

Note.—Lemon and rose tablet can be made in the same way, substituting white loaf for brown sugar, and essence for the ground seasoning.

Fruit Marzipan

Ingredients—

1 lb. Loaf Sugar.	½ lb. Ground Almonds.
1 table-spoonful Fruit Pulp.	A pinch of Cream of Tartar.
½ gill Water.	Glacé Icing.

Method.—Put the sugar, cream of tartar and water into a saucepan and boil to 250°. Then add the almonds and the fruit pulp. This latter must be sieved and of a very thick consistency—apricot pulp is very suitable for the purpose. Then stir over a slow fire until the mixture is thick and draws away from the sides of the pan. Turn out on a slab, and when cool roll out to quarter of an inch in thickness. The mixture may be coloured if wished and flavouring may be added. Coat the top with some thin glacé icing (see p. 225), sprinkle with finely chopped pistachio nuts, and cut into fancy shapes with a very sharp knife.

Marzipan Potatoes

Ingredients—

Almond Paste.	Orange-Flower Water.
Crystallised Cherries.	Grated Chocolate.

Method.—Prepare some almond paste the same as for caramel walnuts or for fruit marzipan, and flavour it with orange-flower water or any other flavouring preferred. Remove any hard sugar from the cherries by placing them in hot water for a minute; then form the paste into shapes resembling very small new potatoes, and place a cherry in the centre of each. They must not be too large. Roll them in finely powdered chocolate and mark a few eyes in each. Small pieces of other preserved fruits may be used instead of the cherries, but there must, of course, be no stone in the fruit, and it must not be hard nor too much crystallised.

Opera Creams

Ingredients—

1 lb. Loaf Sugar.	Cream.
1 gill Water.	Icing Sugar.
2 oz. Glucose.	Flavouring.

Method.—Put the sugar, water and glucose into a saucepan and melt slowly over the fire, stirrring all the time until the sugar is melted. Skim well and wash any scum off the sides of the saucepan with a small brush. Then boil with the thermometer to 245°. Pour on a slab and work until white, first with a wooden spoon or spatula and then with the hands. Then put this fondant back into the saucepan, add a little cream and enough icing sugar to bring it back to the right consistency for shaping. Flavour to taste and put out again on the slab. Form into a square, using a little icing sugar to prevent it sticking to the hands. Then roll out to one inch in thickness, making the mixture as smooth and even as possible. Leave until cold and set, and then cut in squares with a very sharp knife.

These creams are great favourites, and they may be made in a variety of colours and flavours.

Peppermint Creams

Ingredients—

1 lb. Icing Sugar.	Oil of Peppermint.
1 White of Egg.	1 table-spoonful Water.

Method.—Sieve the icing sugar into a basin and moisten with the white of egg and water. Work with the hands into a smooth, soft paste, flavouring with a few drops of oil of peppermint. When the paste is pliable and free from cracks, roll it out to one-eighth of an inch in thickness on a board that has been sprinkled with sieved icing sugar. Cut out into rounds with a small cutter and place aside on a sheet of white paper sprinkled with castor sugar, and let them remain until dry. The cutter should be dipped into castor sugar to prevent it sticking to the paste. The scraps ought to be pressed together and rolled out again until all are used.

Another Method

Ingredients—

1 lb. Icing Sugar.	A few drops Oil of Peppermint.
¾ tea-sp. Cream of Tartar.	
2 or 3 table-sp. of Cream.	

Method.—Sieve the sugar into a basin, add the cream of tartar, and when thoroughly mixed add enough cream to form a stiff paste. Turn out on a sugared board and knead with the hand until smooth and pliable, working in the peppermint flavouring. Then cover the paste over and let it rest for an hour. Finish off as above.

Chocolate Peppermints

Make some peppermint creams as above, then dissolve a quarter of a pound sweet chocolate in an earthenware saucepan. This must be done very slowly and stirred all the time; no water is required, and it must not be allowed to become too hot. Dip the peppermint creams into this, and lift them out with a wire fork and place them on paper to drain. This must be done as quickly as possible.

Peppermint Cushions

Ingredients—

1 lb. Loaf Sugar.	Essence of Peppermint.
1 gill of Water.	A pinch of Cream of Tartar.

Method.—Put the sugar, water and cream of tartar into a lined saucepan and boil to 270° F., removing any scum that may rise. Pour this out on a marble slab and sprinkle over it a few drops of peppermint. Great care must be taken not to flavour too strongly.

Fold over and over with a wooden spatula, and when cool enough pull out with the hands until quite white and firm and in the shape of a long roll. Cut in pieces with a strong pair of scissors.

Russian Toffee

Ingredients—

¼ lb. Brown Sugar.	1 gill Cream.
¼ lb. White Sugar.	1 table-sp. Golden Syrup.
¼ lb. Butter.	Vanilla flavouring.

Method.—First dissolve the butter in a lined saucepan or sugar boiler, then add the other ingredients and flavour nicely with vanilla. Boil all together until the toffee feels crisp when tested in a little cold water. It must be stirred all the time, and when ready it will draw away from the sides of the pan. Pour the toffee into a well-greased shallow tin. Mark it across in squares, and when nearly cold cut in pieces with a very sharp knife. Wrap the pieces in waxed paper.

Walnut Molasses

Ingredients—

1 lb. Brown Sugar.	2 oz. Shelled and Chopped Walnuts.
1 gill Water.	1 oz. Butter.
A pinch of Cream of Tartar.	

Method.—Toast the walnuts in the oven for a few minutes and then chop them somewhat roughly.

Put the water, sugar and cream of tartar into a lined saucepan and boil with the thermometer to 280° F., adding the butter just before it reaches this point. Pour out on a marble slab into a long shape, sprinkle with the walnuts, and fold over with a wooden spoon or spatula. When slightly cool roll with the hands and pull out until about the thickness of a thin walking-stick. Then cut quickly in pieces with a pair of strong scissors, allow the pieces to cool, and twist them into small pieces of waxed paper. If this sweetmeat is left exposed to the air, especially in damp weather, it becomes sticky.

Note.—Chopped hazel nuts may be used instead of walnuts.

OPENING A TYPEWRITING OFFICE

There are many typewriting offices in London and other large towns which are doing very good business, whilst others have proved unmistakable failures.

It is true that, as compared with the conditions prevailing some seven or eight years ago, there is a great deal of competition in this particular business, and as is the case with every other calling, it is the pioneers who have reaped the most benefit from it; but there is no reason why a new typewriting office should not be established successfully by the woman who has had a thorough training in typewriting, shorthand, and general business methods, and who has good experience of all kinds of copying work.

Training.—To learn the ins and outs of every branch of the business it is always better to spend a few months in a first-class typewriting office after the regular business training has been completed. Be careful, however, to select a really good office doing brisk business with an extensive and varied clientele. There are usually vacancies to be found in most copying offices for those who are willing to work at a moderate salary—or to give their services in return for the experience afforded.

The learner should take special pains to get practice in reading badly-written MSS. Caligraphy of all kinds has to be deciphered in a typewriting office, and it would go ill with the office where such writing could not be copied from without serious mistake. Training in all the various kinds of copying work is also necessary; specifications, scientific work, legal work, verse, authors' MSS., plays, parts of the characters in plays—all have to be copied in a distinctive style, whilst special paper has to be used and special ruling made in many cases. Then the various processes of stencil duplicating will have to be mastered. Speed, accuracy, and neat work are the great objects to be aimed at. Good work always proves the best advertisement in this as well as in every other line of business. A good practical knowledge of languages is also necessary, for translation is another important branch of a typewriting business. Those who are able to add research work and indexing to the ordinary typewriting office routine work will find that these are two useful and remunerative additions to the business.

Prospects.—It is always better for two friends, or sisters, to start a business of the kind, beginning in a small way, for this will save the cost of paid assistance. They should have enough capital to ensure at least the first year's rent and working expenses, light, telephone, &c., in addition to paying for the furniture and fittings.

The amount of the capital necessary will depend upon the locality selected, as rents are much higher in some places than in others. It will be necessary to start in a central district, and upon the district chosen will depend to a large extent the kind of work taken to the offices. In some places, such as in the neighbourhood of the Strand and near Bedford Street and its environs, theatrical work will predominate. In busy city districts business typing and letters will be the chief work; in legal and parliamentary environs law work will predominate. An office should always be chosen in some such centre of activity where, to begin with at any rate, some crumbs of work may fall to the share of the new typewriting office, even if the whole loaf or at least a good half of it cannot be had at first. It is worse than useless to start an office far from any centre of activity. Those who start under the most favourable auspices are women who have managed to establish a small connection for type-copying work at home before launching out into business. At first all the work can be undertaken by the principals. Then as the business increases it will become necessary to add to the staff. A very remunerative branch of the work consists of taking in and training pupils—but a word of warning in this respect. Never entrust responsible work to a mere beginner, even in times of stress. The work sent out by some typewriting offices is notoriously bad, because to save expense it is nearly all entrusted to young girls who are learning the business. This is a very false method of economy—a method which will do more than anything else to bring the business into disrepute, and which has been the cause of the failure of many offices which might have been flourishing to-day if more honourable business methods had been adopted. It does not follow, however, that pupils should not be made to prove themselves useful—especially as the best method of learning from their point of view is by practical experience—but let their capabilities be well tested before they are entrusted with important work.

All the work should be under the personal supervision of the principal, who should see that nothing but good work leaves the office. In this way alone can success be attained.

It is always better to have a ground floor or a first floor for offices, at any rate until one is known, but this will depend a great deal upon circumstances and according to where the offices are situated. It is advisable to begin with two rooms at least.

Neat little price-lists should be made out for the use of clients, and should be distributed amongst business firms and other possible clients. It is a good idea to print on the back of these price-lists any testimonials received in regard to efficiency and accuracy of work. Terms should be strictly cash.

The following is a guide to the prices charged for various kinds of typewriting :—

	£	s.	d.
Legal and general copying, per folio (72 words)			1½
Verse and scientific copying, per folio			2
Authors' MSS. under 3000 words, per 1000		1	3
Authors' MSS., in quantities of 3000 words and over, per 1000 words		1	0
Authors' MSS., if over 10,000 words, per 1000			10
Plays, per Act of 18 pp. (4to. typed)		5	0
Plays, after 18 pp., per page			2½
Actors' parts, per page (size of page, half foolscap)			1½
Typing from French, German, Spanish, Italian, per folio			2½
Typing plays from above languages, per Act, 18 pages		8	0
Addressing envelopes, per 1000		7	6

Each Carbon Copy half price.

Dictation

	£	s.	d.
Typing from dictation, per hour (Carbon copies half price.)		3	6
Hire of typewriter and operator, per hour		3	6
Hire of typewriter and operator, per day *from*		12	0
Hire of typewriter and operator, per week by arrangement.			

Stencil Duplicating

Letters, Circulars, Specifications, Balance Sheets, Abstracts of Titles, Drafts, &c.

	£	s.	d.
Per 25 pages. Quarto size		2	6
,, 50 ,, ,, ,,		3	6
,, 100 ,, ,, ,,		4	6
,, 500 ,, ,, ,,		18	0
,, 25 pages. Foolscap size		3	0
,, 50 ,, ,, ,,		4	6
,, 100 ,, ,, ,,		6	0
,, 500 ,, ,, ,,	1	1	0
,, 25 pages. Draft size		4	0
,, 50 ,, ,, ,,		5	9
,, 100 ,, ,, ,,		8	6
,, 25 pages. Brief size		5	0
,, 50 ,, ,, ,,		6	9
,, 100 ,, ,, ,,		8	6

Shorthand

	s.	d.
Attendance for letters, &c., per hour	3	6
Transcribing notes, per folio		2

Translations

	s.	d.
French, German, Spanish, Italian into English, per folio	1	0
English into French, German, Spanish, Italian, per folio	1	6

A well-managed office opened in a suitable locality should be made to pay expenses by the end of the first year. A type-copying business is essentially one where periods of great activity, followed by intervals of slackness of work, occur. The proprietor of the office should regulate her expenditure accordingly, and make provision for those periods when work is scarce.

CANVASSERS

Women canvassers are largely employed by firms who wish to introduce their work to the public, also by advertisement managers and agents and by publishers.

The calling is not one which will appeal to the majority of educated women, although the clever canvasser can make a very good income indeed. Tact and persuasive power are the two most important assets of the canvasser. She must have a good amount of the quality called "push," being slow to take a rebuff; above all she must not be sensitive. The unduly sensitive woman is totally unfit for a position of the kind.

Canvassers may be required to travel—their travelling expenses being paid, of course—or to work in their own town. They are paid in two ways. Most often they are paid by commission only; in this case the commission being a large one, from 20 to 25 per cent. In other cases they receive a small salary of from £1, 10s. to £2 a week, with a small commission ranging from 5 to 10 per cent.

The experienced canvasser prefers the large commission and no salary basis, as this represents to her a greater income, and although business is often dull for even the best of canvassers, she can save out of her earnings when business is brisk to tide her over the dull times. Many women, however, prefer a sure and steady income, however small, and the woman canvasser who has not had much experience would do well to try and obtain work on the salary and small commission basis.

Boarding-House Proprietress.—A boarding-house may turn out a very profitable investment for the business woman who manages to get together a good connection. Sufficient capital to pay the first year's expenses will be necessary, the amount depending a great deal upon locality, size of the house, and rental. The most paying investment is to be found in the large boarding-house where things are done on a generous scale. It is a mistake to furnish a house poorly, and give indifferent food with a low tariff. These methods will never attract the right sort of people. Everything in a boarding-house should be well done, the rooms should be tastefully furnished, the cooking good, and the service above reproach. The tariff also should be kept at a figure that will allow for good catering. In London the terms should never be less than two guineas a week for full board, and £1, 10s. a week for partial board. At the seaside two and a half guineas a week should be the minimum charge during the season, a charge of £1, 10s. being made during the slack time at places where visitors are only attracted in large numbers during one or two months of the year. Extra is always charged for meals served in bedrooms, and also for fires in bedrooms.

The best advertisement for a boarding-house is essentially that obtained by good cooking and strict attention to the comfort of the guests. It is important also that meals should be served with strict punctuality. In the dining-room should be a number of little tables, as the different family parties, as a rule, will prefer to have a table to themselves. Table linen should be fresh and clean, and silver brightly polished. Some flowers should be arranged in vases on each little table. For dinner one or two menu cards should be placed on each table. The waiting should be quickly and quietly done, and there should be at least three maids waiting where there are thirty guests.

Good wages should be paid to the servants. As a rule, servants prefer life in a boarding-house, owing to the addition to their wages in the way of gratuities, and they will got through an amount of hard work quite cheerfully in these circumstances. A considerate mistress, therefore, should be able to keep her servants with little difficulty, for nothing tends to upset the ordinary routine than constant changes in the staff.

It is essential that a boarding-house keeper be a good housewife. She should herself attend to all the ordering of provisions. Special terms are granted to boarding-house keepers as far as these are concerned. Care must be taken, however, to see that all the provisions are of the best, and custom should be at once withdrawn when satisfaction is not given in this respect.

At the seaside and other pleasure resorts the boarding-house keeper should also be able to organise amusements for her guests. One or two dances might be given during the season, for which a small subscription of from 7s. 6d. to 10s. each from all who wish to be present should be asked. Picnics to places of interest in the neighbourhood should also be arranged. The seaside boarding-house keeper should be able to count on the return year after year of some of her visitors, at least, and by strict attention in every way to their amusement as well as to their comfort she can count upon keeping together a regular clientele.

Several qualities besides mere business ability will be found to contribute to the success of the proprietress of a boarding establishment. The lady of accomplishments and refinement, who has an abundance of tact to enable her to deal successfully with the many different types of character with which she must necessarily in such a business come into contact, will prove more successful than the hard-working commonplace woman who does all the cooking herself, and is nothing more than a mere domestic drudge.

CIVIL SERVICE AND PUBLIC WORK

THERE are openings for women in many departments of the Civil Service, the Post Office in particular affording good opportunities, and giving employment to many thousands of girls and women throughout the kingdom. The principal appointments in the Post Office are open to public competition, whilst appointments in other branches of public work are subject to nomination or are open to limited competition only. This is a fact to be borne in mind by women who aim at an Inspectorship or some other similarly high Government post. In this article the various branches of Civil Service and public work are described and full information given in regard to the prospects offered in each individual branch.

THE POST OFFICE

As a career for girls and women the Post Office presents many advantages—chief amongst which are regular employment and a pension after a long period of service. Girls and women in the employ of the Post Office may be either :—

Clerks
Telegraphists
Counter Clerks and Telegraphists
Sorters
Telephonists
Postmistresses
Learners.

There is a great deal of misunderstanding in regard to the scope and character of the employment offered by the Post Office to women, and for this reason a large number of girls are deterred from entering upon a career which has the double advantage of security with a pension to come at the end of a long term of service. The prevailing notion is that to be in the service of the Post Office entails selling stamps or taking telegrams behind the counter of any branch office. This is quite a fallacy. Learners and counter-women have to do this, it is true, but the Post Office employees falling under the general designation of the word "clerk" never come into contact with the public at all. They are employed in the Accountant-General's Department, the Money Order Department, the Savings Bank Department, or the Telephone Exchange.

Post Office clerks are much better off in every way than clerks in business houses. The hours are short, not numbering more than seven daily —a yearly holiday of one month is allowed, also all the public holidays. Not only are pensions granted to those who retire after a long term of service, but all female clerks who have been in the service of the Post Office for a term of six years receive a dowry when they resign their positions upon marriage.

The training of girls for clerkships in the Civil Service should begin quite early, as they are not eligible for any of the entrance examinations after the age of twenty. No girl under sixteen or over eighteen is eligible for the examination for "girl clerkships," and no girl under eighteen or over twenty is eligible for the examinations for women clerkships, whilst candidates for learnerships and sorterships must be between the age of fifteen and eighteen years. Competitive examinations for these positions are held every six months or every year. There are certain conditions relative to the employment of women in the Civil Service which must be complied with. All clerks and other Post Office employees are required to pass a medical examination, and to be re-vaccinated if it is thought necessary. They must have good references as to character, and reside with their parents or guardians or with any relatives or friends approved of by their parents or guardians. They must also be natural born or naturalised British subjects and at least five feet in height. Post Office female employees must also be single, and with the exception of post-mistresses are required to resign their appointments upon marriage.

Women Clerkships.—There are abundant prospects in the Civil Service for the clever girl who is a good worker and who has made up her mind to get on. Women clerkships are divided into two classes. In the second class the salary is £65, rising at the rate of £5 a year to £110. In the first class the salaries begin at £115 and rise to £140. But the chances of promotion do not end here. A first-class clerk may be promoted to the position of principal clerk, with a salary of £150, rising by annual increments of £10 to £200. Then she may rise to be an assistant superintendent, with a salary of £210 to £260. Deputy superintendents receive salaries of from £270 to £330, and superintendents, £280 to £500. There are not so many vacancies in the higher positions, and as the competition for them is very keen, only women of great intelligence and ability will succeed in working their way up to posts of this kind.

Girl Clerks.—Girl clerks must be between sixteen and eighteen years of age. The commencing salary is £42, rising at the rate of £3 per annum to £48. At the end of the two years competent girl clerks are promoted to women clerkships as soon as the necessary vacancies occur—or if they are not deemed sufficiently competent for the promotion they may be transferred to the class of "sorters."

Examinations for Girl and Women Clerkships.—Those who enter for the Civil Service examinations for girl clerkships must be between the ages of sixteen and eighteen, and those who enter for the examinations for women clerkships between the ages of eighteen and twenty. Candidates must send in their names to the examiners as wishing to enter for the examination within the time specified by the Civil Service Commissioners. Examinations are, as a rule, held every six months, and the examination fee is 10s. Candidates for both clerkships will require to satisfy the examiners in the following subjects :—

English Composition.
Arithmetic (general).
Geography (general).
Latin, French, German — Only two of these subjects may be taken.
English History, Mathematics, Shorthand — Only two of these subjects may be taken.

Girl and women Post Office clerks are not employed in the provinces. Clerkships are only to be had at the large central offices in London, Dublin, and Edinburgh.

Other Advantages of Post Office Clerkships.—Girl and women clerks at the General Post Office are treated with the utmost consideration. To begin with the hours are short and regular, every provision is made for their comfort, and as employees are not allowed out in office hours meals are supplied upon the premises at the most moderate charges, a good luncheon being obtainable for a few pence. Though the authorities are very strict in regard to the rules for the medical examination upon entry, insisting upon a perfect bill of health, if by chance an employee should fall ill every consideration is shown to her. In the case of a long illness full pay is granted up to six months, if there is a reasonable chance of the patient's recovery to good health.

In most occupations open to both men and women there is a certain element of uncertainty—changes constantly occur in the management of offices, which entail changes in the staff, so that an employee, except in rare instances, cannot feel absolutely safe. In regard to the Post Office, the position of a girl or woman of average capability who does her work well is secure, whilst the chances of promotion are many. Should a woman wish to retire after ten years' service, she is eligible for a pension; and the marriage dowry after six years' service, consisting of one month's salary for each year she has served, are gifts not by any means to be despised.

Taking all things into consideration, there are few careers for women which present better all-round prospects than that offered by the Post Office.

Sorters.—Though the commencing salary of a girl sorter is small, a good chance of promotion to a clerkship is to be had, inasmuch as candidates who are successful in the sorters' examination secure an extension of the age-limit of entry for the woman clerkship examinations to twenty-five. The duties of female sorters consist principally in sorting and arranging official papers relating to Savings Bank, Money or Postal Order business, and they are mostly employed in the Savings Bank Department and in the Money Order Department. The age limits are fifteen to eighteen. The hours of attendance are eight daily between 6 A.M. and 5 P.M. The salary commences at 14s. a week rising to 22s., and an annual holiday of three weeks is given. Candidates require to satisfy the examiners in—

Reading and copying MS
Handwriting
Spelling
Arithmetic (first four rules simple and compound)
Geography of the United Kingdom.

Female Learners, Telegraphists, and Counter Clerks.—These positions involve coming into contact with the public at any Post Office. Candidates for learnerships must be between fifteen and eighteen years of age, and pass an examination in English composition, arithmetic, and geography. The examination fee is 4s. The commencing salary for learners is 7s. on entry, 10s. 6d. a week when proficiency in instrument duty is reached, and 14s. a week after one year's service at 10s. 6d. if still under the age of eighteen. In the provinces 5s. a week is the initial salary, rising to 13s. 6d. The probationary period of learnership is usually about a year, at the end of which competent learners are given appointments as telegraphists, or counter clerks and telegraphists, as soon as the requisite vacancies occur. In London, telegraphists and counter clerks receive a commencing salary of 16s. a week, rising to 30s. and 40s. In the provinces the rate of pay is from 12s. or 13s. to 36s. The working hours are eight daily. Employees are paid for overtime work.

Typists in the Civil Service.—Appointments in the Civil Service as female typists are not open to public competition. Candidates must be nominated by the head of the office in which they are to serve; they must not be younger than eighteen years of age or older than thirty, and are required to pass an examination in writing, spelling, composition, copying, arithmetic, typewriting, and shorthand, if required. A limited competition may in some cases be held. The salary of a woman typist in the Civil Service begins at £1 a week, rising at the rate of 2s. a week yearly to £1, 6s. a week. Superintendents receive salaries of 35s. to £2 a week. Typists retiring upon superannuation are eligible for a pension, and a dowry is granted upon marriage after six years' service. Female typists are employed in the Post Office, the offices of the Board of Education, the Scottish Education Department, the Colonial Office, the Board of Agriculture and Fisheries, Customs, Foreign Office, Local Government Board, the War Office, the Public Works Office, and in all the principal Government offices.

Training.—Emphasis has already been laid upon the necessity of beginning to train early for the Civil Service examinations. The ordinary school training is not sufficient; a special course of study is necessary, varying in extent from six months to one year, and sometimes longer, in accordance with the capabilities of the pupil. In some exceptional cases three months' preparation have been found sufficient, but successful students in these circumstances possessed talents greatly above the average. As a rule, it will be found advisable to extend the training over the year, though many successes have been achieved after six months' special study.

Whatever the extent of the training may be, too much stress cannot be laid upon the importance that it should be a special one for the Civil Service, and taken under the guidance of some person or persons who make preparation for the Civil Service examinations a special feature of their curriculum. Private coaching may be taken, or a course undergone at one of the business and Civil Service training colleges, such as Clark's College, London. The cost of training for girl and women clerks averages £7, 16s. for six months, and £14 for one year. For evening classes only, £3 for six months and £5, 10s. for a year's training.

PUBLIC WORK

Women now occupy salaried positions in many departments of public work. The number of these appointments, however, is necessarily limited, although there is every indication that the opportunities in this direction will be extended. The chief Government appointments are mostly filled by nomination, and to obtain them some influence is therefore necessary.

Factory Inspectors under the Home Office.—There are now seventeen women factory inspectors under the Home Office, and in London, Glasgow, Manchester, Birmingham, and Belfast a senior woman inspector is stationed at the head of an office and staff. Candidates for these inspectorships must be nominated by the Secretary of State before they can enter for the examination to the Civil Service Commissioners which they are required to pass. All the necessary information may be obtained from the Secretary of State, the Home Office, S.W.

The work of these inspectors is of the utmost importance in securing the welfare of the many thousands of girl and women factory workers. The work includes the inspection of the places where dangerous machinery or dangerous processes of manufacture are used, caring for the health of the workers and seeing to the general sanitary conditions, investigating accidents, enforcing the education of children employed in factories and workshops, and supervising hours of employment, conducting prosecutions where necessary, &c. The inspectors work under the general supervision of the chief lady inspector at the Home Office.

After passing the preliminary examination two years' probation must be undergone, at the end of which a final qualifying examination has to be passed in the law relating to factories and workshops and sanitary science as applied to factories and workshops. The age limit is twenty-five to forty.

The commencing salary is £200 a year; senior inspectors earn from £300 to £400, whilst the salary of the chief inspector at the Home Office begins at £400, rising to £550.

Poor Law Inspectors (under the Local Government Board). This is quite a new field for the woman worker, there being now only six inspectors under the direction of the lady superintendent, and three of these (all trained nurses) were appointed as recently as 1910. There is every prospect, however, that as the usefulness of the work of these ladies is demonstrated the number of appointments will be increased.

An amount of evidence collected by the Woman's Local Government Society from Boards of Guardians throughout the country, bearing upon the necessity of appointing women inspectors, has been put before the Royal Commission on the Poor Laws, and it is to be trusted that this may result in the appointment of a large number of inspectors.

The work includes the inspection of workhouses, especially in regard to women and children, infirmaries, schools and certified homes, lying-in wards, the inspection of boarded-out children, &c. There is as yet no complete organisation of the work, nor any definite rules for appointment. Candidates, however, should be trained hospital nurses, and have had some experience in administrative posts. The commencing salary is £200 a year. All the necessary information in regard to these appointments may be obtained from the Secretary, Local Government Board, Whitehall, London, S.W.

School Inspectors.—Women school inspectors are appointed by the Board of Education. The appointments are by nomination, and there are no set rules in regard to qualifications, although inspectors should be women of good education and show the necessary aptitude for the work. The inspector of schools should have a good knowledge and understanding of educational work, be a good critic of teaching, and able to recognise the methods most fitting for the end in view, and, above all, they should have experience in the actual educational work of schools which are to come under their notice.

Women inspectors are appointed to inspect elementary, secondary, and training schools, technical schools including schools of domestic science under the Board, and training colleges for preliminary and secondary teachers. There is also a needlework directress and an assistant directress of needlework.

Prospects.—The salaries of women inspectors are at the rate of from £200 to £400 per annum, the chief woman inspector receiving from £400 to £500 a year. The needlework directress receives a salary of £300, and the assistant directress a salary of from £80 to £150 per annum.

School Attendance Officers.—There are also openings for women school attendance officers under a number of County Councils. A preliminary examination must be passed, and successful candidates must undergo a medical examination before they are finally approved. The work consists in seeing that all the children in the district attend the public elementary schools unless their education is being well cared for in another way. The attendance officer has to report all cases of absence from school, and if these are not due to illness or other sufficient cause it is her duty to prosecute the parents at the police court where necessary.

The school attendance officer should have an intimate knowledge of the prevailing local conditions of the district in which she works, and she should have a good fund of tact to enable her to deal satisfactorily with the people with whom she must come into contact.

Prospects.—Salaries vary according to the different local authorities. In London the salaries range from £80 to £156 per annum. The age limit is from twenty-five to thirty-five.

Other Salaried Public Appointments.—There are several other paid public appointments available to women which, though at present limited in number, promise to increase in the future. In connection with the Labour Exchanges Act women officials are appointed upon the various labour exchanges at salaries commencing at £130 a year. There are also women registrars in England, Ireland, and Scotland. Medical officers and sanitary inspectors are also appointed by local authorities (see under Medicine). At present there are six women relieving officers in London and eleven in the provinces. In London the salary commences at £80 per annum. (See also Sanitary Inspectors and Health Visitors.)

ARTS AND CRAFTS

In this article the various branches of art and music which offer opportunities to talented women are carefully considered, together with those minor arts and crafts which offer a fair means of livelihood to the painstaking worker.

Emphasis must be laid upon the fact that in the higher ranks of the artistic professions only those who have great talents, combined with an abundance of energy and capacity for hard work, can hope to attain success.

MUSICAL PROFESSION

Performers.—Exceptional talents and capabilities are required by the girl who wishes to take up any branch of the musical profession as performer with any measure of success, and the girl of average capabilities had better pause before she embarks upon a career in which even genius has a hard struggle before it attains recognition. Many girls rush headlong into the profession, either as pianists, violinists, or vocalists, only to find that there is no room for those with mediocre gifts, and that the vast army of moderately capable artists who have by some means obtained a footing find it exceedingly difficult to earn a bare subsistence. The clever girl with talent must be prepared to throw her whole heart and soul into study for her profession. This study must necessarily begin very early; the fingers of the pianist must have acquired suppleness from childhood onwards. The earlier a violinist acquires the rudiments of her art the more skilled musician will she make. A child should be made to practise her piano and her violin at least one hour every day. As she gets older two hours should be given to practice, and when she is completing her studies, at least four hours' practice daily should be taken. This is necessary in order to obtain good technique. The singer, on the other hand, must not strain her voice in childhood, but her training, when it does begin, must be painstaking and thorough. No girl, however clever, should attempt to earn a living by music alone, unless she has some small income which will help her to tide over the time when she is struggling to make a position for herself. For the pianist and the instrumentalist especially are these difficulties in the way. There must be something distinctive about the performance, something characteristic about the personality of an unknown artist for her to be able to attract public notice. Without this she may spend large sums of money in giving concerts without avail. By the influence of her concert agent perhaps she may be successful in procuring one or two minor engagements, but of what avail will these be as a means of livelihood—she will discover too late that she would have done better to devote the time spent on music to training for a more money-making career. Even the girl with talents above the average should not rely upon making a sufficient income as a performer at first; she should in all cases combine her work with that of teaching until she has become sufficiently well known to command a large number of regular engagements. The vocalist has perhaps more scope than the instrumentalist in many directions. In addition to the concert platform there are openings in comic opèra and musical comedy for the well-trained singer, and if her voice be above the average then in grand opera she may find her goal. For the last, needless to say, she must have a voice of great power and wide compass, and she must undergo a training which will be necessarily long and expensive, usually finishing with a term of study abroad. She will require to have a good knowledge of French, Italian, and German, for she may be called upon to sing in opera in any of these languages. When her training is complete she will often require to have years of experience in both singing and acting before she succeeds in attracting any measure of notice.

In regard to comic opera there is less difficulty, although talent for acting, a good appearance, and charm of personality are necessary. The great difficulty in this branch of the professiou is to get a fair start. If a girl begins through the medium of the chorus, and has all the qualities mentioned, she will rise to a higher position in time, but the chances are that years will elapse before she obtains recognition, and in the meantime her voice will probably have deteriorated in quality by reason of the severe strain to which it has been subjected by chorus work.

For the girl who is not ambitious and is content with earning a moderate income, there are many minor branches of the profession in which opportunities are to be had. She may form a connection for "At Home" engagements, dinner concerts at hotels and restaurants, or she may join one of the ladies' orchestras which play at "At Homes," tea-rooms, restaurants, and also at bazaars and other similar functions. In good and well-established orchestras fair salaries are to be had, but in many cases the work is intermittent.

The Accompanist.—One of the most promising fields for the pianist of average talents is that of the accompanist, but curiously enough it is the one branch of the musical profession that few are anxious to enter. The accompanist has no scope for individual display; her performance must be subservient to that of the singer—and yet it is an art to be a good accompanist, an art in which very few excel. The accompanist must have had a good musical training, for she must be able to read at sight, and even to transpose if needs be. She must be able to adapt herself to the methods of each different singer, always keeping time with, and slurring over any mistakes made by the vocalist. It is not such an easy matter as one would imagine for an accompanist to accompany singers whom she has never seen before, and of whose methods she is entirely ignorant, but this she is often called upon to do. When once an accompanist has proved her capabilities, engagements are not slow to follow. Singers remember the names of those who accompany well—very often they will always retain the services of one accompanist whose value they have proved. It is better for a beginner who has no friends or influence in the concert world to register her name at a good concert agent as soon as she is ready to accept engagements. A small percentage will be deducted from her fees for commission in this way, but this is well worth while if good engagements result. Fees paid to accompanists at concerts average from one to two guineas for the evening.

Teachers of Music.—This presents the most favourable means to the well-trained musician of earning a regular income. A thorough training concluding with success at examinations for the A.R.C.M. or the L.R.A.M. or some other recognised qualification is necessary. There are good posts in schools for teachers of piano, violin, and singing. Higher posts are to be had in schools and colleges of music. Good connections as visiting teachers may also be formed. Salaries in schools vary to a great extent, but an advanced music mistress may earn as much as £120 a year from one school alone, and augment her income considerably by private lessons. For the higher posts as teachers in colleges and *Schools of Music* the highest musical honours and also a certain amount of experience are necessary. For teaching, an A.R.A.M. or an A.R.C.M. degree, or a degree of music awarded by one of the universities will be found most useful. A teacher's diploma is very desirable now that such a high standard of efficiency in teaching is exacted.

There is a great opening for teachers of singing under the tonic sol-fa system in the schools under local authorities. Candidates for posts of the kind should prepare for the School Teacher's Certificate of the Tonic Sol-fa College. The London County Council also recognises the tonic sol-fa music certificate as a qualification for teachers of singing and music in secondary schools and pupil teacher centres. Salaries in some cases amount to £200 a year. Full information in regard to training may be obtained from the Secretary, Tonic Sol-fa College, Finsbury Square, London, E.C.

Training.—A great deal of the expense of training may be saved by gaining one of the many scholarships which are awarded in the musical profession by the various music academies and colleges. The best centres for training are undoubtedly in London and other large towns. In all of these are special hostels where music students can get board and lodging at moderate fees. The following are the chief institutions where training may be obtained:—

The Royal Academy of Music, Tenterden Street, London. Entrance fee, £5, 5s.—£1, 1s. payable for entrance examination and £4, 4s. on becoming a pupil. There is a very full course of study which must extend over three terms, including instruction in theory, harmony, and counterpoint. Fees for ordinary course are £11, 11s. per term; for special studies, in accordance with the subjects taken. Examinations are also held twice a year for music students trained independently of the Academy, and successful candidates are entitled to use the initials L.R.A.M. Successful students trained at the college are entitled to the distinction A.R.A.M., and those who distinguish themselves after quitting the institution may be elected by the Directors Fellows of the Royal Academy of Music and are entitled to use the letters F.R.A.M.

There are sixty scholarships in connection with the Academy, full particulars of which may be obtained upon application to the lady superintendent. They are usually tenable for three years, and provide for free instruction during that period.

At the Royal College of Music, South Kensington, London, W., at least a year's course must be taken. The entrance fee for examination is £2, 2s., and fees for ordinary course are £12, 12s. a term. There is also a department for students under sixteen at which the fees are exactly halved. A number of scholarships are awarded, in connection with some of which, in addition to free musical education, special grants towards maintenance are made. Many prizes, consisting of musical instruments or medals, are given annually. A student desiring to join the College should write for an application form, and when this has been filled up, the entrance fee and one term's fees should be paid. Among the subjects taught are the piano, solo singing, viola, cello, double bass, organ, harp, wind instruments, theory, languages, elocution, &c. One principal and one secondary subject is generally chosen, and an entrance examination is held in order to ascertain the degree of proficiency in each subject. A second principal subject may be taken by paying an extra fee. Such subjects as dancing, deportment, and dramatic action are extras. Frequent lectures are given, fully illustrated by voices or instruments. In order to be able to write the letters A.R.C.M. after her name, a student must, on the completion of her training, pass a final examination, the fee for which is £5, 5s.

Alexandra House, Kensington Gore, is a well-known place of residence for lady students at the college. The number of music students received, however, must not exceed fifty. Each student has her own bedroom and shares a sitting-room with another student, and has also the use of the drawing-room, library, and concert-room. The terms for board are sixty guineas a year, with £1 extra per term for washing. Full particulars may be obtained upon application to the college.

Associated Board of the Royal Academy and Royal College of Music.—Local Centre Examinations and School Examinations in music are held by the Associated Board of the Royal Academy and Royal College of Music. These examinations, which include both theoretical and practical music, are held throughout the United Kingdom and in the Colonies. The subjects include primary theory, rudiments of music, harmony and grammar of music, counterpoint, pianoforte, organ, violin, viola, cello, double bass, harp, wind instruments and singing.

Six exhibitions are offered by the Board tenable for three years at the Royal Academy or the Royal College of Music.

At the Guildhall School of Music, Victoria Embankment, London, a very good training may be had in every branch of music. The entrance and deposit fees are each 5s. There is a term fee of 2s. 6d., and fees for singing and music range from £1, 11s. 6d. to £6, 6s. a term. There are a number of scholarships in connection with the school, and examinations are held for the Associateship of the school and for teachers' certificates.

Special teachers' diplomas are granted by the London College of Music, Great Marlborough Street, W., Trinity College, London, and the Royal Manchester College of Music. There are a number of other colleges and schools of music throughout the country where fees are moderate and students are prepared for the L.R.A.M. of the Royal Academy. This degree is most useful for teachers, and the would-be teacher should strive to prepare for it or for one of the special teachers' diplomas awarded by other colleges. Examinations are held by Trinity College at a number of local centres, for which any student may enter. Full particulars of these may be obtained upon application to the Secretary, Trinity College of Music, Mandeville Place, Manchester Square, London, W. Women can also take the degree of Bachelor of Music and Doctor of Music at the Universities of London, Edinburgh, Manchester, Durham, Dublin, and Wales. They are not allowed to take the Oxford and Cambridge degrees. They can enter for the examinations, however, and successful candidates receive certificates.

THE STAGE

Most girls are apt to be "stage struck" at some period of their lives; that is to say, they develop a desire to go upon the stage, and no matter how little histrionic capability they may have, their determination to enter the dramatic profession cannot be shaken. Not all the advice of their parents or friends can turn them from their purpose, with the result that valuable time, which might have been spent to advantage in the pursuit of some other calling, is irretrievably wasted, until by dint of rebuffs and disappointments the crestfallen aspirant is brought to realise that it is only talent supplemented by thorough training and hard work that can open the doors of the dramatic profession to any newcomer. The best training for the stage is that of actual experience:—most of our noted actors and actresses have been acting almost since childhood; they have had to rough it in "fit up" companies at small provincial towns—often they have found themselves stranded far away from home, the finances of the management having suddenly collapsed. Many and various are the stories related of hardships endured and vicissitudes encountered—stories which should be enough to deter any budding aspirant after stage fame who has an idea that the dramatic profession is synonymous with a life of ease and comfort.

Where dramatic talent is present, however, the stage should be its natural outlet. It is very seldom that a person who has the decided dramatic temperament will make a success in any other calling. But she must not have the idea that she has merely to step forward and grasp without any effort the laurels which others often much more talented than she is have worked so hard to attain. She must take into account also the present overcrowded state of the profession, and remember that as far as newcomers are concerned preference is nearly always accorded to the young members of old theatrical families who have lived in a stage atmosphere almost since birth, who have gone through a thorough course of training under their parents' guidance, and who, in addition, can boast of names which their parents have made famous. There are therefore many disappointments which the young beginner will have to face; but there is an old saying that "talent will out," and if she is really gifted, and is prepared for years of hard work, there is no doubt that one day, sooner or later, her chance will come.

Training.—A thorough training is absolutely necessary. The earlier this training begins the better, for the sooner will the novice's dramatic apprenticeship be served. A girl should begin training before her twenty-first year if possible. Carriage and deportment must necessarily take an important part in an actress's education. A beginner will find it difficult even to walk gracefully across the stage—how much more so then if her acting has to include a fall or a faint. We all admire the suppleness and litheness of a Bernhardt, for instance, but suppleness of the kind must be acquired early, before the bones are set, otherwise this part of the training will be exceedingly difficult to other than a naturally graceful girl with a supple figure. Sixteen is a very good age to begin training. If before this a girl has made some preliminary study of elocution and dancing so much the better.

There are several good dramatic schools over the country at which thorough training may be had. In some cases pupils are given actual stage experience in the course of their training. This is the case with pupils of Mr. E. F. Benson, whose provincial Shakespearian companies are well known. They are rehearsed with the professionals by Mr. Benson and are allowed to appear in stage crowds, choruses, &c., at the different theatres visited. This gives them valuable practice in stage deportment.

There are other advantages which may be derived from training at a thoroughly good school. Introductions to managers may be obtained, and on many occasions engagements are procured which in other circumstances would be very difficult to obtain.

The chief dramatic schools are:—

The Academy of Dramatic Art, 62 Gower Street, London, W.C.

This school was founded by Sir Herbert Beerbohm Tree in 1904, and many of the students there have found their way into this well-known actor-manager's companies, thus embarking upon their theatrical careers under the most favourable auspices. Each student is required to pass an entrance examination, which usually consists of a short recitation which the student may choose for herself. The fee for this examination is £1, 1s. Eighteen months represents the average course necessary, but this must necessarily depend upon individual capabilities, some students taking longer than others to complete their training. The year is divided into three terms, and the fees for tuition are £12, 12s. per term. Instruction is given in every branch of stage work, including voice production, elocution, deportment and dancing, fencing and acting in general.

The Ben Greet Academy of Acting, 3 Bedford Street, is another successful theatrical school. There is no entrance examination necessary. Fees for full course of forty-eight lessons, £10, 10s. to £15, 15s.

At the Neville Dramatic Studio, 524 Oxford Street, Marble Arch, six private lessons of one hour each are given for £4, 4s.

The young girl who has completed a course of training at one of the recognised theatrical schools, and who has succeeded in winning the approbation of her tutors, must not make the great mistake of thinking that she will at once step into a big part in a production at one of the London theatres. She must recognise that with the completion of her studies her apprenticeship is only just beginning. Years of hard work in the provinces may be before her before she finally reaches that Mecca of every young actress, the London stage. There are one or two exceptions to this rule, but these exceptions can only be ascribed to chance which favours the few at the expense of the many. The young stage aspirant must therefore be prepared for a great deal of hard and plodding work, and for many heart-breaking disappointments and disillusions before her turn comes; but this period of hard work will give her that experience which is necessary before everything else—if she is to make a success of the career of her choice.

A small income independent of her earnings is almost a necessity for the girl who wishes to enter the dramatic profession. Engagements at first are difficult to procure; very often she will only be working four or five months out of the twelve, and how can she live during the other months if she has not a little money of her own to fall back upon. It may, indeed, be said that lack of means has been responsible for half the failures of girls who seemed to have had most promising stage careers before them at the outset. On the other hand, I do not wish to suggest that girls with comfortable incomes, who have no need whatever to earn their living, should go upon the stage. Such a course of action is manifestly unfair to those other women to whom the dramatic profession represents their sole means of livelihood. Nevertheless, a girl should think twice before she embarks upon a career which has probably more "ups and downs" than any other calling, unless she has some small sum put by which will help to tide her over those months of the year during which she is out of an engagement. Without this she will find many difficulties in her way. As in any other profession, appearances count for a great deal, and the chances of the girl who is forced to go about shabbily dressed are materially lessened when it comes to the question of seeking an engagement. There is also the danger of her health giving way if life resolves itself into a mere hand-to-mouth struggle for existence, and with the loss of health she must needs say good-bye to her last chance of success, for in the pursuit of this profession, even more than in that of any other, good health and a sound constitution are indispensable if any headway is to be made.

ART

It is only those who are endowed with the rare and wonderful genius of the artist who can ever hope to make a living by painting pictures—and even genius has at times to forsake the higher walks of art for by-ways that are more remunerative. Successful artists have devoted their lives to their work, and often success has only come to them after years of endeavour to obtain just that touch of originality which serves to raise them above their fellows.

There are many of the lesser branches of art, however, at which a clever and talented girl can earn a very good living if she possesses the essential qualities of perseverance and keen aptitude for catering to the taste of the public. In poster and advertisement designing, catalogue illustrating and fashion-drawing there are many prospects for the girl who has had a thorough training and can use her pencil with skill.

Training.—There are a number of schools and institutions at which a good training may be had, and at which all branches of painting and colouring should be studied before specialising for any particular art career. The following are some of the principal art schools:—

The Royal Academy Schools, Burlington House; the Royal College of Art, South Kensington, W.; the Slade School of Drawing, Painting and Sculpture; The Byam Shaw and Vicat Cole School of Art; University College, Gower Street, S.W.; The School of Art, Edinburgh.

Royal Academy Schools.—Tuition is free, but before admission students must submit certain specified works as a test of their ability. Such specimens, however, need not be submitted by those who can show certificates of proficiency from the Royal College of Art and certain other institutions. Successful candidates are admitted for three years.

Royal College of Art (see p. 688).

The Byam Shaw and Vicat Cole School of Art, Camden Street, Campden Hill, Kensington. The purpose of the school is to provide a thorough art training for students of both sexes. The building has been expressly erected as an art school. It contains three studios about thirty-two feet square. It is lit by electricity, warmed by hot-water radiators, and well ventilated. The school is situated on the top of Campden Hill—five minutes' walk from Notting Hill Gate Stations (Metropolitan Railway and Central London Tube).

Work is carried on for forty-four weeks in the year, the school only being closed for a week at Christmas and Easter and six weeks in the summer. Students are not bound by fixed terms, but may enter the school at any time. Students who join before the summer holidays continue their term when the school re-opens. The work is strictly progressive. Students must pass in antique drawing and elementary painting before attending the advanced classes. New students submit work to qualify for the Life class. Beginners as well as advanced students are invited to join. Students are prepared for the Royal Academy Schools.

The working day is from 10 A.M. to 6 P.M. with intervals for lunch and tea. The schools close at 4 P.M. on Saturdays. Supplementary classes are held in the evening for students who are unable to join in the day-time. No entrance fee is charged. Students must provide their own easels. These and other materials can be purchased in the school at the usual discount prices. A Scholarship (value £23) is offered yearly for competition. The school is always under the supervision of one or both the principals. During the absence of either of them his place is taken by one of the augmentary staff. The curator attends daily during working hours. Students must conform to the rules of the school and to the ruling of the curator, who is responsible for their observance.

Fees.—By the year (10 A.M. to 6 P.M., ten months' tuition), from date of joining to the same date in the following year . . £19 19 0

	£	s.	d.
Six months (10 A.M. to 6 P.M.)	14	14	0
Three months " "	8	8	0
One month " "	4	4	0
Three months " " (3 days per week)	5	5	0
Sketch class (4.30 to 6 P.M.) (free to day students) 2 months	3	3	0

These fees are reduced by 20 per cent. for the sons and daughters of professional artists and students engaged in teaching. All fees are payable in advance. No fees will be returned. Time lost through illness (only), if exceeding one week and certified by a doctor, may be made up.

The Heatherley School of Art, Newman Street, is one of the oldest art schools in London. The course is suitable for beginners as well as for more advanced pupils, and pupils are encouraged to work from the living model. Special instruction is given to those students who intend to become illustrators. There are both day and evening classes, and a ticket admitting to all the classes costs 25 guineas, or for the day classes only, 3 guineas per month. Special classes can also be taken, and private lessons are given. Fuller particulars can be obtained by writing to Mr. Massey, the principal of the school.

After their general training has been completed, people of limited means will find abundant facilities for special training by attending evening classes at one of the technical schools and schools of handicrafts under local authorities.

If the training can be completed by spending a year or two in a Paris studio, it will be very much to the advantage of the art student. Instruction in Paris does not cost much, and by studying economy in living, £100 a year can be made to cover expenses, while with an extra £50 the life can be quite comfortable.

All information regarding art schools and studios may be obtained by applying to the Secretary of the Franco-English Guild, 6 Rue de la Sorbonne, while board on very reasonable terms can be had at one of the houses run in connection with the Y.W.C.A., or several students may club together and take a small *appartement*, and by doing their catering the cost of living may be still further reduced.

As a rule, three lessons a day will be given in the large studios, one from 8 A.M. to midday, a second from 1 P.M. until 5 P.M., and a third in the evening, but it is not usual to attend more than one or two of these. The pupils work in class under the direction of a professor. Private lessons can also be obtained from many of the well-known Paris artists, but, as a rule, a student prefers the life of the larger studios where there is more opportunity for criticism.

Poster and Advertisement Designing.—For the girl with original ideas and a keen eye for effects there are many opportunities in this direction. It has been abundantly proved that talent utilised in commerce brings in the best returns, and the successful poster and advertisement designer can count upon making a very fair income. The woman who makes her name in this direction and becomes known for her skilful treatment of advertising ideas can always command a good price for her work. Some instinct for advertising, for bringing out the most striking points of a proposition is necessary. In poster designing especially a girl must strive to strike out upon original lines in addition to executing work of artistic merit.

Designing advertisements for reproduction in papers and magazines, designing show-cards and covers and illustrations for trade catalogues are all remunerative branches of the designer's art. Striking ideas which will serve to advertise their wares are always welcomed by business firms who are willing to pay well for really good work.

The woman who wishes to become a successful designer must have had a thorough training at a good art school. This should take at least four years and should be supplemented by a study of the business side of the question, including the various methods of reproduction and the different costs entailed. A short course at a good college of advertising will also be most useful. Experience in the business side of art is best obtained by either paying a premium for the opportunity of learning the work with a firm of illustrators and designers, or a position may often be obtained in a studio of the kind at a small commencing salary. Here the student will get experience in all kinds of black and white work, line-drawings and wash-drawings, also colour work, and will soon be initiated into the mysteries of the technical and business part of her calling. It may happen also that she will find her opportunity in the studio at which she takes this part of her training, for designers are always willing to keep willing and capable artists who have made themselves really useful to the firm.

At the New Art School, 3 Logan Place, Earl's Court Road, London, S.W., especially good training is given in poster designing and work for the press generally. The student has also the advantage of tuition under Mr. John Hassall, the most successful poster artist of the day.

Book and Magazine Illustration.—Black and white work and colour work for book and magazine illustration is also very profitable once an artist has established a good connection. To do this she must have the capabilities and push of a good business woman. She should keep a selection of drawings in her best style to submit to the various editors of magazines and periodicals; she will also have to have something of the instinct of a journalist to make this branch of her calling a success. She will have to become familiar with the style of illustration adopted by individual publications and adapt her works to suit this style. Clever suggestions are always welcomed by editors, and she must lose no opportunity of making these. Very often she will be given an article or a story to illustrate. Generally the various passages to be illustrated will be pointed out to her. She may be given an idea of what is required, or she may be asked to do the work according to her own ideas. In regard to black and white work for magazines and papers, promptitude in delivering the drawings is essential; and very often the artist will have very little time in which to put her ideas into form. This is a feature of the work which must not be lost sight of. The girl who is quick at her work and can keep her promise in regard to time of delivery will make much more headway than the girl who, however talented, cannot get a drawing ready to time or who never fulfils her promise in this respect.

Lady artists in colour illustration are employed a great deal by publishing firms who make a speciality of colour work.

Fashion Drawing.—The clever fashion artist, once she obtains a footing, has every prospect of success before her. There is scarcely a day or an evening newspaper nowadays which has not its fashion page, whilst ladies' fashion papers vie with each other in being up to date in their dress designs. It is true that most papers have their own fashion artists upon their staffs, but there is always room for good ideas and good work. Besides, vacancies will occur, and then who is more likely to step into them than the girl or woman who has made her work known and who is ever watchful for her opportunity. The fashion artist should first of all be *au fait* with the fashions and their various possibilities. She should be essentially a woman with ideas in regard to dress. She should make herself acquainted with the personalities of leaders of fashion and take every opportunity of sketching the toilettes of leaders of society upon interesting social functions. She should regularly submit work to the fashion editress of the principal ladies' journals and also to those of the ladies' pages of daily or weekly papers. If she can begin by becoming assistant to a fashion artist, her path will be made all the easier for her.

A fashion artist may either obtain work as a free lance with various papers, or she may obtain a post on the staff of a paper. In the latter case she will be given a salary. A capable and experienced artist employed by a paper of standing will often earn as much as from £300 to £500 a year, and a really capable artist may calculate upon earning £250 a year when she first obtains a salaried post, for none but efficient workers are employed on first-class publications, and these always can obtain their price.

The free-lance must necessarily be paid by piece-work, and prices obtainable average from 3s. 6d. to 10s. 6d. per single figure. When an artist is given a number of drawings to do at once, as, for instance, several small illustrations for a fashion book, she would be asked to do them at an inclusive charge, which would work out at a lower sum per figure. The artist who is employed on the staff of a paper has as strenuous a life as a journalist in every sense of the word. She is, in fact, a journalist of the pencil. Her working days are long—often she has to go far afield for the subjects of her sketches, and very often the time allowed in which to work them out for press is all too short. But there are many compensations; the work, besides being remunerative, is full of fascination and interest.

Teaching.—There are many openings for teachers of art in art schools and technical institutions under local authorities, also in private schools for those who have had a thorough art training. Teachers must obtain the art teacher's certificate of the Board of Education. Full training may be had at the Royal College of Art, South Kensington, London, which was first established for the training of art masters and mistresses as a college in which recognised art students could take their training, and it can be entered free by means of scholarships. Valuable training scholarships are offered giving free tuition and a maintenance grant from 12s. 6d. to 43s. 6d. a week, and also a number of free studentships. The fees charged to the general public range from 5s. to £5 a term, according to the course taken. A prospectus of the college may be obtained post free 4d.; in this full information in regard to scholarships, conditions of admission, &c., will be found.

The art teacher's certificate is almost a necessity to those who wish to teach in any of the municipal schools or classes, or in the best secondary schools which are under the Board of Education, but those who have received their art instruction in any of the famous schools of the country would have many posts open to them.

MINOR ARTS AND CRAFTS

Photography.—Photography affords excellent opportunities for the woman with artistic tastes combined with good business capacity and the requisite amount of capital with which to start a business of her own. The minor posts in photography, such as retouching, &c., are very poorly paid, and a woman is ill-advised to train with only a post of this kind in view. The best salaries are paid to those who are termed receptionists. Their duties are to be in the studio, to receive clients, make appointments, and to keep the books. They may also be required to do some retouching, photograph tinting, &c. A receptionist will get a salary of from £1, 10s. to £2, 10s. a week, whilst the salary of a retoucher seldom averages more than from 10s. to 15s. weekly.

Training.—A professional course of photography may be taken at the Polytechnic, Regent Street, London, for £52, 10s. The course comprises the scientific as well as the operative part of photography. Another way of training is to become a paying student in a high-class studio. Opportunities of practice are of first importance, and if the student can fit up a studio in her own home, practising her art with her friends as sitters, this will give her a great experience of the practical part of the work as well as of its artistic side.

Artistic photography should be the aim of every photographer who sets up in the business for herself. She should aim at making studies of her pictures. Women photographers, as a rule, are experts in the art of pose, and all women who have followed this profession with any success are renowned for their artistic photographs.

The principal of one of the most fashionable studios in London is a lady who has made her name for artistic work. Her clientele consists mainly of the upper classes and her income is a large one. It is a good plan to specialise in children's photography where possible, for this is a very paying branch of the profession.

Little capital is necessary to start a studio in a country district. In London and other large towns from £200 to £300 would be required, and in order to set up in a fashionable district any sum of from £500 to £1000 would be necessary. The girl who wishes to carry on photography as a home occupation for profit may try her hand at writing articles for magazines and periodicals and illustrating them with her photographs.

Dancing Mistress.—This is a career well suited to girls of refinement who are also graceful in their movements and lithe and supple of figure. The dancing mistress must begin her training very early if she is to attain not only grace of movement and proficiency in her art, but also efficiency in teaching. The best method of training is to serve an apprenticeship of at least two years in a first-class dancing academy. For this a premium of £50 and upwards will have to be paid; even more in some of the most select schools of dancing. In this time every branch of ball-room dancing and the chief fancy dances will be learnt, also Swedish or other simple physical exercises. After the apprenticeship has expired it is better to remain on with the same dancing teacher as assistant in order to gain experience. The assistant will receive a small salary of 10s. a week at first, but this will rise in proportion as her usefulness increases, and at the end of the first year, if her services are retained, she will probably receive a salary of from £1, 10s. to £2 a week. Very often, however, the dancing mistress has to take an enforced holiday during the summer, as few classes are held in this season, and this is a point to be remembered.

Given a thorough training and good experience as assistant, a woman can quite easily open a class of her own. She might aim first at getting a good appointment as visiting dancing mistress in a girls' school, and gradually extend her connection until she is able to hire a hall in which to hold her classes.

HANDICRAFTS FOR HOME WORKERS

There are a number of arts and crafts in which the woman worker can engage at home, and by the pursuit of which she can add materially to her income. Needless to say, a thorough training in each particular handicraft is necessary before it can be utilised for monetary consideration.

Metal Work and Enamelling.—This proves a most fascinating occupation for the woman who has artistic perception and skill of design. Beautiful work can be executed in the production of brooches, chains, clasps, and other jewellery, ornamental buttons, hair-combs, also fire-screens, frames, lamps, and all other articles to which this art may be applied. The girl who wishes to take up the study of metal work and enamelling with a view to profit should have some idea of drawing and design, and also good business capacity, for she will have to estimate the costs of materials and put upon her work a sufficient price for it to yield a profit. The home worker should also remember that the smaller articles, such as jewellery, hair-combs, &c., are most often easier to sell than the larger ones.

The metal and enamel worker must necessarily have an outfit of the tools and an enamelling stove. The latter cannot be had under £5, but this is the most expensive item. The enamels cost about 4d. per ounce; a brush and a pestle and mortar are also necessary. Extra tools will be required for chasing work. A girl should therefore have a little money not only for the purchase of the outfit, but for materials such as gold, silver, &c.

Training.—Lessons in metal work and enamelling may be had at most of the art schools and polytechnics. Excellent training may be had at Alexander Fisher's Studios, 17 Warwick Gardens, Kensington, London. At the Birmingham School of Art a particularly good training is given. At the art schools and polytechnics the training is exceptionally cheap, amounting to only a few shillings a session, but then only one or two lessons per week are given. Another way of training is to become apprenticed to a metal worker for six months to a year. For this premiums vary, some firms demanding more than others. This second method of training, though more expensive, is certainly more effective, as the student in this way gains practical experience of every branch of the work, and a keen insight into costs, proper scales of prices, &c., &c. An expert designer will be able to complete her training in the course of a few lessons.

Prospects.—When the training is ended the best way to attract general notice to one's work is to send exhibits to the exhibitions organised by the various arts and crafts societies. These exhibitions are held in almost every large town. In London the Arts and Crafts Exhibition Society holds a yearly exhibition of all handicrafts. Exhibits can also be sent to the British Industrial League and United Gentlewomen's Handicraft and Home Industrial Exhibition (address—The Hon. Secretary, 42 Vardens Road, London, S.W.).

Apart from home work posts may be had as designers and workers with firms of metal workers, a good designer earning from £75 to £80 a year. Teachers' posts in county council art schools are also to be had by those with exceptional qualifications.

Leather Work and Wood Carving can also be turned into a profitable home occupation if the worker adopts the methods detailed above to make her work known. Both are taught at most art schools and polytechnics. At the School of Art Wood Carving, Thurloe Place, South Kensington, a good training in wood carving may be had at a cost of £5 a quarter. The time training will take must necessarily depend upon the aptitude of the pupil; the full course extends over three years. A month's training will cost £2 and a year's training £14, reduction being made for each successive year of training.

Bookbinding.—Bookbinding is a most interesting occupation for women, and can prove most remunerative to the woman with a good connection if she can open her own workshop. Apart from this there are not many prospects in regard to paid positions in workshops, for the generality of these are filled by men, and in any case the weekly remuneration is small.

The bookbinder, to do really tasteful and artistic work, should have a knowledge of design. The training, which is an expensive one, costing usually about £70, takes one year, and after this it requires constant practice to become really proficient in the art. The necessary training can be obtained at the establishment of Miss Woolrich, 5 Bloomsbury Square, W.C. Lessons in bookbinding may also be taken at London County Council Central School of Arts and Crafts, Southampton Row, W.C. On the whole, as a career bookbinding does not offer many opportunities for women. The woman, however, who has managed to get a good connection together by means of private work, and who has a fair amount of capital, backed up by skill and business ability, should be able to start a business of her own with fair prospects of success.

Lace-making, Spinning, and Weaving.—There has lately been a revival of the ancient arts of lace-making, spinning and weaving, and some prospects in this direction have been opened out to educated women as well as to the poorer classes. Posts as teachers in county council classes, especially in those villages where the lace industry has been revived to any great extent, may be obtained by the efficient worker. Fine lace-mending and repairing may help to add to her income to a certain extent. The lace worker must be able to turn out work of the first quality and have a certain gift for design. In regard to spinning and weaving it is anticipated that these arts will soon be developed as a field of employment. Full particulars in regard to training may be had from the British and Irish Weaving and Spinning and Lace School, 28 Davies Street, Berkeley Square, London, W.

Needlework.—In needlework itself as a profession there are not many prospects, although good needlewomen may dispose of their work by entrusting it to a society organised for the sale of the work of gentlewomen. Women who are anxious to dispose of their work should communicate with the "Gentlewomen's Work Society," which has been specially founded to help gentlewomen in reduced circumstances who are anxious to add to their incomes by the aid of the needle. This society receives orders for all kinds of fine needlework, including trousseaux and layettes, also for fancy work of all descriptions, lace mending, cleaning, &c. Full particulars may be had upon application to the secretary, 114 Church Road, Norwood, London, E. The Girls' Friendly Society, Victoria Street, London, S.W., also undertakes to assist in the sale of needlework by members. In Edinburgh the Society for the Sale of Gentlewomen's Work and the Princess Helena Society have been founded with the same object, and also the Work Depôt for Irish Distressed Ladies, 20 Dawson Street, Dublin. In fact, in almost every large town there are societies with this laudable end in view. Women with a little capital of their own cannot do better than start a fine needlework shop where every kind of work is undertaken and where work materials, &c., are sold. They should select a suitable neighbourhood, and church work might well be made a speciality.

There are schools of plain needlework, fancy work, and embroidery all over the country, at which the work can be learned. At the Royal School of Art Needlework, South Kensington, lessons in all kinds of embroidery and fancy work may be taken. For terms apply to the secretary.

SOCIAL AND PHILANTHROPIC WORK

THIS article deals with a phase of work for women which is at present little understood and even less appreciated by a large number of women workers. The openings for social and philanthropic workers are, however, steadily increasing, and the paid posts are becoming more and more numerous. This article gives details in regard to the various branches of social and philanthropic work, and the prospects which they offer to educated women workers.

For the woman of leisure and means, as well as for the woman who has to toil for her daily bread, philanthropic work of all kinds should have an absorbing interest. In the many responsible unpaid posts the former may find full scope for ameliorating the lot of those less fortunate than themselves; and the latter, whilst engaged in the task of earning their livelihood, are happy in the knowledge that they are doing good and useful work by following one of the noblest careers open to women.

A great fund of sympathy and understanding of human nature are necessary for the woman who would take up philanthropic work with success. She should be patient and intuitively thoughtful for the feelings of others, and refinement will not prove her least valuable asset. Added to this, a regular course of training should be undergone to fit her for that particular branch of philanthropy which she wishes to take up.

Training.—Those who wish to be efficient workers should take a course of training at one of the recognised training institutions. This course should extend over two years in regard to the more important work. There are many facilities for training nowadays, which some years ago did not exist. At the following institutions instruction in the various branches of the work may be had :—

The London School of Sociology and Social Economics, Denison House, Vauxhall Bridge Road. Fees, twelve guineas the session; the complete course is two years, but shorter courses may be taken.

The Women's University Settlement, 44 and 45 Nelson Square, Blackfriars Road, London, S.E. Fees also twelve guineas per session. The ordinary course lasts one year, and constitutes a training in social work generally, but students who wish to specialise in any particular branch should remain a second year. Resident students pay £60 a year for board and lodging.

Lady Margaret Hall Settlement, Kennington Road, Lambeth. Fees, resident students £48 a year.

Training may also be had at many of the other settlements and at the London School of Economics, Clare Market, W.C. Girls may obtain an insight into practical social work at various branches of the Charitable Organisation Society.

The chief openings for women social workers are as almoners in hospitals, settlement workers, welfare managers, secretaries to philanthropic societies, clubs, &c., rent collectors, relieving officers, Poor Law inspectors (see p. 680), managers of milk depots, &c.

Hospital Almoner.—This is a comparatively new career for women. A few years ago there were no women almoners; and, though their number is not great at present, in all probability it will be added to considerably in the future. Posts as assistants to almoners may be had, in which a very full knowledge of the work may be gained, so that the assistant will in time be qualified to take the post of almoner herself.

The duties of an almoner are many and varied, but they may be classified in one sentence—the supervision of the out-patients' department of a hospital. The work has two different aspects, each of which is of the utmost importance. First, it is the duty of the almoner to check abuse of the charity of the hospital, seeing that only those who are eligible receive free treatment, and so preventing a waste of hospital funds; for often the benefits of the hospital are extended free to those who can afford to pay for medical and nursing aid, a fact which is manifestly unfair to the hospital, the other patients, and to medical practitioners. The almoners' duty it is, therefore, to make inquiries in regard to the circumstances of out-patients, to receive recommendations from medical men in regard to deserving cases, and to advise those applicants who are in work to make provision for times of illness by subscription to Provident Dispensaries. Then it is her duty to provide eligible patients with all the help in her power, seeing that they carry out religiously the treatment prescribed, visiting their homes if necessary, or getting into communication with the district visitor of that particular locality, and gaining her co-operation, asking her to report upon any case in her district. She should also be in touch with the various charitable organisations, enlisting their help where necessary on the behalf of deserving cases.

It will be seen, therefore, that the work of a hospital almoner is no sinecure. Every moment of her day is practically mapped out for her. On the other hand, her work is full of variety and interest, and her scope for doing good among poor patients is practically unlimited.

Training.—The hospital almoner should first of all have had a thorough general education. She should have, in addition, a good knowledge of book-keeping, management of money and business methods generally. She should also possess that tact so necessary for dealing with the different classes of people with whom she will have to come in contact. The girl who wishes to become an almoner should write to the secretary of the Almoners' Training Committee, Denison House, Vauxhall Bridge Road, for full information in regard to training, prospects, &c. The principal part of the training is usually to be had from hospital almoners, who train pupils in the actual work of the out-patients' department, usually free of charge. In all cases £5 covers the cost of both theoretical and practical training. Candidates for training must be under thirty-five years of age.

Prospects.—The openings at present are few, but there is every prospect that they will increase. There is nothing to prevent every hospital appointing an almoner in time, when the usefulness of their work is fully appreciated. Salaries vary according to circumstances; they are rarely less than £100 a year, whilst in many cases much higher salaries are paid.

The Social Secretary.—The duties of a secretary to a philanthropic institution or society represent a very large sphere of social work. Most of the social secretaryships are now paid posts, although a great number of these secretarial posts are filled by voluntary workers. The scope of the work is wide and varied, as the many charitable associations deal with so many different phases of charitable work. Thus we have societies dealing with holidays for invalid workers and children, others engaged in rescue works; then we have the girls' and boys' clubs and societies for improving the conditions of the poor generally, &c., &c. In each case the secretary must have a thorough knowledge of her duties, have had a good general education, supplemented by special secretarial training as well as training in the particular branch of social work which she takes up. She must be a good organiser and have plenty of self-reliance and power of initiative. No mere routine worker, who can only do as she is told and not be able to think or act for herself, can successfully take up a post of the kind.

An Honorary Secretary does a great deal of work for no pay, and if capable, conscientious, and enthusiastic, is one of the most useful members of society. She is generally elected to the office on the ground of special fitness, owing either to her interest in the particular work of the association, her social influence which can enlist subscribers and desirable members, or her enthusiasm and persuasive advocacy, a qualification which has much to do with the prosperity of a public cause. The combination of these three recommendations makes an ideal secretary, whether honorary or paid.

One of the first duties of the secretary will be the drafting and issuing of appeals. Now considerable skill is required for this. Then she will have special duties in connection with the organisation and arrangement of committee meetings and public meetings, seeing to all the preliminaries in connection with each. It will also be her duty to inform the local press of the place, day, and hour of public meetings, sending cards of invitation for the occasion so that the proceedings can be well reported. She must be careful to show all courtesy to the reporters who go to her for information and give them all the assistance they require.

The duties of a secretary to a philanthropic institution or association cover a very wide field of activity for the voluntary as well as for the paid worker. It will be realised, therefore, that a thorough training and some amount of experience of the work are necessary for the women who wish to fill a position of the kind with success.

Training.—Good training may be had at the different schools of sociology and at a number of the women's settlements. Excellent training is also given by the Charity Organisation Society. The cost of training varies at the different institutions, and the intending social worker should write to the settlement or society of her choice asking full particulars as to terms, varying courses of training, &c.

Prospects.—Very good secretarial posts may be had with rich philanthropists who make good works their hobby—such posts, as a rule, are the most highly paid. Salaries to be had from charitable institutions are not, as a rule, high, though they vary to a great extent, £80 to £100 or £150 being the average; whilst the salaries paid by private philanthropists often reach the sum of £250 a year.

Welfare Work.—This is a very important branch of social work, and one which is of comparative recent growth. Many of our largest and wealthiest of manufacturers have realised the importance of improving the social and general conditions of their employees, realising that pleasant, happy, and comfortable surroundings form the best incentive to good and conscientious work on the part of the workers; and it has been abundantly proved that the employer who takes an interest in the well-being of his employees is paid many times over by the willingness and appreciation displayed by the workers, who are always grateful for any kindness exercised on their behalf.

It is the duty of the welfare manager (or social secretary, as she is often called) to see that the best is done in promoting the welfare of the employees in every conceivable way. She must see that they work under the best conditions in regard to sanitation and comfort, and that good meals are provided at a nominal cost. Also that these meals are taken in pleasant and cheerful surroundings, so that the dining-hour is one of the most cheerful hours of the day for the workers.

She organises entertainments, encouraging the workers to form entertainment clubs and committees. It is her duty to receive and deal with all complaints in regard to their food or surroundings. Another important part of her work is to promote thrift amongst the employees. Some large manufacturers have founded savings banks for their employees, giving a fair rate of interest, and the welfare manager encourages the girls to save in this way. The health of the employees is also under her supervision. She sees that a girl who is taken ill receives proper attention, and visits her home to make inquiries as to her progress and to afford any little help that may be necessary. In most factories where welfare workers are employed, there are playgrounds and gardens for the employees. The welfare manager must see to the organising of outdoor sports. Usually she will organise a games club, of which she will encourage all employees to become members. Very often a reading library will be under her direction, and she will be required to organise instructive lectures for educational purposes.

There is practically no limit to the scope afforded to a welfare manager for doing good, provided she has those personal qualities which are so necessary to win the respect and affection of the workers. Tact and sympathy, combined with firmness and a sense of strictly impartial justice, are the qualities which will stand her in best stead. The woman who is suited to the work will find it full of interest and variety, and will leave no stone unturned to promote the welfare of those under her charge.

Training should be taken preferably at a settlement. Good advice upon the best method of training may be received from the Hon. Secretary, The British Institute of Social Service, 4 Tavistock Street, W.C., or from any of the Social Settlements.

Prospects.—The posts are well paid—£150 a year representing a fair average.

Settlement Workers.—Settlement workers are engaged in carrying out social and educational work amongst the poor—religious work also being undertaken in this connection. In regard to social work, many of the duties are similar to those of the welfare manager, only they are applied to a more varied community, for the work is amongst the poor generally. The organisation of clubs, thrift societies, the providing of entertainments, and organisation of play centres for children, the conducting of educational work in the form of lectures and classes, district visiting, and last, but not least, religious work, all come within the scope of the charitable work directed by the various settlements. Another important branch of settlement work is the training of all kinds of social workers. Each settlement is under the direction of a warden, who receives a salary of from £50 a year and upwards. Some of the chief settlements for the education of workers have been mentioned in the first part of this article. Amongst other settlements which do a large amount of work amongst the poor are the following:—

The Canning Town Woman's Settlement, East London.

Passmore Edwards Settlement, Tavistock Place, W.C. (No resident women workers.)

The Bermondsey Settlement, 187 Bermondsey Street, London, S.E., for the benefit of the factory girls of Bermondsey.

The work of the following societies are especially deserving of mention in regard to religious as well as philanthropic work among the poor.

The Greyladies.—This is a society of ladies which devotes itself to religious and philanthropic work, whose headquarters are the Greylands College, near Blackheath. The members of the society can either be resident or non-resident, and three months' probation is generally required before one can be formally enrolled as a member. The fees for resident members are £50 per annum, to be paid in quarterly instalments. The college, which is most comfortably fitted up, is under the superintendence of Miss Wordsworth, and there is nothing ascetic about the life.

The Greyladies do district visiting, hold meetings and classes, give lectures and addresses, organise clubs and excursions—in fact, all kinds of parish work, with the exception of nursing. The Bishop of Southwark is president of the college, and the work is carried on under the incumbents of the diocese, each member of the society being given the work which seems best suited to her capabilities.

The aim of the society is to bring together ladies who wish to devote themselves to Church work, and enable them to carry it out on some definite plan and on community lines.

The Biblewomen and Nurses' Mission.—The headquarters of this society are at Ranyard House, 25 Russell Square, so called from the founder, Mrs. Ranyard. The aim of the mission is to send workers into the homes of the poor and give them religious teaching and nursing when required. The Biblewomen are trained mission visitors who live in different districts of London, and generally work in connection with some church or chapel. They try to introduce the Bible into the homes they visit, and encourage the poor to buy it on an instalment plan. Candidates for the post of Biblewomen should be between the ages of twenty-five and thirty-five, and a short training and probation is given in the hostel, Ranyard House, under trained workers, the time varying according to the needs of the worker. A salary is afterwards given according to the kind of work that is undertaken.

The Ranyard nurses must be fully trained, and they have generally a few weeks' probation before being formally accepted. The nurses also receive a salary, varying according to their capabilities, and work under the direction of a superintending sister.

Both nurses and Biblewomen meet at the headquarters for devotional services and to give in reports of the work. Needless to say, only women who are prepared to live a very simple life, and who can manage their own housekeeping if necessary, besides having a special love for the work in hand, should think of taking a post of the kind. Further particulars can be had by applying to the secretary of the mission.

House Management, or, as it is most commonly known, "rent collecting," also affords good scope for the trained social worker; and since the first organisation of this particular work by Miss Octavia Hill, a number of women have taken it up with success. The work consists of transacting all kinds of business in connection with house property of the poorer classes, and the house manager will require a good knowledge and experience of the people among whom she will have to work. The houses under her direction will be almost exclusively those let at weekly rentals, and in connection with these she will have to see to the arranging of improvements and repairs when necessary—reporting upon any defects in sanitation or other matters requiring attention. This is all in addition to the actual work of rent collecting, which of course also falls to her share.

The house manager should have a good knowledge of the law of landlord and tenant as applied to weekly tenancies; she should also have some knowledge of sanitation, sufficient for her to advise upon defective sanitary conditions and suggest improvements where necessary. A knowledge of book-keeping and business methods is also essential, as various accounts in connection with the property have often to be kept by the house manager.

Training.—A good course of social training, supplemented by training in business methods and sanitation will be necessary. It is always best to train in a settlement, and to supplement the training by a few months' actual experience with a house manager. The student should also take a short course at the Sanitary Institute or the National Health Society (see Sanitary Inspectors).

Prospects.—Salaries vary—£40 per annum being, as a rule, the minimum figure. The Ecclesiastical Commissioners and many other large companies owning houses for the poorer classes employ lady house managers, as do also other property owners. As a field of work for women, house management promises further development in the future.

Relieving Officers.—This branch of social work for women is as yet in its infancy, as there are only one or two unions which have appointed women relieving officers. A number of unions have, however, appointed women as assistant relieving officers, and there are therefore much better prospects to be found in this minor position. The duties of the women relieving officers are principally among women. They have to visit those who are receiving relief and to arrange for the reception of those women who wish to enter the maternity wards. A good knowledge of social work is necessary for the relieving officer to be able to deal efficiently with all the applications coming under her notice. Salaries range from about £100 for assistant relieving officers, and from £120 for relieving officers.

Manager of Municipal Milk Depots.—Municipal milk depots have now been inaugurated in various towns throughout England for the supply of pure milk to the poorer classes. So much good has been done by these institutions that there is every prospect that their number will be increased. Women managers are employed in the milk depots at fairly good salaries, though these vary in different localities. Training may best be had by actual experience under a manageress.

Children's Care Committees.—The new Acts in regard to the medical inspection and feeding of school children are responsible for the evolution of another field of activity for the social worker—that of the supervision of Children's Care Committees.

These committees deal with the work of providing meals for necessitous school children. They are required to see, however, that discrimination is exercised in this respect by only administering the charity where real need for it exists. They also watch over the health of the children. They employ health visitors to visit their homes and give advice to their parents in regard to health and hygiene. The London County Council has appointed two organisers and twelve lady assistant organisers to supervise this work. The work of health visiting under the committees is apportioned out amongst its members, each being responsible for a certain district.

Posts as school nurses or health visitors and sanitary inspectors are to be had in London under the London County Council, in addition to those to be had in connection with these committees (see p. 637).

Women in Local Government.—By the Qualification of Women (County and Borough Councils Act), 1907, women are now eligible for service on borough and county councils. As is well known, all administrative work in local government is unpaid, but such work offers unlimited opportunities for many well-educated women who are not obliged to work for their livelihood, and enjoy incomes of their own. (For paid official appointments under local authorities, see Civil Service and Public Work.)

WOMEN IN POLITICS

In this article a comprehensive survey is taken of the part played by women in politics at the present day. The various ways in which women may help their part at election time are detailed, and hints are given in regard to the special training needed to become a successful canvasser, platform speaker, or an efficient worker in committee rooms.

The information in regard to the actual progress of the Women's Suffrage movement, which is included in this article, will be welcomed by those who have not hitherto studied the question, as it gives them the knowledge they lack in a simple and easily intelligible form.

THE WOMAN CANVASSER

In the ranks of all political parties nowadays the woman electioneer plays a prominent part, —a more prominent part, in fact, than at any previous period of our political history, although women have always exerted a certain influence in politics, an influence which has gone a long way towards deciding the fate of many an election.

In former times the weapons employed by the gentler sex to secure votes for their favourite candidate were those of fascination and charm, and many a recalcitrant voter was brought to a sense of his duty as an elector by the persuasive smile of some noble dame who often knew little of the political principles which she had pledged herself to advocate.

With the canvasser of to-day methods have changed; the woman canvasser is a trained worker, and not only an ardent disciple of her cause, but also one who is entirely conversant with the principles which that cause embodies. She can argue like an expert upon tariff reform, free trade, socialism, or any vital point at issue, and knows to a nicety the kind of argument which will have most force with the particular voter she wishes to capture. Her arguments, what is more, are based upon a thorough knowledge not only of the cause she has espoused, but also of the claims put forward by the opposing party; and with all the tact of a trained politician she points out the flaws in the political programme of her opponents. Tact, that greatest of feminine attributes, is absolutely necessary to convert opponent or "doubtful" voters to one's own political opinions. Tact, therefore, is not the least effective weapon in the armoury of the woman canvasser.

The importance of the rôle played by successful women canvassers at elections has received widespread recognition, and the establishment of classes for canvassers conducted by political organisations, in which women can learn the principles and practice of electioneering, is now one of the outstanding features of the preparation for elections. In these classes inexperienced women are initiated into the art of canvassing and all the principles governing election procedure.

THE WOMAN SPEAKER

There are speakers' classes, too, for women who wish to aid their cause by speaking at political meetings, and the number of these classes is more than ever typical of the important part played by woman in politics, and the still more important part which she may in the future be called upon to play. Not only is the student initiated into the mysteries of intonation and correct delivery, but she is also made to realise the importance of that simple, direct, yet forcible style of speaking which carries conviction, and does more than anything else to obtain the sympathy of an audience and hold its attention and interest. The woman who is a naturally gifted speaker will do well to attend these classes; by doing so she will acquire a self-confidence and a finish which will stand her in good stead. Attendance at a speakers' class is doubly necessary for the woman who is not naturally gifted for platform oratory, but whose duties, nevertheless, will call upon her at times to speak in public; for though she may never become a brilliant speaker, at least by taking instruction at classes she will learn to say what she has to say audibly, clearly, and as convincingly as possible.

Some knowledge of the procedure at public meetings is also essential. It often falls to the lot of a woman to take the chair at some political meeting, and much of its success will depend upon the manner in which her duties as president are fulfilled.

WOMEN ORGANISERS

But there are many other important parts played by women in helping the success of their cause beyond that of speaking and actual canvassing. Nowadays, careful organisation is the most characteristic feature of our elections, and often the failure of a particular candidate at the polls is largely ascribed to some defect in the electioneering machinery. Women nowadays enter largely into the actual organisation of the campaign of their party. Thus in many women's committee rooms we find capable women in authority, carrying on work for the election agent, attending to important details in regard to statistics in connection with voters, &c., and directing a large number of voluntary women workers who see to all important detail work in regard to correspondence, filing of records, making appointments, &c. The work of these women is of the utmost value, and cannot but be productive of the best results.

The woman who embarks upon any of the branches of election work above described, and who does her work earnestly and conscientiously, may rest satisfied that she is acting up to her political principles by helping in the smooth running of the organisation of the campaign of her party; in fact, that she is doing her best to help it in every way, whatever may be the ultimate results of the contest in which the parties are engaged.

WOMEN'S SUFFRAGE MOVEMENT

The question of women's rights is one of the most passionate questions of social reform of our day. The character of the women who are leading the movement, the determined way in which the arguments are being fought out, the great impression produced in Parliament, and the deep and almost unexpected response which the cry of revolt has produced throughout the masses of women of the country, all go to prove that this is a question that must be seriously faced and dealt with.

Women, like men, have the desire to expand their realm of intelligence, to take part in the affairs of the world, which bear upon their lives, and the restraint and force of mere tradition, prejudice, or caste, have become intolerable to them. Women want freer lives because they want freer development; they want more capable minds and increased capacities for grappling with the increasing difficulties of modern civilisation.

The agitation for women's rights is no new thing; in many respects it has the air of the recovery of privileges once enjoyed. In feudal days women who possessed lands held them on the same terms as men, and exercised the right of taking part in the election of members of the House of Commons. Even as far back as 1739 it was proved that women who held the freehold of a landed property should vote for Parliament. In that year, however, the Court decided against the claims of women. Even as late as 1867 the law was still uncertain in regard to a number of these questions, and in that year 230 women were on the List of the Voters of Manchester, and the matter was re-argued before it was definitely decided that they should not exercise the vote.

There have been many champions of women's rights long before those with whose names we are familiar at the present day. Mary Astell, for example, was one of the great pioneers of the movement, and her "Serious Proposals to Ladies" is overflowing with wit and wisdom. Another, still later and better known, is Mary Wollstonecraft, and her "Vindication of the Rights of Women" affords admirable reading. The next great name is that of John Stuart Mill. His famous book, "The Subjection of Women," made a stir in its time, and brought the question of Women's Rights within the range of practical politics, but his movement was defeated.

Following John Stuart Mill we find Benjamin Disraeli in 1873 advocating Women's Rights in a letter to a friend.

Of late years the movement has been steadily growing. Petition after petition, signed by thousands of women, has been presented in Parliament, many societies have been founded throughout the country, and several members of Parliament have made themselves conspicuous in advocating the cause. The movement is organised; it is becoming consolidate, efficient, and very powerful. Amongst the multitude of helpers may be mentioned such influential bodies as:—

The **National Union of Women's Suffrage Societies**, comprising over 200 societies—which is the parent of all—14 Great Smith Street, London. President: Mrs. Henry Fawcett, LL.D.

National Women's Social and Political Union.—Founder and Hon. Sec.: Mrs. Pankhurst, 4 Clement's Inn, London.

Conservative and Unionist Women's Franchise Association, 48 Dover Street, London, W.—President: Countess of Selborne.

London Society for Women's Suffrage, 58 Victoria Street, S.W.—President: Lady Frances Balfour.

The New Constitutional Society, 8 Park Mansions Arcade, Knightsbridge.—President: Mrs. C. Chapman.

The Actresses' Franchise League, 2 Robert Street, Strand.—President: Mrs. Forbes Robertson.

The Church League for Women's Suffrage,

Irish Women's Franchise League, Free Church League for Women's Suffrage, Men's Political Union for Women's Enfranchisement, and many others.

All these movements have been conducted on "constitutional" principles, except that of the Social and Political Union, over 300 of whose members have suffered varying terms of imprisonment. How far the daring but self-sacrificing efforts of these ladies have "kept back the cause for twenty years," or given it a reality, a vim, an impetus, and a hopefulness, it must be left to each reader to form her own judgment.

In 1910 all the Suffrage Societies united in support of a Bill (introduced by Mr. Shackleton, M.P.) to extend the vote to those women who now vote municipally. This Conciliation Bill was carried on its second reading on July 12, 1910, by a majority of 110, and was sent to a general committee of the whole House, but was "shelved." Sir George Kemp will submit a new Bill of a slightly amended form for its second reading on May 5.

The text of this new Bill, which is known as the Conciliation Bill, 1911, is the following:—

1. Every woman possessed of a household qualification within the meaning of the Representation of the People Act (1884) shall be entitled to be registered as a voter, and when registered to vote for the county or borough in which the qualifying premises are situate.

2. For the purposes of this Act, a woman shall not be disqualified by marriage for being registered as a voter, provided that a husband and wife shall not both be registered as voters in the same Parliamentary Borough or county division.

The militant suffragists, as well as the constitutional suffragists, are absolutely at one in their intention of giving all possible support to this Bill.

What have women to expect as a result of their enfranchisement? Certainly not the "Golden Age," nor a sovereign remedy for all ills, but rather a lever to help them slowly so that in time many of the laws which affect them may be improved. Thus by the exercise of the vote working women expect gradually to improve their conditions of work and wages as men have done by their enfranchisement. The present restricted range of women's labour is another they hope to see removed in time, and no matter what the character of their work may be, to have it judged by its true market value and not by the sex of the worker.

There are various other matters which closely affect women, such as the housing of the poor, prison reform, relief of the poor and needy, &c., all of which ought to come somewhat within their jurisdiction.

There are also certain existing laws which they would have altered, more especially the divorce laws, which, as they stand, are a crying injustice to women.

To remove the stigma now placed upon all women by including them in such categories as lunatics, criminals, paupers, aliens, and minors, and in this way to raise the status of woman, is another of the aims of the suffragist. This is a stigma which every self-respecting and thoughtful woman must resent, and so must any man who is forced to swear before the altar that he will "honour" his wife.

Granting the franchise to women will also remove that anomaly of taxation without representation, which we declare in the case of men to be tyranny, and it will increase the honesty of our claim to be a free nation.

It is not only to elevate the position of all women and to aid the wage-earner and the poor that the suffragists desire a particular share in the legislation of the country. By introducing a new and practical interest into the narrow lives of that large section of women whose ideas at present do not extend beyond their attire, their household, and their domestic or love affairs, or those of their acquaintances, they hope gradually to do away with the pettiness, the narrowness which generations of such limited interests have engendered.

One notable and most desirable effect of this demand for the elevation of women which is already perceptible, is the drawing together of women of all classes of society and politics in one common bond. In the suffragist processions are to be seen walking together the peeress and the laundry girl, the university woman and the factory hand, the mistress and the maid. There is nothing of condescension or servility on either side, and this condition is characteristic of the whole movement.

It will be seen then that the granting of the suffrage to women would produce no great political or social revolution. The demands are all moderate, just and elevating, for man and woman alike. Women desire to forward the progress of humanity towards a higher and purer civilisation which will include the whole race. Thus the modern woman having shaken off much of her dangerous ignorance, her helplessness, her weak sentimentality and artificiality, will become an ennobling and straightening influence in national as well as domestic life.

MISCELLANEOUS FACTS AND FIGURES

WOMEN'S SOCIETIES AND INSTITUTIONS

POLITICAL ASSOCIATIONS

The Women's Liberal Federation, 72 Victoria Street, London, S.W., and nearly 700 branches.

Women's Amalgamated Unionist and Tariff Reform Association, 13A George Street, Hanover Square, and many branches.

Women's National Liberal Association, 138 Palace Chambers, London, S.W.

Scottish Women's Liberal Federation, 7 West George Street, Glasgow.

Women's Free Trade Union, 185 Palace Chambers, Westminster.

The Primrose League, 64 Victoria Street, London, S.W.

LOCAL GOVERNMENT

Women's Local Government Society for the United Kingdom, 17 Tothill Street, Westminster.

Women Guardians and Local Government Association, 8 Kinnaird Road, Withington.

Yorkshire Ladies' Council of Education, 7 Cookridge Street, Leeds.

Appointment of Women to Public Boards, 83 Bath Street, Glasgow.

Irish Women's Local Government Association, 125 Lunster Road, Rathmines, Dublin.

WOMEN'S NON-POLITICAL ASSOCIATIONS

The International Council of Women, with which national councils in all parts of the world are affiliated. This Association provides a means of communication between women's societies in all countries. The British Branch is known as :—

The National Council of Women of Great Britain and Ireland.—Parliament Mansions, Westminster, London. There are also many branches.

Women's Industrial Council, 7 John Street, Adelphi, London, W.C. Its aim is to improve the industrial conditions of women.

Scottish Council for Women's Trades, 58 Renfield Street, Glasgow.

Women's Co-operative Guild, 66 Rosslyn Hill, London, N.W.

Women's Institute, 92 Victoria Street, London, S.W., for women and others engaged or interested in professional, educational, and other work, lectures, conferences, &c.

Victoria League, 2 Millbank House, London, S.W. An association of British men and women formed with the object of promoting a close understanding between British subjects all over the world.

Society of Women Journalists, 1 Clifford's Inn, London, E.C.

National Union of Teachers, 67 and 71 Russell Square, London, W.C.

Teachers' Guild of Great Britain and Ireland, 74 Gower Street, London, W.C.

Association of Head Mistresses, 92 Victoria Street, London, S.W.

Joint Agency of Women Teachers, 74 Gower Street, London, W.C.

Association of Assistant Mistresses in Secondary Schools, 23 Berners Street, London.

Women's Agricultural and Horticultural Union, 64 Sloane Street, London, S.W.

Association of Women Pharmacists, Gordon Hall, Gordon Square, London, W.C.

Association of Registered Medical Women, New Hospital for Women, Euston Road, London.

Scottish Association for Medical Education of Women, Edinburgh.

Women's Sanitary Inspectors' Association, to protect the interest of sanitary inspectors and health visitors. Honorary Secretary, Miss M. Portlock, 42 Lordship Park, London, N.

PHILANTHROPIC SOCIETIES

Women's Imperial Health Association, the object of which is to teach women and girls the importance of personal and domestic hygiene. Caravan tours are conducted through rural districts for this purpose.

London Biblewomen and Nurses' Mission, 25 Russell Square, W.C.

Society for the Relief of Distressed Widows, 32 Sackville Street, London, W.

Associated Societies for the Protection of

Women and Children, 60 Haymarket, London, S.W.

Governesses' Benevolent Institution and Registration Offices, 47 Harley Street, London, W.

Society for the Relief of Widows and Orphans of Medical Men, 11 Chandos Street, Cavendish Square, London, W.

Little Sisters of the Poor, St. Joseph's House, Portobello Road, Notting Hill, London, W. A Roman Catholic order which undertakes the care of the aged poor.

Heartsease Society, 17 Moore Street, Cadogan Square, London.

Gentlewomen's Work Society, 55 Church Road, Norwood, S.E. For gentlewomen of limited means.

TEMPERANCE ASSOCIATIONS

British Women's Temperance Association, 47 Victoria Street, London, S.W. President, the Countess of Carlisle.

Women's Total Abstinence Union, 4 Ludgate Hill, London, E.C.

World's Women's Christian Temperance Union.—President, the Countess of Carlisle.

United Kingdom Band of Hope Union, 60 Old Bailey, London, E.C.

Young Abstainers' Union, 33 Henrietta Street, Strand, London, W.C.

FOR CHILDREN AND YOUNG GIRLS

National Society for the Prevention of Cruelty to Children, Leicester Square, London, W.C.

Children's Country Holidays' Fund, 18 Buckingham Street, Strand, London, W.C. It was founded with the view of affording country holidays to children attending public elementary schools when needed.

Children's Protection League, 8 More's Gardens, Cheyne Walk, Chelsea, London, S.W. The aim of the society is to help in the carrying out of existing legislation in regard to child life and to promote further legislation towards rescuing children from dangerous surroundings.

Girls' Friendly Society, 39 Victoria Street, Westminster, London, S.W. A society for girls and young women to encourage mutual help and good citizenship; has homes and employment bureaux for girl workers.

National Society of Day Nurseries, 1 Sydney Street, Fulham, London, S.W. Organised to promote the efficiency of crèches throughout the kingdom.

Guild of the Brave Poor Things, University Settlement, Farncombe Street, S.E., to help crippled men, women and children.

National Vigilance Association and International Bureau for the Suppression of the White Slave Traffic, 161A Strand, London, W.C. This Society has national committees all over Europe actively engaged in furthering its objects. A feature of the work is the sending by the Society of ladies to the chief railway stations and ports in England to meet girls travelling alone to or from this country and give them any assistance they may require. Inquiries are also made by the Society on behalf of girls about to take situations abroad, in regard to the character of their employers.

Ragged School Union and Shaftesbury Society, 32 John Street, Theobalds Row, London, is engaged in all kinds of charitable work for children.

Santa Claus Society, Cholmely Park, Highgate, London, N., provides gifts for sick people in the hospitals and toys for the children.

Girl Guides.—Honorary Secretary Miss Baden-Powell, 116 Victoria Street, London, S.W. The aims of the organisation correspond with those of General Baden-Powell's Boy Scouts, namely, to teach girls the duties of good citizenship and practical self-help.

Travellers' Aid Society, 3 Baker Street, London, W. A society for the protection of young women and girls travelling alone. These may be met by arrangement at railway stations and ports by ladies employed by the society, who will see them to their destination and engage rooms for them, if necessary.

Young Women's Christian Association, 25 and 26 George Street, Hanover Square, London, with branch offices all over the kingdom and also abroad.

LONDON RESIDENTIAL HOMES AND CLUBS

Alexandra House, Kensington.

Boarding-House for Governesses, &c., 223 Elgin Avenue.

Brabazon House, Moreton Street, S.W. Single rooms from 7s. 6d., double rooms 18s. 6d., cubicles 5s. to 7s. Full board 10s. 6d. a week. Breakfast and dinner only with full board on Sundays, 8s. 6d. a week.

Hall of Residents for Students and Professional Gentlewomen, 33 Cheniston Gardens, Kensington, S.W.

Hopkinson House, 88 Vauxhall Bridge Road. Under same management as Brabazon House.

Rudyard House, 52 Longridge Road, Earl's Court. Nine single rooms with board from £1, 1s. weekly. Cubicles from 18s. 6d.

Connaught Club, 134 to 136 Elgin Avenue. Entrance fee 5s. Rooms, furnished and unfurnished, 4s. 6d. to 12s. Board 9s. 6d.

St. George's Hostel for Ladies, 77 and 79 Gloucester Street, Warwick Square, S.W. Board and lodging (cubicles) from 14s. Rooms (single) 19s. to 21s. Bed-sitting-r[illegible] from £1, 2s. 6d.

St. Monica's Hostel, 19 Brooke Street, Holb[illegible] Cubicles with board 12s. 6d., rooms from 14s.

Residential Home and Club.—Miss Lena As[illegible]

well's scheme to provide a home for women connected with the dramatic, musical and artistic professions bids fair to be fulfilled. A large house has been taken in Marylebone Road, and it is anticipated that it will be ready in September. It will provide accommodation for a hundred ladies. The residential rates will be from 15s. to 25s., including cubicle or bedroom, breakfast and dinner.

20th Century Club, 24 and 29 Stanley Gardens, Notting Hill Gate. Terms moderate.

St. Andrew's House Club, 31A Mortimer Street. For nurses and ladies engaged in the medical profession.

French Home for Governesses, 18 Lancaster Gate, London, W.

Roman Catholic Home of Residence for Governesses, Brompton Square, London.

Y.W.C.A., Kent House, 89 to 91 Great Portland Street; **Y.W.C.A. Home,** 8 Kemplay Road, Hampstead, and many others.

FLATS AND RESIDENTIAL CHAMBERS IN LONDON

Chenies Street Chambers, Bloomsbury, W.C.

York Street Chambers, Bryanston Square, W.

Waterlow Court, Hampstead Garden Suburb. Rents of flats from £1, 14s. a month.

Holbein House, Sloane Square, S.W. Rents from £1, 11s. a month.

HOSPITALS FOR GENTLEWOMEN

St. Saviour's Hospital for Ladies of Limited Means, Osnaburgh Street, London, N.W. For terms, &c., apply to the Honorary Secretary.

Hospital for Invalid Gentlewomen, 19 Lisson Grove, London, W.

Hospital for Invalid Gentlewomen, 90 Harley Street, London, 25s. to 50s.

CONVALESCENT HOMES FOR GENTLEWOMEN AND MEDICAL AID SOCIETIES

The Buckmaster Memorial Home for Gentlewomen, Broadstairs.

St. Mary's, Dean Park, Bournemouth.

Lady Smyth's Home, Long Ashton, Bristol.

Home of Rest for Necessitous Gentlewomen, Felixstowe.

Teachers' Home of Rest, Hastings.

Governesses' Convalescent Home, Southport.

Medical Aid Society for Necessitous Gentlewomen, 7 St. Catherine's Precincts, Gloucester Gate, London, N.W., provides medical and surgical aid for gentlewomen of limited means and women workers.

LOAN FUNDS FOR WOMEN

These funds help women who are desirous of training in any special subject and have not sufficient means to do so. The loan was to be repaid in instalments when a post has been obtained.

The following societies have instituted Loan Funds:—

(1) **The Society for Promoting the Employment of Women,** 23 Berners Street, Oxford Street, London.

(2) **The Central Bureau for the Employment of Women,** 5 Princes Street, Cavendish Square, London.

(3) **The Women's Institute,** 92 Victoria Street, London, W.

(4) **The Manchester Employment Association,** 1 Ridgefield, King Street, Manchester.

(5) **Scottish Central Bureau,** 25 Queen Street, Edinburgh.

(6) **Irish Central Bureau,** 30 Molesworth Street, Dublin.

(7) **Gentlewomen's Emergency Fund,** Leeds.

(8) **Guild of Service and Good Fellowship,** La Belle Savage, Ludgate Hill, London.

(9) **Educated Women Workers' Loan Training Fund,** St. Stephen's Chambers, Telegraph Street, London.

Note.—There are many other training funds in connection with training schools and employment bureaux throughout the country.

LADIES' CLUBS

See p. 361.

PLACES OF INTEREST IN LONDON

ART GALLERIES, &c.

Academy, Royal, Burlington House, Piccadilly, W. Open from 1st Monday in May to 1st Monday in August, from 8 A.M. to 7 P.M. Admission 1s. Evenings last week, 6d.

Doré Gallery, 35 New Bond Street, W. Private Gallery.

Dulwich Gallery, Dulwich College, S.E. Free. Open every day from 10 A.M. to dusk. Sundays, July to September, from 2 to 5 P.M.

French Gallery, 120 Pall Mall, S.W. Private Gallery.

Goupil Gallery, 5 Regent Street, S.W. Private Gallery.

Grafton Gallery, Grafton Street, Bond Street, W. Private Gallery.

Guildhall Art Gallery, the Guildhall, King

Street, Cheapside, E.C. Free. Open daily from 10 A.M. to dusk.

Hanover Gallery, 47 New Bond Street, W. Private Gallery.

Leighton House, 2 Holland Park Road, Kensington, W. Tuesdays and Saturdays free; other days 1s. by ticket. Open 10.30 A.M. to 5.30 P.M.

National Gallery, Trafalgar Square, W.C. Thursdays and Fridays, 6d., 11 A.M. to 4 P.M.; other days free from 10 A.M. to 4, 5 or 6 P.M. Sundays from 2 to 4, 5 or 6 P.M.

National Gallery of British Art (Tate Gallery), Grosvenor Road, Millbank, S.W. Tuesdays and Wednesdays, 6d., from 11 A.M. to 4 P.M.; other days free from 10 A.M. to 4, 5 or 6 P.M. Sundays from 2 to 4, 5, or 6 P.M.

National Portrait Gallery, St. Martin's Place, W.C. Thursdays and Fridays, 6d., from 10 A.M. to 4 or 5 P.M.; other days free from 10 A.M. to 4, 5 or 6 P.M. Sundays from 2.30 to 5.30 P.M., or until dusk in winter.

New Gallery, 121 Regent Street, W. Admission 1s.

Royal Institute of Oil Painters, 195 Piccadilly. Admission 1s.

Royal Institute of Painters in Water Colours, 195 Piccadilly, W.

Royal Society of Painters in Water Colours, 5A Pall Mall East, S.W.

Royal Society of British Artists, Suffolk Street, Pall Mall East, S.W. Admission 1s.

Wallace Collection, Hertford House, Manchester Square, W. Tuesdays and Fridays, 6d.; other days free. Open from 10 A.M. (excepting Monday 12 noon) to 4, 5 or 6 P.M. Open Sundays from 2 P.M.

CATHEDRALS, CHURCHES, &c.

Brompton Oratory, Brompton Road, South Kensington, W. This well-known Roman Catholic Church is a fine example of the Italian Renaissance style of architecture, and is noted for the beautiful musical services held there.

Chapel Royal, Color Court, St. James's Palace, S.W.

Chapel Royal, Savoy, W.C.

City Temple, Holborn Viaduct, E.C. Was built for the late Dr. Joseph Parker. The present minister is the Rev. R. J. Campbell. A service is held every Thursday at 12 noon in addition to the Sunday services.

Great Synagogue, St. James's Place, Aldgate, E.C. Chief Rabbi: Rev. Hermann Adler, D.D.

St. Bartholomew Church, Smithfield, E.C. The oldest and one of the most interesting churches in London. Open daily from 9 A.M. to 5 P.M.

St. George's Cathedral, St. George's Road, Southwark, S.E. Roman Catholic.

St. Paul's Cathedral. The main entrance looks down Ludgate Hill, E.C. This magnificent and colossal edifice took thirty-five years to build, and was completed in 1710. It contains the remains of some of our most famous naval and military heroes and other eminent men. The nave and transepts are open free. Admission to view the Whispering Gallery, Stone Gallery, Clock, and Library, 6d.; Crypt, 6d.; Golden Gallery, 1s.; Ball, 1s.

St. Peter's (Italian Church), Clerkenwell Road, E.C. Roman Catholic.

Southwark Cathedral, lately St. Saviour's, Southwark.

Temple (The) Church, situated in The Temple, off Fleet Street, celebrated for its musical services. Orders for service on Sunday at 11 A.M. may be obtained by writing to the Master of the Temple. Afternoon service at 3 P.M. without orders. Master, Rev. H. G. Woods, D.D.

Westminster Abbey, Old Palace Yard, Westminster, S.W. A magnificent ecclesiastical edifice, founded in the seventh century. From the reign of Edward the Confessor to the present day, without a break, the Sovereigns of England have been crowned in the Abbey; and here also are the tombs and monuments of many of England's monarchs and of numbers of the leading men in English history. Open daily. Ambulatory and Royal Chapels, admission 6d., except Mondays and Tuesdays, which are free days. From November to February the Abbey is closed after the afternoon service.

Westminster Cathedral, Ashley Gardens, S.W. Roman Catholic. When completed, this superb cathedral will be one of the finest of its class in existence. The foundation stone was laid in 1895.

Tabernacle, Metropolitan, Newington Butts (close to Elephant and Castle). In the original building enormous congregations were attracted by the preaching of the late Rev. C. H. Spurgeon. Burnt down in 1898 and rebuilt in 1900.

MEMORIALS, MONUMENTS, &c.

Albert Memorial, facing the Albert Hall, Kensington Road, W. A handsome monument, with gilt bronze statue of Prince Albert and over 150 figures in marble. Erected by Queen Victoria and the people of England in memory of the Prince Consort, at a cost of £120,000.

Cleopatra's Needle, Victoria Embankment, S.W. This famous obelisk, which originally stood before the Temple of Heliopolis, is 68 feet high. It was presented to the nation by Mehemet Ali in 1819, and conveyed to this country by Dr. Erasmus Wilson.

Duke of Wellington's Statue, opposite Apsley House, Hyde Park Corner.

Duke of York's Column, St. James's Park, S.W. A column 120 feet high, surmounted by a statue in bronze of the Duke of York, second son of George III.

Marble Arch. This sculptured arch, with its handsome bronze gates, forms the north-east entrance to Hyde Park, and cost over £80,000. It was designed by George IV. as a porte-cochère to Buckingham Palace, but was re-erected in its present position in 1851.

Monument, at the northern approach to London Bridge. A fluted column of Portland stone, 202 feet high, and ascended by a spiral staircase of 345 steps. It was erected to commemorate the Great Fire of London of 1666, which started at this spot. Admission 3d.

Nelson Column, Trafalgar Square, W.C. A granite Corinthian column 150 feet high, surmounted by a statue of the hero of Trafalgar, erected by the nation to commemorate Nelson's great victory.

Queen Victoria Memorial, in front of Buckingham Palace. Unveiled May 1911.

MUSEUMS

Bethnal Green (Branch of the Victoria and Albert Museum), Cambridge Road, E. Free. Open Mondays, Thursdays, and Saturdays, from 10 A.M. to 10 P.M. Tuesdays, Wednesdays, and Fridays, from 10 A.M. to 4, 5 or 6 P.M., according to the time of year. Sundays from 2 P.M. to dusk.

British, Great Russell Street, Bloomsbury, W.C. Free. Open week-days from 10 A.M. to 6 P.M. Sundays, 2 P.M. to 4, 5, or 6 P.M., according to the time of year.

Carlyle's House, Cheyne Row, Chelsea, S.W. Open daily from 10 A.M. to sunset. Admission 1s.

Horniman, London Road, Forest Hill, S.E. Free. Open daily; week-days, 11 A.M. to 6 or 8 P.M. Sundays, 3 to 9 P.M.

Imperial Institute, South Kensington, W. Opened by Queen Victoria in 1893. Contains interesting collections representing the industries of the British Colonies. Open daily, except Sundays, from 10 A.M. to 4 or 5 P.M. Admission free. The main portion of the building is occupied as the headquarters of the London University.

Indian Museum (part of Victoria and Albert Museum), Exhibition Road, South Kensington, S.W. Free. Open daily. Hours same as Victoria and Albert.

Natural History (Branch of the British Museum), Cromwell Road, South Kensington, S.W. Free. Open week-days from 10 A.M., and on Sundays from 2.30 P.M. Time of closing varies from 4 to 8 P.M.

Practical Geology, Jermyn Street, Piccadilly, S.W. Free. Open week-days 10 A.M. to 4 or 5 P.M. Mondays and Saturdays to 10 P.M. Sundays from 2 P.M. till dusk.

Royal United Service Association, Whitehall, S.W. Admission 6d. (Sailors, Soldiers, and Policemen in uniform free). Open from 11 A.M. to 4 P.M. in winter and 11 A.M. to 6 P.M. in summer.

Science Museum.—Exhibition Road and Imperial Institute Road, South Kensington. Free. For times when open refer to Victoria and Albert.

Sir John Soane's, 13 Lincoln's Inn Fields. Free. Open daily, excepting Mondays and Saturdays, from 10.30 A.M. to 5 P.M. from March to August inclusive.

Victoria and Albert, South Kensington, S.W. Open Mondays, Thursdays, and Saturdays from 10 A.M. to 10 P.M. free. On Tuesdays, Wednesdays, and Fridays, 10 A.M. to 4, 5 or 6 P.M., according to the time of year. Admission 6d. Sundays free from 2 P.M. to dusk.

PRINCIPAL THEATRES

Adelphi, 410 Strand, W.C.
Aldwych, Aldwych, Strand, W.C.
Apollo, Shaftesbury Avenue, W.
Comedy, Panton Street, S.W.
Court, Sloane Square, S.W.
Covent Garden, Bow Street, W.C.
Criterion, Piccadilly Circus, W.
Daly's, Leicester Square, W.
Drury Lane, Catherine Street, W.C.
Duke of York's, St. Martin's Lane, W.C.
Gaiety, 345 Strand, W.C.
Garrick, 2 Charing Cross Road, W.C.
Globe, Shaftesbury Avenue, W.
Haymarket, 7 Haymarket, S.W.
His Majesty's, Haymarket, S.W.
Imperial, Tothill Street, S.W. (closed).
Kingsway, Great Queen Street.
Little Theatre, John Street, Adelphi.
Lyceum, Wellington Street, Strand.
Lyric, 29 Shaftesbury Avenue, W.
New, St. Martin's Lane, W.C.
New Royalty (Théâtre Français), 73 Dean Street, Soho, W.
Playhouse, The, Northumberland Avenue, S.W.
Prince of Wales's, Coventry Street, W.
Princess's, 152 Oxford Street, W. (closed).
Queen's Theatre, Shaftesbury Avenue, W.
St. James's, King Street, S.W.
Savoy, Strand and Embankment.
Scala, Charlotte St., Fitzroy Square, W.
Shaftesbury, Shaftesbury Avenue, W.
Terry's, 105 Strand, W.C. (now a "Picture Palace").
Vaudeville, 404 Strand, W.C.
Whitney, Aldwych, E., Strand, W.C.
Wyndham's, Charing Cross Road, W.C.

CHIEF VARIETY THEATRES

Coliseum, St. Martin's Lane, W.C.
London Hippodrome, Cranbourne Street, W.C.
Palace, Shaftesbury Avenue, W.C.
Palladium, Oxford Circus, W.

OTHER PLACES OF ENTERTAINMENT

Agricultural Hall, Royal, Upper Street, Islington, N. Trade and other exhibitions and shows are held here, Cattle Show, Dairy Show, and Horse Shows.

Albert Hall, Royal, South Kensington, S.W. Concerts and large Meetings. The hall holds from 8000 to 10,000 people and contains one of the largest organs in the world.

Alexandra Palace, Muswell Hill, N. Exhibitions and various Entertainments. The palace stands in delightful grounds.

Crystal Palace, Sydenham, S.E. Exhibitions, Concerts, &c. Beautiful grounds of 200 acres. First-class Cricket and Football grounds and Athletic tracks. The final tie for the Association Football Cup is held here. Headquarters of the London County Cricket Club, which is managed by Dr. W. G. Grace.

Earl's Court, W. Summer Exhibitions.

Horticultural Hall, Vincent Square, S.W. Exhibitions and Shows held here.

Madame Tussaud's, Marylebone, N.W. Celebrated Waxwork Exhibition.

Olympia, Addison Road, Kensington, W. Large Spectacular Exhibitions, including Military Tournament.

Queen's Hall, Langham Place, W. Concert Hall.

Steinway Hall, Lower Seymour Street, W. Concert Hall.

St. George's Hall, Langham Place, W. Maskelyne's Home of Mystery.

White City, Shepherd's Bush. Annual Exhibitions held here.

Zoological Gardens, Regent's Park, N.W. Extensive and interesting collection of animals, birds, reptiles, &c.

OFFICIAL BUILDINGS

Bank of England, Threadneedle Street, E.C. The premises are guarded every night by the military.

Central Criminal Court.—It is built on the site of Newgate prison, and takes the place of "The Old Bailey."

Custom House, Lower Thames Street, E.C.

General Post Office, St. Martin's le Grand and King Edward Street, E.C. Here are situated, in a group of lofty and extensive buildings, the headquarters of the enormous postal and telegraphic business of this country.

Greenwich Hospital (now known as the Royal Naval College). The Painted Hall contains a collection of naval relics and pictures. May be viewed free daily.

Greenwich Observatory.—This famous observatory is not open to the public, and cannot be viewed except by special permission of the Astronomer Royal.

Government Offices.

Admiralty, The	Whitehall and St. James's Park.
Board of Trade Offices	
Colonial Office	
Foreign Office	
Home Office	
Horse Guards	
India Office	
Privy Council Office	
The Treasury	
War Office	

Guildhall, King's Street, Cheapside, E.C. Noted for its great civic functions and receptions to foreign potentates and distinguished persons. On the 9th November each year the Lord Mayor's Banquet is held in this historic and interesting building. An excellent Museum and Art Gallery and Free Library are contained in the Guildhall, and are open to the public free daily.

Houses of Parliament, Westminster, S.W. Visitors are admitted to view these beautiful and stately buildings on Saturdays from 10 to 4, except when Parliament is assembled. Admission to the Strangers' Gallery of the House of Commons, when sitting, can be obtained by an order from a Member of Parliament.

Lambeth Palace, Lambeth Palace Road, close to Lambeth Bridge. The town residence of the Archbishops of Canterbury. May be viewed by permission of the Archbishop's Chaplain.

Law Courts, Strand, W.C. A magnificent block of buildings, opened by Queen Victoria in 1872. Visitors are admitted to the public galleries when the Courts are sitting, or may view the Central Hall during the vacation upon application to the Superintendent.

Mansion House, Queen Victoria Street, E.C. This historic building, which dates back to the year 1739, is used as the Official Residence of the Lord Mayor of London.

Mint, Tower Hill, E.C. Upon application, by letter, to the Deputy-Master of the Mint, admission may be obtained to inspect this establishment, where the gold and silver coinage of the realm is produced by wonderful machinery.

Record Office, Chancery Lane, W.C. A splendid block of fire-proof buildings of Tudor architecture, containing priceless national records and State papers, including the celebrated Domesday Book. The public are admitted free of charge.

Royal Exchange, Threadneedle Street and Cornhill, E.C. May be viewed by any one wishing to do so, except during business hours—3.30 to 4.30. Part of the building is occupied by "Lloyd's," known the world over in connection with underwriting and ship insurance.

Royal Hospital, Chelsea, for old and disabled soldiers. Founded 1682.

Somerset House, Strand and Victoria Embankment, W.C., contains numerous Government offices, including Probate Registry Office,

Inland Revenue Office, Audit Office, Office of the Registrar General of Births, Deaths and Marriages, &c. It is a remarkably fine building and one of the largest in London. It cost about £1,000,000 to build.

Stock Exchange, Capel Court, Bartholomew Lane, E.C. The money market for buying and selling Stocks, Shares and Securities. Not open to the public.

Tower of London.—Tower Hill, E.C. This ancient fortress has a most interesting history dating from the time of William the Conqueror. Open daily (Sundays excepted). Mondays and Saturdays free. Admission to view the Armouries, 6d., and the Crown Jewels, 6d.

Westminster Hall.—The entrance to the Houses of Parliament. Originally built by William Rufus, it is one of the oldest and grandest architectural structures in the Metropolis.

Woolwich Arsenal.—Open for inspection by British subjects on Tuesdays and Thursdays by card, to be obtained at the War Office, Pall Mall.

ROYAL PALACES

Buckingham Palace, St. James's Park, S.W. Built by George IV. The London Residence of their Majesties the King and Queen. Not open to the public, but permits to inspect the Royal Stables may be obtained from the Master of the Horse.

Hampton Court Palace, Hampton, Middlesex. This imposing mansion, erected by Cardinal Wolsey, with its beautiful grounds and park, is situate on the Thames, 15 miles from London. The State Apartments, with a choice collection of pictures, are open to the public free of charge daily (except Fridays), Sundays from 2 P.M.

Kensington Palace, Kensington Gardens, W. This Palace is of particular interest as the birthplace of Queen Victoria. The State Rooms are open to the public free daily (except Wednesdays, Christmas Day and Good Friday). Sundays 2 to 6 P.M.

Marlborough House, Pall Mall, S.W. The town residence of Queen Alexandra. It was built in 1708.

St. James's Palace, St. James's Street, S.W. Built by Henry VIII. The official town residence of the Court since the fire at Whitehall in 1698. The Park of the same name was originally the grounds of the Palace, but was opened for the public in 1829.

Windsor Castle, Windsor, Berks. Has been a residence of the British sovereigns since the time of the Conqueror, who began the first building. Many monarchs have added to and altered the original building. When the King is not in residence, the State Apartments are open to the public on Tuesdays, Wednesdays and Thursdays from 11 A.M. to 3 or 4 P.M. The Stables daily from 1 to 2.30 P.M. St. George's Chapel daily, excepting Wednesdays, from 12.30 to 3 or 4 P.M.

THE ROYAL FAMILY

His Most Excellent Majesty George the Fifth, by the Grace of God of the United Kingdom of Great Britain and Ireland, and of the British Dominions beyond the Seas, King, Defender of the Faith, Emperor of India; second son of his late Majesty Edward VII. and Queen Alexandra, born 1865, married 1893 the Princess Victoria Mary of Teck, only daughter of the Princess Mary Adelaide (of Cambridge) by her marriage with Francis, Duke of Teck, succeeded to the throne May 6, 1910, and has issue:—

(1) H.R.H. Edward Albert Christian George Andrew Patrick David, Prince of Wales—born 23rd June, 1894.
(2) H.R.H. Albert Frederick Arthur George—born 1895.
(3) H.R.H. Victoria Alexandra Alice Mary—born 1897.
(4) H.R.H. Henry William Frederick Albert—born 1900.
(5) H.R.H. George Edward Alexander Edmund—born 1902.
(6) H.R.H. John Charles Francis—born 1905.

DESCENDANTS OF QUEEN VICTORIA

(1) H.I.M. Victoria, Empress Frederick of Germany—born 1840, married 1858 Crown Prince, afterwards Emperor of Germany, and left issue of whom the eldest is William II., Emperor of Germany, born 1859, married 1881 to Princess Augusta Victoria of Schleswig Holstein.

(2) The late King Edward the Seventh.

(3) H.R.H. Alice Maud Mary—born 1843, married 1862 to H.R.H. Louis IV., Grand Duke of Hesse, died 1878 and left issue. Alice Victoria, the youngest, born 1872, married 1894 H.I.M. the Czar of Russia. They have four daughters and one son.

(4) H.R.H. Alfred Ernest Albert, Duke of Edinburgh, and Duke of Saxe-Coburg-Gotha—born 1844, married 1874 the Grand Duchess Marie Alexandrovna of Russia, died 1900, and left issue one son and four daughters. The eldest daughter, Marie, married Ferdinand, the Crown Prince of Roumania.

(5) H.R.H. Helena Augusta Victoria—born 1846, married 1866 to Prince Frederick

Christian, C.A. of Schleswig-Holstein, and has issue.

(6) H.R.H. Louise Carolina Alberta—born 1848, married 1871 the Marquis of Lorne, now Duke of Argyll.

(7) H.R.H. Arthur William Patrick Albert, Duke of Connaught—born 1850, married 1879 Princess Louise Margaret of Prussia, and has issue. The eldest daughter, Margaret, married 1905 the Crown Prince of Sweden.

(8) H.R.H. Leopold George Duncan Albert, Duke of Albany—born 1853, married Princess Helen, daughter of the late Prince George of Waldeck, died 1884 and left issue—Leopold, Duke of Albany and Duke of Saxe-Coburg, and Princess Alice Mary (Princess Alexander of Teck).

(9) H.R.H. Beatrice Mary Victoria Feodora—born 1857, married 1885 to Prince Henry Maurice of Battenberg, who died 1896, and left issue. The only daughter, Victoria Eugenie, married 1906 H.M. King Alphonso of Spain, and has issue two sons and one daughter.

DESCENDANTS OF EDWARD VII.—ALEXANDRA OF DENMARK

(1) H.R.H. Albert Victor Christian Edward of Wales, Duke of Clarence and Avondale—born 8th January, 1864, died 14th January, 1892.

(2) H.M. King George V.

(3) H.R.H. Louise Victoria Alexandra Dagmar, Princess Royal, Duchess of Fife—born 1867, married 1889 to the Duke of Fife. They have two daughters—H.H. Princess Alexandra, born 1891, and H.H. Princess Maud, born 1893.

(4) H.R.H. Victoria Alexandra Olga Mary—born 1868.

(5) H.R.H. Maud Charlotte Mary Victoria—born 1869, married 1896 to Haakon, King of Norway. They have one son, Alexander Edward Christian Frederick (Olaf), born 1903.

(6) H.R.H. Alexander John Charles Albert, born 6th April, died 7th April 1871.

THE CONSTITUTION AND ADMINISTRATIVE GOVERNMENT OF THE BRITISH EMPIRE

The country is governed by a Sovereign Parliament consisting of three interdependent parts—the Crown, the Lords, and the Commons. From a legal point of view it should be remembered that Parliament includes the King as well as the two Houses.

The Crown.—The King has certain rights, powers, and prerogatives which enable him to do certain things without the concurrence of the Lords and Commons. He has the right of making treaties with foreign sovereigns and states, although in practice the King never makes any treaty except on the advice of his Ministers. The King has also the prerogative right of making war on foreign states, although he does not exercise this right except through the instrumentality of his Ministers. The creation of Peers, conferring of the order of knighthood and various other orders and titles, together with the regulation of the order of precedence, also form part of the royal prerogative, although in practice appointments are made and honours conferred by the King after consultation with his Ministers.

When the owners of land die intestate and without heirs, the Crown succeeds to the property. The Crown has also a prerogative right to gold, silver, or other treasure found in the soil in cases where the true owner is unknown.

The Crown has also the right of pardoning persons convicted of crimes—a right, however, which is only exercised upon the advice of the Home Secretary. It is also a constitutional precept that "The King can do no Wrong," consequently it is impossible to take any proceedings against the King for any crime or tort. If, therefore, property has come into the possession of the Crown which rightly belongs to a subject, the latter can only proceed by way of petition, which is drawn up and left at the Home Office for His Majesty's fiat (permission to proceed). When the fiat is granted the petition is heard in the High Court of Justice and judgment given upon it in the same manner as in the case of actions between subject and subject.

House of Lords.—The House of Lords or the Upper House of Parliament consists of the Lords Spiritual and Temporal. The number of Peers who sit in the House of Lords is not fixed. Peers are members of the House of Lords by hereditary right. Hereditary peerages are continually becoming extinct through the death without heirs of the holders, but this continual and gradual decrease in their numbers is more than made up again by the creation of new Peers. The House of Lords has the power of amending or rejecting a Bill passed by the House of Commons. They cannot, however, amend a "Money Bill," and their legal right to reject this is practically obsolete. The refusal of the House of Lords in 1909 to pass the Budget until a General Election had taken place upon it raised the great constitutional question whether the House of Lords had the right to reject the Budget. In 1910 a conference of the Government and the Opposition met to consider the question so raised, but they failed to arrive at an agreement, and the reform of the House of Lords is a matter now under consideration.

The House of Commons.—The House of Commons consists of 670 members who are elected to represent their constituencies. At the opening of Parliament the Commons are called to the bar of the Upper House and directed to elect a Speaker, and the first duty of members after the election of their Speaker is to take the oath of allegiance. The House arranges its own sittings and can always alter the arrangements. Of the three portions of our Sovereign Parliament the so-called Lower House is undoubtedly constitutionally the most important. The Commons are an elected body, and since the electors are drawn from practically every class of the community, the political opinions of the House of Commons fairly represent, as a rule, the opinions of the majority of the nation. In fact, it may be said that the House of Commons rule the country subject to the power of the Crown and the House of Lords to check party and ill-considered action.

Party Government.—It has always been the practice of the various individuals who constitute the two Houses of Parliament to organise themselves into parties for the purpose of securing legislation according to their opinions, as opinions are only passed into law when backed by strong majorities. From the larger of the two leading parties in the House the executive Government is formed, the duty of criticising their policy and administrating Acts falling to the smaller party known as the "Opposition."

Cabinet and Premier.—The Cabinet is a body composed of the heads of the chief executive department who are jointly responsible for the government of the country. The chief of the Cabinet and the head of the Parliamentary executive is called the Prime Minister.

The Ministry.—His Majesty's Ministers are now always appointed on the advice of the Premier, and consist of some forty or more persons, rather less than half of whom form the Cabinet. The Ministry is drawn from the predominant party in Parliament, the majority being chosen from the House of Commons. If the Secretary of State for any of the great departments is a member of the House of Lords, it is usual for the department to be represented in the House of Commons by the corresponding Under-Secretary, whose duty it is to answer questions respecting the policy of the department.

COLONIAL GOVERNMENT

Different colonies are governed in different ways; all are under the Crown, but they are not all subject to the control of the British Parliament.

Sir William Anson in his "Law and Custom of the Constitution" groups the systems of government for different colonies into four great classes:—

(1) *Colonies with no legislature.* For these the Crown legislates by means of Orders in Council, usually counter-signed by the Secretary of State, the executive powers being vested in a governor appointed by the Crown on the advice of the Ministry. Gibraltar is perhaps the best-known instance of this class of colony.

(2) *Colonies with a nominated legislature.* In each of these there is a governor and executive and legislative councils, all the members of which are nominated either by the Crown or by the governor. The best-known instance of this class are the Straits Settlements of Singapore, Penang, and Malacca.

(3) *Colonies with an elected legislature and a nominated executive.* Even in these colonies, of which the Bahamas are an instance, a portion of the legislature is nominated by the Crown.

(4) *Colonies with responsible government.* In these the Crown is represented by a governor, who is assisted by two chambers, generally called the Legislative Council and the Legislative Assembly. The assembly is wholly elected by the colonists, whilst the members of the legislative council are in some colonies elected, and in others appointed by the governor on the advice of the executive council, a body nominated not by the Crown but by himself. To this class of colonies belong Canada, Newfoundland, Australia, New Zealand, and United South Africa.

The Home control of the colonies is exercised on behalf of His Majesty by the Colonial Office, through its Secretary of State, and this right of control is exercised over all the British possessions except the Isle of Man, the Channel Islands, and the Indian Empire. Indian affairs are under the control of the Secretary of State of the India Office. The Secretary of State is assisted in advising the Crown by a council of twelve members, none of whom may sit or vote in Parliament. The major part of the council is chosen from persons who have spent at least ten years in India.

PRINCIPAL COLONIES AND THEIR GOVERNORS

Component Parts.	Form of Government.	Government Representative.
British India—	Crown Colony.	Lord Hardinge, G.M.S.I., G.M.I.E., Viceroy and Governor General.
Ceylon	Crown Colony.	Col. Sir H. E. McCallum, R.E., G.C.M.G., Governor.
British America—		
Canada	Self-governed.	Earl Grey, C.M.G., Governor General.
Newfoundland	Self-governed.	Sir R. C. Williams, K.C.M.G., Governor.
British Honduras	Crown Colony.	Col. Sir Eric John Eagles Swayne, K.C.M.G., Governor.
British Guiana	Representative Government.	Sir F. Mitchell Hodgson, K.C.M.G., Governor.
British Australasia—		
New South Wales Victoria Queensland South Australia Western Australia Tasmania	Forming the Australian Commonwealth, a federation of self-governed states.	Earl of Dudley, G.C.M.G., Governor General.
British New Guinea	Administered by the Commonwealth Government.	
New Zealand	Self-governed.	Lord Islington, K.C.M.G., Governor.
British Africa—		
(1) South Africa Cape of Good Hope Natal Orange River Colony Transvaal	Forming the Union of South Africa, a federation of self-governed provinces.	Viscount Gladstone, G.C.M.G., Governor General.
Basutoland	Crown Colony.	
Rhodesia	Administered by Chartered Company.	
Bechuanaland	Protectorate.	

Of the smaller possessions the West Indies, including Bahamas, Jamaica, Windward Islands, Leeward Islands, Barbadoes, Trinidad, and Tobago, are Crown Colonies. In West Africa, Gambia, Sierra Leone, the Gold Coast are Crown Colonies. Northern Nigeria is a Protectorate, and Southern Nigeria a Crown colony and Protectorate. In East Africa we have the East Africa Protectorate, Uganda, Zanzibar, Nyassaland Protectorate, and Somali Coast Protectorate. Gibraltar, the Maltese Islands, and Cyprus in the Mediterranean are Crown Colonies. In the Atlantic Ocean, the Bermuda Islands have a representative government. St. Helena, Tristan da Cunha, Falkland Islands, and South Georgia are Crown Colonies. Ascension Island is governed by the Board of Admiralty. Our possessions in the Indian Ocean include Aden, the Straits Settlements, the Federated Malay States, and several groups of islands. In the Pacific Ocean the British possessions include British Borneo, Hong-Kong, and several island groups.

The self-governed colonies possess legislative assemblies, the members of which are elected by the colonists. The Governor is appointed by the Crown, and is the only official controlled by the Home Government. Crown Colonies are under the direct control of the Imperial Government, and the administration is carried on by governors and officials appointed by the Home authorities. Dependencies are subject to the Government of the colony to which they are subordinate, and are administered by officials appointed by such Government. Protectorates retain a considerable measure of internal independence, under the general influence and direction of British officers, but in their external relations they are completely under British control.

EMPIRE DAY—24TH MAY

On the 24th of May, 1904, a meeting was held in St. James's Hall, London, to establish an Empire Day Festival. Previous to this an Empire Day had been observed as a legal holiday in the Dominion of Canada. Under the name of "Victoria Day" it had been legalised in Natal, Barbadoes, Jamaica, and the Straits Settlements; under the name of "Empress Day" in India, and under the name of "Empire Day" in New Zealand and Newfoundland, but the first Imperial Celebration was held in May 1904. The day chosen is the birthday of our late Queen Victoria, and its aim and object is to develop those bonds of friendly feeling and imperial sentiment which could never be embodied in any treaty or commercial agreement, and to train the rising generation in patriotism and their responsibility towards others.

The great supporter of the movement in Great Britain is the Earl of Meath, who has taken considerable pains to explain the proposal, and to enlist the support of the Home Government and that of the British colonies. The "League of the Empire" has done much to forward the establishment of an Empire Day Festival in all the schools of Great Britain by promoting co-operation between the different colonies in educational affairs. The movement has spread with wonderful rapidity, and the 24th of May is now looked upon throughout the Empire as the birthday of the Empire, and is celebrated as such.

HINTS TO AUTHORS

PREPARATION OF MSS.

The printer's charges for Author's corrections are frequently the cause of great annoyance and dispute, but if the following rules are carried out in preparing the MSS., a considerable amount, if not all, of this annoyance may be prevented.

Use large post quarto or foolscap quarto, as this is the most convenient size of paper for the printer to work from.

Have the paper ruled with lines wide apart to allow of alterations being made distinctly; or a good plan is to have the lines rather close together, and write on every other line.

Have a wide margin on left-hand side for instructions to printer, &c.

When making alterations, strike out the part to be altered and re-write above it. If a long piece is to be altered, it is well to strike out the old part and say, "See (A)," and re-write on a separate sheet, marking the new part "To go at (A), sheet. . . ."

Number the sheets as you go along.

Write on one side of the paper only.

Do not crowd a number of lines at foot of a sheet after the last ruled line. Start a fresh sheet if only for two or three lines.

Write as plainly as possible, giving special attention to proper names, foreign words, &c., and all words that the compositor may easily mistake.

Typewritten copy is the most easily read.

Give full instructions to the printer as to type to be used, and the marks you use for his guidance (*e.g.* set in minion, words underlined to be in italics, those doubly underlined in clarendon). This should be put on the first sheet of every portion of copy sent. It is best to write all instructions in red ink.

Put extracts quoted from other works in the *next size* smaller type.

Remember that the compositor will follow your punctuation, use of capitals, spelling (of words that are spelt in two different ways, as almanack, &c.), unless you instruct him otherwise.

Fasten the sheets together, being careful that they are all there and in order.

Mark distinctly on the MS., or "copy," what it is for and by whom sent. Also give instructions where the proofs are to be sent when ready.

PRINTERS' TECHNICAL TERMS

Broadside.—A sheet of paper not folded, but printed as one page the whole size of the sheet.

Composing.—Setting up the type ready for printing. The mechanic who does this is called a Compositor.

Distributing.—Breaking up the type after the printing is done and returning each type to its proper box. This takes about half as long to do as the composing.

Folio.—The number of a page. The size of a sheet of paper folded once, making two leaves or four pages.

Forme.—When the make-up is complete, a number of pages (generally sixteen or some multiple of sixteen) are brought together and *locked up* into one complete, rigid piece, ready to place on the machine. This is known as *a Forme*, and from this the actual printing is done.

Fount.—A batch of type of the same size with the proper proportions of the different letters, &c. (*i.e.* so many a's, so many b's, &c.).

Headline.—The top line of a page, usually containing the title of the book or chapter, and the folio.

Imposing.—Arranging the pages on the machine so that when printed and the sheet is *folded* the pages will come in proper sequence.

Imprint.—The name of the printer or publisher, or both, at the end of the publication and on the title page.

Inset.—Pages that are sometimes printed as alterations or additions, after a publication has been printed, and inserted during the binding operations.

Make-up.—When the whole of the matter for a publication has been set up into type, it has to be arranged into pages. This is called the *make-up*, and is done by the author and sent to the printer.

Octavo (8vo).—Denotes a sheet of paper folded three times, making eight leaves or sixteen pages.

Proof.—When the author's copy has been set up into type, a *proof* is printed from the type and sent to the author. This proof is corrected by the author and returned to the printer, who makes the corrections and sends a *revised proof* to the author. If necessary, this process is gone through again (there may be second and third revised proofs), but when the author is finally satisfied with the proof he marks it *press*, and this is the *press proof* from which the publication is printed.

Quarto (4to).—Denotes a sheet of paper folded twice, making four leaves or eight pages.

Register.—The printer has to put the type for the different pages on the machine in the exact position that they should print on the sheet, and in such a way that the pages on the opposite sides of the sheet should exactly back one another. This is called the *Register*.

Set off.—Sheets that are just printed sometimes come in contact with other sheets, and the wet ink makes an impression on these other sheets. This is called a *set off*.

Signature.—A sign (usually a letter or figure) on the first page of each sheet to show the binder the sequence of the sheets.

Stet.—If any part of a manuscript or proof is struck out by mistake, the word *stet* placed against it shows that the part struck out should stand.

SIZES OF TYPE

The size of a type is the depth of the type and gives the number of lines that can be got on a page. Each size, however, is made with what is known as a different "face," *i.e.* the letters are of different widths, and therefore one style of any size of type will give more words to a line than another style of the same size.

The examples given in the opposite column are all of the same "face."

The name of a type is its size, and each size has at least three different styles; these are "Roman," "Clarendon," and "Italics," and each of these three has its Large Capitals and Small Capitals. The "Roman" is the ordinary type, the others being used to emphasise any words or sentences.

Excepting the last four, the examples given in the following column are "Roman," the first letter "T" being a Large Capital. The last three examples show the Roman Small Capitals, Clarendon, and Italics of Minion type.

There are various styles for headings and titles, but it is better to arrange these with the printer from what he has in stock or can obtain.

The Typewriting Type is an imitation of typewriting copy and is used for Circular Letters, &c.

Printers measure the length of a line by the number of ems that the line will take. Although the types vary in width it may be taken that

$4\frac{1}{3}$	ems of	Great Primer	=	1 inch.
$5\frac{1}{2}$	,,	English	=	,,
6	,,	Pica	=	,,
7	,,	Small Pica	=	,,
$8\frac{2}{3}$	,,	Long Primer	=	,,
$9\frac{1}{2}$	,,	Brevier	=	,,
12	,,	Nonpareil	=	,,
$17\frac{1}{3}$	,,	Diamond	=	,,

It can also be reckoned that

One line of	Double Pica	=	2 lines of	Small Pica.
,,	Great Primer	=	,,	Bourgeois.
,,	English	=	,,	Minion.
,,	Pica	=	,,	Nonpareil.
,,	Long Primer	=	,,	Pearl.
,,	Bourgeois	=	,,	Diamond.

DIAMOND.

The size of a type gives the number of lines that can be got on a page.

PEARL.

The size of a type gives the number of lines that can be got on a page.

NONPAREIL.

The size of a type gives the number of lines that can be got on a page.

MINION.

The size of a type gives the number of lines that can be got on a page.

BREVIER.

The size of a type gives the number of lines that can be got on a page.

BOURGEOIS.

The size of a type gives the number of lines that can be got on a page.

LONG PRIMER.

The size of a type gives the number of lines that can be got on a page.

SMALL PICA.

The size of a type gives the number of lines that can be got on a page.

PICA.

The size of a type gives the number of lines that can be got on a page.

ENGLISH.

The size of a type gives the number of lines that can be

GREAT PRIMER.

The size of a type gives the number of lines that

DOUBLE PICA.

The size of a type gives the number of

TYPEWRITING TYPE.

The size of a type gives the number of lines that

MINION SMALL CAPS.

THE SIZE OF A TYPE GIVES THE NUMBER OF LINES THAT CAN BE GOT ON A PAGE.

MINION CLARENDON.

The size of a type gives the number of lines that can be got on a page.

MINION ITALICS.

The size of a type gives the number of lines that can be got on a page.

HOW TO MARK A PROOF FOR CORRECTION.

1. OATMEAL is to to many people indigestible, very/though nourishing
2. if it can be digested
3. OATMEAL water is made by placing a hanpful of oatmeal in a
4. muslin bag andallowing it to soakin a gallon of water and then boiling
5. for twenty minutes. The upper portion is then poured off gently.
6. OBESITY literally on account of eating "—is the term used to denote
7. an undue accumulation of fat in the body. thecauses of obesity vary;
8. heredity is responsible in some cases, but unsuitable
9. diet in most cases. The anæmic shop-girl or draper's assistant, whose
10. mid-day meal is t ea and buns instead of meat, is often fat. Many
11. other examples will occur to the reader. OPHTHALMIA. In-
12. flammation of the inner surfac of the eyelids. (See Eye.)
13. OPIUM is the dried juice of the white poppy. It contains resin, and other bodies.

THE ABOVE PROOF AFTER CORRECTION.

OATMEAL is to many people indigestible, though very nourishing if it can be digested.

OATMEAL WATER is made by placing a handful of oatmeal in a muslin bag and allowing it to soak in a gallon of water for an hour and then boiling for twenty minutes. The upper portion is then poured off gently.

OBESITY, literally "on account of eating"—is the term used to denote an undue accumulation of fat in the body. The causes of obesity vary; heredity is responsible in some cases, but unsuitable diet in most cases. The anæmic shop-girl, whose mid-day meal is tea and buns instead of meat, is often fat. Many other examples will occur to the reader.

OPHTHALMIA. Inflammation of the inner surface of the eyelids. (See *Eye.*)

OPIUM is the dried juice of the white poppy. It contains morphine, codeine, resin, and other bodies.

EXPLANATIONS OF THE CORRECTIONS.

Corrections In Copy	In Margin	Explanation	See Lines
		Delete or omit the words or letters, &c., struck out	1, 8, 9, 10
	Small Caps	Put words underlined in small capital letters	3
	#	Divide the words	4, 7
	Eq	Equalize the spaces shown	5
		Insert the words or letters, &c., shown in the margin	4, 6, 12
		Insert inverted-commas or asterisk, &c., where shown	6
	X	Take out bad letter and replace with good one	7
	=	Put straight	8
		Correct word or letter, &c., as shown in margin	6, 9
	⊙	The full-stop is shown in a circle	11
		Close up	10
	wf	Wrong fount, i.e. a wrong-sized type is used and must be altered	10
	⊏	Bring the word or letter, &c., to where shown	11
	tr	Transpose	1
		Reverse letter	3
	l.c.	Lower case, i.e., use small letters, not capitals	5
	? Space	See if there is too much (or too little) space between these lines	5, 6, 10, 11
	Cap	Letter underlined should be a capital	7
	Clar	Put words underlined in clarendon type	7
	run on	Continue in the same line	8, 9
	N.P.	This word should start a new paragraph	11
	Italics	Put words underlined in italics	12
	stet	Do not omit the parts struck out	13

When the ends of the lines are uneven, draw lines as shown on right hand margin. If there is not room opposite the line, in the margin, a correction can be put anywhere, but a line must be drawn from the error to the correction . . 13

MEANING OF GIRLS' CHRISTIAN NAMES

H=Hebrew. G=Greek. L=Latin. K=Keltic. T=Teutonic.

Abigail (H.), father's delight, exultation.
Ada or **Adah** (H.), ornament, happiness.
Adelaide (H.), noble maiden.
Agatha (G.), good.
Agnes (L.), a lamb, pure, chaste.
Aileen or **Eileen** (G.), light.
Alice (T.), noble.
Alexandra (G.), a helper of men.
Amelia (T.), industrious, energetic.
Amy (L.), beloved.
Angelina (G.), angelic.
Anna, Anne, Annie (H.), grace, mercy.
Augusta (L.), majestic.
Aurora (L.), dawn.
Barbara (G.), foreign, strange.
Beatrice (L.), making happy.
Bella (L.), beautiful.
Belinda (L.), charming, a serpent.
Bertha (T.), bright.
Blanche (F.), white, fair.
Bessie, from " beth" in *Elizabeth*.
Caroline, Carlotta, Charlotte, fem. of *Carolus* (L.), for Charles, noble spirited.
Catherine (G.), pure.
Charity (G.), love.
Christabel (G.), following Christ.
Christine, Christiana, fem. of *Christian*.
Clara (L.), clear, bright.
Clarissa (L.), most bright.
Claudia (L.), lame.
Constance, fem. of *Constantine*.
Cora (G.), a maiden.
Cordelia (K.), a sea-jewel.
Cornelia (L.), horn.
Daphne (G.), a laurel tree.
Deborah (H.), a bee.
Denise (G.), a reveller.
Diana (L.), a goddess; the moon.
Dinah (H.), judged.
Dora (G.), a gift.
Dorcas (G.), a gazelle.
Dorothea, Dorothy (G.), the gift of God.
Elizabeth, oath (solemn promise) of God.
Ellen, a form of *Helen*.
Emily, a form of *Amelia*.
Eric (T.), kingly.
Estelle, star.
Esther (H.), a star.
Ethel (T.), noble.
Euphemia (G.), well spoken of.
Eva, Eve (H.), life.
Evangeline, a bearer of good news.
Eveline, short form of **Evangeline**.
Felicia, happy.
Flora (L.), flower.
Florence (L.), flourishing, blooming.
Frances (T.), free woman.
Frederica (T.), peaceable.
Georgina (G.), a rustic.
Geraldine, skilful with the spear.
Gladys (K.), a fair maiden.
Grace (L.), favour.
Gwendolen, Gwendaline, (K.), white bow, new moon.
Hannah (H.), grace.
Harriet, ruler of the home.
Helen, Helena (G.), torch, fire-brand.
Henrietta (T.), home ruler.
Hilda (T.), warrior maiden.
Hortensia (L.), fond of gardening.
Irene (G.), peace.
Isabella, fair *Eliza*.
Jane, from *Genoa*.
Janet, Janette, little *Jane*.
Jemima (H.), a dove.
Joan, Joanna, Johanna, the Lord graciously gave.
Josephine, may He add.
Kate, Katharine, Kathleen (G.), pure.
Laetitia (L.), joy, gladness.
Laura (L.), bay, laurel.
Lilian (L.), a lily.
Lucy (L.), bright, shining.
Madeline, form of *Magdalen*.
Magdalen (H.), of Magdala.
Margaret, Margery (G.), a pearl.
Martha (H.), a lady.
Mary, Maria, Marian (H.), a form of **Miriam**, that is, bitterness.
Mildred (T.), mild in counsel.
Miranda (L.), one to be admired.
Nancy, form of *Annie*.
Naomi (H.), pleasant.
Octavia (L.), eighth.
Olive, Olivia (L.), olive, peace.
Paulina, Pauline, little.
Phœbe (G.), light.
Phyllis (G.), foliage, a dish of herbs.
Priscilla (L.), ancient.
Psyche (G.), the soul.
Rachel (H.), a ewe-lamb.
Rhoda (G.), a rose.
Rosa, Rosalie (L.), a rose.
Rosabella (L.), a lovely rose.
Ruth (H.), a friend.
Sara, Sarah (H.), a princess.
Selina (G.), the moon.
Septima (L.), seventh.
Sibylla (G.), a prophetess.
Sophia (G.), wisdom.
Stella (L.), a star.
Susan, Susannah (H.), a lily.
Theodora (G.), gift of God.
Theresa, a gleaner.
Una (L.), one.
Ursula (L.), a little bear.
Vera (L.), true.
Victoria (L.), victory, success.
Viola, Violet (L.), a violet.
Virginia (L.), maidenly, chaste.
Wilhelmina (T.), a defender.
Winifred (T.), winning, peace.
Zoë (G.), life or lively.

MEANING OF BOYS' CHRISTIAN NAMES

H=Hebrew. G=Greek. L=Latin. K=Keltic. T=Teutonic.

Aaron (H.), lofty, inspired.
Abijah (H.), one to whom God is a father.
Abraham (H.), great father.
Absalom (H.), father of peace.
Adolphus (T.), noble wolf.
Alan or **Allan** (K.), harmony.
Alexander (G.), a helper of men.
Alfred (T.), all peace.
Algernon, with a beard.
Ambrose (G.), immortal.
Amos (H.), one who bears a burden.
Andrew (G.), a man.
Anthony (L.), worthy of praise.
Archibald (T.), brave and bold.
Arnold (T.), strong and swift.
Arthur (K.), of high birth.
Athelstan (T.), stone of honour.
Augustin, Austin, Augustus (L.), majestic, imperial.

MEANING OF BOYS' CHRISTIAN NAMES—*Continued.*

Baldwin (T.), bold in battle.
Barnabas (H.), son of a prophet.
Bartholomew (H.), a friend.
Basil (G.), royal, kingly.
Bede (T.), a prayer.
Benedict (L.), blessed.
Benjamin (H.), son of the right hand.
Bertram (T.), fair, illustrious.
Boniface (L.), a benefactor.
Caesar (L.), with much hair, blue-eyed.
Caleb (H.), a dog.
Cecil (L.), with dim sight.
Charles (T.), a man, noble spirit.
Christian (L.), a follower of Christ.
Christopher (G.), bearing Christ.
Clarence (L.), illustrious.
Claude, Claudius (L.), lame.
Clement (L.), mild, gentle.
Conrad (T.), resolute, bold in counsel.
Constant, Constantine (L.), firm, steady.
Cornelia (L.), horn.
Cuthbert, known to fame.
Cyril (G.), lordly.
Daniel (H.), God is judge.
David (H.), beloved.
Denis (from Dionysius), the God of wine.
Donald (K.), proud chief.
Douglas (K.), dark, grey.
Duncan (K.), a dark-complexioned chief.
Ebenezer (H.), stone of help.
Edgar, happy in honour.
Edmund, rich protection.
Edward, defender of property.
Edwin, a winner of possessions, rich.
Egbert (T.), bright eye.
Eldred, fierce in battle.
Eleazar (H.), helped by God.
Erasmus (G.), worthy of love.
Eric (T.), kingly.
Ernest (G.), earnest.
Eugene (G.), well born.
Eustace (G.), strong, healthy.
Evan, Welsh for John.
Everard (T.), brave, strong as a boar.
Felix (L.), happy.
Ferdinand (T.), brave, valiant.
Francis, Frank (T.), free.
Frederic, Frederick (T.), peaceful ruler.
Gabriel (H.), hero of God.
George (G.), a farmer, a rustic.
Gerald (T.), skilful with the spear.
Geoffrey, same as Godfrey.
Gilbert (T.), bright as gold.
Godfrey (T.), God's peace.
Godwin (T.), good in battle.
Godwin, fortunate in war.
Gregory (G.), watchful.
Griffith, ruddy.
Guy (G.), good sense, a leader.
Harold, leader of men.
Harry (T.), ruler of the house.
Hector, brave defender.
Henry (T.), see *Harry*.
Herbert (T.), a bright warrior.
Honor (L.), honour.
Horace, Horatio (L.), worthy behold.
Hubert (T.), bright in spirit.
Hugh (T.), high, lofty.
Humphrey, support of peace.
Ivan, Russian for *John*.
Jacob (H.), a supplanter.
James, Jacques, see *Jacob*.
John (H.), the Lord graciously gave.
Jonathan (H.), the Lord hath given.
Joseph (H.), may He add.
Joshua (H.), a Saviour.
Justin (L.), just.
Kenneth (K.), a leader.
Lambert, endowed with land.
Lancelot, little warrior.
Laurence, Lawrence (L.), crowned with laurels.
Leonard (T.), brave as a lion.
Lewis, Louis (T.), brave in battle.
Lionel (L.), a little lion.
Llewellyn (K.), lightning.
Lucius, Luke (L.), bright, shining.
Marcus, Mark (L.), a hammer.
Martin (L.), martial.
Matthew (H.), gift of the Lord.
Maurice, dark in colour, Moorish.
Michael (H.), who is like God.
Nathan (H.), He hath given.
Nathaniel (H.), God hath given.
Nicolas (G.), victorious.
Noël, relating to Christmas.
Norman (T.), a northman, or from Normandy.
Octavus (L.), eighth.
Oliver (L.), olive, peace.
Patrick (L.), of noble birth.
Paul (L.), little.
Peter (G.), a rock.
Philip (G.), a lover of horses.
Ralph, Rodolph (T.), hero of renown, or wolf.
Reginald (T.), powerful ruler.
Richard (T.), stern king.
Robert (T.), famous in counsel.
Roger (T.), powerful, able in counsel.
Roland, Rowland (T.), famous.
Rupert, same as *Robert*.
Samson (H.), sunny.
Samuel (H.), asked of God.
Saul (H.), asked for.
Sebastian (G.), to be reverenced.
Septimus (L.), seventh.
Sidney, a conqueror.
Silas, short for *Silvanus* (L.), sylvan.
Simon, Simeon (H.), famous.
Solomon (H.), peaceful.
Stephen (G.), a crown.
Theodore (G.), gift of God.
Theophilus (G.), a lover of God.
Thomas (H.), a twin.
Timothy (G.), one who fears God.
Tristram (L.), grave, sad.
Uriah (H.), the Lord is light.
Valentine (L.), strong, healthy.
Valeria (L.), a sort of eagle.
Victor (L.), a conqueror.
Vincent (L.), conquering.
Walter (T.), a leader.
Wilfred, strong and peaceful.
William (T.), a defender.

RELATIVE HEIGHT (1) OF MEN, (2) OF WOMEN

A glance at the table below will give a fair idea of what people's weight should be in proportion to their height. The average man or woman grows stouter with advancing years, and slimness is becoming to the young, but to be well-proportioned the fully-developed man or woman should conform to the following standard :—

WOMEN

		Stones.	Pounds.
Five feet	about	7	5
Five feet one inch . . .	,,	7	10
Five feet two inches . .	,,	8	0
Five feet three inches . .	,,	8	7
Five feet four inches . .	,,	9	0
Five feet five inches . .	,,	9	7
Five feet six inches . .	,,	9	13
Five feet seven inches . .	,,	10	6
Five feet eight inches . .	,,	10	12
Five feet nine inches . .	,,	11	2

MEN

		Stones.	Pounds.
Five feet two inches . .	about	9	0
Five feet three inches . .	,,	9	7
Five feet four inches . .	,,	9	13
Five feet five inches . .	,,	10	2
Five feet six inches . .	,,	10	5
Five feet seven inches . .	,,	10	8
Five feet eight inches . .	,,	11	1
Five feet nine inches . .	,,	11	7
Five feet ten inches . .	,,	12	1
Five feet eleven inches .	,,	12	6
Six feet	,,	12	10

POSTAL INFORMATION

INLAND RATES OF POSTAGE

(*United Kingdom, Channel Islands, Orkney, Shetland, and Scilly Isles*)

LETTERS

Not exceeding 4 oz. in weight, 1d. ; for every additional 2 oz., ½d.

Double postage will be charged on delivery for letters posted unpaid, and double the deficiency for letters not sufficiently paid.

Letters may not exceed two feet in length or one foot in width or depth, excepting those to or from a Government Office.

LATE FEE LETTERS

To catch the night mails, inland letters for the country and abroad must be posted in London before 6 o'clock, and in suburban places from half-an-hour to an hour and a half earlier. If, however, an extra ½d. be affixed to the letter, it will be forwarded by the night mails when posted after that hour. The late fee posting time is 7 P.M. at most town branch offices ; 7.30 at General Post Office, and 7.45 at Mount Pleasant. Letters bearing an extra ½d. stamp may also be posted in the letter-boxes affixed to all mail trains to which sorting carriages are attached.

RE-DIRECTION OF LETTERS, &c.

No charge is made for the re-direction of letters, halfpenny packets, post-cards and newspapers, provided they are re-posted not later than the day after delivery (Sundays and public holidays not counted), and that they do not appear to have been opened or tampered with.

Re-directed registered letters must not be dropped into a letter-box, but must be taken to a post-office to be dealt with as registered. No additional postage or registering fee will be charged, provided they are presented for re-registration not later than the day after delivery.

Re-directed parcels are liable to additional postage at the prepaid rate for each re-direction, except in those cases where the original corrected addresses are both within a delivery from the same post-office.

Letters, &c., will not be officially re-directed for a person leaving home temporarily, unless the house be left uninhabited, nor will they be re-directed when addressed to Clubs, Hotels, Boarding-houses, or Lodgings.

NOTICE OF REMOVAL

Notices of removal and applications for letters, &c., to be re-directed by the Post Office authorities must be duly signed by the persons to whom the letters are addressed. Printed forms can be obtained from the post offices, and when filled up and signed should be given to the postmaster or to the postman. Separate notices must be filled up for parcels and telegrams. The Post Office will continue to redirect letters, &c., for a period of one year, but the time may be extended, if desired, on payment of 1s.

POSTE RESTANTE

Letters, &c., addressed to a Poste Restante, to be called for, are retained for one month. If not called for by the end of that time they are sent to the Returned Letter Office to be disposed of. If, however, a letter be addressed to a post office at a seaport town for a person on board a ship bound for that port, it is kept two months. The Poste Restante is only intended for the accommodation of strangers or travellers who have no permanent abode in the town.

Persons applying for Poste Restante letters or parcels should be able to produce some proof of identity. Foreigners should produce their passports.

REGISTRATION OF LETTERS AND PARCELS

The ordinary registration fee for each inland letter, parcel, or other postal packet is 2d., in addition to the postage. The payment of this fee secures compensation in the event of loss or damage up to £5. Compensation up to a limit of £400 may be obtained on the following scale: Fee of 2d., compensation £5; 3d., £20; and after this every additional penny on the fee adds £20 to the amount of compensation, up to the limit of £400.

Registered letters must be handed to an agent of the Post Office, and a receipt obtained. They must not be posted in a letter-box.

Letters containing money must be posted in an envelope supplied for registered letters by the Post Office.

EXPRESS DELIVERY OF LETTERS AND PARCELS

There are three systems for the special delivery of letters and parcels :—

1. *By special messenger the entire distance*, for which the charge is 3d. per mile, or part of a mile (ordinary postage is not charged). Special charges are made where the packet is heavy or bulky, and for long distances where no ordinary public conveyance is available. This is the quickest service, and letters, &c., for Express Delivery are accepted at all the more important post offices. They must bear the word "Express" in the top left-hand corner of the cover.

2. *By special messenger after transmission by post*. By this system letters and parcels are forwarded in the regular course of post, and on arrival at the office of delivery are sent out by Express Messenger. The charge is 3d. per mile, or part of a mile, from the office of delivery, in addition to the ordinary postage. There are special charges as in system No. I.

3. *By special delivery in advance of the ordinary delivery*. Any persons wishing to receive their letters, &c., in advance of the ordinary delivery may have them delivered by special messenger on payment of 3d. per mile for one packet, and a further charge of 1d. for every ten, or less, additional packets.

HALFPENNY PACKETS

Printed or written matter not in the nature of a letter may be transmitted by the halfpenny packet post. The packet must not exceed 2 oz. in weight, and the regulation size is the same as that of letters.

Rules Concerning Halfpenny Packets.—A halfpenny packet must be posted without a cover, or in an unfastened envelope, or cover which can be easily removed to allow of examination. It may be tied with string for security. It must not contain any communication in the nature of a letter. Should any of these regulations not be complied with, the packet will be treated as a letter. If posted unpaid, double postage will be charged.

NEWSPAPERS

The postage is ½d. for every registered daily or weekly newspaper, whether posted singly or with others in a packet. The newspaper must be posted without a cover, or in a cover open at both ends, and must be folded in such a way as to show the title. Nothing in the nature of a letter must be enclosed, but the name and address of the sender may be written on the wrapper, a request for return in case of non-delivery, and a reference to any page in the newspaper to which the sender wishes to call attention.

PARCEL POST

Not over 1 lb.	3d.	Not over 8 lbs.	8d.
" " 2 lbs.	4d.	" " 9 lbs.	9d.
" " 3 lbs.	5d.	" " 10 lbs.	10d.
" " 5 lbs.	6d.	" " 11 lbs.	11d.
" " 7 lbs.	7d.		

Regulations.—No parcel may exceed 11 lbs. in weight, 3 feet 6 inches in length, or 6 feet in length and girth combined. Parcels must not be posted in a letter-box, but must be handed over the counter of a post office, or given to a rural postman, and the postage must be prepaid by postage stamps affixed by the sender. The words "Parcel Post" should be written in the left-hand corner above the address. The sender's name should be on the cover or inside the parcel. A certificate of the posting of a parcel may be obtained at the time, if so desired.

FOREIGN AND COLONIAL POSTAGE RATES

LETTERS

From the United Kingdom (1) to British Possessions generally and to Eygpt, the United States of America, and the places in Morocco where there are British Post Office Agencies the rate of postage is 1d. per ounce; and (2) to all other countries it is 2½d. for the first ounce, and 1½d. for each succeeding ounce or fraction thereof.

REPLY COUPONS

Coupons exchangeable for stamps of the value of 25 centimes (2½d.) each in any country participating in the arrangement can be purchased at any Money Order Office in this country at the price of 3d. each for the purpose of prepaying replies to letters. The coupons can be exchanged by the addressees of such letters at the post office of the place of destination for local postage stamps.

Coupons received from other countries may be exchanged for postage stamps at any Money Order Office in the United Kingdom.

POST-CARDS

Official post-cards are transmissible to all parts of the world, 1d. single, 2d. reply. Inland post-cards may also be used, provided the additional postage is supplied by means of postage stamps. Private post-cards may be sent abroad if they are of the same size and substance as the official cards and have the words "Post Card" printed or written on the address side. Plain cards without any inscription cannot be sent abroad as post-cards.

A post-card from a place abroad, if unpaid, is chargeable with a postage of 2d.; and if partially paid, with double the deficient postage.

PRINTED PAPERS AND SAMPLES

Printed Papers comprise newspapers, books (stitched or bound), periodical works, pamphlets, sheets of music, proofs of printing, plans, maps, engravings, photographs, &c. Printers' proofs, corrected or not, and the corresponding manuscripts when included in the same package, are admitted as "printed papers," but not the products of the copying press and typewriter.

The rate of postage on printed papers for all places abroad is ½d. per 2 oz., and on commercial papers is 2½d. for the first 10 oz., and ½d. per 2 oz. thereafter.

Packets must be posted without a cover, or in an ordinary envelope left entirely unfastened, or in a cover wholly open at both ends. To ensure the safety of the contents, however, the ends of the packet may be tied with string, but it must be easy to unfasten.

Packets must be prepaid; if wholly unpaid the packets will be stopped; if not fully prepaid, double the deficiency will be charged on delivery.

Canadian Magazine Post.—The postage rate on British Newspapers, Magazines, and Trade Journals intended for Canada is 1d. per lb.; on packets not exceeding 2 oz. it is ½d. Such packets must be posted in covers open at both ends and easily removable.

Sample Post.—The rate of postage for all places abroad is 1d. for the first 4 oz. and ½d. per 2 oz. thereafter. Packets containing goods for sale, or articles sent by one private individual to another, cannot be forwarded by Sample Post.

Samples must be sent in such a manner as to be easy of examination and, when practicable, must be sent in covers open at the end. In order to secure the return of packets which cannot be delivered, the names and addresses of the senders should be printed or written outside.

FOREIGN AND COLONIAL PARCEL POST

The rules and regulations for foreign and colonial parcels are similar to the rules for inland parcels, but the sender of each parcel must make a declaration as to its contents for Customs purposes. This declaration must be made on a form provided by the Post Office for the purpose. The sender can prepay all charges to certain countries and places by paying a fee of 6d., signing an undertaking to pay on demand the amount due, and making a deposit of 1s. for each 10s. and fraction of 10s. of the value of the parcel (to Canada and U.S.A. 1s. for each 4s. with a minimum deposit of 5s.), otherwise the Customs and other charges must be paid by the addressee. The size limit to some places abroad differs from that for inland parcels. All parcels must have the fastenings and knots on string carefully sealed.

The rates for postage and also for insurance can be obtained at any post office.

CASH ON DELIVERY

Arrangements have now been made whereby the senders of postal packets exchanged between the United Kingdom and certain British Possessions and Egypt can have the value of the contents collected from the recipients and remitted to them by money order or postal order.

MONEY ORDERS

INLAND

At every Money Order Office Money Orders can be obtained between the hours of 8 A.M. and 8 P.M. The poundage for these orders is:—

For sums not exceeding

£1	£3	£10	£20	£30	£40
2d.	3d.	4d.	6d.	8d.	10d.

No order may contain a fractional part of a penny.

No single Money Order can be issued for more than £40.

A Money Order may be crossed like a cheque for payment through a bank.

TELEGRAPH MONEY ORDERS, INLAND

Money may be transmitted by Telegraph Money Order from any Money Order Office in the United Kingdom, which is also a *despatching* office for telegrams, and may be made payable at any Money Order Office which is also an office for the *delivery* of telegrams.

The charges for Telegraph Money Orders are a Money Order poundage at the ordinary rate for inland Money Orders, with an additional fee of 2d. for each Order and the cost of the official telegram of advice.

POSTAL ORDERS

Postal Orders are issued and paid at all Money Order Offices in the United Kingdom during the ordinary hours of business on week-days, and in certain British Colonies and places at which British Postal Agencies are maintained.

Orders may be had for every 6d. up to 19s. 6d.; and for 20s. and 21s. Those for 6d. up to 2s. 6d. cost ½d. each; after that, up to 15s. the charge is 1d.; after that, to 21s. the charge is 1½d.

By affixing stamps (perforated ones not allowed), not exceeding 5d. in value nor three in number, to the face of any one Postal Order, odd amounts may be made up, but not fractions of a penny. An Order not cashed within three months from the last day of the month of issue will be charged a fresh commission.

FOREIGN AND COLONIAL MONEY ORDERS

For sums not exceeding—

£1	£2	£4	£6	£8	£10
3d.	6d.	9d.	1s.	1s. 3d.	1s. 6d.

and for countries on which Orders may be issued for a larger sum than £10 the charge is 3d. for every additional £2 or portion of £2.

TELEGRAPH MONEY ORDERS

Foreign and Colonial

Telegraph Money Orders may be sent to or from certain places. The charges for those issued in the United Kingdom are the ordinary foreign and colonial Money Order poundage, with the addition of a fee of 6d. and cost of official telegram of advice.

TELEGRAMS

Inland

For the first twelve words, 6d.; for every additional word, ½d. Figures are counted at the rate of five to a word.

Stamps in payment must be affixed by the sender. The address of the receiver is charged for, but not that of the sender, if written on the back of the telegraph form.

The charge includes delivery, provided the address be within the Town Postal limits, or within three miles of a head office. When the address is beyond the free delivery limit, a charge of 3d. for each mile is made, reckoned from the office door. This charge to be prepaid by the sender. Replies not exceeding forty-eight words in length may be prepaid by the sender.

Telegraph forms are of two kinds, the A form (given gratis) with no stamp; and the A1 form embossed with a stamp, which may be purchased singly, or in a book of twenty, price 10s. 2d.

Any one may register an abbreviated address on payment of a fee of 21s. per year.

Telegrams re-directed by wire to a second address are liable to an additional charge.

The usual hours of attendance at Telegraph Offices on week-days are from 8 A.M. to 8 P.M. The usual Sunday attendance in England is from 8 A.M. to 10 A.M.; in Scotland from 9 A.M. to 10 A.M., and in Ireland from 8.25 A.M. to 10.25 A.M.

A few special offices are always open.

CANCELLING TELEGRAMS

The sender may have his telegram cancelled, and if it be cancelled before the commencement of transmission the sum paid will be returned at the time, less a fee of 2d. for cancelling it; but if transmission has commenced, the sum will not be returned. If transmission has been completed, an official telegram, prepaid by the sender, will be sent to the Postmaster at the Terminal Office. If the official telegram should arrive too late, the sender will be informed that the attempt to cancel his telegram has failed, but the sums paid will not be refunded.

FOREIGN AND COLONIAL TELEGRAMS

The following are a few of the charges for the transmission of telegrams abroad.

[Where more than one price is given, the charge varies according to the route, or to the part of the country to which the telegram is sent.]

	Rate per word. s.	d.		Rate per word. s.	d.
Aden	2	0	Italy	0	2½
Algeria	0	2½	Jamaica	3	0
Argentine Republic 3s. 3d. and	3	7	Japan . 4s. 7d. and	4	10
Australia 2s. 9d. and	3	0	Madeira	1	0
Austria	0	2½	Malay Peninsula 3s. 3d. and	3	6
Belgium	0	2	Malta	0	4
Brazil . . . 3s. to	6	5	Morocco . . 3d. to	0	4
British Central Africa	2	11	Natal	2	6
British East Africa 2s. 6d. and	2	9	New South Wales .	3	0
Canada . . . 1s. to	3	2	New Zealand 2s. 9d. and	3	0
Cape Colony . . .	2	6	Norway	0	2½
Ceylon . 1s. 11d. and	2	1	Orange River Colony	2	6
China . . 4s. 2d. to	4	7	Portugal	0	3
Costa Rica	4	2	Rhodesia 2s. 8d. and	2	11
Denmark	0	3	Roumania	0	3
Egypt . . . 1s. to	1	4	Russia	0	4½
France	0	2	Spain . . 3d. and	0	5
Germany	0	2	Sweden	0	3
Gibraltar	0	3	Switzerland	0	2½
Holland	0	2	Transvaal	2	6
Hungary	0	2½	Turkey	0	6
India . 1s. 10d. to	2	0	United States . 1s. to	2	9

Special forms are provided for Foreign and Colonial Telegrams.

TELEPHONES

The Telephone Trunk Lines which connect the various Telephone-Exchange areas throughout the country are the property of the Postmaster-General, and are worked by his officers. The Trunk lines can be used by callers at Post Offices which are connected with the Trunk Telephone system as well as by subscribers and callers using Telephone Exchanges.

The fees for the use of the Trunk lines are as follows :—

For 25 miles or under . . .	Threepence.
" 50 " " . . .	Sixpence.
" 75 " " . . .	Ninepence.
" 100 " " . . .	One Shilling.
" Every additional 40 miles or fraction thereof . .	Sixpence.

The period of conversation is three minutes from the time when the caller has been informed that the connection is completed; but any person, by prepaying a double fee, may secure either the uninterrupted use of a Trunk line for six minutes, or the option of continuing it at the end of three minutes. In the latter case the fee for the second period is refunded when the call is completed in three minutes. No person is entitled to use a Trunk line continuously for more than six minutes.

The charge for a six minutes' conversation between 7 P.M. and 7 A.M. is the same as for a conversation of three minutes' duration in the day-time. All sums payable for the use of a Trunk line must be prepaid. Callers are required to pay the Call Office fee in addition to the Trunk fee.

RADIOTELEGRAPHIC SERVICE

Radiotelegrams are accepted at any Telegraph Office for transmission to ships equipped with wireless telegraph apparatus through different coast stations in the United Kingdom or abroad. The usual charge for a radiotelegram sent through a British Coast Station is 10½d. a word. Further particulars can be had at any Telegraph Office.

TELEPHONE EXCHANGES

The Postmaster-General has Telephone Exchanges in London and at a large number of provincial towns. The rates of subscription in London for the *Ordinary Message-rate Service* (including one telephone at the subscriber's premises) are as follows :—

(*a*) For connection with any Exchange *in* the County of London within two miles of the subscriber's premises, annual subscription £5.

Message Fees : (1) One penny for each call to a subscriber on any Exchange in the County of London. (2) Twopence for each call to a subscriber on any Exchange outside the County of London.

(*b*) For connection with any Exchange *outside* the County of London within two miles of the subscriber's premises, annual subscription £4.

Message Fees : (1) One penny for each call to a subscriber on the same Exchange. (2) Twopence for each call to a subscriber on any other Exchange.

N.B.—The minimum yearly amount payable by each subscriber for Message Fees is 30s.

Any person can use a Call Office in London for a fee of twopence.

TELEPHONIC DELIVERY OF LETTERS IN LONDON ON SUNDAYS

A message posted in the provinces or in London in time to ensure arrival at the General Post Office, London, on Sunday, can be delivered by telephone to a subscriber in the London Exchange area. For the special conditions inquire at any Telegraph Office.

SENDING TELEGRAMS AND EXPRESS LETTERS BY TELEPHONE

Any subscriber to a Telephone Exchange may telephone messages (except those for transmission at Press rate) to many post offices which can be reached through the local Exchange System, or by means of the Post Office Trunk wires, in order that the message may be written down and dealt with as telegrams or express letters or ordinary letters. For special regulations inquire at any Telegraph Office.

TELEPHONE COMMUNICATION WITH FRANCE AND BELGIUM

London and certain provincial towns in England can communicate by telephone with Paris, Brussels, and certain provincial towns in France and Belgium. The fee is from 8s. to 10s. for a conversation of three minutes, the same conditions and regulations in this case as in that of ordinary Trunk line conversations.

PROVINCIAL SYSTEM

The Postmaster-General has Telephone Exchanges at a large number of provincial towns. The terms for Telephone Exchange circuits, and for circuits to post offices for use in connection with the Telephone Trunk lines, may be ascertained on application to the local post office or to the Secretary, General Post Office.

GENERAL INFORMATION

THERMOMETER

To convert Centigrade into Fahrenheit, multiply by 9, divide by 5, and add 32; Réaumur into Fahrenheit, multiply by 9, divide by 4, and add 32; Fahrenheit into Centigrade, deduct 32, multiply by 5, and divide by 9; Fahrenheit into Réaumur, deduct 32, multiply by 4, and divide by 9.

$$F = \tfrac{9}{5}\,C + 32° = \tfrac{9}{4}\,R + 32°.$$

$$R = \tfrac{4}{9}\,(F - 32°) = \tfrac{4}{5}\,C.$$

The following are equivalent degrees:—

Cent.	Fahr.	Réau.	Cent.	Fahr.	Réau.	Cent.	Fahr.	Réau.
100	212	80	60	140	48	20	68	16
95	203	76	55	131	44	15	59	12
90	194	72	50	122	40	10	50	8
85	185	68	45	113	36	5	41	4
80	176	64	40	104	32	Zero	32	Zero
75	167	60	35	95	28	5	23	4
70	158	56	30	86	24	10	14	8
65	149	52	25	77	20	15	5	12

THE SEASONS

Spring commences March 21st and lasts 92 days 21 hours (*Vernal Equinox*).

Summer commences June 22nd and lasts 93 days 14 hours (*Summer Solstice*).

Autumn commences September 23rd and lasts 89 days 17¾ hours (*Autumn Equinox*).

Winter commences December 22nd and lasts 89 days 1 hour (*Winter Solstice*).

The longest day is the 21st of June. The shortest day is the 21st of December. Two days in the year are equally divided into day and night, viz., the 21st of March and the 23rd of September.

FOREIGN AND COLONIAL MONEY

Countries.	Chief Coins.	Approximate value in British money. s.	d.
Argentina	Peso (paper)* = 100 centisimos	1	9
	,, (gold)	4	0
Austria-Hungary	Krone or Crown = 100 heller	0	10
Belgium	Franc = 100 centimes	0	9½
Brazil	Milreis (paper)* = 1000 reis	1	3¼
B. Honduras	Dollar (gold) = 100 cents	4	1
Bulgaria	Leva = franc = 100 stotinkis	0	9½
Canada	Dollar (gold) = 100 cents	4	1
Ceylon	Rupee = 16 annas	1	4
Chile	Peso (paper)* = 100 centavos	0	10
	,, (gold)	1	6
China	100 candareens = 10 mace = tael of silver (a weight)	2	4½
Cuba	Dollar (gold) = 100 cents	4	1
Denmark	Krone = 100 öre	1	1¼
Egypt	Egyptian £ = 100 piastres	20	6¼
Finland	Markka = 100 penni	0	9½
France	Franc = 100 centimes	0	9½
Germany	Mark = 100 pfennige	0	11¾
Greece	Drachmè (paper)* = 100 lepta	0	9
Holland	Florin or Gulden = 100 cents	1	8
India	Rupee = 16 annas	1	4
Italy	Lira = franc = 100 centesimi	0	9½
Japan	Yen = 100 sens	2	0½
Mauritius	Rupee = 16 annas	1	4
Mexico	Dollar (gold) = 100 centavos	2	0
Newfoundland	Dollar (gold) = 100 cents	4	1
Norway	Krone = 100 öre	1	1¼
Peru	Sol = 100 centismos	2	0
Portugal	Milreis = 1000 reis	3	10½
Roumania	Ley = franc = 100 banis	0	9½
Russia	Rouble = 100 copeks	2	1½
Servia	Dinar = franc = 100 paras	0	9½
Spain	Peseta = franc = 100 centimos	0	8½
Straits Settlmnts.	Dollar (silver)	2	4
Sweden	Krone = 100 öre	1	1¼
Switzerland	Franc = 100 centimes	0	9½
Turkey	Turkish £ = 100 piastres	18	0
United States	Dollar (gold) = 100 cents	4	1
Uruguay	Peso (gold) = 100 centimos	4	2

* The exchange value of paper money fluctuates considerably in countries where it is not readily convertible, at its face value, into gold

STANDARD TIME

In Great Britain Greenwich Time is adopted as the *Standard Time* all over the country. The same is also adopted over Belgium, Holland, and Spain. In France, Paris time (now the same as Greenwich) is the standard. In countries of great extent it is impossible to adopt one *Standard Time* and meridians 15° apart have been chosen, and each place within 7½° of these meridians have the same *Standard Time*. Thus, Mid Europe (Sweden, Denmark, Germany, Austria, Switzerland, Italy, and Servia), 1 hour *fast* of Greenwich; East Europe (Roumania, Bulgaria, Turkey, Egypt), 2 hours *fast* of Greenwich; Cape Colony, 1½ hours *fast* of Greenwich; Natal, 2 hours *fast* of Greenwich; India, 5½ hours *fast* of Greenwich; Burma, 6½ hours *fast* of Greenwich; Japan, 9 hours *fast* of Greenwich; West Australia, 8 hours *fast* of Greenwich; South Australia, 9½ hours *fast* of Greenwich; New South Wales, Queensland, Victoria, and Tasmania, 10 hours *fast* of Greenwich; New Zealand, 11½ hours *fast* of Greenwich; America—Newfoundland 4 hours, Eastern 5 hours, Central 6 hours, Mountain 7 hours, and Pacific 8 hours *slow* of Greenwich.

TELEPHONES

The Telephone Trunk Lines which connect the various Telephone-Exchange areas throughout the country are the property of the Postmaster-General, and are worked by his officers. The Trunk lines can be used by callers at Post Offices which are connected with the Trunk Telephone system as well as by subscribers and callers using Telephone Exchanges.

The fees for the use of the Trunk lines are as follows :—

For 25 miles or under . . .	Threepence.
„ 50 „ „ . . .	Sixpence.
„ 75 „ „ . . .	Ninepence.
„ 100 „ „ . . .	One Shilling.
„ Every additional 40 miles or fraction thereof . .	Sixpence.

The period of conversation is three minutes from the time when the caller has been informed that the connection is completed; but any person, by prepaying a double fee, may secure either the uninterrupted use of a Trunk line for six minutes, or the option of continuing it at the end of three minutes. In the latter case the fee for the second period is refunded when the call is completed in three minutes. No person is entitled to use a Trunk line continuously for more than six minutes.

The charge for a six minutes' conversation between 7 P.M. and 7 A.M. is the same as for a conversation of three minutes' duration in the day-time. All sums payable for the use of a Trunk line must be prepaid. Callers are required to pay the Call Office fee in addition to the Trunk fee.

RADIOTELEGRAPHIC SERVICE

Radiotelegrams are accepted at any Telegraph Office for transmission to ships equipped with wireless telegraph apparatus through different coast stations in the United Kingdom or abroad. The usual charge for a radiotelegram sent through a British Coast Station is 10½d. a word. Further particulars can be had at any Telegraph Office.

TELEPHONE EXCHANGES

The Postmaster-General has Telephone Exchanges in London and at a large number of provincial towns. The rates of subscription in London for the *Ordinary Message-rate Service* (including one telephone at the subscriber's premises) are as follows :—

(*a*) For connection with any Exchange *in* the County of London within two miles of the subscriber's premises, annual subscription £5.

Message Fees: (1) One penny for each call to

GENERA[illegible]

THERMOMETER

To convert Centigrade into Fahrenheit, m[illegible] ply by 9, divide by 5, and add 32; Réaumur Fahrenheit, multiply by 9, divide by 4, and 32; Fahrenheit into Centigrade, deduct multiply by 5, and divide by 9; Fahrenh[illegible] Réaumur, deduct 32, multiply by 4, and d[illegible] by 9.

$F = \frac{9}{5} C + 32° = \frac{9}{4} R + 32°.$

$R = \frac{4}{9} (F - 32°) = \frac{4}{5} C.$

The following are equivalent degrees:—

Cent.	Fahr.	Réau.	Cent.	Fahr.	Réau.	Cent.	Fahr.
100	212	80	60	140	48	20	68
95	203	76	55	131	44	15	59
90	194	72	50	122	40	10	50
85	185	68	45	113	36	5	41
80	176	64	40	104	32	Zero	32
75	167	60	35	95	28	5	23
70	158	56	30	86	24	10	14
65	149	52	25	77	20	15	5

THE SEASONS

Spring commences March 21st and las[illegible] days 21 hours (Vernal *Equ*[illegible]

Summer commences June 22nd and las[illegible] days 14 hours (*Summer Sol*[illegible]

Autumn commences September 23rd and 89 days $17\frac{3}{4}$ hours (*Autumn Equ*[illegible]

Winter commences December 22nd and 89 days 1 hour (*Winter Sol*[illegible]

The longest day is the 21st of [illegible] shortest day is the 21st of D[illegible] days in the year are equally divided [illegible] night, viz., the 21st of March and [illegible] September.

INDEX

2 z

Accidents,
Accompanist
Accountancy
Accounts, h
Addressing
Administrat
Advertiseme
ing, 666;
Africa, infor
Afternoon "
Afternoon t
Agents, hou
Agriculture,
Air-cushions
"Aid, first,"
Air gas, 9
Almond pas
Almonds for
Ammonia, f
Anemones,
Annuals, ga
Annuities,
immediate
Ants, exterm
Apoplexy, 5
Apple cream
Apple ginger
Apples and
Apples, vari
Aprons, 313
Armorial bea
Arms, how t
Army, how
the, 643
Arrowroot fo
Art schools,
Artichokes, c
Artist, the ca
Arts for wom
Asparagus, c
Associations
Assurance, 3
Asters, 586
"At Home"
"At Homes,"
tions to, 33
Attendance of
Auction game,
Auriculas, 552
Authors, hints
Aviary, the, 51

Baby, the, 473
476, 478, 479

INDEX

ACIDENTS, first aid in, 573
Acompanist, the, 683
Acountancy as a profession, 666
Acounts, how to balance, 363
Adressing persons of rank, mode of, 354
Aministrators of will, 375
Avertisement designing, 687; hints on answering, 666; writing, 628
Arica, information on South, 663
Aternoon "At Homes," 252; etiquette of, 339
Aternoon tea, 251
Aents, house, women as, 667
Ariculture, women in, 647–657
Ar-cushions, 553
"Aid, first," 548–579
Ar gas, 9
Amond paste, 225
Amcuds for cakes, 225
Amonia, for laundry work, 276
Aemones, 590
Anuals, garden, 581
Anuities, deferred, 371; Government, 372; mmediate, 371
Ats, extermination of, 80
Aoplexy, 573
Aple cream for invalids, 559
Aple ginger, 229
Aples and nuts, game of, 535
Aples, various dishes with, 196
Arons, 313
Amorial bearings, 354, 384
Ams, how to whiten, 450
Amy, how to address officers of, 355; nurses in the, 643
Arowroot for invalids, 559
At schools, 686
Atichokes, cooking of, 149
Atist, the career of the, 686; the fashion, 688
As for women, 682
Aparagus, cooking of, 149
Asociations for children and young girls, 700
Asurance, 371
Asers, 586
"At Home" day, the, 334
"At Homes," 252; etiquette of, 339; invitaions to, 332
Atendance officers, women as, 681
Action game, 533
Ariculas, 582
Athors, hints to, 709
Aiary, the, 514

BABY, the, 473; and the bath, 479; feeding of, 76, 478, 479; weaning of, 477
Baby's basket, 470; binder, 472; clothing, 470, 471; headgear, 444, 445; outfit, 469; vest, 472; washing of clothing, 297
Bacon, treatment of, 100
Badminton, 547
Baking powder, 214
Ball gowns, 304
Balls, county, 341; etiquette of, 340; invitations to, 332; public, 341
Bandeaux, 433
Bank of England, the, 369
Bank manageress, how to become, 666; notes, 366; rate, 369; Savings (Post Office), 369
"Bank Return," the, 369
Banking account, how to open, 366; hints on, 366–370
Bankruptcy, law of, 370
Barracoat, the, 473
Baseball, game of, 546
Bassinette, baby's, 469; cost of, 469; how to trim a, 469
Basting of garments, 388
Bath, baby's, 480; child's, 479; hip and sponge, 448; hot air, 564; how to enamel, 607; mustard foot, 564; soda, 564; steam face, 451; sulphur, 564; vapour, 564
Bath-room, the, 33; cleaning of, 61
Baths, 447; in illness, 564; rubber camp, 448; salt (at home), 448; sea, 448
Beans, cooking of, 150; French, how to cook, 152; haricot, how to cook, 153
Beauty specialists, 669
Bed covers, 259; cradle, 560; how to make patient's, 551; linen, 257; pans, 560; rest, 560; sores, 567; table, 560
Bedding, 31; in sick-room, 549
Bedroom, decoration of, 32; furniture, 29, 32; spring cleaning of, 81; ventilation of, 453; colour schemes for, 16
Beds, care of, 68; making of, 67; water, 553
Bed-sitting-room, furnishing a, 33
Bedsteads, cleaning of, 68
Beef, collops, 168; creams, 169; darioles of, 179; how to choose, 107; how to serve, 245; juice, 558; olives, 169; roast, 168; roll, glazed, 179; Russian steaks, 170; salt, boiled, 167; sandwiches for invalids, 559; steak, 168; steak and kidney pie, 181; steak and kidney pudding, 181; tea, 558; use of different joints, 108
Bee-keepers' Association, 655
Bee-keeping for women, 654
Beetles, extermination of, 78
Beetroot, cooking of, 150

INDEX

ACCIDENTS, first aid in, 573
Accompanist, the, 683
Accountancy as a profession, 666
Accounts, how to balance, 363
Addressing persons of rank, mode of, 354
Administrators of will, 375
Advertisement designing, 687; hints on answering, 666; writing, 628
Africa, information on South, 663
Afternoon "At Homes," 252; etiquette of, 339
Afternoon tea, 251
Agents, house, women as, 667
Agriculture, women in, 647–657
Air-cushions, 553
"Aid, first," 548–579
Air gas, 9
Almond paste, 225
Almonds for cakes, 225
Ammonia, for laundry work, 276
Anemones, 590
Annuals, garden, 581
Annuities, deferred, 371; Government, 372; immediate, 371
Ants, extermination of, 80
Apoplexy, 573
Apple cream for invalids, 559
Apple ginger, 229
Apples and nuts, game of, 535
Apples, various dishes with, 196
Aprons, 313
Armorial bearings, 354, 384
Arms, how to whiten, 450
Army, how to address officers of, 355; nurses in the, 643
Arrowroot for invalids, 559
Art schools, 686
Artichokes, cooking of, 149
Artist, the career of the, 686; the fashion, 688
Arts for women, 682
Asparagus, cooking of, 149
Associations for children and young girls, 700
Assurance, 371
Asters, 586
"At Home" day, the, 334
"At Homes," 252; etiquette of, 339; invitations to, 332
Attendance officers, women as, 681
Auction game, 533
Auriculas, 582
Authors, hints to, 709
Aviary, the, 514

BABY, the, 473; and the bath, 479; feeding of, 476, 478, 479; weaning of, 477
Baby's basket, 470; binder, 472; clothing, 470, 471; headgear, 444, 445; outfit, 469; vest, 472; washing of clothing, 297
Bacon, treatment of, 100
Badminton, 547
Baking powder, 214
Ball gowns, 304
Balls, county, 341; etiquette of, 340; invitations to, 332; public, 341
Bandeaux, 433
Bank of England, the, 369
Bank manageress, how to become, 666; notes, 366; rate, 369; Savings (Post Office), 369
"Bank Return," the, 369
Banking account, how to open, 366; hints on, 366–370
Bankruptcy, law of, 370
Barracoat, the, 473
Baseball, game of, 546
Bassinette, baby's, 469; cost of, 469; how to trim a, 469
Basting of garments, 388
Bath, baby's, 480; child's, 479; hip and sponge, 448; hot air, 564; how to enamel, 607; mustard foot, 564; soda, 564; steam face, 451; sulphur, 564; vapour, 564
Bath-room, the, 33; cleaning of, 61
Baths, 447; in illness, 564; rubber camp, 448; salt (at home), 448; sea, 448
Beans, cooking of, 150; French, how to cook, 152; haricot, how to cook, 153
Beauty specialists, 669
Bed covers, 259; cradle, 560; how to make patient's, 551; linen, 257; pans, 560; rest, 560; sores, 567; table, 560
Bedding, 31; in sick-room, 549
Bedroom, decoration of, 32; furniture, 29, 32; spring cleaning of, 81; ventilation of, 453; colour schemes for, 16
Beds, care of, 68; making of, 67; water, 553
Bed-sitting-room, furnishing a, 33
Bedsteads, cleaning of, 68
Beef, collops, 168; creams, 169; darioles of, 179; how to choose, 107; how to serve, 245; juice, 558; olives, 169; roast, 168; roll, glazed, 179; Russian steaks, 170; salt, boiled, 167; sandwiches for invalids, 559; steak, 168; steak and kidney pie, 181; steak and kidney pudding, 181; tea, 558; use of different joints, 108
Bee-keepers' Association, 655
Bee-keeping for women, 654
Beetles, extermination of, 78
Beetroot, cooking of, 150

Begonias, 597
"Best Man," the, 347
Bibs, baby's, 473
Bilious attack, 567
Bills, checking amd filling of, 366
Binding, method of, 403
Birds, cage, 512; ailments of, 515; various kinds, 514
Births, registration of, 376
Biscuits, cocoa-nut, 219; milk, 220; oatmeal, 220; various kinds, 218
Bite, frost, 576
Bites, dog, 573; insect, 573; snake, 573
Black eye, cure of, 574
Blackheads, 567
Blanc-mange coffee, 205
Blanket stitch, the, 398
Blankets, 261, 262; how to mend, 415; washing of, 288
Bleaching, 278
Bleeding, nose, 576; of rectum, 577; of stomach, 577
Blind man's buff, 531
Blinds, 21, 22; cleaning of, 70; how to make, 608
Blisters, 566
Blood-spitting, 577
Blouse, 496; directions for making, 421
Blue, for laundry work, 276
Boarding-houses, 501
Boating-parties, 344
Boiler, burst, 607
Boils, 567
Bolster slips, 258
Bonnet, baby girl's, 444
Bonnets, 308, 309
Bookbinding, 690
Book illustration, 687
Book-keeping, 666; system of, 363
Books, cleaning of, 72; for children, 488
Boot cupboard, 610
Bootees for baby, 473
Boots, 309; care of, 314; choice of, 452; cleaning of, 78
Borax, for laundry work, 276
Botanic Society's school, 648
Bottles, hot-water, 560
Bottling of fruit, the, 232–235
Bouts Rimés, 535
Bow, the Alsatian, 438; the butterfly, 438; for hat, 437
Bowls, 547
Bows, the making of, 437; sewing on of, 440; of velvet, silk, &c., 438
Boxes for windows, 600
Boys' Christian names, meaning of, 712
Braid, how to, 404
Brain, concussion of, 574
Brass, cleaning of, 72
Brawn, how to make, 173
Bread, brown, 214; household, 214; treatment of, 101; Vienna, 215
Breakfast, how to serve, 249, 250
Breakfast-room, colour schemes for, 16; furnishing of, 28
Breakfast sets, 238
Breathing, the art of, 454
Bridal procession, the, 348; trousseau, the, 321
Bride's dress, 347
Bridesmaids, 347
Bridge drives, 542; parties, etiquette of, 340; teas, etiquette of, 339
British Empire, administrative government of, 706; constitution of, 706
Bronchitis, 568
Bronze, cleaning of, 73
Brooches, how to clean gold, 312
Broth, how to make, 119; various kinds of, 120, 121
Bruises, 573
Brushes, care of, 78; care of paint, 606; hair, 456; how to wash, 457
Bugs, extermination of, 79
Building society, 2
Bulbs, cultivation of, 587; for garden, 582
Bunion, 568
Buns, how to make, 216; rice, 218
Burns, cure of, 574
Business, women in, 665–677
Butler, the, 54
Butter, treatment of, 100
Button-holes, 400
Buttons, how to sew on, 400

CABBAGE, cooking of, 150
Cabinet and premier, the, 707
Cages, care of bird, 512
Cake, angel, 220; cherry, 220; Christmas, 221; Easter, 221; holiday, 221; iced, 223, 224; invalid, 222; luncheon, 222; Madeira, 222; orange, 223; Scotch seed, 223; sponge, 224
Cakes, 211–218
Cakes, chocolate, 216; Coburg, 216; decoration of, 224; ginger, 218; girdle, 217; how to bake, 213; icing of, 225, 226; queen, 218; tea, 216; tins, how to prepare, 212
Calceolarias, 596
Calf's feet, 175; liver, 174; sweetbreads, 175
Calico seams, different, 391
Calls, etiquette of making, 330; paying and receiving, 333
Calves' brains, 174
Canada, information concerning, 663
Canaries, varieties of, 512
Canary, breeding, 513; cage for, 513; food for, 513; how to choose a, 513; taming of, 514
Candy, how to make American, 672
Candytufts, 585
Canvassers, income of, 676
Cape, evening, 429
Caramel walnuts, how to make, 672
Cards, gentlemen's, 331; visiting, 329
Cards and fortune telling, 538
Carnations, 582, 591
Carnival, roller skating, 542
Carpet, Axminster, 20; beating of, 62; Brussels, 20; choice of, 18, 19; Kidderminster, 20; kinds of, 20; measurements for, 19; stair, 20; sweepers, 61; tapestry, 20; to remove stains, 62; to revive colour of, 62; velvet pile, 20; Wilton, 20
Carriages, licences for, 384
Carrots, cooking of, 150
Carving, hints on, 244
Cash book, specimen page of, 364; use of, 363
Cash box, use of, 363
Cashiers, women as, 666
Castor-oil enema, 561

Caterers, how to select, 340
Caterpillars, destruction of, 602
Cats, common ailments of, 512; care of, 511; different kinds of, 512
Cauliflower, cooking of, 151
Ceilings, cleaning of, 69
Celery, how to curl, 161; how to fry, 151
Chairs, cleaning of, 64
Chairs, re-upholstering of, 613
Charades, 528
Charity, entertainments for, 541
"Charts," "feeding," 477
Cheese cakes, 197; custard, 186; soufflé, 187; treatment of, 101
Chemise, how to iron and fold a, 284
Chemists, women, 639
Cheque-book, the, 367
Cheques, alteration of, 367; cashing of, 368; crossing of, 367; dishonoured, 368
Cherries, with cream, 205
Chestnuts, how to cook, 151
Chicken, à la Cardinal, 177; and ham pie, 182; chaudfroid of, 176; for invalids, 558; potted, 180
Chiffon, how to wash, 292
Chilblain, 568
Child, the, 466–497; the bath, 479; feeding of, 476; training and education of, 485–487; weaning of, 477
Child's hair, the, 480; exercise, the, 482
Children, advantages of reading, 487
Children's ailments, 483–485; clothing, 495; clothing, washing of, 297; endowments for, 371; literature, 487; millinery, 444; nurses, 661; pocket-money, 486; punishment of, 486; shoes, 497; stockings, 497
Chills, danger of, 484
Chimney on fire, regulations as to, 382
Chimneys, care of, 65
China for table, 237; how to mend, 607; washing of, 76
Chintz, how to wash, 294
Chocolate caramels, how to make, 673; peppermints, how to make, 674
Choking, treatment in case of, 574
Christening fees, 350; lunch, 350
Christenings, 349, 350
Christmas parties, 536; postman, 536; tree, the, 536
Chrysanthemums, 585, 591
Church decoration, 360
Circular notes, 368
"Circulator," 7
Cisterns, 7
Civil Service, the, 493, 678–681
Clarkias, 585
Clergy, how to address the, 355
Clerks, lady, 665; in post office, 678
Clothes, care of, 313; care of men's, 315; cleaning of, 316; dyeing of, 316; horse and pully, 273; ropes, pins and poles, 273; storing away of, 314; children's, 495; choice of, 451; colour of, 451
Clubs, ladies', 701
Coal gas, 9
Coal, various kinds of, 98
Coats and wraps, 306; motoring, 306
Cocoa-nut drops, how to make, 673; slices, 217
Codicils to wills, 375
Coffee caramels, how to make, 673; how to serve, 250; pot, 536
Coiffure, the, 458, 460
Coke, use of, 98
Cold in the head, 568
Collars, how to wash, 295; of dress, 311
Colleges for girls, 494; of cookery, 660
Colonial government, 707; outfit, hints on, 664
Colonies and their governors, 708; work in the, 663
Combinations, how to iron pair of, 286
Combs, how to wash, 458
Commission agents, 383
Compensation Act, Workmen's, 370
Complexion and skin, the, 448; general hints, 451; influence of health on, 449; "making up" of, 465; use of powder for, 465
Composite drawing, 530
Concussion of brain, 574
Condy's fluid, 464
Consequences, game of, 530
Constipation, 468, 568; in children, 484
Construction of house, 3
Consultations, 551
Continent, holidays on the, 502; hotels on, 503; pensions on, 503
Convalescence, 556
Convalescent homes for gentlewomen, 701
Convent education, 494
Conversation, the art of, 352; topics for, 352
Convulsions, treatment for, 484
Cook, the, 48; duties of, 49, 50
Cookers, electric, kinds of, 97
Cookery classes, 659; guide to, 116–235; teachers, dress of, 660; teaching of, 659
Cooking by electricity, 97; on oil-stoves, 97
Cooks, lady, 661
Coral stitching, 397
Cornice poles, 22
Corns, destruction of, 568
Corset, the, 451
Costumes, outdoor, 303
Cot, baby's, 469
Cottages, country, 501
Cotton material, how to darn, 411
Cough, 569
Counter clerks in post office, 679
Counterpanes, 259
Country, holidays in, 501; house parties, 336
Court dress, 360; presentation at, 358, 359
Covenants, 379
Covers, toilet, 260
Cradle, baby's, 469; bed, 560
Crafts for women, 682
Cramp, 569
Cream, treatment of, 101; ices, 209
Creams, opera, how to make, 674; various kinds of, 201–204
Credit, 367
Creepers, 598
Crests, 354
Cricket, rules for game, 544
Crimping of linen, 283
Crocuses, 588
Croquet, 546
Croup, treatment of, 484
Crown, the, 706
Crullers, 217
Crumpets, 215

Cuffs, how to wash, **295**
Cup, spit, 563
Cupboard for boots, 610
Curling-pins, use of, **459**
Curtains, 21; arrangement of, 22; casement, 22; how to make, 610; how to wash, 291; the drop, 526; various kinds, 610
Cushions, air, 553; water, 553
Custard, caramel, 204; chocolate, 205; orange, 206
"Customs," inspection by, **505**
Cutlery for table, 236

Dadoes, 15
Daffodils, 588
Dahlia, the, 592
Dairy work for women, **654**
Damp, cause of, **4**
Dances, etiquette of, 340; fashionable, **341**; invitations to, 332; various kinds, 342
Dancing mistress, 689; value of art of, **491**
Darning, the art of, 408, 410, 412
Deaf, teaching of, 618
Death, 566
Deaths, registration of, 376
Debt, actions for, 370; recovery of, 370
Début of daughter, 495
Decoration of church, **360**; of houses, 667; of table, 253
Degrees, medical, 634
Dental hospitals, 640
Dentistry for women, 640
Deposit account, the, 366
Designing of advertisements, 687; of garden, 649; of posters, 687
Dialogues, 526
Diamonds, how to clean, 312
Diarrhœa, 569; in children, 484
Diet, Allenbury, 556; and health, **452**; chart for baby, **478**; for patients, 556; in convalescence, 557
Dining-room, colour schemes for, 15; furnishing of, 26
Dinner invitations, 332; party, 240; service, 238
Dinners, etiquette of, 337; serving, **238, 239**
Discharge of bankrupt, 370
Diseases, infectious, 382
Dislocation, **574**
Dispensing, 639
Distemper, **14**
Distempering, 605
Distress Amendment Act, 381
"Distress," levy of, 380
Divinations by tarocs, **540**
Djibbah, the, 497
Doctor, the, 473, **550**; and consultations, **551**
Doctors, cost of training, 634; women as, 633–646
Dog collars, 385, 509; kennels, **508**; licences, 385
Dogs, ailments of, 510; and railway companies, 386; exercise for, 509; how to feed, 508; management of, 507; various kinds of, 507
Domestic science, 658–664
Domicile, 374
Dominoes and fortune telling, **539**
Door-steps, cleaning of, 73
Drain pipes, **5**
Drainage, **5**; earth system, 6; testing, 6
Dramatic profession, the, 684; schools, 685
Drawers for baby, **473**; how to iron pair of, 285
Drawing, black and white, 687; fashion, 688
Drawing-room, colour schemes for, 15; furnishing of, **23, 24**
Dress, accessories of, 311; allowances, 319; allowances, specimens, 320; buying at sales, 319; collars, 311; etiquette of, 335; for holidays, 502; for nurse, 549; for presentation at Court, 360; for woman worker, 305; its choice and care, 301–324, evening, **304**; morning, **429**; style and colour, 302
Dress bodice, how to wash, 294
Dresses, dinner, 304; summer, 304; theatre, **304**
Dressing, the art of, 301
Dressing-gown, 430
Dressmaking, 668; at home, 419–431; general hints, 425; tools for, 420
Dressing-room, decoration of, **32**
Drill, teaching of, 621
Drivers, licence of, 385
Driving, etiquette when, 327
Drowning, **574**
Druggists, women, 639
Duck, roast, 177
Ducks, how to choose, **112**
Dumb crambo, game of, **529**
Dust-bin, kinds of, 94
Dusting, directions for, **63**
Duty, house, 382
Dyspepsia, 570

Ear-ache, 569
Ears, care of the, **464**; foreign body in, **575**
Earwigs, destruction of, 601
Eating, etiquette of, 327
Editing, sub, 627
Editor, exchange, 625; society, 625
Editors, women as, 624
Education of children, 489; university, **493**
Egg cutlets, 185; drink for invalids, 559
Egg-plant, how to cook, 152
Eggs à la Chartres, 183; depots for collecting, 655; in bread sauce, 183; poached, 185; scrambled, 185; treatment of, 101; with green peas, **184**; with shrimp sauce, **184**; with tomatoes, 184
Electric light, 9; fittings, 10
Electricity, cooking by, **97**; in nurse's work, **646**
Electrolysis, **451**
Electro-plate, 237
Embroidery by hand, **426**
Empire Day, 708
Enamelling, 689; of wood, 606
Endive, how to cook, 152
Endowments for children, 371
Enema, castor oil, 561; glycerine, 562; olive oil, 561; salt, 561; starch and opium, 561; turpentine, 561
Enemata, 561; nutrient, 562
Engagements, 345; breaking off of, **345**
Entertaining, etiquette of, 337
Entertainment, indoor, 524
Entertainments for charity, **541**
Epilepsy, **575**
Eschscholtzias, 585
Estate agent's commission, 383

Etiquette, general hints on, 328; guide to, 325–361; for visitor, 333; in olden times, 326; of eating, 327; of introductions, 328; of the table, 327; of to-day, 327; of visiting, 335; of visiting cards, 329; out of doors, 327; wedding, 345; when driving, 327
Examinations for teachers, 616
Exchange editor, 625
Excise licences, 384, 385
Exercise, value of, 454
Exercises, chart of, 455; physical, 454–456
Executors of will, 375
Eye, cure of black, 574; foreign body in, 575
Eyes, care of the, 462
Eyebrows as aids to beauty, 463
Eye-cup, use of the, 463
Eyelashes as aids to beauty, 463
Eyelet holes, 402

FACE, the steam bath, 451; how to wash the, 449; massage of, 450; use of powder for, 465
Factory inspectorships, 680
Fainting, 575
Fan fight, the game of, 533
Farmers, women as, 652
Fashion and dress, 301; drawing, 688
Fastenings, 400
Feather stitching, 397
Feathers, how to wash, 318; sewing on of, 439
"Feeding charts," 477
Feet, care of the, 464
Felling of garments, 390
Ferns, 599
Fever, hay, 570
Finger, crushed, 573
Fire, conduct on outbreak of, 85
Fire-guard, the, 474
Fireplaces, cleaning of, 64, 65
Fires, how to light, 65
"First Aid," 548–579
Fish cakes, 133; calendar of same in season, 111, 112; cream, 133; curry, 134; custard puddings, 134; cutlets, 134; how to boil, 130; how to broil, 131; how to choose, 111; how to clean, 130; how to fry, 130; how to serve, 248; how to skin and fillet, 131; how to steam, 130; omelet, 134; pie (Russian), 139; pies, 135; puddings, 135; rules for cooking, 130; scalloped, 136; smoked, 136; steamed for invalids, 558; treatment of, 100; various kinds, 131–140
Fixtures, landlord's and tenant's, 380
Flageolets, how to cook, 152
Flannel seams, 393
Flannels, how to wash, 287; prevention of shrinking, 288
Fleas, extermination of, 79
Flies, extermination of, 80
Flooring, 18
Floor-cloth, cleaning of, 66, 67; coverings, 18
Floors, polished, care of, 66; scrubbing of, 66; staining of, 607; tiled, care of, 67
Florists, women as, 651
Flowering plants, 600
Flowers for decoration, 253; sewing on hats of, 440
Fomentation, laudanum, 566; turpentine, 566
Food and health, 452; and the kitchen, 87–115; Benger's, 556; patients', 556; treatment of, 100
Footman, the, 54
Forks, care of, 76
Foreign languages, teaching of, 618
Forfeits, 529
Fortune telling by cards, 538; by dominoes, 539
Foundations, 3
Fowl, curried, 177; fricassée of, 176; how to roast a, 175; how to serve, 247; how to steam a, 176
Fowls, keeping of, 517–523
Fractures, 576
"Free Lance," the, 627
Fritters, various kinds of, 195
Frock for baby, 473; the yoke, 496
Frost-bite, 576
Fruit and the complexion, 453; bottling of, 228, 232–235; calendar of same in season, 114; how to choose, 114; how to serve, 256; marzipan, how to make, 673; preserving of, 228; salads, 206, 207; storage of, 102
Fuchsias, 597
Fuel, kitchen, 98
Funerals, formalities of, 350
Furnished house, letting, 40
Furnishing, estimates of, 35
Furniture, arrangement of, 24; cleaning of, 63; choice of, 16; distinctive styles in, 34; purchase of, 17
Fur, how to cut, 442; how to join, 442; in millinery, 442
Furs, 307; how to clean, 319; storing away of, 315

GAME, calendar of same in season, 113; how to choose, 112; how to serve, 247; salmi of, 178; treatment of, 100
Games for parlour, 529–536; indoor, 524; outdoor, 542–547; teaching of, 621
Garden annuals, 581; arrangement of beds, 584; borders, 590; designing, 649; fences, 597; parties, invitations to, 332; the suburban, 580; tools, 602, 603; walls, 597
Gardeners, 531; lady, 647
Gardening, French, 651; Glynde School of, 648; home, 580–603; jobbing, 650; landscape, 649; market, 650; schools of, 647; teachers of, 651
Gas escapes, 608; fittings, 10; heating by, 11; stoves, 95
Gathering of garments, 390
Geese, how to choose, 112
General information, 719
General Post, game of, 531
General servant, 53
Gentlemen's cards, 331
Gentry, how to address, 354
Geranium, the, 596
Gingerbread, 221
Ginger tablet, how to make, 673
Girl clerkships in post office, 679
Girls, accomplishments for, 491; Christian names, meaning of, 712
Glass for table, 237, 238; washing of, 75
Glaze, how to make, 119
Gloves, 309, 310; baby's, 473; how to keep clean, 305; how to mend, 417; how to wash, 295

Glycerine enema, 562
Goffering of linen, 284
Golf, 547
Goloshes, 310
Goose, how to serve, 247; roast, 177
Governess, the, 492, 619
Gowns, evening, 305; for balls, 304
Grafting in repairing garments, 410
Grass plots, 581
Green-fly, destruction of, 601
Groceries, ordering of, 106; storing of, 104
Grubs, destruction of, 602
Gruel, oatmeal, 559
Guest, etiquette of, 335
Gum-boil, 570
Gymnastics, teaching of, 621; value of, 491

HÆMORRHOIDS, 571
Hair brushes, choice of, 456
Hair, care of patient's, 554; care of the, 456; dyeing the, 458; how to comb the, 456; how to dress the, 459; how to strengthen growth, 458; how to wash the, 457; lotions, 458; use of false, 458; waving and curling of the, 459
Hairdressing, 669; styles of, 460
Hall boy, the, 55
Hall, cleaning of, 60; colour schemes for, 16; furnishing of, 25
Ham, how to boil a, 172
Handicrafts for home workers, 689
Hands, care of the, 461; how to dry the, 461; how to keep clean, 461
Hare, jugged, 179
Hares, how to choose, 113
Hat, a river or country, 440; baby boy's, 445; for little girl, 445
Hats, 308; care of, 314; care of men's, 316; how to clean felt, 318; straw, 318, 442, 443; straw, how to cover brim, 443; straw, trimming of, 443
Headache, 570
Head-linings, 432
Health and cleanliness, 447; and diet, 452; and exercise, 449; and food, 452; how to retain, 447; importance of good, 447; influence on appearance, 447; visitors, 637
Heartburn, 468, 570
Height of men and women, relative, 714
Hemming of garments, 389
Hem-stitching, 399
Hen-house, the, 517
Hens, keeping of, 517
Herbs, storage of, 102
Herring-boning, 397
Hiccough, 570
Hieroglyphics, game of, 533
Hire-purchase system, the, 383
Hoarseness, 570
Hockey, rules for game, 545
Holiday abroad, the, 501; the annual, 498; the woman worker's, 500; dress for, 502; in the country, 501; on the continent, 502; the children's, 499; the question of, 498, 506
Holland, how to wash, 294
Home nursing, 548–579
Home workers, handicrafts for, 689
Honeysuckles, 598
Hooks, how to fasten, 401
Horticulture, schools of, 647; women in, 647–657
Hospital nursing, 641
Hospitals, dental, 640; for gentlewomen, 701; list of chief London, 642; list of lying-in, 645
Hostess, etiquette of, 336
Hotch-potch, 121
Hotels, continental, 503
Hot-water pipes, 12; supply, 7
House, the, 1
House-agent's commission, 383; women as, 667
House, aspect of, 5; decoration, 12, 13, 14, 667; duty, 382; furnished, 381; general condition of, 12; heating of, 10; lease of, 1; locality for, 2; on shutting up a, 85; purchase of, 1; site, 3
House *versus* flat, 2
House of Commons, 707; of Lords, 706
Household accounts, payment of, 365; expenses, 365; repairs, 604–614; work, guide to, 58
Housekeeper, the, 54
Housekeepers, 662
Housekeeping without a servant, 56, 57
Housemaid, the, 50, 51
House-parlourmaid, duties of, 51
Housewifery, 41, 660; teaching of, 659
Housing Act, 380
Hyacinths, 588
Hygiene, importance of, 447
Hysterics, fit of, 577

ICE applications, 566
Ice-cream, 207, 209
Iced, puddings, 210
Ices, 207; cream, 209; how to serve, 210; water, 208
Icings, 225, 226, 227
Illness, symptoms of child's, 483
Incandescent gas, 9
Income, allotment of, 362
Indexing, 631
Indigestion, 570
Infants' clothing, washing of, 297
Infectious cases, 555; diseases, 382
Infirmary nurses, 643
Influenza, 570
Inhalations, 562
Injection, saline, 562
Insects, destruction of, 601
Inspectors, factory, 680; medical school, 637; sanitary, 637; school, 681; under Poor Law, 680
Insurance, 370–374; accident, 372; burglary, 374; endowment, 371; fire, 373; Government, 372; interest, 372; of servants, 373; with profits, 371
Insure, how to, 372
Interest, how to reckon, 366; insurance, 372
Intestacy of husband, 375; wife, 376
Introduction, letters of, 329; etiquette of, 328
Invalid, consideration for, 554
Invitations, 332, 333; acceptance and refusal of, 332; general hints, 333
Iron-stand, 274
Ironing boards, 274; general directions, 280; irons for laundry work, 273, 274
Ivory, cleaning of, 73

"JAEGER" underwear, the, 451
Jam, hints on making, 228; various kinds of, 230
Jasmine, 598
Jellies, 199, 200; hints on making, 228; how to make French, 673
Jelly, apple, 229; aspic, 176; coffee, 200; orange, 201; port wine, 201; with bananas, 200
Jewellery, 312
Journalism, 623; training for, 628
Judges, how to address, 355

KENNELS, dog, 508
Kettle, steam, 562
Kidneys, curry of, 171; grilled, 171
Kindergarten teaching, 618
Kitchen, how to clean, 91; how to furnish, 87; price list of utensils, 90; range, the, 89; utensils, 90
Kitchen-maid, the, 55
Knickerbockers, washing of, 299
Knives, care of, 76

LABOUR Exchange Acts, 681
Lace bows, 438
Lace, cleaning of, 317; how to wash, 290; quills, 438
Lace-making, 690
Lady cooks, 661; salaries of, 661; servants, 660
Lady's maid, the, 54
Lamb cutlets, 172
Lamb, how to choose, 107; how to serve, 246; use of different joints, 110
Lamb's fry, 172
Lamps, care of, 77; gas, 10; oil, 10
Land tax, 383
Landings, furnishing of, 25, 26
Landlord and tenant, law of, 378
Landscape gardening, 649
Languages, teaching of foreign, 618
Larder, the, 99; economy in, 101
Laundry-maid, the, 55
Laundry manageress, 662; utensils, 272–275; price list of, 275; work, guide to, 271–300; teaching of, 659; training in, 662
Lavatory, cleaning of, 61
Lawn tennis, 542
Layette, the, 470; on making the, 471
Leather work, 690
Leases, 379
Lecturers, women as, 619
Ledger, the, 364
Leeks, how to cook, 153
Legal guide, 362–386; notes, 374
Lentils, how to cook, 154
Letter-writing, the art of, 353
Letters, business, 353; of condolence, 351; of introduction, 329
Letting a furnished house, 40
"Lever embossing press," 354
Liability, husband's, 374
Library, colour schemes for, 16; furnishing of, 29; work, 631
Lice, destruction of, 571
Licences, 384, 385
Lighting, 8; artificial, 8
Linen, crimping of, 283; airing of, 284; cupboard, the, 264, 267; drying of, 279; estimates of prices of, 268–270; folding of, 279, 284; for bed, 257; goffering of, 284; how to darn, 411; how to mark, 265, 405, 406; inventory, 266; press, 264; household, 257; mangling of, 279; mending of, 267; scenting of, 265; table, 262; washing of, 278
Linings, 432
Linoleum, 21; cleaning of, 66; how to lay, 610
Literary work, 623–630
Literature for children, 487
Loan funds for women, 701
Lobelias, 596
Lobster cutlets, 137
Local Government, 699
Lodger's property, 381
London, cathedrals, churches, &c., 702; flats and residential chambers, 701; memorials, monuments, 702; museums, 702; official buildings, 704; places of entertainment, 704; places of interest in, 701; principal theatres, 703; residential homes and clubs, 700
Lounge hall, the, 26
Luggage, treatment of, 335; question of, 504
Lumbago, 571
Luncheons, 251; etiquette of, 338

MACAROONS, 219, 220
Machine, the sewing, 417
Machines for washing, 272
Magazine illustration, 687
Maintenance, legal notes on, 374, 376
Mangle, the, 272
Manicure, 461
Manners, as mark of good breeding, 325
Mantelpiece decoration, 22; drapery, 609
Manuscripts, sending of, 626
Marble, cleaning of, 71
"Marcelle" wave of hair, the, 459
Marigolds, 586
Market gardening, 650
Marketing, hints for, 105
Marmalade, 230, 231
Marriage by banns, 345; by ordinary licence, 346; by registrar, 346; by special licence, 346; expenses, 347; fees, 346; forms of, 345; settlement, 374; in Scotland, 346
Marzipan potatoes, how to make, 674
Massage, 450, 451; for scalp, 457; in nurse's work, 646
Matrons, 662
Matting, Indian, cleaning of, 67
Mattresses, care of, 68; covers, 258; how to remake wool, 608
Mayors, how to address, 355
Meat, boiling of, 166; braising of, 166; broiling or grilling, 167; calendar, 108; dishes, 165–183; frozen, 111; frying of, 166; how to bake or roast, 165; how to choose, 107; how to glaze, 119; scallops, 180; steaming of, 166; stewing of, 167; treatment of, 100; use of different joints, 108; with pastry, 181–183
Medical aid societies, 701; degrees open to women, 634; missionaries, 637; school inspectors, 637
Medicine as a profession, 633–646; chest, 579; glasses, 563

Medicines, 563, 564
Mending and sewing (plain), 387–418; the art of, 407
Mental nursing, 644
Menu, drawing up a, 243
Metal goods, cleaning of, 75
Metal work, 689; and enamelling, training for, 689
Mice, extermination of, 79, 602
Midwife, the, 473
Midwifery, 644
Midwives Act, the, 645; salaries of, 645
Mignonette, 585
Migraine, 567
Mildew, how to remove, 277
Milk, Horlick's malted, 556; treatment of, 101
Millinery, 668; children's, 444; equipment, 432; home, 432–446; preliminaries of, 435
Mincemeat, 198
Mince pies, 198
Ministry, the, 707
Mirrors, cleaning of, 72
Missing ring, game of, 535
Missionaries, medical, 637
Mistress and servants, 41–57; duties of the, 41
Money equivalents in travelling, 503; foreign and colonial, 719; management of, 362–386
Money orders, foreign and colonial, 717; inland, 717
Morning-room, furnishing of, 28
Motherhood, preparing for, 466, 467
Mother's requirements, the, 468
Moths, extermination of, 79
Motor cars, licences for, 384; registration of, 385; regulations for light, bells, &c., 385
Mourning cards, 352
Mourning, formalities of, 350; notepaper, 352; periods of, 351
Mouth, care of child's, 481
Muffs, 443; black satin and fur, 444; fashions in, 443
Mushrooms, 154
Music, Royal Academy of, 683; Royal College of, 683; teachers of, 683; training in, 683
Musical chairs, game of, 530
Musical profession, the, 682
Muslin, how to mend, 415; how to wash, 289
Mutton cutlets, 171
Mutton, how to choose, 107; how to serve, 246; roast shoulder, 170; scrambled, 180; use of different joints, 110

Nails, care of child's, 481; care of finger, 461; how to manicure the, 462
Name divinations, game of, 534
Napkins, 472
Narcissi, 588
Nasturtiums, 585
Nature study, teachers of, 651
Navy, how to address officers of, 355; nurses in the, 643
Neck, cure of stiff, 573; how to whiten, 450; massage of, 450
Needlework, 690
Net, how to wash, 291
Neuralgia, 571
Night-dress, how to iron a, 287
Nobility, how to address, 354
Non-political associations, women's, 699
Nose bleeding, 576; foreign body in, 576
Note-paper, choice of, 354; how to stamp, 354
Notice, on giving, 381
Nurse, the, 475, 476, 549; and night duty, 550; children's, 661; choice and qualifications, 475; co-operation, 645; day's work, 555; dress of, 549; duties of, 476; in army, 643; in colonies, 646; in infirmaries, 643; in navy, 643; monthly, 473; professional, 550; training of hospital, 641; village, 646
Nursery, the, 474, 475
Nursery College, Hampstead, 477
Nursery cupboard, 474
Nursery, furniture of, 474; recipes, 478; rusk, 479; the night, 475
Nursing as a profession, 633–646; district, 646; home, 548–579; infectious cases, 555; mental, 644; private, 645
Nut omelet, 155
Nuts and nut foods, 154

Oatmeal gruel, 559
Office, typewriting, 675
"Official receiver," the, 370
Oil fittings, 10
Olive-oil enema, 561
Omelet, cheese, 186; ham, 186; plain, 185; savoury, 186
Oven, regulation of, 213; gas, 96
Overalls, 313; child's, 496
Overcasting for seams, 391
Overdrafts, 368
Ox-tail, haricot of, 169
Oyster soufflés, 138

Pack, hot and cold, 564
Packing, hints on, 506
Paint brushes, 606
Paint, how to wash, 70
Painting, 14; of wood, 606
Palms, 599
Palpitation of heart, 571
Pancakes, 192
Panelling, 15
Pansies, 593
Pantry, the, 236
Papering of rooms, 604
Papiers poudrés, 465
Parlour games, 529–536
Parlour-maid, the, 52
Parqueterie, 18
Parrots, care of, 514; kinds of, 515
Parties, boating, 344; children's, 342; Christmas, 536; dinner, 240; etiquette of evening, 339; garden, 342; invitations to garden, 332; juvenile, 342; tea, novel, 537
Partridge, braised, 177; broiled, 178
Party government, 707
Pass-book, the, 367
Pastry, genoise, 217; flaky, 163; how to make, 162; puff, 163; rough-puff, 164; short crust, 164; suet, 164; to make patty cases, 165
Patches, various kinds of, 413, 414
Patching, method of, 412
Patient, care of the, 551; food for, 556; how to feed helpless, 557; treatment for insensible, 554; hair, care of, 554; teeth, care of, 553; toilet, the, 553

Patterns for dressmaking, 419, 426; illustrations of, 426, 427
Patties, sweetbread, 183
Paying-in book, the, 367
Peas, green, how to cook, 153; sweet, 586
Pease pudding, 155
Pelargoniums, 596
Pen, play, 474
Pensions, continental, 503
Peppermint creams, how to make, 674; cushions, how to make, 674
Persons of rank, how to address, 354
Pests, extermination of, 78
Pets, home, 507–576
Petticoats, 307; how to wash cotton, 294; the baby's, 473
Pharmaceutical society, 639
Pharmacy, 639
Philanthropic societies, 699; work, 691; training for, 691
Photography as an art, 688
Piano, care of, 73; choice of a, 25
Picnics, 343
Pictures, cleaning of, 71
Pie, chicken, 182; pigeon, 182; Roman, 182; mince, 198
Pigeon for invalids, 559
Pigeons, how to choose, 112
Pilches, 472
Piles, 571
Pillow shams, 259; slips, 258; how to remake feather, 608
Pinafores, washing of, 298
Pipes, burst, 607
Piping, method of, 394
Plackets, 424
Plants for decoration, 253; for rooms, 599; for suburban garden, 581; for windows, 599
Play, the pastoral, 527
Play-pen, 474
Plays, choice of, 526; for "grown-ups," 527
Pleating, method of, 404; various kinds of, 404, 405
Pneumatic gas switch, 9
Poisoning, cases of, 577
Poisons, kinds of, 577
Political associations, 699
Politics, women in, 696
Poor Law inspectors, 680
Poppies, 586
Pork cutlets, 172
Pork, how to choose, 107; how to serve, 247; use of different joints, 111
Postage, inland rates of, 714; foreign and colonial, 715
Postal information, 714; orders, 717
Poster designing, 687
Post-office clerks, 678; employment in, 678; savings bank, 369
Potato chips, 156; fritter, 156; pie (sweet), 158
Potatoes, how to steam, 155; mashed, 156; new, 156
Poudrés, papiers, 465
Poultice, bread, 566; charcoal, 566; jacket, 565; linseed, 565; linseed and mustard, 565; mustard, 565
Poultices, 565, 566
Poultry, breeding of, 520; calendar of same in season, 113; common ailments, 522, 523; cooking of, 100; fattening of, 521; food, 518, 519; how to buy, 519; how to carve, 247; how to choose, 112; how to feed, 518, 519; how to kill, 522; keeping, 517–523; keeping for women, 655; runs for, 518; varieties of, 520
Poultry Organisation Society, 655
Precedence, rules of, 356
Pregnancy, 466, 467
Presentation at Court, 358
Preserve fruits, how to, 228
Press for trousers, 315
Primroses, 593
Printers' technical terms, 709
Prints, how to wash, 293
Professions for women, 615
Prolapse, treatment for, 485
Pronunciation, 352
Property Acts, Married Women's, 374
Property of lodgers, 381; of married women, 374
Proverbs, game of, 531
Provisions, ordering of, 106
Pruning of shrubs, 583
Public work, employment in, 680
Pudding, cabinet, 190; chester, 190; chocolate, 191; Christmas plum, 191; date, 191; fig, 191; ginger, 192; orange, 198; Yorkshire, 193; hot, 190; iced, 210
Pulley for patient, 560
Pulse, the, 563
Puppies, care of, 509
Purées, 124–129; vegetable, 125, 129; with nuts, 126

QUARANTINE officers, 637
Quilling, 437
Quills, lace, 438; sewing on of, 439
Quilts, how to wash, 289
Quinsy, 572

RABBITS, how to choose, 113; stewed, 178
Radiators, electric, 11
Radiotelegraphic service, 718
Railway tickets, coupon, 502
Rates, 379; gas, 383; water, 383
Rats, extermination of, 80
Reading aloud, the art of, 353
Reading for children, 487
"Receiving Order," the, 370
Recreations, 524–547
Refuse, removal of, 6; treatment of kitchen, 94
Registry office, 44
Relief work, 15
Removal, notice of, 381
Removals, how to conduct, 83–85
Rent, 379
Repairs to property, 380
Reporting, social, 625
Respiration, 563
Rhubarb mould, 206
Ribbon, how to finish ends of, 438; rosettes, 439
Ribs, broken, 577
Rice, to boil for curries, 157
Ring, fixed (removal of), 577
Ringworm, 485
Rissoles, 180
Roller-skating carnival, 542
Roses, 582, 593; kinds of, 595; pruning of, 594 soil for, 594

Rosettes, how to make, 437; kinds of, 439; of narrow ribbon, 439; ribbon, 439; silk, 439; tulle, 439
Rouleau, a, 435; sewing on of, 440
Rounders, game of, 546
Royal Family, the, 705
Royal palaces, 705
Royalty, how to address, 354
Ruching, 436; sewing of, 440
Rugs, cleaning of, 62, 63
Running of garments, 390

Salad basket, 159
Salad, cucumber, 161; dressing, 160; fish, 161; how to serve, 160; mixed, 162; oyster, 162; tomato, 162
Salad-making, 159
Salads, fruit, 206, 207; various kinds, 161, 162
Sales, how to buy at, 319
Salmon, 139
Salsify (to fry), 157
Sandwiches, 187–189; beef, 188; jam, 222; nut, 189; tomato, 189
Sanitary inspectors, 637; regulations, 382
Sauce, anchovy, 141; apple, 141; apricot, 146; brandy, 146; bread, 142; butter, 142; caper, 142; celery, 142; chestnut, 143; cranberry, 143; custard, 146; directions for making, 140; egg, 143; gooseberry, 143; horse-radish, 144; jam, 147; lemon, 147; melted butter, 144; mint, 144; mushroom, 144; onion, 145; orange, 147; oyster, 145; parsley, 145; savoury, various kinds, 141–146; sweet, 146–147; tomato, 145
Saucepans, kinds of, 90; the cleaning of, 92
Scalds, cure of, 574
Scalloping, 398
Scalp massage, 457
School attendance officers, 681
School, choice of girls', 492; inspectors, 681; inspectors, medical, 637
Schools, boys', 492; dramatic, 685; girls' high, 494; grammar, 493; of art, 686; private, 493, 494, 619; preparatory, 492; public, 493; secondary, 617
Sciatica, 572
Science, domestic, 658–664
Scones (bread), 211–216; materials for, 211; various kinds, 215
Scullery, how to furnish, 87
Scullery-maid, the, 55
Seaming of garments, 390
Seams, different calico, 391; flannel, 393; how to press, 425
Seasons, the, 719
Secretarial work, 630, 632; training for, 630
Secretary to editor, 625
Seed, how to sow, 584
Servant and master, law as to, 376
Servants, bedrooms of, 47; character giving to, 45; characters, 377; dismissal of, 377; duties of, 48; engaging of, 44; food allowances of, 45; holidays of, 46; injuries, 377; lady, 660; licences for, 45, 384; on giving notice to, 377; treatment of, 46; wages of, 45
Serviettes, 263
Serving, hints on, 244
Sewing and mending (plain), 387–418
Sewing-machine, the, 417
Shadows, game of, 531
Shawls, washing of, 288
Sheets, materials for, 257; price and size of, 257
"Sheringham Valve," 8
Shirts, how to wash, 296
Shivering, 572
Shoes, 309, 310; care of, 314; children's, 497; choice of, 452; cleaning of, 78
Shortbread, 218, 223
Shorthand typist, the, 665
Shrimp patties, 139
Shrubs, 582
Sick, food for, 556
Sick-room, the, 548, 549; ventilation of, 548
Sickness, morning, 468
Silk, how to mend, 417; how to wash, 292
Silver, care of, 74, 75; for table, 236
Sinks, cleaning of kitchen, 94
Sitting-room, cleaning of, 59
Size, how to make, 605
Skating carnival, roller, 542
Skin and complexion, the, 448
Skin food, use of, 450
Skirts, how to make, 422, 423
Slang, avoidance of, 352
Sleep, for children, 481; need of, 453; periods of, 453
Sleeplessness, 468, 572
Sleep-walking, 485
Slops, emptying of, 68
Slugs, destruction of, 602
Smocks, washing of, 299
Snowshoes, 310
Soap for laundry work, 275
Soap-jelly, how to make, 287
Social guide, 325–361; reporting, 625; work, 691; training for, 691
Societies and institutions, women's, 699
Society editor, 625
Socks, washing of, 288
Soda for washing, 275
Soil for shrubs, 583
Soils, 3
Somnambulism, 485
Sorbets, 211
Sore throat, 572
Sorrel, 157
Sorters in post office, 679
Soufflé, apple, 194; apricot, 194; how to make, 193; lemon, 194
Soup, almond, 126; artichoke, 125; bean, 127; cabbage, 122; calf's tail, 122; carrot, 125; chicken, 127; cream of barley, 128; fish, 127; green vegetables, 129; hare, 128; how to make, 116; lentil, 127; lettuce, 123; macaroni, 128; mock turtle, 123; onion, 125; oyster, 123; pea, 127; potato, 126; sorrel, 124; tomato, 126; turtle, 124; various kinds of, 119, 120; vegetable marrow, 126; thickened, 122
Spider, destruction of red, 601
Spinach, 157
Spinning and weaving, 690
Spirits, care of, 105
Spit-cups, 563
Spitting blood, 577
Splinters, 578
Sponges, care of, 448

Sponging, cold and tepid, 565
Sprains, 578
Spring cleaning, 80–83
Stage, the, 684; training for the, 685
Staining of floors, 607
Stains, how to remove, 276, 317
Staircase, cleaning of, 60; furnishing of, 25
Stair rods, 21
Stamps on policies of insurance, 372
Starch, for laundry work, 276; how to make, 280; use of, 280–282
Steam, applied, 562; face bath, the, 451; kettle, 562
Steel, cleaning of, 72
"Steriliser" for fruit-bottling, 233
Stew, Dutch, 171
Stitches, fancy, 397; hints on simple, 388
Stitching, 390
Stock, how to make, 117
Stock-pot, the, 118
Stocking web tissue, 410
Stockings, 311; children's, 497; the mending of, 408; washing of, 288
Stocks, 586
Stones, symbolism of precious, 312
"Stoppeur," the, 417
Store indicator, 103
Store-room, arrangements of, 102
Stoting, the use of, 416
Stove, how to black-lead, 92
Stoves, 11; care of, 77; cooking with oil, 97; gas, 95; gas, cleaning of, 97; gas, directions for use, 95, 96; oil, 12
Stories, short, 626
Strangulation, 578
Strings, 402
Stroke, 573
Stroking of garments, 395
Student teachers, 616
Stye, cure of, 573
Sub-editing, 627
Sub-letting a house, on, 381
Suet, how to choose, 108; how to keep, 100
Suffocation by gas, 578
Suffrage, women's, 697
Sugars, coloured, 224
Suits, boys' sailor, washing of, 299
Sulphur bath, the, 289
Sunstroke, 578
Supper, how to serve, 252
Surgeons, women as, 638
Suspenders, 311
Sweet-making, 671
Sweet recipes, 672–675
Sweets, hot and cold, 189–211
Syringe, Higginson's, 561

Table, the, 236–256; cloths, 263; cutlery, 236; decorations, 253; etiquette of the, 327; linen, 262; setting the, 239; silver, 236; serving at, 243, 244; waiting at, 241
Tableaux vivants, 527
Tacking of garments, 388
Tact, 325
Tapes, 402, 403
Tapioca, for invalids, 559
Tarocs, divinations by, game of, 540
Tart, apple, 197; gooseberry, 197
Tartlet cases, 199; chocolate, 197; strawberry, 199
Tax, land, 383
Taxes, 379
Tea, afternoon, 251; how to serve, 250
Tea-parties, novel, 537;
Tea-room, opening a, 670
Tea sets, 238
Teas, book, 537; etiquette of bridge, 339; general knowledge, 537
Teachers in Scotland, 618; of domestic subjects, 659; of gardening, 651; of nature study, 651; high school, 617
Teaching profession, the, 615
Teeth, care of child's, 481; care of, 464; care of patient's, 553
Teething, 484
Telegrams, 532; cancelling, 717; inland, 717; foreign and colonial, 717
Telegraph money orders, 717
Telegraphists, 679
Telephone exchanges, 718
Telephones, 718; provincial system, 718
Temperance associations, 700
Temperature of body, 563
Tenancies, varieties of, 378
Tenancy, termination of, 381
Tennis, lawn, 542
Theatricals at home, 524, 525
Thermometer, 719; clinical, 563
Throat, sore, 572
Thrush, 484
Tickets, combined coupon, 502; season, 503
Tidings, game of, 532
Tie, how to wash gentleman's, 292
Time, standard, 719
Tips after sea voyages, 503; subject of, 336, 337
Toe nails, care of, 464
Toffee, how to make Russian, 674
Toilet, the, 447–465; child's, 479; patient's, 553
Toilet covers, 260
Tomatoes, how to cook, 158
Tongue, boiled, 170
Tonsilitis, 572
Tools for garden, 602, 603; for house, 604
Toothache, 468, 573
Tooth powder, 464
Toques, flower, 441; fur, 442
Tourists, advice to, 501
Tours, general hints on, 503
Towels, 260, 264; kitchen, 264
Travel, 498–506; foreign, as an educator, 504; general hints on, 503; luggage in, 504
Trays, Japanese, cleaning of, 72
Trees for garden, 583
Trimmings, 426; sewing of, 439
Tripe with tomatoes, 170
Trouser press, 315
Trousseau, the bridal, 321; estimates of cost of, 322
Trunk, how to pack a, 506
Tubs, washing, 272
Tucking, method of, 393
Tulips, 589
Tunic, boy's, 496
"Turban" coiffure, the, 460
Turkey, how to choose, 112; how to serve, 247; roast, 178
Turnips, how to cook, 159

Turpentine for laundry work, 276
Tweed cloth, how to mend, 416
Type, sizes of, 711
Typewriting office, opening a, 675; price list in, 676; prospects in, 675; training in, 675
Typist, the shorthand, 665; in civil service, 680

ULCERS, how to cure child's, 484
Umbrellas, care of, 314
Underclothing, 306
Underskirts, 307
University education, 493, 494
Upholstery, 604–614

VACCINATION, 376
Valet, the, 55
Varicose veins, 573
Vases, for table decoration, 254
Veal and ham cutlets, 174; cream, 173; for invalids, 558; galatine of, 175; how to choose, 108; how to serve, 247; jellied, 173; kidney, 174; olives, 173; steamed, 173; use of different joints, 109
Vegetable "cookers," 148; marrow, 159
Vegetables and salads, 147–162; calendar of same in season, 115; cooking of, 148; curried, 151; how to choose, 114; preparation of, 148; storage of, 101
Vegetarianism, 148
Veils, 309, 446; various kinds, 446
Veins, varicose, 468, 573
Velvet, how to raise the pile, 318; use of, 434
Velveteen, how to wash, 289
Venison, how to choose, 108; use of different joints, 111
Ventilation, 7
Vermin, destruction of, 508
Violas, 593
Visiting cards, 329
Visiting, etiquette of, 335; general hints, 335
Visitor, etiquette for, 333
Vomiting blood, 577
Voyages, tips after sea, 503

WALKING as an exercise, 454
Wall-papers, 14
Walls, cleaning of, 69
Walnut molasses, how to make, 673
Warts, 573
Wash-stand, care of, 68
Washing day, preparation for, 276; directions for home, 271; machines, 272; sending out the, 266
"Washing up" directions for, 73
Water-beds, 553; closets, 6; cushions, 553; ices, 208; for laundry work, 275; how to soften, 449; supply, 6
Waxworks, 535
Wedding anniversaries, 349; cake, 349; cards, 349; day, fixing the, 345; etiquette, 345–349; luncheons, 349; reception, the, 348; trip, the 349; golden, 349; invitations to, 332; silver, 349
Whipping of garments, 396
Whist drives, 542
Whitewash, how to make, 605
Wife as husband's agent, 376
Will, how to make a, 375; in Scotland, 375
Window-boxes, 600
Windows, cleaning of, 69
Wines, care of, 104, 105; how to serve, 248
Wiring (in millinery), 437
Wizard photography, 535
Women, legal position of married, 375
Wood, as fuel, 99; carving, 690
Wool mattress, how to remake, 608
Woollen articles, how to wash, 287; clothing, 451
Work-basket, the, 387
Workmen's Compensation Act, 370
Worms, cure for, 485; in pots, destruction of, 602
Worry, 468
Wounds, 578
Wraps, evening, 305
Wringer, the, 272
Wrinkles, cause of, 448
Writer, the special, 627

YOKE frock, the, 496

Printed by BALLANTYNE, HANSON & Co.
Edinburgh & London